Encyclopedia of Nineteenth-Century Thought

Encyclopedia of Nineteenth-Century Thought

Edited by Gregory Claeys

Routledge
Taylor & Francis Group

LONDON AND NEW YORK

First published 2005
by Routledge Car
2 Park Square, Milton Park, Abingdon, Oxon OX14 4RN
Simultaneously published in the USA and Canada
by Routledge
270 Madison Ave., New York, NY 10016

Routledge is an imprint of the Taylor & Francis Group

© 2005 Routledge Ltd
Typeset in Times New Roman by
Newgen Imaging Systems (P) Ltd, India
Printed and bound in Great Britain by
TJ International Ltd, Padstow Cornwall

British Library Cataloguing in Publication Data
A catalogue record for this book is available from the British Library
Library of Congress Cataloging in Publication Data
A catalog record for this book has been requested

ISBN 0–415–24419–6

Contents

Editors

Volume editor

Gregory Claeys
Professor of History,
Royal Holloway, University of London

Consultant editors

F.C. Beiser
Syracuse University
(Germany)

Christopher Duggan
University of Reading
(Southern and Eastern Europe)

Pamela Pilbeam
University of London
(France)

Chushichi Tsuzuki
Hitotsubashi University
(Japan and East Asia)

Contributors

Evelina Barbashina	Malcolm Hardman
F.C. Beiser	Jennifer Harrison
Fritz Breithaupt	Clive E. Hill
Anthony Brewer	Alan D. Hodder
Robert Brown	H.S. Jones
Gavin Budge	Pierre Kerszberg
Evgenia V. Cherkasova	Alan R. King
Gregory Claeys	Tim Kirk
Gill Cockram	Detmar Klein
N.D. Daglish	D.M. Knight
Simon Dentith	Timothy Larsen
Michael S. Dodson	Oliver Leaman
Christopher Duggan	Kyoo Lee
Peter Field	Michael Levin
David Gladstone	Andre Liebich
Olaf Hansen	Sandy Lovie

Elizabeth McCardell	Martin Simpson
Donal McCartney	Franz Solms-Laubach
Erin McKenna	Sue Stedman-Jones
Takashi Mitani	Shannon Stimson
John Morrow	Dan Stone
Kathryn Oliver Mills	C. Takeda
John S. Partington	Sheila Thomas
Pamela Pilbeam	Noel Thompson
Liz Potter	Kathryn Tomasek
Simon J. Potter	Lyman Tower Sargent
John Pratt	Keith Tribe
Pamela Ralston	Chushichi Tsuzuki
David Rose	Karine Varley
Roland Sarti	Georgios Varouxakis
David A. Shafer	Richard Whatmore

Introduction

'The Wonderful Century': the idea of the nineteenth century and its critics

Viewed at its culmination, the nineteenth century appeared incontestably to have been the most extraordinary epoch that had ever occurred. In it, as Alfred Russel Wallace insisted in *The Wonderful Century. Its Successes and its Failures* (1898), humankind had progressed as far as in the whole of preceding human history.[1] Principally this was a function of science and technology. It was an age richer in inventions than any other: steam-power, railways, gas illumination, electricity, refrigeration, the telegraph, the internal combustion engine, the phonograph, vaccination, anaesthetics, photography, radiation – to name but a few. Comforts increasingly abounded, and those who could enjoy their benefits found their lives immeasurably enriched. The world shrank rapidly: travel and communication were vastly easier; telescopes reached out into the universe, while microscopes and scalpels divulged a new world within. Life-expectations were greatly extended. Perceptions were sharpened, and urbanity and sociability expanded. These changes were intimately bound up with the fact that Europeans, in particular, left the land in ever-greater numbers for the bright lights of ever-larger cities, where, if they were well off, their standard of living and life-chances advanced steadily, while if they were not, they might well decline. But for all classes the experience was astonishing, bewildering and provocative.

The epoch could not but be an age equally richer in ideas than any other, and self-consciously, from the outset, an age of transition, where the rest of human history became the 'old', to be swept away, along with most of its best-loved certainties, by the brave new world of modernity. To describe the new, and to appraise its development, required new ideas: revolution, social welfare, the international market and division of labour, race, democracy, equality, feminism, industrialism, rationalism, capitalism, Romanticism, utilitarianism. Linking the two great achievements, political and technological, of the epoch, were the *nouveaux riches*, the triumphalist middle class or bourgeoisie, throughout the civilized world enriching itself, promising affluence to others, and everywhere disdainful of both the 'idle', 'parasitic' ruling landed elite above them, whose titles and privileges they coveted, and those among the hapless workers and peasants beneath them who were unwilling to enlist under the banner of the new order. Justifying their economic rights by the new political economy, for which capital accumulation was the *raison d'être* of modernity, and their political rights by the need to protect and foster this wealth, the middle classes increasingly embraced a secular, hedonistic, world-view in which the pursuit of pleasure became the highest aspiration of humankind, and modern standards of taste became increasingly those of the mass of consumers. Yet the new ideal met with fierce resistance from Romantics, some evangelicals, some conservatives, socialists and others, to whom a fragmented, atomized individualism coupled to an exploitative factory system and decaying, impoverished urban existence held out no hope of real human amelioration. It was, thus, a century of widespread strife, social and economic as well as intellectual, in which the concept of struggle would finally emerge as the master-metaphor of the epoch, and war fought with the newly invented machine-gun and tank, and in the air and under the water, would be seen by some as a desirable way of testing and improving national virtues. And it was the age in which the greatest utopian ideal ever conceived, an internationalist communist order, would by 1900 increasingly be seen as the sole alternative to capitalist exploitation, inequality and militarism.

Eight leading ideas held sway over the imagination of the period: revolution, nationalism, industrialism, liberalism, socialism, evolutionism, scientific and technical progress, and, finally, civilization, which binds many of the rest together.

The nineteenth century's moment of initial self-definition was indisputably the French Revolution, with its sweeping assault on corrupt privilege and feudal unfreedom, and its bold assertion of equality, natural rights and personal freedom. Following close upon the American Revolution, the fall of the Bastille heralded an uncompromising assertion of popular sovereignty, and of national, ethnic and personal liberation. Man, Rousseau had said, had been born free, but found himself everywhere in chains; this was the century, revolutionaries asserted, in which humanity was to be unshackled. But, though Florence Nightingale recalled an 'old legend' 'that the nineteenth century is to be the "century of women"', the female sex largely remained enchained throughout it. Enslaved peoples regained their liberties by stages through the period, though not necessarily any recognition of their common or fundamental humanity, or security from conquest and bondage masquerading as 'the White Man's Burden' – possibly the most cynical concept of the epoch.

The ideology of liberty, exported throughout Europe by French armies, helped inspire one of the central developments of the epoch, nationalism, in Germany, Italy, Hungary, Poland, Greece, Ireland, South America, Egypt, India and elsewhere, and then throughout much of the rest of the world. By the end of the First World War three empires, Russia, Germany and Austro-Hungary, had fallen; the British, French, Belgian and Dutch would soon follow. The proclamation of the right of national self-determination assumed many forms, radical as well as conservative, secular as well as religious. Through Fichte, Schleiermacher, Ranke, Michelet, Mazzini and a host of others the 'state' and the 'nation' became imbued with higher, spiritual, even mystical, collectivist qualities, and yoked to Darwinism, Romanticism, Idealist philosophy, racialism and many other ideas. With it came a historicist appreciation, first heralded by Burke and Herder in the late eighteenth century, and applauded by Meinecke in the nineteenth century, of the uniqueness of national histories, and the need to celebrate and preserve their distinctive individuality.

But the rights of revolution and national self-determination were also often understood by most Europeans as anchored in a discourse on civilization, thus as applicable to 'civilised' but not to 'backward' nations. Non-Western peoples not only had no right of self-rule, but, it was widely felt, ought to welcome the extension of commerce, Christianity and civilization that Europeans graciously offered. By mid-century revolutionary ideas of the brotherhood of man jostled beside new theories of fundamental human inequality, notably in the racialist theories of Gobineau. By 1900, however, anti-imperialism was gathering momentum. Resistance movements, like Mahdism in the Sudan, scored some notable triumphs over imperial forces, and heralded the enduring attraction of tradition and custom to many non-European peoples. Japan became the first non-Western nation to achieve technological parity with Europe, and European formal domination over most of the world would soon be ended.

Because it gained the largest empire, began the Industrial Revolution and was the leading mercantile power of the period, Britain stamped its image squarely upon the nineteenth century. The result of Waterloo, the exhaustion of Britain's great rival, gave her unprecedented sway until German unification introduced a late contender for European and imperial hegemony. The British constitutional model, the spirit of gentlemanly conduct, innovations in science and technology, the great British navy, all excited wonder, envy and emulation elsewhere. But the 'Pax Britannica' hardly implied peace for the non-Western world; the struggle for imperial supremacy brought constant warfare, from China and Burma to India and Turkey, to Egypt, Sudan and eventually much of the rest of Africa. And the scent of Britain's imperial success excited bloodlust elsewhere, until by 1900 even Japan and the USA had joined the scramble for empire. The growth of racialism after 1850, too, provided an even stronger justification for the invasion of non-European peoples than had the concept of civilization, particularly in relation to Africa. 'Greater

Britain', as John Seeley famously put it, 'in a fit of absence of mind',[2] became, with the other empires, increasingly intolerant of aboriginal peoples, and unconcerned about their probable extinction, notably in parts of Australasia.

The British model also represented two of the other great ideas of the epoch: liberalism, both economic and political; and industrialism, for until late in the century Britain was indisputably the most important industrial power in the world. The two were widely regarded as intimately inter-related: the growth of commerce in the early modern period had engendered a conflict of power between the towns and the countryside that had resulted in that limitation of executive power and system of constitutional checks and balances which Britons associated with the 'Glorious Revolution' of 1688. As commercial success fostered industry, the mercantile and manufacturing middle classes made still further demands for a share of political power, which was extended to them in three parliamentary reform acts (1832, 1867, 1884). By 1900 the social and political power of the aristocracy had been substantially eclipsed, and the last vestiges of feudalism swept away. A monarch had lost his head in seventeenth-century constitutional struggle; none need do so in the nineteenth century. While Continental Europe was periodically convulsed by revolutions, Britons smugly congratulated themselves on their 'matchless constitution'. The basis of liberal thought might shift; in the last decade Platonic and Hegelian neo-Idealism would make inroads on empiricism, and a trend towards collectivism, resisted by individualist critics, like Herbert Spencer, would reshape attitudes towards the state. The scope of state interference expanded greatly, to encompass old-age pensions, factory legislation, compulsory education and much more. The electorate grew steadily, as it did elsewhere. But despite these changes the liberal order itself seemed the crowning achievement of modernity, and to many historians it was the 'progress of liberty' that thus essentially defined European, and indeed world, history in the period, and which marked it as the culminating epoch of human development.

As two of the greatest thinkers of the age, John Stuart Mill and Karl Marx, both acknowledged, the ruling ideas of the age were the ideas of its dominant classes. Yet both liberalism and industrialism met with a substantial challenge from the most important critical strand of thought in the period, socialism. Emerging simultaneously in the major European nations as a reaction to poverty, unemployment, and poor living and working conditions for the majority, socialism achieved international significance as the major alternative system of ideas with the Continental revolutions of 1848. Thereafter its earlier manifestations, notably Owenism, Fourierism and Saint-Simonism, were supplanted by Marxian socialism, which was more intent on industrial development than many earlier types of socialism, and much more revolutionary. By the 1880s various forms of liberalism had come to compromise with socialist proposals for a much more interventionist role for the state, and by 1900 many of the leading components of the twentieth-century welfare state, such as unemployment and old-age insurance, were being introduced not only in Europe, but also in New Zealand, Australia, Scandinavia, the USA and elsewhere. If the two great contending ideals of the era were non-interventionist liberalism and statist socialism, a substantial accommodation between these had been reached in principle by 1914. Everywhere writers began to herald the ideal of community, to deride or attempt to modify liberal individualism as destructive of the social virtues, and, like Emile Durkheim, to praise as preferable a condition of organic solidarity and mutual interdependence, while querying its sustainability in modern society.

It is often assumed that the single idea hegemonically dominating nineteenth-century thought was 'progress', in the sense of the increasing improvement of the quality of individual life, and, at least until a *fin de siècle* sense of degeneracy and malaise became pervasive, this is hardly surprising. The idea of progress was already well established by the French Revolution, but was lent enormous impetus by scientific discoveries and inventions, and a steadily rising standard of living, at least for the middle classes but, by the end of the century, often the working classes as well. Liberal political economy posited an indefinite growth of wealth through capital accumulation and the expansion of production and demand, a vision tempered only by the permanent spectre of working-class overpopulation, which would force wages down to the subsistence level. Liberal political thought acknowledged the gradual but probably inevitable growth of democracy. Socialists often envisioned a cataclysmic end to the old society, but then portrayed in rosy hues the quasi-perfectionist attributes of the new. Saint-Simonism and Positivism gave special stress to the role played by industry in transforming the old society, and shaped the views of left and right alike. As geology, palaeontology and other sciences advanced, it became evident that sacred chronologies had to be abandoned in favour of a much longer time-frame. New sciences of society, history, anthropology, philology and archaeology arose. Crowning and uniting all of the progressive sciences was the idea of civilization itself, with its sharp demarcation between 'advanced' and 'backward' societies, its boasted rapprochement of science and Christianity, its vaunted superiority of customs, morals and manners. Yet even here there was ambiguity, the nagging fear that classical Greece, or the Roman Empire, or the medieval community, or some lost golden age, or primitive people, had penetrated more deeply into the inner secrets of human aspiration or more successfully captured the elusive condition called 'happiness'. Beneath the surface modern society was, some feared, like its produce, shoddy, hastily mass-produced, tawdry and vulgar, inauthentic and deeply unhappy, deprived of its spiritual essence and incapable of finding self-realization in mere consumerism. For writers like Goethe or Matthew Arnold 'culture' was to be the antidote to the 'anarchy' of lower middle-class self-assertion and self-definition. Others sought meaning in reversion to religion, or fashioning some substitute for it; this was also common outside industrializing countries.

In mid-century, like a great storm bursting upon a tranquil afternoon, there came Darwin – or more precisely, Spencer, Darwin, Wallace, Huxley, Sumner and a variety of other evolutionist thinkers, whose world-view when combined with other trends in religious criticism was deeply unsettling to theologians and moral philosophers in particular, but increasingly also to the wider public. No longer the benign extension of the deity, nature was now, in one popular view of Darwinism, an unlimited arena of free competition, in which the fittest survived, and the rest succumbed. Harmony gave way to incessant conflict, Christ became man, but man fell even further, from angel to ape. God became a mere hypothesis, or gave way to the worship of power. The meaning of human life, for some, became construed as an act of will-power, the will to live, Schopenhauer suggested, the will to power alone, Nietzsche insisted, predominating. Bishops mocked evolution, but pews emptied. The anti-clericalism of Voltaire and the eighteenth-century Enlightenment, seemingly in retreat after 1815, surged forward. The great edifice of religious belief, for conservatives the very basis of social order itself, which had so often been repaired throughout the course of the century by legions of evangelicals, theists, pantheists, mystics and others, now teetered anew and even threatened to come crashing down. As churches weakened, secular forces seized the moment; *Kulturkampf* between Church and State broke out in the 1870s in Germany; in 1905, separation of Church and State occurred in France. The worship of science heralded by the new Enlightenment associated with Positivism was continued by Ernst Haeckel and others. And Marxism moved ever closer to the claim to represent the cause of natural science clothed in the garb of historical inevitability.

Darwinism was thus dual-edged, supportive of the enlightening propensities of empiricism and the scientific method on the one hand, but also of the predominance of the darker forces of animality and instinct over reason on the other. A further blow to reason came from the discovery of the psychology of the instinctive and the unconscious, beginning as early as von Schubert's study of the *Symbolism of Dreams* (1814), the poetry of Blake and others, and developed in E. von Hartmann's *Philosophy of the Unconscious* (1869) and later in Jung and others. There rapidly emerged that central role posited for sexuality in the shaping of human behaviour, which we associate principally with Havelock Ellis, and Freud. The world within, it was increasingly evident, was disturbed, if not aberrant; it might be controlled, but would never, like the outer, be tamed or mastered; the struggle must be constant. The passions, as some Enlightenment thinkers had conjectured, would not bow before reason; now the erotic threatened virtually to subvert it. While some claimed that science could still promote species-progress, notably through eugenics, others dismissed such appeals as 'the meddlesome interference of an arrogant scientific priestcraft'.[3] It was, certainly, widely evident that the period from 1880–1914 marked a clear loss of confidence in the idea of the progress of rational, harmonious, human self-control. Even the Romantic ideal of the self, with its emphasis on the creative passions, seemed disturbed and unhappy, buoyed by the liberating rebellion against bourgeois morals of the period, but anxiously peering into the abyss of bottomless self-unknowability. Conscious mythologizing became in some quarters the order of the day; the masses or 'crowd', their collective psychology diagnosed as herdlike, needed heroes – the shadow of Bonaparte fell long into the century – and equally ideas by which they could be manipulated, and the period is often referred to as commencing the age of ideologies. But if it was the age of the masses, the championship of elites was never far away, whether in Nietzsche's Superman or Pareto's assertion, based on a critique of Marx, that elites naturally emerged to steer any mass movement. But still others, notably anarchists like Michael Bakunin, resisted the claim that such elitism was inevitable.

The decade of the 1890s, then, has usually been seen as marking an important psychological watershed, where the sense of *fin de siècle* is pervaded with irrationalism, mysticism, disillusionment, various forms of neo-Romanticism and Social Darwinism. At root seemed to lie the sentiment that the promise to mankind of rational scientific control over the world was being subverted by deeper passions, psychologically, and their mirror social pathologies, especially nationalistic militarism. The solid edifice of civilization seemed increasingly like a papier mâché frontage or Potemkin village. Civilised mores appeared as a mere pastiche of civility, a fig-leaf barely restraining the lustful or blood-letting instincts: Rousseau enjoyed a renaissance. But if the passions were savage, their discovery could also be liberating and empowering, the overthrow of libidinal guilt marking a new epoch of sexual freedom for women. Literature, drama and painting all began to link ideas of artistic creativity to the assault on bourgeois respectability, and through Wedekind, Zola, Wells and a host of others the artist became the symbol of rebellion *par excellence*. Painters like Van Gogh and Gauguin exalted the primitive, the everyday, the humble, the fleeting, momentary, unrepeatable impression. Poets like William Morris, imbued with a guiding hatred of modernity, evoked the beauty and inner spiritual calm of the medieval world. Romantics of all stripes began a concerted rebellion against bourgeois conformism. But counter-attack was never far away, and works like Max Nordau's *Degeneration* (1895) assailed the new aestheticism as decadent, corrupt and escapist. Painting moved still further into abstraction, music into atonality. The idea of the modern, in all its richness, pain and ambiguity, was emerging. The world had begun to move beyond a male, white, repressed, European bourgeois meta-narrative of progress towards something much more uncertain but clearly less restrictive.

The end of the 'long' nineteenth century, bounded by the French Revolution and the First World War, demonstrated all too clearly the bleak, horrifying, destructive, lemming-like aspect of modernity. As one catastrophe followed another after 1914, many blamed the voluntarist philosophies of Nietzsche, Bergson and others, with their stress on energy and power as principles, perhaps supra-moral principles, of neo-pagan, Social Darwinist, irrationalist self-assertion. To the pious this was only the logical consequence of the uncertainty created by scientific questioning, and of Darwinism in particular; science, as Francis Power Cobbe put it, was 'essentially Jacobin', and would leave no king dethroned.[4] Man had been returned to nature, and now began to act naturally, freed of the restraints provided by both divinity and civility. Particularly where the state became identified with this force, no long as the incarnation of a higher spiritual ideal, as in Hegel, but as a self-expanding collective will, a shark amongst minnows, as it was in Treitschke, international violence was sure to follow. With a fear of species degeneration came the apprehension of a creeping barbarism, first noticed by some at the time of the Armenian massacres from 1894–6, about which Leonard Hobhouse later recalled that:

> It was not so much the actual cruelty and outrage, bringing the worst horrors of the seventeenth century into the midst of a supposedly humane and ordered civilisation. It was the indifference of Europe in face of such deeds that affected every one with the least touch of imagination'.[5]

Following close on this came a war between Turkey and Greece, another in Cuba, and then the South African conflict. Nations, as one observer put it, 'intoxicated with patriotism', became 'wild beasts, who looked upon a large part of the world as undivided prey'.[6] The new Great Powers, the USA, Germany and Japan, in particular, anxious to expand their power, began to cut away at the pre-existing imperial structure. The catastrophe of 1914, which we often presume to have marked the end of the century, came as less of a surprise to many observers than we might imagine today, and its eventual consequence, the greater catastrophe of 1939, seemingly followed inevitably. The technology of destruction, now wedded to racial arrogance, began to unleash its full potential. The 'Wonderful Century', its ideals and confidence exhausted, closed with the near-dissolution of the world-order that had dominated and defined it, and the prospect that its alluring promises would fade into mere collective delusion.

Notes

1 A.R. Wallace. *The Wonderful Century. Its Successes and its Failures* (1898), p. 150.
2 J.R. Seeley, *The Expansion of England* (1883), p. 8.
3 James Marchant. *Alfred Russel Wallace, Letters and Reminiscences* (2 vols, 1916), vol. 2, p. 247.
4 Frances Power Cobbe, *The Scientific Spirit of the Age and Other Pleas and Discussions* (1888), p. 27.
5 L.T. Hobhouse, *The World in Conflict* (1915), p. 10.
6 Havelock Ellis, *The Nineteenth Century. A Dialogue in Utopia* (1900), p. 24.

Acknowledgements

This collection of essays does not represent an intellectual history of the period as such, but a series of incursions into a vast, complex and ever-contested arena of ideas. No two editors will ever see such a diverse panoply of ideas the same way, but while responsibility for this volume is entirely mine, it is presented in the hope that readers in perusing it will want to explore further the mysteries, delights and perplexities of such an extraordinary era.

While editing a volume of this type is akin to marshalling an army of cats, my co-editors and collaborators in this dictionary have on the whole performed admirably to specification, and have produced an exciting, interesting and informative reference work. I owe much to the calm efficiency of my editor, Dominic Shryane, an adept feline-tamer, and to Fred Beiser, Christopher Duggan, Pamela Pilbeam and Chushichi Tsuzuki for their assistance in the sometimes daunting task of matching topics to suitable contributors. Finally, as ever, I am grateful to my family for patiently enduring absences, flights of fancy, and an unhealthy obsession with making software work properly.

Gregory Claeys
London
April 2004

A

ACTON, JOHN EMERICH DALBERG (1834–1902)

John Emerich Edward Dalberg, 1st Baron Acton, eminent British historian, was born on 10 January 1834 at Naples, the son of a Roman Catholic baronet. Educated at Oscott under Dr, later Cardinal, Wiseman, he studied at Edinburgh, then at Munich under Döllinger, who inspired him to become a historian. His great aim was to write a 'History of Liberty', but this was never achieved. He spent several years as a Member of Parliament (1859–65), where he adhered to William Gladstone, and developed a reputation as an individualist, free-trading Liberal. Disputing the view that slavery had caused the American Civil War, he supported the Southern states' right of secession. But his real love was Catholicism: 'The one supreme object of all of my thoughts is the good of the Church,' he wrote to his wife. Acton thus exerted much energy as the editor of the Catholic monthly, *The Rambler*, which merged with the *Home and Foreign Review* in 1862, though as a liberal Catholic he was isolated even from most British Catholics, and was nearly excommunicated (Döllinger was) because of his opposition to papal infallibility. He helped to found the *English Historical Review* in 1886, and became Sir John Seeley's successor as Regius Professor of History at Cambridge in 1895. Following the success of his inaugural lecture, 'The Study of History', he gave two courses of lectures, on the French Revolution and on Modern History, and achieved a reputation as a remarkable tutor.

Relatively little of Acton's historical work was published during his lifetime. The essays on 'The History of Freedom in Antiquity' and 'The History of Freedom in Christianity' do not develop adequately his Tocquevillian worries about the threat of democracy to modern liberty. His journalism, though deeply partisan (he took issue with 'the materialist' Buckle in *The Rambler* over the role of both free will and Providence in history, for instance, on overtly Catholic grounds), offers as much insight into the key theme of his political philosophy, the interpenetration of religious and political liberty, and the need to secure both by abridging the power of the state. Acton's account of liberty as 'the highest political end' is abstract, Burkian and Whiggish; he defines liberty as 'the assurance that every man shall be protected in doing what he believes his duty against the influence of authority and majorities, custom and opinion.' Acton seemingly ignored the great debates on the reshaping of liberalism towards a 'New Liberal', interventionist ideal, during the 1880s and 1890s. Nonetheless he conceded the compatibility of Christianity and socialism, and agreed that the poor should be aided where private enterprise had failed them. Both his liberalism and his Catholic cosmopolitanism also led him to warn of the destructive effects of nationalism, notably in the well-known essay on 'Nationality' (1862). Acton died on 19 June 1902.

Further reading

Acton, John (1906) *Lectures on Modern History*. London: Macmillan.
—— (1907) *The History of Freedom and Other Essays*, London: Macmillan.
—— (1907) *Historical Essays and Studies*, London: Macmillan.
Fasnacht, G.E. (1952) *Acton's Political Philosophy*, London: Hollis & Carter.
Hill, Roland (2000) *Lord Acton*, New Haven, CT: Yale University Press.

Gasquet, Dom (1906) *Lord Acton and His Circle*, London: George Allen.

SEE ALSO: historiography and the idea of progress; liberalism

GREGORY CLAEYS

AESTHETICS, PAINTING AND ARCHITECTURE

The history of aesthetic thought in the nineteenth century has been little investigated by modern scholars, and is still largely unknown territory. In the Anglophone world, at any rate, this is attributable to the long reaction against Victorianism, which dominated the first five or six decades of the twentieth century. From a modernist point of view, the Victorian tendency to moralize made it practically impossible for a serious investigation of the proper objects of aesthetics to take place, a state of affairs of which modernists regarded the supposed corrupt sentimentality of Victorian art as a symptom.

This twentieth-century dismissal of the dominant nineteenth-century tendencies in aesthetics was in large part the culmination of a process that began in the later nineteenth century. The development of a scientific, and eventually laboratory-based, psychology in Britain, Germany and the USA during the last 30 years of the nineteenth century effected a transformation in the discourse of aesthetics, in that it became increasingly difficult to invoke final causes in the discussion of aesthetic questions. This problematization of the theological argument from design, in part a result of the intellectual impact of evolutionary theory, affected thinking about aesthetics particularly profoundly because an appeal to natural beauty had been in many ways the last bastion of religious providentialism.

The late nineteenth-century call for a scientific aesthetics was accompanied by a change in the definition of aesthetics itself, a change that had profound consequences for the way in which the history of nineteenth-century aesthetics was written (or, more frequently, left unwritten). JOHN RUSKIN, early on in the second book of *Modern Painters*, objected to the very term 'aesthetics' itself, as a description of the philosophical study of beauty, because it focused attention on the role played by the senses in appreciation of the beautiful, rather than on what the mind perceived by means of the senses. The later nineteenth-century psychologization of aesthetics, coupled with Whistler's impressionist-influenced proclamation that the only criterion by which a painting could legitimately be judged was its sensuous immediacy, fulfilled Ruskin's fears that use of the term 'aesthetics' heralded a behaviouristic redefinition of beauty purely in terms of sensory inputs.

Consequently, in order to understand the development of nineteenth-century aesthetics we must expand our category of 'the aesthetic' beyond what most twentieth-century commentators have understood by the term. This means that we must abandon the assumption that the appeal to an extra-artistic reality, characteristic, for example, of Victorian narrative painting, is necessarily aesthetically incoherent, or merely 'sentimental'. The characteristic twentieth-century attitude that pronounces reference outside the artwork itself aesthetically illegitimate is a reflection of a relativistic philosophy for which reality, outside the structuring systems of human aesthetics and culture, is essentially chaotic; reference to such a reality by a work of art must in this view be either an exercise in falsification, or in contravention to the work's own principles of aesthetic order. For the majority of nineteenth-century thinkers, however, there is no such conflict between intrinsic aesthetic qualities and external reference, so that aesthetic order can be understood as corresponding to an order that really exists outside the work of art, and which can be referred to by the artist in its support.

The philosophical perspective that justified this predominant nineteenth-century view of art, as indicative of a reality which transcended it, may be identified with that of the so-called Common Sense school of philosophy founded in the eighteenth century by Thomas Reid. Common Sense philosophy was a protean intellectual tradition that continued to be an important influence in all major European countries, and also in North America, until the 1870s. It thus constituted the philosophical frame within which arguably the majority of nineteenth-century aesthetic thought took place, and whose rejection lay behind the scientific psychology of such figures as Alexander Bain and James Sully, and the Decadent aesthetics of Pater.

The Common Sense tradition has been little studied by twentieth-century scholars, who have generally found its insistence on philosophical realism unappealingly dogmatic (although a revival of interest in the realist position among philosophers during the 1990s has led to a corresponding upturn in the academic fortunes of Thomas Reid). The widespread nature of the influence of Common Sense philosophy has therefore attracted little recognition even in studies of the nineteenth-century British intellectual tradition. It has however been shown that in Germany Scottish Common Sense philosophy formed the matrix from which the philosophy of Kant and the German Idealists emerged, and that in France its influence was perpetuated by the philosophical eclecticism of Cousin and his pupil Jouffroy. In both Britain and France Common Sense philosophy was heavily implicated in the development of nineteenth-century faculty psychology and studies of the physiology of the brain, as well as in popular movements such as phrenology and mesmerism. The Scottish Enlightenment inheritance of educational systems in North America has been well known for some time, and Common Sense philosophy represented an important part of that inheritance, influencing EMERSON and the transcendentalists. Because of the overlap between Common Sense philosophy and German Idealism, many nineteenth-century ideas of great importance for aesthetic theory (such as that of the essential activity of the mind in the process of perception), which have usually been attributed to the influence of German Idealism in twentieth-century scholarship, are more correctly viewed as belonging to the Common Sense tradition's intellectual heritage; this has been shown to be the case, for example, for THOMAS CARLYLE, often regarded even in his own day as an essentially 'German' thinker, but whose actual acquaintance with German Idealist philosophy appears to have been scanty at best.

Common Sense philosophy's importance for nineteenth-century thinking about aesthetics lies in its development of Berkeley's account of perception. Thomas Reid, in his 1764 *Inquiry into the Human Mind on the Principles of Common Sense*, analysed each of the senses in turn in order to show that human perception was essentially dependent on the interpretation of divinely ordained sensory signs, as Berkeley had claimed. Reid argued, in an anticipation of Kant, that Hume's demonstration of the insufficiency of reasoning based on the data available to the senses to justify common human beliefs, such as that in a world external to the mind,

made it necessary to suppose that these beliefs represented fundamental intuitions that were inherent in the mind's capacity to apprehend the world. Such intuitions (collectively entitled 'common sense' by Reid) were the enabling conditions that allowed the mind to form a coherent interpretation of the perceptual cues, or signs, presented by the world, and were comparable to the basic assumptions about the structure of experience that for Reid were embodied in the grammar of every language.

The Common Sense philosophy of Reid insisted on the irreducibility of the mind's perceptions of the world to mere sense-data, an argument that was intended to refute the materialist associationism of Hume. Later developments in the Common Sense tradition, however, tended to combine this account of foundational transcendent intuitions with associationist arguments. An early example is Archibald Alison's *Essays on the Nature and Principles of Taste*, first published in 1790, but influentially popularized by FRANCIS JEFFREY in the *Edinburgh Review* in 1811, which went on to be a standard nineteenth-century text on aesthetics and was later read by Marcel Proust. Alison's work is normally described as an example of associationism, but as is made clear by the conclusion to its second volume, where Alison cites Reid's Common Sense philosophy, Alison's associationist analyses take as their basis the kind of foundational intuitions described by Reid (who returned the compliment, writing a commendatory letter to Alison). This tendency to combine Reidian Common Sense philosophy with associationism was taken to an extreme by the later Common Sense philosopher Thomas Brown who controversially argued in the 1810s that there was no inherent conflict between the philosophy of Reid and that of Hume, and proceeded to elaborate an essentially Humean analysis of the methodological problems of the physical sciences. Brown's combination of Reidian intuitionism with Humean associationism is reflected in his notion of unconscious 'suggestion', which proved to be influential on much subsequent nineteenth-century aesthetic discussion.

The Common Sense tradition's potential for combining Berkeleyan immaterialism with the materialist implications of Humean psychology meant that its intellectual legacy to nineteenth-century aesthetic thought was fundamentally ambiguous. On the one hand, Reid's claim for the semiotic basis of perception pointed the way towards various varieties of symbolist doctrine, a trend that extended from the symbolist poetics of writers such as Carlyle, Emerson and Elizabeth Barrett Browning right up to the French *Symbolistes* at the end of the nineteenth century. On the other hand, Reid's insistence on the fundamentally immaterial nature of perception, as an interpretative act of the mind, prompted scientific inquiry into the physiological basis of perception, a tendency foreshadowed by Reid's own investigations into the nature of sensation and that ultimately led to the physiological aesthetics of 1870s writers such as Grant Allen.

It would be a mistake to regard this physiologically orientated research, particularly in the early part of the nineteenth century, as necessarily motivated by a materialist agenda; the study of involuntary physiological processes, it was thought, could help to demonstrate the essentially immaterial nature of mind and its independence from the body. Charles Bell's *Essays on the Anatomy of Expression*, first published in 1806 and, in its many revised editions, a major influence on the pre-Raphaelite painters, is an example of this kind of immaterialist-orientated physiological investigation. The ultimate effect of such research, however, was to emphasize the physiological workings of the brain to such an extent as to suggest that the individual characteristics of works of art could be traced back to peculiarities in the dietary habits and physical organization of the artist. The early reception of Edgar Allan Poe's writings in France affords an example of this physiological reading of aesthetics, with critics explaining Poe's artistic idiosyncrasies as the inevitable result of his alcoholic temperament.

One of the major facets of Common Sense philosophy's influence over aesthetic thought in early nineteenth-century Britain was its encouragement of a typological approach to art. The extent to which Victorian art was typological in orientation, in the sense that it included apparently realistic detail that was intended to be interpreted allegorically as significant of a spiritual world transcending what could be represented, has been commented on by many critics. A well-known example is Holman Hunt's painting *The Awakening Conscience*, where the minutely rendered bourgeois parlour contains many indicators both of the young woman's status as a kept mistress, and of her newly aroused moral capacity to redeem herself

through repentance. The critic F.G. Stephens, in his anonymously issued 1860 memoir of Hunt, furnished a lengthy interpretation of the painting *The Light of the World* in these terms, objects such as the unusual seven-sided lantern that Christ carries being assigned quite specific theological significance.

That the architecture of the Gothic Revival was also understood by the Victorians as possessing typological significance is suggested by the writings of its first great exponent, Augustus Welby Pugin, who argued that the Gothic style was the only appropriate one for a church, because its use of height was, by a natural typology, indicative of the Resurrection. A similar kind of typological reading of church architecture, though applied to a very different theological purpose, is to be found in the eccentric late Victorian occultist Hargrave Jennings. Chris Brooks, in his 1984 study *Signs for the Times: Symbolic Realism in the Mid-Victorian World*, has advanced typological interpretations of a number of specific Victorian churches.

Although the prominence of typological interpretation in early Victorian aesthetics has often been attributed by late twentieth-century commentators to the influence of evangelicalism, the recourse to a typological aesthetics is found in nineteenth-century writers belonging to a number of theological persuasions. John Keble, the prominent Tractarian, advanced as early as 1814 his view that the effect of poetry could be understood as deriving from its use of natural 'types' of the divine that had been authorized for the Christian by their appearance in the Bible, a view that he expounded at length in Tract 89 ('On the Mysticism Attributed to the Early Fathers of the Church') and in his *Oxford Lectures on Poetry*. The striking proliferation of arguments from natural typology in early nineteenth-century Britain is probably to be attributed to the use made of Common Sense philosophy by orthodox defenders of Trinitarian theology, such as Bishop Magee, in their controversies with the Unitarians during the 1790s.

Common Sense philosophy encouraged an aesthetics based on a natural typology in which hidden correspondences were identified between the realm of Nature and that of spirit (rather than just between separate passages of the Bible) because in its view perception itself was based on just such unexplainable correspondences. For the Common Sense school, the sensory cue of the perceptual sign was recognized, through the human mind's intuition, to correspond to an intelligible perception of the external world, just as a linguistic sign might be recognized to correspond to a concept, without the connection between the two being amenable to rational analysis. Since from this perspective all perception was a form of typological correspondence, religious typologies were easily understood as an aspect of everyday experience, however much they might be disregarded in the course of the normal business of life. In this intellectual context, SAMUEL TAYLOR COLERIDGE's German Idealist-influenced theorizing about the nature of the 'symbol', often regarded by modern critics as the chief source of Keble's and Carlyle's aesthetic thought, may be understood as merely one aspect of a wider British intellectual preoccupation with the implications of the relationship between perception and signification. Coleridge certainly attempted to modify his contemporaries' understanding of perceptual and linguistic signification, in that he suggested a biological model of assimilation and digestion might serve as a paradigm for the process whereby the connection between sign and concept was formed, but he did not originate the basic parallel between language and perception that underlies the majority of nineteenth-century British aesthetic thinking, as has sometimes been claimed.

The aesthetic writing of John Ruskin is the most sustained exposition of Victorian typological aesthetics, the developing crisis in which is reflected in changes of view at various stages in his career. Ruskin seems to have encountered Common Sense philosophy through his Scottish parents, and its influence is reflected in the view, forcefully articulated from the outset of *Modern Painters*, that painting is essentially a kind of language whose effects may be compared to poetry. Ruskin derived from this position his characteristic claim that the aim of painting should not be imitation, but communication of truth. This Ruskinian argument follows on from the Common Sense School's Berkeleyan account of perception as a process of interpretation of signs. For Ruskin, the painter's weighty moral calling was to learn how to manipulate the divine language of visual signs, success in which would supply immediate evidence of the existence of God. Painterly imitation of the materiality of objects, on the other hand, led, in Ruskin's view, directly to atheism, since it substituted an unmeaning sensuousness for this typologically charged visual language.

Ruskin's later writing, on the other hand, from book three of *Modern Painters* onwards, accords much greater weight to the role of individual association in aesthetic appreciation. In part this reflects developments within the Common Sense tradition on which I have already commented, but it also appears to stem from a decrease of confidence in the stability of natural 'types' that can be linked to the development of evolutionary thought. The natural typology on which Ruskin had founded his account of painting as a divinely instituted visual language was based on the assumption that Nature, and natural species, had remained essentially unchanged since God's creation of the world, and so ultimately represented an embodiment of ideas in the mind of God. The perspective of evolution challenged the notion that there was anything inevitable or necessary about the categories that could be discerned in the natural world, an idea on which the Victorian typological aesthetic relied for its credibility.

The development of aesthetic thought in North America during the nineteenth century closely parallels trends in Britain, being based on many of the same intellectual sources. Transcendentalist aesthetics, as presented by Emerson in his essays, may be regarded as a version of the typological aesthetics I have described as characteristic of early nineteenth-century Britain, where Nature is regarded as full of spiritual correspondences that can be perceived by the intuition of the contemplating mind; it prepared the way for an enthusiastic reception of Ruskin during the 1850s. Although the Transcendentalists had an interest in German Idealism, their actual knowledge of it appears to have been largely mediated through French sources such as Victor Cousin, which assimilated it to the Common Sense tradition (a tendency that is also apparent in reception of German Idealism in Britain up till the late nineteenth century). Transcendentalism is probably best characterized as a reaction against the tendencies within the Common Sense tradition that were tending to equate it with Humean associationism; in this respect it might be compared to the position represented by William Hamilton in Britain, whose popularization of Kantian thought was coupled with an attempt to renovate the Common Sense philosophy of Reid. This is an interpretation that is supported by a comment of the nineteenth-century historian of Transcendentalism, Octavius Brooks Fotheringham, equating the Transcendentalist movement with the English philosophy of Butler, Reid and Coleridge.

From the 1860s onwards, German intellectual influences, especially Hegel, appear to have played a more substantial role in US aesthetic debate, figuring in the work of writers such as James Eliot Cabot, who expressed dissatisfaction with the anti-systematic nature of Ruskinian aesthetics. The tenor of discussion, however, remained directed towards modifying Ruskin in the direction of a quasi-Coleridgean organicism rather than in rejecting his typological aesthetics altogether; Leopold Eidlitz's 1881 *The Nature and Function of Art, More Especially of Architecture* is representative of this tendency. Ruskinism was eventually replaced during the 1890s by a physiologically and psychologically based aesthetics in the work of Henry Rutgers Marshall and George Santayana.

Aesthetic thought in France during the nineteenth century also presents considerable similarities with the narrative I have outlined of the development of a typological aesthetics in Britain, although in the latter part of the century the intellectual prestige of BERGSON appears to have inhibited the development of a scientific aesthetics. The promotion of Common Sense philosophy by PIERRE PAUL ROYER-COLLARD and, later, by his pupil Victor Cousin formed part of the Napoleonic backlash against Idéologues such as Destutt de Tracy; this intellectual tendency was continued by Théodore Jouffroy, who translated the works of Reid and his pupil DUGALD STEWART as well as producing original work on aesthetics. The prominent status of all these figures in French academic life ensured that the Common Sense tradition dominated French aesthetics for a large part of the nineteenth century; it underlies, for example, Charles Lévêque's *La Science du Beau* [The Science of Beauty], published in 1861.

The aesthetic thought of Charles Baudelaire in many ways sums up the opposing tendencies I have identified in the Common Sense tradition. On the one hand, an essay such as *The Painter of Modern Life* is quite clearly based on a view of art as the manipulation of a transcendentally significant visual language, a view that can be compared to Ruskin's (although Baudelaire is prepared to find more value in the man-made world of fashion than the early Ruskin). On the other hand, Baudelaire's writings on Poe elaborate an aesthetic of nervous stimulation and exhaustion that owes much to contemporary medical physiological investigations. Eugène Delacroix's ideas about art seem similarly indebted to the Common Sense tradition; in a famous passage in his journal, Delacroix describes art as a kind of 'hieroglyphic' that forms a bridge between the perceptions of the artist and those of his audience, a characterization that, once again, recalls the Common Sense emphasis on perception as a process of interpretation of divine visual signs.

The later enthusiasm for the philosophy of Schopenhauer among French *Symbolistes*, such as the art critic Albert Aurier, may be understood as a continuation of this intellectual heritage, rather than a radical break with it. Schopenhauer's conception of art as the intuition of the Ideas underlying phenomena is not very remote from the typological conception of art I have described, and his interest in physiological modes of explaining mental phenomena is also akin to elements in the Common Sense tradition, with which Schopenhauer was probably familiar as a result of his English education.

Aesthetic thought in Germany, at least in the area of the visual arts, seems after the end of the Romantic period in about 1815 not to have been greatly influenced by Idealist philosophy until about mid-century. The aesthetic theorist F.W. Schlegel, for example, abandoned Idealist scepticism in favour of a fideistic position that could be identified with the *Glaubensphilosophie* [philosophy of faith] of F.H. Jacobi, essentially a restatement of some of the central positions of Common Sense philosophy. Jacobi's influence on Romantics such as Novalis suggests that it might be possible to interpret German Romanticism itself as a reaction against aspects of post-Kantian idealism in favour of a philosophically realist position akin to Common Sense philosophy; this certainly seems to be how Heinrich Heine interpreted Romanticism in his well-known 1836 essay *The Romantic School*. The major movement in German art during this period, the Nazarene school of painters led by Peter Cornelius, certainly subscribed to a similar religious fideism, expressed by Cornelius in his cultivation of a monk-like persona. Nazarene painting was also characterized by a typological aesthetic very similar to the one underlying early pre-Raphaelite art in Britain, in which painting was understood as a language of visual signs that transcended the material world.

The German development that did most to shape aesthetic thought in Europe and North America was in fact the reaction against Hegelian Idealism represented by the work of Johann Friedrich Herbart. Herbart brought about a revival of Kant's formalist aesthetic that permeated the physiological and psychological research done into perception in the latter half of the nineteenth century by Hermann Helmholtz and Gustav Fechner; Helmholtz's work in particular was widely known among physiologically orientated aestheticians in Britain. Hermann Lotze, Fechner's pupil, rejected this formalist emphasis, insisting, in company with Friedrich Theodor Vischer, on empathy as the essential characteristic of art, a position that can be related to the development of expressionism in Germany. Lotze's work was known in the USA, where it was an important early influence on the philosophy of George Santayana.

Reference

Fotheringham, O.B. (1959) *Transcendentalism in New England: A History*, 122, New York: Harper.

Further reading

Budge, G. (ed.) (2003) *Aesthetics and Religion in the Nineteenth Century*, Bristol: Thoemmes Press.
Frank, M.B. (2001) *German Romantic Painting Redefined: Nazarene Tradition and the Narratives of Romanticism*, Aldershot: Ashgate.
Ikonomou, E. and Mallgrave, H.F. (eds) (1994) *Empathy, Form, and Space: Problems in German Aesthetics, 1873–1893*, Santa Monica, CA: Getty Centre for the History of Art and the Humanities.
Manns, J.W. (1994) *Reid and his French Disciples: Aesthetics and Metaphysics*, Leiden: Brill.

SEE ALSO: psychology, the emergence of; religion, secularization and the crisis of faith; Social Darwinism

GAVIN BUDGE

AMERICAN THOUGHT IN THE NINETEENTH CENTURY

For many, the greatest achievements in American thought pre-dated the nineteenth century. The creation of a 'city on a hill' and its intellectual defence, the philosophical and theological writings of Jonathan Edwards (1703–58), the popular and scientific writings of Benjamin Franklin (1706–80), the political writings of the framers of the US Declaration of Independence and Constitution, particularly John Adams (1735–1826) and THOMAS JEFFERSON (1743–1826), and the defence of the Constitution by the writers of *The Federalist Papers* (1787–88), particularly Alexander Hamilton (1757–1804) and James Madison (1751–1836) all demonstrate that there was a lively and significant intellectual life on which nineteenth-century thinkers could build, either through development or rejection.

The thinkers of the first half of the nineteenth century had to face an issue that their forerunners had largely chosen to set aside, slavery. Those in the second half of the century had to confront the aftermath of the way that slavery had been handled, which often meant following in the footsteps of eighteenth-century thinkers and setting aside or ignoring the issues involved. And slavery was symbolic of another major issued that has bedevilled American political thought throughout its history, the relations between the national government and the governments of the states. The Civil War, still called the War Between the States by many Southerners, was fought at least as much over this issue as it was over slavery, and while the issue of slavery was formally ended by the war (only to be replaced by discrimination and segregation), the debate over the locus of power continues to this day.

Perhaps due to these overriding issues and their continued relevance throughout the century, much of the thought in the period can be at least loosely labelled social thought. Philosophy in the sense the term is used today was generally weak until the end of the century, and, for much of the period, was closely related to religious thinking. When it did develop, it was often written in social terms. Theology was also often concerned with human relations on this earth as much as it was concerned with relations between people and God.

It is also important to recognize that there was a strong anti-intellectual current in the nineteenth century, which continues. This current led to regular attacks on almost all the thinkers discussed here, but, during this period, particularly on the scientific thought stemming from Darwin.

Religion

The eighteenth century had seen the ending of the complete dominance of Puritanism and

Congregationalism and the growth of Unitarianism and Deism, and the initial inroads of Methodism and Baptism. By the end of the eighteenth century and the beginning of the nineteenth, Unitarianism dominated in intellectual circles. Denying the Trinity did not, however, imply a rejection of the active intervention of the divine in human life, as symbolized by miracles. This would lead to various challenges to the dominance of Unitarianism and its gradual demise as an intellectual force throughout the century, being challenged initially by Transcendentalism and ultimately replaced by both science and more conservative religious doctrines that did not reject Trinitarianism.

The nineteenth century witnessed a series of religious revivals and the development of new Protestant denominations and both the development of significant alternatives within the mainstream of Christianity and various radical challengers that saw themselves as Christian but were virtually heterodox. The tour of the USA by John (1703–93) and Charles Wesley (1707–88) in 1736 ultimately led to the rapid expansion of Methodism, which by the beginning of the twentieth century was the largest Protestant denomination in the USA. John Wesley represented a branch of Perfectionism that has waxed and waned in the USA, one that emphasizes the need to be personally saved, as Wesley believed he had been. With this awareness of one's personal salvation, this 'Second Blessing', it became possible to live a good life on this earth. Followers of Wesley in the USA tended to support a double standard of morality for men and women because women did not have to go out into 'the world' with its dangers of corruption.

More radical movements included the continuation of the Shakers, or the United Society of Believers in Christ's Second Coming, who, although there remain a few adherents in the twenty-first century, reached their peak in the first half of the nineteenth century. The Shakers believed in a quadripartite God (the Trinity plus Holy Mother Wisdom) and that Christ's second coming had already occurred in the form of their founder, Ann Lee (originally Lees – 1736–84). The Shakers practised celibacy and community of goods, aimed at gender equality, and were extremely successful.

The Shakers radical perfectionism then taught that it was possible for human beings on this earth to attain or at least approach perfection. The best-known exponent was JOHN HUMPHREY NOYES (1811–86). A less well-known exponent of Perfectionism, Adin Ballou (1803–90), illustrates the common drive to social reform inspired by the doctrine. Ballou founded a community, called Hopedale, in Massachusetts, which was quite successful economically, but it was his argument that we must make the teachings of Christianity real through our lives that illustrates an important thread in nineteenth-century thought. He wanted, as the title of one of his periodicals has it, to develop *Practical Christians*. Later in the century, using similar language but outside the Perfectionist camp, thinkers like Edward Everett Hale (1822–1909), best known as the author of 'Man without a Country' (1863), pastor of the famous South Congregational Church of Boston from 1856 to 1909, and Chaplain of the US Senate from 1903–9, proposed very similar ideas. In *Ten Times One is Ten* (1870), Hale suggested that if each person taught another person the truth of Christianity, in roughly 27 years the world could be transformed. His *How They Lived in Hampton* (1888) was subtitled *A Study in Practical Christianity* and argued for the need to apply Christianity to economic relations.

Spiritualism was another popular movement in the nineteenth century. The belief in the ability to communicate with the dead or with more advanced beings on other planets also gave rise to a very popular, as measured by book sales, belief in what came to be known as the 'domestic' heaven or an afterlife little different from life before death but better. Elizabeth Stuart Phelps's (1844–1911) *The Gates Ajar* (1868), *Beyond the Gates* (1883) and *The Gates Between* (1887), and a number of imitators all described contact with those who had died and were living comfortable middle-class lives in heaven.

Other radical religious movements included the Millerites, followers of William Miller (1782–1849), who believed that the end of the world was imminent. While Miller was never specific as to the date, Joshua V. Himes (1805–95), who became the publicist for the Millerite millennium, initially said March 1843 or 1844 and then 22 October 1844. When all these dates passed, most Millerites, who had, in their thousands, sold their worldly goods, rejected the message. But a few remained, and the Millerite phenomenon ultimately produced the denomination today known as the Seventh Day Adventists. The belief in the imminent end of the world or the nearness of the Second Coming is a common feature of US religious history and, for all of the popularity of Miller, this belief may well have been more popular in the seventeenth and eighteenth centuries, and it again became popular near the end of the twentieth century, particularly as the year 2000 approached.

Transcendentalism

The most important movement in the first half of the nineteenth century that was both philosophical and theological, and dealt with social issues was Transcendentalism. Its foremost spokesperson was RALPH WALDO EMERSON (1803–82), who, after Edwards and Franklin, was among the earliest US thinkers to have a contemporary influence outside the USA.

In addition to Emerson, transcendentalist thinkers included Orestes Brownson (1803–76), who searched the religious spectrum and ended his life as a Roman Catholic; Margaret Fuller (1810–50), the most outspoken feminist among the Transcendentalists; George Ripley (1802–80), the founder of Brook Farm (1841–7), a communal experiment that briefly attracted Nathaniel Hawthorne (1804–64) among others; and Bronson Alcott (1799–1888) and Elizabeth Palmer Peabody (1804–94), educational theorists. But it was Emerson who was the central figure and primary theorist of Transcendentalism, in part because he directly challenged the then dominant Unitarian orthodoxy of the Boston intellectuals of his day. The leader of the Unitarians was William Ellery Channing (1780–1842), who had challenged the earlier Puritan/Congregational orthodoxy by insisting that reason be applied to religion. This led to the 'higher criticism' that became the basis for serious Biblical scholarship, but it also led to a 'cold' religion that failed to attract the Transcendentalists, who also believed that there was a fundamental contradiction in Unitarianism's insistence on the compatibility of reason and the belief in miracles. A movement that had similar objections to Unitarianism but later joined with it was Universalism. Led initially by Hosea Ballou (1771–1852), Universalism has often been called the rural version of Unitarianism and stressed the power of God's love.

Emerson, who was an ordained minister, refused to give communion in his church, thus rejecting the miracle of transubstantiation, lost his pulpit and in 1838 gave a speech at Harvard Divinity School that was in many ways the founding moment of Transcendentalism. He was not invited back until after the end of the Civil War. Emerson's new religion was based on 'the infinitude of the private man' and stressed self-reliance, but not a self-reliance that would be recognized by the proponents of the 'self-made man' of capitalism and the Social Darwinists. Emerson's self-reliant person would be active in the world as a reformer.

Pre-war reform

The main debates over the Constitution were completed with its ratification in 1787 followed by the adoption in 1791 of the first ten amendments to the Constitution, known as the Bill of Rights, plus the adoption in 1798 and 1804 of two further amendments of a more technical nature. There followed a period in which the energies that had been expended in the constitutional debates seemed to move to more general social reform. As Emerson wrote to THOMAS CARLYLE (1795–1881) in 1840, 'We are all a little wild here with numberless projects of social reform. Not a reading man but has a draft of a new Community in his waistcoat pocket. I am gently mad myself, and am resolved to live cleanly' (*The Correspondence of Thomas Carlyle and Ralph Waldo Emerson 1834–1872*, 2nd edn, 2 vols, ed. Charles E. Norton. [Boston, MA: James R. Osgood, 1883], pp. 308–9).

These reforms included the abolition of slavery and the enfranchisement of women as well as much more wide-ranging programmes of social transformation. These latter movements gave rise to the establishment of Brook Farm, Fruitlands, Oneida and many other intentional communities/communitarian experiments, many inspired by either ROBERT OWEN (1771–1858) or CHARLES FOURIER (1772–1837).

The best-known result of the pre-war reform is an essay by HENRY DAVID THOREAU (1817–62), 'On the Duty of Civil Disobedience' (1849), which influenced MOHANDAS K. GANDHI (1869–1948) in India and, through Gandhi, Martin Luther King, Jr (1929–65) in the USA. Thoreau argued that one has a duty to disobey unjust laws. Thoreau is also known for his *Walden, or Life in the Woods* (1854), which recounts a period of self-reliance at Walden Pond where Thoreau demonstrated that one could live both fully and cheaply by withdrawing from the competition to do better than one's neighbours and living simply.

Another aspect of pre-war reform was feminism. Although feminism in the USA clearly pre-dates the nineteenth century, it was in the nineteenth century that it had its first real flowering. Feminist thought of the period included arguments for education of women and votes and equal rights for women. Women like Margaret Fuller, whose *Women in the Nineteenth Century* (1844) was an early feminist text, and Frances Wright (1795–1852) wrote and spoke in favour of such changes and tried to live lives reflecting their desire for the changed status of women, although they did not always do so successfully. The best-known document of the period was the 'Declaration of Sentiments' of 1848, adopted by the first women's suffrage convention held at Seneca Falls, New York. The 'Declaration of Sentiments' was modelled on the 'Declaration of Independence' with a virtually identical statement of basic principles followed by a list of grievances and insisting on the franchise as a way of solving these grievances. The other well-known document was the speech 'Ain't I a Woman' that was given by Sojourner Truth (1797–1883) in 1851 at another women's rights convention. In this speech the ex-slave reflects on the image of women as weak and refutes it using her experience as a slave, manual labourer and mother.

After the war, the female suffrage movement was defeated because the advocates of votes for male ex-slaves thought that including women would lead to the defeat of the attempt to expand the franchise. This did not end the campaign and in 1873 Susan B. Anthony (1820–1906) was found guilty of voting, and in a famous speech to the court challenged its right to try her. Other women, like Elizabeth Cady Stanton (1815–1902) tried to ensure that feminists sought a more wide-ranging equality than the franchise, but as a movement, it tended to become a single-issue campaign. At the end of the century, Charlotte Perkins Gilman (1860–1935) published *Women and Economics* (1898), a pioneering analysis of the economic disadvantages that women worked under and an argument for significant improvement.

Union/states' rights/slavery

The lead up to the Civil War focused on the related issues of slavery and the locus of power, related because if power was in the states, the South could protect its 'peculiar institution.' But if power was in the national government, the inevitable expansion of the USA west into areas where slavery was not economically feasible would upset the balance of power found at the beginning of the century and produce a system where non-slave states dominated. Thus, those thinkers who supported states rights or the supremacy of the union over the states supported those thinkers who supported or opposed slavery.

Slavery was defended and attacked on biblical grounds, but it was also defended by George Fitzhugh (1806–81) in his *Cannibals All!* (1857) as being a better system than the wage slavery of the North. While Fitzhugh romanticized slavery and assumed that all slave owners behaved as the best of them did, certain of his criticisms of the northern industrial system were well-taken, and near the end of the century, critics of industrial capitalism made many of the same points that Fitzhugh had made.

The opponents of slavery ranged across a wide spectrum in their attitudes toward slaves, with many of them believing that the slaves were inherently inferior. But they all agreed that owning another human being was wrong, whether from a humanitarian or a religious perspective. And the opponents of slavery, who included ex-slaves like Frederick Douglass (1817–95) and Sojourner Truth, did not have the delusions of a George Fitzhugh regarding the behaviour of slave owners. They knew that slaves were beaten, raped, ill-fed, clothed and housed, and often assumed to be and treated like animals.

Whether intending primarily to protect slavery or based on a principled belief in states' rights over against national power, the defenders of the states rarely mentioned slavery. The Constitution of the Confederate States of America (1861), which is almost identical to the United States Constitution and includes the Bill of Rights in the main text, barely refers to slavery, differing mostly on political and economic issues.

The most important theorist of states' rights was John C. Calhoun (1782–1850), whose theory of 'concurrent majorities' is now often equated with the consociational democracy being tried in countries like Lebanon. Calhoun argued for a system in which a group that constituted a majority in a particular place would have, in effect, a veto on a policy designed to be adopted nationally. All potential majorities would have to concur for a law to be passed.

Other defenders of states' rights argued, as many had at the time the Constitution was ratified, that the states had formed the national government and were, therefore, superior to it. Defenders of the Union argued, as had Alexander Hamilton, that something new had been created that took precedence over the states. The issue has not yet been entirely settled.

Reconstruction

During and after the war, there was a brief period when radical theorists proposed not merely ending slavery and giving male ex-slaves the vote, but went so far as to propose the enfranchisement of women and the integration of ex-slaves into the wider society. The intellectual leader of the Radical Republicans was Thaddeus Stevens (1792–1868), who was particularly concerned with the possibility of redistributing Southern land to ex-slaves so as to develop a black yeomanry because he believed that in addition to the vote, which he considered a minor issue, blacks needed equality of opportunity and equality before the law.

During the war, the Freedmen's Bureau was established with a view of bringing the ex-slaves into national life. Led by Robert Dale Owen (1801–77), a son of Robert Owen, the Freedmen's Bureau report proposed education, land and family stability as means of solving the problems brought on by the end of slavery. The focus of most was much more limited, the legal abolition of slavery and votes for male ex-slaves. With the assassination of Abraham Lincoln (1808–65), the focus turned to the reintegration of the South into the Union and concern with the ex-slaves virtually disappeared for some years, only to be resurrected by African Americans themselves.

At the turn of the century, two major African American thinkers emerged, BOOKER T. WASHINGTON (1856–1915) and W.E.B. DU BOIS (1868–1963), who represented diametrically opposed approaches to the racial situation in the USA. Washington counselled accommodation and acceptance of the reality of segregation and Du Bois counselled opposition. Washington's Atlanta Exposition address of 1895 argued that African Americans, then known as Negroes, were willing supporters of capitalism and that they accepted being primarily

agricultural and manual skilled workers. As head of Tuskegee Institute, Washington provided the type of education needed for these goals, while rejecting any comparison to white education, even rejecting the label 'college' for Tuskegee. At the same time, Washington also founded the National Negro Business League to encourage entrepreneurship, and he encouraged the development of black bankers, funeral directors, lawyers, physicians, teachers and so forth to serve the black community.

Du Bois, who had a doctorate from Harvard University, was a scholar and activist, publishing many books on the situation of African Americans in the USA. Du Bois changed his approach over his lifetime, becoming a Marxist and adopting a class analysis, but at the time of his disagreement with Washington, he argued that those blacks that were able, the 'talented tenth', should get the best university education possible. They should demonstrate that they were inferior to no one and then work to help achieve change for all African Americans.

Philosophy

In the last quarter of the nineteenth century and the first years of the twentieth, a tradition of US philosophy emerged, mostly from Harvard University. The founder of what came to be known as pragmatism was Charles Sanders Peirce (1839–1914), who, in 1877–8, published the first articles that gave rise to the tradition. Peirce, who was a pioneering thinker in logic and the philosophy of science, did not develop his original insights, and in fact later tried to separate himself from what became known as pragmatism. William James (1842–1910) developed Peirce's ideas, initially in his 'Philosophical Concepts and Practical Results' (1898) and then more fully in *Pragmatism* (1907). James, who had been first a scientist and then a professor of psychology before turning to philosophy, argued that philosophy should be concerned with the actual, concrete results of acting on philosophical concepts and that the success or failure of such action could be a test of their truth or falsity. JOHN DEWEY (1859–1952) applied the principles of pragmatism to education, arguing that the school should be both experimental and democratic, and include the pupils in the democracy. As a result, US conservatives blame Dewey for much of what they perceive to be wrong with US education.

The other significant US philosopher at the end of the nineteenth century, Josiah Royce (1855–1916), rejected pragmatism. Royce had been inspired by Georg Wilhelm Friedrich Hegel (1770–1831), as had Dewey early in his career. Royce, unlike Dewey, remained an Idealist and argued for a religious philosophy in works like *The Religious Aspect of Philosophy* (1885), a defence of theism, *The World and the Individual* (2 vols; 1899, 1901) and *The Problem of Christianity* (1913). In the last, he is somewhat less Hegelian, replacing his earlier insistence on the Absolute with a stress on the Universal Community.

Social Darwinism

A central issue for all thinkers in the latter part of the century was the impact of Charles Darwin (1809–82). For some the issue was evolution, for some it was the possible conflict between science and religion, and for others it was how to use Darwin's insights. There was, and still is, a strong anti-evolutionary current in US thought based on the belief that the Bible does not support evolution. But for most nineteenth-century thinkers, the question was how to reconcile science and religion, and, given the emergence of the 'higher criticism', many thinkers had no serious problem with rejecting a literal interpretation of the Bible in light of scientific evidence to the contrary.

One aspect of Darwin's language came to predominate in social theory, 'the struggle for survival'. What came to be called Social Darwinism was used to justify ethnic and racial discrimination, capitalism and the division between the rich and the poor. Social Darwinists argued that those who did well deserved to and those who failed also deserved to, and, in particular, that those who failed were not owed assistance by those who succeeded. They had no one to blame but themselves. The most important thinker taking this position was William Graham Sumner (1849–1910), whose essay 'The Absurd Effort to Make the World Over' (1894) can be taken as emblematic of the position.

The main spokesperson of the opposition to Social Darwinism was Lester Frank Ward (1841–1913), one of the founders of the discipline of sociology in the USA. He argued that evidence showed that co-operation and the ability to plan ahead were human characteristics. Thus people are disposed to and perfectly capable of modifying the natural and social environment for the betterment of all. Another opponent of Social Darwinism was Jane Addams (1860–1935), whose Hull House in Chicago and the settlement house movement that it inspired were based on the premise that it was social conditions, not inherent personal flaws, which produced poverty.

A critic of capitalism coming from a somewhat different perspective was Thorstein Veblen. His *The Theory of the Leisure Class* (1899) stressed the role in the operations of US capitalism of waste and 'conspicuous consumption', a phrase that came to be commonly used.

Utopianism

Among those social theorists who adopted the language of evolution for radical purposes was EDWARD BELLAMY. While utopianism has a strong presence throughout US thought, the most utopian moment in US history followed the publication in 1888 of Edward Bellamy's (1850–98) novel, *Looking Backward: 2000–1887*. It was followed over the next 25 years by over a hundred other utopias that responded to Bellamy directly, either positively or negatively, or, stimulated by the popularity of the form, provided alternative visions of the good life or the horrors of a potentially worse future. Some, like Ignatius Donnelly (1831–1901) and Jack London (1876–1916), provided both. Donnelly's *Caesar's Column* (1890) was almost wholly negative, depicting a class war and its results, while his *The Golden Bottle* (1892) presented a populist utopia in which readily available money frees the farmers and small businessmen from the dominance of capitalism. London's *The Iron Heel* of 1907 and 'A Curious Fragment' of 1908 presented the terrible future, including, as in Donnelly, class war, to be brought about by capitalism, while his 'Goliah', also from 1908 showed the better future to be achieved through socialism.

Socialism and anarchism

Although he downplayed the centralizing and non-democratic elements when he wrote *Equality* (1898), a sequel to *Looking Backward*, Bellamy's vision was based on state socialism, which he called nationalism because socialism had such negative connotations in the USA. But the main tradition of US socialism is democratic. While mostly a phenomenon of the post-First World War period, it had its roots in the late nineteenth century. The leader and theorist of democratic socialism during this period was Eugene V. Debs (1855–1926). The revolutionary socialists, a very small number, were led by Daniel De Leon (1852–1914).

While many commentators trace the origins of US anarchism to Thoreau, it is more accurately seen as first identified with Lysander Spooner (1808–87) and the immediate post-Civil War period. While Spooner had little immediate impact, he is of particular importance in that he developed a theory of anarcho-capitalism, which is arguably the chief US contribution to anarchist theory, albeit mostly in the late twentieth century. Spooner and other anarcho-capitalists believed that only capitalism fits with anarchism, that any collective system, such as those proposed by PIETR KROPOTKIN (1842–1921) or EMMA GOLDMAN (1869–1940), undermines personal freedom. Only personal, individual consent to collective arrangement is permissible. BENJAMIN R. TUCKER (1854–1939), writing later in the century, began a continuous US tradition of anarchism. Tucker's writings were close in spirit to Spooner's. While most modern anarchists are collectivists rather than individualists like Tucker or anarcho-capitalists like Spooner, US anarchism has always had a strong component stemming from these thinkers, together with a more collectivist strain stemming from Goldman.

The issues of the nineteenth century, particularly the relations of the states and the national government, the position of African Americans and women, and the benefits and problems of competition, remain in the twenty-first century. Religion as an important factor in US thought remains, although the specific issues are different. Philosophy has become more and more technical since the end of the nineteenth century but has also played a significant role in a wide variety of debates in US thought. Thus, the issues and ways of addressing them have changed in detail but often not in substance.

Further reading

Blanchard, Paula (1978) *Margaret Fuller: From Transcendentalism to Revolution*, New York: Delta/Seymour Lawrence.

Davis, William C. (1991) *Jefferson Davis: The Man and His Hour*, New York: HarperCollins.

DeRosa, Marshall (1991) *The Confederate Constitution of 1861: An Inquiry into American Constitutionalism*, Columbia: University of Missouri Press.

Faust, Drew Gilpin (ed.) (1981) *The Ideology of Slavery: Proslavery Thought in the Antebellum South, 1830–1860*, Baton Rouge: Louisiana State University Press.

Foner, Eric (1988) *Reconstruction: America's Unfinished Revolution 1863–1877*, New York: Harper & Row.

Francis, Richard (1997) *Transcendental Utopias: Individual and Community at Brook Farm, Fruitlands, and Walden*, Ithaca, NY: Cornell University Press.

Garvey, T. Gregory (ed.) (2001) *The Emerson Dilemma: Essays on Emerson and Social Reform*, Athens: University of Georgia Press.

Haynes, Stephen R. (2001) *Noah's Curse: The Biblical Justification of American Slavery*, Oxford: Oxford University Press.

Hofstadter, Richard (1955) *Social Darwinism in American Political Thought*, rev. edn, Boston, MA: Beacon Press.

—— (1963) *Anti-intellectualism in American Life*, New York: Alfred A. Knopf.

Kateb, George (1995) *Emerson and Self-Reliance*, Thousand Oaks, CA: Sage.

Kuklick, Bruce (1977) *The Rise of American Philosophy: Cambridge, Massachusetts 1860–1930*, New Haven, CT: Yale University Press.

Mabee, Carleton, with Susan Mabee Newhouse (1993) *Sojourner Truth: Slave, Prophet, Legend*, New York: New York University Press.

McCardell, John (1979) *The Idea of a Southern Nation: Southern Nationalists and Southern Nationalism, 1830–1860*, New York: W.W. Norton.

Myerson, Joel (ed.) (2000) *Transcendentalism: A Reader*, Oxford: Oxford University Press.

Nelson, Bruce C. (1988) *Beyond the Martyrs: A Social History of Chicago's Anarchists, 1870–1900*, New Brunswick, NJ: Rutger's University Press.

Niven, John (1988) *John C. Calhoun and the Price of Union: A Biography*, Baton Rouge, Louisiana: Louisiana State University Press.

Peters, John Leland (1956) *Christian Perfectionism and American Methodism*, New York: Abingdon Press.

Rose, Anne C. (1981) *Transcendentalism as a Social Movement, 1830–1850*. New Haven, CT: Yale University Press.

Sargent, Lyman Tower (ed.) (1997) *Political Thought in the United States: A Documentary History*, New York: New York University Press.

Stauffer, John (2002) *The Black Hearts of Men: Radical Abolitionists and the Transformation of Race*, Cambridge, MA: Harvard University Press.

Veysey, Laurence (ed.) (1973) *The Perfectionists: Radical Social Thought in the North, 1815–1860*, New York: John Wiley & Sons.

Yellin, Jean Fagan and Van Horne, John C. (eds) (1994) *The Abolitionist Sisterhood: Women's Political Culture in Antebellum America*, Ithaca: Cornell University Press Published in co-operation with the Library Company of Philadelphia.

LYMAN TOWER SARGENT

ANTHROPOLOGY AND RACE

Although it is never possible to explain to our ultimate satisfaction why a particular idea comes to the fore, there are many reasons why late eighteenth- and nineteenth-century thinking, especially in Europe and the USA, became steadily fixed on the idea of race. The development of science generally, especially natural science; the secularisation of Europe that went hand in hand with the discovery that man could be classified with the animals; and the subsequent development of the theory of evolution are all major turning points. Nevertheless, it is also important to note that for centuries notions such as the 'noble savage' and the 'wild man' had fed the European imagination, fuelled the desire for travel (and embellished the tales of travellers) and driven the colonial adventure. Now science was not only providing rational explanations for the natural world, including human beings, but also giving credence to long-standing fantasies about different, non-European peoples. Sometimes – as in Thomas More or Michel de Montaigne – these early-modern theories of difference had been quite open to 'otherness'; one of the striking things about the race-thinking that developed in the nineteenth century is its hardening of lines of difference, its drawing of racial distinctions that was no less inquisitive about 'the other', but that sought to establish clear demarcation lines. One of the things that needs explaining, in other words, is how a theory that necessitated the coming into contact of different peoples (necessary for ethnological research) aimed at classifying types and drawing rigidly maintained boundaries, and went hand in hand with a fear of pollution and miscegenation, finally developing into a theory of racial hierarchy that – like the closely allied fields of primitivism and orientalism – was more a reflection of the 'self' than it was an attempt to understand the 'other'.

The attempt to draw up a natural history of mankind, classifying human groups in the same way as plants and animals were now being classified – according to kinship rather than external similarity – began in the late seventeenth to mid-eighteenth centuries with the pioneering work of John Ray (1627–1705), regarded as the father of natural history, Carolus Linnaeus (1707–78), Georges-Louis Leclerc (1707–88), Conte de Buffon (1707–88) and Johann Friedrich Blumenbach (1752–1840), among others (for example François Bernier, Francis Willughby, Georges Dagobert, Baron Cuvier). Though both still creationists, Buffon, in his *Histoire naturelle, générale et particulière*, and Linnaeus, with his *Systema Naturae*, sought to understand human beings as simply part of the world of natural occurrences. Linnaeus distinguished different races on their ability to use reason, with *Homo Europaeus* at the top; Buffon believed that God had created man in his image, and that the different races were marked by their deviation from the norm, which he considered to be the white European. Both theories are significant in that, although they see reason as the faculty that distinguishes human beings from animals, they nevertheless feel comfortable classifying man with the animals. These ideas were taken further by Johann Gottfried von Herder (1744–1803), IMMANUEL KANT (1724–1804), Barthold G. Niebuhr (1776–1831), Johann Wolfgang von Goethe (1749–1832), Johann Gottlieb Fichte (1762–1814) and Carl Gustav Carus (1789–1869), to the point at which the idea of fully created species had been replaced with natural history, and pre-Darwinian theories of evolution.

Despite the theoretical sophistication of Kant and Goethe (who did not reduce human beings to their physicality, unlike many modern race-scientists), it is Blumenbach who is accredited as the father of modern anthropology. His *De Generis Humani Varitate Natura* (*The Natural Variety of Mankind*, first edition 1775) was the first study that argued for the importance of skull shape in determining racial classification, a claim that endured for more than a century and a half (and is currently becoming fashionable again in certain quarters).

Blumenbach's inquiries inspired the work of many followers, among them James Cowles Prichard (1786–1848), considered the founder of English anthropology, with his *Eastern Origins of the Celtic Nations* (1831) and *Researches into the Physical History of Mankind* (1836–47), and Jean Baptiste, Chevalier Lamarck (1744–1829), author of the *Philosophie zoologique* (1809). The development of this type of anthropology – aimed primarily at measuring physical characteristics – was furthered by the studies of men such as the Swede Anders Retzius (1796–1860), who introduced the cephalic index to anthropology; Paul Broca (1824–80), the French craniologist and brain surgeon; Robert Knox (1791–1862), Edinburgh anatomist and author of *The Races of Man* (1850); JOSEPH COMTE DE GOBINEAU (1816–82), foremost proponent of the fixity of racial differences whose *Essay on the Inequality of the Human Races* (1853–5) made him the hero of a later generation of racists; T.H. HUXLEY (1825–95), leading British evolutionist; and Rudolf Virchow (1821–1902), the anti-Darwinian craniologist who carried out extensive surveys of the physical characteristics of German schoolchildren.

A recognisably modern, scientific race theory first emerged in the 1850s and 1860s. None of its proponents can be considered anthropologists in the sense we mean that word today; first and foremost they were zoologists, botanists, philologists, anatomists, archaeologists, physicians and lawyers. What they were interested in was explaining the physical origins of mankind, in particular how mankind diverged into different 'stocks' or 'races'. Many were polygenists, that is, in contrast to the biblical tale of creation, they believed in the existence of several distinct human species. And they took for granted the idea that these races were of unequal worth.

Polygenism was challenged by the view that the races were not separate species, but that they had evolved and interbred. CHARLES DARWIN's *Origin of the Species* (1859), along with the work of HERBERT SPENCER, was the cause of much debate, and eventually a reorientation of the discipline. Yet the eventual eclipse of polygenist thinking (which took longer than one might suspect, especially in the USA where it was a useful justification for white supremacism) did not mean a rejection of the hierarchical race-thinking that accompanied it. Quite the contrary; the rise to prominence of monogenism actually strengthened the racist case. Furthermore, Darwinism – contrary to the implications of Darwin's thinking on the meaning of species – did not mean an overturning of conventional methods of human classification; the broad outlines of racial evolution had already been suggested by Kant and many others, and the *a priori* assumption that races could be distinguished and then placed in a hierarchy of value remained in place. What Darwin and Spencer accomplished was to suggest that the laws of social life were subject to the same trends of evolutionary change that characterised natural history.

Hence towards the end of the nineteenth century, the emphasis of thinkers such as Kant and Hegel (see HEGEL AND HEGELIANISM) on race as only one part of the human animal – the other part being reason or spirit – was overturned so that the emphasis was squarely placed on physical characteristics alone. 'Race is everything,' said Houston Stewart Chamberlain, echoing Disraeli, 'there is no other truth. And every race must fall which carelessly suffers its blood to become mixed.' This final statement reveals that understanding race theory solely through the writings of 'great men' does not suffice; actually, for all the clashes between supporters and opponents of Darwin, or between polygenists and monogenists, the idea of 'race' held connotations that were extremely widely shared in the nineteenth century, meshing as it did with notions of European superiority that accompanied industrialization, technologization and imperialism. The hardening of attitudes to race that occurred at the century's end was connected to the challenges to that instinctive sense of superiority being brought about by the rise of mass politics, feminism, immigration, fears of racial degeneration, 'restless natives' and economic decline.

In all of these developments in race-thinking the early anthropological societies played a key part. They promoted the new science, gradually turning it from an amateur pursuit into a discipline in its own right. The history of anthropology's institutionalization in Britain is perhaps the best illustration of the development of the discipline during the nineteenth century. The earliest such society was the Ethnological Society of London (ESL), formed at the end of 1843 by Richard King (1811–76) and Thomas Hodgkin (1798–1866) out of the remains of the earlier Aborigines Protection Society (APS). The latter, a group led by evangelicals and Quakers, was a humanitarian body that campaigned against slavery in the colonies, and much of this sentiment accompanied the interest of the ESL in studying 'savage' and 'primitive' societies. The ESL sought to explain the origins of human beings through culture, language and archaeology, as well as through physical traits. It believed, in other words, in evolution, and in the unity of mankind.

Only a few years after its foundation, the ESL's premises were being challenged by the new emphasis on the analysis of physical characteristics. In opposition to the ESL, the Anthropological Society of London (ASL) was set up in 1863. Its founder, James Hunt (1833–69), a student of human speech, was much influenced by the racial theories of Knox; after three unsatisfying years of membership of the ESL (he joined in 1856) Hunt left and set up the ASL. Hunt's polygenist assumptions, which he derived from Knox, are revealed most clearly in his famous essay 'On the Negro's Place in Nature' (1863), a classic statement of mid-nineteenth-century Anglo-Saxon supremacism.

After several years of wrangling, however, the two groups compromised and merged (though not without continued strife) to form the Anthropological Institute of Great Britain and Ireland in 1871. With a membership rarely exceeding 500, its members crossed the spectrum from the amateurs interested in prehistoric archaeology and folklore to the military men who had encountered 'primitives' during their service in the colonies, to a minority of medics and natural scientists who made up the scholarly end of the society. What is striking is that, in the context of post-Darwinian evolutionary theory, the Institute (which became the Royal Anthropological Institute in 1907) moved steadily away from the humanitarian premises that accompanied the dominant 'ethnological' approach of the 1870s and moved ever closer to a biological determinism after the mid-1880s. Scientists had always assumed the existence of a connection between physical and mental attributes, and the developments in anthropological methods of the 1880s onwards seemed to breathe new life into established patterns of race-thinking. Lorimer notes that the acceptance of an international definition of the cephalic index; developments in psychology, especially the 'localization of functions of the brain'; the growth of anthropometry (testing the sensory and motor functions); and the application of statistical methods to biological criteria (biometry) all revivified the tradition of physical anthropology. Photography also played a major role in objectifying 'primitive' people in the field. Although the polygenists eventually lost out to the Darwinians, their debates ensured that within the multiplicity of discourses about race in the late nineteenth century, there was an increasing tendency towards biological determinism, accompanied by a rigidification of the boundaries between the 'races'. Yet it is important to bear in mind that, until the late 1890s, the Anthropological Institute had ties with the Folklore Society and the Society of Antiquaries; only in the twentieth century would the distinctive trait of modern anthropology – fieldwork – give the discipline the rigour it required. The Cambridge University trip to the Torres Straits (1898) organised by Alfred Cort Haddon (1855–1940) is generally considered to be the first major example of anthropological fieldwork.

George Stocking, the pre-eminent historian of anthropology, sums up the three phases of the discipline's history in Britain during the nineteenth century: first, an older, 'ethnological' tradition that derived from the APS a humanitarian instinct, and that sought to investigate 'primitive' culture, language and archaeology – as well as bodies – as a way of understanding the common origin of human beings; second, the growth of an 'anthropological' tradition with an emphasis on more narrowly physical characteristics, which sought to provide a polygenist account of the emergence of 'human races in the context of a pre-Darwinian tradition of comparative anatomy'; third, an emerging 'evolutionary' tradition at the end of the century, which sought to account for 'the problem of the discovery of human remains in the context of Darwinian biological evolutionism'. The third group were, by contrast to the second, still 'ethnologicals', that is to say, they were not radical, racist polygenists. Rather, they were scientifically more sophisticated, and had close links to the scientific establishment. Nevertheless, their emphasis was, unlike the first group, firmly on the physical; hence men such as Augustus Lane Fox (1827–1900), John Lubbock (1834–1913), William H. Flower (1831–99), John Evans (1823–1908), John Beddoe (1826–1911) and even E.B. Tylor (1832–1917) contributed to the hardening of race theory that took place at the end of the century by stressing the dominance of nature over nurture and by failing to call into question the racial typologies (as opposed to their evolution) that had been in place for more than a century. The logic of evolution lost out to a rhetoric of heredity, that is, a return of the belief in the immutability of racial types.

By the end of the nineteenth century, then, anthropology had become synonymous with physical anthropology. The mere description of living peoples was considered ethnology, which was interesting as a first step, but basically a highbrow form of travel writing usually accompanied by an unscientific and effete humanitarianism. What anthropologists were interested in was the origin of human beings. They believed that societies could be classified on a trajectory of evolutionary development that ran: savage–barbaric–primitive–civilized. Hence the idea of race was so attractive to anthropologists, who saw 'primitive' peoples as 'stuck' at a stage of development that reminded them of European children, and thus legitimized their 'disappearance' at the hands of white colonial settlers as a 'natural' consequence of racial pro-gress. Many colonial genocides were justified and swiftly forgotten on that basis, with the total eradication by the British of the Tasmanians, the archetypal 'Naturvolk', being an excellent example. The European tradition of the 'noble savage', once biologized and refracted through the lenses of race theory, became less a romantic tale of repulsive but sympathetic Calibans and more an obstacle to the spread of white civilization. 'Primitives' simply had to be eradicated, as the laws of Nature had revealed. Penetrating the 'heart of darkness' and expediting Nature's work for her was considered to be humane for all concerned, as Daniel Brinton, a leading US anthropologist put it:

> The Bechuana kraal which refuses to have a grand opera house and electric lights, if the European sees fit to put them there, will be wiped out of existence. So will every tribe, every nation, every race, which sets forth to oppose the resistless flow of civilised progress.

Hence, the hardening of race theory at the end of the century was not solely a result of developments in science and methodology, but also owed much to the rapidly changing social and political context of the 1880s and 1890s.

The histories of other anthropological asso-ciations also tell a story of a biologization of anthropology towards the end of the century. The French split between the Société Ethnologique de Paris and the Société d'Anthropologie de Paris remained in place far longer than that of their London equivalents, however. Nevertheless, the work of such thinkers as Gobineau, Broca and Georges Vacher de Lapouge (1854–1936, author of *Les Selections sociales* in 1896 and *L'Aryen* in 1900) did much to encourage an intuitive link between anthropology and a belief in rigid racial schemas. The French obsession with pro-natalism was encouraged by anthropological race-thinking, which fed by the end of the century into the science of puericulture, the French equivalent of eugenics.

Yet the work of Gobineau and Lapouge was more influential in Germany than in France. Although it took much longer for anthropology to become institutionalized in Germany, once it did so the country soon became one of the leading centres of research into primitive societies and race. The discovery of the Neanderthal skull in 1856, suggesting that Germany was the birthplace of mankind, was an enormous boost to the nascent science. When the Berlin Anthropological Society was founded in 1869 at its head was Rudolf Virchow, a critic of Gobineau's and Lapouge's Aryanism. Yet the popularization of anthropology through museums such as Berlin's Museum für Völkerkunde (1886), along with the rise of Social Darwinist thinking epitomized by men such as Otto Ammon (1842–1916), who measured the skulls of nearly 28,000 military recruits in Baden and uncovered racial differences between Germanic long-heads and Asiatic round-heads within the population, did much to overturn this initially relatively liberal consensus in a fairly short space of time. Indeed, despite generally being regarded by historians as an enemy of anti-Semitism, Virchow's own massive study of the racial characteristics of German schoolchildren, which explicitly separated Jews from non-Jews on the basis of hair, eye and skin colour, paved the way for thinking in terms of Jews and Germans as separate races.

The rise of Nordicism and race-hygiene in Germany – especially epitomized by the work of Alfred Ploetz (1860–1940), Fritz Lenz (1887–1976), Erwin Baur (1875–1933), Ernst Rüdin (1874–1952), and Eugen Fischer (1874–1967) – continued apace in the early twentieth century even while anthropology elsewhere (especially in Britain) was beginning to question the racist assumptions it had developed throughout the nineteenth. Perhaps the relatively small size of the German empire (which it lost altogether in 1918) meant that, whilst British anthropologists could discover in the field that their theories bore no relation to the people they were studying, German anthropologists turned inwards to focus on 'degenerates' at home. Cer-tainly the theories of Gobineau, Ammon and Chamberlain were important in helping Alfred Rosenberg (1893–1946, Nazi philosopher and Minister for the Occupied Territories of the Soviet Union after 1941) and Hans F.K. Günther (1891–1968, known as 'der Rassen-Günther' because of his obsession) formulate their explicitly Nazi race theories. And the continuity of personnel from Felix von Luschan (1854–1924, the first Professor of Anthropology in Berlin in 1900) to Fischer (who began his career studying the so-called Rehoboth Bastards in German Southwest Africa and even-tually became head of the Kaiser-Wilhelm Institute for Anthropology, Human Heredity and Eugenics in Berlin during the Third Reich), to Otmar von Verschuer (1896–1969, who worked with Fischer on the issue of Jewish *Mischlinge*, or 'mixed-race' individuals) and Josef Mengele (1911–84, a student of Fischer's and the 'angel of death' of Auschwitz) is well-documented.

The standard textbooks of anthropology that became fashionable in the years before 1900 illustrate this drift towards biological determinism. E.B. Tylor's *Anthropology* (1881), unlike his more famous *Primitive Culture* (1871), gave considerable space to racial determinism. And Augustus Keane (1833–1912) wrote two popular textbooks, *Ethnology* (1895) and *Man, Past and Present* (1899), which, like many other books of the period, provided descriptions of the characteristics – both physical and mental – of the world's racial groups. A similar approach was taken by John Beddoe, in his *The Races of Britain* (1885), which sought to distinguish racial types according to his 'index of nigrescence'; Paul Topinard (1830–1911), in his *Anthropology* (French edn 1874; English edn 1894), which distinguished ethnography ('the general science of nations') from anthropology ('the branch of natural history which treats of Man and of the races of Man'); Daniel Brinton, whose *Races and Peoples* (1890) argued that the 'leading race in all history has been the white race'; Joseph Deniker, librarian of the natural history museum in Paris and author of *The Races of Man* (1897); and William Z. Ripley, author of *The Races of Europe: A Sociological Study* (1899), which argued that 'Race denotes what man *is*; all these other details of social life represent what man *does*.' The examples could be multiplied many times over. Yet however these writers chose to divide up the races (most followed the pattern: Caucasian, Mongoloid, Ethiopian, American and Malayan), the most benign conclusion was that such pure races did once exist, even if they were now interbred, and the most radical that the racial types are immutable and easily ranked in terms of quality and achievement. An increasing hereditarian obsession with skin colour tended to favour the latter conclusion, despite the difficulties in establishing clear lines between one pigment and another.

All of these trends – physical anthropology, race-hygiene, Social Darwinism, biometrics, anthropometry, the growing obsession with race defined by skin colour – coalesced at the end of the nineteenth century with the eugenics movement. In Britain, where the term eugenics was coined by Darwin's cousin Francis Galton (1822–1911), the movement had both a scholarly wing, led by Karl Pearson at University College London, and a popularizing wing in the Eugenics Education Society, led for some years by Darwin's son Leonard. Although its interests dovetailed with broad public concerns about racial degeneration, crime, immigration and 'national efficiency', it made little headway in terms of legislation, mainly thanks to the existence of a public welfare bureaucracy. In the USA, however, under the influence of Charles B. Davenport, Henry H. Goddard, Paul Popenoe, Roswell Johnson and other scientists, the eugenics movement was responsible for sponsoring legislation in more than half of the states of the union that ended in the sterilization of thousands of supposedly 'feeble-minded' or 'congenitally ill' people. The same is true for the Scandinavian countries, where the sterilization campaigns prove that eugenics was by no means simply a concern of the right; for these countries all had progressive, technocratically minded, social democratic governments. Eugenics movements were influential in Russia, Italy, France, Romania, Latin America and China. Especially in Germany, eugenics, particularly in its 'hard', racist form, grew in influence after the Great War, and informed policy during the Weimar and Nazi years. Research into race in these years ended not just by stigmatizing and sterilizing criminals, alcoholics and epileptics; it was also one of the strands of thought that fed the Holocaust.

It has been generally assumed that in the rest of the world at this time, this 'hard' form of 'mainline' eugenics declined in importance. But this decline in eugenics has been much exaggerated. After all, even up to the outbreak of the Second World War, British left-wing scientists such as J.B.S. Haldane (1860–1936) and Lancelot Hogben (1895–1975), who protested about the abuse of science by the Nazis, nevertheless continued to accept that research into race *per se* was perfectly valid. They continued to use the basic textbook *Human Heredity* by Lenz, Baur and Fischer that took for granted the assumption that race was a meaningful term, and failed to see the implication of modern genetics that race, basically defined as groups of different colour, had no scientific validity, since genetic differences *within* any chosen population group are always greater than genetic differences *between* any chosen population groups. In the USA, revised editions of Paul Popenoe and Roswell Johnson's standard textbook *Applied Eugenics* continued to appear into the 1940s. Furthermore, the aspirations of eugenics – the creation of 'better babies' – continued to echo in popular culture, as they still do.

Nevertheless, the rise of cultural anthropology, especially in the USA, had a decisive impact on eugenics and on the practice of physical anthropology. This attack on physical anthropology was led by a man trained in the discipline, Franz Boas. Although later on other scholars such as Jacques Barzun, Ashley Montagu, A.C. Haddon and Julian Huxley also explicitly took on the notion of race, Boas's wide-ranging studies on race, language and culture, and his devotion to political activity fighting racism, ensured that his school of cultural anthropology gradually came to dominate US academic anthropology. His demonstration that the children of immigrants to the USA had larger heads than their parents effectively exploded the myth that the physical characteristics that supposedly defined race were immutable. He took on Lothrop Stoddard and Madison Grant, the most outspoken defenders of racist physical anthropology, and worked hard to ensure that his students, among them Alfred Kroeber, Margaret Mead and Ruth Benedict, were all well-placed within academia. In Britain, physical anthropology gave way to the functionalism of Bronisław Malinowski, A.R. Radcliffe-Brown and Edward Evans-Pritchard. Even though it was shaped by the colonial adventure, this school developed (almost unintentionally) from its own methods a critique of that adventure that has assured the continued relevance of anthropology in the post-Second World War period. Indeed, it has left the self-reflexive and self-critical anthropological community better placed than many other disciplines to resist the 'return of racial science' that has, in the shape of socio-biology, evolutionary psychology and genetic counselling, according to many, marked the start of the twenty-first century.

References

Beddoe, John (1885) *The Races of Britain: A Contribution to the Anthropology of Western Europe*, Bristol: J.W. Arrowsmith.

Brinton, Daniel G. (1890) *Races and Peoples: Lectures on the Science of Ethnography*, New York: N.D.C. Hodges.

Chamberlain, Houston Stewart (1912 [orig. 1899]) *The Origins of the Nineteenth Century*, London: John Lane, The Bodley Head.

Lorimer, Douglas (1988) 'Theoretical Racism in Late-Victorian Anthropology, 1870–1900', *Victorian Studies* 31, 3: 405–30.

Ripley, William Z. (1899) *The Races of Europe: A Sociological Study*, London: D. Appleton & Company.

Stocking, George W., Jr (1971) 'What's in a Name? The Origins of the Royal Anthropological Institute (1837–71), *Man*, new series, 6, 3: 369–90.

Topinard, Paul (1894 [orig. 1874]), *Anthropology*, trans. Robert T.H. Bartley, London: Chapman & Hall.

Further reading

Arendt, Hannah (1979), *The Origins of Totalitarianism*, new edn, San Diego: Harcourt Brace.

Brantlinger, Patrick (1995), ' "Dying Races": Rationalizing Genocide in the Nineteenth Century', in Jan Nederveen Pieterse and Bhikhu Parekh (eds) *The Decolonization of Imagination*, 43–56, London: Zed Books.

Hannaford, Ivan (1996) *Race: The History of an Idea in the West*, Baltimore: Johns Hopkins University Press.

Stepan, Nancy (1982) *The Idea of Race in Science: Great Britain, 1800–1960*, Basingstoke: Macmillan.

Stocking, George W., Jr (1982), *Race, Culture, and Evolution: Essays in the History of Anthropology*, Chicago: University of Chicago Press.

Voegelin, Eric (1940) 'The Growth of the Race Idea', *Review of Politics*, 2: 283–317.

SEE ALSO: anti-colonial movements and ideas; Boas, Franz; Darwin, Charles; Disraeli, Benjamin; Galton, Francis; Gobineau, Joseph; Hegel and Hegelianism; historiography and the idea of progress; Huxley, T.H.; Kant, Immanuel; Social Darwinism; Spencer, Herbert

DAN STONE

ANTI-COLONIAL MOVEMENTS AND IDEAS

During the nineteenth century, few Europeans believed that the indigenous inhabitants of overseas colonies constituted nations with a right to immediate self-government. Even white settlers were seen as members of essentially colonial societies that would retain a link with the mother country for many years to come. As a result, most contemporaries took it for granted that multi-ethnic overseas empires were a legitimate and enduring form of government. Opposition to colonialism was limited, and even critics of empire such as free traders and humanitarians believed that, although open to abuses, colonial rule was ultimately a necessity. As a result, criticism of colonial rule centred largely on particular examples of perceived misgovernment, seeking to reform rather than abolish errant colonial states. Even in the colonies, for most of the period anti-colonial movements attacked the form that colonialism took in particular instances rather than colonialism itself. Coherent anti-colonial ideologies did not emerge until the very end of the nineteenth century, when Liberals in Britain and Marxists in Europe began to portray colonialism as the result of basic inequalities in Western society, an illegitimate form of rule that served the interests only of small parasitic groups of capitalists. At the same time, truly anti-colonial movements began to emerge in some colonies in the form of organized and politicized nationalism, posing a serious challenge to imperial rule.

It was once argued that in Britain, the nineteenth century could be divided up into periods of imperialism and anti-imperialism. In particular, it was argued that the mid-nineteenth century saw the emergence of a general lack of enthusiasm for and even hostility towards empire, led by free-trade thinkers such as Richard Cobden and John Bright. For free traders, the ideal world order was not one based on hostile competition between mercantilist empires seeking to control more and more colonial territory. Rather, a global economy based on international free trade offered the prospect of a peaceful order based on co-operation and mutually beneficial exchange. Empire was an unwelcome obstacle to this pacific future, and Cobdenites attacked the commercial interest groups who perpetuated mercantilism and criticized the record of British colonial administration in India. Free traders also argued that money spent on fighting for and administering colonies was essentially wasted, and supported the granting of self-government to Britain's settler colonies.

However, this critique was not entirely novel. In the wake of the Napoleonic Wars some had been particularly disapproving of the expense and corruption associated with the 'old colonial system'. Moreover, it is widely recognized that even if thinkers like Cobden were opposed to colonialism in theory, in practice they never pressed for the end of empire. Most called only for reform that would eliminate the more corrupt aspects of colonial administration, and for an end to mercantilist protectionism. Indeed, free trade became an essential part of British imperialism, not its antithesis (see IMPERIALISM AND EMPIRE).

Similarly, humanitarian criticism of colonial rule in the nineteenth and early twentieth centuries was aimed more at the reform than the abolition of empire. This tendency can be traced to the legacy of EDMUND BURKE, who in the late eighteenth century had emphasized the concept of trusteeship (see IMPERIALISM AND EMPIRE). Together with the evangelicalism of the Christian missionary movement that flourished from the late eighteenth century onwards, humanitarianism influenced most nineteenth-century critics of empire. However, what these people challenged was not the legitimacy of imperial rule itself, but rather the way that particular colonies were run.

This reflected the limitations of the concept of trusteeship, which saw colonialism as a legitimate form of rule, in the short to medium term at least. For in order for Britain to fulfil the duties of trusteeship, and to ensure that indigenous peoples were protected from the damaging effects of the expansion of white settlement and Western commercial enterprise, it was vital that colonial regimes remain in place, and even that they assume greater responsibilities. While humanitarians proved highly critical of colonial regimes that failed to protect indigenous peoples from Westerners, or even co-operated in their exploitation, they believed that colonial states were ultimately a necessity. As a result, some humanitarians found themselves arguing that the extent of colonial rule and the scope of colonial intervention should if anything be increased, in order to better fulfil the duties of trusteeship.

Humanitarians continued to adopt this position even at the end of the nineteenth century, when hardening European racial attitudes and heightened competition between rival imperial powers led to much more vicious forms of colonial exploitation. This was certainly true in the case of the British journalist E.D. Morel, who played a crucial role in the formation of the Congo Reform Association, which sought to expose King Leopold II's ruthless regime in the Congo. The Association targeted in particular the array of coercive methods sanctioned by the state to force local peoples to help extract primary produce from the region, including inter-tribal war, slaving, human mutilation and cannibalism. Rather than attack colonialism itself, however, Morel worked within the parameters of British free-trade imperialism, and was supported by merchants who sought to free the Congo from Leopold's exclusive trading regime. The Congo Reform campaign also drew on substantial support from the Protestant missionary movement, which was not only appalled by the depredations of Leopold's colonial state, but was also threatened by the expansion of rubber production, which took potential converts out of the missions and into the colonial economy. Gathering international protest eventually obliged the Belgian government to take control of the Congo away from Leopold in 1908.

Another notable humanitarian critic of rapacious colonialism was the British civil servant, Sir Roger Casement. Acting in the capacity of a British consular official and aided by local missionaries, Casement undertook his own investigations in the Congo, reporting his findings in 1903. He went on to expose abuses in the Amazonian rubber trade, and was knighted for his work in 1911. However, like Morel, Casement failed to develop a coherent critique of the nature of colonialism and its evils. Indeed, his growing commitment to the Irish nationalist cause led him (after resigning from the British civil service in 1913) to support German imperialism, despite its genocidal consequences in Southwest Africa, as a means of toppling British power. Casement transformed himself from a humanitarian seeking to use British imperial influence as a means to correct local colonial abuses, into a revolutionary Irish nationalist fundamentally opposed to British overseas rule. Perhaps as a result of the ambiguities and contradictions of his position, few have been able to satisfactorily explain the volte-face that eventually led Casement to support armed rebellion in Ireland in 1916, resulting in his execution by the British government. Casement's life and death provide us with an illustration of the difficult relationship between humanitarianism and imperialism. They also remind us of the links between anti-colonial movements and the growth of nationalism in what some would describe as Britain's oldest colony, Ireland.

It was only at the beginning of the twentieth century that British critics of empire began to move beyond the limits of humanitarianism, and develop theories of colonialism that attacked the very basis of colonial rule. Perhaps the most significant figure in this regard was the radical Liberal journalist, economist and political thinker J.A. HOBSON, who forwarded what has proved to be one of the most influential and enduring theories of the causes of imperialism.

In his classic text *Imperialism, a Study* (1902), Hobson attacked the 'New Imperialism' that had emerged in the last decades of the nineteenth century as the Western powers set about partitioning Africa and Asia into colonies (see IMPERIALISM AND EMPIRE). Unlike humanitarian critics of empire, Hobson argued that colonial rule in these areas was basically illegitimate, as Western imperialists had no real intention of spreading 'civilisation', despite their stated intentions. Rather, the new colonies had been annexed merely in order to allow certain parasitic interest groups to pursue their own selfish ends. This argument was based on a conspiracy theory that Hobson had picked up from Cape Liberals while visiting South Africa in 1899, and which he developed in his subsequent writings about the origins of the South African War. Hobson argued that the war was the result of the machinations of gold and diamond mining capitalists, who had misled the British government and public into supporting their scheme to oust the government of the Transvaal and establish a more pliant colonial government that would protect their economic interests. In *Imperialism*, Hobson extended this analysis, claiming that a range of 'economic parasites', particularly financiers and investors, were urging governments to conquer new colonies.

Hobson argued that the roots of imperialism were essentially economic, the result of the unequal distribution of the profits of nineteenth-century industrial growth. Capitalists had retained and saved the lion's share, denying their workers a proper wage. As a result, Hobson claimed, the masses had little money to spend on consumption, and could not provide a domestic market big enough to sustain industrial expansion. Profit thus became 'surplus capital' that could not find sufficient returns from domestic investment. Instead, investors sought overseas opportunities where returns would be higher, and encouraged governments to engage in the imperialist struggle to monopolize profitable investment markets.

As a Liberal, Hobson believed that surplus capital, and thus imperialism, could be eliminated without toppling the overall capitalist system. Domestic policies aimed at confiscating excess profits and redistributing wealth would enable the workforce to spend their income on the products of domestic industry, creating outlets for domestic investment and removing the need for imperial domination. A more radical interpretation was provided by European Marxist thinkers (see MARX AND MARXISM) who, while agreeing with Hobson's definition of the causes of imperialism, often differed as to what the final result of imperial expansion would be, and as to how the colonial order would come to an end.

During the early twentieth century a number of Marxists developed theories intended to explain the 'New Imperialism' that were implicitly, and often explicitly, anti-colonial. One of the earliest Marxist thinkers to develop a serious critique of colonialism was Karl Kautsky. Like Hobson, Kautsky stressed that imperialism was the result of 'underconsumption' in Western capitalist countries. However, while he did give some consideration to the role of investment, Kautsky argued that industry rather than finance was the motivating force behind imperial expansion, as industrialists sought overseas markets for goods that could not be sold at home. Kautsky believed that the capitalist system could survive the search for overseas markets by developing peaceful ways to divide the world into agreed spheres of influence.

The German Marxist ROSA LUXEMBURG posited a more revolutionary alternative in her *Accumulation of Capital* (1913). Like Hobson and Kautsky, Luxemburg argued that Western capitalism was producing 'surplus value' that was being exported to the non-capitalist world. However, Luxemburg argued that this export of surplus was gradually destroying the non-capitalist societies of the colonial world. When there were no more non-capitalist societies left to eliminate, no more colonies left to annex, then the capitalist system would collapse, ushering in the socialist revolution. Luxemburg was one of the few early twentieth-century critics of empire to escape the Eurocentrism and racism shared by most contemporaries, of whatever political hue, and to stress the damage that imperialism did to indigenous peasant societies.

However, in the short term at least, the Austrian Marxist Rudolph Hilferding provided a more influential discussion of colonialism in his *Finance Capital* of 1910. Hilferding argued that, in an age of growing corporate ownership and industrial concentration, the banks and credit institutions that funded the cartels and trusts had become a powerful force in their own right, even coming to dominate the forces of industrial capital. According to Hilferding, the new breed of finance capitalist sought to protect profits by creating national and international monopolies, and by supporting a strong state that would set up tariff barriers around both internal and colonial markets. As states competed with each other for colonial territories, seeking to monopolize access to markets and supplies of raw materials, warfare and opportunities for socialist revolution would follow.

Hilferding's work provided much of the inspiration for perhaps the most widely read Marxist analysis of imperialism, V.I. LENIN's *Imperialism, the Highest Stage of Capitalism* (1916). Drawing on Nikolai Bukharin's *Imperialism and the World Economy* (1916), which refined some of Hilferding's ideas, Lenin emphasized the role of 'monopoly capitalism', banks, trusts and cartels. Lenin also drew on Hobson's work, claiming that the primary aim of monopoly capitalism was not to export surplus goods, but rather to invest surplus capital in 'backward countries' where returns would be high. According to Lenin, monopoly capitalism sought exclusive access to these markets, turning them into colonies and leading to international competition and war. For Lenin, the First World War was proof that capitalism had reached its 'highest stage', and was in a crisis that could be resolved only by a combined proletarian and colonial revolution.

However, even during the early twentieth century, it seldom seemed that the prospects for colonial revolution were good. Not only were anti-colonial movements rare, but also those colonial opponents of empire that did exist tended not to develop coherent ideologies. As in the metropole, many colonial critics of empire focused on reform.

In Britain's colonies of settlement, there was little criticism of the imperial link itself. Local leaders could prove particularly hostile to the Colonial Office, which was perceived to be too remote from and ignorant of local concerns, or to the decisions of individual British governments on particular issues. However, this seldom amounted to serious questioning of the legitimacy of the imperial link. One of the few occasions when rebellion did break out in a colony of settlement was in 1837, when ethnic tensions between French, British and Irish settlers in Lower Canada (modern Quebec) erupted into violence. The rebellion, led by the French Canadian Louis Joseph Papineau, primarily reflected disagreement as to the form that political institutions within a British colony should take, and to the relative weight given to different groups in society in the decision-making process, rather than basic hostility to the imperial link. Similarly, the Canada First movement of the early 1870s, led by English-speaking Canadians, espoused only a mild nationalist agenda, calling for Britain to cede treaty-making powers to the

Canadian federal government. Most members of Canada First were careful to stress their loyalty to the empire, and while one member, Goldwin Smith, espoused Canadian union with the USA, others remained firmly committed to the imperial bond. Some even backed imperial federation. For men like G.T. Denison, imperial unity was rendered attractive due to an antipathy towards the USA that sprang in part from United Empire Loyalist traditions cherished since the American Revolution. This historic animosity was compounded by a fear of US economic and territorial expansion, and dislike of US political institutions. It was only the French Canadians who developed an anti-colonial identity in the years before the First World War, articulated by Henri Bourassa in response to the heightened English Canadian pro-empire sentiment that accompanied the South African War.

Similarly, anti-colonial thought in Australia was shallow and of little lasting significance. Perhaps the most important opponent of the imperial link in the 1880s was the Sydney *Bulletin*, a magazine that developed a more-or-less coherent anti-imperial ideology. Much of this was based on the argument that Australian links with Britain had been tainted from the outset by convictism, and rested on the economic exploitation of Australia for the benefit of British capitalists and warmongers. Anti-imperialism was part of the magazine's democratic, republican ethos, and fell on fertile ground during the lean years of economic depression. Some historians have questioned the significance of the *Bulletin's* anti-colonial views, however, and it is important to note that, by the end of the 1890s, the *Bulletin* had lost much of its anti-imperial tone. The federation of the Australian colonies into a single Commonwealth in 1901 was accompanied by little hostility towards the imperial link.

In tropical colonies, anti-colonial sentiment again lacked ideological coherence. For much of the century, resistance to the increasingly powerful colonial state, and to the demands of plantation agriculture, took place on an unorganized, non-political and largely non-ideological daily basis, as individuals engaged in acts of passive resistance and sabotage. Resistance often continued to run though traditional channels, as the dissatisfied attacked local figures of authority and indigenous collaborators, rather than targeting the colonial system as a whole. In some areas, resistance

to colonial rule was sharpened by religious sensibilities. Islam provided one of the most powerful mobilizing ideologies of resistance, and led to some notable triumphs for those who sought to challenge colonial rule, such as the Mahdist movement in Sudan. In some areas, resistance was inspired by millenarian beliefs, often with disastrous results for indigenous participants, as in the case of the Xhosa cattle killing of 1856 in the eastern Cape, and the Maji Maji rising in German East Africa in 1905.

However, resistance seldom boiled over into outright rebellion. When it did, as in the 1865 Morant Bay Rebellion in Jamaica, it did not generate coherent anti-colonial ideologies. Even the Indian Mutiny and Rebellion of 1857 reflected a range of specific grievances, including the resentment of local leaders recently displaced from positions of power, the economic grievances of peasants, and fears among Indian troops that they would be forced to break religious observances while in army service. Mutineers and rebels were not united by an overarching anti-colonial ideology, a factor that in part explains the lack of organization and eventual failure of the rising. More successful was the Maori King movement, which matched British claims to sovereignty in New Zealand by installing an indigenous monarch. This provided an enduring focus for Maori organization in the King Country of the North Island.

However, only at the very end of the nineteenth century, in two specific areas, did anything approaching an anti-colonial ideology emerge in the colonial world. In South Africa, the late nineteenth century saw the efflorescence of a fiercely anti-British, republican nationalism led by President Paul Kruger of the Transvaal (also known as the South African Republic). Kruger sought to rally the support of what he viewed as an Afrikaner nation. Krugerite nationalism bore more in common with later resistance movements in the tropical dependencies than with the national identities that were emerging in the other colonies of settlement. Convinced of the hostility of the British towards his republic, and disgusted by the pusillanimity of the Cape Dutch, Kruger sought to build on a heroic set of myths dating back to the Great Trek of 1835–8, when a number of Dutch-speaking settlers, the *Voortrekkers*, had moved away from the British-controlled Cape Colony and into the interior of the continent, setting up the Transvaal and the Orange Free State. Kruger developed what has been called the 'Afrikaner

Civil Religion'. This combination of state-sponsored ceremony and nationalist mythology drew on Calvinist imagery in order to present the *Voortrekkers* as God's chosen people, who with divine aid had triumphed over their Zulu enemies during the Battle of Blood River (1838). Kruger's efforts were supported by burgeoning cultural organizations such as the Genootskap van Regte Afrikaners (Fellowship of True Afrikaners). Boer nationalism was also given a fillip by the Transvaal's victory over the British during the First Anglo-Boer War in 1881, a year that also saw the first major celebration of the anniversary of Blood River.

The anti-colonial side of this nationalist ideology became increasingly apparent as, following the discovery of gold near Johannesburg in 1886, the British government sought to increase its control over the affairs of Southern Africa. This process culminated in the Second Anglo-Boer War of 1899–1902, now usually referred to as the South African War. During the war, Boer tracts such as *Eene eeuw van onrecht* (*A Century of Wrong*, first published in Dutch in 1899) by Jan Christiaan Smuts and J. de Villiers Roos, argued for the existence of a century-long antagonism between Boer nationalism and British imperialism, brought to the boil by the machinations of the region's cosmopolitan mining capitalists. This strand of thought remained a powerful influence over the subsequent emergence of Afrikaner nationalism, and would ultimately help legitimate South Africa's withdrawal from the British Commonwealth in 1961.

It is important to note however that, in the wake of the war, some Afrikaners argued that Boer and Brit would have to be reconciled under the aegis of the British Empire, in order to secure their mutual interests. Even Smuts, who would later become one of the great heroes of the empire, was by 1902 calling for the reconstruction of South Africa on the basis of white unity. The ambiguity of Afrikaner responses to the British Empire also perhaps helps account for the inability of the African National Congress, founded to resist the increasingly segregated racial order of twentieth-century South Africa, to either enlist British humanitarian support or develop along unequivocally anti-colonial lines before the First World War.

The second area where anti-colonialism became a significant force during the early twentieth century was India. Here, criticism of colonial rule became politicized and ideological, as high-caste Hindus (who had undergone Western education in preparation for careers in the lower echelons of the colonial administration) began to question the established order. Western education helped spread the idea that Indians would eventually enjoy constitutional self-government and full civil rights in their own country. Most significantly, such ideas were expressed by the Indian National Congress, founded in 1885 as the first all-India political organization.

Initially, Congress was keen to stress its loyalty to the empire, and its activities focused on gaining greater scope for Indian participation in the running of the colonial state. In some ways, Congress in its early years could be seen as a means to allow high-caste Hindus to gain more opportunities for collaboration, rather than as a means to challenge the colonial order. This began to change however following the appointment of Lord Curzon, who acted as the British viceroy in India between 1898 and 1905. Curzon pushed through a range of administrative and economic reforms that rode roughshod over Congress, making a mockery of the idea of consultation. By the end of Curzon's period in office, criticism of British rule had reached unprecedented proportions. G.K. Gokhale, the president of Congress, argued for example that British rule in India had become subordinated to selfish military, economic and civil service interest groups. Similarly, a growing body of work such as Dadabhai Naoroji's *Poverty and Un-British Rule in India* (1901) and R.C. Dutt's *The Economic History of India in the Victorian Age* (1906) argued that British rule had involved the drain of wealth from the Indian countryside, as taxes were levied in order to pay for imperial military and administrative expenditure, and to service debt repayment to British capitalists. As a result, it was argued, Indian industry had been crushed. Such writing inspired radicals such as B.G. Tilak to break away from the moderates in Congress, and turn to direct, violent action in order to challenge British rule.

In conclusion, it can be argued that the nineteenth century saw the emergence of few serious challenges to colonialism. In the case of Britain, criticism of empire was limited by the basic precepts of free trade and humanitarian ideology. It was only at the beginning of the twentieth century that Liberal thinkers in Britain, and Marxists on the Continent, began to challenge the essential legitimacy of colonial rule. This had little effect on imperial policy, however, in much the same way that anti-imperial republican rhetoric in the USA did not prevent the annexation of the Philippines in 1898. Similarly, in the colonies themselves, critics of empire often pursued particular schemes of reform, or engaged in non-political resistance at the local level, rather than challenge the overarching colonial system. It was only with the rise of nationalism in South Africa and India that serious challenges to imperial rule emerged. Given the fact that nationalist movements were also beginning to emerge in many other African and Asian colonies by the eve of the First World War, this did not bode well for the future of empires. Finally, it is interesting to note that in Britain, Europe and the colonies themselves, Liberal, Marxist and nationalist critics of colonialism all drew on common themes, in particular the idea that imperialism was essentially economic in its origins, and that the colonial order served only narrow, parasitic interests groups. This latter argument can be traced back to eighteenth- and early nineteenth-century attacks on the mercantilist order, and it remained one of the pillars of anti-colonial ideology throughout the twentieth century.

Further reading

Brown, J.M. (1994) *India – The origins of an Asian democracy,* Oxford: Oxford University Press.

Fieldhouse, D.K. (1973) *Economics and empire, 1830–1914,* London: Weidenfeld and Nicolson.

Moodie, T.D. (1975) *The Rise of Afrikanerdom,* Berkeley, Los Angeles and London: University of Califonia Press.

Porter, A. (1999) 'Trusteeship, Anti-slavery, and Humanitarianism', in A. Porter (ed.) *The Oxford History of the British Empire Volume 3: The Nineteenth Century,* 198–221, Oxford: Oxford University Press.

SEE ALSO: Bolivar, Simon; Gandhi, Mohandas K.; Hobson, J.A.; imperialism and empire; Lenin, V.I.; the nation, nationalism and the national principle

SIMON J. POTTER

ARNOLD, MATTHEW (1822–87)

The most important British interpreter of the concept of 'culture' as a critique of vulgar democracy and overzealous evangelicism, Arnold was born at Laleham, near Staines, on 24 December 1822, the eldest son of the Rev. Thomas Arnold, historian and headmaster of Rugby School. Educated at Winchester, Rugby and Balliol College, Oxford, he was elected a Scholar in 1840, won the Newdigate Prize for English verse in 1843 on the subject of Cromwell, and became Fellow of Oriel College in 1845. In 1851 he became one of the Lay Inspectors of Schools, under the Committee of Council on Education, which post he retained until 1886. He published several volumes of poetry, and became Professor of Poetry at Oxford in 1857. There followed a comparative study of the educational systems of France, Germany and Holland, which Arnold had been sent to study in 1859–60. A further visit instigated by the Royal Commission on Middle-Class Education in 1865 resulted in another volume on the subject. Amongst his other later works were *Lectures on the Study of Celtic Literature* (1868), *Literature and Dogma; an Essay towards a better Apprehension of the Bible* (1873) and *Saint Paul and Protestantism* (1873). Arnold became, consequently, an extremely influential literary critic.

Though he was increasingly anti-clerical, Arnold was apprehensive of the threat of radical social and political reform, particularly when allied to a puritan spirit. As early as 1848 Arnold warned, during the Chartist riots of that year, 'the hour of the hereditary peerage and eldest sonship and immense properties has struck', a consequence of which was that 'a wave of more than American vulgarity, moral, intellectual, social' was 'preparing to break over us'. This signalled the dominant theme that was central to his most important work, *Culture and Anarchy* (1869). Prior to this, however, Arnold published *A French Eton; or, Middle Class Education and the State* (1864), which argued against the prevailing *laissez-faire* individualism of the mid-Victorian period that it was necessary for the state to act as a mediating agency, rising above the conflicts of social class, and engaging in the cultural guidance of substantial parts of the population. The model to be used here was the French 'Republic of Letters', with an Academy centrally engaging in a constant process of cultural criticism, and promoting and organizing the most talented intellects in order to guide public opinion in a suitable direction.

The extension of the franchise promoted by the 1867 Reform Act, and the threat it announced of the growing social and political power of middle- and lower middle-class Dissenters, forms the immediate backdrop to *Culture and Anarchy. An Essay in Political and Social Criticism*. Arnold's attack commenced with his last Oxford lecture, on 'Culture and Its Enemies', in 1867. The preface to the book states its purpose as being 'to recommend culture as the great help out of our present difficulties', defining culture as 'the pursuit of our total perfection by means of getting to know, on all the matters which most concern us, the best which has been thought and said in the world; and through this knowledge, turning a stream of fresh and free thought upon our stock notions and habits'. Arnold denied that culture was 'bookish, pedantic, futile', insisting it could be derived even from reading newspapers. This 'total perfection', moreover, was not only individual, but also the development of a 'harmonious perfection' in the entire society. The enemy of 'many-sided development' or 'totality', correspondingly, was the 'Hebraising' tendency to sacrifice all sides of the personality to religiosity: this was the besetting sin of the smug, narrow, provincial Nonconformists. At the opposite extreme, however, Benthamism, or 'an inadequate conception of the religious side in man', is also criticized. Arnold noted that the USA already exemplified a society well advanced down this road; he later lectured there in 1883–4, and seemingly met few prepared to refute this view.

In Chapter One of *Culture and Anarchy*, 'Sweetness and Light', Arnold emphasized that things of the mind could be desired both for their own sake, for the 'genuine scientific passion' of seeing them in their true light, and for the sake of the 'love of perfection', which involved 'clearing human confusion, and diminishing human misery, the noble aspiration to leave the world better and happier than we found it'. The goal of culture is thus social perfection, not resting content with what each 'raw person may like', but getting 'ever nearer to a sense of what is indeed beautiful, graceful, and becoming, and to get the raw person to like that'. The dominant ethos of the era is addressed in the second chapter, 'Doing As One Likes', or the 'assertion of personal liberty', which Arnold associates with the Manchester School of political economy. More important than liberty, he contends, 'is to like what right reason ordains, and to follow her authority'. But no traditional state, and certainly not one led by either the aristocracy or middle class, is capable of offering such leadership, only a state composed of 'our collective best self, of our national right reason'. In Chapter Three Arnold delineates the chief characteristics of the main classes, the barbarians (aristocracy), philistines (middle classes) and populace (working classes) in order to ascertain where the 'best self' in each class is located. Chapter Four, 'Hebraism and Hellenism', contrasts the ideal of puritan zealousness to that of the Greek theory of culture, with its emphasis on perfecting both individual and society in this life, and upon the creation of works of beauty, a theme continued in the fifth chapter. Arnold concludes by examining some of the reform agenda of the upcoming middle classes, though this contributes little to his central argument. Arnold died on 15 April 1887.

Further reading

Allott, K. (1955) *Matthew Arnold*, London: Longmans, Green.

Carroll, J. (1982) *The Cultural Theory of Matthew Arnold*, Berkeley: University of California Press.

Collini, Stefan (1988) *Arnold*, Oxford: Oxford University Press.

Harvey, C. (1931) *Matthew Arnold: A Critic of the Victorian Period*, London: J. Clarke.

McCarthy, Patrick (1964) *Matthew Arnold and the Three Classes*, New York: Columbia University Press.

SEE ALSO: intellectuals, elites and meritocracy; novels, poetry and drama; Romanticism, individualism and ideas of the self; theories of education and character formation

GREGORY CLAEYS

B

BABEUF, GRACCHUS (1760–97)

Gracchus Babeuf was a sheep turned wolf, a feudal tax lawyer before 1789, a radical journalist after, who came to the view that the political revolution would fail unless it was accompanied by social revolution. The 1789 revolution, civil and foreign war led to desperate food shortages in the early 1790s and serious unemployment. Babeuf struggled with a blueprint for a solution. He toyed with a variety of ideas: land might be redistributed equally, which he calculated would give every head of household 14 acres, a progressive tax could be introduced to have a similar impact on the redistribution of wealth, or private ownership might be eliminated. The Jacobins instituted a maximum price for food to try to alleviate shortages. Babeuf proposed that distribution should be collectivized to stop hoarding. Money, individual trade and competition should be abolished. A central store for food and other necessities should be set up and goods given to everyone, in return for the work that he or she had done. He argued that these changes had to be forced upon society by violent revolution, followed by a short period of dictatorship. Babeuf believed that his ideas were fundamentally in harmony with those of Robespierre and the Jacobins; and much later Buonarroti popularized this view, but it is very unlikely that the Jacobins of the 1790s would have agreed.

Babeuf was one of the first to assert that modern society was driven by warfare between the classes, to use the term proletarian and to believe that planned revolution was the solution. He hoped to exploit class hostility to bring about revolution. As editor of the *Tribun du peuple*, Babeuf claimed he was the head of a 'plebeian army', a vanguard party that would spearhead revolution and engage mass worker support. Instead, in the spring of 1796 one of the police spies in his Society of Equals denounced them. Babeuf was guillotined.

Babeuf was forgotten by Thiers and the early historians of the Revolution. That he was remembered was due to the popularization of his ideas by his fellow conspirator, Philippe Buonarroti. In 1828, years after his release from prison, Buonarroti published an account of the conspiracy that was regarded by the early socialists, as PROUDHON later said, as 'our Bible'. In the 1920s the Russian Communists were charmed to identify their ideas with Babeuf, although lively ideological disputes developed about which faction could claim him as their own. It has been suggested that, far from being the first communist, Babeuf was a backward looking pessimist who did not realize that capitalism would bring an expanding economy and who, at best, hoped that his plans would lead to equalization of misery. A message couched in these terms would have found few takers, even in a bad year like 1796. The Equals actually promised their supporters happiness for all. Babeuf's message that the proletariat was naturally revolutionary was taken up by BLANQUI in the 1830s.

Further reading

Birchall, I.H. (1998) *The Spectre of Babeuf*, Basingstoke: Macmillan.

Rose, R.B. (1978) *Gracchus Babeuf. The First Revolutionary Communist*, Stanford: Stanford University Press.

Sewell, W. (1989) 'Beyond 1793: Babeuf, Louis Blanc and the Genealogy of "Social Revolution"', in F. Furet and M. Ozouf, *The French Revolution and the Creation of Modern Political Culture*, vol. 3: *The Transformation of Political Culture 1789–1848*, 509–26, Oxford: Pergamon Press.

Thomson, D. (1947) *The Babeuf Plot: The Making of a Republican Legend*, London: Kegan Paul, Trench, Trubner & Co.

SEE ALSO: Blanqui, Louis-Auguste

PAMELA PILBEAM

BAGEHOT, WALTER (1826–77)

Walter Bagehot is probably the most quotable of nineteenth-century British political thinkers and writers. His pithy, often provocative, and some-times aphoristic statements have proved eminently long-lived, even memorable. He has been called '[t]he Greatest Victorian' by G.M. Young, and early twentieth-century US President Woodrow Wilson, an avid reader of Bagehot himself, has remarked that 'To ask your friend to know Bagehot is like inviting him to seek pleasure.' This is not as much of an exaggeration as it may sound to readers familiar only with his more 'serious' major works. Much of Bagehot's journalistic writing, to say nothing of his correspondence, displays a refreshing facetiousness that was not common among Victorian writers. His most ambitious work was *Physics and Politics* (1872), but he is more remembered to subsequent generations as the author of *The English Constitution* (1867), a work that proved particularly influential in some respects (both books were first published in several instalments as articles and later in book form). Yet, Bagehot was not a systematic political thinker or philosopher, but rather primarily a journalist with philosophical interests. Perhaps the most accurate description of the nature of the bulk of Bagehot's work has been given by himself while categorizing the writings of another Victorian, Nassau W. Senior, after the latter's death. He wrote that Senior was 'a publicist', which meant:

> He devoted much of his time to temporary politics, but has always dealt with them in an abstract and philosophical manner. He always endeavoured to deal with the permanent aspects of them, he addressed only thoughtful men, he was a 'didactic member' of the republic of letters; and this we suppose is the idea of a publicist.
>
> (Bagehot 1965–86, Vol. II: 374–86)

Born on 3 February 1826 at Langport, Somerset, the son of a Unitarian banker, Bagehot was edu-cated at Langport Grammar School and then at Bristol College. Due to his Unitarian background, he could not study in Oxford or Cambridge, so he went to University College London in Gower Street instead (UCL being, since its founding by Benthamite Radicals, secular and welcoming to all, independently of religious affiliation). During his student years he developed a close friendship with R.H. Hutton (later to become the editor of the *Spectator* as well as Bagehot's co-editor of the *National Review* between 1855 and 1864). At UCL Bagehot was awarded a BA with first-class hon-ours in Classics (1846) and an MA (accompanied by a gold metal) in Philosophy (1848). Between 1848 and 1852 he studied Law; as a result he was called to the Bar but never practised. Between the summer of 1851 and the summer of 1852 the young Walter (twenty-six now, indecisive about his future direction and somehow depressed) spent a year in Paris, a sojourn which worked wonders for his moods. Besides observing French life and mores, he had the chance to witness the events associated with the *coup d'état* of President Louis Napoleon Bonaparte in December 1851. He was favourably disposed to the President's action (as he reported in a letter:

> I wish for the President decidedly myself as against M. Thiers and his set in the Parlia-mentary World; . . . and also as against the Red party who, though not insincere, are too abstruse and theoretical for the plain man. . . . I am in short what they would call a *reaction-naire*, and I think I am with the majority – a healthy habit for a young man to contract.
>
> (Bagehot 1956–86, XII: 327)

It was from Paris that he sent his notorious 'Letters on the French *Coup d'Etat*', a series of seven letters to the *Inquirer*, a Unitarian paper (between 10 January and 6 March 1852). The provocative lightness of tone of these letters incurred a great deal of criticism; even his close friend Hutton admitted that 'They were light and airy, and even flippant, on a very great subject' (quoted in Varouxakis 2002: 87). Bagehot's main argument in these letters – to the horror and disgust of mainstream liberal opinion back in Britain – was that, first of all, Louis Napoleon's *coup d'état* was necessary and therefore justified, in order to end the constitutional uncertainty and the paralysing fear of the comfortable classes about imminent revolution; and, second, that, regarding the overall and long-term issue of the appropriate constitutional settlement for France, what the President seemed to be proposing, a system with a strong Head of the Executive accompanied by a representative body with only a consultative role, without legislative or veto powers, was ideal for France given the attributes of the French 'national character'. The French were 'a vain, a volatile, an ever changing race', 'a *mobile*, a clever, a versatile, an intellectual, a dogmatic nation'. Due to these traits, French parliamentary assemblies were always bound to be quarrelsome and divisive, as compromise was anathema to the French mind (Varouxakis 2002: 86–90). In articles-letters with titles such as 'On the Aptitude of the French Character for National Self-Government' (Bagehot 1965–85, IV: 50–3, 54–62) he depicted these national character traits, offering a memorable comparison and contrast between what he presented as the 'clever'-yet-unsuccessful French character and the 'stupid'-yet-successful English national character (Varouxakis 2002: 119–22).

He was, however, to change his mind about the appropriateness of Louis Napoleon's system even for the 'volatile' French themselves, let alone as a model for other nations, such as newly emerging nations like Italy (even including Britain, as some were arguing in the 1860s). In a great number of articles in *The Economist* during the 1860s, Bagehot offered what has been perhaps the most classic and the sharpest description of the political system embodied by Louis Napoleon (now Emperor Napoleon III), what he called 'Caesarism'. His grasp of how exactly this system worked, and what were the reasons for its popularity as well as its major weaknesses, was not the least of Bagehot's achievements as an observer of the contemporary European political scene (Varouxakis 2002: 90–6, 98–99, 164–70).

In 1861 Bagehot became editor of *The Economist*, succeeding his father-in-law, founder and proprietor of the paper, James Wilson, MP – whose daughter Eliza he had married in 1858. Besides his leading role in the running of *The Economist* and the *National Review*, he was also one of the people (including, among others, George Eliot and G.H. Lewes) who established the Liberal *Fortnightly Review* in 1865. Both *The English Constitution* and *Physics and Politics* were first published as series of articles in the *Fortnightly*

Review before they came out in book from (*The English Constitution* starting from May 1867; *Physics and Politics* starting from November 1867). He was on intimate terms with the leaders of the Liberal Party and he tried several times (unsuccessfully) to enter Parliament as a Liberal MP. He was respected as an authority in financial matters (no lesser a figure than Gladstone asked for his advice at least twice).

As befits a man as influenced by Burke as he was, Bagehot has been claimed by some as a Conservative and by others as a Whig (Jones 2000: 68). He clearly was not a democrat. Like many Victorian Liberals as well as Conservatives, he feared the consequences of universal manhood suffrage, of giving power proportionate to their numbers to the ignorant 'multitude'. However, this does not mean that Bagehot had no wish to have them educated gradually – but rather just take advantage of their ignorance as has been argued (Smith 2001: xxii, xxvi–xxvii). It has to be remembered that 'Bagehot's cast of thought... was dynamic', which is the reason why he was critical of static views of 'the foundations of communal cohesion' (Jones 2000: 67). Thus, Bagehot argued that liberalism – with which he identified – consisted in a quest for equilibrium between the 'predominance of the politically intelligent' and the 'gradual training of the politically unintelligent' (Jones 2000: 70). In the same spirit, in a review of MILL's *Considerations on Representative Government* in *The Economist* (11 May 1861), Bagehot 'defined liberalism as "the faith in the possibility, nay the duty, of constant political expansion – of drawing a larger and larger portion of the population into the circle of political duties which connect them with the government, give them a control over it, and interest in what it does"' (Jones 2000: 70).

Bagehot is most remembered for some of the arguments he put forward in *The English Constitution*. Among those arguments two stand out. In the first place, he dismissed what he presented as the orthodox misreading of the Constitution, the 'literary theory' of the Constitution, as he called it, to the effect that power was divided between separate branches, legislative, executive and judicial (separation of powers) or balanced in a mixed system (crown, Lords and Commons). Most subsequent commentators agree that he overplayed the prevalence of these views, which were already becoming obsolete before he wrote. This being as it may, clearly it was he who most famously proposed the alternative view that in fact the 'efficient secret' of the British Constitution was cabinet government, that is, 'the close union, the nearly complete fusion of the executive and legislative powers', which was effected by the cabinet, which joined them together. According to Bagehot the cabinet was 'a committee of the legislative body selected to be the executive body'. As a result, it was the House of Commons (which was in a position to choose and dismiss the cabinet) that was the ruling body, exercising the effective sovereign power (Jones 2000: 66–7; Smith 2001: xi–xii).

In the second place, Bagehot is still remembered and quoted in textbooks for having formulated the distinction between the 'dignified' and the 'efficient' parts of the constitution. The efficient parts were the House of Commons with the cabinet, which had to do the business of government, and the dignified parts were the monarchy and the House of Lords, which provided the former with the legitimacy they needed in order to rule, thanks to the instinctive and unreflecting deference of the masses to the monarchy and, more generally, to the *theatrical show* of society'.

Bagehot has been charged 'that he seriously – and influentially – misread the nature of the constitution in a way that masked the full potential power of government in the British system' (Smith 2001: xxvi). On the other hand, Vernon Bogdanor has seen in him a 'founding father' of British political science, in 'groping towards something very much like the modern notion of "political culture", basic elements of which were those norms and values which affected behaviour' (quoted in: Smith 2001: xxvi).

Finally, there is a most important aspect of Bagehot's thought that needs to be examined and highlighted here. He was, next to Mill, one of the two Victorian thinkers most keen to establish a 'scientific' study of what they called 'national character'. For, as we have already seen, although today he is remembered mainly thanks to *The British Constitution*, his most ambitious work, and therefore the most important in his own eyes, was *Physics and Politics.* The latter book was 'one of the earliest attempts to work out the implications of Darwinism for social thought' (Jones 2000: 67), and directly dealing with national character. In *Physics and Politics* Bagehot addressed explicitly and head on the question (which, he wrote, had 'puzzled' him a lot) whether there is *one* character for an entire

nation and how it came to be formed and to change. The book was subtitled: *Or thoughts on the application of the principles of 'Natural Selection' and 'Inheritance' to political society.* And Peter Mandler is right in maintaining that this title (and for that matter its opening pages) have misled commentators into taking it as clear evidence of the biologising effect of Darwinian thought' (2000: 234). Yet it was not, for Bagehot (whatever he may have written earlier, in his youth) explicitly rejected biological racial inheritance as well as climate as explanations of how each national character was formed or changed. So, what accounted then for the diversity among nations and national characters that he thought was obvious and indisputable? 'But what are nations? What are these groups which are so familiar to us, and yet, if we stop to think, so strange; which are as old as history . . . ? What breaks the human race up into fragments so unlike one another, and yet each in its interior so monotonous?' (Bagehot 1965–86, VII: 65). He discarded the commonplace explanation that such distinctions could be accounted for 'by original diversity of race'. He retorted that there might have been originally distinct great racial groups, but that this could not account for subsequent differentiations. Instead, Bagehot argued that nations were the product of two great processes: 'one race-making force which, whatever it was, acted in antiquity, and has now wholly, or almost, given over acting'; and 'the other the nation-making force . . . which is acting now as much as it ever acted, and creating as much as it ever created' (Bagehot 1965–86, VII: 67).

According to Bagehot, national character was the result of chance predominance of some types and 'unconscious imitation' by the rest. What was at work was the principle of 'elimination', the 'use and disuse' of organs that naturalists spoke of. 'At first a sort of "chance predominance" made a model, and then invincible attraction, the necessity which rules all but the strongest men to imitate what is before their eyes, and to be what they are expected to be, moulded men by that model' (Bagehot 1965–86, VII: 37–8). It was not easy, he conceded, to understand the effect of ordinary agencies upon the character: 'We get a notion that a change of government or a change of climate acts equally on the mass of the nation, and so we are puzzled – at least I have been puzzled – to conceive how it acts.' But such changes, he maintained, did not at first act equally on all people in the nation. 'On many, for a very long time, they do not act at all. But they bring out new qualities, and advertise the effects of new habits.' As a result, 'the effect of any considerable change on a nation is thus an intensifying and accumulating effect'. It acted with its maximum power only on 'some prepared and congenial individuals'; in them 'it is seen to produce attractive results, and then the habits creating those results are copied far and wide' (Bagehot 1965–86, VII: 80; cf. ibid. 121).

References

Bagehot, W. (1965–86) *The Collected Works of Walter Bagehot*, ed. N. St John-Stevas, 15 vols, London: The Economist.
Jones, H.S. (2000) *Victorian Political Thought*, Basingstoke and London: Macmillan.
Mandler, P. (2000) '"Race" and "Nation" in Mid-Victorian Thought', in S. Collini, R. Whatmore and B. Young (eds) *History, Religion, and Culture: British Intellectual History 1750–1950*, 224–4, Cambridge: Cambridge University Press.
Smith, P. (2001) 'Editor's Introduction', in W. Bagehot, *The English Constitution*, vii–xxvii, Cambridge: Cambridge University Press.
Varouxakis, G. (2002) *Victorian Political Thought on France and the French*, Basingstoke: Palgrave.

Further reading

Burrow, J.W. (1983) 'Sense and Circumstances: Bagehot and the Nature of Political Understanding', in S. Collini, D. Winch and J.W. Burrow, *That Noble Science of Politics: A Study in Nineteenth-Century Intellectual History*, 161–82, Cambridge: Cambridge University Press.
Sisson, C.H. (1972) *The Case of Walter Bagehot*, London: Faber & Faber.
St John-Stevas, N. (1959) *Walter Bagehot: A Study of his Life and Thought together with a Selection from his Political Writings*, London: Eyre & Spottiswoode.
Vile, M.J.C. (1967) *Constitutionalism and the Separation of Powers*, Oxford: Oxford University Press.

GEORGIOS VAROUXAKIS

BAKUNIN, MIKHAIL (1814–76)

Mikhail Aleksandrovich Bakunin, revolutionary anarchist, is now best known as an opponent of Karl Marx (1818–83) (see MARX AND MARXISM). He was born into the Russian nobility, and, although the family was not wealthy, he led an idyllic life on the family estate outside Moscow until, in 1828 at age 14, he was sent to the Artillery School in St Petersburg. Expected to follow family tradition and have a military career, Bakunin chafed under military discipline and was dismissed

from the school in 1834, and, after brief service, he retired from the military in 1835. From then on Bakunin led a peripatetic existence moving to Moscow and then to Germany, ostensibly for an education that would allow him to teach Philosophy. Bakunin rejected the discipline of education almost as much as he had that of the military, and instead began a life-long commitment to the European radical and reform movements. He moved to Zurich, then to Paris, then to Belgium, in each case having to leave the country because of his political activities. He was sentenced to death in Saxony, which commuted the sentence and sent him to Austria, where he was again sentenced to death. The sentence was again commuted, and he was sent to Russia, which had earlier stripped him of his titles of nobility, and was imprisoned in St Petersburg. Family influence combined with illnesses brought on by 6 years in prison allowed him to be exiled to Siberia. Four years later, he escaped from Siberia and travelled to Europe via Japan and the USA. In Europe he travelled from revolt to revolt, country to country, living off friends and publishers' advances for books he never completed. Bakunin was, for much of his life, a professional revolutionary. Bakunin began to formulate his anarchist theories in about 1864–5 and wrote most of the works he is remembered for between 1867 and 1874. In 1874, near the end of his life, Bakunin concluded that statist forces had temporarily won the battle, and that, while they could be resisted, they would dominate for 10 to 15 years.

Bakunin is notorious for the last sentence in his first published article, 'The Reaction in Germany' (1847), that 'The passion for destruction is a creative passion, too' (Bakunin 1973: 58) and his involvement with Sergei Gennadievich Nechaev (1847–82) in writing the notorious 'Catechism of a Revolutionary' (1869), now known to have been almost entirely the work of Nechaev. Bakunin was a revolutionary, and believed that the state and Church must be destroyed in the process of creating a free society, but he did not believe in violence for its own sake. His frequent references to destruction related to his belief that revolution would be based on the mass uprising of those with nothing to lose. They would be a truly destructive force, but such destruction would be creative in that it would sweep away all the institutions of oppression and make way for the new way of life of the future society.

Much of Bakunin's current reputation comes from his opposition to Marx, but his writings are full of remarkable insights, rarely fully developed, that place him among the foremost theorists of anarchism. While he wrote vast amounts, he finished almost nothing, and the text of his that is best known, *God and the State*, was a part of a massive and massively disorganized final work, *The Knouto-Germanic Empire and the Social Revolution*, which was partially published in French in 1871. Élisée Réclus (1830–1905) published *God and the State* separately in 1882.

Bakunin's thought is notoriously unsystematic. It can be best understood under the headings of anarchism, or anarchy as he called it, as a theory of political action, his insistence that equality and liberty must go together, and his analysis of the structure of society after the revolution. Much of his thought was developed through his critique of Marx and his critiques of religion and politics, capitalism and state socialism, and intellectuals.

For Bakunin action is more important than thought and analysis. While Marx argued that the real point was to change society not analyse it, Bakunin embodied the position. Partially this was simply a reflection of his personality; his childlike enthusiasm made him in person an immensely effective propagandist. But it was also a response to his romantic belief that all that was needed was to somehow inspire the masses, and they would overthrow their oppressors. As a result, he helped inspired 'propaganda by the deed', which produced the stereotype of the anarchist as bomber. In Bakunin's case, this is not necessarily a false image.

Bakunin's argument that equality and liberty belong together is at the basis of his critiques of other thinkers and social institutions. For Bakunin, equality must come first and liberty next, but they belong together because equality without liberty is likely to produce despotism. While anarchists like MAX STIRNER (1806–50) argued for liberty alone, Bakunin argued that any liberty without equality creates a privilege that limits the liberties of others. Bakunin insisted that women should be equal to men, and that they should have the same liberties as men.

The structure of the future would be from the bottom up rather than the top down. This would become possible with the abolition of the state, private property and the legal system. They would be replaced with individuals coming together into communes. These communes would form a federation that would allow co-operation on issues that affected a larger area. PIETR KROPOTKIN

(1842–1921) made a similar argument in his development of anarchist theory.

In the future anarchist society, everyone would work. Bakunin explicitly rejected the idea that distribution would be based on need; it would be based on contribution. At birth every person, both men and women, would have the means of fulfilling their full humanity using their different skills and talents. Society must be structured so that exploitation is impossible.

Historically, the most important part of Bakunin's life was his conflict with Marx over the leadership of the First International. While they actually agreed on many things, they disagreed fundamentally on the way the International should be organized, over what was at the basis of the current system of oppression, and how to bring about the desired revolution. Marx was a much more effective fighter within such organizations, and Bakunin was expelled.

Bakunin's differences from Marx were both theoretical and tactical. He rejected the economic inevitability of Marx's theory and believed that there were no preordained historical laws. He argued that a dictatorship of the proletariat would be like any other dictatorship and thought it foolish to assume that the proletariat, or their leaders, would be any more likely to give up power than the leaders of any other dictatorship.

Bakunin also rejected Marx's idea of a revolutionary party as the primary tactic of the revolution. He utterly rejected involvement in the contemporary political system as a tool of the revolution. Bakunin argued that only libertarian means could ever produce libertarian socialism, and he can be read as having predicted what was called Eurocommunism and the recent metamorphosis of Communist parties into Social Democratic parties. For Bakunin, such parties would have meant the failure of the revolution.

Bakunin also rejected Marx's plan to centralize authority in the International. He argued that a federation of local, autonomous groups was the right model. Such groups would be the basis of the future society and were the appropriate means of bringing it about. He believed that the revolution would come about through an uprising of the masses, particularly the peasantry and urban mobs, the *lumpenproletariat*, the very people who Marx saw as unlikely to be revolutionary. Bakunin believed that these groups retained the vigor that would make an uprising possible. Revolution, for

Bakunin, would come from those with nothing to lose. The *proletariat* he saw as having achieved enough that they had an investment, however small, in the current system. They would be part of the revolution, but they were unlikely to start it.

According to Bakunin, the central institutions oppressing people are religion and the state. Authority was the problem, whether spiritual or temporal. In *God and the State*, Bakunin argued that the entire social apparatus that oppressed the masses was based on their believing in God. Such belief acted as a safety valve that allowed the oppressors to direct attention away from their oppression by both convincing people that God had established the existing hierarchy and promising them their reward after death. He argued that if God exists, then humans are slaves, and since humans must be free, God cannot exist. Humanity must choose between freedom and God.

For Bakunin, the revolution had to begin with the elimination of the state and its various appendages, such as the police, the military and the courts, and the transfer of all social capital to the workers' organizations. This aspect of Bakunin's thought gave rise to anarcho-syndicalism, which was particularly important in France and Spain.

Bakunin was certain that a state in the hands of communists would be no different from a state in the hands of capitalists. Bakunin was particularly concerned about the danger emerging from the left and well before there was an absolutist socialism to point to, he warned against it. He contended that a state that was truly in the hands of the people would not need to be abolished, and if a state must be abolished, it could never have been other than an oppressor of the people.

Bakunin also contended that the authority of scientists, or more broadly intellectuals, was dangerous. He believed that science was incapable of recognizing individuality and was prone to dictatorship. He pointed particularly to the followers of AUGUSTE COMTE (1798–1857) and Marx as wanting to force variety into uniformity. At the same time, he recognized the authority of science in its own sphere and believed that everyone should be educated in science so that they could not be oppressed in their ignorance by an educated elite. The authority of knowledge was acceptable to Bakunin, but it should not be allowed to dictate to others.

Bakunin's critique of Marx, particularly his prediction of the dual possibilities of an absolutist socialism and a Communism that is merely another political party competing within the system of oppression, reveal him as a prescient thinker. Also, Bakunin, rather than Marx, was right about where the revolutionary classes would originate. The twentieth-century revolutions in Russia and China were not proletarian revolutions; they came from the masses that Marx disparaged.

Finally, Bakunin's argument for the essential combination of equality and liberty would also reject not only the individualism of Stirner but also equally the anarcho-capitalist and libertarian writers of the late twentieth and early twenty-first centuries, like Ayn Rand (1905–82) and Robert Nozick (1938–2002), who see equality among humans as not merely unnecessary but dangerous. Bakunin saw such thinking as simply another tool used by the oppressors to stay in power.

Further reading

Avrich, P. (1974) *Bakunin and Nechaev*, London: Freedom Press.
Bakunin, M. (1883) *God and the State*, trans. Benjamin R. Tucker, Tunbridge Wells: Science Library.
—— (1950) *Marxism, Freedom and the State*, trans. and ed. with a Biographical Sketch by K.J. Kenafick, London: Freedom Press.
—— (1953) *The Political Philosophy of Bakunin: Scientific Anarchism*, comp. and ed. G.P. Maximoff, New York: Free Press of Glencoe.
—— (1972) *Bakunin on Anarchy: Selected Works of the Activist-Founder of World Anarchism*, ed. and trans. Sam Dolgoff, New York: Alfred A. Knopf.
—— (1973) *Selected Writings*, ed. Arthur Lehning, trans. Steven Cox and Olive Stevens, London: Jonathan Cape.
—— (1990) *Statism and Anarchy*, trans. and ed. Marshall Shatz, Cambridge: Cambridge University Press.
Carr, E.H. (1937) *Michael Bakunin*, London: Macmillan.
Kelly, A. (1982) *Mikhail Bakunin: A Study in the Psychology of Politics and Utopianism*, Oxford: Clarendon Press.
Pyziur, E. (1955) *The Doctrine of Anarchism of Michael A. Bakunin*, Milwaukee, WI: Marquette University Press.

SEE ALSO: intellectuals, elites and meritocracy; liberalism; Marx and Marxism; utopianism

LYMAN TOWER SARGENT

BARRÈS, MAURICE (1862–1923)

Maurice Barrès, writer, politician, member of the Académie Française and Déroulède's successor as leader of the Ligue des Patriotes (Patriot League)

was a key figure in the evolution of modern French nationalism. Credited with coining the term 'nationalist' in a newspaper article of 1892, Barrès has been identified as the father of modern nationalism. In the context of Boulangism and the Dreyfus Affair, French nationalism lost its republican universalism and became increasingly associated with anti-Semitism, xenophobia and a discourse of decadence and corruption. This transition from a republican 'open' nationalism of the left to a 'closed' nationalism of the right is embodied in Barrès' career and literary legacy.

Barrès was born in Lorraine in 1862, but moved to Paris at the age of 20, determined to make his mark on the literary scene. The tension between pride in his Lorraine roots and a life spent in Paris was just one of the many contradictions within Barrès. Indeed, Barrès's thought lacked coherence; despite the concordances between their ideas, Barrès and CHARLES MAURRAS of Action Française (French Action) were poles apart in their intellectual approaches. Whereas Maurras was a doctrinaire positivist who arrived at monarchism through reason, Barrès, who rejected monarchism, developed an aesthetic approach to nationalism. Indeed Barrès introduced the term 'intellectual' in a pejorative sense, owing to his belief that society was not founded on logic or reason but prior necessities.

Barrès's first 'Culte de Moi' (cult of myself) novels sponsored unrestrained individualism in search of self-development and Barrès exalted action and 'energy'. This dynamism drew him to Boulangism and a politics of anti-parliamentarian, anti-bourgeois revolt, attacking the opportunist republic in the name of the people's tradition of 1789, 1830 and 1848. Barrès opposed the parliamentary republic in the name of a regenerated national republic and developed a syncretic nationalism, integrating the military glories of the French republic into the long history of French greatness. The same went for Napoleon, saluted as a 'professor of energy', at whose tomb the young Lorrainian protagonists of Les Déracinés (The Uprooted, 1897) are inspired with will, audacity and appetite. It was precisely this energy that France lacked under the parliamentary republic, which symbolized France's decadence. A discourse of sickness and decadence was central to this new nationalism, which stressed internal sources of corruption. In the 'national energy' novels Barrès portrayed the Opportunist republic

as in thrall to the Frankfurt-born Jewish banker Jacques de Reinach.

Anti-Semitism and xenophobia, the dominant characteristics of the nationalism of the 1890s, made Barrès an anti-Dreyfusard, joining the Ligue de la Patrie française (League of the French Fatherland). For Barrès the issue at stake was that of national greatness; the Dreyfusard intellectuals had demoralized the army, weakening the French nation, as revealed by Fashoda, where the French army was forced to withdraw before the British. Barrès's analysis chimed with that of Maurras, concluding the Dreyfus was capable of treachery on account of his race. Barrès's anti-Semitism however was not racially based, but an expression of his new conception of nationalism. This is best illustrated with reference to Alsace-Lorraine. Whereas JOSEPH-ERNEST RENAN, in keeping with the political voluntarist tradition of the Revolution, held that the people of Alsace-Lorraine were French because they wanted to be French, Barrès claimed that their history and traditions made them French. For Barrès Alsace-Lorraine was a Gallo-Roman and Catholic region that had consistently opposed German barbarism. Nationalism for Barrès was based on 'la terre et les morts', the land and the dead. To be a nationalist was to be aware of this spiritual communion and accept the role ascribed by birth. Thus the eponymous heroine of Colette Baudoche (1909) breaks off her engagement to a German on realising her French identity through her community's commemoration of the dead of 1870.

This conception of nationalism led Barrès to stress regional identity. The Third Republic's error was over-centralization, a centralization that led the schooling system to neglect to teach children to love their region, creating a nation of déracinés (uprooted). Moral unity was to be found through an awareness of one's roots, an intimate connection to the locality and the past, symbolized above all in the graveyard. Barrès developed a cult of ancestors and provinces, involving the heroes of the national past, particularly the dead of 1870 and the very landscape. Barrès's France exhibited a geography of patriotism, patterned by sites of national memory such as Donrémy or, for Lorrainers, Metz.

Barrès's admiration for the fixity of the past drew him in a conservative direction, affirming the necessity of a shared religion, despite a personal lack of faith and purely aesthetic appreciation of

Catholicism. Nationalism took Barrès from the socialist left to the conservative right. The young Barrès, elected as a Boulangist socialist at Nancy in 1889, tried to define a French socialism, distinct from German-Jewish materialism, as editor of the newspaper *La Cocarde* (The Cockade) and in his 1898 Nancy programme linked nationalism to socialism through an appeal to protectionism, restrictions on immigration and hostility to naturalized citizens. The Barrès who was elected as a deputy for Paris in 1906 (a seat held until his death) became a conservative member of the Union Sacrée (Sacred Union) of 1914 and appealed for national unity above all. Ultimately Barrès's personal evolution was the evolution of a modern nationalist, from the cult of the self to the submergence of the self in the nation, from anti-bourgeois rhetoric to an emphasis on tradition, from left to right. Some see a more sinister development: the language of decadence and internal corruption, the exaltation of energy and action, anti-Semitism and an arational determinism make Barrès a precursor of fascism.

Further reading

Curtis, M. (1959) *Three against the Third Republic: Sorel, Barrès and Maurras*, Princeton: Princeton University Press.
Gildea, R. (1994) *The Past in French History*, London: Yale University Press.
Sternhell, Z. (1972) *Maurice Barrès et le nationalisme français*, Paris: Armand Collin.
Winock, M. (1988) *Nationalism, Anti-Semitism and Fascism in France*, Stanford: Stanford University Press.

SEE ALSO: conservatism, authority and tradition; Maurras, Charles; the Nation, nationalism and the national principle

MARTIN SIMPSON

BAUER BRUNO (1809–82)

Historian and theologian Bruno Bauer was a leading member of the 'Young Hegelians' in the pre-revolutionary ('*Vormärz*') Berlin during the late 1830s and early 1840s. He was primarily concerned with the theological implications of Hegel's philosophical method, and he managed to reposition him as a theological radical, establishing the revolutionary interpretation of Hegel that was adopted by the left Hegelians of the 1840s. He did this by publishing a conservative critique of Hegel as a rationalist and atheist (*Die Posaune des jüngsten Gerichts über Hegel den Atheisten und Antichristen: ein Ultimatum*, 1841) that parodied contemporary theological orthodoxy. He adopted a similar position the following year in *Hegels Lehre von der Religion und Kunst von dem Standpuncte des Glaubens aus beurtheilt.* At the centre of Bauer's work throughout the 1830s was a critical reinterpretation of the scriptures. He distinguished between the essentially legalistic relationship in the earlier books of the Old Testament between an authoritarian God and a subordinate humanity, and the higher form of religious consciousness evinced in the later books. He emphasized the discontinuity between the Old and New Testaments, and publicly rejected the contemporary orthodoxies of the Christian churches. His increasingly radical position is reflected in his critiques of St John's gospel and of the Synoptic Gospels (1840–2), in which he argued that the gospels were literary works produced by religious experience with no foundation in historical fact. Outside the gospels, he claimed, there was no evidence for the existence of Jesus of Nazareth in contemporary writers. This led him to conclude that Christianity had been a necessary stage in human development, but was now redundant, and had been superseded by autonomous self-consciousness, and his conclusions had direct political relevance, leading him to argue that no institution should survive that could not withstand rational criticism. He denounced both the contemporary Prussian state and its liberal constitutionalist opponents as defenders of particularist interests, whether spiritual or material, criticizing, for example, the state's restrictions on the Jews as an injustice founded on specious religious arguments. He also opposed liberal demands for emancipation as such, arguing that both Jews and Christians should forgo their particularist religious attachments. His critique of liberalism – and with it a critique of socialism – was further developed in his work on the French Revolution in the late 1840s (*Geschichte der französischen Revolution*, 3 vols, 1847), a time of increasing fractiousness among the Left Hegelians. The failure of the 1848 revolutions, which Bauer identified with a failure of the dominant ideas of the Enlightenment and the end of philosophy, proved a watershed in his thinking, prompting him to abandon his earlier republican ideals. Anticipating later political and intellectual developments he foresaw the emergence of a new, global order of competing imperialisms led by culturally disinterested elites with no specific national loyalty. European culture was a spent force for him, and he cited the evidence of Jewish influence as evidence of its demise, now interpreting the difference between Jews and Christians in racial rather than other terms. Bauer died in 1882, largely forgotten, according to Engels's otherwise very positive – if not uncritical – obituary.

Further reading

Moggach, Douglas (2003) *The Philosophy and Politics of Bruno Bauer*, Cambridge: Cambridge University Press.

Stepelvich, Lawrence S. (ed.) (1983) *The Young Hegelians*, Cambridge: Cambridge University Press.

SEE ALSO: Hegel and Hegelianism; main currents in philosophy

TIM KIRK

BAX, ERNEST BELFORT (1854–1926)

Ernest Belfort Bax made an original Marxist contribution to British socialism. The son of a wealthy garment manufacturer, Bax was educated by private tutors from 1864 to 1875. While studying music and philosophy in Germany and London (1875–81), he met German socialist exiles who 'converted' him from Positivism to their political perspective (1879). From 1882 to 1918, Bax was a successful freelance journalist, author, translator and a leading figure in the Social Democratic Federation (SDF) and Socialist League. The last 8 years of his life were spent in semi-retirement in London and Nice.

Although he never met Marx (see MARX AND MARXISM), Bax wrote a sympathetic review of *Capital* in 1881, stressing its Hegelian dimension. He subsequently established a close friendship with Engels, but eventually concluded that a *via media* was required between materialism and Idealism: the economic factor was 'not by itself necessarily the determining cause in social evolution' (Bax 1918). Bax argued that intellectual, moral and other non-material phenomena helped shape both human history and 'consciousness': issues that he sought to explore in *A Handbook of the History of Philosophy* (1886), *The Problem of Reality* (1892) and *The Roots of Reality* (1907).

The political consequence of Bax's anti-economism was a significant emphasis on socialist education. Many of his early writings – collected as *The Religion of Socialism* (1886) and *The Ethics of Socialism* (1889) – stressed the importance of ethical propaganda, although he countenanced the possibility that violent, minority revolution could be a viable path to communal ownership of the means of production. Bax left the SDF in a dispute over electoral tactics (1884) but he never rejected parliamentarism entirely. In 1888 he was one of the first dissidents to return to the Federation from the Socialist League (which had become a quasi-anarchist group).

Nevertheless, Bax's socialism was of the 'root-and-branch' variety; he preferred socialist propaganda to trade unionism and never countenanced joining the Labour Party. However, a historical work, which he composed with WILLIAM MORRIS (*Socialism: Its Growth and Outcome*, 1893), acknowledged that collectivist reforms might be a necessary prerequisite of 'revolutionary administration' in the advanced capitalist countries – a case of education through practice, not propaganda. In the 1880s, Bax recognized that 'the Scramble for Africa' was reinvigorating capitalism (cheap resources, new markets, etc.) and his later works were increasingly pessimistic about the prospects for socialism in his own time. One 'crotchet' in the toolbox of Baxian arguments was an extremely strident anti-feminism: for example *The Fraud of Feminism* (1913). In self-justification, Bax always claimed that he was against sex 'privilege' within capitalism, and in favour of 'real' sexual equality, but an unhappy family life (plus his philosophical admiration for Schopenhauer) may contribute to an explanation of his unusual position.

Further reading

Cowley, J. (1992) The Victorian Encounter with Marx: A Study of Ernest Belfort Bax, London and New York: British Academic Press.

Pierson, S. (1972) 'Ernest Belfort Bax: The Encounter of Marxism and Late Victorian Culture', The Journal of British Studies, 12, 1: 39–60.

SEE ALSO: Marx and Marxism

CLIVE E. HILL

BEBEL, AUGUST (1840–1913)

August Bebel is best known as a founder member of the German Social Democratic Party and as the author of *Die Frau und der Sozialismus* (*Woman and Socialism*), first published in 1879 and still popular until after the First World War. He was born in Cologne, received only an elementary education, commenced work as a wood-turner and soon became active in trade union organizations. In 1864 he met WILHELM LIEBKNECHT, who introduced him to Marxism and became his life-long political associate. In 1869 they founded the German Social Democratic Workers' Party, the first Marxist party in the country.

In 1867 Bebel was elected to the Reichstag of the North German Confederation but in 1870 he made it clear that his brand of socialism was incompatible with conventional parliamentary practices. With Liebknecht he declared that the Social Democratic Party participates in parliamentary elections solely for purposes of agitation. They had no intention of allying or compromising with other parties. Nevertheless, once German unification was achieved, Bebel was a member of the Reichstag for nearly all of its existence, from 1871–81 and then again from 1883 until his death in 1913. Unsurprisingly, over these years he gradually modified his opposition to parliamentarism.

Though not without nationalist sentiments, during the Franco-Prussian War Bebel joined Liebknecht in abstaining from voting the war credits. For this, and for their support of the 1871 Paris Commune, both were sentenced to two years' imprisonment on a charge of high treason. This was just one of numerous prison sentences, invariably on charges such as insults against the Chancellor and the army. He used the time to augment his initially scanty education.

In 1875 Bebel accepted the Gotha Progamme by which his party united with Ferdinand Lassalle's General German Labour League to form the Social Democratic Party of Germany (SPD), which exists to this day. Marx wrote a famous denunciation of the compromise programme ('Critique of the Gotha Programme'), which he saw as too much of a victory for Lassalle's ideas over his own. It is, in fact, largely through the comments of Marx and Engels that Bebel is known at all outside of Germany. For years Bebel and Liebknecht were watched from afar by Marx and Engels with rather closer scrutiny than they may have desired. Engels once described Bebel, rather unfairly, as 'a quite efficient chap who has however this one handicap': not even 'a smattering of theoretical education'. Yet when Engels died, Bebel, with Bernstein, was made his literary executor.

Bebel's *Woman and Socialism* was published in 1879. Here, in a manner typical not only of Marxism but of much wider strands of nineteenth-century social thought, Bebel outlined the stages of historical development from primitive communalism through to the presumed arrival of communism. As the title implies, he saw female emancipation as intrinsically linked with the development of socialism and so led to German social democracy accepting the ideas of female emancipation and equal rights. Women were to be delivered from the tyranny of the private kitchen, which would be superseded by large catering establishments in which machines performed the most mundane and onerous tasks. Bebel's vision of the future, though clearly based on the Marxist prognosis, is, for better or worse, clearly more detailed than anything supplied by Marx and Engels themselves. Bebel was pessimistic about capitalism, which seemed doomed, but optimistic about the eventual outcome once it was replaced. Under socialism science would at last be applied to all fields of human activity. Although, unlike in bourgeois society, everyone would have to work, they would not have to do so for long, for a two-hour working day would be possible. There would also be a free choice of activity. Thus there would be no permanent positions or occupational hierarchies. The chosen organizers would be comrades quite unlike the managers of the capitalist epoch. Yet even so, partially due to economies of scale, productivity would grow enormously. Bebel was confident that the fuller use of electricity could easily cope with the world's energy needs. Furthermore, the potential of solar power 'removes the fear that we shall ever run short of fuel'. Times of shortage, crisis and unemployment would vanish; money would disappear as also would big towns, thieves, tramps, vagabonds and religious organizations. By the year 2000 wars will have been abolished. This can now, of course, easily be dismissed as naïve but remains instructive as an instance of the prevailing optimism that so differentiates Bebel's age from ours. It furthermore offered a beacon of bright light to people living in dark times.

In the 1890s Bebel, with Karl Kautsky, became a main opponent of EDUARD BERNSTEIN'S revisionist attempts to modify Marxism according to the changed socio-economic conditions. At the 1899 party conference in Hanover Bebel delivered a six-hour speech rejecting Bernstein's views. Bebel and Bernstein had long been friends and although Bebel remained, on the whole, fairly civil, he did for a time recommend that Bernstein be expelled from the Social Democratic Party. He thought, almost certainly wrongly, that 99 per cent of the party differed from Bernstein, who had thus abandoned social democracy entirely. In his later years Bebel distanced himself from anti-militarism and anti-nationalism. By now he and Kautsky could be placed in the centre of the party as a more radical left was emerging around ROSA LUXEMBURG, Karl Liebknecht, Clara Zetkin and Franz Mehring. Bebel didn't quite live long enough to witness the crunch moment of August 1914 when the party he had founded voted the war credits and later split into three separate groupings.

Further reading

Bebel, A. (1910–14) *Aus meinem Leben*, 3 vols, Stuttgart: Dietz. Abridged version ed. W.G. Oschilewski (1976), Berlin: Dietz.
—— (1917) *Woman and Socialism*, New York: Socialist Literature.
—— (1976) *Society of the Future*, Moscow: Progress Publishers. Forms the latter part of *Woman and Socialism*.
Carsten, F.L. (1991) *August Bebel und die Organisation der Massen*, Berlin: Siedler Verlag.
Lidtke, V.L. (1966) *The Outlawed Party. Social Democracy in Germany, 1878–1890*, Princeton: Princeton University Press.

SEE ALSO: Bernstein, Eduard; Liebknecht, Wilhelm; Marx and Marxism

MICHAEL LEVIN

BELLAMY, EDWARD (1850–98)

Edward Bellamy, who is remembered primarily as the author of the utopian novel *Looking Backward 2000–1887* (1888), was born and died in the same small town, Chicopee Falls, Massachusetts, and spent most of his short life in New England. After a brief legal career, Bellamy turned to journalism, and edited a newspaper in Springfield, Massachusetts, from 1872–7, but he found his calling as a writer. Novels such as *The Duke of Stockbridge* (1879), *Dr. Heidenhoff's Process* (1880) and *Miss Luddington's Sister* (1884) were well received and established his reputation.

But *Looking Backward* brought him prominence. In *Looking Backward*, Bellamy combined the traditional utopia with the sentimental novel and produced a bestseller, which has never since been out of print. The hero, Julian West, who has had trouble sleeping, is put to sleep in an underground room in Boston in the year 1887 and wakes up in the year 2000. West was a wealthy Bostonian who was worried about industrial relations and poverty, and was, therefore, a sympathetic observer of the future Boston.

When West awakes, Boston has been transformed. The old buildings are gone and replaced with tree-lined boulevards, squares and cul-de-sacs, and new buildings designed to fit the new life and reflect its grandeur. Even the air is cleaner since the city is now smoke-free.

But the real changes in the future are in economics and politics, particularly in the ownership of the means of production and the organization of labour. Through the development of monopoly capitalism, enterprises became larger and larger, and were simply taken over by the state. No one has to worry about a job or food, clothes or housing; therefore, everyone has the time and energy to pursue a great diversity of intellectual interests. The future is a bit bland and middle class, but it would be a paradise to all but the wealthy of 1887 Boston.

This new Boston was brought about through gradual change not violent revolution. Bellamy recognized that there would be opposition to the takeover, but he argued that given the choice of losing their property violently or losing it peacefully, the monopolists would choose to lose it peacefully and enjoy its benefits rather than lose it violently and perhaps perish with it.

In addition to the change in the ownership of production, the central change in Bellamy's society was in the organization of labour, which was also nationalized. The labour system, the industrial army, is organized like an army – the term of service is 24 years, from 21 to 45, with a workday averaging six hours. Shortening or lengthening the workday equalizes occupations.

Everyone starts their service in the same way as common labourers. Then each individual can chooses an occupation, but whether they get their first choice depends on a combination of need and aptitude. Professional training is open to everyone until age 30; again, though, the combination of need and aptitude must be correct.

Each person in Bellamy's future Boston receives an equal income, which is not transferable and cannot, except in very unusual circumstances, accumulate from year to year. As a result, consumption fuels the economy.

The entire structure is unchanging and little legislation is passed. Bellamy contends there is little needing legislative decisions because fundamental laws are in place and work. Since there is no conflict in society, and there are no special interest groups to be appeased or paid off, there is little for a legislature to do.

The political organization is primarily administrative and in the industrial army. The administration works under democratically established limitations. It cannot, for example, eliminate a product for which there is any demand whatsoever. It can raise the price to cover costs but not punitively. It also must produce any product requested as long as a certain level of consumption (indicated through a petition system) is expected. Thus, according to Bellamy, a centrally planned economy can be much more efficient in responding to demand than a free-market system and can provide greater freedom of choice.

In *Looking Backward* women are members of the industrial army but leave when they become pregnant. As a result, most women serve some 10 to 15 years in the industrial army; those without children serve the entire 24 years. Bellamy says that women's work is lighter, with shorter hours and more frequent vacations, and was criticized more for these paternalistic sentences than for any other part of the book.

One form of gender differentiation is built into the system. Women's work is separate and has a separate hierarchy under a woman 'general-in-chief' chosen by women. Also, in legal cases where both parties are women, the judge is a woman; where there is one man and one woman, both female and male judges must agree on the result. Thus, in *Looking Backward* Bellamy clearly discriminates against women while trying to balance that discrimination by empowering them in a separate sphere that actually institutionalizes their political inferiority.

The society envisioned by Bellamy appealed to many people, and a movement began to encourage the adoption of many of the proposed reforms. This movement, the Nationalist Movement, developed initially in New England, and quite a few Nationalist Clubs were established there in the first years after the publication of *Looking Backward*. The Nationalist Movement was largely made up of members of the middle class, and many members were also Theosophists. From 1889 to 1891, *The Nationalist* was published in Boston as a means of fostering Nationalist ideas and communication among the Clubs, and from 1891 to 1894 Bellamy edited and published *The New Nation*. *Looking Backward* also produced Nationalist movements throughout the world, and Nationalism was particularly strong in Europe and the Antipodes.

The initial focus of the Nationalist Movement in the USA was municipal ownership of utilities, and, since this coincided with widespread corruption in the utilities, and a movement already existed arguing for municipal ownership, they had some successes. Bellamy, though, took the movement into the national political arena and brought it into close affiliation with the People's Party. When that party was soundly defeated in 1896, the Nationalist movement in the USA began to collapse. Nationalist movements in other countries continued well into the twentieth century.

Over the 10 years he lived after the publication of *Looking Backward*, Bellamy and others responded to criticisms of the book, and, finally, Bellamy decided to write a sequel that included changes in important institutions. *Looking Backward* had been particularly criticized for its treatment of women, and for its authoritarian structure, and Bellamy addressed both these issues.

Bellamy came to see women as full partners in his new society. Machinery, he argued, allows women to take on even the most physically demanding jobs, but also in the future women will be physically much stronger than they were in the Boston of his day. Women in the Boston of the year 2000 spend a great deal of time in physical exercise. In fact, everyone must participate in obligatory exercise at least until age 24.

Other changes in *Equality* also signal Bellamy's changed attitude toward women. In *Looking Backward* he had taken jobs such as washing, ironing and sewing out of the home, but in *Equality* he got rid of such jobs altogether. He did this by using paper clothes, which are recycled rather than washed. Rugs, sheets and all other household materials are discarded rather than cleaned, and he devised a water bed and air-stuffed pillows so that feathers, and other stuffing for pillows, mattresses, chairs, etc., which produce dust, are unnecessary.

Bellamy also made significant changes in the political system. In *Equality* the people have much more direct control than they did in *Looking Backward*. Bellamy still left much of the political system unclear, but a shift is obvious. In *Equality* all elected officials are liable to be recalled at any time. And all major legislation is referred to the people before being passed. Thus, there is much more political participation possible for people of the 1897 version of Bellamy's future Boston.

By limiting the hours of daily work and reducing the years of labour, Bellamy has radically redefined the role of labour in a person's life. Leisure activities become the defining characteristic of human life, not work, and there are no official or financial limitations on leisure activities. Hence, an area of life in Bellamy's future may be in a limited sense authoritarian while all the rest of life is freely under personal control.

WILLIAM MORRIS argued that Bellamy was mistaken to design his society around the reduction of labour. Morris, who wrote *News from Nowhere* (1890) in response to *Looking Backward*, argued that the goal should be to make labour more pleasurable. Bellamy did not directly respond to Morris's criticism.

Worn out from his 10 years of prominence, Bellamy died of tuberculosis in 1898.

Further reading

Bellamy, E. (1888) *Looking Backward: 2000–1887*, Boston, MA: Ticknor and Company.

Bowman, S.E. (ed.) (1962) *Edward Bellamy Abroad: An American Prophet's Influence*, New York: Twayne Publishers.

Lipow, A. (1982) *Authoritarian Socialism in America: Edward Bellamy and the Nationalist Movement*, Berkeley: University of California Press.

Patai, D. (ed.) (1988) *Looking Backward, 1988–1888: Essays on Edward Bellamy*, Amherst: University of Massachusetts Press.

SEE ALSO: democracy, populism and rights; Marx and Marxism; Morris, William; utopianism

LYMAN TOWER SARGENT

BENTHAM, JEREMY (1748–1832)

Born in 1748, Jeremy Bentham was an author whose notable writings displayed many of the rationalist assumptions of the Enlightenment. By his death in 1832, the development of these biases into fully fledged system building had become part of the 'spirit of the age'. This article outlines Bentham's life, his ethical theory (commonly known as utilitarianism), his writings on legal, administrative and penal reform, his reaction to the French Revolution, his general theory of legislation and his later work on representative government.

Often seen as the founder of modern British jurisprudence, Bentham was a child prodigy – educated privately and later at Queen's College, Oxford (1760–64). His father and grandfather were both attorneys and a legal training at Lincoln's Inn followed (1764–72). Although Jeremy was called to the bar, he never practised law (or got married) and instead sought to establish himself as both an author of legal criticism and a practical prison reformer. The latter ambition involved an unsuccessful expedition to Russia with his brother Samuel, in the 1780s, and a long and futile campaign to persuade the British Government to adopt his panopticon proposal (see below). Moreover, during most of his lifetime, Jeremy was significantly more productive as a writer of manuscripts than he was as an author of published texts and he lived on a *rentier* income. Bentham's *A Fragment on Government* was first published anonymously in 1776; his *Panopticon* pamphlet had a very limited circulation in 1791 and the more analytical text of *An Introduction to the Principles of Morals and Legislation* was no more of a publishing success in 1789. He only attracted significant public attention with the provocatively titled 1787 tract, *Defence of Usury*, which attacked statutory restrictions on the lending of money at interest. From c.1780–1808 Bentham moved in Whig circles, but in later life he became aligned with parliamentary and extra-parliamentary Radicals who favoured a more 'democratic' liberal system. Bentham's researches on the law of evidence and judicial procedure, undertaken in the early 1800s, were eventually edited for publication by the young JOHN STUART MILL as *Rationale of Judicial Evidence* (1827), but the work received poor reviews.

After Bentham's death, the first attempt to bring both his published and unpublished work to public attention – *The Works of Jeremy Bentham* (1838–43), edited by John Bowring – was both incomplete and of highly uneven quality. Hence, during the late twentieth century, an ongoing project was established at University College London, dedicated to the publication of the *Collected Works of Jeremy Bentham*. More than twenty volumes have been produced for the new series, and it must be assumed that total coverage will eventually be achieved.

On the very first page of his first publication (*A Fragment on Government*), Bentham observed that 'it is the greatest happiness of the greatest number that is the measure of right and wrong'. Happiness (or utility) was understood by Bentham as pleasure (or the absence/minimal presence of pain) and to be capable of measurement. Moreover, he made the additional assumption that individuals frequently sought to maximize their own pleasure (where no countering force applied), which in turn explained the 'natural' order of – and the capacity of legislators to regulate – society. Bentham seems to have maintained these ethical and psychological positions throughout his long and varied career, but – towards the end of his life – he sought to make his normative utility principle philosophically more rigorous (see below). In the 1822 edition of *An Introduction to the Principles of Morals and Legislation*, Bentham proposed to substitute the terms 'greatest happiness principle' and 'greatest felicity principle' for the term 'principle of utility', but the change of terminology failed to catch on. (His school was never redesignated 'felicitarian'!) The principle of utility was egalitarian in that it gave equal consideration to the happiness of each individual member of the community, but it could (in theory) be applied to legislation by an undemocratic government – such as an 'enlightened' despotism – although his later works questioned this assumption (see below). Finally, in his 1831 pamphlet, *Parliamentary Candidate's Proposed Declaration of Principles*, Bentham expounded a more rigorous and complete conception of his ethico-political position:

> I recognise as the *all-comprehensive*, and only right and proper end of Government, the greatest happiness of the members of the community in question: the greatest happiness – of all of them, without exception in so far as possible: the greatest happiness of the greatest number of them, on every occasion on which

the nature of the case renders the provision of an equal quantity of happiness for every one of them impossible: it being rendered so, by its being matter of necessity, to make sacrifice of a portion of the happiness of a few to the greater happiness of the rest.

Bentham's *œuvre* of publications and manuscripts (taken as a whole) indicate a further presumption that legal structures were more or less identical with social structures. Consequently, Bentham inferred that utilitarian ethics implied legal and political reform, undertaken by a single legislator (a person or a group) who was endowed with complete legal sovereignty – as a trust exercised on behalf of the citizens of any given state. A single 'legislative will' implied coherence of legislative action – 'In every political state, the greatest happiness of the greatest number requires, that it be provided with an all-comprehensive body of law' – and Bentham devoted much energy to the production of general and comprehensive legal codes that sought to indicate how his ideas on crime, punishment, property, reward, surveillance, policing, judicial organisation, political and administrative organization and public service could be linked together in a logical and practical manner. This concern with *codification* links manuscript works from the 1780s, such as *Of Laws in General* – which asserted that 'as yet no complete code of statute law is anywhere to be found' – with published texts such as *Codification Proposal Addressed by Jeremy Bentham to All Nations Professing Liberal Opinions* (1822) and the 1830 version of the *Constitutional Code*, which included references to further work on civil and penal codes. Furthermore, in 1811, Bentham had offered to codify the laws of the USA and (in 1814) had made the same offer to the Russian Empire, although neither proposal was accepted!

Bentham's famous 'panopticon' proposal took the form of a plan for a prison/workhouse/factory of circular design, with a central observation point from which a superintendent could maintain continuous surveillance of the establishment. This novel conception of a penitentiary (originally developed in Russia in the 1780s) sought to achieve deterrence, moral reformation and secure imprisonment of prisoners as well as ensuring economy of expenditure for government(s). When panopticist ideas were applied to poor relief and factory production in *Pauper Management Improved*

(1797), the emphasis fell upon the deterrence of indigents from seeking relief and the fiscal economy that would arise from supervised production, although the inculcation of habits of self-reliance (a type of reform) was also part of the overall plan. Although twentieth-century critics as diverse as Foucault and Himmelfarb have emphasized the totalitarian possibilities implicit in the panopticon schemes, it should also be noted that Bentham's 'lenity principle' involved full respect for a prisoner's health and nutrition requirements *within* the institution, while his 'severity principle' was only used to justify *incarceration* (Bentham was a consistent opponent of the common practice of manacling). 'Economy', the third principle of Bentham's penology, was to be achieved through commercial contracts – which could be terminated on humanitarian grounds – between the supervisors of the new institutions and government(s), plus a variety of ingenious schemes to maximize the productivity of the labour of the inmates and to minimize expenditure on their (very limited) enjoyments.

At its outbreak, Bentham was sympathetic to the French Revolution. His private manuscripts show that between 1789 and 1792 he conceived representative democracy (rather than enlightened despotism) as the best mechanism for the achievement of a rational governance that accepted the principle of utility, but, during the 1790s, he became disillusioned with this view. His main concern was that democratically elected assemblies were unlikely to provide the careful definitions of terms and the consistent use of language that were necessary if the calculation of community happiness was to become an exact science. In *Anarchical Fallacies* (1796), Bentham attacked the 'Declaration of the Rights of Man' as a 'perpetual vein of nonsense' that arose from an unscientific view of language and politics, and which involved numerous self-contradictions, such as the advocacy of both unbounded natural rights of liberty and property on the one hand, and criminal laws and taxes on the other.

Although Bentham's general principles of legislation gave priority to negative liberty over other legislative goals (see below), in his overarching philosophy, personal liberty was subsumed within a more general category of 'Security'. In a manuscript of the 1790s, known as *Principles of the Civil Code (PCC)*, he contended that it was the ethical duty of a legislator to measure and balance the claims of 'Subsistence', 'Abundance', 'Equality' and 'Security' as the objectives of civil (and criminal) law – using the principle of utility as a guide. Despite the technocratic bias of the panopticon project, in *PCC*, Bentham argued against what is now known as social engineering, on the grounds that the advocate of 'a coercive law ought to be ready to prove, not only that there is a specific reason in favour of this law, but also that this reason is more weighty than the general reason against every law', namely 'that such a law is restrictive of liberty'. While Bentham favoured measures against inherited wealth (see below), he claimed that doctrinaire egalitarianism involved the danger of removing the incentive to maintain and possess abundance, so that if 'all property were to be equally divided, the certain and immediate consequence would be, that there would be nothing more to divide'. Bentham's increasing concern with the logic of private property in this period was also reflected in manuscripts on the principles of *laissez-faire* economics (for example his 'Manual' and 'Institute of Political Economy') and pamphlets such as *Supply without Burthen* (1795), which argued for a kind of inheritance tax that would only fall on estates where no close relatives stood to benefit, thereby greatly reducing the disincentive effect associated with other forms of public revenue collection.

Bentham's work on British legal procedure helped him to conclude that the defeat of his panopticon project was no accident, but instead due to what he came to describe as 'sinister interests'. In particular, he adjudged that a 'conspiracy among the high and opulent to support one another against the low and indigent' was the most profound obstacle to utilitarian reform and he now sought allies outside the charmed circle of the British Establishment. Bentham became increasingly concerned with parliamentary reform (e.g. *Bentham's Radical Reform Bill*, 1819) and as a result of extending the economic assumption that every individual was best judge of their particular self-interest to the realm of politics, he came to the conclusion that universal suffrage was a fundamental precondition of good government. On grounds of efficiency and social order, however, Bentham always favoured representative democracy over direct democracy, as the former allowed a special role for the expert legislator and he was keen to avoid the charge of Jacobinism. In principle, Bentham favoured female as well as male suffrage, but he concluded that even enlightened public opinion could not accommodate this degree of radicalism and he chose to work with the advocates of adult male suffrage. During Bentham's 'democratic period' (roughly 1808 to 1832) he formed strong personal links with a variety of 'self-made men' who were in broad sympathy with his aims, if not always with the minutiae of his utilitarian philosophy. This Benthamite group (with subsequent offshoots) became known as 'the Philosophic Radicals' and included figures such as Samuel Romilly (1757–1818), Francis Place (1771–1854) and JAMES MILL.

Bentham's *Constitutional Code* project, which began in 1822, was not completed in his lifetime. Only one of the three projected volumes was published, although a vast array of manuscripts was produced. The work was both a concrete expression of Bentham's internationalism (for he hoped, but failed, to see it enacted in Portugal, Spain or Greece) and a conceptual development of the liberal aspects of his earlier thought. The *Constitutional Code* was a republican constitution, based on the separation of powers, but endowed with an active executive branch led by a 'Prime Minister', who was directly elected by a full male suffrage. Fourteen ministries and sub-departments dealt with elections, legislation, the army, the navy, 'preventive service' (public works), interior communication, indigence relief, education, 'domain' (public buildings), health, foreign relations, trade and finance – all according to the dictates of the greatest-happiness principle. Yet, elections were a necessary, but not a sufficient condition for this to be achieved, for good government also needed to be transparent. Bentham had subscribed to an 'interest–duty junction' principle (that equated the duties of rulers with the common interest) since the 1770s, but it was only in his later works that he concluded that radical, democratic measures were necessary to ensure that ministers, civil servants, legislators and judges did not mistake their self-interest for their duty. In the *Code*, both adult male suffrage and genuine freedom of the press were necessary preconditions for the existence of a 'Public Opinion Tribunal' (otherwise, an active citizenry) as an additional check on the pernicious exercise of political power.

In popular debate, Bentham has been commonly associated with a narrow legalism and a *laissez-faire* approach to economics. However, not even the popularization of his work during the early nineteenth century – by such close followers as Pierre Etienne Dumont (1759–1829) – clarified the distinction between Bentham's empirical and normative assumptions about human happiness or indicated the breadth of his project of legislative and administrative reform. Hence, despite the famous claim by the influential liberal historian, A.V. DICEY, that, in the period 1825 to 1870, 'the teaching of Bentham obtained ... ready acceptance among thoughtful Englishmen', scholarship in the final quarter of the twentieth century has tended to suggest that the rationalist and doctrinaire style, and the technical and abstract terminology of much of Bentham's writing (e.g. his 1818 tract on religious education, *Church-of-Englandism*), prevented specifically Benthamite – as opposed to generally utilitarian ideas – from becoming common currency. Finally, it should be noted that Bentham was a child of the 'radical Enlightenment' in that his philosophy was materialistic and discreetly sceptical of religion. Despite the authoritarian aspects of his panopticon, his unpublished manuscripts indicate an iconoclastic interest in extending democracy and applying the greatest-happiness principle to questions of race, gender and animal welfare. As Bentham's full corpus becomes generally available, these novel aspects of his thought may even become central topics for twenty-first-century Bentham studies.

Further reading

Campos Boralevi, L. (1984) *Bentham and the Oppressed*, Berlin and New York: De Gruyter.
Dinwiddy, J.R. (1989) *Bentham*, Oxford: Oxford University Press.
Rosen, F. (1983) *Jeremy Bentham and Representative Democracy*, Oxford: Clarendon Press.
Thomas, W. (1979) *The Philosophic Radicals*, Oxford: Clarendon Press.

SEE ALSO: democracy, populism and rights; intellectuals, elites and meritocracy; liberalism; theories of law, criminology and penal reform; theories of the state and society: the science of politics

CLIVE E. HILL

BERGSON, HENRI (1859–1941)

Henri Bergson was the foremost European philosopher of his age. While his ideas have lost favour today, especially among Anglo-American philosophers, in the era immediately before the First World War he enjoyed a huge public renown and an intellectual reach of the kind few technical philosophers can command. He was one of the philosophical leaders of the *fin de siècle* revolt against rationalism, and sought to construct a philosophical rationale for the rehabilitation of instinct and intuition as sources of knowledge of the world.

Bergson was born in Paris, the son of a Polish Jewish musician and an Anglo-Irish woman. He was educated at the Lycée Condorcet and the École Normale Supérieure, where he studied philosophy and graduated top of his year. He held various posts teaching philosophy in *lycées* before being appointed to a post at the école Normale Supérieure in 1898. From 1900 to 1921 he held the chair of Philosophy at the Collège de France, where his public lectures became hugely popular society events, especially for Catholics. He was elected to the Academy of Moral and Political Sciences in 1901 and to the Académie Française in 1914. By no means an ivory-tower philosopher, he played a minor role in the negotiations that brought the USA into the war in 1917, and from 1921 to 1926 was president of UNESCO's forerunner, the Commission for Intellectual Co-operation of the League of Nations. Shortly before his death from bronchitis in 1941, Bergson expressed in several ways his opposition to the Vichy regime: notably, he refused the regime's offers to exempt him from the operation of its anti-Semitic laws. Bergson, who was not a practising Jew and was strongly attracted to Catholicism, declined to convert at the end of his life chiefly because he wished to show his solidarity with French Jews at a time of persecution. One of the great literary stylists among major philosophers, he was awarded the Nobel Prize for Literature in 1928. His major works included *Time and Free Will* (*Essai sur les données immédiates de la conscience*, 1889); *Matter and Memory* (*Matière et mémoire*, 1896); *Creative Evolution* (*L'Evolution créatrice*, 1907); and *The Two Sources of Morality and Religion* (*Les Deux Sources de la morale et de la religion*, 1932).

Bergson once said that each great philosopher has only one thing to say. For Bergson, that one thing, which he restated in a whole series of influential works over half a century, was summed up in the proposition that time is real. What did this mean?

Bergson thought that the great conundrums of the Western philosophical tradition – free will versus determinism, for example, or idealism versus realism – were unsolved and unsolvable because they had been misstated. His distinctive method was to juxtapose the rival solutions that had been offered to a particular problem, to identify where they overlapped, and then to expose that overlap to expose a confusing misstatement of the problem. Specifically, he argued that a whole range of philosophical conundrums were rooted in a basic confusion of time and space; or, to put it differently, a tendency to think about time as if it were simply another dimension of space. For Bergson real time or duration – '*la durée*' was the French term he used – cannot be grasped by abstract reason, but only directly, by intuition, as one of the 'immediate data of consciousness'. Crucially, once we take seriously the proposition that time is real, we can see that the future does not yet exist. This may seem obvious, but to Bergson it was fundamentally at odds with philosophical determinism, which rested, he thought, on the assumption that events simply unfold a reality that already exists. For the philosophical determinist, Bergson thought, the future exists in the same sense as China exists for someone who has never been there. Bergson maintained that this was a fundamental error. Determinism was radically incompatible with freedom, and yet we know that we are free.

Bergson's aim was to combat scientific determinism and to liberate our understanding of the world from the grip of a mechanical and analytical mode of reasoning. Bergson was no crude exponent of the 'bankruptcy of science': he had a close knowledge of the scientific thought of his day, making a particularly close study of the technical literature on the brain in connection with aphasia, and took on Einstein in public debate on the implications of the theory of relativity. But he questioned the capacity of the analytical intellect to gain a comprehensive understanding of the world. He thought that mechanistic thinking exercised a stultifying influence. So in his most famous work, *Creative Evolution*, he engaged with Darwinism (see DARWIN, CHARLES) and evolutionary ideas more generally, but rejected what he saw as positivist or deterministic theories such as the Darwinian theory of evolution by natural selection. Instead, he saw the evolution of the universe as a creative process pervaded by a 'life force' that ensured (as natural selection did not) that evolution entailed progress.

Bergson's works had a wide and deep impact on the European intellectual world of his time; and his impact on literary culture was probably greater than his influence on philosophical circles narrowly defined. Proust's *Remembrance of Things Past* derived its central concern, the unseizable nature of time, from Bergson; while GEORGES SOREL, who like Proust attended Bergson's lectures and on Bergson's own admission understood his ideas 'perfectly', was profoundly influenced by his critique of determinism in the name of freedom and creativity. Finally, while Bergson's works were placed on the Index by the Vatican in 1914, he had a notable influence on the Catholic modernists.

Further reading

Hanna, T. (ed.) (1962) *The Bergsonian Heritage*, New York: Columbia University Press.

Hughes, H.S. (1959) *Consciousness and Society: The Reorientation of European Social Thought. 1890–1930*, London: MacGibbon & Kee.

Kolakowski, L. (1985) *Bergson*, Oxford: Oxford University Press.

Lacey, A.R. (1989) *Bergson*, London: Routledge.

SEE ALSO: main currents in scientific thought; religion, secularization and the crisis of faith; Social Darwinism

H.S. JONES

BERNSTEIN, EDUARD (1850–1932)

Eduard Bernstein, the main figure in the German socialist revision of Marxism, was the son of a train driver. While still working as a bank clerk he joined the German Social Democratic Workers' Party, the more left wing of the two German socialist groupings and the first Marxist party in any country. However in 1878 Bismarck's Anti-Socialist Law made it necessary for him to flee to Switzerland. From there he edited *Der Sozialdemokrat* (The Social Democrat), the official newspaper of the German Social Democrats. Exile, however, did not produce security, for in 1887 pressure from Bismarck led the Swiss authorities to close the party offices. So, like Marx (see MARX AND MARXISM) and Engels before him, Bernstein moved to London where he continued his journalistic activities. Marx had died 4 years earlier but

Bernstein worked closely with Friedrich Engels and also made contact with the Fabians and with Henry Hyndman's Social Democratic Federation.

Meanwhile in Germany the Anti-Socialist Law (1878–90) served to push the Social Democratic Party in a Marxist direction, for it seemed to validate the supposition that liberal freedoms would be annulled if they threatened to facilitate a transition to socialism. Thus the first congress of the re-legalized party laid down a policy perspective in broadly Marxist terms. This Erfurt Programme of 1891 remained the party orthodoxy for decades to come. Bernstein had played his part in its drafting and was at that time a convinced Marxist, so it posed no immediate problem for him. However, during the course of the decade the shift was to occur that made him the most vilified man in world socialism.

In 1896 Bernstein began a dispute with the English Marxist ERNEST BELFORT BAX on colonialism. Both shared the prevailing analysis that graded societies at various stages along the path from barbarism to civilization but took a different stance on the plight of those they termed savage and barbarian. Bax thought such peoples should not be subjugated; Bernstein that they should, in order to bring them up to the norms of a higher civilization. The clear intimation of later disputes was already evident, for Bax despised modern civilization and wanted it replaced; whereas Bernstein admired it and wanted it further developed. In the course of this exchange Bax became the first person to pronounce on Bernstein's breach with Marxism. Such a charge must have appeared extraordinary at the time. Bax was a minnow, a member of a small British Marxist group; Bernstein was a big fish in the largest socialist party in the world. He also enjoyed the immense prestige of being the executor of Engels's estate and his joint literary executor. Yet, as we shall see, Bax led where more famous socialist theoreticians were soon to follow.

In the same year Bernstein published a number of articles in *Die neue Zeit* (The New Time), edited by Karl Kautsky, the leading Marxist theoretician of the age. Here Bernstein attempted to situate the party within the prevailing socio-economic context. In view of later developments it needs stressing that no challenge to Marxism was originally intended or perceived. Bernstein, through his link with Engels and his senior position within the party, seemed in many ways an embodiment of ideological rectitude. However, his positing of Marxist presuppositions against current realities revealed some significant anomalies; for example although there had been no major economic downturn for about a quarter of a century, the official party theory declared capitalism prone to recurrent crises. Furthermore it seemed that the working-class population was not yet qualified to meet socialist assumptions concerning participation in administration. The level of public knowledge still made it inevitable that decisions would be taken by trained specialists. Bernstein thought it quite wrong to attribute revolutionary attributes, participatory inclinations or administrative capabilities to the working people. He also noted that the working classes were not solidifying into one homogeneous mass with similar interests. On the contrary, they were becoming ever more differentiated and stratified. Over the 1890s, then, Bernstein slowly came to the conclusion that Marx and Engels's analysis was of its time; that its time was over, and that the socialist movement's analyses and aspirations were, consequently, implausible. This he viewed not as a breach with Marxism but as an updating that embodied the open-minded approach of the founders themselves. Editor Kautsky must have been getting increasingly uncomfortable for in 1898 he wrote of Bernstein's regression in theory and doubted whether they could go on working together. In the same year Kautsky was among the majority who rejected revisionism at the party's Stuttgart conference. Kautsky and LIEBKNECHT joined many others in suggesting that Bernstein's views derived from the conditions of his English exile. In their opinion English circumstances were unique and so no general conclusions could be drawn from them. This point certainly had credibility, for the gradualist approach clearly had a better chance in Britain's parliamentary system than in Germany's more authoritarian and monarchical regime.

In 1899 Bernstein responded to pressure to present his views in systematic form and produced *The Preconditions of Socialism*, which has become the classic statement of parliamentary socialism. Bernstein's fundamental point was that the situation Marx and Engels had described decades earlier, and which furnished the basis for their proposals, no longer applied. For Marx and Engels the anarchy of capitalist production made the economy inherently unstable; the swings of the trade cycle would result in dislocation and collapse. This Bernstein rejected on the basis that the growth of trusts and cartels had stabilized capitalism and so had overcome its anarchy of production. Marx and Engels, unsurprisingly, had been overinfluenced by the large-scale economic crises of 1825, 1836, 1847, 1857 and 1873. These were unlikely to recur. Consequently capitalism was not obviously approaching its terminal phase; it might have its crises, its stops and starts, but none of them looked like being fatal to the whole system.

Furthermore the class polarization presumed in the 1848 *Communist Manifesto* was not verified by later developments. The possessing classes were actually increasing in number. Middle-sized firms were not declining; they survived easily alongside large undertakings. Furthermore large industry actually gave life to smaller and medium trades. Consequently the middle class was not getting smaller. The presumed proletarianization, which should so fundamentally fortify the social base of the revolutionary class, was not occurring. In Marxist theory the revolutionary force was that of the immense majority. This democratic credential now seemed unlikely to accrue.

Marxist theory was first formulated at a time when the working classes had not got the vote and when their trade union activity was either illegal or severely circumscribed. In this context workers had only very limited means of furthering their aims and so revolutionary tactics seemed the only realistic possibility. By the 1890s, however, this situation no longer prevailed. In the major countries of Europe democratic advance was evident. In Germany the 1871 constitution granted the vote to all men over the age of 25. In this situation the need for revolution had to be re-examined. The idea of revolution had a central place in the ideology of German socialism. The movement was seen by both friends and foes as culturally outside of its society: 'vagabonds without a fatherland' in the eyes of their opponents. Opposition, then, was total, so transformation should be total. To Bernstein this mentality was myopic. Revolution seemed a purely negative act. It removed the barriers to social improvement but, in itself, did nothing to ensure that better arrangements would be forthcoming. Furthermore the Marxist recommendation of proletarian revolution was based on a false historical analogy. The Marxist system was one that attempted to tidy up history into neat patterns of change. Thus, just as the rising bourgeoisie had needed to rise up against feudal encumbrances, so would the proletariat have to revolt against the constraints of the capitalist system. This is what Bernstein rejected. He acknowledged that feudalism had to be brought down by revolution because its unbending structures allowed no alternative. LIBERALISM, however, was not like this. Its flexible arrangements facilitated reforms and provided opportunities for participation. These opportunities should be taken. Liberalism, seen by Marx and Engels as the ideology of the exploiters, was viewed by Bernstein as a doctrine that could lead in a socialistic direction. The task, then, was not to oust liberalism but extend it. Its theories of consent and participation should be utilized to place workers into positions of influence. Revolution for Marxists was part of the neo-Hegelian dialectic of history; encrypted into the socio-genetic code of social advancement. Bernstein rejected both the determinism and the economic materialism of this approach, which he replaced with a neo-Kantian moral imperative. Individuals were now to be seen as the creators of their own destinies in their own ways. For this reason Bernstein can be classified with the more usual nineteenth-century progressive doctrines of linear development.

A further impediment to revolution and its presumed socialist aftermath was the nature of the working class. Not even in England (where he was living), let alone in Germany and France, did this class seem capable of planning, regulating and administering their respective societies. By and large workers were poor and uneducated, lived in squalid and overcrowded conditions, and were almost entirely bereft of the cultural standards that socialism required. At their current stage the working class seemed quite incapable of taking over the economy, let along the state. They still had a long way to go and Bernstein recommended that they make a start, but not in the way that most Marxists presumed. Their task was not to man the barricades and produce a dictatorship of the proletariat but to get elected into trade union, co-operative and local government positions. In this way the working class would develop administrative expertise and experience, and so socialism would be achieved gradually and peacefully.

This, for Bernstein, was socialism: a society in which workers ran their own affairs. In contrast not only to Marx and Engels, but also to such contemporaries as BEBEL and Kautsky, he had scant focus on the new society that socialism should introduce. He declared himself not concerned with the distant future but only with the present and immediate future. For him socialism was not the delivery of a plan or a blueprint but just the implementation of a principle. This refusal to envisage and explicate the 'final aim' was contrary to the whole culture and social psychology of German Marxism, which held before the workers an appealing vision of a liberated society.

These proposals seemed like an immense shift of focus for the movement. For Bernstein, in contrast, it was only a change in their ideology but not in their practice. He thought the two had come into contradiction. The theory was one thing and the practice another. The platform rhetoric was of revolution but the everyday activity was of reform and compromise. Social democrats talked of revolution but actually they had made electoral alliances with the middle class and had co-operated with employers. From this perspective Bernstein was merely raising the practice of Social Democrats to a theoretical level and asking them to abandon a theory that no longer conformed either to prevailing conditions or to the realities of their behaviour. German social democracy, in short, should emancipate itself from an outworn phraseology and recognize itself for what it really was, a democratic, constitutionalist movement of gradual, incremental reform.

Bernstein, then, told the German socialists what they were really like rather than what they imagined they were like; to some of them this was unforgivable. During these years the German Social Democratic Party was not merely overwhelmingly the largest socialist party in the world; it was also regarded as the most revolutionary. Its proceedings were not only closely monitored by supporters within the country, but also watched from afar by socialists everywhere. The charge that the Social Democratic Party had never really acted as a revolutionary force was not something its leading intellectuals wished to hear. There was particular hostility to Bernstein's idea that the movement was everything and the final goal nothing. This cut deeply into the utopian optimism of the party, which significantly based its appeal on its supposed ability to lead the working class into a transformed and superior existence.

The crusade of polemics against Bernstein began with the Russian journalist Parvus (Alexander Helphand) and with ROSA LUXEMBURG. For the latter Bernstein had abandoned Marxism rather than updating it. In 'Social Reform or Revolution?' she argued that the essential core of Marxism included the presumption of an inevitable capitalist crisis that made socialism objectively necessary. Bernstein's Kantian ethics placed him entirely outside of this framework. Soon most of the major figures of European socialism joined in the attack; Kautsky, Plekhanov, Bebel, LABRIOLA, Jaurès, Adler and Clara Zetkin all voiced their disapproval. The issues Bernstein raised cut deeply into the movement's self-image and would not go away in a hurry. At the 1903 party conference in Dresden a resolution condemning the attempt to change the policy based on class struggle was passed by 288 votes to a mere eleven. In 1917, 18 years after the publication of *Preconditions*, LENIN, in *State and Revolution*, still felt it necessary to voice his anger, denouncing Bernstein as a philistine, opportunist, renegade and ex-Social Democrat.

Presumably, if Bernstein was so wrong, he could have been safely ignored. That he wasn't indicates that he had touched a raw nerve. The party, and even more the trade union movement, was engaged in piecemeal adjustments and compromises to a greater extent than they liked to acknowledge. Furthermore if Bernstein's revisionism was anti-Marxist he could certainly find Marxists who showed similar tendencies. This started with the founders themselves. Though clear advocates of revolution, Marx and Engels never fully rejected the parliamentary path. They never criticized the parliamentary focus of the English Chartists, nor that of the German Social Democratic Party. In an 1872 speech Marx imagined that England, the USA and possibly Holland might achieve socialism peacefully. In the years after Marx's death, and on the basis of a male working-class franchise, Engels clearly shifted in a constitutionalist direction. In a sense that his detractors were loath to recognize, Engels opened the door for Bernstein, as the latter was pleased to demonstrate in the foreword to *Preconditions*. Of the later leaders of German socialism, August Bebel and Wilhelm Liebknecht had also moved towards gradualism, combining their declared hostility to constitutionalism with active parliamentary work. *The Preconditions of Socialism* made Bernstein immediately notorious rather than simply famous throughout world socialism. The polemical responses to his work are now almost forgotten. *Preconditions* itself is not nearly as well known as it deserves to be, for it can now be seen as

the basic theoretical statement of the parliamentary socialism that for over a century was characteristic of Western liberal democratic societies.

Any supposition that *Preconditions* marked Bernstein's departure from the political left is not borne out by his later actions. In 1901 he was allowed to return to Germany for, on the basis of the revisionism dispute, the authorities believed his presence would do more to divide than to fortify German socialism. He became a Social Democrat deputy in the Reichstag from 1902–6 and 1912–18, and then a member of the parliament of the Weimar Republic between 1920 and 1928. In 1914 he opposed the First World War and a year later voted against the war credits. In 1917 he left the Social Democratic Party to join its more left-wing offshoot, the USPD (Independent Social Democratic Party of Germany). After the war he rejoined the main party and argued strongly against turning the German revolution of 1918–19 in a Bolshevik direction. Bernstein lived just long enough to witness the Wall Street crash of 1929. The consequent global economic crisis brought Germany Nazism rather than socialism. He died just six weeks before Hitler seized power. Nazi thugs destroyed the urn that contained his ashes.

Further reading

Bernstein, E. (1993, first published 1899) *The Preconditions of Socialism*, Cambridge: Cambridge University Press.

Gay, P. (1962) *The Dilemma of Democratic Socialism. Eduard Bernstein's Challenge to Marx*, New York: Collier Books.

Nettl, J.P. (1973) 'Social Democracy in Germany and Revisionism', in P.P. Wiener (ed.) *The Dictionary of the History of Ideas*, Vol.4, 263–76, Scribner: New York.

Tudor, H. and Tudor, J.M. (1988) *Marxism and Social Democracy. The Revisionist Debate 1896–1898*, Cambridge: Cambridge University Press.

SEE ALSO: Marx and Marxism

MICHAEL LEVIN

BLANC, LOUIS (1811–82)

Louis Blanc was the only early socialist to enter government. He was regarded as a Jacobin socialist, partly because he looked to the state to facilitate social reform, but mainly because he admired the Jacobins, and praised Robespierre's Declaration of the Rights of Man at a time when few could separate them from the Terror.

The son of a legitimist who lost his pension in 1830, Louis was a scholarship boy at the *collège* in Rodez. After a brief spell as a tutor, he embarked on a career as a radical journalist, first in 1834 for the *Bon sens*, a weekly paper directed at workers; in 1839 he helped found *La Revue du progrès politique, social et littéraire*. In 1840 a selection of these articles became *L'Organisation du travail*. Within two weeks 3,000 copies had been sold and the next printing disappeared equally fast, probably helped by a government confiscation order. By 1847 it was in its fifth edition. It was Blanc's solution to poverty, buttressed by evidence from social commentators such as Guépin, Villermé and Buret. He argued that poverty was the consequence of capitalist exploitation, itself a product of the bourgeois revolutions of 1789 and 1830, a phenomenon ultimately as damaging to the bourgeoisie as to the proletariat. The government had to act as banker to the poor to compensate for the fact that capitalism had robbed the poor of the means of production. Governments should lend capital to artisans to create co-operative social workshops. After the first year the workers would pay back the state, which would then adopt a more distant, supervisory role. Blanc was confident that through education people would lose their selfishness and develop a sense of common purpose. He then wrote *Histoire de dix ans*, a damning account of the mistakes of the Orleanist monarchy, and helped found and run the most socially radical paper of the day *La Réforme*. In 1847 came the first two of his fifteen-volume history of the 1789 Revolution.

After the February Revolution, 1848, the provisional government made Blanc its secretary and president of the innovative Commission of Workers. Elected representatives of Parisian workers and employers met to debate solutions to the economic crisis and endured repetitive orations from Blanc. They arbitrated between masters and men, prevented strikes in a number of key trades including baking, and got the roofers on the new Constituent Assembly building back to work. Although it had no budget it helped create co-operative workshops, a 2,000 strong tailors' group to make National Guard uniforms, an embroiderers' workshop to make the insignia and a saddlers' workshop. Blanc felt side-lined. He was excluded from the national workshops set up by the Provisional government. They were merely short-term dole schemes like those introduced after earlier revolutions. Blanc's call for a Ministry of Labour was rejected by the Constituent Assembly and his Commission was disbanded. Blanc was unjustly blamed when he made a speech to the crowd during the occupation of the Assembly on 15 May and, second, for the outbreak of the June Days. He was sentenced to deportation, but had already fled to Britain, where he continued his prolific historical writing – and his arguments with other radicals. He returned to France in 1870, opposed the Paris Commune and was a member of the Chamber of Deputies until his death in 1882. He is usually considered as one of the main founders of radical socialism, the centrist federation that was developed into the fulcrum of Third Republic politics.

Further reading

Blanc, J.J.L. (1913) *Organisation du travail*, in J.A.R. Marriot, *The French Revolution of 1848 in its Economic Aspect* I, 14, Oxford: Oxford University Press.

Loubère, L.A. (1961) *Louis Blanc; His Life and his Contribution to the Rise of French Jacobin Socialism*, Evanston, IL: Northwestern University Press.

Pilbeam, P. (2000) *French Socialists before Marx: Women, Workers and the Social Question in France*, Teddington: Acumen.

SEE ALSO: early socialism

PAMELA PILBEAM

BLANQUI, LOUIS-AUGUSTE (1805–81)

Louis-Auguste Blanqui was an unusual early socialist, being a conspiratorial revolutionary and spending half his adult life in prison as a consequence. Blanqui had a middle-class moderate republican background. He and his elder brother, Adolphe, were educated at the expensive and selective *lycée* Charlemagne. Both graduated to the *charbonnerie* from whence his brother became a highly successful civil servant and a liberal economist, opposed to everything Auguste held dear. Auguste was decorated after the 1830 revolution and quickly turned to perpetual insurgency, inspired by Buonarroti. He became totally absorbed in his clandestine existence, constantly fearful of spies and government agents. He always asked friends to destroy letters he sent them and tried to eat incriminating documents on his arrest in 1836.

In 1832 he was charged with inciting the poor to rebel by his role in the *Friends of the People* club. He defended himself in a speech that summarized his philosophy and earned him his first jail sentence, although the charge against him was dismissed. He categorized socio-economic relations as a class war, in which the rich constantly oppressed the poor, with, among other inequities, prohibitive indirect taxes, in whose definition and collection the poor had no voice. He was less concerned with questions of unemployment and low wages than other early socialists. Blanqui insisted to the president of the court that his profession was 'proletarian' and that this was indeed a profession, since it described nearly 30 million French people. He questioned the competence of the court. Blanqui proceeded to tell the court what he wanted: universal suffrage and social equality. In this speech Blanqui laid the parameters for his revolutionary socialism, reminiscent of, but more radical than, the ideas of BABEUF and Buonarroti.

On his release Blanqui remained a conspirator and a journalist, notably arrested in 1836 for organizing the Society of the Families, and failing to raise the Parisian 'masses' in the rebellion of the society of the Seasons in May 1839. On both previous occasions he had profited from amnesties after only a year in prison, but this time he was incarcerated for the rest of the July monarchy. Throughout his life he remained convinced that violent revolution in Paris orchestrated by a small group of devoted insurgents was the only route to a socialist republic. The vast majority of the educated elite shared his belief that the masses were innately revolutionary and successive regimes feared his influence, despite all evidence to the contrary.

In the spring of 1848, liberated by the revolution, Blanqui organised a radical club, took part in demonstrations, notably 15 May, and was jailed for 11 years, followed by a 4-year sentence for conspiracy against the Empire and exile in Belgium on his release in 1865. Back in Paris in 1870, he was arrested after an abortive coup on 31 October, thus missing the participation of his followers in the Paris Commune. Despite the total failure of all his efforts, he inspired his Blanquist followers and was apparently also a mentor to Russian revolutionaries.

Further reading

Bernstein, S. (1971) *Auguste Blanqui and the Art of Insurrection*, London: London: Lawrence & Wishart.
Spitzer, A.B. (1957) *The Revolutionary Theories of Louis-Auguste Blanqui*, New York: Columbia University Press.

SEE ALSO: Babeuf, Gracchus; early socialism

PAMELA PILBEAM

BOAS, FRANZ (1858–1942)

Boas is widely regarded as the founder of twentieth-century US cultural anthropology. He is lauded as the man whose 'scientific activism' successfully fought off the white supremacist Nordicism of the US physical anthropological tradition (epitomized by Madison Grant and Lothrop Stoddard) by demonstrating the cultural achievements of African Americans and showing in his renowned paper 'Changes in Bodily Form of Descendants of Immigrants' (1910–13) that, contrary to received wisdom about the permanency of skull shape (and hence the skull as a marker of racial difference), the children of immigrants to the USA had larger heads than their parents. Yet the nineteenth-century foundation of Boas's thought must not be overlooked. His studies focused on three key areas: race, language and culture, and it is the former that is key. Boas trained as a physicist (like that other *émigré* founder of modern anthropology, Bronislaw Malinowski) and geographer, and worked in Berlin with Rudolf Virchow, the well-known anti-Darwinian physical anthropologist. He only moved to the USA in 1885 when his Jewish origins prevented him from working in Germany, a country to which he felt a life-long attachment, as manifested in his protests against US involvement in the Great War, for which he was branded a traitor and removed from office in the American Anthropological Association. In other words, Boas trained and thought as a physical anthropologist, shared its assumptions about racial classification, and provides a classic example of how a discipline is reshaped not by outside criticism but by someone on the inside, deeply immersed in its traditions and methods. Thus, he shared many assumptions about the degenerate condition of blacks, but claimed that this was a result not of innate racial characteristics but was 'due to social surroundings for which we are responsible'; and he believed the main problem facing the USA was the possibility of assimilating immigrants and different racial groups to US life. Always convinced of the relevance of science for politics, Boas's public activities culminated in vigorous anti-Nazi campaigning in the last years of his life, centred on the American Committee for Democracy and Intellectual Freedom, which he founded in 1939.

But whilst he was an insider to the physical anthropological tradition, Boas's critique of evolutionism marked him out. Like Malinowski, he insisted on the importance of fieldwork, and spent numerous periods among Native Americans such as the Kwakiutl. He also focused on language, art and mythologies as key tools for understanding human societies, and proposed the concept of *Geist* (spirit) or 'the genius of a people' in unifying culture as a counterweight to biological determinism. His *The Mind of Primitive Man* (1911) brought these themes together, though his wide-ranging research is best approached through his numerous essays.

Boas's stance can be seen as a commitment to scientific rationalism, empiricism and universalism, combined, as with Malinowski, with a Central European romanticism that sought to validate cultures that resisted absorption, like the Inuit of Baffinland whom he first studied in 1883. Along with a belief in universalism, progress and scientific truth went a sense of the intrinsic worth of alternative cultures. In this sense he was very much a product of the nineteenth century: the term 'culture' for which Boas is so famous was, in the relativistic sense that anthropologists use it today, developed less by him than by his students, Margaret Mead, Ruth Benedict, Alfred Kroeber, Clyde Kluckhohn, Melville Herskovits and others. It also enormously influenced post-Second World War US sociology in the shape of Talcott Parsons, David Riesman and the 'Culture and Personality' school. Yet without his lead, the internal critique of anthropology that he pioneered, which ended in the overturning of the discipline's fundamental presuppositions about race, might not have taken place.

Reference

Boas, Franz (1911) *The Mind of Primitive Man*, New York: Macmillan.

Further reading

Boas, Franz (1980 [1940]) *Race, Language and Culture*, Chicago: University of Chicago Press.
—— (1986 [1928]) *Anthropology and Modern Life*, New York: Dover Publications.
Stocking, George W., Jr (ed.) (1974) *The Shaping of American Anthropology, 1883–1911: A Franz Boas Reader*, Chicago: University of Chicago Press.
—— (1992) 'Anthropology as *Kulturkampf*: Science and Politics in the Career of Franz Boas', in *The Ethnographer's Magic and Other Essays in the History of Anthropology*, 92–113, Madison, WI: University of Wisconsin Press.
—— (ed.) (1996) *Volksgeist as Method and Ethic: Essays on Boasian Ethnography and the German Anthropological Tradition*, Madison, WI: University of Wisconsin Press.

SEE ALSO: anthropology and race; Darwin, Charles

DAN STONE

THE BODY, MEDICINE, HEALTH AND DISEASE

The development of modern medicine is not a simple linear affair from a brute past to an elegant present, but is a dense field of often conflicting ideas and practices jostling for academic and popular acceptance. An account of it must situate its knowledge within particular cultural and philosophical ideas as well as day-to-day events. Nineteenth-century Europe and North America saw increased urbanization and industrialization, revolution, civil, and other wars; the downgrading of religious influence in secular matters (see RELIGION, SECULARIZATION AND THE CRISIS OF FAITH), changing concepts of death, the influence of the philosophy of René Descartes (see MAIN CURRENTS OF PHILOSOPHY), and so on. This was also a time when trade unions and colleges of education were forming to consolidate and moderate the knowledge gained by their graduates. Resistance to such academic pressure, as well as disagreement as to subject matter taught in these places, gave rise to splinter groups. Diverse theories of the human body and the nature of disease coexisted among doctors, apothecaries, herbalists, and other healers and lay people. Some clung to religious ideas about pain and disease, accepting them as the will of God; folk remedies, perhaps effective perhaps not, were sought by many; some, following the ancient

Greek physician, Hippocrates, and Galen's later version, insisted on understanding bodily health in terms of the balance (homeostasis) of bodily fluids (humours: blood, phlegm, yellow bile and black bile) appropriate to each person – disease or 'fevers' being defined as having a plethora of a single humour (relievable by blood-letting, the use of leeches, purges and enemas); other ideas current were based only on clinical observation without anatomical reference; while still others were manufactured away from actual patients, theorized without reference to bodily symptoms at all. The nosological work of Philippe Pinel (1745–1826) is an example of this. Pinel, a somewhat transitional figure in late eighteenth- and early nineteenth-century medical thought, was innovative where his psychiatric patients were concerned (he is reputed to have released them from their chains, even though this was, in fact, the work of a hospital administrator). He also wrote a book cataloguing a large number of 'fevers' characterized by their visible symptoms and classified according to theoretically artificial criteria that did not take account of new methods of patient examination or discoveries that work on autopsies yielded. The nineteenth century, though, was also a time when scientific medicine began to develop as a driving and mainstream force. Statistical analysis of symptoms; measurement of medication; experimentation on animals; the use of microscopy, using newly developed coal tar-derived staining materials (originating from the Londoner, William Perkins's 1856 discovery of aniline dyes), to define the nature of micro-organisms; diagnostic tools such as the stethoscope and, later, X-rays; the development of anaesthesia; and changes in medical education all witness to this. Changes in the hospital system and public health benefited from the development of a scientific medicine.

Cartesian thought, already influential since the eighteenth century, considered the body a very complex machine with the mind or soul separate from it. The soul, it was thought, equated with conscious rationality. It should be noted that Descartes's claim that the soul/mind and the body belonged to distinctly different categories cut right across earlier ideas about the nature of human beings. In seventeenth-century thought, the body was the instrument of the soul. This new idea was very popular throughout Europe at the beginning of the eighteenth century, and adhered to by many throughout the nineteenth century, assimilated Newtonian philosophy where the body was seen as a machine consisting of fluids in tubes. Another dominant idea was vitalism (the idea that something accounts for life other than the matter of the physical body). The seventeenth- and eighteenth-century arguments for vitalism may be traceable to Cartesian dualism via the metaphysical foundations of G.E. Stahl (1660–1734). Others tempered their vision with conjectural accounts of eugenic theory under the impulse of Darwinian evolutionary thought (see DARWIN, CHARLES). Jean-Martin Charcot (the 'father' of neurology) and his pupil Gilles de la Tourette (c.1887) working at the Salpêtrière Hospital of Paris, much influenced by Darwinian thought, considered the ticcing condition now known as Tourette's Syndrome a 'degeneracy'. Charcot based his reasoning on the supposition that people with the syndrome occupied a lower position on the human phylogenetic scale. Tourette physically suspended patients to straighten such 'primitives' to aid them to become modern *Homo erecti*.

As in other fields of endeavour, Romanticism (see ROMANTICISM, INDIVIDUALISM AND IDEAS OF THE SELF) and Rationalism both had adherents in the medical field. Medical Romanticism saw the clinician as a charismatic figure who healed by charm alone. The practice of mesmerism (following the work of the Viennese physician Franz Anton Mesmer [1734–1815]), or suggestion, began to be used in the treatment of the mentally ill; a practice that transgressed beyond medicine to entertainment. Homeopathy, developed by Samuel Hahnemann (1755–1843), is another example of Romantic medicine. The basis of Homeopathy is the belief in the 'law of similars' where the vibration of a substance (a much watered down version of the original substance) is administered that has the same characteristics as the disease process. Romantic medicine, though, had a valuable side: it continued to listen to the experiences of patients, where mainstream scientific medicine often failed. Experiences are, after all, not easily measurable. The psychoanalytic techniques of Sigmund Freud (1856–1939) and Carl Jung (1875–1961) incorporated the experiential aspects of this Romantic medicine, as well as the Germanic fascination for mythology.

Rationalism came to dominate the development of a scientific medicine. This medicine is scientific in the sense of incorporating the systematic collection of data, its measurement and controlled experimentation. Previously, deference to tradition, empiricism and a concentration upon symptoms ruled. The development of scientific medicine coincides with the realization that contrary to the notion of disease as a single entity, there are many diseases with many causes, many symptoms and many treatments.

The realization of the multiplicity of disease processes impacted upon an understanding of public health. The escalating industry of the nineteenth century brought more workers to towns, putting increasing pressure upon limited fresh water and sewage resources. Town councils were forced to provide inexpensive housing, schools and churches for industrial workers. Poverty became visible and social classes discernable. Diseases came to be seen as bad for the national interest and, for a time, a sign of individual irresponsibility and a failure to abide by the well understood rules of modern hygiene, though, by the late 1880s and 1890s the germ theory of disease and understanding of bacteriology had clouded the issue of individual responsibility for illness.

The formation of a scientific medicine had to fight free from religious control and dogma. This meant a cultural climate willing to let go of the past. The post-French Revolution period provided exactly this climate for change.

Old-style medical training facilities in France were abolished during the French Revolution. Learned societies were condemned as being elitist in the name of liberty and equality. Religious-run institutions had to abandon them to the state. What sprung up from the ashes were medical institutions and three schools of health in Paris, Montpellier and Strasburg, accountable to the state. Thus France, unlike other parts of Europe, could truly be scientifically independent. French, rather than the traditional Latin, became the language of discourse. Professors were appointed and paid by the state, chairs for the individual disciplines and set numbers of students were instituted.

There was a great number of innovative thinkers and medical inventions in France at this time, all contributing to a scientific medicine.

Jean-Nicolas Corvisart (1755–1821) – Napoleon's physician – recommended percussion to diagnose thoracic complaints. A student of his, Theophile-Rene Laennec (1781–1826), invented auscultation with a tube placed on the female chest. To put one's ear to a woman's chest was deemed lacking in decorum. This was the forerunner of the stethoscope. In Vienna, Karl Rokitansky (1804–78) and his pupil Josef Skoda (1805–81), both heads of medical schools, adopted this French practice of 'listening to the chest' by means of percussion and auscultation.

Pierre-Charles Louis (1787–1872) introduced what he called 'the numerical method' (a precursor of what is now called 'medical statistics'), This was the scrupulous observation of symptoms, their repetition and frequency, from which he drew diagnostic and prognostic conclusions. In this way, the results he obtained were carefully quantified so as to ascertain their effectiveness. The results, likewise, of therapy were also quantified, this measurement determining the effectiveness of the therapy. While criticized by his contemporaries, this careful comparison of symptoms and lesions allowed doctors to associate a particular disorder with a particular sign and symptom.

François Magendi (1783–1855) argued against animism and vitalism, and urged experimentation on animals, thus causing outrage among the protectors of animals. Magendi viewed the body as a complex machine and animals as nothing more than automata. Using animals, he studied the peristalsis of the oesophagus, the formation of the image on the retina, the effect of absences in one's diet, and did considerable work on the nervous system.

Pierre Bretonneau (1778–1862) identified in typhoid fever a whole range of pathological symptoms (sore throat, pink rash, joint pain, peritonitis due to the perforation of the small intestine, haemorrhaging, liver and renal and possible heart problems). Bretonneau realized that this litany of conditions had a single origin in the abnormal patches on the mucous membrane of the intestine. Bretonneau's work contributed to a basic medical precept: specificity. The concept of specificity in medicine is this: a disease is specific in that it has a cause and seemingly unconnected symptoms that have a single prognosis. In this way, diagnosis is simple and treatment must be tailored to the disease.

A Prussian-born doctor Rudolf Virchow (1821–1902) explored particularity of medical disorder to specific organ dysfunction. He developed the science of pathological histology (the study of tissues), noting that each form of tissue has its own particular cell type and that cells belonging to the various organs are alive in their own right, are nourished by the blood and discharge waste, and are born from a similar cell. This observation built upon the earlier work of the Frenchman François-Xavier Bichat (1771–1802). Bichat, without the use of microscope, had identified classes of tissues according to structure and function. Bichat pushed for the study of physiology – work continued by Claude Bernard (1813–78). Claude Bernard contributed much to the study of physiology, especially to knowledge of the secretions of the pancreas. He established the concept of 'function', that is, the role fulfilled by each tissue or organ in the human physiology to maintain life. He described the physico-chemical substance that bathes bodily tissues, inside the blood vessels and outside them, so that a change in the medium can have repercussions on a remote organ.

Medical training in France consisted of dissections and regular and compulsory visits to hospitals. The effect of this was to ensure that hospitals became places of learning and no longer ones where the sick were left to languor. Furthermore these state-run institutions ensured that health care was egalitarian. The new institutions swelled the numbers of hospitals, patients and medical students. In 1830, Paris boasted thirty hospitals with 20,000 patients, and training 5,000 medical students.

The progress of scientific medicine was enmeshed with changing ideas about the nature of death and life. The development of these ideas allowed for a radical change in the way medicine was practised. This is elaborated below.

The examination of pathological anatomy essential to the kind of medical education taught in France, and later elsewhere, helped redefine the theoretical nature of disease and changed the way such disease was treated. The examination of cadavers also changed the way death was understood. No longer was death seen as a battle of life lost as was believed in previous times, but the corpse itself came to be understood as the putrefying site of different life forms. This shift in understanding life and death is reflected in the writings of Jean-Nicolas Corvisart, who considered the normal functioning of the living organism was to become increasingly and intrinsically pathogenic. Such an understanding permitted a number of valuable discoveries: two, for instance, being the nature and pathology of disease causing micro-organisms in wound infection and disease process and the development

of anaesthetics that could be used to induce death-like states while surgery could be performed.

Louis Pasteur (1822–95) noted that the destruction of organic materials was due to the multiplication of living creatures and life appearing in a new form. Some of his first work was on fermentation of beer, wine and vinegar. He applied the same rationale to disease processes. By use of the microscope (previously underused by medical researchers, even though already improved by Leeuwenhoek in the seventeenth century), he identified the micro-organism responsible for fowl cholera. Realizing the implications of the presence of micro-organisms, Pasteur insisted on the sterilization of surgical instruments.

Some micro-organisms were found to protect a person against more serious diseases. The important work of Edward Jenner (1749–1823) needs to be mentioned here. Through study of smallpox and cowpox (a much less serious disease), Jenner noticed the similarities between the two. He inoculated a young boy with cowpox material, demonstrating that this vaccination technique protected against smallpox.

Pasteur's association of putrefaction and wound infection led to the germ theory of disease and to a veritable weaponry of poisonous substances introduced into the body to destroy disease. Later work by Paul Ehrlich (1854–1915) continued this technique of introducing poisonous substances into the body to combat disease. He illustrated his technique by reference to a German folktale about a Magic Bullet that when fired blindly would unerringly find its target.

An English doctor, Joseph Lister (1827–1912), introduced antiseptic surgery, which was not generally adopted until the twentieth century.

As already noted, France led medical education at least in the first half of the nineteenth century. Surgical studies and internal medicine were on the curriculum for both doctors and surgeons. Previously and elsewhere in Europe and North America, surgeons had a different education and a different life path. Practical surgery was a craft often combined with barbering learned by being apprenticed to a master and was controlled by a trade guild, though there is evidence that some surgeons were university trained as was true in Padua, Italy. Surgeons studied anatomy, dissected corpses and performed autopsies to ascertain a person's death. The use of cadavers was generally illegal, so surgeons paid grave robbers to supply them with corpses. These disinterred putrefying corpses killed off a number of young surgeons.

Doctors, on the other hand, had previously only studied philosophy and Latin. They did not study anatomy, or physiology. Many doctors of the period never even touched their patients, merely ascertaining the disease from symptoms alone. Cadaver examination came to be seen as most valuable for the training of doctors as well. Many Americans and other foreign students travelled to Paris to study this new medicine. Gradually other medical schools similarly amalgamated the training of internal physicians and surgeons.

Women in certain parts of Europe (Paris, Zurich and Berne) were not excluded from medical study, even though they often found it difficult to practise as doctors because of prevailing gender-specific prejudice against them. The first woman university trained physician, Dorothea Christiane Erxleben-Leporin, Prussian-born, was granted her doctorate in 1754. The social conditions that allowed women to become doctors in these places, but not in England for many years, appears to be linked to the climate of Nonconformist Protestantism, their links with international anti-slave movements and feminism (see FEMINISM AND THE FEMALE FRANCHISE MOVEMENT). All medical doctorates awarded women were non-British until the 1870s. In 1876, an act was passed allowing women to sit for medical examinations. Dublin's King and Queen's College of Physicians was the first to admit women and seven did so in that year.

The situations of war also brought the professions of surgery and internal medicine closer together. The sheer numbers of injured meant that a common knowledge base of both professions was needed: not all limbs needed to be amputated and there were infections to deal with. It was also in war that the nursing profession came to its own through the ministrations of the British reformer, Florence Nightingale (1820–1910). Trained at an Institute for Protestant Deaconesses in Kaiserwerth, Germany (one of the first formal nursing training institutions), Nightingale became superintendent of the Hospital for Invalid Gentlewomen in London. When the Crimean War broke out, she went to the battlefield to direct nursing operations at the command of the minister of war. With thirty-eight nurses, she instigated sanitary conditions in the military camps that were otherwise antagonistic to the healing process. In this way, the mortality rate among the soldiers was greatly reduced. Though popular sentimental accounts of Florence Nightingale depict her as a gentle lady with a lamp, she was a steely administrator with reformist ambitions. When the Crimean War ended in 1860, she founded the Nightingale School and Home for Nurses at Saint Thomas' Hospital in London. This school was the first to train nurses in a professional manner.

The changing concepts of death, plus viewing the body asleep as insensate machinery, impacted upon the development of anaesthetics for surgery. Surgeons began inducing death-like states with various substances so as to explore previously forbidden interior bodily zones such as the abdomen. Anaesthetic was generally not thought of as ameliorating pain even though Humphrey Davy (1778–1829) had already suggested that the pain and shock of surgical operations might be relieved if patients inhaled nitrous oxide.

Ether, whose starting materials are sulphuric acid and alcohol, had long been known. It was used as a sedative in the treatment of tuberculosis, asthma and whooping cough, and as a remedy for toothache. Its anaesthetic potential, though, had never been exploited and its introduction was gradual.

In the USA in 1846, William Morton demonstrated the surgical applications of ether, using a hastily rigged apparatus to deliver the substance to the patient. The new technique was to revolutionize surgical practice, enabling surgeons to develop finer skills and life-saving invasive procedures.

Chloroform was introduced by James Young Simpson (1811–70), a Professor of Midwifery at Edinburgh, to replace ether with its disagreeable and persistent smell. He began using it to relieve women's pains of childbirth and incurred the wrath of those holding to the biblical view that 'In sorrow thou shalt bring forth children.' After Queen Victoria chose to be anaesthetized in 1853 for the birth of Prince Leopold and again in 1857 for the birth of Princess Beatrice, the practice became common among the upper and middle classes.

By the 1880s anaesthesia, with aseptic surgical technique, was standard practice in US and European surgical theatres. Middle-class patients, used to receiving medical care at home, sought admission to hospitals for operations, and hospitals were transformed from charitable asylums for the poor into consumer-oriented service institutions. While the surgeon's prestige and power soared, the anaesthetist was a mere assistant – a nurse, intern or medical student. The development of the independent medical speciality of anaesthesiology did not occur until the early twentieth century.

What of the nature of surgery? As noted above, the introduction of anaesthetics allowed the surgeon to operate within the body cavity. Much of the first internal surgery was conducted on women. Indeed, gynaecological surgery led to gynaecology becoming the specialized field of medicine it is today and the development of modern surgery itself. Much of this early gynaecological surgical work was practised in the US South during the Revolutionary and Civil wars on black female slaves by the 'father' of gynaecology, J. Marion Sims (1813–83). Many of the women had suffered injury as a result of difficult or mismanaged births. Sims operated on these women to fix such injuries sometimes with anaesthetics, sometimes without.

Anaesthesia was not considered in terms of pain amelioration for some time. Pain was dealt with by a variety of substances: opiates, alcohol, mandrake, belladonna from the deadly nightshade and marijuana. In 1897, Felix Hoffmann discovered another compound, Acetylsalicylic acid, found naturally in willow tree bark, which also had analgesic properties. This was packaged and sold under the trade name 'Aspirin'.

Sensitivity to pain was attributed to higher evolutionary creatures – men feeling more pain than women. Non-Europeans, following eugenic ideas, were thought of as having little capacity to feel pain. Babies were thought to have no capacity for pain, no emotions and no mind to interpret their experiences, in other words, as pre-human.

By the 1890s, physiological and medical concepts of pain, as of the body and of disease generally, had become mechanistic, localized and empirical. The experimental findings of physiologists in France, Germany and England supported mechanical models of body functions, though barely any explanation for differing perceptions of pain. The work of Charles Bell and François Magendie showed that the posterior roots of the spinal nerves responded to sensations whereas the anterior roots appeared to be associated with motor responses, thus laying the groundwork for the idea of a specific neural pathway of pain sensation, elaborated in 1839 by Johannes Müller's theory of 'specific nerve energies'. Further confirmation came from the work of Edouard Brown-Séquard on the pain pathway in the spinal cord; from the contributions of John Hughlings Jackson and others, suggesting specific locations of various function in the brain; and from the experiments of Max von Frey, who in 1896 identified 'pain spots' on the skin.

The insights of human anatomy learned through surgery, plus the conception of the body as an organic machine, allowed for the conceptual development of X-rays. The German scientist Wilhelm Röntgen (1845–1923) noticed that a barium platincyanide screen fluoresced whenever he passed a high electrical current through a near empty tube, demonstrating the ability of these mysterious rays to pass through metal. He took a photograph of the image of his wife's hand complete with wedding ring. Interestingly, cinematography was developing simultaneously with X-ray technology. Building on the work of Röntgen, Marie Curie (1867–1934) and her husband, Pierre, explored the use of radium as the fluorescing element of choice in the development of X-rays. The X-ray machine proved to be a most valuable diagnostic tool and allowed access to a view of the body hitherto unimagined. X-ray technology became very popular, albeit dangerous in those early days; many technicians dying of cancer, including Marie Curie herself. Marie Curie was awarded the 1911 Nobel Prize in Chemistry for her work in discovering radium and polonium, and in isolating radium. The Curies earlier shared the 1903 Nobel Prize in Physics with the French physicist Antoine Henri Becquerel for fundamental work on radioactivity.

Reinterpreting death as continuing life in new forms and the Cartesian model of the body as machine were driving forces in the development of a scientific medicine. It allowed for the experimentation upon the body, it opened up the possibility of internal surgery, the exploration for effective anaesthetics and painkillers, and it encouraged the use of microscopy and X-ray technology for systematic examination of the body and diagnosis of disease and injury. The realization of what putrefaction meant encouraged aseptic surgery and scrupulous cleanliness in hospitals and the personal hygiene of medical staff. Understanding micro-organisms better allowed for their possible use against some disease itself. Public health became an issue to be reckoned with. Medical education for doctors and surgeons came to be recognized as absolutely essential; an education that included clinical rounds, the study of anatomy and physiology, the examination of cadavers, mathematics, physics and chemistry. The systematic education of nurses, too, became important. Scientific medicine was established and became mainstream, thus continuing to expand our understanding of the body, health and disease.

Further reading

Bynum, W.F. and Porter, Roy (eds) (1993) *Companion Encyclopedia of the History of Medicine*, Vols 1 and 2, London: Routledge.
Dally, Ann (1991) *Women under the Knife, A History of Surgery*, London: Hutchinson Radius.
Shryock, Richard Harrison (1979) *The Development of Modern Medicine, An Interpretation of the Social and Scientific Factors Involved*, Madison, WI: The University of Wisconsin Press.
Sournia, Jean-Charles (1992) *The Illustrated History of Medicine*, London: Harold Starke.

SEE ALSO: main currents in philosophy; main currents in scientific thought

ELIZABETH McCARDELL

BOLIVAR, SIMON (1783–1830)

Simon Bolivar was a South American soldier and statesman whose revolutionary struggles against Spain resulted in the independence of the countries now known as Venezuela, Columbia, Ecuador, Panama, Peru and Bolivia. Bolivar was born at Caracas, Venezuela, on 24 July 1783, and died at Santa Marta, Columbia, in 1830. Born to a noble land-owning family, Bolivar was sent to study in Madrid, and during a trip to Paris met an old tutor, Simon Rodriguez, who encouraged him to study Locke, Hobbes, Montesquieu, Rousseau and other thinkers, amongst whom the latter two were to prove most influential on his thought. In 1805, at Rome, he dedicated himself to securing the independence from Spain of her South American colonies. He helped to gain Venezuela's independence in 1811, while opposing the decentralized, federal constitution that it adopted. Moving to Nueva Granada in 1812, he pitted his 800 men against 15,000 Royalists, and on victory was styled 'The Liberator'. Reaching Caracas in August 1813, he proceeded to further victories until being defeated at La Puerta in June 1814, which resulted in the Spanish reconquest of Venezuela. In exile in Jamaica in 1815, he wrote the most important political statement of his career, the 'Letter from Jamaica', which proposed the establishment of constitutional republics throughout Spanish America modelled on the British system, with a hereditary upper house, an elected lower house and a president elected for life. The latter feature derived in part from his own election as dictator after his initial successes in Venezuela, but has been frequently criticized. Though he wished to abolish slavery and secure civil liberty, Bolivar's republicanism was strongly oligarchical, with property qualifications limiting the electorate and a strong executive ensuring the centralization of power. Socially he anticipated that the deaths of so many white soldiers during the revolution might bring about the rule of a mixed-race elite or 'Pardocracy'.

Returning to Venezuela in 1817, Bolivar commenced a lengthy campaign that resulted in a major defeat for the Spanish forces in August 1819, another in June 1821, and in several battles in 1823–4. Bolivar became President of Gran Columbia, the unified states of Ecuador, Venezuela and Columbia. Fearing that political fragmentation would follow victory, Bolivar proposed a permanent confederation of the newly sovereign states, with an assembly of plenipotentiaries that would act as mediator and conciliator in resolving disputes between the states. A constitutional convention in February 1825 established the first political organization of the new republic, but by 1828 centrifugal forces had seriously weakened the union, and Bolivar resigned the leadership of Nueva Granada after 14 years. He spent most of 1829 suppressing a Peruvian incursion into Columbia, and died on 30 December 1830. In his latter years he made various efforts to unify other Latin and South American republics by treaty. At a congress held at Panama in 1826, for instance, a common army and navy, and the resolution of disputes by arbitration, were planned for Mexico, Columbia, Peru and Central America. Bolivar's reputation remains dogged by accusations of authoritarianism, though he remains indisputably the most important theoretician of the South American independence movement, and of a system of unified government for the region.

Further reading

Belaunde, Victor (1938) *Bolivar and the Political Thought of the Spanish American Revolution*, Baltimore: Johns Hopkins University Press.

Bolivar, Simon (2003) *El Libertador: Writings of Simon Bolivar*, Oxford: Oxford University Press.

GREGORY CLAEYS

BONALD, LOUIS DE (1754–1840)

Count Louis de Bonald was a dominant force in the French counter-revolution, both as a theorist and as a political figure. Although he lacked the polemical skills of his contemporary, JOSEPH DE MAISTRE, Bonald developed a set of social theories that exercised a powerful influence on both counter-revolutionary and sociological thought in the nineteenth century. His organicism drew the attention of HENRI DE SAINT-SIMON and his one-time disciple AUGUSTE COMTE, credited as the founder of sociology. Comte honoured Bonald with an entry in his positivist calendar and echoed Bonald in his recognition of the need to study society as a collective phenomenon. Although his key theoretical works, the three-volume *Théorie du pouvoir politique et religieux dans la société civile, démontrée par le raisonnement et l'histoire* (Theory of Political and Religious Power in Civil Society, Proved by Reasoning and History, 1796), *Essai analytique sur les lois naturelles* (Analytical Essay on Natural Laws, 1799) and the three-volume *Législation primitive* (Primitive Legislation, 1802) were little read, and little appreciated, Bonald was a prominent counter-revolutionary journalist, a contributor to the *Mercure de France*, the *Gazette de France* and a co-founder of CHATEAUBRIAND's *Le Conservateur*. Bonald's organicism exercised a strong influence on the discourse of Legitimists (the supporters of the ousted Bourbon monarchy), who contrasted an *ancien régime* characterized by a harmonious system of corporate bodies with the individualistic post-revolutionary order. In the late nineteenth century, Catholic traditionalists René de La Tour du Pin and Albert de Mun put forward Bonaldian views, believing corporatism, in the form of 'organized professions', to be a remedy for the corrosive individualism born out of the Revolution. Arguably the organicism championed by Pétain's Vichy regime bore the stamp of such ideas.

Louis-Gabriel-Ambrose de Bonald was born into a wealthy provincial noble family with a tradition of municipal service in the local town of Millau. His education at the prestigious Oratorian Collège de Jully brought him into contact with both the modern ideas of Buffon, Bayle, Malebranche and Newton, and the austere Jansenist strain of Catholicism. After a brief stint in the exclusive but anachronistic Musketeers Bonald returned to his estates in Rouergue, and, in accordance with family tradition, became mayor of Millau. A supporter of the 'aristocratic revolution' of 1787–8, Bonald looked to a revival of provincial estates, seeing in them a solution to what he identified as a noble crisis of identity. In the context of the revolutionary agitation of August 1789 he proposed a confederation of the towns of the Rouergue, a proposal he later sent to the National Assembly as a blueprint for provincial representation. Despite Bonald's concern for noble leadership, his break with the Revolution came relatively late, precipitated by the issue of the enforcement of the Civil Constitution of the Clergy, a project to which he was in principle sympathetic.

Although initially enlisted in an *émigré* force, Bonald soon settled in Heidelberg to serve the counter-revolution with his pen. The result was *Théorie*, which appeared in 1796 to general indifference. In 1797 Bonald made a clandestine return to France and became active in the Parisian counter-revolutionary circles. His interests in science and affinity to the Idéologues (a group concerned with establishing empirical social sciences) made for a difficult relationship with mainstream counter-revolution, typified by Chateaubriand for whom the counter-revolution was a literary and aesthetic movement. As with many counter-revolutionaries, Bonald entertained certain hopes about the Napoleonic state, but was ultimately disappointed. He nonetheless served Napoleon, accepting a position on the Grand Council of the University in 1810.

The moderate nature of the Restoration was a further disappointment, although Bonald enjoyed an influential political career among the ultra-royalists, becoming a minister of state in 1821, followed by elevation to the Chamber of Peers in 1823 as the Vicomte de Bonald. Convinced of the unworkability of the constitutional monarchy established by the Charter, Bonald urged a return to absolute monarchy. His repressive and intolerant attitudes were expressed in his sponsorship of the infamous Sacrilege Law, which proposed the death penalty for sacrilege. Bonald even recommended that the condemned should be forced to make a public confession and beg for forgiveness. This idea of a ritualized punishment is quite as unpleasant as anything encountered in Maistre's writings, although Bonald lacked Maistre's dark fascination with bloodshed and expiation. However with the fall of the Bourbon monarchy in the July Revolution Bonald's counter-revolutionary career effectively came to an end. He withdrew from politics and the only major work he produced in the last decade of his life was his *Réflexions sur la révolution du Juillet 1830* (Reflections on the Revolution of July 1830, 1988), a testament to an old man's bitterness at the perceived inadequacies of the Restoration, 'a fifteen year farce'.

The long and repetitious *Théorie* indicates the systematic cast of Bonald's thought and his scientism. In its modes of argument, with frequent appeals to history and reason, and in its system-building pretensions it was a work of the Enlightenment, but in its conclusions it looked to the re-establishment of a revitalised *ancien régime*. It represented Bonald's attempt to construct a science of political society, what he referred to as 'moral or social science'. This endeavour diverged from Enlightenment science in significant ways, having a religious conception of man at its heart. Bonald's reason was metaphysical, and he ultimately stood more in the Cartesian tradition than in the Enlightenment tradition. Thus for Bonald Condorcet's ideas were flawed, not because of his notion of 'social mathematics,' but because he possessed a materialistic and sacrilegious view of human nature.

Bonald's emphasis lay on the organization of society; indeed, organization was identified as the defining characteristic of human life. The divine power constituted society as series of interlocking social structures that contained the destructive human tendencies of egoism and individualism. Thus, as Bonald put it, man did not constitute society, but society constituted man. In a strikingly original insight Bonald also saw language as constituted by society and hence of divine not human origin. The laws, institutions and customs of the *ancien régime* were an expression of the divine organizing power, a set of necessary and legitimate social relations. The revolutionaries were therefore profoundly mistaken in their endeavour, opposing the natural order and ultimately God. The truth of this theory was proved by an appeal to history, which revealed that violence and instability were intrinsic to republics.

Bonald's focus on the organization of society meant that he lacked Maistre's obsession with the Revolution. His observations about the Revolution were nonetheless significant, revealing fundamental aspects of his thought. This analysis was most powerfully expressed in *Considérations sur la révolution française* (Considerations on the French Revolution, 1818) written to refute MME DE STAËL's account. First Bonald rejected de Staël's analysis of the *ancien régime*. Her image of unhappy and oppressed France was inaccurate. The *ancien régime* was only a time of oppression in one respect, oppressed by the false doctrines and impious writings of the Enlightenment *philosophes*. True oppression came with the Revolution. Second, Bonald dissected the Revolution. His starting point was to note that the spirit of the Reformation was active in modern revolutions, which rejected authority and attacked the Catholic political society. The spirit of Calvinism was the spirit of democracy. Whereas the revolutions of antiquity had been motivated by ambition for political power, modern revolutions had a moral dimension, an ambition for spiritual power. The Revolution, which Bonald revealingly identified as still active in Europe, had a religious not a political thrust; the intent to de-royalize was intrinsically linked to a project to de-Catholicize. Overall, opined Bonald, the Revolution represented the negation of all social power, political and religious atheism, the destruction of all ideas of power, duty, justice, divinity, humanity and society. It was moral evil at its most powerful.

Yet Bonald also located a further cause of the revolution: the decline of the nobility, which amounted to a loss of the active power of the monarchy. In France, as in every naturally constituted society the nobility represented what Bonald described as 'the action of power'. The service nobility were evidently a central part of the monarchical state, and Bonald placed a corresponding value on the territorial wealth that buttressed this aristocracy, noting that liquid assets led to democracy. Bonald was intensely hostile to industrialization and urbanization, as conducive to individualism and egoism, identifying a fatal shift away from the landed system beginning at the turn of the sixteenth century. Bonald's restoration envisaged a radical reconstruction of society, which necessarily included a return to France's agricultural traditions.

As has been seen, Bonald identified the revolution as an ongoing phenomenon; his considerations on social organization were concerned with the great question of how to bring the revolution to a close and undo its evils. Arguably this made his thinking on state centralization and the role of the state confused. His ideas appear to have either to have undergone substantial change or to be fundamentally inconsistent and contradictory. Certainly Bonald has been interpreted in diametrically opposed fashions on this issue. One interpretation sees Bonald as essentially a traditional counter-revolutionary, anti-individualist and anti-statist, looking to a reconstituted *ancien régime* 'shorn of its abuses'. This was a vision of the *ancien régime* as a hierarchy of social groups (under noble guidance) that would mediate between the individual and the state. In this reading Bonald possessed a pluralistic theory of authority. The rival interpretation sees Bonald as a believer in unrestricted state power, a theorist of absolutism.

The vision of Bonald-as-absolutist rests partly on the second volume of *Théorie*, which presents a vision of a reconstituted *ancien régime* with *intendants*, no provincial assemblies, an infrequently convened Estates-General and a much-strengthened monarch whose powers would include appointing the members of the *parlements*. This is evidently at odds with Bonald's indictment of the haughty central administration in the first volume, blamed for alienating the nobility, leading to apathy and a loss of enthusiasm for public service. His *Du divorce* (On Divorce, 1801) reinforces this idea of Bonald as a champion of an all-powerful state; the state should possess the right to regulate the family. Bonald's Restoration politics also support such an interpretation; in his review of de Staël's work Bonald commented that in the context of the weak democratic constitution an absolutist administration was necessary. He supported the exceptional laws of the 1820s on the grounds that the stability of the state overrode any other considerations and urged stricter censorship, reiterating the arguments in favour of censorship he had made under the Empire, namely that God himself was 'supremely intolerant'. There seems little trace of the man who had supported the aristocratic revolt and envisioned a return to provincial assemblies. On the other hand, it is notable that Bonald attacked the fiscal system of the Restoration, blaming high taxation on the mistaken practice of the state provision of public services. Such matters apparently should be left in the hands of the landed bodies of the Church and nobility, traditional providers of charity and education.

A possible way to resolve this argument is to look at Bonald's position on the nobility. The systems that Bonald constructed were premised on a belief that there was an underlying natural triadic order, from the three estates to the Holy Trinity. Bonald's image of society was thus expressed in the formula power, minister, subject; power was identified with the monarch, the ministers with the nobility as royal agents, through whom the state power acted on the subjects. Bonald was absolutely unequivocal on the issue of the nobility's special role as 'the action of power'. Bonald supported the traditional concept of *dérogance*, the loss of noble status for those who became involved in commerce, declaring that such activities made nobles unfit for public service, concerned with particular interests. The privileges that the nobles had enjoyed were justified by the nobles' disinterested service of the state, renouncing lucrative professions and the need to strengthen landed wealth on which the aristocratic state rested. The nobility were thus conceived as a caste apart, albeit a caste into which it was possible to rise, a feature of the *ancien régime* that Bonald upheld as proof that true liberty and equality were enjoyed. In *Théorie* Bonald suggested that nobles should wear special insignia and share certain rituals to bind them together. The sons of the nobility would be educated for state service at special schools and his vision even encompassed a 'Temple of Providence' at which national festivals would be celebrated to inculcate a 'religion of society'. Bonald's stress on the collectivity thus led him to a distinctly Rousseauist idea. Yet this should not necessarily lead us to a conclusion that Bonald believed in an all-powerful state forcing men to be free. First, we should note Bonald's assertion that a monarchical state, even if ruled by a tyrant, could never rival the oppressive power wielded under the Revolution; Bonald distinguished absolute power that respected the laws from arbitrary power, the result of popular sovereignty. As Maistre had argued, the monarch was only absolute in the sphere allotted to him by the law. Second, this conception of a service nobility connects back to long-established ideas of the nobility as mediating between monarch and locality. Bonald's ideal was to reintegrate the nobility into the state. His vision of society was certainly authoritarian and presumed unity – pluralism was not part of Bonald's agenda – but hardly proto-totalitarian.

At the heart of Bonald's thought lay God, and a conception of the constituted society as divinized. Men encountered God in the legitimate social forms; power was constituted independently of men, according to natural laws of a divine nature. In the family the power of the father was thus of a divine nature. Legitimacy was nothing other than conformity to God's laws, society as willed by God, an eternal order that could be found in the primitive and fundamental laws of human society. This conception of society meant that liberty of expression was dangerous licence, and moderation dangerous indifference: this was the criminal error of the Restoration governments. Legislation should prescribe sacred and indispensable duties. In a trope subsequently celebrated by Catholics and Legitimists, Bonald declared that the Declaration of the Rights of Man had opened the Revolution and a Declaration of the Rights of God would close it.

Further reading

Beik, P. (1970) *The French Revolution Seen from the Right: Social Theories in Motion, 1789–1799*, New York: Howard Fertig.

Klinck, D. (1996) *The French Counter revolutionary Theorist Louis de Bonald*, New York: Peter Lang.

Nisbet, R. (1944) 'De Bonald and the Concept of the Social Group', Journal of the History of Ideas 5: 315–31.

Reedy, W.J. (1979) 'Conservatism and the Origins of the French Sociological Tradition: A Reconsideration of Louis de Bonald's Science of Society', *Proceedings of the Sixth Annual Meeting for the Western Society for French History* 6: 264–73.

SEE ALSO: Chateaubriand, François; Comte, Auguste; conservatism, authority and tradition; Maistre, Joseph de; Saint-Simon, Henri de; social theory and sociology in the nineteenth century

MARTIN SIMPSON

BOSANQUET, BERNARD (1848–1923)

Bosanquet was born at Rock Hall, near Alnwick, Northumberland, on 14 July 1848 and died in London on 8 February 1923. Educated locally and then at Harrow School (1862–7), he entered Balliol College, Oxford, in 1867 and was among the most brilliant of T.H. GREEN's students. Bosanquet was a Fellow of University College, Oxford, from 1870–81. Thereafter, except for a period as Professor of Moral Philosophy at the University of St Andrews (1903–8), he devoted his time to private study and a range of characteristically late-Victorian political and intellectual activities: 'charity organization'; the Aristotelean Society; ethical society, adult education and art education lecturing. His intellectual interests were broad ranging and informed by current developments in philosophy, psychology and sociology in France, Germany and Italy.

Bosanquet's earliest book-length publications were in logic (*Knowledge and Reality* [1885]) and aesthetics; *A History of Aesthetic* (1896) was the first British contribution to modern philosophical treatments of the subject. Having published a number of essays on social and political philosophy in the late 1880s and 1890s, Bosanquet made a major contribution in these fields with *The Philosophical Theory of the State* (1899). This book was reviewed widely, issued in three new editions before his death, and kept in print for more than half a century. The metaphysical basis of Bosanquet's work on aesthetics, logic and political philosophy, a form of 'absolute idealism' that was much indebted to F.H. BRADLEY's *Appearance and Reality* (1893), was presented in his Gifford Lectures of 1911–12 and 1912–13, published as the *Principle of Individuality and Value* and the *Value and Destiny of the Individual*.

Bosanquet was highly critical of the bifurcation of the individual and society that he identified with an English tradition of political thinking in which JEREMY BENTHAM, J.S. MILL and HERBERT SPENCER were prominent. In response to these theories of the 'first look', Bosanquet conceptualized the modern state as a complex network of legal institutions and voluntary agencies. Individuals realized themselves by participating in the life of their community at a number of geographical and functional levels, creating and sustaining thereby a 'concrete' universal expressing the authentic organicism of 'identity in difference'. Since the state and the range of less complete wholes that were incorporated within it were made through the action and thought of individuals, Bosanquet argued that it was essential for citizens of the modern state to retain the capacity for self-willed action, a stipulation that underwrote his life-long commitment to charity organization.

This association placed Bosanquet among the critics of 'new liberal' and socialist proposals for a more extensive welfare role for the state and gave rise to accusations of conservatism. At the same time, his organicism seemed to fly in the face of conventional liberal concerns for the autonomy of individuals. More recently, however, scholars have noted Bosanquet's contributions to a more broadly conceived new liberal attempt to develop accounts of liberalism as a non-individualistic doctrine. Radical features of Bosanquet's political thinking – his commitment to democracy, to classless, participatory forms of community organization, and his endorsement of JOHN RUSKIN's and WILLIAM MORRIS's ideas on the 'decorative arts' – lend credence to these reconsiderations of his location and significance.

Further reading

Bosanquet, B. (2000), *The Collected Works of Bernard Bosanquet*, 20 vols, ed. W.L. Sweet, Bristol: Thoemmes Press.
Morrow, J. (2000) 'Community, Class and Bosanquet's "New State"', *History of Political Thought* 21: 485–500.
Nicholson, P.P. (1990) *The Political Philosophy of the British Idealists: Selected Studies*, Cambridge: Cambridge University Press.
Simhony, A. and Weinstein, D. (eds) (2001) *The New Liberals*, Cambridge: Cambridge University Press.
Sweet, W.L. (1997) *Idealism and Rights*, Lanham: University Press of America.
Vincent, A. and Boucher, D. (2000) *British Idealism and Political Theory*, Edinburgh: University of Edinburgh Press.

SEE ALSO: Green, T.H.; intellectuals, elites and meritocracy; liberalism; theories of the state and society: the science of politics

JOHN MORROW

BRADLAUGH, CHARLES (1833–91)

A renowned secularist, republican, radical and birth-control advocate, Charles Bradlaugh was born at Hoxton, London, on 26 September 1833. Successively an errand-boy, coal-dealer, Sunday-school teacher and free-thought lecturer, he enlisted in the 7th Dragoon Guards in 1850, and became further radicalized by witnessing peasant evictions and distress in Ireland. On his discharge, he became a solicitor's clerk and secularist lecturer, often writing under the pseudonym of 'Iconoclast'. After three attempts to enter Parliament he became MP for Northampton in 1880, and immediately became a *cause célèbre* through his refusal to take the oath of allegiance. Deprived of his seat three times, by judicial decree, expulsion from the house and resignation to appeal to his constituency, Bradlaugh was each time re-elected. Finally allowed to take his seat, he played a prominent role in Parliament in establishing a Labour Borough, represented the interests of the Indian National Congress and was a prominent opponent of socialism.

Continuing a tradition associated with Thomas Paine and Richard Carlile, Bradlaugh rose to prominence in company with G.J. Holyoake, Charles Watts and Annie Besant, as one of the leading secularists of the era. Like Paine, he stressed inconsistencies in the Bible, popularizing these views in the *Freethinker's Text Book* (1876) and other works. His weekly radical newspaper, the *National Reformer*, was founded in 1860, and here Bradlaugh opposed the monarchy and imperial expansion, promoted land reform, including the confiscation of untilled land (the case is stated in *Compulsory Cultivation of Land* (1887), and see also *The Land, the People, and The Coming Struggle* [1877]). He also supported the case for Irish home rule and Indian administrative reform, and attacked state regulation of wages and hours of labour. He also opposed Sabbatarian legislation. Bradlaugh's radical individualism places him close to Herbert Spencer at points. Unusually for a radical, he was a Malthusian (see *Jesus, Shelley and Malthus* [1861]), arguing that overpopulation was the cause of low working-class wages. While hostile to governmental interference (see, e.g., *The Eight Hours' Movement* [1889]), he supported labour's own right to combine through trade unions, friendly societies and co-operative associations (see, e.g., *Capital and Labor* [1886]). State Socialism, where all property was held in common and all labour controlled by the state, he condemned as 'totally hostile to the institutions of a free democracy', and prone thus to despotism (see *Socialism: Its Fallacies and Dangers* (1887) and *Debate between H.M. Hyndman and Chas Bradlaugh. Will Socialism Benefit the English People?* [1884]). Bradlaugh became President of the National Secular Society in 1866, and was frequently in legal difficulties for his advocacy of the cause, most notably in 1877, when he and Annie Besant were tried for publishing the birth-control manual, *The Fruits of Philosophy*. Equally dramatic was his plea for republicanism, most popularly developed in *The Impeachment of the House of Brunswick* (1871). Bradlaugh died on 30 January 1891.

Further reading

Bonner, Hypatia Bradlaugh (1895) *Charles Bradlaugh. A Record of His Life and Work*, 2 vols. London: C.A. Watts.

Bradlaugh, Charles (1891) *Labor and Law*. London: R. Forder.

—— (1895) *Speeches*, 2nd edn. London: Bonner.

—— (1970) *A Selection of the Political Pamphlets of Charles Bradlaugh*, New York: Augustus M. Kelley.

GREGORY CLAEYS

BRADLEY, FRANCIS HERBERT (1846–1924)

Francis Herbert Bradley was born on 30 January 1830 in Clapham, London, and died in Oxford on 24 September 1924. Educated at Cheltenham College (1856–61), Marlborough College (1861–3), and University College Oxford (1865–9) he was elected in 1870 to a life fellowship at Merton College, Oxford. This appointment carried no teaching duties and Bradley devoted his time to philosophy. As an undergraduate Bradley attended T.H. GREEN's lectures on moral philosophy, and although he was an independent thinker his work is usually associated with the British Idealist movement. Bradley and BERNARD BOSANQUET shared many intellectual interests and admired each other's work in metaphysics and logic. Bradley's major contributions in these fields were *Principles of Logic* (1883, second edition 1922) and *Appearance and Reality* (1893).

Bradley's thought was marked by a characteristically Idealist hostility to empiricism and hedonistic utilitarianism. The former was the starting point for Bradley's earliest substantive publication, *The Presuppositions of Critical History* (1876), in which historical facts were held to be linked to the belief system of the historical thinker; utilitarianism was the initial target of *Ethical Studies* (1876). In these essays Bradley criticized both utilitarianism and the formal ethics of Kant on the grounds that they rested on 'abstract' one-sided conceptions of the 'self' whose realization formed the focus of ethical enquiry. The self was neither a collection of particular feelings nor an abstract universal but a 'concrete universal' that had to be understood in relation to the 'moral organism' of which it formed a part. In the essay entitled 'My Station and Its Duties' Bradley identified the scope for self-realization that was made possible by fulfilling one's role in increasingly universal social entities: the family, society and the state. In the next two chapters, however, Bradley identified the limitations and contradictions of conventional morality and looked beyond this, first to ideal morality, and finally to religion in which contradictions are overcome because goodness is conceived to have been realized in some world. These conditions were dialectical advances on social morality, not a negation of it since their fruits served as the basis for refining conceptions of the moral possibilities and requirements of social life.

Although *Ethical Studies* was the first book-length study of ethical and social philosophy written from the standpoint of British Idealism Bradley did not advance a systematic statement of his political philosophy. Nor did he see his writings in this area as part of a reform programme in the way that both Bosanquet and Green did. *Ethical Studies* was the subject of a markedly hostile review by HENRY SIDGWICK who accused its author of lacking the sympathetic insight necessary for a well-informed critic, but this work, together with Bradley's collected essays and *Appearance and Reality*, remained in print long after his death. Bradley's writings probably attracted more interest from philosophers in the twentieth century than those of other Idealists, or Sidgwick.

Further reading

Bradley, F.H. (1999) *The Collected Works of F.H. Bradley*, 12 vols, eds C. Keane and W.J. Mander, Bristol: Thoemmes Press.

Nicholson, P.P. (1990) *The Political Philosophy of the British Idealist. Selected Studies*, Cambridge: Cambridge University Press.

Wollheim, R. (1959) *F.H. Bradley*. Harmondsworth: Penguin.

SEE ALSO: Green, T.H.; main currents in philosophy

JOHN MORROW

BROUGHAM, HENRY (1778–1868)

Henry Peter Brougham was first baron Brougham and Vaux, lord chancellor, educational reformer and proponent of social science. From 1802, with FRANCIS JEFFREY and SYDNEY SMITH, he was a principal *Edinburgh Review*. The outstanding parliamentary lawyer of his generation, moments of dishonesty and excessive self-praise damaged his reputation.

Stemming from impecunious northern gentry, Brougham had little sympathy with working-class radicalism, or the pretensions of landed grandees. The anti-slavery arguments of his *Inquiry into the Colonial Policies of the European Powers* (1803) ingratiated him with the Hollands and other leading Whigs; by 1810 he was in Parliament, promoting free trade, low taxation and other policies favourable to commerce. His bills of 1820 for parochial schools in England and Wales on the Scottish model fell foul of denominational vested interests; but his *Observations on the Education of the People* (1825) went through twenty editions; and his Society for the Diffusion of Useful Knowledge promoted mechanics' institutes and science teaching; and in 1828 he helped found the (secular) London University; while his law reform schemes of that year modernized real property law and the workings of the common law. Lord Grey raised him to the chancellorship, 22 November 1830, and Brougham was able to make sweeping reforms, establishing the Central Criminal Court and making the case for county courts. His highest point was the speech of 7 October 1831 in support of the second reading of the parliamentary reform bill. However, his betrayal of party confidences excluded him from political office after 1834; though he sat constantly in the court of appeal and on the judicial committee of the privy council, and pursued reform through the Law Amendment Association and *The Law Review*, courts of conciliation and a justice ministry being among his pet schemes.

His speeches defending Queen Caroline against the bill designed to end her marriage to George IV (1820) made him a hero of middle-class liberalism, with their argument against any right of the Lords to prevail over the mandate of the people. This popularity was consolidated, from 1857, through the National Association for the Promotion of Social Science, anticipatory of WEBB socialism in its view of government as a practical, and humanitarian, science. Unsurprisingly, Brougham was no friend to Romanticism (see ROMANTICISM, INDIVIDUALISM AND IDEAS OF THE SELF). In attacking Tory interests in the north of England he crossed swords with Wordsworth and de Quincey; he famously savaged the poetry of Lord Byron; and his Benthamite (see BENTHAM, JEREMY) contempt for the supposedly 'sacred' rights of landed families distressed S.T. COLERIDGE. Product of an earlier Enlightenment – Newton and Voltaire remained his heroes – Brougham gave his name to the rapid light carriage ('brougham') popular with well-to-do Victorians dashing to and from railway stations: a fit symbol of his ambiguous link with a more egalitarian future.

Further reading

Brougham, Henry Peter (1855–61) *Collected Works*, 11 vols, London & Glasgow: R. Griffin & Co.
Ford, Trowbridge H. (1995) *Henry Brougham and his World*, Chichester: Barry Rose.
Stewart, Robert (1985) *Henry Brougham 1778–1868: His Public Career*, London: Bodley Head.

SEE ALSO: liberalism; main currents in scientific thought; political economy

MALCOLM HARDMAN

BUCKLE, HENRY THOMAS (1821–62)

An influential mid-Victorian historian, Buckle was born in London on 24 November 1821, into a ship-owning family. A delicate child, he was educated chiefly at home; he discovered an aptitude for languages when travelling abroad, which he came to regard as the chief component of education, and by 1850 could read nineteen languages and converse fluently in seven. Politically he began to move towards radicalism and free trade. Independent at his father's death, Buckle took up the study of history, and, since he disliked libraries, he acquired a library of 22,000 volumes in the process. He laboured for 14 years with the aim of producing a history of civilization in general, but had to settle with confining it to Britain. Volume 1 of the *History of Civilisation in England* appeared in 1857, Volume 2 in 1861 and Volume 3 in 1864. It was an instant success. Distracted for a time in 1859 by his defence of a prominent blasphemy case, Buckle's health became strained, and in 1861 he resolved to travel in the Middle East. He succumbed, however, to a fever, dying at Damascus on 29 May 1862.

Buckle's substantial reputation rests both upon his attempt to impose a scientific method on historical study, and the vast breadth of reading evidenced in the thick undergrowth of annotation that accompanies the text. His starting-point is the causal influence on human society of natural laws, and the relative unimportance of free will. Four types of physical cause primarily shape society: climate, food, soil and the general natural environment. The emergence of civilization in Europe stems chiefly from the greater labour required to conquer nature, and its relatively benign climate. The primary cause of the progress of civilization within Europe Buckle regards, like J.S. MILL, as intellectual advancement, which is intimately intertwined with moral improvement. Moral truths, however, are stationary:

> To do good to others; to sacrifice for their benefit your own wishes; to love your neighbour as yourself; to forgive your enemies; to restrain your passions; to honour your parents; to respect those who are set over you: these, and a few others, are the sole essentials of morals; but they have been known for thousands of years.

Progress is thus primarily intellectual, and its practical application is the increase of happiness in this life through the mastery of science. The specific circumstances that rendered England's rise to civilization more orderly than elsewhere then become a major focus for Buckle, and here greater freedom, and the relative absence of the 'protective principle', whose strength in France is explored at length in Volume 2, are vital. Volume 3 is devoted entirely to Scotland, and particularly to the more pronounced 'deductive' spirit characteristic of its intellectual endeavours, which Buckle attributes largely to the influence of the clergy on the educational system.

Further reading

Buckle, Henry Thomas (1872) *The Miscellaneous and Posthumous Works of Henry Thomas Buckle*, 3 vols, London: Longmans.

Huth, Alfred Henry (1880) *The Life and Writings of Henry Thomas Buckle*, 2 vols, 2nd edn, London: S. Low Marston Searle & Rivington.

Robertson, John Mackinnon (1895) *Buckle and His Critics*, London: Swan Sonnenschein.

GREGORY CLAEYS

BURCKHARDT, JAKOB (1818–97)

Best known for his treatment of Italian culture in *Die Kultur der Renaissance in Italien* (*The Civilization of the Renaissance in Italy*, 1867), Jakob Burckhardt was born at Basle on 25 May 1818, and died there on 8 August 1897. From 1839–43 he studied at Berlin and Bonn, notably under the art historian Franz Kugler. He became Professor of History at Basle in 1845, and remained in the post for most of the period until 1893. His main works are *Die Zeit Konstantins der Grossen* (1853) (*The Age of Constantine the Great*, 1949), *Der Cicerone, eine Anleitung zum Genuss der Kunstwerke Italiens* (1855), a study of Italian art that took the form of a travel guide, and *Geschichte der Renaissance in Italien* (1867). *Griechische Kulturgeschichte* (1898–1902), *Erinnerungen an Rubens* (1898), *Beiträge zur Kunstgeschichte von Italien* (1898; 'Contributions to the Art History of Italy'). Two other posthumous publications (*Weltgeschichtliche Betrachtungen* 1905; *Force and Freedom: Reflections on History*, 1943), along with the *Historische Fragmente* ('Historical Fragments', 1929, in *Gesamtausgabe*; *Judgments on History and Historians*, 1958), which includes selections from his lectures, demonstrate his contribution to wider historiographical debates.

In his early writings Burkhardt portrayed the decline of the classical world sympathetically, but acknowledged the inevitability of the rise of Christianity, and its centrality to the cultural self-definition of the Middle Ages. Burckhardt's main study, *The Civilization of the Renaissance in Italy*, established the Renaissance as a fixed historical period, and the period in which, focusing on the fifteenth century, the medieval person passed over into the modern. It is divided into six sections: 'The State as a Work of Art'; 'The Development of the Individual'; 'The Revival of Antiquity'; 'The Discovery of the World and of Man'; 'Society and Festivals'; 'Morality and Religion'. While he celebrated its achievements, Burckhardt did not portray the Renaissance as uncompromisingly progressive; his description of its politics stresses the more mechanistic and instrumental elements to emerge to the fore in modern politics. Indeed, he has been seen as foreshadowing theorists of the totalitarian state of the twentieth century. Yet the 'modern Italian spirit' was for Burckhardt not singularly political, but a totality of elements cast from the contribution of antiquity, the influence of the Church and religion, and the political influence of northern institutions. From these there emerged both a world-view and a 'national spirit' (both *Geist* and *Kultur*, used in a wider sense than the English 'culture', coalesce here), a state of mind or motivation, the theoretical exposition of which remains Burckhardt's most enduring achievement. Its most important expression is in the beginning of Part Two, 'The Development of the Individual', which defends the sweeping proposition that 'Man was conscious of himself only as a member of a race, people, party, family or corporation – only through some general category', whilst in the Italian Renaissance 'man became a *spiritual* individual and recognized himself as such'. This dual consciousness of self and the objective world brought Burckhardt thus famously to proclaim his subjects 'the first-born among the sons of modern Europe'.

Further reading

Howard, Thomas Albert (2000) *Religion and the Rise of Historicism. W.M.L. de Wette, Jacob Burckhardt, and the Theological Origins of Nineteenth-Century Historical Consciousness*, Cambridge: Cambridge University Press.

Kahan, Alan (1992) *Aristocratic Liberalism. Social and Political Thought of Jacob Burckhardt, John Stuart Mill and Alexis de Tocqueville*, Oxford: Oxford University Press.

SEE ALSO: aesthetics, painting and architecture; historiography and the idea of progress

GREGORY CLAEYS

BURKE, EDMUND (1729–97)

Edmund Burke, politician, thinker and propagandist, is best known for his massively influential *Reflections on the Revolution in France* (1790). At the age of 61 Burke suddenly became the foremost defender of the old order in its hour of greatest danger. That he could play this role was far from obvious from his earlier political campaigns. Burke rejected a career in the law and turned to politics, becoming the Member of Parliament for Wendover (1765–74), Bristol (1774–80) and Malton (1781–94). He also became Secretary to Lord Rockingham, who was twice Prime Minister (1765–6, 1782). For someone of Burke's background it was a remarkable achievement to rise so high in the British establishment. He was a commoner and an Irishman with Catholic connections on his mother's side, whereas the political class was overwhelmingly aristocratic, English and Protestant.

Furthermore, Burke made only a limited effort to accommodate himself to the prevailing political realities. One might say that he often denounced the political practice of his time for failing to live up to the declared norms. It is this that gives his apparent early radicalism the conservative base that only later becomes fully apparent. Nowhere is this more evident than in his bold attacks on the growing powers of the Crown. As a Whig, Burke was committed to the settlement of 1688, when James II fled the country to be replaced by William and Mary. This 'Glorious Revolution' had curbed monarchical power, established the rights of Parliament and assured the Protestant succession. Nearly a century later it seemed to Burke that once more the monarchy was subverting the British constitution by its excessive influence over Members of Parliament. In the 1770s Burke was also on the anti-monarchical side in the dispute with the American colonies. He thus became identified with radicals like THOMAS PAINE who favoured American independence. This was misleading, for Burke supported the colonists not in what they were for but in what they were against – a government in London that looked more to force than to conciliation.

In the 1780s Burke worked prodigiously to secure the impeachment of Warren Hastings, the Governor-General of Bengal. Hastings appeared to be at the apex of British exploitation, whereby Indian principalities were impoverished by officials whose wealth then corrupted the politics of their own home country. Burke believed that the East India Company had ruined every prince and state who trusted it. He wrote more on India than on any other issue and his powerful indictment of British rule by the East India Company significantly prefigured some of the themes of *Reflections*. The British in India seemed scarcely less revolutionary than the Jacobins later in France in their disregard for established norms and practices.

Burke is also known for attempting to remedy the grievances of Irish Catholics and for the classic statement of the view that a Member of Parliament cannot be mandated by his constituency but should vote according to what seems best for the country as a whole. Burke, then, had been in the thick of political life prior to 1789. His earlier campaigns no doubt steeled him for his greatest battle, for he became the spokesman of the European traditional order against the ideas of the Enlightenment and the French Revolution. Many who later turned against the revolution had at first welcomed it as a long-awaited synthesis of theory and practice, and a liberating springtime of mankind. Burke, however, saw the revolution presciently, less as it then was and more as it was to become. His *Reflections on the Revolution in France* read as if the great terror of 1793–4 had already occurred, though it still lay 3 years in the future. As the first major attack on the revolution, the book made an immediate impact. In little over a year it sold 30,000 copies and went through eleven editions; quite extraordinary figures both in view of the length and style of the work itself and of the relatively low population and literacy levels. Burke unwittingly initiated the greatest political debate in British literary history. The responses from Tom Paine and Mary Wollstonecraft were just the most famous of the many publications answering Burke. Within a few years the *Reflections* had been translated into French, German and Italian, and were to have a significant influence on emerging European conservatism.

To the radicals, Burke seemed a deserter from the radical cause. Paine began his *Rights of Man* (1791–2) with the grievance of abandonment. Thus began a strand of radical thought, reaching through to Cobbett and Marx, which assumed Burke was a bought man who changed his opinions as he changed his paymaster. What actually caused Burke to adopt an explicitly conservative position was that the social order of Europe seemed more fundamentally endangered than ever before.

One aspect of this related to France itself, the country where aristocracy seemed the most resplendent, where the 'sun king' Louis XIV had established the magnificent palace of Versailles. France at the time was the most populous country of Europe and already set the fashion in food, philosophy and much else. More significantly it was too close for comfort and had supporters on the English side of the Channel. The book's full title continues as follows: *Reflections on the Revolution in France and on the Proceedings in Certain Societies in London Relative to that Event. Reflections*, then, is a book about both France and England. It is written for an English readership, warning them against those like the Rev. Richard Price, the Welsh Nonconformist minister, who had shocked Burke by blasphemously preaching from the pulpit in support of the French Revolution. Burke immediately realized that what made the French Revolution attractive outside of its own country was a peculiarity of its doctrine. In their appeal to 'The Rights of Man' the revolutionaries proclaimed a universal ideology that transcended all particular and local attachments. National frontiers, religious allegiances and class interests all seemed threatened by the contagion of revolutionary ideas. For Burke these ideas constituted 'an armed doctrine' that had supporters in every country. Burke regarded the origins of the revolution as intellectual. The ideas derived from the thinkers of the Enlightenment; from such men as Voltaire, Diderot, Rousseau and D'Alembert, who had, ironically, been granted a prestigious platform by the aristocracy they were so busy undermining. According to Burke these men believed that rationality alone provided a basis for government and that it began with themselves. Everything from the past seemed mere superstition. Thus their followers pushed aside all respect for tradition and plotted against the traditional order of state and church.

For Burke it was sheer, unwarranted presumption to discard ancient wisdoms. The rules of acceptable social life had been forged by all our ancestors over many generations and had been slowly adapted to society's practical needs. Yet these guidelines were being torn asunder in the name of a spurious rationality. Burke's rejection of the Enlightenment is sometimes taken as an attack on rationality itself, yet from his perspective it was more rational to stick to tried and tested methods than for people to treat their country as empty terrain upon which they might construct whatever they fancied. Society, then, was there to be accepted and not to be treated as a subject of experiment. To Burke the revolutionaries were like sailors who had thrown their compass overboard in mid-ocean. Their self-conceit allowed them to elevate their own particular ideas above the wisdoms embodied in the traditional culture. In contrast Burke considered that the general principles of government had already been fully understood long previously. In consequence he recommended a more modest style of politics than the revolutionaries were attempting. Each generation, then, had the primary obligation of merely holding and transmitting the heritage that it had acquired. This, of course, assumed the fundamental importance of continuity. The revolutionaries believed that the old regime was based on oppression and superstition, and so introducing the rights of man required a clean break. Burke declared himself acquainted with the faults of the previous French government but suggested that the country build upon its sound and established foundations rather than tear them down for replacement by a merely experimental structure.

The core of Burke's case is that the revolutionaries were guided by theory rather than practice. Their maxim was 'liberty, equality and fraternity'. In respect of the former, Burke merely saw liberties being taken. Was he to congratulate an escaped convict on attaining his liberty? Of fraternity there was no sign. It was the impact of equality that he took most seriously and so it is to that topic that we must now turn. Though Burke did not separate them in this way, he provided two different arguments rejecting equality, each of which can stand or fall on its own. We shall turn first to the sociological answer before considering the theological one.

The sociological case against equality is based on the revolutionary transition necessary to achieve it. Burke was keenly aware that unprecedented social mobility was occurring in France and that, as a consequence, the traditional and hierarchical 'natural order of things' was being perverted. The old aristocratic class had been trained to rule; their very socialization from their earliest years had accustomed them to the breadth of vision and the leadership that a great country requires. It seemed instead that village idiocy had come to town for the new men knew of little outside of their own restricted localities. The results were bound to be disastrous. Men of theory there certainly were, and in abundance, but none with any practical experience in affairs of state.

The inevitable result of entrusting government to those with theory but without knowledge was that they would disregard specific realities and solely try to apply their blueprints. In their approach the situation counted for too little and their ideals for too much. In Burke's opinion governments should act more in accord with the circumstances and dispositions of their own unique culture. The importance of experience is thus a strong factor for leaving things as they are, for any change of ruling personnel can only elevate inexperience and so lead to deterioration. Thus Burke viewed with contempt the provincial attorneys and minor civic dignitaries whose grandiose plans were in inverse proportion to their ability to actually implement them. Such men were bound to become intoxicated by their unprepared and rapid elevation. So, on this aspect of what is wrong with equality, Burke thought it ludicrous to discard ancient wisdoms. Experience was the truest guide, but the revolution had abandoned it. Burke was sure that the attempt at levelling would fail. It was

against nature. Bringing down one class would merely lead to the rise of another, and Burke was not alone in predicting that when all authority is undermined then force would prevail, and soon the head of the army would become the ruler of the country. The theological argument against equality is that there is a natural order of things of which the human hierarchy, and Burke specifically singles out the state, is a part. It is all God's creation. A social order that is divinely ordained is one in which people are obliged to accept their place. Thus one's social position and political obligations are determined in advance by the structure and institutions of the society one grows up in. Against this, neither metaphysical reasoning nor individual consent should be of any consequence. Burke's arch-enemy Rousseau put all the major political problems of the state directly to each individual conscience. There are no representatives. All must apply their individual reason. Burke's view was directly contrary to this. For him problems of allegiance and affiliation should not arise. Individuals find themselves in a particular social situation and are merely obliged passively to act out the social role they inherit.

To Burke the levellers were blasphemous and atheistical in trying to undo God's work. Thus Burke claimed to be protecting Christian civilization as such. In spite of pages devoted to the loss of Church lands, Burke avoided confining his argument to the local level of defending French Catholicism. That would not have been convenient in rallying the English against the revolution. He glossed over the differences between Catholicism and Protestantism, and presented the revolution as an attack on Christianity as a whole. It is hardly surprising that someone as polemical as Burke should have received a mixed reception. To the lower orders he became notorious for his denigration of them as a 'swinish multitude'. However, as the Napoleonic Wars continued Burke's reputation grew, for he had been the first to proclaim the cause of counter-revolution. He has been regarded as a significant influence on such conservative thinkers of the next generation as Wordsworth, COLERIDGE, Gentz, Müller, MAISTRE and BONALD. Many Victorians regarded Burke as Britain's greatest political thinker. Here we include not just conservatives. Many Victorian liberals co-opted him to their cause, emphasizing his suspicion of the Crown and his writings on the dispute with the American colonies. However, of all Burke's concerns it was the French Revolution that sent the main shock waves into the nineteenth century, particularly as lesser versions were re-enacted in 1830, 1848 and 1871. So Burke provided the basis of defence against all those in the nineteenth century who dreamt of overthrowing established systems and starting anew, or imagined that rationality alone provided sufficient criteria for political choice. Of such approaches there were many, as parts of this *Dictionary* testify, and so, for the conservative side, much use that could be made of Burke's counter-arguments. Thus it was that a man who initially appeared as the scourge of the Establishment became its foremost defender when it was under greatest attack. To argue for Burke's continued relevance, his conservatism must be shown as more than the defence of the traditional European agrarian and aristocratic order. One argument is that Burke impartially defended the 1688 settlement in England, local self-government within an imperial framework in the American colonies, autocratic monarchy in France and Hindu institutions in India. Burke, then, in each instance, defended what was traditional for that particular society. A procedure that had stood the test of time, which had developed gradually through a long historical process of small adjustments and changes, had, by virtue of that process, and whatever its precise content, become proper for the people and society in question. It is this approach that has enabled Burke's writings to be used through to our own time as a general conservative philosophy, even by those living in societies very different from anything he could personally have envisaged.

Further reading

Burke, E. (2001) *Reflections on the Revolution in France*, ed. J.C.D. Clark, Stanford, CA: Stanford University Press.

Hampsher-Monk, I. (1987) *The Political Philosophy of Edmund Burke*, London: Longman.

Lock, P.F. (1985) *Burke's Reflections on the Revolution in France*, London: Allen & Unwin.

O'Brien, C.C. (1993) *The Great Melody*, London: Sinclair.

SEE ALSO: conservatism, authority and tradition; Paine, Thomas; the nation, nationalism and the national principle;

MICHAEL LEVIN

C

CABET, ETIENNE (1788–1856)

Cabet was a curious mixture of a utopian and a practical reformer, an egalitarian but illiberal democrat. Through his newspaper, *Le Populaire*, and his Icarian movement, he became the most influential socialist in France in the mid-1840s and in 1848 headed the largest political club created after the February revolution. Yet in 1856 he died a forgotten exile in the USA and left no legacy to later socialist groups.

Cabet was the son of a master cooper in Dijon. A member of the *charbonnerie* while he was a student qualifying as an *avocat*, he took part in the 1830 revolution and was briefly *procureur-général* in Corsica, before being elected to Parliament. He was prosecuted five times for his book in which he asserted that the Parisian artisans had been robbed of the revolution. In June 1833 Cabet started *Le Populaire*, a newspaper partly owned and written by artisans. In less than two months its circulation had reached 12,000. At 10 francs for an annual subscription it was massively cheaper than other papers. In 1834 when the Orleanists launched a consolidated attack on the opposition press, Cabet preferred exile in London to a punitive fine and jail sentence. As a consequence of his links with Owenites in 1839 he returned to Paris a socialist, dubbing himself a communist.

In 1840 he published *Voyage en Icarie*. It was a blueprint for an egalitarian society. All property was held in common and its proceeds shared equally. There was no money. Icarians were all provided with similar housing, furnishings, clothing and food. Icarie had a machine-age economy, with railways and canals. It was a democracy, but no liberal republic. Cabet abhorred the individualism of the 1789 Declaration of Rights, arguing that the rights of the community were paramount and the idea of 'liberty' was 'a mistake, a sin, a grave evil'. There was one official newspaper and freedom of the press was unknown.

Cabet elaborated in detail on social organization. Women were educated in mothercraft. Up to five children were reared by both parents. They went to school from 5 to 18 where they were taught the natural sciences, but not Latin or Greek. At 18 boys and girls worked a seven-hour day. Women did the housework in addition to their regular job. There was no established religion, but society was guided by basic moral principles. Cabet's 'Divinity' was basically Voltairean. Icarians were taught about the various world religions and left to choose. Cabet's utopianism was an Enlightenment-inspired confidence in the pre-eminence of reason developed by education. The rich would sympathize with his community and give up their property. He argued that most revolutions strengthened the status quo or allowed a self-interested dictator to take over, although he conceded that the Jacobins initiated an embryonic popular revolution. By 1848 *Icarie* had been re-printed five times, perhaps because its fairy tale orderliness contrasted with real life.

Le Populaire, revived in 1841, focused on the practical problems faced by working people, who provided three-quarters of its shareholders. For 3 months in 1842 it ran a detailed survey of working practices based on evidence supplied by workers. By 1846, with a circulation of 4,500, it was out-selling other radical papers. Cabet headed the first mass workers' movement, *Le Société pour fonder l'Icarie*, about 100,000 strong in 1844. Paris and Lyon were the focuses, with groups in seventy-eight departments. Most Icarians were traditional artisans and their wives; only about 4 per cent were middle class. Icarianism had a particular appeal to cabinet-makers, textile workers, shoe-makers; trades in which the craftsmen felt their skills were being undermined by the development of machines and new methods of production. Such craftsmen were prominent in popular upheaval and revolutionary activity in these years. Of the twenty-two cities where there were subscribers to *Le Populaire*, only three were modern industrial centres. Icarianism was spread by Cabet's publications. The Orleanist regime banned clubs and meetings.

In the mid-1840s Cabet became more assertive in proclaiming the equality of men and women, and in equating his ideal society with Christianity. He began to present Jesus as the champion of the suffering workers, the first communist. In 1846 his *Le Vrai Christianisme* sold 2,000 copies in 20 days. In line with his new messianic Christian message, Cabet abandoned his notion that Icarie would develop gradually and joined Owen in a project to establish a community in the USA. Icarians may have liked to read about Icarie, but few wanted to live there. By November 1847 *Le Populaire* had lost nearly a third of its subscribers and only sixty-nine Icarians agreed to set sail, many resenting the autocratic constitution proposed by Cabet for the community. The colonists had to supply 600 francs towards a homestead of 320 acres in the Red River area, but it emerged that the land was actually owned by the state of Texas. Cabet was waiting to answer a fraud charge in February 1848, when the settlers arrived in the USA, and France erupted again into revolution.

Cabet realized that many of his artisan supporters initially placed great hope in the revolution. His club, the *Société fraternelle centrale*, became the largest of the many clubs at the time, with meetings of 5,000 men and women. He urged respect for the rights of the people and campaigned for a living wage for women workers. He helped to organize the demonstration of 17 March when 150,000 people gathered to demand that elections for a Constituent Assembly be delayed while people learned what voting and the republic could mean for them.

Cabet's communism and his popularity among Parisian workers were initially seen as a real threat by fellow republicans. Disappointed with the republic, he set sail for Nauvoo, Illinois, ignoring attempts to found Icarian co-operatives in Lyon and elsewhere in France. He tried to rally the colonists ravaged both by cholera and personal and ideological wrangles, but his autocratic attitudes led to his exclusion from Nauvoo, which survived until the end of the century. Cabet moved to another settlement near St Louis, but died shortly afterwards. None of his major writings was translated into English.

Further reading

Johnson, C.H. (1974) *Utopian Communism in France. Cabet and the Icarians 1839–51*, Ithaca: Cornell University Press.

Pilbeam, P. (2000) *French Socialists before Marx: Women, Workers and the Social Question in France*, Teddington: Acumen.

SEE ALSO: early socialism; utopianism

PAMELA PILBEAM

CARLYLE, THOMAS (1795–1881)

The 'Victorian Sage', perhaps the most influential critic of *laissez-faire* political economy and utilitarian philosophy in Victorian Britain, Thomas Carlyle was born 4 December 1795 at Ecclefechan, Scotland. From his father he received a commitment to education; from his mother, a sense of original sin and the virtue of piety. Precociously adept at languages, and enamoured of fiction, he attended Edinburgh University from 1809–12 with the aim of becoming a minister, but found the city contemptibly sinful and his fellow students riotous and libertine. By 1815, his religious faith plagued by scepticism, mentally agitated and depressed, he considered other careers. By 1820, animated by reading Schiller and Goethe, he conceived German Idealism to provide an answer to his spiritual problems. Moving to London, he gained work as an essayist and translator, and became one of the foremost interpreters of German thought to his contemporaries. In the early 1830s he came under the influence of the Saint-Simonians (see SAINT-SIMON, HENRI DE), and sympathized with their proposals to end the exploitation of the poor, and to guide society and organize industry meritocratically, while reviving a spiritual variation of Christianity. He also found of interest the Saint-Simonian philosophy (see MAIN CURRENTS IN PHILOSOPHY) of history, with its emphasis on the necessary historical progression from feudalism to industrialism, and the resulting supersession of existing institutions by rule based on science and wisdom rather than privilege and land-ownership. Accordingly he translated Saint-Simon's *Nouveau Christianisme*, while dismissing the effort to revive Christianity without God as senseless. In 1827 he married Jane Welsh; despite a wedding-night fiasco they remained together for 40 years.

Many of Carlyle's leading social themes were outlined in an early essay, 'The Signs of the Times' (1829), in which he condemned an 'Age of Machinery' which placed its faith in nostrums, reform programmes and secular philosophies like utilitarianism and materialism, rather than reinforcing individual endeavour, internal perfection, a politics founded in moral goodness rather than a Benthamite (see Bentham, Jeremy) calculation of profit and loss, and a truly spiritual religion that reveals the superiority of 'a higher, heavenly freedom' above mere civil and political freedom. In his essay 'Characteristics' (1831), similarly, Carlyle indicated a willingness to wed mystical, religious and metaphysical arguments to practical proposals for government guarantees of employment for the working classes. Carlyle's first publication, *Sartor Resartus* [The Taylor Reclothed], 1834, was an elaborate semi-autobiographical excursus into the perils of religious scepticism, the belief in the universe as a mere mechanism, and the need to rediscover the essence of divinity by renouncing hedonism and materialism, and realizing that the essence of humanity lay in embracing the spiritual world. Its quaint combination ('Carlylese', it would later be called) of Germanic prose, Idealist philosophy and anguished introspection met with scant approval, though its delineation of a Godless world as quintessentially a modern outlook would find many subsequent adherents, notably among the twentieth-century existentialists. Carlyle here sees mankind solely as an embodiment of spirit, 'a soul, a spirit, and divine apparition' merely disguised by bodily and external arrangements. Virtue, he insists, cannot be derived from the pursuit of happiness: the 'soul is not synonymous with pleasure'. A universe devoid of purpose is a life devoid of purpose, and of the essential grounds of sociability, which are for Carlyle also founded in religious belief, because mutual respect and care was founded on the recognition that all people were 'temples of the Divinity', and belonged to the 'Communion of Saints'. The liberal ideal of maximizing the 'independence' of individuals from each other is thus for Carlyle mistaken; independence

was mere rebellion, while hierarchy, if those above were worthy to govern and those beneath worthy to obey, was the ideal to be maintained. Obedience and 'hero-worship', two of the key Carlylean themes, are thus first explored and justified in detail in *Sartor Resartus*, as is the notion that the purpose of life was 'to do some work therewith', that 'the end of man is an action, & not a Thought, though it were the noblest'.

Carlyle's first great success, a quirky, colossal history of the French Revolution, appeared in 1837, and immediately won him acclaim. His influential essay on 'Chartism' (1839), which condemned the 1834 Poor Law Amendment Act as regarding the poor as a bothersome nuisance, acknowledged the justice of the labourer's claim to a 'fair day's wages for a fair day's work', but dismissed both *laissez-faire* and democracy – being anarchical variations on the same theme – as viable solutions in favour of government by a 'real aristocracy ... a corporation of the best and the bravest', who would recognize that work was 'the mission of man on this earth', and secure the just obedience of the working classes in return for assisting them. Practically, Carlyle advised both universal education and large-scale emigration to ease the problem of overpopulation. This established his peculiar melange of political principles: he opposed democracy (see democracy, populism and rights) and *laissez-faire*, and supported the reinforcement of authority, but of a non-traditional form, and with the aim of creating an interventionist and regulatory government closer to socialism than any other contemporary ideal. As a non-socialist and non-radical critic of political economy, Carlyle had now succeeded in creating a distinctive critical niche for himself.

In the spring of 1840 Carlyle gave a series of public lectures, published as *Heroes and Hero-Worship*. It was the perspective here presented that led mid-twentieth-century commentators to view him as the grandfather of fascism, through the degeneration of the cult of the hero in NIETZSCHE and later National Socialism. Though it is true that Carlyle sought to reinforce authority, this is largely a misplaced charge. In presenting history as an account of the actions of great individuals, *Heroes* had two essential aims: to delineate those qualities accounted 'heroic' throughout the ages, offering an account of heroic types chronologically and thematically from the semi-mythical and divine (the Scandinavian divinity Odin) through the prophetic

(Mahomet) and poetic (Dante, Shakespeare) to the hero as priest (Luther and Knox) and on to more modern forms of leadership, religious, literary and political (Cromwell, Napoleon); and to suggest why and how leaders continued to affect the masses – in other words, why liberal individualism would constantly be undermined by leader-worship and the inevitable emergence of hier-archies. In light of twentieth-century cults of leadership, particularly in totalitarian societies, this remains one of the most important pre-socio-logical accounts of the problem of authority in the modern world, and an important precursor to the studies of Le Bon and others, and the philosophy of GEORGES SOREL in particular. A tertiary goal in the work is a more precise accounting of the displacement of the authoritative role played his-torically by the priesthood in the modern world by 'the organization of men of letters'. This new his-toric type, having emerged in the eighteenth cen-tury, and defined by the qualities of 'originality, sincerity, genius' (compare J.S. MILL, *On Liberty*, ch. 3) was capable of discerning 'the Divine Idea of the World', and of becoming 'the world's priest'. 'The man of intellect as the top of affairs: this is the aim of all constitutions and revolutions, if they have any aim' proclaimed Carlyle. But Carly-le's discussion of his chief examples, Rousseau, Johnson and Burns, is convoluted by an attack on Bentham, which reveals that not all intellectuals have accepted Carlyle's mandate, or aim at self-annihilation and spiritual affirmation. At bottom there is a vitalist or activist philosophy expressed here that condones both simple action as such, and following 'true sovereigns, temporal and spiritual', or great men, as such, more because of their faith in themselves than in what they substantively had faith in. 'A world all sincere, a believing world' remains Carlyle's ideal, but it is a nostrum that encourages following virtually any charismatic leader at all, and it is difficult to be persuaded that there is 'no nobler or more blessed feeling [that] dwells in man's heart' because people raises them-selves 'by revering that which is above' them. It is the sociological fact of hero-worship and the light his discussion sheds on this vital facet of mass society, rather than Carlyle's explanation of its value, which remain important for modern readers.

To contemporaries Carlyle's next major work was more immediately applicable to the difficult circumstances of the economic depression of the early 1840s, now frequently referred to as the 'Condition of England problem'. *Past and Present* (1843) remains of interest to later readers for two chief reasons. First, it approaches contemporary problems through an examination of medieval social and political attitudes, by recounting a lengthy tale of a twelfth-century monastery fallen on hard times and under poor management, but saved by prudence, justice, frugality and other virtues enjoined by a worthier leader. Thereafter Carlyle would come to be seen as the architect of the medieval revival, and the notion that a close-knit, homogeneous medieval community, bound by *noblesse oblige* from above and a sense of the sacred duty of obedience from below, had been torn asunder by modern competition and indivi-dualism, but might yet be revived in some form. Aspects of this vision were to be developed by two of Carlyle's most important successors, JOHN RUSKIN and WILLIAM MORRIS.

The second reason *Past and Present* remains influential derives from its social and economic analyses and prognoses. Taking up the main themes of both 'Chartism' and *Heroes*, Carlyle acknowledges that the plea for 'a fair day's wages for a fair day's work' was 'as just a demand as Governed men ever made of Governing... the everlasting right of man'. No simple legislative nostrums, nor any further adhesion to the 'Gospel of Mammonism' would help, but an 'aristocracy of talent' could provide a solution thereto, and heal the wounds that the reduction of society to a mere 'cash nexus' had opened. But this could not be the old aristocracy, who now abjured their responsi-bilities and were content to receive price supports for their agricultural produce through the Corn Laws. Nor could it be the existing government, which merely policed public order, without offer-ing true leadership. The 'millocracy' or 'working aristocracy', by contrast, had the capacity of self-reform, and could recognize, Carlyle argued, that 'overproduction' was a mere economic concept, and could renounce the ceaseless 'underselling' that rendered the market more cruelly competitive. The possibility of reform, thus, lay in first assisting the industrial lords to learn 'that Mammonism was not the essence of his or of my station in God's universe', and to aspire to a new definition of lib-erty, where the worker would 'learn, or to be taught, what work he actually was able for; and then by permission, persuasion, and even com-pulsion, to set about doing of the same'. The older definition of liberty as 'not being oppressed by others', while still of value, had thus to be supplanted by a new conception driven by the development of industrial society. But, as in 'Chartism', the 'working millions' were again advised not to seek a solution in democracy, which would merely embody 'no-guidance' of another, and potentially even more destructive, type. Saint-Simonism, rather than Jacobinism, offered a worthier ideal.

The practical reform programme outlined in Book 4 of *Past and Present* is one of the most extraordinary proposals, outside of the socialist camp, of the period. Besides pleading for a new aristocracy and priesthood, a reinforcement of the role of the monarch as 'pontiff-king' (Victoria, of course, was Queen), and an acknowledgement of the governing role of the 'industrial aristocracy', Carlyle proposes an 'organization of labour' into industrial armies, led by captains of industry, who would instil a new sense of chivalry and just subordination. To ensure obedience from below, workers would be offered a permanent labour contract, subject to working properly, and potentially some share in the management of industrial enterprises. To secure the protection of the workforce, legislation should ensure conditions of safety and comfort. 'Interference has begun; it must continue, must extensively enlarge itself, deepen and sharpen itself', proclaimed Carlyle: factory regulations, mine regulations, sanitary regulations, parks for workers, the right education and free emigration, were all to be incorporated into the social programme of the future. This was an extraordinary set of proposals that helped to popularize a collectivist approach to economic problems, which would become much more widely accepted by the 1880s. The classification of his mature social theory defies easy categorization, however, indebted as it is to certain forms of authoritarian conservatism, to the socialism of the Saint-Simonians and, in part, the Owenites, to liberal assumptions about meritocracy and the worth of the rising middle and industrial classes, and to a Saint-Simonian philosophy of history wedded to his own understanding of the meaning of the supernatural.

Carlyle's writings after *Past and Present* did not contribute substantially to his reputation. His essay on 'The Nigger Question' (1849) brought offence for its ever-shriller authoritarianism. *Latter-Day Pamphlets* (1850) was similarly poorly received, being illiberal on the slavery issue, and dismissive of *laissez-faire*, again, just as free trade seemed to be ascendant and successful. Here

Carlyle recommended that the Prime Minister, Peel, whom he fêted as a new Cromwell, should choose the ten best men in the country and place them in charge of ten new ministries supervising all vital areas of public life. In the early 1850s he began to acquire serious followers, notably John Ruskin, whom he met in 1851. Elected Rector of Edinburgh University in 1865, Carlyle supported Governor Eyre's ruthless suppression of the Jamaican slave rebellion that year. His final great historical study, of the life of Frederick the Great, appeared in eight volumes between 1858–65, while a magisterial edition of Cromwell's letters and speeches offered similar homage to one of his heroes. He supported the South during the American Civil War, though at least partly in the view that emancipation would prove a cruel deception, and in the 1870–1 Franco-Prussian War took the German side. In 'Shooting Niagra' he contended against the Reform Act of 1867. Declining a knighthood offered by Disraeli in 1874, and the offer of a Grand Cross of the Order of the Bath in 1875, he died on 4 February 1881. His reputation in the late nineteenth century was more as a literary figure and semi-prophetic moralist than as a social theorist, but the light *Past and Present*, in particular, sheds on the more collectivist strands of liberalism after 1880 and the turn towards 'positive' conceptions of liberty indicate that Carlyle remains a necessary reference point in any evaluation of Victorian LIBERALISM.

Further reading

Campbell, I. (1974) *Carlyle*, London: Hamish Hamilton.

Carlyle, Thomas (1899–1901) *The Works of Thomas Carlyle*, 30 vols. London: Chapman & Hall.

Cofer, David (1931) *Saint-Simonism in the Radicalism of Thomas Carlyle*. College station: English Publishing Co.

Froude, J.A. (1885) *Thomas Carlyle*. London: Longmans, Green.

Harrold, C. (1934) *Carlyle and German Thought*, New Haven, CT: Yale University Press.

Kaplan, Fred (1983) *Thomas Carlyle*, Ithaca: Cornell University Press.

LaValley, A. (1968) *Carlyle and the Idea of the Modern*, New Haven, CT: Yale University Press.

Le Quesne, A. *Carlyle* (1982). Oxford: Oxford University Press.

Lehman, S. (1928) *Carlyle's Theory of the Hero*, Durham: Duke University Press.

Roe, Frederick (1921) *The Social Philosophy of Carlyle and Ruskin*, London: George Allen & Unwin.

Rosenburg, P. (1974) *The Seventh Hero: Thomas Carlyle and the Theory of Radical Activism*, Cambridge, MA: Harvard University Press.

SEE ALSO: conservatism, authority and tradition; democracy, populism and rights; early socialism; historiography and the idea of progress; intellectuals, elites and meritocracy; liberalism; religion, secularization and the crisis of faith; theories of the state and society: the science of politics

GREGORY CLAEYS

CARPENTER, EDWARD (1844–1929)

Edward Carpenter, advocate of homosexual equality and socialist writer, was born on 29 August 1844 in Brighton, son of a naval officer. He studied at Brighton College and in 1864 entered Trinity Hall, Cambridge. Upon his graduation in 1868 he was elected to a clerical fellowship in his college and served as curate to F.D. MAURICE in St Edward's Church, Cambridge. In the intellectual climate of advanced liberalism in Cambridge he came to admire Walt Whitman's *Leaves of Grass* and its gospel of manly comradeship. In 1874 he relinquished his clerical fellowship, at once joined the University Extension Scheme begun a year before, and lectured to the workers and women in the north. About the poor but proud working men of Sheffield he wrote to Whitman whom he had visited at Camden, New Jersey, in 1877. In 1883 appeared his book of poems *Towards Democracy*, certainly Whitmanesque but largely autobiographical, a hymn of democracy spiritual and personal attained by his sexual liberation due to living with working-men friends in Sheffield. In the same year he acquired a farm and a cottage at Millthorpe near Chesterfield, which became a rendezvous of socialists of all sorts while his idea of democracy became increasingly socialistic. He began to advocate a simple life and co-operative production, joined the Democratic Federation and provided the fund to start its organ *Justice*. Disappointed with its internal divisions he was attracted to the Fellowship of New Life, the parent body of the Fabian Society, but felt more at home with the Sheffield Socialist Society set up in 1886. He wrote 'England Arise: A Socialist Marching Song' (1886) for the new movement, and his Fabian 1889 new year lecture was published as *Civilization: Its Cause and Cure* (1889), which described commercial civilization as moral and social disease. In 1892 he defended the Walsall anarchists tried for an attempt to manufacture

bombs for the Russians and assisted the Humanitarian League set up by Henry Salt in 1891, taking part in its campaigns against vivisection, against capital punishment and for prison reform. An emphasis on spiritual freedom in *Towards Democracy* was derived from his reading the *Bhagavadgita*, and he sought to reinvigorate his faith by visiting Ceylon and India in 1890–1. Meanwhile, he collaborated with John Addington Symonds and HAVELOCK ELLIS for sexual studies and appeared prominently, though anonymously, in the latter's studies in *The Psychology of Sex* (1897). He himself wrote a series of pamphlets on sex in a free society in 1894–5. His *Intermediate Sex* (1908) had seminal effects both in Britain and abroad. Among those influenced by his works were Siegfried Sassoon, Robert Graves, E.M. Forster and D.H. Lawrence. He supported the Suffragette movement, especially its moderate wing led by Mrs C. Despard. His mature thought on Syndicalism can be found in his *Non-Governmental Society* (1911) and during the First World War he wrote a vigorous anti-war poem 'Never Again' (1916) as well as *The Healing of Nations* (1915), which advocated the United States of Europe. In his later years he moved to Guildford, Surrey, where he died in January 1928.

Further reading

Carpenter, Edward (1916) *My Days and Dreams*, London: George Allen & Unwin.
Tsuzuki, Chushichi (1980) *Edward Carpenter: Prophet of Human Fellowship*, Cambridge: Cambridge University Press.

SEE ALSO: Marx and Marxism

CHUSHICHI TSUZUKI

CHATEAUBRIAND, FRANÇOIS RENÉ AUGUSTE (1768–1848)

François René Auguste, Vicomte de Chateaubriand, an inaugural member of the Romantic movement in literature, was born at St Malo in Brittany on 14 September 1768. Raised at his family's medieval chateau, he attended grammar school at Rennes and finished his education at Dol College. Unsure of the direction to take in life after years of preparation for the priesthood, he joined the army in August 1786. Disillusioned by the aims of a military life, he embarked for the USA on

7 April 1791 in an attempt to discover the North-west Passage. This trip would become fodder for much of his work and inspired his idyllic portrayals of nature. He had only been in the USA for several months when he heard of the arrest of King Louis XVI at Varennes, and he returned to France on 2 January 1792 to fight for King Louis XVI and the royalist army. This return resulted in marriage, and his joining the army of Conde. Wounded in battle in Thionville, he escaped to England for 8 years, a period marked by scepticism and disillusionment, and works such as *Essai historique, politique et moral sur les révolutions anciennes et modernes considerées dans leurs rapports avec la révolution française*, published in 1797. His tone changed after the death of his mother in 1798, and the nineteenth-century Chateaubriand began to emerge. His exile in England was a period of misery for Chateaubriand, and when he was able to return to France, it was only under an altered name.

His contributions to the Western canon included *Le Génie du christianisme* (1802), which centred around Chateaubriand's argument that conceptual reasoning was no longer sufficient in an age of power play and argumentation. Although somewhat exaggerated in tone, Chateaubriand may have single-handedly helped revive an interest in religion since the publication of *Le Génie du christianisme* coincided with the re-emergence of Roman Catholicism in France. This work attracted Napoleon, who appointed Chateaubriand secretary to the Rome embassy in 1802, the beginning of a life in politics for Chateaubriand. However, on 21 March 1804, he resigned from the diplomatic service in order to make a pilgrimage to the Holy Land. His travels became the inspiration for his 1811 work, *Itinéraire de Paris à Jérusalem et de Jérusalem à Paris, en allant par la Grèce, et revenant par l'Egypte, la Barbarie, et l'Espagne*. After its publication in 1811, Chateaubriand's political career occupied centre-stage. He became the French ambassador to Berlin, a delegate at the Congress of Verona, and Minister of Foreign Affairs. In 1815, he had been honoured as a peer of the realm, a post that he relinquished in 1830, unwilling to dedicate himself to Louis Philippe. This event essentially marked the retirement of Chateaubriand, and he dedicated the remainder of his life to his *'raison d'être'*, his *Mémoirs d'outre tombe*, published posthumously in pamphlet form from 1849 to 1859. His political life, however, can be succinctly divided into three eras, specifically

the royalist period when he was an officer fighting in the names of King Louis XVI and Napoleon, a loyalty that lasted until 1824, when his political career took a marked turn towards liberalism, which lasted until he relinquished his post as peer of the realm in 1830, and the political leaning towards ideal republicanism that lasted until his death in 1848.

Chateaubriand can be credited with facilitating the transition from the classical school to the Romantic style, and it was a characteristic he did not take lightly. Not surprisingly, his influences included George Washington, Napoleon, Pius VII and Burke, each of whom influenced Chateaubriand's work ethic: 'freedom is preserved only by work, because work produces strength…the strength of the body is maintained by physical exercise; once labour is lacking, strength disappears' (*Mémoirs*, p. 373). This inspired much of Chateaubriand's work, as well as his life. His urge to explore the exotic had led him to the USA in 1791, and the writing of *Atala*, the 'painting of two lovers who walk and talk in solitude; all lies in the picture of the turmoil and love in the midst of the calm of the wilderness' (Preface to *Atala*). Keeping in mind that Chateaubriand believed that thoughts made the man, he created Chactas, the Indian protagonist, who was unable to assimilate to the civilized world, and Atala, the white female, who was torn between her desire for Chactas and her desire for home. Yet this was also a tale of brotherhood, a work representing the state of nature and the problems of populating it. In *Atala*, Chateaubriand invested his two protagonists, *'les deux sauvages dans le désert'*, with great wisdom, essentially elevating them to the status of priests. The mythic elements of the story make this story a rite of passage, and the inclusion of the Catholic priest, Father Aubry, serves as the catalyst for the introduction of republican values based primarily on natural religion.

Chateaubriand imbues Chactas with a sense of quiet superiority; he refers to a man like other men, yet a man who had become a respected patriarch. *'Il y avait parmi ces Sauvages un vieillard nommé Chactas'*, one who had lived a fulfilled life. The narrator, in both the Prologue and Epilogue, attempts to determine *'la sagesse des temps'*, or essentially the purpose of life, with the themes of death, war and exile occurring in a reoccurring movement in the text. The narrator reveals the paradox of the tale – those who speak of reason may not be reasonable in the end, yet even he could not determine what led to the harmony the 'old men' felt; '*je ne sais quelle mystérieuse harmonie*'.

The introspective tone and egotism so expressive of the '*mal du siècle*' found in many of the writings in *Le Génie du Christianisme*, is also found in *Rene*, also published separately in 1807. Self-titled, this work is the tale of a man imprisoned in himself; it is the tale of a man on a mission to find true happiness. It is the ultimate tale of *ennui*, the story of a man so self-absorbed that he ignores his wife and children, as well as the world around him. His mental anguish mirrored his incapacity to deal with the end of the ancien régime, and only in nature, or physical exile, could the answers be found. This was a tale in which man's suffering was central to the story line, but in which religion and faith remained victorious. Father Souel, the Catholic priest, supported Rene through his toughest times, an event that perhaps mirrored the French Catholic revival in early nineteenth-century France.

Centred around the search for self-expression, and the momentous scene of the main character, Rene, sitting on the edge of a volcano, '*un jeune home plein de passions, assis sur la bounce d'un volcan*', *René* expresses the Romantic attitude towards life and self. The volcano is the symbolic expression of the internal struggle characteristic of Romanticism, and suggests symbolic interpretations such as creativity, fear and fire. The eruption of the volcano can be interpreted as the crisis of the conscious mind. René's climb up the summit of Mount Etna occurs as he nears the end of his journey for meaning in life, a journey that was a direct result of his father's death, and just before the isolation of his return to France, where he contemplates suicide. The volcano has been seen as a 'waking dream' by Mircea Eliade, in which René distanced himself from the outer, 'physical' world and allowed his inner thoughts to emerge after years of submission. There was no specific explanation provided for why René needed to climb Mount Etna; it appears that he is drawn instinctively to Etna. The narrator notes, '*un jour, j'étais monté au sommet de l'Etna*' (199), which corresponds to his emotional turmoil; the appearance of the volcano, '*un volcan qui brûle au milieu d'une île*' represents what some critics have referred to as Rene's 'psychological geography'. The symbolism of the fire, and, in a sense, the Promethean

myth, explains the courage that such creativity requires, as well as the ability to 'open' oneself to the unknown, as Rene did in his self-explorative narrative at the entrance to the volcano. Yet, this also invokes the symbolism of fear, specifically the fact the sensitive and creative Rene was very conscious of how alone he is in the world. Rene's journey is one that exemplifies the Romantic quest for insight into the inner world of the self.

Chateaubriand popularized the notion of the individual with the publication of *René*. Yet, he also highlighted the role of space in his *Mémoires d'outre tombe*, his description of Combourg, his family home, and a patriarchal tale of the father's dominance, and the mother's passive resistance. The concept of 'space', another example of Romanticism, defines René's personal voyage to determine what was important to him in life. Therefore, Combourg occupied the focal point in the text, particularly with the pervasive presence and image of the negative father, referred to by Chateaubriand in non-specific terms as '*Monsieur mon pére*'. He refers to his father in cold terms, using words such as 'rigidity', 'austerity', 'coldness' and 'introversion'. His mother, on the other hand, to whom he refers as '*ma mére*', is described using words such as 'imagination', 'elegance' or 'lively humor'. Her only expression of resistance, however, was her sighs (her '*soupirs*'), only a passive attempt to deflect her husband's negativity. There was a certain rivalry between father and son, despite his cruelty, which Chateaubriand refers to as violent ('*cette maniére violente de me traiter*'), yet, due to his mother's faith in the power of God, he begins to challenge his father. In order to achieve – and discover – his own identity, François-René is forced to leave Combourg, making the *Mémoires* a powerful expression of the relationship between space and time, and the exploration of the concept of Self.

Similar to other nineteenth-century authors and thinkers, Chateaubriand felt the torment of religious conflict. Despite his moral difficulties, Chateaubriand maintained his belief in Christianity, although that belief wavered during his period in the USA. It took the death of his mother in 1798 to reconcile him to his faith, which had been his mother's dying wish. He explained this abandonment of his faith in his 'Essai sur les revolutions', and again in the preface to the first edition of *Le Génie du christianisme*, in which he wrote, 'I wept...and I believed.' Yet, his constant doubting of his faith would also be a theme throughout his life, although, despite his scepticism, he remained true to Christianity. In the latter work, subtitled 'Beauties of the Christian Religion' in the first edition, Chateaubriand wrote:

> Though we have not employed the arguments usually advanced by the apologists of Christianity, we have arrived by a different chain of reasoning at the same conclusion: Christianity is perfect; men are imperfect. Now, a perfect consequence cannot spring from an imperfect principle. Christianity, therefore, is not the work of men.

It is with this work that Chateaubriand is credited with reinvigorating Christianity in France.

His writing was an attempt to justify the events of the two centuries in which he lived. In altering between royalist and republican notions politically, and writing in the Romantic style, Chateaubriand was a man caught between two centuries, a turmoil revealed in his writing. He noted:

> I have found myself caught between two ages, as in the conflux of two rivers, and I have plunged into their waters, turning regretfully from the old bank upon which I was born, yet swimming hopefully towards the unknown shore at which the new generations are to land.
> (*Mémoires* xxiv)

Nevertheless, Chateaubriand's contribution to the concept of 'self' in works from *Le Génie du christianisme* to *Mémoires d'outre tombe* demonstrates his niche in nineteenth-century thought.

Further reading

Barthes, Roland (1980) *New Critical Essays*, New York: Hill & Wang.

Bowman, Frank Paul (1990) *French Romanticism: Intertextual and Interdisciplinary Readings*, Baltimore: Johns Hopkins University Press.

Chateaubriand, Francois Rene (1902) *Mémoires d'outre tombe*. Vol. 1, trans. Alexander Teixeira de Mattos, xxiv–vi, 373, London: G.P. Putnam's Sons.

—— (1966) *Le Génie du christianisme*, 1, 58, Paris: Garmier-Flammarion.

Eliade, Mircea (1978) *The Forge and the Crucible*, trans. Stephen Corrin, Chicago: University of Chicago Press [reprinted in 1962 edn in English].

Freed, Marianne T. (1996) 'La "Sagesse des temps": le trésor d'Atala', *The Romantic Review* 87, 2 (March): 225–38.

George, Albert J. (1964) 'Transition', in *Short Fiction in France: 1800–1850*, 23–9, Syracuse: Syracuse University Press.

Hamilton, James F. (1996) 'The Gendering of Space in Chateaubriand's Combourg: Archetypal Architecture and Patriarchal Object', *Symposium* 50, 2 (summer): 101–14.

—— (1998) 'Rene's Volcano, Creative Center and Gendered Periphery', *Romanic Review* 89, 2 (March): 187–98.

Roulin, J.M. (1996) 'Chateaubriand: l'exil et la gloire', *French Studies* 50, 3: 338–50.

Wang, Ban (1997) 'Writing, Self, and the Other: Chateaubriand and his *Atala*', *French Forum* 22, 2 (May): 133–48.

SEE ALSO: Conservatism, authority and tradition; Romanticism, individualism and ideas of the self

JENNIFER HARRISON

CHINESE THOUGHT IN THE NINETEENTH CENTURY

The Qing dynasty that ruled China from the middle of the seventeenth century was established by the Manchurian conquest. In order to suppress any attempt by Chinese intellectuals to criticize the system of government, it strictly controlled public opinion, and prohibited many publications. However, it also patronized the study of old documents, and mobilized many researchers for the compilation of the encyclopaedia of the Kangxi Dictionary or the Complete Library of the Four Treasuries. For this reason, most of the intellectuals were absorbed in the bibliographical study of the sacred books on Confucianism and historical books known as Evidential Research, which removed them from the real problems of the world.

However, at the beginning of the nineteenth century, the political regime began to be shaken and destabilized by peasant revolts, such as the White Lotus Society (Bai-lian jiao), in various parts of China. Moreover, the advancement by invasion of European countries, especially Britain, was perceived by the Chinese as disturbing the traditional East Asian order, where China was situated at the centre, and every other country was subsumed to Chinese civilization. China grew weaker as a result of imperial penetration. Especially, the rise in the price of silver due to the secret opium trade that resulted in the outflow of silver from China brought about social anxiety, as it was used as a means of payment of taxes. Opium addiction among the civil servants and army officers also weakened the bureaucratic system and the army, leading to fears of a crisis in the Qing dynasty itself. This led to a neo-Confucian reaction, and the formation of a group called 'the school of statecraft', which became increasingly influential.

At this time, some intellectuals such as Wei Yuan (1794–1857), who belonged to the school of statecraft, came together around Lin Tsehsu (1785–1850). Lin took up his new post as an Imperial Commissioner in Canton in 1839 and confiscated and discarded opium, which resulted in the Opium War as a result of his firm stand against the British government. At the same time, he ordered his men to collect large quantities of foreign literature, and encouraged them to learn foreign languages, in order to understand the outside world. Following China's defeat by Britain, the Nanking Treaty in 1842 ceded Hong Kong to Britain, opened five ports to foreign trade, paid compensation and abolished trade restrictions. In the same year, fifty volumes of the *Illustrated Gazetteer of Maritime Countries* (Hai-kuo tuchih) written by Wei Yuan were published. They were based on materials regarding foreign countries that his friend Lin had ordered collected. His aim was to learn the superior technology, skill and techniques of the barbarians (Westerners) in order to control them. This indicates his wedding of traditional Chinese thought with the recognition of the superiority of the West in military technology. The main characteristics of the books were that they reconstructed 'the West that the Westerners themselves talked about' through literature written by Westerners themselves. But Wei also developed a strategic theory of Chinese defence and diplomacy based on his recognition of the power of the 'maritime world' outside of China. The revised and enlarged editions of the books turned into 100 volumes and were published in 1852. These books, however, had little influence on Chinese intellectuals in those days, though when they were introduced in Japan, they had a strong impact on intellectuals like Shoin Yoshida and Shozan Sakuma, who were conscious of Japan's need to modernize as well.

The opening of five ports in conformity with the Nanking Treaty changed the society in the southern part of China's coastal areas profoundly. It hastened the decline of the Qing dynasty's prestige, the depression of handicrafts caused by the influx of cheaper goods made in other countries, the greater outflow of silver and heavier taxes, caused by the payment of compensation, which made the people's lives poor and miserable. Poverty led to riots, and then, in 1851, the Taiping Rebellion started in the mountain areas of Guangxi province, which destabilized Qing rule. The leader, Hung Hsiuchuan (1813–64) was a third son born in a Hakka peasant family in Guangtung province. Since the time of the Opium War, Guangzhou (Canton) was the only port city open to the world. It was also a place where there were great opportunities to have contact with foreigners as well as Western civilization, and where their threat to China was accordingly more obvious. It was a big city situated farthest from the capital city of Beijing. Thus it was not by chance that the three main reformers – Hung Hsiuchuan, Kang Youwei and Sun Yat-Sen, whose aim was to change the old regime of 60 years since the opening of the ports, were all from Guangtung province.

Hung failed the imperial examination four times, although he received great help from his relatives, who had high hopes that he would become a bureaucrat. When he failed the third time, he became ill with severe fever and lost consciousness. Then, he had a dream that later came to be popularly known as Hung's visions. In that dream, an old man ordered him to save mankind from the devil, and another middle-aged man helped him, and killed the devil with a sword. The content of the dream was said to have coincided with the Protestant leaflet handed out in the streets of Guangzhou (in Canton) in 1834: 'Good words to admonish the age' (*Chuangshih liangyen*), a selected comment from the Bible. The old man was the heavenly father – Jehovah; the middle aged-man was the heavenly elder brother – Jesus Christ; and he himself was the younger brother; the devil was idols of Buddhism and Taoism that cheated on people. After his failure in the examination on the fourth try, he started a religious society called: 'God-worshipping Society' (Bai Shang-di hui) in 1844. Though the peasantry disliked such challenges to their beliefs, Hung and a friend travelled to the mountain areas of Guangxi province to seek their support. The local bureaucrats there were also against them because they destroyed Buddhist idols and shrines, and did not allow any kind of idols. In the year 1850, a severe starvation broke out in the Guangxi province that drove large numbers of people towards Bai Shang-di hui. In the next year, in January 1851, at the time of the celebration of Hung's 37th birthday, the people decided to rebel in public against the Qing dynasty, and declared the establishment of the Heavenly Kingdom of Great Peace (Taiping Tianguo), with Hung ascending the throne as the 'Heavenly King'. The Taiping troops gradually gained adherents everywhere, especially from amongst the poor, and advancing towards the north, and occupying Nanking, which they renamed the 'Heavenly Capital'. By this time, the Bai Shang-di hui had about 2 million members. Its ideals were as follows: worship of 'God' as the only one god, the principles of equality of all people and compliance with ascetic rule of Decalogue (the ten commandments of Moses). This rebellion was different from traditional Chinese peasant revolts in that it challenged the existing political regime publicly. We can clearly understand why Hung, having failed the imperial examination, condemned Confucian textbooks as 'incoherent', and how he utilized Christian texts as a theoretical weapon against Qing rule. However, while establishing their substantial state power in central-south China, their ideals were gradually transformed: ascetic rule was loosened, an aristocracy of leaders arose and there were bloody internal conflicts. This led to weakening of their armed forces, and their defeat in 1864 by a local voluntary army and mercenaries – the former organized by local bureaucrats and the latter directed by Westerners in Shanghai.

The fact that the Taiping army defeated Qing's army revealed the weakness of the latter. Qing's leaders did not deal with the rebellion by themselves and depended on the local voluntary peasant power organized by bureaucrats. Two of the most famous examples are the Hunan Army organized by Zeng Guofan (1811–72) and the Anhwei Army organized by Li Hongzhang (1823–1901). Zeng appealed to the intellectuals in Hunan province as his ally, arguing that the Taiping rebellion would destroy the Confucian order entirely. The Hunan Army was a kind of personal armed network with Zeng at the centre, whose power had to be acknowledged by the Qing government to maintain local order. Thus central-south China became gradually more independent, and the local authorities gained substantial power over army finance and personnel.

In the autumn of 1860, the allied forces of Britain and France occupied Beijing at the end of the second Opium War and concluded the Beijing treaty with the Qing government. As a result of a *coup d'état* in Beijing in the following year, 1861, the Manchuria aristocrats who insisted on an exclusionist policy were executed. After that, a group comprising Prince Gong (1832–98) and the Empress Dowager (1835–1908) held political power. Their external policy was compromise with the West, while internally they sought to suppress the revolts in co-operation with bureaucrats like Zeng Guofan and Li Hongzhang, and to promote the Self-Strengthening Movement. According to Prince Gong, the purpose of this movement was stated in terms of two diseases that were hurting China. First, internal revolts such as the Taiping Rebellion were like a heart disease, an internal and fatal disease. Second, the conflicts with Britain and Russia were like diseases of the arms and legs. Hence British influence – a mild disease – could be utilized to suppress internal revolts – a more serious threat; while importing Western weapons and developing an armaments industry would strengthen China's power both to suppress revolts and oppose Britain and Russia in future. Thus while the superiority of Western military technology was recognized after two defeats, adopting Western technology in unity with Chinese principles in practice implied 'Chinese learning for the substance and Western learning for function'. That is, traditional Chinese thought should remain fundamental to the political regime, while Western knowledge and technology should be absorbed as long as it does not contradict against the former. Thus Feng Guifen (1809–74), an adviser of Li Hongzhang, said that 'making the Chinese Confucianism as the foundation which if reinforced according to the scientific technique that made the west rich and powerful, would achieve the best effect'. He insisted on the acquisition of Western knowledge and technology, especially calendar studies, mathematics and physics, fostering translators and so on. Besides, the promoters of the Self-Strengthening Movement explained that, after all, the introduction of Western learning, especially natural science, was the only way to recover China's own learning and tried to persuade even those who opposed this idea. In this manner, the Qing government pushed forwards to industrialize itself by concentrating on military industry in order to suppress the rebellions. However, it became clear later that when the Qing dynasty suffered a crushing defeat in a war with Japan, which was also going through a period of Meiji restoration around the same time, that the efforts they made were insufficient.

At this time, the theory of social evolution introduced in China by Yen Fu (1854–1921) had a strong influence on intellectuals. Yen Fu was the son of a doctor in Fujian province. After graduating from a naval school, he went to England in 1877 for a period of 2 years as the first Chinese to be dispatched as a foreign student abroad, especially to West Europe. There he became anxious to ascertain the real causes of China's decline, and equally of the wealth and power of Western countries, while learning naval technology at the same time. After returning to his country, in 1898 he published the translated version of Thomas Huxley's *Evolution and Ethics* while working as a teacher in a navy school. This became the first work on modern European thought to be introduced to China, apart from the works relating to Christianity. The idea that all things are in the process of evolution, involving a severe struggle for existence and failure for those incapable of adapting, seemed to match the crisis of a ruined country after the defeat in the Sino-Japanese War. Later on, Yen Fu also translated the works of J.S. MILL, Adam Smith, Montesquieu and others.

Kang Youwei (1858–1927) boldly criticized the Self-Strengthening Movement and became the leader of a younger generation of intellectuals. Kang advised the emperor to carry out fundamental reforms to change the political system and not merely rely on minor reforms and modernizing the military, if China was to compete with other countries. According to him, Confucius was not a defender of tradition, but a reformer. The continuation of reforms would realize Confucius's dream of the future ideal society (*Ta-t'ung*), and the responsibility of a faithful follower of Confucius's teachings was thus to pursue those very reforms, not to imitate the West. His pupil, Liang Qichao (1873–1929), popularized Kang's thoughts through the new medium of the press, and won the sympathy of many young men such as Lu Xun, Mao Tsetung and so on. Liang, who also came from an intellectual family in Guangtung, was of the opinion that Freedom, Democracy and Evolution were the three main principles for the cause of

wealth and power in Western countries. Therefore, he energetically introduced the Western political and philosophical theories of Rousseau, Hobbes, Spinoza and others into China. Tan Sitong (1865–98) in Hunan province also attempted to implement a curriculum based upon Western studies. In his *An Exposition of Benevolence* he insisted on breaking down the discrimination on the basis of status and sex that supported the ruling system of the Qing dynasty. This book is a complex philosophical mixture of natural science and Confucianism, Buddhism and Christianity. It was radical in its insistence on breaking down all political and social restrictions. Although Tan came from a high bureaucratic family, he widened his horizons by travelling alone in various parts of China in his youth, and had also learned martial arts. In 1898, Kang Youwei and others who obtained the Emperor's trust began many reforms aimed at transforming the despotic system of government into a constitutional monarchy. But, due to the *coup d'état* by conservatives led by the Empress Dowager, it broke down after 100 days.

At this time, in the rural agricultural region of Huabei, violent anti-foreign movements involving the destruction of Christian Churches and killing of Christians were being promoted by participants in the Boxer Rebellion. Since the Empress Dowager and others had intended to curtail foreign influence in China, they officially recognized the Boxer Rebellion and went to war with various countries. However, they were defeated by the allied forces of many countries, which led to the occupation of Beijing. Kang and Liang then escaped to Japan and Tan was executed. After being defeated in that battle, from 1901 onwards they tried to solve the problem of reform by following the plans of Kang Youwei and others, but again met with no success.

Sun Yat-Sen (1866–1925), the planner of the first armed uprising aimed at overthrowing the Qing dynasty in 1895, also came from Guangtung province like Kang Youwei. Unlike Kang, however, he belonged to a peasant family, and also spoke English, having been educated at a mission school in Hawaii. According to the first declaration (establishing a united government) made when Sun first established the revolutionists' society in Hawaii in 1894, aiming to overthrow the Qing dynasty, his first political aim was to establish a democratic state like that of the USA. Sun's revolution, based on the military strength of the

Heaven and Earth Society and the economic support of Chinese merchants abroad, began with armed revolts in the remote southern area near his native place. In 1905, when the Chinese Revolutionary League was formed by gathering revolutionaries from various parts of China, Sun's Three People's Principles, which became the platform, were: overthrowing the Manchuria dynasty (nationalism); the establishment of republican government (people's rights); restrictions on concentration of land and capital (people's livelihood). Sun had actually seen the widening of gap between rich and the poor in Western countries and the unrest it entailed, and wanted to removed this evil in advance of China's social revolution. A dispute however developed between the Revolutionary League and factions of the constitutional reformers such as Kang Youwei and Liang Qichao, in political asylum in Japan, which was the base for the League's activities, over whether China should go for a 'revolution' or for a 'reform'. Liang insisted that violent revolution merely invited foreign intervention, and was not a condition for achieving a republican system in China, and promoted instead an enlightened monarchy. As a result, the young people from the progressive group who earnestly desired a radical revolution gave up on him. In regard to this, E. Balazs has stated: 'Their tragedy consisted in the rapidity with which the efforts of the Chinese progressives became outdated. It took more courage to declare oneself a constitutional Monarchist in 1890 than to become a Republican in 1910, or confess to being a Communist in 1930' (1964: 163).

Inside of the Revolutionary League, Sun's internationalism, which expected the sympathy and support of Western countries and Japan towards the Chinese Revolution, was subjected to severe criticisms from Zhang Binglin (1869–1936) and Sung Chiaojen (1882–1913), and others, who anticipated foreign interference in any revolution. The revolution sought by Zhang Binglin, a learned academician of Chinese traditional studies, was the overthrow of the Manchu dynasty, while fending off imperialism in a nationalistic and spiritualistic manner, and also avoiding Western-style democracy. Zhang Binglin's ideal was a world where there was no rule of the people by the powerful, of weaker nations by the stronger, or of poor people by the rich. In 1911, when the revolution planned by Sung Chiaojen and others in central China through the revolt of the army spread all over the country much earlier than expected, the fact that Sun Yat-Sen only learned of the beginning of the revolution through a newspaper during his stay in the USA, very well exemplifies his kind of position in the Revolutionary League at this time.

As a consequence of the alienation of the local forces from the Qing dynasty, the Chinese Empire that had continued for 2,000 years collapsed. Although the Chinese Republic was established the following year, Sung was assassinated by Yuan Shikai, which left the development of the Republic and still more the revolution unfinished. As a result, in 1915, a movement by the young generation, with Beijing University in the centre, was started under the slogan of 'Democracy and Science', with the aim of completing the tasks of the revolution.

Further reading

Balazs, Etienne (1964) *Chinese Civilization and Bureaucracy*, trans. H.M. Wright, New Haven: Yale University Press.

Chang, H.P. (1964) *Commissioner Lin and the Opium War*, Cambridge, MA: Harvard University Press.

Elman, Benjamin A. (1984) *From Philosophy to Philology: Intellectual and Social Aspects of Change in Late Imperial China*, Cambridge, MA: Harvard University Press.

Fairbank, John King (1994) *China: A New History*, Cambridge, MA: Harvard University Press.

Jen, Yuwen (1973) *The Taiping Revolutionary Movement*, New Haven: Yale University Press.

Leonard, Jane K. (1984) *Wei Yuan and China's Rediscovery of the Maritime World*, Cambridge, MA: Harvard University Press.

Schwartz, Benjamin (1964) *In Search of Wealth and Power: Yen Fu and the West*, Cambridge, MA: Harvard University Press.

Wong, Young-tsu. (1989) *The Search for Modern Nationalism, Zhang Binglin and Revolutionary China, 1869–1936*, Oxford: Oxford University Press.

Wright, Mary C. (1957) *The Last Stand of Chinese Conservatism: The T'ung-chih Restoration, 1862–1874*, Stanford, CA: Stanford University Press.

TAKASHI MITANI

CIESZKOWSKI, AUGUST (1814–94)

August Cieszkowski was a leading Polish national thinker and a cosmopolitan intellectual of considerable originality. In Poland, his monumental Polish-language work *Our Father* has placed him in the forefront of the ideological current known as messianism, though he must rank as a most untypical messianist. Abroad, attention has focused largely on his German-language *Prolegomena zur Historiosophie*, a critique of Hegel (see HEGEL AND HEGELIANISM) that first formulated the concept of *praxis* picked up and elaborated by Marx (see MARX AND MARXISM). Cieszkowski's mainly French-language publications on social and economic issues, notably *Du Crédit et de la circulation*, have attracted less scholarly interest though they were among his most popular writings in his own time.

August Cieszkowski was born to a wealthy and moderately prominent landowning family in central Poland. He always used the papal title of 'count' acquired by his father. After having, allegedly, taken part as a parliamentary scribe in the Polish insurrection against Russian rule in 1830/1831, Cieszkowski undertook studies in philosophy. These led him to the University of Berlin, then completely under the influence of the recently deceased Hegel. Cieszkowski's closest association here was with two Old Hegelians, the centrist Karl-Ludwig Michelet (1801–93), with whom Cieszkowski maintained a life-long friendship, and the progressive Ludwig Gans (1798–1839).

Cieszkowski soon demarcated himself from his mentors with his *Prolegomena zur Historiosophie* (1838). Although conceived within a Hegelian framework this slim book represented an early and radical challenge to Hegel's philosophy. According to Cieszkowski, Hegel had provided insight into the totality of history but he had erred in his interpretation and periodization of history. As Cieszkowski argued, mankind was now entering a third synthetic historical era. This third era was to be post-theoretical and socially oriented. He named its identifying concept *praxis* and its concrete manifestation, the *deed*.

The *Prolegomena zur Historiosophie* stirred interest, even in distant Russia where they constituted ALEXANDER HERZEN's introduction to Hegelianism. In Berlin they were soon overtaken by the radicalisation of the Young Hegelian School. The historiographical question that has arisen is that of Cieszkowski's role in shaping the Marxian concept of *praxis*. Most historians have concurred that Cieszkowski's influence was real but indirect, transmitted through Marx's teacher, Moses Hess, an admirer of the *Prolegomena*.

From Berlin Cieszkowski moved to Paris, where he soon published a substantial economic treatise, *Du Crédit et de la Circulation* (1839). Its specific proposals for interest-bearing notes based on land

values greatly impressed PIERRE-JOSEPH PROUDHON. Its broader aim of finding a proper balance between liberalism and protectionism, between the public and the private sphere, attracted positive attention both from academic economists and from Fourierist socialists (see FOURIER, CHARLES).

In the 1840s Cieszkowski engaged in one of the more esoteric debates among Hegelians with a polemical work on the immortality of the soul entitled *Gott und Palingenesie* (1842). He continued to write on topical issues, notably on the social question, and he put forward various policy propositions. These ranged from educational projects through land credit schemes. The most sustained such proposal was his *De la Pairie et de l'aristocratie moderne* (1844) a reform project for the French Upper House that, in fact, formulated a meritocratic theory of elites for the modern state.

During this decade Cieszkowski's focus turned back to his native Poland, though restrictions in tsarist-occupied Warsaw made him transfer his activities to Prussian-held Poznan. There he undertook a life-long engagement in promoting social reform and in building up civil society. During the momentous events of 1848 Cieszkowski also plunged into political activity. He was elected to the new Prussian National Assembly, set up a pressure group modelled on the British Corn League, so successful that it was banned in 1850, and he addressed the pan-Slavic congress in Prague. Even after hopes raised in 1848 has been dashed, Cieszkowski remained a deputy in the Prussian Diet, with a few years' interruption, until 1866 and a leader of the Polish parliamentary faction.

Cieszkowski's *Our Father* is a monumental meditation on the Lord's Prayer, understood as a prophetic announcement of the coming future era of true social reconciliation. Its reputation as an expression of Polish messianism, the idea that Poland represented a 'Christ of Nations' whose suffering would redeem mankind, rests upon its eschatological expectations as well as its intermeshing of religious vocabulary and Christian themes with worldly concerns. In fact, the message of Cieszkowski's *Our Father*, in contrast to that of traditional messianists, is resolutely meliorist rather than apocalyptic. Indeed, the *Our Father* may be seen as an alternative to messianism rather than an expression of it. Its vast and dramatic historical fresco underpins a peaceful programme of social, economic, and moral, reform and development. Salvation through modernization is its underlying message. Its national Polish dimension is embedded in a vision marked by pan-Slavism and cosmopolitanism. Cieszkowski appears to have worked on *Our Father* virtually all his life, though he published only one volume in his lifetime. His reluctance to allow broader publication was due, undoubtedly, to its incomplete character – it was unfinished at his death – but also to his fear of violating Catholic doctrine.

Cieszkowski's life and thought cover a wide span of nineteenth-century history and ideas. Although he contributed to several major intellectual currents he never identified himself completely, in ideological terms, with any of them. As a result, he stands out as a paradoxical figure, a thinker who is both representative of his times and out of step with them.

Further reading

Liebich, Andre (1979) *Between Ideology and Utopia: The Politics and Philosophy of August Cieszkowski*, Dordrecht: Reidel.
—— (ed.) (1979) *Selected Writings of August Cieszkowski*, Cambridge: Cambridge University Press.
Walicki, Andrzej (1982) *Philosophy and Romantic Nationalism: The Case of Poland*, Oxford: Oxford University Press.

ANDRE LIEBICH

COBBETT, WILLIAM (1763–1835)

William Cobbett was a non-commissioned officer, grammar teacher, political and agricultural writer, parliamentary reporter and (from 1832) MP for Oldham. Son of a small tenant farmer and innkeeper in Surrey whose own father had been a day-labourer, Cobbett's own ambitions took him to a lawyer's clerk's job in London and thence into the British army, where he improved his education, travelled to Nova Scotia and rose as far as possible for one of his background, i.e. to regimental sergeant-major. He would remain a partisan for the working population of the agricultural southern counties, but also for the traditions of monarchy and the Church of England; advocate of all those forms of social and political enablement (including self-motivated education) whereby men of modest means might rise to positions of influence; a hater of the spurious liberalism of the commercial middle classes; and (which remains his chief influence) a prose-poet of what would now be called an 'ecologically sustainable' pattern of human life.

On honourable discharge from the army (1791), he failed in England to right various army-related wrongs by legal means, and after a spell in France began in Philadelphia from 1792 and later in New York his life-long career as political pamphleteer, taking the battle home to England from 1800. He at first lampooned, then came to revere, THOMAS PAINE, sharing with him an English ambiguity in regard to Washington's party and the French Jacobins, who were both, for Cobbett, middle-class partisans of a fake and parasitical 'liberty'. His radical conservatism (see CONSERVATISM, AUTHORITY AND TRADITION) would lead him to attack the population theories of MALTHUS, and the Arkwright system of factory labour, while perpetrating stereotypes of usurious Jews and backward 'blacks'. His love of the land, hatred of railway speculation and nostalgia for medieval charitable institutions anticipated CARLYLE, RUSKIN and MORRIS; yet (unlike the latter two) he had no time for trade unions, seeing them as the refuge of urban malcontents. Detesting BENTHAM and BROUGHAM, he nevertheless implemented an idea cherished by those intellectualist reformers, that of reporting 'Parliamentary Debates', his publication of that name (from 1803) being taken over by Hansard from 1812. In 1830, his long-running *Political Register* advocated universal manhood suffrage, and other reforms dear to the Chartists, including (what would remain anathema to middle-class reformers like J.S. MILL) the secret ballot.

Something of a John Bull in appearance, Cobbett's personal courage was never in doubt. He faced prosecution for attacking government corruption in Ireland, and imprisonment and financial ruin for his opposition to military flogging. Since his death, he has increasingly been respected for his advocacy, and evocation, of ecologically sustainable life patterns, in his most enduring work, *Rural Rides*.

Further reading

Derry, John (ed.) (1997) *Cobbett's England*, London: Parkgate Books.
Dyck, Ian (ed.) (2001) *William Cobbett: Rural Rides*, London: Penguin.
Nattrass, Leonora (ed.) (1998) *William Cobbett: Selected Writings*, 6 vols, London: Pickering & Chatto.
Thompson, Noel, and Eastwood, David (eds) (1998) *The Collected Social and Political Writings of*

William Cobbett, 17 vols, London: Routledge/Thoemmes Press.

SEE ALSO: democracy, populism and rights; political economy

MALCOLM HARDMAN

COBDEN, RICHARD (1804–65)

Richard Cobden was born in Dunford, Sussex, on 3 June 1804 and died in London on 2 June 1865. Educated locally and at a private boarding school in Yorkshire, he worked in a London warehouse and then entered the textile trade in Lancashire. Involvement in radical politics in Manchester was the prelude to Cobden's rise to national prominence as a leading figure (with John Bright, with whom his name is invariably linked) in the Anti-Corn Law League, an organization dedicated to seeking the removal of legislation that favoured domestic wheat producers and their landlords at the expense of the urban working classes and the manufacturing interest. He was MP for Stockport (1841–7), the West Riding of Yorkshire (1847–57) (losing his seat as a result of his opposition to the Crimean War) and Rochdale (1859–65).

Cobden's political ideas were forcefully and effectively expounded in speeches (many of which were published) and pamphlets. They focused for the most part on two related themes: 'free trade', and the injustice and expense of Britain's conventional colonial, foreign and defence policies. In both cases, aristocratic control of the state was seen as a means of furthering the interests of this class by sacrificing the moral and economic well-being of the rest of the community. Cobden had originally held high hopes of the middle classes, but their willingness to continue deferring to the aristocracy encouraged him to look to 'respectable' sections of the working classes and to promote extensions of the franchise in order to increase their political effectiveness.

The campaign against the Corn Laws came to a successful conclusion in 1846 but for Cobden this achievement was but one step along the road to 'freedom of trade'. Cobden claimed that government interference in domestic and international markets disrupted a spontaneous and generally beneficial order, raising the price of goods, hindering the profitability of industry and lowering the returns to labour and capital.

This line of argument was applied to the relationship between the metropolitan country and its colonies, as well as to foreign countries. When colonies were forced into restrictive and exclusive trading relationships with the imperial power, their interests as well as those of producers and consumers at home, were sacrificed to provide opportunities for amusement, employment and military heroism for the aristocracy, their surplus offspring and hangers-on. The protection of commerce by military means was necessary only because colonies were forced to trade with the 'mother country'. When trade was free, cheapness and honesty were the best guarantors of prosperity and security.

Cobden argued that British colonial policy demonstrated many of the weaknesses of conventional foreign and defence policies. In all these cases, the upper classes' self-serving penchant for military display and diplomatic and armed aggression were concealed by appeals to disinterest and general benefit. In one of his earliest publications Cobden turned this critique against the shibboleth that British policy towards Europe was dictated by a desire to maintain a 'balance of power' on the Continent. Cobden deployed his considerable argumentative powers against the confusions and delusions found in statements of this position and came to the conclusion that the term 'balance of power' was a synonym for a line of policy that was manipulative, self-interested and hypocritical: 'England has, for nearly a century, held the European scales – not with the blindness of the goddess of justice herself, or with a view to the equilibrium of opposite interests, but with a Cyclopean eye to her own aggrandisement' (Cobden 1903: 201).

Commerce and peace would secure the dual benefits of cheap government and mutually advantageous exchange, both of which were threatened not by the fundamental antagonism of the citizens of other states, but by the self-interests of an aristocratic-military complex that was able to exploit the class bias of British political institutions and the manipulative skills of a mercenary and supine press. Cobden argued that the ability of the latter to create and sustain 'panics' – over non-existent Russian and French threats, for example – made it possible for a very narrowly based and exclusive section of the population to rally popular support for its bellicose, expensive and self-serving diplomatic and military adventures.

In his earlier writings Cobden had relied on free trade as the instrument for transforming international politics, but he later paid increasing attention to developing modes of international co-operation that were integrated into the patterns of interaction between states. Free-trade treaties (such as the 1860 'Cobden–Chevalier' Treaty between Britain and her long-time bogey France) were one example of this strategy. It also embraced mechanisms for international arbitration and arms limitation, and the development and utilization of a body of international law to manage inter-state relations.

Cobden's claims for free trade made him vulnerable to charges that he was a proponent of extreme *laissez-faire*, while his enthusiasm for commerce as a means of fostering international co-operation and banishing militarism gave his pronouncements a utopian air. THOMAS CAR-LYLE, for example, was hostile to Cobden on both scores, dismissing one of his pacifistic initiatives by scornful references to Cobden's 'calico millennium'. These objections have a certain plausibility. It should be noted, however, that Cobden was never committed to uncondi-tional *laissez-faire*: some members of the community would need to be protected by government and it might also be necessary to make public provision for education in order to ensure that the population as a whole would be equipped to exercise political rights. Moreover, many of the ideas of international co-operation that he promoted played an important role in twentieth-century history. In a nineteenth-century context Cobden is perhaps best seen as a proponent of a strongly progressive ethos that was deeply suspicious of the continuing cultural, social and political influence of aristocracy, and resistant to rising tides of imperialism and jingoism. This ethos was important in the late Victorian Liberal Party and it also provided the context for the more sophisticated and overtly philosophical accounts of 'advanced' liberal politics put forward by thinkers such as T.H. GREEN and L.T. HOBHOUSE.

Reference

Cobden, R. (1903) *The Political Writings of Richard Cobden*, 2 vols, 4th edn, London: T. Fisher Unwin.

Further reading

Cain, P. (1979) 'Capitalism, War and Internationalism in the Thought of Richard Cobden', *British Journal of International Studies* 5: 229–49.

Cobden, R. (1903) *Speeches on Questions of Public Policy*, eds John Bright and James E. Thorold Rogers, 2nd edn, London: Macmillan.

Howe, A. (1998) *Free Trade and Liberal England, 1846–1946*, Oxford: Clarendon Press.

SEE ALSO: anti-colonial movements and ideas; ideas of war and peace; imperialism and empire; liberalism; theories of the state and society: the science of politics

JOHN MORROW

COLERIDGE, SAMUEL TAYLOR (1772–1834)

Coleridge was born in Ottery St Mary, Devonshire, on 21 October 1772 and died in Highgate, London, on 25 July 1834. He was educated at Christ's Hospital and at Jesus College, Cambridge. Destined originally for the Church, he was attracted in the mid-1790s to both radical (although not revolutionary) politics, and to Unitarian religion. Except for a brief spell in the British administration in Malta (he proved a very able public servant), Coleridge's career was entirely literary. Best known as a poet, he was also at times a prolific and accomplished political journalist, and produced a range of works on literary criticism, theology, logic and political and social philosophy.

Coleridge's earliest prose works took a sharply critical view of the English Church establishment, war and the morally corrupt condition of contemporary society, but from the late 1790s his radical ardour cooled. He never, however, became a conventionally conservative thinker. In common with proponents of eighteenth-century opposi-tionist 'Country Party' ideology, Coleridge insisted that constitutions where the possession of political rights was closely related to the distribution of property produced a generally beneficial integration of political power and the cultural and social structure of the community. These requirements were satisfied by the role ascribed to landed elites in the traditional English constitution, but Coleridge emphasized that this constitution should be flexible enough to incorporate new interests – particularly those identified with the growth of 'commercial society' – with the potential to make significant contributions to the material and moral well-being of all members of the community. On this reading, the English constitution provided a political framework for balancing what Coleridge termed the forces of 'permanence' and of 'progression'.

In addition, however, the constitution embraced the established Church, an institution that could bring its moralizing influence to bear on the conduct of secular elites and was able to play this role because it was endowed with property holding that ensured its independence of those who wielded economic and political power. This body (the 'clerisy') was of vital importance in relation to the second dominant theme in Coleridge's thought, his insistence on the intellectual and moral inadequacy of modes of thinking and action that were underwritten by mechanical and utilitarian assumptions about the world and humanity's place in it. The spurious appeals of political economy as a guiding principle of public policy were attributed to a mechanistic cast of mind that had become increasingly entrenched in England since the time of John Locke. Coleridge argued that it was the role of the clerisy to replace these malign influences with the moral and religious fruits of a way of thinking that had always had a presence in life of Christendom, but had been almost completely neglected by his countrymen since the halcyon days of the Cambridge Platonists of the seventeenth century.

Further reading

Coleridge, S.T. (1976 [1829]) *On the Constitution of the Church and State, According to the Idea of Each*, ed. J. Colmer, *Collected Works of Samuel Taylor Coleridge*, X, Princeton: Princeton University Press.
Hedley, D. (2000) *Coleridge: Philosophy and Religion*, Cambridge: Cambridge University Press.
Morrow, J. (1990) *Coleridge's Political Thought. Property, Morality and the Limits of Tradition*, London: Macmillan Press.

SEE ALSO: conservatism, authority and tradition; intellectuals, elites and meritocracy; main currents in philosophy; Romanticism, individualism and ideas of the self

JOHN MORROW

COMBE, GEORGE (1788–1858)

George Combe, the well-known nineteenth-century popularizer of phrenology, was born in Edinburgh on 21 October 1788. From humble beginnings as one of seventeen children born into a family of brewers, Combe raised himself through a long process of self-education and service as an articled clerk to become by 1812 'a writer to the signet'. Thereafter, he set himself up in his own practice, a career he combined with his burgeoning interest in phrenology, the interest growing quickly to encompass lecturing, writing and publications on the subject. Combe's first book *Elements of Phrenology* appeared in 1824, the widely popular *The Constitution of Man in Relation to External Objects* following in 1828. Earlier, in 1822, Combe had joined with others to form the Phrenological Society, which also published its own *Phrenological Journal. Constitution of Man, etc.*, the book that made Combe's reputation, was published in numerous editions, including a print run of 50,000 copies aimed at what he called 'the industrious classes'. Subsequently, the demands on Combe as the public face of phrenology in Britain grew to such an extent that by 1836 he had made a decision to retire from business entirely and spend the rest of his life propagating phrenology.

Phrenology was developed in Vienna by Franz Joseph Gall (1758–1828) and Johann Caspar Spurtzheim (1776–1832). Prior to publishing his own work on phrenology Combe attended lectures given by Spurtzheim in Edinburgh, visiting him in Paris in 1817. The basic idea of phrenology was that a variety of traits and abilities – faculties – were differentially located within the brain, and that the relative dominance of these could be identified by examining the shape of a subject's head, relating its topography to that found in specially prepared phrenological charts. Combe's contribution to the subject was to take the original ideas and make them both accessible and relevant to daily life, principally by using the outcomes of phrenological examination as a guide to advice on maximizing a person's potential. Thus, through understanding the strengths and weaknesses of one's character as revealed by phrenology a person might conduct his affairs in the world more successfully, thereby achieving personal happiness and harmony with his fellow beings.

Combe's 'theory of mind' was an interesting mix of *nature* and *nurture*, partly developmental as well as being fixed, in the sense that although 'different individuals possess the faculties in different degrees' it was also the case that in order for a man to act harmoniously and achieve happiness he must train himself. As Combe put it in *Constitution, etc.*, 'the sources of knowledge are observation and reflection, – experience, – and instruction by books, teachers and all other means by which the Creator has provided for the improvement of the human mind'. This tension between having a fixed potential but some ability to make choices and develop allowed Combe and other phrenologists to propose a wide range of interventions including: advice on physical and mental hygiene, the selection of an appropriate marriage partner, advice on the hiring of servants, the determination of racial characteristics, education in its broadest sense and the reform of criminals.

Phrenology achieved a wide following in the 1830s, particularly it seems among young people and those attempting to rise in the world. Lectures on the subject were popular and many societies were formed. However, phrenology also had its critics, principally among those concerned at the continuing failure and likely impossibility of identifying either the location or the number of faculties in the brain. In addition, adherence to phrenology raised serious religious questions at the time, for example its seeming concentration on achieving happiness in this life as opposed to the hereafter, and also for the way in which appropriate conduct was being derived from observation and the Natural Law without recourse to religious teaching or the Scriptures. Ultimately, phrenology as a movement within society was to fail but not before many thousands had derived reassurance and consolation from having a programme to follow that gave direction to their lives together with confidence that the direction they were taking was based on what appeared to them as sound principles.

Further reading

Combe, George (1937) *Dictionary of National Biography*, Vol. 4, 883–5. Oxford: Oxford UK.
Gibbon, Charles (1878) *The Life of George Combe*, 2 vols, London: Macmillan.

SEE ALSO: main currents in scientific thought; psychology, the emergence of

ALAN R. KING

COMTE, AUGUSTE (1798–1857)

The French philosopher and pioneer sociologist was born Isidore-Auguste-Marie-François-Xavier Comte. Comte was the author of the 'positive philosophy', or Positivist approach to science, and the study of society and its history. The foundation of this philosophy was empiricist, in that all knowledge had to be based on observation and experience. From empirical evidence Comte formulated general laws of intellectual change and progress, in the manner of Condorcet's *Sketch for a Historical Picture of the Progress of the Human Mind* (1795). The most important branch of positivism with respect to 'social philosophy', as opposed to astronomy, physics, chemistry or biology, was termed 'political science' in the early 1820s, 'social physics' and in 1838 'sociology'.

Sociology derived from the law of historical development termed the 'law of the three stages', stating that humanity was progressing from the theological stage to the metaphysical stage and on to the final positive stage of social organization. While the first stage was characterized by monarchical-theological-military power, and the movement from fetishism and polytheism to monotheism in religion, the second was a stage of revolutionary transition. The metaphysical stage substituted abstractions in place of divine will. It was characterized by the sovereignty of the people in politics and the sovereignty of individual reason in intellectual culture. The goal of humanity was to speed the arrival of the third positive stage in which the vain search for first causes would be abandoned in favour of laws 'of relations of succession and resemblance'. In this stage science became a vocation; government would be undertaken by scientists and industrialists. With respect to politics and religion, the positive stage was the culmination of thousands of years of historical development. It would be an age of peace and rationality, and of consensual economic progress. Comte's aim was to restore the sense of community lost when individuals abandoned themselves to the dictates of independent reason and the unregulated market. At the same time he accepted that the clock could not be turned back to the old moral communion of the pre-Reformation *pax Christiana*. Industry, production and science had to be embraced not as forces for social division but as sources of social harmony.

These ideas were first outlined in a work supervised by the unorthodox philosopher SAINT-SIMON in 1822–4, the *Plan of the Scientific Work Necessary for the Reorganisation of Society* (*Plan des travaux scientifiques nécessaires pour réorganiser la société*) and were developed in the *Course of Positive Philosophy* (*Cours de philosophie positive*). The latter work commenced as a series of lectures in 1826. It was suspended during Comte's mental breakdown and attempted suicide, continued from 1829, and finally published in six volumes between 1830 and 1842. Many writers, led by J.S. MILL, have argued that Comte's later work, exemplified by the *System of Positive Politics* (*Système de politique positive*, 1851–4), must be distinguished from his earlier *Course* because it raised imagination and sentiment above reason. Positivism became a spiritual rather than a philosophical doctrine. The best evidence of this was Comte's attempt to replace Christianity with the worship of humanity: Comte was the self-appointed high priest presiding over a clerical hierarchy, a calendar of positivist saints, new sacraments and festivals celebrating aspects of the positive society. Comte's focus on spiritual power did mark his later years. Many commentators have traced this to the fact that after the age of 40 he disdained the reading of anything other than poetry, describing this decision as 'cerebral hygiene'. Studies of Comte in the 1990s have focused on the unity of his early and later writings. It is certainly the case that the role of the spiritual power was emphasized in his first work, which was indebted to Saint-Simon's related musings on the possibility of social unity through religious innovation, teaching the universal love of mankind.

Of a bourgeois, Catholic and royalist family, Comte was born in Montpellier and attended the local *lycée* before entering the École Polytechnique at Paris in 1814. With the rest of the student body he was expelled in 1816 for criticism of the Restoration authorities. In 1817 he replaced Augustin Thierry as secretary to Saint-Simon, and worked on the journal *L'Industrie* (*Industry*) founded in 1816. Saint-Simon was then arguing that social progress depended on intellectual development, to be ensured by the application of the scientific method to social problems. Applying this method made clear that the nineteenth century was to be the 'industrial century' because an elite of scientists, bankers and industrialists would regulate and manage public affairs. To ease the transition to this age of authority

founded on scientific knowledge, a new spiritual authority had to be founded. All of these themes continued to play a leading role after Comte broke with Saint-Simon in 1824, shortly before the latter's death. The following years were complicated by Comte's recurring physical ill health, a complicated relationship with his wife, Caroline Massin, who he later accused of being a prostitute, and lack of an adequate income. All of these factors contributed to Comte's mental collapse between 1826 and 1828. The publication of the *Cours* from 1830 brought him wider public notice, and financial difficulties were eased by an appointment as Admissions Examiner at the École Polytechnique in 1836. They returned in 1844, after the breakdown of his marriage, when his post was not renewed. Mill was among those who organized a subscription fund to supply financial aid. Between 1844 and 1846 Comte conducted an intense relationship with Clotilde de Vaux. The nature of her religious beliefs, and the effect on Comte of her early death, were significant factors in the decision to found the Positivist Society, and the subsequent creation of the Positivist Calendar as part of the Religion of Humanity.

Placing Comte's ideas in historical context requires scrutiny of the intellectual consequences of the French Revolution. By 1799 it was evident that the attempt to create a republic in a large state had failed. The instability of the Directory, and its fall with Bonaparte's Brumaire *coup d'état*, itself the prelude to the establishment of the first French Empire, convinced many intellectuals that endless constitutional innovation was of little use if reform was to be lasting. The enjoyment of liberty, it was now argued, was not necessarily directly related to the form of government. Rather, it depended on political culture more generally, the *mœurs* or manners of the leading citizens, and the capacity of this elite to transform the culture of the people in general. The revolutionaries of 1789 had failed to maintain the liberties they had enshrined in constitutional law because the culture of the nation had been corrupted by monarchy, Church and aristocracy. Reversing the tendency of the French people to involve themselves in political violence, to venerate demagogues and to foster political division was not the work of a national convention as PAINE believed. Instead, the people had to be made more rational, or persuaded to make the practice of certain positive social virtues habitual, by education, civic instruction, public festivals and the example of their leaders. Such arguments had first been made in the early 1790s by Rœderer, Condorcet, SIEYÈS and other critics of the constitution of 1791 and later of the Terror. Under the Directory and the Consulate, their ideas were embraced by the Idéologues, the prominent intellectuals of the National Institute, the STAËL salon and the numerous scientific and educational institutions gracing Paris at this time.

Two particular themes of Idéologue discussion particularly influenced Saint-Simon, who was then avidly attending public lectures given by leading scientists. In turn they influenced Comte. The first was the physician Cabanis's claim that if human well-being was precisely defined then it would be possible to prescribe forms of living to different types of individuals, with the certain knowledge that it was in their best interest to follow such social practices. His most important statement was that liberty would be safeguarded because such interests were capable of scientific definition. Cabanis called the subject that defined healthy human living physiology; one of its central branches was hygiene. Many other scientists, physicians and philosophers of the day were working towards the same goal, including Bichat, Pinel and Tracy. The second theme was whether forms of religious practice could be discovered that might bring the French nation together, challenging the divisions that had characterized the nation under Catholicism, and also the time since 1789 when religious toleration had been established in law but reversed in practice. It was recognized by all writers that the Revolution had inaugurated a period of spiritual uncertainty, without directly intending to do so, from the time of the enactment of the Civil Constitution of the Clergy. Opponents of Revolution, such as BONALD and MAISTRE, argued that the Revolution represented the abandonment of Christianity, and explained the turbulence of the 1790s by reference to the social collapse that was bound to accompany divine wrath. For survival and redemption it was essential to return to political and religious orthodoxy. The revolutionaries agreed that religion was a social glue vital to national unity in a war-torn republic. Under the Directory many of the Idéologues were involved in attempting to establish the rational religion of Theophilanthropy. By the early nineteenth century across the political spectrum, from CONSTANT to CHATEAUBRIAND, it was recognized that modernizing the French state necessitated that attention be paid to the contribution of religion to social order. Few writers, such

as SAY, argued that religion could be replaced as a social force. A greater number were content to see Napoleon reintroduce the Catholic governance of education and popular mores with the Concordat.

The other significant intellectual development of the revolutionary years that influenced Comte centred on the science of political economy. The revolutionaries had accepted that increasing commerce was important for any state intending to improve the economic conditions of its populace while defending itself against aggressive commercial monarchies. At the same time they did not want to follow the British example and create a mercantile state devoted to fostering kinds of commerce at odds with republican morality, which they believed ultimately explained why the British spent so much time at war. The leading political economists of the Empire and Restoration, such as Say and SISMONDI, accepted that the project of tying commercial progress to republican government had to be abandoned. The French republics had been able to defend themselves against external challenge but could not guarantee domestic order. At the same time the political economists adhered to the view that commerce, if it was to avoid becoming a force for social division and moral corruption, had to be made conducive to social harmony. Laws could be used to forbid the most dangerous forms of commerce, such as slavery. But government was not to be allowed to involve itself in production. Rather, the moral education of the populace became the key to combating luxury and prodigality. In addition, it was necessary to foster the skills of the working classes in wider trades, in order to create a commercial society characterized by moderate wealth, rather than by the extreme inequalities typified by British experience. Say's great hope was that the advancement of industry could be rationally organized to ensure its maximum benefit to the citizens and also to a French state revivified to vanquish the British arch-enemy.

Approaching Comte from these perspectives makes clear that he was in many ways continuing the revolutionary debates of the 1790s, in the wake of his tutor Saint-Simon. There was certainly little original in attacking excessive commerce for creating social disharmony and inequality, or in seeking solutions to the problems of the French state in the reform of religious belief and practice. Too many historians have made liberalism into the straw man of Restoration intellectual life, when in fact liberals such as Constant shared Comte and Maistre's fascination with the possibility that religion could restore the moral communion lost with unbridled social and economic development. Like Constant and the political economists, Comte accepted that the division of labour was an irreversible aspect of the modern world, and that the upheavals of the previous generation could be traced to the emancipation of the communes and the consequent rise of the middle classes. It was from these classes that the leaders of science and industry were most likely to arise. Most Restoration writers also shared Comte's opposition to democracy, accepting that the Terror had proved that the people must play a passive and subordinate role in political life. He differed from them, however, in his view that representative government was not the end-point of the Revolution of 1789, because it was no more likely to bring stability than the experiments in republicanism of the revolutionary decade. Terminating the Revolution could only be achieved by formulating a determinate common purpose for humanity. The liberal ideal of a society characterized by a multitude of ends and opinions was to Comte a recipe for anarchy and unhappiness.

The division of labour in politics that Comte favoured maintained the technocratic management of individuals favoured by the Saint-Simonians. In the new industrial world people were to be directed rather than commanded. The self-evident rationality of scientists and industrialists was a key to the positive order. Where he differed from the Saint-Simonians was in the absolute separation of temporal from spiritual power. While politics became management, the spiritual power guaranteed social order. It ensured this by the control of education, part of which was to assert the dogma of the religion of humanity in an absolute and unquestionable form. While many accused Comte of erecting a dictatorship of self-perpetuating oligarchs, his counter-argument was that the bankers or industrialists in politics had limited authority because of the existence of the spiritual power. This was why in later life he argued that sociology was better termed 'sociocracy' or 'sociolatry'. Its aim was to provide an education for the modern priesthood, the countervailing institution that prevented the rich or intelligent from exercising despotism. Distinguishing between the two spheres of social life was Comte's improvement upon the separation of the legislative and executive so pronounced in republican and liberal theory.

Further reading

Baker, K.-M. (1989) 'Closing the French Revolution: Saint-Simon and Comte', in F. Furet and M. Ozouf (eds) *The French Revolution and the Creation of Modern Political Culture: The Transformation of Political Culture 1789–1848*, 3 Vols, vol. 3, 323–39, Oxford: Pergamon.

Comte, A. (1998) *Early Political Writings*, ed. and trans. H.S. Jones, Cambridge: Cambridge University Press.

Mill, J.S. (1991) *Auguste Comte and Positivism*, in *Utilitarianism*, ed. H.B. Acton, London: Dent.

Pickering, M. (1993) *Auguste Comte and Positivism: An Intellectual Biography*, Cambridge: Cambridge University Press.

SEE ALSO: industrialism, poverty and the working classes; liberalism; Saint-Simon, Henri de; social theory and sociology in the nineteenth century; theories of the state and society: the science of politics

RICHARD WHATMORE

CONSERVATISM, AUTHORITY AND TRADITION

The three principles that Anthony Quinton (1978) identifies with 'English Conservatism' – traditionalism, organicism and political scepticism – apply also to conservative thinking in a broader European context. These principles are inter-related parts of a single edifice but the value attached to tradition provides the cornerstone of it. The transmission of sources of viable political and social authority reflects the organic character of historically stable communities by linking past, present and future, while scepticism about the reliability of reason is frequently counterbalanced by reliance on the fund of experience embodied in traditional ideas, institutions and practices. Customary institutions and ideas are treated as authoritative in a given community; this status is also often conferred on the classes or individuals who have played a central role in them.

Continuous and discontinuous traditions

Appeals to tradition are invariably appeals to history. They represent the present as the result of a long process of transmission that may be likened to a chain of bequests. Continuity is seen as a sign of the robustness of the chain: its integrity has never been successfully challenged because it has continued to serve the interests of the community whose existence it has anchored. The idea of tradition as continuity plays a central role in British conservative political thinking in the nineteenth century. Even here, however, it was sometimes displaced by theories premised on historical discontinuity that were similar structurally to some 'radical' political thinking in the early modern period. Thus one finds, as in the seventeenth- and eighteenth-century utilization of the idea of the 'Norman Yoke', appeals to history that treat the more or less recent past as unwelcome interruptions to a desirable state of affairs that had once been part of tradition. Transformative political action will reclaim traditional institutions, ideas and practices that stood in pristine splendour at the point of rupture and have become at best marginal to the life of the community since that time. This line of argument assumes the timeless moral integrity of the wholesome fruits of a disrupted tradition. For this reason, institutions and practices that have become established since the rupture are held to be part of a counter-tradition, a tainted heritage of malignancy that needs to be purged.

Given the implications of this position for the integrity and value of the status quo, its generically conservative status is clearly problematic. But while such theories point to a need to modify the status quo, they may still embrace the organic and sceptical perspectives integral to conservatism. They do not venerate the present or the recent past but they still regard some aspects of the history of the community as a source of moral and political authority relevant to the present generation. Moreover, the radical potentialities of theories of discontinuity may be blunted by their incorporation of the assumption that a desirable condition can be recovered without disturbing many of the salient features of the prevailing distribution of social, political and economic influence. The transformation of the present is largely behavioural and moral rather than economic or institutional. Finally, in the late eighteenth and early nineteenth centuries, these theories confront doctrines whose implications are radically transformative, and in which appeals to history and the values associated with it are either non-existent or completely marginal.

The conservative reaction to radical natural-rights theory

In the latter part of the eighteenth century the three primary principles of conservative political thinking were challenged by the deployment of natural-rights theory for avowedly radical, reconstructive ends. The salience of such language in the revolutionary turmoil that wracked France, Italy and parts of Germany in the 1790s ensured that a critical reaction against natural-rights theory played a significant role in later conservative political thinking. This reaction continued long after natural rights had ceased to be a staple of radical politics, a delayed effect that reflected a widespread and persistent belief among conservative thinkers that appeals to natural rights epitomized perspectives on the nature and source of political authority that were anathema to those who looked to the past to legitimize the present.

Natural-rights theory played a challenging and radical role in Anglo-American political thinking in the 1770s and was resisted by those who supported the British government in the conflict with its North American colonies. The conservative reaction against natural rights theory came to a head in the 1790s when it was associated closely with the later writings of EDMUND BURKE, particularly *Reflections on the Revolution in France*, *Letter to a Noble Lord* and *Letters on a Regicide Peace*. Burke argued that while claims concerning natural rights might account for the origins of government, they could not generate valid criticisms of prevailing ideas, institutions or practices, or justify alternatives to them. This argument was grounded in a religiously motivated scepticism that played a significant role in eighteenth-century Anglican thought. (Hampsher-Monk 1987: 33–4) It also brought fashionable ideas about the role of association in human cognition to bear on the distinctive experience of particular communities. Seen from this perspective, the past appeared as a virtually infinite number of associations that provided the cumulative substance of the mind of the community and its members. The products of this process were likened to a 'second nature', a non-voluntaristic basis of habit and thought that displaced any ideas or interests ascribed to 'natural' human beings. Claims based upon natural rights were thus held to be irrelevant to the evaluation of contemporary political institutions, or to attempts to specify the duties of rulers or the rights of subjects.

In place of what he took to be an intellectually flawed and dangerous appeal to natural rights, Burke extolled a system of government that was the finely wrought outcome of a tradition of human interaction, not a conscious product of human legislation. This conception of British government had strong parallels with the language and frame of mind identified with the common law. In both cases, custom and precedent were endowed with legal and symbolic privilege. They were 'coterminous' with the community and the longevity of the institutions ascribed to them was due to their proven capacity to meet its needs by addressing an infinite range of problems that had arisen in the course of its history. Burke likened the transmission of rights and institutions through the stable medium of the traditional constitution to a process of inheritance. This perspective at once evoked the reality of a constitutional structure in which political rights were closely related to property holding, the hereditary transmission of monarchical office and hereditary title, fundamental biological processes and familial relationships. The fact that inheritance was seen as entailed meant that all its advantages would be jeopardized if its disposal or alteration was left to the passing whim of a single generation.

When communities sought to dispense with the entail attached to their inheritance, they lost the protection afforded by what Burke called the 'cloak of custom', leaving themselves exposed to the vicissitudes of aggregated private judgements. The hazards of such a rash move were increased immeasurably when the least rational, most passionate and most economically desperate sections of the community played a determining role in political deliberations. Indeed, such a state of affairs contradicted the very idea of government: coercive agencies were necessary for productive human life precisely because of the intellectual and moral shortcomings of the lower classes, and the pressing need for them to be subject to forms of regulation that they were incapable of framing for, or of applying to, themselves.

Burke's traditional constitution was essentially that of the Revolutionary Settlement of 1688–9. In opposition to radical accounts that treated this event as a revolutionary act of recreation, Burke argued that it was significant because it restored the nation to a trajectory from which it had been deflected by the misconduct of James II. In Burke's writings from the 1790s increasing stress was laid on the civilizing role of an independent Church of England, an institution that was contrasted with the dependent body resulting from the seizure of Church property in France and the creation of a state-salaried clergy.

As in all appeals to tradition, Burke's was partial and to some degree prescriptive of tradition itself. Thus while he was sympathetic to Roman Catholicism in Ireland on the grounds that it was capable of playing the same role there as Anglicanism did in England, he was strongly antagonistic towards what he saw as the insolently assertive and independent tendencies in English dissent epitomized by the Reverend Richard Price, the preliminary target of the *Reflections*. Similarly, while Burke celebrated the capacity of the English constitution to absorb and utilize 'men of talent', he was dismissive of the underemployed doctors, barristers and 'political' men of letters who dominated the French Constituent Assembly. This attitude to elite recruitment reflected an insistence that an appeal to tradition was not a prescription for intransigent resistance to change. Rather, beneficial change took place, as it had in 1688–9, within a framework supplied by precedent and ancient institutions. One of the cardinal sins of the revolutionaries in France was that they had wilfully destroyed a structure that was capable of appropriate reform and had, indeed, shown encouraging signs of this over the course of the eighteenth century. In Burke's view, however, France was merely the first victim of a distemper that threatened a traditional European order made up of a community of nation-states.

Burke's *Reflections* was translated into German soon after publication and attracted considerable attention in the German states. While some of this notice was sharply critical, reminiscent of the response of radicals in Britain, much of it was strongly positive. To some degree the ground had been prepared for Burke in Germany by Justus Möser's defence of the historically evolved political and social structure of the principality of Osnabrück. However, the timing of Burke's *Reflections*, and the fact that it focused on a large and powerful European state rather than a petty principality (Aris 1936: 255), lent additional force to his argument. Certainly, in the 1790s and well into the nineteenth century, Burke's writings were a common reference point for conventional conservatives in Germany and for their less conventional, Romantically inclined, compatriots. These thinkers invoked an image of 'Europe' as a coherent moral and political order, although Romantics such as Novalis (Frederick von Hardenberg), Joseph Görres and FRIEDRICH SCHLEGEL did not think that this ideal had been realized in early modern Europe. Novalis's 'Europa' looked back to a medieval world where moral leadership was provided by the papacy. Both Görres and Schlegel thought that Protestantism had had a harmful impact on the tradition of universal authority that they identified with Roman Catholicism. For these writers, the idea of an order of European states under the moral direction of the Pope was an alternative to republican cosmopolitanism that erroneously privileged the universal over the particular and local. By contrast, the conservative order was made up of discrete national communities with their own traditions and their own distinctive political and social structures. These structures were integrated in a historically derived network of relationships and dependencies that constrained and moderated the interactions of its members.

Tradition and discontinuity

Romantic attitudes towards Europe reflected a more general tendency to seek authentic models of political authority in the distant past, treating the early modern period as a regrettable disruption of a tradition that needed to be recovered. This view of the eighteenth century stood in sharp contrast to that of Burke. German Romantics pointed to unsettling parallels between the assumptions underlying late seventeenth- and eighteenth-century monarchical absolutism, and those of the proponents of the 'rights of men and citizens' in the 1790s. In each case, sociability and individuality were seen as fundamentally antithetical. Sovereign power was an expedient necessary to protect the interests of bearers of natural rights, but it did not generate collective values or political cultures capable of capturing the transformations that individuals underwent as a consequence of their integration in a range of complex social relationships. Romantics argued that when political life was explained in these terms, the state assumed a cool, instrumental and conditional character that made it unable to withstand either criticisms about

its value to individuals, or the alluring prospects of reinvigorated and engaged social life advanced by the champions of liberty, equality and fraternity. Given their atomistic starting-point and hostility to existing forms of collective life, these aspirations proved tragically false; yearnings for fraternity were obliterated by the fratricidal practice of revolution. By 1800 German Romantics had become stern critics of the revolutionary movements sparked by events in France. Over the following decades they became increasingly hostile to even the most modest constitutional aspirations of reformers in France and elsewhere. It is important to note, however, that the Romantic critique of absolutism was just as sharp as its reaction to constitutional government and rested on much the same grounds.

This critique was exemplified in Novalis's characterization of Frederick the Great's Prussia as a 'factory' state presided over by a 'state mechanic' committed to the hopeless task of squaring the circle of his own and his subjects' self-interest. Other Romantics focused on the shortcomings of exclusively juristic conceptions of the state. Frederick Schlegel, for example, drew a contrast between 'rational' and 'natural' law and claimed that the latter was a necessary feature of a true political community. Since rational law began with the idea that individuals were bearers of pre-political rights, it could not evade the conclusion that state membership compromised rather than reconciled the interests of individuals. By contrast, natural law was the product of systems of authority that had their origins in the family; it thus integrated interests that were based on affection and sociability rather than those juristic constructs that were premised on the fiction that natural human beings lived in isolation from one another. This formulation reflected the Romantics' stress on reconceptualizing the relationship between subjects and rulers so that fear of coercion and the pursuit of self-interest was replaced by exchanges based on admiration, affection and respect. Relationships of this kind were not possible under absolute monarchy, but nor could they be expected to emerge under constitutional regimes that reduced the monarch to the status of a paid servant of the public, or an empty symbol. Romantics tended to see monarchs as independent political actors bound to their subjects by strong ties of identity and emotion, and presiding over a network on institutions akin to traditional estates.

Estates provided advice for rulers without impugning their sovereign authority and a focal point for subjects to participate in the state through institutions that reflected other aspects of their life as members of the community.

French conservatives and the challenge of the revolutionary past

While German writers had to contend with aspects of eighteenth-century government that were not considered part of a viable tradition, conservative thinkers in France faced the problem of how to respond to the events of the 1790s and the period of Napoleonic rule that had followed them. One response was to regard these events as interruptions to a tradition that was endowed with many of the virtues that Burke had ascribed to his countrymen's inheritance. JOSEPH DE MAISTRE, a loyal and long-suffering subject of the King of Piedmont and Sardinia, one whose intellectual interests focused on France, adopted this position. He looked to the restoration of the Bourbons in 1814 as the occasion for a return to a system of royal authority whose legitimacy and practical value was demonstrated (to those not beguiled by the spurious and dangerous attractions of 'enlightened reason') by its integration within a social and political culture whose longevity was a sure sign of its fitness for the needs of the French people and of divine approbation. LOUIS DE BONALD, a contemporary of Maistre's who held office under the Restoration, thought that revolutionary ideas had acquired a sufficiently firm hold on the mind of his countrymen to pose as an alternative tradition to that of the *ancien régime*. He sought to shake off this incubus by stressing the congruence of the model of royal government of the Bourbons and fundamental, divinely ordained patterns of authority embedded in the traditional family.

Bonald and Maistre wished to purge the government of post-war France of innovations that resulted from the Revolution. For some French conservatives, however, the Restoration was welcomed as providing an opportunity to fuse the substantive advantages of the old regime with the spirit of freedom that was the most important legacy of the Revolution. This hope provided the focus of FRANÇOIS CHATEAUBRIAND's post-war works. While rejecting the excesses of the revolutionary period, Chateaubriand also condemned the Napoleonic regime as the 'saturnalia of monarchy'. He appealed to the Bourbons to fortify aspects of traditional government with conventions drawn from constitutional monarchy. The aim was to secure freedom by making arbitrary rule impossible, while preserving the benefits associated with images of social and political order imbued with the lustre and warmth of a long tradition of monarchy.

When these hopes were dashed by the intransigence of the Bourbons and the stifling and tawdry ethos of the July monarchy, other romantic figures (such as LAMARTINE and LAMENNAIS) turned away from monarchy and sought salvation in republican democracy. As the century progressed, however, it was more common for conservative thinkers to follow Bonald's example and to see the Revolution as the starting-point of a malign counter-tradition that needed to be sternly resisted. This line was prominent in the writings of right-wing thinkers active in the closing decades of the century who were fortified in their traditionalist faith by the impact of the military humiliations of 1870, the revolutionary spectre raised by the Paris Commune of 1871 and the perpetuation of centralization and anti-clericalism under the Third Republic.

In response to this state of affairs CHARLES MAURRAS extolled the virtues of the tradition of political and religious authority embodied in the Bourbon monarchy and the Roman Catholic Church. The former would shun any attempt to adopt a constitutional guise and would rule instead as the unquestioned (and indeed unquestionable) head of a state whose members would be incorporated in a range of functional, geographical, professional and occupational and religious corporations. A return to what Maurras depicted as *the* traditional French state would relieve subjects (who republicans foolishly treated as sovereigns as well) of the constant interference that was the hallmark of republican government. As subjects of a Bourbon king, ordinary French men (women were subsumed in patriarchal families) would be at liberty to deal with their own affairs under the direction of a monarch whose power was untrammelled and openly acknowledged. These arrangements recognized universal and hence natural patterns of subordination in ways that took account of the distinctive character and historical experience of the French people.

Institutional continuity and intellectual and moral discontinuity in British conservatism

In the immediate post-war period in Britain the traditional 'constitution in church and state', and the social structure identified with it, continued to be the primary focus of conservative political thinking. As in France and Germany, important statements of conservativism came from figures identified with Romantic tendencies in literature. William Wordsworth espoused an idea of 'second nature' that owed much to Burke and extolled the moral, political and personal virtues of practice that relied on unreflective tradition. This stance favoured the local, particular and immediate over the abstract and self-conscious, seeing these as the basis of personal life and of an organic community where legitimate authority was focused in the established Church and in social and political institutions that were historically attached to it. Wordsworth's mature political position was formulated in the face of a range of destabilizing political, economic and religious developments that followed in the wake of the successful conclusion of the Napoleonic War. Concern at these developments – closely associated with, but not exhausted by, responses to economic stagnation after the war, the attempts to extend the franchise and to repeal political penalties imposed on both Roman Catholics and Protestant Dissenters – was shared by ROBERT SOUTHEY and SAMUEL TAYLOR COLERIDGE. Like Wordsworth, Coleridge and Southey extolled the virtues of social and political forms that might be seen as part of the fabric of the community, but in Coleridge's case stress was also laid on the need to productively incorporate dynamic impulses. Both the forces of 'permanence' (associated with landed property and the gentry) and those of 'progression' (stimulated by the growth of commerce and the opportunities opened up by economic development) were represented in the House of Commons. He argued, however, that the moral and practical viability of this structure rested on its capacity to resist the corrosive moral influences of an unchecked 'spirit of commerce'. Coleridge looked to the Church of England to provide elites with both an education and an ongoing moral and intellectual culture that would ensure their commitment to an ethic of Christian humanism. In the recent past such commitment had been lacking, largely because of the impact of an ethos of philosophical materialism that Coleridge traced to the writings of John Locke. He sought to counteract this by urging the clerisy to reattach itself to a tradition of indigenous Christian Platonism that had flourished up until the late seventeenth century.

While Coleridge thus seemed to endorse many conventional conservative views on the role of tradition, his stress on its intellectual dimensions meant that his position was distinctive. One important result of this feature of Coleridge's political and social thinking was that later appeals to intellectual traditions were often made in support of liberal and progressive positions (as in the cases of F.D. MAURICE, MATTHEW ARNOLD and T.H. GREEN), and tended to diverge from those adopted by political conservatives. Between about 1835 and 1850, for example, BENJAMIN DISRAELI and his associates in the Young England movement attempted to transform conservative thinking in England in ways that (unconsciously) echoed the ideas of Romantics in Germany. They were dismissive of the supposed triumphs of eighteenth-century development and distinctly cool towards the Glorious Revolution. In place of what they saw as the corrupt self-serving ethos of the Whig ascendancy, they sought to recover a medieval ideal of monarchy and aristocracy (courageously but unsuccessfully defended by the Stuarts) that would secure the loyal obedience of members of the lower class through its protection of their interests and its engagement of their (appropriately respectful) affections. These thinkers were also attracted by what they saw as the warmth and cultural colour of the medieval Church and by its capacity to provide a unifying focus for the community. In the modern world these roles might be taken up by the Church of England, but first it would need to be purged of strains of Calvinism that had tainted it since the seventeenth century, and freed from the shackles of law and convention that had turned it into a complacent adjunct of the Whig state. Although Young England had a sentimental preference for peasantry (one that made it particularly sympathetic to the plight of the Irish lower classes) they sought to apply their ideas to social and moral problems arising from industrialization, urging the upper classes to use their political power to protect the urban working classes and to curb the worst excesses of the commercial spirit. In addition, however, they saw literature as a way of stimulating sentiments that supported their political, social and ecclesiastical ideals, and of reasserting a tradition that had been in a condition of partial eclipse for much of the early modern period.

Conclusion: conservatism without tradition in the late nineteenth century

By the closing decades of the nineteenth century the relationship between conservatism and tradition had become increasingly tenuous. In Britain the Marquis of Salisbury made a case for preserving aristocracy as a disinterested bulwark against the forces of politically armed self-interest launched on the country by the democratization of the electoral system, but he lacked the confidence in tradition that had inspired his predecessors. The only other late nineteenth-century British conservative thinker of any note, W.H. MALLOCK, abandoned his youthful faith in aristocratic culture and followed the plutocratic tendencies of contemporary political conservatism. In Mallock's later writings, conservatism was increasingly seen as a defence of property and inequality against the inroads of socialism and reformist liberalism. Maurras's attempt to resuscitate a strongly localized image of tradition was inspired in part by an attempt to exclude 'alien' elements (Protestants and above all Jews) from the body politic. This gave rise to a style of politics (identified with the Action Française) that had much in common with that adopted by his radically non-traditional contemporary MAURICE BARRÈS. Significantly, Maurras was shunned by the representatives of the House of Bourbon and by the papacy. The fact that these figures continued the century-long campaign against the Revolution and natural-rights thinking provided some continuity to French conservatism. By contrast, the status quo in Germany had been so radically transformed by the political and military events of the years 1860–70 that ideas of conservation lost all contact with any coherent or plausible notion of tradition as a source of inherited ideas, institutions and practices.

References

Aris, R. (1936) *History of Political Thought in Germany*, London: Allen & Unwin.
Hampsher-Monk, I. (ed.) (1987) *The Political Philosophy of Edmund Burke*, London: Longman.
Quinton, A. (1978) *The Politics of Imperfection*, London: Faber & Faber.

Further reading

Beiser, F. (ed.) (1996) *The Early Political Writings of the German Romantics*, Cambridge: Cambridge University Press.
McClelland, J. (ed.) (1970) *The French Right: From Maistre to Maurras*, London: Jonathan Cape.
Menczer, B. (ed.) (1952) *Catholic Politic Thought, 1789–1848*, London: Burns Oates.
Morrow, J. (ed.) (1990) *Young England. The New Generation*, London: Leicester University Press.
—— (ed.) (1991) *Coleridge's Writings: On Politics and Society*, Princeton: Princeton University Press.
Reiss, H.S. (1955) *Political Thought of the German Romantics*, Oxford: Basil Blackwell.

SEE ALSO: Bonald, Louis de; Burke, Edmund; Carlyle, Thomas; intellectuals, elites and meritocracy; industrialism, poverty and the working classes; Maistre, Joseph de; Maurras, Charles; the nation, nationalism and the national principle; Romanticism, individualism and ideas of the self; Social Darwinism; Spencer, Herbert; theories of the state and society: the science of politics

JOHN MORROW

CONSIDÉRANT, VICTOR (1808–93)

Victor Considérant created and led the Fourierist movement in France. He was a leading socialist radical in 1848, increasingly out of tune with the conservative trend of the Second Republic. Forced into exile in June 1849 to escape prosecution, he became involved in a number of utopian settlements in North America. Considérant made virtually no contribution to later socialism and was almost forgotten by historians until the end of the twentieth century.

Considérant, a native of the Franche-Comté, was first introduced to FOURIER's ideas when, as a *lycée* pupil, he lodged with Clarisse Vigoureux in Besançon. He joined the army engineering corps in Metz after training in the Ecole Polytéchnique. He relieved the boredom of barracks life by reading Fourier, whom he first met in March 1830. At the end of 1831 when the Saint-Simonian movement began to implode, Considérant took the lead in attracting disillusioned acolytes to Fourier's ideas. In early 1832, with the financial backing of Clarisse Vigoureux, he launched *Le Phalanstère*, a Fourierist journal committed to creating a *phalange*.

Although the experiment at Condé-sur-Vesgre, near Paris, failed, Considérant successfully developed a Fourierist movement. It attracted men and women, but soon drew away from Fourier's more extreme ideas. Fourierists seem not to have believed that, once the shackles of conventional society were removed, people would be naturally good. Women had a notable influence in developing Fourierist morality. Many Fourierists had abandoned Saint-Simonianism because of ENFANTIN's ideas on temporary sexual unions, and reverted to conventional notions of the family. Fourier rejected traditional religion, whereas many Fourierists drew close to Catholicism.

Considérant became the leader of the movement and married Clarisse Vigoureux's daughter, Julie. His main contribution was to substitute the state for the *phalange* as the agent of social reform. In some respects he made Fourierism more practical, with closer links to current politics. He placed less emphasis than Fourier on the division of society into many human types and focused, before Louis Blanc, on the idea that society should recognize the right to work. In August 1843 he founded a daily, the *Démocratie pacifique*, which became a central part of his socialist publicity, together with public lectures and a library.

Considérant believed that his ideas, and those of his master, were based on rational observation and constituted a social science. In the year of Fourier's death Considérant published his *Destinée Sociale*, which he dedicated to Louis-Philippe. He explained and justified Fourier's theory of *phalanges*. Fourier's plan was to make the country anew, a single community at a time. Fourierists were not a political party and at first did not envisage large-scale reform. The societary commune, the term Considérant tended to use rather than *phalange*, presumably because the commune was already the basic unit in France, would be the cornerstone of society, if its organization could be perfected. Work would be agreeable. The individual would be free, his faculties would be expanded, everyone would work in harmony, although class divisions would remain. Unlike Fourier, Considérant did not expect family structures to disappear, nor did he believe that harmony would exist instantly when a *phalange* was formed, Considérant thought that it would emerge gradually as society became more receptive to the benefits of co-operation.

Considérant analysed the present, where, he claimed, a great deal of effort was wasted; on military expenditure and defence, on evils such as gambling, whores, beggars and prisoners; on the legal system, police and prisons; on idlers *'oisifs'*; on the fiscal system; on metaphysicians and philosophers; and, finally, on commerce. Trade was parasitical. None of these would exist in his ideal world. Like Fourier, Considérant believed that humanity had developed according to a general law of nature in which society passed through stages, akin to those of the individual; hence, birth, infancy, youth, maturity give way to decline, decrepitude and death. Current notions of property, based, he asserted, in the right of conquest, were illegal. He thought equal subdivision was impractical and was entirely opposed to a revolutionary redistribution as Babeuf had suggested. He was not against hereditary rights as such but believed that ownership should be based on the right to work. As Considérant developed his concept of a right to work, he began to see the state as the initiator of reform. The government should make a scientific assessment of the economy from which it would create an industrial framework within which it would guarantee that there would be enough work for all. He claimed that such an endeavour could be achieved without political reform or legal changes. Such state-directed reform would have been anathema to Fourier.

Fourierist groups formed in Paris, Lyon, Bordeaux, Nantes, Metz, Orléans, Besançon and Dijon. Fourierism also gained sympathizers world-wide, in Britain and elsewhere in Europe, in Australia, but especially in North America. A substantial number of accounts of Fourierist ideas were published in English, although most of Fourier and Considérant's own work was not translated.

The Revolution of 1848 seemed to offer Considérant the chance to promote his theories. However, although known as a journalist and a member of the Luxembourg Commission, he struggled to be elected to the new Constituent Assembly for the Loiret, and more on a democratic than a socialist ticket. He became a member of both the Labour and the National Workshops subcommittees. He argued the right to work vociferously and unsuccessfully, was entirely opposed to the June 1848 rising against the closure of the workshops and supported Cavaignac's military repression. He was elected to the Legislative Assembly as a *démocrat-social*. On 13 June with Ledru-Rollin and others he urged violent resistance to Louis-Napoleon's decision to send an expedition to Rome to restore papal authority.

Following their failure, Considérant left for exile in Belgium and was condemned in his absence by the high court in Versailles.

He spent the next 20 years with Clarisse and Julie trying to help run utopian socialist communities in the USA. The group at La Réunion, Red River Texas, collapsed on the outbreak of the Civil War. Considérant returned to France in 1869, lived in poverty and never re-entered politics. Fourierist socialism fizzled out in 1849, despite a brief attempt to revive its ideals of 'solidarity' in 1871.

Further reading

Beecher, J. (2001) *Victor Considérant and the Rise and Fall of French Romantic Socialism*, Berkeley: University of California Press.
Vernus, M. (1993) *Victor Considérant*, Dole. Carevas Editeur.
An extensive list of Considérant's books and accounts of Fourierism in English in Pilbeam, Pamela (2000) *French Socialists before Marx: Women, Workers and the Social Question in France*, Teddington: Acumen.

SEE ALSO: early socialism; Fourier, Charles, Saint-Simon, Henri de

PAMELA PILBEAM

CONSTANT, BENJAMIN (1767–1830)

Benjamin Constant de Rebecque was best known in his lifetime as a politician and political journalist, but he acquired a largely posthumous reputation as a Romantic novelist that for long overshadowed his political reputation. With the resurgence of interest in liberal ideas in France in the 1980s, however, his importance as a political theorist began to be appreciated. Formerly he was often dismissed as a political adventurer, who at different times expressed sympathy for the Jacobins, constructed equally principled defences of the liberal republic against monarchy and of constitutional monarchy against republicanism, and also briefly rallied to Napoleon during the Hundred Days. Now he is increasingly regarded as one of the outstanding theorists of nineteenth-century LIBERALISM. He is best known for his searching distinction between ancient and modern liberty, but this has to be set in the context of his broader enquiry into the nature of the modern self.

Constant was born in Lausanne in 1767. His mother was from an old French Protestant family who had sought refuge in the Vaud for religious reasons; she died after giving birth. His father, Juste, was a colonel in a Swiss regiment in the service of Holland. Constant was educated at the University of Erlangen in Bavaria in 1782–3, and at the University of Edinburgh, where he spent two formative years in 1783–5 and was an active member of the Speculative Society. At Edinburgh he came into contact with the central ideas of Scottish political economy, and these were to have a profound impact on his political thought, for the idea that the advent of commercial society must bring about a new kind of politics was an enduring theme in his writings, shaping both his defence of representative government and his concept of the liberty of the moderns.

Constant was in Paris in 1785–6, living in the house of the distinguished critic Jean-Baptiste Suard. He returned to Lausanne in 1786. In 1788 his father obtained for him the post of Gentleman of the Chamber at the court of Brunswick, which he held until 1794. The failure of his marriage in May 1789 to the Baroness Wilhelmina von Cramm, a lady-in-waiting at the same court, led to his return to Switzerland. There, in September 1794, he met and fell in love with MME DE STAËL, whom he accompanied to Paris in May 1795. Their relationship was to endure, intermittently, for a decade and a half, and Constant probably fathered Staël's daughter Albertine, subsequently Duchesse de Broglie, who was born in 1797. In the same year as he met Staël he bought the property of Hérivaux, near Luzarches, as the precondition for acquiring French citizenship. Constant was thus a Frenchman by choice, and in a sense he was drawn to France by the world-historical significance of the French Revolution. From the outset he welcomed the revolution: he acknowledged that much revolutionary politics consisted of 'knavery and folly', but preferred to be on the side of the folly that destroyed injustice than to be on the side of those, such as BURKE, who as Constant saw it defended injustice and absurdity.

In the late 1790s Constant met and won the patronage of that great survivor of French revolutionary politics, EMMANUEL-JOSEPH SIEYÈS. Sieyès, another political activist whose reputation as a theorist began to blossom at the end of the twentieth century, both promoted Constant's political career and had a powerful influence on his political thinking. He was instrumental in securing Constant's election to the Tribunate in January 1800, but Constant's advocacy of freedom of speech antagonized Bonaparte, who dismissed him in 1802. He spent the years 1802–14 in exile with Staël, whom Bonaparte had expelled from France. He had prolonged stays both at Staël's family estate at Coppet, near Geneva, and in Germany (Weimar 1803–4, Göttingen, Brunswick and Hanover 1812–13). In 1808 he married Charlotte von Hardenberg, with whom he had had a prolonged if irregular relationship since their first meeting in 1793. He finally broke with Mme de Staël in 1811.

Constant lived predominantly in France from 1814 onwards, apart from a spell in London from January 1816 to the summer of 1817. He served as a deputy for various constituencies from 1819 to 1822 and from 1824 to 1830, and championed such causes as the freedom of the press, the abolition of the slave trade and Greek independence. He lived to see the advent of the July Monarchy, but died in December 1830. He is often viewed as a thinker of the Restoration, since it was during this last period that he published most; but in fact his political views had taken a more or less definitive form by 1806. From that time he dissociated the question of the form of government from that of liberty: in other words, he came to believe that political liberty was compatible either with monarchy or a republic. The location of sovereignty was less important than its limits.

Constant was the author of a short novel, *Adolphe* (1816), which enjoyed some success during his lifetime but has subsequently become recognized as something of a classic, not least for its innovative introspective narrative style. It recounts the relationship between the hero and a somewhat older woman named Ellénore, a Polish exile. Along with a posthumous novel, *Cécile* (1951), and his autobiographical works also published posthumously from manuscripts, *Adolphe* articulates a powerful sense of the importance of personal independence.

His chief political works, however, remained unpublished in his lifetime. The most important were two manuscript drafts towards a projected treatise on political theory: the *Principes de politique applicables à tous les gouvernements* (Principles of Politics Applicable to all Governments), which was completed in draft in 1806, and *Fragments d'une constitution républicaine dans un grand pays* (Fragments of a Republican Constitution in a Large Country), which was composed between 1795 and 1807. Constant drew on these manuscripts for a number of smaller pieces, including his celebrated speech on ancient and modern liberty.

Constant was criticized, in his lifetime and after, for his political inconsistency: the man who supported the modern republic against advocates of a monarchical restoration under the Directory would later, during the Restoration, defend the superiority of constitutional monarchy; and the man who, in *The Spirit of Conquest and Usurpation* (*De l'esprit de la conquête et de l'usurpation*), developed a fundamental critique of Napoleonic rule, would later, briefly, rally behind Napoleon's Hundred Days. But Constant always insisted that constitutional forms – the contest between hereditary monarchy and republic – meant little in comparison with the need to establish constitutional guarantees for individual freedom. Along with Staël he was among the first to articulate the post-revolutionary liberal critique of the French Revolution: he saw that the transfer of a formally unlimited sovereignty from king to people offered little guarantee of individual freedom. The lesson of the Terror was that popular. The lesson of the Terror was that popular sovereignty could pose a still deadlier threat to liberty than absolute monarchy. The principle of popular sovereignty, for Constant, had a negative significance; it stipulated that no individual or group may subject the body of citizens to its particular will. But the principle that all legimate power must belong to the body of citizens does not imply that they may use that power however they wish. Opression does not become legimate just by virtue of being committed by a majority against a tiny minority. Here he drew on a distinction Sieyes had drawn between the 're-publique' and the 'ré-totale' and anticipated nineteenth-century liberalism's quest to limit the scope of the public authority. Furthermore, Constant was never a mere defender of the status quo. On the contrary, during the period of the Restoration Constant showed an unusually perceptive insight in his analysis of parliamentary monarchy. He saw, for instance, that it required ministerial responsibility; that this responsibility must be collective and not merely individual; and that collective ministerial responsibility required an organized opposition and hence disciplined political parties. He saw, for instance, that it required ministerial responsibility; that this responsibility must be collective and not merely individual; and that collective ministerial responsibility required an organized opposition and hence disciplined political parties.

Constant's most important contribution to political theory was his distinction, which has become classical, between the liberty of the ancients and the liberty of the moderns. This was expounded in a famous lecture he gave at the Athénée Royal in 1819, but it was not a product of the immediate circumstances of the Restoration, for the essential distinction may be found in the 1806 manuscript of his *Principes de politique*. It was clearly influenced by similar ideas developed by Mme de Staël in her *Des Circonstances actuelles qui peuvent terminer la Révolution et des principes qui doivent fonder la République en France* (The Present Circumstances which Might Close the Revolution in France and the Principles that Should Underpin the Republic in France) written in 1798–9 though not published until 1906. Drawing on Condorcet's pronouncement that the ancients had no notion of individual rights, Constant followed Staël in arguing that ancient liberty consisted in active participation in the public affairs of the state, whereas the distinctive characteristic of the modern concept of liberty was the far greater emphasis on negative rights against the state. Although Constant has been read – for example, by Sir Isaiah Berlin – as an advocate of the negative concept of liberty, his position was in fact much more complex. His central point was the historical one that it is impossible for the moderns to recapture the ancient concept of liberty in its integrity, for the growth in the size of modern states, the shift from a society geared to war to a society geared to commerce, and the demise of the institution of slavery had combined to undermine the social foundations of ancient liberty. When the moderns sought to rediscover ancient liberty, as the Jacobins did under the influence of Rousseau and Mably, the result could only be despotism and terror. So Constant was not arguing that one understanding of liberty was right and the other wrong, or that one was better or more conceptually precise than the other. His point was that each was tied to a given kind of social order. In this respect Constant's political theory was profoundly historicist. Moreover, Constant certainly did not give up on political participation. He saw that it was instrumentally important to the protection of individual liberty; but, more importantly still, he also felt profoundly that there was something noble about active citizenship, and that the political

theorist should be concerned not solely with the maximization of happiness but also with self-development. It was important not just that our actual wants should be satisfied, but that we should become better and fuller human beings.

Why did Constant cherish liberty with such passion? Our understanding of the sources of his political beliefs has been deepened by being studied in the light of his long-standing interest in religion and its history: this project, conceived in the 1780s, remained incomplete at his death, although at the end of his life he published a five-volume study, *De la réligion* (On Religion). When he conceived the project as a young man he undoubtedly intended to produce a sophisticated defence of toleration in which he would defend the radical Enlightenment proposition that the polytheism of antiquity had been more conducive to religious toleration than had Christianity. But the final work abandoned this position, for he came to see ancient toleration as a consequence of indifference. Modern toleration, by contrast, rested on a sense of the radical importance of religious belief to personal identity, and hence on a profound respect for individual belief. Under the influence, no doubt, of German Romanticism (see ROMANTICISM, INDIVIDUALISM AND IDEAS OF THE SELF), Constant had become deeply conscious of the claims of personal integrity and authenticity, and his main point now was not so much to defend the individual's right to freedom of worship as to advocate an ideal of emotional authenticity. He thought this was impeded by the authority of the institutional Church.

Further reading

Constant, B. (1988) *Political Writings*, ed. B. Fontana, Cambridge: Cambridge University Press.

Fontana, B. (1991) *Benjamin Constant and the Post-Revolutionary Mind*, New Haven and London: Yale University Press.

Holmes, S. (1984) *Benjamin Constant and the Making of Modern Liberalism*, New Haven & London: Yale University Press.

Pitt, A. (2000) 'The Religion of the Moderns: Freedom and Authenticity in Constant's De la Religion', *History of Political Thought* 21, 1: 67–87.

Wood, D. (1993) *Benjamin Constant*, London & New York: Routledge.

SEE ALSO: intellectuals, elites and meritocracy; liberalism; Staël, Mme de

H.S. JONES

CROCE, BENEDETTO (1866–1952)

Benedetto Croce is perhaps the best-known Italian philosopher of the twentieth century. Although his influence today is most strongly felt in the fields of aesthetics, philosophy of history and literary criticism, his theory of art was merely a part of his whole philosophical system that embodied aesthetics, logic (conceptual knowledge), economics and ethics.

As the son of wealthy landowners in the Abruzzi of Italy, Croce was born into the enviable position of never having to earn money in order to support his scholarly pursuits. For this reason, he never held an academic teaching post although he did twice serve as Minister for Education for the Italian government, once in 1920–1 and again after the Second World War. After being injured in the earthquake that killed his parents, Croce spent three years in Rome before moving to Naples in 1886 where he lived until his death. He had a long friendship with Giovanni Gentile and they collaborated together on the journal *La Critica*, but their relationship finally dissolved when Croce openly criticized the fascist government for whom Gentile had become the official philosopher. Croce, oddly enough, was tolerated by the fascist authorities, becoming the most well-known critic of the regime and, in the eyes of the Italian people, the champion of liberty.

The system of spirit

Croce's whole philosophical system began from the consideration of aesthetics and, in particular, the problems of literature and history. Above all, he was primarily fascinated by the debate over whether history was an art or a science. The answer he was to offer would radically revise the relationship between art and science by promoting art to the level of knowledge. Life and reality were, for him, history and nothing but history and this 'historical idealism' was an attempt on his part to make intelligible the Hegelian aspiration to identify what is rational with what is historically actual or real. In framing and responding to his own question in this way, Croce aligned himself with his major influences, Vico and Hegel, and like them held a position counter to the prevailing ideas of the Enlightenment: truth is not to be described in abstract terms independent of history, but it is rather historical through and through. His thought

was an Idealism because reality is constructed by the power of the knowing mind and it was specifically a form of Hegelian Idealism because the historical rationalization of reality is truth. When one is aware of the historical process of truth, one recognizes one's philosophy as part of this development and this, according to Croce, is spirit. Spirit is perhaps best comprehended as a harmony between the knowing mind and reality, when the knowing subject knows what is the case and why historically it is the case.

The system of spirit describes the development and ascent of knowledge and is primarily separated into the traditional division of theoretical reason (describing what is) and practical reason (describing what should be). Theoretical reason is either aesthetics (the cognitive experience of the particular) or logic (cognitive experience of the universal), whereas practical reason is divided into economics (practical experience concerned with the particular) and ethics (practical experience concerned with the universal). Art for Croce – as it was for both Vico and Hegel – is a primitive form of knowing but – unlike them – he did not believe it to be rational. However, philosophy and logic are dependent on and determined by aesthetic expressions of reality since these supply the raw material from which the mind is able to conceptualize objects. Philosophy or logic, in turn, supplies the language for economics or the sphere of knowledge in which man renders his wants, volitions and needs intelligible. The main characteristic of economic practical reason is that it describes objects as useful or not in terms of the purposes of men. Finally, the practical knowledge of ethics, that is, the universal nature of volition and knowledge of good and bad independent of utility, is derived from the subject's experience of the more primitive economic volitions. Ethics describes what is universally good independent of particular or group purposes. The Good is not to be understood in terms of some universal and impersonal moral law because all truth is ultimately historical; the Good is understood in terms of the historical processes of spirit.

In order to complete the circle of spirit, one would assume that our new, sophisticated account of the Good would feed back into our understanding of art and begin the progression at a higher level and, although Croce does sometimes seem to suggest this, at others he suggests that knowledge of the Good raises the knowing subject to the level of historical knowledge and truth proper. The full elaboration of this progressive schema is perhaps the best way to elucidate Croce's philosophy.

Aesthetics

The first moment of universal spirit is artistic; knowing, in short, begins with art. Art is the expression of intuitions, but intuition is to be understood in terms of Kant's *Anschauung*: a manifold of experience, which is to say that, even at this level, the mind is active and not passive. One can understand the artistic moment as the attempt on the part of the subject to fix what is real and dissect it from what is mere appearance, thus it is a cognitive expression and not a value judgement: the artist is not aiming at beauty, nor some moral judgement, but he is aiming at the truth of the particular (much like the expressivist artist).

Art must be expressed in a particular medium, hence the divisions of poetry (words), plastic arts (colour, matter, etc.), music (sounds) and so on, but all are equally ruled by feeling. It is feeling in the sense of mood or emotion that structures the form of the image and the image which allows a feeling to be expressed. The active element of a representation at this non-conceptual level is human spirit expressing itself in the way it structures the experience it is given. It is an immediate and aesthetic experience of reality. However, to equate Croce with the Romantic elements in Hegel's early philosophy is to make a mistake; the feeling or emotion at stake is a particular manner of knowing reality for the subject, and it is not a moment of primitive reason that needs to be overcome and reified as Hegel held. Artistic expression is the a priori synthesis of feeling and representation, and it is equally an immediate, vital and non-conceptual awareness of knowing what is real.

Croce also departed from Hegel's influence in one other major way: the realms of expression and reason are distinct, and the dialectic of the distincts is not one of opposition (as it was for Hegel in which art would be overcome by more reified ways of knowing such as religion). Intuition is distinct from pure concepts, much as in Kant the faculty of intuition is distinct from the faculty of understanding, rather than an opposition that can be resolved. The concepts of reason require intuitions as raw material from which to form objects; but aesthetics, when concerned with beauty, requires the pure concepts of logic. The dialectic operates between the borders set by the knowledge of pure intuition (aesthetics) and the knowledge of pure concept (logic).

Logic

From the particular expressions with which the knowing subject represents the world aesthetically, one can abstract general concepts that can then be used in science and other realms of knowledge. Although the human being's faculty of logic is separate from his faculty of intuition or immediate experience, the former is incapable of operation without the material supplied by the latter. The central and most controversial claim of Croce's philosophy of knowledge was the identification of truth with history, although this thesis was already well known to Hegelians. Logic is defined as the knowledge of the universal that uses the particular knowledge of intuitions to form objective truth. Croce held that since any philosophical assertion is made by a subject and that subject exists concretely and historically, and not as some abstract entity, then the assertion itself must be historical: when I say, 'My laptop is on' the truth of this statement can be established because it is a matter of historical fact.

The awareness of the historical nature of concepts, that is, their relationship to the development of spirit, brings the subject to a new kind of knowledge, that is, spirit itself. However, art was not a primitive form of reason but the faculty of intuition, that is, the way in which the subject immediately apprehends the world. Logic, then, is the faculty of understanding, and the categories that determine the truth of the subject's conceptual objects are not abstract universals but the categories of historical knowledge that determine the four ways in which one can evaluate statements: intuitively, rationally, economically and morally.

Croce dismissed the idea of abstract universals in knowledge because they were, according to him, always in the service of some deeper practical aim. Error arises due to the confusion of pseudo-concepts for concepts proper. A pseudo-concept, such as egoism in economic systems of explanation, does not describe some universal aspect of human nature. Egoism is true of men only in so far as we are interested in predicting the effect of market forces and regulations on a country's economy. Croce does not deny the practical applicability of pseudo-concepts but he maintains that, in the final instance, one is mistaken when one raises them to the level of truth when they are more properly conceived in pragmatic terms. The evaluation of pseudo-concepts in terms of utility is not dissimilar to the Marxist critique of ethics: what is good depends on deeper structures, viz. economics. What is true in science depends on deeper structures and aims: our scientific concepts often change in tune with our practical, historical aims. Truth, for Croce, is a predicate of statements made by concrete individuals in particular, historical situations.

Economics

Economics covers the sphere of the operations of practical reason concerned with the matter of the individual: his or her needs, desires and volitions. Any concept employed in the satisfaction of these needs would of course be a pseudo-concept that could not be universalised. Economic operations presuppose the immediate knowing of the world present in aesthetic experience as well as the conceptual knowledge of logic.

Controversially for an Idealist, Croce locates politics and law within the realm of economics: what is legally right is what is useful; law is essentially amoral. The state, for Croce, is nothing but a process of purposive actions by a group of individuals or within the group of individuals, and laws are adopted in order to bring about these useful ends. He saw politics as the dialectical struggle between the distinct entities of power and consent as well as authority and liberty: a view that is hardly surprising given the fascist structure of Italy that he experienced.

Morality could play no part in politics because the moral life of the individual is not geared towards the useful. Croce here follows Machiavelli rather than Hegel and his rather odd brand of liberalism can perhaps be understood as descending from his compatriot rather than the ethico-political holism of the German. In many ways, he was a liberal by default since difference, individuality and tolerance were necessary for his dialectic of the distincts, and liberalism was the only way to secure these values. As far as the democratic ideals of fraternity, liberty and equality were concerned, he viewed them as pseudo-concepts rather than moral ideals: that is, concepts useful for attaining an end rather than prescribing or describing universal values.

Ethics

In the sphere of economic practical reason, Croce reduces all goods or concepts to pragmatism: they are useful in so far as they bring about the end aimed at by the agent. However, usefulness as a value only makes sense if there is some good or end aimed at, which the science of economics cannot evaluate or supply. It is for this reason that ethics occupies the highest echelon of Croce's system: it gives us universal knowledge of the Good so that we can aim at it. However, Croce was more Machiavellian than Hegelian: he did not see that the moral life could lead to the ethical whole of the state and that law was ultimately economic and not moral. So what is the nature of the Good that ethics makes possible?

The moral point of view is when the economic interests of the agent are trumped by some supreme value that obliges him to act in accordance with it rather than pragmatism. The only origin of such a value is not the Hegelian ethical state, nor the Kantian moral law, but spirit understood as historical experience. One sees Good is the progress of spirit to ever more adequate ways of understanding the world, and the truth of a political state can only be experienced historically by the progress of spirit. Thus, Croce seems to be committed to at least a minimal conservatism: one can only evaluate the actions of men in terms of the progress of history and not from some universal, moral standpoint.

Croce's philosophy often suffers by being understood as a derivative of Hegelian Idealism, an accusation that is unjust given the obvious differences listed above. Croce combined elements from Hegel with Vico, but also Kant and his own original insights, in order to produce a unique form of historical Idealism that is much more than a mere theory of aesthetics.

Further reading

The complete works of Croce are available in Italian and the works have been translated separately into English. The major philosophical ideas can be found in *Aesthetic* (*Estetica come scienza dell'espressione e linguistica generale*, 1902), *Logic* (*Logica come scienza del concetto puro*, 1902) and *Philosophy of the Practical* (*Filosofia della pratica, economia ed etica*, 1909).

Moss, M.E. (1987) *Benedetto Croce Reconsidered*, Lebanon, NH: University Press of New England.

Verdicchio, Massimo (2000) *Naming Things: Aesthetics, Philosophy and History in Benedetto Croce*, Naples: Instituto Italiano per gli Studi filosofici.

DAVID ROSE

D

DARWIN, CHARLES (1809–82)

Charles Darwin, the English natural historian, revolutionized biological theory in the nineteenth century, although – following the general prejudice of the period – he always presented himself as a thoroughgoing empiricist. Darwin did not invent 'evolution' – the theory that simple life-forms were once the ancestors of modern, complex organisms – but he did explain the mechanism of evolution in terms of a hypothesis – 'natural selection', or the preservation of well-adapted, variant organisms in an ongoing 'struggle for existence' – that has remained central to biological science ever since. The following paragraphs outline Darwin's intellectual life, the content of his theory of natural selection, some historical issues raised by the ongoing popularity of alternative theories of evolution during the period (despite Darwin's fame) and the impact of his work on social science. Particular reference is made to his most famous books, *The Origin of Species* (1859) and *The Descent of Man* (1871).

Charles Darwin was born in Shrewsbury in 1809 and first educated at the local public school (Shrewsbury School) from 1815 to 1825. His father, Robert, was a physician and, as a youth, Charles intended to join this profession until he failed to make a success of medical school in Edinburgh (1825–7). He moved to Cambridge University (1827–31) with the intention of becoming a clergyman, but, apart from the works of William Paley, Darwin disliked academic theology, and devoted more time to his hobby of natural history – both through reading and through collecting insects and fossils. His interest in the subject had been aroused in Scotland and later made more rigorous through an association with an Edinburgh physician, Robert Edmund Grant. His paternal grandfather, Erasmus Darwin (1731–1802), had also been a naturalist and was the author of *Zoonomia* (1794–6). (Scholars differ regarding the extent to which Erasmus Darwin's ideas about evolution anticipated Charles Darwin's theory of natural selection, given that the main thrust of the earlier theory followed the path outlined by the radical biologists of the French Enlightenment – see below – and stressed 'acquired characteristics'.)

On graduation, Darwin accepted the unpaid post of naturalist aboard the geographical survey ship, HMS *Beagle*. The most famous episodes in this 5-year voyage (1831–6) were his visits to South America and to the Galapagos Islands in the Pacific Ocean, where he observed many unusual plants and animals. Already sceptical of the 'creationist' account of the origins of life, the voyage inspired Darwin to invent his own theory of biological evolution, but 23 years elapsed between his return to England and his decision to make his ideas public. Darwin's mother, Susannah (who died in 1817), was a daughter of Josiah Wedgwood, the potter, and in 1839 Charles married another Wedgwood, his cousin Emma. This family wealth helped to sustain Darwin's lengthy research programme for many years prior to the commercial success of *The Origin of Species.*

In 1838 Charles became Secretary of the Geological Society and in 1839 he published a *Journal of Researches* from his voyage to the southern hemisphere. He subsequently published monographs on coral reefs, on volcanic islands and on South America. From 1846 to 1851, he worked on a significant problem of biological classification and this led to the publication of a four-volume study of both fossil and living barnacles (1851–4). Thus, Darwin became known as an accurate and thorough *descriptive* naturalist, although he had already begun a programme of breeding *experiments* on domestic animals, designed to investigate the transmission of inherited characteristics.

Fifteen years earlier (between 1837 and 1839) Darwin had organized his evidence and drafted his theory of evolution in roughly 900 pages of private notes (*The Notebooks on Transmutation of Species*) and much of his subsequent work involved seeking to verify the central hypotheses of natural selection. In 1844 he completed a lengthy essay expounding the theory (which was never published in his lifetime) and this gained the support of two notable scientific friends, the botanist, Joseph Hooker (1817–1911), and the geologist, Charles Lyell (1797–1875). The deeply hostile public reaction to a popular work on evolution by Robert Chambers – *Vestiges of the Natural History of Creation* (1844) – discouraged Darwin from publishing his ideas, but in 1856 he started work on a fully fledged exposition of the theory of natural selection. However, this work was cut short in 1858 by the discovery that another British naturalist, ALFRED RUSSEL WALLACE, had reached the same conclusions regarding the *mechanism* of evolution and intended to publish the theory – which he did, shortly afterwards. This challenge encouraged Darwin to publish an abstract of his fully fledged theory as *The Origin of Species by Means of Natural Selection.*

Darwin held back from stating directly in *The Origin* that not only the animal kingdom, but also mankind itself, must be a product of natural selection and biological evolution – and this view was only made explicit in one of his later works, *The Descent of Man.* Nevertheless, *The Origin* was bitterly contested in public controversy as a blasphemous, anti-Christian work, and took more than a decade to acquire general acceptance. In the 1860s, he continued his scientific work in relative seclusion in Kent, while a colleague, THOMAS HUXLEY, took the lead in 'the Darwin debate'. In later life, Darwin published several further works that elaborated various aspects of his theory, such as *The Variation of Animals and Plants under Domestication* (1868), *The Expression of the Emotions in Man and Animals* (1872) and *The Effects of Cross and Self-Fertilisation in the Vegetable Kingdom* (1876). Having suffered poor personal health since the 1840s, Darwin finally died at Down House in Kent in 1882.

Why was Charles Darwin's theory so contentious? In the eighteenth century, educated Europeans had generally assumed that the earth was only a few thousand years old and that the natural world was divided into a large, but finite, number of independently created species. Biblical authority was usually cited to justify such a perspective and this world-view remained commonplace in the mid-nineteenth century. Darwin's theory relied upon recent geological ideas about the great antiquity of the earth in order to provide time for long sequences of minor variations between parents and offspring to produce the great variety of observable flora and fauna, and the prior succession of species shown by the fossil record. Darwin applied Malthusian ideas about competition for scarce resources to explain the extinction of certain variations and even of whole species, but he did not invent the general idea of evolution – the theory that simple life-forms were once the ancestors of modern, complex organisms was as old as the Greeks. The credibility of his theory was assisted by the fact that, during the Enlightenment, evolutionist ideas had acquired limited acceptance amongst professional scientists, thanks to the work of figures such as Georges-Louis Buffon (1707–88) and Jean-Baptiste Lamarck (1744–1829) on the 'transmutation' of species through the acquisition of functionally useful characteristics.

Darwin was sceptical whether the biological category of 'species' was ontologically different from that of 'variety' – such categories were imposed on data by naturalists for the sake of convenience – and so his research focused upon behavioural and physiological change within 'breeding populations'. The theory of natural selection assumed that a multitude of chance variations were always present in the behaviour and, more importantly, the physiology of such breeding populations, and that these variations were transmitted across generations by a mechanism of inheritance. Without a workable theory of genetics, Darwin assumed that most variations were randomly distributed, although some took the form of 'acquired characteristics'. Each breeding population was subject to 'selection pressures' (e.g. changes in habitat, climate, the presence/absence of predators and internal competition within the population for scarce resources) and these pressures had differential effects favouring some variations at the expense of others. Darwin concluded that environmental change tended to favour the survival of variants (within a breeding population/species) that were well adapted to hostile changes, while other, less well-adapted variants died out over the generations. The long-term consequence of this process was the complete transformation of biological life from simple to complex forms, otherwise known as 'evolution'. In the revised, fifth edition of *The Origin* (1869), Darwin referred to the medium-term survival of species (of those that were more or less satisfactorily adapted to both their old and new environments) as 'the survival of the fittest' – thereby adopting a phrase coined by SPENCER and creating additional controversy regarding the morality of his doctrine.

As noted earlier, Darwin addressed the question of 'whether man, like every other species, is descended from some pre-existing form' in *The Descent of Man and Selection in Relation to Sex* – the second topic being highlighted on the grounds that it was 'highly probable that sexual selection has played an important part in differentiating the races of man'. Following earlier work by Huxley, Darwin argued that the resemblance between the bodily structures of adult humans and primates, the resemblance between human and primate embryos and the presence of common rudimentary organs that served no modern purpose all pointed towards descent from common ancestors. By stressing the role of 'sexual selection' (mating according to an implicit standard of beauty) in enhancing the physiological differences between the 'so-called races of man', Darwin was able to confute the theories of 'polygenists', such as James Hunt (1833–69), who had considered the different races to be separate species – descended from a number of 'original pairs'. Although *The Descent* is often criticized today for unreflectively assuming the activity of males, and the passivity of females, in courtship and for accepting at face value a variety of 'travellers' tales' regarding non-European cultures, it is no more (and no less) subliminally 'sexist' or 'racist' than many other notable Victorian texts.

It should be noted that, like most other theories, Darwin's theory of evolution was itself the product of an 'intellectual evolution'. Perhaps the four most important influences on Darwin's scientific thought were Paley, Lyell, Lamarck and MALTHUS. Through the study of William Paley's *Natural Theology* (1802) while an undergraduate, Darwin came to appreciate the particular significance of the adaptation of animals and plants to their immediate environment; this was

a recurring theme in all his works. Before he met Lyell in person, Darwin read Lyell's *Principles of Geology* (1831–3) and was particularly impressed by the book's uniformitarian theory of geology and its summary of the theory of Lamarckian evolution (although Lyell concluded that the evolutionism was not proven). Darwin certainly acquired much of his knowledge of European 'nature philosophy' at second hand, but he considered Lamarck to be a 'justly-celebrated naturalist' – having been introduced to his evolutionary ideas initially by Grant in the 1820s. In the early stages of his career, Darwin made frequent reference to Lamarck's *System of Invertebrate Animals* (1815), which included the (now famous) contention that all modern species are descended from other species.

Originally hesitant to embrace evolution, Darwin moved towards 'transmutationism' while reflecting on his Galapagos Islands data. In 1838 he read Malthus's *Essay on the Principle of Population* (1798) and drew novel conclusions. The application of Malthusian theory to biological life, in general, led Darwin to deduce that competition for ecological resources could intensify selection pressures to the point where favourable variations might so transform a breeding group that its members could no longer interbreed with other descendants of common ancestors (who had formed another breeding group/'species'). As noted previously, on further reflection, Darwin concluded that (at least among the higher organisms) the most well-adapted individuals tended to mate with other well-adapted individuals ('sexual selection') and this constituted an important causal factor in both the preservation of 'favoured races' and in physiological differentiation within races. This paralleled the well-recorded tendency of human horticulturists and farmers to breed from 'superior' individuals and to 'weed out' less-favoured plants and animals. 'Selection by nature' was thus a metaphorical extension of selection by mankind, but Darwin's works always attributed some causal influence in natural history to 'the conditions of life' (the environment) and the 'use and disuse' of parts of the organism (as well as to purely inherited variations). Thus, Darwin's theory of evolution (taken as a whole) combined a major hypothesis – that of Malthusian 'natural selection' – with several auxiliary hypotheses of a more Lamarckian character.

Although there were a significant number of objections to Darwin's theory from within the scientific community, the strongest reaction against his work came from all parts of the Christian church (Anglican, Catholic, Non-conformist). This seems to have been mainly due to a long-drawn-out upsurge of biblical literalism after the French Revolution. However, two distinguished Christian critics, Samuel Wilberforce (1805–73) and St George Mivart (1827–1900) also raised scientific objections to *The Origin* of some value, which adumbrate a variety of possible anti-Darwinisms. More famous for a polemical confrontation with Huxley – 'The Oxford Debate' of 1860 – Wilberforce deployed a most telling anti-Darwinian argument by pointing out the absence of cases where domestic selection had created *new* species. Mivart, on the other hand, reasserted the case for Lamarckian, saltatory evolution in *On the Genesis of Species* (1871), and this is just one example of the continued popularity of non-Darwinian evolution – further exemplified by figures such as Spencer and Ernst Haeckel (1834–1919).

Twentieth-century commentators (so numerous that their activities are often referred to as 'the Darwin industry') have often assumed that there was some connection between the continued popularity of Lamarckian ideas after 1859 and the relative importance to Darwin's own theory of both natural selection and the maintenance of the idea of acquired characteristics. An example of the latter is Darwin's hypothesis of 'pangenesis' – proposed in *The Variation of Animals*, but now refuted – which suggested that minute 'gemmule' cells (from *adapted* organs) circulated in the body and eventually affected reproduction. Other commentators have placed greater emphasis on Darwin's original uniformitarian geology (rather than a definite commitment to Lamarckism) and have argued that, during his latter years, he felt obliged to 'speed up' evolution, for he was unable to deal with an objection (again now refuted) to his chronology by the physicist, William Thomson (1824–1907). (In 1862, Thomson, later Lord Kelvin, published thermodynamic calculations to the effect that the earth was only about 1 million years old.) Finally, it must be noted that both Darwin and the Lamarckians had a significant impact on the social sciences in the late nineteenth century, although the term 'SOCIAL DARWINISM' – which has also generated a massive literature – is a catch-all phrase, encompassing many different applications of evolutionary, hereditarian and organicist concepts to human society. In *The Descent*, Darwin expressed a certain sympathy for the eugenicist ideas being developed by his cousin, FRANCIS GALTON, as well as seeking to demonstrate some (limited) continuity between biological evolution and mechanisms for change in contemporary human society.

Further reading

Desmond, A. and Moore, J. (1991) *Darwin*, London: Michael Joseph.
Harrison, J. (1971) 'Erasmus Darwin's View of Evolution', *Journal of the History of Ideas* 32, 2: 247–64.
Oldroyd, D.R. (1980) *Darwinian Impacts: An Introduction to the Darwinian Revolution*, Milton Keynes: Open University Press.
Young, R.M. (1985) *Darwin's Metaphor: Nature's Place in Victorian Culture*, Cambridge: Cambridge University Press.

SEE ALSO: Galton, Francis; Kidd, Benjamin; main currents in scientific thought; Social Darwinism; Wallace, A.R.

CLIVE E. HILL

DEMOCRACY, POPULISM AND RIGHTS

In the momentous years between 1789 and 1918, liberals, democrats, populists, socialists and conservatives were all important actors on the stage of international history. This article seeks to outline some of the most important institutional and theoretical questions raised by both supporters and critics of representative democracy – including the so-called 'populists' – and the notable three-way debate about rights between the 'liberal', 'historical' and 'socialist' positions. In the interests of brevity, arguments to the effect that non-human subjects (e.g. animals, forests or buildings) can enjoy rights are not considered, as these had little currency in the nineteenth century. European and North American sources predominate, but some reference is made to South American, Asian and African writers as well.

While political slogans may not tell the reader very much about the detailed intellectual history of the nineteenth century, it is perhaps worth noting a few as signposts in a complex historical landscape. In Paris, in 1789, the National Assembly of France declared the 'sacred' significance of the 'Rights of

Man and of Citizens'; in 1848, in Seneca Falls (New York), a Woman's Rights Convention protested the 'entire disenfranchisement of over-half [of] the people' (women and slaves) from these same liberal rights; and, in 1917, the President of the USA (Woodrow Wilson) argued in Washington, DC, that 'the world must be made safe for democracy' through warfare. Meanwhile, in 1843/4, an obscure German journalist named Marx had denounced the whole concept of 'rights', but only a few years later came to argue that it was essential for Communists to 'win the battle of democracy' (see MARX AND MARXISM).

Although Karl Marx used the latter phrase in the (implicit) context of a debate with radical anarchists, who wanted to abolish the state as well as to resolve 'the social question', his presence in the foregoing list reminds us that in Europe, in particular, democracy was often seen as the ideological reflex of industrialization. Marx certainly knew his audience, for, during most of the century, the idea that democratization would involve *social* change (greater economic equality, wider and more 'integral' education, etc.), as well as political/institutional change, was generally accepted by both sceptics (e.g. TOCQUEVILLE, ARNOLD) and enthusiasts, such as the Chartists and Jacksonians. In the Western world, however, it seems that by 1900 democracy had lost many of its negative associations with 'mob rule' and its more positive associations with 'active citizenship' had become increasingly disassociated from challenges to economic hierarchies (despite the strength of the movement known as '*social* democracy') and was in the process of being redefined as a relatively simple method of selecting governments through party-political competition. Instead, at the end of our period, the language of rights was increasingly co-opted in certain discourses (e.g. 'New Liberalism' and 'Progressivism') to address the economic and social concerns of ordinary people; concerns such as education, employment, leisure and social security (the so-called 'social rights'). It was in this context that we can perhaps best understand the less familiar slogans of 'populists' (amorphous groups of protesters whose ideas never solidified into a single ideology, even within individual countries), slogans such as 'a pair of boots is worth more than Shakespeare' (Russia in the 1870s) and 'the people must be the sovereign' (the USA in the 1890s).

The idea of 'popular sovereignty' was no doubt implicit in the theory (if not the practice) of Ancient Greek democracy and early-modern republicanism, but it was not formulated in a recognizably modern way until Jean-Jacques Rousseau published his *Du contrat social* in 1762. After his death, Rousseau was criticized by those to his 'right' for formulating the doctrine at all (e.g. by MAISTRE), and by those to his 'left' for failing to make an adequate case for universal male, or just universal, voting rights (e.g. by PAINE, Condorcet and Wollstonecraft) or a feasible model of *representative* government. However, the phrase 'the sovereignty of the people' was popularized on both sides of the Atlantic by intellectuals and politicians such as BENJAMIN CONSTANT and Thomas Jefferson, and the most famous linkage between the political slogan and a new model of cultural analysis (which examined the manners of ordinary people) was provided by de Tocqueville in *De la démocratie en Amerique* (1835–40). Nevertheless, familiarity did not entirely remove the contempt once expressed in the famous comment about the 'swinish multitude' made by EDMUND BURKE in 1791, and may help to explain the increasing scepticism regarding voting reform displayed by liberal 'intellectuals' (such as SPENCER) as the century progressed. Yet, while it remained common for the traditional, and even the new, elites of nineteenth-century society to reject the capacity of ordinary men and women to judge technical issues of governance and legislation, it was more difficult for those who espoused the causes of patriotism and nationalism to ignore the 'voice of the people' completely. Hence, there was the periodic use of plebiscites to seek political legitimacy (or to reconcile religious differences) as exemplified by the practice of the two French Empires, and of nineteenth-century Switzerland.

So, were there any 'genuine' democracies in existence during the nineteenth century? If we define a 'genuine' democracy as a state in which the will of the majority of the adult citizens – ascertained through universal suffrage elections and periodic referenda on major issues – is treated as hegemonic by the whole apparatus of government, then very few, if any, nineteenth-century governments pass the test set for them. For example, the exclusion of women, native peoples and former slaves (through judicial convention, special treaties and 'grandfather legislation') clearly weakens the claims of the so-called 'Anglo-Saxon republics': Australia, New Zealand and the USA in the late nineteenth century. Moreover, the almost universal maintenance of various 'emergency' and extra-constitutional powers by governments of all types certainly qualified the extent of the juridical freedoms of movement, expression, assembly and association enjoyed by their subjects/ citizens throughout the period. In this sense, very few people enjoyed all of the necessary rights and powers that are deemed the prerequisites of democratic politics, as we commonly understand it today. However, thanks to a series of liberalizations in the years immediately before the First World War, we can perhaps designate Finland, Norway, New Zealand and Australia as 'genuine democracies' by 1914, and describe nations such as France, Switzerland, Italy and the USA as limited ('male') democracies by the same date. Yet the debate about democracy in the nineteenth century, *taken as a whole*, was largely one about aspirations, rather than practice, and these aspirations constitute the main subject of the next section of this essay.

For anti-democrats, of course, the political violence associated with the French 'Jacobin constitution' of 1793 only served to confirm the dreadful truth of Burke's polemics, but the famous 'People's Charter', issued by the London Working Men's Association in 1838, embodied more humane aspirations that had been the stock-in-trade of British Radicals since the 1780s – universal male suffrage, secret ballots, equal-sized constituencies, abolition of the property qualification for (and payment of) representatives plus annual parliaments. The so-called 'Knowledge Chartists' favoured female suffrage as well and were willing to negotiate compromises with liberal reformers in pursuit of their goals. Regarding the 'democratic aspirations' noted earlier, the Chartists, who were a radical coalition rather than a political party in the modern sense of the words, might be said to have aspired to greater political participation, to greater accountability of national leaders and to material improvements following on from their proposed reforms.

In mainland Europe, however, both sides of the debate were more intransigent. Democrats were generally unwilling to set aside their 'Jacobin' heritage – and the associated vision of 'militant virtue' – until after their defeats in 1848/9, while the consequences of later, 'more realistic' policies were not always as expected: for example the famous association of MAZZINI and Garibaldi with the creation of the liberal (but undemocratic)

Kingdom of Italy in 1861. Consequently, Paine's earlier assertion of the incompatibility of democracy and monarchy was still generally accepted and the American Republic retained a talismanic quality for many democrats living on the other four continents.

Ironically, during the period under consideration, a significant amount of North American intellectual ingenuity was devoted to qualifying (and even debunking) the power of the citizen majority, and not to celebrating it. This was the case from the years of the *Federalist* debate (the 1780s) right up to the *fin de siècle* period of the 1890s, when the founders of political science in US universities (e.g. Burgess and Bentley) accepted many of the assumptions of the European elitists. The fact that a significant number of Americans were Jacksonians, abolitionists, feminists, socialists and even anarchists at different points along the timeline of the nineteenth century only enhanced these anxieties, so that, for example, the system of indirect presidential elections was defended as a bulwark against 'popular despotism'. Moreover, the concept of 'state's rights' (the autonomy of the sub-national governments of the USA) underwent a significant change during the same period. Thus, having been originally associated with the ideal of a virtuous, homogenous agrarian democracy in the years between the American Revolution and the Jacksonian period (1829–37), the slogan of 'state's rights' became associated with conservative, anti-Indian and pro-slavery sentiment in the period leading up to the Civil War. Even the famous Gettysburg Address of 1863 by ABRAHAM LINCOLN ('government of the people, by the people [and] for the people') avoided *the word* democracy, while the eponymous *Democracy: A American Novel* (by Henry Adams, 1880) turned out to be a veritable jeremiad against the practice of the post-bellum congressional system.

However, direct experience of the early years of the American Republic did at least inspire the patriotic efforts of the Venezuelan general, Francisco de Miranda (1750–1816), as he unsuccessfully sought independence for his homeland through rebellion against Spain in both 1806 and 1811. Later, Miranda's protégé, SIMON BOLIVAR, led further (and successful) Latin American revolutions across most of the continent between 1813 and 1824. Nevertheless, the republican (as opposed to the *democratic*) aspects of Bolivar's vision – encapsulated in his support for 'life-presidents' elected by limited adult suffrage – became the dominant motif of South American politics for many decades, although Costa Rica did achieve a form of stable, multi-party politics in the 1890s.

The ideals of the American Republic were also exported to Liberia in 1821, a small West African colony that declared itself independent of the USA in 1847. In practice, it too became a fiefdom of a Europeanized elite (in this case, one made up of liberated US slaves and their descendants) at the expense of the native peoples. Yet the idea of a 'dark continent' is too simplistic if we consider Africa as a whole, for it is worth noting that in many territories the common tradition of tribal gatherings (a limited direct democracy, often known by the Zulu word '*indaba*') survived into the twentieth century, and that Britain's Southern African colonies saw the opening scenes in the story of the 'experiments with truth' (and democracy) that made up the career of MOHANDAS GANDHI. Moving northwards, moreover, the West Africa of the 1860s and 1870s domiciled a notable opponent of polygenism and advocate of African self-government, James Africanus Horton (1835–82), while late nineteenth-century Egypt was the home of another important thinker, the Islamic modernist scholar, Muhammad Abduh (1849–1905), who argued at length (and with some success) that Islam was compatible with *democratic* institutions, scientific inquiry and the liberation of women.

The vice of 'demagogy' was well known to nineteenth-century critics of democracy, but the term 'populist' did not acquire this particular, unsavoury connection until the late twentieth century. Although academic students of *populism* have made no specific linkage between East Asian democratic thought and the much more famous examples of 'populist' ideology found in Russia and North America, there seems to be at least a certain family resemblance between the political ideas of the Chinese Revolutionary Alliance (led by Sun Yat-Sen), the Narodniki and the Farmer's Alliance/People's Party. Following the 'Russian' socialism of HERZEN, the Narodniki of the 1870s and 1880s celebrated the purity of the Russian peasantry at the expense of the city elites, and advocated a federation of communes (*obshchina*) instead of a moralized empire or a Western, liberal nation state. The North American populists of the 1880s and 1890s were mainly self-reliant (but increasingly commercial) farmers, who saw

themselves as forming the productive and dutiful heartland of a nation, a people whose moral leadership had been usurped by the sinister interests of financiers and industrialists from the eastern seaboard. US populism accepted liberal political forms, but gave expression to dissatisfaction with both material insecurity and the lack of moral content in representative politics highlighted in *Democracy: An American Novel*. Finally, Sun's famous 'Three Principles of the People' – 'Nationalism, Democracy, Livelihood' – stressed the 'purity' of the Han Chinese peasants at the expense of their 'corrupt' Manchurian leaders and recommended a panacea for their economic woes, namely the 'single Tax' policy associated with the US economist, Henry George (1839–97). Moreover, although Sun did not become an advocate of 'direct' democracy until 1916, his earlier reticence on the issue may have been part of a strategy to appear 'moderate' – and to distance himself from the extreme violence associated with the Taiping and Boxer rebellions – by seeming to endorse Western representative government. If populism had a core intellectual meaning (and this is open to some doubt) it was perhaps the form that nineteenth-century democratic aspirations took in certain societies where the agrarian interest remained sufficiently strong to resist (at least temporarily) the imperatives of industrialism.

The idea of rights as universal entitlements emerged in seventeenth-century Europe out of the early-modern concept of 'natural right', a privilege or immunity sanctioned by natural law, and therefore ultimately endorsed by God. In shorthand terms, this is often called the 'liberal' view of rights, although, as we shall see, this usage is somewhat misleading. In contrast, the 'historical' view of rights is a very different conception; rights are seen as entitlements that are always specific to a particular time and place (via the mechanisms of custom and donation). This was also a commonplace of the nineteenth century, although the newly developed 'liberal view' often took centre-stage, particularly in the form of the 'Rights of Man', which were now enjoyed (or at least recommended) thanks to the assumption of a universal human capacity to exercise 'right reason'.

The argument that the 'natural' rights of life, liberty and property were originally enjoyed by mankind in a primeval state of nature, before government was created to better protect those self-same rights (as civil rights), was developed by John Locke in the seventeenth century and was later implicit in the US Declaration of Independence of 1776. But while Locke carefully minimized the circumstances in which resistance to actually existing governments was justified, both the 'Founding Fathers' and the authors of The Declaration of the Rights of Man and of Citizens of 1789 placed greater weight upon the right of 'resistance to oppression' as an adjunct of the right of liberty. If the right of liberty was taken to include a self-justifying right of acting according to one's own 'private judgement' (or conscience), it could even become part of an argument for anarchism, as it did in the writings of WILLIAM GODWIN.

It was this association between political disorder and the language of rights that concerned many liberals and, to give just one example, led to the famous attack on the French Revolutionary doctrine of the 'Rights of Man' as 'nonsense on stilts' by JEREMY BENTHAM. Bentham was both a utilitarian and a legal positivist but his 'intellectual godson', JOHN STUART MILL, was more sympathetic to the idea of 'moral rights' as imperative 'social utilities'; that is, as part of a general utilitarian theory of justice. Mill associated strenuous defence of one's rights with the energetic personal character that he valorized in *On Liberty* (1859) and *Considerations on Representative Government* (1861), although he was also concerned to stress the importance of performing one's duties to individual men and women, and of protecting minorities. In the USA, the assumption that utilitarianism and rights *were* compatible was much more commonplace because, 20 years prior to Bentham's protests against it, the idea of natural rights had been extended to include 'the pursuit of happiness' by the Declaration of Independence. Several more pragmatic aspirations were embodied in the Constitutional Amendments known as 'The Bill of Rights' (1791) and the language of rights became part of the warp and weft of US politics in the early nineteenth century. However, as we saw earlier, this was a political culture wracked by severe tensions; in the 1840s, HENRY THOREAU asserted the right of private judgement as a justification for disobedience to immoral legislation and Elizabeth Cady Stanton (with others) satirized the language of the 1776 Declaration in their own 'Seneca Falls Declaration' of the rights of women. Later in the century, US radicalism did not disappear, but the language of rights became more closely associated with the idea of

a conservative, 'rugged individualism' expressed by writers such as WILLIAM GRAHAM SUMNER and Edward L. Youmans.

A hundred years earlier, the 'historical view' of rights had originally been expounded by Burke, who emphasized the general importance in human affairs of custom, particularly as the legitimate means of sanctioning specific rights and privileges in individual polities (the doctrine of 'prescription'). In his opinion, as well as being contrary to the 'organic' principle of political evolution (which allowed for limited reform through a process of trial and error), the universalist theories of rights associated with the French Revolution were speciously egalitarian and metaphysical. As another conservative, de Maistre, observed (with irony) in 1797: 'I have seen Frenchmen, Italians, [and] Russians.... But as for *Man*, I declare that I have never in my life met him; if he exists he is unknown to me.' Shortly afterwards, in 1803, the German legal scholar, Karl von Savigny (1779–1861), argued that the study of Roman and European feudal history indicated an important distinction between 'property' and 'possession' that undermined any assumption of an 'absolute' right of private property such as the one enshrined in the Napoleonic legal Code. Although formulated in opposition to the French Revolution, and the radically universalist aspirations of some of its supporters, the influence of the 'historical view' can be traced into the latter part of the century as well; for example elements of it can be found in the theories of HENRY MAINE and WALTER BAGEHOT.

Of course the 'liberal view' of rights was open to socialist criticism too, and the most famous example of this is found in Karl Marx's 'On the Jewish Question' (1843–4). Here, Marx argued that 'the so-called rights of man' were actually the rights of an 'egoistic man' living in a bourgeois society that sought to hide real, economic inequality behind legal, 'abstract equality'. Referring to the four principal rights enshrined in The Declaration of the Rights of Man and of Citizens, Marx criticized liberty as the right to 'withdraw into oneself' (at the expense of our distinctively human and social qualities), property as 'the right of selfishness', equality as the right to be treated 'without discrimination . . . as a self-sufficient monad' while security was simply 'the assurance' of the egoism assumed in the discussion of the other three rights. Combining the historical view of rights associated with Savigny with the humanist critique of self-interest he had learnt from FEUERBACH, Marx argued that the 'abstract' individual of liberalism was wrongly 'separated from the community' as a whole, just as 'a lord and his servants' were once 'cut off from the people' under the feudal regime of 'seignorial right'.

In fact, the argument that a liberalism that emphasized individual rights at the expense of material and social needs was an impoverished liberalism was put forward by many eighteenth- and nineteenth-century writers, notably those from mainland Europe. The importance of Christian humanitarianism (later known as 'Christian Democracy') was stressed by SAINT-SIMON, LAMENNAIS and Pope Leo XIII (*De Rerum Novarum*, 1891); more secular concepts of *duty* were emphasized by KANT, COMTE and MAZZINI, while LOUIS BLANC coined the slogan 'the right to work'. Furthermore, it was commonly held that it was not only possible for individuals but also for groups to enjoy rights. The argument that every (linguistic/cultural) nation has a 'right of self-government' was explained (to his own satisfaction) by Fichte, while the idea that both subordinate 'corporations' and the state itself have rights – the latter in its role as guarantor of the collective interest of society as a whole – can be found in the writings of Hegel and his various disciples (see HEGEL AND HEGELIANISM).

In late-Victorian Britain, for example, the philosophical defence of rights became less closely related to individualism and more closely associated with the general project of moralizing society, as espoused by the Oxford Idealists. Hence, although T.H. GREEN acknowledged that the ultimate ground of rights was simply membership of the human race (a fact that had been increasingly recognized in recent history), he also argued that the state had rights in relation to its citizens over and above a simple right to punish those who transgressed the legal claims of innocent parties. In particular, the ultimate value of developing the human personality was deemed to trump the right of personal liberty with reference to issues such as compulsory education and the regulation of alcoholic beverages. Green's ideas prefigured those of the British 'New Liberals' and US 'Progressives' of the early twentieth century, while the more conservative *Ethical Studies* by F.H. BRADLEY expounded the Victorian ideal of 'duty' only three years before it was so mercilessly satirized in Gilbert and Sullivan's famous operetta, *The Pirates of Penzance* (1879).

Leaving humour to one side, thanks to the inhumanities of empire, to late twentieth-century decolonization and the various historical analyses that accompanied those phenomena, one of the least-admired components of 'Victorian deontology' has been 'the White Man's Burden'; the idea of a civilizing mission that was often used to justify European (and US) colonialism in the nineteenth and early twentieth centuries. The values of self-sacrifice and respect for custom were certainly maintained in the indigenous societies of Asia, Africa and Latin America, but with reference to educated elites, this observation must be qualified by noting an increased awareness of the leading characteristics of Western philosophies and ideologies – as we have already seen with respect to 'democracy'. The traditional hierarchical collectivism of many of these societies was certainly antipathetic to liberal and individualistic conceptions of rights, but this tendency was often exaggerated in the polemics of conservative, European anthropologists such as Maine. Indeed, by the close of the period considered by this volume, the language of rights was being increasingly well used in a number of anti-colonial discourses, such as Indian nationalism and the campaign to protect 'Aboriginal Rights' in West Africa. For example, in the early 1900s, the Indian sociologist, Shyamji Krishnavarma (1857–1930), used Spencer's 'law of equal freedom' – a fusion of evolutionary and Kantian ideas about rights – to criticize the British Raj, while the Ghanaian intellectual, Caseley Hayford (1866–1930), engineered a sophisticated defence of the West African system of family property rights in works such as *Gold Coast Native Institutions* (1903) and *The Truth About the West African Land Question* (1913).

In the nineteenth century, many traditional patterns of social deference declined and new political loyalties and rhetorics were invented. Returning to the topic of mottos and slogans, it can be argued that two of the most famous ('the sovereignty of the people' and 'the sovereignty of the individual') seek to invest the bearers of citizenship and of rights with a dignity once reserved for royalty alone, while the anti-democratic slogan, 'the tyranny of the majority', seeks to ascribe the vices of usurpers to the masses. Intellectual historians have become increasingly aware that the cultural identity of 'a people' is itself structured by questions of politics, economics and gender, although the otherwise valuable treatment of our topic in Roper (1989) ignores the third dimension entirely.

Discussions regarding the cultural conditions that allowed liberalism to develop have stressed factors such as warfare, urbanization, associational culture and (industrial) commerce. According to some commentators, 'external' dangers and cheek-by-jowl living mitigated conflicts about the distribution of both rights and material goods; democracy became a more 'natural' way of conducting politics. By the same token, if association with persons outside of one's immediate family and locality became 'natural' (thanks to the development of 'civil society' and the market economy), investing 'strangers' with universal rights became an intelligible philosophical move. There is some resonance here with Macpherson's well-known argument that liberal democratic theory was originally 'protective' (and was simply opposed to arbitrary government), but subsequently became 'developmental' and aspired to create a moral community. However, one of the main problems with this line of reasoning is that even in the most liberal nations, the mothers, daughters and sisters of citizens (who were clearly never 'strangers') met great resistance to their case for political equality. On the other hand, if the male citizens of the nineteenth and early twentieth centuries really did believe that both 'commerce' and the 'rights of man' were 'natural', perhaps we can at least understand why so many gave their support to the dictatorships of Bonapartism and of fascism; in extreme conditions, it seemed 'natural' to trade 'liberty' for 'security'.

Reference

Roper, J. (1989) *Democracy and Its Critics: Anglo-American Democratic Thought in the Nineteenth Century*, London: Unwin Hyman.

Further reading

Canovan, M. (1981) *Populism*, London: Junction Books.
Eley, G. (2002) *Forging Democracy: The History of the Left in Europe, 1850–1900*, Oxford: Oxford University Press.
Herbert, G.B. (2002) *A Philosophical History of Rights*, New Brunswick and London: Transaction Publishers.

CLIVE E. HILL

DEROIN, JEANNE (1805–94)

Jeanne Deroin was a world pioneer in her campaign for votes for women in France. A seamstress with little formal schooling, in 1831 Deroin was introduced to the Saint-Simonian sect by her future husband, Desroches, the bursar of an old people's home. All acolytes were required to sign a statement of their beliefs and most wrote a fairly standard single sentence. Deroin covered forty-four pages in a school exercise book in the cramped and variable script of someone to whom writing did not come easily. She asserted that gender inequalities were mere inventions of male-dominated society. Contemporary marriage consecrated their inferior status. 'A slave can at least hope for freedom. A woman finds hers only in death.' Saint-Simonianism restored her faith that universal fraternity could be achieved, with its opposition to privileges of birth, the call for the liberation of women and the moral, physical and intellectual progress of working people. On the other hand, even at the outset, she was alarmed at the hierarchical structure of the movement and disenchantment was swift.

In 1832 Deroin joined a number of former Saint-Simonian working women to run the first-ever newspaper for women, *La Femme libre*. She spent the rest of the July Monarchy raising her three children, attending evening classes, qualifying and practising as a teacher. Some of her fellow journalists became Fourierists and after the 1848 Revolution they reunited to run a feminist newspaper and club, *La Voix des femmes*. They pressed for higher wages for women, nurseries and better education for girls but Deroin was almost alone in petitioning for votes for women to match male suffrage. She was not prepared to tolerate that half the nation be left under the domination of the other half. This demand and the attempt to restore the right to divorce were scorned by the conservative press. The *Voix des femmes* club and newspaper were attacked for their support for divorce with such force that the paper was suspended and both were shut down.

Deroin launched a 'Course on Social Law for Women' and she and Desirée Gay briefly set up the Association Mutuelle des Femmes and a new paper, *La Politique des femmes*. This was succeeded in August 1848 by Deroin's *L'Opinion des femmes*, which was forced to close in August 1849 by an increase in caution money to 5,000 francs.

The brief of *L'Opinion des femmes* was to secure political and full legal rights for women together with better working conditions. Deroin also founded an Association of Socialist Teachers, which included men and women.

Deroin stood as a candidate in the 1849 legislative elections. She tried to attend the hustings and the workers in Saint-Antoine were sympathetic. The Comité Démocrate Sociale added her to their list of candidates. However, the most well-known woman socialist, George Sand, continued to consider female suffrage premature. Apart from CONSIDÉRANT, few male socialists were supportive. PROUDHON was totally hostile.

Like most early socialists Deroin was convinced that the answers to social and economic problems were education and association. She gave classes in her Women's Mutual Education Society. She started a Fraternal Association of Democratic Socialists of both sexes for the liberation of women. In July 1849 she and Gay were granted 12,000 francs to set up an association of women seamstresses making ladies underwear from the fund established by the National Assembly to encourage workers' associations.

Her most ambitious project was the formation with Pauline Roland of an Association Fraternelle et Solidaire de Toutes les Associations. Linking together over a hundred existing workers' associations, it aimed to provide tools, raw materials and interest-free loans for its members. Deroin hoped to add mutual aid benefits, nurseries and schools. However, after the June Days, 1848, the right of association was progressively withdrawn. In May 1850 the association's offices were raided and forty-six members were arrested. Whilst in prison Deroin continued her political activities, in particular vainly defending the right of women to petition Parliament. When she was released in June 1851, she supported herself by teaching, and struggled to reunite her family. Her husband had developed a serious mental illness from which he never recovered. Warned that she was likely to be rearrested, in August 1852 she fled to England with her two younger children, one of whom was a permanent invalid. Fellow exiles found her work teaching and embroidering. Her husband developed typhoid fever and died before he could join her.

Deroin remained in London for the rest of her life. In 1861 she set up a tiny girls' boarding school, but it did not survive. Deroin charged very low fees and gave free places to girls from poor families. When most of the exiles returned to France in 1870–1, they persuaded the new republican regime to grant Deroin a pension of 600 francs a year. Deroin maintained a lively correspondence with feminist reformers in France, sometimes writing during lesson time and occasionally submitting newspaper articles written on school exercise-book paper.

She published three women's almanacs during her exile. The first was published in Paris in 1852, the second and third in London and Jersey in 1853 and 1854. All were published in French and the second also appeared simultaneously in English. The tone of her feminism became increasingly spiritual. Women, she asserted, had a crucial role as social evangelists in workers' co-operatives and mutual-aid groups. She believed that women alone, reborn by the spirit of love, liberty and justice, could reform society and turn social science into a new universal religion uniting all of humanity in love.

Léon Richer, who founded the Association for the Rights of Women in 1870, publicized the almanacs in the *National de l'ouest* and other newspapers. Through him Deroin made contact with Madame Arnaud. In 1886 she corresponded with Hubertine Auclert (1848–1914), a leading young feminist, but socialist feminism meant very different things to Auclert. In her eighties Deroin became involved in WILLIAM MORRIS's Socialist League. He gave the oration at her very well-attended civil funeral.

Further reading

Gordon, F. and Cross, M. (1996) *Early French Feminisms 1830–1940*, Cheltenham: Elgar.

Pilbeam, P. (2003) 'Jeanne Deroin: French Feminist and Socialist in Exile', in S. Freitag (ed.) *Exiles from European Revolutions: Refugees in Mid-Victorian England*, 275–94, Oxford and New York: Berghahn Books.

SEE ALSO: Considérant, Victor; early socialism; Enfantin, Barthélemy-Prosper; Fourier, Charles

PAMELA PILBEAM

DEWEY, JOHN (1859–1952)

John Dewey is one of the best-known philosophers of the twentieth century. A central figure in the philosophy of US Pragmatism, he was also a well-known public intellectual. He travelled around the world speaking on topics such as education reform, women's suffrage, labour issues, and war. His publications, which appeared in both academic and popular forums, come to more than forty volumes in the *Collected Works of Dewey* published by Southern Illinois University Press.

Dewey's philosophy is as relevant today as when he was writing. Dewey's philosophical perspective is one that acknowledges that we live in a constantly changing world. Rather than fear or seek to avoid such change, Dewey focuses on the idea that increased understanding will allow us to go with and/or direct change more intelligently. Dewey's perspective was influenced by the work of CHARLES DARWIN. Darwin's theory draws a picture of a world in flux. Adaptations are a constantly evolving phenomenon. What works in one time or place may not work in another. Being flexible becomes a key notion. Dewey suggests that taking this perspective with regard to social concerns will result in the creation of flexible individuals who can critically reflect on a problematic situation, with an open mind, and arrive at workable solutions. These solutions will eventually become problematic themselves and require further reflection and change. This ongoing process of deliberation guiding action is the adaptability of the human species. This experimental method is the process of democracy. To fail to approach problems in this way will, Dewey believes, result in recourse to violence. He championed critical inquiry over reactionary patriotism in the face of the violence of two world wars. The twenty-first century, with its increased globalization, needs such critical and reflective citizens if peace is to be an option.

It is difficult to identify a single topic as central for Dewey, or to pick the few central texts from his life's work. However, there are consistent themes in his writing. Dewey's pluralistic approach results in his view being one that is open and attentive to marginalized perspectives. For instance, during his lifetime he was an active supporter of the NAACP, women's suffrage, birth control and immigrant rights. His philosophy is one that has appeal to liberatory groups. During his years at the University of Chicago (1894–1905) Dewey was involved with Jane Addams and her work at Hull House, and with the lab school run by his wife Alice Chipman Dewey. He credits such experience

as teaching him about life and informing his philosophy in important ways. For example, the women of Hull House were dealing daily with the realities of poverty, racism, sexism and the struggles of the labour class. Long before the feminist theory of the 1960s and 1970s Dewey saw the problem of divorcing theory and practice. As a result, he took on the issues of his day and argued that philosophy had a public role to play, especially with regard to education.

With regard to education, we have yet to take Dewey seriously and implement his suggestions. Dewey is often blamed for a perceived failure of public education, but since his philosophy of education, properly understood, has never been widely implemented this seems unfair. While Dewey advocated taking the interests of children seriously, and finding ways to engage their native curiosity and active minds, he was not an advocate of a child-centred approach. Far from letting individual interests be the primary guide or goal, he sought to bring about a heightened awareness of our social embeddedness. It is the realization of our interconnectedness that, for him, motivates the desire to employ critical reflection that includes multiple viewpoints in order to solve problems and sustain community. Only when the citizenry develops the habit of critical and flexible reflection can democracy be sustained.

Dewey's notion of democracy is not that of a specific political organization. Democracy is a type of faith. For Dewey:

> Democracy is belief in the ability of human experience to generate the aims and methods by which further experience will grow in ordered richness.... Democracy is the faith that the process of experience is more important than any special result attained, so that special results achieved are of ultimate value only as they are used to enrich and order the ongoing process.
>
> (LW 14: 229)

He sees democracy as a way of life; it is a condition and habit of participation joined with corresponding responsibilities. We are responsible for the social conditions under which we live. These conditions also set boundaries on what is possible for us. Since there is this interplay between humans and their social environments, it is very important for us to continually critique and modify our social environments so these environments expand rather than limit our possibilities. It is an open-ended process, capable of being reformed and redirected. Democracy is the experimental method (what Dewey calls the method of intelligence) applied to social concerns. It is a method for directing the future and enriching experience so that one sees the interconnectedness of all things. This is what Dewey call the aesthetic experience.

In *Art as Experience*, Dewey speaks of aesthetic experience in the following way: '[I]ts varied parts are linked to one another, and do not merely succeed one another. And the parts through their experienced linkage move toward a consummation and close, not merely to cessation in time' (LW 10: 61). Such experience enables us to act with intelligent foresight and apply the method of intelligence to how we live. This is lived experience. In contrast anaesthetic or ordinary experience lacks this cohesiveness, this unity, this consummation. Dewey says:

> For in much of our experience we are not concerned with the connection of one incident with what went before and what comes after. There is no interest that controls attentive rejection or selection of what shall be organized into the developing experience. Things happen, but they are neither definitely included nor decisively excluded, we drift.
>
> (LW 10: 46–7)

Dewey also calls this received experience. With received (as opposed to lived) experience we remain passive spectators who are not prepared to act with intelligent foresight or to apply critical intelligence to how we live. Dewey seeks to move people from accepting a life of received experience to seeking lived experience. In other words, aesthetic experience needs to become more common.

Aesthetic or lived experience can also be described as religious experience, though clearly distinguished from religion for Dewey. In *A Common Faith* he says if the religious:

> were rescued through emancipation from dependence upon specific types of beliefs and practices, from those elements that constitute a religion, many individuals would find that experiences having the force of bringing about a better, deeper and enduring adjustment in life are not so rare and infrequent as they are commonly supposed to be. They occur frequently in connection with many significant moments of living.
>
> (LW 9: 11)

Dewey finds the religious in everyday experience just as he finds the aesthetic in everyday objects and experience. He warns us not to elevate the religious and aesthetic to the rare and untouchable, but to understand that much of our everyday lives can be experienced in these ways and that we should try to have this level of integration, awareness and unity as much as possible.

In the aesthetic (or religious) experience things hold together in a way that they do not in the anaesthetic experience. There is an integrity and unity to the aesthetic experience that moves the live creature to understand that experience, and life in general, in a more intense way. It is this kind of deep or lived experience that makes intelligence possible and democracy desirable. In contrast, anaesthetic experience does not organize experience in this cohesive way. For Dewey anaesthetic experience and specific religions tend to encourage rigid habits of mind, unthinking obedience, reverence and worship. For Dewey, we need to embrace and seek to have experiences on the level of the religious and the aesthetic. Such experiences encourage critical engagement with, and transformation of, the world and ourselves. Such experiences encourage democracy.

Democracy requires that we see beyond our limited self-interest. It requires that we see the interconnectedness and unity of live creatures and their environments. Ideal democracy is a method of living in the present with regard to the future. Democracy tries out institutions and modifies them as needs and interests change, not expecting a final form of society to eventually emerge, but embracing the potentiality of intentionally controlled change. Democracy's focus on the process of improving the future through intelligent guidance both necessitates and results in a deeper appreciation of the interconnectedness of live creatures and their environments. It necessitates and makes possible a deeper experience of life. This understanding is dynamic and changing. Without this sense of connectedness it is much more likely that society will splinter into mere associations. It is this understanding of social embeddedness and interconnectedness that makes a functioning democracy possible and it is democracy that demands us to move beyond the rigid habits of either/or thinking.

This habit of thinking is not easy to change. Given a world of flux many people seek certainty by creating fixed and transcendent metaphysical, epistemological, ethical and political systems. Dualistic thinking is simple and clear, and can be quite comforting (see Dewey's *The Quest for Certainty*). However, it reinforces false dichotomies and promotes a rigid and oppositional way of thinking. It is not a productive approach for solving real problems of socially embedded people. To do that we need to encourage people to have experiences that involve creating and sustaining an awareness of the interconnectedness of the fluid, dynamic and processive universe. Awareness of our interdependence makes us aware of our dependence on things beyond our control. Again, this vulnerability spawns a variety of responses. We fear this dependence. We seek control. We become obedient to a 'superior' power. We become fatalistic and passive. Alternatively, Dewey suggests we embrace a natural piety that begins with a:

> sense of nature as the whole of which we are parts, while it also recognizes that we are parts that are marked by intelligence and purpose, having the capacity to strive by their aid to bring conditions into greater consonance with what is humanly desirable.... It trusts that the natural interactions between man and his environment will breed more intelligence and generate more knowledge.... There is such a thing as faith in intelligence becoming religious in quality.

> (LW 9: 18–19)

Faith in intelligence is central to Dewey's theory of democracy. Democracy is not, for Dewey, about institutions or hard and fast rules or methods. It is best understood as an attitude toward life; it is an attitude that forms the foundation for critical intelligence. Dewey is often accused of being naïve and/or overly optimistic. One of the common charges is that he is overly optimistic about the average person's intelligence and willingness to see beyond themselves and their 'individual' interests. However, Dewey was very aware of this danger. This is why so much of what he writes is aimed at bringing us to understand the nature and importance of the ethical, democratic, aesthetic and religious attitudes toward life. Without these attitudes towards, and understanding of, the processive nature of life and society democracy is at best a dream and at worst a nightmare. Education is his main means of transforming and sustaining democracy.

For Dewey, education is what prepares people for social and political participation. He promotes a process of education that will develop what he calls the method of intelligence. The method of intelligence begins when something is encountered as a problem. Old habits are no longer working. The problematic situation is examined and alternative approaches are imagined and tried out. Each 'solution' is only temporary and generates new problematic situations that require the same kind of examination and thoughtful inquiry. The process is an ongoing one. The method of intelligence needs to become the one habit on which we rely. We are free only when we act with knowledge and foresight so his education will encourage observation, reflection, flexible judgement and vision.

As with his view of democracy, Dewey's views on education are not endorsements of specific kinds of institutions or curricula. These will vary with time, place and the emerging needs of communities. Education needs to help promote flexible and open habits of mind (see Dewey's *Democracy and Education*). Education is to build on natural curiosity to retain and develop the capacity of self-reflection, rather than replace that with a reliance on authority. Dewey says:

> (w)hen the school introduces and trains each child of society into membership within such a little community, saturating him with the spirit of service, and providing him with the instruments of effective self-direction, we shall have the deepest and best guarantee of a larger society which is worthy, lovely, and harmonious.

> (MW 1: 19–20)

For education to prepare people to govern themselves, to help people learn to form and voice their own judgements, to enable them to think experimentally, to encourage them to co-operate socially it must educate the 'mass of citizens ... for intellectual participation in the political, economic, and cultural growth of the country and not simply certain leaders' (MW 15: 275).

Dewey is clear that democracy is not a viable option if people are educated into a reliance on authority. He believed that reliance on political and/or religious authorities has, throughout history, resulted in oppression, stagnation and loss of individuality. It is important to note that while Dewey rejects the atomistic and antagonistic notion of the individual that emerges from classical liberal theory and embraces instead a notion of a socially embedded individual, he does not subordinate the individual to social concerns. The individual and individuality are essential to a real community and working democracy. What distinguishes a community from mere association is effective participation by a diverse range of people, a mutual recognition of individual needs and desires, and the development of conjoint activity (see Dewey's *The Public and Its Problems*). Community, and democracy, requires individuals and groups with flexible habits of mind and an awareness of their social embeddedness and interconnectedness.

Humans are born dependent beings, and remain social and interdependent throughout their lives of growth and change (see Dewey's *Experience and Nature*). Education must prepare people to deal with this connectedness, growth and change by means of providing intelligent direction rather than falling back on authority and/or dualistic thinking. Dewey views education as the best means for encouraging the kind of independent and critical thought that will make democracy both possible and desirable. This makes philosophy, as understood by the pragmatist tradition, key to social activism and public discourse:

> Faith in the power of intelligence to imagine a future which is the projection of the desirable in the present, and to invent the instrumentalities of its realization, is our salvation. And it is a faith which must be nurtured and made articulate: surely a sufficiently large task for our philosophy.
>
> (MW 10: 48)

In sum, Dewey's theory of democracy uses education to encourage people to see their interconnectedness with other beings and their environment. This sense of connectedness allows for a deeper, richer experience of life (an aesthetic and/or religious) experience. Only when such 'lived experience', rather than a more passive 'received experience', becomes the guiding experience of life, are people prepared to handle the diversity and complexity of our increasingly global and constantly changing world. With 'lived experience' as a guide people can apply Dewey's method of critical intelligence and productively engage in democratic discourse and action. Only then will we be prepared to address the causes of social, political, economic and environmental problems.

References

Dewey, John (1976) 'The School and Society', in *John Dewey: The Middle Works, Vol. 1: 1899–1901*, ed. Jo Ann Boydston, 5–237, Carbondale: Southern Illinois University Press.

——(1980) 'The Need for the Recovery of Philosophy', in *John Dewey: The Middle Works, Vol. 10: 1916–1917*, ed. Jo Ann Boydston, 3–48, Carbondale: Southern Illinois University Press.

——(1983) 'Report and Recommendation upon Turkish Education', in *John Dewey: The Middle Works, Vol. 15: 1923–1924*, ed. Jo Ann Boydston, 275–97, Carbondale: Southern Illinois University Press.

——(1986) *A Common Faith*, in *John Dewey: Later Works, Vol. 9: 1933–1934*, ed. Jo Ann Boydston, Carbondale: Southern Illinois University Press.

——(1987) *Art as Experience*, in *John Dewey: Later Works, Vol. 10: 1934*, ed. Jo Ann Boydston, 224–30, Carbondale: Southern Illinois University Press.

——(1987) 'Creative Democracy', in *John Dewey: Later Works, Vol. 14: 1939–1941*, ed. Jo Ann Boydston, Carbondale: Southern Illinois University Press.

Further reading

Alexander, Thomas M. (1987) *John Dewey's Theory of Art, Experience, and Nature: The Horizons of Feeling*, New York: State University of New York Press.

Campbell, James (1992) *The Community Reconstructs: The Meaning of Pragmatic Social Thought*, Urbana: University of Illinois Press.

Eldridge, Michael (1998) *Transforming Experience: John Dewey's Cultural Instrumentalism*, Nashville: Vanderbilt University Press.

Green, Judith (2000) *Deep Democracy*, Lanham, MD: Rowman & Littlefield.

McKenna, Erin (2001) *The Task of Utopia: A Pragmatist and Feminist Perspective*, Lanham, MD: Rowman & Littlefield.

Pratt, Scott (2002) *Native Pragmatism: Rethinking the Roots of Pragmatism*, Bloomington: Indiana University Press.

Seigfried, Charlene Haddock (1996) *Pragmatism and Feminism: Reweaving the Social Fabric*, Chicago: The University of Chicago Press.

Stuhr, John J. (1997) *Genealogical Pragmatism: Philosophy, Experience, and Community*, New York: SUNY Press.

Sullivan, Shannon (2001) *Living across and through Skins: Transactional Bodies, Pragmatism, and Feminism*, Bloomington: Indiana University Press.

Westbrook, Robert B. (1991) *John Dewey and American Democracy*, Ithaca: Cornell University Press.

SEE ALSO: aesthetics, painting and architecture; Darwin, Charles; democracy, populism and rights; James, William

ERIN McKENNA

DICEY, A.V. (1835–1922)

One of the foremost jurists and constitutional historians of late-Victorian Britain, Albert Venn Dicey was born at Lutterworth on 5 February 1835, the son of a Whig newspaper proprietor, and died at Oxford, 7 April 1922. Educated at Oxford, he was a fellow of Trinity College between 1860–72, and, with a break to develop his legal career in London, became Vinerian Professor of English Law in 1882. Close to Bryce, Green, Goldwin Smith, Acton, Sidgwick and other liberal luminaries of the era, Bryce published his first law book, *The Law of Parties to Action*, in 1870. There followed his *Treatise on Domicil* (1870), his *Introduction to the Study of the Law of the Constitution* (1885) and *Digest of the Law of England with Reference to the Conflict of Laws* (1896). Politically he was involved in the 1860s and 1870s in the anti-slavery movement, offering vigorous support for the North during the American Civil War, the campaign to unify Italy and agitation against the dictatorship of Louis Napoleon. Despite his liberalism he opposed Gladstone's policy of Home Rule, and wrote several tracts against it, notably in the *The Case of England against Home Rule* (1886).

Dicey's chief contribution to the period was his *Lectures on the Relation between Law and Public Opinion in the Nineteenth Century* (1905), sometimes described as the '*Esprit des Lois*' of the epoch. Inspired by Leslie Stephen's studies of eighteenth-century thought and Utilitarianism, and having closely studied US democracy at first hand, Dicey vowed to describe the 'revolution in beliefs' that had taken place in nineteenth-century Britain. This he principally views as a movement from 'individualism' to 'collectivism', which is analysed in terms of three chief stages, (1) the period of 'old Toryism or legislative quiescence' (1800–30); (2) the period of Benthamism or individualism (1825–70); and (3) the period of collectivism (1865–1900). The causes assigned for this development are five-fold: (1) the impact of Tory philanthropy and the factory reform movement of the 1840s; (2) the changed attitude of the working classes following the failure of Chartism, and their engagement with more collectivist strategies; (3) the growing sympathy for socialism, and criticism of *laissez-faire* political economy, after mid-century; (4) the changing nature of the commercial system, and increasing interference by the state, notably in railway development; and (5) the

extension of the suffrage in 1867 and 1884, which produced a current of thought, defined by *The Radical Programme* (1885), strongly in favour of state protection of the poor and the labouring classes. By the 1890s, for Dicey, thus, there was widespread adherence to the ideal of collectivism, defined as 'faith in the benefit to be derived by the mass of the people from the action or intervention of the state even in matters which might be, and often are, left to the uncontrolled management of the persons concerned'. This the lectures traced in terms of the extension of the idea of protection, the growth of restrictions on freedom of contract, a preference for collective action, especially in trade union bargaining, and an increasing public commitment to social equality, notably through education.

Further reading

Dicey, A.V. (1905) *Lectures*, London: Macmillan.
Rait, Robert S. (1925) *Memorials of Albert Venn Dicey. Being Chiefly Letters and Diaries*, London: Macmillan.

GREGORY CLAEYS

DILTHEY, WILHELM (1833–1911)

The turn of the century witnessed the birth of a philosophy focusing on the idea and concept of 'life' with its characteristics of the flowing, the irrational, the individualistic, unrepeatable. In France its most famous protagonist was BERGSON with his biologistic-metaphysical concept of *élan vital*, stressing that nothing 'is' but everything 'becomes'. In Germany it was most notably the philosopher Wilhelm Dilthey whose *Lebensphilosophie* – philosophy of life – referred to all of man's mental states, processes and activities, be they conscious or unconscious, and investigated all manifestations of life in the realm of the 'human sciences', i.e. those sciences covering the reality of history and society, and not pertaining to the realm of natural sciences. Dilthey tried to come to an understanding of 'phenomena of the mind' as represented in philosophy, psychology, pedagogy, literature, art or history. Contending that all reality was nothing but life and that life could only be understood out of life, he concluded that man's understanding of himself needed to be based not just on his intellect but his whole being. Within this conceptual framework he analysed the process of 'understanding' the 'meaning' of the phenomena of the human mind, developing a theory of hermeneutics without taking refuge to any a priori, metaphysical or moral preconditions. He put history at the very centre of his philosophy: 'The human being knows itself only in history.' This pre-eminence of history in the life of man was the nucleus of Dilthey's 'historicism', which saw life as being historically conditioned and thus subject to variability and relativity of values: history as the story of the creative struggle of man to come to terms with reality. Dilthey's thinking has had a profound influence on German philosophy in the twentieth century, particularly on existentialists such as Jaspers and Heidegger, and on thinkers in the realm of hermeneutics such as Gadamer.

Dilthey was born in the Rhineland, as the son of a Protestant clergyman. He felt strongly drawn towards philosophy, history and questions of epistemology, of processes of attaining knowledge. Decisive impulses came from KANT, Goethe, COMTE and Schleiermacher. His academic career as a professor of philosophy started in Basel in 1867, from where he moved to the universities of Kiel, Breslau and finally Berlin, where he taught from 1882 until 1905. His life-long occupation was to write a *Critique of Historical Reason,* an undertaking that he never completed but which can be pieced together from a number of works published during his lifetime and a multitude of fragments. Dilthey never created a fully fledged philosophical system but made countless contributions to the theory of knowledge, to moral philosophy, aesthetics, sociology, psychology and the philosophy of history. His collected writings comprise twelve volumes (*Gesammelte Schriften,* partly trans. as *Selected Works, 1985–2002*). Amongst his major works are the *Introduction to the Human Sciences* (*Einleitung in die Geisteswissenschaften: Versuch einer Grundlegung für das Studium der Gesellschaft and der Geschichte,* 1883, trans. 1988) and *Hermeneutics and the Study of History* (*Der Aufbau der geschichtlichen Welt in den Geisteswissenschaften,* 1910, trans. 1996).

How to get knowledge of the human-historical world: this side of epistemology, both the science and art of hermeneutics, became Dilthey's major concern, with the concept of 'understanding' as leitmotif. To him, hermeneutics was not just the interpretation of written records but of all fixed and enduring expressions of mind. Since 'meaning' was the relationship between 'sign' and 'signified',

such an 'understanding' required a deciphering of the signs. Interpretation – grammatical, linguistic and historical – was based on 'understanding' as a projection of the self into the other, which he saw as an imaginative act: as a 'rediscovery of the I in the Thou', encompassing both thinking and feeling of the understanding subject. To understand, says Dilthey, is to reproduce (*nachbilden*) someone else's experience in one's own consciousness and thus to relive it (*nacherleben*): despite the relativity of values through the ages man can do so because all men share the same mental structure and general psychological make-up, someone else's actual experiences being one's own potential experiences that, in turn, can be actualized via the process of 'understanding' and thus enrich the life of the understanding subject.

Dilthey deemed each period of history to be centred upon itself (akin to LEOPOLD VON RANKE's dictum of each period being 'immediate to God'), not to be a merely preliminary stage to our own time. In Dilthey's eyes, history was not a victorious march of liberal progressivism, nor was it the unfolding of a divine plan or the metaphysical process of an absolute transcendental subject coming to self-consciousness. History, like all the other human sciences, was not governed by deterministic laws as was the case in the natural sciences. Natural phenomena could be 'explained' in terms of causality by means of outer observation and experiment, whereas phenomena of the human realm were to be 'understood', requiring in addition to outer observation and classification a certain insight from within. He would, however, concede that certain explanations in the realm of history could be made, based on the findings of natural sciences or statistics – but never on historical laws as such. Dilthey's 'philosophy of understanding' was the foundation for both grasping history's individualistic and unique character and following Leopold von Ranke's tenet of depicting history 'as it actually was'. Dilthey asked the historian to conduct his research in a mindset of 'empathy' and base it on historical sources, and then come to an 'understanding' via three stages: first to understand events from the point of view of the original actors, then to understand the meaning which their actions had on their contemporaries, and finally to assess this meaning in the light of the historian's own age, taking into account the effects actions had for subsequent historical times and thus circumventing the danger of an excessive antiquarian compilation of facts. The historian would thus serve as a mirror in which the minds and experiences of historical protagonists are reflected.

Further reading

Dilthey, Wilhelm (1961) *Meaning in History: Wilhelm Dilthey's Thoughts on History and Society*, ed. and intro. H.P. Rickman, London: George Allen & Unwin.
Ermarth, M. (1981) *Wilhelm Dilthey: The Critique of Historical Reason*, Chicago: University of Chicago Press.
Hodges, H.A. (1952) *The Philosophy of Wilhelm Dilthey*, London: Routledge & Kegan Paul.
Makkreel, R.A. (1992) *Dilthey: Philosopher of the Human Studies*, Princeton: Princeton University Press.
Plantinga, Th. (1992) *Historical Understanding in the Thought of Wilhelm Dilthey*, Toronto: Toronto University Press.
Rickman, H.P. (1988) *Dilthey Today: A Critical Appraisal of the Contemporary Relevance of His Work*, New York/London: Greenwood.

SEE ALSO: historiography and the idea of progress; Romanticism, individualism and ideas of the self

DETMAR KLEIN

DISRAELI, BENJAMIN (1804–81)

The son of the literary historian Isaac D'Israeli, Benjamin Disraeli was born in London on 21 December 1804, and trained as a solicitor. The success of his first novel, *Vivian Grey* (1826), gave him the opportunity to travel for three years in Spain, Italy and the Middle East. After several attempts he entered Parliament in 1837, and in a variety of works both literary and philosophical he crafted a new variety of conservatism that, in the wake of the 1832 Reform Act, did much to redefine an older Toryism devoted to the landed aristocracy and resistant to working-class claims into a populist, pro-imperialist ideal with considerable plebeian appeal. An early satire, *The Voyage of Captain Popanilla* (1828), attacked utilitarianism in particular. In *A Vindication of the English Constitution* (1835), abbreviated as *The Spirit of Whiggism* (1836), he insisted, against the alliance of the Whigs with wealth generated by urban commercial and manufacturing interests, that the Tories were the only genuinely democratic party, because they represented the nation as a whole. Three remarkable novels – *Coningsby* (1844), *Sybil* (1845) and *Tancred* (1847) – extended this vision, looking back nostalgically at an epoch of *noblesse oblige* and the guardianship by the Church of England of popular morals, and exploring, particularly in *Sybil*, the difficulties of working-class life in the 'Hungry Forties', which Disraeli had himself witnessed on a tour with the 'Young England' leaders Lord John Manners and G. Smythe. The claims of the Chartists and other radicals he also defended in Parliament in a speech in July 1839 on the submission of the first Chartist petition, when he declared that 'the rights of labour were as sacred as the rights of property'. *Coningsby* in particular urged a more paternalist care for the industrial poor, supporting Shaftesbury's plea for factory reforms and better working-class housing, and appealing to the new 'cotton lords' to unite with the older aristocracy in the cause of reform. A much later novel, *Lothair* (1870), described conservative party organization in the period.

Though he had opposed Peel's determination in 1846 to repeal the Corn Laws, in 1848 Disraeli became his party's leader in the Commons, and after serving as Chancellor of the Exchequer under Derby, he became Prime Minister in 1868, and again between 1874–80. In this latter period he cemented imperialism to Victorian conservatism, expanding British interests in Egypt by acquiring a controlling interest in the Suez Canal, conferring on the Queen the title of Empress of India, and representing Britain at the Congress of Berlin following the Russo-Turkish War of 1877–8, which aimed to exclude Russia from the Mediterranean but also gained for Britain the island of Cyprus.

Further reading

Disraeli, Benjamin (1882) *Selected Speeches of the Late Right Honourable the Earl of Beaconsfield*, 2 vols, London: Longmans, Green & Co.
——(1913) *Whigs and Whiggism. Political Writings by Benjamin Disraeli*, London: John Murray.
Gorst, Harold (1900) *The Earl of Beaconsfield*, London: Blackie.
Moneypenny, William, and Buckle, George (1910–20) *The Life of Benjamin Disraeli*, 6 vols, London: John Murray.
O'Connor, T.P. (1884) *Lord Beaconsfield. A Biography*. London: Unwin.

GREGORY CLAEYS

DOSTOEVSKY, FEODOR (1821–81)

Feodor Mikhailovich Dostoevsky was one of the most prominent and controversial Russian novelists of the nineteenth century. Dostoevsky's harsh, tumultuous life provided ample material for his deeply troubling, emotionally charged fiction that explored fundamental questions of human destiny and vocation. A prolific writer and active public intellectual, Dostoevsky earned the reputations of a keen psychologist, religious prophet, the father of existentialism and inventor of a new literary style. His novels have been described as 'polyphonic' because they encompass ideas, convictions and destinies conveyed through a great variety of fictional voices. Prominent themes in Dostoevsky's work included exploration of the irrational and destructive in human nature, intricate analysis of freedom and responsibility, and powerful depictions of the dangers of political radicalism and totalitarianism. The rich and engaging philosophical content of Dostoevsky's work shaped the thinking of future generations of philosophers, writers, psychologists and political theorists.

Dostoevsky was born in Moscow on 30 October 1821 into the family of a military physician. At the age of 17 Feodor entered the School of Military Engineering where he received rigorous education in the sciences. In 1844 he abandoned his military career and devoted himself to literature. Dostoevsky's first novel, *Poor Folk* (*Bednye liudi*, 1846) enjoyed a warm critical response and was even considered the first attempt ever at a social novel in Russia. Although it was written in a Romantic tradition, the novel already contained a germ of Dostoevsky's celebrated psychologism.

The young novelist's attraction to utopian socialist ideas and his involvement with the Petrashevsky circle – an ill-fated secret society of young intellectuals – resulted in his arrest, imprisonment and a subsequent death sentence that, however, was commuted at the very last moment to four years of hard labour in Siberia. The terrifying experience of being subjected to a mock execution and believing that he had only a few minutes left to live haunted Dostoevsky for the rest of his life. By his own account, it taught him to appreciate life even at the most unbearable moments of loss and despair. Profound meditations on life and death as well as passionate expressions of life affirmation were to appear conspicuously in his post-Siberian writings.

While in prison Dostoevsky underwent a profound spiritual transformation: he renounced his earlier socialist liberal views and came to see Christianity as the ultimate expression of truth, freedom and love. Despite the extreme hardship of imprisonment, Dostoevsky, a careful observer and intense thinker, dared to transform his experiences into a work of art. In 1861, upon his return to St Petersburg he published *Notes From the House of the Dead* (*Zapiski iz mertvogo doma*) – a thrilling fictional account of his Siberian experiences, offering unique insight into the criminal psyche, its violent and self-destructive impulses, and its all-too-human longing for appreciation. This book was soon followed by Dostoevsky's celebrated *Notes from Underground* (*Zapiski iz podpol'ya*, 1864) – a peculiar blend of confession, psychological struggle, buffoonery and philosophical dispute, written from the perspective of a spiteful 'anti-hero' who rages against the contemporary rationalist, determinist and socialist-utopian projects. Because of its uncompromising exploration of the irrational in human nature and its precise, if bizarre, formulation of the paradoxes of freedom, *Notes from Underground* is considered a classic of existentialist literature.

While working on *Notes from Underground*, Dostoevsky sadly endured the death of the two people closest to him – his wife Maria and his brother Mikhail. In addition, his journalistic projects, undertaken earlier with Mikhail, failed and left the novelist with an enormous financial debt. Astonishingly, in the midst of these misfortunes, which were intensified by his very poor health, Dostoevsky found strength and courage to live and work. In *Crime and Punishment* (*Prestuplenie i nakazanie*, 1866) he portrayed an ambitious young hero who, preoccupied by Napoleonic fantasies, attempts to test his ability and right to kill an allegedly evil old woman. Ideas of spiritual superiority, utilitarianism and rational egoism, which the hero uses intermittently to justify his deed, all fail in the face of sheer horror and guilt experienced by the unfortunate murderer.

In 1867 Dostoevsky remarried and spent the next four years in Europe avoiding his creditors. During this time he wrote *The Idiot* (1868–9), a tragic story of a Christ-like figure, Prince Myshkin, whose naïve involvement in the convoluted affairs of other people lead to catastrophic consequences for himself and everyone around him. Dostoevsky returned to Russia in 1871 and in the following decade published two monumental novels, *The Possessed* (*Besy*, 1871–2) and *The Brothers Karamazov* (*Brat'ya Karamazovy*, 1879–80), as well as numerous essays, stories and socio-political commentaries. While his own political views expressed in his monthly one-person periodical *Diary of a Writer* (*Dnevnik pisatelya*, 1873–81) were quite eccentric and nationalistic, in *The Possessed* he offered a penetrating and witty critique of all the major developments of political radicalism in nineteenth-century Russia.

The monumental *The Brothers Karamazov*, staged around the tragedy of parricide, raised the questions of guilt and moral commitment, religious faith and disbelief, individual freedom and universal accountability. In this novel, finished just two months before the novelist's death, Dostoevsky's artistic creativity reached its height as he portrayed the characters' struggle with the unbearable reality of human suffering, their rebellion against God's creation and rediscovery of life's splendour and beauty.

Dostoevsky died in January 1881, considered by many a national hero and an unsurpassable literary genius.

Further reading

Dostoevskii, F.M. (1912–20) *The Novels of Fyodor Dostoevsky*, trans. C. Garnett, 12 vols, rept, New York: Modern Library, 1950; rept, New York: Dutton, 1960.
——(1993–4) *A Writer's Diary*, trans. K. Lantz, 2 vols, Evanston, IL: Northwestern University Press.
Frank, J. (1983) *Dostoevsky: The Years of Ordeal, 1850–59*, Princeton, NJ: Princeton University Press.
——(1986) *Dostoevsky: The Stir of Liberation, 1860–65*, Princeton, NJ: Princeton University Press.
——(1995) *Dostoevsky: The Miraculous Years, 1865–71*, Princeton, NJ: Princeton University Press.
——(2002) *Dostoevsky: The Mantle of the Prophet, 1871–81*, Princeton, NJ: Princeton University Press.

SEE ALSO: early socialism; novels, poetry and drama; Russian thought in the nineteenth century; utopianism

EVGENIA V. CHERKASOVA

DU BOIS, W.E.B. (1868–1963)

William Edward Burghardt Du Bois (1868–1963) was the leading intellectual in the African American community in the first half of the twentieth century. Arguably the most prolific writer and thinker of black letters, Du Bois is considered the founder of Black Studies in the USA. His rise to prominence is marked by a series of 'firsts' at the close of the nineteenth century: his dissertation, *The Suppression of the African Slave-Trade to the United States* (1895), was the first volume in Harvard Historical Series; his speech 'The Conservation of the Races' at the inaugural meeting of the American Negro Academy (1897) gained him major recognition; and he wrote the first sociological study of the African American community published in the USA, *The Philadelphia Negro* (1899). Over the next 70 years, Du Bois would examine racial politics from a variety of perspectives: early segregationism and support of BOOKER T. WASHINGTON, later integrationism, pan-Africanism and even later an embrace of socialism and Afrocentrism. At the close of the nineteenth century, however, Du Bois was the emergent thinker of the most sophisticated ideas concerning race, African Americans and cultural dualism, an idea begun in 'The Conservation of the Races' and evolving into the more profound assessment of the state of the Negro in the USA as 'double consciousness' in his most famous work, *The Souls of Black Folk* (1903), which would come to support his struggle for racial integration in the USA.

Born in Great Barrington, Massachusetts, on 23 February 1868 to Mary Burghardt Du Bois and Alfred Du Bois (who later deserted the family), Du Bois was raised in a family that encouraged him. Du Bois later described his education in an integrated school system as one unmarked by racist discrimination. He graduated with honours in 1884, and in 1885 he travelled south to Fisk University in Nashville, Tennessee, to learn more about his black heritage. Here Du Bois was exposed to southern racism, and, more importantly, he experienced his first full immersion into the lives of African Americans. He graduated from Fisk with his bachelor's degree in 1888. In a story he details in *The Souls of Black Folk*, he briefly became a teacher at a black school in rural Tennessee, where he experienced a level of poverty and a lack of education for which he was unprepared by his own experience. He also learned, however, about the great resourcefulness of the people he came to know well. Following this experience, Du Bois applied and won for a scholarship at Harvard University. Graduating in 1890 with a second bachelor's degree and a master's degree in 1891, he travelled to Germany for two years of study at the University of Berlin. During his time at Harvard, Du Bois studied under WILLIAM JAMES and Albert Bushnell Hart, one of the founders of sociology. Returning to the USA, he graduated with his doctorate in history from Harvard in 1895.

Du Bois sought work as an academic, landing his first position at Wilberforce University, founded by the African Methodist Episcopal Church in Ohio, where he met Alexander Crummel, one of the leading black intellectuals, who later invited the young scholar to speak at the inaugural meeting of the American Negro Academy (1897). After a year on the faculty, during which time he met and married Nina Gomer, Du Bois took a research position at the University of Pennsylvania, where, despite inadequate resources, he completed the research on the Philadelphia black community that resulted in *The Philadelphia Negro* (1899). In 1897 he joined the faculty of Atlanta University, where he spent the next 13 years engaging in issues concerning race in the USA.

During his time as an academic, Du Bois came to be recognized as a leading public intellectual. As he came into his own, he began to separate himself from the Washingtonian stance of co-operation and accommodation of southern white leadership. As his resistance and reservations grew, Du Bois came to publicly challenge Washington and his followers, including in *The Souls of Black Folk* a lengthy chapter entitled 'Of Mr. Booker T. Washington and Others', where he chided the leader for his passive position, creating a national audience for what would become an unstinting campaign for civil rights. In 1905, he met with twenty-eight other black leaders in Fort Erie, Ontario, Canada, to organize a more militant movement. The resulting Niagara Movement became a vehicle for Du Bois to work actively against Washington's position. Washington responded with direct pressure, ruining the careers of some of the Niagaraites through his use of political prestige. The Niagara Movement imploded in 1908, resulting, however, in the beginnings of a new organization. The movement had drawn the attention of a small group of progressive whites who joined forces with the remaining members to create the biracial movement, the National Association for the Advancement of Colored People (NAACP). Du Bois was one of the few black members to occupy a position of power

in the first two decades of the NAACP. In 1910, he resigned his position at Atlanta, moved to New York and came into his own politically. He founded *The Crisis*, the monthly journal of the NAACP, fought for editorial control of the journal and for the next 24 years had a forum available to promote all his ideas. During the Harlem Renaissance, *The Crisis* published numerous new artists' work, creating a literary phenomenon. Growing more radical in a battle against imperialism, he embraced pan-Africanism and socialism, and came into disagreement with Walter White, head of the NAACP; he resigned as editor of *The Crisis* in 1934.

While Du Bois was a staunch integrationist for most of his life, he came to embrace ideas of nationalism later in life, ultimately leaving the USA for Ghana in 1961, where he became a citizen and lived until his death in 1963.

Further reading

Byerman, Keith (1994) *Seizing the Word: History, Art, and Self in the Work of W.E.B. Dubois*, Athens: University of Georgia Press.
Du Bois, W.E.B. (1996 [1903]). *The Souls of Black Folk*, New York: Penguin.
Lewis, David Levering (2000) *W.E.B. Du Bois: The Fight for Equality and the American Century*, New York: H. Holt.
Schneider, Ryan (2002) 'Fathers, Sons, Sentimentality, and the Color Line: The Not-Quite-Separate Spheres of W.E.B. Du Bois and Ralph Waldo Emerson', in Cathy Davidson and Jessamyn Hatcher (eds) *No More Separate Spheres! A Next Wave American Studies Reader*, Durham: Duke University Press.
Wintz, Cary D. (ed.) (1996) *African American Political Thought, 1890–1930: Washington, Du Bois, Garvey, and Randolph*, Armonk, NY: M.E. Sharpe.

SEE ALSO: anthropology and race; anti-colonial movements and ideas

PAMELA RALSTON

DURKHEIM, EMILE (1858–1917)

Life and university career

The father of the French school of sociology, if not of sociology itself, was born in 1858 in Epinal in Lorraine, France. His father, himself the son and grandson of rabbis, was the Chief Rabbi of the Vosges and Haut Marne. Durkheim was destined for the rabbinate, but decided against this whilst still a schoolboy. He began his studies at the Ecole Normale in 1879, as part of a brilliant generation including Jean Jaurès (the future socialist leader and life-long close friend of Durkheim's) and HENRI BERGSON. He passed his aggregation in 1882 and began his career as a philosophy teacher in the French *lycée* system. He began work on his principal doctoral thesis in 1883, which was destined to be his first book.

In 1885–6 he visited Germany on a scholarship from the French Government to study its latest scholarly and scientific work. He was impressed by the influence of Kantianism and the development of a science of morality – particularly in the work of Wilhelm Wundt; from the German school Durkheim claimed that he acquired his 'sense of social reality, its organic complexity and development'. His articles on *philosophy* and social science attracted attention, and he was appointed to a course on social science and pedagogy specially created for him (under the influence of the Minister of Education, Louis Liard) at the University of Bordeaux. So began his academic career and his life-long struggle to establish the viability and intellectual credibility of the new, then as now hotly debated subject, sociology.

He was married in 1887 to Louise Dreyfus with whom he shared, together with their two children, a happy and contented family life. He taught at Bordeaux from 1887–1902, where he began his work on the concept of moral education, which became a life-long concern. Although he worked also on educational psychology, it was the beginning of his sociology of education that was significant at this time. He stressed the importance of education as a social reality, as intimately linked to each society's social structure, and the cultural relativity of educational ideas. He also offered public lectures on the nature of social solidarity – understood as the 'bonds which unite men one to another' – considerations that were to be the basis of his first book, *The Division of Labour in Society* (1893).

He gave a public lecture course on the subject of suicide in 1889–90. His book *Suicide* was subsequently published in 1897, based on the research and statistical analysis he undertook with the help of his nephew, Marcel Mass. One of his most famous and contested works, this study was for Durkheim proof of both the reality of society and of the importance and significance of sociological explanation. These considerations he formulated into his treatise on sociological method, *The Rules of Sociological Method* (1895). Equally at Bordeaux he gave his first lecture course on religion in 1894–5, where he began his life-long preoccupation with the role of religion in social life and the functional importance of religious institutions. And in 1895–6 he gave a series of lectures on the history of socialism – which applied the sociological and historical method to the study of the socialist idea; this was published posthumously in 1928 as *Socialism*, known in translation as *Socialism and St Simon* (1958).

In 1896 and in 1900 he gave a public course on morality and political questions, particularly the state, studied sociologically, which was published posthumously in 1950 and translated as *Professional Ethics and Civic Morals* (1957). Treated under the rubric of civic ethics, he analysed different types of state according to the degree of conscious awareness and communication between the government and the governed; the highest degree of this is found in the democratic state, which he took to be 'normal' for modern industrial society. In 1896 he decided to found the journal, so distinctive of the Durkheimian school, *L'Année sociologique*, where he was assisted by his nephew, Marcel Mass, together with (amongst others) Francis Simiand, Henri Hubert and Paul Fauconnet – the most well known now amongst that brilliant first group of Durkheimians.

When the Dreyfus affair occurred Durkheim was an instigator and supporter of the 'Ligue des Droits de l'Homme'. This, together with the influence of Jaurès, was fundamental to the Dreyfusards, who were so influential in fighting the case of the falsely accused army captain. In his *Individualism and the Intellectuals* (1898) Durkhein turned the tables on the anti-Dreyfusard case formulated by Ferdinand Brunetière. This was anti-intellectual, pro-army and established social order and hierarchy. Durkheim argued it was they who were threatening the country with anarchy through first denying freedom of thought, central to intellectual life, and second denying individualism, which he held to be the only system of beliefs that could henceforth ensure 'the moral unity of the country'. Stephen Lukes rightly holds that this article conclusively refutes a widespread interpretation of Durkheim as an illiberal and anti-individualist right-wing nationalist, and a forerunner of fascism (Lukes 1973: 338).

By the time that Durkheim moved to Paris to teach at the Sorbonne in 1902 the themes and intellectual preoccupations of his life's work were set. These were the overriding concern with morality and the sense of the moral crisis of modern society, which can only be resolved through justice and equality; the study of solidarity through different social and historical forms; the social phenomenon of suicide; the reality of social facts and the possibility of a scientific study of them; the centrality of religion to human life and its importance as a social institution; the concern with education of the child; and with understanding of different social forms of punishment.

He took the chair of the Science of Education at the Sorbonne, unwillingly at first, since his interest at the time was limited to moral education. His *Moral Education* was published posthumously in 1925; here he stressed the importance of both autonomy and discipline in the education of the child. However, he went on to give an annual lecture course (from 1904–13) on 'The History of Education in France', where he stressed its historical and sociological aspects. This was published in 1938 by Maurice Halbwachs and translated as *The Evolution of Educational Thought* (1977). He continued his teaching on morality and the social institutions associated with it (the family); his book, *Morality*, remained unfinished at his death. He wrote *The Determination of Moral Facts* (1906) and *Value Judgements and Judgements of Reality* (1911). These, together with *Individual and Collective Representations* (1898), have been published as *Sociology and Philosophy* (1974). He taught a lecture course on Pragmatism during 1913–4. This was published posthumously as *Pragmatism and Sociology* (1955). Although there he argued that there was much to be admired in the Pragmatism of JAMES and DEWEY, he nevertheless criticizes Pragmatism's attack on rationalism and the concept of truth, which Durkheim argued cannot be reduced to the useful. His crowning achievement, and possibly the book for which he is most famous, is *The Elementary Forms of the Religious Life* (1912).

The outbreak of war in 1914 found Durkheim as busy and engaged as ever, and he threw himself whole heartedly into the war effort. He wrote an analysis of the German mentality, shown in the writings of TREITSCHKE. *Germany above All Else* criticizes its militarism and views of the state, which he contrasts to a humanitarian morality and democratic state. He died in 1917 at the age of 59, it is said, heartbroken by the loss of his son André in the war, through which he also lost many of his colleagues and collaborators in the Année Sociologique.

His major works

The *Division of Social Labour* (1893) is addressed to his life-long problematic – that of solidarity. It concerns the social and historical nature of solidarity; he argues that in the transformation from pre-industrial to industrial societies solidarity is not left behind, but is transformed by the division of labour. Whilst the pre-industrial world was bonded through common ideas and feelings, the industrial world was united in a different way – by the specialization of function and the dependence that this entailed. For Durkheim, the paradox of modern society is that while we are more autonomous, we are also more dependent on society; this shows a complex interweaving between personal individuation (the mark of the modern) and social dependency. This, in contrast to the mechanical solidarity that characterized the old world, Durkheim called 'organic solidarity'. He opposed AUGUSTE COMTE, who argued that a strong state is required to offset the dispersive effects of the division of labour. Equally he opposed HERBERT SPENCER, who argued that the free play of economic interests in exchange is enough to establish society. Just as he replied to the latter that social bonding does and must transcend the fleeting nature of exchange relationships, so he argued against the former that a strong state is incompatible with the democratic and individualistic aspirations of modern society.

However, all is not well with modern society for Durkheim: in Book III he identifies inegalitarianism as the block to the development of organic solidarity, and the fundamental source of social pathology. The 'constraining' division of labour is characterized by injustice and inequality seen in class war.

'Anomie' characterizes the other aspect of modern social pathology and this indicates where the true forms of functional integration have not been generated in work relations. Anomie does not mean 'disorder', but lack of solidarity – shown in the conflict between labour and capital (Besnard 1987).

The *Rules of Sociological Method* (1895) remains one of Durkheim's most controversial books. During the recent anti-scientific movements in the social sciences it was vilified for its stress on the scientific and its apparent opposition to interpretative/hermeneutic approaches to social phenomena. The method he used acknowledged the objective reality of social facts. The specificity and reality of the social is seen not just in the interaction of agents, but also in the reality of the social milieu. He insists not only on human action, but also on the facts of social morphology that are found through analysis of the 'volume' and 'density' of society; the former is the number of social units, and the latter 'the degree of concentration' of the 'mass' of social phenomena. The concepts of the normal and the pathological Durkheim argued are crucial to the examination of the health of society. He insisted on the comparative method, which involves the examination of social types, and held that adequate explanation in the social sciences, in addition to functional analysis, must finally involve causality. 'The method of concomitant variation is the instrument, par excellence, of sociological research' (1895: 131).

Suicide (1897) was an occasion to prove the principles of The Rules. The phenomenon of suicide proved the existence of social reality – shown in the suicide rate; both its 'permanence' and its 'variability' reflect the 'rhythm of social life'. Suicide rates, which are discovered statistically, vary as a function of different social concomitants – which represent different social milieu; the sociological explanation of suicide lies in social forces generated here. Suicide is the negative side of solidarity, for it shows where these bonds have broken down. The degree of social integration is the crucial factor: egoistic suicide results from 'excessive individuation', altruistic suicide from 'insufficient individuation' and anomic suicide from the breakdown of an established moral framework, that is, the scale that regulates our needs and desires. This is seen in both crises of poverty and sudden wealth. So rejecting physiological or psychological explanations, he postulates a correlation between the will to live and society, and in so doing addresses the question of European social malaise.

Although it was in 1895 that Durkheim was aware of the essential role of religion in social life, it was not until 1912 that he completed his masterpiece on religious life, *The Elementary Forms of the Religious Life*. Acknowledging a debt to Robertson Smith's ideas of clan totemism as the most primitive form of religion and of the communal function of religion, he also took up William James's idea of the truth of religion. Durkheim argued that religion is not an illusion, but its truth concerns the underlying reality of society. In contrast to MAX WEBER and William James, he argued that the essential features of religion are most clearly displayed in the simplest and the most primitive: Australian totemism is the test case for a general theory about religion. Through the analysis of this material (contested, as was his hypothesis), he offers a sociological explanation of religion. God and the soul are born of society and are symbolical representations of it: dependency on the sacred beings that are believed in and worshipped in ritual action being a derivative of our dependence on society. Sacred beings are created out of collective thought – in particular collective representations and forces, and he stressed the moments of collective effervescence as the birthplace of religious ideas and indeed of moments of social change. The sacred/profane dichotomy was also fundamental to his explanatory apparatus.

Together with his 1901 work with Mass, *Primitive Classification*, *Elementary Forms* is also an exercise in the sociology of knowledge – shown in Durkheim's Kantian stress on categories of knowledge; unlike KANT he, of course, offers a sociological account of knowledge, that is of the social determination of knowledge by stressing the social origin of both the necessity and forms of classification central to knowledge, together with social and historical diversity of these.

Reaction to his thought

Durkheim's work has always provoked controversy. These began with the attacks on the new science of sociology, still suffering from association with the bizarre ideas of the later Comte. Whilst he continues to be viewed as a conservative thinker through the interpretation of him imposed by the US sociologists – Robert Nisbet, Talcott Parsons and Lewis Coser – at the time his new subject was seen to be too close to socialism and thus incurred the opposition of conservatives, Catholics, anti-Dreyfusards and some philosophers – particularly Bergson and the eclectic philosophers then in the ascendancy in the university.

From that day, his thought has been subject of many criticisms – many beside the mark: the most widespread among students is that he is a conservative theorist of order and a Positivist in his theory of knowledge and approach to social phenomena. Durkheim claimed on the contrary that he was a rationalist and stressed the representational and relational nature of society. He acknowledged that he was a socialist, although neither a Marxist nor a revolutionary. However controversial, his works are still pored over by scholars of the social sciences. But his influence is profound and still widespread; it stretched from the British anthropologists Radcliffe Brown and Evans Pritchard, to Claude Lévi-Strauss, the Annales School, and to George Bataille, Roger Caillois and the Collège de Sociologie (in Paris between the war), and to Michel Foucault.

References

Besnard, Philippe (1987) *L'Anomie*, Paris: Presse Universitaire de France.
Lukes, Stephen (1973) *Emile Durkheim, His Life and Work*, Harmondsworth: Penguin.

Further reading

Allen, N., Pickering, W.S.F. and Watts Miller, W. (eds) (1998) *On Durkheim's* Elementary Forms of the Religious Life, London: Routledge.
Filloux, Jean-Claude (1977) *Durkheim et le socialisme*, Geneva: Librairie Droz.
Gane, Mike (ed.) (1992) *The Radical Sociology of Durkheim and Mass*, London: Routledge.
Giddens, Anthony (ed.) (1986) *Durkheim on Politics and the State*, Cambridge: Polity.
Pearce, Frank (1989) *The Radical Durkheim*, London: Unwin Hyman.
Pickering, S.F. (ed.) (2000) *Durkheim and Representations*, London: Routledge.
——(1984) *Durkheim's Sociology of Religion*, London: Routledge and Kegan and Paul.
——(ed.) (2001) *Emile Durkheim Critical Assessments Vol. 1–4*, London: Routledge.
——(ed.) (2002) *Durkheim Today*, New York: Berghahn.
Stedman Jones, Sue (2001) *Durkheim Reconsidered*, Cambridge: Polity.

SEE ALSO: intellectuals, elites and meritocracy; social theory and sociology in the nineteenth century; theories of the state and society: the science of politics; Marx and Marxism

SUE STEDMAN-JONES

E

EARLY SOCIALISM

By 'early socialism' is here meant the leading pre-Marxian socialists chiefly active prior to 1848, and often derogatorily termed 'Utopian Socialists' to distinguish them from the 'scientific Socialism' of Karl Marx and Friedrich Engels (see MARX AND MARXISM), which is however usually termed 'communism'. The three leading schools of early socialists were the Owenites, or followers of ROBERT OWEN, in Britain; the Fourierists, or followers of CHARLES FOURIER, in France; and the Saint-Simonians, or adherents to the views of HENRI DE SAINT-SIMON, also in France. Several German and US socialists are also discussed here, as are several other non-Marxian forms of socialism from the later nineteenth-century.

The term 'socialism' comes into currency in the major European languages in the middle and late 1820s to denote a system of thought defined by its opposition to liberal individualism, especially in political economy, and its support for both communal and collectivist forms of property-holding, and the reorganisation of society into small-scale communities. Socialism thus inherits early traditions of communal property holding, such as monasticism, as well as the specifically utopian tradition, associated with Plato's *Republic* and Thomas More's *Utopia* (1516), of reorganising an entire society along communistic lines. In addition, republican discussions of the limitation of private property in land by an agrarian law are an important source for socialist discussions of limiting ownership. Attempts to describe poverty as rooted in the wage relationship rather than unjust taxation, as is attempted in Charles Hall's *The Effects of Civilization on the People in European States* (1805), also form a starting point for

socialist economics. Though the pre-Marxian forms of socialism tend to be displaced after 1848 by Marxism, they continue to exert a limited influence in Europe through writers like WILLIAM MORRIS; Fourierism in particular remains important in the USA until the 1870s.

Owen and Owenism

Robert Owen (1771–1858) gained fame as a cotton-spinner at New Lanark, near Glasgow, and as a sympathetic employer who endeavoured to improve conditions in his factory. After Waterloo, social dislocation and unemployment convinced him that limited reforms, such as restricting the hours of child labour, were insufficient. Instead, by 1820, Owen became convinced that increasing mechanization would destroy the character of the working class, and that a 'new moral world' should be created based upon small-scale communities of no more than 2,500 persons, living and working in common, aiming at self-subsistence, and alternating between manufacturing, agricultural and other forms of labour. The 'social system' (from whence 'socialism' is coined) was to promote a spirit of common enterprise and public spirit, and a harmonization of economic interests. As the movement developed in the 1830s and 1840s, and several communitarian experiments were attempted (notably at New Harmony, Indiana, and Queenwood, Hampshire), an increasingly liberal view of women, marriage and the family was added to Owen's original agenda. (The most important feminist tract of the first half of the century, William Thompson's *Appeal on Behalf of One Half the Human Race*, 1824, emerges from Owenism.) Politically, Owen himself tended towards paternalism, but would eventually, in *The Book of the New*

Moral World, 1836–44, propose the reorganisation of society according to age group, with all passing through the same routine, and thus becoming governors in due course. This would avoid elections in particular, which Owen thought elicited some of the worst passions in human nature.

The Owenite movement produced a number of penetrating works of economic analysis, of which the best known are John Gray, *A Lecture on Human Happiness* (1826), and *The Social System* (1831); William Thompson, *Inquiry Concerning the Distribution of Wealth* (1824), and *Labor Rewarded* (1827); and John Francis Bray, *Labour's Wrong and Labour's Remedy* (1839). These writings developed themes first explored at length by Owen in his *Report to the County of Lanark* (1820). Owenites usually argued that the working classes were the principal producers of value, but were deprived of their reward by the capitalist wage system. If society were reorganized on a co-operative basis and far more labour were made productive, idleness abolished, and the invention of machinery turned to useful purposes rather than generating further unemployment, the working day could be reduced, and the working classes would enjoy a far higher standard of living. By the early 1830s, Owenism had a fairly detailed analysis of recurrent economic crises, and insisted that these were endemic to capitalism, and would contribute to the increasing poverty of the working classes.

Two major economic issues divided the early British socialists: whether it was desirable to restrict needs, and live at a more primitive level, in order to reduce working hours, or whether production should expand with needs, but goods be distributed more justly; and whether the scope of organization should be the community, or could be extended to the nation-state. In addition, Owenites disagreed as to whether competition should be abolished completely, or only partially. Owen himself preferred some restraint of needs, and insisted that the communitarian model alone suited socialist aims; John Gray in particular inaugurated the view that a national system of economic planning could be designed and successfully implemented. Owen's insistence on communitarianism, however, had a crucial moral component: only in community, where individuals lived face to face and knew one another, could substantial moral improvement be achieved, and the abolition of coercive organizations like the

police and army be achieved through a regime of mutual moral supervision.

Politically, more of Owen's followers were democrats, like the Chartists, with whom they often competed from 1836–45. But they disagreed with radical assessments of the origins of poverty, which concentrated on the effects of unjust taxation, and on the continuance of private property under any reformed system. The most frequently used example urged here was the USA, which, Owenites argued, had by the 1830s generated a new class of urban poor. And they largely agreed on seeing national politics as epiphenomenal, or a function of class conflicts between the landed and mercantile and manufacturing orders, such that parliamentary politics plays no major role in any Owenite vision of the future.

Fourier and Fourierism

Charles Fourier (1772–1837) stemmed from an affluent Lyon merchant family, but by the late 1790s had come to react against the dullness of bourgeois life, the 'anarchic' competition of the commercial system, and the growing promise of equality popularized by the French Revolution. Aspiring to become the Newton of the social sciences, Fourier proclaimed his discovery of the law of 'passionate attraction' governing all nature, which, when fully understood and practically applied, would form the basis of a new society based upon the harmonization of the passions, rather than their mastery by reason. This ideal Fourier elevated into a grand, sometimes eccentric, metaphysical system, as well as a comprehensive plan, often referred to as a 'social science', of an ideal form of small-scale communal organization that by 1800 he referred to as the 'Phalanx', whose hallmark was to be the harmonization or reconciliation of individual desires, as well as the abolition of poverty and the promotion of the communal good. Fourier's first main work was the *Theory of the Four Movements* (1808); there followed the *Traité de l'association domestique-agricole* (2 vols., 1821), the most important of his writings published in his lifetime, and then *Le Nouveau Monde industriel et sociétaire* (1829) and *La Fausse Industrie* (1835–6). His very liberal views on sexuality and marriage or 'enslaved monogamy', which he wished to abolish, and his insistence on the value of universal, polymorphous sexual gratification, with a guaranteed 'sexual minimum' like a minimum wage, and a 'Court of Love' regulating sexual congresses, were regarded as too extreme by most of his followers, and were not published in full until the late twentieth century.

Like Owen, the chief focus of Fourier's account of commerce was upon its deleterious effects on morality, and the promotion of lying, cheating, hoarding, usury, speculation and parasitism. Fourier also wished to reduce unproductive labour, such as that of monks, soldiers and lawyers, to a minimum, and saw as one of the principal advantages of community life the vast savings achieved by shared resources, compared to each isolated household. Though he condemned unpleasant and degrading factory labour, a central element in Fourier's system is his essentially romantic, creative approach to work as central to life. If at least 800 persons associated together, work in the Phalanx could be based upon the principle of the 'attractive association' of 'compound groups' organized voluntarily in a 'passional series' linked by mutual likes, but also a sense of friendly rivalry. Instead of being merely 'profitless boredom', work would become 'attractive labour' by a system of rotation of up to eight tasks daily, with no more than two hours devoted to any one task, and each person contributing to as many as forty types of work. Manufacturing would be limited to no more than a quarter of working time, but is still essential; Fourier was no primitivist and disbelieved in 'the virtues of the shepherds'. Labour was thus to become an essentially 'free' activity. A typical day, Fourier suggested, might consist of five meals, a concert, reading in the library, hunting, fishing, gardening and agriculture, the main job in the Phalanx. For much larger projects industrial armies would be formed.

Unlike Owen, Fourier did not insist upon complete communism in the Phalanx. He did seek to instil 'the spirit of societary or compound property', but contended that the community's profits should be divided between capital (receiving four-twelfths), labour (five-twelfths) and talent (three-twelfths). A minimum wage would prevent poverty amongst the less well-off, but drudgery would be better paid than normal work, even though the wealthy could avoid certain unpleasant tasks.

Social relations in the Phalanx were equally to be governed by the 'law of passionate attraction', the exact science of which involved for Fourier an intricate categorization of the forms and varieties of passions and their interrelationships, which

Fourier thought resulted in some 810 basic personality types. These were dependent on the predominance of particular passions, of which anywhere from one to seven might prevail in any individual. Human happiness was contingent in particular on the free expression of three 'distributive' or 'mechanising' passions, which were the 'Butterfly' or variety, the 'Cabalist' or intriguing and the 'Composite' or mixture of physical and spiritual elements. Fourier has often been seen as anticipating Freud in his insistence that a healthy human life must avoid repression of the passions, and particularly those of a sexual nature.

Like Owen, Fourier anticipated that politics would play little role in the Phalanx. Everyday decisions would be taken by a 'Regency' consisting of the wealthiest and most learned members, and the chief task, the organization of production, would be supervised by the Areopagus, or Supreme Council of Industry, which was made up of the leaders of the main industrial series, plus a few shareholders and other respected persons. Its injunctions, however, would not be binding, though Fourier thought they would generally be followed. Fourier did design a complex hierarchy of offices and honours in order to assuage the natural 'lust for honour' that would still exist. But such offices were to be largely ceremonial, and without responsibility. Some minor disciplinary measures are anticipated, with ostracism from particular series or groups the most severe; otherwise crime and disorder are largely anticipated to have disappeared.

The Fourierist movement resulted in the founding of a few experimental communities in France, and rather more in the USA. The most influential of Fourier's French disciples was VICTOR CONSIDÉRANT, a pacifist and advocate of direct democracy, while in the USA Albert Brisbane, author of *The Social Destiny of Man* (1840), was widely read. Important communes included Brook Farm and the North American Phalanx. Fourierism also made some impact in Russia and Eastern Europe.

Saint-Simon and Saint-Simonism

The most influential form of early socialism, as far as mainstream social and political thought is concerned, was Saint-Simonism. Its founder was Henri de Saint-Simon (1760–1825), a French nobleman who fought in the American War of

Independence, and renounced his title at the French Revolution. Thereafter he became involved in canal construction and land development, but was ruined financially in 1804. His main writings, published between 1803–17, are neither communitarian nor, strictly speaking, socialist; it was his chief followers who extended his ideas in this direction, or who, like his secretary, AUGUSTE COMTE, build upon his analysis of industrial society, which is influential on THOMAS CARLYLE, JOHN STUART MILL, Karl Marx and others. His endeavour to provide a new form of spiritual authority, or 'new religion', called 'Physicism' (or, sometimes, 'Positive Philosophy'), which would be based upon science rather than theology, and take Newton as its founder, was also taken up by Comte in particular, and developed into the system called 'Positivism'. (Prior to its public acceptance, however, Saint-Simon counselled deism as a popular religion.)

Saint-Simon's chief contribution to socialism was his account of 'industrialism' (a term he coined) and its implications for the reshaping of the modern world, notably in L'Industrie (1816–18). Society is categorized in terms of three main classes, scientists, writers and artists; proprietors; and toilers. Spiritual power should reside with the former, temporal power, or control of the state, with the proprietors, and the right of election with all workers. All useful workers are 'industrialists', according to Saint-Simon, since work is the basis of all virtue, and all incomes not based on work were essentially robbery. The failure of the French Revolution lay in the assumption of power by the most ignorant, and an over-concentration on perfecting the mechanism of government, when the chief aim should have been the subordination of government to administration. Here we see that the analysis of politics is vastly more important to Saint-Simon than to Owen or Fourier, or for that matter most other nineteenth-century socialists. For Saint-Simon the present was an age of transition, in which the natural progress of society was from a governmental, or a feudal, military or predatory regime, to an administrative or industrial regime, in which the functions of government will be minimized to the prevention of any disruption of useful work, while the class of industrialists would promote the greatest production of useful things. This is, for Saint-Simon, a meritocratic ideal, and one hostile to feudal privilege and economic interference; as such it is close in some particulars to the liberal economics of 'the immortal' Adam Smith. (Saint-Simon also believed that taxes would be much reduced in the juster industrial system.) Much more important than political participation, thus, was economic participation, and Saint-Simon anticipated a growing interdependence in the productive process, which would promote a greater harmony of interests between the various types of industrialists, with decision-making being based less on command and obedience than persuasion and argument. National parliaments would formulate an economic 'plan', but this respected public works only; as a whole the economy itself was to remain independent of political control in order to maximize efficiency and minimize parasitism and interference. This was outlined at length in L'Organisateur (1819). Having subverted the idea of government from an economic viewpoint, Saint-Simon went on to propose, in Concerning the Reorganization of European Society (1814), the further diminution of the powers of the separate European states by the creation of a European parliament composed of two houses, one of nobility, the other of businessmen, scientists, administrators and magistrates. Saint-Simon's Le Politique (1819) also advocated the abolition of standing armies. Only in his last works, notably the Système industrial (1821), does Saint-Simon move towards socialism, mainly by arguing that the government should guarantee the right of work.

Saint-Simon's followers were interested not only in his philosophy of history and theory of industrial society, but also the practical application of his ideas. Positivism proposed an influential replacement for Christianity, echoing Saint-Simon's view that the reinforcement of spiritual power was crucial to the transitional age, particularly during an intermediary stage when theology was still widely approved. Saint-Simon's followers addressed this in the chief interpretation of his writings, The Doctrine of Saint-Simon (1828–9), which also argued for greater equality for women, the increased facility of divorce, an expansion in national education, and both greater freedom of trade and closer integration of the state and the system of production, especially through a remodelling of the banking system. Such views were popularized in the 1820s and 1830s by men like Olinde Rodrigue, BARTHÉLEMY-PROSPER ENFANTIN, Philippe Buchez, Saint-Amand Bazard, Gustave d'Eichtal and Michel Chevalier. By the late 1830s they had made a substantial impact on intellectual life in Britain, Germany and elsewhere. The movement began to split, however, in part over the issue of whether a female Messiah was needed to reveal the next stage of doctrine, upon which Enfantin insisted. By the 1840s its influence had dwindled, though its philosophy of history and account of industrial society were developed by various thinkers, including Marx.

Other forms of non-Marxian socialism

Amongst the other influential forms of non-Marxian socialism during the nineteenth century, mention should be made of the proposals of ETIENNE CABET (1788–1853), author of the *Voyage en Icarie* (1840), who founded a series of colonies in the USA, and proposed a highly rationalist, and decided authoritarian, system of social organization. It attracted as many as several hundred thousand adherents in France during the 1840s for its proposals for non-violent, gradual change towards egalitarian socialism. Another Frenchman, LOUIS BLANC (1811–82), became prominent through his *Organisation du travail* (1840), which urged state guarantees for working-class employment, and is regarded as a founder of state socialism.

Among the early German socialists, the principal thinker was the tailor Wilhelm Weitling (1808–71), whose first tract, *Mankind as It Is and as It Ought to Be* (1838) was composed under the influence of a secret revolutionary society based in Paris, the League of the Just. Here he projected a future system of organization based upon units of 10,000 families, subdivided into units of 1,000 families that were in turn subdivided. Each unit would elect delegates to administer its own affairs, who would in turn elect administrators to the next higher level. Industry was to be similarly organized on the basis of an ascending series of elected bodies representing major occupational groups. Weitling's main work, however, was *Guarantees of Harmony and Freedom* (1842), which offered an account of the loss of a 'golden age' or state of nature prior to the creation of private property, and of the emergence of the modern industrial proletariat. Weitling's proposals for a communist society detailed those needs (which he classified in terms of a need for acquisition, for pleasure and for knowledge) that would be satisfied, including the assurance of intellectual development, and the extension of freedom to all. Basic subsistence needs for all, including housing, clothing and food, were to be assured; any luxuries wanted could be laboured for by additional units of work. The production of unnecessary surpluses would be regulated by denying labour-credits to their producers until stocks were depleted. An industrial army, modelled on the military, would be the main unit of labour organization, and the means by which large-scale projects could be completed. Money and private property, the bane of modern existence, were to be eliminated, and the system of exchange instead based upon labour-time, as Owen and the US individualist (but former Owenite) Josiah Warren had proposed. Critical of both the Fourierists and Saint-Simonians for not pursuing equality sufficiently, Weitling nonetheless followed Saint-Simon in assuming that 'administration' of the productive process would supersede politics as such, and that future progress was contingent upon scientific development in particular. His system of planned organization, however, tended to be based upon the small workshop model of the artisan, rather than the larger factory in which the proletarian was employed. Against Owen and Fourier, he placed greater stress on family life, while recognizing the need for easier divorce, and the extension of employment rights to women. Before Marx he proposed that a period of popular dictatorship would follow the revolution and precede the ultimate creation of communism.

Like many early socialists Weitling also sought to found his views on a radical interpretation of Christianity, as explained in *The Poor Sinner's Gospel*. His views, however, were much more millenarian than those of the Owenites, Fourierists or Saint-Simonians, and assumed that the primitive happiness once enjoyed in an ideal 'golden age' could be recaptured in the future. Exiled after the failed revolutions of 1848, he attempted to found colonies in the USA and, amongst other activities, mostly as a journalist, projected a new universal language, and helped to organize co-operative banks. Equally important as his socialist proposals was Weitling's willingness to counsel violent revolution as the means of implementing them, which separates him from the majority of pre-Marxian writers. His argument for the establishment on a national scale, rather than only in small-scale communities, also clearly paves the way for Marx's proposals. Nonetheless he and Marx fell out in 1846, with Moses Hess siding with Weitling, and no further collaboration proved possible.

Other German socialists of note include some who contributed to theories of revolutionary strategy and tactics like Karl Schapper and Auguste Willich, who were linked with the French revolutionary Auguste Blanqui in the League of the Just, which after 1847 became the Communist League. The Young Hegelian Moses Hess (1812–73) is a theoretician of minor influence, and author of *The European Triarchy* and other works. Other 'True Socialists', mostly now remembered in Marx and Engels' caustic dismissal of their views in 1845–6 in 'The German Ideology', included Karl Grün and Georg Kuhlmann.

Another German, John-Adolphus Etzler (1796–c. 1860), wrote a number of works, notably *The Paradise within the Reach of All Men* (1833), proposing a technologically innovative form of socialist society.

Two late nineteenth-century US writers had considerable influence on collectivist ideologies. The first, EDWARD BELLAMY (1850–98), published an extremely influential utopia, *Looking Backward* (1888), which created a world-wide movement known as Nationalism. Bellamy described a future in which industrial organization was highly centralized, forming one great corporation, the state, and where labour was universal and mandatory for 21 years, and distribution was equal. Money has been abolished, and replaced by a universal credit system. The advantages of technological innovation (air cars, television) are stressed. Crime has nearly disappeared, and there is no need for an army. A sequel, *Equality* (1897), was also published.

A journalist born in Philadelphia, HENRY GEORGE (1839–97), expanded a pamphlet entitled *Our Land and Land Policy* (1871) into an enormously successful book, *Progress and Poverty* (1877), which contended that all forms of taxation except that on land should be abolished, since land ownership was invariably a function of monopoly power.

In Russia, where Saint-Simon and Fourier were especially influential, ALEXANDER HERZEN (1812–70) was one of the most important figures to develop the socialist tendencies in the Decembrist movement, which focused principally upon an exposition of the communal nature of the Russian peasant community, or *mir*.

Further reading

Beecher, Jonathan (1986) *Charles Fourier. The Visionary and His World*, Berkeley: University of California Press.
Butler, E.M. (1926) *The Saint-Simonian Religion in Germany*, Cambridge: Cambridge University Press.
Claeys, Gregory (1987) *Machinery, Money and the Millennium. From Moral Economy to Socialism, 1815–1860*, Princeton, NJ: Princeton University Press.
—— (1989) *Citizens and Saints. Politics and Anti-Politics in Early British Socialism*, Cambridge: Cambridge University Press.
Cole, G.D.H. (1962) *A History of Socialist Thought, vol. 1: The Forerunners*, London: Macmillan.
Guarneri, Carl (1991) *The Utopian Alternative. Fourierism in Nineteenth-Century America*, Ithaca, NY: Cornell University Press.
Iggers, Georg G. (ed.) (1972) *The Doctrine of Saint-Simon: An Exposition. First Year 1828–29*, New York: Schocken Books.
Johnson, Christopher (1974) *Utopian Communism in France. Cabet and the Icarians, 1939–1851*, Ithaca, NY: Cornell University Press.
Lattek, Christine (2005) *Revolutionary Refugees: German Socialism in Britain, 1840–1860*, London: Routledge.
Lichtheim, George (1969) *The Origins of Socialism*, New York: Praeger.
MacNair, Everett (1957) *Edward Bellamy and the Nationalist Movement*, Milwaukee: Fitzgerald Company.
Manuel, Frank (1956) *The New World of Henri de Saint-Simon*, Cambridge, MA: Harvard University Press.
Noyes, John Humphrey (1870) *History of American Socialisms*, Philadelphia: J.B. Lipincott & Co.
Van Davidson, Rondel (1988) *Did We Think Victory Great? The Life and Ideas of Victor Considerant*, Lanham: University Press of America.
Wittke, Carl (1950) *The Utopian Communist. A Biography of Wilhelm Weitling*, Baton Rouge: Louisiana State University Press.

SEE ALSO: Hegel and Hegelianism; industrialism, poverty and the working classes; Marx and Marxism; religion, secularization and the crisis of faith; social theory and sociology in the nineteenth century; utopianism

GREGORY CLAEYS

ELLIS, HAVELOCK (1859–1939)

A pioneering psychologist, theorist of sexual behaviour and advocate of eugenics, Ellis was born 2 February 1859 to a lower middle-class London family. Given an intensive religious education by his mother, he travelled round the world twice with his father, spending four years in Australia. While at medical school, he joined the Fellowship of the New Life, from which the Fabian Society later evolved. Befriending Olive Schreiner, Eleanor Marx and the eugenicist Karl Pearson, his interests turned towards the 'woman question', sexual relations, and birth regulation and control. Commencing an unorthodox marriage to Edith Lees in 1891, Ellis published *Man and Woman: A Study of Human Secondary Sexual Character* (1894), which developed eugenicist themes respecting the necessity of the 'fit' to reproduce in order to improve the race. Turning to examine homosexuality, on the study of which he collaborated with John Addington Symonds, and took advice from his friend EDWARD CARPENTER, Ellis began the series entitled *Studies in the Psychology of Sex* (1900–28). Amongst the controversial topics it explored was the view that marriage was simply a variation on prostitution, and that female sexual desire was no less ardent than the male.

Ellis seems to have become interested in eugenics by the early 1890s, and in 1909 contributed an article to the *Eugenics Review* on 'The Sterilization of the Unfit', wrote in support of euthanasia and later even supported Hitler's views on sterilization. In the earlier period such views were less controversial, given widespread assumptions about racial degeneracy and the progressive role played by hereditary intelligence in the evolution of the human species. He published studies on the effects of war on eugenic prospects, while condemning the glorification of conflict as such. His chief scientific contribution to the subject, continuing the focus begun by FRANCIS GALTON (*Hereditary Genius*, 1869) was *A Study of British Genius* (1904). Here he examined the range of distribution of different types of ability across Britain, and attempted to correlate with genius such factors as age and size of family, health and personal appearance. Like Galton and even more Karl Pearson, Ellis was concerned to develop the collectivist and statist implications of eugenics. At the time of a series of parliamentary enquiries into medical treatment in the early 1890s, Ellis in *The Nationalisation of Health* (1892) began to advocate the 'nationalization' of the British health system, condemning the chaos and waste of the existing system respecting such areas as blindness, typhoid fever and maternity, and pointing to the advantages of a general registration of diseases for control, and the need to supervise dangerous occupations, such as lead-manufacture, for debilitating diseases. These themes were broadly stated in *The Problem of Race Regeneration* (1911), which concentrates on the need for maternal care and the regulation of feeble-mindedness, and in *The Task of Social Hygiene* (1912). He remained fascinated by the question of the interrelationship between genius and insanity. Ellis died on 8 July 1939.

Further reading

Ellis, Havelock (1898) *Affirmations*, London: Constable & Co.
—— (1914–23) *Impressions and Comments*, 3 series, Constable & Co.
—— (1932) *Views and Reviews*, 2 vols, London: Harmsworth.
—— (1933) *Psychology of Sex*, London: Heinemann.
—— (1939) *My Life. Autobiography of Havelock Ellis*, London: William Heinemann.
Peterson, Houston (1928) *Havelock Ellis: Philosopher of Love*, Boston: Houghton Mifflin.
Rowbotham, Sheila and Weeks, Jeffrey (1977) *Socialism and the New Life. The Personal and Sexual Politics of Edward Carpenter and Havelock Ellis*, London: Pluto Press.

SEE ALSO: anthropology and race; the body, medicine, health and disease; psychology, the emergence of; Social Darwinism

GREGORY CLAEYS

EMERSON, RALPH WALDO (1803–82)

Ralph Waldo Emerson ranks as perhaps the most famous intellectual in US history. Many millions of people have read one or another of his famous essays such as 'Self-Reliance', 'Experience' or 'Fate,' which have been translated into dozens of languages. In his own day Emerson became a household name in the USA, where he was identified with the amorphous intellectual movement called Transcendentalism. For parts of five decades Emerson embarked on annual lecture tours that consistently drew large and enthusiastic audiences. Although his publications never sold particularly well, they established their author's reputation among the key literary figures of the Anglo-American community. In 1848, at the peak of his popularity, Emerson made a triumphant speaking tour of England and Scotland, where he attained almost celebrity status. After the American Civil War, despite the fact that his intellectual powers were greatly diminished and his publications all but ceased, Emerson remained popular enough to deliver well-subscribed series of lectures throughout much of the country. By his death, in April 1882, Emerson had become an American institution.

Emerson's reputation has endured in the six score years since his death. To this day school-age Americans read his essays and learn about the Transcendentalists.

Despite the post-modern turn away from the canon in recent times, Emerson's lustre remains untarnished, especially within academic circles. A veritable cottage industry exists devoted to the scrutiny of every aspect of his life, as well as that of HENRY DAVID THOREAU and others of the Transcendentalist circle. Library shelves groan under the weight of hundreds of specialized studies of every size and dimension, with Emerson's writings alone filling some forty volumes. Highlighted by the new Harvard University Press *Collected Works of Ralph Waldo Emerson* (five volumes of which have appeared to date), scholars can now consult virtually complete collections of everything Emerson wrote.

In his lifetime Emerson published almost a dozen volumes, including *Nature,* two books of poetry, a series of biographical vignettes called *Representative Men*, a study of England called *English Traits,* as well as edited versions of his favourite public lectures and orations. Emerson is best known for essays, published in two volumes in the 1840s, which are unmatched for their beauty and poetic style. His poetry is neglected and *Nature* only rarely read, but the essays endure, with generations of readers discovering in them one of the USA's great literary achievements. 'Self-Reliance', 'The Poet', 'Circles' reveal a gifted essayist and wordsmith, who is at once a poet, preacher and thinker of the first order. Romantic and ecumenical, intellectual and accessible, American and yet not insular, Emerson emerges from his essays as a strangely compelling national prophet. Ninth in a line of Congregationalist ministers, Emerson eschewed the Puritan 'fire and brimstone' Jeremiad so effectively and famously deployed by revivalists from George Whitefield and Charles Grandison Finney to Billy Sunday and Billy Graham. Instead he resigned his Unitarian pastorate and left the Church in order to be the nation's irenic pastor of the Deutero-Isaiah type. Simultaneously Emerson was avuncular, stern, passionate, patriotic and protreptic – all without pandering to a US people intent on being alternately praised and entertained. The essays continue to reflect powerfully the elemental honesty and vitality of the man.

For all that, it is difficult to establish precisely what Emerson's essays and other writings profess. It remains perhaps an insuperable challenge to nail down what one might call the Emersonian philosophy to which multitudes have responded so enthusiastically. It may well be the Concord sage's enduring popularity derives from his opacity, from the fact that admirers can read into him what they like. Optimist, pessimist, sooth-sayer, realist, idealist, Puritan, pragmatist, conservative, radical, Emerson in his essays can be all and none of these. What is beyond cavilling is that the essays are beautifully written and have the power to move their readers, although what in particular is written therein is not exactly clear. No other US author proves to be at once so quotable and utterly impossible to synopsize.

Emerson's private writings hardly offer more philosophical unity than his essays and other published works. As with his essays, so his correspondence and journals are famously elusive, often exasperatingly so. Not surprisingly, the person who declared 'mad contradictions flavour all our dishes' never fetishized consistency. Eclectic in the extreme, Emerson despised systematic analysis, preferring instead to read highly selectively, sampling here and there, and purloining whatever he found useful. Emerson biographer Stephen Whicher probably had it right when he noted that to reconstitute Emerson, one should:

> take a quantity of Kant; add unequal parts of Goethe, Schiller, Herder, Jacobi, Schleiermacher, Fichte, Schelling, Oken, and a pinch of Hegel; stir in, as Emerson did, a generous amount of Swedenborg; strain through Mme De Staël, Sampson Reed, Oegger, Coleridge, Carlyle, Wordsworth, Cousin, Jouffroy, Constant; spill half and season with Plato.

What holds for Emerson's writings is equally true of the public lectures and orations for which he was so famous in his own day. When it came to summarizing the substance of an Emerson lecture, reviewers found themselves utterly at a loss, such as a writer for the Providence, Rhode Island, *Manufacturers' and Farmers' Journal* who confessed 'there was much that he said that I could not possibly understand'. Emerson himself confided to his wife how a typical review aptly called his latest lecture 'very fine & poetical but a little puzzling'. Ready to acknowledge his culpability for many of the difficulties readers had grasping his overall argument, Emerson confessed in 1839: 'I need hardly say to any one acquainted with my thoughts that I have no System.'

That he was a key figure in the Transcendentalist circle is true but clarifies little, suggesting at best a family resemblance to the German Idealist philosophy of Kant and Schelling. The late scholar Perry Miller claimed that at the heart of Transcendentalism lurked a religious mysticism in which, as another scholar suggested, Plato had displaced Christ. Emerson read the mystics and the Platonic corpus throughout his life; he subscribed to a two-world credo and a eudemonistic ontology whose intellectual pedigree runs from fourth-century Athens through to the present and includes Plotinus, Augustine and the Church Schoolmen, the Cambridge Platonists and much of Continental philosophy. An admirer of many of the nineteenth century's most esoteric philosophical schools, Emerson derived much of his ideas from his European contemporaries, Carlyle, Coleridge, Schleiermacher, Swedenborg and Goethe primary among them. The most mature expression of his half-digested Idealism is contained in his essays 'Compensation' and 'The Over-Soul', in which the author articulates less a philosophy than an eclectic religious affirmation, composed of elements of the Western Idealist tradition, Eastern mysticism and Quaker pietism.

An Emersonian ethos, if not a full-fledged philosophy, does emerge from the sum of his writings, the overall tenor of which prove far more consistent than the individual parts. The Emersonian ethos combines idealism and scepticism in a compelling yet ultimately unsatisfactory fusion. As its author discarded the doctrines of traditional Christianity, he came to appreciate how truth emanated from intuition and a shared individual mental experience. 'We learn that God IS; that he is in me; and that all things are shadows of him . . . that all nature is the rapid efflux of goodness executing and organizing itself.' Knowledge of the real was simultaneously universal and personal. It was accessible to all but sufficiently elusive that the genuine thinker required the healthy scepticism of all claims to knowledge in the world of things in which we live. Emerson did not reject empiricism, materialism or Lockean psychology so much as he asserted their profound limitations. With Kant, Emerson understood that once all the unimpeachable statements about the phenomenal world had been assimilated, humankind had comprehended very little about reality. Truly useful knowledge about the human condition of the type that he sought to convey demanded a new genre altogether. More poet than philosopher, Emerson begs to be read as the unique poet–preacher–prophet that he sought to become.

Fully aware of his own limitations when it came to 'systematic philosophy' (he was hopelessly inept at mathematics), Emerson turned vice into virtue by celebrating his freedom from philosophical rigor. Preferring poetry to precision, he famously remarked that 'a foolish consistency was the hobgoblin of little minds'. This disdain for systems means that when it comes to explaining a great many of his ideas one must come to terms with the multitude of vagaries and inconsistencies in his prose. From the most profound issues, such as his explication of human nature, the conduct of life, and the origins and legitimacy of private property to more trivial matters such as the presidency of Andrew Jackson and the vacuity of the contemporary press, Emerson's writings, both public and private, can be maddeningly ambiguous. Even when he is not contradictory, the Concord sage almost never defines his terms, preferring instead to gesture at them with general descriptions, fanciful allusions and the generous employ of metonym and metaphor. Even such vitally Emersonian terms as individualism, idealism and the over-soul fail to elicit 'each and only' denotations; in undertaking an examination of Emerson's ideas, it is virtually impossible to pin down precise definitions.

In so far as he comprehended that he was not up to systematic logical analysis on any sophisticated level, Emerson readily granted to others the task of refuting, for example, the radical empiricism of David Hume or resolving the great technical puzzles of academic philosophy. Some college papers excepted, Emerson did not write philosophical discourses or analyses; and though his essays and lectures have a certain similarity to those of FRIEDRICH NIETZSCHE and his prose, like that Ludwig Wittgenstein's *Philosophical Investigations*, can baffle us with the contents of our broom closet, we ask too much to read Emerson as philosophically precise. Without publications remotely equivalent to either Nietzsche's systematic refutation of Schopenhauer or Wittgenstein's austere and exact *Tractatus Logico-Philosophicus*, it seems to strain credulity to embrace Emerson as a rigorous or precise philosophical thinker. Even as a precursor to Pragmatism, as Cornel West and Richard

Poirier eloquently lay out, Emerson barely gets passing marks. Like JOHN DEWEY he sought to broaden the appeal and provenance of the 'public philosopher', but, unlike Dewey, he produced nothing comparable to *Experience and Nature* or *Reconstruction in Philosophy.* He simply was not up to it.

Emerson should be considered a vital and original contributor to the Western intellectual tradition but for reasons having nothing to do with systematic exposition. His awesome breadth of reading, life-long dedication to intellectual inquiry, preoccupation with ethics and his very Wittgenstein-like devotion to an unimpeachable intellectual honesty make Emerson a philosopher in the broad sense of the term. In fact his lack of analytical ability proved to be a blessing, as a great deal of his popularity in his day and his continued relevance in our own stems from his monumental imprecision as well as his affection for the plain language study of everyday life that nature's necessity determined would be his lot. His greatness arose from his lyrical sympathy for the beautiful, comprehensible, useful and pedestrian.

Never a systematic philosopher, Emerson sought a much broader audience than an academic elite. He became the commanding figure of nineteenth-century US culture as a public lecturer. In his day that inexpressible brilliance, which still shines so brightly in his essays, emanated from his public lectures delivered over four decades to many thousands of Americans from all walks of life. Only a few read his books or heard one of his sermons; multitudes more attended his lectures. From the lecture platform and in the lyceums Emerson came to be recognized as he attempted to create himself – as a unique, irenic prophet to the US people. Americans of his day frequently found his peculiar turns of phrase to be inspirational, able to bring hope to the forlorn, strength to the weak and confidence to the insecure. An Emerson lecture could be akin to a conversion experience for those who found their churches, as Emerson put it, 'dead ponds' destitute of their once-great power to transform people's lives. Emerson's friend and fellow Transcendentalist Bronson Alcott had it right when he declared that 'there was no public lecture until Emerson made it'. The Concord sage single-handedly created that 'American invention [which] serves the country with impulse and thought of an ideal cast and conquering virtue. The lyceums are properly *Emersonia*, and we must

substitute the founder's name for the thing he has invented.' Alcott's hyperbole notwithstanding, Emerson and the novel cultural agency of the public lecture produced each other.

Emerson readily grasped the democratic promise of the lecture hall. At the lectern he found himself before an audience more diverse, inquisitive and hungry for conversion than he had at the pulpit of New England's Unitarian churches. The lyceum seemed a remarkably egalitarian agency that, as Donald Scott has suggested, 'appeared to make knowledge readily accessible to the common man'. Lectures, delivered day after day in cities and towns throughout the nation, afforded the prospect of achieving the impact and notoriety that resulted only from mass appeal. 'A lecture is a new literature, which leaves aside all tradition, time, place, circumstance, & addresses an assembly as mere human beings,' Emerson declared. 'It is an organ of sublime power.'

In the more democratic learning situation that characterized lyceums and public lectures Emerson brought culture, or a message of self-culture, to the nation by means of an evangelical medium. By self-culture, Emerson hoped to suggest something akin to the German *Bildung*, by which he meant personal striving for the intellectual and spiritual complement to material pursuits. Borrowed from von Humboldt via Goethe, the Romantics employed *Bildung* to convey their belief in the virtually limitless human capacity for development of their spiritual faculties through the study of culture. Like his sermons, Emerson's original lectures were always hortative, attempts to inculcate a highly syncretistic kind of conversion experience in his audiences, a rebirth not in Christ, but as self-reliant individuals, who readily grasped the spiritual elements in their everyday lives. Wrapped in an ethos of sincerity so essential to his unique charismatic appeal, Emerson dispensed his philosophical-prophetic wisdom through an egalitarian agency. His lay pulpit represented the site where intellectual high culture strove to meet without condescension the fickle demands of US bourgeois tastes.

From the late 1830s until the last decade of his life, a span of almost 40 years, Emerson regularly delivered lectures, often as many as seventy in a year. He consistently ranked at the very pinnacle of his adopted profession. 'It is a singular fact, that Mr. Emerson is the most steadily attractive lecturer in America,' James Russell Lowell pronounced. 'Mr. Emerson always draws.' Between his first public address in 1833 and his last in 1881, across the USA, from Portland, Maine, to St Paul, Minnesota, to San Francisco, California, Emerson carefully crafted his adopted vocation of public speaker, reading one or another of his resplendent lectures an astonishing 1,500 times. His oratorical career proved to be, as William Charvat astutely noted almost a half-century ago, 'one of the most extraordinary phenomena in the history of American culture'.

Crucial to Emerson's allure was the fact that everything about Emerson suggested that here was a teacher who lived precisely as he lectured. The Concord sage possessed an exemplary personal demeanour and strength of character that disclosed themselves wherever he ventured. Typical are the words of Lowell who remarked that 'the whole life of the man is distilled in the clear drop of every sentence, and behind each word we divine the force of a noble character'. Those enchanted by Emerson felt wholeheartedly that his full measure was contained in his lectures, that the word and the man were one. His utter lack of hypocrisy, or even the semblance of it, was critical to his emerging status as one of the nation's leading public figures. In Emerson, the words and the man were of a piece.

Emerson's enduring renown ultimately stems from the unique combination of man and message, from the conjunction of inner and outer lives. He lived the self-reliant life that he preached, famously rejecting the expected, the obvious, the philistine and the traditional. The USA's avatar of self-reliant individualism, Emerson both coined the term and followed its dictum. At the youthful age of 29 Emerson had quit his comfortable, well-paying post at Boston's fashionable Second Congregational Church with its annual salary of $1,800. Later in the decade, self-reliance dictated that Emerson deliver two revolutionary public orations that served as a clarion call for his intellectual colleagues to break away from, as he put it, 'that early ignorant & transitional *Month-of-March* in our New England culture' and its sickly dependence on stale European sources. In the first, called the 'American Scholar' and delivered at Harvard in 1837, Emerson had dismissed the effete high culture of the day (which his own father had done so much to foster), instead calling for an indigenous literature free from toadying to European models. Emerson himself lacked the talent to become that 'poet of democracy', but his appeal directly inspired Walt Whitman, who dedicated his 1855 *Leaves of Grass* to the Concord sage. The USA was becoming the vanguard nation of the world, Emerson insisted, and this responsibility demanded the fostering of a class of poets and literary prophets commensurate with US political and economic power, and dedicated to the rising glory of democratic individualism.

Emerson's second great public address of the 1830s, delivered before the graduating class of Harvard Divinity School, marked the key turning point in Emerson's career. Just as 'American Scholar' proved to be the nation's declaration of intellectual independence, so Emerson's 1838 Harvard 'Divinity School Address' was its religious analogue. Having resigned from his prestigious pastorship in Boston in 1832, Emerson essentially quit Unitarianism and disavowed formal religion altogether in 1838. The Address accused the Unitarians of engendering the 'famine of our churches' that had left 'the worshipper defrauded and disconsolate'. The ministers of the Unitarian church, Emerson lamented, 'accept another man's consciousness for their own, & are in the state of a son who should always suck at his mother's teat'.

Like most organized, institutionalized religious sects, Unitarianism, Emerson loudly proclaimed, 'was founded on nothing & led to nothing'.

The address on the 'evil of the church now manifest' represented the great turning point in Emerson's professional life, thrusting the aspiring intellectual into the role of chief critic of the Unitarian elite of eastern Massachusetts into which he had been born and who earlier in the decade he had seemed destined to join. The address in Divinity Hall proved to be nothing less than an American intellectual parricide in which Emerson urged the Harvard Divinity graduates to follow him by following their own inner path towards enlightenment and spiritual truth. Forsake the past for the present, he declared; 'show us that God is, not was; that he speaketh, not spake'. Typically Emersonian in its measured radicalism, this call to look within for meaning, for hope, for God resonated in 'The American Scholar', in his first book, *Nature* (1836), and would in his subsequent works. 'Let me admonish you, first of all,' he urged, 'to go alone.'

Numerous critics have noted that Emerson's particular brand of radicalism, as expressed in *Nature*, 'The American Scholar', the 'Divinity School Address' and later in abolitionist speeches and lyceum lectures, hardly deserves to be called radical at all. As accurate as this criticism seems, it misses the point. Emerson did not advocate the overthrow of capitalism any more than he described humans as 'Homo faber'. For Emerson-the-idealist and author of the essay 'Man Thinking', which articulates a sociology utterly antithetical to Marxian materialism, economics was a decidedly secondary consideration. His was a radicalism of individuality, or as he stated it, of the 'spiritual primacy and inviolable sanctity of the self'. A bourgeois radical, Emerson insisted that the only revolution that mattered was internal. '*Intra te quaere Deum,*' Emerson insisted: 'seek God within.' The renowned Boston doctor and poet Oliver Wendell Holmes perfectly observed how Emerson 'outflanked the extreme left of liberalism'; yet was 'so calm and serene that his radicalism had the accents of the gospel of peace'.

Born in Boston, a graduate of Harvard and a Unitarian preacher by his mid-twenties, Emerson was the consummate insider who revolted against his social and intellectual inheritance. That he utterly eschewed wanton destruction and carefully, publicly explained his disenchantment with his brahman elitist heritage seemed to add immeasurably to his impact in his own day and the continued relevance of his message in ours. This 'iconoclast without a hammer', as Holmes suggested, readily confessed that he had no positive doctrine; he could never endorse socialism, Fourierism, phalanxes or any of the other procrustean solutions bandied about in the era of Romantic reform. Every person had to find their own exalted ends, which were always broadly ethical. Emerson followed Socrates who in the *Republic* reminds his interlocutors that the genuine teacher can lead only so far, that the student had to go the final steps alone. Seeking the good is a solitary quest.

Emerson rejected his elite brahman heritage and abandoned his 'predestined' path into the Unitarian ministry in the name of US democracy. Just as his parents, parishioners, teachers and erstwhile colleagues abhorred and decried the nation's democratic turn in the age of Jackson, so Emerson embraced the nation's middle classes and their elemental creative powers. The US nation was profoundly flawed, its politics shameful, its materialism poisonous and its jingoism destructive, but its multitudes represented for Emerson, as for Lincoln, 'the last, best hope of mankind'. In its theoretical celebration of the common man, as seen in its procedural politics, its freedom and its *laissez-faire* vitality, democracy inculcated in everyone an elemental self-respect that was, Emerson believed, the sole reliable source of a virtuous society. US free institutions and procedural democracy provided the best environment for the incremental development and exercise of the individual moral faculty of the common person. Emerson joined ALEXIS DE TOCQUEVILLE in seeing democracy for what it was, warts and all, but also in understanding that the US republic represented the future. Ever the optimist, Emerson sought to devote himself to his nation's democratic future.

Emerson sought to become a prophet to the US people, simultaneously a celebrant of their greatness and an exhorter to do better, to self-reliance and self-improvement. As a lecturer, during his annual treks across much of the nation, twenty-three states and Canada in all, and of 'rough riding' and of taking 'the last & worst bed in the tavern' Emerson put himself and his talents to national use. 'On the highway,' where John Dewey insisted 'all truth lies,' Emerson rescued himself from a Boston-bred ennui by ferreting out a *métier* – no matter how unsuited to his talents and natural inclinations – that enabled him to achieve the relevance he craved and had failed to find 'in the dead pond which our church is'. As a public lecturer heard by thousands upon thousands of Americans Emerson empowered his genius. He earned his living observing the salubrious development of the nation and exhorting his fellow Americans to put the same energy into their intellectual, cultural and moral development that they put into seeking the best chance. This was Emerson's greatness. Well-born, highly educated and brilliant, Emerson rejected the anti-democratic sour grapes of his region and social class to create a novel vocation, the democratic intellectual he called for in his 'American Scholar' address in 1837 and in the ensuing decades. As a poet-prophet-exhorter to the people, Emerson simultaneously established himself as one of the nation's greatest public servants and created an enduring archetype of the US democratic intellectual. Emerson would surely have agreed with the architect Louis Sullivan, when he declared that 'in a democracy there can be but one test of citizenship, namely: Are you using such gifts, such powers as you possess . . . for or against the people?'

Reference

Whicher, Stephen E. (1953) *Freedom and Fate: An Inner Life of Ralph Waldo Emerson*, Philadelphia: University of Pennsylvania Press.

Further reading

Allen, Gay Wilson (1981) *Waldo Emerson: A Biography*, New York: Viking.

Cabot, James Eliot (1887) *A Memoir of Ralph Waldo Emerson*, Boston: Houghton Mifflin.

Field, Peter S. (2002) *Ralph Waldo Emerson: The Making of a Democratic Intellectual*, Lanham: Rowman & Littlefield.

Gougeon, Len (1990) *Virtue's Hero: Emerson, Antislavery, and Reform*, Athens: University of Georgia Press.

Kateb, George (1995) *Emerson and Self-Reliance*, Thousand Oaks, CA: Sage.

McAleer, John (1984) *Ralph Waldo Emerson: Days of Encounter*, Boston: Little, Brown & Co.

Porte, Joel and Morris, Saundra (eds) (1999) *The Cambridge Companion to Ralph Waldo Emerson*, New York: Cambridge University Press.

Richardson, Robert (1995) *Emerson: The Mind on Fire*, Berkeley: University of California.

PETER FIELD

ENFANTIN, BARTHÉLEMY-PROSPER (1796–1864)

Barthélemy-Prosper Enfantin was the charismatic leading figure in the Saint-Simonian movement and also played a major part in destroying it.

Enfantin was one of the founders of the movement and joint editor with Olinde Rodriguès of its first journal. He wrote articles suggesting how to equalize wealth, including a proposal for death duties. Enfantin soon challenged the democracy of Saint-Simonianism and turned it into a fanatically hierarchical mystical religious sect. He seems to have had a compelling and attractive confidence that he held the secret of how to achieve their objectives of liberating women and workers. During 1831 he became increasingly autocratic and dismissed middle-class women leaders.

In November 1831 at an acrimonious assembly he announced that their immediate strategy was to find the one special woman who would unlock the secret of how their 'church' should develop. She was to occupy the vacant throne for the new female 'pope', next to him, the self-declared male pope. Enfantin introduced the notion of 'progressive' or experimental marriage. This shocked some of the original membership, which had consisted of middle-class couples. Enfantin argued that it was women's passions or flesh, rather than their low wages, that prevented their liberation. Contemporary society was fragmented because the power of love was not realized. Women were the emotional heart of the basic social unit, the male–female couple. Christianity was at fault in demanding that people deny their sensual selves. Love should not be constrained by the rules of conventional marriage. Temporary unions should replace monogamous marriage.

The vast majority left the movement. Enfantin's doctrine looked suspiciously like a rationalization of his own sex life with Adèle Morlane, mother of his son, whom he never married because, although he liked to be adored, the more someone loved him, the more distant he became. Enfantin exerted an almost hypnotic influence over women similar to that of Mesmer, who, in his violet robes, had charmed numerous wealthy Parisian ladies before the French Revolution.

Enfantin tried to organize the rump of his church. The remaining disciples were obliged to adopt a uniform of red waistcoat, white trousers and blue jacket, complete with beret. The jacket buttoned at the back, to emphasize human interdependence. Enfantin's shirt was marked 'Father' and he toyed with the idea of wearing violet. An all-male retreat was held at Enfantin's home, Ménilmontant, where the men peeled potatoes and washed their uniforms. Wealthy reformers began to prefer more practical causes. The government banned their public meetings, which had brought converts and money. Enfantin and Michel Chevalier were accused of corrupting public morality and embezzlement, and were sentenced to a year's imprisonment.

A few remaining members sailed away to seek the missing female half of the papal duo in the 'Orient' and eventually Enfantin joined them. He resumed his career as an engineer, working on plans for the colonization of Algeria (1843) and for a canal through the isthmus of Suez (1845). He helped to secure the route and concession for the Paris–Lyon railway. An embarrassing anachronism of Romanticism, he continued to believe that he held the secret of a sort of holy grail and corresponded with a few former supporters.

Further reading

Pilbeam P. (2000) *French Socialists before Marx: Women, Workers and the Social Question in France*, Teddington: Acumen.

SEE ALSO: Deroin, Jeanne; early socialism; Fourier, Charles; Saint-Simon, Henri de

PAMELA PILBEAM

F

FAWCETT, MILLICENT GARRETT (1847–1929)

Millicent Garrett was born in June 1847 into a wealthy business family with strong liberal connections. She grew up in a feminist milieu, though Millicent's own formal education ended at the age of 15. In 1867 she married Henry Fawcett, the blind Professor of Economics at Cambridge, Liberal MP for Brighton and one of the leading parliamentary spokesmen for women's suffrage. It was a cause with which Millicent Garrett Fawcett was also associated, especially in her role as President of the National Suffrage Societies between 1897 and 1918.

Both before and after her husband's death in 1884, she was also involved in a variety of other reforming and political movements. These include issues of women's employment (where, in the light of the experience of the First World War, she modified her earlier position on the role of the market in setting wages for women's work, in favour of equal pay for equal work), their access to higher education and the campaign to secure for married women the legal right to their own property. She was the author of numerous articles, of texts in political economy published in the 1870s and of a volume of reminiscences in 1924. She was made a DBE in 1925 and died in London in August 1929.

It is for her leadership of the constitutional section of the women's suffrage movement that she is best remembered. She became a member of the first women's suffrage committee in 1867 and made her first public speech on the subject the following year. For Fawcett, women's suffrage was an important precondition for other reforms and improvements in the status of women in an almost exclusively masculine state. These were the broad tenets of the suffragists: those who sought to achieve votes for women on the same terms as men by means of rational argument conducted through speeches and pamphlets, and pressure on politicians by petitions. Such constitutional and legal methods set the National Union of Women's Suffrage Societies apart from the Women's Social and Political Union founded in 1903 by Mrs Pankhurst and her daughter, whose members, known as suffragettes, engaged in more sensational and violent action, especially against property.

Both organizations suspended their campaigning on the outbreak of the First World War, but Millicent Fawcett was a prominent lobbyist when in 1916 a conference was called by the Speaker of the House of Commons to examine a variety of issues concerning the parliamentary franchise. The subsequent legislation – the Representation of the People Act 1918 – extended the vote to women over 30 with a basic property qualification. Ten years later, and only one year before her death, Millicent Fawcett was in the gallery of the House of Lords to witness the final reading of the Equal Franchise Bill, which finally made male and female voters equal before the law at a uniform age of 21.

Further reading

Fawcett, Millicent Garrett (1924) *What I Remember*, London: T Fisher Unwin.
Rubinstein, David (1991) *A Different World for Women: The Life of Millicent Garrett Fawcett*, Brighton: Harvester Wheatsheaf.

SEE ALSO: feminism and the female franchise movement

DAVID GLADSTONE

FEMINISM AND THE FEMALE FRANCHISE MOVEMENT

The longstanding *querelle des femmes* of Western literature and philosophy became a significant political issue in the nineteenth century, engaging the thought and action of women in the USA, Great Britain, Europe and their colonies. Ushered in by the political revolutions of the final quarter of the eighteenth century, women's rights movements culminated in women gaining the right to vote in many parts of the world by the mid-twentieth century.

These movements drew on multiple traditions in political thought, and justifications for claiming women's rights changed with shifting intellectual, ideological and political contexts. Women claimed rights ranging from the franchise to economic and personal autonomy, including a woman's right to control her body. The grounds for these claims ranged from natural-rights arguments rooted in republican ideology, to egalitarianism derived from socialism, to assertions of women's moral superiority founded on evangelical notions of separate spheres. Women often claimed rights based on their equality with men and just as often based on their differences from them.

The diverse interests of women contributed to the variety of issues that movements for women's rights took up throughout the nineteenth century. By mid-century movements that addressed questions of women's citizenship and political rights frequently focused on related issues that were of concern primarily to white women of the emerging middle classes: efforts to expand women's educational opportunities, campaigns to secure married women's property rights, attempts to open the professions to women, and debates about marriage, divorce and sexuality. Many advocates of women's rights began their political activism in the anti-slavery and labour movements, but early women's rights movements frequently failed to attend to concerns of women of colour or to those of poor or working-class women: equal opportunities and fair treatment for free black women, subsistence and fair wages for poor and working women, tribal sovereignty and self-determination for indigenous women. Even movements for black rights and socialist and trade union movements failed to support fully the rights of women of colour or working-class women. In

fact, by the end of the nineteenth century, movements for women's suffrage focused as much on efforts at class and racial exclusions to voting as on middle-class and elite women's efforts to gain the franchise. The winning of suffrage in the twentieth century left much unfinished business and many inequities, which feminists continue to address.

Revolutions, citizenship and sexual difference

Much of the inspiration for the women's rights movements of the nineteenth century lay in the political ideologies that influenced the American and French Revolutions. In British North America, colonists employed Lockean notions about consent of the governed and Rousseauian concepts of natural rights and republicanism to justify resistance to reinvigorated imperial rule between 1763 and 1783. These ideas and the disruptive effects of resistance and revolution shaped the actions of large portions of the general population. People of colour found inspiration in the rhetoric of liberty, and those who were enslaved took advantage of numerous opportunities created by wartime disorder, including aiding both the British and American forces, to free themselves. Some middling and elite white women remained loyal to British rule; others took up the cause of resistance and revolution. In neither case did women necessarily follow the lead of the men of their families. Many white women formed sewing circles to aid the war effort; others took action based on their roles as consumers. Poor and working women, concerned about the effects of wartime hoarding, set off food riots. A group of elite women in Edenton, North Carolina, issued a statement of support for the non-importation agreements in 1775. A similar group of elite women in Philadelphia collected the money they saved by limiting their consumption of luxury goods and used it to benefit George Washington's army in 1780.

Abigail Adams echoed women's public activism in her now well-known private letter to her husband John Adams. Writing to him while he was serving in the Continental Congress in 1776, she urged him and his colleagues to 'remember the ladies' as they made laws for their new nation. Abigail Adams considered the guarantees of life, liberty and pursuit of happiness mentioned in the Declaration of Independence to be as much her rights as her husband's, but John Adams did not take her admonition seriously. Nor did subsequent legislators; neither the 1783 Articles of Confederation nor the 1787 Constitution addressed the question of women's rights in the new nation.

Like their sisters in the USA, women who participated in the French Revolution considered liberty, equality and fraternity to be as much their rights as those of men. Working-class women marched on Versailles to bring the king to Paris in 1789, and they instigated bread riots in the city. The Society of Revolutionary Republican Women (1793), the first group to organize for women's rights, saw themselves both as consumers responsible for feeding their families and as citizens equal to men in their capacity to bear arms. They demanded price controls and argued for women's right to carry arms in defence of their country.

Other advocates of women's rights in France saw the Revolution as an opportunity to remake entirely notions of equity, justice and citizenship. They sought to equalize the status of women and men, both by instituting political equality and by changing policies regarding education, marriage and sexuality. The Marquis de Condorcet, one of the only men to speak in favour of women's rights, called for full suffrage; he also advocated women's education and sought to legalize birth control and homosexuality. Etta Palm d'Aelders, a Dutch woman who participated in the French Revolution, called first on the Estates General and later on the Assembly to include women in the political life of the nation. She also campaigned especially for divorce laws. Both Condorcet and d'Aelders saw contemporary ideas about marriage and sexuality as detrimental to women and in need of change.

This opinion of marriage and sexuality was shared by one of the best known of the women's rights activists of the French Revolution, Olympe de Gouges. A self-made woman of letters, de Gouges explicitly opposed the identification of the rights of citizenship with masculinity. Seeking equal citizenship rights for women, she adapted revolutionary rhetoric to make the argument for women's rights. De Gouges rewrote the seventeen articles of the *Declaration of the Rights of Man and Citizen* (1789) in her *Declaration of the Rights of Woman and the Female Citizen* (1791), replacing the word 'man' with the words 'woman and man' and pointing out the significance of certain rights

for women. Freedom of speech, for example, would aid women's sexual autonomy and enable them to demand support from the fathers of their children, eliminating the shame of illegitimacy and giving women leverage in non-marital sexual relationships. De Gouges also proposed replacing marriage with a simple and easily dissolvable civil contract, a model for which she appended to her declaration.

When the Jacobins took control of the French government, women's participation in politics came under attack, and de Gouges found herself in direct conflict with revolutionary gender ideology. The Jacobins saw women's value to the Republic in their nurturing abilities as mothers, and Jacobin emphasis on femininity as motherhood precluded any public role for women. For the crime of trying to assume a masculine political role, Olympe de Gouges was guillotined in 1793.

Most women avoided such fatal rejection of their political activism in the revolutionary era, and, in fact, some saw significant changes. In Massachusetts, a woman and man known as 'Bett' and 'Brom' used the concept of natural rights to sue for their freedom. Their suit brought an end to slavery in that state in 1781. Some women had limited voting rights by the beginning of the nineteenth century. In New Jersey, for example, tax-paying determined voting rights, and legislation affirmed inclusion of women voters in 1790. In France, marriage became a civil contract in 1791, and divorce became legal in 1792.

Most gains, however, were soon lost. Though several states followed Massachusetts in abolishing slavery, federal laws in the USA continued to sanction the institution until the Civil War in the 1860s. In France, the Napoleonic Code rolled back revolutionary reforms regarding marriage and divorce in 1804. And New Jersey legislators revoked women's suffrage in 1807.

In fact, by the beginning of the nineteenth century, married white women in both the USA and France held only an indirect relationship to the state. The roots of their condition lay partly in republican political theory and partly in their legal status, both of which defined women as dependants in republics that valued the autonomy of the individual citizen. As described in such works as Jean-Jacques Rousseau's *Émile* (1762), the abstract individualism of the republican citizen required reason, virtue and independence, all of which were based on sexual difference. Reason was a masculine trait. Since Rousseau's Sophie could not use reason to control her passions, she lacked the capacity for republican virtue, and therefore for full citizenship. Even Emile's virtue could be ensured only through a stable home life grounded in marriage and family. And, finally, republican virtue also required economic independence so that the citizen could set aside his own self-interest and use his vote in the interest of the common good. Rousseau thus defined the individual (male) citizen in relationship to others – the women, children and other dependants of his family and household. Those others failed to meet the criteria for citizenship at least in part because the (male) citizen's virtue was predicated on both his difference from them and their dependence on him.

Mary Wollstonecraft famously took issue with Rousseau's attitude towards women in her influential *Vindication of the Rights of Woman* (1792). Addressing Rousseau's notion that women were not equipped to function as republican citizens, Wollstonecraft maintained that any deficiencies women exhibited were the result of poor education and lack of opportunity rather than innate capacity. If women were vain and self-serving as Rousseau claimed, Wollstonecraft argued, it was because a society controlled by men had limited them to subordinate roles. This male-dominated society had taught women that feminine behaviour was their only route to power or influence. To rectify this situation, Wollstonecraft urged, women should be recognized as 'reasonable creatures' and taught to think for themselves. Provided with educations equal to that of men, women could become as good citizens as men.

Wollstonecraft's critique of Rousseau addressed only part of the problem that political ideology posed for women at the end of the revolutionary period; seeing women as reasonable creatures did not necessarily change their dependence on men, an element of both republican ideology and French and US legal systems. These legal systems limited married women's economic and personal autonomy by defining them as dependants. The Napoleonic Code established women's legal status in France and its colonies, and English Common Law remained part of the legal system in the USA long after the American Revolution. English jurist William Blackstone described women's legal status under the Common Law when he explained coverture in his *Commentaries* (1765). Women gave up certain rights when they married, losing their legal

identity because husband and wife were seen as one person – the husband – at law. That is, a woman's legal identity was covered by that of her husband during the term of the marriage. Since most women were married at some point in their lives, at any one time the great majority of women in the USA and Great Britain had no independent identity at law, leaving them unable to make contracts, to sue or be sued, or to own property in their own name. They were, in a manner of speaking, legally dead. Similarly, the Napoleonic Code denied married women's property rights. It also eliminated divorce and modified adultery laws. Coupled with republican ideology, these legal systems ensured that only certain self-supporting, property-owning, white men could meet the criteria for full citizenship – including the franchise – in France and the USA.

Thus defined out of the category of republican citizenship, women were to adopt the position of republican womanhood in its stead. This indirect relationship to the state made them responsible for its continuation by maintaining its moral integrity. The ideal republican woman was modest and well educated. She was to remind her husband to focus on the common good rather than on self-interest, and she was to train her sons to be virtuous republican citizens. She was not to take any active political role.

One positive result of the ideal of republican womanhood lay in new opportunities for education. Condorcet in France, Wollstonecraft in Britain and Judith Sargent Murray in the USA: all advocated improving women's education. And in the USA, for example, numerous academies were established for the education of girls and young women at the turn of the century. The curricula at these academies went well beyond the music, art and languages of earlier finishing schools, teaching girls of the middling classes such academic subjects as mathematics and history, which had previously been reserved for boys. Girls, however, still lacked the opportunity to prepare for the professions by learning Latin and Greek. The goal of education for women lay primarily in enhancing their domestic role, making them good spouses and mothers for men and boys, who were the true citizens of the republic.

Socialism, labour, evangelical reform and public speaking

In socialism women could find a promise of equal treatment unavailable in republican womanhood.

CHARLES FOURIER decried the revolutionaries in France for failing to carry new divorce laws to the logical conclusion of eliminating marriage altogether, and he is often noted for having declared in *Theory of the Four Movements* (1808) that one could determine a society's level of progress by looking to the condition of its women. His plan to treat all members of his phalanxes as individuals promised women economic autonomy denied them under either the Napoleonic Code or the Common Law. Fourier shared his disdain for marriage with ROBERT OWEN; both saw it as a system in which women prostituted themselves, exchanging sex for financial support. In Owen's New Moral World, as in Fourier's Harmony, co-operative housekeeping would free women from the drudgery of housework, and communal nurseries would assume the burdens of childcare. Women could choose for themselves the work they found most fulfilling. Similarly, the Saint-Simonians encouraged recognition and cultivation of the talents of individuals, including women in their movement's leadership hierarchies.

Women joined enthusiastically in the Owenite, Fourierist and Saint-Simonian movements, engaging in propaganda, lecturing, communities, co-operatives and trade unions. And in many instances, these activities brought them face to face with the limits of socialist egalitarianism. In Owenite and Fourierist communities, women often found their workloads increased rather than decreased, as they replaced caring for the needs of their families with seeing to the needs of their entire communities. Sexual divisions entered the Saint-Simonian movement when Prosper Enfantin ascended as its leader in 1831. Under Enfantin, Saint-Simonian ideas about women's rights narrowed to sexual liberation and notions that men should be responsible for women's emancipation.

All three socialist movements suffered from gender assumptions they shared with the dominant cultures they sought to replace. The individualism at the core of Owen's and Fourier's theories shared with Rousseauian republicanism an underlying masculine ideal of the individual. In contrast, the Saint-Simonians saw the individual as a dual being with masculine and feminine halves, epitomized by the heterosexual couple. They therefore endorsed complementarity between women and men, but notions of gender difference inherent in such complementarity led them back to a paternalism that alienated many women from their movement.

Women's participation in socialist movements coincided with expansion of their opportunities for economic autonomy. By the second quarter of the nineteenth century, economic changes were creating new employment opportunities for white women of the emerging working and middle classes. Factory labour or needlework offered alternatives to domestic service for working-class women, and teaching became the first profession open to middle-class women. Such opportunities ran counter to prevailing notions of women's dependence on men and to definitions of masculinity that were founded on such notion. Cultural anxieties – among the emerging middle class about the amoral nature of a market-place in which self-interest was necessary for success, among the emerging working class about men's status as providers and heads of household, and among free people of colour about men's authority in the face of racial discrimination – led to distinctive, class- and race-inflected gender ideologies that defined women's place as in the home.

White working men's dilemma provides perhaps the best-known example. At the same time that demand for cheap labour increased women's employment opportunities, entrepreneurialism threatened the status of skilled working men, who sought to hold onto their artisan identity and craft privileges by opposing women's employment.

Working men argued that women's wage labour drove down their own wages, making it impossible for them to support their families. Such arguments ignored the fact that, in most industries, women and men already worked in a gender-segregated labour market. Tailoring was one of the only trades in which women's cheapened labour threatened men's employment. Men continued to dominate in construction and mechanical trades for the next 150 years. Nevertheless in both Britain and the USA, trade unions promoted a new working-class domestic ideal associated with a so-called family wage, which would enable male breadwinners to become their families' sole support. In their efforts to promote the interests of working men as heads of household, trade unionists presumed that all women lived in male-headed households, and new working-class gender ideologies thereby overlooked the situations of female heads of household, widows and single women. Similarly, middle-class domestic ideals belied families' reliance on the paid labour of women to fund education that would ensure sons' upward mobility and white-collar careers. Free black women encountered even more complex pressures, as the stability of their incomes made them primary wage earners in many male-headed households and their communities often expected their so-called feminine behaviour to counter the racial assumptions of the white majority.

In the USA, tensions were also mounting over the question of women's right to speak in public before mixed or 'promiscuous' audiences of women and men in the second quarter of the nineteenth century. Women had spoken in religious settings, especially in prayer groups and Quaker meetings for at least the past 200 years. The first to do so outside of religious contexts was Scottish Owenite and freethinker Frances Wright. After the collapse of Nashoba, her Owenite community in Tennessee, Wright moved to New York City, where she worked with Robert Dale Owen to promote workers' rights and free thought. Wright's outspoken advocacy of anti-slavery, free thought and marriage reform turned her name into a metaphor for the impropriety of women's public speaking by the end of the 1820s.

Similar criticism descended on Maria Stewart when she tried to inspire the women and men of her free black community in Boston in the early 1830s. Stewart, the first US-born woman to speak before mixed audiences of women and men, was also a friend of David Walker, militant advocate of racial justice and author of *David Walker's Appeal . . . to the Coloured Citizens of the World* (1829). After Walker's untimely death, Stewart felt a religious calling to continue his work. She encountered sympathetic audiences when she spoke of the injustices and limited opportunities faced by free black women. When, however, Stewart echoed Walker's *Appeal* and called on black men to act as men and defend their rights and those of black women, she violated the standards of her community. Her audacity in publicly impugning the masculinity of black men resulted in such harsh denunciations that Stewart gave up public speaking in 1833, less than two years after she had begun.

Concerns about women's economic independence, their public speaking and the notion of women's rights in general also came into open conflict with emerging gender ideologies when textile workers went on strike in Lowell, Massachusetts, in the mid-1830s. As they struggled to define their position, the strikers saw themselves less as dependent women than as part of the republican tradition of independent workers. They referred to themselves as 'daughters of freemen', invoking the memory of the American Revolution and claiming equality with mill owners and managers. In their references to freemen, they also invoked the working man's claim to property in his labour, implying that mill owners and managers threatened their competency, the means of support on which freemen based their voting rights. Thus, far from seeing themselves as dependent members of male-headed households, the striking mill workers made their claims in their own right, as self-supporting workers. But local newspaper editors saw them differently, as women stepping out of their place. The editors compared the mill operatives to Mary Wollstonecraft, recalling not only her work as the author of *A Vindication of the Rights of Woman* but also her embrace of sexual freedom, including the fact that she had borne a child outside of marriage. The editors thus not only suggested that the mill workers advocated inappropriately radical ideas about women's rights, but they also impugned the operatives' sexual respectability. The latter became an increasingly common tactic used against women who dared to enter the public sphere.

Anti-egalitarianism was as evident in political reforms as in the class- and race-based gender ideologies encountered by Wright, Stewart and the Lowell strikers. Neither the July Revolution in France nor the English Reform Bill of 1832 extended the franchise to women. In the USA, political reforms resulted in the extension of the franchise to most white men and the elimination of most property qualifications for voting. At the same time, most free black men lost the franchise, and women of all classes and races went unmentioned. And the aims of the Chartist movement in England tended more to emphasize the interests of male heads of household than to engage with questions of women's rights.

Along with the experiences of socialists, working women and women who spoke in public, another strong source of both separate-spheres ideology and claims for women's rights lay in evangelical religion and reform. Whereas certain biblical interpretations led ministers to promote subordinate roles for women in their churches and families, evangelicalism also emphasized the duty of the individual believer to lead others to salvation. And in combination with women's longstanding responsibility for such benevolent activity as sewing societies, orphan asylums and relief for indigent women, evangelical teachings ushered many white women of the emerging middle class into intensified efforts on behalf of their society's most downtrodden.

Such evangelical ideas led some anti-slavery activists to conclude that the only moral course lay beyond gradualism, in the immediate abolition of slavery. British anti-slavery advocate Elizabeth Heyrick introduced this concept in *Immediate, not Gradual Abolition* (1824), and US editor William Lloyd Garrison took it up when he began to publish his *Liberator* in 1831. In her *Appeal in Favor of that Class of Americans Called Africans* (1833), US author Lydia Maria Child presented a comprehensive picture of US laws on slavery, discussing emancipation movements in the rest of the Western hemisphere, and noting the complicity of northern capital in the southern institution. Child also wrote of the sexual exploitation faced by enslaved women, touching on a subject that respectable white women were not to discuss, according to middle-class gender ideals. Her colleague, Maria Weston Chapman, argued in the *Liberator* that women had a special obligation to support the anti-slavery cause. White women did join the cause in large numbers, gathering signatures on petitions to Congress and raising money for lecturers through anti-slavery fairs.

Compassion for women suffering sexual exploitation also contributed to the movement for moral reform, in which white evangelical women sought to mobilize their alleged moral superiority to attack the double standard of sexual morality, hoping to eliminate both prostitution and the demand for it. Employing only women as agents and staff, Magdalene societies focused on the sexual vulnerability of young white women who left their fathers' homes to earn their living in mill towns and growing cities. Numerous local moral reform societies spread throughout the northeastern USA in the 1830s, located in urban and rural communities that found themselves most affected by economic change. Agents of the societies visited brothels to reform prostitutes and to collect the names of patrons, which they then threatened to publish in such periodicals as the *Advocate of Moral Reform*. The moral reform movement attacked masculine immorality with unprecedented militancy, but the movement faded after the early 1840s, as clergymen urged moral reformers to refocus their efforts on moral education within the home.

But the clergy could not control all of the women who used religious arguments to defend their public activism. When Sarah and Angelina Grimke,

members of a slaveholding family from South Carolina and converts to the Society of Friends, toured New England communities as agents of the American Anti-Slavery Society in 1837, Congregational ministers responded by issuing a pastoral letter in which they warned against women who forgot their place. The ministers declared that women's power lay in their dependence and that they should restrict themselves to praying and running Sabbath schools. Further, the ministers denounced women who presumed to present themselves as lecturers or teachers and who spoke about such sexually suggestive material as the particular burdens of enslaved women. Sarah Grimke, who had proven her theological prowess in her *Letters on the Equality of the Sexes and the Condition of Women* (1837), responded that women should look only to God when they undertook public reforms and concern themselves only with whether they did His will. Grimke's view was grounded in beliefs regarding women's ministry within the Society of Friends. She believed that women were responsible for their own actions, and she did not think they were required to heed the chiding of ministers who sought to impose restrictions on their discharge of their moral obligations.

Women's rights at mid-century: an international movements

The origins of the first international movement for women's rights lay in the British Owenite and French Saint-Simonian movements of the 1820s and in the US and British anti-slavery movements of the 1830s. Irish socialist Anna Wheeler provided important links between radicals in Ireland, Owenites in England and Saint-Simonians and Fourierists in France. She worked with Irish radical William Thompson to compose their *Appeal of One Half the Human Race, Women, Against the Pretensions of the Other Half, Men, to Retain them in Political and Thence in Civil and Domestic Slavery* (1825). Responding to JAMES MILL's argument against the enfranchisement of women, Thompson and Wheeler pointed out the considerable conflicts between the interests of women and the husbands and fathers who supposedly represented them. They also decried marriage as an unjust institution that enslaved women. Wheeler went on to publish numerous pieces in the Owenite press.

Anna Wheeler also recognized the importance of alliances among women *as* women. In 1829, she called for a women's movement, and, in 1833, a group of women in London joined together in a cross-class alliance that they called the Practical Moral Union of Women of Great Britain and Ireland. When a group of Saint-Simonians styled themselves the 'New Women' and began to publish their own newspaper, the *Free Woman*, Wheeler translated their work for English audiences. The New Women assumed a critical attitude towards the Saint-Simonian movement and its presumption that women needed to be saved by men, eventually shifting away from Saint-Simonism and renaming their newspaper the *Women's Tribune*.

Women from the USA entered the international network of women's rights advocates through the anti-slavery movement in the 1840s. After the debates over the Grimke sisters' lecture tour, the question of women's proper role continued to be an issue in the anti-slavery movement both domestically and internationally. When Abby Kelley became a member of the business committee of the American Anti-Slavery Society in 1840, many abolitionists walked out in protest, concerned that the issue of women's public activism would divert the movement from its primary cause, the abolition of slavery. These dissidents formed their own organization, the American and Foreign Anti-Slavery Society, splitting the movement in the USA. The woman question also led to disputes at the World Anti-Slavery Convention in London later that same year. Organized by the British and Foreign Anti-Slavery Society, which itself excluded women from leadership positions, the convention seated women delegates in a separate ladies' gallery rather than on the floor of the convention.

The World Anti-Slavery Convention brought women from the USA into contact with women who were part of the developing international women's rights movement in Europe. US Quaker and Philadelphia anti-slavery activist Lucretia Mott met British Quaker and abolitionist Anne Knight, and Knight corresponded with the Grimke sisters about the events in London. Mott also met fellow US and future women's rights leader Elizabeth Cady Stanton at the convention, and Stanton met members of the Bright and Priestman families, British Quakers and abolitionists whom she would visit on her return to England in the 1880s. In 1840, Stanton was in London on her honeymoon, having married abolitionist lecturer

and politician Henry B. Stanton, who was a delegate to the World Anti-Slavery Convention. Sitting together in the ladies' gallery, Lucretia Mott and Elizabeth Cady Stanton agreed that women needed a movement in defence of their own rights.

It would be eight years before Mott and Stanton met again and acted on their resolve, and in the mean time Transcendentalist Margaret Fuller developed an argument for women's rights that addressed the economic dependence and lack of opportunities women suffered under the political ideals and legal systems that prevailed in the USA, Britain, France and elsewhere. In *Woman in the Nineteenth Century* (1845), Fuller argued for women's opportunity to develop their full human potential, seeking for women a version of the self-reliance promoted by her fellow Transcendentalist, RALPH WALDO EMERSON. Fuller found support for her ideas in the Romantic literature of Goethe, the religious thought of Swedish mystic Emmanuel Swedenborg and the economic theories of Charles Fourier. She concluded that women could only achieve their full potential if they were economically autonomous, if they had the freedom to discover their own interests, if they had the opportunity to pursue whatever occupations suited them. Fuller's essay influenced the issues discussed at the first women's rights convention, held in Seneca Falls, New York, in 1848. Fuller did not attend the convention herself, but she did take advantage of international networks to meet socialists and revolutionaries when she travelled in Europe as a correspondent for the New York *Tribune*, and she stayed in Rome when the Italian Revolution began.

During the democratic revolutions that erupted in Europe in 1848, women participated as fully as they had in the French Revolution 60 years earlier. They marched in demonstrations, built and defended the barricades, died in the fighting. In Baden, such women as Amalie Struve and Mathilde Franziska Anneke rode beside their husbands in battle. In France, British abolitionist Anne Knight called for the elimination of all forms of privilege, including that based on sex, and she declared that only the full franchise would bring true social and political change. Pauline Roland, a former Saint-Simonian, tried to vote in municipal elections. Together the Society for the Emancipation of Women and the Committee for the Rights of Women called on the French government to bring about equality for women in all areas of life, including politics, work and the family. And in 1849, former Saint-Simonian JEANNE DEROIN ran for a seat in the Legislative Assembly, even though her action was unconstitutional.

When Lucretia Mott and Elizabeth Cady Stanton met again in Western New York in the summer of 1848, they once more discussed the need for an independent movement for women's rights. Mott, Stanton and several other women decided to send out a call for a women's rights convention, to be held on 19 and 20 July at the Wesleyan Chapel in Seneca Falls, New York. Only women were admitted on the first day; men were allowed to attend on the second. The convention drew about 300 participants, both women and men.

A Declaration of Sentiments drafted by Stanton and the organizing committee followed the format of a revolutionary document, the Declaration of Independence (1776). The Seneca Falls declaration replicated the original text's format: an introductory statement of principles followed by a list of grievances and a proposal for action. The first paragraph repeated that of the original word for word, changing only the phrase 'all men are created equal' to 'all men and women are created equal'. The new text replaced the original's grievances against the King with woman's grievances against man. He had usurped her citizenship rights, taxing her without allowing her to vote, and there was much more. He had prevented her training for and practice of the professions, kept her from the pulpit, limited her educational opportunities, restricted her property rights and denied her rights to divorce and to custody of her children. The convention voted on eleven resolutions based on these grievances, and ten were approved unanimously. Only the suffrage resolution encountered resistance, with Lucretia Mott warning that people would ridicule the convention for claiming the franchise for women. Even this resolution was eventually approved by a majority of those attending the convention.

A second local women's rights convention was held in Rochester, New York, two weeks later, and the first national women's rights convention assembled on 23 and 24 October 1850, in Worcester, Massachusetts. Local and national women's rights conventions continued to be held in the northeastern and midwestern USA throughout the 1850s, and the regularity of these events contributed to the strength of the international women's rights movement. News of the conventions in the USA spread to Europe, and women who had participated in the revolutions of 1848 claimed sisterhood with women's rights advocates in the USA.

Women in Europe could also look to Britain for inspiration in the 1850s. Harriet Taylor published her call for 'The Enfranchisement of Women' in the *Westminster Review* in 1851, and a group of women led by Barbara Leigh Smith (later Bodichon) lobbied Parliament for a married women's property bill in 1855. Smith also participated in the formation of the Association for the Promotion of the Employment of Women in 1857, and British women established their contribution to the international women's press in 1858. The *English Women's Journal* became the focus of an expanding network of British women campaigning for higher education, entry into the professions, married women's property rights and the vote.

In contrast to women in the USA and Great Britain, many European women encountered repression and censorship when their revolutionary governments collapsed. Jeanne Deroin and Pauline Roland, for example, sent a letter of solidarity to the women of the Worcester convention from a prison cell in Paris. As they combated official prohibitions on their political activities, German and French women relied on the international ties that they had developed over the preceding decades. Their network of support and information included numerous newspapers edited by women, and in these newspapers they could read reports of continuing women's rights activism throughout North America and Europe. Repressed at home, they could take comfort in the fact that their allies kept up the struggle for women's rights abroad.

NATIONAL MOVEMENTS

The international focus of women's rights movements faded after 1860, and activists concentrated on legal and political struggles at the national level. The British movement enjoyed the greatest degree of continuity, as the expansion of women's rights activism of the 1850s merged with the growth of political liberalism to create a broader base of support for women's suffrage in the 1860s and 1870s. The ability to campaign openly for the franchise was a privilege limited to women who lived in politically stable nations where they enjoyed relative freedom of speech. In France, developments in the 1860s paralleled those in Britain, but the Franco-Prussian war and its aftermath, including the Paris Commune and the subsequent establishment of the Third Republic, led to concerns about the stability of the state that overshadowed the movement for women's rights. In Germany, women's political activity was forbidden by law, and, in the USA, civil war interrupted the campaign for women's rights between 1861 and 1865. After the Civil War, many black women in the USA faced the threat of racial violence if they tried to speak out for their own rights or for those of the men of their communities.

In Britain, several distinct sets of political activists addressed the question of women's rights in the 1860s and 1870s. The Langham Place group, connected to Barbara Smith Bodichon and the *Women's Journal*, carried on the work that they had begun in London in the 1850s. The circle of intellectuals and politicians associated with JOHN STUART MILL constituted another London group. This group, which included Henry and Millicent Fawcett as well as Mill's stepdaughter Helen Taylor, advocated women's suffrage as a component of their progressive liberalism. Finally, provincial groups in major cities – Manchester, Edinburgh, Birmingham and Bristol – also advocated women's rights. These groups included such well-known figures as Lydia Becker, leader of the Manchester group, and such lesser-known but influential women as members of MP John Bright's family circle, including the women of the Priestman family of Newcastle. The latter linked these provincial groups to a radical Quaker tradition that dated to the Anti-Corn Law League and anti-slavery activism. All of these groups participated in developments that brought the issue of women's suffrage to national attention in the 1860s. The first London and Manchester suffrage societies were formed in 1866.

In Britain, taxpayers' rights made the most compelling argument for the franchise, since both the Reform Bills of 1832 and 1867 had expanded the franchise to various groups of property holders. Thus, British suffragists chose the strategy of gaining the franchise for single women ratepayers even though their approach left out the important question of suffrage for married women. They supported their claims in a variety of ways. Single-women ratepayers should be granted the franchise, Lydia

Becker argued, because women had voted in earlier periods in English history. Becker also claimed that the 1867 Reform Bill had used the word 'man' rather than 'male person' in expanding the franchise and therefore included women as part of the generic group 'man'. Neither claim brought success.

John Stuart Mill was an important but less than fully reliable ally in the British struggle for women's rights. He presented the first women's suffrage petition to Parliament in 1866, and he tried unsuccessfully to amend the 1867 Reform Bill to extend the franchise to women. In his *Subjection of Women* (1869) he pointed out the legal disadvantages of married women under English Common Law, comparing women's status under coverture to slavery. He argued in favour of equality between women and men within marriage and for women's freedom to choose their occupations and to control their property. Justice, he urged, required the extension of basic human rights to women. But Mill himself did not work well with strong-minded women and preferred to be in control of political alliances. When Manchester activists organized the first central, national suffrage committee in 1871, Mill and Helen Taylor blocked their London society from participation and split London suffragists in the process.

In the USA, suffragists split over the question of black rights. Links between the women's rights and anti-slavery movements had initially created a powerful group of allies for women's suffrage. Women's rights advocates demonstrated the strong bonds between the two movements when they suspended activism for their own cause during the Civil War in order to focus on supporting the Union. In 1863, Elizabeth Cady Stanton and Susan B. Anthony organized the National Women's Loyal League to conduct a petition drive in support of the Thirteenth Amendment to the US Constitution, which banned slavery.

When the war ended, Stanton and Anthony expected women to receive the franchise as a reward for their loyalty to the Union, but they were disappointed when their former political allies placed women's voting rights in false opposition to those of black men. For Stanton and Anthony, the Fourteenth and Fifteenth Amendments to the US Constitution represented the ultimate betrayal on this score. Guaranteeing the right to vote in federal elections for all male citizens over 21 years of age, the Fourteenth Amendment associated voting with sex for the first time and created the necessity for a constitutional amendment to enfranchise women. The Fifteenth Amendment failed to meet this need. It guaranteed the right of US citizens to vote regardless of 'race, color, or previous condition of servitude', but it failed to mention sex. Stanton and Anthony's opposition to the Fifteenth Amendment dominated the 1868 convention of the American Equal Rights Association (AERA), a universal suffrage organization that included former anti-slavery activists and women's rights advocates.

Making a decision that followed the logic of many previous women's rights advocates, Stanton and Anthony concluded that the only hope of success for women's suffrage lay in an independent movement devoted to that cause. In 1869, they used the AERA convention to recruit women to a separate meeting aimed at creating such a movement. They established an independent organization, the National Woman Suffrage Association (NWSA), to work for a constitutional amendment to enfranchise women. The rival American Woman Suffrage Association (AWSA) worked for women's voting rights at the local and state levels. Stanton and Anthony's actions and those of their former allies split the women's rights movement in the USA for the next 20 years.

The split did not deter women's rights activists. Several tried to claim the right to vote in the presidential election of 1872. Sojourner Truth in Michigan, Virginia Minor in Missouri and Susan B. Anthony in New York sought to test the premise that they had been granted the franchise under the 'privileges and immunities' clause of the Fourteenth Amendment. Anthony was arrested, tried and convicted for illegal voting. Since she refused to pay her fine, she could not take her case to the US Supreme Court and Minor sued the registrar of voters in St Louis for denying her one of the privileges and immunities of citizenship when he refused to allow her register to vote. In *Minor v. Happersett* (1875), the US Supreme Court affirmed women's citizenship but denied Minor's claim that voting was one of the privileges and immunities guaranteed to citizens in the Fourteenth Amendment. In fact, the Court found no connection between citizenship and voting for women.

Even in the wake of *Minor v. Happersett*, Susan B. Anthony continued to claim the franchise as a right of citizenship for women. In her 'Declaration of Rights for Women' (1876), Anthony called for impeachment of the federal government of the USA,

claiming multiple violations of women's rights, including denial of the right to trial by a jury of one's peers, unequal laws for women and men, and taxation without representation. Among the many offences for which Anthony indicted the US government were laws and practices that disadvantaged women and violated their rights to personal and economic autonomy. Such autonomy lay beyond the grasp of married women who sought divorce and custody of their children, of respectable working women who sought living wages and even of prostitutes, according to Anthony. These examples echoed her own experiences in defence of women's rights. She had hidden a runaway wife and her daughter from an adulterous husband in the 1850s, comparing her action to those of abolitionists who aided fugitive slaves. In the 1860s, she had formed a Workingwomen's Association in New York City and tried to establish a training programme for women printers. Along with Elizabeth Cady Stanton, she had defended Hester Vaughan, a British immigrant abandoned by her lover and accused of infanticide. And during an 1871 lecture tour in the western USA, Anthony had made explicit the connections she saw between women's subordinate status and the murder trial of Laura Fair, a prostitute accused of killing her lover. If men really protected women in the ways they claimed, Anthony had declared, such cases would never occur. Women's economic and personal autonomy were a matter of simple justice for Anthony. And only the franchise could guarantee that autonomy.

Reform feminism

Whereas Anthony held to a broad notion of individualism, equality and human rights as the foundation for her suffrage activism, in the final three decades of the century other women's rights advocates began to focus on issues that emphasized the differences between women and men. The reform feminism of this period emphasized women's supposed moral nature and led to many campaigns aimed at correcting or cleaning up mistakes allegedly made by men. Settlement houses, the peace movement and clean-government campaigns in cities were examples of such reform feminism, as were efforts to change sexual practices through the social purity movement's attempts to create laws to protect women from men.

The lectures that British activist Josephine Butler presented in response to the Contagious

Diseases Act of 1869 (CDA) offer one example of reform feminism and its concern with protecting women. The CDA introduced to Britain a French system to regulate prostitution and police the sexual health of prostitutes. Under the CDA, prostitutes would be examined regularly for signs of venereal disease and, if found to be infected, hospitalized until they were found to be free of disease. Upon release, they would continue to be required to submit to regular physical examination. Butler and other anti-CDA activists objected to the CDA on numerous grounds, not least that it reinforced a sexual double standard, encouraging prostitution by purporting to make illicit sex safe for male patrons and then punishing prostitutes as carriers of venereal disease. Butler claimed that since the act allowed the police to arrest women on suspicion, whether or not they had a record of engaging in prostitution, the CDA put all British women in danger of this assault on their freedom. Perhaps the most effective argument that Butler and other anti-CDA activists made lay in their opposition to the 'instrumental rape' of women arrested under the CDA with specula, examples of which the speakers displayed at their lectures. In 1871, Butler and her colleagues presented a petition to Parliament, protesting the CDA. The Contagious Diseases Acts were repealed in 1886.

Similar political action was the goal of English women's rights advocate Frances Power Cobbe. In 'Wife-Torture in England' (1878), Cobbe identified the injustice of women's position within marriage as the root of domestic violence. Claiming that the practice was at its worst among the labouring classes of the industrial north, Cobbe blamed negative cultural attitudes towards wives, especially the notion of the wife as property of the husband, for the phenomenon. Such attitudes were reflected in legal traditions that classified acts of wives against husbands as petty treason. The seventeenth-century principle that men could use any 'reasonable' instrument to chastise their wives, Cobbe noted, had remained a part of English law until 1829. She called for a bill to make divorce easily accessible to women of all classes, to grant custody of children to women and to require husbands to pay for the maintenance of their ex-wives and children.

Before the 1870s, only the temperance movement had offered an arena for mention of domestic abuse, and even there such discussion had been couched in more general rhetoric about the sufferings of the drunkard's family. After 1874, the temperance movement again opened the way to women's activism on numerous issues. The Women's Christian Temperance Union (WCTU) was founded in that year in Chicago, and, after Frances Willard became its leader in 1879, the WCTU grew into the premier women's organization, both nationally and internationally. Under Willard, the temperance movement became a prime example of reform feminism, a women's movement that focused on sex difference as the main argument for suffrage. Enlisting ideas of home protection and maternalism, the charismatic Willard chose as her motto 'Do Everything', and under her leadership the WCTU expanded beyond anti-alcohol campaigns to a much broader agenda, which included departments focused on peace, labour reform, social purity, health and city welfare work. Members could participate at the local, state or national level, and after Willard joined with British temperance leader Lady Henry Somerset to found the World Women's Christian Temperance Union (WWCTU) in 1884, they could focus on the international level as well. An ardent suffragist, Willard used the notion of home protection to persuade women that they needed the vote in order to defend their homes and families from the evils of drink. Most temperance workers were suffragists, and the WWCTU promoted women's suffrage efforts throughout the world, especially in New Zealand and Australia, the first two countries to grant women's suffrage at the national level.

Winning suffrage

As suffragists continued to struggle for the full parliamentary franchise in Britain and for voting rights at both state and national levels in the USA, the first significant gains in the international movement for women's rights came in the western USA and the Antipodes. Women in Wyoming Territory gained full suffrage in 1869, and the first appeal for women's suffrage was published in New Zealand in that year. In both of these areas, white settlers' responses to the issue of women's suffrage expressed their racial anxieties. Granting the franchise to women became a way to solidify the position of whites in relation to displaced indigenous populations and other non-white groups, including African Americans and Asians, whom white settlers perceived as potential challengers to their power.

Women won full national suffrage first in New Zealand and Australia. Settler anxiety about race affected both nations, but the position of the Maori in New Zealand differed from that of the Aborigines in Australia. Since the Maori had adopted Christianity and, perhaps more importantly, had the capacity to mount a military defence against settlers, the settler government in New Zealand included Maoris, first in male suffrage and then in granting women the national franchise in 1893. The status of Aborigines differed in each of the Australian colonies, and the 1901 Australian Constitution created a status for Aborigines separate from that of white women on the national level. Only white women gained full national suffrage in the Commonwealth of Australia in 1902.

The WWCTU played a significant role in these suffrage campaigns, and WWCTU missionaries' willingness to adapt their propaganda to local racial attitudes contributed to their success. Jessie Ackerman and Mary Leavitt were particularly successful WWCTU organizers in Australia and New Zealand. Their international ties and access to Anglo-American suffrage ideas, particularly those of John Stuart Mill, lent them considerable appeal in settler societies on the periphery of the British Empire. After 1902, white Australian women followed the implications of Ackerman and Leavitt's work, seeing themselves as missionaries of the suffrage movement. Since their own racial and gender positions were a product of racial imperialism, white Australian women identified with British and US women, and they outspokenly sympathized with US women about the so-called negative effects of immigration.

The willingness of WWCTU activists to adapt to local political and racial contexts, white Australian women's views of their role in an international suffrage movement, and the priority that many suffragists gave to gaining the franchise for white women over women of other races and ethnicities: all signalled the strength of such divisive factors as race, ethnicity and class as suffrage campaigns continued. In Great Britain, class-inflected arguments had characterized the thought of John Stuart Mill and Thomas Hare in the 1860s. Mill had recommended educational tests for voting and plural votes for better-educated voters, and Hare had advocated proportional representation to encourage the election of such talented men as Mill and his colleagues. In the USA, the class position of suffragists contributed to anti-immigrant feeling

in the north and anti-black sentiment in south. In 1890, the same year that US suffrage groups, the NWSA and AWSA, reunited to create the National American Woman Suffrage Association (NAWSA), Mississippi and other southern states began to develop legal methods to prevent black men from voting. Within the women's rights movement, black women were expected to keep to the margins and avoid offending racist white suffragists.

Black women combated the increasingly racialized climate of the international movement for women's rights and challenged white women to look past race and reform feminism as they sought liberation. Many of their arguments revolved around questions of sexuality. At the World Columbian Exposition in Chicago in 1893, Fanny Barrier Williams and Anna Julia Cooper addressed the question of black women's moral integrity. Sexual immorality, they argued, was not the fault of black women but of white men who continued to attack them. Williams asserted that the threat of sexual exploitation lay behind the decisions of many black women to leave their homes in the south and migrate to northern cities. Investigative journalist and anti-lynching activist Ida B. Wells (later Wells-Barnett) published evidence to counter claims, such as those made by WCTU leader Frances Willard, that lynching constituted white men's retaliation for black men's assaults on white women. Lynching more often resulted from economic competition than sexual assault, and, in fact, black women were more vulnerable to sexual exploitation at the hands of white men than the reverse. Wells confronted Willard publicly, and Willard eventually supported anti-lynching legislation. Willard, however, represented only one of the more powerful voices of reform feminism.

In fact, white feminists' racial biases ran deep, and many subscribed to trends in racial thought that supported the notion that blacks and other non-whites were naturally inferior to whites. US journalist, fiction writer and social purity advocate Charlotte Perkins Gilman expressed the prevailing racial thought in her *Women and Economics* (1898). Relying heavily on Friedrich Engels's *Origin of the Family, Private Property, and the State* (1884) for her notion of how the gender division of labour had developed, Gilman combined principles of socialism and Darwinism to argue that women suffered from an overdevelopment of their sex-function. Correcting the problem would serve the interests not only of women but of the Anglo-Saxon race as well. Seeking an evolutionary answer to women's subordination, Gilman claimed that economic independence for women and professionalization of housekeeping and nurseries would have an eugenic effect. Such a conclusion necessitated ignoring the labour of women of colour, the majority of women receiving wages as domestic workers at the time. When Gilman addressed 'the Negro problem', she suggested that most African Americans would need to correct their 'primitive' characteristics through service in industrial armies; those who could prove that they were civilized could avoid such service.

As racial divisions continued, socialism and the growth of suffrage militancy strengthened the renewal of the international suffrage movement. Such well-known figures as German socialist Clara Zetkin and Russian socialist Aleksandria Kollontai tried to strike a balance between combating the sexism of socialist men and the class interests of bourgeois suffragists. A strong network of socialist women and support for women's rights in Finland's Social Democratic Party played a significant role in making Finland the first nation in Europe to grant the national franchise to women in 1906. In Great Britain, the activism of Lancashire textile workers in the 1890s contributed to the climate for the founding of the Women's Social and Political Union (WSPU) by the Pankhursts. Organized in Manchester in 1903, the WSPU emphasized public agitation, working-class organization and links to the Labour Party. After moving from Manchester to London in 1906, the WSPU concentrated on organizing mass public demonstrations. By 1911, militancy dominated the British suffrage movement.

British militancy influenced suffrage movements in both Europe and the USA. French women disavowed militancy, but an organized movement for women's suffrage began in France by 1906. L'Union Francaise pour le Suffrage des Femmes was formed in 1909 and affiliated with the International Woman Suffrage Alliance (IWSA), which had been formed between 1899 and 1902. In the USA, British militancy had a particularly notable effect on the activism of Alice Paul, a Quaker suffragist who learned militant tactics in England and brought them back to energize the movement in the USA after 1913. Paul and her colleagues attacked the Democratic Party in the USA, urging supporters to oppose the Democrats and renewing consideration of a national suffrage

amendment in Congress. Carrie Chapman Catt, leader of the NAWSA, preferred to lobby for women's suffrage at both the state and national levels. Catt's winning strategy finally achieved success in 1920, when the fact that women had gained the franchise in a majority of the states ensured the victory of the Nineteenth Amendment in Congress and its ratification by the states.

Western women won the franchise gradually through the first half of the twentieth century. After Finland, Norway granted women a limited franchise based on an economic qualification in 1907, and conferred full suffrage in 1913. Iceland granted suffrage to women aged 40 and over in 1915, and Denmark extended the franchise to all women in that year. In 1917, Canada granted the federal vote to white women who were in the armed forces or were close relatives of soldiers. In Great Britain, married women, women householders and women university graduates aged 30 or over gained the franchise in 1918. Irish women won full suffrage in 1922, and the UK extended full suffrage to women in 1928. French women did not receive the franchise until 1944, just one year before women in Japan and Italy. White women gained the vote in the USA in 1920, but various legal strictures in some states deprived black women of the franchise until the Voting Rights Act of 1965. Racial restrictions also limited the voting rights of American Indians and Australian Aborigines until the 1960s.

Feminism and the female franchise

Some historians have argued that feminist activists have been some of the most creative theorists of citizenship, as they struggled to define and combat women's economic and legal disadvantages in political systems that were predicated on gender systems that defined women as other, lesser or subordinate to men and that denied them a connected historical narrative of women's achievements and thought. Making the argument for women's rights based either on equality with men or difference from them presented considerable challenges throughout the century.

Once women gained the franchise, they did not vote in blocs or otherwise exercise their influence in the ways that some suffragists had predicted. Some historians have argued that the franchise lost its value as soon as women gained it, since, for example, the political culture of the USA shifted away from electoral politics in the 1920s. Other historians have claimed that the very move away from electoral politics and towards the welfare state was the result of women's growing political influence from the middle of the nineteenth century forwards. Indeed, some historians have argued that reform feminism laid the groundwork for the welfare state, urging governments to take responsibility for the lives of their citizens.

The franchise was only one goal of the woman's rights movement. Its concerns and achievements were many: expanded opportunities for women's education, greater access to certain occupations and professions, fuller legal rights. The word feminism came into general use only late in the period, when it was coined by French suffragist Hubertine Auclert in the 1890s. By the turn of the century, racial and class divisions within the movement were more apparent than they had been earlier and those divisions point to some of the shortcomings of the movement. Campaigning solely on the basis of gender deprived the movement of a broader definition of justice that might have lent itself to a more comprehensive movement for liberation. The fact that women's rights activism returned to the political stage in the second half of the twentieth century attests to women's continued desire for full citizenship, and continued critiques from women of colour and working-class women testify to the movement's unfinished business.

Further reading

Anderson, Bonnie S. (2000) *Joyous Greetings: The First International Women's Movement, 1830–1860*, New York: Oxford University Press.
Daley, Caroline, and Nolan, Melanie (eds) (1994) *Suffrage and Beyond: International Feminist Perspectives*, New York: New York University Press.
Newman, Louise Michele (1999) *White Women's Rights: The Racial Origins of Feminism in the United States*, New York: Oxford University Press.
Wallach Scott, Joan (1996) *Only Paradoxes to Offer: French Feminists and the Rights of Man*, Cambridge, MA: Harvard University Press.

SEE ALSO: Deroin, Jeanne; Early Socialism; Fourier, Charles; Goldman, Emma; Mill, John Stuart; Pankhurst, Emmeline; Utopianism

KATHRYN M. TOMASEK

FEUERBACH, LUDWIG (1804–72)

Ludwig Feuerbach is often seen as a mere precursor of Marx and Engels (see MARX AND MARXISM), and as the purveyor of the aphorism

'man is what he eats', a pun in German – '*der Mensch ist, was er isst*' – which had not even been invented by him. Whilst it is true that his critique of Hegel's idealistic-metaphysical system (see HEGEL AND HEGELIANISM) is one of the major elements of the groundwork on which Marxism is based, he is more than just a transitional figure between Hegel and Marx. From 1839 onwards Feuerbach became one of Hegel's foremost critics amongst the Young Hegelians (Left Hegelians). He vigorously attacked Hegel's 'theological idealism' and proclaimed an empiricist, senses-based, materialism that rejects God or any other idealistic, metaphysical projection. His critique of religion hit the theological-philosophical community of the 1840s 'like a thunderbolt': this was the assessment of his fellow Young Hegelian DAVID FRIEDRICH STRAUSS whose *Life of Jesus* had shaken the foundations of theology in the preceding decade. Feuerbach's importance lies equally in the development of a philosophical anthropology and in the investigation into the psychological aspects of the genesis of religion. In this regard he has had a great influence on the existentialist movement, on thinkers such as Martin Buber and on twentieth-century theologians such as Bultmann or Karl Barth.

Feuerbach, son of a jurist who had achieved fame through the reform of criminal law in Bavaria, first studied theology before going to Berlin to continue with philosophical studies under Hegel. His early work of 1830, *Thoughts on Death and Immortality* (*Gedanken über Tod und Unsterblichkeit*, ed. and trans. J.A. Massey, Berkeley: University of California Press, 1980), was an irreverent assault on theology and ruined his prospects of an academic career, forcing him to lead a rather frugal life as a private writer that was only affordable due to his wife's financial assets. Although initially an ardent admirer of Hegel, he soon broke with the latter's metaphysical idealism. Feuerbach's critique of religion and notion of materialism were developed in a series of works, starting with his *Kritik der Hegelschen Philosophie*, published in 1839 in the *Hallische Jahrbücher für deutsche Wissenschaft und Kunst*, which marked his break with Hegel. His most famous work was to become *The Essence of Christianity* (*Das Wesen des Christentums*, 1841, trans. 1843), a critique of religion that was elaborated upon in subsequent works such as *Principles of the Philosophy of the Future* (*Grundsätze der Philosophie der Zukunft*, 1843, trans. 1966), *Das Wesen der Religion*

(*The Essence of Religion*, published 1846 in *Die Epigonen*), *Lectures on the Essence of Religion* (*Vorlesungen über das Wesen der Religion*, 1851, trans. 1967) and *Theogenie* (1857), an encompassing survey of the 'genesis of gods', the genesis of religious thinking in Ancient Greece and Rome, Judaism and Christianity. In his last major study, *Das Geheimnis des Opfers oder der Mensch ist was er isst* (*The Mystery of Sacrifice or Man is What He Eats*, 1862), Feuerbach stressed the common materiality of man and nature.

Feuerbach was thrilled by the French Revolution of 1848 but seemed to be less enthusiastic about the German. Although he was the idol of the revolutionary students who asked him in 1848/9 to hold public lectures in Heidelberg's town hall – later-on published as *Lectures on the Essence of Religion* – he himself was, from the very beginning, deeply sceptical about the political maturity of the Germans and thus about the chances of a successful democratic revolution; that is why he did not even bother trying to get elected into the German revolutionary Paulskirche parliament in Frankfurt. In one of his *Lectures* he pointed out that he did not give a damn for political liberty if man still stayed a slave of religious illusions, and he stressed that true freedom was only where man was also free from religion. Still, he was favourably inclined to Marx's *Kapital*, and 2 years before his death he joined the German Social Democratic Workers' Party.

What is the origin of religion? There is no doubt for Feuerbach that religion is nothing but illusion. His conception of sensuous materialism, according to which man can only gain experience and knowledge from sense perception, leaves no room for a senses-based experience of God. He does not deny the existence of a historical Jesus who became the trigger for the Christian religion, but he does deny that this Jesus was a Christ, a God or Son of God, born of a virgin and working miracles: to him, this Jesus Christ is nothing but a fantasy. In the *Essence of Christianity* Feuerbach explores the relationship between man and this Christian idea of God. Man projects his qualities that in him are limited into infinity and objectifies them, giving them an independent divine existence. But there is no external reality to God; the most real being, the *ens realissimum*, is man's essence. Feuerbach characterizes the true relationship between God and man as follows: 'Man is the God of man. That man exists at all he has to thank nature, that he is man he

has to thank man.' God is nothing but hypostatised, i.e. 'essential man': in a complete reversal of the biblical message, it has always been man creating God in order to overcome his finitude and find child-like comfort and reassurance. God's infinity is in reality the infinity of the capacity or potentiality of the human species, of 'generic man', as opposed to the finitude of the human individual. In the same vein, Christ is in reality nothing but the consciousness of species unity: whoever loves man for the sake of man, who rises to the universal love adequate to the nature of the species, is a Christian, is Christ himself. In the *Principles of the Philosophy of the Future*, God as the 'epitome of all realities or perfections' is defined as 'nothing other than a compendious summary devised for the benefit of the limited individual, an epitome of the generic human qualities distributed among men in the self-realisation of the species in the course of world history.' God is reduced to man; eliminating God means realizing man's potential and thus concretizing man: but it is important to stress that Feuerbach is not speaking about individual but 'generic' man. Distinguishing in the *Essence of Christianity* between the 'true or anthropological essence of religion' and the 'false or theological essence of religion', Feuerbach does not denigrate religion as such; he just reinterprets religion as an ontological concept, as a discourse that in truth is not about – a non-existent – God but about man. The language of religion – although meaningless with regard to the external reality of its object – still gives an insight into man's inner being and thus makes sense if reinterpreted as a discourse about man. *The Essence of Religion*, his brochure of 1846, and the subsequent *Lectures on the Essence of Religion*, elaborate on the same topic, but they bring in an additional point of view: they stress the genesis of religion out of man's attempt at overcoming his fear of nature upon which he totally depends, at trying to tame it by making it into God(s). In the *Lectures* he succinctly summarizes his world-view in two words: 'nature' and 'man'. These two terms also constitute the epistemological condition for the dialectic process of man getting to know himself. Man needs both nature and fellow man as the 'other', as the *Thou* that man's *I* has to refer to as way of coming to terms with the world and gaining self-knowledge.

The 'essence of man' exists not on its own but only in community, as Feuerbach stresses in §§ 59, 60 and 63 of the *Principles of the Philosophy of the Future*: 'The single man for himself possesses the essence of man neither in himself as a moral being nor in himself as a thinking being. The essence of man is contained only in the community and unity of man with man'; 'solitude is finiteness and limitation; community is freedom and infinity. Man for himself is man (in the ordinary sense); man with man – the unity of *I* and *Thou* – is God'; 'the secret of the Trinity is the secret of communal and social life'.

How does Feuerbach see the role of theology and philosophy respectively? The very conditions of human life, the biological needs of individual and species survival – water, air, food and sex – as well as the psychological needs for law, creativity, love and hope are expressed in religious terms brought about by sensuous imagination that objectifies and projects them onto a God. Theology turns these forms, by means of abstraction, into an esoteric, otherworldly edifice of thought evolving around a personalized God; philosophy, on the other hand, abstracts them once again, casting them in a fully abstract form of metaphysical discourse, in a sort of 'abstract theology' using terms such as *Essential Being* or *Absolute Spirit*. Both theology and metaphysical-speculative philosophy are means of man's quest for self-knowledge, so the very essence of theology and philosophy is anthropology. Only the science of anthropology is doing justice to a genuine understanding of man, thus overcoming man's alienation of himself. So man's image of God is his ideal image of man as a universalized social, as a species being; the *God* of the theologians and the *Being* or *Absolute Spirit* of the metaphysicians are nothing but the human consciousness of its own nature. In the beginning, there is man with religion as illusion, as self-deception that forms part of a historically necessary! – dialectic that brings about a process of self-revelation and results in man becoming fully conscious of himself. Feuerbach reduces God to man whilst not denying the role of the 'religious' in mankind's quest for self-knowledge. In this process truth is neither materialism nor idealism, neither physiology nor psychology; truth is only anthropology: transcending the dualism of body and soul, Feuerbach affirms the totality of mind–body identity. Man consists of head and heart and stomach; feeling, willing and thinking constitute man's consciousness, as his essential nature.

One of the key terms of Feuerbach's philosophy is 'alienation'. Since Feuerbach sticks to the premise that man remains determined by nature, it is not the transformation of nature and society, not man's activism that constitutes an end to his alienation. Alienation in Hegel's system is the theory that man whose true nature is divine falls short of the divine in his actual existence: to the extent that man has not realized himself as divine he is estranged from his true, authentic self. To Feuerbach, alienation has a diametrically opposed meaning: man's condition of alienation is caused by his projecting part of his being onto another – imaginary – being and thus becoming estranged from his complete being; God as a fantasy is thus the cause of man's alienation. Man's liberation lies in an inward reorientation in his consciousness, in abandoning his illusions of the exterior reality of any *God* or abstract notions of *Being*, *Logos* or *Absolute Spirit* – only through turning to man and to man alone man becomes fully 'real' and truly free. This does not mean, however, that Feuerbach condones a resigned attitude of man *vis-à-vis* his environment. Activity is called for, but in his eyes it is not a *conditio sine qua non* for the ending of man's alienation, as posited by Marx and Engels. Feuerbach clearly sees the ill effects of religion in practical life and castigates religion as an obstacle to man's material improvement; he identifies religion as a reactionary form that protects the status quo due to its negating the value of earthly life and shifting man's hopes and aspirations from this life to an illusionary after-life. How much Feuerbach valued the importance of earthly conditions for man is most famously encapsulated in the dictum 'man is what he eats'; he would conclude that if life is the precondition of thought and food the precondition of life, then food is the precondition of thought: '*primum vivere, deinde philosophari*' – first, to live, then to think or philosophize. So, if one wants to better people they should be given better food. But this demand stays on a philosophical level, not tackling the active side of this notion – which Marx would make to one of the centrepieces of his programme when explicitly criticizing Feuerbach on this very point in his *Theses on Feuerbach*, written in 1845: 'The philosophers have only interpreted the world, in various ways; the point is to change it.' Feuerbach was criticized by Marx and Engels for inconsistent materialism. Marx praised him for having proven that philosophy was nothing else but religion expounded by thought, i.e. another form and manner of existence of the estrangement of the essence of man. But Marx and Engels go beyond Feuerbach by demanding the removal of the social conditions that made man create God and religion in the first place, transforming thus the critique of religion into a critique of economics and politics, the only level they deem appropriate for man's alienation to be overcome by means of turning individual man into an active, revolutionary agent with the aim of becoming fully 'concretized', fully 'real'. To Feuerbach, outer change can only be effected from within. He strongly opposes the effect of religion leading man to expect salvation and happiness only in Heaven and to accept and reconcile himself to his suffering from poverty and injustice on earth. In this sense religion is regarded as counter-productive to the emancipation and liberation of the huge class of the under-privileged, impeding their struggle to better their lot and get their due, thus perpetuating the dominance of the privileged classes. The only solution, in the eyes of Feuerbach, is for the underprivileged class to reject God and become atheistic. Only by doing so, by effecting inner change first, their alienation can be overcome on all levels, including the socio-economic one.

Was Feuerbach truly a-theistic? In his work *Ludwig Feuerbach and the End of Classical German Philosophy* Engels enthusiastically praised Feuerbach for his materialistic view that nothing existed outside nature and man, and that the higher beings our religious fantasies had created were only the fantastic reflection of our own wishes, our own essence; to Engels, the liberating effect of Feuerbach's *Essence of Christianity* in the sense of breaking the spell of Hegel's idealistic system was such that it made him and other Young Hegelians at once into Feuerbachians. On the other hand, Engels commented on Feuerbach as being in his lower half a materialist but in his upper half an idealist. It could be argued that in Feuerbach's thinking God comes back through the backdoor of humanism, in the form of a humanist religion. 'The purpose of my writing,' says Feuerbach in his *Lectures on the Essence of Religion*:

is to convert people from theology to anthropology, from love of god(s) to love of their fellow human beings, from being candidates for life after death to being students of this life; to free them from religious and political servitude to heavenly or earthly monarchies and

aristocracies; to make them into self-confident citizens of the Earth.

Radical twentieth-century theologians also departed from such an anthropological stance in their re-evaluation of religion, endorsing Feuerbach's statement of '*homini homine nihil pulchrius*' – nothing is more beautiful to man than man. By identifying God with the 'essence of man' God is simultaneously dethroned and reinstated as an evolving 'human species being'; the reduction of God to man means the death of God to individual man, but does it really negate God as far as 'generic man' is concerned? Isn't the 'essence of man' a religious concept? Not to mention the problems that arise in connection with this concept if one considers the notion of 'evil'!

Feuerbach wants to make God human, but he does not really escape God. Even if he kills off God as God, he connects man with the divine. Replacing the love of God through the love of man is characterized as the 'only true religion' in the sense that it is the only link from man to man which makes man truly human. Feuerbach's philosophy is a critique of religion and philosophy as well as a humanist religion.

At the very end of his *Lectures* he reiterates his goal of turning men to 'full men' rather than keeping them in a state of 'half animal, half angel' as viewed by the Christians. Before deciding on the final title of *Essence of Christianity* Feuerbach had thought of entitling it with the Greek *Know Thyself* – his philosophy is indeed a reflection of man's self-discovery, providing us to this very day with lots of 'food for thought' about the being of man and his *raison d'être* on this earth.

Further reading

Feuerbach, Ludwig (1957) *The Essence of Christianity*, trans. G. Eliot, intro. K. Barth, New York, London: Harper & Row.
—— (1966) *Principles of the Philosophy of the Future*, trans. and intro. M.H. Vogel, Indianapolis: Bobbs-Merrill.
—— (1972) *The Fiery Brook: Selected Writings of Ludwig Feuerbach*, trans. Z. Hanfi, New York: Doubleday.
Harvey, V.A. (1995) *Feuerbach and the Interpretation of Religion*, Cambridge: Cambridge University Press.
Johnston, L. (1995) *Between Transcendence and Nihilism: Species-Ontology in the Philosophy of Ludwig Feuerbach*, New York: Peter Lang.
Wartofsky, M.W. (1982 [1977]) *Feuerbach*, Cambridge: Cambridge University Press.

DETMAR KLEIN

FOURIER, CHARLES (1772–1837)

Charles Fourier was the first of the French early or 'utopian' socialists (see EARLY SOCIALISM). The outlines of his 'scientific' conception of society were first published in book form in 1808, entitled *The Theory of the Four Movements.* The book itself was an oddity with his theory hidden amongst complex and bizarre dialogue. The reader was presented with details of his discovery alongside a critique of 'civilization', fantastic pronouncements about copulation between planets, promises about a new religion and an outline of amorous and gastronomic delights to come. Yet despite the obscurity of its presentation the book told of the most fantastic utopia of the nineteenth century. In addition it was the first work to define and discuss the 'the social problem' which later occupied socialists. Since it was the reader's task to extract 'the pearl in the mud' (Fourier's metaphor for his great scientific discovery), many simply ignored the work, and the little attention it did receive was ridicule. Fourier remained neglected until the 1830s when socialists seeking a solution to the social question 'resurrected' his works. A small and dedicated band of followers, led by VICTOR CONSIDÉRANT, presented a bowdlerised and simplified version of Fourierism, which omitted his more radical ideas. Additionally Victor Considérant's wife held back the *cahiers* announcing a new amorous world and these were not published until the 1960s. Such was the appeal of Fourierism that an impressive number of simplified versions of Fourier's theory appeared in the 1830s and 1840s. One such example is *The Phalanstery or Attractive Industry and Moral Harmony* written by Zoë Gatti de Gamond. Fourier's call for women's liberation attracted the respect and support of a number of leading feminists following their disenchantment with Saint-Simonianism (see SAINT-SIMON, HENRI DE). Indeed Pamela Pilbeam has shown that the high level of mostly middle-class female assistance was crucial to the financing and development of his theories, making Fourierism a significant socialist movement during the years 1820–48.

Like the Fourierists, later socialists, such as Marx and Engels, found it problematical presenting Fourier as both the founding father of a socialist tradition and the creator of a fantastic theory. So over the years various attempts have been made to acknowledge Fourier's socialist and critical foresight whilst also explaining why his theories were enmeshed in a bizarre dialogue. Consequently he has been portrayed as a solemn humanitarian, a social reformer, a satirist and even a precursor of surrealism. However, the translation of *The Theory of the Four Movements* by Gareth Stedman Jones and Ian Patterson allows individual assessments to be made regarding just how serious Fourier was about his theory.

From the outset of *The Theory of the Four Movements* Fourier was keen to tell the reader that this first work would only give us a glimpse of his theory, a taster of things to come. He claimed that should he unveil all the good things to come it would be more that civilization could bear in its unhappy state. However, Fourier warned that not everyone was capable or serious-minded enough to appreciate the finer details of the theory. Furthermore, patience was needed and the five preliminary chapters of the 'General Destines' must be read at least twice, or preferably three times to fully understand the concept. Aware that many people would simply not understand his complex theory Fourier lowered his expectations to raising an awareness of the 'absurdities of civilised politics' and the existence an exact science. Fourier argued that God gave every globe the problem of solving the puzzle of the General System of Nature. And only by solving this puzzle could humanity be happy. Philosophers and governments had failed to find the key to happiness because they had not been studying an exact science. Prejudice, closed minds and self-interest had served to blind them of the real solution to society's ills. The constraints of space limit a full discussion of the more magical aspects of Fourier's theory: copulating planets, anti-lions, restoration of the earth's Northern Crown, pink lemonade seas, humans growing tails, and an identical climate throughout the globe. Thus only the bare mechanics of the scientific aspects of his theory will be discussed here.

Fourier acknowledged that Newton and Leibniz were on the right track but had only partially uncovered the discovery. Fourier furthered their idea that there were laws governing the physical world by suggesting that there were parallel laws governing social relationships. Thus he theorized 'there is a unified system of movement for the spiritual and material world', therefore 'the analogy of the four movements, material, organic, animal and social'. Fourier claimed that he alone had solved the problem of the General System of Nature by discovering an absolute divine order through the study of Agricultural Association, the Theory of Passionate Attraction, and the Analogy of the Four Movements. According to Fourier there were several phases and periods in the progress of social movement. The society he lived in had become stuck in the fifth stage 'civilization' simply because it had not followed the God-given theory. In order to effect the leap from 'Chaos' to 'Harmony', from present society to a utopia, society needed to organize themselves into autonomous associative communes, or phalanxs. Fourier asserted that 'man was composed of twelve passions', the liberation of which would lead to happiness and order. So essential to the success of the commune was the correct combination of passional types. Fourier's ideal phalanx would be a group of 1,620; a figure chosen because it represented the double number of 'passional' types he identified in human society. Once correctly organized, man's natural instincts would be released, and a return to a state of nature would bring instant perfection and universal love.

Associated Households and Attractive Industry equalled continually increasing wealth. Although claiming that the phalanx was based on the passions Fourier constantly stressed the viability of his system. Since everything in the phalanx would be made and sold communally Fourier expected profits to be four times bigger than those in existing enterprises in 'civilization'. Additionally communal living made economies of scale possible and waste would be stamped out. The commune would be democratic, with a community committed to social improvement and the displacement of capitalism. But whilst the commune would eradicate capitalism it would not be communist and consequently land and property would still belong to individuals. Children from the age of 3, men and women would be shareholders; no one would be a wage earner. The annual profit would be divided amongst the group in twelfths. So five-twelfths would be dispensed for labour performed, four-twelfths to capital invested and three-twelfths according to talent displayed. Class would not disappear but would be made less noticeable as everyone in harmony would be satisfied.

Since the commune's driving force would be love not discipline Fourier envisaged that such a peaceful state would not require laws or moral codes. So whilst Fourier accepted a God, his was all-knowing but not all-powerful. For him God was the source of knowledge and understanding of the pre-ordained social order, the one who held the key to a divinely ordained destiny. However, once God had revealed to Fourier how society should be organized his work was at an end. Therefore there would be no need for a judicial structure or the need for a God to uphold moral principles, especially a God who was bound by the rules of universal order and had no power to bend or remake them. Thus Fourier's deity was an impersonal concept, which explains why there was no provision in the phalanxs for a church.

Central to Fourier's doctrine was the freeing of the passions and the liberation of women, including their sexual liberation. Fourier argued that until women were liberated social progress was impossible and he ensured that life in the phalanx offered a practical solution to their subordination. This resulted in women being assured the right to an education, the right to work and the right to choose sexual partners. Since marriage and the family were central to women's subjection in civilization there would be no place for either in Harmony. He railed that following the French Revolution the Convention had not gone far enough in 'trampling down all prejudices' because it had not destroyed marriage. Marriage stifled the passions that needed to be expressed collectively ensuring unhappiness for both parties. He asserted that men entered marriage under duress only to be rewarded with at least eight universal sources of annoyance, including monotony, random happiness, expense and cuckoldom. But however wretched marriage was for men it was nothing compared to the slavery endured by women. Moreover in the absence of any productive employment marriage remained the only option for women, which was effectively prostitution by another name. Fourier observed that once married the rules were clear, a lifetime of bondage and obedience to a husband, and moral servitude to the family. Moreover the ever-present knowledge that she would have to attract a buyer-sponsor in the form of a husband had a damaging effect on the personality of a growing girl and caused most women to develop vice-ridden characters, marked by 'servility and deviousness'.

Fourier's invective on the subject of marriage was matched by his feelings regarding the family. He described family feelings as the Judas among the twelve passions. Fourier continued, arguing that after much observation he had not found a single joyful family. There was no gaiety and no happy moments to be found in family life, which resulted in family members seeking escape at the first opportunity.

In short, the family in civilization represented an unnatural arrangement and it was this division into families that had caused fragmentation of the modern social order, or 'chaos'. Consequently the commune not the family was the basic social unit in Fourier's Harmony. Later in life Fourier does modify his hostility to marriage, accepting that it could be possible if developed by degrees becoming permanent only after the birth of children, as love and paternity were the last of the passions to be brought to the phalanx.

Fourier unlike his contemporaries believed that both men and women possessed sexually passionate natures. Therefore in the phalanx men and women of all classes would be free to choose and change sexual partners as their desires dictated. Sex was integral to life in Harmony and as necessary as food. A system of 'amorous guarantees', or the 'amorous corporation', would ensure that every member had access to a sexual minimum of fulfilling sex. A complex incentive system would allow even the old and ugly to participate in an amorous life. Jealousy and other 'illegal voluptuousness' would disappear because everyone would have a fully satisfying love life. The elderly were not forgotten and their assistance was required in giving advice on sexual matters.

In Fourier's teaching there were three sexes, male, female and the neuter sex. Children would be the immature or neuter sex and it was Fourier's wish to prolong this 'neutrality' or their chastity for as long as possible. To this end he did not want them to study material that might give them premature sexual information; this even included observing intercourse among animals. As from the age of 16 all young people would start in the group of vestals, virgins as the name implies. Half of the group would then progress to form the parallel group of damsels. Vestals would be composed of two-thirds young women and one-thirds young men, while the reverse would be true of damsels. Fourier envisaged that the specific contribution of the vestals would be to attract men into the industrial armies. Industrial soldiers would compete for the loveliest vestals and as an added attraction there would be nightly amorous festivals.

Perhaps as a result from pressure from his followers, Fourier wrote less about love in his later works. To the extent that he even acknowledged that initially the phalanx would have to be established without the proper organization of love, since this would be more acceptable to man and woman brought up in civilization. This contradiction of on the one hand criticizing 'civilization' for its sexual abuses of women whilst presenting the idea that women would act as tactile bait to men in Harmony has raised doubts as to the nature of women's liberation. It is this element of Fourier's vision that caused Marx to complain that Fourier's suggestions result in making women a piece of communal property, thus moving from private marriage to general prostitution.

Fourier was the first to claim that access to an education and work was a natural right. No one in the commune would be disbarred from either due to gender or class. Everyone was given a chance in spite of capability and inclination; indeed Fourier envisaged that the phalanx would form one vast school of mutual instruction.

It was Fourier's design that work in harmony should be a constant delight. He argued that it was God's intention that work should not be a trial and due to the law of passionate attraction people need only to participate in work they were drawn to. Thus work would no longer be forced or distasteful. Such was the organization of work that people need only work at one task for as long as their concentration lasts, which is usually an hour, thus workers were fresh and motivated throughout their working day. Since the organization of work and the organization of pleasure were inextricably linked Fourier devised a system of gastronomic and sexual rewards to act as incentives. Presumably this came in useful when really horrible jobs needed doing.

Aware that both education and work were fundamental to women's independence Fourier ensured that his system offered a practical solution to their subordination. Moreover he argued that the existing enslavement of women was uneconomic because it prevented them from making their rightful contribution to society. Accordingly in Harmony women would be freed from the responsibilities of childcare and household duties leaving them able to pursue an education and a career. Children, although belonging to the mother by right, are the ultimate responsibility of the community. Infants and babies were to be looked after in communal nurseries by women passionately drawn to such work. No woman should be excluded from any work for which talent and strength qualified her. Accordingly half the jobs were to be reserved for women and all attempts must be made not to relegate them to the thankless and servile roles they had become accustomed to. Whilst expecting that some women would be drawn to 'traditional' work, such as looking after children and household cares, he also believed that women's talents did not end there. Acknowledging that women had talents for the arts, the sciences and industrial works, Fourier anticipated that women would make up two-sixths of the industrial armies. These women would travel the world undertaking Herculean tasks such as reclaiming the Sahara Desert, living an itinerant lifestyle and enjoying the great festivities. Thus in Harmony no longer would prejudice pressure women out of every gainful employment except prostitution or marital subjugation.

Fourier died in 1837 just as his ideas were becoming known more widely. The wealthy benefactor needed to fund a full-scale phalanx never appeared, but Fourier did become involved in an experimental commune at Condé-sur-Vesgre (Rambouillet). The venture failed, as did the attempt at Citeaux in which Gatti de Gamond was actively involved. Despite these failures Fourierism grew with groups founded across Europe and North America. The significance of Fourier's work is that he was the first raise issues such as the liberation of women, the right to work and the evils of capitalism, issues which were later and indeed still today occupy socialists and feminists alike.

Further reading

Beecher, J, (1986) *Charles Fourier. The Visionary and His World*, Berkeley: University of California Press.

Fourier, C. (1996) *The Theory of the Four Movements*, trans. and eds. G. Stedman Jones & I. Patterson, Cambridge: Cambridge University Press.

Gamond Gatti de, Z. (1841) *The Phalanstery or Attractive Industry and Moral Harmony*, London. an edition translated into English by an anonymous 'English Lady' is located in the Goldsmith's Collection, Senate House Library, London.

Goldstein, L. (1982) 'Early Feminist Themes in French Utopian Socialism: The St. Simonians and Fourier', *Journal of History of Ideas*: Vol. 43, 240–67.

Pilbeam, P. (2000) 'Dream Worlds: Religion and the Early Socialists', *Historical Journal* 43: 499–515.

—— (2000) *French Socialists before Marx*, Teddington: Acumen.

SEE ALSO: Cabet, Etienne; Considérant, Victor; early socialism; utopianism

SHEILA THOMAS

FRANCE, ANATOLE (1844–1924)

Anatole France, the pseudonym for Jacques Anatole Thibaut, was born in Paris on 16 April 1844, and died on 12 October 1924 in Tours. A writer and critic, France became a leading Dreyfusard and social commentator. His writing was both inspired by and likened to that of Voltaire, and was characterized by scepticism and acute historical observation.

The son of a Paris book dealer, France began writing in the late 1860s. Under the Second Empire, he wrote several anti-Bonapartist poems, including *Denys, Tyran de Syracuse* (Denys, Tyrant of Syracuse) and cited HIPPOLYTE TAINE as one of his greatest influences. The events of *l'année terrible* (1870–1) profoundly affected his political perspective. France served as a national guard during the Franco-Prussian War, but it was the events of the Paris Commune that transformed the young writer into a bourgeois conservative. In the early years of the Third Republic, his writing was marked by his opposition to republicanism, parliamentarianism, radicalism and socialism.

France's first major success as an author came in 1881 with *Le Crime de Sylvestre Bonnard* (*The Crime of Sylvestre Bonnard*), which received a prize from the Académie Française. Four years later, he was appointed as literary critic for the moderate republican *Le Temps*, where he crusaded against naturalism and anti-militarist literature. By the mid-1880s, France's politics had evolved into intransigent patriotism and anti-internationalism.

France's own literary output was predominantly historical: initially evoking early Christian civilization, then depicting the eighteenth century in his most famous novel, *LaRôtisserie de la Reine Pédauque* (*At the Sign of the Reine Pédauque*), which was published in 1893. In the years 1897–1901, France turned to a more contemporary subject matter in four novels published under the title *L'Histoire contemporaine* (*Contemporary History*), in which the principle character, Professor Bergeret, represented France himself. In 1896, France was elected to the Académie Française, only to withdraw from it only four years later owing to differences of political opinion.

The Dreyfus Affair triggered the second major transformation in France's political beliefs. He became a leading Dreyfusard and ally of Emile Zola, while in 1904 he joined the central committee of the Dreyfusard Ligue des Droits de l'Homme.

France's writing reflected his changed political views, as he began to analyse social conflict in *L'Affaire Crainquebille* (*Crainquebille*) (1901) and abuses of liberty in *Les Dieux ont soif* (*The Gods are Athirst*) (1912). His political journey towards the left was marked by his participation in the socialist newspaper *L'Humanité* in 1904, and it culminated in his support for the Russian Revolution in 1917.

In 1920, France married his second wife, Emma Laprévotte, after his first marriage to Valérie Guérin de Sauville in 1877 ended in divorce 16 years later. The following year, his prolific and celebrated literary output was rewarded with the Nobel Prize for Literature. Following his death in 1924, France's complete works were republished in twenty-five volumes over the years 1925–35.

Further reading

Bancquart, M. (1984) *Anatole France: un sceptique passioné*, Mayenne: Calmann-Lévy.

SEE ALSO: Conservatism, authority and tradition

KARINE VARLEY

FREUD, SIGMUND (1856–1939)

Sigmund Freud was the founder of psychoanalysis and it would be no exaggeration to say that his ideas have exerted an influence on our understanding of the individual comparable with that of the influence of Marx's ideas on the social realm. In fact, almost all aspects of the twentieth century, from science to art, from sociology to ethics, were profoundly dominated and determined by the radical nature of the intellectual challenges to conventional thinking originating from these two Jewish thinkers.

Freud's writings are a testimony to the ongoing development of his ideas since he remained, throughout his life, a practising scientist aware of the fact that any hypothesis offered had to be both explanatorily useful and empirically verified in the process of analysis. Due to this, his central concepts are often tuned, revised or even discarded as new facts present themselves, making it difficult to offer a characterization of Freud's thought that is not, in some way, contradictory with some phase of his work. Yet, it is perhaps this very feature of his writings that makes them so inspiring and relevant almost 100 years later.

Freud was born in Freiberg in the Austro-Hungarian Empire (now part of the Czech Republic), but moved to Vienna at the age of 3 and remained there for most of his professional life. At university, he studied medicine, specializing in neurology but it was during his time in Paris (1885–6) under the celebrated French physician Charcot that the seeds of his future direction were sown as the experience turned Freud's attention to the psychological aspects of his vocation. He married in 1886 and the youngest of his six children, Anna, became a distinguished psychoanalyst in her own right. The last 16 years of his life were marked by the deterioration of his health due to cancer and the rise of the Nazi regime with its anti-Semitic legislation, which eventually forced his exile to London in 1938 (leaving behind his four sisters who were all killed) where he died a year later. Throughout this period, he not only continued to practise but also produced some of his most speculative meta-psychological works.

From Charcot and his work on hysteria, Freud learnt some fundamental lessons, most notably that ideas, rather than just physical processes, had to play a significant role in hysterical symptoms and that the mind, rather than the body, was responsible for the disease. Under the influence of Breuer, a Viennese colleague, Freud began to develop an alternative therapy to hypnotism: if the patients were able to talk about the idea that was the origin of their symptoms, these symptoms often disappeared. From these two influences, psychoanalysis began to arise, Freud began to substitute the directive and suggestive nature of hypnotic cures in favour of a diagnostic process and the 'cathartic' method of free association. The central aim of psychoanalysis was fixed: it was to be a form of therapy that removed symptoms of mental disorder through the power of words and which would bring patients to an awareness of those ideas at the root of their ailments.

In his pursuit of the cathartic method, Freud was soon to discover another fact significant to the development of his theory of mind: free association revealed resistance, that is, at a certain point in the therapy, the patient would fall silent and refuse to answer questions or attempt to direct the conversation away from the crucial topic. Freud postulated that this was due to the fact that the idea which was becoming conscious was so repugnant to the patient's moral being, that he or she refused to face it. He saw this as the symmetrical opposite to repression and he began to formulate explanations on the origins of psychological disorders. He postulated that patients were conscious of experiences (that, more often than not, were sexual in nature) that they found disgusting and sought to forget. For Freud, mental states were composed of two elements: an idea and energy; and, although the idea could be forgotten, the energy had to be redirected and discharged in another way, hence the symptoms of mental disorders.

Freud's early thoughts on psychological disorders were concentrated on showing that an event causing trauma in early life (the primal scene) is repressed by the infant but recalled in adolescence, only for it to be so repugnant to consciousness that it is repressed once more, but the energy of that idea seeks discharge through other channels causing neurotic symptoms. However, Freud slowly realized that if such a theory were true, sexual abuse had to be rife in Viennese society and that even his own sister was a victim of seduction by an adult. One of his most radical ideas, one that he resisted for so long, had then to be postulated: the event in childhood was not fact but fantasy and this fantasy was due to infantile sexuality. The traumatic event was, therefore, replaced by an unfulfilled wish or desire on the part of the infant. Sexuality was becoming more and more prominent in the instinctual constitution of a human being. Neurotic behaviour was to be interpreted as meaningful because manifest symptoms could be explained in terms of deep, unconscious wishes and desires.

Therefore, for Freud, what were traditionally thought to be mere events but not actions of the human being began to take on a new significance. For him, the range of these events included dreams, errors (parapraxes) and jokes. Freud had enlarged the realm of action to involve unconscious intentions that could be made intelligible when the underlying, deep unconscious principles involved were made conscious. Agents were to be held responsible not only for what they knew they wanted, but also what they intended to do but were unaware of wanting. Dreams were perhaps the best illustration of this new account of agency since the interpretation of dreams could supply knowledge of the workings of the unconscious mind. Dreams, in short, are disguised fulfilments of a repressed wish. First, the dream only represents part of the repressed wish (condensation), and it is over-determined, since it may involve the attempt on the part of the mind to fulfil more than one wish. Second, the symbols in dreams obey the same logic as free association: the mind will not directly represent the wish, but symbolically represent it. Third, the conscious mind will try to impose an order on the illogical nature of the unconscious (secondary revision) when it is described to the analyst and also to one's own mind.

The process of analysis soon led Freud to postulate his full theory of the mind that, although constantly revised and never more than a hypothetical tool, formed the cornerstone of his whole theory. He remained a materialist throughout his life, believing that his explanations could ultimately be reduced to physical processes and his first presentation of his theory was largely in materialist terms (*Project for a Scientific Psychology*, 1895), but his later metaphorical explanations are clearer and more adequate. The most significant concept was the unconscious and Freud found evidence for this in the latent nature of ideas: the fact that they can be conscious at one second, forgotten the next and recalled again. He saw it as mere convention to identify the mind with consciousness and he postulated that there existed a part of the mind where a mixture of innate ideas and ideas acquired through the individual's development were present.

Freud divided the mind into the ego (*Ich*) and the id (*Es*): all conscious activity is caused by energy manifest in the id. Even the conscious instincts in the ego that seem to oppose the energy of the id are ultimately derived from deeper instincts. The unconscious is the collection of drives (caused at a deeper level by biological processes) in which each desire seeks its own independent satisfaction. The ego will not allow certain desires to become conscious because they will be harmful to the organism as a whole. Contradictions arise due to the processes of the mind because it begins to seek pleasure (the Pleasure Principle), but the ego instincts seek to safeguard the individual from harm (the Reality Principle). Freud here offers a modern redescription of the traditional dichotomy of hunger and love. The ego's role is to mediate between the claims of the id (to secure satisfaction at all costs) and the objections of the external world. However, a further distinction occurs between ideas capable of becoming conscious and those incapable of becoming conscious, that is, repressed ideas. Thus, within the unconscious we have a section called the preconscious (desires that are latent, that is, capable of becoming conscious) and the unconscious proper (desires that cannot become conscious because they will harm the individual).

Yet, as Freud had already discovered, strong desires will return in other symbolic forms (wish fulfilment), but the distinction between id and ego – that is pleasure and reality – could only account for psychosis, or the conflict between the ego and the external world where the ego is in the absolute service of the id. The explanation of neurosis had to invoke another concept: the super-ego or the internalization of the Oedipus complex. Freud had offered a sketch of the sexual development of the individual whereby he described a general picture of the progress from childhood to adulthood, although the progress was never smooth or absolute. The most important of these stages was the Oedipus complex whereby an infant has fixed its mother as a sexual object but this wish is accompanied by the threat of castration by the father. The mix of fear, respect and love (and the guilt for wanting to remove an object of love) that the infant feels for his father means that the wish for the love of his mother is repressed. This guilt would form the basis of what moral philosophy would refer to as the conscience.

The super-ego is what the ego should truly be (the rules of the society, of family are internalized and become the individual's rules). Whereas fear is connected with the reality principle, guilt is symptomatic of the operation of the super-ego: a psychotic has no fear or fears the wrong things; a neurotic has no guilt or feels guilty about the wrong things. Both fear and guilt lead to repression of desires. The super-ego accounted for neuroses where the patient suffered a conflict between the desires of the id and the ego because the ego was in the service of the super-ego; and also neuroses where the ego was in the service of the id but this generated a conflict between ego and super-ego. Neurosis is the conflict whereby a repressed drive is so intense that it seeks satisfaction through another form of expression (a conflict between the id and the super-ego where the ego may be in the service of one or the other). The psychoanalytic cure resides in sublimation (discharging the wish in another way), repression or satisfaction of the repressed desire that is causing neurotic or psychotic behaviour.

In his most speculative writings, Freud began to question his own dichotomy between love and hunger, and wonder whether the conflicts in the unconscious could be due to instincts that were already acting against one another deep in the id. In *Beyond the Pleasure Principle* (1920), Freud postulated the dichotomy of love and hate, that is, self-preservation (Eros) and the death drive (Thanatos), as a replacement. The death drive was characterized as aggression: the aggressive instincts of the unconscious that are directed at the subject himself. The super-ego took on a new role and a revolutionary one for moral thinking: whereas one normally supposes humans renounce aggression because they have a moral conscience, Freud suggested that human beings have a moral conscience because they renounce aggression (specifically towards their parents when they internalize the Oedipus complex). The super-ego became more than our conscience, it became a historical development not unlike the story told by Nietzsche's genealogy. And, for this reason, Freud was aware that civilization may have helped one to regulate aggression, but at the cost of causing anxiety and frustration when harmless drives are repressed due to civilized sensibilities. In *Civilisation and Its Discontents* (1930), Freud speculated on the evolutionary origin of society: unhappiness stems from the weakness of our bodies, the superior power of nature and finally the inadequacy of the regulations that bind us together in a society since they repress unharmful desires for irrational reasons. The aim of civilization was to minimize the first two forms of unhappiness, but at the cost of creating the third. Some neuroses were, therefore, due to society and its rules, which Freud saw as frustrating perfectly acceptable desires and wishes.

In the final instance, Freud saw that psychoanalysis could reveal not only the repression of harmful wishes by a patient, but also it could reveal those unconscious social rules that frustrate perfectly acceptable wishes. It could, in other words, cure both patients and society. And herein lies perhaps the biggest contradiction of Freud the thinker: a man who believed that human beings were ultimately reducible to deep biological forces, saw reason and responsibility for oneself as the key to a healthy mind. It was reason that was ultimately to regulate desires and not the id or society. Freud described human existence in a revolutionary way and inspired a practice that, despite its detractors, still allows many individuals to overcome conflicts within themselves.

Freud's complete works have been collected and translated in *The Standard Edition of the Complete Psychological Works of Sigmund Freud*, ed. J. Strachey (with A. Freud, A. Strachey and A. Tyson) in 24 vols, London, 1953–4.

Further reading

Ferris, Paul (1998) *Dr Freud: A Life*, Washington, DC: Counterpoint.

Robinson, Paul (1993) *Freud and His Critics*, Berkeley: University of California Press.
Thurschwell, Pamela (2000) *Sigmund Freud*, London: Routledge.

SEE ALSO: psychology, the emergence of

DAVID ROSE

G

GALTON, FRANCIS (1822–1911)

The founder of eugenics, Galton was born on 16 February 1822 in Birmingham, and educated at King Edward's School, King's College, London, and Trinity College, Cambridge, where he read Mathematics but fared poorly owing to bad health. His livelihood secured by an inheritance, Galton embarked on a voyage of exploration to Africa, described in *The Narrative of an Explorer in Tropical South Africa* (1853), which was succeeded by a handbook, *The Art of Travel* (1855). In the 1860s his scientific interests included meteorology, statistics and photography.

Galton is principally known as the creator and developer of eugenics, or the study of the possibility of improving human physical and moral character through selective breeding. This is often seen as among the more important results of the application of Darwinism to human and social evolution. (DARWIN was, indeed, Galton's half-cousin.) The starting-point for these endeavours was Galton's study entitled *Hereditary Genius*, which took up a commonplace mid-Victorian assumption concerning the guiding role an intellectual elite should play in society and politics, and attempted to prove that the qualities we term 'genius' were largely inherited. The most important of these was, broadly speaking, 'intelligence', and it was largely through discussions with Galton that Darwin himself came to view human progress in terms of the promotion of intelligence and civility over ignorance and barbarism. While such views had clearly racialist implications, Galton and most eugenicists were as concerned to assess domestic 'feeble-mindedness' and the propensity to various serious diseases as to apply the concept in an imperial and international context. Though its starting-point – the assessment of 'eminence' as evidenced in the biographical entries in *Men of the Time* (Routledge, 1865) – seems startlingly amateurish today both in the narrowness of its database and absence of any social-historical, class-based explanatory context, Galton was convinced that mental capacity was biologically transmitted, and that this could be proven by close analysis of statistical variation from averages. A second study, *English Men of Science* (1874), extended the same method to the examination of the background and aptitudes of Royal Society members, which also revealed that educational factors might hinder or facilitate natural intelligence, thus modifying the transmission of traits. The mature statement of Galton's theory came in *Inquiries into Human Faculty and Its Development* (1883), which popularized the word 'eugenics', from the Greek *eugenes*, 'namely, good in stock, hereditarily endowed with noble qualities'. Galton here demonstrated the dual focus of the new science, upon the positive development of useful qualities, such as energy, and the restraint of harmful tendencies, such as idiocy. Though he advocated the replacement of 'poor' races by 'better' ones, Galton was chiefly concerned with promoting intelligence rather than eliminating its opposite, and did not succumb to the crude racialism of the period of late nineteenth-century European imperial expansion. *Natural Inheritance* followed in 1889. His later scientific interests including pioneering work in fingerprinting. His eugenics concerns were extended by his chief follower, Karl Pearson. Galton died on 17 January 1911.

Further reading

Forrest, D.W. (1974) *Francis Galton. The Life and Work of a Victorian Genius*, New York: Taplinger.

Galton, Francis (1908) *Memories of My Life*, London: Elek.

Pearson, Karl (1914–30) *The Life, Letters, and Labours of Francis Galton*, 4 vols, Cambridge: Cambridge University Press.

SEE ALSO: anthropology and race; the body, medicine, health and disease; intellectuals, elites and meritocracy; psychology, the emergence of; Social Darwinism; utopianism

GREGORY CLAEYS

GANDHI, MOHANDAS K. (1869–1948)

The Indian nationalist, Mohandas ('Mahatma') Gandhi, rejected his upper-class background to become a 'champion of the oppressed' in both South Africa and India. Between 1893 and 1914 he developed an eclectic socio-political doctrine that synthesized oriental and Western ideas on resistance, reconciliation and 'the good life'. An activist rather than a theoretician, Gandhi wrote few books, but was a prolific journalist.

Gandhi was born in western India in October 1869. His father, a Hindu, was the Prime Minister of the native state of Porbandar, while his mother was a devotee of the Pranami sect, a religion that venerated both the Koran and the cult of Vishnu. Although Gandhi subsequently regretted his child-marriage (1883) and his poor record as a school student, his early life acquainted him with both the 'power politics' of the British Raj and the major Pranami tenets of religious toleration, simplicity of living and the ability of the will to subdue bodily appetites (e.g. through fasting).

In 1888, Gandhi travelled to London to study Law. After three years of training, he became a barrister, although his extracurricular interests in theosophy, Christianity and vegetarianism had a much greater long-term impact on his intellectual development. Gandhi also read TOLSTOY (*The First Step*) during this visit to London. From 1891 to 1893, Gandhi practised law in India before emigrating to South Africa. Once there, he encountered anti-Indian discrimination in both Natal and Transvaal, and began to campaign against various discriminatory laws and policies. Gradually, Gandhi developed a style of non-violent resistance that – from 1908 onwards – he called *satyagraha* ('truth force'). Having won many, but

not all, of his demands, Gandhi returned to India in 1915.

In 1904, Gandhi read *Unto this Last*, by RUSKIN, and concluded that the revival of traditional handicrafts was the necessary economic corollary of his socio-political conceptions of local democracy, a 'minimal state' and 'the simple life'. A more specific goal of Gandhian politics was Indian independence from British rule, and he set out both this specific demand – and his overarching philosophy – in *Hind Swaraj* (*Indian Home Rule*). Originally a newspaper article (1909), this seminal text was republished as a pamphlet in 1910, 1914, 1919, 1921, 1924, 1938 and 1939.

Gandhi had established the intellectual parameters of *satyagraha* in Africa and the final 33 years of his life can be seen as the application/popularization of a nineteenth-century doctrine. This involved personal campaigning *against* both colonialism and 'untouchability', and *in favour* of Hindu–Muslim unity, gender equality, hand-spinning and village self-sufficiency, as well as publishing books such as *The Story of My Experiments with Truth* (1927–9) and *Satyagraha in South Africa* (1928). The main changes to Gandhism, after the Chauri Chaura massacre of Indian policemen (1922), were an even greater emphasis on *ahimsa* ('non-violence') and a less optimistic assessment of the prospects for a harmonious 'end of empire'. During the Boer, Zulu and First World Wars Gandhi supported medical/ambulance assistance to British forces, but in 1942 he launched a 'Quit India' campaign that ultimately contributed to both independence and partition (i.e. the creation of Pakistan). In January 1948, Gandhi's opposition to communal violence led to assassination by a Hindu extremist.

Gandhi's disagreements with other Indian nationalists were not new, and help to explain the different emphases that he placed upon certain aspects of his system at different times. For example, in the Edwardian period, Gandhi stressed his criticisms of industrialism, modernization, terrorism and Hindu chauvinism in order to debunk expatriate socialists and the 'Extreme' wing of the Indian National Congress. His position, as set out in *Hind Swaraj*, was closer to that of the 'Moderate' faction in Congress, in that he shared their admiration for the principles (but not the practice) of the British Constitution, but Gandhi was not a secularist, and saw 'reform of the soul' as a necessary prerequisite of political transformation. Furthermore, the 'oriental' dimension of Gandhi's thought can be seen again in the manner in which he sought to stress continuity between his conception of *dharma* ('natural moral law') as a system of *mutual* obligation, and the more hierarchical concepts of duty propounded in the classical Indian texts that he studied avidly (e.g. *Bhagavadgita* and *Ramayana*). However, Gandhi's religious thought included a more active dimension than was traditional in the subcontinent; this was reflected in his admiration for both Mohammed and Jesus of Nazareth.

As well as biblical Christianity, a number of other Western beliefs helped to shape Gandhi's doctrines. Thus, in *Hind Swaraj*, Gandhi described himself as a follower of Tolstoy, Ruskin, EMERSON and THOREAU. The first three were unorthodox Christians, while Thoreau's more secular doctrine of civil disobedience to unjust laws was nevertheless reliant upon a 'Protestant' conception of individual conscience. Gandhi was particularly indebted to Tolstoy's *The Kingdom of God is within You* (which he read in 1894) for bringing to his attention Christian ideals of personal virtue and non-violence (as expounded in the Sermon on the Mount). Moreover, Tolstoy and Ruskin were advocates of 'the simple life' – and therefore passionate critics of industrial civilization – for not only was such a life preferable for the poor, but also luxury corrupted the moral and aesthetic sensibilities of the rich. This line of argument was frequently taken up by Gandhi in *Hind Swaraj* and elsewhere. Although Gandhi also described himself as a follower of Emerson, this admiration seems to have been largely due to a sense that the American was a 'spiritual' thinker, rather than to any specific concept. There seem to be stronger parallels between Gandhi's attempts to link national and personal regeneration, and those of the Italian nationalist, MAZZINI. Gandhi expressed particular admiration for the latter's *The Duties of Man* (1844).

Further reading

Bondurant, J.V. (1988) *Conquest of Violence: The Gandhian Philosophy of Conflict*, rev. edn, Princeton, NJ: Princeton University Press.

Gandhi, M.K (1997) *Hind Swaraj and Other Writings*, ed. A.J. Parel), Cambridge: Cambridge University Press.

Iyer, R.N (1973), *The Moral and Political Thought of Mahatma Gandhi*, New York, Oxford: Oxford University Press.

SEE ALSO: anti-colonial movements and ideas

CLIVE E. HILL

GARIBALDI, GIUSEPPE (1807–82)

The Italian soldier and freedom fighter Giuseppe Garibaldi was born in Nice in 1807 into a seafaring family. He received little formal education, but was heavily influenced as a young man by Italian patriotic literature and poetry. In 1834 he became involved with GIUSEPPE MAZZINI and his revolutionary organization, *Giovane Italia*, and was sentenced to death for his part in an attempted insurrection in Genoa. Forced into exile, he spent more than 10 years in South America fighting on behalf of the republican rebels of the Rio Grande and Uruguay, and gained an enormous reputation for fearlessness and military skill as commander of the red-shirted Italian Legion. With the outbreak of revolution in Europe in 1848, he returned to Italy, and fought alongside the Piedmontese army against the Austrians. In the early summer of 1849 he orchestrated a brilliant defence of the Roman Republic against the besieging forces of the French army.

Garibaldi's achievements in South America and in Italy in 1848–9, together with his romantic lifestyle, simplicity of character and striking looks (which invited pictorial comparison with conventional images of Christ) gave him massive popular appeal, and during the 1850s (much of which he spent travelling in America and Asia, before settling down in 1857 on the small island of Caprera, off northern Sardinia) he was regarded by many Italian patriots as critical for winning mass support for the cause of Italian unity. Though by instinct a republican, his relations with Giuseppe Mazzini grew increasingly strained, and when war broke out in northern Italy against the Austrians in 1859, he offered his services to King Victor Emmanuel of Piedmont-Sardinia. He was given the rank of general and successfully commanded a corps of volunteers.

The abrupt end of the war and the cession by the Piedmontese prime minister, Count Cavour, of Nice to the Emperor Napoleon III infuriated Garibaldi. In response to entreaties from followers of Mazzini, he agreed to lead an expedition to Sicily in a bid to wrest the initiative from Cavour and complete Italian unification. The campaign in southern Italy between May and October 1860 was an extraordinary military and political feat, and stirred the imagination of liberals and nationalists everywhere. It ended with the annexation to Piedmont of all of Italy, apart from Rome and

Venice. Garibaldi quickly became disenchanted with the new Italian government, and especially with its repressive policies in the south of the country: in April 1861 he entered Parliament (an institution for which he had little regard – he preferred benevolent dictatorships) and accused the prime minister, Cavour, of waging a civil war.

Garibaldi spent much of the last 20 years of his life away from Italian politics on his island of Caprera. He made two abortive attempts to capture Rome – in 1862 and 1867 – and in 1870 he fought for the French Republic against Prussia. An international celebrity (the crowds that greeted him on a visit to England in1864 were unprecedented), he lent his name to many left-wing causes in the 1860s and 1870s, including that of international peace. He wrote no theoretical works, but his *Memoirs* (1872) consolidated his image as the quintessential romantic revolutionary. He died in 1882.

Further reading

Ridley, J. (1974) *Garibaldi*, London: Constable.
Smith, D. Mack (1957) *Garibaldi*, London: Hutchinson.

SEE ALSO: Mazzini, Giuseppe

CHRISTOPHER DUGGAN

GEORGE, HENRY (1839–97)

Henry George was the author of *Progress and Poverty* (1879 with many later expanded editions) and founder of the 'single tax' on land values, a mechanism designed to enhance progress while alleviating poverty. George was born in Philadelphia and ended his formal education there at age 13. Two years later, he signed on as a foremast boy on a 15-month voyage to Australia. On his return, he worked briefly as a printer's apprentice until shipping out as a steward on a ship bound for California, where he lived until moving to New York after the publication of *Progress and Poverty*. In California, he worked variously as a typesetter and printer, prospected unsuccessfully for gold, published and edited newspapers, and, while living at the margins of poverty, gained recognition as a crusading proponent of social reform.

In 1870, George concluded that land values were the key to the fact that progress seemed to be producing poverty, and he began to write and

lecture on the subject, publishing *Our Land and Land Policy* in 1868. He wrote *Progress and Poverty* between 1877 and 1879, which, after considerable difficulty finding a publisher, was printed by the respectable firm of Appleton in New York. Initially, *Progress and Poverty* was ignored and received mixed to unfavourable reviews.

In New York, George wrote for *The Irish World* and published *The Irish Land Question* (1881). The paper sent him to Ireland and Britain where he lectured for a year, gaining support for the views expressed in *Progress and Poverty* but not for his views on Ireland.

On returning to New York, he discovered that the tide had shifted dramatically and *Progress and Poverty* was now considered a major contribution to debates over economic and social reform. George ran for mayor of New York in 1886 and secretary of state of New York in 1887, losing both races. He lectured frequently in the USA, twice more in Europe and made a tour of Australia and New Zealand, where his ideas were particularly influential. On returning from this trip, he suffered a stroke and his health was problematic for the rest of his life. Against medical advice, he ran again for mayor of New York in 1897 and died of a stroke just before the election.

George had concluded that the central problem of the modern era was that growing wealth was combined with increasing poverty. He searched for the cause of this situation and concluded that rises in the price of land were always combined with low wages and that low land prices came with high wages. To make his argument, George used a labour theory of value and attacked the arguments regarding population of THOMAS MALTHUS (1766–1834).

George argued that wages came from expended labour rather than from advances by capital, as was then the common position in political economy. George argued that wages were not advanced from capital or reduced capital. He contended that labour creates capital, part of which is then returned to the labourer in wages. He went so far as to argue that labour employed capital rather than the other way around.

George saw Malthusianism as a potential threat to his ideas, as did many other radicals and reformers in the nineteenth century. He argued that Malthus simply served the interests of the wealthy by justifying disease, hunger and poverty as part of the natural order rather than the result of greed and social maladjustments. He asserted, without examining Malthus's evidence, that population growth had nothing to do with the existence of human misery and argued that a society run on the proper lines was perfectly capable of caring for an increasing population. He contended that in a society based on equality, population growth would make everyone better off.

The reason this is possible is George's discovery that while land is the basis for the production of wealth, rent is the basis for its distribution, and, typically of the time, he tried to state this insight as a scientific law, even developing a formula:

Produce = Rent + Wages + Interest

therefore

Produce − Rent = Wages + Interest
(*Progress and Poverty*: 171)

Wages and interest are what is left when rent is deducted. Thus, rent is what inhibits economic development.

The solution was 'a single tax' on land values. This would radically increase productivity and would redistribute wealth to those who produce and to the community as a whole. Extremes of wealth and poverty would be eliminated, and all would have more than necessary for a good life. This situation would transform society by reducing crime and elevating morality.

George published *Social Problems* in 1883 to take advantage of the popularity of *Progress and Poverty* and to apply his formula to contemporary issues in the USA. He also tied his work to various reform movements, particularly unionization and the Knights of Labor, which he supported, and land nationalisation, which was particularly popular in Australia and New Zealand.

While George did not write a utopia in the traditional sense of depicting an imaginary country, he did spell out the positive effects of his changes, and others wrote utopias depicting these results. Such works were published in Australia, Britain, Canada, New Zealand and the USA. Also, a number of communities were founded in the USA and other countries based on George's ideas, three of them very successfully, Fairhope in Alabama founded in 1895, Arden in Delaware founded in 1900 and Free Acres in New Jersey founded in 1910. All three still exist. While there were single-tax communities established in other countries, there is very little information available about them.

Further reading

Andelson, R.V. (ed.) (1979) *Critics of Henry George: A Centenary Appraisal of Their Strictures on Progress and Poverty*, Rutherford, NJ: Fairleigh Dickinson University Press.
Barker, C.A. (1955) *Henry George*, New York: Oxford University Press.
George, H. (1879) *Progress and Poverty: An Inquiry into the Cause of Industrial Depressions, and of Increase of Want with Increase of Wealth. The Remedy*, New York: Appleton.
Giacalone, J.A. and Cobb, C.W. (eds) (2001) *The Path to Justice: Following in the Footsteps of Henry George*, Malden, MA: Blackwell.
Young, A.N. (1916) *The Single Tax Movement in the United States*, Princeton, NJ: Princeton University Press.

SEE ALSO: Marx and Marxism; political economy; utopianism

LYMAN TOWER SARGENT

GOBINEAU, JOSEPH COMTE DE (1816–82)

Joseph-Arthur Count Gobineau was a French diplomat, writer, ethnologist and social thinker whose works in the realm of racial and racist theories had a profound impact, either directly or indirectly, on the subsequent development of 'race science' and on protagonists of racial and racist thinking such as Richard Wagner or Hitler. He was not so much the 'father' of racist ideology but rather a synthesizer who drew on history, linguistics and anthropology to explain that 'race' (see ANTHROPOLOGY AND RACE) was the key to understand the world and its history.

Gobineau – himself of bourgeois descent, having acquired the title of 'Count' only after his uncle's death in 1855 – was very well educated in languages and in the cultures of the orient. During TOCQUEVILLE's brief term as minister of foreign affairs he served as his secretary, after which he embarked on a diplomatic career. He became well known through fictional writings such as the famous *Pleiads* (*LesPléiades*, 1874, trans. 1928), as well as through scholarly works on the histories and religions of Asia (*Histoire des Perses*, 1869; *Religions et philosophie dans l'Asie Centrale*, 1865) and on *The Renaissance* (1877, trans. 1913). However, it was his early work on *The Inequality of Human Races* (*Essai sur l'inégalité des races humaines*,

1853–5, trans. 1915) that was to become the most famous and influential of all his publications, above all in Germany.

Gobineau saw the true cause of the fall of great civilizations in the adulteration of blood, in the physical and moral degeneration of the people's 'body'.

History was thus not a history of class struggles but of race conflicts, and geography and climate were not seen as influential factors in the fortunes of a people. Nor were government and politics of much significance in determining social existence. What mattered in the lives of peoples was the degree of degeneration caused by 'miscegenation', the cross-breeding between races: Gobineau argued that miscegenation was always a betrayal of superior birth since it was always the respective superior race that had to make the racial sacrifice.

Gobineau distinguished between three fundamental races: white, black and yellow. The whites comprised not only Caucasians but also the Semitic races, and the yellows counted various branches such as the Mongols, Finns or Tartars. There were, however, no more truly pure races because of the ongoing mixing of races; instead, peoples were marked by various degrees of miscegenation. Blacks were marked by an almost animal-like nature with usually very limited intellect but great energy and will-power; they were sensual and musical, but had no concept of true vice and virtue – a 'slave race'. The yellow race was seen as the antithesis of the Negro, showing no physical strength, a certain apathy and a weak desire, a love of utility and business, and respect for the law. Such qualities made the yellows superior to the Negroes, but they were still mediocre *vis-à-vis* the whites.

The white race was considered the only true bearer of culture and civilization. Whites displayed an energetic intelligence, they loved life and liberty but valued honour even more. To Gobineau, the most remarkable branch were the 'Aryans', a 'master race' that was believed to have originated in northern India and migrated to Europe, and which was accredited with all the high civilizations. 'Aryan' was a notoriously multi-faceted term in nineteenth- and early twentieth-century discourse, which was based on linguistic similarities between Sanskrit and most European languages. Race-thinkers had differing notions of which nations or even parts of nations belonged to this alleged 'race' and which rank they occupied in its hierarchy.

Gobineau argued that the Aryans had contributed to the formation of the Hindu, Iranian, Hellenic, Celtic, Slavonic and Germanic peoples; to him, the Germanic stock amongst the European peoples constituted the very top of the racial pyramid. However, the Aryans' chief weakness was their great susceptibility to miscegenation – which he considered a huge problem since he regarded the strength and thus the fate of civilizations as being based on their racial composition. In his system of racial thought the Slavs were at the forefront of miscegenation with the yellow race. Jews, although belonging to the Semitic races and thus to the whites, were not considered a civilizing force in humanity. In his *Essai* he used the image of a textile fabric with regard to the role of races in his system of racial thought: the two most inferior varieties of the human species, the black and yellow races, were the crude foundation, the cotton and wool, made supple by the families of the white race by means of adding their silk; while the Aryan group, circling its finer threads through the noble generations, was designing on its surface a dazzling masterpiece of arabesques in silver and gold.

Gobineau was – despite his praise of the Germanic element – not in praise of contemporary Germans, although he had some hopes for northern Germany. In his view the German people did not contain much of the ancient pure Germanic racial material – an assessment that he applied to varying degrees to all contemporary European nations.

He was deeply imbued with ideas of cultural pessimism, arguing that the ongoing mixing of races was leading to the final demise of the last vestiges of Aryandom and to the universal establishment of societies of mediocre quality. Only in later years, in his work on the *Renaissance* and, most notably, in his novel *Pleiads*, glimmers of hope can be detected: the existence of a tiny number of noble characters – in the *Pleiads* metaphorically also referred to as 'sons of kings' – who have preserved enough racial value to rise with their thoughts and deeds above the surrounding sea of 'fools', 'scoundrels' and 'brutes'. This elite was not bound to any particular nation but rather constituted an inter-national brotherhood of Aryans.

Gobineau did not find much resonance in the French Far Right, which did not appreciate the fact that he did not extol the French 'race'. He became famous only by his later amicable association with

Richard Wagner, who found his own thoughts of race and degeneration confirmed in Gobineau's work, but added his idea of redemption and regeneration to it. After both Gobineau's and Wagner's death the Bayreuth circle was instrumental in popularizing Gobineau in the German-speaking world and in creating a movement called 'Gobinism'. Nationalist and racist associations in Germany adapted Gobineau's ideas to German requirements: Gobineau's fear of the 'yellow peril' from the East stepped back in favour of an aggressive anti-Semitism; the German 'race' was exalted. At the turn of the century Gobineau was thus turned into a prophet of both German racial superiority and the need to defend the German 'race' against its racial enemies.

Further reading

Biddiss, M.D. (1970) *Father of Racist Ideology: The Social and Political Thought of Count Gobineau*, London: Weidenfeld & Nicolson.

Gobineau, J.A. Comte de (1970) *Selected Political Writings*, ed. and intro. Michael D. Biddiss, London: Jonathan Cape.

Hannaford, I. (1996) *Race: The History of an Idea in the West*, Baltimore, MA: Johns Hopkins University Press.

Mosse, G.L. (1978) *Toward the Final Solution: A History of European Racism*, London: J.M. Dent & Sons.

SEE ALSO: anthropology and race; conservatism, authority and tradition; Social Darwinism

DETMAR KLEIN

GODWIN, WILLIAM (1756–1836)

Though the term 'anarchism' was not used in a positive sense until 1840, by the French writer PIERRE-JOSEPH PROUDHON, William Godwin is regarded as the founder of philosophical anarchism. Born at Wisbech on 7 March 1756, Godwin was raised by a strict Baptist father, and became a Sandemanian Baptist minister in 1778. By 1783, however, he had abandoned his religious beliefs and calling for a career as a historian, novelist and journalist. His chief work, the *Enquiry concerning Political Justice* (1st edn, 1793), was the most extensive and serious philosophical appraisal of the first principles of the French Revolution, and escaped prosecution only because of its high price. Rendered famous by its success, and that of his first major novel, *Caleb Williams* (1794), Godwin

married the feminist writer Mary Wollstonecraft, but she died in childbirth in 1797; their daughter married the poet Percy Shelley. Godwin extended and amended certain doctrines of *Political Justice* in both the 2nd and 3rd edns of the work (1795, 1798) and in *The Enquirer* (1797). But his reputation was greatly undermined by the attack on him, and upon all forms of utopian social engineering, in T.R. MALTHUS's *Essay on Population* (1798), and despite publishing a number of later novels and historical works, as well as a response to Malthus, *Of Population* (1820), he never regained prominence.

The reputation of the *Enquiry concerning Political Justice* rests on its treatment of eight themes: (1) philosophical necessitarianism – the foundation of Godwin's optimism is his notion of the pliability, and improvability, of human nature, and his insistence, particularly against the notion of original sin, that individual moral character was derived from the environment, and that the voluntary actions of men were derived from their opinions; (2) theory of justice – in his famous 'fire case', where we are faced with a choice between rescuing an illustrious person who has been or is capable of assisting humanity as a whole, or a comparatively humble individual, Godwin urges us to choose the former; 'my neighbour's moral worth, and his importance to the general weal' are 'the only standard to determine the treatment to which he is entitled'; (3) individualist anarchism – Godwin builds on Swift, PAINE and others to argue that not merely government, but also most forms of co-operative endeavour, including marriage and common labour and meals, hinder the capacity of each individual to form their own judgements (the Nonconformist plea for the right of private judgement, with sincerity as the root virtue, being the root of this view) by compelling compromise; in the first edition of *Political Justice*, in particular, he urged the return to a simple society without government or exchange, law or punishment, where order was to be based on mutual moral supervision without coercion and social organization was to be parish-based; (4) critique of political institutions – Godwin scathingly assails not only monarchy and aristocracy, but equally the negative aspects of democracy, notably its propensity to interfere with private judgement through 'partiality and cabal', and the evil effects of vote-taking to secure decisions; (5) cosmopolitanism – Godwin places much greater value on universal benevolence than the crucial republican virtue, patriotism; (6) rejection of a complex division of labour – particularly in the 1st edn of *Political Justice*, Godwin (here largely following Rousseau) pleads for simplicity in work, with all being cultivators primarily, and condemns the propensity of separate professions (physicians and lawyers, but especially soldiers) to develop an interest separate from that of the public; (7) theory of property – again particular in the 1st edn., Godwin opposes all exchange and all significant inequality of property, on the principle that 'there is nothing more pernicious to the human mind than the love of opulence'; if all superfluity were abolished, and labour shared equally, it would be reduced, Godwin thought, to a few hours a day, with time then available for intellectual speculation. War and selfishness, moreover, Godwin also saw as the offspring of unequal property. The system of distribution proposed was also linked to his theory of justice, all property being viewed by Godwin as held as a 'trust' that must be expended in the most just manner; (8) perfectibility – Godwin famously speculated that reason would eventually conquer the passions, especially sexual desire, that life might be greatly prolonged; besides abolishing law, government and war, human tempers would improve, to the point to which there would be no 'disease, anguish, melancholy, nor resentment; nor would there be no reason to fear that overpopulation would undermine the system of economic organisation' (this was the starting-point of Malthus's critique not only of Godwin but also Enlightenment optimism generally).

The changes in the three editions of *Political Justice* published in Godwin's lifetime involved a reinforcement of his arguments against violence and revolutionary change, and a shift from relying upon reason as the basis of voluntary action to the feelings. In keeping with his breach with his agitator friend, John Thelwall, a popular lecturer among the London working classes, Godwin by 1797 stressed that the working classes would not be ready for universal suffrage for many years. He also moved sharply away from the embracing of simplicity, condoning even luxury, which he now associated with refinement and knowledge, in *The Enquirer*, so long as it was not exclusively enjoyed by the few to the burden of the many. He also conceded to Burke in particular, moreover, that benevolence was best practised not by an abstract and universal principle, but according to the

'nearness to ourselves' of persons and things. This gave greater stress to the value of and virtues associated with the domestic affections, as well, which no doubt owed something to both the personal and intellectual influence of Mary Wollstonecraft on Godwin.

Further reading

Clark, John P. (1977) *The Philosophical Anarchism of William Godwin*, Princeton: Princeton University Press.
Locke, Don (1980) *A Fantasy of Reason. The Life and Thought of William Godwin*, London: Routledge & Kegan Paul.
Marshall, Peter H. (1984) *William Godwin*, New Haven: Yale University Press.
Monro, D.H. (1953) *Godwin's Moral Philosophy. An Interpretation of William Godwin*, Oxford: Oxford University Press.
Philp, Mark (1986) *Godwin's Political Justice*, London: Duckworth.
—— (ed.) (1993) *Political and Philosophical Writings of William Godwin*, 8 vols, London: William Pickering.

SEE ALSO: early socialism; intellectuals, elites and meritocracy; theories of the state and society: the science of politics; utopianism

GREGORY CLAEYS

GOLDMAN, EMMA (1869–1940)

Emma Goldman is the best-known US anarchist. Goldman was a leading activist and lecturer for anarchist causes, as well as an advocate for birth control, women's rights and free speech, and she was a popularizer of the arts, particularly modern drama.

Goldman was born in Kovno, Lithuania, into a middle-class Jewish family, emigrated to the USA in December 1885 and was radicalized by the Haymarket bombing in May 1886 and the execution in November 1887 of four of the innocent men who had been found guilty of the bombing. About this time, and after an unhappy marriage, she moved to New York and met Alexander 'Sasha' Berkman (1870–1936), who became her lover and with whom she remained close for the rest of his life. She also met Johann Most (1846–1906), who was editor of *Freiheit*, a paper intended for German-speaking workers. Most was notorious as an advocate of violence and the author of *Revolutionäre Kriegswissenschaft* (1885), a pamphlet on bomb-making. Most became Goldman's mentor, and his advocacy of violence may have led her, together with Berkman, to attempt the assassination in 1892 of Henry Clay Frick (1849–1919), the manager of the Carnegie steel mills in Homestead, Pennsylvania, who was notorious for his anti-union activities. The attempted assassination was a fiasco, with Frick only slightly wounded, but Berkman served 14 years in prison, an experience that gave rise to his famous *Prison Memoirs of a Revolutionist* (1912).

Goldman apparently learned from this experience and avoided violence. Earning her living as a nurse, Goldman turned to writing and lecturing, which ultimately provided her an income. She edited a significant journal of anarchist thought and agitation, *Mother Earth* (1906–17). This was edited by Berkman after his release from prison and was followed by eight issues of *Mother Earth Bulletin* (1917–18).

In general Goldman followed the theories of KROPOTKIN, and was more of a publicist and activist than theorist. Her most important contribution to anarchism was her book *Anarchism and Other Essays* (1910). Her other writings included *The Social Significance of Modern Drama* (1914), which, together with her lectures, helped introduce US audiences to Ibsen, Strindberg and Hauptmann.

Goldman was deported from the USA to Russia in 1919. She was welcomed as a great revolutionary, but became a critic of the Soviet experiment. Radicals hoping that the Soviet Union would live up to expectations did not welcome her critique. She left Russia after only two years, and she had trouble finding publishers for her analysis of the situation in the Soviet Union. *My Disillusionment in Russia* was published in 1923 with the last twelve chapters missing, which were published as *My Further Disillusionment in Russia* a year later. After she left Russia, she wrote her autobiography *Living My Life* (2 vols, 1931). At the end of her life she became an advocate of the anarchists during the Spanish Civil War. Her writings on Spain have been collected as *Vision on Fire* (1983).

Further reading

Drinnon, R. (1961) *Rebel in Paradise: A Biography of Emma Goldman*, Chicago: University of Chicago Press.
Goldman, E. (1910) *Anarchism and Other Essays*, New York: Mother Earth Publishing Co.
——(1931) *Living My Life*, 2 vols, New York: Alfred A. Knopf.
Wexler, A. (1984) *Emma Goldman: An Intimate Life*, New York: Pantheon.

SEE ALSO: Bakunin, Mikhail; Kropotkin, Pietr

LYMAN TOWER SARGENT

GREEN, T.H. (1836–82)

Thomas Hill Green was born on 7 April 1836 in Birkin, Yorkshire, and died in Oxford on 26 March 1882. He attended Rugby School from 1850 to 1855 and then entered Balliol College, Oxford. Green was elected to a fellowship at Balliol College in 1860 and to the Whyte's Professorship of Moral Philosophy in the University of Oxford in 1878. He promoted the reform of university education, its extension to provisional centres and access by women, and was also active in movements to promote popular education and reform of educational provision for the middle classes, serving as an Assistant Commissioner on the Taunton Commission on Secondary Education and later on the Oxford School Board. His service on these bodies, together with his active role in temperance at both the local and national levels, demonstrated Green's principled commitment to practical politics and to an ethic of universal citizenship. He identified with the 'advanced' wing of the Liberal Party and was elected in 1876 (as a City rather than University representative) to the Oxford City Council. With the exception of a few articles and pamphlets, and a book-length introduction to the Green and Grosse edition of *The Philosophical Works of David Hume*, the bulk of Green's writings appeared posthumously. The most important of these works were the *Prolegomena to Ethics* and the *Lectures on the Principles of Political Obligation*.

Throughout Green's career at Oxford, his college was dominated by Benjamin Jowett, a liberal (on some views a dangerously liberal) figure in Victorian theological controversy, the translator of Plato and Aristotle, and an early admirer of G.W.F. Hegel's philosophy (see HEGEL AND HEGELIANISM). Like Jowett, Green was committed to liberal Anglican theology and to a strongly positive view of the importance of Ancient Greek political thought and philosophy. But while Jowett later regretted the enthusiasm for Hegel that he had helped foster, this view was not shared either by

Green, BERNARD BOSANQUET or F.H. BRADLEY, younger members of what came to be seen as an 'English' or 'British' school of philosophical Idealism.

Green's philosophy embraced a characteristically Idealist argument concerning the subject and object in knowledge, which was directed against the sceptical impasse into which empiricist accounts were always driven. For Green, however, human consciousness could be explained only by reference to the 'eternal consciousness' (or 'God'), the source of knowledge of the physical and moral world. This formulation gave philosophical support to Green's religious views and was welcomed by some of his contemporaries for this very reason. It also provided the basis for a system of ethics in which the end of human conduct was thought to entail the progressive 'realization' of a conception of self that has its origin in the 'eternal consciousness'. But while Green placed a premium on self-directed action as the only basis for moral perfection, insisting that the standard of worth must relate to the 'good of persons', he stressed that such an idea of the good was shared or 'common' and could be realized only within a social context in which individuals were motivated by the desire to further the 'common good'.

The idea of the 'common good' entailed a conception of social life in which the realization of each individual was harmonized with that of others. In advanced stages of moral development realization took place through the freely willed actions of socially conscious beings committed to perfecting themselves in the course of enhancing the range of opportunities for autonomous action available to other members of a given society, and ultimately of humankind. The emphasis on moral self-development, and the consequent stress on free action, connected Green's political thinking with important currents in mid-Victorian liberalism and, indeed, with the highly moralized liberal nationalism of European figures such as GIUSEPPE MAZZINI. At the same time, however, his understanding of the 'common good' as a progressive development of consciousness, the dependence of consciousness upon mutual recognition and his focus on the embodiment of a community's consciousness of its good in a succession of political and social institutions was reminiscent of parts of Hegel's political philosophy.

From this perspective, Green can be seen as reformulating core liberal ideas so that liberty was given a positive cast that focused on creating the conditions in which moral autonomy would be more likely. Rights delineated the possibilities of autonomous action, but they did so in relation to claims whose recognition reflected judgments on the historically specific requirements of the common good. These judgements were incorporated in law, the source and guarantor of which was the collective moral sense of the community, more or less imperfectly incorporated in the institutions and actions of the 'state'. A reconsideration of the character and role of the 'state' was central to Green's project. His stressed that its coercive capacities rested ultimately on the 'will' of its members, reflecting their understanding of its moral significance and giving heightened effect to this as it freed itself from class bias and became more participatory and democratic. In this and other respects, Green's political views were markedly radical. He was a proponent of free trade but insisted that this objective needed to be conditioned by the requirements of a positive view of freedom that, under prevailing conditions, justified the mobilization of the legal powers of the state to promote education, public health, temperance and to eliminate the consequences of historical injustices inflicted by the aristocracy on the lower classes of both Britain and Ireland. In foreign affairs, Green was opposed to militarism and imperialism.

While the obloquy attracted by Bosanquet's political philosophy in the early twentieth century did not extend to Green, his ethical and metaphysical theories were subjected to severe criticism in the 1930s by H.A. Prichard and J.P. Plamenatz. Since the appearance of Melvin Richter's intellectual biography in 1964, however, Green's political and ethical philosophy have become the focus of extensive and generally sympathetic scholarly treatment.

Further reading

Dimova-Cookson, M. (2001) *T.H.Green's Moral and Political Philosophy: A Phenomenological Perspective*, London: Palgrave.

den Otter, S.M. (1996) *British Idealism and Social Explanation*, Oxford: Clarendon Press.

Green, T.H. (1986) *Lectures on the Principles of Political Obligation and Other Writings*, eds P. Harris and J. Morrow, Cambridge: Cambridge University Press.

——(1997) *The Collected Works of T.H.Green*, ed. P.P. Nicholson, 5 vols. Bristol: Thoemmes Press.

Nicholson, P.P. (1990) *The Political Philosophy of the British Idealists. Selected Studies*, Cambridge: Cambridge University Press.

SEE ALSO: intellectuals, elites and meritocracy; liberalism; main currents in philosophy; Romanticism, individualism and ideas of the self; theories of the state and society: the science of politics

JOHN MORROW

GUESDE, JULES (1845–1922)

In the history of nineteenth-century political thought, Jules Guesde is not recognized for the originality of his ideas. However, he remains a significant figure in the history of French socialism. His personal ideological metamorphosis mirrored the evolution of French socialist thought from being premised on an association of independent producers to the collectivization of resources. More importantly, Guesde contributed to the growth and development of French socialism through the dissemination and popularization of Karl Marx's ideas. In addition, Guesde reorientated the apolitical stance of the late nineteenth-century French workers movement towards political activism and party formation.

Born Jules Bazile on 11 November 1845 in Paris, the future Jules Guesde first entered political discourse as a journalist in 1867. An advocate of republicanism during the waning years of Louis Napoleon's Second Empire, Guesde adopted his mother's family name in order to protect his family. Before being sentenced to five years in prison for his writings in defence of the Paris Commune (his support was predicated less out of an affinity for communard doctrines, than out of a distrust of the 'republicans' at Versailles), Guesde fled France, first for Geneva, then for Rome and Milan.

When he went into exile, Guesde was a republican, but not yet an adherent to socialism. His more seasoned compatriots viewed Guesde as an ideological neophyte, still adhering to the centralized statism and social democracy identified with French Jacobinism. However, contact with other French exiles, as well as European socialists who had participated in the First International, exposed Guesde to concepts that he later distilled into his ideas. Exiled socialists were divided between Karl Marx's collectivist theories (see MARX

AND MARXISM) and MIKHAIL BAKUNIN's anarchism that promoted a stateless society as the end result of a spontaneous social class revolution. The latter's apolitical tendencies was more consistent with Proudhonian-inspired French socialism's triad of associationism, mutualism and federalism (see PROUDHON, PIERRE-JOSEPH). Guesde's move to Milan in 1874 appears to have represented a personal and ideological turning point. He married Mathilde Constantin, an intellectual soulmate who was fluent in five languages. Ideologically, Guesde broadened his ideological foundations beyond anarchism's anti-statism. Under the influence of the works of Théodore Dézamy, a communist during France's July Monarchy, and Russian utopian socialist Nicolai Chernyshevsky, Guesde's writings between 1875 and 1876 reflected a burgeoning interest in collectivism.

Returning to France in 1876, Guesde encountered a republic dominated by monarchists who passed laws that restricted the development of socialism. The workers' movement largely eschewed political measures, let alone revolutionary activities. Although Guesde, in 1878, still drew upon French socialism's anarcho-federalism's emphasis on a revolutionary federation of municipal councils and trades, he no longer believed that workers were capable of leading a socialist movement. By contrast, the lead role reserved by Guesde for an intellectual, revolutionary elite provided rudimentary evidence of his exposure and receptivity to Marx's ideas.

Surrounded by a cadre of revolutionary intellectuals, including Marx's son-in-law, Paul Lafargue, Guesde soon attracted Marx's attention and confidence as a potential leader of the French socialist movement.

However, Guesde faced formidable obstacles in achieving his primary goal – attracting support for a separate workers' party. Until 1879, defence of the beleaguered Third Republic was a more compelling message than the advancement of a social class agenda. The Republic's stabilization in 1879, followed by its neglect of the socialist agenda, appeared to substantiate Guesde's revolutionary, as opposed to co-operative, brand of socialism. At the national labour congress held at Marseilles in 1879, Guesde spoke of how the irreconcilability of class interests rendered reform within the existent system impossible, thus mandating that workers build their own political organization. However, until a unified party emerged in 1905 French socialism was bedevilled by internecine warfare between reformists and revolutionaries, associationists and collectivists. Although little separated Guesde's programme from that of the majority, Guesde's continued reliance on revolutionary messianism and a centrally organized party led by an intellectual elite distanced him from French socialism's traditional message and constituency. Consequently, in 1882, Guesde formed the Workers' Party, which served as a vehicle for his introduction of the principal tenets of Marxism to the French political landscape. Recognizing that skilled workers could not be weaned off of their penchant for associationism, Guesde directed his message to the burgeoning, though unorganized, unskilled proletariat, particularly in the industrial north of France.

During the 1890s, the Workers' Party (renamed the French Workers' Party), taking advantage of an increase in labour militancy, became France's largest socialist party. Guesde's election to the Chamber of Deputies from a constituency in the northern industrial town of Roubaix demonstrated the growing strength of his party. Guesde's electoral defeat in 1898 demonstrated his vulnerability to nationalist attacks that his embrace of Marxism had tied him too closely to German socialists and ideologies, a particularly potent message when the Dreyfus Affair was reaching its crescendo.

Guesde's trademark rigidity in refusing to abandon his revolutionary rhetoric rendered him a less than efficacious political figure. Yet in spite of his penchant for doctrinaire stances, Guesde was, at times, plagued by pragmatism; personally repulsed by the misogynistic impulses of French socialism, Guesde's fears over alienating male voters and enfranchising conservative female voters muted his support for feminism.

By 1900, Jean Jaurès eclipsed Guesde as French socialism's most identifiable face. Though re-elected to the Chamber of Deputies in 1906, 1910, 1914 and 1919, Guesde's insistence on revolutionary orthodoxy (including opposition to nationalization of key industries because it did not entail outright expropriation), socialist abstinence from participation in bourgeois governments (though Guesde served as minister 'without portfolio' during the First World War) and subordination of every conceivable issue to class struggle (including his characterization of the Dreyfus Affair as being of little relevance to the working class and his responses to war in 1914) marginalized him from the socialist mainstream. In

the twentieth century, Guesde was too militant for the increasingly conciliatory Socialist Party, while his open hostility to the Russian Revolution rendered him too distant from new currents of communism.

Further reading

Geary, Dick (ed.) (1989) *Labour and Socialist Movements in Europe Before 1914*, Oxford: Berg.
Mayeur, Jean-Marie, and Rebérioux, Madeleine (1984) *The Third Republic from its Origins to the Great War, 1871–1914*, Cambridge: Cambridge University Press.
Moss, Bernard (1976) *The Origins of the French Labor Movement*, Berkeley: University of California Press.
Willard, Claude (ed.) (1970) *Jules Guesde. Textes choisis, 1867–1882*, Paris: Éditions Sociales.
——(1991) *Jules Guesde, l'apôtre et la loi*, Paris: Les Éditions Ouvrières.

SEE ALSO: Blanc, Louis; Blanqui, Louis-Auguste; Marx and Marxism; Proudhon, Pierre-Joseph

DAVID A. SHAFER

GUIZOT, FRANÇOIS (1787–1874)

François-Pierre-Guillaume Guizot, a leading French historian and conservative liberal politician during the July Monarchy (1830–48), was born on 4 October 1787 in Nîmes, and died on 12 October 1874 in Val-Richter. Guizot's father had been executed during the Revolution, and he returned with his mother after six years of exile in 1805, immediately involving himself in anti-Bonapartist circles. Appointed Professor of History at the University of Paris in 1812, Guizot became known as a defender of constitutional monarchy, his views being associated with the group known as Doctrinaires, who sought a *juste milieu* between absolutism and democracy. These ideals he explained in *Du gouvernement représentatif et de l'état actuel de la France* (1816; On Representative Government and the Present Condition of France). Guizot's main historical works appeared between 1820–30, namely the *Histoire des origines représentatif* (1821–2; History of the Origins of Representative Government); the *Histoire de la révolution d'Angleterre depuis Charles I. à Charles II.* (2 vols, 1826–7; History of the English Revolution from Charles I. to Charles II); the *Histoire de la civilisation en Europe* (3 vols, 1828; General History of Civilization in Europe) and the *Histoire de la civilisation en France* (5 vols, 1829–32; The History of Civilization in France). He also translated Gibbon's *Decline and Fall of the Roman Empire*.

In his political ideas Guizot remained from 1814 wedded to the Bourbon restoration, and to restricting further extensions of the franchise; his main parliamentary opponent was ADOLPHE THIERS, who wanted more substantial bourgeois involvement in the regime. From 1822–8 he was a liberal opponent of the government of Charles X. Increasingly conservative after 1830, Guizot became during the July Monarchy (1830–48) first Minister of Education (1832–7), and passed the famous Guizot Law (1833), guaranteeing secular primary education to all. Briefly Ambassador to England, he became in 1840 Foreign Minister under Soult, and the *de facto* leader of the government, which he came to head in 1847. Guizot had some success in foreign affairs, notably in averting war with Britain. Tensions mounted, however, over Guizot's insistence on a narrow franchise based upon a substantial property qualification, at a time when demands for universal suffrage were increasing. After two years of economic crises Guizot was forced to resign on 23 February 1848, the day before the monarchy was abolished and a republic declared. In exile he moved to England, and published *Histoire de la république d'Angleterre et de Cromwell* (2 vols, 1854; History of the English Republic and of Cromwell) and *Histoire du protectorat de Cromwell et du rétablissement des Stuarts* (2 vols, 1856; History of the Protectorate of Cromwell and the Restoration of the Stuarts). In retirement he wrote *L'Histoire de la France, depuis les temps les plus reculés jusqu'en 1789* (5 vols, 1872–6; The History of France from the Earliest Times to the Year 1789) and a lengthy memoir-cum-contemporary history, *Mémoir pour servir à l'histoire de mon temps* (9 vols, 1863).

Further reading

Crossley, Ceri (1993) *French Historians and Romanticism. Thierry, Guizot, the Saint-Simonians, Quinet, Michelet*, London: Routledge.
Johnson, Douglas (1975) *Guizot: Aspects of French History 1787–1874*, Westport, CT: Greenwood Press.

SEE ALSO: democracy, populism and rights; historiography and the idea of progress; liberalism

GREGORY CLAEYS

H

HARRISON, FREDERIC (1831–1923)

The foremost interpreter in Britain of the Positivist philosophy of AUGUSTE COMTE, Harrison was born in Muswell Hill, London, on 18 October 1831. Educated at King's College School and Wadham College, Oxford, he was admitted to the bar, but an interview with Comte in Paris persuaded him that studying the Comtean system, which emphasized three successive social stages (theological, metaphysical, positive), offered higher rewards. Commencing the study of mathematics and natural science, he taught at the Working Men's College, and began to publish essays, reviews and newspaper articles, often promoting the causes of working-class education and political rights. (Harrison opposed extending the franchise to women, however, and argued against JOHN STUART MILL on this issue, as well as what he regarded as the overly strong individualism of *On Liberty*.) He met JOHN RUSKIN in 1862, and despite differences did much to extend Ruskin's reputation among the working classes.

In the first of some thirty books, *The Meaning of History* (1862), he took up the characteristically Comtean theme of the need to understand history as the unfolding of rational laws, and emphasized the centrality of the French Revolution to defining the last great stage of historical evolution. In 1867 he helped to found the Positivist Society, to which he was the principal lecturer, and the *Positivist Review*, which he edited. His principal study in political thought, *Order and Progress* (1875), defended republicanism when introduced by gradual rather than revolutionary means. But, in the light of the extension of the suffrage in the 1867 Reform Act, he contended that 'order' required a reinforced executive, and that social authority should rest on intellectual meritocracy, not anarchic democracy. Harrison's anti-imperialist views, extended by his fellow Positivists E.S. Beesley and Richard Congreve, were also introduced here. In 1877 he became Professor of Jurisprudence and International Law at the Inns of Court, but rarely wrote on the subject. Though he disagreed with Congreve and others on the strict ritualism of the Positivist religion, Harrison acknowledged that the essence of the Comtean religion was the promotion of the moral substance of the Bible, while denying its divine origins, and the possibility of miracles. Harrison thus remained a moral relativist, and denied that any knowledge of ultimate reality or absolute truth was possible. This rationalist theism was thus similar in some respects to the notions of ROBERT OWEN and HENRI DE SAINT-SIMON.

Harrison's writings include a number of biographies, notably of Oliver Cromwell (1888), John Ruskin (1902) and the Earl of Chatham (1905), and more than half a dozen collections of essays, of which the most important are *The Creed of a Layman* (1907), *The Philosophy of Common Sense* (1907), *National and Social Problems* (1908) and *Realities and Ideas* (1908). *On Society* (1918) offers a final summary of his finished views on the Religion of Humanity. He died on 14 January 1923.

Further reading

Harrison, Frederic (1911) *Autobiographic Memoirs*, 2 vols, London: Macmillan.
Vogeler, Martha (1984) *Frederic Harrison. The Vocations of a Positivist*, Oxford: Oxford University Press.
Wright, T.R. (1986) *The Religion of Humanity. The Impact of Comtean Positivism on Victorian Britain*, Cambridge: Cambridge University Press.

SEE ALSO: historiography and the idea of progress; intellectuals, elites and meritocracy; religion, secularization and the crisis of faith; social theory and sociology in the nineteenth century

GREGORY CLAEYS

HEGEL AND HEGELIANISM

Absolute Idealism

Seen from a broad historical perspective, Hegel's philosophy was the last great attempt since Kant to rehabilitate metaphysics, that is, the attempt to know through pure reason the absolute or unconditioned. Through his dialectic, Hegel believed that he could overcome the limitations of traditional metaphysics, surpass the Kantian critical limits of knowledge and provide a new rational foundation for moral and religious faith. It is striking that Hegel himself defined his own philosophy in these terms. In the introduction to his *Encyclopedia of Philosophical Science* (*Enzyklopädie der philosophischen Wissenschaften*) he characterized his philosophy by its opposition to three major currents of his age: the old metaphysical rationalism, the critical philosophy of Kant and the philosophy of feeling of F.H. Jacobi and the Romantics. While the old metaphysical rationalism was correct in postulating a rational knowledge of the absolute, it did not have the proper dialectical methodology but remained stuck in the old deductive model of demonstration. Though Kant was right in his critique of this model of demonstration, he went too far in concluding that there could be no rational knowledge whatsoever of the absolute. Jacobi and the Romantics were justified in rebelling against the Kantian constraints upon knowledge, but they went astray in thinking that they could be overcome by replying upon aesthetic or religious feeling and intuition alone. In agreement with the older rationalism, Hegel stressed that knowledge of the absolute would have to be rational, conceptual or demonstrative, but he recognized that there could be no return to the old deductive methodologies of classical rationalism, which had been undermined through the Kantian critique of knowledge. Hegel therefore saw the distinctive contribution of his philosophy as his new methodology for metaphysics: the dialectic. In stressing the need for a rational comprehension of the absolute, Hegel attempted to restore the sovereign role of reason in philosophy against the Romantic faith in aesthetic experience. His philosophy was therefore an attempt to restore – through a new means – the legacy of the Enlightenment against the currents of Romanticism.

Like Descartes, Spinoza and Leibniz, Hegel stresses that metaphysics is the foundation of the sciences, and it indeed provides the basis for every part of his system. Hegel first sketched his metaphysics in his late Frankfurt years (1799–1800), then developed it during his collaboration with Schelling in his early Jena years (1800–4); he gave it its first mature exposition, only after breaking with Schelling, in his 1807 *Phenomenology of Spirit* (*Phänomenologie des Geistes*). The chief exposition of his metaphysics is his *Science of Logic* (*Wissenschaft der Logik*) (1812–13), a more condensed form of which appears in the first part of his *Encyclopedia*.

Hegel himself described his metaphysics as *absolute Idealism*. Put very simply, the central thesis of absolute Idealism is that everything in nature and history is an appearance or manifestation of the absolute idea. Hegel understands the absolute idea in teleological terms: it is the single self-realizing and self-organizing purpose or end of all things. To say that everything is an appearance of the idea therefore means that everything acts or exists for the sake of this purpose or goal. This goal or purpose is the realization of spirit (*Geist*), where spirit consists in mutual or intersubjective self-awareness, where the self knows itself through the other as the other knows itself through the self. Spirit is 'an I that is a We and a We that is an I'.

There are three more specific theses behind absolute idealism. The first thesis is *monism*: that the universe consists in not a plurality of substances but in a single substance. Such monism opposes not only *pluralism,* the doctrine that there are many substances, but also *dualism*, the doctrine that there are *two* kinds of substance, the mental and the physical, the ideal and the real. For Hegel, the mental and physical, the ideal and real, are simply different appearances or manifestations of the single universal substance. The second thesis is *organicism*: that reality forms a living whole, or consists in a single living process. According to Hegel, this process consists in three basic moments or movements: inchoate unity (identity), differentiation (difference) and the unity of the two previous moments in a more organized and differentiated unity (identity-in-difference). The third thesis is *rationalism*: that this living process has a purpose, or conforms to some form, archetype or idea. Putting all these theses together, absolute idealism is the doctrine that everything is a part of the single universal organism, or that everything conforms to, or is an appearance of, its purpose, design or idea.

Although Hegel's absolute Idealism is monistic, it does not maintain that reality is pure oneness, an undifferentiated unity without difference within itself. Hegel was critical of any definition of the absolute as pure identity, as if it could be an identity that excludes difference. He insisted that absolute Idealism had to explain the reality of the finite world, the fact that there are differences between things. Accordingly, the absolute had to be conceived not simply as unity but as the unity of unity and non-unity. Such a conception of the absolute is expressed in his organicism: If the absolute is life, then it must realize itself through self-differentiation.

What, more precisely, makes absolute *Idealism*? The Idealist dimension of absolute Idealism comes from its rationalism. The ideal does not refer to something mental or subjective but to the archetypical or intelligible. Hence the absolute Idealist's claim that everything is ideal does not mean that everything is an appearance of some cosmic mind or super-subject. Such an interpretation of Hegel's absolute Idealism is a serious misrepresentation, since it understands the absolute in one-sided subjective or mental terms. Since Hegel understands the idea as an archetype or form, it manifests itself in both the subjective and objective, the mental and material.

There are two fundamental differences between Hegel's absolute Idealism and the transcendental Idealism of Kant and Fichte. First, Hegel's absolute idealism is much more realistic since it is compatible with the existence of material objects independent of the awareness of them. Even if nothing subjective yet exists, it still manifests the absolute idea. Second, absolute Idealism is much more naturalistic, explaining all subjectivity as one part or manifestation of nature. The realization of spirit is indeed the goal of all nature and history, the highest organization and development of all the powers of nature, but it still does not transcend nature and history, existing in some self-sufficient noumenal or intelligible realm.

Religion

Hegel's absolute Idealism was a self-conscious attempt to rationalize – to preserve the truths and to negate the errors – of traditional Christianity. Hegel held that philosophy is the rational comprehension of the content of religious belief. What art and religion grasped on the level of intuition and feeling, the philosopher would formulate on the higher level of concepts or systematic thought. The absolute was Hegel's technical philosophical concept for the traditional religious idea of God. His absolute has some of the traditional Christian attributes: it is infinite, spiritual and self-creating, its essence involving its existence. Hegel's teleology rehabilitated the traditional concept of providence: God's governance of the universe now meant that everything conforms to the absolute idea. And his organicism rationalized the traditional doctrine of the trinity: the father represents the moment of unity, the son the moment of difference and the holy spirit the moment of unity-in-difference.

In other respects, however, Hegel's absolute Idealism involves a sharp break with traditional Christian theism. Hegel rejects the doctrine of a transcendent God, a deity that exists in a supernatural realm apart from nature and history. He insists that the absolute cannot transcend nature and history because it comes into existence only in and through them; apart from the specific events of history and the concrete things of the natural world, God would be nothing more than an abstraction. Because of its severe rationalism, Hegel's absolute Idealism left no room for supernatural revelation. The Bible was replaced by philosophical comprehension; miracles could not exist in a universe governed strictly according to laws. Finally, because it denies the existence of a supernatural spiritual realm beyond the earth, absolute idealism undermined the traditional Christian doctrine of personal salvation. In the tradition of Machiavelli and Rousseau, Hegel criticized the traditional Christian ethic of salvation because it undermined the virtue or public spiritedness required for a republic.

Some of Hegel's more orthodox contemporaries accused him of pantheism, a serious charge in his day because pantheism was commonly associated with atheism. However, Hegel protested against this charge, rebutting it on two grounds. His first rebuttal consists in a *defence* of pantheism. To equate pantheism with atheism is a misunderstanding, Hegel argues, because the pantheist never identifies God with the totality of finite things. The pantheist holds that God is the *substance* or *essence* of all finite things, which are only appearances of it; so rather than giving divinity to finite things, the pantheist makes finite things disappear in the divine. It would be better to call such a doctrine 'acosmism', Hegel contends, meaning by that term the disappearance of the finite in the infinite. Hegel's second rebuttal is that, though pantheism is not atheism, he is not a pantheist after all. The problem with pantheism, in Hegel's view, is not that it is false but that it is incomplete. He agrees with the pantheists that there is a single universal substance that is the essence and source of all finite things, but he disagrees with them in two fundamental respects. First, he does not think that the realm of finitude *disappears* in the absolute; rather, he insists that this very realm *reveals* the absolute, and indeed that the absolute comes into being only through it. Second, he holds that the infinite is not only substance but also subject; this means that it reveals itself not only in nature, but also especially in the sphere of culture and history; and that it is not only organic but also spiritual, consisting not only in life but also the self-awareness of life. What is distinctive about Hegel's pantheism is that he extends the divine to the historical world and does not, like Bruno, Schelling and Spinoza, limit it to the natural world. For Hegel, the fundamental place for the realization of God in the world is in history.

Dialectic

Since absolute Idealism is a full-blown metaphysics, Hegel had to face the challenge of Kant's critique of metaphysics. In the *Critique of Pure Reason* Kant had limited all knowledge to sense experience, and argued that metaphysics, in the sense of a knowledge through pure reason of the absolute or unconditioned, is impossible. Hegel's response to this challenge was his famous dialectic. The dialectic was Hegel's method to revive metaphysics, to achieve a rational comprehension of the absolute that would do justice to the Kantian demand that we critically examine all claims to knowledge.

The inspiration for Hegel's dialectic was the antinomies of the *Critique of Pure Reason*. Kant's four antinomies demonstrated that reason gets involved in contradictions whenever it goes beyond the limits of experience. These contradictions have a similar form: on the one hand, a thesis where we *must* bring the series of conditions to an end with the unconditioned (a final cause, an ultimate unit of analysis) to escape an infinite regress; on the other hand, an antithesis where we *cannot* bring the series of conditions to an end, because we can always determine further the conditions for anything. Hegel agreed with Kant that the antinomies have this form, and that they arise of necessity whenever we go beyond the limits of experience. He disagreed with Kant, however, about the number and solution of the antinomies. For Hegel, there were not only four antinomies because they are endemic to all reasoning, and the solution of the antinomies is not to limit knowledge to experience but to grasp the whole upon which experience depends.

According to Hegel's account in the *Encyclopedia*, there are three moments or aspects of the dialectic. The first is the moment of abstraction, which is the correlate of the Kantian thesis. Here the understanding assumes that some concept is unconditioned or self-sufficient, perfectly intelligible in itself, in abstraction from everything else. The second is the negative moment, which corresponds to the Kantian antithesis. The understanding now finds that its concept is not self-sufficient after all, because it is comprehensible only through its relations to other things. It finds that it must seek the reason or condition for what it first thought to be unconditioned. Now the understanding is caught in a contradiction: it must assume something unconditioned to complete the series of conditions, but it also cannot assume the unconditioned, because it must find its condition. The third is the speculative or positively rational moment, which resolves the contradiction by seeing the unconditioned not as one thing alone but the whole of which all finite things are only parts. If we make this move, we still save the central claim of the thesis – that there is something self-sufficient or unconditioned – but we also recognize the basic thrust of the antithesis – that any one thing is somehow dependent. We avoid the contradiction by ascending to a higher level, to the standpoint of the whole, of which the concept and its opposite are only parts. The contradiction arose by seeing the unconditioned simply as *one part of the whole*, whereas the only thing that can be unconditioned is the whole, of which the unit and that on which it depends are only parts. Thus the dialectic attempts to vindicate Hegel's holistic paradigm of reason, according to which the whole precedes its parts (since only the whole is unconditioned, not its parts).

Political thought

Hegel's political thought is best understood as an attempt to liberalize the classical Greek concept of the community. Hegel revives some of the central theses of classical political thought: that the state is an organic whole prior to its parts, and that the individual has its identity only within the state. He is therefore critical of the contractarian tradition of Hobbes and Locke, which held that the state can be formed by a contract between self-sufficient individuals. Reviving Aristotle's dictum that man is a beast or god apart from the *polis*, Hegel contends that there are no individuals apart from the state. The very identity and worth of the individual rests upon his performing his role within the state and political life. Nevertheless, Hegel was also critical of the classical state for its failure to recognize individual rights and freedoms. The modern state would have to overcome this limitation, ensuring every individual certain basic rights and the freedom to pursue its self-interest in the market-place.

In the tradition of Rousseau and Kant, Hegel maintains that the foundation of the law is the concept of freedom. The justification for law is not that it ensures happiness, still less that it has been established by tradition or force, but that it guarantees freedom. Hegel has two concepts of freedom: subjective freedom, which consists in the power and right to pursue my self-interest independent of constraint by others or the government; and objective freedom, which consists in moral autonomy, acting according to the principles of morality. While Hegel stresses the value of moral autonomy, he insists that the specific content of morality has to be provided by the community and cannot be supplied by the reason of the individual alone. This has led to charges of authoritarianism, but such criticisms neglect the great value that Hegel places upon subjective freedom. Hegel stresses that there are certain fundamental constitutional truths, certain basic rights, which

should be given to every individual simply as a free and rational being.

Although Hegel was inspired by the republics of antiquity and stressed the value of individual rights, he was still sceptical of modern mass democracy. He doubted the wisdom of the masses as well as the value of universal suffrage. Nevertheless, he still affirmed the importance of public participation in government, stressing that the state had to reflect the general will of its people. Such participation would take place indirectly through the channels of corporations, which would represent the interests of their members. Hegel also stressed the value of a bicameral legislative body, whose members would be elected from corporations and local governments. Although he valued a monarchy, he also insisted that the monarch should be bound by the constitution, and that his policies should be formulated according to the will of the legislative body.

While Hegel recognized the importance of a single central power in the modern state, he was also highly critical of too much centralization at the expense of local autonomy and independent groups. He deplored the absolutist states of the *ancien régime* and the government of revolutionary France for attempting to control everything from above. A healthy constitution permitted individual initiative, independent corporations, and local government and popular participation in affairs of the state. Rather than a machine that controls everything from above, the state should be an organism that has some independent life in its individual parts. These intermediate or independent groups played a pivotal role in Hegel's attempt to reconcile the demands of community and liberty: they would ensure community as a source of belonging for the individual, and they would uphold liberty by limiting control from above.

Hegel's political philosophy has been notorious for its Prussianism, for its attempt to rationalize the reactionary Prussian state. This interpretation has been based upon Hegel's notorious dictum that 'the actual is rational, the rational is actual', and his famous claim in the preface to the *Philosophy of Right* that the purpose of philosophy is not to prescribe how the state ought to be but to comprehend the reason within the present. Yet Hegel himself explained that the actual should not be conflated with whatever exists but only what realizes the ideals of reason. If Hegel preached reconciliation to the facts of history this was mainly because he believed that history was progressing towards its ultimate goal, the self-awareness that every human being is free. Rather than an apology for a reactionary Prussian state, Hegel's political philosophy is better understood as a defence of the Prussian reform movement, which attempted to liberalize and modernize the Prussian state by creating more local government, economic freedom, popular participation and a constitution ensuring fundamental rights.

Hegelianism

In the preface to his *Philosophy of Right* Hegel wrote in some famous lines that every philosophy is only the self-awareness of its age. This dictum applied to Hegel's philosophy too, which was only the self-awareness of its age, the era of the Prussian Reform Movement. This movement dominated Prussian political life during the reign of Friedrich Wilhelm III from 1797 to 1840. Although many of its ideals were far from reality, and although hopes for reform were disappointed time and again in the 1820s and 1830s, many hoped that their monarch would finally deliver on his promises for reform. As long as hope remained, the Hegelian philosophy could claim to represent its age, at least in aspiration if not in reality.

Hegel's rise to prominence began in 1818 with his appointment at Berlin. Hegel was called to Berlin by the Prussian Ministry of Culture, and more specifically by two powerful ministers, Baron von Altenstein and Johannes Schulze. They supported Hegel's philosophy largely because they saw it as the medium to support their own reformist views against reactionary court circles. In 1827 Hegel's students began to organize themselves, forming their own society, the Berliner kritische Association, and editing a common journal, *Jahrbücher für wissenschaftliche Kritik*. For almost all the Young Hegelians before 1840, Hegel's philosophy represented the *via media* between reaction and revolution. It seemed to be the only alternative for those who could not accept the reactionaries' appeal to force and tradition or the Romantic revolutionaries' appeal to sentimental patriotism.

Despite these shared sympathies, there were always deep tensions among Hegel's followers. Battle lines began to form only in 1835, when DAVID FRIEDRICH STRAUSS published his *Das Leben Jesu,* which argued that the biblical story of Jesus was essentially mythical. Some regarded Strauss's argument as a betrayal of Hegel's legacy, while others saw it as its fulfilment. The basic issue at dispute concerned the proper relationship of Hegel's philosophy to religion. To what extent can Hegel's philosophy rationalize the traditional Christian faith? The opposing answers to this question gave rise to the famous division of the Hegelian school into a right wing, left wing and centre. This distinction was made by the Hegelians themselves. According to Strauss, there were three possible positions regarding this issue: either all, some or none of the traditional Christian beliefs could be incorporated into the Hegelian system. The right wing held that all, the centre that some, and the left that none, could be rationalized by the system. Among the chief right-wing Hegelians were Henrich Hotho (1802–73), Leopold von Henning (1791–1866), Friedrich Förster (1791–1868), Hermann Ninrichs (1794–1861), Karl Daub (1765–1836), Kasimir Conradi (1784–1849), Phillip Marheineke (1780–1846) and Julius Schaller (1810–68). Among the moderate or centre Hegelians were Karl Michelet (1801–93) and Karl Rosenkranz (1805–79). And among the prominent left-wing Hegelians were LUDWIG FEUERBACH (1804–72), Arnold Ruge (1802–80), David Friedrich Strauss (1808–74), MAX STIRNER (1806–56) and, in his later years, BRUNO BAUER (1808–82). The second generation of left-wing Hegelians included Karl Marx, Friedrich Engels and MIKHAIL BAKUNIN.

Although the battle lines between the Hegelians first became explicit and self-conscious over a theological issue, their religious differences ultimately arose from deeper political ones. These political tensions had been present in the early 1820s, but they became more apparent in the 1830s. The basic question at issue concerned the extent to which existing conditions in Prussia realized Hegel's ideals. Here again the Straussian metaphor proved useful to describe the various positions in the debate. The right held that most, if not all, conditions in Prussia fulfilled Hegel's ideals; the centre claimed that some did; and the left believed that few, if any, did. Although there was an apparent chasm between right and left, the dispute between them still took place within the broad confines of Hegel's system. All parties remained true to Hegel's basic principles and ideals, and simply quarrelled over the extent to which they were now realized in Prussia. It is misleading, therefore, to see the split between right- and left-wing Hegelians as a conflict between radicals and reactionaries. Throughout the 1820s and 1830s, the division between radicals and reactionaries was only between opposing wings of a reformist programme. The radical currents of left-wing Hegelians developed only in the 1840s, after the accession of Friedrich Wilhelm IV.

What finally dissolved Hegelianism was not its internal disputes but Prussian history. In 1840 the Prussian Reform Movement came to an end. In that year Altenstein and Friedrich Wilhelm III died. Hopes for reform were again raised with the accession of Friedrich Wilhelm IV, but the new king's personal politics were very reactionary. He advocated government by the old aristocratic estates, disapproved of the plans for a new constitution, insisted upon protecting the state religion and even defended the divine right of kings. In 1841 Friedrich Wilhelm showed his political colours by inviting SCHELLING to Berlin 'to combat the dragonseed of Hegelianism'. Then, in 1842, the government began to impose censorship, forcing the Hegelians to publish their work outside Prussia. For any Hegelian in the 1840s, then, this course of events could be only profoundly discouraging. Rather than marching forwards, as Hegel prophesized, history seemed to be moving backwards. By the late 1840s, Hegelianism was essentially dead as an intellectual movement in Germany. The owl of Minerva flew to England and the USA, where the spirit of Hegel reincarnated itself in the systems of BOSANQUET, BRADLEY and Royce.

Bibliography

Science of Logic (1969), trans. A. Miller, London: George Allen & Unwin.
Lectures on the Philosophy of World History (1975), trans. H. Nisbet, Cambridge: Cambridge University Press.
Phenomenology of Spirit (1977), trans. A. Miller, Oxford: Oxford University Press.
Lectures on the Philosophy of Religion (1984–6), trans. P. Hodgson and R. Brown, Berkeley: University of California Press.
The Encyclopedia Logic (1991), trans. T. Garets and W. Suchting. Indianapolis: Hackett.
Elements of the Philosophy of Right (1991), trans. H. Nisbet. Cambridge: Cambridge University Press.

Further reading

Avineri, S. (1972) *Hegel's Theory of the Modern State*, Cambridge: Cambridge University Press.
Taylor, C. (1975) *Hegel*, Cambridge: Cambridge University Press.

Toews, J. (1980) *Hegelianism: The Path Toward Dialectical Humanism, 1805–1841*, Cambridge: Cambridge University Press.
Wood, A. (1990), *Hegel's Ethical Thought,* Cambridge: Cambridge University Press.

F.C. BEISER

HERZEN, ALEXANDER IVANOVICH (1812–70)

Alexander Ivanovich Herzen was an outstanding Russian thinker and public activist. His talent and vast erudition manifested themselves in science and philosophy, journalism and literature. His works greatly influenced the thought and social movements of Europe and Russia.

Herzen was born on 6 April 1812 in Moscow. He graduated from the Department of Physics and Mathematics of Moscow University in 1833. The radicalism of his views on Russia's present and future led to his deportation from Moscow. Herzen was sent into exile to the provinces where he spent a considerable part of his life (1835–40, 1841–3).

Herzen kept abreast in scientific developments and paid particular attention to the methodology of science. His works *Dilettantism in Science* (*Diletantizm v nauke*, 1843) and *Letters on the Study of Nature* (*Pisma ob izuchenii prirody,* 1845) became the first works on the philosophy of science in Russia. His first attempts at fiction were the novels *Who Is to Blame?* (*Kto vinovat?* 1845–6) and *Doktor Krutsov* (*Doctor Krutsov*, 1847), which were devoted to the themes of human dignity and individual responsibility.

In 1847, Herzen and his family emigrated for Europe. During the 1850s he published his brilliant memoirs *My Past and Thoughts* (*Byloe i Dumy*) that maintained the value of individual life and freedom. His novel *From the Other Shore* (*S togo berega,* 1850), first published in German, was designed to make European readers aware of the peculiarities of Russian life and way of thinking.

In 1852 Herzen moved to London where he founded the Free Russian Press. He launched a series of periodicals, including the *Polar Star* magazine and a newspaper *The Bell* (*Kolokol*), which were the first uncensored publishing enterprises in Russian history. Working as an editor and a publisher, he also wrote a number of articles on the social problems of contemporary Europe and Russia.

Hezen's diverse activities were united by the question of the future of Russia. He found it necessary to adapt the principles of Western socialism to the Russian local and historical conditions: peasant communes, with their collectivism, the habit of mutual assistance and the absence of private property. He called his vision of the new social order 'Russian socialism', being – together with N. Chernyshevsky – a major theoretician of this political doctrine.

Herzen's protean personality and his versatile talents of poet and politician, theoretician and public activist, Slavophile and Westernizer, influenced the development of scientific and political though both in Russia and Europe. His novels have proved their high artistic stature and remain widely read.

Herzen died on 27 January 1870 in Paris, and was buried in Nice.

Further reading

Herzen, A.I. (1956) *Selected Philosophical Works*, trans. L. Navrosov, Moscow: Foreign Languages House.
—— (1968 [1924–6]) *My Past and Thoughts*, trans. C. Garnett, 5 vols, rept, New York: Knopf.
Malia, M. (1961) *Alexander Herzen and the Birth of Russian Socialism: 1812–1855*, Cambridge: Harvard University Press.
Zimmerman, J. (1989) *Midpassage: Alexander Herzen and European revolution 1847–1852*, Pittsburgh: University of Pittsburgh Press.

SEE ALSO: early socialism; Russian thought in the nineteenth century

EVELINA BARBASHINA

HISTORIOGRAPHY AND THE IDEA OF PROGRESS

The writing of history, and the reconceptualization of the idea of history itself, were central to the unfolding self-identity of the leading nineteenth-century nations. The sense of the emancipatory and character-building capacity that knowledge of the past might provide was inherited from the Enlightenment, and linked to the emerging profession of the intellectual. In this period were written many of the most important national histories of the modern era, often by political conservatives, such as FRANÇOIS GUIZOT's *History of Civilisation in France* (4 vols, 1830), HEINRICH VON TREITSCHKE's *History of Germany in the Nineteenth Century* (1879–96), William Stubbs's *The Constitutional History of England* (1874–8) or Henry Hallam's conservatively Whiggish *Constitutional History of England* (1827), but also by liberals, like George Bancroft (1800–91) in the USA (*History of the United States*, 10 vols, 1834–74). As earlier, popular history in particular often served nationalist aims, becoming increasingly jingoistic in the last decades of the century. The biography of great figures remained both a scholarly and popular focus of historical interest; US historiography commences with Jared Sparks's editing of Washington's works in 12 volumes (1833–7). The growth of literacy helped to make history a widely popular subject for the first time. And though some, like Wilhelm Windelband (1848–1915) in Germany, and BENEDETTO CROCE (1866–1952) in Italy, denied that history could rise to an equivalent level of generality as natural science, this was for historians in particular the great age of 'scientific history', in which laws could be discovered and methods applied that would bring certainty and even predictability to historical study. Academic and professional history, while obsessed with the unique qualities of the age, endeavoured increasingly to earn for the subject the coveted legitimacy attached to the natural sciences, and with it the right to claim universal application and validity based upon an established uniformity of human experience and an agreed interpretation of what 'evidence' was suitable for generalization.

The institutionalization and professionalization of history in both the public and academic realms that mark the century had a great impact on its conceptualization, notably through the confrontation with theology by the application of historical methods to the study of religion, especially by examining the life of Jesus and through biblical criticism. By the end of the century, the study of historical method had been greatly systematised; see, e.g., for France, the *Introduction to the Study of History* of Charles V. Langlois and Charles Seignobos (1898), or for Britain, Edward Freeman, *Methods of Historical Study* (1886). A few individuals, notably LEOPOLD VON RANKE (1795–1886) in Germany, who wrote extended studies of Prussian, French and British history, were able to exert a profound influence as teachers upon the creation of academic history; of considerable academic influence in Britain was LORD ACTON (1834–1902), who insisted that history had 'to be critical, to be colourless, to be new'.

By the beginning of the period, notable attempts had already been made to integrate national histories into a secular scheme of human evolution generally, notably by Johann Gottfried von Herder (1744–1803; *Ideen zur Philosophie der Geschichte der Menscheit*, 1784–91) and the Marquis de Condorcet (1743–94; *Esquisse d'un tableau des progress de l'esprit humain*, 1795). By 1900 disciplinary subdivision had established economic, social, intellectual, political, legal, comparative and technological histories, amongst others. 'Modern history' as such had come fully into its right, for instance in the work of JULES MICHELET (1798–1874), whose *Chronological Table of Modern History* appeared in 1825. All of the major interpretations of history in the period acknowledge the centrality of commercial and industrial developments, and their fundamental redefinition of many of the parameters of human life. European historians tend to focus also on the nature and effects of the French Revolution, with THOMAS CARLYLE (1795–1881) its greatest historian in English. This article will survey the chief trends in the period, focusing particularly on Britain, France and Germany. It will examine theories of history as such, rather than advances in particular forms of evidence, such as philology, archaeology and palaeontology, the opening and cataloguing of archives, or reappraisals of the problems of bias or objectivity, and in reference to theories of the modern period, rather than medieval or classical scholarship.

From conjectural history to the Whig interpretation of history

The most important late eighteenth-century historical school to define the emergence of modernity emerged from the leading writers of the Scottish Enlightenment, notably David Hume (1711–76; *History of Great Britain*, 1754–62), William Robertson (1721–93), Adam Ferguson (1723–1816) and John Millar (1735–1801). 'Conjectural' or 'philosophical' history for the Scots involved tracing and assessing the stadial development of humanity through, frequently, four main stages: hunting and gathering, pastoralism, agricultural and commerce. This progress from 'rudeness' to 'refinement' entailed both an economic narrative, in which the founding of private

property, and later the emergence of the urban trading classes, were key moments, and a political narrative, in which the creation of free political institutions, specifically in Britain, demarcated the emergence of the ideal modern polity. History, thus, focused on the factors that stimulated wealth-creation, from which the new science of political economy emerged in the last decades of the eighteenth century, and the embracing of liberty, the analysis of which became central to the emerging science of politics. Conjectural history purported to be universally applicable, because based upon a science of human nature. This provided an account of natural, but ever-expanding, human wants, the satisfaction of which through the improvement of material conditions provided the motive-force for movement from one stage to the next. The development of commerce and manufactures causally introduced a 'good' or 'regular' government of free political institutions, which in turn promoted further commercial freedom as the middling orders grew more powerful. While the broad trend of this school, represented by Hume and Adam Smith in particular, was overwhelmingly optimistic about commercial society, stressing both increasing opulence and sociability, some writers, notably Ferguson, expressed greater ambiguity, contending that progressive economic specialization threatened the loss of both martial and civic virtue, risking both the degeneracy of artisan character and a relaxation of national public-spiritedness.

Successive generations of British historians in the nineteenth-century refined this approach in a variety of ways. Large numbers were, as Herbert Butterfield noted, Protestant, progressive and Whig, and were concerned to celebrate the achievements, liberty, stability and prosperity, of a Protestant constitution whose roots could be traced back to 1688, or 1649, or 1215, or even earlier. The tendency to see history generally as the 'story of liberty', as Croce put it, which is perhaps the dominant interpretation of the later modern period, dates from this era. Such 'Whiggish' history put the past at the service of the present, and condemns, moralizes or applauds according to its perceived contribution to the Victorian constitution. It is opposed in particular by the historicism of FRIEDRICH MEINECKE (1862–1954), which contends that each age must be understood solely in terms of its own internal principles, not by reference to the present. Such Whiggishness for Butterfield reached its apogee in Acton: it does not define the age as such. The two leading British historian of the era were THOMAS BABINGTON MACAULAY (1800–59) and HENRY THOMAS BUCKLE (1821–62). Macaulay's whose *History of England* (1848–61) was phenomenally successful. Though he avowed his willingness to plot national disasters, and even worse, great crimes and follies, as well as triumphs, Macaulay's Whig politics brought him to side with his partisan forebearers in his discussion of seventeenth-century developments, and to trace much further back the three factors that contributed most to British liberty, the limitations on executive power, the absence of a 'caste-like' nobility and the failure to develop a military establishment that threatened popular liberty. But first and foremost his intent was to defend the claim that 'the history of our country during the last hundred and sixty years is eminently the history of physical, of moral, and of intellectual improvement'. Not only had resistance to monarchical and ecclesiastical encroachment been successful, but also Britons were rich, and their scientific and technological achievements had brought about a considerable rise in the standard of living of even ordinary people, a focus crucial to the earlier Scottish writers.

In the chief work of BUCKLE, *History of Civilisation in England* (1857–61), the emphasis on the emergence of British freedom is less on institutions and politics, and more on intellectual and natural factors. There is a more pronounced effort to proclaim history as a science based upon the assumption of regularity and uniformity in human motivation and action, based on laws 'permeated by one glorious principle of universal and undeviating regularity' that are of divine design. But, at root, Buckle's is still a history of liberty as such, and of the relative absence of the 'protective spirit' in Britain by comparison with her Continental neighbours. Britain possessed, Buckle noted, a 'love of liberty, which for many centuries has been our leading characteristic, and which does us more real honour than all our conquests, all our literature, and all our philosophy put together'. Its final great product was Smith's *Wealth of Nations*, which was for Buckle 'eminently a democratic book'. A similar effort to ascertain the sources of modern individualism was *The Civilisation of the Renaissance in Italy* (1860), by the Swiss historian JACOB BURCKHARDT, and to recount the emergence of modern European liberty, the *History of the Italian Republics* by JEAN CHARLES SIMONDE DE SISMONDI (1773–1842), which appeared in 16 volumes between 1803–18.

The Hegelian Philosophy of History

The German philosopher Georg Wilhelm Friedrich Hegel (1770–1831) established one of the most influential philosophic systems and historical schools in this period (see HEGEL AND HEGELIANISM). As evidenced in the *Lectures on the Philosophy of World History*, published in 1840, the aim of Hegel's philosophy of history was to define world history as the progress of the consciousness of freedom, the end of the historical process being the freedom of the subject to follow its own consciousness and morality. This Hegel identifies broadly with the modern liberal, constitutional state. While teleological, this scheme purports to explain why people desire freedom more than they have ever done so before. But it is also an attempt to deny the full reality of mere sense-experience, by arguing that the 'idea' or 'spirit' of freedom, a notion indebted but not confined to the notion of a Christian Providential deity, manifests itself in particular nations at particular times, then degenerates and must be reborn at a higher level elsewhere. The development of the idea of freedom is traced through four main historical stages: the oriental world, in which there is no consciousness of freedom as such, and only the ruler is free, and which thus formally lies outside 'true' history; the Greek world, which first demonstrates the consciousness of freedom, though limiting it by the institution of slavery and the inadequate development of individual conscience; the Roman world, in which the political constitution and legal system recognize individual right, but the state still eventually crushes individuality; and the Christian world, which accords primacy to the spiritual over the natural world, militates against slavery and, after the Reformation, stresses the capacity of individuals to achieve their own salvation, and recognizes the principle that all men as such are destined to be free, and that social and political institutions would have to alter to reflect this fact. At each stage spirit moves from a less coherent to a more complete form of knowledge, and from a more particular to a more universal conception of freedom. In his *Philosophy of Right* (1821) Hegel describes the ideal modern polity, in which commercial freedom is limited by the rational monarchical state arbitrating between the conflicting interests in civil society, with the bureaucracy representing the universal interest, such that extreme poverty in particular is prevented and social stability assured.

The Saint-Simonian Philosophy of History

The theory of history associated with the writings of HENRI DE SAINT-SIMON (1760–1825) focuses on the analysis of the emergence of modern industrial society. Building on the ideas of Turgot in particular, Saint-Simon contended that there were two main stages in human intellectual development, that of theological conjecture, in which human beings were subject to the will of one or many gods, and that of positive knowledge, beginning with Bacon and Descartes, in which natural laws are seen as controlling human life. All history involved an oscillation between organic periods, when widely shared assumptions dominate and underpin stability, and critical periods, when older notions are thrust aside and continuity broken. The nineteenth century, Saint-Simon believed, was a critical period whose special mission was the reorganization of society in order to promote the most efficient form of modern industrial production, and the supplanting of older systems of political rule by a meritocratic system in which the industrial class, which included workers as well as capitalists, concentrated on maximizing production, thus removing the need for most functions traditionally called 'political'. Power and authority would also be developed at a transnational, European level, in order to avoid the damaging effects of previous national rivalry. The universality of labour and abolition of parasitism would promote universal opulence, while the decline in religious belief and increasing embrace of positive ideas based on natural science and a secular system of morals would help ensure greater intellectual, and thus social, harmony. Late in life Saint-Simon contended that the state would also play an increasingly powerful role in, for instance, guaranteeing the subsistence of the poor.

Historical studies influenced by these concepts include the *Introduction to the Science of History*, (2nd edn, 1842) by Philippe Buchez (1796–1866). In Britain, the idea of the problem of authority in the modern critical period was developed in a Saint-Simonian vein by Thomas Carlyle, who in *Heroes and Hero-Worship* (1841) states the case for viewing the class of 'men of letters' as inheriting the traditional role played by priests and warriors.

Auguste Comte and Positivism

AUGUSTE COMTE (1798–1857) served for a time as secretary to Saint-Simon, and extended his ideas particularly through the proposition that there were three stages of historical development both of humanity and of particular systems of ideas: the theological, the metaphysical and the scientific. These corresponded broadly to three main stages of social development: oriental society, which was predominantly theological, and politically militaristic; classical antiquity and the medieval period, in which law and metaphysics became increasingly strong; and the industrial stage, in which myth and superstition are finally displaced by science. These stages also correspond to a sequence of conceptions of volition, commencing with a reliance on external objects or supernatural beings, then upon a conception of abstract force residing in the object, though independent of it, and finally, in the positive state, in reference to external laws. The aim of the positive philosophy was specifically to facilitate the unfolding of the third historical stage by delineating the inadequacies of the preceding stages and the advantages of a unified philosophical system based on science. The analysis of society was in turn divided into two main areas, the statical, concerning the laws of order, and the dynamical, respecting the laws of progress. These ideas are developed in *The Principles of a Positive Philosophy* (1830–42) and *The Principles of a Positive Polity* (1851–4) in particular. Following Saint-Simon, Comte was early on concerned to define and justify a new spiritual power, separate from the temporal, and assuming, especially, the role previously played by the Catholic Church. He also felt that an improvement in the condition of women, which would facilitate their civilizing influence on men, was essential to progress.

Comte influenced many historians, including HYPPOLYTE TAINE in France, FREDERIC HARRISON in Britain, Franklin Giddings in the USA and Karl Lamprecht in Germany, as well as more historically based sociologists, including EMILE DURKHEIM in France and WILHELM DILTHEY in Germany.

Marx and the materialist conception of history

The school of history associated with Karl Marx (1818–83) and Friedrich Engels (1820–95) developed an economic, determinist model of historical development first outlined in the unpublished 'German Ideology' (1845–6), and first offered to the public in the *Manifesto of the Communist Party* (1848). The model focuses on describing the economic basis, or mode of production, in any society, which is defined by the system of property ownership, classes and the division of labour. From this basis there emerges a superstructure, which includes law, religion, the state and other social institutions, which reflect the existing distribution of property and are in many respects 'caused' by it. Part of the aim of this schema was to reject any independent role for ideas or a Hegelian 'spirit' in history: the mode of production is primary, and ideas have no independent existence. Much influenced by Scottish writers, Marx and Engels delineate a series of successive historical stages, commencing with tribal property, moving to ancient communal and state ownership, then the feudal system, and finally capitalism. The 'end' of history is not a Hegelian realization of the 'self-consciousness' of 'spirit', but the development of contradictions in the capitalist stage to the point at which, through a final series of severe commercial crises, a proletarian revolution abolishes the system of private property entirely and, after a revolutionary stage of the 'dictatorship of the proletariat', introduces communism. At every stage, however, the motor force of historical development is class struggle, which ends only with the abolition of classes.

Not surprisingly, much nineteenth-century Marxist historiography, which began to develop in the 1880s, was concerned with the development of peasant and labour movements, and the emergence of capitalism and its development through imperialism (for instance in LENIN's study of the Russian economy). In Britain, for instance, H.M. HYNDMAN wrote, besides works of political agitation, a study of Indian administration (*The Bankruptcy of India*, 1886), an account of Asian resistance to colonial rule (*The Awakening of Asia*, 1919), an evaluation of capitalist crises (*Commercial Crises of the Nineteenth Century*, 1892) and *The Historical Basis of Socialism in England* (1883), while ERNEST BELFORT BAX wrote at length on the French Revolution, the German Reformation and other subjects. In Germany AUGUSTE BEBEL published important studies of women and of the English Revolution.

The concept of progress

It is usually conceded that the idea of progress comes to dominate nineteenth-century historiography and social theory alike, but equally that, despite the plethora of inventions, discoveries and technological innovations in the last decades of the century, it was under considerable assault from several quarters by 1900, as increasing pessimism about the future united with nostalgia about past ways of life being rapidly destroyed. The modern idea of progress, a gradual, steady, lineal and indefinite improvement in the lives of the majority, was certainly widely accepted by mid-century, and few writers advert to any notion of cyclical progress and then decline, even though the examples of classical Greece and Rome were always prominent in European minds in particular.

Though notions of direct divine intervention had generally receded, the theory of progress is not secular as such, but is often wedded to Providentialist ideas of God's will, for instance in US developments of the idea of 'Manifest Destiny', or in the popular blending of such themes in Britain in the liberal Anglican view of history. The specific contribution of natural science and technology plays a prominent role in most accounts of progress: the century was steam-powered, iron-clad, telegraph-linked, gas-lit, inoculated, photographed, irradiated and anaesthetized. Such achievements undermined efforts to romanticize any preceding period of the past; Macaulay notably lambasted the fashion of placing 'the golden age of England in times when noblemen were destitute of comforts, the want of which would be intolerable to a modern footman'. They also separated the 'civilized' inhabitants of the 'advanced' nations much more rigidly than had been the case a century earlier, and increasingly provided a rationale for the conquest, exploitation and even extermination of 'backward' peoples and races in the name of 'progress'. With the rise of anthropology, and especially after DARWIN, primitive peoples became increasingly seen as having failed in an evolutionary race towards successful modernization. To bring them commerce, civilization and Christianity became virtually an imperious necessity: without these tools, native peoples were destined to disappear.

The creation of a pan-European ideal of progress, in which European peoples were seen as linked by a common inheritance, or common racial characteristics, encouraged renewed efforts to trace European history back to a Greek, then a Roman, source, to a common 'Teuton' or 'Saxon' ancestry and institutions, and even further, perhaps, to an 'Aryan', or Indo-European, origin in Central Asia, a claim derived from philology in the first instance. The emergence of democracy from the Greek *polis*, and to a lesser degree the Roman republic, was particularly important politically. Christian moral propriety was everywhere seen to be superior to the mores of savages, and often the perceived scurrility and laxness of the ancients. By mid-century the notion of a 'science of society' based on progressive laws came increasingly to be augmented by metaphors, analogies and theories drawn from the natural sciences. Of enormous influence here was HERBERT SPENCER (1820–1903), whose 'law of progress' plotted the evolutionary development of societies from the simple, homogenous and indeterminate to the complex, heterogenous, differentiated and individualistic. This process of transformation for Spencer made the modern *laissez-faire* state the best guarantor of an optimal evolutionary outcome, since interference, notably to assist the poor, impeded the 'survival of the fittest' (which phrase Spencer coined). An enormous impetus was given by Darwin's account of natural selection, together with related discoveries in geology, palaeontology and other sciences, to the extension of historical time and enormous elongation of human history, as well as to the notion that human society was based upon an inevitable struggle for scarce resources. This was widely used to justify militarism and imperial conquest, and to bolster the pre-existing account of the superiority of civilization over savagery.

The critique of the idea of progress

In the last decade of the century the virtually unqualified optimism of the preceding half-century began to give way in face of a series of nagging doubts about the true nature and eventual future of industrial civilization. The growing popularity of socialism forced a widespread reassessment of the central liberal virtues of liberty, and particularly the system of freedom of trade, as well as the value of democratic institutions whose advantages were increasingly seen as at least partially nullified by social inequality. Some forms of socialism, moreover, were either overtly or partially anti-industrial, such as the ideas of EDWARD CARPENTER and WILLIAM MORRIS in Britain. At the other end of the political spectrum, conservatives like Guizot, Treitschke and W.E.H. LECKY warned of the overt dangers posed by the increasingly imminent arrival of democracy. Already by the late 1870s Darwinism, too, had helped to provoke an unsettling secularism and agnosticism, and could also,

as in FRIEDRICH NIETZSCHE's (1844–1900) thought, be utilized for overtly anti-democratic ends. The Pax Britannica seemed less secure following Prussia's defeat of France in the 1870–1 war, suffered constant threats from a trans-European arms race and imperial scramble, notably over Africa in the 1880s, and was dented by what was widely seen to be an ignominious stalemate in the Boer War (1899–1902).

But there were many other sources of the perception that social, political and economic progress required revaluation by the end of the century. Certain forms of Darwinism in particular suggested the potential physical degeneration of the human species, and the requirement, as eugenists urged, to avoid replication of 'unfavourable' variants in the species. The philosophy of Nietzsche lent credence to the notion that only an elite of 'supermen' capable of imposing their will on the hapless mass could stem the tide of decay and decline. Certain styles in art and architecture helped to promote a medievalist ideal as morally and aesthetically superior to the industrial age. The literary and aesthetic movement associated with the concept of 'decadence', or the intense expression of artistic beauty, was popularized by the poetry of Charles Baudelaire (1821–67), the flourishing of impressionism in art, and the drama of Henrik Ibsen (1828–1906), and the music of Richard Wagner (1813–83). The aesthetic and artistic rebellion against bourgeois conventionalism was matched by the sexual rebellion of a revived, and increasingly radical, feminism in the 1880s and 1890s, in which the 'new woman' claimed an increasing range of social, political and sexual rights. Everywhere the old certainties seemed to be dissolving; after 1914, the world would be made anew, and at enormous cost, only to break down again almost immediately. There was now scant scope for the apparently vapid optimism of the mid-nineteenth century.

Adding to the increasing rejection of reason as the supposed controlling factor in individual and collective destinies were the psychological theories of Sigmund Freud (1865–1939), whose account of the unconscious mind, of the primacy of sexuality in infantile development and of the proneness of civilizations to large-scale aggression, built on earlier conceptions of the mentality of the crowd, and helped to promote an already increasing eroticism throughout Europe and elsewhere. Freud had been prefigured by writers like E. von

Hartmann, whose *Philosophy of the Unconscious* (1869) pointed to a similar incompatibility between civilization and human happiness. Similarly anti-rationalist themes predominated in the social theory of the French syndicalist and socialist GEORGES SOREL (1847–1922), who contended that the great lesson of Greek antiquity was that a 'myth' underpinning a warrior mentality of struggle was necessary to avoid the degeneration of society into merely consumerist hedonism. This theme he applied to the working-class movement in *Reflections on Violence* (1908), which stressed the creative aspects of will-power and energy against rationalist approaches to social order. In *The Illusions of Progress* (1908), most notably, Sorel argued that the idea of progress had been used to justify the extension of state power in liberalism as well as socialism, and that this undermined the capacity of the working classes to organise themselves and to resist oppression from above. The work of the French philosopher HENRI BERGSON (1859–1941), notably *Creative Evolution* (1907), similarly lent weight to the idea that the existence of a supra-rational 'life force' could alone explain the secrets of human development. The popularity of mysticism and oriental religions assisted the sapping of faith in a tradition of European rationalism. The old fixed reference points providing a sense of certainty and continuity were thus rapidly disappearing. At the end of our period, Oswald Spengler's *The Decline of the West* (1918–22), which described the decline of a 1,000-year-old 'Faustian' culture, essentially feudal, in the face of modern materialism, democracy and collectivism, and gave a fillip to anti-rationalist, apocalyptic and authoritarian theories after the First World War. 'Progress' would be re-established in the following century, but on a much more tenuous and conditional basis.

Further reading

Barnes, Harry Elmer (1937) *A History of Historical Writing*, London: Constable.

Bowler, Peter (1989) *The Invention of Progress. Victorian Historians and the English Past*, Oxford: Basil Blackwell.

Burrow, J.W. (1981) *A Liberal Descent. Victorian Historians and the English Past*, Cambridge: Cambridge University Press.

Bury, J.B. (1921) *The Idea of Progress*, London: Macmillan.

Butterfield, Herbert (1950) *The Whig Interpretation of History*, London: G. Bell.

Collingwood, R.G. (1946) *The Idea of History*, Oxford: Clarendon Press.

Croce, Benedetto (1941) *History as the Story of Liberty*, London: George Allen & Unwin.

Gooch, G.P. (1913) *History and Historians in the Nineteenth Century*, London: Longmans, Green & Co.

Merz, John Theodore (1912) *History of European Thought in the Nineteenth Century*, 4 vols, Oxford: Blackwood.

Simon, William (1963) *European Positivism in the Nineteenth Century*, Ithaca, NY: Cornell University Press.

von Arx, Jeffrey Paul (1985) *Progress and Pessimism. Religion, Politics and History in Late Nineteenth-Century Britain*, Cambridge, MA: Harvard University Press.

SEE ALSO: anthropology and race; conservatism, authority and tradition; intellectuals, elites and meritocracy; mythology, classicism and antiquarianism; the nation, nationalism and the national principle

GREGORY CLAEYS

HOBHOUSE, L.T. (1864–1929)

An eminent British sociologist, Leonard Hobhouse was born on 8 September 1864 in St Ives, and educated at Oxford, where he became fellow of Merton College in 1887 and Corpus Christi in 1890. He was active in Liberal politics, served as secretary to the Free Trade Union in 1903–5, and was a journalist with the *Manchester Guardian* for five years and political editor of *The Tribune* from 1905–7. In 1907 he became Martin White Professor of Sociology at the University of London (the first chair in the field in Britain), and in 1908 became editor of the *Sociological Review*. As a prominent 'New Liberal' he was instrumental in bridging the gap between the *laissez-faire* ideals of Gladstonianism and the Manchester School, and the interventionism of radicals and socialists. Though he was suspicious of Fabian socialism as tending to promote bureaucracy, he nonetheless believed that liberals and socialists should unite 'against the growing power of wealth, which, by its control of the Press, and of the means of political organisation, is more and more a menace to the healthy working of popular government' (*Democracy and Reaction*, 1904: 237). A determined opponent of imperialism, he believed it had spawned militarism, and squandered resources that should have been used 'to improve the condition of the people'. He remained sympathetic to the internationalism of COBDEN and Bright, and wrote against harmful nationalism in *The World in Conflict* (1915) and elsewhere. His liberalism stressed the need to uphold an organic ideal of society in which social duties balanced individual rights, and individualism was balanced by mutual aid and collective action. The role played by organized labour in such a state was assessed in *The Labour Movement* (1893).

Though his first major book was on epistemology (*The Theory of Knowledge*, 1896), intellectually, Hobhouse had wide interests that spanned sociology, psychology, philosophy, history and social theory, but his writings are linked by a devotion to both analysing and promoting social progress as defined by the application of evolutionary theory. A basic statement of his first principles may be found in *Development and Purpose. An Essay towards a Philosophy of Evolution* (1913). These are developed in ethics in *Morals in Evolution* (1915) and *The Rational Good* (1921), and applied to political thought in *The Metaphysical Theory of the State* (1918) and *The Elements of Social Justice* (1922). With *Social Development* (1924), which evaluates the nature of progress both psychological and social, these last three works were reissued as the *Principles of Sociology*. Hobhouse gave a brief restatement of his leading political and intellectual ideas in *Social Evolution and Political Theory* (1911), which also includes a critical evaluation of eugenics. Though unsympathetic to SPENCER's politics, Hobhouse develops his theory of evolution. Other important influences include MILL's utilitarianism and T.H. GREEN's idealism. He died on 21 June 1929.

Further reading

Collini, Stefan (1979) *Liberalism and Sociology: L.T. Hobhouse and Political Argument in England 1880–1914*, Cambridge: Cambridge University Press.
Freeden, Michael (1978) *New Liberalism. An Ideology of Social Reform*, Oxford: Oxford University Press.
Owen, John (1974) *L.T. Hobhouse. Sociologist*, Columbus: Ohio State University Press.

SEE ALSO: liberalism; Social Darwinism; social theory and sociology in the nineteenth century

GREGORY CLAEYS

HOBSON, J.A. (1858–1940)

The most prominent of the 'New Liberal' writers who from the 1880s began to argue for substantially more state intervention in the British economy, J.A. Hobson was born in 1858 in Derby, and educated at Derby School and Lincoln College, Oxford. Early influenced by MILL and SPENCER, Hobson's faith in *laissez-faire* was shaken by reading HENRY GEORGE and William Booth, which led him to be convinced that poverty was 'a social disease, and not . . . an individual fault or misfortune'. When a schoolteacher in Exeter, he met A.F. Mummery, and together they wrote *The Physiology of Industry* (1889), which contended that an economy could be damaged by oversaving leading to insufficient demand, particularly under conditions of high unemployment. The market, he now conceived, was an intrinsically unfair mode of distribution prone to concentrate wealth in the form of unearned income. The only remedy was increased taxation of 'social property'. In the *Evolution of Modern Capitalism* (1894), Hobson first sketched his views of modern machinery, the emergence of the modern proletariat and its loss of control over conditions of work. Encountering RUSKIN's *Unto this Last* in the mid-1890s, Hobson became convinced that political economy should concern itself with humanist issues, and promote 'a standard of life not based upon present subjective valuations of "consumers", but upon eternal and immutable principles of health and disease, justice and injustice'. Hobson's growing radicalism and rationalism now placed him in close proximity with writers like T.H. GREEN, and Herbert Samuel, who coined the term 'New Liberalism' to emphasize a greater commitment to equality and fraternity than mid-Victorian liberalism had demonstrated.

During the Boer War Hobson reported as a correspondent for the *Manchester Guardian*, and produced *The War in South Africa* (1900), *The Psychology of Jingoism* (1901) and *Imperialism* (1902). In the latter, his best-known work, Hobson gave increasing stress to the role of financiers in militarism, and to imperialism as the effect of underconsumptionism at home, and the search for outlets for 'surplus' capital through foreign investment. It had a substantial impact on V.I. LENIN's *Imperialism, the Highest Stage of Capitalism*. After the war Hobson concentrated on popularizing a new ideal of sociology, with the assistance of L.T. HOBHOUSE in particular, which urged the study of society 'as an evolving unitary system', and assessed social development by the criteria of 'ethical standards of value', defined particularly in terms of 'a new utilitarianism in which physical, intellectual and moral satisfactions will rank in their due places'. During the First World War he wrote *Towards International Government* (1915) in order to assess the role of imperial rivalry in causing the war, and of economic inequality in perpetuating international rivalry. Hobson's other major works include *Problems of Poverty* (1891), *The Problem of the Unemployed* (1896), *The Economics of Distribution* (1903), *The Crisis of Liberalism* (1909), *The Science of Wealth* (1911), *Problems of a New World* (1921) and *Democracy and a Changing Civilisation* (1934). His autobiography, *Confessions of an Economic Heretic*, was published the year of his death, in 1940.

Further reading

Freeden, Michael (1978) *The New Liberalism. An Ideology of Social Reform*, Oxford: Oxford University Press.
—— (ed.) (1990) *Reappraising John Hobson*, London: Unwin Hyman.

SEE ALSO: anti-colonial movements and ideas; imperialism and empire; liberalism; social theory and sociology in the nineteenth century; theories of the state and society: the science of politics

GREGORY CLAEYS

HUGO, VICTOR (1802–85)

Victor Hugo was a French poet, novelist, playwright, leader of French Romanticism and for much of his time an immensely popular political figure. He was a man of extraordinary ambition (already in his teens he exclaimed: '*Je veux être Chateaubriand ou rien*'), which, fortunately for him, was matched by extraordinary talents, imagination and energy. Born in Besançon to parents who were to divorce a decade later, his father was a Bonapartist army officer. In 1822 Victor married his childhood friend, Adèle Foucher. By 1830 they would have five children. By that time, though, it was no longer a secret that Adèle had formed an amorous liaison with his friend, the famous critic Sainte-Beuve.

Hugo's feverishly hard work in the 1820s, aided by royalist family sympathies, earned him prizes and favour with the reigning Bourbon family. By the time he published *Cromwell* (1827), Hugo had come to be recognized as the leader of the young Romantics, assembling around himself a distinguished coterie of young writers. He met with a real apotheosis on 25 February 1830, at the premiere of his play *Hernani,* a milestone in French literary history. In 1841 he would be elected to the Académie Française.

Hugo shifted his political loyalties more than once: from a staunch royalist, supporter of the Bourbons in his early years, he had come by the late 1820s to Bonapartism and, moreover, he contributed greatly to the success and popularity of the Napoleonic legend. Then, during the 1830s, he was torn between his sympathy for the new Orléans King, Louis-Philippe, and his growing republican views and sensibilities. In 1847 he wrote one of his most socially sensitive works, the novel that was, much later, in 1862, to be published as *Les Misérables.* Meanwhile, in 1845, King Louis-Philippe had made Hugo a Peer of France. His speeches in the Upper House showed his sensitivity to the popular discontent that was to bring the Revolution of February 1848. He accepted the moderate Provisional Government of the Second Republic and in June 1848 he won a by-election and became a member of the National Assembly. He actively supported the candidature of Louis Napoleon Bonaparte, who was elected President of the Republic in December. By 1851, however, he was disillusioned and attacked the President. After the *coup d'état* of December 1851, he narrowly escaped arrest by fleeing to Brussels. From there he castigated the new dictator with such powerful pamphlets as *Napoléon le petit.* A few months later, he moved to Jersey. From there he came to be seen as a leading figure of French republican opposition to the Second Empire. Once the Empire fell in 1870 and he returned to Paris, it was not difficult for revered Hugo to be elected a deputy with a huge number of votes. The failure of the battling factions of the Assembly to take seriously his proposal for a 'United States of Europe' led him to resign some weeks later. Hugo was passionately attached to the ideal of European unity and wrote some very powerful and evocative texts supporting it. He was probably the most enthusiastic prophet of European unity in the nineteenth century. He was elected again as a senator in 1876. An enormous crowd flooded Paris to attend his funeral in 1885, in one of the biggest funerals in French history, and his ashes were taken to the Pantheon.

Further reading

Hugo, V. (2001) *Écrits politiques,* ed. F. Laurent, Paris: Librairie Générale Française.

Maurois, A. (1956) *Victor Hugo,* London: Jonathan Cape.

Pena-Ruiz, H. and Scot, J.-P. (2002) *Un Poète en politique: les combats de Victor Hugo,* Paris: Flammarion.

Robb, G. (1997) *Victor Hugo,* London and Basingstoke: Picador.

SEE ALSO: novels, poetry and drama; Romanticism, individualism and ideas of the self

GEORGIOS VAROUXAKIS

HUMBOLDT, ALEXANDER, FREIHERR VON (1769–1859)

The scholar and explorer Friedrich Wilhelm Heinrich Alexander von Humboldt was born in Berlin. The son of an officer, Humboldt was educated by private tutors along with his brother Wilhelm von Humboldt. He studied at Frankfurt an der Oder, Berlin and Göttingen, and then at the mining school in Freiberg, Saxony. He left without completing his studies to work for the Prussian state. He now developed his research in a number of emerging scientific disciplines grouped around 'physical geography', including geology and mineralogy, climatology, botanical and zoological geography. In 1797 he resigned in order to embark on a voyage of exploration to South America, which was then more or less closed to the outside world. After several years of exploration collecting empirical data – he mapped over 2,000 kilometres of the Orinoco – Humboldt and his colleague, the French botanist Aimé Bonpland, sailed to Mexico, and then went to the USA before returning to Paris, where Humboldt wrote up and published his material between 1804 and 1827. Humboldt was not a professional philosopher so much as a dedicated empirical geographer, whose impact is measured as much through his methodology as through abstract hypotheses. He believed that the earth was an organic whole, that its natural phenomena were interconnected and that this necessitated studying the relationships between them within specific contexts on the basis of accurate measurement and observation. Only once the particular facts had been established on the basis of rigorous fieldwork could generalizations be posited. His approach went beyond the observation,

recording and classification of his predecessors, and did much to define geography as a scholarly discipline. The impact of his contribution was reinforced by the sheer scale of his publications. His *Voyage aux regions équinoxiales du Nouveau Continent* appeared in thirty volumes and his *Relation Historique du voyage aux regions équinoxiales du Nouveau Continent* comprised a further three. He returned to Berlin when his financial resources were exhausted. There he attended court, was a member of the Privy Council and was tutor to the crown prince. He gave lectures at the university and organized one of the first international scientific conferences. In 1829 he undertook a second, much shorter journey of exploration, this time to the little-known Central Asian regions of the Russian empire. He spent the last 30 years of his life in Berlin, much of it writing the five volumes of his last and most ambitious work, *Kosmos*, a popular and accessible account of the structure of the universe as it was then understood. Humboldt has been called the last of the universal scientists (and the last of the affluent amateurs), necessarily interdisciplinary in his intellectual interests at a time when modern academic disciplines, and modern scholarly methodology, were only just beginning to emerge. His findings contributed to a number of fields.

Further reading

Booting, Doulas (1973) *Humboldt and the Cosmos,* London: Joseph.

Meyer-Abich, Adolf (1969) *Alexander von Humboldt,* Bonn Bad Godesberg: Inter Nationes [in English].

Sweet, Paul Robinson (1978–80) *Wilhelm von Humboldt. A Biography,* 2 vols, Columbia: Ohio State University Press.

SEE ALSO: anthropology and race

TIM KIRK

HUMBOLDT, WILHELM, FREIHERR VON (1767–1835)

The philologist and educational reformer, and elder brother of Alexander, Karl Wilhelm von Humboldt was born in Potsdam and studied at Göttingen and Jena. He visited Paris in 1789 and briefly worked in the Prussian civil service (1790–1) before marrying and retiring in order to pursue his intellectual interests. He worked closely with Goethe and Schiller, and established a reputation as a literary critic and translator of classical poetry. In 1802 he resumed his public career, this time as a diplomat, and was appointed Prussian minister in Rome, where he remained until 1808. The following year he joined the reforming administration of Freiherr vom Stein as director of culture and education in the newly reorganized interior ministry.

Humboldt's reforms effectively established the modern German education system at all levels. His ideas reflected the times and his own experience: he had visited Paris in 1789 and lived through the disorder of the Napoleonic Wars. He had explored the theme of the relationship between the individual citizen and the political authority of the state in a number of essays on constitutional problems, notably *Ideen zu einem Versuch, die Grenzen des Staates zu bestimmen,* written in 1792 but first published in 1851, where he argued that the state had the responsibility to ensure the development of the citizen's individual strengths, and state authority should be limited if it threatened to hinder this. Earlier grounds for limiting individual freedom for the benefit of the nation now no longer applied because a point had been reached where further human development could no longer be achieved by state decrees, but only by the undirected activity of individuals. Citizens on the other hand should be responsible enough to place their developed talents at the service of the community. He was committed to the notion of *Bildung* – education as the free development of a cultivated individual according to humanistic values. Accordingly, he aimed to extend educational opportunity and educate Germans as cultivated and responsible citizens. Primary education was improved by raising standards of teaching training, and was to draw on the liberal pedagogical principles of the contemporary Swiss educationalist Pestallozzi. The humanistic *Gymnasium* with its classical curriculum became the standard secondary school of the educated middle classes, and Berlin University, in whose foundation Humboldt played a pivotal part, not only served as a model for other German universities founded in the nineteenth century, but also profoundly influenced the modern understanding of research and scholarship.

Humboldt resigned his ministerial position in 1810. As ambassador to Vienna (from 1811) he helped persuade Austria to rejoin the coalition against Napoleon. At the Congress of Vienna he was an advocate of a liberal constitution for the German Confederation, and of civil rights for Jews. Although he held other positions in the state service after 1815 he was out of place in the new conservative order of restoration Germany and was relieved of all his duties in 1819 after opposing the Karlsbad Decrees. He spent the rest of his life in retirement at the family estate.

Further reading

Sweet, Paul (1978) *Wilhelm von Humboldt: A Biography*, Columbus: Ohio State University Press.

SEE ALSO: theories of education and character formation

TIM KIRK

HUXLEY, T.H. (1825–95)

The most important of CHARLES DARWIN's followers in Britain, Huxley was born on 4 May 1825 in Ealing, London, the son of a schoolmaster. Interested in engineering and metaphysics as a youth, he studied medicine, becoming a surgeon in 1845. He joined a surveying ship, HMS *Rattlesnake*, which charted the waters between Australia and New Guinea, and by its return in 1850 had made various studies of tropical marine life. His account of polyps, in particular, brought him widespread recognition, and he was elected Fellow of the Royal Society in 1851. Already interested in evolutionary theory, he still limited its application to internal progression within great natural groupings, despite HERBERT SPENCER's endeavours in 1852 to persuade him to adopt a more general theory. In 1854 he became lecturer at the School of Mines, and in 1855 naturalist to the Geological Survey. In 1858 his account of 'The Theory of the Vertebrate Skull' was widely acknowledged to have contributed to the demise of the deductive method in anatomy. After Darwin's *Origin of Species* appeared in 1859, Huxley (who reviewed it in *The Times*) quickly assented to the general application of evolutionary theory, rejecting in particular Richard Owen's contention that the anatomical structure of the human brain indicated the uniqueness of the human by comparison with any animal species. Huxley's case was summarized in *Man's Place in Nature* (1863; *Collected*

Essays, vol. 7), in which he linked humans to apes. By this time Huxley had moved into palaeontology and in particular the study of fossil reptiles and fishes. In the 1870s and 1880s Huxley served on a variety of Royal Commissions, became secretary to the Royal Society, and then its president (1881–5); he was also a member of the London School Board, and from 1892 a Privy Councillor. His health was frail after 1885, however, and he died after a long illness at Eastbourne on 29 June 1895.

In his role as 'Darwin's bulldog', self-consciously an outsider and even a 'plebeian', Huxley was prominently associated with the secularist, 'agnostic' (a term he coined in 1869) implications of Darwinism. Although as late as 1856 he had argued that the design of the universe pointed to a governing 'Infinite Mind', *Origin of Species* effected a conversion to the view that nothing whatsoever could be known about the ultimate nature of the universe. But, while denying that atheism was philosophically tenable, Huxley also contended that there was no firm scientific evidence for any God, and condemned as immoral any doctrine not resting on firm scientific evidence. His views brought him into conflict with many leading public figures, including the Archbishop of Oxford, Samuel Wilberforce, who attacked Darwinism in 1860, and the leading Liberal politician, W.E. Gladstone, with whom he engaged in a lengthy controversy in *The Nineteenth Century* between 1885–91. Huxley's opposition to the possibility of miracles led him to write a study of David Hume, published in 1878 (*Collected Essays*, vol. 6), but he denied (in 'Science and Morals', *Collected Essays*, vol. 9) being a materialist, regarding the 'substance of matter' as an unknown metaphysical quantity, not necessarily a non-existent one. Knowledge of the life and teachings of Jesus, however, he regarded as uncertain, and established Christian doctrine he frequently assailed as an implausible hybrid of paganism and Judaism, while still commending Bible reading as suitable for children. Morality, instead, he viewed as resting on an innate moral sense, and one plausible principle, 'do as you would be done by'.

This deduction led Huxley to make a substantial contribution to the social application of Darwinian principles of his own, arguing that no precise set of moral precepts could be deduced from natural selection, or indeed existed in the 'cosmic process' as a whole. But if nature exhibited no moral purpose as such, the 'survival of the fittest', while necessarily governing the lower stages of human evolution, needed to and could be superseded by a co-operative ideal in the higher. Human beings were thus capable of rising above the evolutionary process; this was the chief message of *Evolution and Ethics* (1893). A strongly ethical man who believed that the substance of religion consisted in acting justly and mercifully, Huxley argued here that 'ethical nature, while born of a cosmic nature, is necessarily at enmity with its parent'. The ethical progress of society thus consisted in combating the 'gladiatorial theory of existence', which could only be reintroduced if overpopulation engendered a new struggle for scarce resources. The state had the duty to educate the poor to help ensure this did not occur. It also could instil that sense of virtue which, for Huxley, would inculcate self-restraint in place of ruthless self-assertion, and promote the survival of the many rather than merely the 'fittest', thus 'curbing the instincts of savagery in civilized men', but also restraining the destructive aspects of 'insatiable hunger for enjoyment'. Much of this he saw as achievable through the force of public opinion, rather than law. But if 'intervention' was clearly called for in many spheres, Huxley did not take this principle as far towards socialism as A.R. WALLACE, and was as critical of the a priori method of HENRY GEORGE respecting natural rights as of that of Rousseau. He did, however, concede that if 'the abolition of property would tend still more to promote the good of the people, the State will have the same justification for abolishing property that it now has for maintaining it'. Scathing of evangelical schemes such as 'General' William Booth's 'Salvation Army', which he attacked in *The Times* in 1890–1, Huxley was equally dismissive of the 'administrative nihilism' of Herbert Spencer, arguing that the complexity of a high stage of civilization by definition required more widespread interference. The answer was neither anarchy nor regimentation, but some compromise between them based, minimally, upon an 'irreducible minimum of wages' necessary for survival.

Further reading

Desmond, Adrian (1994, 1997) *Huxley*, 2 vols, Boulder, CO: Perseus Books.

Huxley, Leonard (ed.) (1900) *Life and Letters of T.H. Huxley*, 2 vols, London: Macmillan & Co.

Huxley, T.H. (1898) *Collected Essays*, 9 vols, London: Macmillan.

SEE ALSO: anthropology and race; main currents in scientific thought; religion, secularization and the crisis of faith; Social Darwinism

GREGORY CLAEYS

HYNDMAN, H.M. (1842–1921)

Henry Mayers Hyndman, leader of the socialist revival in Britain in the 1880s, was born on 7 March 1842 in London, the son of a West India merchant. Matriculated at Trinity College, Cambridge, in 1861, Hyndman attended lectures by Henry Fawcett, read J.S. MILL and AUGUSTE COMTE, and graduated BA in 1861. During the Italian war for Venice he followed the Garibaldian forces as a war correspondent of the *Pall Mall Gazette,* later visited the exiled MAZZINI in London and absorbed the nationalist aspirations of the Risorgimento. Meanwhile, his journey to Australia in 1869–70 strengthened his belief in the mission of the empire. He also wrote several articles on the 'drain' of wealth from India in connection with the Indian famine of 1876–8.

He sought to put into practice his pet idea of a reformed empire and stood for Marylebone in the general election of 1880 but had to withdraw owing to an opposition from the radical workers. He visited BENJAMIN DISRAELI who cautioned him against his entertaining the idea of Tory Democracy. From early 1880 he made several visits to Karl Marx (see MARX AND MARXISM) at Hampstead, read *Das Kapital* in French during his business trip to the USA and on his return informed Marx of his intention to revive the Chartist movement. He presided over the inaugural conference of the Democratic Federation held in June 1881 in London and distributed among those present copies of his book entitled *The Text-Book of Democracy: England for All.* Though largely a summary of *Capital*, the book suppressed the name of the author, annoying Marx and estranging him from Hyndman.

The Federation adopted its first socialist manifesto *Socialism Made Plain* with a nationalization programme in 1883, while Hyndman published *The Historical Basis of Socialism in England* in the same year, emphasizing the British origins of the movement. In January 1884 was established *Justice,* the organ of the movement, which was to last 41 years. At the annual conference of 1884 the Federation changed its name to the Social Democratic Federation (SDF) but the difference of opinion over socialist tactics and international co-operation led to the split in December of WILLIAM MORRIS and his allies, who then formed the Socialist League. Hyndman's SDF was remembered for its role in the West End Riot of the unemployed in 1886 but John Burns and Tom Mann of his party who led the London Dock Strike of 1889 soon broke away.

Hyndman fought four parliamentary elections (1895, 1906, January 1910 and December 1910) without success. The SDF's attitude to the Labour party in whose inauguration conference in 1900 it participated, however, remained ambivalent as the party was a creation of the trade union movement and the Independent Labour Party. Hyndman and his followers formally joined it after it had adopted a socialist programme in 1918. He had worked well with SIDNEY WEBB on the War Emergency Workers' National Committee and also espoused nationalist causes in East Europe during and after the Great European War. He died of pneumonia in London on 22 November 1921.

Further reading

Hyndman, H.M. (1911) *The Record of an Adventurous Life*, London: Macmillan.
—— (1912) *Further Reminiscences*, London: Macmillan.
Tsuzuki, Chushichi (1961) *H.M. Hyndman and British Socialism*, Oxford: Oxford University Press.

SEE ALSO: Marx and Marxism

CHUSHICHI TSUZUKI

IDEAS OF WAR AND PEACE

Prior to the eighteenth century, few voices had been raised against war. War had been seen as an inevitable aspect of the human condition and of relations between princes. During the Renaissance some stirrings of anti-war sentiment had appeared: the great humanist, Erasmus, had called Mars 'the stupidest of all the gods'; and his friend, Thomas More, had described war as a base and inglorious (if inescapable) activity. In the early seventeenth century the Dutch jurist Hugo Grotius had responded to the protracted carnage of the Wars of Religion by calling for relations between states to be regulated by the application of international law. But his call for the codification of a body of rules that all governments could agree to subscribe to had fallen largely on deaf ears. In the absence of any higher tribunal, war was considered a necessary evil, a corollary of social organization, which was itself necessary to prevent even greater evils.

In the course of the eighteenth century this view began slowly to be modified. War may indeed have been the product of social organization, but that did not justify it. Rather it provided grounds for examining society itself and, if need be, changing it. Jean-Jacques Rousseau, like a number of other leading Enlightenment philosophers, maintained that man in the state of nature was a pacific creature and that it was largely the vested interests of princes and governments that brought about war. Rousseau had little faith in security mechanisms to ensure peace. He posited the idea of a strong federation of European states, but he did not see this as very practicable or necessarily very effective. The only certain way to bring about a permanent end to belligerence, he argued in *L'Etat de guerre*, was to dissolve the social contract and destroy the state.

The arguments of Enlightenment philosophers about the need to restructure society in order to prevent war converged, in the course of the second half of the eighteenth century, with the arguments of economists. The ruinous cost of military campaigns during the early part of the century had led various writers, especially in France, to argue against the idea that war paid: it was only arms manufacturers and a few contractors, they said, that benefited. More importantly, the investigations of François Quesnay and his fellow Physiocrats in France and of Adam Smith in Britain into the workings of agriculture, manufacture and trade laid the foundations for a new theory of international relations. Far from being divided through competing economic demands, mankind, it appeared, was linked by reciprocal needs. War and government intervention in markets disrupted the 'natural order', which, if left to its own devices, would generate greater wealth and bring the various peoples of the world ever closer together.

This liberal belief that mankind was bound together by a set of underlying laws, and that wars would end once these had been fully comprehended, was set out most influentially by JEREMY BENTHAM in his *Plan for a Universal and Perpetual Peace* (1789). His programme, which was to remain the basis of British liberal policy right down to the First World War, had as its cornerstones free trade, reduced arms spending, the abandonment of colonies and abstention from entanglement in alliances. It also proposed a practical mechanism for the resolution of disputes between nations, a Common Court of Judicature, whose deliberations, Bentham believed, could be made binding on governments through pressure of public opinion, not coercion. All that was needed was for the Court to ensure freedom of the press in each state.

Bentham's faith in the reasonableness of public opinion, the beneficence of commerce and the pacific inclinations of 'the people' was shared by other leading liberal intellectuals in the late eighteenth century. In Prussia the great philosopher IMMANUEL KANT argued in his pamphlet *Perpetual Peace* (1795) that an essential precondition for the permanent cessation of war (the most terrible scourge to afflict human society, in his view) was the establishment of republics in place of monarchies: while kings were at liberty to 'declare war as a sort of pleasure on the slightest provocation', free citizens would naturally 'think long before embarking on such a terrible game'. Kant's contemporary, THOMAS PAINE, was equally convinced that a root cause of war would be eliminated with the overthrow of monarchies. Republics, he felt, operating a system of free trade, would enable mankind to gravitate towards peaceful intercourse and prosperity. It was princely governments alone that divided humanity, accusing each other of 'perfidy, intrigue and ambition', and deliberately 'heating the imagination of their respective Nations and incensing them to hostilities'.

Paine hoped that the French Revolution would bring a new international order based on peace. In fact it brought 20 years of savage wars, with 'the people' of France and other countries galvanized by the newly potent idea of 'the nation'. This might have been expected to undermine the optimistic theories of Bentham and other Enlightenment philosophers. However, in Britain and France, and increasingly in the USA too, the decades after 1815 saw fresh attempts to find a lasting cure for war along traditional liberal lines. The utilitarians in particular trumpeted the claims of industrial and commercial progress, and the growing power of the middle classes to guarantee peace. 'It is commerce,' wrote JOHN STUART MILL confidently in 1848:

which is rapidly rendering war obsolete, by strengthening and multiplying the personal interests which act in natural opposition to it. And it may be said without exaggeration that the great extent and rapid increase of international trade, in being the principal guarantee of the peace of the world, is the great permanent security for the uninterrupted progress of the ideas, the institutions, and the character of the human race.

This idea, that economic progress and the remorseless march of democracy would lead to the decline of the belligerent aristocratic elites and the ascendancy of the pacific producing classes, encouraged the initiatives of liberal reformers after the Napoleonic Wars. The year 1816 saw the simultaneous foundation of a Peace Society in New York and a Society for the Promotion of Permanent and Universal Peace in London. The latter aspired, in Benthamite fashion, to the peaceful resolution of differences between states by means of a Congress of Nations. In 1843 an International Peace Convention was held in London, and another in Brussels five years later. Meanwhile the idea that differences between states might be settled through arbitration gained ground, and governments came under systematic pressure to insert into international agreements clauses stipulating recourse to a third party to resolve any disagreements arising. Between 1828 and 1899 some forty bipartite treaties of arbitration were signed.

The belief that society was destined for ever-greater peace received a measure of 'scientific' underpinning from the influential writings of the French positivist school of SAINT-SIMON, AUGUSTE COMTE and their followers. Saint-Simon believed passionately in technological progress. In works such as the *Reorganisation of European Society* (1814), he maintained that the world was passing in the early nineteenth century from an era dominated by religion and militarism to one based on industry and science. He envisaged a future of increased prosperity, literacy, planning and ever-widening levels of 'association': the core unit of mankind had grown over the centuries from the family and the tribe, to the city and the nation-state; and in due course there would be a universal human community dominated by love, harmony and peace. Comte had a similarly optimistic teleology (though like Saint-Simon he accepted that human will could influence the laws of history). He saw mankind's historical evolution as divided into three phases, of which the last, dominated by empirical science, would be characterized by concord, altruism and the 'religion of humanity'. Industry would replace war as the main instrument for the creation of wealth.

The confidence of positivists and middle-class liberals in France, Britain and the USA after the Napoleonic Wars was not always shared in other quarters. The French Revolution had released from the bottle a dangerous genie: the nation.

While in France 'the people' had initially defined themselves in 1789–92 in opposition to the monarchy, very soon it was through war against foreign enemies that '*la patrie*' came to feel most fully and vitally expressed. The exuberance of patriotism elided easily with bellicosity. And as the *grande armée* swept through Southern, Central and Eastern Europe, subjugating states in the name of liberty, fraternity and equality, nationalist feelings were stirred among peoples that had not hitherto felt the need for political self-assertion. A new and potent source of conflict had been created: the idea that a 'nation' had a right, duty even, to assert itself and attain freedom, if necessary by war.

In Germany, the galling experience of defeat at the hands of Napoleon led a number of influential writers and philosophers to stress the importance of educating the people to nationhood. They were products of Romanticism. They saw Germany's failure against the revolutionary armies of France as essentially one of will, and from their perspective war could be considered not, as Kant and his fellow Enlightenment liberals would have it, as an unmitigated evil to be avoided at all costs, but as an instrument necessary for generating national consciousness and driving out foreign oppressors. True freedom would only come through struggle, and though peace might in some respects be intrinsically desirable, in the short term at least it could prove unwholesome and corrupting. As Hegel put it (and his views were to be echoed by a long line of nineteenth-century Prussian historians): 'Just as the blowing of the winds preserves the sea from the foulness which would be the result of a prolonged calm, so also corruption in nations would be the result of a prolonged, let alone "perpetual", peace' (see HEGEL AND HEGELIANISM).

The idea that war might be beneficial and welcome was of course not confined to Germany. Indeed, everywhere in Europe and South America – and, in the second half of the century, increasingly in Asia and Africa, too – where nationalist ideas took hold, it was widely accepted that war in the cause of independence was justified, even 'holy'. This was a variant of liberalism that in Britain the likes of Bentham, Mill and their friends found troubling. The great Italian ideologue of nationalism, GIUSEPPE MAZZINI, envisaged a future order of free nations living at peace with one another; but that order – which he saw as divinely ordained – would only come about through the shedding of blood: 'Insurrection... is the true method of

warfare for all nations wishing to emancipate themselves from a foreign yoke.... It constitutes the military education of the people and consecrates every inch of the national soil through memory of some warlike deed'. Mazzini's most famous disciple, GIUSEPPE GARIBALDI, encapsulated the paradoxes of this mid-nineteenth century liberal nationalism: after a career dedicated to warfare in two continents, he became closely associated in the 1860s and 1870s with organizations such as the International League of Peace and Liberty.

The willingness with which nationalists looked to armed conflict to achieve their goals was partly a consequence of the fact that war continued to be regarded throughout the nineteenth century as a rational and manageable human activity. Neither the monstrous scale of the later Napoleonic campaigns, nor the protracted carnage of the American Civil War, did much to alter the belief of most European military thinkers that success could be achieved through a decisive victory, and that this would be secured through good organization and command structures, and a thorough understanding of tactics. It was certainly accepted that armies were getting bigger, and that technological advances – such as the introduction of rifling, smokeless powder and breech-loading mechanisms – were making weapons steadily more powerful and accurate; but the old view of eighteenth-century Enlightenment theorists, that war was a science based upon discoverable universal principles, continued to hold sway.

This was evident in the writings of the two most important military theorists of the nineteenth century, the Swiss Antoine de Jomini, and the German Karl von Clausewitz. Jomini's voluminous studies, published in the 1820s and 1830s, were based upon the author's direct experience of the early Napoleonic campaigns. Their central premise was that the art of war as practised by Napoleon was still essentially that of the era of Frederick the Great. The same timeless principles applied: mobility, the capacity to outmanoeuvre the enemy by threatening his flanks, rear and lines of communication, and above all the concentration of superior numbers at the decisive point in an engagement. Jomini remained enormously influential in military circles right down to the outbreak of the First World War, more so, in all probability, than Clausewitz. Much of his influence was due to the reassurance that he afforded conservatives in his suggestion that Napoleon's victories owed little or nothing to the revolution out of which they had sprung. War was still a high-powered game for generals and princes; political, social and economic factors were of only incidental importance.

The principal source of inspiration for Clausewitz's great study, *On War*, published post-humously in 1833, was the later rather than the earlier campaigns of Napoleon. These were campaigns in which the armies involved were massive – well over half a million troops at the Battle of Leipzig in 1813 – and the interaction of manœuvre and combat far less evident. A passionate admirer of Romantic literature, Clausewitz approached war more from the perspective of art than of science, and highlighted the complex and often unpredictable ways in which a range of forces – moral, emotional, social and political – could affect the character and conduct of fighting. But (and for many of his nineteenth-century readers this was probably crucial) he retained a sense that war was as an inherently rational activity, to be understood and thereby controlled. He spoke of the tendency of conflict to escalate towards what he called 'absolute war', but he tempered this with his famous assertion that war was 'a continuation of political activity by other means'. Limited objectives, in other words, could still produce limited wars. Napoleonic excess was by no means inevitable.

Like Clausewitz, politicians in the nineteenth century continued to look upon war as a legitimate tool of government, and they were thus reluctant to countenance proposals for collective security or disarmament. Nonetheless, the idea that states should seek, where possible, to work with one another to find peaceful solutions to problems steadily gained ground. The principle was embodied in the Concert of Europe, set up in 1815 to enforce the decisions of the Congress of Vienna; and the ensuing series of international congresses at Aix-la-Chapelle, Troppau, Laibach and Verona provided a model for similar gatherings later in the century in London, Paris and Berlin. At the same, co-operation between states was fostered by the setting up of functional organizations such as the International Telegraph Bureau (1868), and above all by the development of international law through multilateral treaties. In 1864 the first of a long series of Geneva Conventions declared that that those helping the wounded in a conflict should be regarded as neutral, while four years later, in the preamble to the St Petersburg Declaration banning explosive bullets, the principle that a war was essentially a struggle between states, not peoples, was laid down. Law on the conduct of war was further developed at conferences in The Hague in 1899 and 1907.

Such developments notwithstanding, and despite the ardent hopes of liberals that the progress of the economy would bring to the fore less bellicose social groups, an ethos of militarism persisted in many states. If anything, indeed, it intensified in the last decades of the century. The Franco-Prussian war of 1870, and its legacy of bitter enmity between France and Germany, the onset of colonial rivalries in the 1880s and growing friction between Austria and Russia, Britain and Russia, and Britain and Germany, all contributed to an atmosphere in which conflict seemed to many observers inevitable. Economic problems added to the sense of insecurity. Faith in free trade was undermined by the onset of prolonged recession, and protective tariff barriers sprang up almost everywhere in Europe from the 1870s. At the same time, the dissemination of socialist ideas and mounting unrest among industrial and agricultural workers encouraged the idea that war might provide a possible solution to domestic difficulties.

Belief in the inevitability of war received powerful sustenance from the 1870s from new currents of biological and sociological thought. The ideas of CHARLES DARWIN, often vulgarized and distorted, were especially important, and militarists frequently invoked his name to back up their contention that conflict was not only 'natural', but also an agent of evolution. The bestselling German author, Friedrich von Bernhardi, for instance, argued that war was a 'fundamental law of development', which exemplified the Darwinian struggle for existence, where nature ruled 'by the right of the stronger' and the weak were selected out. His fellow countryman, Helmuth von Moltke, was equally persuaded of the virtuous necessity of war. 'War,' he declared in 1880, echoing Hegel before him, 'fosters the noblest virtues of man: courage, self-denial, obedience to duty, and the spirit of sacrifice. Without war the world would stagnate and sink into materialism'. Nor were such ideas confined to Germany. A respected British journal had no difficulty in declaring shortly before 1914 that 'the only court in which nations' issues can and will be tried is the court of God, which is war'.

Darwin himself was much more circumspect about the role of war in human development than the advocates of militarism liked to suggest. If pugnacity was an instinct, so too – and possibly more so, in his view – was sociability. In addition he emphasized the capacity of intelligence, education and culture to mould and temper behaviour. In *The Descent of Man* (1871), the work in which he addressed most fully the relationship between war and the human instincts, he argued that aggression and predation were aspects of man's social and mental evolution, not just of any innate urges. Out of the conflict between tribes, cities and then nations, he suggested, had developed – and would continue to develop – higher ethical values and a growing sense of altruism that would serve to curb any proclivity to war. In the end, indeed, war would become obsolete – though Darwin did qualify this position by accepting that a continuing struggle for existence was necessary to the development of mankind, and by allowing for the possibility of retrogression, or even a complete halt, in human evolution.

The intense debates over instinct, aggression, competition and evolution that Darwin's ideas fostered in the late nineteenth century influenced ideas of war and peace in complex ways, and opponents of militarism as well as militarists could find in them support for their views. Generally speaking, in those countries where liberalism had strong roots – such as Britain or the USA – the tendency was for the new currents of biological and sociological thought to be deployed in a broadly pacific direction. This was evident in the eugenics movement, dominated from the 1880s by Darwin's cousin, FRANCIS GALTON. The belief that human behaviour had genetic determinants, and that these could be understood scientifically, encouraged the hope that evolution might now be shaped by human self-control rather than by the lottery of war. Most British and US eugenists were of the view that the highly indiscriminate nature of modern weaponry, and the selective character of mass armies, meant that war was inherently 'dysgenic' and would jeopardize the development of mankind.

Even Social Darwinism – widely seen as promoting the idea of the naturalness of brutal struggle – was far from lending itself automatically to militarism. Indeed its most prominent exponent, HERBERT SPENCER (who coined the phrase 'the survival of the fittest'), shared the views of many liberals and positivists that modern economic development was impelling humanity away from primitive bellicosity and egoism, towards an era of growing altruism and peace. War had undoubtedly served a useful evolutionary function: it had promoted social cohesion and thereby laid the bases for nations and states. But industrialization and capitalism were creating a higher, more individualistic, phase of civilization, one in which war would be redundant. Spencer was not an outright pacifist, but he loathed militarism, and in his last years became embittered by what seemed an increasingly jingoistic climate in Europe. 'In all places and in all ways,' he said in 1902, 'there has been going on during the last fifty years a recrudescence of barbaric ambitions, ideas and sentiments and an unceasing culture of blood-thirst.'

Spencer's feeling that the advance of capitalism would make the world an ever-safer place received powerful support, albeit from another angle, in the work of a highly influential group of economic rationalists. Their arguments, developed from the 1890s, chiefly within liberal and socialist circles in Britain, France and Italy, was that the sheer cost of any modern conflict, and the complexity of the international economic system, made war unthinkable. Their case was most powerfully set out by a Polish-born banker and railroad magnate, Jan Bloch, in a six-volume study of 1898, *The Future of War* – a work that immediately made the author a hero in European pacifist circles. Bloch predicted with chilling accuracy the protracted and brutal character of any forthcoming war, with armies bogged down in extended front lines and millions of casualties. It would be total war, and the financial burdens placed on domestic economies would be intolerable. The world system of distribution and supply of food, and the structure of international finance would be disrupted, with devastating consequences. Any future war, he felt, would bring in its wake chaos and anarchy.

Bloch's conclusions were echoed and developed in the years leading up to the First World War by a string of academics and publicists on both sides of the Atlantic. The idea that the world was facing a 'natural decline of warfare' (a phrase coined in 1898 at the time of Tsar Nicholas II's peace proposals) appeared indeed to be gaining momentum and credibility the closer war came. While the French-trained sociologist Jacques Novicow and the prominent US scientist David Starr Jordan exposed the biological destructiveness and waste of war, British intellectuals such as Norman Angell rammed home the message of Bloch that conflict in the modern age would be economically ruinous. Like Bentham and other middle-class liberals a century earlier, they were buoyed up by their faith in the rationality and peaceful inclinations of the great mass of the population. 'From the Ural Mountains to the Atlantic,' wrote Novicow in 1912, 'the Europeans have the utmost horror of conscription and war', while 2 years later the economist H.N. Brailsford said in a much-acclaimed work that the elimination of commercial rivalries and the desire of most businessmen for peace, would render the world an ever-safer place: 'In Europe the epoch of conquest is over.... My own belief is that there will be no more wars among the six Great Powers.'

Socialists were certainly far less confident about the pacific inclinations of the business classes. Many ascribed to the view, famously set out by J.A. HOBSON in his *Imperialism* (1902), that colonial rivalries between European states were in large measure the result of industrialists, desperate for new markets, pressurizing their governments into acquiring foreign territories. In the era of Fashoda, the Boer War and the Moroccan crises of 1905 and 1911, such arguments could appear persuasive. Another thesis, widely accepted in socialist circles, was that avaricious weapons manufacturers ('merchants of death') were driving on the arms race and pushing the world towards the precipice. In these circumstances, they argued, peace depended on the good sense and instinctive anti-militarism of the working classes. 'Do you know what the proletariat is?' asked the French socialist leader Jean Jaurès at a rally on the eve of the First World War. 'Masses of men who collectively love peace and abhor war!'

The confidence of socialists such as Jaurès, and economic rationalists such as Angell and Brailsford that war would be averted by the good sense of the majority, proved unfounded. The extraordinary explosion of mass enthusiasm that greeted the outbreak of war in August 1914 showed just how deeply darker passions and currents of thought, linked to nationalism, had penetrated into the fabric of society. Nor had the sombre warnings of Jan Bloch done much to alter the belief of military strategists that a modern war could be won relatively quickly through rapid mobilization, good command structures and a decisive battle. Many generals, indeed, faced with the brutal realities of the machine gun and high explosives had perversely convinced themselves that the instinct

for self-preservation would make war if anything swifter and less bloody than before. In French military circles it had even become fashionable to claim that *élan* was more important than material factors in military success. The result of such paucity of imagination was to be four years of carnage and stalemate in the trenches.

Further reading

Best, G. (1982) *War and Society in Revolutionary Europe*, London: Fontana.

Crook, P. (1994) *Darwinism, War and History*, Cambridge: Cambridge University Press.

Gallie, W.B. (1978) *Philosophers of Peace and War. Kant, Clausewitz, Marx, Engels and Tolstoy*, Cambridge: Cambridge University Press.

Gat, A. (1989) *The Origins of Military Thought. From the Enlightenment to Clausewitz*, Oxford: Clarendon Press.

Howard, M. (1976) *War in European History*, Oxford: Oxford University Press.

—— (1978) *War and the Liberal Conscience*, London: Temple Smith.

Nelson, K. and Olin, S. (1979) *Why War? Ideology, Theory and History*, Berkeley: University of California Press.

SEE ALSO: anti-colonial movements and ideas; historiography and the idea of progress; imperialism and empire; the nation, nationalism and the national principle; Social Darwinism; utopianism

CHRISTOPHER DUGGAN

IMPERIALISM AND EMPIRE

At the end of the Napoleonic Wars, the world was dominated by the British Empire. Based on military and aristocratic values, and an autocratic political system, this empire was run through the application of ideas about trade and government that had been inherited on the one hand from seventeenth-century European mercantilism, and on the other from indigenous non-European political, social and economic institutions. It was only as political and economic change proceeded in Britain during the 1830s that contemporaries began to apply new ideas to the running of empire, bringing a commitment to humanitarianism, education, free trade and responsible self-government. This did not lead to an overnight revolution in colonial policy, however, or to the emergence of a coherent ideology of imperial rule. Outside the empire of white settlement, the implementation of new ideas was often delayed and limited. Indeed, it was only the resurgence of old imperial rivalries and the emergence of new ones in the last decades of the nineteenth century that forced British thinkers to systematically consider how to run an empire. As new colonial possessions in Africa and Asia were drawn into European, US and Japanese empires, thinkers around the world began to consider why there was a need to stake out territorial claims and control colonial resources. The 'new imperialism' of the late nineteenth and early twentieth centuries thus brought new ways of thinking about empire, but also contained echoes of the aggressive and interventionist thinking of the early nineteenth century.

In discussing nineteenth-century thinking about empire, it is important to note that the word 'imperialism' was not used to describe European overseas expansion until the later decades of the century. Moreover, for most of the period contemporaries tended to do little abstract thinking about empire. J.R. Seeley's claim that the British Empire was acquired in 'a fit of absence of mind' ignored the ruthless determination with which many policy-makers, colonial administrators and opportunistic 'men on the spot' went about expanding and consolidating imperial frontiers. It did however accurately describe the relative absence of serious discussion of the nature and purpose of overseas expansion that was a feature of most of the period. The history of nineteenth-century thought about empire is largely the history of pragmatic and businesslike discussion of the everyday realities of colonial trade and administration.

The early nineteenth-century British Empire was a by-product of the expansion of the English fiscal-military state, a process that reached its apogee during the Napoleonic Wars. The creation of government structures capable of raising large amounts of money through taxes and loans, and able to spend the vast bulk of that revenue on the army and navy, buttressed an aristocratic and aggressively expansionist order. The consolidation of a 'British' state with the power to rule the distinct societies of the UK was accompanied by the acquisition of new colonies in Southern Africa, Australia, India and the Far East. This 'second British Empire' provided compensation for the Thirteen Colonies lost during the American Revolution. Although important colonial possessions remained in British

North America and the Caribbean, the empire's centre of gravity shifted eastwards.

However, although the construction of this empire was accompanied by pragmatic new administrative and commercial arrangements in many areas, few contemporaries were encouraged to think about colonial rule in drastically innovate ways. In the sphere of political economy, mercantilist ideas, first codified in the seventeenth century, continued to dominate. According to this school of thought, trade between colony and mother country had to be closely regulated in order to ensure that Britain benefited. An 'old colonial system' had been constructed accordingly, with a whole host of laws, regulations and protective tariffs designed to control trade. During the Napoleonic Wars, measures like the Navigation Acts, designed to encourage the development of a strong merchant navy, were supplemented by the introduction of timber and sugar duties in order to encourage the production of key raw materials in British North America and the West Indies.

Ideas about colonial rule also drew on what were seen to be traditional, even age-old precepts. British policy-makers and administrators justified the authoritarianism of British rule in India and the Far East in terms of the concept of 'oriental despotism', the idea that indigenous peoples were used to being governed by arbitrary states and had to be treated accordingly. Officials of the ruling East India Company also sought to harness other aspects of perceived Indian tradition, seeking through the *ryotwari* or 'peasant-wise' system to create a more settled system of commercial agriculture amenable to taxation. Old village councils or *panchayat* were also revived as a means of reinforcing local communities dominated by landed wealth. How far such thinking led to the preservation of genuinely traditional societies, and how far it in reality pushed indigenous peoples into new moulds that proved useful for the colonial state, is still a matter for debate.

In temperate zones, British outposts of empire meanwhile generally took the form of colonies of settlement, enclaves of European migrant agriculture and trade. Here, as in the tropical colonies, trade policy was still shaped by mercantilism, while political institutions continued to reflect older ways of thinking about colonial representation and rule. Only in the penal colonies of Australia were societies created along new, innovative lines, as contemporaries attempted to put into practice (albeit with limited success) the strictures for rational punishment laid down by JEREMY BENTHAM.

The ideological underpinnings of this early nineteenth-century, mercantilist, autocratic British Empire were never immune from assault. Central to imperial thinking in this period was the idea that the British constituted a 'governing race', with a right and a duty to spread their ideals and institutions to others, a view expressed in documents such as the *Report of the Select Committee on Aborigines* (1837). Patriotic and racial beliefs merged, and were fed by growing Anglican and Nonconformist missionary activity. However, such ideas were also tempered by the concept of trusteeship, developed during the 1780s by EDMUND BURKE. According to Burke, Europeans only held power over indigenous peoples in trust, until the governed were able to govern themselves. Colonial administration thus had to take the welfare and development of the indigenous subject as its first priority, preparing colonial populations for eventual self-government through British parliamentary institutions.

Such arguments provided ideological underpinnings for the claims of some British thinkers that colonial policy should aim to promote 'civilization', extending British political structures to colonial government. This thinking also reflected the influence of the 'stadial' view of history advocated by Scottish Enlightenment thinkers such as Adam Smith. This model, based on the idea that societies progressed towards modernity through a number of intermediate stages, was taken by some as applicable to the future development of indigenous societies, which seemed to be at stages analogous to those experienced previously by Western countries. If this was true, then colonial subjects could also progress towards 'civilization', and be encouraged to move in the right direction. Men like THOMAS BABINGTON MACAULAY thus argued that indigenous peoples should be educated along Western lines, preparing them for a time when they would run British-derived institutions for themselves. The colonial state would in the mean time stamp out indigenous customs abhorrent to Western eyes, including Indian practices such as suttee (widow burning) and female infanticide.

These changing attitudes towards colonial rule over indigenous peoples in turn reflected a broader transformation in the nature of political discourse in Britain. Particularly important was the campaign that led to the repeal of the Corn Laws in 1846, delivering a crushing blow against the idea that the state should privilege particular economic interest groups through legislation. Even before repeal, William Huskisson and Robert Peel had begun to dismantle the protectionist structure, and in 1849 the Navigation Acts were finally eliminated. The fate of mercantilism was effectively sealed as Britain moved towards a more regimented system of bureaucratic government that intervened less in daily life, but when it did intervene, was more efficient in so doing.

During the mid-nineteenth century, mercantilism gave way to a new form of free-trade imperialism based on the belief that a dynamic British manufacturing economy could naturally secure British international political hegemony. Peripheral areas of the world could be nudged into a British-dominated global trading system either through gentle pressure, for example the free-trade treaties signed with many Latin America governments, or through the deployment of limited but decisive force such as the 'gunboat diplomacy' used to open China up to international trade. Elsewhere Britain would annex key enclaves, including Singapore, to form the focuses of expanding regional trade networks. This policy was perhaps most closely associated with the British foreign secretary and prime minister, Lord Palmerston, who in his speeches set out a policy of opening up international trade through minimal government intervention on the one hand and the constant threat of force on the other.

Ideas about the role of the colonies of settlement also began to change in this period of free-trade imperialism. This was in part due to the influence of a loosely connected group of 'colonial reformers', of whom the most prominent, even notorious, was Edward Gibbon Wakefield. While serving a sentence in Newgate Prison for abducting and attempting to marry an underage heiress, Wakefield developed an interest in Britain's overseas empire. In 1829 he published *A Letter from Sydney*, which purported to be written by an Australian colonist, and which advocated a policy of 'systematic colonization'. Wakefield argued that a simple complementarity existed between the economic and social needs of the mother country and the settler colonies. Migration from an overcrowded Britain to the wide open spaces of the colonies would end the physical and moral degradation of the working classes in British urban slums and create prosperous new settler societies on the labour-starved periphery. These colonies would in turn supply raw materials and consume British manufactured goods, helping to raise the living standard of those left in Britain's cities. This idea of a complementarity of interest between colony and mother country would resurface in various guises over the decades that followed, and exert a powerful influence over generations of thinking about the relationship between Britain and the colonies of settlement.

Wakefield also argued that British governments should not allow emigration to continue on its existing haphazard basis. Neither should the government simply 'shovel out paupers' by sending the degenerate underclass to the colonies, a policy which would recreate British social problems abroad. Instead, Wakefield envisaged the state-supported export of the entire British social hierarchy. The migration of peasants, workers, bourgeoisie and landed gentry in correct proportion would supposedly allow the replication of British values in the colonies of settlement. Wakefield's vision represented the optimism of contemporary colonial reformers who dreamed about the potentially transformative powers of the modern state.

Wakefield and his followers had some impact on British colonial policy, particularly in the new colonies founded in South Australia and New Zealand. It is possible to exaggerate the extent of his influence however. For the Colonial Office was unwilling to undertake the programmes of large-scale state intervention envisaged by the colonial reformers. Instead, by the mid-nineteenth century, it was increasingly leaving the administration of the settler colonies to local parliamentary institutions and political elites. This reflected the export to the colonies of new British ideas about government.

While apparent for many years, the difficulties of managing diverse local populations in the colonies of settlement, and the inadequacies of existing political arrangements, were made particularly obvious by the rebellions that took place in Upper and Lower Canada in 1837. The British government responded by sending a new governor general, Lord Durham. On his return Durham published a report on conditions in the Canadas, including suggestions for reform that bore the imprint of Wakefield's thinking. While later generations came to see the report as setting the colonies of settlement on the path to 'responsible self-government' and ultimate independence, revisionist studies in the 1970s demonstrated that the impact of the Durham report was in reality limited. Much more important were practical shifts that occurred in the nature of government in Britain, particularly the final ascendancy of Parliament over the Crown that was guaranteed in 1841, when the government of Lord Melbourne was forced out of power by the Commons, even though it enjoyed Queen Victoria's continued support. It was necessary to hammer out the basis of responsible government in Britain before it could be extended to the colonies of settlement.

Outside the colonies of settlement humanitarianism also brought new ways of thinking about empire, building on the Burkean heritage. This was perhaps most clearly expressed in the anti-slavery movement. Since the later eighteenth century, genuine moral outrage at the maintenance of slavery in an empire that prided itself (however hypocritically) on British liberties had been reinforced by growing Anglican and Nonconformist evangelical opposition to human bondage. Humanitarian opposition helped bring about the end of the slave trade in the British Empire in 1807, and in 1823 the Anti-Slavery Society was established in London to press for the emancipation of those who remained enslaved. Growing pressure from Caribbean slaves themselves, and a number of slave rebellions, strengthened this movement, and emancipation finally came at midnight on 31 July 1834 (although compulsory apprenticeship for freed slaves continued until 1838).

Humanitarianism subsequently suffered a severe blow however in the form of the 1857 Indian Mutiny and Rebellion. The violence and scale of the rising seriously damaged confidence in the ability of British institutions to create 'civilized' Western societies in the colonies. The point was rammed home by other instances of indigenous resistance to British rule, such as the New Zealand Wars. As a result, contemporaries became increasingly pessimistic about the capacities of indigenous peoples for reform, and more conservative in their proposals for change. Many came to argue that the transformation of indigenous societies could be but a slow, gradual process. In the mean time, it was claimed, traditional political, social and economic structures had to be maintained. Burke's concept of trusteeship began to be interpreted in terms of a passive duty to prevent interference with native traditions and customs, rather than as a mandate to 'civilize' indigenous peoples.

These changes also widened the perceived gap between the two different types of colony, temperate-zone white settler colonies and tropical colonies populated predominantly by indigenous peoples or non-European migrants. While attitudes towards the so-called tropical dependencies became more pessimistic, the rapid economic growth of the colonies of settlement in the second half of the nineteenth century, secured through massive inputs of human and financial capital from Britain, encouraged contemporaries to start thinking in new ways about what came to be known from the late 1860s as the 'Dominions' of white settlement.

This departure corresponded with a period in which Britain's mid-Victorian international commercial lead began to disappear. As relative decline set in, contemporaries began to look at the world around them in a new light. In Britain, Halford Mackinder of the London School of Economics argued that international rivalries had to be examined through the lens of geopolitics. Mackinder believed that in the future large, effectively organized states would dominate. The late nineteenth century had seen the unification of Italy, Germany, Russia and the USA into powerful new states controlling substantial military and economic resources. These new continental empires threatened to overwhelm island nations. In geopolitical terms, a maritime power like Britain could only find a solution to this predicament by turning to the people of the settler colonies. Here, early inspiration was provided by Sir Charles W. Dilke's *Greater Britain*, published in 1868, which stressed the potential of the 'Anglo-Saxon' community created by the settler diaspora of the previous decades. Such ideas did not really take off until the 1880s, however, when they were popularized by a series of lectures delivered at Cambridge University in 1883 (subsequently published as *The Expansion of England*) by Sir J.R. Seeley. Seeley argued that Britain and the Dominions could only meet future challenges if unified under the umbrella of a single state, and bound together by a single imperial identity.

The need to recruit the human and material resources of the Dominions into a more unified imperial structure led some to suggest reform of the existing constitutional basis of empire. From 1884 the Imperial Federation League agitated for parliamentary reforms that would give the Dominions some form of representation at Westminster. Although imperial federation was rejected by Gladstone's government in 1893, debate continued, feeding into controversy over Irish Home Rule and resurrected during the early twentieth century by Lionel Curtis's Round Table movement.

However, not all those who wished to recruit the resources of the Dominions agreed that the best way to do so was through constitutional reform. 'Constructive imperialists' instead argued that policies designed to promote the emergence and consolidation of complementary economies in Britain and the Dominions were necessary before any constitutional realignment could be contemplated. This movement corresponded with the resurgence of protectionist thought in Britain, partly in response to the imposition of tariffs in the USA and some European countries as a result of the collapse of agricultural prices during the Great Depression of 1873–95. In 1903, Colonial Secretary Joseph Chamberlain launched his Tariff Reform campaign, which sought to bring the Dominions to the aid of the British 'weary Titan' through a system of imperial tariff preferences.

For Tariff Reformers, political or constitutional unity could only work if it came naturally, as the product of economic integration. This in turn reflected a new way of thinking about the nature of the communities that had emerged in the Dominions, enshrined in the writings of the British imperial theorist Richard Jebb. In *Studies in Colonial Nationalism* (1905), Jebb argued that national identities were emerging in the Dominions, and that imperial policy had to be carefully adjusted to take this into account. Dominion nationalism could be harnessed to imperial unity, but only if British policy-makers accepted that the empire would have to become an alliance of equal nations. Such views were reiterated by Sir C.P. Lucas, the Assistant Under-secretary of State for the Colonies, in *Greater Rome and Greater Britain* (1912). Lucas highlighted the importance of the Crown as the key link between Britain and the self-governing Dominions, a theme that would remain important throughout the twentieth century.

Lucas also recognized that, in the tropical dependencies, the link with Britain rested less on sentiment and more on force. To some extent, this reflected the novelty of colonial rule in many areas of Africa and Asia, which had only become colonies during the 1880s and 1890s under the pressure of heightened imperial competition. Prior to this period, limited colonial expansion for pragmatic purposes had seemed to contemporaries to require little in the way of ideological justification. French imperial expansion in Cochin China and North Africa, often accomplished by maverick military leaders in defiance of civil authorities in Paris, was supported by only flimsy ideological underpinnings that went little further than vague claims about *la mission civilisatrice*. In the Congo, annexed by the Belgian King Leopold II in 1884, similar claims failed to conceal gross exploitation. While Leopold's colonial state launched expeditions to punish those Africans who failed to provide sufficient labour or commodities, European concessionaires were allowed to operate unchecked. Unreconstructed mercantilism meanwhile survived in the Dutch East Indies, in the guise of the 'cultivation system'. Colonies were obliged to devote one-fifth of their land to the production of export commodities, which were given to the Dutch government in return for a nominal fee. This fee was then paid back to the government in the form of taxation.

However, the Scramble for Africa and other late nineteenth-century outbursts of imperial rivalry did help modify contemporary thinking about empire. Particularly important in this regard was the wider spread of SOCIAL DARWINISM, overturning the free-trade belief in an international order based on peaceful co-operation. Social Darwinism posited a world of cut-throat competition for national survival, in which the acquisition of colonies became a means of demonstrating the virility and fitness of a nation, and also of providing the resources and opportunities needed to participate in the struggle.

By the later decades of the nineteenth century, this new way of thinking about the role of colonies in sustaining the mother country had begun to take hold in some of the older imperial powers. In Britain, interest in tropical conquest as a means to promote national greatness was perhaps most closely linked with Prime Minister BENJAMIN DISRAELI. In France, the Comité de l'Afrique Française began to discuss the integration of French possessions in Africa into an efficient and powerful whole. It was in the case of the newcomer imperial powers that such thinking was most important however. The imperial enthusiasms of German pressure groups such as the Kolonialverein (founded in 1882) and the Gesellschaft für Deutsche Kolonisation (founded in 1884 – the two subsequently merged to form the Deutsche Kolonialgesellschaft in 1887) were stoked by a sense of *Torschlusspanik*, or fear that the door of colonial opportunity might soon be closed, denying Germany great-power status. Similarly, in a rapidly changing Japan, Social Darwinist ideas were imported along with other Western ideas about state and society. For thinkers like Tokutomi Soho, Japanese imperial expansion into Korea and China was a means to assert equality with the Western powers. For others, imperialism would help bring domestic social unity, deemed vital if Japan was to replicate Western industrial expansion. Even in the USA, Social Darwinism helped encourage Americans to take up 'the white man's burden', turning the ideas of Manifest Destiny developed during westwards expansion into justification for the conquest of the Philippines.

As the carve-up of Africa and Asia proceeded apace, contemporaries began to grapple with the question of what to do with these newly acquired tropical colonies. In general, the response was to attempt to encourage the production of commodities for export markets. In German Southwest Africa, this was pursued through policies designed to rapidly develop a settler, pastoral economy, involving the near eradication of the indigenous Herero peoples. In other German colonies, attempts to encourage the production of food and raw materials took the less malevolent form of the application of advances in scientific understanding to colonial health and agriculture through the foundation of institutions designed to eradicate human, animal and plant diseases, and encourage the adoption of more efficient agricultural practices. Similar tendencies could be observed in the Dutch empire, where an 'ethical' policy of improvement in education, administration, public health and agriculture was adopted in 1901. Similar programmes were introduced by US and French governments, who also sought to tie colonial economies more closely to the metropole through tariff preferences. In Britain, Joseph Chamberlain and his successors at the Colonial Office pushed through economic and administrative reforms, but proved unable to overcome *laissez-faire* principles and introduce a system of tariff preference. It would not be until after the First World War that contemporaries would begin to think about the development of the tropics in earnest.

Further reading

Burroughs, P. (1999) 'Imperial Institutions and the Government of Empire', in A. Porter (ed.) *The Oxford History of the British Empire Volume 3: The Nineteenth Century*, 170–97, Oxford: Oxford University Press.

Porter, A. (1999) 'Trusteeship, Anti-Slavery and Humanitarianism', in A. Porter (ed.) *The Oxford History of the British Empire Volume 3: The Nineteenth Century*, 198–221, Oxford: Oxford University Press.

Ward, J.M. (1976) *Colonial Self-Government: The British Experience 1759–1856*, London: Macmillan.

SEE ALSO: anti-colonial movements and ideas; ideas of war and peace; the nation, nationalism and the national principle; Social Darwinism

SIMON J. POTTER

INDIAN THOUGHT IN THE NINETEENTH CENTURY

It is difficult to enumerate the full range of Indian thought during the course of the nineteenth century, and, indeed, to elucidate the depth and complexity of this vast region's intellectual movements. After all, by the late nineteenth century, the Indian subcontinent was home to well over 200 million people, many of whom lived in highly literate urban centres. Indian thought encompassed deliberations upon topics ranging from political theory, logic and metaphysics to ethics, theology and science. Moreover, the region incorporated not only a majority Hindu population, but also sizeable minority communities with distinctive socio-intellectual traditions such as the Sikhs, and Sunni and Shi'a Muslims. It is impossible, therefore, not to be highly selective when discussing the intellectual history of the subcontinent. As such, this essay seeks instead to identify just a few of the most important trends and debates within South Asian intellectual life during this period, primarily with reference to northern India. In particular, it will interrogate the impact of British colonialism upon the region's intellectual production; the relationship of intellectual movements to religious and cultural change; and, importantly, the emergence of nascent forms of nationalism by approximately the 1870s and beyond.

The nineteenth century was, of course, a time during which important transformations took place in the Indian subcontinent. The century's commencement was marked by the presence of numerous powerful regional states, such as the Marathas of the Deccan. Yet British political control was gradually extended throughout the region, so that by the mid- to late nineteenth century Britain effectively dominated India politically and militarily. Many of the historical accounts of this process written before the post-colonial era have emphasized the intellectual and civilizational 'improvement' wrought by British rule, and have thereby acted as a species of justification for that rule. To take but the crudest example, T.B. MACAULAY noted in 1835 that colonial rule, and more specifically the imposition of English education, would serve to produce 'a class of persons Indian in blood and colour, but English in tastes, in opinions, in morals and in intellect'. The purpose assumed by Macaulay was, of course, the 'intellectual improvement of the people' that would lead eventually to the emergence of India as a full 'partner' to Britain in the wider world. Yet even during much of the twentieth century, very similar preconceptions about British colonial rule drove the analysis of the intellectual, social and religious activities of Indians during this period. As such, Indian intellectual productivity came to be viewed by many historians as the symptoms of an enforced modernization, necessary for the subcontinent's emergence into the world of self-determining nation-states.

This is quite clearly an unacceptable way to conceptualise the trajectory of Indian intellectual and cultural activity during the nineteenth century, for it not only adheres to an overtly imperialist developmental model, but it also fails, significantly, to grasp the complexities inherent in the diversity of Indian intellectual production at this time. Moreover, the subversive, and distinctly anti-imperial, component of many Indians' engagement with Western knowledge forms can be easily underestimated by this mode of investigation. Even so, contemporary historians are still largely divided upon the best way to theorize the intellectual and cultural impact that British colonialism had upon the subcontinent, and, by extension, the roles that British ideas and ideals played in the trajectory of Indian thought. Speaking broadly, the debate turns upon the issue of the measure of continuity that can be perceived in Indian social and cultural forms from the pre-colonial era into the period of British rule, and the attendant power of the colonial state to remould India in its preferred image. While cruder historical portrayals of absolute British power and intellectual hegemony in the subcontinent have now been largely discounted or qualified, there remains for historians the challenge of producing a complex intellectual history of India during the nineteenth century. This should be a history that is able to trace the diverse influences, cross-pollinations and effective genealogies of Indian intellectual movements; Indians' own understandings of their historical and civilizational heritage and its relationship to that of Europe; as well as the impacts of these sets of ideas upon the emergence of Indian identities and nationalisms at the end of the century. Only in this way can the intellectual history of nineteenth-century India be said to evoke a substantive Indian agency, and, further, place the influence and impact of Western knowledge upon Indians into a more nuanced perspective.

A wide variety of intellectual movements can be adduced in early nineteenth-century Calcutta, the seat of British political power in the subcontinent and arguably the most important interface between Indians and Britons during this period. The topic that dominated much of the work of Indian intellectuals and social activists, however, was the notion of India's 'decline', specifically the religious practices of Hinduism and Islam, as well as the need for their 'reform'. During the eighteenth century, Britons had attempted in their orientalist scholarship to discern 'value' in Indian intellectual heritages, and, indeed, this had been necessitated largely by the mandate of governmental rule according to India's 'ancient constitution', which had marked the Governor-Generalship of Warren Hastings (1773–85). But the second decade of the nineteenth century was then witness to the more aggressive expansion of the Company's rule into the subcontinent, the introduction of Christian missionary activity from 1813 and governmental imperatives to introduce Western ideals and knowledge in the name of 'improving' Indian society. During the regime of Governor-General William Bentinck (1828–35), for example, the influence of British liberalism, the utilitarianism of JAMES MILL and the evangelicism of Charles Grant all came to bear upon British governmental policy in India. For example, educational institutions were to prioritize Western learning in their curricula, and legal measures were taken to curtail a variety of cultural practices deemed 'immoral', most notably that of suttee, or the burning of a Hindu widow upon the funeral pyre of her husband.

So how did members of the Indian intelligentsia in Calcutta respond to these attempts at Anglicization? At the most radical level, members of the Young Bengal movement, led by the Eurasian Henry Derozio (1809–31), advocated that Indian society and religion should be judged by the dictates of European rationalism. As a teacher in English Literature at the Hindu College in Calcutta, Derozio drew on the writings of Hume and Maine, for example, and advocated the wholesale adoption of British culture and European rational thought. Other Bengalis such as K.M. Banerjea (1813–85) converted to Christianity, and spent their lives promoting its teachings as a regenerative force for Indian society. Most Indians, however, took a rather more measured view. Ram Mohun Roy (1772–1833), for example, an influential member of the Bengali *bhadralok* (the emerging middle class, lit. 'respectable people') attempted to promote a vision of an 'improved' and 'enlightened' monotheistic, rational Hinduism based in the ancient Sanskrit texts known as the *Upanishads* (i.e. the *vedanta*). Without a doubt, Roy viewed Western knowledge as a principal source of rational thought, and thus advocated Indian education in it, even making a direct request to government in this regard in 1823. Yet the longer-term trajectory of Roy's thought amply illustrates his engagement with a variety of intellectual influences, and thus most likely reflects the long tradition of cultural and intellectual syncretism within pre-colonial India. Indeed, Roy was himself a brahman knowledgeable in Sanskrit, Persian, Arabic, Bengali and later in English. Roy's early Persian work, *Tuhfat-ul-Muwahidin* (1804), for example, drew upon contemporary Islamic rationalism (see below) to promote his ideas on monotheism, while in later works one can discern not only a deeper appreciation of the *advaita* (non-differentiated) *vedanta* of the eighth-century philosopher Shankaracharya, but also the teachings of European deism and Christian ethics. Yet Roy in no way 'aped' Christian thought, for he subjected it to a searching critique based in reason, criticizing the notion of Christ's divinity, for example. Ram Mohun Roy founded a series of organizations, including the influential Brahmo Samaj in 1828, to promote his highly textualized and rational vision of Hinduism, and to help purge Hindu religious practice of accreted 'degraded' practices, such as idolatry and overly elaborate ritual, which he viewed as being largely the product of priestly intervention. In this regard, Roy's reappraisal of Hindu religious doctrine included a specifically social element, for he believed that religion must not only be inherently rational, but also supportive of an egalitarian social order. As such, the Brahmo Samaj introduced a series of social reforms, including the abandonment of caste and a revised marriage ritual.

The emphasis of Ram Mohun Roy and the Brahmo Samaj upon the authority of textual sources and the exercise of reason in the understanding of religious doctrine drew criticism from a variety of sources, including bewildered Christian missionaries and self-styled defenders of Hindu 'orthodoxy'. Nowhere were the conflicting understandings of 'Hinduism' more pronounced in this period than over the debate surrounding the cultural and religious validity of the practice of suttee. Roy argued in an 1818 tract against the practice upon the basis of Sanskrit scriptural authority, characterizing it instead as a product of contemporary Hindu degeneracy. Others, however, such as the religious conservative Radhakant Deb, a founding member of the Calcutta Dharma Sabha ('society for [the preservation of] religion'), argued for the cultural importance of suttee as an integral component of religious practice. In this regard Deb also argued from the basis of Hindu scriptural authority, but he wished to reinvigorate Hindu religious practice by an appeal to 'tradition', thereby insulating it from undue outside influence, whether from Christianity or radical reformers such as Roy.

It is important to note here that it is possible to discern something of a double genealogy for many of the principal ideas that Bengali reformers drew upon. The prevalent notion of Indian civilizational 'decline' can be traced to late eighteenth-century orientalist writers, and which then became institutionalized in one way or another in most nineteenth-century discourse on India. Scottish mathematician and astronomer John Playfair (1748–1819), for example, believed that Indian knowledge of astronomy had once been considerable, but that over time it had been largely forgotten. In this way, the orientalist model conformed broadly to a biblical conception of knowledge as Providential. Yet Hindu thought also conceptualized the trajectory of human civilization by reference to a cyclical decline, and it was widely understood that we live in the last of the four great eras, the *Kali Yuga*, in which the

proper observation of religion and its dictates is said to become increasingly scarce. In addition, it is apparent that the focus upon the cultural authority of textual forms, and the need to return to a more directly Sanskritic religious practice, reflected both European orientalist preconceptions of a 'religion of the book' as well as the religious importance granted to Sanskrit (as a divine language) and the corpus of Sanskrit literature by the elite brahmans of India. Indeed, the very centrality of religion to discussions of Indian identity and history was based not only upon European orientalist imaginings of India as 'inherently religious', but also derived from the concerns of the brahmans and maulavis (the *religious* elites of India) whom the colonial government came to rely upon for authoritative cultural and social information.

In addition to Calcutta, the older cities of northern India also witnessed during the early part of the nineteenth century socio-intellectual movements to assert forms of revivalist religion. Attempts to revive a 'true' understanding of Islam, for example, traced their intellectual heritage to Shah Waliullah (1703–63) of Delhi, and the Madrassa-i-Rahimiya. But rather than interaction with the West, Waliullah's brand of reformism found its inspiration from within Islamic intellectual traditions, and from the Arabian peninsula in particular. Waliullah desired a restoration of Islam to its former position of power and influence in the subcontinent, and so advocated an understanding of Islamic belief and practice with reference to its most authoritative sources: the Koran and the *hadith* (sayings of the Prophet). Simultaneously, he wished to cleanse Islam of what he considered to be its debased practices and beliefs, by moving away from many of the populist teachings and customs of Sufism, such as saint worship. In effect, Waliullah understood the authority of religious knowledge to lie in the key texts of Islam, rather than popular custom or belief. Key to his thought, however, was the notion that the 'gates of reason' had not closed (*ijtihad*) – an innovation to Sunni orthodoxy – and that qualified Islamic scholars could, as such, apply their learning and reason to the Koran and the *hadith* so as to return Islam to its original purity. Waliullah's views are systematized in his Arabic commentary, *Hujjat-allah al-Baligha*, but so as to promote the 'original' source of Islamic knowledge throughout India, Waliullah translated the Koran into Persian, and one of his sons even translated it into Urdu, the vernacular of northern India.

Waliullah's successors, particularly his son Shah Abdul Aziz (1746–1824), and Sayyid Ahmad Barelvi (1786–1831), successfully popularized his ideas throughout northern India, and brought to them an overtly political imputation. Abdul Aziz, for example, declared India to no longer be *dar ul-Islam*, a land under Islamic political control, in a famous 1803 *fatwa* that followed the East India Company's conquest of Delhi. This opened the door for the declaration of *jihad* by the leader of the Tariqat-i-Muhammadiya movement, Sayyid Ahmad Barelvi, and an unsuccessful attempt to assert direct political control of northern India by way of armed conquest. In Bengal, Shariat Allah (1781–1840), leader of the Faraizi movement, similarly drew upon Waliullah's teachings and those of the Wahhabis of the Arabian peninsula to lead a series of violent peasant uprisings against the largely Hindu landlord class. Here it may be seen that religious thought was translated into a rationale for direct political action based on the desire for economic redistribution.

The elaboration of a public sphere in India during the first decades of the nineteenth century, and particularly the adoption of printing technology by Indians for vernacular languages, allowed such intellectual discourse to impact relatively widely, though of course at this early juncture such impact must be considered as being limited largely to literate elites. Originally introduced by Christian missionaries for the production of Bible translations, the printing press was utilized by Indians to produce not only books (including school textbooks in English as well as editions of Bengali, Persian and Sanskrit literature) but also a wide variety of journals, newspapers and polemical pamphlets. Indeed, the debate over the 'legality' of suttee was conducted largely through the production of pamphlets, and one can also find instances of overtly anti-Christian polemics in print produced by members of the Bengali intelligentsia. Moreover, although Muslim reformers such as Sayyid Ahmad Barelvi were amongst the most successful at popularizing their views beyond intellectual elites, it is significant that they also made use of print media, issuing a variety of books and polemical pamphlets in both Persian and Urdu. As the nineteenth century reached its middle years, print and other informational media continued to expand in the subcontinent, most notably in the form of 'native newspapers'. Taken together with the increased patronage of literary and educational activities by the emerging middle classes, wealthy merchants, pensioned-off Indian princes and the British government itself, this led to a substantial widening of intellectual discourse and its cultural impact, and renewed debate about the nature of Indian religion, history and the nation.

One can perceive in the early nineteenth-century intellectual movements and religious debates discussed above much which foreshadows the intellectual productions of the later decades of the century. Indeed, the whole of the later nineteenth century may largely be characterized as a time during which Indian religious and historical thought was progressively, and more aggressively, systematized, and thereby formulated for deployment in a variety of social, cultural and political projects by Indians. In particular, visions of Hinduism's exalted ancient status, as well as its inherent rationality and spirituality, popularized by a variety of religious reformers, would take on important resonance for the production of a national identity deemed sufficient to substantiate claims to political independence from Britain. Yet thought about the nature of Hinduism and Indian civilization also became substantially fractured during this later period, reproducing the gross dichotomy of reform/tradition witnessed in earlier Bengal-centred debates. Simultaneously, Muslim thinkers increasingly began to engage with the intellectual impact brought by Britain's colonial presence in India, often advocating a programme of modernization by reference to Western knowledge and values. Yet mirroring the dichotomy present within debates about the nature of Hinduism, Islamic thought also fractured into several identifiable trajectories.

Indian attempts to systematically define the nature of 'Hinduism' as well as the cultural significance of Hindu religious thought and practice were often carried out in a context of politically charged intellectual disputation. In the middle of the century, Christian missionaries and their supporters developed increasingly sophisticated arguments to combat the myriad attractions of Hindu belief systems. For example, the Scottish administrator John Muir (1810–82) published in 1839 a text entitled *Matapariksha* ('an examination of [religious] doctrine'), in which he attempted to demonstrate the rational basis of Christianity in comparison with the irrationality of Hinduism.

Writing in Sanskrit, Muir argued, for example, that the miracles of Christ were confirmed by the weight of testimony and historical evidence, while the recorded deeds of Hindu deities were clearly 'born from delusion'. Indians, and in particular the traditional Hindu intelligentsia, the *pandits* ('learned men'), now actively engaged with Christian polemics. In response to Muir's text, for example, the *pandit* Nilakantha Shastri (1825–95) argued in his 1844 *Shastra-tattva-vinirnaya* ('a verdict on the truth of the *shastra* [the Sanskrit corpus]') that the tenets of Christianity could not be established by reference to reason, as the Bible contained many more palpable contradictions than Sanskrit texts did. Moreover, Nilakantha argued that the proper place of reason should be to more fully understand a body of scripture, and in this regard he also outlined the way in which the distinct 'traditions' within Hinduism simply represented different paths to the same ultimate goal. In so doing, Nilakantha effectively broke the British attempt to monopolize important intellectual values for Christian doctrine, such as conformity to reason, and declared an overarching unity to Hindu thought.

Yet British educators such as James Ballantyne (1813–64), the superintendent of the government's college in Benares between 1846 and 1861, continued to promote a vision of Christianity's exclusive relationship with the dictates of reason and Western scientific knowledge. In essence Ballantyne conceptualized Hindu metaphysics and science as being at a lower stage of intellectual development than that of Europe, and so he intended to co-opt the traditional cultural authority of the *pandits* employed by the college to promote an 'improving' educational curriculum in Western 'useful' knowledge through the medium of Sanskrit and Hindi. Ultimately, he intended this curriculum as preparatory to Indians' 'rational' acceptance of Christian doctrine. Yet it is possible to discern in the scholarship of the *pandits* who worked with Ballantyne not only a serious intellectual engagement with Western knowledge, but also, significantly, a resituating of it outside a colonial ideology steeped in India's need for 'improvement'. For example, *pandit* Vitthala Shastri (d. 1867) wrote a long commentary on Francis Bacon's *Novum Organum*, effectively adopting it into the corpus of Sanskrit-based logic, and also authored a text on Western chemistry, in which he claimed that this system of knowledge,

far from being 'foreign' to India, was instead perfectly consistent with doctrines of scientific methodology advocated by Hindu intellectual traditions. Vitthala Shastri and many of the other *pandits* of Benares College actively promoted their views in a variety of journals and through active involvement in literary clubs. This process, which we can see mirrored also in the cities of Poona, Calcutta and Delhi, for example, served to make available to a wider audience these understandings of the significant connections between Hinduism, rationality and scientific discovery.

Throughout the remainder of the century two principal groups of Hindu intellectuals were active in northern India. The *pandits*, increasingly, seem to have strayed from a direct engagement with Western thought, and instead emerged as promoters of an idealized vision of *sanatan dharma* (the 'eternal religion' of Hinduism). These largely 'conservative' movements drew upon the sanctity of 'tradition' to authorize their particular visions of Hindu religious thought, and most often promoted this vision through their membership in a *dharma sabha*. For example, *pandits* associated with the Kashi Dharma Sabha, centred in Benares, undertook in the 1870s a systematic enquiry into the various fields of Sanskrit literature in order to pronounce authoritatively upon the textual basis of Hinduism. Others, such as Raja Rama Shastri and Bala Shastri, wrote socially conservative texts that argued against the permissibility of widow remarriage (a topic of interest to social reformers) by reference, again, to authoritative Sanskrit texts. Then, in 1887, *pandit* Din Dayalu Sharma (b. 1863) founded the Bharat Dharma Mahamandala, an umbrella organization designed to provide unity to the variety of local *dharma sabha*s that had sprung up across northern India. High on the agenda of this organization was the perceived need to protect the symbols of Hindu orthodoxy, including the cow, brahman privilege and pilgrimage sites, and it worked to actively promote an understanding of the 'traditional' Hindu social order, *varnashramadharma*, as sanctioned in the Sanskrit *shastra*.

But perhaps the true inheritors of the spirit of active engagement with, and critique of, Western colonial modernity first exemplified by *pandits* Nilakantha Shastri and Vitthala Shastri are the more radical late-nineteenth-century Hindu reformers such as Swami Dayananda Saraswati (1824–83), the founder of the Arya Samaj ('society of Aryans') based in northwestern India, as well as Swami

Vivekananda (1863–1902) of Bengal. Dayananda Saraswati, much like Ram Mohun Roy, advocated a return to a purified version of Hinduism, cleansed of its later priestly accretions such as image worship and caste divisions. In this regard, Dayananda understood the ancient Sanskrit texts, the Veda, to be the foundational texts of Hinduism, and so by returning Hindu practice to conformity with them, Dayananda believed he would cleanse it of later degenerative practices. To expound his views, Dayananda wrote *Satyarth Prakash* ('the light of truth'), and engaged in relentless debate with his opponents. Among his strategies was the promotion of an understanding of Christianity as an irrational body of knowledge, and the superior 'truth' of the Veda, given the latter's conformity to the principle of reason and the findings of scientific enquiry. Indeed, one of Dayananda's followers, Guru Datta Vidyarthi (d. 1890), went so far as to translate the Veda into English in such a way as to confirm to British critics their inherently scientific, rather than mythological, nature. In contrast, Swami Vivekananda, a follower of the seer Ramakrishna (1836–86), turned away from a purely rationalist vision of Hinduism, and instead promoted Ramakrishna's focus upon devotion. In essence, Vivekananda emphasized Ramakrishna's notion of the universality of all religions, but, equally, the superiority of Hinduism, given its emphasis upon spirituality and tolerance. Interestingly, it has been argued that the entrance of the notion of 'tolerance' into characterizations of Hinduism derived from Vivekananda's time in the USA, where he would have encountered the exalted place of this value in the discourse of Western democracy and modernity.

In each of the examples outlined above, whether of 'reformists' or 'traditionalists', it is possible to identify many common points of reference in their respective thought. These may include the productive relationship of the Hindu religion with reason and the findings of Western science; the textual basis for authoritative understandings of Hinduism; the exalted antiquity of Hindu-Indian civilization; the notion of Hinduism's relative decline and therefore need for strengthening through systematization; and, finally, the impression of Hinduism as being under siege both from within and without. While none of the intellectuals discussed here were overtly nationalists, in the sense that none were active in political engagement with the colonial state, they did, however, popularize

a variety of understandings of Hinduism forged in defence of largely Western critiques. These would then become important for the twentieth-century construction of a nationalist Hindu-Indian identity. For example, the Arya Samaj, while largely unsuccessful in popularizing its views on Hinduism, did, however, stress the importance of a systematic belief system set out within an identifiable body of text, and, moreover, the importance of Hinduism's rational and scientific character. This would become an important element in the development of a nationalist vision of Hindu scientific practice, exemplified in the work of Brajendranath Seal and Prafulla Chandra Ray. Vivekananda's vision of Hindu spirituality, in turn, was utilized by M.K. GANDHI, as well as the chauvinist Rashtriya Swayamsevak Sangh (RSS), to express India's superior claim to nationhood over the materialist West. Indeed, so pervasive has this idea become that it informed Indian nationalist understandings of pre-colonial religious syncretism in India, as well as nationalist historiography that viewed the partition of the subcontinent as an 'aberration' of that syncretism. This is not to mention, of course, India's 'spiritual' character being a principal selling point for contemporary Western tourism to the subcontinent.

Finally, it must be mentioned, however briefly, that very similar debates were taking place within the sphere of South Asian Islamic thought during the mid- to late nineteenth century, and followed much the same trajectory as well. Following the ideals outlines by Shah Walliullah and his intellectual descendants, later Islamic 'traditionalists' associated with the Deoband *madrassa* (school), such as Muhammad Qasim Nanautawi (1833–77) and Rashid Ahmad Gangohi (1829–1905), were drawn from the established class of Muslim theologians, the *'ulama*. The Deoband *madrassa* was a 'modern' educational institution that emphasized the importance of the Koran and the *hadith* as the true source of Islamic knowledge, as well as the explanations of these by qualified *'ulama*. The Deobandis also participated in debates with Christian missionaries and the Arya Samaj to defend their vision of Islam. Yet other Muslims in India began an active engagement with Western knowledge forms. Sayyid Ahmad Khan (1817–98), for example, who was in active service to the British Government, and who remained loyal during the Mutiny/Rebellion of 1857, became convinced of the need to reinvigorate the Indian

Muslim community by reference to Western knowledge and education. As an acknowledged 'modernizer', Sayyid Ahmad advocated a knowledge of Western science, as well as the adoption of British values such as discipline and order. In this regard, he drew upon the notion of *ijtihad*, and argued that, as lived circumstances changed, the interpretation of Islamic religious norms must also change. This view hardly endeared Sayyid Ahmad to the traditional *'ulama*, yet he nevertheless promoted his ideas through the Muhammadan Anglo-Oriental College established in Aligarh in 1875. Here Sayyid Ahmad hoped to prepare young Muslims to work within the British governmental service, and, ultimately, to bring them into positions of political power that would enable them to protect the Indian Islamic community.

The nineteenth century in India is witness to an intellectual diversity and vitality that defies the demands of imperial rhetoric. Yet this is also a period of intellectual history that has been shackled by historiographies primarily concerned with either reproducing that rhetoric, or analysing the pervasiveness of British colonial power and representational authority. As such, there remains much work yet to do in order to restore a pervasive historical understanding of Indian intellectual and cultural agency.

Further reading

Bayly, C.A. (1988) *Indian Society and the Making of the British Empire*, Cambridge: Cambridge University Press.

Dalmia, V. (1997) *The Nationalization of Hindu Traditions: Bharatendu Harischandra and Nineteenth-Century Banaras*, Delhi: Oxford University Press.

Dodson, M.S. (2002) 'Re-Presented for the Pandits: James Ballantyne, "Useful Knowledge", and Sanskrit Scholarship in Benares College during the Mid-Nineteenth Century', in *Modern Asian Studies* 36, 2: 257–98.

Jones, K.W. (1989) *Socio-religious Reform Movements in British India*, Cambridge: Cambridge University Press.

—— (ed.) (1992) *Religious Controversy in British India: Dialogues in South Asian Languages*, Albany: SUNY Press.

Metcalf, B.D. (1982) *Islamic Revival in British India: Deoband, 1860–1900*, Princeton: Princeton University Press.

Powell, A.A. (1993) *Muslims and Missionaries in Pre-Mutiny India*, Richmond: Curzon.

Prakash, G. (1999) *Another Reason: Science and the Imagination of Modern India*, Princeton: Princeton University Press.

Trautmann, T.R. (1997) *Aryans and British India*, London: University of California Press.

Van der Veer, P. (1994) *Religious Nationalism: Hindus and Muslims in India*, London: University of California Press.

Young, R.F. (1981) *Resistant Hinduism: Sanskrit Sources on Anti-Christian Apologetics in Early Nineteenth Century India*, Vienna: De Nobili Research Library.

MICHAEL S. DODSON

INDUSTRIALISM, POVERTY AND THE WORKING CLASSES

The nature of the inter-relationship between industrialization and the material well-being of the working class has been and remains a matter of considerable controversy. This has been particularly so in Britain where a so-called 'standard of living' debate originated with the onset of industrialization itself and has continued to the present day. Thus for nineteenth-century social commentators such as CARLYLE, SOUTHEY, RUSKIN and others, industrialization impoverished materially, socially, culturally, spiritually and morally. In particular, it ruptured paternalistic and harmonious social relationships, it debased taste, it destroyed the possibility of artistic expression and it created an egotistical materialism that demoralized the population. Even where, as with Ruskin, critics accepted the material advances that industrialization had delivered, these were usually seen as outweighed by the social, psychological and ethical diseconomies that had eventuated. Thus while, for Ruskin, 'it [was] a good and desirable thing truly to make many pins in a day', he considered it was too often forgotten 'with what crystal sand their points [were] polished, sand of human soul' (Ruskin 1904: 196). The early nineteenth-century socialists, and later Marx and Engels, also recognized the material triumphs of industrialism. 'The bourgeoisie, during its rule of scarce one hundred years, [had] created more massive and more colossal productive forces than [had] all preceding generations together' (Marx and Engels 1976: 85). But for all that such achievements were both consequent upon, and offset by, the material impoverishment of the working class.

Yet, contemporaneously with such commentators, there were those such as Ure, Chadwick, MACAULAY and many others who celebrated the process of industrialization and who considered that it not only increased material prosperity but also, through mechanization, liberated the working class from the enervation and mental atrophy of physical drudgery. For such writers industrialization improved the economic condition and also the mental, moral and social tone of society.

In the twentieth century the debate assumed a new vigour within academic circles, becoming the most sustained single controversy in British economic history. This phase of the debate originated with Clapham's *Economic History of Modern Britain*, which used real-wage data to construct an essentially optimistic view of the impact of industrialization on labour; a view that was challenged by J.L. Hammond in an essay on 'The Industrial Revolution and Discontent', which contended that quantitative gains in terms of increased consumption were more than outweighed by the quality-of-life losses that industrial capitalism inflicted on the working class. This division between the meliorists and the pessimists was to be further accentuated in the 1950s and 1960s by the Hartwell/Hobsbawm exchanges, with the debate assuming a more rigorously quantitative form relating to the impact of industrialization on the level of wages, patterns and levels of consumption and the size and distribution of the national income.

In the last three decades of the twentieth century there has been no diminution in its intensity with major contributions from a number of economists and economic historians. What emerged in this period was a more statistically sophisticated consideration of the evidence and also an attempt to factor into the equation a much wider range of quantitative evidence than previously – for example on unemployment, inequality, transportation, housing, recreation, mortality and longevity. In addition, there have been attempts to give quantitative expression to evidence of a qualitative nature, while there was also an increase in the number of studies making use of disaggregated data to consider standard-of-living issues in relation to the experience of particular regions and specific occupational groupings. This latter research was important given the regional concentration of industrial development. Yet, as regards this general proliferation of data, such a multiple-indicator approach to the issue of living standards was seen by some as, at best, conveying an essentially impressionistic sense of the standard of living while, at worst, involving

poorly quantified series that generated conflicting perspectives on what is happening to living standards.

The last two decades have also seen a more systematic and sophisticated use being made of physiological evidence relating to stature and body/mass ratios. The use of anthropometric observations as the basis for assessments of the welfare of working populations has a long history. Auxology, the study of growth, can be traced back at least as far as French physiologists of the 1820s who commented on the impact of general environmental conditions on the health and stature of the French worker; while later, Marx, in the first volume of *Capital*, made reference to the auxological work of Liebig when explaining the factory acts as the product of a recognition that an unregulated labour market had precipitated a significant deterioration in physical condition of the British working population.

Most anthropometric data was, and is, gleaned from records on the physiological state of naval and military recruits and convicts, and it has allowed historians to draw conclusions about access to material sustenance and the physical and psychological environment that the working class confronted with the onset of industrialization. In effect, stature, in contrast to the multiple-indicator approach, represents a composite index reflecting, amongst other things, factors such as the availability and quality of foodstuffs, the prevalence of disease, the quality of housing, the intensity of labour and its working conditions. Such evidence on the physiological state of populations has been particularly abundant for European nations where compulsory military service required the annual medical examination and measurement of the entire population of young male adults of conscription age. But it has also been amassed for military and naval recruits in Britain where a voluntary system prevailed. Such anthropometric material provides a useful summary of the outcome of a variety of environmental influences. However, it should be noted that even if we accept that there is a significant connection between stature and well-being, such evidence says something about welfare and welfare trends only over the period of physical growth.

There have also been attempts in the last two decades to construct other composite indices of well-being combining manifestly quantitative and more obviously qualitative data. In part this came out of a recognition of the deficiencies of simply using per capita national income, real wage and consumption data as the basis for statements about living standards. Thus it was increasingly recognized that even if such evidence was available and reliable, translating it into statements about human welfare was still highly problematic. In part too the search for composite indices that combined the quantitative and qualitative was also the product of an upsurge of interest in social accounting, in the 1960s and 1970s; a period when the positive and, more often, the negative externalities of economic growth were becoming matters of increasing concern. In this context use has been made by historians of the Human Development Index (HDI) that came out of a United Nations Human Development Report published in 1953; an index that understood underdevelopment in terms of lack of certain basic capabilities, rather than simply a lack of purchasing power, and that had three basic components – longevity, knowledge (measured by reference to adult literacy and years of schooling) and income.

Focusing on the notion of 'capabilities', some commentators also sought to construct an index of well-being that encompassed political rights and civil liberties. Others have suggested a physical-quality-of-life index compounded of infant mortality, life expectancy at year one and literacy rates, while still others have proposed the use of gender-related development indices. At times, indeed, it has almost seemed as if there has been in the late twentieth century a resumption of the nineteenth-century quest for the Holy Grail of a felicific calculus.

Much of the controversy surrounding the impact of industrialization on the working class has therefore inevitably revolved around the nature of the data deployed, its mathematical manipulation, the weight given to particular components of that evidence, the indices it has been used to construct and the weight given to the components of which those indices are comprised. However, underlying debate of this kind there has lurked even more fundamental differences of opinion that stem, in part, from divergent perceptions of what is of value and worth in human existence. For there are those who have seen in the demise of a pre-industrial society the loss of a system of values, a social ethos, a material environment, a pace and a rhythm of life, even an aesthetic; losses of inestimable worth that could not be compensated for by the industrial manufacture of material abundance. In this regard too late twentieth-century disillusionment with the consequences of the affluent society, the growth of environmentalism and the emergence of green politics have also all served to influence the nature and the intensity of the expression of this kind of view. By the same token many commentators, from Adam Smith onwards, have seen in the growth of a commercial and industrial society a transformation of the material possibilities available to mankind; the creation of a new world where the material dearth of the pre-industrial one has been eliminated and where the material well-being of most has changed decidedly for the better. And when, like this, the relative merits of a world lost and a world gained are juxtaposed the problem of incommensurability is always likely to engender more heat than light.

However, leaving aside the difficulties involved in estimating well-being, what does the available evidence, with all its deficiencies and provisos, tell us about the impact of industrialization on the living standards of the working class. Here, to begin with, it is useful to consider the experience of some early industrializers, specifically, Britain, the USA and France.

In the case of Britain while, as noted above, there are clearly problems with simply considering data on real wages and per capita national income, it is nonetheless important to note that these measures of living standards do show an upward trend for the early phase of industrialization. Thus recent work points to an increase in real wages of 37.8 per cent for blue-collar workers in the period 1781–1827. Also, a personal consumption series suggests an increase of 1.51 per cent, per annum between 1819–51; figures that are consistent with the buoyancy of mass-production industries aimed at the working-class consumer market. And such evidence has led some to conclude that given that the average worker was better off in any decade from the 1830s onwards than he/she had been in any decade prior to 1820, the debate over real wages is effectively over. In addition, when efforts have been made to factor in other variables to a standard of living equation such as changes in the terms of trade, the diseconomies of urbanization and the incidence of unemployment, the results have suggested that the meliorist view still holds. Of course there remains the question of how these gains were distributed between regions, within classes, by gender and even within households, and it is important to distinguish between the mean labourer and the median labourer, but even so evidence of this kind certainly has provided grist for the mill of the optimists.

In addition, use of the HDI index points to a relatively favourable assessment of the trajectory of well-being during the Industrial Revolution period, as a consequence of improvements in literacy, schooling and life expectancy. More generally, quality-of-life measures of this kind, despite the foreboding of J.L. Hammond and subsequent writers, have furnished further evidence that can be used to substantiate the meliorists' case.

Yet the mortality evidence points less obviously in an optimistic direction. Wrigley and Schofield estimated that while life expectancy in England improved from 35 to 40 years between 1781 and 1826, there was then little improvement for the next 50 years. In Scotland the second quarter of the nineteenth century was a period characterized by frequent mortality crises. There is also evidence that indicates a more rapid increase of infant than adult mortality rates in the second quarter of the nineteenth century in England. The evidence on mortality and morbidity therefore suggests that there was some deterioration in both the late eighteenth century and, in particular, in the second quarter of the nineteenth century. Further, comparative evidence suggests that in comparison with Europe, mid-century mortality in Britain was relatively high and life expectancy relatively low; something that was clearly related to the urbanization attendant upon the growth of industrial capitalism.

Also, and most significantly, the British population experienced a decline in height in the second quarter of the nineteenth century and one that persisted amongst those born in the 1850s and 1860s. Thus between 1820 and 1850 it has been estimated that the stature of the British population declined by 5.4 cm. Indeed, on the basis of the available evidence it has been concluded that it was not until 'the cohort born just before the First World War' that 'it is likely that the mean heights had recovered and perhaps slightly surpassed the levels reached in the birth cohorts of the 1820s' (Floud *et al.* 1990: 306). For some, such evidence on stature, comprehending as it does a composite of factors relating to real income, diet, the incidence of disease, living and working conditions and intensity of labour, suggests that whatever

gains in working-class real incomes or real wages occurred in the second quarter of the nineteenth century were more than outweighed by other adverse environmental conditions. So here we have significant evidence to support a pessimistic view of the impact of early industrialization on the working class. In this context it is also interesting to note that in Britain, as elsewhere in Europe in the eighteenth and throughout most of the nineteenth century, the stature of the population was greater in rural than in urban areas and that, for a large part of the nineteenth century in Britain, urban areas were actually characterized by falling stature in relation to rural areas.

Of course reasons other than the impact of industrialization can be given for this decline in stature: the pressure on resources created by a rapidly growing population, war, social conflict and unenlightened statesmanship and legislation may all have contributed to this trend. Nevertheless it would seem that an increased exposure to pathogens and pollution, a deterioration in housing conditions, an intensification of the labour process and the psychological and physiological diseconomies associated with this, the adverse dietary consequences of an increasing tendency to food adulteration and other factors, integrally connected to the interrelated processes of industrialization and urbanization, can all be regarded as having had deleterious consequences for stature.

As regards the experience of another early industrializer, the USA, the trajectories of health and economic growth seem, in many respects, to have paralleled those of Britain. Thus in the early industrial period the income gains that came from rising output were not matched by a comparable trend in health. On the contrary whether it is measured by stature, by mortality rates or by the body/mass index, health in this phase of industrialization seems to have deteriorated. As regards stature, for instance, the decline has been estimated at around 4.0 cm in the period 1830–90.

As to the reasons for this, a number are certainly connected with the industrialization occurring in this period. Thus the growth of inter-regional trade, together with migration and immigration, meant that previously isolated populations were exposed to disease strains of a kind that they had not previously encountered. In addition the increase in the number of public schools concentrated juvenile populations in a way that facilitated the spread of disease, as did rapid urbanization for the population more generally. The economic difficulties caused by the Civil War may also have had an impact on the health of the US population but here, of course, we have a factor unrelated to industrialization. By the twentieth century, though, for the USA as for all other Western industrial nations, economic growth and health trends were moving in the same positive direction.

Finally, amongst the earlier industrializers, the French experience would seem to have been different from both that of either Britain or the USA. Thus, in France, the evidence suggests that physical indicators and the conventional economic indicators do *not* run in contrary directions. Here the evidence suggests that there was a slow and steady increase in height of the French population between 1820 and 1913, with a gain of 2.5 cm over that period; while between 1820–60 real wages increased rapidly. As regards the distribution of income there was, though, in this period, a shift away from the manual working class.

For the later industrializers it can be said that, in general, growth of per capita GDP and incomes tended to be more rapid than for those who experienced an early start. Further, in the case of countries such as Sweden, the Netherlands and Japan, these indicators also tended to move in the same direction as those measuring stature and health more generally. In effect, these countries experienced a sustained increase in a range of quality-of-life measures during their initial phases of industrialization. That said, in the case of Japan, while the height of Japanese military recruits from industrial areas grew by an average of 4.1 cm, 1899–1937, and that of recruits from agricultural areas grew by only 2.8 cm in the same period, industrial areas had higher rates of mortality than agricultural.

In contrast, in the case of Germany, we have a late industrializer that, although enjoying a rapid growth in per capita national income in the last quarter of the nineteenth century, together with a small increase in literacy rates and a fall in mortality rates, still experienced a decline in the stature of its population in the 1880s. And, indeed, in the period 1866/67–1892/3, it has been argued that, for the population as a whole, there was no significant improvement in net nutrition. It is true that if we take the period 1890–1914, there was certainly a significant improvement in all indicators. Even so, it was the case that the profound macroeconomic difficulties of the 1870s and early 1880s, rising income inequality and rapid urbanization, seem to have produced, for a time, a stagnation and possibly even a decline in the health and living standards of the average German. On balance though it seems to have been the case that, as regards living standards, earlier industrializers suffered more negative repercussions than those industrializing later.

Nineteenth-century industrialization does not seem, therefore, to have produced a uniform impact on the working populations of Britain and other European countries. However, there were some common factors and developments that, to a greater or lesser extent, seem to have influenced the material outcomes of the process. Thus given the increased understanding of the role of germs in the spread of disease and the impact that had on public policy, later industrialization was attended by less adverse repercussions in terms of the increased exposure of working populations to pathogens. In this regard more efficient sewage disposal, the improved quality of the water supply and the improved housing that attended public investment and increased epidemiological knowledge in the late nineteenth century helped to mitigate those adverse consequences for longevity, mortality and stature that were apparent in countries such as Britain and the USA that had industrialized earlier and where, in relation to such public goods, investment as a proportion of national income was clearly at a sub-optimal level. It was also the case that, in general, later industrializers benefited from more rapid economic growth and more rapidly rising incomes, and were more likely to enjoy the benefits of some kind of social safety net, as was the case in Bismarckian Germany.

The extent and pace of urbanization also played a part in terms of the epidemiological environment. In Britain, where urbanization with the onset of industrialization was rapid (a rise in the urban population of over 25 per cent per decade, 1801–51), and encompassed a significant proportion of the population, there were major problems. Indeed this unusually rapid industrialization is considered one of the main reasons why mortality conditions in mid-century Britain compare unfavourably with those in Europe. In contrast, in France, where urbanization was slower, and the greater part of the population remained rural throughout the nineteenth century, the impact on mortality and morbidity was considerably less; one reason certainly why there was no loss of stature amongst the French population during its early phase of industrialization.

The existence or non-existence of abundant land resources also affected the material consequences of industrialization. Lower population density diminished the spread of disease, while the size of the agricultural sector that land resources permitted influenced the availability and quality of food. For example, it has been argued that the high level of urban meat consumption in nineteenth-century France helped to mitigate the negative environmental consequences of industrialization and urbanization in that period. Also where, as in Sweden and the Netherlands, industrialization occurred in essentially rural areas, the adverse consequences for public health were considerably reduced. In this regard too the differential in stature of rural as against urban populations in nineteenth-century Europe is significant.

Limitations of family size, as in nineteenth-century France, also improved the health and physical growth of young children during the industrialization period. It did so first, because it reduced the pressure upon resources within the family unit, thereby affecting the level and quality of consumption; second, because smaller family size restricted the spread of communicable diseases; and, third, because low marital fertility may have permitted greater per capita investment in the health of children. In contrast to France's low fertility and slow population growth, Britain was characterized by a rapid and accelerating growth of population in the late nineteenth and early twentieth century and it has been suggested by some that this exerted considerable downwards pressure on living standards and was a major cause of poverty in this period. In general, therefore, it can be suggested that a rapidly growing population seems to have been a factor that exacerbated the adverse consequences of nineteenth-century industrialization

The character of industrialization also impacted on health. Thus the spread of disease was more likely and more rapid where industry was characterized by the emergence of large units of production, such as factories, rather than small workshops. In addition, the length and intensity of the working day also had a bearing on health and stature as did the nature of the working environment – humidity, ventilation, effluvia – which affected the prevalence of pathogens. Furthermore, where industrialization involved the expansion of inter-regional and international trade, opportunities were created for the more effective transmission of disease along trade routes, as was the case in the USA.

Clearly, then, in general terms the material experience of industrialization by the working class was determined by its character, pace and timing, by the nature of the migration and urbanization that it precipitated, and by the kind of industrial processes that attended it, i.e. by factors related to industrialization itself. But it was also determined in part too by other factors that can be seen as largely exogenous to it, for example the state of epidemiological knowledge, government policy, social attitudes to leisure and consumption and population growth. Of course, in practice, it is not always easy to distinguish the former from the latter.

References

Floud, R., Wachter, K. and Gregory, A. (1990) *Height, Health and History, Nutritional Status in the United Kingdom, 1750–1850*, Cambridge: Cambridge University Press.
Marx, K. and Engels, F. (1976) *The Communist Manifesto*, Penguin: Harmondsworth.
Ruskin, J. (1904) *The Stones of Venice*, in E.T. Cook and A. Wedderburn (eds) *The Works of John Ruskin*, 39 vols, London: Allen & Unwin, Vol. 10.

Further reading

Cannadine, D. (1983) 'The Present and Past in the English Industrial Revolution', *Past and present* 103: 131–72.
Crafts, N. (1997) 'The Human Development Index and Changes in Standards of Living: Some Historical Comparisons', *European Review of Economic History* 1: 299–322.
Steckel, R. and Floud, R. (1997) *Health and Welfare during Industrialisation*, Chicago: University of Chicago Press.
Taylor, A. (ed.) (1975) *The Standard of Living in Britain in the Industrial Revolution*, London: Methuen.

SEE ALSO: early socialism; historiography and the idea of progress

NOEL THOMPSON

INTELLECTUALS, ELITES AND MERITOCRACY

An emphasis on sociological continuity in history suggests that the social hierarchy of medieval and early modern Europe was modified, rather than overturned, by industrialization. Many elite groups, including the '*philosophes*'/'*men of letters*' of each national society, were able to renegotiate their position *vis-à-vis* other groups and to retain many important privileges. (The invention of a new terminology – '*intellectuals*'/'*intelligentsia*' – at the close of our period should not be allowed to disguise this.) The elite status of 'the professions' and of specialist writers as 'experts' was challenged, but not lost, thanks to the growth of literacy, as this change was a necessary prerequisite of the growth of a mass market in printed literature. At opposite ends of the political spectrum, radically anti-elitist ideas were expounded by anarchists and communists, while an academic theory known as '*elitism*' or '*elite theory*' was developed after 1880, most notably in Italy and Germany. However, the latter theory was far from being entirely novel, given that belief in the virtues of *aristocracy* (whether traditional and/or commercial) was a commonplace of many conservatives throughout the period under consideration.

A plethora of arguments regarding the concept of 'the intellectual' that originated in the twentieth century (some liberal and some Marxist in character) has made it difficult to discuss the nineteenth-century category of 'man'/'woman of letters' without anachronism. The same accusation can be made against a framework that views such figures as participants in wider debates on *nationality*, *gender* and *class*, but as these ideas are unavoidable within contemporary historiography, it seems necessary and desirable that intellectual history should recognize the importance of these categories.

During the twentieth century, the idea that good education is the *only* true qualification for the legitimate exercise of political power has become known as the case for 'meritocracy'. In fact, this word was unknown prior to the 1950s, but for the period 1830–1914 the term 'clerisy' was a close match. In the context of imperialism, the argument that a process of 'educating' the colonised was the best justification of empire (rather than *Realpolitik*) could be linked to meritocratic ideas, and usually involved attempts to co-opt non-European elites into European culture, rather than seeking to create an 'educational democracy'.

In medieval and early modern times, the traditional elites of European society were aristocrats, churchmen and (to a lesser extent) lawyers. In monarchical systems, a core elite' of courtiers surrounded the monarch – and sometimes royal courts recruited 'talent' from outside of the dominant elite families, for example the Tudor statesman, Thomas Cromwell (*c.*1485–1540). Republican systems, such as the Italian city-states of the Renaissance, conferred elite status upon a commercial stratum, so it is sometimes possible to speak of a 'merchant elite'. Although standing armies were far from universal (and were usually replaced by militias in republics), there were numerous examples of 'military elites' throughout the pre-industrial epoch. Moreover, this pattern was at least recognizable outside of Europe, although in the case of China, the mandarinate – which administered the whole country on behalf of the Emperor – was an important example of a bureaucratic elite.

Returning to Europe, and proceeding to the turn of the nineteenth century, it seems that while traditional members of the elite such as courtiers, the nobility (in general), religious leaders and military officers were being challenged for authority by the *nouveaux riches* of the bourgeoisie, the newly established role of the '*philosophes*' or 'men of letters' was also open to renegotiation. Apart from the fact that many '*philosophes*', 'illuminati' and other educated members of society were themselves nobles, support for the aristocracy had been commonplace, because aristocrats had become the major source of patronage for both individuals and universities as the role of the Church in society declined. In the new century, writers came from a wider variety of social backgrounds and the 'republic of letters' became a battleground between different ideologies and world-views.

Although the nineteenth century was a period in which scholarly inquiries tended to become more specialized (partly due to the development of specialist syllabuses in universities) the popularization by intellectuals of relatively esoteric doctrines (e.g. by DARWIN and RENAN) was notable and important. The questioning of traditional Christianity from scientific and historical perspectives had a clear impact on popular attitudes, as well as acting as a catalyst for experiments in existential and liberal theology – for example by KIERKEGAARD and Frederick Temple. Yet, if the nineteenth century was an age where religion was both important and contested, the doctrine of Christian poverty was rarely practised by choice – from this perspective, figures such as BOOKER T. WASHINGTON and GANDHI made a virtue of necessity for their followers. Instead, Europe and North America began to develop the characteristics of modern consumer societies and an international community of political economists (e.g. RICARDO, LIST, JEVONS, Francis A. Walker and Leon Walras) charted the parallel development of a 'science' of the production of *wealth*. As we now know, however, an account of how and why commodities are produced under certain conditions cannot answer the question of whether or not the various 'players' in a market-place *deserve* the rewards they receive.

Meanwhile, the growth of literacy and the spread of education also raised problems of *status* within 'the professions' and amongst writers – although it was these very phenomena that created a much-expanded market for printed matter. BURKE even suggested that the French Revolution of 1789 was due to the machinations of the 'inferior, unlearned, mechanical, merely instrumental members' of the legal profession in the National Assembly. In response to this charge, a multi-causal explanation of the Revolution – that it was not caused by a single factor, but by 'an incessant chain of [oppressive] events' – was expounded by GODWIN. His *Enquiry concerning Political Justice* (1793) also proposed a communistic 'system of equality', which would ensure that 'all men were admitted into the field of knowledge' and 'all were wise'. Furthermore, while Godwin implied a residual role for 'geniuses', during the same decade in France, the ideal of a communist society with *no elites whatsoever* was put forward by BABEUF. Hence, although Marx and Engels enjoy a unique place in the intellectual history of nineteenth-century Europe, their work drew upon established traditions of revolutionary agitation and radical anti-elitism (see MARX AND MARXISM).

It was probably the relative success of the new revolutionary tradition in Europe before 1870, and its perceived failure to establish a 'true democracy' after 1870, which created the preconditions for the rise of analytical and normative *elitism* as identifiable schools of thought. On one side of the coin, ultra-democratic doctrines continued to enjoy a measure of support, which provoked moderates and reactionaries to rebut them, and, on the other, the absence of a viable counter-example to the claim that 'all societies are hierarchies' encouraged the development of a more general set of elitist concepts. From the 1880s onwards, the Italian scholar, MOSCA, contended that in every society an organized minority ('the political class') ruled over the disorganized majority. As the twentieth century began, the political economist, PARETO, argued that this minority was usually divided into a governing elite, who exercised political power directly, and a non-governing elite, who merely enjoyed political influence. In the modern world, this non-governing elite was, in fact, a group of 'elites', such as political parties and professional groups, who might aspire to

exercise political power themselves. In order to describe circumstances where these aspirations were realized, Pareto coined the phrase 'the circulation of elites'. The changing role of elites in every part of the world certainly added plausibility to these hypotheses. Italian elite theory was – at one level – a reaction against radical egalitarianism (as noted above), but it *was* egalitarian in the limited senses that it respected 'freedom of opportunity' as a cause of social mobility and treated all members of an elite as more or less significant. In Germany, by contrast, liberal elite theorists (such as WEBER) paid greater attention to the 'charismatic' role of individual leaders in political life, while in France the two Bonapartes had encouraged both a 'cult' of their own personalities and a 'nobility of merit'.

In essence, normative elitism is belief in the virtues of an aristocracy and this normative position retained a number of reputable supporters throughout the period. In the early decades of the nineteenth century, SAINT-SIMON and COMTE advocated government by a strictly organized 'new elite' of natural and social scientists (with support from bankers and industrialists), while, in the 1840s, CARLYLE concluded that the energy of the new 'Captains of Industry' made them the best available candidates for social leadership, although he still hankered after a place for literature in an 'aristocracy of talent'. Later, at the *fin de siècle*, NIETZSCHE despaired of both the new and the traditional European elites, but he outlined a programme for a future generation of artistic individualists ('the *übermensch*') who might one day achieve a 'transvaluation of all values'. Yet, whether organization, energy or insight was the most valued characteristic of small-group leadership, it had to be acquired through education, so there is a 'natural' connection between the question of elitism and the 'self-identity' of the educated classes of the nineteenth century.

The use of the word 'intellectual' as a noun seems to have begun in seventeenth-century England, but the term was originally synonymous with 'thinking being'. In the early nineteenth century, the noun acquired currency as a term for a programmatic politician, but it was only in the 1840s that the plural acquired its portmanteau quality as a description of writers, scientists and artists in general. Nevertheless, Heyck (1998) has shown that such usage was very rare and did not indicate 'a prevailing way of thinking about cultural activities'. The popularity of the term in Continental Europe dates from the Dreyfus

Affair, and the famous 'Manifeste des intellectuels' published by Emile Zola and his supporters in January 1898. Four notable schools of interpretation have dominated discussions about intellectuals since that time, each of them defined by a particular view, namely: the view that intellectuals 'speak' for the ruling class, the view that intellectuals 'speak' for society as a whole, the view that intellectuals *should* 'speak' for those who cannot 'speak' for themselves and the view that intellectuals *should* withdraw from public affairs and simply pursue 'truth'. Each of these will now be examined briefly.

During the early twentieth century, LENIN adapted Marxist theory in order to endow the concept of 'ideology' with greater explanatory power and the Russian term '*intelligentsia*' acquired popularity. While Marx and Engels had written in 1840s that the 'prevailing ideas of a period have always been simply the ideas of the ruling class', it subsequently became commonplace for Marxists to explain the content, as well as the orientation, of intellectual life with reference to the capitalist economic system. Nikolai Bukharin's *Historical Materialism* (1921) argued that the intelligentsia (viewed as 'ideological labourers') developed norms that were always conducive to the preservation of capitalist society. Consequently, intellectuals enjoyed a 'monopoly of knowledge' which ensured that they enjoyed 'a greater share of the social product than their subordinates'. Connections between the 'ruling class' and 'the intellectuals' in the nineteenth century were certainly commonplace, but they were also more complicated than most Marxists have allowed.

Nineteenth-century theories of history that accorded primacy to the *production* of knowledge (e.g. the theories of Hegel (see HEGEL AND HEGELIANISM) and COMTE) were the precursors of twentieth-century theories of society that accorded privilege to the *producers* of knowledge – for example the theories of Karl Mannheim (1893–1947). According to Mannheim, the 'free intelligentsia' of the modern period were the direct successors of the medieval clergy (a view he shared with COLERIDGE) and they enjoyed special responsibility for moulding 'society's world-view'. The same assumption of the potency of abstract theorizing was reflected in Julien Benda's negative assessment of 'the values of action' (which the European intelligentsia were alleged to have

espoused in the period between 1890 and 1927) but the ideal of Socratic independence expressed in *La Trahison des clercs* (1927) can be found much earlier; in JOHN STUART MILL, for example. Events such as the Governor Eyre Controversy and the Dreyfus Affair drew attention to the claim that writers, scientists and artists had a special duty to espouse causes that were unpopular with both 'the political class' and society at large. Here, intellectuals were resisting, rather than moulding, the 'spirit of the age'. As for the ideal of complete separation from politics, it is certainly worth noting that Gustave Flaubert advocated 'Art for the Sake of Art' from the 1850s to the 1870s and that EMERSON had urged his fellow scholars to 'leave governments to clerks and desks' in his lecture on *The American Scholar* as early as 1837.

To risk stating the obvious, nineteenth-century men (and women) of letters did not define themselves with reference to Soviet or Mannheimian definitions of 'the intellectual'. The French Revolution inspired some (but not all) to set aside apparently disinterested pursuit of knowledge for political partisanship and to create a new category, the revolutionary agitator. Within more traditional political discourse, Plato's ideal of the 'philosopher-king' still had appeal for some, while others aspired to the more 'realistic' role of advisers to their political masters. Slightly more technical questions with a wide-ranging significance were 'Could humanity's ever-widening knowledge be integrated into a single system?' *and* (but with very different implications) 'Should the multiplication of disciplines be accepted and even welcomed?' The answers that intellectuals gave to these questions were sometimes explicit, and sometimes the answers must be inferred from their practice by the historians of today. The central preoccupations of the nineteenth century – at least in Europe – appear to have been wealth, power and spirituality, with class, gender, race and nationality also enjoying strong claims for attention by the intellectual historian. While the practice of 'gendered readings' of apparently 'gender-free' texts has become commonplace since the 1960s, it can be argued that even quite 'technical' literature should be read with reference to nationality. It was often through the deployment of concepts of 'national character' that judgements regarding the appropriate distribution of political power were surreptitiously introduced into 'non-political' discourse.

There were, of course, many *explicitly* nationalist and proto-nationalist movements in the period 1789 to 1914 and – since the 1960s – the Czech historian, Miroslav Hroch, has argued that many of these movements emerged according to a definite *sequence*. Hroch contends that in the early stage of a nationalist movement ('Phase A'), scholarship – as practised amongst a social elite – values the culture, language and history of an ethnic group, but it is not evangelical regarding the centrality of this value. In the next stage ('Phase B'), new activists join in the intellectual movement and make use of its proto-nationalist scholarship as a resource for *agitations* designed to spread 'national consciousness' throughout their ethnic community. Where such an agitation is successful, a consensus emerges that national identity is especially valuable. This is expressed through a mass movement ('Phase C'). The 'Hroch sequence' is a useful explanatory device, but more contingent factors, such as diplomatic strategies, also played an important role in the political history of the nineteenth century.

This is not to deny that frequently nationalistic ideologies were closely associated with processes of state-building, but where an already well-established political entity existed, other questions – such as the 'ruler/adviser' question – were more prominent. Plato's ideal of the 'philosopher-king' concept may not have been directly applicable to Europe in the nineteenth century, but intellectual expertise was co-opted into the highest echelons of government with some regularity. Gladstone, DISRAELI and Henry Fawcett enjoyed significant reputations as novelist, Classical scholar and political economist respectively – and all were chosen as British ministers. Yet John Stuart Mill, an archetypal Victorian polymath, only served a short period as an MP (1865–8). In contrast, the French historian, GUIZOT, served as both a minister of education (1832–7) and a foreign minister (1840–7), although his short-lived premiership (1847–8) ended in the famous February Revolution. An intellectual could become a politician, but by no means every politician was an intellectual.

Outside the political 'establishment', the leadership of various socialist and nationalist societies often fell into the hands of privileged, educated, but disaffected, persons and the model of the revolutionary secret society was 'exported' to Asia – where it meshed with already existing traditions of revolutionary conspiracy. Nevertheless,

self-taught working men ('autodidacts') such as Josef Dietzgen and PROUDHON could make a significant contribution to the philosophical and political culture of the time through their own efforts. Furthermore, the desire to be a political figure was by no means universal and so it must be asked whether the absence of a formal education was an insurmountable obstacle to more modest forms of social promotion. Clearly from an empirical perspective, the answer varied greatly from country to country and continent to continent, but the assumption that such promotion was possible was very commonly held – and helps to explain the international popularity of a work such as *Self Help* (1859) by Smiles.

One of the most notable prejudices of the period, shared by most men and by a significant number of women too, was that mental labour was generally unsuitable for the female sex. The logical consequence of this was that many held that a woman *could not be an intellectual*. However, at the very beginning of our period, a challenge to this viewpoint was certainly implicit in the activities of (Germaine) DE STAËL, who worked with Tracy to establish a short-lived role for the '*idéologistes*' in post-Jacobin France. Of course, de Staël's aristocratic background insulated her from most of the pressures of family life and domestic labour that – alongside the formal restrictions of the law and the academy – placed great limitations on the ability of many women to contribute to the intellectual life of the nineteenth century. The career of her less socially privileged contemporary, Mary Wollstonecraft, illustrates these constraints in microcosm. The subsequent growth of an emancipation movement in Europe and North America, which challenged the 'masculinity' of the intelligentsia in the name of equal citizenship, is now well known, but, once again, vocabulary changed more slowly. The term 'feminism' was not coined as a description of the movement's theory of gender equality until the 1890s, but, in Britain alone, figures such as Mary Ann Evans (George Eliot), Jane Harrison, HARRIET MARTINEAU and Mary Somerville made significant contributions to both imaginative literature and scholarship.

Assumptions of racial inequality were other commonplaces of the period, but a few educated men in North America, South Africa and British India were able to challenge the view that physiological differences between Europeans and non-Europeans predetermined the intellectual inferiority of the latter. The careers of Booker T. Washington, W.E.B. DU BOIS and Mohandas Gandhi had this effect, but they also reflected more general questions regarding intellectual leadership during our period. Washington's politics relied upon the assumption that existing 'interests' could be reconciled by gradual dissemination of more enlightened views; Du Bois's politics presumed that social science (later Marxism) could provide a conceptual grid within which a challenge by the oppressed to their oppressors would lead to a social transformation through which new (more harmonious) interests would arise; while Gandhi's doctrines of non-violent resistance and peasant self-sufficiency offered a half-way house between accommodation and revolution. Moreover, Gandhi's Tolstoyan politics involved no claim that education should be specially rewarded; in this too he was outside of the nineteenth-century mainstream.

The term 'intellectual' existed throughout the nineteenth century, but – as was noted – it only acquired its modern resonances at the close of the period. In contrast, the word 'meritocracy' was not coined until the late 1950s to describe government by people selected on merit through a competitive education system. The term first appeared in *The Rise of the Meritocracy, 1870–2033* (1958) – a dystopian 'history of the future' in the style of WELLS or Orwell – by the sociologist Michael Young (1915–2002): this was a work composed principally as a satirical critique of educational segregation in mid-twentieth-century Britain. However, the word 'meritocracy' has acquired a secondary meaning in the last 40 years, as a term for any ruling or influential class of educated people. This usage is much closer to the nineteenth-century concept of 'clerisy', although the terms are not exactly synonymous because a great deal of European speculation from the earlier period had religious connotations and assumed that it was more important to develop the 'higher faculties' of those who already enjoyed power and influence, rather than to recruit 'new blood' through formal education.

Of course, meritocratic thinking in the nineteenth century was far from homogenous. For example, the claim by an educated class to legitimate power and influence was sometimes justified on the basis of an alleged ability to stabilize society, and sometimes on the basis of an alleged ability to radically change and improve social affairs. For those Europeans and Americans who

emphasized the importance of social stability, higher learning might be best deployed to reconcile the material interests of others, to defend orthodox religion or to debunk the theories of those intellectuals who took a revolutionary path.

In Imperial China, on the other hand, the dominant Confucian ideology was not perceived to be under threat. Its supporters continued to stress the importance of recruiting talented individuals to bolster, rather than reform, the mandarinate – although Weber argued that, in practice, corruption ensured that social mobility was much more limited than in liberal capitalist America, as did the regulations that excluded women, merchants, entertainers and brothel-keepers (!) from participating in the classical examination system. In Africa, meanwhile, the traditional elites did not enjoy even the limited respect from Europeans that Asian elites received; in particular, religious conversion to Christianity was generally expected as a precondition of education for a subordinate, administrative role in the local imperialist structures, while no such strictures were applied to Muslims or Hindu brahmans by the British in India after 1858. In the context of imperialism, the education of the colonized was often presented as a justification for *Realpolitik*; although this generally involved a strategy of co-opting non-European elites into the norms of European culture, rather than creating an 'educational democracy'.

During the period under consideration, only Latin America succeeded in emulating the USA by achieving political independence from European colonialism. Despite the originally liberal inspiration of the anti-colonial movement, resistance was led by the 'Bonapartist' SIMON BOLIVAR – and the military *caudillo* became the archetypal South American contribution to the political ecology of the nineteenth century. Across the continent as a whole, a military elite generally held formal power, while a landed elite enjoyed economic privilege; both groups were of European descent, while indigenous peoples remained clearly subordinate and social mobility was minimal. European intellectual disputes were sometimes mirrored in political life – the first Brazilian Republic adopted the Comtean slogan 'Order and Progress' as its national motto, Paraguay provided a home for Bernard Förster's anti-Semitic colony in the 1890s and Otilio Montaño assisted Emiliano Zapata in drafting the 'Plan of Ayala' in 1911 – but these were exceptional interventions. There were no 'velvet revolutions' in the nineteenth century: Bolivar and Bismarck, Zapata and the Paris Commune all made history using 'blood and iron'. As the Venezuelan author, Simón Rodriguez, observed:

> Rare indeed is the military man who can distinguish among men of letters, but rarer still is the literary man who will do justice to a soldier.

Further reading

Heyck, T. (1998) *The Transformation of Intellectual Life in Victorian England*, London and Canberra: Croom Helm.

Hroch, M. (1992) 'Social and Territorial Characteristics in the Composition of the Leading Groups of National Movements', in A. Kappeler, F. Adamir and A. O'Day (eds) *The Formation of National Elites*, 257–276, Aldershot: Dartmouth.

Knights, B. (1978) *The Idea of Clerisy in the Nineteenth Century*, Cambridge: Cambridge University Press.

Said, E. (1994) *Representations of the Intellectual*, London: Vintage.

SEE ALSO: anthropology and race; conservatism, authority and tradition; democracy, populism and rights; liberalism; Romanticism, individualism and ideas of the self; Social Darwinism; social theory and sociology in the nineteenth century; theories of the state and society: the science of politics

CLIVE E. HILL

ISLAMIC THOUGHT IN THE NINETEENTH CENTURY

The Islamic world in the nineteenth century was under both physical and ideological attack. The Ottoman Empire was in retreat, and European colonialism encroached progressively on the Islamic world. What seemed an even greater threat to many was the identification of progress and the idea of the modern with Europe, in effect with the leading Christian countries, and the implication that Islam represents backwardness and the past. Some leading Islamic thinkers developed the theory that Islam thought compatible with science, and that Islamic society should be reformed to incorporate the desirable aspects of modernity. There were also attempts at developing models of the state that would incorporate the strengths of religion with the benefits of some form of popular representation.

The *Nahdah* (renaissance)

One of the most important events in the nineteenth century in the Islamic intellectual world was the creation of the *Nahdah* (rebirth, renaissance). This really started in Syria but achieved its real momentum in Egypt, then as subsequently the intellectual engine room of Islamic intellectual life. The *Nahdah* movement represented an attempt to do two things. One was to introduce some of the main achievements of Western culture into the Islamic world. The other was to defend and protect the major positive features of Arab culture and revive them despite the assaults of Western imperialism (see IMPERIALISM AND EMPIRE). The important aspect of the movement is the attempt to combine these policies, to react to the apparent decadence of the Arab world not by rejecting Arab culture but by purifying it and introducing in the Arab world aspects of modernity from without that were seen as acceptable from an Islamic point of view.

The main *Nahdah* thinkers were al-Tahtawi, al-Afghani and 'Abduh, who in their different ways sought to confront modernity not by rejecting it or by rejecting Islam, but by effecting some kind of synthesis. Although we are only concerned here with the nineteenth century, it is worth pointing out that later remained this significant topic in the Islamic world, and indeed in earlier centuries also it was very much on the intellectual agenda. Islamic culture has often sought to revitalize itself in response to the criticisms of other systems of thought that appear capable of presenting a more attractive or modern view of the world. Some areas of the Islamic world have on occasion totally rejected the importation of foreign ideas, and also sometimes completely given itself up to them. The Renaissance movement suggested that this was a false choice, one could accept some ideas and reject others, thus preserving tradition while adopting modernity at the same time.

The *Nahdah* movement argued that Islam is itself a profoundly rational system of thought, and has no problem in accepting science and technology. So there is no reason for Muslims to abandon their faith while at the same time accepting the benefits of Western forms of modernity. On the other hand, the significance of reviving Islam or Arabism played a considerable part in the political rhetoric of the time. Some thinkers sought to reject the carving up of the Middle East into nation-states by Western imperialism, and argued for the Islamic world to be formed into an international *ummah* or community as it was originally, at least as ideally perceived. On the other hand, the Ottoman Empire, which represented one way of doing this, was a generally unsatisfactory alternative to the idea of the nation-state, since that empire was characterized by the very decadence so criticized by many of the *Nahdah* thinkers. Perhaps, though, if the empire was revived in a more modern form it would be capable of resisting the encroachments of the West on its territory, and only something like a revival of the former caliphate was likely to be able to muster sufficient force and support for such resistance to be a viable policy.

The most important intellectual figure in this movement was undoubtedly Sayyid Jamal al-Din Afghani (1838–97), who as his name suggested had close connections with Afghanistan, where part of his early education took place. He seems to have been deliberately unclear about his precise ethnic origins to prevent that from being a divisive factor in his attempts to address the whole Islamic community. A similar question hangs in the air as to whether he was a Sunni or Shi'a Muslim, doubtless for the same motive of transcending deep divisions in the Islamic world. At the age of around 18 he moved to India where he came across the thoroughly modernist ideas of Sayyid Ahmad Khan (1817–98), which he was later to attack in his *Refutation of the Materialists*. Ahmad Khan bent over backwards in his writings to show the British rulers of India that Islam was a religion capable of accepting rationality, and it was this apologetic tone at which al-Afghani directed his barbs. In 1870 he visited Egypt and Turkey, and was welcomed by the Ottoman authorities and thinkers who were involved in the *Tanzimat* changes designed to modernize the empire, and regarded al-Afghani as having a like mind. In 1883 he spent some time in London and Paris, summoning to the latter city Muhammad 'Abduh from Lebanon to work with him on a journal. While in Paris his refutation of the views of the famous orientalist ERNEST RENAN is important in establishing a view of Islamic culture that is independent of that current in the West. In 1886 the Shah of Iran invited al-Afghani to advise him, but political differences caused him to leave for Russia and he ended up in Istanbul where

he spent his last six years, sometimes supported by the Sultan 'Abd al-Hamid II and often under suspicion of involvement in subversive activities.

The internationalist nature of al-Afghani's career is significant; it represents nicely his belief that the Islamic world should be united. But his arguments were not based on Islam alone; they also borrowed a great deal from what he regarded as science and philosophy. Islamic philosophy is perfectly compatible with modern science and technology, and should encourage Muslims to acquire the necessary skills in order to resist the impact of Western imperialism, he argued. Part of the Islamic Renaissance ideology is that there should be a rebirth and rediscovery of the main intellectual and political achievements of the Islamic world during its heyday. At that time, as the supporters of the movement never tired of reciting, there was an openness to new ideas, wherever they came from, which was sadly, in their view, lacking in the decadent years of the nineteenth century.

Al-Afghani wrote very little, but it had considerable impact. His *Refutation of the Materialists* suggests that the source of evil is materialism, the philosophical doctrine that argues that the world has developed out of a set of material preconditions. He also criticizes the theory of evolution, which he sees as denying God's role in designing the world. His critique has a social aspect also in that materialism is held to reject founding society on any common moral values, and in being critical of religion as such, and of Islam in particular. This sort of critique of what is seen as Western culture has since the nineteenth century become quite common in the Islamic world.

In his response to Renan, al-Afghani tries to show that the Arabs and Islamic civilization are capable of producing philosophy and science. Al-Afghani argues that Muslims had in the past been in the forefront of science and philosophy, and there is no reason to think this would not be repeated in the future. On the other hand, he accepts that religion and philosophy are in constant conflict, but suggests that Muslims could catch up with Christians who rejected aspects of their religion after the Enlightenment. It is not clear from his response how much of traditional Islam is expected to survive such a transformation of intellectual life, and al-Afghani set up the issue in such a way as to dominate the continuing discussions of this topic in the Islamic world through the nineteenth and subsequent centuries.

The influence of his ideas was amplified by the efforts of Rashid Rida (1865–1935), who founded in 1898 the journal *al-Manar* (The Lighthouse) in Cairo. The central theme of the journal was that there is no incompatibility between Islam on the one hand, and modernity, science, reason and civilization on the other. It might be said that Rida tended to emphasize religion and was a firm opponent of secularism, the latter doctrine always being a tempting prospect for the thoroughgoing modernist. This general compatibility thesis was supported in various forms by a variety of Arab intellectuals, and it was instituted in the framework of Arab society in various ways. For example, Rifa'ah Rafi 'al-Tahtawi (1801–73) was sent to Paris in 1826 to find out what Western culture was all about. He was at that time a teacher at al-Azhar, the ancient Islamic university in Cairo, but had also started reading Western books and learning French, a language of which he became an able translator. One of the most important things he brought back to Egypt from his experience of Europe was the desire to establish a European-style university in Egypt, a university that would base itself on universal knowledge, not just the Islamic sciences, and which would study seriously the intellectual contributions of the West. It is worth pointing out how far his efforts here were supported by the state; the ruler of Egypt Muhammad 'Ali encouraged al-Tahtawi's efforts, and promoted him within the state structure. Although changes of regime did lead to occasional hiccups in the modernization campaign, al-Tahtawi did manage to place that campaign firmly within the bureaucratic structure of the state, going so far as to initiate the education of girls.

One of the links he managed to make was not only between modernity and Islam, but also between nationalism and Islam. He took control for a period of Egyptian antiquities, and opposed their transfer abroad, arguing that there is no incompatibility between the universal message of Islam and the desire of an Egyptian to celebrate his country's heritage. Of course, within the context of the Ottoman Empire nationalism turned out to be a much more dangerous doctrine than modernity. Modern Arab commentators on al-Tahtawi often criticize him for being too close to the West, but they fail to recognize his situation as an Egyptian intellectual within a distinct imperialist environment, that of the Ottoman Empire, for whom what the West had to offer was in part an escape from

that empire. Although al-Tahtawi was definitely not a thinker of the stature of al-Afghani and his entourage, he was perhaps more effective in that he spent his life within the administrative structure of Egypt and helped bring about material changes in that structure, especially in its educational institutions. A similarly placed bureaucrat in Tunisia, Khayr al-Din al-Tunisi (1810–89) also initiated secular education in his country, based on the same ideas that progress meant science and was not incompatible with Islam. This spirit of reform was widespread throughout the Middle East, and small groups of intellectuals campaigned in favour of both science and liberalism, seen to be part and parcel of the same ideological movement.

Muhammad 'Abduh (1849–1905) used his position as head of al-Azhar, the leading theological university in the Sunni Islamic world, to propound the message of the *Nahdah* that the Islamic world should accept modernity while at the same time not rejecting Islam. The period of stagnation that he identified with the tenth to the fifteenth centuries CE was a time when the early scientific and philosophical progress of the Islamic cultural world came to an end and the political and religious authorities had a mutual interest in maintaining control by restricting the intellectual curiosity of those over whom they ruled so effectively. What was now needed, he argued in the nineteenth century, was reform of all the institutions of the Islamic world, while preserving the timeless truths of Islam itself. He suggests that the connection between religion and modernity, in particular between Christianity and modernity, is entirely misplaced. After all, as he argues, Christianity advocates belief in the transience of everyday life, not the concern for possessions and comfort so characteristic of modern industrial societies. Yet it found no inconsistency in combining the religion with modern ways of operating, so this need not be a worry for Muslims either. The effective broadcasting of his views throughout the Islamic world through the media, and the liberal *futuwa* (legal rulings) from al-Azhar, played a leading role in defining a relevant role for Islam within the framework of the modern state.

Tanzimat and the Ottoman Empire

Perhaps the area of the Islamic world that felt threatened by modernity most acutely was Turkey and Istanbul, the headquarters of the Ottoman

Empire. The Turkish historian Ilber Ortayli called the nineteenth century the longest century of the empire. The empire was seemingly set on a period of decline that led to its role as the 'sick man of Europe', and to much discussion within Turkey itself as to the future role of the empire, if any, in the developing structure of Europe and the Middle East. The Young Ottomans were a group of Turkish intellectuals who met at a picnic in 1865 and tried to produce a theoretical and practical plan to preserve the empire. It is worth pointing out that all these intellectuals were part of the state bureaucracy, and were trying to reform the system of which they were a part. Some of them went so far as to be critical of Islam, while others were more sympathetic to traditional religion, but they all tried to find some version of religion that would not compete with material and social progress. The *Tanzimat* (regulation) period (1836–78) was one of intellectual ferment in Turkish political ideology, and it played a large part in the future history of Turkey and the lands of the Ottoman Empire beyond the nineteenth century.

It is interesting to note that the source of discontent of the Young Ottomans were 'Ali and Fuad Pasha, and yet these individuals who were important decision-makers in the Government were themselves struggling with the attempt to modernize and improve the situation of the empire. The outlying areas of the empire were keen on independence, and this was supported by the Christian powers, or at least by some of them such as Russia, and there were demands for all the citizens of the empire to be given equal constitutional rights. Up to this time a complicated system whereby each religious community was more-or-less allowed to run its own affairs had persisted, but legally Muslims in the empire had more rights than the other religious groups, although in practice this did not lead to a great deal of unfair treatment in Ottoman society. The Ottomans were unable to hold onto their territories through military power, their armies proved increasingly ineffective, and financially the state proved to be less productive given the inroads of capitalism and imperialism from without. It is always difficult to manage a period of protracted decline, of course, and with hindsight the rulers of the Empire do not seem to have done too badly, but for those living at the time the actions of the government were perceived as being disastrous, although the reasons for the disaster were variously identified.

Some thought that the empire was not sufficiently aggressive, others that it was too Islamic, and some argued it was not Islamic enough. There was not just one 'Young Turkey' movement, and the production of political theory during this period took many different forms.

Even within the Islamic world the empire was losing its grip, and yet the Sultan nominally represented the caliphate, the Islamic world as a unified political entity. It is hardly surprising that the decline of the Ottoman Empire brought about a lively discussion about the role of Islam in the state and the compatibility of religion with science and technology. It is important to appreciate that in many ways the leading advocates of such a discussion was the state itself, and its officials.

Other responses to colonialism and modernity

In the Dutch East Indies, now Indonesia, improved communications brought reformist ideas from Egypt into the country, and the Muhammadiyah movement was set up by Ahmad Dahlan (1868–1923), someone who had lived in Egypt and met 'Abduh. On the other hand, it was not difficult for the ideas of the *Nahdah* to be taken in another direction, as they were by 'Abd al-Rahman al-Kawakibi (1854–1902) who lived for most of his life in Syria. He advocated modernity and liberalism, and also pan-Islamism, but within the context of leadership by the Arabs, not the Ottomans, criticizing the latter for their love of despotism and conservatism. The expansion of Russia south and wars with Iran created many new Muslim subjects for the Tsar, and also much discussion among Muslim intellectuals as to how to respond effectively to the onslaught from the north.

One set of ideas that had a good deal of currency in the nineteenth century was that of Mahdism. The mahdi is someone who is divinely chosen to deliver the community from danger, and the increasing pressure of the industrial West on the Islamic world lead to many mahdis appearing, especially in Africa. Commerce had traditionally been concentrated on the cross-continental routes, but the influence of colonialism lead to the competing power of the coastal ports. In an area between Guinea and Senegal 'Umar ibn Sa'id ruled between 1852–64, trying to stay out of the way of the French, and also fight against them when absolutely necessary. In Libya the Sanusi clan, and in particular Sayyid al-Mahdi al-Sanusi established their rule while Muhammad Ahmad ibn 'Abdullah in the Sudan drove out the Turks and the Egyptians, killed General Gordon in Khartoum, and for a short time ruled that huge country. At the end of the century the Somalis discovered a mahdi in Muhammad 'Abdallah Hasan who went on to resist the British and later the Italians. The crisis as traditional Islamic cultures were overwhelmed by colonialism led to the rapid growth of such millennial movements who offered a potent message of resistance, religion and salvation.

But the search for a mahdi was not limited to Africa; it occurred also in Persia and India, leading to the construction of highly heterodox sects such as the Bahai and the Ahmadiyya movements. The former originated with Sayyid 'Ali Muhammad who came from Shiraz and was declared by some to be the Bab or door through which humanity would be united with the concealed imam, who himself is the link between this world and the divine realm. The movement was fiercely resisted by the Persian regime and the Bab himself was shot, along with many of his supporters, but it took a strong hold in the form of followers of Mirza Husayn 'Ali or Baha' Ullah (Glory of God), and turned into a complex religious movement that over time has become more and more distinct from orthodox Islam, even of the Shi'a variety.

In India Mirza Ghulam Ahmad in 1891 declared himself to be the mahdi (and Christ) and acquired a large number of followers. Some of the latter regarded him merely as a reviver of Islam, but others as a prophet, which goes against the basic Islamic principle that the Prophet Muhammad was the last prophet. As one might imagine, these groups have often not been treated well by the Muslim communities in which they live, but the early persecution does not seem to have prevented them from growing into relatively large and successful movements.

Islam and the Islamic world saw itself as definitely in retreat in the nineteenth century. The expansion of the Christian colonialist powers continued to dominate the world economically and militarily. The Ottoman Empire, whose ruler was formally the head of the Sunni Islamic world, the caliph, was in retreat and widely regarded as a crumbling and corrupt edifice. Modernity in the form of science and technology was the brainchild of the Christian countries, and its slow acceptance in the Islamic world caused much questioning about how far Muslims could adopt such alien ideas. The Islamic world attempted to react to the encroaching influence of competing ideas and influences by reinventing itself to incorporate many but not all of those ideas within itself. It established radical resistance movements, and new sects that developed highly original versions of orthodox Islam.

Further reading

Hourani, A. (1982) *Arabic Thought in the Liberal Age 1798–1939*, Cambridge: Cambridge University Press.

Keddie, N. (ed.) (1972) *Scholars, Saints and Sufis*, Berkeley: University of California Press.

—— (1983) *An Islamic Response to Imperialism: Political and Religious Writings of Sayyid Jamal al-Din 'al-Afghani'*, Berkeley: University of California Press.

Kedourie, E. (1966) *Afghani and Abduh: An Essay on Religious Unbelief and Political Activism in Modern Islam*, London: Frank Cass.

Kurzman, C. (2002) *Modernist Islam: A Source Book*, New York: Oxford University Press.

Mardin, S. (2000) *The Genesis of Young Ottoman Thought: A Study in the Modernization of Turkish Political Ideas*, Syracuse: Syracuse University Press.

SEE ALSO: anti-colonial movements and ideas; main currents in scientific thought

OLIVER LEAMAN

J

JAMES, WILLIAM (1842–1910)

William James is best known as the torch bearer of the new US psychology *c.* 1890, but one might also think of him as a committed medical researcher and physiologist who developed a strong and persisting love for philosophy, and then used the skills and knowledge acquired from each area to recast psychology as an admixture of the two. One should also note his strictly secular, and hence entirely untypical, view of US psychology at the time. Thus, where most nineteenth-century US psychologists and educationalists looked to European and Scottish moral and mental philosophy for their ideas, James's inspiration was provided by the agnostic figures of Alexander Bain and JOHN STUART MILL, and the empirical insights supplied by physiology and German psychology. There was, in addition, the new US philosophy of Pragmatism (described rather pragmatically by James as 'a method of conducting discussions', see Bjork 1988: 249), whose practical, relativistic and adaptive message can be found on most pages of his psychological masterwork of 1890, *The Principles of Psychology* (see also Putnam 1997 for recent comments on both James in general and on his Pragmatism).

William James was born on 11 January 1842, into a privileged New York family whose wealth had been assured by his paternal grandfather's successful investment in projects such as banking and the building of the Erie Canal. James's father, Henry James Sr, was, therefore, in theory able to lead any kind of life that he wished, including one of complete idleness. Instead, he married, helped raise and eccentrically educate five children (including the leading US novelist of the day, Henry James Jr), and took up the study and dissemination of Sandemanian and Swedenborgian mystical philosophy, mainly on the grounds that reading it had helped cure him of the anxiety attacks (or 'vastations') that had plagued his early married life. William James's upbringing was, therefore, intensely intellectual, dizzyingly cosmopolitan and entirely unsettling. Indeed, his MD from Harvard Medical School was the only formal qualification that he ever earned, and even that had been taken after many stops and starts from 1864 to 1869. This period, for example, had included over a year off on a specimen-collecting expedition to Brazil organized by the Harvard biologist Agassiz (1864 to 1865), and an equally lengthy, partly curative, partly intellectual visit to France and Germany during 1867 and 1868, where the journey had been undertaken to alleviate a recurring back pain (termed 'dorsal insanity' by James and thought to run in his family). The European trip was also marred by a partial blindness brought about by an attack of smallpox during his time in Brazil.

More seriously for his intellectual development, however, was that from 1870 onwards he suffered, like his father, from disabling anxiety attacks. Most commentators have interpreted this condition as the physical reaction to his attempt to reconcile his pessimistic views about the deterministic nature of the world as revealed to him by his beloved science with his equally strong wish for self determination and personal freedom (see, for instance, Fancher 1990: 245–6; also Lawrence and Shapin 1998 for recent analyses of the 'embodiment' of scientific knowledge).

These two positions are, of course, ultimately irreconcilable and, as a consequence, James was always destined to twist and turn on their contradictions. But by erecting a barrier between the universal ('this is how the world *mechanically* operates') and the individual ('but *I* am free to choose over matters of personal action and belief'), he hoped to stop the one from overwhelming the other (see Myers 1986: xiv–xv on the essentially personal nature of James's philosophy). Most commentators have timed the discovery of James's moderating views on personal freedom to 29 April 1870, when he had read an essay on that very topic by the French philosopher Charles Renouvier. However, while this did not mean an end to his sufferings, it did grant him enough self confidence in 1872 to embark on a 35-year-long career as Harvard teacher and luminary, initially as a physiologist, then as a philosopher and finally as a psychologist. And his successful marriage to Anne Gibbens in 1878 also helped, both physically and psychologically.

The major task during his first two decades at Harvard was to compile his textbook on psychology *The Principles of Psychology*, a work commissioned by the publisher Henry Holt as early as 1878. In the event, it took James 12 years to come up with the 1,000 pages required, which also incorporated the numerous journal articles written as multiple *Prolegomena* to the *Principles*. (James is reputed to have described the work to Holt as 'the enormous *rat* which … ten years gestation has brought forth' – see Fancher 1990: 250). Less well known, but just as personally significant, was James's deep interest in the paranormal that also dates from the early 1870s, and which some have argued links the *Principles* with James's late masterpiece *The Varieties of Religious Experiences* (1902), in part through his discussion of what constitutes, and what links, consciousness and reality (see Bjork 1988: 210–13).

It is often claimed that after the ordeal of the *Principles*, James moved back into philosophy. However, while it is the case that, post-1890, his goals were a little less overtly psychological, it is also true that what constituted scientific psychology for James was not the etiolated empiricism that it has become. Consequently, his shortened version of the *Principles* (*Psychology: Briefer Course*, also known familiarly as the *Jimmy*) appeared in 1892 to popular acclaim, while he maintained his support of the growing field of psychology in the USA; he served, for example, as President of the American Psychological Association on no less then two occasions. There was also his continuing work on the paranormal and his quasi-psychological treatment of religion in the

Varieties, with its emphases on psychopathology, the value of *personally* transcendent experience and the empirical exploration of religious feelings. In addition, he felt the need in 1907 to spell out what *he* took to be Pragmatism, as against what his fellow members of the long-defunct Metaphysical Club such as Charles Peirce had thought was its nature; but, according to James, this was little more than an explication and extension of what had long been implicit in the *Principles* and elsewhere in both his and other people's writings. However, all this furious activity ceased abruptly on 26 August 1910 when, amidst universal mourning and tributes to his achievements, James died from a chronic heart condition.

References

Bjork, D.W. (1988) *William James: The Center of his Vision*, New York: Columbia University Press.
Fancher, R.E. (1990) *Pioneers of Psychology*, 2nd edn, New York: Norton.
Lawrence, C. and Shapin, S. (eds) (1998) *Science Incarnate: Historical Embodiments of Natural Knowledge*. Chicago: University of Chicago Press.
Myers, G.E. (1986) *William James: His Life and Thought*, New Haven: Yale University Press.
Putnam, R.A. (ed.) (1997) *The Cambridge Companion to William James*, Cambridge: Cambridge University Press.

Further reading

James, W. (1890) *Principles of Psychology*, 2 vols, New York: Holt.
—— (1892) *Psychology: Briefer Course*, New York: Holt.
—— (1902) *The Varieties of Religious Experience*, New York: Longmans.
—— (1907) *Pragmatism*, New York: Longmans.

SEE ALSO: psychology, the emergence of; theories of education and character formation

SANDY LOVIE

JAPANESE THOUGHT IN THE NINETEENTH CENTURY

The background

The mid-nineteenth century witnessed a dramatic end of Japan's ancient regime and the beginning of its modernization. The political shape of the regime that began in the late twelfth century was formed by a central warrior government called *bakufu*, headed by its hereditary chief *shogun*, deriving his power nominally from the Emperor, and local lords, large and small (numbering some 260 in 1861), enjoying autonomy of their fiefs. The country, after a long period of domestic warfare and instability, came to live in comparative peace under the Tokugawa *shogunate* (1603–1867), which enforced the ban on Christianity and foreign trade. The closing of the country was formally completed in 1635–41 except for a small outlet at Nagasaki for the Dutch and the Chinese. Its social form was marked by a strict status system created by sword hunts coupled with land surveys of the late sixteenth century, which prohibited peasants from holding weapons and tying them to a plot of land as cultivators. The ideological support for this feudal order was provided by neo-Confucianism justifying it as derived from eternal 'nature'.

Isolation and domestic peace helped the economy to mature with a national market formed for an important crop, rice, a unified currency and a banking system. The growth of money economy and the rise of the merchants entailed a relative impoverishment of the ruling samurai (warrior) class while encouraging small manufacturing industries and mining, as well as the reclamation of agricultural lands. Owing to the penetration of money economy into rural areas feudal bonds began to slacken, and agrarian revolt spread.

The stability of the ancient regime was also shaken by threats from outside. Japan was perhaps too far away to be affected by the Industrial Revolution and the French Revolution, though Russian attempts to open trade from the north led to armed conflict in the Kurile Islands early in the nineteenth century. The Napoleonic Wars played a role in the Far East by the British effort, though not successful, to dislodge the Dutch from Nagasaki.

The ancient regime in serious trouble presented a backcloth against which ideas, new and old, defensive and offensive, were to delineate the course Japan would take in the century, which turned out to be one of nation-building for many countries.

The beginning of Western Studies

After the lifting in 1720 of the ban on the import of Western books except those on Christianity, 'Western Studies' or 'Dutch Studies', studies of medicine, astronomy and gunnery, were quickly disseminated among the educated classes. In due course appeared political treatises dealing with domestic economy, foreign trade and even overseas expansion. Honda Toshiaki (1743–1820), a schoolteacher, in his major work *Tales of the West* (*Seiiki monogatari*) (1798) argues that the poverty of the peasants was due to the faster growth of population than an increase in rice produced and also to a rise in the number of the unproductive people other than the peasantry, and that the remedy was to be sought in an expansion of the country. He suggests a new Japan as wealthy and strong as Britain, extending from Kamchatka in the north, to Ryukyu in the south and to Manchuria in the west, a trading power to be created by commerce and colonization (not by military conquest). Two decades later a bolder treatise in terms of expansionism was written by Sato Nobuhiro (Shin-en) (1769–1850), a medical doctor. His work *The Secret Policy of Mixing and Blending* (*KondoHisaku*) (1823) proposes the use of armed ships and of the skill of distant navigation for the creation of a vast empire covering East Asia, Siberia, Southeast Asia and the Indian subcontinent, foretelling Japan's military aggression in the twentieth century.

National Learning

Both Honda and Sato were versed in Western Studies whose opposite was 'National Learning' (*Kokugaku*) represented by Motoori Norinaga (1730–1801), another medical man who sought to restore natural Shinto, which he deemed to have existed in the mind of the Ancient Japanese before it was corrupted by their contact with Buddhism and Confucianism brought from China. Ando Shoeki (1703–62) before him had developed similar arguments. What mattered to Shoeki was the pristine Way of Nature preserved in human labour, while to Norinaga it was the creation of the country by the godly imperial ancestors, a myth, which in the form of emperor-worship remained the core of Japanese nationalism. This was strengthened by nationalist scholars of the Mito school who sought to Japanize Confucianism, setting forth the order of reverence from the Emperor at the top to *bakufu*, local lords, and their vassals, replacing the virtuous rule of the Chinese sages. Thus arose a theory of national polity with Japan as the middle kingdom superior to barbarian foreigners. Aizawa Seishisai

(1782–1863), a Mito samurai and the protagonist of these ideas, in his work *New Thesis* (*Shinron*) (1825) upheld the *bakufu's* 1825 edict to expel foreign ships. Enforced till 1842, the edict produced critics and martyrs, and it soon became apparent that xenophobia would not work as a national policy.

Opening of the country and the Meiji Restoration

The Opium War of 1839–42 was a timely warning to the seclusionists, and the Western pressure on Japan to open the country culminated in Commodore Matthew C. Perry's success in his gunboat diplomacy of 1853–4. Commercial treaties signed with the USA and other Western powers in 1858 were 'unequal' with their stipulations on extraterritoriality and tariff regulation. As soon as foreign trade started in 1859 attacks on foreigners and foreign ships began, and these led to the British bombardment of Kagoshima, Satsuma, in 1863 and also to the destruction of the Choshu forts at Shimonoseki by US, French, British and Dutch naval forces in 1863–4. Yet Satsuma and Choshu were the two great *han* (territory under a local lord or *daimyo*) that along with *bakufu* sent students to Europe to study subjects varying from naval engineering to political economy. Fukuzawa Yukichi (1834–1901), the founder of Keio School (later University), who visited Europe on a *bakufu* mission (1862), was impressed with the wealth and strength of the Western nations as much as with the liberty they enjoyed. The Meiji slogan (Meiji being an era name, 1868–1912) of 'enriching and strengthening the country' was a sentiment shared by all other students sent abroad at the time.

It was again Satsuma and Choshu that took the lead in overthrowing *bakufu* in the civil war of 1867–8 in collaboration with the scheming court nobles who aspired to reassert the imperial power. Thus began the great political and social upheaval called the Meiji Restoration. The Charter Oath of Five Articles (1868), a statement of the principles of the new government, emphasized among others the need of public debate in an assembly, replacement of obsolete customs by acts agreeable to international justice, and search for knowledge all over the world in order to strengthen the imperial polity. This was sworn by the young Emperor not to the people or to the aristocracy, but to his ancestral gods. Japan's modernization thus began

under the aegis as it were of the spirit of imperial Japan.

The Meiji government initiated reform measures to put an end to feudal land tenure and social statuses: a modern system of local government was introduced, a nation-wide system of education adopted and modern conscription enforced, while key factors of industrialization were promoted under state sponsorship and by privatization of government-owned resources.

One-half of the government ministers went abroad as the members of the Iwakura Embassy (1871–3), which was encumbered at first with the premature hope of revising unequal treaties. They spent 19 months studying the processes of modernization in the USA and Europe, and Kume Kunitake (1839–1931), the historian and compiler of its record, emphasized that European wealth and power dated from around 1800 and Japan's progress would take less time. In his account of the Vienna Exposition of 1873, itself an epilogue to the massive record of the embassy's observation of Western politics, industry and culture, he was quick to perceive that small nations such as Belgium and Switzerland were as impressive as the large, prosperous nations like Britain and France, though elsewhere Bismarck appeared prominently with a German model of development. The choice of models was still open and western ideas poured in.

The introduction of Western ideas

In the forefront of Japan's westernization stood Fukuzawa Yukichi, already mentioned. In his writing entitled *An Encouragement of Learning* (*Gakumon no susume*) (1872–6) he declared for egalitarianism of a sort in which useful knowledge acquired would only contribute to social distinctions among the people. He highly praised the spirit of independence and responsibility and the progressiveness of the pluralistic Western civilization, while deploring the passivity of the hierarchical Eastern civilization (see his *Outline of a Theory of Civilization* (*Bunmeiron no gairyaku*) 1875). Nakamura Masanao (1832–91), formerly professor of the *bakafu* academy, who had taken *bakufu* students to London on the eve of the Restoration civil war, provided another source of westernization of ideas by translating into Japanese Samuel Smiles's *Self Help* (1871) and J.S. Mill's *On Liberty* (1872). Kato Hiroyuki (1836–1916), another *bakufu* professor before

Meiji, produced a Lockean treatise titled *General Principles of True Politics* (*Shinsei tai-i*) (1870) describing the role of government as the defence of the people's right to life and property. Western works translated into Japanese in those days included *De l'esprit des lois* by Montesquieu (1876), *Du contrat social* by J.-J. Rousseau (1877) and *Social Statics* by Herbert Spencer (1877).

Jiyu-Minken movement

Japan's 1870s can be called a decade of reform in the world of ideas as well as in administrative measures, while politically a series of rear-guard actions intended for the preservation of samurai autonomy had to be put down by the new government. The decade was best represented by the movement for Jiyu-Minken (Liberty and People's Right), which began with the 1874 memorial for a popular assembly. The Meiji government in its early years consisted of state ministers and councilors, and important posts were practically in the hands of the politicians of Satsuma–Choshu origins, the state of affairs referred to as 'autocracy by officials'. Four former state councilors including Itagaki Taisuke (1837–1919) of Tosa, who had found himself in a minority on the Korean issue (of whether to chastise the Sinophile Koreans), together with four associates signed the above memorial denouncing the meddling by the officials who placed themselves between the Emperor and the people, and advocating the establishment of 'a council-chamber chosen by the people'. Itagaki regarded the Meiji Restoration not merely as the restoration of the imperial right but also as that of the people's right, a view widely held at the time. Meanwhile, intellectual ferments for reform took the shape of an academic society called Meirokusha (The Sixth Year of Meiji (1873) Society) founded by Mori Arinori (1847–89), a former Satsuma student sent to London who acted as a consul-general in the USA after the Restoration, and whose zeal for Western civilization went so far as to advocate the spread of Christianity and the adoption of English as an official language in Japan. The society published its own journal edited by Fukuzawa Yukichi and contributed to by many other able scholars. Though they took a moderate line as to Itagaki's memorial, Mori and Nishi Amane (1829–97), formerly a *bakufu* student sent to Holland and later the compiler of the imperial rescript to the soldiers, argued against its

egalitarian assumptions, while Kato Hiroyuki considered it premature for ignorant people.

The initiative taken by Itagaki and the concerted efforts by local activists like Ueki Emori (1857–92) of Tosa developed into a powerful movement, supported by 100,000 petitioners by 1880, while several Minken groups joined together to form the Liberal Party in 1881. This was the peak year of Jiyu-Minken, when as many as thirty-nine drafts of a Japanese constitution were prepared including one by Ueki Emori upholding the right to resist an oppressive government.

The government for its part announced in an imperial decree of October 1881 that a constitution was to be granted prior to a national assembly promised for 1890. This coincided with an attempt to force resignation from the government of a liberal state councilor Okuma Shigenobu (1838–1922), who had favoured a British-type constitution. These authoritarian measures were meant to cope with the spread of the Popular Right movement throughout the country, especially among the common people in east and northeast Japan, where opposition to the Satsuma–Choshu hegemony had been strong, and the government policy of economic retrenchment hit hard the peasants and small traders engaged in sericulture. Local branches of the Liberal Party were also involved. A series of popular uprisings ensued, at Fukushima (1882), Mt Kaba, Lida and Nagoya, all in 1884. One at Chichibu in the same year took the magnitude of a peasant war involving over 10,000 men in one district, with their nucleus formed in a Party of Sufferers (Konminto), though they were besieged and overwhelmed by the government troops. The decline of the movement was hastened by government measures such as the deportation of radical leaders from the metropolis.

Setback of liberalism

The 1880s saw the defeat of the People's Right movement and the subtle change of emphasis in the ideas of its protagonists. Nakae Chomin (1847–1901), a student of the Iwakura Embassy who had earlier parted company with the official body and had seen some of Paris and Lyon of the post-Commune days, came to believe in republicanism. In 1881 he edited a radical newspaper and in the following year brought out his own translation of Jean-Jacques Rousseau's *Du contrat social*, which inspired the participants of the Chichibu peasant war. In an analysis of the movement that had come to a deadlock (*The Discourse of Three Drunkards on Government* (*Sansuijin-keirinmondo*), 1887) he seems to have accepted the *fait accompli* by the government, and argued that the people's right once granted should grow through care and energy into a people's right as magnificient as the one won by the people. Baba Tatsui (1850–88), Fukuzawa's student and Chomin's friend, who had spent several years in England studying law, became an editor of the *Liberal Newspaper* (*Jiyu shinbun*) (Chomin was another editor) in which he wrote extensively on freedom of thought and action. When such freedom was denied to him by government suppression, he chose the life of a political exile in the USA, where he met an early death. Some chose the life of the apostate. Kato Hiroyuki, whose reference to the Emperor as a man was strongly repudiated by a nationalist scholar of the Mito school, soon recanted and in his new writing on people's right (1882) attacked the idea of natural right, upholding the Spencean theory of natural selection and calling for efforts to extend 'the influence of the imperial throne'.

Indeed the collapse of the popular movement turned some of its theorists to nationalism and expansionism, which had existed as an undercurrent in their aspirations. Oi Kentaro (1843–1922) belonged to the radical wing of the Liberal Party and stood by the poor and downtrodden, advocating what virtually amounted to universal suffrage. At the height of the movement, he was involved in an unsuccessful plot (known as the Osaka Incident of 1885) to help the Korean reformers.

After a period of imprisonment he founded a new party called the Oriental Liberal Party (*Toyo jiyuto*) in 1892, which advocated a tough foreign policy to enhance 'national right' and to extend popular rights. Fukuzawa Yukichi, who had deplored the daring and sometimes violent acts of the local agitators at the time of the radicalization of the movement, began to approve the role of the throne as a focus of people's loyalty, paying increasingly greater attention to the need for national 'independence'. He aired such loyalist sentiments in a newspaper of his own, *News of Contemporary Affairs* (*Jiji-shinpo*) in the eighties. In 1884–5, at a time when an attempt by progressive Koreans, some under Fukuzawa's influence, to set up a reformist government in Seoul proved abortive and Japan and China were brought to the brink of war over Korea (it was avoided by a compromise reached by the Tientsin treaty of April 1885), Fukuzawa wrote an important article titled 'Exit Asia, Enter Europe' (*Datsua-ron*) in his newspaper. There he argued that Japan had liberated itself from Asian narrowness and obscurantism, and had moved into the Enlightenment of Western civilization, while China and Korea remained fettered by their Confucian code of life and were destined to be divided up by the advanced Western powers. So Japan 'should treat China and Korea not with special favour as neighbouring countries but in the same way as the western powers would treat them'. On one level this would mean that feudal values were to be replaced by utilitarianism. On another it meant more: the East Asian international order with China at its centre (Middle Kingdom), to which Korea subscribed and which Japan had opposed with its own version of a Japan-centred middle kingdom, was to be replaced by the Western order of international relations based on international law but increasingly assuming the character of imperialist rivalries.

Rise of nationalism and German influence

CREATION OF A STATE IDEOLOGY

Reaction set in after the reformist 1870s: government control of education was tightened with textbook censorship by the Ministry of Education and a Shintoist revival starting with the establishment of a state shrine for the war dead (only those who died on the government side in the Restoration civil war and other similar wars). The nationalist revival of the 1880s provided an atmosphere congenial to the government attempt to prepare a new constitution based on ideas appropriate to an authoritarian state that was emerging.

Inoue Kowashi (1844–95), a bureaucrat in the justice department, exerted a decisive influence on the course of framing the constitution. When in 1882 Ito Hirobumi was sent to Europe to study constitutions, Inoue strongly urged him to concentrate on a monarchy of the Prussian type. Ito chose Germany as the base of his constitutional studies. Bismarck welcomed him, and both Rudolf von Gneist, law professor of Berlin University, and Lorenz von Stein of Vienna University taught him to place the monarchical right above the legislative power. After his return Ito created the House of

Peers in 1884 as the bulwark of the throne and in the following year started the cabinet system with himself as the first prime minister.

Hermann Roesler (1834–94), professor at Rostock University and a legal adviser in the Japanese Foreign Ministry since 1878, shared von Stein's views on 'social monarch' and became a close adviser to Ito on constitutional matters. At the opening of the deliberation on the draft constitution Ito declared that the centre of unity in Japan was the imperial house, just like Christianity in the West, which bonded all classes, high and low. The constitution promulgated in February 1889 was framed largely under German tutelage. It was accompanied by the Imperial Rescript on Education issued in October 1890, an intimate address by the Emperor to the nation on the virtues of a good subject, a Confucian-Shintoist document and a consummation of the National Learning (of the Mito School) of the early nineteenth century. A state ideology was now born.

Persecutions of the Christians reappeared in the early years of Meiji and it was only in 1873 that the ban on Christianity was lifted. Christian missionaries, especially US Protestants, succeeded in setting up several strongholds throughout the country, and Uchimura Kanzo (1861–1930), educated at Sapporo, one of such strongholds, launched a Non-Church movement for churchless Christianity, taking up various causes of peace and reform. Christianity soon came into conflict with the state ideology introduced by the Education edict. When Uchimura made a light courtesy bow instead of the deep bow of worship at a ceremony to revere the edict early in 1891, he was accused of *lèse-majesté,* and forced to resign from his school.

Japanese Christians stood on the defensive again, facing the increasingly nationalistic requirements imposed on their schools and the pressure on their churches.

MEIJI NATIONALISM IN FULL SWAY

Already in the 1880s some of young publicists felt that Japan's Westernization had gone too far. In 1888 a fortnightly magazine called *Nipponjin* was founded by Miyake Setsurei (1860–1945), Shiga Shigetaka (1863–1927) and others, Miyake seeking to combine Western philosophy and his own Asian studies, and Shiga depicting a New Japan in the tradition of Honda and Sato. Japan's 'uniqueness' was their favourite topic. Kuga Katsunan (1857–1907), another publicist of

a similar hue, stood for 'Japanism' in his own newspaper *Nippon* (started in 1889), which would accept Western civilization solely for Japan's welfare. Meiji nationalism was growing fast.

The last decade of the nineteenth century in Japan was marked by the beginning of constitutional politics, still weak and confused, and by the first modern war for Japan, a war with China (1894–5). Japanese victory in the war was followed by the Triple (Russian–German–French) Intervention (1895) to compel Japan to return to China the ceded territories on the Liaotung peninsula and also by Japan's first colonial war to subjugate Taiwan, another ceded territory. The rise of modern nationalism that had begun in the 1880s was now accelerated. Tokutomi Soho (1863–1957), a student of Herbert Spencer, who had portrayed the Meiji Restoration as a process of evolution from feudal aristocratic militarism to popular productionism in his book *The Future Japan* (*Shorai-no-Nihon*) (1886), now declared that Japan was fighting to determine her position in the world, in other words to expand its influence and territories. Formerly a Christian himself, he was now converted to 'the gospel of power'. *Nipponjin*, the aforementioned magazine, under the new title *Asia*, began to advocate a 'Great Asian Alliance' for which Japan should defeat the 'arrogant' China, a foretaste of the war of 1931–45. It was in 1901, the first year of the following century, that an exceedingly aggressive society called the Amur River Society (Kokuryukai) was organized, calling for war with Russia. Japan's victory without indemnity in the Russo-Japanese war (1904–5) brought the popular rage to a feverish pitch. The twentieth century seems to have intensified and highlighted the key ideas and aspirations born of the experiences in the preceding century.

Industrialization and its critics

Socialism was born of the rapid progress of industrialization in Meiji Japan. Although Japan remained an agricultural country, mining and industrial production grew more than four times during the 30 years from 1885. The proportion of textiles in the total manufacturing products reached its highest (41 per cent) around the turn of the century. Lacking factory legislation, the conditions of the workers were atrocious in the mining, pitiable in the textiles and barely tolerable in other branches of manufacturing.

River pollution caused by a copper mine (at Ashio) affected the rural population in a wide area.

Sporadic attempts to organize workers began in the 1880s and 1890s, and in 1898 Takano Fusataro (1869–1904), an AFL organizer while in the USA, started an association to promote trade unions in Japan, a Japanese AFL in embryo, but the Public Order Police Act of 1900 nipped it in the bud. Katayama Sen (1859–1933), who helped Takano, had visited Toynbee Hall, London, and started a similar institution, Kingsley Hall, in Tokyo in 1897.

Katayama was also prominent in the first socialist body in Japan called Society for the Study of Socialism (Shakaishugi-Kenkyukai) (formed in 1898) whose founders were all Christian or Christian socialists. This led to an attempt to start a Social Democratic Party in 1901, which was at once declared illegal because its programme demanded universal suffrage and a legal status for trade unions. In 1901 Kotoku Shusui's (1871–1911) work entitled *Imperialism: The Monster of the Twentieth Century (Teikokushugi: Nijusseiki-no-Kaibutsu)* came out, which condemned Japanese imperialism in China along with many other prototypes in the world. Kotoku and his anarchist associates were executed in the Treason Trial of 1910–11, but this is to anticipate. Events at the turn of the century foreshadowed the main currents of ideas and their evolution in the years to come.

Further reading

Beasley, W.G. (1990) *The Rise of Modern Japan*, London: Weidenfeld & Nicolson.
Jansen, Manus B. (ed.) (1989) *The Cambridge History of Japan*, Vol. 5 *The Nineteenth Century*, Cambridge: Cambridge University Press.
Tsuzuki, Chushichi (2000) *The Pursuit of Power in Modern Japan*, Oxford: Oxford University Press.

SEE ALSO: anti-colonial movements and ideas; conservatism, authority and tradition; imperialism and empire; liberalism; the nation, nationalism and the national principle

CHUSHICHI TSUZUKI

JEFFERSON, THOMAS (1743–1826)

The third President of the USA, Jefferson was born on 13 April 1743 in Shadwell, Virginia, the son of a prosperous civil engineer, and remains best known for his promotion of democratic ideals during and subsequent to the American Revolution. Admitted to the bar, he entered the Virginia House of Burgesses in 1769, the first Virginia Convention in 1774 and the Continental Congress in 1775. Though he is said never to have made a speech, he rose quickly to prominence through force of character and literary skill. His *A Summary of the Rights of America* (1774) attacked the actions of both Crown and Parliament towards the American colonists, and contended that the colonies possessed a substantial degree of autonomy. These arguments were extended in the *Declaration of Independence* (1776), which Jefferson drafted, and which established him as the foremost leader of the revolutionary movement. Returning to Virginia, now with a substantial estate as a propertied country gentleman, he assisted in the reconstruction of her constitution and laws, arguing in particular for the eradication of all traces of aristocracy in both the legal and landholding systems, and the establishment of a truly republican government, which in his view necessitated the abolition of the laws of entail and primogeniture, the disestablishment of the state church and the introduction of a system of general education. In many of his proposals he was considerably more radical than the public opinion of the period, notably in his proposals for the expatriation and emancipation of slaves (of which he owned at one point 150), and the prohibition of their importation. He also helped to revise the penal code, and restricted capital punishment to treason and murder. His reform proposals were summarised in the *Notes on Virginia*.

After independence Jefferson served in France, first as Franklin's assistant, then Minister, when he helped the National Assembly to draft a constitution. His very liberal religious opinions – deist rather than atheist – were derived in part from this period of residence. Upon his return he became Secretary of State under Washington, and crucially intervened to ensure that the new Constitution contained a Bill of Rights designed to protect citizens from governmental intrusion. His antagonism towards Alexander Hamilton assisted in the formation of the political parties of Federalists and Democrats, with Hamilton favouring stronger centralized powers. Though isolationist in his diplomacy, predictably Jefferson was much more sympathetic than Hamilton towards the French Revolution, which did not diminish his faith in democracy; indeed he famously commented on a taxpayers' revolt that 'a little rebellion now and then is a good thing', a doctrine abhorrent to the legalistic and order-minded Hamilton. Though he retired in 1793 to devote himself to experimental farming, Jefferson was elected Vice-President in 1796 under the Federalist John Adams, and resolutely resisted the passage of the Alien and Sedition laws during the anti-French reaction of the period. He became President in 1801, and was re-elected in 1804. As President he eschewed pomp and ceremony, with the aim of republicanizing the institution. In his last years Jefferson thus remained as resolutely egalitarian as ever, as committed to freeing the slaves and as rooted as ever in an agrarian ideal hostile to urban and manufacturing growth, and in favour of the small-scale proprietor. 'Cheap land', it has been said, was the basis of his political thought, but his democratic outlook also rested on a rooted faith in popular sovereignty and the common man. Many facets of these ideals were taken up and extended by Andrew Jackson 30 years later, and ABRAHAM LINCOLN in the 1860s.

Further reading

Jefferson, Thomas (1853–4) *Writings of Thomas Jefferson*, 9 vols, Washington: Taylor & Maury.

Mayer, David N. (1995) *The Constitutional Thought of Thomas Jefferson*, Charlottesville: University of Virginia Press.

Sheldon, Garrett Ward (1993) *The Political Philosophy of Thomas Jefferson*, Baltimore: The Johns Hopkins University Press.

GREGORY CLAEYS

JEFFREY, FRANCIS (1773–1850)

Jeffrey was a founding editor in 1802 of the *Edinburgh Review*, a journal that exerted a strong influence on British intellectual activity for many decades. A lawyer by profession, Jeffrey edited the *Review* for its first 26 years, contributing to it more than 200 essays on philosophical, political, historical and literary subjects. He was a Whig Member of Parliament twice between 1830 and 1834 and, like his life-long friends SYDNEY SMITH and HENRY BROUGHAM, an important figure in the late Scottish Enlightenment.

Jeffrey was born in Edinburgh on 23 October 1773, the son of a law clerk and was educated at Edinburgh High School and Glasgow University.

He then attended lectures in Edinburgh on law, history and those of DUGALD STEWART on political economy. From 1794 he practised law but his liberal anti-Tory sympathies hindered his career until his writings and forensic abilities gradually brought his practice recognition. He became a judge and Lord Jeffrey in 1834, and served until his death in Edinburgh on 26 January 1850.

Jeffrey wrote rapidly but lucidly on a great variety of topics and subjected some of the Common Sense tradition of Scottish philosophy, which in general he supported, to criticism. He argued against Thomas Reid, for example, that our unshakeable belief in the existence of an external world might be mistaken. Even if it did not exist we could still have all the present evidence of our senses that it did. This belief is highly probable but could be overturned by new evidence. Yet the fact that we could possibly be mistaken is not a good reason for believing that in fact we are mistaken. Good evidence need not be conclusive.

In ethics, Jeffrey criticized Bentham's utilitarianism. For if the distinction between right and wrong is whether something gives us more pleasure or pain, we need to compare their quantity; but Bentham gives us no way of doing so, and no method for calculating the total pleasure and pain that an action creates in a community. In the science of mind, Jeffrey criticized both Reid and Dugald Stewart for claiming that mental behaviour could be studied by using the experimental procedures of the sciences. We cannot manipulate mental events and processes, said Jeffrey, as we can physical and chemical properties. We can only observe and record our present knowledge of our mental life. The psychologist can only systematize what we already know from daily experience. Although Jeffrey was regarded as a severe critic, he praised the work of Archibald Alison in aesthetics and welcomed John Millar's discussion of social ranks. He expressed unflattering views of some of both Wordsworth's and Byron's poetry, but still managed to be regarded favourably by them and by such other critics as CARLYLE, MACAULAY and Sydney Smith.

Further reading

Cockburn, Henry Lord (1852) *The Life of Lord Jeffrey*, 2 vols, Edinburgh: Adam & Charles Black.

Greig, J.A. (1948) *Francis Jeffrey of the 'Edinburgh Review'*, Edinburgh: Oliver & Boyd.

Jeffrey, Francis (1844) *Contributions to the Edinburgh Review*, 4 vols, London: Longmans, Brown, Green & Longmans.

SEE ALSO: Brougham, Henry; liberalism; main currents in philosophy; political economy; Stewart, Dugald

ROBERT BROWN

JEVONS, WILLIAM STANLEY (1835–82)

Stanley Jevons is today known chiefly as the author of *The Theory of Political Economy* (1871), a work that broke with the Classical theory of production and distribution in linking the formation of prices to subjective choices formed by a calculus of pleasure and pain. Now linked with the names of the Austrian Carl Menger and the Frenchman Leon Walras as the originator of the 'marginal revolution' that in the 1870s founded the neoclassical framework that underpins modern economics, Jevons's principal contribution was to turn the idea of subjective utility into mathematical form. In so doing he drew upon a wider interest in formal logic and the sciences that preceded his foray into economic reasoning. Besides the *Theory* he contributed to debate on the exhaustion of natural resources by arguing in *The Coal Question* (1865) that coal reserves would quickly become exhausted, and also to the early analysis of economic fluctuations by making a link between the trade and the sunspot cycles.

Jevons was born in Liverpool on 1 September 1835, son of Thomas Jevons, an iron merchant, and Mary Ann, daughter of William Roscoe, a banker prominent in the cultural life of a city then second only to London in prosperity. His early life was however overshadowed by the death of his mother in 1845, the onset of his eldest brother's mental illness in 1847 and the collapse of the family business in 1848. After beginning his schooling in Liverpool he was sent to the school attached to University College London (UCL), which he then entered in 1851 to study Mathematics and Chemistry. The Unitarian faith of his family barred him from entering existing English university institutions – Oxford, Cambridge and King's College, London – since entry or graduation required a formal declaration of religious conformity. In

1853, however, he was offered the post of assayer at the Sydney Mint, and given the reduced state of his family's finances he took the post without graduating, staying in Australia from 1854–9. During this time he studied botany and meteorology, from 1857 developing an interest in social and economic issues, his interest in a mathematical approach to economic argument being prompted by reading Lardner's *Railway Economy* (1850).

Re-entering UCL in 1859 he earned his BA in 1860 and an MA in Logic, Philosophy and Political Economy in 1862. He sent two papers to Section F of the 1862 British Association meeting, one of them outlining a mathematical approach to economic reasoning, the other discussing seasonal price fluctuations. Neither paper attracted attention, and Jevons turned back to work on symbolic logic, publishing his own *Pure Logic* in 1863, the first of a series of publications that established his reputation. His cousin, Harry Roscoe, now a Professor of Chemistry at the newly opened Owens College in Manchester, suggested that he take a vacant post there as tutor preparing candidates for entrance to the college; Jevons accepted, and it was during this period that he published *The Coal Question*, which brought him national recognition as a political economist.

This was reflected in his appointment as Professor of Political Economy and Mental and Moral Science in 1866, although this was not a full-time post. While at Manchester he continued to work on both logic and political economy, publishing in 1874 his important *Principles of Science: A Treatise on Logic and Scientific Method*, and in 1875 both *Money and the Mechanism of Exchange* and his first essay on sunspots and price fluctuations in the journal *Nature*. In 1876 he left Manchester for a chair in Political Economy at UCL, likewise not a full-time appointment, but with duties lighter than those he had borne in Manchester. Nonetheless, he gave up this post in 1882 so that he could devote all his efforts to research and writing. He drowned while holidaying with his family on the south coast near Hastings in mid-1882.

The novelty of Jevons's approach to political economy was rooted in his understanding of mathematics and logic. He contributed significantly to the development of the latter, having been taught by Augustus De Morgan at UCL and proposing that logical problems can be solved symbolically through their expression as algebraic equations. In 1870 he presented to a Royal Society meeting his 'logical piano', a primitive computer capable of replacing the thought processes involved in logical procedures. His *Principles of Science* presented a theory of scientific inference designed to resolve JOHN STUART MILL's empirical method whose precision required an unattainable degree of completeness in the statement of premises. In its place he proposed a conception of probabilistic reasoning, suggesting a way of measuring a reasonable expectation that an event would occur. This conception was to become of revolutionary significance for statistical analysis, but Jevons never made the link between this idea and his interest in prices and economic fluctuations. In any case, his chief concern in studying the latter was to establish the regularity with which highs and lows recurred, rather than identify the inherent causes of fluctuations. Although he believed there to be a causal linkage between the sunspot cycle and climatic variation, this linkage served to identify periodicity, rather than underlying economic variables.

Jevons's contributions to logic, important enough at the time, were later eclipsed by the work of Frege and Whitehead. His new approach to the principles of economics had a similar fate, chiefly for lack of a wide enough audience. Although he had been, in part at least, a Professor of Political Economy in Manchester and in London, there was at this time a very limited demand for the systematic teaching of Political Economy to which his work contributed. He was known chiefly as a writer – a popular yet gifted and innovative thinker. It was not until the 1890s that teaching Political Economy in Manchester became a full-time occupation. It was ALFRED MARSHALL, not Stanley Jevons, who stamped his name on the new British academic economics, publishing in 1890 his own *Principles of Economics,* and in 1903 founding at Cambridge the first three-year university course in economics.

Further reading

Black, D. Collison and Konekamp, R. (eds) (1981) *The Papers and Correspondence of William Stanley Jevons,* 7 vols, London: Macmillan.

Jevons, W.S. (2001 [1871]) *The Theory of Political Economy,* eds B Mosselmans and M.V. White, Basingstoke: Palgrave.

—— (1874) *The Principles of Science,* London: Macmillan.

—— (1864) *Pure Logic or the Logic of Quality apart from Quantity: With Remarks on Boole's System and on the Relation of Logic and Mathematics,* London: E. Stanford.

Peart, S. (1990) *The Economics of W.S. Jevons,* London: Routledge.

Schabas, M. (1990) *A World Ruled by Number: William Stanley Jevons and the Rise of Mathematical Economics,* Princeton: Princeton University Press.

KEITH TRIBE

K

K'ANG YU-WEI (1858–1927)

K'ang Yu-Wei was born in a traditional well-read family in Nanhai county of Kwangtung province. As a child, he studied the teachings of Confucianism. Later, when he stayed in Hong Kong and Shanghai, he observed European habits, and read many books about Europe and America situations translated into Chinese by missionaries. He was also strongly influenced by T.H. HUXLEY's work *Evolution and Ethics*, introduced in China by Yen Fu, which led him to believe that China was facing a profound crisis. In the year 1895, K'ang was deeply shocked by the defeat of the Q'ing dynasty in the Sino-Japanese war. So, he called on the examinees assembling in Beijing for the imperial examination, and together they issued a joint petition to the Emperor against the signing of the humiliating peace treaty. After that, his existence came to be noticed with keen interest by the central government of the Q'ing dynasty. In 1889, K'ang, who had won the trust of Emperor Guang Xu, began to realize the need for the political reform of the Q'ing dynasty, and so he started reform (Bianfa) along with one of his pupils, Liang Qichao, as well as with other younger intellectual groups. The purpose of this reform (Bianfa) was to establish a new political system capable of adapting itself to international economic and imperial competition. Moreover, this reform was an attempt to avoid the crisis of China being divided into many parts and also in order to change the autocratic monarchical system of government into a constitutional monarchy. K'ang severely criticized the previous trivial reformations made during the 'self-strengthening' movement, and insisted more on fundamental reforms. The concrete reform policies considered by him included developing non-official commercial industries, enforcing the universal conscription system and implementing a compulsory education system for elementary and junior high schools. These policies, according to him, would help in the national enrichment and reinforcement of the military system. K'ang wrote several books in which he mentioned the reforms of Peter the Great of Russia and the Meiji Restoration of Japan, describing them as models for his reforms. He persuaded the Emperor to carry out these policies, but the conservative wing with the western Empress Dowager as its central force, and the bureaucrats ruling the local governments in the provinces, opposed them. K'ang's reform policies thus failed after about a hundred days. As a result, K'ang left China for Japan and took political asylum there, leaving China in a critical political situation. The revolutionists who wanted to overthrow the Q'ing dynasty and who realized the need of establishing the republican system regarded K'ang as a reactionary ringleader. Therefore, K'ang became the main target for their criticism.

Further reading

Kung-ch'uan, Hsiao (1975) *A Modern China and a New World, Kang Yu-wei Reformer and Utopian 1858–1827*, Seattle: University of Washington Press.

SEE ALSO: anti-colonial movements and ideas

TAKASHI MITANI

KANT, IMMANUEL (1725–1804)

It has become an overused cliché to describe a philosopher as the most significant since Plato, but there is perhaps no better pretender to the throne than Immanuel Kant. The guiding theme of Kant's philosophical project was the problem of objective knowledge: he wanted to overcome what he saw as the errors in both rationalism and empiricism whilst preserving their true insights. For him, neither experience nor reason alone could adequately provide a basis for knowledge. He himself described his thought as a 'Copernican Revolution' in that the appearance of an object has to be understood as a product of the activity of the subject, but whereas Copernicus's astronomy took man out of the centre of the universe, Kant's philosophy placed the knowing subject right at the heart of his system.

Kant's philosophical career was due more to chance than design; two contingent incidents determined his path rather than free choice. First, as the fourth child of nine in a poor family in the Prussian town of Königsberg (renamed Kaliningrad by Stalin), he had to rely on the benevolence of a local pastor who recognized his undoubted intelligence and arranged for a scholarship at a Pietist school. Second, he could so easily have been a professor in Mathematics or Natural Science, but was offered the Chair in Logic and Metaphysics by his local university in 1770. Kant passed his whole life in Königsberg, entering the university there at 16 and leaving six years later to begin working as a private tutor. He obtained his first – unsalaried – post when he was 31 and his lectures were very well attended. By this time, he had already published works on dynamics and mathematics, but once installed in his chair his sense of duty drove him to concentrate solely on philosophy.

Kant remained unmarried, although he twice considered it, and his private life was notoriously uneventful; his Pietist upbringing installing in him a sense of duty and routine that was parodied by Heine's remark that the housewives of Königsberg would set their clocks by Kant's daily walk. Politically, he was no radical – once promising the King of Prussia to cease writing on matters of religion in case his thought was seen as subversive – but he sympathized with both the American and French revolutions, and also the political thought of Rousseau. However, it was not his life but his thought that would carve his place in history.

The works of Kant were initially concerned with natural philosophy and mathematics, and these publications won him a great reputation in academic circles. It was, however, after a period of relative silence that his greatest work appeared. *The Critique of Pure of Reason* was first published in 1781, the product of 12 years of careful reflection, but five months hurried writing. Due to this Kant attempted to clarify some of the ideas in the *Prolegomena to Every Future Metaphysic* in 1783 and rewrote parts of the *Critique* for its second edition in 1787. His major works on morality, *The Groundwork to the Metaphysics of Morals* and *The Critique of Practical Reason*, appeared in 1785 and 1788 respectively. The final *Critique of Judgement*, the less well known of the three, was published in 1790 and revised in 1793.

Epistemology

Kant's mature philosophical project began with the consideration of the problem of reality or, put more precisely, how it is possible for a subject to have objective knowledge. Kant, schooled and immersed in a tradition of Leibnizian rationalism, was to be awoken from his 'dogmatic slumbers' through the influence of Hume's empiricism. Rationalism held that all knowledge could be derived from the exercise of reason alone because the human mind was able to intuit the rational order of things, whereas empiricism argued that all knowledge comes to the subject through experience and therefore knowledge claims were generated by things impinging on our senses and causing perceptions. Kant, however, was aware of a certain gap in both epistemological accounts: What is it specifically about the human mind which means that its representations happen to map snugly on to reality? In other words, why do we assume that there is an unquestionable harmony between reality and our representation of it?

His response to this was the Critical Philosophy, or the attempt to synthesize the seemingly contradictory claims of rationalism and empiricism. For Kant, judgements are either analytic, that is the negation of this judgement will involve a contradiction ('a bachelor is male') or synthetic, that is they join two concepts together in order to form a new item of knowledge ('the table is round'). Judgements are also either *a priori*, that is not derived from experience, or *a posteriori*, that is derived from experience. Hume supposed that the distinctions were the same and that all analytic judgements are *a priori* and all synthetic judgements are *a posteriori*, thus the only way the subject can know things that are not definitions or tautologies is via experience. Kant was unhappy with this for the simple reason that, according to him, there exist three classes of judgements: analytic *a priori*; synthetic *a posteriori*; and, in contradiction of Hume, synthetic *a priori*. These judgements are most readily employed in mathematics, scientific statements such as 'every event has a cause' and moral judgements. Kant's argument for this consists in showing that an analytic *a priori* statement such as 'a bachelor is male' is a simple tautology, whereas with '$5 + 7 = 12$', the concept $5 + 7$ only states the idea that five and seven are to be united but says nothing about what that new concept will be. (This view of mathematics would be criticized by Frege.) Similarly, the idea of event does not contain the concept of cause and one cannot experience all events, therefore the statement 'every event has a cause' is synthetic but derived from reason and not experience. Synthetic *a priori* judgements allow the subject to make objective judgements about the world; that is, judgements that are true for all rational beings and not just true for the subject having the experience.

The aim of Kant's first critique was two-fold: to demonstrate that synthetic *a priori* knowledge is possible (which Hume's empiricism denied) and to examine the claims of metaphysics, demonstrating that reason employed without any input from experience will lead to illusion. The book itself is split into three main parts, each corresponding to a different faculty or power of reason: the Aesthetic is concerned with how the subject can have knowledge of objects of experience; the Analytic concentrates on the conceptual elements of reasoning and how the subject forms synthetic *a priori* judgements; and, finally, the Dialectic wants to discover the boundaries of the subject's possible knowledge and demonstrate that transcendental knowledge of reality as it is in itself (the thing-in-itself or noumenon) is impossible.

Rather than trace the arguments of the first critique, in such a brief account it would be more pertinent to sketch Kant's basic epistemological position. It can perhaps be best summarized by his own words in that 'Thoughts without concepts are empty; intuitions without concepts are blind.' In other words, contrary to the rationalist, knowledge cannot depend on reason alone, since the concepts of the mind need to be applied to intuitions (*Anschauung*) otherwise – as he shows in the Dialectic – it is possible to generate two valid arguments starting from the same

premise whose conclusions are contradictory. Put simply, intuitions are necessary to constrain thought processes. Similarly, contrary to the empiricist, knowledge cannot depend on experience alone, otherwise synthetic *a priori* judgements would not be possible and no judgement could be objectively true.

The solution which Kant offers is that of the transcendental idealist: the knowing mind has a certain structure that makes it possible for the subject to make judgements from the intuitions given to it by reality. A useful – though ultimately unsatisfying analogy – is to describe a subject who has impaired sight and can only have (visual) experience when he is given a pair of glasses to wear. For him to have any experience at all, he must wear the glasses, but unfortunately the lenses of these glasses are tinted pink. Without the glasses, he can have no experience, but with the glasses his experience is influenced by a factor that does not belong to the object itself. For Kant, human reason plays the same role as the glasses: it is impossible to have any experience at all without applying certain *a priori* categories to that experience, categories which belong to the knowing subject and not the object. Kant's epistemology, therefore, consists of transcendental arguments: given that one has the experience 'x', what *a priori* concepts make it possible for one to experience x?

The best way in which to comprehend Kant's transcendental idealism is to divide reason into its three moments: one, the faculty of intuition receives a manifold of intuition, that is intuitions unified by their appearance in space and time; two, the faculty of imagination reproduces (schematizes) the object of experience for the faculty of understanding; and, three, the faculty of understanding applies the proper concepts to the object in order to form a judgement. Thus, it is firstly necessary that intuitions be given in space and time; the 'pure intuitions' as Kant calls them because they are not concepts but are produced by the knowing subject and not from reality itself. For this object to become an object of thought, it must be rendered explicable in conceptual terms, thus the correct concepts must be applied to it. Kant then asks himself: What are these *a priori* concepts by virtue of which objects of experience are constituted? By interrogating the judgements of the mind, Kant was able to list the twelve pure concepts (divided into four categories) involved in making judgements: the category of quantity: unity, plurality, totality; the category of quality: reality, negation, limitation; the category of relation: inherence-and-subsistence, causality-and-dependence, reciprocity; and the category of modality: possibility, existence, necessity-and-contingency.

These fundamental concepts make it possible for the knowing subject to form judgements because without them he would be unable to know anything at all. Synthetic *a priori* judgements are only possible according to Kant because the knowing subject can apply the categories to the *a priori* contents as well as the empirical contents of the mind.

Kant's transcendental idealism commits him to assuming that objects are empirically real in that they are true for any rational being who employs the categories of understanding. This means that science is not affected by his idealism and neither is knowledge at an everyday level since judgements can be objectively true for every rational being. However, objects are transcendentally ideal, that is it is impossible to say anything of reality independent of the human mind, since that is beyond our powers of knowing. Having demonstrated that the empiricist who believes the knowing subject to be passive is unable to explain how our subjective representations agree with each other in this objective sense, Kant now turns his attention, in the Dialectic, to the rationalist where he shows that speculative metaphysics, that is the use of reason without it being constrained by intuitions, leads to false or, at best, indefensible positions. Transcendental illusion results when principles not meant for use outside experience are used as if they were. Concepts need to be constrained by intuitions and are only applicable if they can be judged in accordance with those outside objects. Sensibility (the faculty of intuition) is this constraining restriction and without this constraint reason can go wild. Kant demonstrates this with regard to three very specific metaphysical problems: the Idea of the soul, the Idea of cosmology and the Idea of God. His conclusion might seem to favour a reduction of metaphysics to matters of science, but his aim is quite different in that the Ideas of reason are concepts that it is right for us to have (given our subjective constitution) but which there is no scope for employing in forming judgements. Unlike, say, causality, the Idea of human freedom or God is not used to constitute a judgement, but they regulate the free use of reason so that the knowing subject aims at truth and full explanation. It was to these ideas that Kant's moral philosophy was to return.

Ethics

Given Kant's admiration for the Newtonian view of the universe, he immediately saw a problem for moral philosophy. If the whole universe is determined and the agent and his actions are part of that universe, then the human subject cannot be responsible for his own actions because they are merely the result of natural causation. The distinction between the transcendentally ideal and the empirically real again plays a part in Kant's moral theory that was elaborated in the *Groundwork* and the second critique.

It is beyond our cognitive powers to state that the universe is wholly determined since causality is a concept the subject applies to intuitions, a concept without which he or she would be unable to represent objects in the understanding. Objects and agents, then, are phenomenally subjects of natural causation, but noumenally it is impossible to say whether human agents are free or determined. Kant believes that the Idea of freedom is a regulative concept for moral action: agents do not know what their freedom consists in, but they know they are free because they are moral agents. With theoretical knowledge, the categories of reason constituted the object of thought. What, then, is required for the agent to be able to formulate objective practical principles, that is synthetic *a priori* judgements that do not represent what is the case, but what ought to be the case? Kant's answer was that the Idea of freedom regulates and makes possible moral judgements. To make moral judgements about what ought to be, the knowing subject must presuppose that agents are free or autonomous.

Kant is interested in the reason for an action: if an action is caused by processes in the phenomenal world, including desires and passions, it is not free and therefore morally without worth. This is a description of action that is apt only for theoretical knowledge. Hypothetical imperatives or intentions that depend on the particularity of the agent can have a reason for action, but not an objective one since it applies only to that agent at that time. The only actions that have moral worth are those freely performed and arising from a maxim (the underlying principle that justifies the particular intention) that is in conformity with the moral law. The idea of freedom allows Kant to deduce what then constitutes a free, objectively binding maxim: the maxim of my action conforms to the moral law if and only if I can will it to become a universal law. By willing it to be a universal law, I claim for it an objectivity as a duty for all rational beings because it does not depend on my identity, culture or situation, but is equally applicable to all rational beings.

These duties that should determine the behaviour of all rational beings are, depending on the specific interpretation of Kant's words, either generated by, derived from or tested by the formula for universal law. Kant offers three differing formulations of the moral law and it is debatable whether at times he is trying to reformulate or add to it, but the overarching aim of his moral theory is to justify an objective morality that is true for all rational beings based on the Idea of freedom.

The Critique of Judgement

Kant's final critique seemingly has various themes, which leads to some confusion concerning his overarching aim. On one level, Kant wants to show that the scientific project is regulated by the Ideas of reason; that is, the desire to offer an ultimate explanation of the universe is motivated by the regulative concepts of reason. On another level, the book is a work of aesthetics concerned with the problem of beauty in so far as aesthetic judgements are an expression of subjective opinion but also claim universal assent. In other words, if one's aesthetic pleasure depends solely on the particular agent, how is it possible that it can be a judgement in Kant's robust sense of that word? The answer was, not surprisingly, that aesthetic judgements were synthetic *a priori*: the judgement of beauty is based in pleasure but this pleasure ought to be universally valid. For Kant, aesthetic judgement became the paradigmatic example of the faculty of imagination because it reflects the process of systemization of intuitions into conceptual objects. However, since the object conceptualized is not dependent on a purely impersonal, rational being, the imagination engages in 'free play' and rejoices in its own creative power. The subject is pleased by beauty not because of a property belonging to the object, but because he or she experiences the harmonious working of his rational faculties and his power to project that harmony on the world. The final section of the work interrogates the concept of purpose and its scientific validity.

Kant's influence was to dominate, first, German philosophy in the reactions of the subjective Idealists (Fichte and Schelling) who took Kantian philosophy one step further by rejecting the role of the thing-in-itself. Reality was, for them, purely the product of mental activity. It is also certain that without Kant, there would be no Hegel and his absolute Idealism and it is perhaps arguable that philosophy in the twentieth century would not be as it is without the man from Königsberg.

Further reading

Allison, Henry E. (1999) *Kant's Transcendental Idealism*, New Haven: Yale University Press.
Cassirer, Ernst (1981) *Kant's Life and Thought*, New Haven: Yale University Press.
Guyer, Paul (1992) *The Cambridge Companion to Kant*, Cambridge: Cambridge University Press.
Williams, Howard (1983) *Kant's Political Philosophy*, Oxford: Basil Blackwell.

SEE ALSO: Hegel and Hegelianism; main currents in philosophy

DAVID ROSE

KIDD, BENJAMIN (1858–1916)

A leading British sociologist and Social Darwinist, Kidd was born at Bandon, Ireland, on 9 September 1858. His career was in the civil service, principally in the Inland Revenue office, but he was also a journalist and writer. Kidd's most important work was *Social Evolution* (1894), which became the best-known Social Darwinist text of the era. Denying that educational and moral attributes as such were inherited, Kidd preferred Weissman's view that 'there can be no progress except by the accumulation of congenital variations above the average to the exclusion of others below'. Kidd's argument that religion played an important progressive role in promoting altruistic behaviour, such as philanthropy, and in regulating social conduct, was unusual, but important to his critique of the limits of materialism and secular ethics, and description of the irrational basis of species progress. Here, thus, he departed strikingly from the emphases of T.H. HUXLEY, in particular. The central thrust of Kidd's argument was liberal and meritocratic. Competition is valued, and should be increased in efficiency, but the poor required 'equality of opportunity' (it is claimed he coined the term) in order to rise to their maximum capabilities, and this required alleviating the most extreme forms of poverty. Socialism is rejected as undermining incentive systems and failing to deal with overpopulation; the best form of social organization is that which promotes 'the most effective subordination of the individual to the interests of the social organism with the highest development of his own personality'.

In *The Control of the Tropics* (1898), Kidd contended that the end of the nineteenth century witnessed a period of 'instinctive rivalry' for key raw materials, such as rubber, which necessitated control over tropical peoples, who were incapable of developing their own resources, but who could not expect 'good government, in the European sense' from their conquerors, though Kidd denied that there was any scientific 'warrant for speaking of one race as superior to another'.

In *Principles of Western Civilisation* (1902) Kidd applied evolutionary theory to modern European development, and described the large-scale obsolescence of much of the inheritance of European thought, including utilitarianism, radicalism and *laissez-faire*, and their supersession by an evolutionary thought that dictated 'protracted efficiency' as the key to race survival, and the promotion of the strongest interest in any society, which Kidd felt was being undermined by monopoly capitalism. His ideas on group-selection were expanded in two pamphlets, *The Principal Laws of Sociology* (1907–8) and *Individualism and After* (1908). His last work, *The Science of Power* (1919), builds upon NIETZSCHE, DARWIN and others to contend that a new paganism, based upon the worship of force, that 'Might is Right', had arisen in Western civilization that rested upon collective emotion, rather than reason. Civilization had now been revealed to be little more than 'glorified savagery'; the antidote was to craft a new form of more humane collectivism, in which, for Crook, women, who were more closely attuned to species needs than men, would play a central role. Kidd died on 2 October 1916.

Further reading

Crook, D.P. (1984) *Benjamin Kidd. Portrait of a Social Darwinist*, Cambridge: Cambridge University Press.

GREGORY CLAEYS

KIERKEGAARD, SØREN AABYE (1813–55)

One person, many faces: an introduction to a resonant life

Søren Kierkegaard was born on 5 March 1813 and died on 11 November 1855. A young Danish man, the sensitive son of an aggressively Lutheran father, he lived a four-dimensional life. He was, to begin with, a prolific literary writer, whose life-long achievements will be made fully evident by the projected fifty-five volumes of *Søren Kierkegaards Skrifter* that includes twenty-seven volumes of commentary on his work, all to be completed by 2009; also worth noting is the Hongs' impressive English translation (Princeton editions, twenty six volumes so far). He was an intensely self-critical, as well as critical, philosopher, too, whose focused if only fragmented attack on the nineteenth-century scientism and impersonal speculation virtually paved a way, 'leapingly', into post-Hegelian (see HEGEL AND HEGELIANISM), twentieth-century philosophies of the self that, in the wake of troubled universalism, struggle in various ways to relocate 'the individual,' the responsive and responsible subject. Still best known, however, as a rebellious believer and practitioner of Christian religion, still best studied, therefore, by the theological type Kierkegaard himself despised with passion, he embodies the paradox of disbelief, disbelief as an irreducible form of belief, philosophical or otherwise: when encountering existentially and ecstatically unthinkable impossibilities such as Jesus the man-God, one *becomes* – not is – a true Christian, he stressed. Then, the fourth face? Kierkegaard remains all three at once: an aesthete, a philosopher and a religious thinker. The full dimension and implications of this short, intense life dedicated to writing, often pseudonymous and so multi-voiced, are yet to emerge. In what follows, I am going to construct a story of Kierkegaard, focusing mostly on how the patently 'Kierkegaardian' theme, 'three – aesthetic, ethical and religious – stages', itself reflects the three-fold dimension of his life and work, and conclude by showing how that theme is also mirrored, on a more macro-level, in the recent trends of Continental philosophy vitalized by the 'turn to aesthetics, ethics and religion'. Let me begin by noting three preliminary points.

The first turning point (1840) was disengagement with fiancée, Regine Olsen (1822–1904): realizing that he had made a mistake, Kierkegaard broke off the engagement abruptly. Willing to take all the blame, he could not, however, articulate the source of his own anxiety: the chronic melancholia induced by religious dread (the fear of dying before hitting 34, the Christian age of sacrifice) and the self-critical disdain for bourgeois happiness, reinforced by physical weakness, were the surface reasons, but the mystery surrounding this turn remains the same. This stranger started writing prolifically (feverishly to the deadline) after this traumatic experience, this event, this guilt.

The second turning point (1845) was 'the *Corsair* affair' (December): Kierkegaard's contemporaries ignored or else ridiculed him as a loner, a loser, especially during and after his pen fight with P.L. Møller, a mere acquaintance from his student days, whose professorial opportunism led him to mount a scathing, moralizing attack on Kierkegaard's *Stages on Life's Way* (1845) 'edited, complied and discovered by Hilarius Bookbinder', which consists of reflections of three different or differently named author-character(s), William Afham ('by himself'), Judge William and Frater Taciturnus ('taciturn brother'), who had to break his (their) engagement(s) with his (their) lover(s). Alas, Kierkegaard made a fatal mistake, again, of responding even more personally to Møller by publishing his sharp retorts in the *Corsair*, a satirical weekly for the gossip-hungry Copenhagen intellectuals, to which Møller had been contributing regularly. Having damaged Møller's reputation quite successfully, Kierkegaard, in turn, had to face the longer, more relentless public humiliation engineered, this time, by the editor who decided to be offended by Kierkegaard's implicative accusation of shady journalism; the memory of this affair, on top of the failed love affair, left a deep scar in Kierkegaard's psyche, the already wounded soul, who withdrew further into the private world of nameless, pseudonymous thoughts. The task, theme and trope of unmasking or debunking – central to, for instance, FRIEDRICH NIETZSCHE's anthropological de-mystification of Western metaphysics and especially German Idealism, Karl Marx's forensic analysis of socio-political ideology behind nineteenth-century Western capitalism (see MARX AND MARXISM), and Sigmund Freud's vertiginous exploration into the realm of the unconscious and the uncanny – are all characteristic of that period, the spirit of the time; and yet, what is strikingly uncanny (confusingly obscure) about Kierkegaard, as with Nietzsche, is that he did unmasking while masking himself *afham*.

The third turning point (1930s and 1940s) was a century later: Kierkegaard suddenly came into prominence, discovered and reinvented as the forefather of 'existentialism', the intellectual movement that defines and reflects the ambiguous mood of wartime Europe, 'existence precedes essence' (Jean-Paul Sartre), which is at once resigning and resolute, alternatively political as well as intensely personal. His diary prophecy has been fulfilled. The posthumous global fame of this provincial thinker who wrote in Danish deliberately as well as naturally is a direct consequence of the Central European (mostly French café) intellectuals' attempts to locate the seats of their tested, scarred humanism against the receding background of the Enlightenment project cast, pursued and expanded by the German Idealists such as KANT and/through Hegel, whose consciously 'modern', Protestant beliefs in reason, whether circumscribed (Kant) or absolutized (Hegel), were once seemingly justified, unshakably and unstoppably. A more literary reception and appreciation of Kierkegaard's work by Anglo-American writers working around this time, slightly later, is clearly evidenced, for instance, by W.H. Auden's edited volume, *The Living Thoughts of Kierkegaard* (1952). This way, Kierkegaard became plural again.

Stages on Life's Way: from aesthetic, via ethical, to religious

One: why do we, after all, believe that a 'proper' name alone is proper? It is a question of authenticity or irreducible individuality, the locus of responsibility, legal or otherwise: all the pseudonyms above refer to one person, the one and only Kierkegaard, whatever *he* says or claims, humorously or seriously. That's the idea, the numerically objectified 'idea of existence', as he puts it. We just, and do have to, assume we can talk about *this* man, Kierkegaard, and end up organizing all his writings, the linguistic traces of his existence, into one tidy encompassing system, a nameable spot – even against his will, *his* will.

The ghostly force of objectification is at work in our most basic act, need of naming or identifying; what is ironic, however, is the more fundamental evasiveness of the *I* as such, its 'existence' *per se*, simply unidentifiable. And that is annoying. And that irony is what troubled as well as amused the young Kierkegaard for long. On 1 January 1838, for instance, in his diary (posthumously complied into *Journals*), which he started keeping almost religiously from 3 December 1833, age 20, he writes: 'Irony is an abnormal growth; like the abnormally enlarged liver of the Strassburg goose it ends by killing the individual.' Arguably the most unfortunate, almost literal example is Socrates, on whom Kierkegaard wrote his dissertation (Copenhagen Univ., Theology and Philosophy, 1840) entitled *Concept of Irony: with Continual Reference to Socrates* (1841), his second major publication after *From the Papers of One Still Living* (1838, the year his father died). Why did, Kierkegaard asks, the Athenians bother to execute the Socrates that is not even an executable entity, to begin with? What they killed, or rather thought they had done, is the 'idea' of his existence, that infinite irritation:

Most men think, talk, and write as they sleep, eat and drink, without even raising the question of the relation to the idea; this only happens among the very few and then that decisive moment has in the very highest degree either the power to compel (genius), or it paralyses the individual with anxiety (irony).

(6 September 1839)

Irony is the fusion of a passionately ethical view, which inwardly lays infinite stress upon the self – and of education which outwardly abstracts infinitely from the personal I. The result of the latter is that no one notices the former; therein lies the whole art of irony, and that is what conditions the infinite stress of the first.

(Undated 1845)

Socrates the existential and 'ethical' subject, laid bare, moved forward infinitely, who does not know himself and therefore keeps saying 'Know thyself' incessantly, is precisely that which survives the cut: that which undercuts any possibility of historical victimization or dialectical subjugation of a finite being that engenders, or justifies, the vision of Hegelian *scala paradisi*, a spiral ladder to heaven – to absolute knowledge. The figure of Socrates as the master artist of irony, highlighted in *Concept of Irony*, is indeed a lasting legacy of Western philosophy taken as ongoing acts of the intellect's midwifery that is caring, of course, but

cutting, cuttingly ironic: 'Listen to the cry of a woman giving birth, look upon the death struggle at its height: and then say whether what begins and ends thus can be intended to be pleasure' (December 1854).

Two: immediately after completing *Concept of Irony*, which presented the triplet of his life-long themes in an ironic, cryptic style that caused the immediate and temporary raising of the academic eyebrows, Kierkegaard spent five years churning out books on the human mode of existence, 'the existence spheres/stages' of life. Such early 'aesthetic' works – aesthetic not in the sense of 'looking pretty, dandy' but more technically in the sense of relating to, and itself being, 'drifty, inwardly passionate and outwardly playful', sensation-mediated and imagination-inducing – include, first, *Either/Or* (1843, by A (Young Man), ed. Victor Eremita). Here, those he calls 'reflective aesthetes', viz., the German Romantics (see ROMANTICISM, INDIVIDUALISM AND IDEAS OF THE SELF) and more archetypal characters such as 'the Wandering Jew', Don Juan and Faust, all disbelievers or believers in reflective pleasures, 'play' with their life instead of constructing it, with escapist humour or irony drawn from the experiences of the forbidden, that is, in subtle avoidance of ethical and religious tests they face; sharply opposed to that attitude, still today, is the Hegelian mode of life that strives to synthesize irreconcilable contradictions – e.g. to marry OR not to, to be ugly & good OR rather, to be pretty & evil – into a firmer, higher ground for informed recognition and resolution. An 'ethical' decision against and triumph over aesthetic seduction has to be made, with Hegel concludes Kierkegaard in the end. But more importantly, what Kierkegaard saw in aesthetics is not its sub-jugated inferiority to speculative philosophy or theology but an inaugural passivity that cannot simply be 'negated' or 'incorporated', dialectically or not; what Kierkegaard demands is not a tran-sitional dialectic but a 'leap' of action, of faith.

Then, *Fear and Trembling* (1843, Johannes de Silentio) would follow and did follow. In this work that curiously echoes Hegel's use of Antigone, the defiant Hellenic sister torn between bio-familial inclination (aesthetic) and observance of the *polis* law (ethical), Kierkegaard, by contrast, retells the Hebraic legend featuring Abraham the man, old but still tempted, who, at God's command, nearly sacrificed his only son, Isaac. The action of this father is not only callous (unaesthetic) but also unjust (unethical). It is justifiable only in a 'higher' realm of un-thought: as the narrator says in *Exordium*, 'he (Abraham) was not a thinker. He did not feel any need to go beyond faith', or could not climb higher than the top of Mountain Moriah, where he sets up his altar. Again, this allegory points to that shaky ladder to faith, not a sentimental medium but a brutal state, edgy (life-or-death), which Kierkegaard describes and spot-lights in terms of 'the theological suspension of the ethical'; and such a sense of suspension, frighten-ingly intense rather than coolly empty, unfolds repeatedly in *Repetition* (1843, by Constantin Constantius) that subverts Plato's view of knowl-edge acquisition as a form of 'recollection', too static, in Mr Constantinus's view, for its irrever-sible temporal orientation towards the past. Despite the evidence that he has, in a sense, over-come the 'stage' thinking, Kierkegaard went on to write *Stages on Life's Way* (1845), which, as the sequel to *Either/Or*, vividly and summarily re-illustrates those jagged steps by staging the mock-dialectically related three figures (noted earlier). Then, last, this 'aesthetico-ethical' stage (1840–5/6) saw the publication of *Concluding Unscientific Postscript* (1846, by Johannes Clima-cus, ed. S Kierkegaard), a fragmented companion to the previous *Philosophical Fragments* (1844, by Johannes Climacus, ed. S. Kierkegaard), where 'John the climber' sets out to question religious belief in a way that revisits and complicates – i.e. parodies – the path of thinking René Descartes opened up two centuries back in *Meditations*, especially in his God-thinking, and that of Hegel's *Science of Logic* taken here as a purely ontological equivalent to *Meditations* stripped bare of empiri-cal or psychological contents. The *Concluding* heralds Kierkegaard's more explicitly 'religious' phase, where the immovable centrality of human faith in the divine and Christian God's insur-mountable superiority or offensiveness to reason are affirmed.

Intermission: the *Corsair* affair

Three: as many readers observe it, the majority of Kierkegaard's later religious or 'single-mindedly' spiritual text (1846–55) bear his real name, even symbolically in the case of the much celebrated *Upbuilding Discourses in Various Spirits* (1847) where the lyrical evocation of 'purity of heart' seems, indeed, clearly indicative of a new beginning.

What we see is however not necessarily the Augus-tinian kind of 'return of', say, 'a repentant playboy' to the bosom of God, the ultimate source of one's authenticity. The nominal oneness does not guar-antee the oneness of the named but could, on the contrary, further disguise the actual complexity of the person's psychological identities. When, in 1850, Kierkegaard writes:

> Socrates did not possess the true ideal, nor had he any notion of sin, nor that man's salvation required a crucified God.... He therefore retained irony which simply expressed his superiority to the world's folly. But for a Chris-tian, irony is not enough, it can never answer to the terrible truth that salvation means that God is crucified, though irony can still be used for some time in Christendom, to arouse people
> (*Journals*, undated)

he sounds, looks, different, indeed. But has he discarded irony entirely? Would the eradication of irony be enough? Note: his later text is equally, heuristically, 'arousing'. Kierkegaard, one must remember, questioned in every step of the way any dogmatic, self-servingly pietistic, institutionalized talk of a one-time rebirth or redemption. The force of religious belief, manifest ever more intensely in his later works, is in the very transformative or trans-substantive becoming of a person: repeatedly practised, not merely held, faith makes one 'one-self', the self being, as Anti-Climacus says in *Sickness unto Death* (1849), practically 'a relation which relates itself to itself'. The Kierkegaard used selectively by French existentialists later was just that self.

Four: curiously, the late Michel Foucault, the late twentieth-century thinker, who creatively revived traditional asceticism, also held a similar view: ethics as a self-relation rather than, more moral-mechanically, self-regulation. As with many 'post-modern' or 'post-Hegelian' philosophers (e.g. Jacques Derrida), who pointedly resist universal-izing the concrete stance of the autobiographical I, Foucault's so-called 'quasi-religiosity' has Kierkegaardian resonances. The last two decades have been seeing 'dead-locked' limit-philosophy's articulated turn to ethics and religion, which resembles, and seems even to be anticipated by, Kierkegaard's 'stages'. Inspired by Emmanuel Levinas's radical, ethico-theological reworking on the phenomenological tradition of modern philosophy, Continental philosophers of religion, today, such as Jean-Luc Marion and John Caputo, are debating the very possibility of the Gift (*Gave*), that which is, in the idiom of the later Kierkegaard, 'absurdly' given from God – as opposed to *a priori* given as a condition (Kant) – which it is always wrong for us humans (or Christians) not to accept. The task (*Opgave*), for Kierkegaard, is to realize it, every time the gifting happens to the believer. The task, for us readers, would be to receive the Kierkegaardian gift of thought, critically.

Further reading

Auden, W.H. (ed.) (1999) *The Living Thoughts of Kierkegaard*, New York: NYRB.

Eagleton, T. (1999) 'Absolute Ironies: Søren Kierkegaard', in *The Ideology of the Aesthetic*, 173–95, Oxford, UK, Cambridge, USA: Blackwell.

Gardiner, P. (2002) *Kierkegaard: A Very Short Introduction*, Oxford: Oxford University Press.

Hong, H. and Hong, E. (eds) (2000) *The Essential Kierkegaard*, Princeton, NJ: Princeton University Press.

SEE ALSO: main currents in philosophy

KYOO LEE

KINGSLEY, CHARLES (1819–75)

One of the leaders of the mid-Victorian Christian Socialist movement, Charles also achieved renown as a philosopher, novelist and, to a lesser degree, a historian. Born on 12 June 1819 at Holne Vicarage, Devonshire, Kingsley wrote sermons in imitation of his clergyman father at the age of four. Entering Magdalene College, Cambridge, in 1838, he read COLERIDGE, CARLYLE and MAURICE with interest, and was ordained in 1842. Presented with the living of Eversley, he witnessed first hand rural poverty and ignorance in the mid-1840s. Meeting F.D. Maurice, whose *Kingdom of Christ* assuaged his religious doubts, in 1844, Kingsley reacted similarly to the 1848 revolutions, and, with Thomas Hughes and others, contributed as 'Parson Lot' to *Politics for the People* (1848), *Tracts on Christian Socialism* (1850) and *The Christian Socialist* (1850–1). Here a leading theme was the denial that 'selfish competition' was necessarily founded in human nature, and that the rights of private property were absolute, or unbounded by duties proportionate to rights, which views were clearly much indebted to Carlyle's *Past and Present* in particular. Becoming

Professor of English Literature at the newly founded Queen's College, London, Kingsley wrote his first two novels, *Yeast* (1848) and *Alton Locke* (1850), against the background of the revolution. Their portrayal of the distress of the rural labourer and urban artisan made them amongst the most important 'social' novels of the period. But while Chartists found much of appeal in his writings, despite his opposition to Feargus O'Connor's Land Plan, Kingsley's own politics were Toryish in their sympathy with country squires, whose case for agricultural protection he reiterated, and clergymen, whom he wished to assist the poor rather than submit to the loss of their own privileges. His later novels included *Hypatia* (1853), which aimed to describe Christianity as 'the only truly democratic creed', *Westward Ho!* (1855), *Two Years Ago* (1857), on the Crimean War, and *The Water Babies* (1863).

Appointed to the professorship of Modern History at Cambridge in 1860, he held the post for nine years; a popular lecturer, he never engaged systematically with the subject. His inaugural lecture, 'The Limits of Exact Science as Applied to History', stressed the importance of biography to historical understanding, but, while paying lip-service to political economy, managed to avoid confronting any controversy about actual historical development. In his later years he took a pronounced interest in natural science, and in a lecture entitled 'The Theology of the Future' and elsewhere attempted a reconciliation between science and theology, especially Darwinism, which he believed did not contradict Christian teaching. His later theology was much inspired by Maurice, while he proclaimed himself a 'Platonist' in philosophy, with a taste for mysticism, and was in agreement with JOHN STUART MILL, whose promotion of co-operation he also supported, on the cause of women's suffrage.

He died on 23 January 1875.

Further reading

Kingsley, Charles (1855) *Sermons for the Times*, London: John W. Parker.

—— (1860) *The Limits of Exact Science as Applied to History*, London: Macmillan.

—— (1880) *Sanitary and Social Lectures and Essays*, London: Macmillan.

Mrs Kingsley (1877) *Charles Kingsley. His Letters and Memories of His Life*, 2 vols, London: Henry S. King.

GREGORY CLAEYS

KROPOTKIN, PIETR (1842–1921)

Prince Pietr Alekseevich Kropotkin (1842–1921) was born into the Russian aristocracy but spent most of his life in exile in France and England. He was a widely acclaimed scientist and earned his living as a writer but is remembered today as one of the foremost anarchist theorists of the late nineteenth and early twentieth centuries.

In 1857, Kropotkin joined the Corps of Pages in Moscow. In 1861, he became a Personal Page to Tsar Alexander II, who, at that time, Kropotkin idolized, but his personal experience of the Tsar brought disillusionment. After his time as a Page, Kropotkin turned down positions in prestigious regiments and asked to be posted to an obscure regiment in Siberia where he tried to assist in the reform movement. Again disillusioned, this time with local corruption and bureaucratic ineptitude and interference in Moscow, he turned to science, particularly physical geography. Kropotkin led a number of scientific expeditions in Siberia, the results of which gained him acclaim as a scientist and, much later, contributed to the scientific basis of his anarchism.

Offered the position of secretary to the Russian Geographical Society in 1871, he turned it down and chose a career of social reform rather than science. In 1872, he travelled in Switzerland and Belgium, and was much influenced by his experiences with the anarchists of the Jura Federation. Returning to Russia, he became active in reform circles and was arrested and imprisoned. After a spectacular escape two years later, he left Russia and settled in Switzerland, where he founded the anarchist newspaper *Le Révolté*, which became, in France, *La Révolte* and then *Les Temps nouveaux*. Expelled from Switzerland in 1881, he was arrested in France and jailed for three years. On his release in 1886, he moved to England, where he helped found the newspaper *Freedom*, which is still published.

He published a pamphlet, *Appeal to the Young*, in 1880 and his first book, *Paroles d'un révolté* (recently translated as *Words of a Rebel*), written while in prison in France in 1885. These works were followed, in French or English, by *Law and Authority* (1886), *In Russian and French Prisons* (1887), *The Conquest of Bread* (1892 in French, 1906 in English), *Fields, Factories and Workshops* (1898 in French, 1899 in English), *Memoirs of a Revolutionist* (1899), *Mutual Aid* (1902), *Russian*

Literature: Ideals and Realities (1905), *The Great French Revolution* (1909), *Modern Science and Anarchism* (1909), *Ethics* (published posthumously in 1925) and many pamphlets and articles. Kropotkin lived simply and earned his living from his writings, declining to try to recover the family fortune in Russia.

Until 1914, Kropotkin was treated as the leading anarchist spokesperson, but, in that year, he supported the Allied position in the First World War and was rejected by many anarchists. In June 1917, Kropotkin returned to Russia and was given a hero's welcome. Even after the Bolsheviks seized power, Kropotkin was, for a time, treated as a grand old man of the Russian Revolution and had access to LENIN. But Kropotkin remained an anarchist, and he was close to Nestor Makhno (1889–1934) and the anarchist rebels in the Ukraine, and supported amnesty for the leaders of the White Army. In ill health, Kropotkin was marginalized by the Bolsheviks and had to live off the food he and his family could grow, combined with support from the anarchists. As EMMA GOLDMAN (1869–1940) discovered when she visited Kropotkin, they could only afford to heat one room of their house. But Kropotkin continued to send Lenin letters of advice, which were ignored, until shortly before his death.

While on his explorations of Siberia, Kropotkin noticed what he believed to be co-operative behaviour within species and concluded that the 'struggle for survival' hypothesized by CHARLES DARWIN (1809–82) was flawed. Eventually, this insight led to Kropotkin's book *Mutual Aid,* which provided a scientific basis for his anarchism. Kropotkin's anarchism is usually labelled collectivist or communist anarchism and focuses on the community, in contrast to the anarchism of individualists like MAX STIRNER (1806–50).

In a famous article in the 11th edition of the *Encyclopaedia Britannica* (1910), Kropotkin defined anarchism as a theory of society without government in which free agreements among individuals and groups produce harmony. As an anarchist, Kropotkin saw the state and law as one of the central barriers to social change.

In his major theoretical works, *The Conquest of Bread* and *Fields, Factories and Workshops*, Kropotkin argued that modern technology applied to both agriculture and industry could easily produce sufficient goods to eliminate hunger and poverty. The problem with the current system was with distribution, not the inability to produce enough. But the current system of production and distribution benefits those holding power, and it will take a revolution to change the system. While Kropotkin did not reject revolutionary violence, he did not emphasize it either, and his own position regarding violence remains ambiguous.

For Kropotkin, the solution was the socialization of production and distribution under community control with a federation of communities acting together regarding issues that were beyond the scope of the local community. Based on his experiences with the Jura Federation, Kropotkin argued that self-regulating communities were the best means of ensuring both quality and quantity of production, and fairness in distribution.

Kropotkin's approach to anarchism remained influential throughout the twentieth century. In 1974, Colin Ward (1924–), a leading twentieth-century anarchist theorist, published a revision of *Fields, Factories and Workshops* with *Tomorrow* added to the title in which he updated Kropotkin's statistics and argued that Kropotkin's dream of community control industry and agriculture could still be realized.

Further reading

Cahm, C. (1989) *Kropotkin and the Rise of Revolutionary Anarchism 1872–1886*, Cambridge: Cambridge University Press.

Kropotkin, P. (1899) *Fields, Factories and Workshops*, London: Hutchinson.

—— (1902) *Mutual Aid: A Factor of Evolution*, London: William Heinemann.

—— (1906) *The Conquest of Bread*, London: Chapman & Hall.

—— (1906) *Memoirs of a Revolutionist*, Boston, MA: Houghton, Mifflin & Co.

—— (1974) *Fields, Factories and Workshops Tomorrow*, ed. Colin Ward. London: George Allen & Unwin.

Miller, M.A. (1976) *Kropotkin*, Chicago: University of Chicago Press.

Woodcock, G. and Avakumović, I. (1950) *The Anarchist Prince: A Biographical Study of Peter Kropotkin*, London: T.V. Broadman.

SEE ALSO: Bakunin, Mikhail; theories of the state and society: the science of politics; utopianism

LYMAN TOWER SARGENT

L

LABRIOLA, ANTONIO (1843–1904)

Labriola was born in Cassino near Naples on 2 July 1843 in a modest middle-class family (his father was a high-school teacher). After obtaining a degree in philosophy at the University of Naples he taught for a while and dabbled in journalism while seeking an academic appointment. His early essays on Hegel and on Plato, and the support of his university tutor, the great Hegelian scholar Bertrando Spaventa, got him a position at the University of Rome in 1874.

Labriola is generally regarded as the founder of Italian Marxism, but he became a Marxist only towards the end of his life. In his later correspondence with Engels he gave himself a curriculum more in keeping with that of Marx himself: first the encounter with Hegel, followed by the overcoming of Hegel and finally the commitment to historical materialism.

In reality for most of the 1870s and 1880s he was a 'bourgeois' moderate, committed to a secular culture, to the separation between Church and state, and above all to the expansion of education to the working classes. It was in recognition of his educational concerns that in 1877 he added to his chair the job of director of the Museo dell'istruzione e di Educazione – a state appointment he owed to the reform-minded minister of education Ruggero Bonghi.

Labriola was one of a rare breed of people who, with age, moved to the left. By 1886 'moderate' was no longer adequate a description for someone who had become critical of liberalism, espoused the extension of the suffrage, advocated welfare support for the poor and the disabled, and promoted mass schooling. Like most of the (left) Italian intelligentsia he was also an enthusiastic 'social' imperialist, and believed that the conquest of Libya would enable Italy to catch up with the other European countries. He became increasingly involved in political agitation, which included addressing steelworkers on 'Le idee della democrazia' – the text has unfortunately gone lost. By the end of the 1880s he had produced his main work: *Saggi intorno alla concezione materialistica della storia* (1895) (Engl. title: *Essays on the Materialist Conception of History*). Engels's positive verdict ('*Alles sehr gut*' – It's all very good) and their publication in French in the journal *Le Devenir social* edited by Sorel enhanced his wider fame. In fact, he had become one of the first academic Marxists in Europe.

His mode of exposition contained many of the virtues and defects of subsequent Italian Marxism: a rejection of dogmatism, a disdain for the overarching *summa* so loved by German socialists such as Kautsky and a refusal to see the connection between the economic base and the political and ideological superstructures as automatic. At the same time the opaque prose, the lack of precision and the absence of systematic analysis of the subject matter made it difficult to use his 'genetic' (a term he favoured over the fashionable 'dialectical') method for solidly grounded empirical analyses. These remained the prerogative of positivist sociologists. His relationship with the Italian Socialist Party and particularly with its leader, Filippo Turati, was often fraught and he was disappointed by Croce's idealist turn against Marxism. He died of cancer in 1904 in Rome. Later in the twentieth century he was championed by both Gramsci and Togliatti but remained little known outside a narrow circle of academic specialists.

Further reading

Labriola, Antonio (1959–62) *Opere complete*, 3 vols, ed. L. Dal Pane, Milan: Feltrinelli Milan.

Dal Pane, L. (1975) *Antonio Labriola nella politica e nella cultura italiana*, Turin: Einaudi Turin.

Piccone, Paul (1983) *Italian Marxism*, Berkeley: University of California Press.

Miller, J.E. (1990) *From Elite to Mass Politics. Italian Socialism in the Giolittian Era, 1900–1914*, Kent, OH: Kent State University Press.

CHRISTOPHER DUGGAN

LAMARTINE, ALPHONSE DE (1790–1869)

For very brief periods of time, Alphonse de Lamartine was the most important figure in nineteenth-century French poetry, and then in nineteenth-century French politics. First celebrated, then obscure, Lamartine was a poet of the sublime who ultimately preached the virtues of popular literature; an aristocrat who helped to launch France's Second Republic; a man viewing himself as an 'amateur' writer who turned to literary commercialism. This poet and politician's life and work are defined first by drama, then by paradox, irony and contradictions.

Alphonse-Marie-Louis de Prat de Lamartine was born in Mâcon on 21 October 1790. Since five sisters followed, and his father's two brothers had no heirs, Alphonse was to inherit family estates originally acquired along with the patents of the minor aristocracy in the eighteenth century. A profound attachment to ancestral *châteaux* and land remained with Alphonse, to the point even of contributing ultimately to his financial downfall; the family's allegiance to Church and throne, however, did not.

Lamartine's childhood and early adulthood were marked by Catholicism and his family's influence. He attended the Institut Puppier from 1801–3, then the former Jesuit school at Belley from 1803–7. When Alphonse left school, his parents and the uncles from whom he was to inherit prevented him from starting a career, because service to Napoleon was unthinkable, and they also kept a close watch on the suitability of his romantic attachments, since he embodied the future of the family name. That combination of restrictions resulted in a period of dilettantism and mild dissipation. In 1811 Alphonse was sent to Italy to avoid one alliance; there he had a liaison

that later inspired his novella, *Graziella* (1852); his affair with the wife of a neighbour upon returning to Burgundy produced his illegitimate son, Léon de Pierreclos, on 1 March 1813. Visits to Paris in 1812 and 1813 led to extravagance, gambling debts and the need for rescue by his family.

When Napoleon abdicated in 1815, Lamartine was free at last to pursue a career, and his fortunes began to change. He served briefly in the Garde-du-Corps of Louis XVIII, and when his health prompted a visit to Aix-les-Bains in the autumn of 1816 he met the woman who inspired *Les Méditations*, Julie Charles (1784–1817). Very poor, and already consumptive, Julie had married the distinguished physicist J.A. Charles in 1804, when she was 20 and he 58. Although their relations were almost certainly passionate at some point, Lamartine's poetry renders this woman in ethereal and spiritualized terms. By other accounts she was tall, with black hair and dark eyes, lively, and coquettish. The two met when he rescued her from drowning in a boating accident, and professions of love followed almost immediately afterwards. Early the following year Lamartine frequented her salon in Paris, pursuing their relationship and benefiting from her social connections. The pair agreed to meet again at Aix-les-Bains in the autumn, but the illness that soon killed her prevented Julie from joining her lover. Lamartine's most famous poem, 'Le Lac', commemorates that aborted rendezvous.

In one sense a banal story of adultery at a health resort, in another Lamartine's experience with Mme Charles prepared the ground for his literary, religious and political future. Whatever the reality of their relations, Julie Charles became for him 'Elvire', the feminine form of CHATEAUBRIAND's '*bien inconnu*' [unknown good] who defines the melancholic, yearning tone of his most famous collection of poetry. In its turn, Elvire's death and her religious conversion just prior to her death prompted a spiritual crisis and quest in Lamartine, who had abandoned the faith of his youth. He read LAMENNAIS's *Essai sur l'indifférence en matière de la religion* at this time. Finally, the trauma of Julie's death, and probably also the reality of his financial needs, caused Lamartine to seek order in his life. After 1817 he wanted a wife, and he wanted a job in politics.

Lamartine met Maria Anna Eliza Birch (Marianne) (1790–1863) at the marriage of his sister, Césarine de Vignet, in February 1819. After a passionate interlude with Léna de Larche, and unsuccessful attempts at getting a diplomatic post, he saw Marianne again and declared himself two weeks later, on 14 August 1819. Lamartine's letters make it clear that passion was not the motive for this speedy proposal. The only child of a British major, she had a significant fortune. The problem, according to Lamartine, was that she was not beautiful: 'I will have moral perfection itself. She lacks only a little beauty, but I'm happy enough with what there is of it.' Marianne had 'admirable' brown hair, intelligent eyes and a swan neck, but her teeth stuck out, her complexion was blotchy and her nose was too big. However, the standard-bearer of the Romantic movement was prepared, and eager, to make a marriage of reason.

At the beginning of 1820 Lamartine went to Paris again to convince Marianne's mother that he could support a wife. There he promptly fell ill and converted to Catholicism; Marianne did the same, abjuring her family's Protestant faith. In March 1820 Lamartine was granted the position of *attaché* to the Embassy in Naples. On 11 March 1820 the *Meditations*, unsigned, with twenty-four poems, was published. The new Romantic feelings of religious *malaise* and melancholia, already identified by Chateaubriand and GERMAINE DE STAËL, were represented in poetry for the first time, and were immediately accessible in the familiar forms of odes and elegies. This collection created a sensation. Sainte-Beuve wrote that 'from one day to the next the climate and the light had changed . . . it was a revelation'. A youthful VICTOR HUGO heralded Alphonse de Lamartine as the 'real poet' for whom France had been waiting. Audiences were spellbound. Lamennais wanted to meet the author of the spiritual poems. Seven editions of *Meditations* appeared in its first year of publication; 10 years later there were nineteen more. In response to the *Meditations* the Minister of the Interior sent Lamartine a collection of great literary works, and the poet was asked to write a report on the role of the French nobility in a government with two chambers. As of 1820, Lamartine was launched in the political and literary worlds of France. Alphonse married his bride on 6 June 1820.

On 15 June 1820 the couple, accompanied by Marianne's mother, left for Naples. In the next 10 years, Lamartine occupied, and resigned from, several diplomatic postings in Italy. And between 1820 and 1830 Lamartine produced a number of individual works along with two major collections of poetry, the *Nouvelles méditations poétiques* (1823), and *Harmonies poétiques et religieuses* (1830). Although they had admirers, both collections were criticized for stylistic sloppiness. In the years 1820–30 the Lamartines also had two children and were saddened by several deaths. Their son Alphonse was born on 15 February 1821; he died on 4 November 1822. Their daughter Julia was born 14 May 1822. Two sisters of Lamartine died, and on 16 November 1829, 11 days after Lamartine was elected to the *Académie Française*, his mother died, fatally burned by scalding bath water. This period concludes with the crowning of Louis-Philippe, and Alphonse's resignation from the diplomatic service on 15 September 1830.

In 1831 Lamartine failed in his bid to be elected a deputy, in part because of the ambiguity of his platform. He then wrote *La Politique rationnelle* (*Rational Politics*, November 1831) to define his political views. At this stage Lamartine, a liberal, constitutional, monarchist influenced by Lamennais, already believed in the separation of Church and state, the abolition of the death penalty, expanded suffrage, freedom of the press and of education. Following his electoral defeat, Lamartine and his family embarked for the Orient in July 1832, partly with a view to addressing Lamartine's religious questions. The questions remained unanswered. In their stead, Lamartine acquired debts, and more spiritual doubt as a result of Julia's death in Bayreuth on 7 December 1832. In January 1833 Lamartine was elected *in absentia* as a deputy from the city of Bergues.

Throughout his career as a deputy, from 1831–47, Lamartine deliberately balanced between the two parties. His increasingly progressive humanitarian ideas gave him many points in common with the Liberal Party, but he did not break with the King's regime until 27 January 1843, and even then he kept his distance from the leader of the opposition, LOUIS THIERS. Lamartine's critics found his ideas superficial, but over the years he developed a tremendous following with his gift for speaking, and his appeal to both parties. As a politician Lamartine had to fight against the image of a dreamy poet, but he did continue to publish. Lamartine's *Oeuvres complètes* appeared from 1834–43. *Jocelyn* (1836), a long narrative poem about a man who is forced to renounce human love in order to become a priest, was one of Lamartine's biggest popular successes. *La Chute d'un ange*

(*The Fall of an Angel*, 1838), another narrative poem, was about an angel who became human for love of a woman. Recognizing Lamartine's move away from traditional Christianity, Rome put *Jocelyn* and *The Fall of an Angel* on the Index. *Recueillements* (*Contemplations*) was Lamartine's last collection of poetry (1839). Echoing most critics, Sainte-Beuve wrote that with these works Lamartine was 'renouncing his glory'. As an emerging deputy Lamartine also wrote two works in prose to assuage his growing need for money. Proscribed by Rome as well, *Voyage en Orient* (1835) recounted that trip, but inaccurately, according to travelling companions. *Les Girondins* (1847), another popular success, told about revolutionaries who missed their chance to avoid bloodshed. Lamartine informed Molé, the King's minister, that this work was to prepare the next revolution.

Lamartine helped to catalyse that revolution even more directly in February 1848. Over the course of his career he had expanded on the ideas of *Rational Politics*; his belief in the sovereignty of the people had become even more pronounced. On 19 February 1848 Lamartine gave a speech inciting the public to attend a 'Banquet', the means found to get around Louis-Philippe's interdiction against potentially subversive gatherings. The government threatened military intervention, so no one attended, but on 22 February discontented people were milling around in the streets, and the deputies – without Lamartine's signature – voted to impeach the government. On 23 February the King tried to form a new government, but it was too late. Barricades were up on 24 February, and by midday Louis-Philippe abdicated in favor of the Duchesse d'Orléans as regent for her son. That day Lamartine was asked to be head of a government under the regency, but he refused to take part in anything but a republic. It is theorized that Lamartine had been planning this moment all along. The leader of a provisional government, his eloquence alone quelled angry mobs in the revolution's immediate aftermath, and after immense success in that April's elections, he was encouraged – but declined – to become France's dictator. Lamartine represented moderate politics and a republic of progress. But the increasingly riotous mobs in May and June led to military intervention, and on 24 June the Assembly voted General Cavaignac executive powers. In August of the same year the hero of February was falsely accused of appropriating public funds, and that December

Louis Napoleon was elected president of the Second Republic, with Lamartine coming in fifth.

Lamartine anticipated France's move towards a republic, and saved that institution with his courage between February and April. There are different theories for why he was unable to sustain his political vision. ALEXIS DE TOCQUEVILLE thought that Lamartine's dramatic demise resulted from the same coalition of parties that put him into power: ultimately Lamartine could not please everyone. Charles Baudelaire spoke for many when he wrote that in the end 'the people could not find a real idea for the future beneath the poetic thoughts of a great writer'.

Lamartine came to accept Louis Napoleon, but after 1848 the poet-politician was not an active participant in the Chamber, and he formally resigned as a deputy following the *coup d'état* in 1851. The all-consuming preoccupation of Lamartine's last 20 years was money. Over time he had accumulated tremendous debts with a lavish lifestyle, the subsidy of his political life, the acquisition of more land, disastrous speculations and, most touchingly, acts of charity that persisted even in bankruptcy. To pay his creditors, Lamartine wrote about his professional life in *Histoire de la révolution de 1848* (1849). *Les Confidences* (1849) and *Les Nouvelles confidences* (1851) as well as *Raphaël* (1849) pitched his private life to the public. He wrote a play, *Toussaint l'Ouverture* (1850). He produced voluminous histories of Russia (1854) and Turkey (1855), as well as of the Restoration (1851–3). All of his historical and biographical works are notoriously unreliable. Lamartine also produced explicitly popular literature, tales about servants who sacrifice themselves for their families. He cranked out occasional poems and regular articles in a succession of journals he produced for a fee – *Le Conseiller du peuple* (1849–51), *Le Civilisateur* (1852–4) and *Le Cours familier de littérature* (1856–69). Finally, he produced his own *Oeuvres complètes* (1860–6). These works were all obviously written in haste.

By the 1860s Lamartine's fall from 'pure' poetry to hack literature, his shameless use of pathos to market his works, his political oblivion and his desperate financial state rendered him the object of both pity and disdain. In 1860 Lamartine finally started to sell his houses, land and horses. The long-suffering Marianne died on 23 May 1863; in a magnanimous gesture Marianne left her jewels and part of her fortune to Valentine de Cessiat,

Alphonse's niece. Lamartine married Valentine secretly, probably in 1867, after Pope Pius IX had given the necessary dispensation. That year his mind also began to wander, and finally, after rejecting offers twice, he had to accept a pension from the empire that opposed everything for which he had fought. He died on 28 February 1869, with Julie Charles' death-bed crucifix nearby, and his head on Valentine's shoulder. Although offered a national funeral, Alphonse de Lamartine was buried with his family in the Chapel at Saint-Point, the only family estate he still owned.

Lamartine considered himself primarily a politician, but he is best known as a poet. As a poet he is perceived as the first Romantic, but he himself was uninterested in identifying himself with the Romantic movement; in any case Marceline Desborde-Valmore's Romantic collection of poems actually came first, and his forms are classical. Although Lamartine is a fixture of the French canon, even his Pléiade editor remarks that few read or study him. His facility of expression, his volubility, his sentimental scenarios, do not appeal to the modern reader any more than they did to such later contemporaries as Flaubert. Lamartine's best chance of rehabilitation currently comes from traits particularly criticized during his life – his association with popular literature, and the 'femininity' of his writings. Paradox and irony continue to define Lamartine after his death.

Further reading

Lamartine, A. (1963) *Oeuvres poétiques complètes*, Paris: Gallimard.
Lombard, C. (1973) *Lamartine*, New York: Twayne Publishers.
Lucas Dubreton, J. (1951) *Lamartine*, Paris: Flammarion.

SEE ALSO: Chateaubriand, François; democracy, populism and rights; Hugo, Victor; Lamennais, Felicite De; liberalism; novels, poetry and drama; Thiers, Louis-Adolphe; Tocqueville, Alexis de

KATHRYN OLIVER MILLS

LAMENNAIS, FÉLICITÉ DE (1782–1854)

Félicité De Lamennais (or La Mennais) was a priest (from 1816) and the foremost Catholic thinker of Restoration France. From the mid-1820s onwards he moved to liberal Catholicism; when the Church rejected his liberal overtures, he abandoned Catholicism altogether and moved towards his final vocation as a political and social reformer.

Born in Saint-Malo in 1782, Lamennais spent much of his early life as a priest who had gathered around himself a group of young men in his land in Brittany. His first work, *Essai sur l'indifférence en matiére de réligion* (1817), was a vigorous onslaught on the reliance on individual reason propagated by the eighteenth-century *philosophes*, which would usher in social instability and destroy the social fabric, as had happened during the French Revolution. His solution was the acceptance of Catholicism. However, from the mid-1820s onwards Lamennais, conscious of the inevitability of the final overthrow of the Bourbons, started advocating an alliance between the Church and the liberals. He argued that liberalism needed religion in order to achieve order and stability. Following the July Revolution of 1830, Lamennais and some of his associates established the journal *L'Avenir*. *L'Avenir* advocated measures as radical as separation of Church and state, and freedom of education (leaving the choice of kind of education for children to parents). The conservative establishment of the Church was vehemently opposed to these proposals and the journal ceased publication in November 1831. Then Lamennais and his associates shifted their attention to trying to convince the Pope in Rome to endorse their ideas. Pope Gregory XVI instead formally condemned liberal Catholicism. In that context, Lamennais, who had by then become completely disillusioned with the new rulers of July Monarchy France, came to see himself in the role of a champion of the exploited working classes. In 1834 he published what turned out to be his most successful work, the *Paroles d'un croyant*. In apocalyptic style, the book castigated the exploitation of the working classes and prophesied its end. In the next 20 years Lamennais, besides contributing writings explaining his abandonment of the Catholic Church, went on to write works directly aimed at the working classes themselves, and castigating the established social order, such as *Livre du peuple* (1837) or *Esclavage moderne* (1839). His recipes against the exploitation of the workers included universal suffrage, generalized education and workers' co-operatives. His 1840 pamphlet *Le Pays et le gouvernement* was so critical of the government that it earned him a year in prison. After the Revolution of 1848 he was twice elected to the

National Assembly in 1848–9, sitting on the extreme left. Overall, Lamennais was a rather lonely figure, who, nevertheless, had many admirers thanks to his personal example of courage and conviction.

Further reading

Duroselle, J.-B. (1951) *Les Débuts du Catholicisme social en France (1822–1870)*, Paris. Presses universitaires de France.
Gibson, W. (1986) *The Abbé de Lamennais and the Liberal Catholic Movement in France*, New Haven, CT: Yale University Press.
Jaume, L. (1997) *L'Individu efface: ou le paradoxe du libéralisme français*, Paris: Fayard.
Remond, R. (1948) *Lamennais et la démocratie*, Paris.

SEE ALSO: religion, secularization and the crisis of faith

GEORGIOS VAROUXAKIS

LASSALLE, FERDINAND (1825–64)

Ferdinand Lassalle was a socialist leader. Lassalle was born in Breslau into a well-to-do Jewish family. He studied philosophy at the universities of Breslau and Berlin, where Hegel was an early and enduring influence, and one from which – quite unlike Marx – he derived a positive view of the state and its moral function. He also rejected the materialistic view of the world adopted by Marx, retaining a belief in the importance of ideas as the determining force in history, and in the ability of individuals to take action to change it. His own approach to politics was that of an impatient activist. Nevertheless, after graduating he worked on the *Neue Rheinische Zeitung*, was a member of the Communist League and considered himself a follower of Marx, with whom he had a long, if increasingly difficult relationship. He was imprisoned for violent resistance against state officials during the revolutions of 1848–9, but came to favour a pragmatic approach to the present political situation, writing that 'one can never make a revolution; all one can ever do is to endow a revolution which has taken place in the actual conditions of a society with the outward signs of legality, and to give consistency to its course'. After the failure of the 1848 revolutions he anticipated the development of a new revolutionary situation, and saw the national movements of the day as a vehicle for popular democratic aspirations. With the outbreak of the Italian wars of unification, and the development of the political crisis in Prussia, he intensified his political activity, initially in collaboration with left-wing liberals of the Progress Party and the *Nationalverein*. He became frustrated with the Prussian liberals and began to urge workers to form their own political organization. In 1863 he organized the General German Workers' Association (ADAV), effectively Germany's first labour party, and became its president. His two principal aims were contained in his programmatic *Open Letter* to the workers of Saxony (1863): first, a democratic constitutional state based on universal, equal and direct suffrage; and, second, state intervention to bring about social change through economic support of workers' co-operatives. In the hope of achieving universal suffrage and welfare measures within the political framework of the existing state, Lassalle held meetings with Bismarck, then minister president of Prussia, but his hopes of an anti-liberal alliance came to nothing. He was killed shortly afterwards in a duel connected with a love affair. Marx and Engels thought Lassalle's knowledge of economics superficial and his political tactics questionable, but his active interventions in the politics of the labour movement determined its political outlook for a generation. Marx continued to resist his influence even after his death, objecting strongly, and in some detail, to the Lassallean Gotha Programme, which was adopted at the 1875 'unity conference' where the ADAV merged with the Social Democratic Workers' Party (SDAP) to form the German Social Democratic Party (SPD). EDUARD BERNSTEIN's revisionist evaluation, published as the introduction to an edition of Lasalle's collected works in 1893 put his achievements as a radical agitator and inspiring popular leader in a more positive perspective.

Further reading

Bernstein, Eduard (1893) *Ferdinand Lassalle as a Social Reformer*, London: Swan Sonnenschein.
Brandes, Georg (1911) *Ferdinand Lassalle*, London: Macmillan.
Footman, David (1946) *The Primrose Path. A Life of Ferdinand Lassalle*, London: The Cresset Press.

SEE ALSO: Bernstein, Eduard; Marx and Marxism

TIM KIRK

LEBON, GUSTAVE (1841–1931)

Gustave LeBon was a French philosopher and sociologist. He became the founder of 'mass psychology' with his influential book on the *The Crowd* (*La Psychologie des foules*). LeBon also wrote on the psychology of nations. He was good at explaining science to a wider audience, and due to a skilful mixture of popular science and social commentary his works became so fashionable that he could almost live from the sale of his many publications in the realms of medicine, physiology, Eastern civilizations, 'race science' and social psychology. In addition, he invented and developed technical scientific equipment, such as a 'pocket cephalometer' for anthropologists who engaged in the latest fad of racial 'craniology' and its measuring of skulls.

Trained as a medical doctor, he applied his 'diagnosis' to the purported ills of French national life, such as the dramatically falling birth rate or the rise of alcoholic consumption, ills for which he was searching for a remedy, particularly in view of the antagonism *vis-à-vis* Germany and the defeat of 1870. The fear of degeneracy of the 'national body' was closely connected with the issue of the 'masses': the revolutions of 1789, 1830 and 1848, the phenomenon of the Paris Commune, and the increase of the proletariat nurtured a growing concern amongst the educated elites regarding the role of the masses. The intelligentsia became increasingly fearful of the 'mob', and the topic of the crowd turned out to be one of the important motifs in *fin de siècle* discussions. Although this was a Europe-wide phenomenon it was in France where it was most hotly debated.

LeBon attended lectures on hysteria at the famous Salpétrière hospital in Paris; there, in 1870, he also came into contact with neuro-physiologists and anthropologists. In 1881, he published *L'Homme et les sociétés* (Man and Societies), an account of humankind's cultural and physical evolution from its animal origins, and a study which was rooted in Darwinian evolutionary biology (see DARWIN, CHARLES) and imbued with theories of race and their values (see ANTHROPOLOGY AND RACE). The book bears witness of his fascination with hypnotic theory and the phenomena of sleepwalking and hallucinations. It laid the foundation of his life-long elaboration on two concepts – the psychology of race and the crowd mind. A reason for the decadence of civilization was seen not only in the mixing of 'superior' and 'inferior' racial stocks but also in the nefarious egalitarian spirit of democracy that led to chaos and went against the natural law of the inequality of men. LeBon warned of the dangers of racial assimilation of any sort and accused the modern reformers of seducing the masses with their ominous socialist utopia. LeBon's further research into the history and the 'souls' of races was summarized in 1894 in his *Psychology of Peoples* (*Lois Psychologiques de l'évolution des peuples*, trans. 1899), which propagated the urgent need for the regeneration of the French social organism. This work was enormously popular and purportedly became bedside reading for the future US president Theodore Roosevelt. It stated the inferiority of both the non-European peoples and the lower strata of European societies, the superior grades of society being as far apart from its inferior grades as the white man from the black.

Other major works in the realm of social psychology comprise: *The Psychology of Revolution* (*La Révolution française et la psychologie des révolutions*, 1912, trans. 1913); *The Psychology of Socialism* (*Psychologie du socialisme*, 1898, trans. 1899); *Psychologie de l'éducation* (1902); *La Psychologie politique et la défense sociale* (1910); and *Psychology of the Great War: The First World War and its Origins* (*Enseignements psychologiques de la guerre européenne*, 1915, trans. 1916). It was, however, his groundbreaking enquiry into *La Psychologie des foules*, published in 1895, which became world-famous. By 1974, this work on the psychology of the crowd, which set the foundation of social psychology, had been translated into at least sixteen foreign languages (first translated into English as *The Crowd: A Study of the Popular Mind*, 1896) and published in forty-five French editions. In this book he developed further his ideas regarding the crowd mind.

LeBon contended the structural resemblance between the racial (i.e. the people's) mind and the crowd mind: the latter reflecting the atavistic traits or primordial sentiments deeply embedded in the primitive heritage of the race. A study of crowd behaviour was thus the path of enquiry into the people's ancestral mentality.

What are the characteristics ascribed by LeBon to the crowd and its mind? When a crowd forms, it presents new characteristics very different from those of the individuals composing it. Regardless of the qualities of the individual members of a crowd, the fact that these individuals have been transformed into a crowd puts them in possession of a collective mind that may differ very strongly from the individual minds. A crowd is subject to the 'law of the mental unity of crowds', and it is always dominated by considerations of which it is unconscious. Steered by stark images rather than reasoning, easily influenced by suggestion and prone to collective hallucinations, the crowd always tends to go to extremes and does not admit doubt or uncertainty. The crowd is thus moved by a certain religious-like sentiment and most possibly by an intolerant fanaticism that can easily lead to violence. Crowds can be as easily heroic as criminal, and in situations like war be ready for sacrifice. They obey their leaders who by definition need to be despotic and use tactics such as simplistic affirmation, repetition and suggestion – tactics that also apply to the biggest 'psychological crowd', the democratic electorate.

To LeBon, mental contagion and suggestion in the sense of hypnotism were the decisive factors in the genesis of ideas, emotions and beliefs in crowds. Since the entry of the popular classes into the political arena there had been the dawn of the 'era of crowds', which demanded a new art or even 'science' – namely of crowd manipulation – a 'science' that every French statesman needed to know in order to combat pacifistic socialism at home and the German beyond the border, as he pointed out in *La Psychologie politique et la défense sociale*.

LeBon's contribution to race thought exerted a considerable influence on other 'race scientists' such as Houston Stewart Chamberlain or Vacher de Lapouge who both, in turn, influenced Hitler. In the realm of social psychology LeBon's ideas were appropriated by FREUD. Regardless of whether Hitler knew of LeBon's work or not, he was certainly aware of the manipulation of the crowd mind, a topic for which LeBon had laid the theoretical groundwork several decades earlier.

Further reading

Hannaford, I. (1996) *Race: The History of an Idea in the West*, Baltimore, MD: Johns Hopkins University Press.
Malik, K. (1996) *The Meaning of Race: Race, History and Culture in Western Society*, Basingstoke, Hampshire: Macmillan Press.
Nye, R.A. (1975) *The Origins of Crowd Psychology: Gustave LeBon and the Crisis of Democracy in the Third Republic*, London/Beverley Hills: Sage Publications.
Widener, A. (ed.) (1979) *Gustave LeBon: The Man and his Works*, Indianapolis: Liberty Press.

SEE ALSO: the body, medicine, health and disease; psychology, the emergence of

DETMAR KLEIN

LECKY, W.E.H. (1838–1903)

Born near Dublin on 26 March 1838, Lecky was educated at Trinity College Dublin. The publication of two small books, *The Religious Tendencies of the Age* (1860) and *The Leaders of Public Opinion in Ireland* (1861), coincided with his last years at Trinity. He spent most of the 1860s in libraries on the Continent. The result was the publication of *History of the Rise and Influence of the Spirit of Rationalism in Europe* (1865) and *History of European Morals from Augustus to Charlemagne* (1869). These were written while he was under the influence of THOMAS BUCKLE's Positivism. They were pioneering studies in historical sociology and in the search for the laws underlying causation. They incorporated much that appealed to the mid-Victorians: he opposed utilitarian ethics; embraced the idea of progress and the advance of liberty from theological obscurantism and the political tyranny of the Dark Ages; proclaimed the conquest of reason over superstition; and welcomed the increase in political morality, the movement towards democracy and the rights of nationalities. Although the volumes struck a chord with contemporaries, were widely acclaimed and went through several editions they were to lack the more enduring qualities of his later work on the eighteenth century.

Settled in London he published a revised and extended edition of his *Leaders of Public Opinion in Ireland* (1871). Nostalgia for the independent Irish Parliament of the eighteenth century was a strong element in his political philosophy. The eight volumes of his *History of England in the Eighteenth Century* (1878–90) confirmed his reputation as a leading historian. A cabinet edition (1892) devoted five volumes to Ireland and seven to England. The work was welcomed for its impartiality, judiciousness, moral tone and liberal sympathies. The philosophy throughout illustrated how much he owed to EDMUND BURKE, whom Lecky described as the greatest of all modern political philosophers. While nationalist sentiment remained in evidence in the Irish volumes Lecky now argued that the circumstances were not right for the establishment of an independent Irish Parliament.

An Irish landowner himself, he had become horrified by what he regarded as an unholy alliance of nationalism, socialism and democracy in the Land League and Home Rule agitations led by CHARLES STEWART PARNELL. Although his work was extensively quoted by Irish politicians, and by Gladstone and other leading Liberals in favour of Home Rule, Lecky now campaigned in defence of the Union. He sat in parliament for Dublin University (1895–1902) as a liberal unionist. His book, *Democracy and Liberty* (1895), echoed the warnings of J.S. MILL and others against the threats to individual liberty that were posed by democracy and the tyranny of the majority. Lecky died on 22 October 1903. *Historical and Political Essays* was published posthumously in 1908.

Further reading

Lecky, Elisabeth (1909) *A Memoir of the Right Hon. William Edward Hartpole Lecky, by His Wife*, London: Longmans, Green and Co.
McCartney, Donal (1994) *W.E.H. Lecky: Historian and Politician 1838–1903*, Dublin: The Lilliput Press.

SEE ALSO: conservatism, authority and tradition; democracy, populism and rights; historiography and the idea of progress

DONAL McCARTNEY

LENIN, V.I. (1870–1924)

V.I. Lenin, theorist and revolutionary, was born in 1870, the son of a local inspector of primary education. Education, then, was in the family, and though Lenin achieved fame as a man of action, perhaps the most famous revolutionary of them all, he still remained a committed scholar, whose many volumes of *Collected Works* bear witness to his determination to persuade by evidence and rational argument. It seems that Lenin had become a Marxist by the age of 19 and so his first theoretical task was to ascertain Russia's placing within the Marxist historical schema. Serfdom had only been abolished in the decade before his birth.

In terms of the development of industry, the country obviously lay far behind England and Germany. Furthermore the dominant strand of Russian radicals, the populists, denied that the Marxist pattern of development applied to their own country at all. In their view Russian society possessed the unique aspect that remnants of the medieval rural commune had survived into modern times. This, they believed, furnished the basis whereby Russia might transfer straight to socialism without having to go through the capitalist epoch. In such a schema the industrial proletariat had no part. It was, then, a stark alternative to the Marxist notion that the working class would overthrow capitalism and replace it with a communist society.

In *The Development of Capitalism in Russia* (1899) Lenin challenged the populist thesis. He argued that the Russian countryside was already pervaded by capitalist relations, and so its pattern of development fitted the Marxist programme. However, applying Marxism to the specific conditions of Russia was no easy task. The urban working class might be emerging as industry took root, but tsarist autocracy did not allow them to form into a mass party. In *What is to be Done?* (1899–1902) Lenin advocated a dedicated, professional elite party, working in secret. Though in later years this tract became a communist orthodoxy for the nature of the party anywhere, Lenin's text makes it clear that his proposals were specifically geared to the conditions then pertaining in Russia; that a party accessible to the masses would simultaneously be accessible to the police in a regime where the most elementary freedoms could not be exercised.

Following military defeat by Japan in 1905, revolution broke out in a number of Russian cities. There was a general strike and a workers' soviet was formed in Petrograd under the leadership of the young Leon Trotsky. In October Tsar Nicholas II granted a constitution and a parliament whose powers were slight, but gradually the regime seemed to have stabilized itself.

The outbreak of the First World War altered everything. Lenin, in exile in Western Europe, was devastated to learn that the German social democrats, the accepted leaders of world socialism, had turned nationalist and voted for their country's war credits. Under the influence of war Lenin sought to analyse capitalism as an international system. In *Imperialism, the Highest Stage of*

Capitalism (1916) he developed an international theory that became very influential in the 'Third World' for much of the twentieth century. Lenin's context was that by 1900, for the first time, the world was completely divided up, so that in future only redivision was possible. Thus he saw the First World War as a competition for markets between the capitalist powers. The result of this was that the most powerful nations were exploiting the small and weak ones. Nation now vied with class in his analysis and so a change occurred in the relationship between classes in the advanced countries. The bourgeoisie were now able to buy off the proletariat and stifle their discontent by offering their leaders part of the 'super profits' of imperialism. Although it was not fully explicit, Lenin certainly intimated that parts of the Western working classes develop a limited vested interest in imperialism. In terms of Marxist theory this represents the superimposition of a theory of international relations, and one that immensely complicates the simpler model of presumed fundamental antagonism between capitalist and working classes.

Imperialism was the 'highest stage' of capitalism in that it formed the final possibility for the expansion of capital. It represented 'parasitic or decaying capitalism' and so marked the immediate prelude to revolution. Less than a year later, in February 1917, revolution occurred. What fell was not capitalism as such but rather Russia's tsarist regime. Lenin was in Switzerland when he heard the news and while Alexander Kerensky began to introduce a liberal constitution, Lenin prepared plans for an immediate socialist takeover. It was in this phase that he wrote his last major theoretical work, *The State and Revolution*. In it he denounced those who thought socialism could be achieved by co-operation in a parliamentary regime. In his attack on the social democrats of both Russia and Germany, Lenin quoted selectively from Marx and Engels (see MARX AND MARXISM) to insist that the revolution should be violent and avoid any compromise with the existing order. He also placed a significant emphasis on the 'dictatorship of the proletariat', the period of transition following the socialist revolution. Here the state would remain necessary so long as enemies of the new order were still active but would gradually wither away. Once property was collectively owned, there would be no class to suppress and so the state would become redundant. Lenin assumed that administrative tasks would be carried out by anyone with a standard education and that the law and order function could devolve to the armed people.

Within weeks of penning these proposals Lenin and the Bolsheviks seized power in a revolution that determined the shape of world politics for most of the rest of the century. Lenin had presumed that revolution in Russia would be supported by similar transformations in the more advanced countries to the West. These failed to materialize. Russia's socialist experiment was bedevilled by isolation, civil war and foreign invasion. Gradually the relative freedoms of the immediate post-revolutionary situation gave way to the oppressions of Stalinism. The extent to which Lenin can be implicated in the emergence of Stalinism remains a disputed issue. Lenin died in 1924 having been seriously ill for the previous few years. After his death he was granted equivalent status with Marx (hence 'Marxism-Leninism') and his embalmed body became a place of pilgrimage in Red Square, Moscow.

Further reading

Harding, N. (1996) *Leninism*, Basingstoke: Macmillan.
Lenin, V.I. (1992) *State and Revolution*, Harmondsworth: Penguin Books.
——(1996) *Imperialism, the Highest Stage of Capitalism*, London: Pluto Press.
Service, R. (2000) *Lenin. A Biography*, London: Macmillan.

SEE ALSO: ideas of war and peace; imperialism and empire; Marx and Marxism; Russian thought in the nineteenth century

MICHAEL LEVIN

LIBERALISM

The term 'liberalism' was initially derived from an early nineteenth-century Spanish political party (1810–11), but does not become common currency in English until mid-century; the Liberal Party in Britain, which succeeded the Whigs, assumes the name from *c*.1839. From that time it has been broadly associated with political principles and movements that focus upon extending individual and social liberty, civil and political as well as economic. Usually presuming that individuals seek to maximize both their own independence and their own happiness, liberalism in the nineteenth century was often related to and rested upon other principles, including toleration; a faith in rationality; a commitment to meritocracy over inherited privilege; a belief that society generated its own natural system of order; the wish to minimize state power, and to retrench the costs of government; the pursuit of 'balanced' constitutions, or separation of powers, where no one branch could predominate over others; and natural rights, especially the right of private property. It is often associated with the rise to power of the commercial and manufacturing middle classes in this period, the growing predominance of cities and towns over the countryside, and the predominance in public opinion of the press and literate classes. In its more conservative forms liberalism merges with conservatism, which generally upholds established propertied elites, particularly aristocracies and monarchies, more adamantly, gives precedence to prerogative, and seeks to limit the onset of democracy. In its more radical variations it merges with radicalism, which generally implies a commitment to the greater extension of the suffrage towards democracy and popular sovereignty, and, by the late nineteenth century, to social reforms favouring the labouring classes that imply a substantial degree of state intervention. Liberals were thus capable of identifying with socialism, though this is uncommon before the 1870s. At the other extreme, individualist liberalism shares with anarchism a dogmatic suspicion of politics and state power.

Liberalism is usually understood as wedding a political philosophy committed, minimally, to the protection of civil rights and safeguarding against state tyranny, with an economic philosophy dedicated to promoting *laissez-faire*. Both ideas are seen to rest on a similar faith in individual initiative, the desire for self-improvement and the capacity for individuals contracting together in society to produce both opulence and liberty when permitted to do so. Though liberalism is often confused with 'democracy', this formula does not require 'democracy' as such; most nineteenth-century liberals resisted demands for universal suffrage, particularly when applied to women or non-European peoples. Some, notably TOCQUEVILLE, specifically described democracy as a threat to liberty, while regarding its arrival as inevitable. Others, such as J.S. MILL, further contended that the basic principles of liberal society were applicable only to 'civilized' peoples, not 'backward'

societies. A number of leading thinkers in this period, such as G.W.F. Hegel (see HEGEL AND HEGELIANISM), were liberal according to some criteria, but not others. Nor was liberalism necessarily republican, except in the USA, and intermittently in France; rather, it sought the constitutional limitation of monarchical powers, rather than their abolition. Nor, though linked in its origins to Protestantism, was liberalism widely viewed as incompatible with other forms of religious persuasion. It could be intimately intertwined with religion, as in ACTON's confession of his belief 'that political Rights proceed directly from religious duties, and hold this to be the true basis of Liberalism', or scarcely linked at all, as in J.S. Mill's system. And though it frequently allied itself to imperialism, its ranks included some of the most vocal critics of empire.

The historical origins of liberalism lie in the confluence of demands for greater freedom of trade, epitomized in Adam Smith's *Wealth of Nations* (1776); demands for greater religious toleration, freedom of the press and civil liberty, which are particularly pronounced in seventeenth- and eighteenth-century Britain, and are often associated with the writings of John Locke; demands for the limitation of state power by tempering executive power through representative institutions, widely associated with Britain's 'Glorious Revolution' of 1688, famously embellished in Montesquieu's *Spirit of the Laws* (1748); then the American Revolution of 1776, and the French Revolution of 1789. Throughout the nineteenth century liberal principles were identified with Britain and the USA in particular. This article will survey the major national traditions of liberal thought in the period, namely Britain, France and the USA, and summarize trends elsewhere.

British liberalism

Besides the free-trade ideals of Adam Smith, nineteenth-century British liberalism was most indebted to the utilitarianism of JEREMY BENTHAM (1748–1832), whose famous slogan was that society should maximize the 'greatest happiness of the greatest number'. Bentham echoed the presumption of most liberals that individuals were naturally prone to seek their own interest, defined as the pursuit of pleasure and avoidance of pain. Only an adequate system of legislation and education could instil a sense of the duty to prefer the greatest happiness when calculating the effects of actions, which was for Bentham the sole legitimate basis of morality. Practically, Bentham's main concerns were with legal, penal and poor law reform; around 1809 he converted to radicalism, and urged universal suffrage, as well as the disestablishment of the state Church. His most important immediate disciple was the historian and India Office employee JAMES MILL (1773–1836), who helped to link utilitarianism to political economy through his friendship with DAVID RICARDO, and whose *Essay on Government* (1819) posited a science of politics based on Benthamism. This urged the wide extension of the franchise (but not to women), the secret ballot and frequent elections, and argued against the orthodox Whig plea for balanced government, contending that a single assembly might adequately represent the interests of the majority, which Mill largely construed in terms of the middle class. These arguments were famously opposed by the Whig historian T.B. MACAULAY in an article published in the *Edinburgh Review* in 1829, which voiced traditional suspicions about universal suffrage in particular.

The most famous interpreter of Benthamism, and theorist of Victorian liberalism, was James Mill's son, John Stuart Mill (1806–73). By the late 1820s he had come to challenge the Benthamite legacy, arguing that Bentham's world-view was incomplete and overly mechanical, and did not allow, in particular, for the necessity of individuals to form their own character for themselves. This stress on individuality, which was to become a characteristically Millite theme, was wedded to the conviction that social progress generally required a guiding intellectual elite, whose authority was increasingly under attack the more democratic society became. Here Mill was much influenced by Tocqueville's *Democracy in America*. The quintessential defence of this idea was offered in *On Liberty* (1859), in which Mill argued that society had the right to interfere in the actions of individuals only when they harmed others. Freedom of thought, he contended, should be virtually unlimited; limiting action required proving that some 'distinct and assignable obligation' to others had been violated. As with Bentham, a clear concern here is to render legislation more transparent by uniformly applying utilitarian harm principles, and avoiding

the anarchic, unjust effects of popular prejudice, particularly in religious affairs. Mill's plea that all individuals were sovereign in matters that were solely self-, as opposed to other-, regarding, however, was not extended to the inhabitants of backward nations; he had followed his father in to the India Office, and advised that 'despotism' was a legitimate mode of rule over 'backward' nations, provided that it assisted their improvement towards civilization. Besides offering a variety of examples to test the validity of the self/other-regarding distinction, Mill in *On Liberty* gives a vigorous defence of the principle of 'individuality', or the possession of the qualities of genius, creativity, originality and spontaneity, summed up in the capacity of individuals to form their own character. This alone permitted the emergence of new modes of social arrangement, and thus prevented society from slipping into the repetitive incantation of habitual ideas and mores, which Mill thought was an inevitable cause of social decline. Mill here envisioned a particular type of ideal character, vigorous, self-asserting and energetic, but also capable of stoic self-denial, and of the willingness to sacrifice one's own happiness for that of others, which Mill in *Utilitarianism* describes as the 'highest virtue which can be found in man'. However, Mill both in his *Autobiography* (1873) and other works acknowledged a willingness to consider that the existing social ideal of entrepreneurial effort and economic expansion might some day be supplanted by a greater concern with qualitative, cultural and humanist ends.

Mill in two other works of his maturity, *Considerations on Representative Government* (1861) and *Utilitarianism* (1863), approaches elitism from different directions. The former work, while defending representative institutions, contends that majoritarian democracy fails to give due heed to minority opinion, and proposes a scheme for proportional representation popularized by Thomas Hare, in which votes could be transferred to candidates on a national list, such that the eventual composition of an assembly would reflect accurately the division of opinion in society as a whole. This would help to offset what Mill claims are the two main dangers of modern democracy, the low intellectual level of legislators, and the propensity for the working classes to legislate in their own interest rather than those of the whole society. In *Utilitarianism* Mill develops a distinction between 'higher' and 'lower' pleasures in order to contend that a hedonistic philosophy did not degrade human nature, but rather privileged the judgement of those who had a wide experience of a range of pleasures. In his last major political work, *The Subjection of Women* (1869), finally, Mill offers the case for extending the principle of meritocracy to women in the economic sphere, and extending a full range of rights to property, responsibility for their children and the ability to separate, within the institution of marriage. The chief enemy here, as in other works, is paternalism.

Another important strand in mid-nineteenth-century British liberalism was represented by the free-trade agitation of RICHARD COBDEN (1804–65), a Manchester calico-manufacturer, and John Bright (1811–89), a Quaker mill owner, often described as the political face of the 'Manchester School' in political economy. Both helped to found the Anti-Corn Law League in 1839, which brought about the repeal of the Corn Laws, or price supports for landowners, in 1846. Both were committed to political and administrative reform, but opposed governmental interference in trade and industry, including the regulation of hours of labour, except for children. In various works, notably *England, Ireland and America* (1835) and *Russia* (1836), Cobden in particular applied free-trade ideals to the international order, contending that the existing system of a 'balance of power' promoted war, militarism and political despotism. Both were vehement critics of Britain's expansionist imperial policies, and opposed conflict with Russia at the time of the Crimean War. Cobden, in particular, continued the free-trade internationalist tradition begun by Smith and PAINE, in promoting pacifism and universal prosperity rather than free-trade imperialism, and favoured international arbitration and the reduction of armaments. Some of these principles, notably retrenchment at home and avoidance of imperial adventurism abroad, were agreeable to the most important liberal statesman of the century, W.E. Gladstone (1809–98), who was four times prime minister, and who famously described liberalism as 'trust in the people qualified by prudence', as opposed to conservatism, which was 'distrust of the people, qualified by fear'.

A further variation on the stress given to maximizing liberty and reducing state interference was presented by HERBERT SPENCER (1820–1903), an influential philosopher, sociologist and psychologist.

Even before Darwin, Spencer had presented the case for a general theory of evolution, in which human progress is seen in terms of a movement from the homogeneous to the heterogeneous. Having coined the phrase, 'the survival of the fittest', Spencer applied it much more wholeheartedly than Darwin, much less writers like A.R. WALLACE or T.H. HUXLEY. Governmental interference with poverty in particular, he came to argue, would inhibit the basic evolutionary process by which the 'fit' separated themselves from the 'less fit'. Spencer's extreme individualism was outlined most clearly in *The Man versus the State* (1884), which warned against the 'coming slavery' that an accretion of gradual encroachments on individual liberty, such as the regulation of foodstuffs, factory inspection and the growth of state education, would engender.

Spencer's views, however, were out of keeping with much late nineteenth-century British opinion. By 1890, amid depression and considerable poverty, many liberals had come to believe that the predominant individualism and self-help, anti-paternalism of the mid-Victorian period needed to be replaced by an ideal that recognized that the state could play a central and positive role in aiding the poor. By 1910, often driven initially by evangelical humanitarian reformers like Lord Shaftesbury, the scope of state action was progressively extended to the protection of labourers at work, their education beforehand and their security afterwards, by pension and insurance schemes. Amongst the most important of the 'New Liberal' writers to propose such a view of the state was J.A. HOBSON (1858–1940), author of *The Evolution of Modern Capitalism* (1894), *The Problem of the Unemployed* (1896), *The Economics of Distribution* (1900), *The Social Problem* (1901), *Imperialism* (1902) and other works. Hobson wedded a humanist ideal drawn in part from JOHN RUSKIN to a theory of social organism indebted to Social Darwinist writers in order to contend that society collectively, notably in the form of the state, had the duty to improve the lives of its members and guide them towards a higher evolutionary end. Liberty, rather than being seen as a merely negative avoidance of state interference, now was understood in terms of the positive contribution the state could make in developing human potential. Such views were lent substantial support through the influence of the Oxford Idealist philosopher T.H. GREEN (1836–82), who stressed in his *Prolegomena to Ethics* (1883) and other works the social context in which individual freedom could alone be achieved, and the duty of social and political institutions to foster the moral character of individuals.

Continental liberalism

FRANCE

French liberalism after the Restoration of the Bourbons was necessarily deeply influenced by the British model of constitutional monarchy, and often gave a conservative emphasis to the need for social stability, the importance of laws, the limitation of executive power and the restriction of popular participation in politics, notably in the writings of FRANÇOIS GUIZOT (1787–1874), leader of the group, with PIERRE PAUL ROYER-COLLARD (1763–1845), known as the 'Doctrinaires', who sought a middle way between absolutism and democracy. Royer-Collard stressed the importance of preserving freedom of the press, of Parliament and of the judiciary, and regarded religious freedom as the foundation of both society generally and the limitation of Jacobinical or Bonapartist state power in particular. Guizot became much more conservative after the Revolution of 1830, and remained a determined opponent of democracy, finally being forced into exile after the 1848 Revolution. Another prominent theorist of liberalism after the Restoration was Germain Necker, Baronne DE STAËL (1766–1817), who with BENJAMIN CONSTANT (1767–1830) warned of the propensities of both Bonapartism and monarchical absolutism, and advocated emulation of the British constitutional model (see her *Considerations on the French Revolution*, 1818). An anti-Bonapartist, Constant saw freedom of the press as the best security for protecting liberal principles. He was instrumental in bringing Louis-Philippe to the throne in 1830.

A more moderate liberalism emerged after the 1830 Revolution. Its leading intellectual figure, ALEXIS DE TOCQUEVILLE (1805–59), is best-known for his *Democracy in America* (2 vols, 1835–40), which asserted that an overpowering spirit of equality in the USA tended to undermine minority rights and to produce a 'tyranny of the majority' in public opinion. In his assessment of French politics after 1830 Tocqueville stressed the triumph of the middle classes and a concomitant growth in equality of conditions. Regarding the

trend towards governmental centralization and increasing uniformity as inevitable, Tocqueville argued that the state bureaucracy would tend increasingly to act both as a new aristocracy and as caretaker for the needs of the majority, who would gradually cede all powers of self-responsibility to it. These themes were reiterated in his later *The Ancien Régime and the Revolution* (1856). During this period the Positivist doctrines of AUGUSTE COMTE (1798–1857) also influenced liberalism, particularly through their stress on the need for meritocracy. After 1848 a more radical form of liberalism began to emerge. Romantic writers like ALPHONSE DE LAMARTINE (1790–1867) urged a reassessment of the positive elements of the 1789 Revolution, while VICTOR HUGO (1802–85) saw a democratic ideal as an alternative to socialism after 1848. Following Louis Napoleon's *coup d'état* in 1851 conservative and Catholic liberals like Charles de Montalembert (1810–70) again stressed the validity of the British constitutional model. In this period a republican opposition also emerged, which included such thinkers as Hugo, the historian Edgar Quinet (1803–75) and the lawyer Léon Gambetta (1838–82).

GERMANY

German liberals in the early nineteenth century were concerned in the first instance with liberation from French rule, then with avoiding an extreme reaction after the defeat of Napoleon. The movement for national unification did not develop substantially before 1848, but became a central focus for liberal thought thereafter. Prior to this German liberals were concerned with plans for creating popular representative assemblies, introducing freedom of the press and similar rights, and establishing economic freedom. As with France, the British model was particularly important to German writers, but until late in the century social and economic conditions in Germany were not analogous to Britain's, while the strength of the monarchy and landed aristocracy, particularly in Prussia, was more difficult to limit. Republican liberalism, accordingly, remained much weaker than in France, while Romantic conceptions of a common fatherland were correspondingly stronger. Economic liberalism, too, was correspondingly weak, and the protectionist spirit, epitomized in FRIEDRICH LIST's *National System of Political Economy* (1841), stronger. Unless we except Georg

Wilhelm Friedrich Hegel (1770–1831), whose conception of constitutional monarchy outlined in his *Philosophy of Right* (1821) represents at best a very conservative liberalism, Germany produced few liberal thinkers of international stature. Of note, however, are the writings of the Prussian legal reformer Heinrich von Stein (1757–1831); the development of individualism in Wilhelm Humboldt's *Essay on the Limits of the Action of the State* (1851); the constitutionalist programme of the Göttingen professors' protest against the Hanoverian government in 1837; and the various manifestos and programmes issued during the 1848 revolutions, which concentrated on freeing Germany from Austrian influence and founding a new liberal constitution. An important strand of economic liberalism was represented in the co-operative movement founded by Hermann Schulze-Delitzsch (1808–83).

ITALY

Like their German counterparts, nineteenth-century Italian liberals were commonly concerned first with national liberation, then national unification. The best-known figure of the early period is indisputably the radical democrat and republican GIUSEPPE MAZZINI (1805–72), whose secret revolutionary society, Young Italy, sought a unified Italian republic founded on patriotic and Christian principles. Mazzini was however critical of materialist, anarchic and individualist trends in liberalism, preferring an organicist, and populist but anti-socialist, view of society. Most Italian liberals did not go as far as Mazzini towards democracy. The prominent Risorgimento nationalist leader Count Camillio Cavour (1810–61) sought to develop a competitive agricultural economy by ending feudal land tenures and protectionist barriers, and selling Church lands. Two Italian liberal writers active in 1848 of note are Cesare Balbo (1789–1853), an associate of Cavour's, and Massimo d'Azeglio (1798–1866), who became premier of Sardinia, 1849–52. After 1848 the most prominent nationalist figure was Giuseppe Garibaldi (1807–82), who led a series of attempts to establish a republic.

US liberalism

After Britain the USA provided the second most important constitutional model in this period, and one that differed from the British both in its republicanism, its greater democracy and absence of a landed aristocracy, its separation of Church and state, its greater decentralization and protection of states' rights, and its emphasis on natural and civil rights. While virtually all US political thought was, in this sense, 'liberal' (even including pro-slavery arguments, since these had been part of British political discourse until slavery was abolished in 1833), there were important variations within the democratic tradition, and divisions over many issues. The tradition known as Jeffersonian democracy, after Thomas Jefferson (1743–1826), 3rd president of the USA, stressed the USA's commitment to equality, natural rights, the right of resistance to tyranny and the foundation of government in the consent of the governed. These trends were continued in the programmes of Andrew Jackson (1767–1845), 7th president of the USA, whose movement, known as Jacksonian Democracy, stressed the importance of the common man, the sovereignty of the people and the independence not only of small landowners but now also of urban artisans. Jackson's populism resulted in an enhancement of executive power at the expense of the legislative, a general extension of the suffrage from a property qualification to a manhood basis and the widespread abandonment of property and religious qualifications for political office. The most important political difference of the era was of course the question of how far the federal system permitted relative sovereignty to the states, and whether they had a right to secede, which resulted in the American Civil War (1861–5). During this conflict Abraham Lincoln (1809–65), 16th US president, used ideas of natural rights, and particularly natural equality, in order to argue against slavery, which he finally abolished in 1863. During the late nineteenth century US liberalism was influenced by SOCIAL DARWINISM, resulting in a greater emphasis upon individualism, but also by various forms of radicalism, particularly the single-tax movement of HENRY GEORGE (1839–97), and socialism, notably in the form of the Nationalist movement of EDWARD BELLAMY (1850–98). One response to this was a gradual movement towards a more collectivist and interventionist idea of the state, which acknowledged a much wider scope for paternal responsibility than was conceded at the beginning of the century.

Conclusion: liberalism elsewhere

Liberal movements had developed within all of the great autocracies, such as Austro-Hungary and Russia, by the end of this period. Elsewhere in the world, liberalism had an ambivalent reputation, for it was the ideology of empire as well as independence. By the end of the nineteenth century European influence throughout the world was, as a consequence of imperial conquest, at its peak, and the lesson was not lost that European technological superiority, commercial freedom and representative institutions might not be intimately inter-related. European rule did not as such popularize liberalism, because imperialism was intrinsically illiberal. The extension of domestic political institutions through colonies of Britons, for example in Canada or Australia, through the right of self-rule, was increasingly accepted as the century wore on; the right of native populations to a share in that rule was not. The marriage of Western industrial organization to feudal institutions in Japan proved that modernity did not as such generate democracy, and that economic liberalism was not incompatible with authoritarianism of various types. The reaction against the colonial oppressor could also engender anti-modernist, though not necessarily anti-democratic, sentiments, as was the case with MOHANDAS GANDHI's eventual designs for Indian village self-sufficiency and decentralized industry. From the first wave of national independence movements of the period, in South America led by SIMON BOLIVAR (1788–1830), attempts were made to found constitutional republics throughout the region, the British and US models in particular remained attractive to liberals throughout the less developed world. By 1900, however, socialist ideals of economic organization seemed to many colonized peoples more applicable to less industrialised nations, with New Liberals like John Hobson pressing the case against empire at home.

Further reading

Arblaster, A. (1984) *The Rise and Decline of Western Liberalism*, Oxford: Basil Blackwell.

Bellamy, Richard (1992) *Liberalism and Modern Society*, Cambridge: Polity Press.

Hobhouse, Leonard (1911) *Liberalism*, London: Williams & Norgate.

Hobson, J.A. (1909) *The Crisis of Liberalism*, London: P.S. King.

Laski, Harold (1936) *The Rise of European Liberalism*, London: George Allen & Unwin.

Manning, D.J. (1976) *Liberalism*, New York: St Martin's Press.

Robertson, J.M. (1912) *The Meaning of Liberalism*, London: Methuen.

Ruggiero, Guido de (1959) *The History of European Liberalism*, Boston, MA: Beacon Press.

Samuel, Herbert (1902) *Liberalism*, London: Grant Richards.

Sandel, Michael (ed.) (1984) *Liberalism and Its Critics*, Oxford: Basil Blackwell.

Sheehan, James (1978) *German Liberalism in the Nineteenth Century*, Chicago, IL: University of Chicago Press.

Simon, W.M. (ed.) (1972) *French Liberalism 1789–1848*, New York: John Wiley.

SEE ALSO: conservatism, authority and tradition; democracy, populism and rights; Hegel and Hegelianism; intellectuals, elites and meritocracy; the nation, nationalism and the national principle; political economy; social theory and sociology in the nineteenth century; theories of the state and society: the science of politics

GREGORY CLAEYS

LIEBKNECHT, WILHELM (1826–1900)

Wilhelm Liebknecht was at the forefront of the development of socialism in Germany. With August Bebel he founded the Saxon Workers' Party in 1865 and the German Social Democratic Workers' Party in 1869. His political career began with participation in the failed Baden uprising of 1848–9. He then fled to Switzerland where he was imprisoned, following which he went into exile in London until 1862. There he became a regular visitor to the Marx household. His *Karl Marx. Biographical Memoirs* is the fullest direct account we have of Marx's life with his family and London friends. Once Liebknecht returned to Germany, Marx tried to use him to guide the development of German socialism. This was not an enviable situation. Marx and Engels suffered the frustrations of having assumed intellectual leadership while being devoid of actual power. Disciple though he was, Liebknecht did not always do his masters' bidding, or at least not to their full satisfaction. In spite of his loyalty they referred to him as 'that dumb ox', 'donkey' and 'little William'. Liebknecht certainly did not choose the easiest life. He first entered Parliament in 1867 but interspersed the more dignified side of his political career with frequent spells in prison for his insults to the army and the monarchy.

With the outbreak of the Franco-Prussian war Liebknecht showed what use could be made of a public forum and what costs had to be borne. Rather than succumb to the allure of the parliamentary arena, he used his position to express hostility to chauvinism abroad and repression at home. The result was predictable. Following his opposition to the German annexation of the French provinces of Alsace and Lorraine, abstention on the war credits and his sympathetic attitude to the 1871 Paris Commune, Liebknecht, with Bebel, was arrested on a charge of high treason. He used the courtroom as a platform for propagating his political ideas and so, in March 1872, was sentenced to 2 years' imprisonment. In this instance Marx and Engels were delighted with Liebknecht's radical stance. His imprisonment confirmed that he had been doing the right thing: making demands incompatible with the prevailing socio-political order.

For much of his political career Liebknecht managed to combine membership of the Reichstag with the general principle of anti-parliamentarism. However, by the middle 1880s the paradox of his position caught up with him. He suddenly concluded that parliamentary institutions could function as more than mere propaganda platforms; they might also provide instruments for the achievement of socialism.

This change of emphasis sits uneasily with Liebknecht's battle against BERNSTEIN's revisionism. Liebknecht argued that the contradictions of capitalism were actually getting deeper, making it all the more necessary to keep the idea of class conflict in the forefront. Where Bernstein thought the movement was everything and the final goal nothing, Liebknecht saw the two as intertwined. The movement had to be towards the final goal of the overthrow of capitalist society. Liebknecht thought that if Bernstein's proposals were followed the party would no longer be a working-class one. He felt that whereas he had gone to England and become a Marxist, Bernstein had gone there and become a Fabian. It seemed wrong of Bernstein to import English assumptions into Germany. Germany was more backward; its middle class had not won an independent position but had, instead, abdicated political power to the Junkers, the traditional landowning class. It was this contrast between an anachronistic social and political order and the rapid development of modern industry that made fundamental conflict inevitable. It was not, Liebknecht stated, that he personally wanted conflict but rather the recalcitrance of the ruling powers that made it inevitable. This more militant stance was more than replicated in the actions of his more famous son, Karl Liebknecht, who co-founded the revolutionary Spartacist movement in 1916 and the German Communist Party in 1918.

Further reading

Dominick, R. (1982) *Wilhelm Liebknecht and the Founding of the German Social Democratic Party*, Chapel Hill: University of North Carolina Press.

Lidtke, V.L. (1966) *The Outlawed Party. Social Democracy in Germany, 1878–1890*, Princeton: Princeton University Press.

Liebknecht, W. (1901) *Karl Marx: Biographical Memories*, Chicago: C.H. Kerr.

—— (1963) *Briefwechsel mit Karl Marx und Friedrich Engels*, The Hague: Mouton.

SEE ALSO: Bebel, Auguste; Bernstein, Eduard; Marx and Marxism

MICHAEL LEVIN

LINCOLN, ABRAHAM (1809–1865)

The 16th president of the USA, Abraham Lincoln was born on 12 February 1809, and died by assassination on 14 April 1865. He remains famous as the leader who guided Union policy during the American Civil War (1861–5), and in whose famous, and famously brief, Gettysburg Address of 19 November 1863, popularized the notion of 'government of the people, by the people, for the people'. His name remains indelibly associated with the anti-slavery cause.

Lincoln was raised on a farm in Kentucky, but moved to Indiana and then Illinois, where he was elected to the state legislature in 1834. An unassuming Whig congressman between 1845–9, he returned home to further his law practice, but re-entered politics in 1854 by intervening in debates about the extension of slavery to new states, which he unequivocally opposed in a famous debate with Stephen Douglas. Also evident in this period was a deep concern with the poor, and with securing them free or cheap land. Having opposed John Brown's efforts to foster a slave insurrection, Lincoln securing the presidency in the 1860 election, willing to tolerate slavery in the South but not its extension to new states. Although he proclaimed that his 'policy is to have no policy', Lincoln was more than merely pragmatic in his approach to the war. Having survived severe setbacks in the early years of the conflict, Lincoln reinforced the temporary quasi-dictatorial powers of the President during national emergencies, giving greater strength to the executive than previously, by all accounts ruling tyrannically over his cabinet as well, and frequently insisting in public on the need for such powers to be concentrated in the hands of the President. Credited with created a unified command structure geared to mobilizing the entire nation on a war footing by 1863, despite early confusion, Lincoln achieved a remarkable reputation as a commander.

But slavery, which he condemned in 1854 as a 'monstrous injustice' that deprived 'our republican example of its just influence in the world', remained an overriding concern throughout his political career. Yet he was pragmatic in his approach to abolition during the war, overturning early orders of emancipation by his generals in conquered territories, and arguing in August 1862 that his object was 'to save the Union . . . not either to save or destroy slavery'. Nonetheless he offered a tentative Emancipation Proclamation in September 1862, rendered permanent in January 1863. Throughout the war Lincoln nonetheless insisted that the USA remained a federal system in which the North had no right as such to dominate the South. Like his hero Jefferson he regarded slavery, however, as an essentially aristocratic institution hostile to the interests of ordinary people. The Civil War, seen from this viewpoint, was a defence of American democracy and the idea of self-government as such. In a spirit of magnanimity he also proposed a generous reconstruction programme for the South for post-war development.

Further reading

Handlin, Oscar (1980) *Abraham Lincoln and the Union*, Boston: Little, Brown.
Lincoln, Abraham (1899–1906) *The Complete Works of Abraham Lincoln*, New York: Francis D. Tandy
Macpherson, James M. (1991) *Abraham Lincoln and the Second American Revolution*, Oxford: Oxford University Press.

GREGORY CLAEYS

LIST, FRIEDRICH (1789–1846)

Born in Reutlingen, the son of an artisan, the economist Friedrich List was appointed to a chair in government at Tübingen in 1817 and was elected to the Württemberg parliament in 1820. He established his reputation as a liberal opponent of tariffs on behalf of the south German industrialists. As a result he lost his teaching post in 1820 and his seat in the Landtag in 1821. He was imprisoned for his political views, and released only when he undertook to emigrate to the USA, where her edited a German newspaper in Pennsylvania and became a US citizen. List was an unsuccessful businessman, but quickly became a national figure when he became involved with the Pennsylvania Society for the Promotion of Manufactures and the Mechanic Arts, and took up its protectionist cause.

List was influenced by the US school of 'national' economists, who opposed free trade on the grounds that it disproportionately favoured the dominant economic power (then Great Britain) at the expense of emergent manufacturing economies (such as the USA or Germany), which found it difficult to establish themselves under the conditions dictated by classical economic liberalism. His *Outlines of American Political Economy* (1827) argued that an infant industrial economy needed protection.

List returned to Germany in 1834 as American Consul in Leipzig where he became an active supporter of railway construction, and campaigned for protectionist measures to assist German industry through its early stages. He proposed a semi-protectionist 'national system' in Germany, and envisaged its expansion into southeast Central Europe. Austria should be in the German customs union (*Zollverein*), he wrote in 1843; its railway connection to Trieste would bring that port a 'German national' significance. He also proposed subsidies to divert German emigrants from North America to southeastern Central Europe, arguing that emigration to North America constituted a loss of valuable resources to the national economy. The importance to List's thinking of the nation, as the principal subdivision 'between each individual and entire humanity', is reflected in his *National System of Political Economy* (1841), the most important statement of his thinking. As a forerunner of the German historical school of economics List was sceptical of the universal applicability of a theoretical system such as that envisaged in classical economics. International free trade would only work if all nations were at an equivalent stage of economic development, and this was patently not so. Economic 'laws' therefore would necessarily be affected by the social and institutional framework – or national context – within which economic activity took place. Moreover he argued convincingly that although Britain was now a passionate advocate of free trade because it suited British interests, its present position was based on a history of protectionism and encouragement of native manufacturing: 'Had the English left everything to itself… England would have still continued to be the sheep-farm of the Hansards, just as Portugal became the vineyard of England'. Once industries were established, he argued, free trade could then be allowed. His attempts to persuade the political authorities in Germany met with little success and, impoverished and disappointed, he committed suicide in 1846.

Further reading

Henderson, W.O. (1983) *Friedrich List, Economist and Visionary*, London: Frank Cass.
Szporluk, Roman (1988) *Communism and Nationalism. Karl Marx versus Friedrich List*, Oxford: Oxford University Press.

SEE ALSO: political economy

TIM KIRK

LOMBROSO, CESARE (1835–1909)

The Italian criminologist and psychiatrist Cesare Lombroso was born into a Jewish family in Verona in 1835 and studied medicine at the universities of Pavia, Padua and Vienna. While in Vienna he began to develop his life-long interest in the connections between psychology and anatomy, an area of research that was attracting growing academic attention in the 1850s in Europe thanks largely to the work of French doctors such as B.A. Morel and Paul Broca. While Lombroso was not directly influenced by their studies, his own early research made use of similar conceptual suppositions and experimental techniques. One of his first projects involved an investigation of the links between cretinism and diet in Lombardy, in which he demonstrated through careful empirical

research that the degenerative disease pellagra was caused not just by vitamin deficiency but also by poisoning arising from maize rotting while in storage.

Between 1859 and 1863 Lombroso was attached to the Piedmontese army as a surgeon and served in southern Italy. His first-hand experience here of brigandage – at that time a major problem threatening the new Italian kingdom – confirmed him in his belief that mental abnormalities and crime needed to be studied in relation to the physical and biological characteristics of individual criminals rather than in the abstract. This view received further reinforcement during a spell as director of a lunatic asylum in Pavia, where he was able to continue his experimental work on the biological abnormalities accompanying 'alienation'. Lombroso's first studies of insanity and crime, *Genius and Madness* (1863) and *An Experimental and Anthropological Treatise on Delinquent Man* (1872), attracted little interest, but the 1876 edition of *Delinquent Man*, which appeared at a time of intense debate about the nature of Italy's social problems, especially those in the south of the country, proved astonishingly successful. It went through many subsequent editions and was widely translated.

At the heart of Lombroso's view of crime lay a rejection of the whole classical tradition of criminal law, with its notions of free will, morality and individual responsibility. Deviancy, he argued, was not an abstraction but rather a social and human reality brought about by a range of factors, which might vary in relation to each offender and which needed to be approached and studied scientifically. He accepted that social environment, climate, diet and occupation could all contribute to criminal behaviour, but he insisted that the principal determinant was an inherited proclivity. The criminal, like the madman, was the product of biological degeneracy, and the task of the criminologist was to examine and catalogue the external manifestations of degeneracy in order to arrive at a general typology of criminals. This would then be used as the basis for a radical reappraisal of current procedures for punishment and rehabilitation.

Lombroso's views were heavily influenced by contemporary evolutionary theories. The physical peculiarities of criminals – their cranial dimensions, jaw and ear shapes, facial asymmetries, density of body hair (not to mention their penchant for tattoos, slang, alcohol and sexual promiscuity) – were relics, or what he called 'stigmata', from man's primitive past. 'Criminals are neither lunatics nor are they normal beings; they are abnormal beings who bear certain physical attributes of our ancestors, of monkey and carnivores...they are atavistic beings.' However, he was careful to eschew excessive determinism and argued that not all criminals were equally the product of biological degeneracy. He maintained a sharp distinction between casual criminals, who might be drawn into offending as a result of environmental or social pressures, and who might thus be successfully rehabilitated, and 'born' criminals, who were wholly incorrigible and against whom society needed to protect itself.

Lombroso was a strong critic of contemporary penal and police practices in Italy, and argued that since crime was specific to the criminal, the state needed to be more rigorously scientific and targeted in its approach to the problems of deviancy. He called for prison reform, and urged the segregation of casual from habitual offenders in order to avoid the former being vitiated by the latter; and he wanted the penal law to be in general more progressive in its handling of socially determined forms of crime, and more severe in its treatment of 'born' criminals. However, the influence of Lombroso and his increasingly wide circle of followers (among whom was the brilliant and flamboyant young socialist Enrico Ferri) on policy-makers was limited, and the new Italian Penal Code of 1889 failed to incorporate any of their principles. This greatly angered Lombroso. During the 1890s he briefly gave his support to the Socialist Party, and in 1896 he stood as a socialist candidate for the city council of Turin.

From 1876 Lombroso held chairs in Forensic Medicine and Hygiene, Psychiatry and Criminal Anthropology at the University of Turin. Besides new and expanded editions of *Delinquent Man*, and other works on aspects of crime and its causes, he ventured into the field of political criminality in 1894 with a study of anarchism. In this he suggested that anarchists were physically and mentally abnormal – though in different ways to habitual criminals – and that their behaviour might stem from a form of delirium brought about by excessive idealism. No less indicative of the limits of his 'scientific' approach was his study of female delinquency (*Delinquent Woman*, 1893), in which he argued that the natural form of biological degeneracy in women was prostitution, not crime

('primitive woman was impure rather than criminal'), and that prostitutes posed a particularly insidious threat to the social order in as much as they embodied the antitheses of 'normal' female qualities such as chastity, loyalty and graciousness.

Lombroso's work was widely translated and proved highly influential among criminologists and jurists in Europe and parts of South America. He died in Turin in 1909.

Further reading

Gibson, Mary (2002) *Born to Crime. Cesare Lombroso and the Origins of Biological Criminology*, Westport, CT: Praeger.
Pick, Daniel (1989) *Faces of Degeneration. A European Disorder,* c.*1848*–c.*1918*, Cambridge: Cambridge University Press.

SEE ALSO: Social Darwinism; social theory and sociology in the nineteenth century; theories of law, criminology and penal reform

CHRISTOPHER DUGGAN

LUXEMBURG, ROSA (1870–1919)

The revolutionary socialist and theoretician Rosa Luxemburg was born at Zamość in Russian Poland and studied Law and Political Economy at Zurich University, where she gained a doctorate in 1898. Although she was a co-founder of the Polish Social Democratic Party (in Switzerland) and a participant in the Russian Revolution of 1905, she had acquired German citizenship through marriage and had moved to Berlin some years earlier.

Luxemburg made her name during the debates about revisionism within German social democracy during the 1890s, when she responded to Bernstein's critique of a perceived determinism in Marxism with a counter-critique of his reformist position in *Social Reform or Revolution* (1900). Bernstein had observed that society was not changing in the way Marxists had anticipated, and that socialism was not so much a necessary outcome of inevitable historical developments, but a desirable state of affairs, and that improvements in the standard of living of the worker needed to be fought for through economic organizations (the trade unions) and in Parliament. Luxemburg did not deny that this kind of political activity was also necessary under prevailing conditions, but maintained that the crises and contradictions of capitalism would continue as long as the system itself, and that only by taking power for itself and abolishing existing social and economic relations would the workers' movement achieve its ultimate goals. She also continued to intervene in the politics of Russian social democracy. In the wake of the split in the party between Bolsheviks and Mensheviks she criticized Lenin's autocratic approach to leadership, arguing against the 'mechanical subordination and blind obedience of the party membership to the leading party centre'. (*Organisational Questions of Russian Social Democracy*, 1904). Her major theoretical work, *The Accumulation of Capital* (1913) sought to explain the phenomenon of imperialism and its relationship to the capitalist system. She argued that a capitalist economy would be unable to absorb all the surplus value it produced unless it had access to non-capitalist societies. Imperialism was the competition of capitalist systems for the dwindling remains of the non-capitalist world. The imperialist war she anticipated came the following year, prompting her – as a passionate internationalist – to oppose the SPD's initially patriotic stance in the *Junius Pamphlet* (1915), the founding statement of the International Group, later the Spartacus League, which she founded with Karl Liebknecht. Luxemburg spent most of the war in prison, and this gave

her time to write *The Russian Revolution* (1918), in which she expressed her solidarity with the Bolshevik leaders, while remaining critical of their economic policies and overreadiness to clamp down on democracy within the party. She engaged actively in the politics of the German revolution of 1918, as a member of the Spartacus League (which she founded with Karl Liebknecht), and of the KPD (the German Communist Party), she was a participant in the January 1919 uprising in Berlin. She was murdered, along with Liebknecht, by radical right-wing Freikorps members employed by the government to suppress the rebellion.

Further reading

Basso, Lelio (1975) *Rosa Luxemburg: A Reappraisal*, London: Deutsch.
Luxemburg, Rosa (1951) *The Accumulation of Capital*, ed. W. Stark, London: Routledge and Kegan Paul.
Nettl, J.P. (1966) *Rosa Luxemburg*, Oxford: Oxford University Press.

SEE ALSO: Marx and Marxism

TIM KIRK

M

MACAULAY, THOMAS BABINGTON (1800–59)

The English historian, Thomas Babington Macaulay, was born in Leicestershire in 1800. He is best known for *The History of England from the Accession of James II* (1849–61), published in five volumes, but he was also an essayist, a poet and a Whig cabinet minister. He served as an MP three times (1830–4, 1839–47, 1852–6) and was made a peer, Lord Macaulay of Rothley, in 1857. The rest of this entry outlines his career in greater detail, discusses his political and literary ideas, and comments upon his famous 'Whig interpretation of history'. Macaulay assumed that (in general) material, moral and scientific progress was ongoing, provided politicians avoided extremist policies that confused anarchy with liberty, and despotism with civil order.

Thomas Macaulay was the son of Zachary Macaulay, a wealthy Scottish merchant, and Selina Mills Macaulay, the daughter of a prosperous Bristol bookseller. In 1802, the family moved to Clapham, where Zachary, a prominent evangelical campaigner against slavery, could liaise more readily with fellow members of the campaign – the so-called 'Clapham sect' – such as William Wilberforce, Charles Grant and Henry Thornton. In this pious, but rationalistic, context, Thomas Macaulay emerged as a child prodigy, composing a 'Compendium of Universal History' when he was a 7-year-old. However, unlike his slightly younger contemporary, JOHN STUART MILL, Macaulay was sent to boarding school (1812–18) and later to Cambridge University (1818–24). His undergraduate career was chequered, but he was elected to a fellowship at Trinity Hall, which he held until 1831, despite a number of reservations about the academic life.

Indeed, Macaulay's greatest successes before 1830 were qualifying as a barrister in 1826 (although he never practised seriously) and the initiation of his literary career through a series of well-received essays in *The Edinburgh Review*, beginning with 'Milton' (1825). Macaulay also wrote on political issues, acquired political connections and was elected as a Whig MP in 1830. He was a prominent figure in the Reform debate of 1831–2 and upheld the family commitment to the cause of anti-slavery. In 1832, Macaulay became a member of the Board of Control for India (which supervised the work of the East India Company) and was soon promoted to the post of secretary of the Board. Shortly after (in 1834), he undertook a new position as a member of the recently created Supreme Council of India, which had taken over many of the Company's political functions. He voyaged to the subcontinent and played a leading role in creating an Anglophone education system for the native Indian elites, in defending the freedom of the press and in drafting a penal code that stressed the equality of Indians and Europeans before the law and the right of a woman to property in her own person – a right not recognized in England until 1882.

Macaulay returned to London in 1838, was re-elected to Parliament and became Secretary for War (1839–41). In a subsequent Whig government, he served as Paymaster-General (1846–7) but his literary and historical interests came to dominate his career. Macaulay's *Lays of Ancient Rome* was published in 1842 and *Critical and Historical Essays* in 1843. Four volumes of *The History of England* appeared during his lifetime (two in 1848, two in 1855) while the fifth was published posthumously (as edited by his sister, Hannah Macaulay Trevelyan) in 1861. The work was intended to explain the history of England and Britain from 1688 until 1820, but it was written on a scale so extravagant that it only reached the year 1702. Nevertheless, it was generally well received and sold many thousands of copies. At the height of his fame, Macaulay died of heart disease in 1859.

Macaulay's liberalism emphasized individual freedom and the rule of law; he was sceptical of the political ambitions of generals, capitalists and democrats, and – like many nineteenth-century Whigs – he usually argued that a reforming aristocracy (in alliance with a 'decent' middle class) was the best available prophylactic against Jacobinism. Although Macaulay rejected the Calvinist version of 'Original Sin', he was no perfectibilist and assumed a universal need for law and government. His 1824 article on 'Mitford's History of Greece' argued that an ideal society would educate all of its members to exercise political power, but in practice a governing elite was normal. Macaulay's politics, taken as a whole, stressed the benefits of non-intervention, economy in legislation and moderate, proportional punishment whenever discipline proved necessary. A regime of personal freedom was liable to generate socio-economic 'improvements', which could be disseminated, not only within Britain (with its particular 'genius' for political moderation) but also around the world, to the general benefit of mankind. Thus, Macaulay was a free trader, but no pacifist. He was sensible of the economic benefits of empire to both the home country and its colonies, while in the 1850s he gave unambiguous, patriotic support to the Crimean War. However, he also recognized a religious and humanitarian obligation to 'improve' colonial peoples – so that they might one day achieve self-government – although this could be couched in the language of self-interest: 'To trade with civilized men is infinitely more profitable than to govern savages' (1833).

In his youth, the greatest single affront to Macaulay's principles was the continuation of legal slavery (and the associated doctrine of Negro inferiority, which he polemicized against in the *Edinburgh Review* of 1827), but he failed to recognize the parallels between this form of political oppression and the constitutional policies of Britain's own government – he was by no means alone in this. In the 1820s and 1830s, Macaulay argued *against* procedural discrimination against Jews, Catholics and Nonconformists (the 'Emancipation' debates) and *for* the abolition

of the relative privilege of landowners (when compared with other property holders), but insisted hat a pecuniary qualification for the suffrage was a necessary means of excluding 'the uneducated' from a sovereignty that they were bound to abuse if 'universal' suffrage was enacted. The classic statements of Macaulay's case against adult male suffrage were three essays written in 1829 ('Mill on Government', 'Bentham's Defence of Mill' and 'The Utilitarian Theory of Government'), which attacked JAMES MILL's democratic version of 'Philosophic Radicalism'. Macaulay contended that, since Mill's case was the product of an abstract and excessively rationalist method of studying human nature, it failed to recognize the specific, historically contingent threat of a revolution in Britain if universal suffrage was adopted. Although Macaulay favoured both the education of workers and the material improvement of their lives, he set no specific criteria whereby the suffrage might be extended at a future date and he opposed 'protective legislation', such as the Factory Acts, until 1847 (when he was persuaded to vote in Parliament for a Ten Hours Bill).

During his sojourn in India, Macaulay published an essay on 'Bacon' (1837), which praised modern European science at the expense of Ancient Greek philosophy, but he was also a humanist and a great admirer of Dante, Shakespeare and Milton. In the 1820s, Macaulay supported the foundation of London University and many of his literary works strove to popularize esoteric scholarship for the benefit of those who had no access to higher education. Perhaps the most famous example of this was the prefaces to *Lays of Ancient Rome*, in which each of the four poems was linked to the idea of the 'lost ballads' of the early Romans, a hypothesis of Niebuhr. More generally, Macaulay prized conciseness and clarity of language in both his works of imaginative literature and his historical works, while, at the same time, he sought to enlist his reader's imagination with strong, pictorial imagery. Macaulay was a great admirer of Walter Scott (1771–1832) and, as early as 1808, he composed a narrative poem (in the style of Scott's *Marmion*) entitled 'The Battle of Cheviot'. As an adult, Macaulay composed poetry in a variety of styles, and on a variety of topics, such as the 'Battle of Naseby' (1824) and 'The Armada' (1831). Although he frequently expressed antipathy towards Wordsworth and the Lake Poets (because of their democratic sympathies and mystical attitude towards 'transcendental' Nature), Macaulay remained an admirer of Scott (and responded favourably to Byron) on the grounds that feeling and imagination were distinctive human qualities that should be celebrated appropriately and which could contribute to human happiness and development.

The combined weight of these generalizations, and the readily available model of Walter Scott's historical novels, can explain certain aspects of Macaulay's historiography – a topic that will be examined more systematically in subsequent paragraphs. In particular, his emphasis upon characterization (albeit sometimes simplified) and biographical anecdotes (as means of 'interesting the affections' of his readers) help to explain his prolixity; a phenomenon referred to by critics as 'excess of ornament'. Moreover, the presentation of various historical incidents sequentially, and as – in effect – literary scenes, strengthened the parallels between *The History* and a Scottian novel (or a play). An intention to instruct can also be inferred from a vigorous, 'masculine' style that sought to make a strong first impression through the use of emphatic words and hyperbole.

In his review of 'Hallam's Constitutional History' (1827), Macaulay proposed an ideal type for historical writing: a 'compound of poetry and philosophy', whereby 'vivid representation' of the particular – the sphere of historical romance – would be combined with analytical discussions that traced 'the connection of causes and effects' and drew 'general lessons of moral and political wisdom' that, until that date, had been the province of a separate school of historical essayists. Subsequently, the general preface to *Lays of Ancient Rome* stressed the importance of *entertaining* (as well as instructing) readers, and Macaulay's success in achieving this goal was recognized by reviewers of *The History* such as BAGEHOT and MATTHEW ARNOLD. Nevertheless, many passages in *The History* were argumentative, and marshalled numerous corroborative examples in favour of the author's interpretation – a stock-in-trade technique of Macaulay, the political orator and essayist. The reader, once pleased, could often be persuaded, but Macaulay famously misjudged his audience when criticising the Quaker, William Penn (1644–1718), who remained a hero to many Victorians.

In 1828, Macaulay had negotiated unsuccessfully with the Society for the Diffusion of Useful Knowledge regarding a proposal for a popular history of Stuart England. It seems that this plan was the kernel of *The History*, although he did not begin to write the book until 1839. As early as 1824, he had argued that a 'perfectly written' history of Ancient Greece would involve a 'complete record' of Greek poetry, philosophy and arts as well as 'salutary inventions and discoveries' that improved the lives of ordinary people. By implication, the same held true for early-modern Britain, but in *The History* only one chapter out of twenty-five took this agenda seriously. The early chapters charted British history from Roman to Stuart times, before discussing the reign of Charles II and the state of English *society* in 1685. Subsequently, 'high politics' was dominant and five chapters were devoted to the reign of James II, eight to the revolution of 1688 and subsequent civil war, and nine to the reign of William III. Although Macaulay read widely in the political literature of the period, visited the sites of many significant events and was a pioneer in his use of 'oral history' – see Edwards (1988) – he was no student of 'scientific' or 'documentary' history, despite writing a review of 'Ranke's History of the Popes' in 1840. Instead, as noted above, most commentators agree that both Macaulay's essays and *The History* placed much greater stress on the artistic dimension of historical writing.

In the light of this, it may be argued that this artistic emphasis was 'convenient' from the viewpoint of Macaulay's 'Whig interpretation of history' – his alleged tendency to give unjustified praise to Whigs and Protestants, and his assumption that late seventeenth-century England had seen the birth of an 'auspicious union of order and freedom', which was a unique contribution to human civilization – because it allowed him to ignore 'facts' that were 'inconvenient' for the interpretation. Nevertheless, although Macaulay did indeed make a number of empirically inaccurate statements in *The History*, it seems unlikely that the explanation for this was entirely ideological and not, in some respects, methodological. It seems equally plausible that his habit of relying on secondary sources (particularly notable in his early survey chapters) led him to repeat the errors of earlier historians, as well as reiterating a number of judgements made during the eighteenth century, when the animosities associated with 1688 (and its aftermath) were still widespread and politically significant. Furthermore, it is by no means certain that the adjective 'Whig' is itself a fair description of Macaulay's perspective, as the following arguments show.

A common defence of Macaulay in the nineteenth century (given charges of political partisanship) was that *The History* honoured the principled conduct of dissident bishops – such as Thomas Ken (1637–1711) – and of other Tories; and that, consequently, the text was Williamite, that is anti-Stuart, and not a 'Whig' history at all. On the other hand, twentieth-century scholars (notably Joseph Hamburger) have argued that Macaulay did not celebrate Whiggism for slightly different reasons. Instead, *The History* has been presented as a vindication of 'trimming' (the seventeenth-century term for balancing the claims of political parties in the national interest) by stressing the role within the narrative of George Savile, Marquess of Halifax (1633–95). Moreover, the theme of 'balance' can also be identified in the first chapter of *The History*, in which 'great national crimes and follies' were acknowledged – with reference to the history of the USA and Ireland – as well as favourable references being made to domestic political harmony, commercial success and the 'splendid' Indian empire.

It is at a more philosophical level, however, that it seems impossible to deny Macaulay's Whiggism, provided that this term is understood to refer to a generalized 'Enlightenment' optimism. For example, in the same introductory chapter of *The History* noted above, Macaulay claimed that British history (over the preceding 160 years) was 'eminently the history of physical, of moral and of intellectual improvement'. Taken as a whole, it seems that his works *were* a form of special pleading for the superiority of English bourgeois culture and British parliamentary liberalism, and, by treating the events of the 1680s and 1690s as more significant for nineteenth-century Britain than those of the 1640s, he may well have done his compatriots a disservice. Although Macaulay had read the great Scottish historians of the eighteenth century (and discussed their conceptions of 'rude' and 'refined' societies in the 1820s) his works often neglected 'sociological' and 'economic' factors in history, while at the same time failing to *demonstrate* the 'autonomy' of politics.

References

Edwards, O.D (1988) *Macaulay*, London: Weidenfeld & Nicolson.
Hamburger, J. (1976) *Macaulay and the Whig Tradition*, Chicago and London: The University of Chicago Press.

Further reading

Clive, J. (1973) *Thomas Babington Macaulay: The Shaping of a Historian*, London: Secker & Warburg.
Trevelyan, G.O. (1978 [1876]) *The Life and Letters of Macaulay*, Oxford: Oxford University Press.

SEE ALSO: historiography and the idea of progress; liberalism

CLIVE E. HILL

MAIN CURRENTS IN PHILOSOPHY

Nineteenth-century philosophy developed its fascinating momentum by struggling under and against the sway of two giants, IMMANUEL KANT (1724–1804) and Georg Wilhelm Friedrich Hegel (1770–1831) (see HEGEL AND HEGELIANISM). The debate between philosophy and science began here and so did the long and intricate dispute between philosophy and religion. The legacy of Immanuel Kant should prove to be the more resistant to attack in comparison to Hegel, who was already vigorously criticized by contemporaries such as F.W.J. SCHELLING (1775–1854), SØREN KIERKEGAARD (1813–55) and, last not least, Karl Marx (1818–83) (see MARX AND MARXISM). Above all, however, philosophy in the nineteenth century was very much a public affair, sometimes an event. Often the state became involved, the Church was always present, and political factions as well as literary salons spread the word and discussed the most recent developments that were articulated in the lecture hall.

Georg Wilhelm Friedrich Hegel

G.W.F. Hegel was born in Stuttgart, on 27 August 1770. His school years, according to his first biographer, K. Rosenkranz, had prepared him to absorb the general ideas of Enlightenment, on the one hand, and those of ancient philosophy, on the other. Having first toyed with the idea of joining the Jena literary circles, he instead, in 1778, became a student of Protestant theology at Tübingen. There he met Schelling and Friedrich Hölderlin, at the famous Stift, and the three formed a brief friendship and an alliance of giddy speculative Idealism, combined with ideas of freedom and a rejuvenated German state modelled on ancient Athens. The influence of Hölderlin and his all-pervading slogan of '*Hen kai pan*' (one and all) should not be underestimated. The future poet-philosopher had already criticized Fichte's theoretical attempts to transcend the limits of human consciousness, only to radicalize this position by assuming an ontological division of human nature that looked forever for unification. (What must come to mind here is of course RALPH WALDO EMERSON's image of 'man as a broken giant'.) For Hegel, Hölderlin's view was a point of departure already in his early works, long before he began to build his grand systematic work on the logical necessity of unity. Having finished his studies at Tübingen, Hegel earned his living as a private teacher, first in Bern, then in Frankfurt. He won his first appointment as *außerordentlicher Professor* in 1805 in Jena, and later worked as headmaster at the Gymnasium at Nuremberg. (The Napoleonic Battle of Jena had put a stop to the activities of the university.) Apart from his *Differenzschrift* (*Difference between the Philosophical Systems of Fichte and Schelling,* 1801), his first major publication was *The Phenomenology of Spirit* in 1807. Between the years 1812–16, his *Science of Logic* was published; there followed, in 1817, *The Encyclopedia of the Philosophical Science in Outline.* In 1818 Hegel accepted an invitation to Berlin, where he occupied the chair of Philosophy and gained his reputation as Germany's preeminent philosopher. He died in November 1831.

The break between Hegel and Schelling, students and friends in Tübingen and briefly colleagues at the University of Jena, became final with Hegel's publication of his *Phenomenology of Spirit.* In his preface to the *Phenomenology* Hegel, who during the years in Tübingen was probably more influenced by Hölderlin than by Schelling, simply called the 'absolute' as construed by Schelling an 'abyss', and resolutely claimed that Schelling's quest for ultimate unity could only lead into the night where distinctions were no longer possible. The necessary and yet tragic separation of the human mind and the divine spirit, as exemplified in nature, was something Schelling saw as the ultimate principle, from which the unfolding of history derived its dynamics. Reconciliation could only be achieved via the acceptance, however painful, of negation. Hegel, in his *Phenomenology* left the Romantics and especially their religious motivation behind, claiming the world of pure spirit for philosophy, a daring step to take. However, it was Hegel's influence that would prevail, even though Schelling succeeded Hegel in Berlin where he tried to give his audience the impression that Hegel's philosophy was a mere episode in the development of man's thought that he would counter with his own *Philosophy of Revelation* (*Philosophie der Offenbarung,* published posthumously). It is not only ironic that Schelling did not manage to replace Hegel – because he did not have the right enemies, the so called left wing Hegelians (FEUERBACH, Ruge, DAVID STRAUSS, BRUNO BAUER), which kept the spirit of Hegel alive *because* of their criticism – but it is also characteristic of early nineteenth-century thought that philosophy was taking a definite political turn. In Continental Europe this turn had to be achieved against the overwhelming and highly diversified influence of German Idealism, which, unlike in Britain where political and economical thought had long ago achieved philosophical acceptance, did not really want to become involved *practically* in the political sphere. This turned out, in the end, to be the source of its final exhaustion, even though it could claim a considerable longevity in the field of aesthetics and literary theory. The popularization of German Idealism and its literary counterpart, Romanticism, by MME. DE STAËL in her widely read book *De l'Allemagne* (1810) would leave a profound impression in Britain, where CARLYLE picked up the main currents of German metaphysical Idealism and passed them on to US writer-philosophers like R.W. Emerson, and his circle of major and minor Transcendentalists.

The real drama of the Hegelian movement, however, occurred when Karl Marx broke away from the notorious *Doktorklub* of the left-wing Hegelians under the aegis of his radical position that Hegel's philosophy had to be turned upside down, to be put on its feet as he put it, because the task of philosophy was to change the world and not to interpret it. Karl Marx, whose reputation has suffered immensely from his adoption and vulgarization as the official representative of 'scientific socialism' in the communist countries of the world, should not be underestimated because of this adoption. He himself would have not considered any of the states that claimed to practise Marxism, including the Soviet Union as it existed up to its collapse, even remotely socialist or communist. Karl Marx (1818–83) first reacted against Hegel's theory of the state and then proceeded to attack metaphysical Idealism on the basis that any theory worth its while had to be practical. Having written his *Kritik des Hegelschen Staatsrechts* in the early 1840s, a critique of Hegel's concept of the state as the ultimate expression of the objective spirit, Marx proceeded to lay the foundation for his political ideas in his *Parisian Manuscripts*, written in exile in 1844. He was influenced at that time not only by Moses Hess (*Über das Geldwesen*) and by his friend Friedrich Engels's *Umrisse zu einer Kritik der Nationalökonomie*, but also through his association with other German radicals in exile, as well as with French socialists like PROUDHON and BLANC, and the Russian anarchist-revolutionary BAKUNIN. Up to a certain point Karl Marx was still thinking in Hegelian terms, especially when it came to implicit epistemological implications of his anthropology. But the more he became personally involved in the socialist movements of his time, the further he removed himself from his former friends and collaborators, as for example from Bruno Bauer. His definite break with the remnants of theoretical Idealism came with the publication of *The Holy Family* (*Die heilige Familie*), a sarcastic criticism of everything the left-wing or Young Hegelians stood for, in this case Bruno Bauer, Anselm Feuerbach and MAX STIRNER. In 1847 Marx published another polemic, this time an answer to Proudhon's *Philosophy of Misery*, which bore the ironic title *The Misery of Philosophy*. The way of polemically breaking away from theoretical Hegelianism, in the case of Karl Marx, has something forced about it, especially because he always adhered to the dialectical aspects of Hegelianism, even if he considered this particular part of Hegel's philosophy not as a method of inquiry but immanent in the very nature of reality. Marx, without Hegel, to be blunt, can only be a fearful misconception. Throughout all of their writings both Marx and Engels adhered to the idea of the Hegelian concept of negation as the fundamental element of progress, even at the cost of some fairly scholastic intellectual constructs, such as that of the proletariat as the natural avant-garde of revolutionary progress, albeit in need of guidance by intellectuals, a question incidentally over which the First International, which Marx helped to organize, would eventually break up. Marx himself, exiled over and over again, from Germany to Paris to Brussels, back to Germany, where the short-lived revolution of 1848 was being crushed by Prussian troops, back to Paris again, having given up his Prussian citizenship and threatened once more with exile, finally settled in England. There he began to work systematically on what would later become *Das Kapital*, of which he himself only saw the first volume in print. Karl Marx did not leave a school of followers to pursue his work, which in the light of its origins as an effort to combine negative Hegelianism with historical materialism and the economic theories of his time is not really surprising. His influence would manifest itself indirectly, in the variety of the interpretations of his work, whether in the dogmatic readings of his economics in Eastern Europe, in the debates of critical theorists like Max Horkheimer, Th. W. Adorno and Walter Benjamin, or in the French reception of his work as part of an ongoing discussion between neo-Marxists and phenomenologists. One aspect in both Hegel's thought and in the work of Karl Marx should not be forgotten. Both saw themselves obliged to fundamental ideas about the morality and reasonability of the individual, as first expounded by Kant. It is equally true that both Hegel and Marx diverged widely from Kant's original outline, which left neither room for the movement of the spirit to its self-fulfilment (Hegel) nor to utopian self-realization of the proletariat (Marx).

Immanuel Kant

Immanuel Kant was born in 1724, in Königsberg, the fourth of nine children. The family was poor, so Kant needed the financial aid of supporters and friends in order to study at the pietistic Collegium Fridericianum. Working as a private tutor he studied at the University of Königsberg, where he was influenced primarily by Martin Knutzen (1713–51), who held a professorship in Logic and Metaphysics. Two major influences can be singled out, the traditional school of metaphysics as derived from Leibnitz, and the example of Newton whom Kant revered as a paradigm of exact science. Following his father's death, Kant had to leave the university to earn a living as a private tutor, employed by families of the local aristocracy. As early as 1755 Kant submitted his major thesis, and already criticized the central assumptions of traditional metaphysics. After years of holding the untenured position of a *Privatdozent*, working as a sub-librarian at the same time, he was finally appointed to a full professorship in Logic and Metaphysics at Königsberg, a position he held until his death in 1804. The most remarkable of his pre-critical texts is undoubtedly his polemic against Swedenborg, *Dreams of a Ghostseer Explained by Dreams of Metaphysics* (1766), published anonymously, where we encounter a Kant full of irony and venom, anticipating much of what he would later discuss in his major works. In 1781, the *Critique of Pure Reason* was published, in 1788 there followed *TheCritique of Practical Reason* and in 1790 *The Critique of Pure Judgment*. Afterwards the world of philosophy would never be the same; the 'smasher of metaphysics', as he was frequently referred to, had made his mark. Many important texts were published in between, and many form his *opus postumum*, but his three Critiques remain as lasting contribution to the realm of philosophy to this very day.

The legacy of Kant shaped the structural contours of nineteenth-century thought in totally different fashion, last not least because of its epistemological presumptions and simply because its maxim *sapere aude*, the epitome of traditional enlightenment, does not lend itself all that easily to politicization. Kant, as early as in his pre-critical writings, as in *Träume eines Geistersehers,* began to demolish the assumptions of traditional metaphysics, assumptions which in the light of the progress of the natural sciences, represented by Galileo and Newton, in the light also of what logic had achieved, Kant found preposterous and not acceptable. Thus he broke with the tradition of Leibnitz, personified by Christian Wolff, and emphasized the *limitation* of human knowledge rather than its speculative powers. Metaphysics, he claimed from the year 1766 on, was the science of the limits of human reason. To outline these limits was the task of his major work, beginning with the *Critique of Pure Reason* (1781), which was also the first step towards establishing the foundations of his own transcendental philosophy. The term 'transcendental', ancient as it is, assumes a new meaning in the terminology of Kant inasmuch as he refers to criteria that constitute the necessary preconditions of knowledge rather than to everything that is generally presupposed. In his painstaking style Kant reduces the empirical world to the elements of pure space and pure time (as opposed to this *specific* time and this space), and deduces all categories from this concept, showing in his further argument that reasoning, on the basis of categories a priori is possible in an empirically given world. Without a systematic, transcendental deduction of categories, subjective knowledge will never be scientific. Objective judgements are the result of the assumption that all categories are synthetically unified in the shape of *pure reason*, the original 'I think' being conceived of as the transcendental unity that is the precondition of all further judgements. Thus Kant breaks with the traditional metaphysical assumption that the essence of things is accessible, the 'Thing as such' (*Das Ding an sich*) is something that the human mind cannot know. Reason is a *regulative* instrument of knowledge, just as human knowledge is limited.

In his subsequent *Critique of Practical Reason* (1783) Kant followed his own principles in the attempt to establish a final, irrefutable foundation for the necessity of moral action, which would culminate in his famous *categorical imperative*, 'Act only on that maxim through which you can at the same time will that it should become a universal law.' In working out the various formulations of this paradigm of rational action Kant introduced another pair of terms, the juxtaposition of which would have far-reaching consequences, the terms of end and means. The extended version of the categorical imperative therefore implies never to use action as means for a purpose alone but always in a way that can be justified as an end in itself, because the nature of reason is an end in itself, as Kant had so elaborately argued in his first Critique. Kant's theory of action, if we want to call his argument about means and ends by this name, would – as we shall see later on – profoundly affect the development of US Pragmatism and British empiricism. In addition we cannot ignore his influence on modern philosophy, even if only certain aspects of his philosophy are relevant, such as the *categorical imperative*, and not the method of transcendental reasoning of his first Critique. So, to name just one example, John Rawls's *Theory of Justice*, in its passionate plea for certain necessary conditions that make the idea of justice plausible in the first place, relies heavily on the acceptance of Kantian premises, without invoking the whole content of Kant's method. In fact, post-Kantian philosophy has either sought to bring his work to its legitimate fulfilment, or it has offered competing interpretations of Kant.

This is also true of the enormous impact of his third Critique, that of *Judgment*, which more than any given text has influenced consequent aesthetic theories. Formally the *Critique of Judgment* seems to mediate between the faculties of reason and of understanding. But the basic question raised in the

Critique of Judgment addresses the problem of how nature can be seen as the intelligible part of our world that allows as well as necessitates a priori judgments concurring with our cognitive faculties. Kant, therefore, has to qualify both the teleological element in Nature, appealing to our sense of seeing, or judging nature as full of purpose, hence objective, and its appeal to our sentiments, which are purely subjective. But we are nevertheless still within the categories of reasonable judgement when we comment on the beauty of an object, because, as Kant points out, our judgement must be disinterested. Taste is our ability to make disinterested judgements concerning the purposeless beautiful. Kant elaborates on this in great detail, covering the beautiful and the sublime, and their respective relation to reason and freedom, until we end up reading his third *Critique* mainly as his contribution to aesthetic theory, more so in any case than as an integral part of his philosophical system as a whole. But whenever we go into the details of Kant's aesthetics, we are eventually carried back to his original arguments about reason, necessity, ends and means.

As we have already mentioned, nineteenth-century Continental philosophy at first tried to avoid the restrictions Kant had put in the way of speculative philosophy by claiming to absorb him into the grand project of Idealism, which meant to say that Kant had in fact strengthened the status of the subject in the fields of philosophical knowledge, *but not radically enough.* Fichte was the first to claim that his criticism of Kant was in fact a completion of his work. But so did Schelling and likewise Hegel. These claims might, at first sight, strike one as somewhat strange in the light of Kant's anti-metaphysical position and his well-known aversion to the larger aspirations of the individual's transgressions against the limitations of its own capacities to understand the world. They are, however, at a closer look not totally without foundation, even after the demise of absolute Idealism, in the post-Hegelian era, the Kantian project would slip away from future Idealists. Kant, in the eyes of Fichte, had compromised his very own intentions by holding on to the idea of the *Ding an sich*, the thing in itself, which provoked the immediate question of its possible existence without the subject. And this idea inevitably led to the question about the subject's creative capacity in general. Vague as this may sound, and not wanting to make a homogenous mess of the highly refined philosophical systems of Fichte, Schelling and Hegel, each of them differing from one another, and confounding them with German literary Romanticism to boot, a common ground in many respects can and should not be denied. It would be hard, otherwise, to explain the influence of post-Kantian Idealism in France, England and the USA. It would be equally hard to come to terms with the profound dislike that the same kind of Idealism met in the same countries, more or less at the same time. While the influence of Fichte would largely remain within the boundaries of philosophy, Schelling and Hegel both influenced the intellectual community of their time. Schelling's visionary qualities, his demand for a new mythology, a new religion in fact, based on a radicalized version of Spinoza's pantheism, was well understood in literary circles, especially because F.H. Jacobi had drawn Lessing into the debate about pantheism by publishing a series of letters to Moses Mendelssohn that revealed Lessing's turn towards pantheism. Schelling not only took the later writings of Fichte seriously – which abandoned the field of philosophy proper and became increasingly political, arguing as they did against the despotism of Napoleon and trying to lay the foundation of German patriotism based on a renewed interest in language, philosophy and art as constitutional element of a national character – but he also emphasized the political nature of Fichte's *ego* that had replaced Kant's transcendental subject as a kind of first principle, and which in the hands of Fichte had become an ontological principle. It would only be a question of time until this ontological ego, already being characterized as the origin of all knowledge – combining spontaneity, with unity and self-presence – should want to be qualified in more concrete terms. However, it would be a mistake to dismiss Fichte lightly as somebody who simply turned Kant upside down. He called his philosophy '*Wissenschaftslehre*', a 'science of knowledge', and he bitterly fought against misunderstanding his ego, his self-positing 'I', as an empirical self. He clearly wanted to be seen as a follower of Kant, albeit a critical one. Very early in his life Fichte outlined and clarified his own intentions by way of reviewing a work critical of Kant, and had argued that neither a transcendental self that related to something outside of itself could exist, nor could a purely empirical self, in Kant's sense. In each case the self would be fatally divided by fundamental logical contradictions. So Fichte endowed his ego, his intelligent self, with one decisive quality, *energeia*, a form of energy striving towards fulfilment, towards unity with its own potential, a moral energy that would lead the way towards self-fulfilment and the unity with the divine. As if simply trying to integrate Kant into his own system of philosophy, Fichte saw three principles at work in the defining of the self: a desire for knowledge, for praxis and for aesthetics. In fact Fichte talks about *Trieb*, so we might call these defining qualities *instinctive* to the self. If we take all that has been briefly pointed out about Fichte seriously, who stands here *pars pro toto*, we immediately see why he became so popular in his own time, and almost notoriously unpopular in a different political and cultural climate. For his time he addressed the topics everybody wanted to hear about: the scientific character of moral and political philosophy, the virtually limitless potential of the subject, the freedom of the individual, freedom being discussed within the context of the French Revolution and its repercussions throughout Europe. Fichte, who became known in Jena as a kind of German Jacobin, left that town after a turbulent and slanderous debate about his alleged atheism for Berlin. There he was welcomed in the literary salons of Henriette Herz and Rahel Levin, and during the Napoleonic Wars his *Speeches to the German Nation* articulated a moral and cultural sense of mission for Germany, which sense was easily abused at the time of extreme German Nationalism and National Socialism. More or less the same can be said for the general fate of German speculative Idealism in its garb of aesthetic Romanticism. However, its influence would, for better or for worse, lie exactly in this domain.

Søren Kierkegaard and Friedrich Nietzsche

Both Kierkegaard and Nietzsche deserve our attention for their role of dealing with the aesthetic and religious extremes of nineteenth-century thought. Both exercise a lasting influence until today. Søren Aabye Kierkegaard was born in Copenhagen in 1813, the youngest of seven children. He died relatively early, at the age of 42, in 1855. His upbringing was strictly Lutheran-pietistic and following the directions of his father, Michael Pederson Kierkegaard, whose influence upon his son would be problematic throughout his life,

Kierkegaard began his studies with Theology at the University of Copenhagen. Soon disappointed by the rational theology he encountered there he became increasingly interested in philosophy, which in Denmark at that time was heavily influenced by German Romanticism in general and by Hegel's dialectical Idealism in particular. Hegel, however, would become the central philosophical adversary in the unfolding of Kierkegaard's own thought. Hegel the 'objective' thinker, and the architect of seemingly endless and yet programmatic systems, provoked Kierkegaard's equally extreme 'subjective' tendencies, which eventually earned him the dubious, because all too simplifying, title of the founder of modern existentialism. Following his father's death he finished his studies in Theology in 1840 and the same year became engaged to marry Regine Olson, an engagement that he dissolved a year later. This event would become the other life-consuming preoccupation in Kierkegaard's work, the third being his constant struggle with the Danish Church and its official representatives. Kierkegaard's biographers have long since speculated about the reason for Kierkegaard's breaking off his engagement with Regine Olson and his subsequent dealing with his decision. We must be content with the explanation that a severe feeling of Protestant guilt, an acute sense of spiritual crisis, were responsible for this fateful decision.

Having successfully finished his dissertation on Socrates and on the concept of irony, which according to the standards of his time he delivered in Latin, he left for his first visit to Berlin to become more closely acquainted with Hegel, listening also to the lectures of the aging Schelling, whom he at first admired, only to reject him violently later. He returned to Copenhagen in 1842 and began to write in quick succession a large part of his most influential books, while keeping an extensive diary and notebook at the same time. Within the years of 1843 to 1846, he published ten books, most them under a pseudonym, although everybody in Copenhagen knew the identity of the author: *Either/Or* (1843, ps. Victor Eremita); *Fear and Trembling* (1843, ps. Johannes de Silentio); *The Repetition* (1843, ps. Constantin Constantius); in 1844 he published *The Concept of Dread* and *Philosophical Fragments*, followed by *Stages on Life's Way*; the next year saw the publication of the *Concluding Unscientific Postscript*; and in 1849 he published *The Sickness unto Death*. Apart from these major works, Kierkegaard also published some minor writings, mainly addressing questions of religion, reflecting his barely hidden anger at the Danish state Church, which he would attack violently after the death of bishop Mynster, who had been a friend of the family. By that time Kierkegaard had not only emerged as a serious philosopher, not fully understood by his contemporaries, but also as one of the greatest literary stylists of the Danish language, and he had become – unavoidably in the Copenhagen of his time – a figure of public interest; a highly controversial one, the target above all of the leading satirical magazine *The Corsair*, which published highly uncomplimentary caricatures of the slightly hunch backed Kierkegaard. Why is it worth looking at Kierkegaard's life to such an extent? In many ways it reflects the most lasting parts of his work, in fact is often extremely difficult to separate Kierkegaard's life from the content of his thought. Nevertheless, his religious revolt against the temptations of even the most advanced form of pantheism relies on its own and highly specific conceptualizations of the drama of existing under the verdict of separation.

Most of his writing concentrates on the essence of human existence as expressed by the work of being. His profound aversion against Hegel was based on the idea that the Hegelian system was endlessly removed from the realities of human life. The title of his first major publication, *Either/Or*, can also be seen as an ironic comment on what he perceived as Hegel's eternally moving from the positive to its negation and then back again, even if it were on a higher level of comprehension. What seemed so natural to Hegel, if we read the introduction to *Phenomenology of Spirit* even today, namely that human knowledge and experience is based on *necessary* contradictions that can only be overcome by negation in the sense of what Hegel calls *Aufhebung* – the final goal being to make philosophy superfluous, at a stage where the world-spirit would have reached its final stage of self-realization – seemed to Kierkegaard the attempt to put mankind into the position of God. Life as Kierkegaard saw it in *Either/Or* is not the ever ongoing mechanism of dialectical movement, it is a question of choice. In *Either/Or* Kierkegaard juxtaposes the aesthetic way of life with the ethical. A fundamental, an existential choice, because as Kierkegaard elaborates, the seemingly free aesthetic mode of existence, devoted as it is to a full exploitation of the senses and Romantic imagination, leaves the individual incomplete, void of a sense of real purpose. This sense of purpose cannot be conjured into life by thinking about it, what it takes is a *decision*. The ethical way of life accepts this commitment, even if it implies a leap into the unknown. In the end – no great surprise given Kierkegaard's theological and religious background – the ultimate decision is the choice of committing the self to faith. In a breathtaking, literary *tour de force*, Kierkegaard in *Either/Or* plays out the persona of Don Juan (representing the aesthetic stage of consciousness) against Socrates, representing the opposite. The predicament of human existence, as Kierkegaard demonstrates, does not end here. A *commitment* to ethical principles, as in the case of Socrates, may in the end have grave consequences, but there is something strangely archaic about it in so far as it lacks understanding of its own true nature. Kierkegaard has to come to terms with the very same insufficiencies that Hegel ascribed to the 'unhappy soul'. The lack of the tragic heroism of the merely ethical consciousness is absence of a definite understanding of sin. Socrates did choose to put his principles before his life, but when defending himself against his judges, he evoked Achilles as an example of following ones principles! To resolve this insufficiency of the tragic it takes the final, and irrevocable, commitment to God, to a faith that alone can overcome its opposite, despair, the 'sickness unto death'. It is obvious that Kierkegaard's opposition to Hegel was not really based upon an internal criticism of Hegelian philosophical assumption, but on a rejection of what he perceived as the failure of Hegel's 'system' as a whole, regardless of its genealogy or method. Kierkegaard must have realized that the appeal of Hegel's grand design had outlived itself – too many abstractions drew away the attention from the real needs of the living individual. At the same time a more literary approach in philosophy seemed possible. A brief look at Kierkegaard's use of pseudonyms will explain this sudden outbreak of the individual and often idiosyncratic voice in philosophy. We have seen that the names he chose for authorship were not really pseudonyms in a literal sense, for they did not hide Kierkegaard's identity. Their function was often programmatic, as for example in the case, to pick just two of many, the Johannes de Silentio of *Fear and Trembling: A Dialectical Lyric* is the persona of the ultimate paradox of Christian faith, as exemplified in the variations of the story of Abraham and Isaac; that is, variations on a theme. The theme itself is the nature of faith about which philosophy must be silent. As Johannes de Silentio knows 'Even though one were capable of converting the whole content of faith into the form of a concept, it does not follow that one has adequately conceived faith and understands how one got into it, or how it got into one.' And yet the silence is the origin of so many words even if they come from someone who describes himself as '*poetice et elegenter*, an amateur who neither writes the System nor promises of the System, who neither subscribes to the System nor ascribes anything to it'. Johannes is the child of revelation, part of a secret, just as mysterious as God's temptation of Abraham. By putting the far from one-dimensional figure of Johannes de Silentio between himself and his text Kierkegaard also tries to achieve what in a different context he defines as '*authorship without authority*'. He goes all the way back to his dissertation on Socrates and the concept of irony so as to evoke the advantages of the *maieutic* attitude as the golden way from the aesthetic stage of life to the religious as the *telos*, in order to reclaim the notion of authorship as being a stage rather than an end. Hence also the programmatic implications of a pseudonym like that attached to the *Concluding Unscientific Postscript to Philosophical Fragments: A Mimical-Pathetical-Dialectical Compilation, an Existential Contribution* by Johannes Climacus. The origin of this particular pseudonym is the Greek monk St John Climacus, (*c.*525–606), author of *Klimax tou Paradeisou*, translated as *Scala Paradisi*, in English as *Ladder of Paradise*, a collection of spiritual aphorisms (*plakes pneumatikai*), containing advice to other monks of how to achieve Christian perfection. Kierkegaard's Climacus himself is, however, not an accomplished Christian, but someone in transition; he rejects the idea of logical procession in matters of faith, where nothing allows for the Hegelian dialectical movement, there is only the choice to take the decisive, existential 'leap', as Kierkegaard puts it. What all of this eventually entails, apart from Kierkegaard's literary achievements, is that he clearly saw what many contemporaries, more familiar with the genealogy of Hegel's thought out of the religious background of the early time spent in Tübingen, tended to overlook, namely the fact that Hegel, whatever his choice of words might be,

could *not* be seen as concerned with the plights of theology or lived religion. His Absolute was not, in the end, the equivalent of the transcendent Christian God.

Given Kierkegaard's life-long preoccupation with misconceptions of the Hegelian system, it is not at all surprising that his legacy would first and above fall on fertile ground in the context of German 'existential' theology as exemplified by Karl Barth and his followers, just as he profoundly influenced the phenomenological existentialists ranging from Heidegger to Sartre.

At the other spectrum of violent, seemingly totally subjective reaction against the great architects of philosophers we see Friedrich Wilhelm Nietzsche. He was born in 1844, the son of a Lutheran pastor, who died when Nietzsche was in his childhood. He was brought up by his mother and sister, and while attending Gymnasium very early discovered his love for ancient philosophy. He became a professor of Classical Philology at a very early point in his life, at the age of 24, but – influenced by the work of Schopenhauer – soon fell out with his peers in the field and turned to philosophy. By that time he had already broken with Christianity and in his first book, *The Birth of Tragedy* (*Die Geburt der Tragödie aus dem Geist der Musik*, 1872) he pitted what he called the Apollonian versus the Dionysian spirit in Greek life and thought, deducing from it, as would become his habit, a whole set of critical insights into European culture. Already the moralist and polemicist – which he would soon become in the content and style of his writing – he praised the qualities of Wagner's music as aspiring to be what we today call a *Gesammtkunstwerk* and condemned his philistine critics for what he perceived as their misunderstanding of an expression of true genius. Nietzsche's aim can be understood as nothing less than the attempt at a transformation of *all* the values of his time. He set out to do so by writing his *Untimely Meditations* (*Unzeitgemäße Betrachtungen*, 1867–73), the last of which also marked his break with Wagner. At this time Nietzsche drew heavily on the ideas of the French Enlightenment, only to drop this particular influence in order to propagate his own two central ideas, that of the '*eternal return*' and of the '*Übermensch*', the powerful, creative human being, who has managed to rise above the constraints of ordinary civilization. Given his tendency to aphoristic and fragmentary thinking, it is not easy to do full justice to this highly idiosyncratic philosopher, who professed to be an ardent admirer of Ralph Waldo Emerson. (He integrated extensive passages from Emerson's *Essays* into his own writings.) But against all the invitations of being misconstrued, there is a passionate effort in his thought, at the core of which we find the desperate attempts to include Life, with all its torturing self-contradictions, into his philosophy.

Nietzsche abandoned his Basel professorship in 1879, and although the victim of chronic illness began to publish in quick succession the core of his work. What seems most interesting, here, is Nietzsche's concept of truth and his idea of life as opposed to any form of limitation. Truth, as Nietzsche affirms most emphatically in *Beyond Good and Evil* (*Jenseits von Gut und Böse*, 1887), and the writings of that period, which was planned as a work on the philosophy of the future, is just as instrumental as knowledge itself. Absolute truth is therefore a fiction. As he came to claim in the notes, published after his death as *The Will to Power*, truth serves the purpose of the force of life, no less than any other human activity. In a way that many of his followers and exploiters hardly realized, Nietzsche was willing to undercut his own positions just as radically as he attacked the beliefs of others. So he knew that whatever he had to offer even as criticism was in itself provisionary – a prelude at best for things to come. It stands to reason that Nietzsche can not be seen as the founder of a specific philosophical school, but would, as already in his lifetime, find his admirers mainly among critics of culture and aesthetically inclined sceptics in general.

The quest for common sense

Kant had wanted his philosophy to be rational; he almost instinctively reacted against any form of speculation. At the same time, however, he could not give up metaphysics entirely. He had read David Hume and claimed to have been awakened by him from his own 'dogmatic slumber', as he put it in his *Prolegomena to Any Future Metaphysics* (1783), but he was deeply frightened by Hume's scepticism. Given the fact that both philosophers regarded Newton as the essential example of what philosophy had yet to achieve, it is surprising how much their reaction to what they perceived in Newton differed. Hume, so it seems, had understood the methodological implications of

Newton much more intrinsically than Kant. Where Kant was looking for rationality, Hume tried to justify empiricism, embracing from the very beginning of his work the idea of experimentalism, based on 'experience and observation'. If we simply compare the language used by Hume to set forth his ideas, we can understand Kant's effort to go further than Hume. Where Hume in his *Treatise* realized the danger of scepticism, and finally decided that human nature would not fall into scepticism's pyrronic traps, Kant wanted to exclude the possibility of scepticism a priori. This difference is indeed a fundamental one and consequential for the widening gulf between Continental and British thought in the nineteenth century. The great antagonist of radical scepticism, to quote from Hume, is 'ordinary life' itself. Never would Kant have been able to be so self-confident about the robust structures of the ordinary and neither were his followers. If, however, as Hume points out, scepticism cannot be refuted by logic, but can easily be shown to be irrelevant in real life, it is plausible enough to accept that knowledge is both possible and useful, without recurring to transcendental principles. You do not have to prove the possibility of viable knowledge, if you cannot seriously doubt its existence. So what remains to be done is to examine how knowledge comes about as the elementary ingredient of what we call experience. Much more than Kant, Hume was a man of letters, but he did not avoid the intricate questions that the ugly spectre of scepticism raised. He is an empiricist, as the ultimate test for philosophy is everyday life. But this does not mean that we can simply take our perception of life, as we see it, for granted. So quite naturally Hume goes about to lay the foundations for a theory of knowledge, using the categories of 'memory' and 'perception' as his cornerstones, to what eventually would turn out to be the whole content of human experience. He complements his first principles by adding two more categories that make up the nature of perception, namely 'ideas' and 'impressions'. The difference between the two is one of intensity, as Hume claims that even the remotest, the weakest impression is more present to the mind than the most immediate idea. Hume realizes that degrees of intensity in themselves are not sufficient to establish the difference he wants and needs between ideas and perception, and so he goes back to establishing experience as the realm where knowledge becomes evident.

By stressing the many aspects of scepticism, Hume has often and mistakenly been characterized as a latent sceptic himself, but his early opponents (Reid, Beattie) simply missed the point of Hume's seemingly obsessive preoccupation with the varieties of scepticism. He wanted to eliminate it as a problem preventing a grounding of knowledge in common sense and he needed it at the same time for the very same purpose. As we have mentioned above, Hume was as much a philosopher as he was a writer; in fact, his first philosophical attempt, his now famous *Treatise of Human Nature* (1739–40) written to a large extent in France was highly essayistic in style, drawing on sources like Pierre Bayle and failed to make the necessary impression in Britain. As Hume put it 'Never Literary Attempt was more unfortunate than my Treatise. It fell dead-born from the Press, without reaching such distinction as even to excite a murmur among the zealots.' Hume was only partly right. His *Treatise* was read, reviewed and criticized. His critics had taken Hume's emphasis on his own scepticism too seriously, and to a certain extent Hume was correct in his judgement that the misfortune of his *Treatise* was due to the *manner* in which it had been written, which however was exactly the reason for concentrating on certain questions of *matter*. Hume had basically made a great effort to avoid the mistakes he ascribed to philosophers in general:

> When a philosopher has once laid hold of a favourite principle, which perhaps accounts for many natural effects, he extends the same principle over the whole creation, and reduces to it every phaenomenon, though by the most violent and absurd reasoning.
>
> (*The Sceptic*)

Nevertheless his critics, Thomas Reid above all, managed to isolate one particular strand in Hume's philosophy, the fact, as they surmised, that he had carried the errors of Berkeley and Locke to their legitimate and mistaken consequences. The truth however is that Hume did not *avoid* scepticism, but was certain that human nature itself would prevent mankind from falling into the traps of *Pyrronism*.

If anything Hume used scepticism to fortify his version of empiricism or fallibilism. Although frequently given to highly metaphorical examples, he made it quite clear in his *Treatise*, as well as in his later writings, that objects of experience *exist* and have a constancy, even if only by the work of our

imagination and not *necessarily* by logic. If we want to give credit to Hume's achievement, we must acknowledge his capacity for compromise, putting together, for example, the roles of imagination and experience in order to achieve an empirical world. It is exactly the ability to work out liveable forms of compromise that makes Hume so attractive today. Philosophy in his hands became a matter of real life, without negating its inherent contradictions. We may, therefore consider him the first *radical empiricist*. It is simply fascinating to observe Hume first explaining that there is no *necessary* connection between cause and effect in the world we inhabit, only to watch him raising the problem of induction, in order to introduce the category of reason as an overriding principle. In his lifetime Hume earned a considerable reputation, but nobody would have seen him as the great British philosopher. He faced a formidable opposition in the spokesmen of Scottish Common Sense philosophy, who made their points mainly by emphasizing Hume's scepticism. In Reid's opinion, for example, it could only lead to the point where no distinctions were possible. Even if Hume did not immediately establish a school of disciples, his critics had to concede that large parts of his system were coherent and that an empirical approach towards an understanding of human nature was definitely the right one to chose. Without Hume neither the work of Jeremy Bentham nor that of John Stuart Mill would be conceivable and the great history of British utilitarianism would probably never have been written. What indeed would Bentham's work be without its emphasis on the *felicific calculus*, an idea clearly derived from Hume's theory of passions?

However, when Reid attacked Hume on his concept of ideas, he probably brought a whole new set of questions into focus the consequences of which he had no way of anticipating. To criticize Hume's theory of ideas necessarily brought up the question of what an alternative to Hume might look like. Reid had not only failed to convince such relatively minor figures like Thomas Brown (1778–1820), a student and later the successor of DUGALD STEWART. He had also managed to discredit the project of empiricism, to which Brown did by and large and despite some misgivings want to adhere to. So there seemed to be a gap that needed to be filled, and the first one to realize this in a radical way was Thomas Hill Green (1836–82). Green, certainly aided by a *general* change of the intellectual climate of his time – Carlyle must be named here as the essential figure – simply declared the empiricist project to have gone bankrupt as a consequence of its own premises. Hume, according to Green, had done an equally thorough and honest job at dismantling empiricism. He made his position clear in an introduction to Hume's *Treatise of Human Nature*. Using the arguments of Hume he tried to demonstrate that the empiricists could not account for the existence of human knowledge, without ignoring a glaring contradiction in their own argument. If the work of the mind was to accumulate sense data, and if the mind itself consisted of minute sense data, how could it ever go beyond itself? Green also went on to show that empiricism, *constructing* a world from perceived sense data, might end up with a nice construct, but what about its relation to the real world. Once again the old claim was made that empiricism must inevitably lead to phyrronic scepticism. Hume in the eyes of Green was a great thinker, but now the torch had to be passed on to someone else. The most suitable candidate seemed to be – Immanuel Kant. From here on the next steps in Green's argument begin to sound somewhat familiar. Kant's transcendental ego is an ontological entity, in fact it *must* be one, because Kant had preceded Hegel. Not that Green had much use for Hegel himself, but Kant in his hands became thoroughly Platonized. While Green took on the whole of empiricism in great detail, to the point of occasionally seeming pedantic, F.H. BRADLEY embraced speculative Idealism in a totally different manner. F.H. Bradley (1846–1924) is one of the most intriguing figures of the relatively brief period of British Idealism. Unlike Green, whose refutation of empiricism kept him bound to the subject–object relationship, and his softened Hegelianism made him hypostasize the *relation* as such, Bradley wholeheartedly embraced the idea of the *Absolute*. It was not an imitation of Hegel's *Absolute*, but like Hegel Bradley believed in an unfolding reality where each individual error would be overcome at a next step of improved knowledge. Bradley, in other words, sidestepped the dualism of Green and insisted upon the unity of given experience, calling it 'a unified whole within which diverse aspects can be distinguished'. Bradley shared Green's view that developed experience, or conscious experience, was relational, or in his term 'mediated', but he did not belittle the existence, or the importance of, immediate experience. In a way, the beginning of Bradley's most fascinating work *Appearance and Reality*

(1893) resembles in large parts Hegel's introduction and first chapter of the *Phenomenology*, especially as Bradley seems to be one of the few *philosophers* who understood what Hegel had meant by such terms as *Vermittlung* and *Aufhebung*. He could speak of mediation, without inheriting all the problems Green encountered when talking about relations. But it is not the formal distinction between Green and Bradley that makes the reading of *Appearance and Reality* such a breathtaking adventure. It is rather the bold approach that Bradley embraces when facing the problems of his predecessors. Where Hegel sometimes plods along, Bradley, as if inspired by an Ancient Greek optimism, presents his insights, sometimes aphoristically, in sweeping intellectual movements. Thus an object of cognition is 'real' if it is not related to anything else, and that is exactly the way by which we are bound to understand it. Reality is absolute, even if our understanding of the real is not always up to such perfection. Nowhere in his writings does Bradley attempt to *describe* the Absolute. This makes sense, of course, because the *Absolute* as designed by Bradley is beyond description. If readers of Bradley have sensed a mystical streak in him, they must not be totally mistaken, but the real crux lies elsewhere. We can always explain that which in philosophy deals with notions of the Absolute as something close to mysticism, and leave it at that. But Bradley's legacy shows us that the effort of *understanding,* and therefore the work of philosophy, cannot be satisfied in such a facile manner. Had Wittgenstein not known that the opposite was true, he would never have finished his *Tractatus* with the notorious statement 'Whereof one cannot speak, thereof one must be silent.'

Bradley, by pitting with a Spinozistic fervour the Absolute as a necessity against our limited ways of knowledge, opened together with Continental philosophers the road towards the question, 'How can we speak clearly about things?' After all, both G.E. Moore and Bertrand Russell had, in their early years, been admiring readers of F.H. Bradley. The sources for the linguistic and analytic turns in philosophy had many origins, and next to Frege, Carnap and Herbart, a figure like F.H. Bradley should not be forgotten.

The republic of professors

We may take the fact that Nietzsche abandoned his tenure in Basel, in order to be able to pursue his thoughts free from academic pressures, just as

Kierkegaard preferred to live off his inheritance rather than seeking a permanent position within either academia or as a minister within the Church, as a sign that something had changed within the universities themselves. Even if the life of Kierkegaard and the slow descent of Nietzsche into clinical madness are hardly comparable, we can nevertheless say that the authority which someone like Hegel, who was eventually seen as a kind of state philosopher – an accepted spokesman of the world-spirit at its most advanced stage – had ceased to exist by the second half of the nineteenth century. A number of contributing factors are responsible for this development, which became most visible in the changes in Continental philosophy, but also in different ways in England and in the USA.

On the Continent, in Germany and France especially, the sciences had become increasingly dominant in the formulation of what pre-occupied society. France had the Grands Ecoles and Germany, after the liberal reforms instigated by Humboldt, relatively self-reliant universities that governed their own affairs, not in total but in a rather far-reaching form of academic freedom. This meant, of course, that in whatever way one wants to define 'autonomy', a large degree of vested interest had for the time being found its 'adequate' organizational form of expression. Also, in different ways academic freedom had become a class privilege, in both Europe and in the USA. This in itself was not, at first, seen as a class *problem*, but as a natural, even desirable event. The philosopher had been replaced by the Professor of Philosophy; a new intellectual type emerged within and, consequently, outside the universities. As early as in his book *Nature* (1836), in his 'American Scholar' delivered a year later at Harvard and in his *Essays, First Series* (1841) Ralph Waldo Emerson developed the concept of *Man Thinking* as opposed to a world of alienation, just as his friend HENRY DAVID THOREAU complained in *Walden* 'There are nowadays professors of philosophy, but not philosophers.' That the rebellion against the *professionalization* of philosophy, as found in the writings of Emerson, was avidly picked up by Nietzsche has already been mentioned in passing. How, indeed, could he have resisted a passage by Emerson, like this one, taken from 'Circles', which he adopted verbatim, stating only '*Ein Amerikaner muß es ihnen sagen*

[An American may tell them]':

> Beware when the great God lets loose a thinker on this planet says Emerson. 'Then all things are at risk. It is as when a conflagration has broken out in a great city, and no man knows what is safe, or where it will end. There is not a piece of science, but its flank may be turned tomorrow; there is not any literary reputation, not the so-called eternal names of fame that may not be revised and condemned.... A new degree of culture would instantly revolutionize the entire system of human pursuits.'
>
> (*Thoughts out of Season* (*Unzeitgemäße Betrachtungen*), 1875–6)

When William James, looking back late in life, laconically claimed that the academic and the disinterested classes were identical, and hence the only social group capable of looking for the truth, he was only expressing a sentiment that had become the general opinion in academic circles by then:

> In our democracy, where everything else is so shifting, we alumni and alumnae of the colleges are the only permanent presence that corresponds to the aristocracy in older countries ... and unlike them, we stand for ideal interests solely, for we have no corporate selfishness and wield no powers of corruption. We ought to have our own class-consciousness. 'Les intellectuals'!
>
> (William James, 1908)

It would soon become the issue of a great debate, though; even if the young John Dewey, in 1905, would almost for the last time in history reclaim the responsibility for a whole nation of philosophy. James of course looked back at the successful history of Pragmatism, and at the German University, as he had experienced it at a time when it seemed to represent what Charles Saunders Peirce had termed the 'community of investigators'. If we look at the beginnings of Pragmatism, as it emerges out of the genteel atmosphere of the Metaphysical Club, we get a glimpse of what ideally the *Gelehrtenrepublik* might have been about, and certainly we will understand the role of the Gentleman-Scholar. But we shall miss – while overpraising the benign character of William James who popularized the philosophy of Pragmatism more than anybody else – that the original insights of Pragmatism, as outlined by Peirce, were far from simple. To the contrary, they were won over and against Kant, Hegel and British traditional empiricism as exemplified by John

Locke and David Hume. Peirce, the son of the famous mathematician Benjamin Peirce, did not take his logic lightly, and his attempt to turn Kant upside down was a serious exercise in itself. Peirce went to extreme lengths to refute the Kantian 'a priori' categories, claiming that as a result reality, seen as a reality-in-itself, would eventually be unknowable. At the same time he rejected the Hegelian idea that truth could be attained by following a certain logical pattern, defined by the nature of truth itself. In order to get out of what he perceived to be the dilemma of speculative idealism (Hegel) or the fallacy of objectivism (Kant), and in order to escape from fruitless relativism, Peirce introduced the category of belief, as a guidance for action, which when tested by many would lead to truth. In a way, though differing from both Kant and Hegel, Peirce was nevertheless deeply indebted to both of them. From Kant he took the methodical approach and from Hegel the evolutionary approach towards the idea of truth. By placing this inheritance into the hands of a 'scientific community', he could rightly assume to have successfully introduced the idea of fallibilism into the philosophical construction of reality, making thought and action part and parcel of one inseparable activity. Rather than being preordained, as in the case of Hegel, truth, as Peirce put it, was *'fated'* to ultimately happen as the result of the investigation by many. It is obvious that this epistemology, whatever its eventual ramifications might be – and it is not unfair to state that the seminal character of Peirce's work, as a logician, as the founder of modern semiotics, and the father of the various versions of Pragmatism that would follow, is the result of exactly these ramifications – puts a great trust in the social reality of any given community. If we were to push this argument, we could claim that Peirce was already mistaken where his immediate academic surrounding was concerned. Not only was he *not* judged by his peers on the strength of his intellectual abilities, but also by his nonconformist attitudes and behaviour, which barred him from ever obtaining the permanent academic position he so badly wanted, almost turning him into a tragic hero in the annals of academic life. He was also wrong in his belief that a friend like James would adhere to the rigors of his own standards of logical inquiry. James, with a few little known exceptions, which would however seriously harm the career of Peirce, defended his friend in most cases and definitely always in print,

but veered so far from what Peirce had originally envisioned that the latter toyed with the idea of renaming his version of Pragmatism, to put a difference between himself and his followers. James, to make the ideas of Peirce more accessible to a wider audience, drew heavily on his own work as a psychologist; his tome, *Principles of Psychology,* had appeared in 1890, and where Peirce was interested in the scientific proof of a given belief, James judged its validity by its usefulness for the practical life of the individual. The 'cash value' of truth, as he put it, was to be seen in its workability, its suitability, in its *usefulness!* Had he confined all of this to the field of inquiry, Peirce might not have objected, but as a definition of truth this did not work. The more James moved into the direction of seeing the task of philosophy as making life worth living for the individual, the more he distorted the original intentions of Peirce. Thus it was only a small step from a *Pluralistic Universe* (1909), in the sense of James – the title that he gave to the book which would move him closer to a religious view of the world than Pragmatism would ever go – to relativism at the cost of scientific investigation. But then again, we must bear in mind that the *Pluralistic Universe* contained the Hibbert Lectures, given at Oxford in 1908–9, and whenever James talked in public he tended to simplify matters, in order to be understood. Nevertheless, and whatever his intentions, James managed to move Pragmatism away from its epistemological confinements into the world of life as lived. To put this in a totally different fashion, and William James into a different perspective: he had arrived, where *he* had always wanted to be as a philosopher, at the heart of an identifiable US experience, and its specific challenges and demands.

Turmoil

The Great War put an end to the coherence of nineteenth-century thought. If we mention this coherence after having dealt for such length on philosophical divergences, we must explain why we nevertheless tend to see the nineteenth century as a unified whole. The key to this riddle lies in the extreme ability of the great and minor thinkers of the century to absorb and to popularize difficult philosophical material. Neither should we ignore the fact that at a time of enormous social changes and upheavals there was a need for unifying ideas. The lament of Henry Adams in his famous *Education*, written at the end of the nineteenth century, that unity had succumbed to anarchy, only mirrors the general desire of the nineteenth century to see itself as one great intellectual endeavour, dedicated to the fulfilment of the promises of Enlightenment. Charles Saunders Peirce had found the following words for the vision that so many intellectuals in so many different ways shared in the nineteenth century.

> Thus, the very origin of the conception of reality shows that this conception essentially involves the notion of a COMMUNITY, without definite limits, and capable of an indefinite increase of knowledge.

Further reading

Ayer, A.J. (1980) *Hume*, Oxford: Oxford University Press.

Brent, Joseph (1998) *Charles Sanders Peirce: A Life*, Bloomington, IN: Indiana University Press.

Danto, A.C. (1965) *Nietzsche as Philosopher*, New York: Columbia University Press.

Elrod, J.W. (1975) *Being and Existence in Kierkegaard's Pseudonymous Works*, Princeton, NJ: Princeton University Press.

MacIntyre, Alasdair (1981) *After Virtue*, London: Duckworth.

Myers, Gerald E. (2001) *William James, His Life and Thought*, New Haven, CT: Yale University Press.

Norton, D.F. (1982) *David Hume: Common-Sense Moralist, Sceptical Metaphysician*, Princeton, NJ: Princeton University Press.

Paton, J.H. (1948) *The Categorical Imperative: A Study in Kant's Moral Philosophy*, London: Hutchinson.

Richardson, Robert D. (1996) *Emerson: The Mind on Fire*, Berkeley: University of California Press.

Smith, N.K. (1930) *A Commentary to Kant's Critique of Pure Reason*, London: Macmillan.

Taylor, Charles (1979) *Hegel*, Cambridge: Cambridge University Press.

Tucker, R. (1969) *The Marxian Revolutionary Idea*, London: Norton.

Wollheim, R. (1959) *F.H. Bradley*, London: Penguin.

Wright, J.P. (1983) *The Sceptical Realism of David Hume*, Manchester: Manchester University Press.

OLAF HANSEN

MAIN CURRENTS IN SCIENTIFIC THOUGHT

In 1800 Paris was the world's centre of excellence in science. There, a new and rigorous mix of experiment, observation and theory (mathematical where possible) was replacing the natural theology so characteristic of Britain and the infant USA, and the metaphysical systems of Enlightenment *philosophes* and German *Naturphilosophen*, with what AUGUSTE COMTE was to hail as positive knowledge. In the Academy of Sciences, the École Polytechnique, medical schools and the Museum of Natural History with its garden and zoo, Paris contained the institutions to propel this second scientific revolution, leading to specialization, new professions and the rise of scientists as gurus. In Britain, engaged in a world war against the French, an emphasis on careful Baconian induction and its useful applications was politically sound and widely acceptable; here also, as in the mass of states constituting Germany and overrun by the French army, ideas we call Romantic were transforming the old view (prominent in William Paley's *Natural Theology* of 1802) that we are little clocks living in an enormous clock. A dynamic science of forces, and an awareness of change over time, challenged Newtonian mechanical ideas and the determinism of P.S. Laplace. The industrial and imperial wealth of Britain, and the refounded universities of Germany, were during the century to eclipse France and be associated with chemical atomic theory, with a respectable theory of evolution, with conservation of energy and classical physics, and by 1900 with electrons and quanta. By then, there were many centres, science had become an important component in education and its ideas seemed an essential feature of what most saw as a century of progress.

Descriptive science

In the late eighteenth century, the work of Carl Linné (Linnaeus) was as important a model as that of Newton. He had organized natural history (most notably botany) by grouping organisms and minerals on the basis of external characters; previously, Aristotle and his successors had relied on perceiving family groups in a process like connoisseurship. Moreover, the English word 'sycamore' for example is applied to very different kinds of trees: Linnaeus assigned double-barrelled Latin names to plants and animals, so that everyone knew just what was meant. By 1800, his system had been improved in Paris, becoming more 'natural' in taking into account more characters; it was now necessary to dissect in order to classify.

Zoologists caught up with botanists; and particularly Georges Cuvier emphasized Aristotle's principle of correlation. Nature does nothing in vain: all the parts of an organism cohere. The carnivore will have cutting and slashing teeth, powerful shoulders, claws, forward vision and a simple digestive system: Cuvier believed that given a single bone he could determine what it came from. Naturalists had hoped to place all organisms on a single great chain or ladder, from amoebas up to humans (and maybe on up through angels); but Cuvier could not accept this even for zoology, seeing instead a great bush with four main stems from which all animals branched off. The language of families and genera implied relationships, and clearly horses, donkeys and zebras were alike; but for Linnaeus and for Cuvier, species were distinct, variability was limited and the ideal of science was to describe and place them carefully, but not speculate about evolution. Old-fashioned people like J.B. Lamarck and Erasmus Darwin had gone in for that, diverting people from sound positive science: and when as Permanent Secretary of the Academy, Cuvier came to deliver the *éloge* for Lamarck, he was scathing and witty.

It was striking that the fauna and flora of places with similar climates, in Europe, North America, Southern Africa and Australia for example, were very different. This had been taken as evidence of God's delight in diversity; but by 1800 'acclimatizing' had become a major enterprise, a way in which science might improve the world. The First Fleet going to New South Wales had not been expected to survive on a diet of kangaroos and witchity grubs: they took cows and sheep to breed from, and corn and vegetables to sow. Potatoes, tobacco, maize and chilli peppers had come to the Old World from the New; and with the confident and active scientific spirit of the nineteenth century the idea (alarming to us) that species should be transferred around the world gained ground rapidly. Sir Joseph Banks, president of the Royal Society from 1778 to 1820, looked after a flock of merino sheep at Kew, and oversaw the transport of some of them to Australia to found the Botany wool industry. Under Sir Joseph Hooker, Victorian Kew became a great centre of economic botany, serving a mighty empire. He brought back and cultivated Himalayan rhododendrons, transforming Victorian gardens; and supervised the collection and smuggling of rubber and quinine trees from Latin America, which were grown in Kew's great hothouses and then transferred to plantations in British colonies. When the London Zoo was founded in 1827 by Sir Humphry Davy (Banks's successor as president of the Royal Society) and Sir Stamford Raffles, founder of Singapore, one of its aims was the acclimatization of animals: it was hoped that llamas for example might grace the fields of England.

In parallel with this went close studies of particular faunas and floras, in what became the science of ecology. The resources of Spanish America had long been state secrets, until Alexander von Humboldt managed under French auspices a five-year visit from 1799. A universal man, he studied all three branches of natural history, as well as magnetism, astronomy and economics: he perceived that maps can include data of physical geography like isotherms as well as topography, and realized that anyone climbing snow-capped mountains at the Equator goes through all climatic zones up to the arctic. On his return, he spent his fortune in publishing thirty volumes of reports on his discoveries: he had to move from Prussia to Paris to be able to write up his work, and became a great advocate of international co-operation. Under his auspices, the 'big science' of the first half of the nineteenth century, involving expensive ships, equipment and skilled manpower, has been called Humboldtian. This meant global vision, co-operating observatories working in close co-ordination and the tabulation of great quantities of data. Scientific voyages that had begun with Captain James Cook and his contemporaries became a feature of the nineteenth century, especially after peace in 1815. Banks, Hooker, THOMAS HUXLEY and Edward Sabine, who all learned their science on voyages, became presidents of the Royal Society; and in 1849 John Herschel, a great admirer of Humboldt who had spent time in South Africa observing the southern stars and nebulae, edited the *Admiralty Manual of Scientific Enquiry*, which has among others a contribution from CHARLES DARWIN. The French, Russian and US navies also played an important part: but the dominance of Britain meant that from 1884 the zero of longitude went through Greenwich, and that the culminating voyage was that of HMS *Challenger*, in 1872–6, whose fifty volumes of reports were finally completed by an international team in 1895. By 1870 transoceanic telegraphy had shifted attention to the deep sea, previously supposed lifeless.

Historical Science

Critical history, recognizing that the past was genuinely different, came to fruition in Germany, notably with Johann Herder, at the beginning of the century. Cuvier, working on fossils from the quarries of Montmartre, reconstructed past creatures amid great excitement, sorting out different animals from the usually disjointed bones, and recognizing that there were a series of distinct faunas beneath Paris. He inferred that there must have been a series of catastrophes separating the different strata, with the mammoth found quick-frozen in Siberia as a victim of such an event. Charles Lyell in England challenged this view in 1830–3, with his *Principles of Geology: An Attempt to Explain the Former Changes of the Earth's Surface, by Reference to Causes Now in Operation.* Instead of catastrophes, he required ordinary forces over tens or hundreds of million of years. His teacher in Oxford, William Buckland, who had upheld the reality of Noah's Flood, was convinced; and in his geological *Bridgewater Treatise* of 1836 he conveyed the sweep of geological time with a frontispiece over a metre long when folded out. Pre-biblical time did not worry Buckland, his theologian friend Edward Pusey or Adam Sedgwick, his opposite number at Cambridge: but they discerned progress over time, as fish gave way to reptiles, and they to mammals, seeing in this God's providence as the world was prepared for mankind, with a cool climate to be moderated by ingenious use of coal, wood and iron. Lyell rejected evolutionary theory in Lamarck's version; but his refutation made it known, and it filled the notorious and very successful anonymous *Vestiges of the Natural History of Creation*, 1844, written by the Scottish publisher Robert Chambers and used by Alfred Tennyson who coined the famous phrase 'Nature red in tooth and claw.' For Lyell, past time was cyclic rather than progressive; the dinosaurs might come back again under suitable conditions; and there was no real and irreversible historical change, nothing really new under the sun.

For Darwin his disciple, it was different. Returning from his voyage on HMS *Beagle*, he worked out the idea that organisms had developed through natural selection in Thomas Malthus's 'struggle for existence', which generated HERBERT SPENCER's 'survival of the fittest'. Lorenz Oken and other Germans had followed Goethe in seeing behind the common plan of homologies an ideal being realized through time, but there was no credible mechanism for evolution – a word Darwin avoided in *On the Origin of Species*, 1859, because it had overtones of progress. His process was open-ended, and organisms might go up or down in the world: the barnacles upon which he became an authority were cousins of the shrimps and lobsters, who had very successfully adopted the lifestyle of the much humbler limpet. His was a great synthesis, bringing together Linnaeus's taxonomy, Humboldt's biogeography, Cuvier's palaeontology and the experience of stockbreeders and pigeon-fanciers. Although there were many gaps, pointed out by scientists like Richard Owen (the first superintendent of the Natural History Museum in London, who had earlier reconstructed the moa from a single bone) as well as by Bishop Samuel Wilberforce, those armed with Darwin's theory could go beyond descriptive science and explain why creatures were the way they were. This might seem a just-so story, not rigorously testable, but history is not like physics, where experiment isolates one cause, but a messy business, unpredictable in detail, of multiple causes and conditions. Resisted at first especially in France, evolutionary theory had generally prevailed by the time Darwin died in 1882; and in anthropology, and even astronomy and chemistry, evolution was the magic word. But the austere and open-ended theory of Darwin and his ally ALFRED RUSSEL WALLACE was rejected by most contemporaries in favour of a more progressive and Lamarckian view.

Scientific method

Many of those who objected to Darwin believed that his ideas were unscientific. Two methods of inference were allowed: induction, generalizing from authenticated facts, and deduction, from axioms to testable conclusions. No animal or plant had ever been seen to change into another species, and so Darwin's conclusions could not be inductive; and they also lacked the logical rigor of Euclidean geometry or mathematical physics. His theory was historical, and statistical: the statistics being informal, based on the idea that in general the individual with some small advantage is more likely to survive and propagate its kind. The great poet is one who expands the sphere of poetry; maybe Darwin's greatness was to expand scientific method into new territory.

Huxley was among those who believed that scientific method could be taught even to those learning little science. Sophisticated induction was described, with examples, by Herschel in his *Preliminary Discourse* of 1831, written to introduce the physical sciences for a series of little books, 'Lardner's Cabinet Cyclopedia' by Longman in London, in the printing and publishing revolution associated with the 'march of mind'. They were cheap, hardbound books: the average price of a book in England fell by 48 per cent in the 25 years after 1827 as they ceased to be items of luxury. Herschel's book was greatly admired by JOHN STUART MILL, whose *System of Logic,* 1843, was a classic statement of inductive philosophy. Early in the century, men of science in Britain had claimed to be followers of Baconian induction, but their practice was not actually in accordance with it. William Whewell in Cambridge, closely connected with those there creating a school of mathematical physics, and aware of German post-Kantian philosophy, proposed in his *Philosophy of the Inductive Sciences,* 1840, the idea that one must intuitively get the right end of the stick before one can begin to collect facts. His version of scientific method was thus much closer to the hypothetico-deductive model. Darwin was by temperament a deductive reasoner, collecting facts to test an idea; the *Origin* is a splendid example of Whewell's method, and Darwin was disappointed that Whewell greatly disapproved of the book.

Handling probability was one of the great triumphs of nineteenth-century science, beginning with Carl Gauss's demonstration that astronomical observations cluster round the true result in a bell-shaped 'error curve', and Laplace's mathematical analysis of probability. In Belgium, Lambert Quetelet was appointed to work at the observatory, but soon perceived that human characteristics also fell on a bell curve, and that in the mass human behaviour was highly predictable. He chilled the spines of readers of his *Essay on Man* (1835, English translation 1842) with murder rates, at just the same time that even backward Britain was collecting what were called vital statistics. These established how unhealthy great cities were compared to the countryside, and became an essential tool of government. In 1859, shortly before the *Origin* was published, James Clerk Maxwell announced his dynamical theory of gases, that they were composed of elastic particles moving on average faster as the gas warmed up. Thus in physics, too, statistics rather than straightforward causality seemed to underlie reality; and with Ernst Mach in the last years of the century, established Newtonian ideas of space and time also came under criticism.

Chemistry

Reorganized by Antoine Lavoisier, chemistry in 1800 seemed the most exciting and fundamental science, promising also to be useful. Davy attracted huge audiences to his lectures at the newly founded Royal Institution (RI) in London's West End, where he and later Michael Faraday competed successfully with other theatrical entertainments, and did their fundamental research in the basement laboratories. Davy, isolating potassium and other elements, showed that chemical affinity was electrical, that chemistry was a science of force as well as matter; while John Dalton at the RI in 1803 and then back in Manchester developed his new chemical atomism, in which each element had its own distinct atom. Chemistry was the science of the secondary qualities, colours, tastes and smells, and the chemist had to develop manual skills well described in Faraday's book, *Chemical Manipulation*, 1827; laboratory instruction gradually entered university courses as chemistry became separated from medicine. The analysis of organic compounds was particularly tricky, but Justus Liebig at the little university of Giessen perfected ways of doing it, and built up a research school of graduate students working for PhDs in a great laboratory. This was one of the great inventions of the nineteenth century, copied at first elsewhere in Germany (with universities newly dedicated to the increase of knowledge, *Wissenschaft*, and to the development of students, *Bildung*) and then abroad. Thus Liebig's star pupil August Hofmann was invited by Prince Albert to start a Royal College of Chemistry in London in 1845 on the Giessen model. There in 1856 William Perkin prepared the first synthetic dye, 'mauve', which marked the beginning of a huge industry – the pupils of Liebig and others ensuring that this research-based business would develop in Germany.

One major problem was to connect the results of analyses with atomic theory to derive molecular structures. Hofmann demonstrated ball and rod models at the RI in the 1860s, but it was impossible to infer unambiguous formulae inductively: there were good arguments for water being HO, for example, or for our H_2O. Auguste Laurent suggested that chemists should work hypothetico-deductively; and this idea was taken up by August Kekulé from 1858, who proposed a ring structure for benzene, and tested its consequences. Structural organic chemistry became a leading part of the science. In 1860 Kekulé called an international conference at Karlsruhe, where H_2O was agreed for water following Stanislao Cannizzaro's advocacy; and this led to an agreed series of formulae, and of relative atomic weights. Using these new and mostly uncontested figures, Dmitri Mendeleev in 1868 constructed a classification system for the chemical elements, the Periodic Table. This grouped them into families, like Linnaeus's plants, and meant that the chemist who knew the properties for example of sulphur could infer those of selenium: there was much less brute fact to learn. Mendeleev had predicted (as botanists could not do!), with what turned out to be astonishing accuracy, undiscovered elements to fill gaps in his table. Chemists who had at first been suspicious about his classification, asking if alphabetical order would be as good, became enthusiasts in the 1880s; and some, notably William Crookes, gave it an evolutionary flavour.

In 1860, in an unusual collaboration between a chemist and a physicist, Robert Bunsen and Gustav Kirchhoff at Heidelberg demonstrated that when substances were heated using Bunsen's burner, and viewed through a prism, they emitted a spectrum that was characteristic of the elements present. Their analyses soon led also to new elements; and the spectroscope became the first 'physical' tool in chemical laboratories dominated by test tubes and other glassware – which by 1900 were made of pyrex glass, and even sometimes fitted together, rather than being connected by glass and rubber tubes with carefully bored corks. The study of slow reactions, and of chemical equilibria, also marked the beginning of physical chemistry, blurring boundaries, and raising the question of whether chemistry might be reduced to physics. Most chemistry in the nineteenth century was done by single investigators, usually with now-forgotten assistants; but by 1900 collective work, by those with complementary skills, was becoming more normal.

The coming of physics

For Lavoisier, heat was a substance, 'caloric'; but by the 1830s the old theory that it was motion of particles was revived. James Joule in Manchester demonstrated this by heating water with a stirrer; and Hermann Helmholtz generalized this in 1847, arguing that heat, light, mechanical motion, electricity, chemical affinity and magnetism were all aspects of indestructible energy, could be quantitatively converted into each other, and be expressed in the same terms of space, time and mass. This great synthesis, the first law of thermodynamics, created the science of classical physics, more fundamental than chemistry: the task of physicists was to determine with great accuracy the exchange rates and constants such as the velocity of light, where the American Albert Michelson was prominent as the USA began to make its mark. The second law of thermodynamics, coming from the reflections of Sadi Carnot in France on the limits to the efficiency of steam engines, was generalized by Rudolf Clausius and by William Thomson to indicate that the universe had a direction to it: the availability of energy was decreasing (or 'entropy' increasing) with the passage of time. We should expect that the Sun will gradually cool, and that eventually the world will end in a 'heat death' of universal tepidity. This antidote to evolutionary, progressive optimism contributed to some *fin de siècle* gloom, as in H.G. WELLS's *Time Machine,* 1895; though the calculations of Thomson (the first scientist to be made a peer, as Lord Kelvin) indicated that there were many million years to come, Kelvin's calculations of the age of the solar system also indicated a relatively short geological past. Assuming that the Sun was made of the best coal and also fuelled by meteors and gravitational collapse, and that the Earth was a cooling sphere, he arrived at a maximum of one hundred million years. Huxley did his best to respond and cast doubt, but arguing with a confident and highly numerate physicist was not easy – though he was right, since Henri Becquerel's discovery of radio-activity in 1896 revealed a new source of energy unsuspected by Kelvin.

This was one of a series of surprises that transformed classical physics. Faraday's work on electromagnetism, put into mathematical form by Maxwell, introduced the idea of a field in place of Newtonian attractions and repulsions between point masses. Following from this, Heinrich Hertz observed radio waves. Crookes meanwhile was studying cathode rays, which J.J. Thomson at the Cavendish Laboratory in Cambridge (set up under Maxwell in 1871) demonstrated in 1897 to be a stream of negatively charged particles, which he first called 'corpuscles' but soon recognized to be the units of charge already called electrons. Those who had supposed that the outlines of physics were known, and only the details remained to be sketched in were wrong; and from 1897 Max Planck found that to account for the radiation from black bodies he had to suppose that energy came in lumps, or 'quanta', rather than con-tinuously. Atoms were complex, and now matter and energy seemed indistinct.

The community of scientists

In 1800 outside Paris science was necessarily a hobby rather than a career for almost everybody. The Royal Society had a small active nucleus but was essentially a club for intellectual gentlemen, whose subscriptions subsidized its publications. Provincial Literary and Philosophical Societies and Athenaeums were similar, at a different social level, while natural historians formed field clubs. Very gradually, the Royal Society began to trans-form itself into something like an Academy of Sciences by 1900. In the 1820s, Oken organized meetings for *Naturforscher* from all over Germany, meeting each year in a different state, and these proved very successful. In 1831 at York the British Association for the Advancement of Science (BAAS) was formed on this model, following widely expressed alarm at the decline of British science, and provincial disdain for London: it was to meet in a different city each year. Cities began to bid for visits, promising to set up libraries, muse-ums or technical colleges as well as host dinners; the vast meetings were organized in sections for different sciences, with some plenary sessions.

Coming in the summer 'silly season', they were well reported, and those going began to feel themselves scientists, the new term coined by Whewell at the Cambridge meeting in 1833. The BAAS, which from its profits made small research grants, was in its turn a model for institutions in the USA and in France. The President for the year would give an address, and might be asked to make representa-tions to government. John Tyndall in Belfast in 1874 used the occasion to claim the whole of cos-mology for science from organized religion; but controversial speeches were not expected or indeed desired.

The surprise Prussian victory over France in 1870 was attributed to German science, and was an enormous fillip to scientific education and influence elsewhere. New industries, regulations and educational bodies required new scientific professions. Scientific ideas were disseminated formally as part of a training, and in research journals that circulated among the elite, and also in lectures and popular publications directed at the general public, which to the puzzlement of professors might well be more interested in the spirits or the reading of character from bumps on the head than in chemical analyses. Tyndall had seen atomism, evolution and energy as the keys to the scientific world-view, and certainly these ideas seem crucial in the development of nineteenth-century science. In many ways, that century was the age of science: new worlds were opening, industrial and social progress seemed apparent, labour and disease were in retreat as science advanced. Acclimatization, fertilizers and explo-sives all appeared thoroughly good and useful; and although science was in fact connected with the development of new weapons, it could still be generally thought in 1900 that it did nobody any harm. With the new century, new ideas were undermining certainty in physics, and science would begin to appear dangerous in the hands of irresponsible Frankensteins.

Further reading

Crosland, M.P. (1992) *Science under Control: The French Academy of Sciences 1795–1914*, Cambridge: Cambridge University Press.
Desmond, A and Moore, J. (1991) *Darwin*, London: Michael Joseph.

Knight, D.M. and Kragh, H. (ed.) (1998) *The Making of the Chemist: The Social History of Chemistry in Europe 1789–1914*, Cambridge: Cambridge University Press.

Nye, M.J. (ed.) (2003) *The Modern Physical and Mathematical Sciences: Cambridge History of Science*, vol. 5, Cambridge: Cambridge University Press.

D.M. KNIGHT

MAINE, HENRY (1822–88)

A leading scholar of historical jurisprudence and theorist of late Victorian British conservatism, Henry Maine was born near Leighton on 15 August 1822, and was educated at Christ's Hospital and Pembroke College, Cambridge. A leading classical scholar, he became fellow of Trinity Hall, and Regius Professor of Civil Law in 1847. Called to the bar in 1850, Maine also wrote for various newspapers and periodicals on contemporary affairs, particularly foreign policy, and French and US politics, and contributing chiefly to the *Saturday Review*. His politics at this point were essentially Peelite. In 1852 he became reader on Roman Law and Jurisprudence at the Inns of Court. His first major work, *Ancient Law* (1861), assessed a variety of ancient codes, and concentrated on the history of the law of nature, of the evolution of testamentary succession, and of the early history of property, contract, delict and crime. It made famous the notion that the movement of progressive societies was from status to contract, and was a pioneering example of the application of the comparative method to historical jurisprudence.

In 1862 Maine left for India to become a legal member of the ruling Council, taking the post once filled by MACAULAY, and in codifying Indian law following the latter's dictum of 'Uniformity when you can have it, diversity when you must have it, but in all cases certainty.' He remained seven years, under the administrations of Lords Elgin, Lawrence and Mayo. On returning he became Corpus Professor of Jurisprudence at Oxford, his first course of lectures being published as *Village Communities* (1891). This attracted attention not only as a work of scholarship, but also in relation to Gladstone's proposed Irish land reforms, and as a more theoretical treatment of the relationship between British social and legal norms and Indian customary practice (notably in relation, for instance, to equality and to systems of land tenure). Another set of lectures, published as *Lectures on the Early History of Institutions* (1875) continued this line of thought, but now focusing as much on recent translations of Brehon or ancient Irish law, and treating themes as diverse as kinship, tribal chiefs, the ancient family, the diffusion of primitive ideas, the emergence of primitive legal remedies, married women's property and early notions of sovereignty. Becoming Master of Trinity Hall in 1877, Maine was increasingly honoured with membership in academies and societies both domestic and foreign. This sequence of writings was completed with the publication of *Dissertations on Early Law and Custom* (1883), which was similarly wide-ranging, containing, amongst the essays, two important essays on religion and law in India, two on ancestor worship, two on kingship and two more on property, and a survey of theories of primitive society generally.

It was at this time that Maine emerged as the leader of conservative reaction to Gladstonian liberalism after the 1884 Reform Act, offering a restatement of its principles in *Popular Government* (1885), which proclaimed his intention to apply the comparative method to contemporary societies. Here his principal concern was to warn of the electoral corruption and intellectual inferiority of popular democratic regimes, and the concomitant necessity for a ruling elite defined by ability and intelligence. Breaking with the tradition of BURKE and COLERIDGE in denying any central role to religion in his conservatism, Maine instead used biological arguments derived from DARWIN to argue a more heredity-based defence of elitism, an emphasis also developed by a younger contemporary, W.H. MALLOCK. The four essays of which *Popular Government* is composed are 'The Prospects of Popular Government', 'The Nature of Democracy', 'The Age of Progress' and 'The Constitution of the United States'. Denying either the political superiority or (against TOCQUEVILLE in particular) historical inevitability of the progress of democracy, Maine takes Rousseau's conception of the state of nature as the fount of natural rights to be the source of most modern democratic theory. Using a variety of modern instances, he attempts to demonstrate the fundamental instability of modern popular regimes, and their proneness to devolve into military dictatorships or mob rule. Civilization, he contends, is inevitably the outcome of aristocratic government alone; barbarism is more likely to flow from popular rule. Fuelled by vulgar prejudices, democracy was rooted in a Benthamite formulation of the inevitability of the pursuit of happiness as self-interest, and thus the corollary that popular government alone could serve the interests of the whole. But for Maine, Bentham had woefully underestimated the virtues of the intellectual elite, and the necessity of public opinion to be informed by the educated few, whose claim to be a natural ruling elite was thus wholly justifiable. Nowhere was this more evident to Europeans than in the history of the French Revolution, whose contribution to the 'Age of Progress' Maine contemptuously dismisses, and, in a wider perspective, in the development of the US polity, whose strengths Maine thought were indebted mostly to imitating British experience, but whose weaknesses would eventually result in a regime of vulgar partisanship, unless restrained by a powerful executive.

Maine's later, brief works include a *Quarterly Review* essay on 'Patriarchal Theory' (1886), and a lengthy chapter in Thomas Humphry Ward's *The Reign of Queen Victoria* (1887), surveying British administration in India, and emphasizing the progressive role played first by the East India Company, then under direct rule, in curtailing customs like suttee, and of the expansion of the infrastructure of roads and railways, of legal codification, and the provision of education. His last book, *International Law* (1888), published posthumously, was a set of lectures examining the emergence and sources of the subject, with most of the work concentrating on the development of the law of war. In the last lecture Maine treats of the problem of international arbitration, and the considerable advantages that would ensue from appointing a permanent court of arbitration whose settlements were enforced by the leading powers. Maine died on 3 February 1888.

Further reading

Grant Duff, M.E. (1892) *Sir Henry Maine. A Brief Memoir of His Life, With Some of His India Speeches and Minutes*, London: John Murray.

SEE ALSO: anthropology and race; conservatism, authority and tradition; democracy, populism and rights; intellectuals, elites and meritocracy; mythology, classicism and antiquarianism; social theory and sociology in the nineteenth century; theories of law, criminology and penal reform

GREGORY CLAEYS

MAISTRE, JOSEPH DE (1753–1821)

Count Joseph de Maistre, born in Chambéry, Savoy, in 1753, was one of the most original and influential of all counter-revolutionary thinkers. His political ideas and above all his interpretation of the revolution profoundly marked the thought of the Legitimist supporters of the ousted Bourbon monarchy in the nineteenth century. Maistre has also attracted interest in the twentieth century due to resonances detected between his thought and, first, that of fascist intellectuals such as d'Annunzio and, second, that of post-modern critics of the Enlightenment. Despite Maistre's undoubted gifts as a writer and polemicist, his more extreme conclusions have repelled both nineteenth- and twentieth-century liberal readers, who have found his insistence on the themes of sacrifice, irrationality, violence and obedience to supreme authority unsettling. This has led to interpretations of Maistre as both an extreme reactionary, a spokesman for absolutism buttressed by violence and as a precursor of fascism with its glorification of violence and irrationality. Maistre was, however, much more than the propagandist of monarchical authority. Whilst his most celebrated work, *Considerations on France* (*Considérations sur la France*) was a violent polemic, the ideas he expressed in this work and explored in his other writings are of lasting significance. Maistre's denunciations of the revolution and the Enlightenment philosophy that he identified at its heart were coupled with a concern to investigate the nature of political order and authority, within a framework of the providential action of God on man and society.

Joseph de Maistre was born on 1 April 1753 in Chambéry, capital of Savoy, the French-speaking province of the kingdom of Piedmont-Sardinia. The Maistre family had risen from trade to law and public service, culminating in the 1778 grant of nobility awarded to Joseph's father François-Xavier, Second President of the Senate of Savoy, for his role in the codification of the Royal Constitutions. Joseph de Maistre duly became a successful magistrate and entered the Senate himself in 1788. His interests however went well beyond the law – in fact it appears from the contents of his library that law was the least of his interests, concentrating instead on *belles-lettres*, arts, sciences, history and theology. Maistre was also drawn to mysticism, a trait that expressed itself in his membership of a highly esoteric illuminist Masonic lodge into which he was initiated in 1778. Other important elements in Maistre's intellectual formation lie in his membership of the Jesuit Congregation of Our Lady and the Confraternity of the Black Penitents, in whose iconography symbols of death featured prominently and whose devotional duties included keeping vigil with condemned criminals awaiting execution. A religiosity that stressed on God's terrible justice, playing upon guilt, fear and punishment, goes some way to explaining Maistre's abiding and almost pathological fascination with sacrifice, bloodshed and expiation. The decisive event in Maistre's life was however the invasion of Savoy by the armies of the French Republic in 1792. It was in response to the revolution, in his self-imposed exile in Lausanne, 1793–7, that Maistre formulated the key elements of his political philosophy and began his literary career. After a brief interlude in Venice and Piedmont he was appointed Sardinian ambassador to Saint Petersburg, 1802–17, during which time he composed what are considered his finest works, above all the *Saint-Petersburg Dialogues* (*Les Soirées de Saint-Petersbourg*) and *The Pope* (*Du pape*). When Maistre died in Turin on 26 February 1821, after a brief spell as a minister of state and head of the magistrature, he left a literary legacy that would nourish and shape counter-revolutionary thought over the rest of the century.

Fundamental to Maistre's political vision was an exceptionally bleak view of man, informed by powerful notions of original sin. Maistre denied that the virtuous suffered; punishment was visited on man, and as irredeemably sinful and corrupt man was always deserving of punishment. Man's nature held within it an insatiable lust for power and an inclination for violence, which found its outlet in warfare, which was no aberration but mankind's habitual state. Maistre's vision of man led to several important anti-Enlightenment conclusions. First, man was a social being; there was therefore no state anterior to society and hence no social contract as postulated by Locke. Second, sovereignty was both necessary and fundamental. History, which Maistre referred to as 'experimental politics', proved that man was not born for liberty. Rousseau, whom Maistre accused of having corrupted politics, had ignored the factual evidence, namely that slavery was the natural state of most of humanity before the introduction of Christianity. Man was however not solely sinful, possessing an instinct of the divine alongside his innate degradation. This meant that men's social impulses could bear the imprint of the divine will and the truths universally accepted by men were to a lesser or greater extent true. Man either acted in accordance with God, in which case his actions were creative, or acted apart from God, in which case his actions were destructive. Legitimate, stable government was therefore aligned with the divine will.

It was with reference to the central question of sovereignty that Maistre embarked upon a biting critique of Rousseau's work in an incomplete manuscript subsequently published as *Study on Sovereignty* (*Étude sur la souveraineté*). That Maistre should attack Rousseau is in itself significant; those who see Maistre as a throwback to the divine-right theories of Bossuet neglect his engagement with the Enlightenment, his consistent efforts to refute Voltaire and Rousseau. This fragment of 1794 reveals the theoretical position that Maistre was to amplify and reiterate in later works. The constitutions of nations were neither the work of man, nor the product of deliberation, nor capable of being written. Constitutions were the political way of life that had been bestowed on a particular nation, and different forms of government were appropriate to different nations. Just as governments were the works of nature, the mode of exercising sovereignty decreed by the Creator, not the work of nations, so men submitted to sovereignty out of an instinctive feeling that it was sacred. This belief in the sacred nature of sovereignty was fundamental: government, Maistre asserted, was a religion that lived through political faith, and called for submission and belief. Just as the application of individual reason to religion annihilated religious sovereignty, so individual discussion of government annihilated political sovereignty. The sovereign, as sovereign, was above judgement. Sovereignty, in whatever way it was organized, was therefore always unequivocal and absolute, and the will of the sovereign was always invincible. To attempt to limit the sovereign was to destroy it. This did not, Maistre stressed, prevent men from instructing rulers of their needs and presenting their grievances. Indeed Maistre himself was a believer in intermediate bodies such as the *parlements.*

One conclusion of these arguments was thoroughly Burkean: national dogmas and useful prejudices, which necessarily included religion, were the secure base on which governments were to be founded. Another was the relativist judgement that the best government possible was that which was capable of producing the greatest amount of happiness and strength for the greatest number of men for the longest time. The third, which has been seized upon by those who wish to identify Maistre as a proto-totalitarian, was that authority should be submitted to without question: patriotism is identified with individual abnegation. When applied to the revolution these arguments amounted to a devastating critique. The attempt to create a constitution *ex novo* on an a priori basis was absurd, an impossibility and the abstract reasoning of the revolutionaries chimerical; neither the concept of universal laws nor than of universal man existed. The concept of the sovereignty of the people and national representation was likewise chimerical; the French Republic only assured a greater level of oppression. As an assault on sovereignty the revolution was a criminal exercise, driven by the Enlightenment loathing of authority. Moreover the Enlightenment had not only made the revolution possible by corroding moral bonds through sapping religion, but it marked the revolution as satanic. The revolution was thus to be interpreted in Manichean terms, as radically evil, a fight to the death between Christianity and Philosophism, as Maistre put it. This interpretation was destined to resonate throughout the nineteenth century.

Yet the scope of Maistre's *Considerations on France* of 1797 went far beyond these arguments. First, it should be noted that it had an immediate

political purpose: to strengthen the royalist cause by proving that the restoration of the monarchy was natural, inevitable and would not be, as liberals such as BENJAMIN CONSTANT argued, a revolution in reverse, but a restoration of peace and stability accompanied by the recognition of liberty and the amnesty of crimes. Maistre marshalled arguments to prove that the French Republic, despite its feats of arms, was destined to collapse. Monarchy was the natural government of France whereas history proved the impossibility of an enduring large republic, a form of government that had never occurred and therefore could never last. Despite his belief that governments underwent modification, Maistre's historical vision was static. Yet when it came to the means of restoration, Maistre advanced a novel argument: not only would the Restoration succeed because it was in harmony with the divine will, but also it would succeed through the operation of the divine will. *Considerations* was not merely a polemic against the revolution, it was an exposition of the operation of Providence, an explanation of the rationality hidden within the irrational. The revolution, paradoxically, was an act of Providence and the revolutionaries were the instruments God had chosen to punish a fallen France. France possessed a national mission, as did every nation, and her deviation from this role as the eldest daughter of the Church marked her out as guilty. The French were the accomplices of the national crime of the revolution, stained with the blood of Louis XVI, and it was their destiny to savour its bitter consequences. If Louis XVI's death was an expiatory sacrifice, the great majority of the victims of the revolution were guilty and it was the destiny of the revolution to accomplish the punishment of the guilty, in contrast to the moderate and merciful justice that the counter-revolution would display. In this reading the revolution became a great regenerative force, designed to purify France. Nor was the revolution confined to France, but a historical watershed; the purification of the corrupt French Church was to prepare a moral revolution across Europe, without which social bonds would dissolve and chaos ensue.

An undercurrent in Maistre's thought, and one that did not appear in *Considerations*, was a far more ominous reading of the revolution. The revolution, he wrote, was not an event, but an epoch. The seeds of the revolution could be found in the revolt of the Reformation, the great rupture in the spiritual unity of Europe, whose doctrines dissolved religious sovereignty and obedience. Closing the epoch of the revolution was therefore far from assured, requiring a wholesale moral revolution. Moreover as an epoch the revolution could not be seen as an aberration, but had to some extent to be accommodated. It was here that Maistre diverged most sharply from the *émigrés*: he held that the counter-revolutionary project to restore the *ancien régime* was as chimerical as the ideals of the revolutionaries. A consistent critic of absolutism, in the tradition of the eighteenth-century *parlementaires*, Maistre therefore deplored the politics of the 'ultras' of the Restoration, despite his own reservations about the *Charte* as a written constitution. The Restoration, it is clear, did not close the epoch of revolution: in *The Pope* Maistre saw the European sovereignty as weakening and the spirit of individualism still working its ravages. At the centenary of the revolution the Catholic right would share this perception of the revolution as an ongoing phenomenon.

Maistre's abiding fascination with the exercise of power and the nature of sovereignty led him to a sustained theoretical investigation of these themes, as always using material from a huge variety of sources, from European monarchies to pagan societies. He did not discard the conceptual framework that he had developed in Lausanne, but rather worked on drawing out the themes that he had identified. His concern was to identify universal laws and patterns in the exercise of power, a concern that ironically marked him out as a man of the Enlightenment tradition. Examination of these themes led Maistre to consider the issues of sacrifice, the social role of the sacred, rituals and subjugation. It is arguably in his vision of the centrality of these issues to the successful exercise of power that the originality of his thought is located. It is unquestionably here that his notoriety is located. A government, Maistre maintained, required either slavery or divine power to operate, leading him to argue against the abolition of serfdom in Russia. Divine power in this context was conceived as performing the function of sacralizing the operations of power; governments had to share in the infallibility of religion and take on the aspects of a power that

judges but cannot be judged. This led Maistre to find a sacred character in the application of justice; the terrible figure of the executioner stands at the heart of the social order. In a related judgement Maistre saw a terrible logic in the pagan practice of human sacrifice, a distorted recognition of the truths of Christianity (for all religions, Maistre held, had elements of truth within them) and went to the point of proclaiming such sacrifices preferable to the anarchy engendered by atheism. The rituals of coronation and the myths surrounding kingship were necessary to impart a sense of awe and veneration; kingship for Maistre should take on the elements of idolatry. Sovereignty, in the last resort, was neither rational nor legitimate and hence required sacralization, an appeal to the irrational. When it came to legitimacy, sovereignty's foundation was always illegitimate, and legitimacy was conferred by the passage of time; every stable established government was therefore good. Ultimately, therefore, despite his arguments that power should be limited, absolute only within a prescribed sphere and despite his assurances that a divine law assured that the illegitimate exercise of power tended towards self-destruction, Maistre was a prophet of irrational submission to power. His fundamental conclusion was:

> There is a point where faith must be blind, there is likewise a point in politics where obedience must be blind; the mass of men are made to be led, reason itself teaches one to beware of reason and the masterpiece of reasoning is to discover the point at which one must cease to reason.
>
> (Bradley 1999: 68)

Reference

Bradley, O. (1999) *A Modern Maistre*, Lincoln, NB: University of Nebraska Press.

Further reading

Lebrun, R.A. (1988) *Joseph de Maistre*, Montreal: McGill-Queen's University Press.
Lebrun, R. A. (ed.) (1988) *Maistre Studies*, Lanham, NY: University Press of America.
Lively, J. (ed. and trans.) (1965) *The Works of Jospeh de Maistre*, London: Allen & Unwin.

SEE ALSO: Bonald, Louis de; Burke, Edmund; Chateaubriand, François; conservatism, authority and tradition

MARTIN SIMPSON

MALLOCK, WILLIAM HURRELL (1849–1923)

William Hurrell Mallock was born into a landed family from Devonshire on 7 February 1849 and died in London in 1923. He was educated privately and then at Balliol College, Oxford, winning the Newdigate Prize for poetry. While at university he undertook work on a series of essays that were published to some acclaim in 1878 as *The New Republic*. This work, a witty satire on a range of eminent elder contemporaries, including Benjamin Jowett, the Master of his college and MATTHEW ARNOLD, was prompted by his dislike of liberal theology. He had already addressed this theme more directly in a series of articles published in the *Nineteenth Century* in 1877–8 and reissued in 1879 as *Is Life Worth Living?* Over the course of the next four decades Mallock wrote a number of novels and a wide range of essays, many of which formed the basis of his books on 'scientific' conservatism. From time to time Mallock lent his services to the Conservative Party, at one stage producing a series of diagrammatic 'visual aids' for party candidates.

In his early writings Mallock promoted an ideal of aristocratic culture in opposition to what he saw as the self-serving vulgarity of middle-class radicalism. This culture was strongly traditional (Mallock was particular sympathetic towards the old Catholic nobility of England, Scotland and remote parts of Continental Europe), combining the social responsibilities and way of life of landed society, with the polished ambiance of the London season. Members of this culture possessed qualities of mind and spirit that were immune to blandishments or challenges of the covertly elitist and oligarchic ethos of the strident middle classes.

From the mid-1880s, however, the focus of Mallock's writings shifted. In response to socialist egalitarianism, he began to extol the progressive benefits of entrepreneurship. The achievements of a very small number of such figures were of far greater significance than the routine labours of the mass of humanity. The danger was that the incentives necessary to prompt entrepreneurial activity would be undermined by redistributive policies promoted by socialists and advanced liberals. Traditional aristocrats were part of a closed system, while this new elite was the product of an open-ended social system that was quite consistent with democratic government, albeit one that was effectively dominated by the elite. The ethos of Mallock's successor to aristocratic culture was strongly materialistic and meritocratic, and appealed to those in Britain and the USA whose image of conservatism was becoming overtly and unashamedly plutocratic.

Further reading

Mallock, W.H. (1878) *The New Republic: Culture, Faith and Philosophy in an English Country House*, London: Chatto & Windus.
—— (1884) *Property and Progress: Or, a Brief Enquiry into Contemporary Social Agitation in England*, London: John Murray.
—— (1920) *Memoirs of Life and Literature*, second edn, London: Chapman & Hall.
Margolis, J. 'W.H. Mallock's The New Republic', *English Literature in Transition* 10: 10–24.
Tucker, A.V. (1962) 'J.W.H. Mallock and Late Victorian Conservatism', *University of Toronto Quarterly* 31: 223–39.

SEE ALSO: conservatism, authority and tradition; intellectuals, elites and meritocracy

JOHN MORROW

MALTHUS, THOMAS ROBERT (1766–1834)

Robert Malthus is known as the originator of 'Malthusianism', a doctrine of population growth according to which the human capacity to multiply at a geometric rate is contrasted with a natural limitation of the means of subsistence to an arithmetical rate of growth. He has therefore become known as an early exponent of the problem of world overpopulation, pointing to an inherent tendency of a population to increase at a rate faster than its means of support. This idea was first outlined in his *Essay on the Principle of Population as it Affects the Future Improvement of Society*

(1798), a single volume expanded into two in a new edition of 1803, with subsequent revisions and additions in 1806, 1807, 1817 and 1826.

There are many qualifications that can be made to this received idea of 'Malthusianism'. Today, the problem of poverty and world population growth is firmly linked to the idea of the demographic transition, the phases of population growth linked to interlocking patterns in the rates of birth, infant mortality and adult life expectancy combined with the deliberate promotion of economic growth by national governments. This understanding of the 'population problem' is a firmly twentieth-century one, but should be noted here since Malthus lived through a period in England's population history that is now understood to be a phase in a long-term transition. How far Malthus appreciated the significance of contemporary changes to Britain's population dynamics, and in what way, will be considered below. Second, Malthus was not so much an 'early demographer' as a late exponent of a link, familiar in the eighteenth century, between national welfare and the size of a population. Malthus, by invoking this linkage, aligned himself with the discourse of eighteenth-century political economy, and was consequently understood by his contemporaries to be a 'political economist'. His arguments on population and subsistence were directed to existing debates concerning the impact of commerce and industrialization on the 'balanced growth' of population and agriculture that had, hitherto, determined the welfare of peoples down the centuries. Further, Malthus counts as the first professional teacher of political economy in Britain: from 1805 to his death in 1834 he was Professor of History and Political Economy at the East India College, for which he received £500 a year, a house to live in, plus coals and candles – no academic British economist has ever since been so well paid. The appointment was made precisely because he was widely considered to be the leading British political economist of the time. From 1811 he became involved, by letter and personal contact, with DAVID RICARDO in discussions concerning the finer points of political economy. Malthus published his own *Principles of Political Economy* in 1820; Ricardo's comments on this and other writings taking up the whole of Volume II of Ricardo's *Works and Correspondence*. The broadly inductivist approach of the *Essay,* reinforced in subsequent revisions, contrasted with Ricardo's own baldly abstract style, although Malthus's own theoretical writings do in fact share much common ground with those of Ricardo. His abiding interest in 'statistics', then understood to be historical, descriptive and numerical information regarding the condition of states, was also evident in the part he played in the creation of a new 'statistical' group in the British Association for the Advancement of Science, 'section F'.

Malthus was born on 13 February 1766 in Surrey, the son of Daniel and Henrietta. His father enjoyed a private income, enabling him to live as a cultured gentleman. In his travels he had met Rousseau, whose work and character he greatly admired; and his freethinking credentials are underlined by his decision to send Robert at the age of 16 to Warrington Academy, a 'Dissenting Academy' run by Gilbert Wakefield. When the Academy closed in 1783 Robert continued to be tutored privately at Wakefield's home, proceeding then in 1784 to Jesus College, Cambridge, where Wakefield had been a Fellow. The fact however that Robert then graduated in 1788 as Ninth Wrangler, the ninth best mathematician of the year, implies that he had, by this time, distanced himself from the influence of Dissent, for until 1856 all graduates of the University of Cambridge had to submit to a religious test of their adherence to the Church of England. Ordained immediately on leaving Cambridge, he was given a curacy by the Bishop of Winchester in 1789 in a small Surrey parish close to his parents' home. His religious conformity was further underlined by his election in 1793 to a non-residential fellowship of Jesus College – a politically significant step given the ill repute into which Jacobinism thereafter fell, further underscored by the outbreak of war between Britain and France in that year. Despite this open avowal of Church and state, and by extension disavowal of Dissent, Jacobinism and Enlightenment culture, he remained living at home when not in college, arguing occasionally over such matters with his father. This we know from the fact that the *Essay,* whose subtitle runs: 'with Remarks on the Speculations of Mr. Godwin, M. Condorcet, and other Writers', was prompted by an argument over the perfectibility of mankind that Robert had with his father some time in 1797. Malthus's exposition of overpopulation as an ever-present threat is part of a larger argument concerning the prospects for the improvement of human welfare. Godwin's

Enquiry concerning Political Justice of 1793 and Condorcet's *Esquisse d'un tableau historique des progrés de l'esprit humaine* of 1795 represent his foils, works espousing a conception of human perfectibility whose attractions Malthus acknowledged, but which he considered unrealisable. The inherent tension in which Malthus placed population and means of subsistence represents his sober rebuttal of such utopian thinking. The stance is also suggestive of the name later given to political economy – the 'dismal science' – as a source of sombre argument deployed against a sanguine faith in the prospect of a better world.

The relation between the size of a population and its general welfare had been a constant theme since the first estimates of population made in England during the later seventeenth century. Some writers suggested that a simple advantage of numbers sufficed to render a ruler more rich and powerful than his neighbours, so that the larger nations would inevitably be richer, absolutely and proportionately, than smaller nations. Others pointed out that Holland was certainly smaller and far less populous than France, but was in important respects as wealthy as France thanks to its location and its place in the world's trading system. The contrast between Holland and France also served to further discussion of the degree to which income from trade and commerce might sustain populations, instead of a reliance on domestic agricultural produce. In turn, once this point had been raised, the cultural consequences of a reliance upon trade became an issue – whether the substitution of commerce for agriculture undermined the moral order of an economy, replacing traditional virtues with those of the market-place. Adam Smith's *Inquiry into the Nature and Causes of the Wealth of Nations* (1776) drew a line under these arguments, identifying the role of the division of labour in the improvement of human productivity, suggesting furthermore that the commercial spirit furthered, rather than undermined, civil virtues. Smith's *Wealth of Nations* became a standard text around which the political economy of the early nineteenth century took shape, and Malthus himself used it as the core textbook in his teaching at East India College.

But the critical issue of commerce and civilisation that Smith's writings addressed was quickly superseded by mechanical argument over the relation of the price mechanism to the value of human labour, and the distribution of income

between the classes of society. Malthus's original *Essay* preserved much of the political argument implicit in Smith, a work that Maynard Keynes in his important biographical essay pronounced much the best of all the editions. The argument is bluntly stated in the first chapter – that the growth of the food supply is constrained to an arithmetical progression, while the unchecked growth of population obeyed geometric proportions. In the second, Malthus demonstrates that efforts to ameliorate the growth of poverty associated with unchecked population increase merely promote further population increase, and hence deepen the misery of the poor.

The *Essay* did not argue that populations did in fact expand geometrically, rather that this potential was everywhere constrained by the much slower growth of means of subsistence. He distinguished, and in later editions elaborated, different kinds of checks to population growth, including changes in life expectancy, poverty, birth control, late marriage and simple restraint. Checks to population growth there had to be; having introduced the tension between subsistence and population growth, the issue became how this tension was in practice resolved. The second edition of the work was more than twice as long as the first, adding evidence in support of the basic theses, seeking to demonstrate that across the world social and moral arrangements were built around this ineluctable tension. Whatever the variety of human institutions, they were ultimately all subordinated to God's providence; and human effort that did not accept this condition would necessarily fail.

Despite the range of evidence adduced in the *Essay*, its theses presuppose an isolated, agrarian economy. The work appeared between two periods of acute grain scarcity, highlighting the crucial role of grain supply in the welfare of the national economy. His demographic arguments presupposed a national population supported entirely from national agriculture, enjoying none of the benefits of commerce outlined by Smith. In modern parlance, Malthus presupposed a closed economy, an autarchic order that consumes all that it produces without trading connections to the rest of the world. Given Malthus's emphasis upon the problem of subsistence, the longstanding argument over the problem of reliance upon other countries that free trade in grains brought with it and the growth of Britain's overseas trade in consumer goods and luxuries, this was not a serious limitation. But at the time Malthus wrote the first version of his essay, these conditions no longer held. The Lancashire cotton industry was beginning its meteoric rise, based on the importation of raw cotton and the export of finished textiles. And since 1793 Britain consumed more grain than it produced, initiating a reliance on net imports of corn that would last for almost 200 years. The population was increasing rapidly, and Britain was quickly becoming an urban, manufacturing nation. Trade and commerce, not subsistence agriculture, would in future provide the mainstay of the population.

In 1800 Malthus published a pamphlet directed to the relation between the level of labouring wages, the level of prices and the effects of welfare provision, themes that belong more obviously to political economy. *An Investigation of the Cause of the Present High Price of Provisions* follows the line of argument already established in the *Essay,* that efforts to improve the condition of the poor through poor relief succeeded only in increasing the price of staple foodstuffs, such as bread, rendering the poor entirely dependent upon relief. Since the supply of grain was fixed in the short run, Malthus argued – here again we have the assumption of a closed economy, but one which had some validity in the light of the disruption to trade arising from the Napoleonic Wars – increasing the purchasing power of the poor simply resulted in a rise in prices, wiping out the initial impact of relief. The first British census was conducted the following year, its results showing that the population was much larger than had been assumed, not least by Malthus himself. This rather suggested that the 'Malthusian trap' was less effective in limiting population than had hitherto been thought; indeed more recent study of European population data indicates that in this period individual welfare improved as population expanded, confounding the principle of population equilibrium that had prevailed down the centuries. Population, nutrition and economic data suggest that, across Europe, a rapid rise in population was linked to increased levels of economic activity, hence contributing to the development of trade and commerce. When in 1814–15 Malthus published three essays on the Corn Laws, arguing for the importance of a domestic surplus in grain and agricultural protection, the argument had moved away from the relationship between population and means of subsistence to a more direct confrontation of agrarian and manufacturing interests. The new theory of political economy was generally linked to argument over the relationship between social classes; Malthus firmly supported the landed interest, distancing himself from the more radical tendencies of his contemporaries.

The appointment as Professor of History and Political Economy to the newly founded East India College however reflected Malthus's high reputation in the early 1800s. The College had been created to train the future administrators of India during what proved to be the last 50 years of the East India Company's private monopoly of trade and government. Throughout his tenure, to his death in service in 1834, Malthus appears to have used as his main teaching text Smith's *Wealth of Nations,* despite the appearance of more didactic works from the likes of David Ricardo, JAMES MILL and J.R. McCulloch. Malthus long harboured an ambition to produce his own edition of *Wealth of Nations,* his own *Principles of Political Economy* of 1820 being constructed as a critical appraisal of some of Smith's key concepts. There is however little evidence that either this work, or smaller treatises written in the 1820s, were related to his regular teaching. In 1836 a posthumous second edition of the *Principles* was published, edited by his friend William Otter from notes made in the 1820s. Malthus continued to write and discuss political economy for almost 40 years after the first publication of the *Essay* – but the impact that this work made has always overshadowed his later writings.

Further reading

James, Patricia (1979) *Population Malthus,* London: Routledge & Kegan Paul.
Keynes, John Maynard (1933) 'Thomas Robert Malthus', *Essays in Biography,* London: Macmillan.
Malthus, T.R. (1970) *An Essay on the Principle of Population,* Harmondsworth: Penguin Books.
—— (1989) *An Essay on the Principle of Population,* ed. P. James, Cambridge: Cambridge University Press.
—— (1989) *Principles of Political Economy,* ed. J.M. Pullen, Cambridge: Cambridge University Press.
Winch, Donald (1987) *Malthus,* Oxford: Oxford University Press.

KEITH TRIBE

MARSHALL, ALFRED (1842–1924)

Alfred Marshall wrote his *Principles of Economics* (1890) to provide a firm foundation for the teaching of Economics in universities; the book quickly became established as the central textbook for the English-speaking world, and was still being read as such in the 1950s. It went through eight editions and numerous reprintings, five times in the 1960s and four in the 1970s. As Professor of Political Economy in Cambridge, he created in 1903 the Economics Tripos, the first specialized three-year course in economics anywhere in the world. Using his Cambridge position he was the moving spirit behind the formation of the British Economic Association in 1891 (from 1902 the Royal Economic Association), a vehicle for the publication of the *Economic Journal* as the central specialist academic journal for the new discipline. Unusually, his intellectual authority in Britain as a theoretical and applied economist was combined with the will and capacity to realize the institutional ambitions that he had for his subject. By contrast, his contemporary at Oxford, Francis Edgeworth, while in some respects a more original economic theorist, lacked entirely both will and capacity to make Oxford the centre of economics in early twentieth-century Britain.

Marshall was born in Bermondsey, London, on 26 July 1842, son of William, a clerk at the Bank of England, and Rebecca Oliver, a butcher's daughter. In 1852 he entered Merchant Taylor's School where he followed a classical curriculum, chiefly of Latin, Greek and Mathematics. In 1861, with some financial help from an uncle who was a successful sheepfarmer in Australia, he entered St John's College, Cambridge, to study Mathematics, with the long-term aim of entering the Church. He graduated Second Wrangler in 1865 – that is, with the second highest first-class degree in Mathematics. After a short spell as a schoolteacher and then as a mathematics coach he was given a college fellowship in November 1865, for which he would have had to attest his adherence to the Church of England. Religious tests of college fellows at St John's were not abolished until 1871, and marriage remained a bar to holding a fellowship until 1882. But by the end of 1867 his interest had turned to metaphysics, and from there to ethics, initiating a progressive shift towards agnosticism and an interest in social issues strongly marked by contemporary discussion of evolution and human development. This change in his interests was recognized in 1868 by the Master who appointed him to a college lectureship in the Moral Sciences, broadly equivalent to the social sciences of the twentieth century. This appointment opened the

way to a focus upon political economy, although his route to the subject meant that he retained a strong interest in social progress and human improvement.

In 1870 Marshall delivered a course of lectures on political economy to women students, the material included in the Moral Sciences Tripos being the only Cambridge degree accessible to young women who, at that time, were generally excluded from the formal intermediate education that would have given them an appropriate working knowledge of classical languages and mathematics. Marshall's lectures were part of an informal arrangement on the part of liberal Cambridge academics that made teaching available to women officially excluded from the university. In this way he came into contact with Mary Paley, who took up residence in Cambridge in October 1871, was encouraged by Marshall to read for the Moral Sciences Tripos and successfully sat the examination as an unofficial candidate in 1874. She returned home to Stamford and began lecturing on her own account there, returning however in 1875 to the beginnings of what was to become Newnham College, Cambridge. Here she began collaboration with Marshall on a textbook for University Extension lectures, published under their joint names as *The Economics of Industry* in 1879. This was the first English introduction to economics written for use as a textbook in teaching, and it quickly became the standard reference work. In 1877 Alfred and Mary married, and as Maynard Keynes rightly notes in his biographical essay, Alfred's dependence upon her devotion became complete. Marshall's early feminist inclinations subsequently withered. In 1892 he replaced the *Economics of Industry* with a dry summary of his *Principles* called *Elements of the Economics of Industry,* and did his best to eradicate the earlier book from circulation. In later life he maintained that economics was a subject unsuitable for the female mind, although it transpired that women students reading for the Economics Tripos Marshall had designed gained degrees consistently above the prevailing average well into the twentieth century.

Alfred's marriage to Mary meant that he had to surrender the St John's Fellowship. University education was however expanding rapidly at this time, among the new foundations being University College, Bristol in 1876. Marshall became its first Principal in 1877, with responsibility also for the teaching of political economy. Mary took over the day classes in 1878 before, in 1879, Marshall fell ill with a stone in the kidneys. Apart from his illness, Marshall disliked his work as Principal, and sought to resign. When in 1881 he was eventually replaced he and Mary went on a long convalescent Continental holiday, the initial work on the *Principles* being completed during a stay in Palermo. On his return he taught political economy for another year at Bristol, moving in 1883 as successor to Arnold Toynbee at Balliol College, Oxford. Part of the motive for this move lay in the imminent retirement of the incumbent Drummond Professor of Political Economy, Bonamy Price, but the death in late 1884 of Henry Fawcett, Professor of Political Economy at Cambridge, opened the way for Marshall's return to his old university. The Marshalls moved back in early 1885, and both lived out the remainder of their lives in the house they built there, Balliol Croft.

Keynes distinguishes three phases in Marshall's intellectual development as an economist: he began studying the subject in 1867; from his wide reading of British and Continental authors he had developed the main features of his doctrine by 1875; by 1883 they were arriving at their final form. Thus when appointed to the Cambridge chair at the age of 44 his understanding of the subject was more or less complete, but he had yet to publish a paper or book that embodied this understanding. The *Principles* was his chosen vehicle for this, although when published in 1890 this was planned as only the first of two volumes – although the material for the second volume, originally assembled in the 1870s, first appeared under the title *Money, Credit and Commerce* in 1923. When Marshall arrived back in Cambridge his principal interest had become the refinement of his understanding into a major book, and the creation of a medium for its teaching. Although he held a fully paid chair, there was little systematic teaching in the subject, and limited interest in it – the latter contrasting with the Oxford he had left. In the mid-1880s Cambridge students typically took ten papers to graduate; and Political Economy represented three papers in the Moral Sciences examinations, and one in History. Given the small numbers taking Moral Sciences, and its relatively elementary level, this represented a weak basis upon which to launch his work, so Marshall set about extending this base on both fronts. By the later 1890s he had determined on the creation of a separate Economics Tripos, his

eventual success in 1903 owing a great deal to the widespread irritation that his long campaign of agitation had engendered. Marshall's political skills lay more in wearing down an opposition than charm and persuasion. Once the new Tripos was established his colleagues in Moral Sciences and History dropped political economy from their own Triposes, and so no longer had to endure Marshall's badgering. The Economics Tripos became, by default, the vehicle for the later development of the social sciences in Cambridge.

Marshall's capacity for antagonizing colleagues is also apparent in the controversy surrounding the succession to the chair in 1908. For many years Marshall had been assisted in his teaching by Herbert Foxwell, Professor of Political Economy at University College London, where, however, there were very few students. As Marshall got older he became increasingly infirm, although the fact that he lived to within a few days of his eighty-second birthday rather indicates a degree of hypochondria. Once the Tripos was established he determined on resigning the chair, and decided that the most suitable successor was Arthur Pigou, a young Cambridge lecturer he had identified as a possible candidate in the early 1900s. However, Foxwell had formed the somewhat unreasonable expectation that, although only seven years younger than Marshall and lacking anything beyond a rather dated and elementary understanding of economics, he should rightfully assume the Cambridge chair. The appointment of Pigou as successor to Marshall in 1908 came as a complete shock to Foxwell and ensured that Pigou's succession was marked with controversy.

Pigou was Marshall's choice; but even if he had not been it is more than likely that he would have been selected as the most suitable candidate. The appointment of Marshall's student did however secure the Marshallian heritage in Cambridge. Marshall lived on in Cambridge, giving advice and supervision to students until his death at home on 13 July 1924. Pigou, although he never engaged in university politics, contributed strongly to the formalization of Marshall's work while still adhering to the social and ethical values that Marshall had brought to it. During the inter-war years, Cambridge economics was Marshallian economics; and since in this period the largest single concentration of British economists was in Cambridge, and not Oxford or the LSE, this ensured that the study of economics in Britain was heavily marked by Marshallian themes until at least the mid-twentieth century.

Marshall's original training in mathematics gave him an understanding of the importance of its principles to the development of economics, but he did not seek to impose mathematical routines on economic reasoning in the way now fashionable. The first edition of the *Principles* opened with a lengthy account of the evolution of human economy, and contained a mathematical appendix to which all formal notation was banished. In his 1885 Inaugural Lecture Alfred Marshall had reviewed political economy since Adam Smith, and in summarizing his differences with this past tradition, he suggested that the chief fault of the earlier English economists had not been that they ignored history and statistics, but that Ricardo and his followers neglected a large group of facts and a method of studying facts that we now see to be of primary importance. Marshall argued that they treated man as a constant quantity, interesting themselves little in human behavioural variation. Economics, he suggested, should not be a formal body of laws, but a means of reasoning, a set of tools that could be used to understand and get the measure of human action. This conception of an *organon,* a means of reasoning, represents the core of the Marshallian heritage, embodied in the *Principles* and passed on in this way into the twentieth century.

Although the *Principles* was much revised and reordered by Marshall, his chief contributions to economics are clear in the first edition of 1890. The analysis was based on the method of partial equilibrium, analysing sectors of human action while holding others constant, a method distinct to the mathematical general equilibrium introduced by Walras that sought to resolve the price mechanism as the interconnection of all markets. Marshall did emphasize the interconnectedness of the economic domain; but the approach that he adopted was not intended to provide a solution to the problem of price formation, rather to illuminate how economies functioned. Accordingly, he recognized the importance of expectations in shaping human behaviour, while at the same time recognizing the real limitations of the conception of optimization as a doctrine guiding economic analysis. With the rise of a formalized and abstract economic science in the later twentieth century much of Marshall's teaching appeared increasingly dated; but the project of turning economics into a mathematically

based model of human action now appears more dated than the fundamentals of Marshall's own approach.

Marshall expressed the hope in his inaugural lecture that a generation of economists with 'cool heads and warm hearts' might arise to carry forward the project of human improvement. Marshall certainly lacked the personal emollience of his colleague Henry Sidgwick, but his colleagues understood that he shared their own liberal values. For many years the genteel details of Marshall's social origins provided in John Maynard Keynes's seminal 1924 obituary essay were assumed to be perfectly reliable, based as they were for the most part on information supplied by his widow and other family members. There is no reason to think that Mary Marshall deliberately misinformed Keynes, nor that Keynes failed in any way to examine the facts as laid before him. But Marshall's background was far more humble than either Mary or Maynard Keynes suspected, a circumstance first demonstrated by Ronald Coase, whose new findings were then elaborated in Peter Groenewegen's biography. Keynes's version of the family history perpetuated a systematic 'gentrification' of Marshall's origins in which he possibly colluded, his progression to Cambridge seeming quite natural. The new picture of his early life shows how much of a social as much as an intellectual achievement this in fact was; and we can only speculate as to quite why Marshall would have wished to obscure this.

References

Coase, R. H. (1994) 'Alfred Marshall's Mother and Father' (1984) and 'Alfred Marshall's Family and Ancestry' (1990), both reprinted in his *Essays on Economics and Economists*, Chicago: Chicago University Press.

Groenewegen, P. (1995) *A Soaring Eagle: Alfred Marshall 1842–1924*, Cheltenham: Edward Elgar.

Keynes, J.M. (1924) 'Alfred Marshall', *Economic Journal* (September), reprinted in *Essays in Biography* (1933). London: Macmillan & Co.

KEITH TRIBE

MARTINEAU, HARRIET (1802–76)

The most important woman prose writer of the mid-Victorian era, and author of some fifty volumes, Harriet Martineau was born at Norwich on 12 June 1802, and died on 27 June 1876. Largely educated at home, Martineau was long plagued by ill health, including a degenerative deafness. She began writing on theological topics, particularly in relation to Unitarianism, in the early 1820s, but went on to become famous as a historian, essayist, novelist and biographer. Her first great success came in the early 1830s, following in the footsteps of Jane Marcet, with *Illustrations of Political Economy* (9 vols, 1832–34), some 10,000 of which appeared, which were succeeded by *Poor Laws and Paupers Illustrated* (1833) and *Illustrations of Taxation* (1834), which were fully attuned to the climate of Whiggish reform of the era of the 1832 Reform Act. One of the most important popularizers of the classical political economists, notably MALTHUS, RICARDO and JAMES MILL, Martineau was fêted by BROUGHAM and other leading Whigs, and attacked by the Tories of the *Quarterly Review*. Several volumes of her moral and literary essays from 1829–32 were published as *Miscellanies* (1836). From mid-1834 to mid-1836 she toured the USA, her observations being published as *Society in America* (1837), a serious account of US social structure and politics that did much to support the anti-slavery movement, and one of the best-known such accounts of the period. Her best-known novel, *Deerbrook*, appeared in 1839. Seeking cures for her increasingly debilitating illnesses, she dabbled in mesmerism in the early 1840s. She contributed several works to the Anti-Corn Law movement of the mid-1840s, including *Dawn Island, A Tale* (1845), and after recovering fully produced her most important single work, the *History of England during the Thirty Years' Peace* (1849), which remains an outstanding account of the post-Napoleonic era, and is usually taken to represent the outlook of the Benthamite or 'Philosophic Radicals', notably James and JOHN STUART MILL, George Grote, Sir William Molesworth and John Bowring, particularly on the era of reform. As such it is somewhat tinged with disappointment, the Benthamites having not fared well in Parliament, though their long-term influence was much more substantial. An introduction to this work, covering the period 1800–15, was also printed separately. In 1851 Martineau published *Letters on the Laws of Man's Social Nature and Development*, written mostly by an overt atheist, Henry Atkinson, which produced a falling out with her brother, the philosopher and theologian James Martineau. Another propagandistic effort of the period was a translation of AUGUSTE COMTE's *Philosophie Positive*, which was completed in 1853 as *The Philosophy of Comte* (2 vols). Her later works included *British Rule in India: An Historical Sketch* (1857), *England and Her Soldiers* (1859), written to assist Florence Nightingale, *Biographical Sketches* (1869) and her posthumous three-volume *Autobiography* (1877), one of the more illuminating memoirs of the period.

Further reading

Martineau, Harriet (1877) *Autobiography*, 3 vols. London: Smith, Elder & Co.
Webb, R.K. (1960) *Harriet Martineau: A Radical Victorian*, London: Heinemann.

SEE ALSO: historiography and the idea of progress; political economy

GREGORY CLAEYS

MARX AND MARXISM

The founder of the most important school of modern socialism, Karl Heinrich Marx was born at Trier, Germany, on 5 May 1818, the son of a Jewish lawyer who converted to Protestantism in 1824. He studied Law, History and Philosophy first at Bonn, then at Berlin, where he encountered the leading philosopher of the period, Georg Wilhelm Friedrich Hegel (see HEGEL AND HEGELIANISM). Here he allied himself with the 'Young' or 'Left' Hegelians, including BRUNO BAUER and MAX STIRNER, who believed that Hegel's conception of dialectical historical development meant that the existing Prussian state was not the final stage of human development, but that the 'spirit' or 'Idea' might realize itself in a higher form. Marx in 1842 became a radical journalist and editor of the *Rheinische Zeitung*, which was suppressed the following year. Marrying Jenny von Westphalen, he emigrated to Paris.

At this time Marx fell under the influence of LUDWIG FEUERBACH, whose materialist philosophy contended that Hegel's idea of 'spirit' was only a reflection of existing social conditions at any one time, and that 'God' was in fact only a projection of human wishes, and an acknowledgement of the absence of control over one's own life. This idea is applied by Marx in his two main writings of this period. In his brief 'Critique of Hegel's Philosophy of Right' (1843), he expressed radical democratic views, and attacked Hegel's devotion to monarchy, as well as his reliance upon the bureaucracy as a 'universal' class capable of mediating between conflicting egoistic interests in civil society. Instead, Marx views universal suffrage as the means of reconciling contending interests. In Paris, however, he encountered both French and *émigré* socialists, notably Wilhelm Weitling, as well as anarchists like PIERRE-JOSEPH PROUDHON and MIKHAIL BAKUNIN. He also met in September 1844 a young Barmen merchant named Friedrich Engels (1820–95), who was resident in Manchester, an enthusiastic supporter of Chartist politics, and a recent convert to socialism. From this point onwards they began a life-long intellectual collaboration, basing their new world-view on a marriage of German philosophy, and particularly the critique of religion, French politics, particularly revolutionism, and British political economy. Engels had already begun to study the latter from an Owenite perspective in Manchester, which assisted the critical analysis presented in his *Condition of the Working Class in England in 1844*, which details the degradation of the urban proletariat, the displacement of manual labour by machinery, the cyclical process of industrial boom and crisis, the resulting 'social war, the war of each against all', and the inevitability of revolution to abolish the existing system.

Already in 1843 Marx had announced that the only class capable of achieving political emancipation in Germany was the proletariat. In 1844 he announced his conversion to communism in an unpublished work, the 'Economic and Philosophic Manuscripts' or 'Paris Manuscripts' (printed in 1932), which also proposed a new critical standpoint, the theory of alienation. Marx's starting-point in the 'Paris Manuscripts' was Adam Smith's account of the division of labour in ch. 1, book 1, of the *Wealth of Nations*. Smith had described increasing economic specialization as the means by which commercial society would prove vastly more productive than any previous stage of economic development, while warning in book 5 of the potential 'mental mutilation' of the labouring class, and their reduction to a near-animal status, if, *en masse*, they were subjected to arduous, repetitive labour without some compensatory education. Marx's critique of Smith relies on Feuerbach's notion of 'species being', or the communal essence of mankind, which has been suppressed or eradicated in commercial society, which

promotes only selfishness and egotism. Applying Feuerbach's notion of religion as the abstract essence of man, Marx describes the alienation of human powers through money, exchange and production. There are four main types of alienated labour: (1) of the process of work from the labourer's essence, since labour is usually forced; (2) of the worker from the product of labour as an alien object over him; (3) from man's species-being, or his ability to relate to himself as a universal and free, 'conscious, vital' being, which turns free activity into a mere means of existence; (4) alienation from other people. Arguing that private property results from alienated labour, Marx contends that only an ending of private property can abolish it, and achieve a 'general human emancipation' in which 'the social relationship of man to man' becomes primary. Communism, however, was not to be a 'levelling-down', but is seen by Marx principally from a humanist viewpoint, as 'the return of man out of religion, family, state, etc. into his human, i.e. social being'. This ideal of communism is not far distant from that of CHARLES FOURIER, in particular, with whom Marx and Engels clearly agreed as to the desirability of a regime of free, creative and varied labour as definitive of the future society. In addition, Marx envisions communism as entailing the abolition of the state, a position that brought him close to anarchist writers like Proudhon.

In the next few years, however, Marx and Engels were concerned to distance themselves from all of their radical and socialist predecessors and competitors, engaging in voluminous polemics that seem tiresome and inordinately drawn-out today. Bruno Bauer and his 'True Socialist' associates are the target in *The Holy Family* (1845), Proudhon in *The Poverty of Philosophy* (1846) and Max Stirner in much of the unpublished 'German Ideology' (written 1845–6). The latter work, however, included a vastly more important section devoted to the positive exposition of what Marx and Engels regarded as their own, new system of analysis, which was termed the 'materialist conception of history', which involves equally a renunciation of many of Marx and Engels's own earlier views, including the Feuerbachian standpoint of the 'Paris Manuscripts'. For now, the manuscript argues, a historical form of materialism supersedes the abstract, humanist materialism of Feuerbach, with its fixed conception of human nature. Social evolution is now defined in terms of a causal, determinist theory of economic development: 'the anatomy of civil society is to be sought in political economy', rather than in any abstract 'spirit' or conception of national character. According to the new analysis, all societies rest upon an economic 'basis', which consists of a mode of production or system of property ownership. Upon this basis there rises in every society a 'superstructure', which includes religion, law, politics and even ideas. Thought, therefore – contra Hegel – has no independent existence, but is derived from actual material conditions: 'Life is not determined by consciousness, but consciousness by life', and the ruling ideas, or ideology, in any epoch are derived from the ruling class of that period, and justify its claims to supremacy. Changes in the economic basis accordingly produce alterations in all aspects of the superstructure. As a materialist model priority is thus given to economic organization over such factors as climate or the distribution of natural resources.

Taking up the conjectural history of the Scottish Enlightenment in particular, which had stressed the passage of all societies through four main stages (hunting and gathering; pastoral; agricultural; commercial) Marx and Engels then describe three main historical forms of property ownership: (1) tribal; (2) ancient communal and state ownership, where slavery exists and private property begins; (3) feudal or estate property, where landed property was maintained by serf labour, but craftsmen and merchants emerge as urban classes; (4) the modern system of capitalist production. The motive-force for the transition from one type to the next, however, is not the natural desire to improve one's condition that dominates Scottish accounts, but is instead the struggle between the chief contending classes in any society. As in the 'Paris Manuscripts', private property is described as emerging out of the division of labour, and as generating the fragmentation of a communal or general interest. The state is described not as mediating between conflicting interests, but as derived from them; the struggle for the extension of the franchise, central to movements like Chartism, thus merely masked the real struggle of classes within civil society. In the future society 'there will be no more political power properly so called, since political power is precisely the official expression of antagonism in civil society'; instead, there is a clearly Saint-Simonian notion here of 'politics' being supplanted by the organization of production, or 'administration'.

Communism is now defined not as an ideal or 'a state of affairs to be established', but as 'the real movement which abolishes the present state of things', the proletariat's conscious desire to supersede the existing system. Communism could not be introduced at an earlier historical stage, but only at the highest stage of modern industrial development, where the existence of a small class of wealthy capitalists and large class of propertyless proletarians is contrasted to the reality of social production and the possibility of 'modern universal intercourse', where individuals can achieve an 'all-rounded' and 'free' development of their potential, where labour becomes the conscious expression of one's own personality. In one of the most famous passages of their writings, clearly indebted to Fourier in particular, Marx and Engels described the future communist ideal:

in communist society, where nobody has one exclusive sphere of activity but each can become accomplished in any branch he wishes, society regulates the general production and makes it possible for me to do one thing today and another tomorrow, to hunt in the morning, fish in the afternoon, rear cattle in the evening, criticize after dinner, just as I have a mind, without ever becoming hunter, fisherman, cowherd or critic.

Although there are thus some elements of continuity between the humanist stance of the 'Paris Manuscripts' and the historical materialism of the 'German Ideology', the breach from Feuerbach also meant that Marx and Engels could not, in theory, use an abstract conception of human nature, particularly communal or species nature, as a critical standpoint. This renunciation of their 'humanism', Louis Althusser in particular has suggested, nullified in Marx and Engels's eyes much of the value of their earlier writings, and meant that no moral or metaphysical standpoint lying outside of actual historical development was any longer possible, which implies, equally, that the ideal communist future could not be described either. In some of Marx's later writings, however, notably the *Grundrisse* (written 1857–8), there is brief discussion of the goals of communist society as including 'attractive labour' and 'individual self-realization' as well as far more free time. It would have been difficult to develop such discussions more fully, however, not only because of constraints imposed by the materialist conception of history, but also because of the rigid distinction between 'utopian', or non-revolutionary, unhistorical socialism, and 'scientific' socialism, which is imposed on most such discussions after 1848. The fact remains, however, that from both the common-language viewpoint and the historical development of a tradition of communal property-holding largely associated with Thomas More's *Utopia* (1516), Marx is the most influential utopian writer of the modern era.

The fully matured historical and political analysis developed by Marx and Engels from 1843–8 is summarized in the best-known and most powerfully formulated of Marx's works, the *Manifesto of the Communist Party* (1848). Written as Europe witnessed widespread revolutionary outbreaks and the first large-scale publicization of a socialist and communist alternative, it was specifically commissioned by the main existing revolutionary organization, the Communist League. Defining the whole of history in terms of class struggle, the *Manifesto* offers a brief account of the rise of the modern proletariat, its necessary and increasing impoverishment, the growth of commercial crises, the increasingly cosmopolitan nature of production and internationalization of the working class, and the necessity of a violent revolution to transform society, which needed to occur simultaneously throughout the industrialized societies. It also describes in brief the post-revolutionary programme of the communists, which includes the centralization of credit, communication and transport in the hands of the state, and the abolition of private property in land and the means of production. The form of government supervising this process is termed the 'dictatorship of the proletariat', by which is meant a democratic mechanism by which the proletariat wields power over the whole society. The ultimate aim of this dictatorship, however, was the transition to a communist society in which classes and political power would have been abolished. The exact nature of this interim form of rule, which Marx likened to the existing rule of the bourgeoisie over the proletariat, was nowhere explored at length, though at the time of the Paris Commune he suggested (in *The Civil War in France*) that the workers' government there was approximately what he envisioned. In light of the experience of 1848 Marx abandoned the notion of revolution by a small conspiratorial elite in favour of the proletariat as a whole, and also the idea that collaboration with the bourgeoisie was necessary for success (see *Class Struggles in France*, and the *Eighteenth Brumaire of Louis Bonaparte*, 1852). Nonetheless it is usually conceded that Marx did not adequately stress the need for democratic accountability in his discussion of the dictatorship of the proletariat. His mature political theory also greatly underestimated the residual strength of nationalism as a source of proletarian loyalty. And Marx's conception of the proletarian 'party', though intended to describe a movement rather than a disciplined organization as such, paid too little heed to the problem of leadership, which would become extraordinarily important in the Leninist, Stalinist and Maoist variations of the communist movement in the twentieth century. Marx was also accused, notably by his great anarchist antagonist, Michael Bakunin, in *Statism and Anarchy* (1873), of dictatorial tendencies, being 'by education and by nature … a Jacobin', and of planning to impose a centralized and necessarily self-perpetuating dictatorship of intellectuals and elite workers over the working classes as a whole, to the detriment of the peasantry in particular.

From 1849 Marx found himself in exile in London, where he remained until his death on 14 March 1883. His time was primarily spent in the British Museum Reading Room, researching on political economy. During the 1850s he laboured in great poverty, making occasional sums from journalism, notably during the Crimean War, where his strongly anti-Russian sentiments were developed. From the mid-1860s he was the leading influence in the International Working Men's Association, which was founded in London in 1864, and addressed or wrote for it on a wide range of subjects, including education and trade unionism. The effects of Bakunin's anarchist agitation in particular forced the transfer of the International to New York in 1872, but it was dissolved 4 years later.

The two main intellectual products of Marx's later years were the *Critique of Political Economy* (1859) and *Capital* (vol. 1, 1867). There is some development here of Marx's theory of commercial crises, amongst other themes. But, if the materialist conception of history is the most important concept of his youth, the theory of surplus value is the great contribution of Marx's maturity. This describes how the capitalist is able to exploit proletarian labour power in order to generate rent, interest and profit from the amount produced by the worker after a subsistence wage has been paid. By analysing the exact contribution of labour to the value of the product, and assessing the varying costs of training a workforce of both skilled and unskilled workers, the percentage of surplus value exploited at any one time in any one process of production can be determined relatively exactly. Marx did not however draw from this account the conclusion that the labourer should receive the 'whole produce of labour', as some earlier socialist and proto-socialist writers, beginning chiefly with Charles Hall, had done. Instead, he insists on the collective social right of the working class as a whole to their aggregate production. The future process of production would continue to reward those engaged in distribution, even though they produced no value as such, because their task was necessary. So too, while the capitalist might perhaps perform a useful task, for instance in supervising production, capital as such added no value to the product.

From the 1860s onwards Marx and Engels began to attract substantial support throughout Europe and beyond, and with the greater circulation of their ideas and development of the international labour movement various questions arose as to the potential modification of the original theory. Engels, who outlived Marx by 12 years, dying on 5 August 1895, had remained with his father's firm from 1850–69, but moved to London in 1870. His most influential later work was *Anti-Dühring* (1878), written against a German socialist, which drew a much closer analogy between Marx's dialectical method and the existence of similar processes of development in nature itself. Engels insisted that three basic laws governed nature, history and human life: the unity of opposites or antitheses, the transformation of quality into quantity, and the negation of the negation. From this work was taken a popular pamphlet, *Social-ism: Utopian and Scientific* (1883). This led Marxist thought to be described systematically as 'dialectical materialism', involving a more intimate association between nature and history than Marx proposes in his main writings. A further development of these themes is in the posthumously published *Dialectics of Nature* (1927). He also applied an account partly inspired by DARWIN's theory of natural selection in *The Origins of the Family, Private Property, and the State* (1884), which was notable particularly for its claim that the development of private property had led to a deterioration of the position of women. One of the problems Marx had to contend with in later years was the suggestion, chiefly put by Russian disciples, who persuaded Marx at least in part, that Russia might establish a communist system based upon the existing semi-feudal system of village communal ownership, thus obviating the need for a bourgeois revolution and lengthy period of capitalist industrialization.

The development of Marxism to 1914

The most important development in Marxist thought from the 1860s onwards was the notion that communism might be attained by electoral means, and state power assumed by the working class through a peaceful transition process. This is identified chiefly with German Social Democracy, and in the first instance with its chief creator, FERDINAND LASSALLE (1825–64), whose supporters' restatement of socialist aims was criticized by Marx in the *Critique of the Gotha Programme* (1875), which rejects that notion that the state can be used as a neutral tool, rather than remaining the chief instrument of capitalist domination. In addition, Marx dismissed the value of moralizing appeals for a more 'just' or fairer society based on abstract ethical standards. Lassalle, however, was willing not only to use the state, once universal suffrage had been introduced, to achieve socialist ends, but also even to negotiate with Bismarck to do so. His main successor, and the chief architect of the theory called Revisionism, was Karl Kautsky (1854–1938), who under the influence of Darwinian evolutionism in particular laid great stress on the determinist elements in the materialist conception of history, and the need to await a ripening of revolutionary conditions through the laws of capitalist development. He also believed that socialism could be introduced via existing parliamentary institutions, through democratic rule. These views were supported by EDUARD BERNSTEIN (1850–1932), whose *Evolutionary Socialism* (1898) stressed the gradualist accomplishment of Social Democratic ends. Bernstein also emphasized the tendency of capitalism to stabilize itself through the growth of large-scale cartels and monopolies, as well as the rise of working-class wages and the growth of the middle classes, all of which indicated that Marx's theory of capitalist crisis required modification. Rejecting the application of the Hegelian dialectic, he preferred to use a Kantian (see KANT, IMMANUEL) moral basis for socialist argument. In *How is Scientific Socialism Possible* (1901), he broke from the ideal that communism must result from the necessary development of capitalism, and instead contended that it was an ideal to be strived for. Amongst the opponents of such views, ROSA LUXEMBURG (1871–1919) notably criticized Bernstein's revisionism, and in *Social Reform or Revolution* (1899) argued that only a revolutionary transformation could introduce socialism. She was also an important critic of Social Democratic support for the German war effort from 1914–18. Luxemburg also emphasized, with New Liberal writers like J.A. HOBSON, the increasing extension of the capitalist search for markets and raw materials through imperialism. Amongst those who also remained much closer to Marx theoretically were AUGUSTE BEBEL (1840–1913) and WILHELM LIEBKNECHT (1826–1900), whose son Karl Liebknecht (1871–1919) was one of the founders of the German Communist Party, and was killed during the abortive revolution that followed the war's end in 1918. Revisionist ideals, though officially rejected at the 1903 party congress, were on the whole extremely influential in the German labour movement.

Other European countries had smaller Marxist movements than Germany, which tended to develop according to their national momentums following the collapse of the First International. In France, following the failure of the Commune, the Parti Ouvrier emerged in 1875–6, led by JULES GUESDE (1845–1922), though tension remained constant between Marxists and both the anarchists and trade unionists. In Britain, the main leader was the prominent anti-imperialist HENRY MYERS HYNDMAN (1842–1921), who helped to found the Social Democratic Federation in 1881, and whose popular works include *England for All* (1881). Another quasi-Marxist group was the Socialist League led by the poet WILLIAM MORRIS (1834–96). Marxism was however less influential on the British labour movement than the Fabian Socialism of SIDNEY WEBB and BEATRICE WEBB, Annie Besant, G.B. Shaw and others, whose definitive viewpoint was outlined in *Fabian Essays in Socialism* (1889).

In both Italy and Russia Marxist ideas were actively combated by anarchists, and Bakunin's followers remained influential through his International Social Democratic Alliance, founded in 1868. Though the Russian Revolution lies outside the scope of this volume, it should be noted that the chief contribution of the Russian Marxist leader, and the most important Marxist revolutionary theorist of the early twentieth century, VLADIMIR ILLICH LENIN (1870–1924), was his theory of the vanguard party of full-time, trained professional revolutionaries, an account of whose mission is outlined in *What is to be Done?* (1902) and *The State and Revolution* (1917). This represented to some degree a reversion to the conspiratorial Blanquism of the Communist League in the period before 1848. It was combated by the other leading tendency in Russian Social Democracy, Menshevism, which split from Lenin's Bolshevik faction in 1903, insisting both that the socialists should create a more open, less conspiratorial party, and that revolution would necessarily ensure only after a lengthy stage of industrialization had created a large-scale proletariat of the type described by Marx in the *Manifesto*. Lenin also completed the first major study of *The Development of Capitalism in Russia* (1899), extended the views of Hobson, Hilferding and others on the extension of capitalism overseas in *Imperialism, the Highest Stage of Capitalism* (1916), and went on, of course, to emerge as the leader of the new Soviet Union after the success of the 1917 revolution. Other Russian Marxist thinkers of note include Georgii Plekhanov (1856–1918), who was the first to contend that a Russian proletariat could become the revolutionary class needed to overthrow the existing system.

Further reading

Avineri, S. (1968) *The Social and Political Thought of Karl Marx*, Cambridge: Cambridge University Press.

Carver, Terrell (1982) *Marx's Social Theory*, Oxford: Oxford University Press.

Cohen, G.A. (1978) *Karl Marx's Theory of History: A Defence*, Oxford: Clarendon Press.

Guttsman, W.L. (1981) *The German Social Democratic Party 1875–1933*, London: George Allen & Unwin.

Hunt, Richard (1974) *Marxism and Totalitarian Democracy*, Pittsburgh, PA: Pittsburgh University Press.

Kolakowski, Leszek (1978) *Main Currents of Marxism*, 3 vols, Oxford: Oxford University Press.

Lichtheim, George (1964) *Marxism: An Historical and Critical Study*, London: Routledge & Kegan Paul.

McLellan, David (1971) *The Thought of Karl Marx*, London: Macmillan.

—— (1980) *Marxism after Marx*, London: Macmillan.

Maguire, John (1972) *Marx's Paris Writings*, New York: Barnes & Noble.

Meszaros, Istvan (1970) *Marx's Theory of Alienation*, London: Merlin Press.

Morgan, R. (1965) *The German Social Democrats and the First International 1864–1872*, Cambridge: Cambridge University Press.

Ollman, Bertell (1976) *Alienation: Marx's Conception of Man in Capitalist Society*, Cambridge: Cambridge University Press.

Parekh, Bhikhu (1982) *Marx's Theory of Ideology*, London: Croom Helm.

Reichard, Richard (1969) *Crippled from Birth. German Social Democracy 1844–1870*, Iowa City: Iowa State University Press.

Tucker, Robert (1961) *Philosophy and Myth in Karl Marx*, Cambridge: Cambridge University Press.

SEE ALSO: early socialism; political economy; social theory and sociology in the nineteenth century; the science of politics; utopianism; theories of the state and society

GREGORY CLAEYS

MAURICE, F.D. (1805–72)

An influential theologian, philosopher and social theorist, F.D. Maurice was one of the founders of the Christian Socialist movement in Britain, which had a substantial influence on attitudes towards the poor and state intervention in the late nineteenth century. Maurice was born at Normanston, near Lowestoft, on 29 August 1805, the son of a Unitarian minister. Intended for the ministry, he entered Trinity College, Cambridge, in 1823, but read for the bar. Beginning to contribute to periodicals on political and topical issues, Maurice followed S.T. COLERIDGE's pantheism and idealism in philosophy, but in politics was an opponent of both Benthamism and Toryism. Becoming editor of the *Athenaeum* in 1829, he favoured the Spanish constitutional party, but then resolved to take orders. Following study at Oxford he was ordained in 1834, and shortly thereafter published a pamphlet, *Subscription no Bondage*, defending the obligatory imposition of a religious test of faith in the Thirty-Nine Articles on Oxford and Cambridge undergraduates. Becoming chaplain of Guy's Hospital in 1836, he began lecturing on Moral Philosophy, and in 1837 published a major theological tract, *The Kingdom of Christ*, which was opposed by the Oxford Movement in particular. In 1840 he was elected Professor of English Literature and History at King's College, London; in 1846 he became chaplain of Lincoln's Inn, and in 1848 helped to found Queen's College.

The revolutions of 1848 proved a turning point in Maurice's ideas. Persuaded that the socialists and Chartists had a good case for a reform in attitudes towards the labouring poor, he nonetheless strongly disputed the secular trend promoted by ROBERT OWEN's followers in particular, most notably, after 1845, George Jacob Holyoake. Christian Socialism was established in order to re-establish socialism on a religious foundation. In conjunction with J.M. Ludlow, Maurice edited *Politics for the People* in 1848, and after a visit to France to study industrial workshops and co-operative techniques, Maurice established a tailors' association in 1850, and a society for promoting similar efforts. A series of *Tracts on Christian Socialism* were published that publicized the history and rules of the association, and proclaimed the moral and economic weakness of 'buying cheap to sell dear' and the necessity of religious restraint for mitigating the excesses of freedom of trade. This helped to secure passage of the 1852 act legalizing co-operative associations, which permitted the rapid expansion of the movement emanating from the Rochdale store of 1844. Soon the centre of theological controversy, Maurice questioned in particular the 'eternity' of future punishment, and was forced to resign his professorship in 1853. He nonetheless went on to found the Working Men's College in 1854, and after the decline of Christian Socialism in that year continued to write on theological themes. Appointed Knightbridge Professor of 'Casuistry, Moral Theology and Moral Philosophy' at Cambridge in 1860, he held the post for nine years. He died on 1 April 1872.

Further reading

Maurice, F.D. (1869) *Social Morality*, London: Macmillan.

—— (1871–2) *Moral and Metaphysical Philosophy*, 2 vols, London: Macmillan

Maurice, Frederick (1884) *Life of Frederick Denison Maurice*, 2 vols, London: Macmillan & Co.

SEE ALSO: early socialism

GREGORY CLAEYS

MAURRAS, CHARLES (1868–1952)

Charles Maurras was a French writer, journalist and political philosopher who, at the turn of the century, became one of the founding fathers of radical nationalism and of the French extreme right, exercising great influence on intellectuals right to the very end of the French Third Republic (1870–1940) and the Vichy regime (1940–4).

After growing up in a traditionalist milieu in the Provence he moved to Paris where he soon frequented literary circles. He started writing for various magazines in which he castigated the excesses and irrationalism of Romanticism and extolled the values of the ancient Greco-Latin world and of a pre-revolutionary, 'classical' France. Under the influence of the novelist MAURICE BARRÈS – often referred to as 'father of French nationalism' – Maurras turned to nationalism, and in the 1890s he joined the anti-Dreyfusards in their campaign against the Jewish officer Dreyfus who was wrongly accused and convicted of being a German spy. Needless to say, Maurras was thoroughly Germanophobe.

Maurras became an ardent federalist and monarchist, arguing that the monarchy prior to 1789 had granted the most liberties to the provinces and communes. His stance in favour of the monarchy and the Catholic Church reflected his hate for anything and anyone considered to be contributing to the disintegration of his 'eternal France' – Romanticism, modernism, liberals, socialists, freemasons, Protestants, Jews, foreigners. His federalism – Maurras stayed attached to his region of birth by participating in the *Félibrige*, the movement for the cultural renaissance of the Provence – led him to demand the thorough decentralization of France in his *L'Idée de décentralisation* (1898).

In 1898/9 a group formed around a periodical called *L'Action Française*, the movement adopting the same name and Maurras being one of its founders. The Action Française attacked individualism, parliamentarianism and abstract human rights; it stood for anti-Semitism and anti-German nationalism, and had links to other movements of the extreme right, such as the Ligue Antisémitique, the Ligue des Patriotes and the Ligue de la Patrie Française. Step by step, Maurras succeeded in persuading the other members of the Action Française to join his royalist platform and create a 'neo-royalist' movement. A wider audience was reached with the creation of a daily newspaper in 1908 – also called *L'Action Française*. Despite ideological affinities and occasional co-operation Barrès and Maurras were never bound in a political alliance: the former did not share the enthusiasm for a monarchical regime.

The return of a hereditary monarchy based on the pillars of army and Catholic Church, as well as the rejection of parliamentary democracy, were propagated in many of Maurras's political-philosophical publications, such as *Enquête sur la monarchie* (Inquiry into the Monarchy, 1900), *L'Avenir de l'intelligence* (The Future of Intelligence, 1905), *La Politique religieuse* (1912), *L'Action Française et la religion catholique* (1913), *Kiel et Tanger 1895–1905, La République française devant l'Europe* (1910). He was equally prolific and successful in the literary realm with works such as *Le Chemin du paradis* (1895), *Les Amants de Venise: George Sand et Musset* (1902), *Anthinéa* (1901), *Le Mystère d'Ulysse* (1923) or *La Musique intérieure* (1925). In recognition of his work Maurras was elected one of the 'immortals' of the Académie Française in the year 1938.

On the eve of the First World War the Vatican issued an – unpublished – decree that disapproved of the Action Française as well as of a few of Maurras's books deemed 'paganistic': in spite of his defence of the Church as to its role in public life he himself was an agnostic. Finally, in 1926, the Pope condemned Maurras and the Action Française publicly for putting politics above religion and misrepresenting the Catholic religion. Although the Catholic hierarchy welcomed the role Maurras played in the 'Catholic renewal', it was nevertheless concerned about the anti-governmental aspects and the militancy of the Action and especially of its youth wing. This youth movement, called Camelots du Roi, consisted predominantly of students, commercial employees and apprentices, and it was much more radical than the elders and engaged not rarely in violent street demonstrations. In 1908, the Camelots occupied the Sorbonne in protest against a professor who had allegedly slandered Joan of Arc. Although Maurras hardly believed in Joan of Arc as a saint he saw in her a potent symbol of all the values of 'eternal France' he did believe in: from the year of her beatification, 1909, onwards he organized, together with Barrès, processions in her honour. Maurras's anti-Semitism found an outer expression in presiding over the Cercle Proudhon, a movement formed in 1911, whose aim it was to take away political power from the 'Jewish gold' and transferring it to 'French blood'.

In his *Enquête sur la monarchie* and in *Kiel et Tanger* Maurras attacked vehemently the idea of democracy. He accused it of furthering only particularistic interests but never the common good; he saw in it the promoter of the reign of money rather than of spirit, thus creating a country divided amongst thousands upon thousands of contradictory interests and undermining morality, family and nation. He argued that a nation was not a sum of questionable, obscure fantasies of 'liberty' entertained by mortal voters but the embodiment of the immortal principle of 'blood and soil', to which all individuals had to submit themselves. What was needed was a state that would overcome the class system and organize the society along the lines of professional representation and local empowerment: in his view only the monarchy could provide the umbrella under which the necessary reorganization of society could take place – if necessary, by means of action of a determined vanguard. The republic, on the other hand, was deemed unsuitable for reaching the aims of what he coined 'integral nationalism', since it would lead to either egotistical anarchy or a potentially stifling kind of military or Caesarean dictatorship. That his idea of monarchy was similar to such a dictatorship was not seen by him: he maintained that the marriage of authority from above was with liberties on the local level, and that his notion of 'integral' nationalism was the true expression of the French nation's will.

Admittedly not all, but still many of Maurras's ideas resemble the concoction of fascism, an assessment that is corroborated by the militant activism of the Action Française and the Camelots du Roi. Maurras did indeed admire Mussolini and support the Vichy regime after France's defeat of 1940. Therefore he can be regarded not only as one of the fathers of radical nationalism but also of fascism.

Further reading

Buthman, W.C. (1970) *The Rise of Integral Nationalism in France: With Special Reference to the Ideas and Activities of Charles Maurras*, New York: Octagon [reprint of 1939 edition].

Curtis, M. (1976) *Three against the Third Republic: Sorel, Barrès and Maurras*, Westport, CT: Greenwood Press.

McClelland, J.S. (ed.) (1971) *The French Right: From de Maistre to Maurras, with an Introduction by McClelland*, New York: Harper & Row.

Mosse, G.L. (1978) *Toward the Final Solution: A History of European Racism*, London: J.M. Dent & Sons.

Sutton, M. (1983) *Nationalism, Positivism and Catholicism: The Politics of Charles Maurras and French Catholics, 1890–1914*, Cambridge: Cambridge University Press.

SEE ALSO: the nation, nationalism and the national principle

DETMAR KLEIN

MAZZINI, GIUSEPPE (1805–72)

Giuseppe Mazzini is now regarded as a saintly figure a founder and chief inspirer of the Italian nation. Behind the hallowed image lies the reality of a life lived with single-minded concentration in pursuit of an ideal. The ideal was that of Italian independence and unity, held on to with stubborn insistence at a time when Italy was considered, in the well-known phrase of Mazzini's arch-enemy, the conservative Austrian Chancellor Klemens von Metternich, a mere 'geographic expression' devoid of political meaning. Among the leading figures of the Risorgimento, Mazzini stands out for a life of sacrifice, for his capacity to inspire and for his broad vision. Another and often overlooked important characteristic of Mazzini was the ability to get the most from the limited means at his disposal. Funds were always scarce, and often came with strings attached to them by donors, the political pamphlets and newspapers that he published had a very limited circulation, and living abroad for most of his life he communicated with his followers in Italy with great difficulty. Yet, for all these disadvantages, again according to Metternich, he was the most dangerous revolutionary in pre-1848 Europe.

A combination of things made Mazzini particularly dangerous in the eyes of conservatives. There was, first of all, his appeal to national sentiment and pride, which in Restoration Europe seemed to be a more potent force that the appeal to class and social sentiments favoured by those groups that were just beginning to be called socialist. But Mazzini was not content with appealing to national sentiments. His appeal to national sentiments was closely linked to a call for political equality and social justice. The independent nations that he envisaged were to be democratic republics in which the voice of the people would prevail. As he defined it, the 'People' (*Popolo* was one of the key words of his political vocabulary that he always spelled with a capital P), consisted of everyone. Rich and poor, educated and uneducated, men and women, were all part of Mazzini's definition of what makes up a people. Their differences were not as important as the similarities of customs, language and history that made them a people.

Mazzini's vision appealed to generous instincts and was not confined to any single people or nationality. Always partial to Italy, he nevertheless regarded the Italian movement as part of something greater. The international scope of his vision, easy to overlook, was an important part of his appeal. Italian unity would be the starting point of a democratic process destined to sweep through Europe and beyond. That liberating process would destroy absolute monarchies and multinational empires, install independent democratic republics, foster forms of social co-operation across class lines and lead ultimately to the peaceful coexistence of independent nations. The crowning achievement would be some form of European unity, which he did not spell out in detail.

Sustaining this vision of a radically new order was the bedrock of religious faith. It was a faith that conformed to no known theology. He believed in God's omnipotence and the immortality of the soul, but not in the Trinity, the divine nature of Christ or the ritual and sacramental aspects of Christianity. He was neither Roman Catholic nor Protestant. Belief in God sustained his sense of certainty. Often when confronted by particularly trying situations and stinging reproaches, he would appeal to God and his conscience as the ultimate justification for his course of action. God was also the logically necessary source of the Law of Progress that he thought would inevitably lead to the new order to which he dedicate his life.

How to achieve that new order was Mazzini's most pressing problem from the moment he discovered his mission in life. Visionary though he was, Mazzini did not lack a sense of the practical. He understood, for instance, that the goals he pursued required a broad strategy of political and social action. In the so-called Age of Revolution, Mazzini proposed political conspiracy, fighting on the barricades and a long-term effort to educate the masses, which he saw as too steeped in ignorance and too impoverished to respond readily to the call for change. His followers, whom he called Apostles, must be ready for all contingencies as conspirators, fighters and teachers. It was a tall order, and Mazzini was known as a hard

taskmaster with little patience for those who strayed from the path he prescribes. Amazingly, he nevertheless managed to gather about him a following of several thousands who were ready to do his bidding.

How this complex figure was formed is the question that has vexed and still vexes his biographers. The vital statistics are clear enough. He was born in Genoa on 22 June 1805. He was the third of four children, the only male, and by far his mother's favourite. A few weeks before his birth Napoleon had incorporated Genoa into the French Empire, making Pippo, as those closest to him always called him, technically a French citizen. Technically only, because Mazzini would grow up to reject nearly everything French, including the French Revolution that others of his generation saw as a great liberating event. The revolution he had in mind had to be Italian, and his. Schooled privately, he entered the University of Genoa at age 14. He graduated with a Law degree in 1827, but the university years were more notable for the love of literature that he developed and for the friendships he made than for his proficiency in law, which he practised only briefly and with no particular distinction. The university years were also those of his political awakening. Shortly after receiving his degree in 1827, he joined the secret society of the Carbonari, conspired to topple the monarchy of the House of Savoy, was arrested, tried, and given the choice of expatriating or accepting confinement to some remote locality where the police could monitor his movements.

Mazzini's chose to go abroad, thus beginning that life of wanderings that took him to France (1831–3), Switzerland (1833–7), and England for the greater part of his remaining years. In Marseilles he founded Young Italy (1831), the political society on which he placed his hopes and with which he is always identified. Young Italy was designed to conspire, promote revolution and educate the masses. It did all three with limited success. It all but dissolved when an attempted invasion of the region of Savoy by conspirators based in France, Switzerland and the Piedmontese navy fizzled out in February 1834. That fiasco greatly complicated Mazzini's life. The Swiss authorities, which until then had tolerated his presence, turned on the pressure and forced him to go underground. That did not stop Mazzini from meddling in Swiss politics, or from launching another political society. Young Europe, founded in Bern in April 1834, was to be the foundation for a 'Holy Alliance of Peoples' that would transcend national differences and point towards European unity. It was torn apart by factions, but the name and concept appealed to a new generation of radicals looking for broader horizons.

Eventually the pressure of the Swiss authorities became intolerable, and Mazzini reluctantly left for England in January 1837. The young, handsome and likable exile eventually gained acceptance in London society. He was befriended by the Carlyles and was on good terms with the Mills. He wrote for French and English radical publications, commented on literature, art and politics, opened a school for the children of Italian workers, made himself a figure to be reckoned with in the world of political exiles. As his international reputation grew, so did his popularity among Italians who chafed under Austrian rule. Mazzini played no direct role in unleashing the revolutions of 1848, but when revolution broke out he rushed to Italy for the first time since 1831 and received a hero's welcome. That changed when he turned to politics. He made enemies in Milan when he put aside his republican sentiments and welcomed the participation of King Charles Albert of Piedmont-Sardinia in the war against Austria.

His moment was in Rome, where he went and took over the Government of the Roman Republic in February 1849. Rome was the stage on which he played his most convincing role as revolutionary and political leader. Universal suffrage, land reform and assistance for the unemployed were among the measures enacted by the Government, but he also showed respect for private property and did his best to maintain law and order. His role in the unequal struggle against the French, Austrian, Neapolitan and Spanish troops sent to suppress the Republic was controversial, but it did not diminish his new prestige. The fact that he had tried and failed to save the Republic by political rather than military means actually improved his image. Before 1848 he had been a conspirator and a political theoretician; after 1848 he had the aura of a statesman who had shown that he could adapt his ideals to the realities of political life.

Mazzini's role changed after 1848. The failure of revolution that year oriented the movement for national unification in a more moderate direction. Moderate or downright conservative elements took the initiative and carried movements of national unification to their conclusion in Italy and Germany. Cavour and Bismarck were the men of the hour. Mazzini remained active, but revolutionary zeal could be counterproductive in the new political environment. Many former supporters turned against him after a botched uprising in Milan in January 1853 provoked a harsh Austrian reaction. Mazzini was left to conspire with extreme zealots like Felice Orsini and Carlo Pisacane. He was still important in Italy's Risorgimento, but more as a symbol than as an actor. Most republicans now placed their hopes on GIUSEPPE GARIBALDI, a former Mazzinian who was turning into a formidable rival. To Cavour, who was more enemy than rival, Mazzini was useful largely as an example of the kind of extremism that moderates could avoid by supporting constitutional monarchy.

Yet, it would be a mistake to dismiss Mazzini as irrelevant after 1848. He continued to play a role in the Italian movement as a spur to action and as a symbol of national identity. Many of Garibaldi's supporters and volunteers were former Mazzinians. After 1860 Mazzini promoted the formation of labour unions, co-operatives and mutual-aid societies. The burgeoning Italian labour movement owed much to his efforts. Internationally, he took up the fight against socialism, a principled position that cost him the support of many young activists, especially after Mazzini condemned the Paris Commune in no uncertain terms as a manifestation of the spirit of materialism and class warfare that he abhorred. By that time he had only a few years left to live. He could have congratulated himself for the role he had played in bringing about Italian unity. Instead, he regarded himself as a failure, a republican defeated by monarchists, a social reformer rejected by socialists, a democrat who had failed to reach the people. He was bitter enough to refuse offers of pardon from the Italian Government that would have allowed him to return to Italy undisturbed. His return under an assumed name was a final act of defiance. He died in Pisa on 10 March 1872. A whole generation had to pass before controversy died down and he could take his place among the officially acknowledged and revered fathers of the nation.

Further reading

Sarti, R. (1977) *Mazzini: A Life for the Religion of Politics*, Greenwood: Westport Press.
Smith, D. Mack (1994) *Mazzini*, New Haven: Yale University Press.

SEE ALSO: Garibaldi, Giuseppe; the nation, nationalism and the national principle

ROLAND SARTI

MEINECKE, FRIEDRICH (1862–1954)

Friedrich Meinecke, German historian, was born in Salzwedel, the son of a Prussian civil servant, and studied German, History and Philosophy in Berlin and Bonn. He joined the Prussian archive service in 1887. He was editor of the prestigious historical journal, *Historische Zeitschrift*, from 1893 to 1933, and was Professor of History at Strasbourg (1901–6), Freiburg (1906–14) and Berlin (1914–28). Meinecke is generally seen as one of the most important founders of intellectual history or the 'history of ideas' (*Geistesgeschichte*). He established his reputation with *Weltbürgertum und Nationalstaat. Studien zur Genesis das deutschen Nationalstaats* (*Cosmopolitanism and the National State, Studies in the Origins of the German National State*, 1896–9), in which he described with some sympathy the transition from the cosmopolitanism of the eighteenth-century middle class to the national pride of the late nineteenth century. In 1916 he argued that British naval power must be broken for the good of international relations, but came to support a negotiated peace and domestic reform. He was an 'intellectual republican' during the 1920s, for pragmatic and patriotic reasons. His second notable work, *Die Idee der Staatsräson in der neueren Geschichte* was published in 1924 (and translated into English as *Machiavellianism: The Doctrine of Raison d'État and its Place in Modern History*, 1954). Meinecke retired form his teaching post in 1932, and was dismissed from the *Historische Zeitschrift* by the Nazis in 1935. He continued to publish, however, and one of his most interesting works, *Die Entstehung des Historismus*, appeared in 1936. The origins and nature of 'historicism' – as used in history rather than the history of art and architecture – had preoccupied German intellectuals since the early nineteenth century. For the most part the term had been used in a negative sense to indicate historical relativism (by FEUERBACH) or the abandonment of theory. In 1913 Ernst Troeltsch defined the term as a recognition that all ideas and values are subject to change, an insight that undermines both medieval faith in transcendental truths and Enlightenment confidence in universal values. In 1915, for Meinecke, the self-awareness associated with historicism was positive: for him it was the highest stage attained in the understanding of humanity. It was also something he identified specifically with the German intellectual tradition in the nineteenth century and there is an implicit assumption, echoing a distinction made by Troeltsch and Thomas Mann, among others, during the First World War between a profound German culture and a superficial Western civilization. At the end of the war Meinecke, now 83 years old, was one of few historians to have lived through all the upheavals in German history from unification to the recent defeat, and he published *Die deutsche Katastrophe*, in which he acknowledged the shame the Nazis had brought on Germany, and abandoned an earlier admiration for Bismarck and *Realpolitik*. His appeal for a return to the humanism of the age of Goethe, however, was seen as naïve, and his attribution of the regime's crimes to Hitler's demonic personality an evasion that reflected the inability of the German middle classes to come to terms with Nazism. Many also felt that he had passed too lightly over Germany's war crimes and the atrocities of the Holocaust. Meinecke was appointed the first rector of the Free University of Berlin in 1948 and his considerable influence on the German historical profession continued long after his death.

Further reading

Antoni, Carlo (1959) *From History to Sociology. The Transition in German Historical Thinking,* London: Merlin Press [Original Italian, Florence, 1940].

Meinecke, Friedrich (1984) *Machiavellism. The Doctrine of Raison d'État and its Place in Modern History*, trans. Douglas Scott, intro. W. Stark, Boulder, CO: Westview Press.

Sterling, Richard Whitney (1958) *Ethics in a World of Power. The Political Ideas of Friedrich Meinecke*, Princeton, NJ: Princeton University Press.

Pois, Robert (1972) *Friedrich Meinecke and German Politics in the Twentieth Century*, Berkeley, London: University of California Press.

SEE ALSO: historiography and the idea of progress

TIM KIRK

MICHELET, JULES (1798–1874)

Born in Paris on 21 August 1798, Jules Michelet emerged as a formidably eloquent and lyrical Romantic historian dedicated, above all, to the cult of France, which, for him, was 'a religion'. Michelet received a good education despite his family's indigence and by 1821 had received a doctorate and passed the *agrégation.* He started his career as History teacher, until, in 1827, he was appointed a lecturer in Philosophy and History at the Ecole Normale. In 1838 Michelet was appointed to the chair of History at the prestigious College de France. It was also in 1838 that he was elected to the Academie des Sciences Morales et Politiques. In 1831 Guizot appointed Michelet archivist of the historical section of the Archives Nationales, a position that greatly facilitated his historical researches.

In the 1830s and early 1840s Michelet published the first six volumes of his major *Histoire de France* (the first two volumes were published in 1833, the sixth in 1844). The overarching theme of the *Histoire de France* was the gradual emergence of the unity of the French nation at the expense of the 'fatalities' of racial, geographical and other peculiarities, in a progressive triumph of civilization over accident (or, as a British contemporary reviewer put it, 'of the power of mind over matter': Mill 1985: 237–8).

In the 1840s Michelet became involved in a fierce confrontation with the Catholic Church in France, whose wish to have control over education in France he was firmly opposed to. In 1843 Michelet delivered a series of lectures on the Jesuits and then had them published as *Des Jésuites,* attacking this religious order and their desire to have a role in French education. His next major campaign was that against what he saw as the threat to the sacred unity of France posed by the existence of class divisions and class hatreds. It was as an antidote to the latter that Michelet wrote *Hé Peuple,* published in 1846, where he called for the reconciliation of all classes in France through the teaching of the patriotic brotherhood of the people in schools.

Louis Napoleon Bonaparte's government suspended Michelet's lectures in March 1851 and when, the next year, he refused to take the oath of allegiance to the Second Empire, he also lost his post at the Archives Nationales.

Between 1847 and 1853 Michelet wrote and published his seven-volume *Histoire de la révolution française.* In this work he tried to 'resurrect' (as he put it himself) what happened in France between 1789 and the fall of Robespierre in 1794. The hero of the book and of the revolution was the people. Although he was not keen on what happened after 1790, and was far from an admirer of Robespierre's fanaticism and extremism, Michelet did still defend the revolution as a whole. It was clear, however, that for him the best part of the revolution was its first year.

Reference

Mill, J.S. (1985 [1844]) 'Michelet's History of France', in J.S. Mill, *Essays on French History and Historians,* eds J.M. Robson and J.C. Cairns [Vol. XX of: *The Collected Works of John Stuart Mill*], 219–55, Toronto, University of Toronto Press.

Further reading

Crossley, C. (1993) *French Historians and Romanticism: Thierry, Guizot, the Saint-Simonians, Ouinet, Michelet,* London: Routledge.
—— (1997) 'Michelet et l'Angleterre: l'antipeuple?', *Litterature et nation* 18: 137–52.
Johnson, D. (1990) *Michelet and the French Revolution* (The Zaharoff Lecture for 1989–90), Oxford: Clarendon Press.
Michelet, J. (1959) *Écrits de jeunesse,* ed. Paul Viallaneix, Paris: Gallimard.
—— (1971–) *Oeuvres complètes,* ed. Paul Viallaneix, Paris: Flammarion.
Monod, G. (1923) *La Vie et la pensée de Jules Michelet,* Paris: Champion.
Viallaneix, P. (1971) *La Voie royale, essai sur l'idée de peuple dans l'oeuvre de Michelet,* Paris: Flammarion.

SEE ALSO: historiography and the idea of progress

GEORGIOS VAROUXAKIS

MILL, JAMES (1773–1836)

James Mill, philosopher and social reformer, was born in Scotland in 1773, the son of a shoemaker. His ability was such that he was recommended to Lady Jane Stuart for financial support to study Divinity at the University of Edinburgh. He was licensed as a preacher in 1798 but failed to find a position and so left for London in 1802. There he made a living out of journalism until he decided that more substantial writing was required to make his name. He allowed himself three years to complete a *History of British India* though it actually took twelve. Its six volumes were published in 1818. It was largely on the strength of them that in 1819 James Mill was appointed an Assistant Examiner for the British East India Company. He remained with the company until his death in 1836, having become Head Examiner in 1830, a virtual Under-Secretary of State for India, with the then substantial salary of £1,900 per year.

Mill never went to India and never thought it necessary to do so. Distance, he imagined, gave his work the quality of objectivity. In fact it bore the marks less of objectivity than of the European Enlightenment. For Mill all societies were to be placed on a developmental continuum that led from original barbarism to advanced civilization. On this scale India occupied a lowly place. For James Mill it was essential that superstition gave way as civilization advances. In India this had not happened. The society was characterized by a more extreme and superstitious theocracy than any yet known. Despotism and priestcraft had produced the 'most enslaved portion of the human race'. Thus whatever its other attributes in terms of industry, art and culture, India bore the prime hallmark of a barbarous people. It was because of their low level of civilization that the establishment of any legislative assembly was inadvisable. The only political form fit for the Indian people was arbitrary government 'tempered by European honour and European intelligence'. This account very much suited the East India Company and Mill's *History* soon became a basic work for its officials.

However, it was not only India that required reform. Great Britain itself seemed in considerable need of improvement, having carried into modern times too many traces of its medieval past. Its social structure, political forms, legal system and public administration appeared all too little changed from previous centuries. Mill had met JEREMY BENTHAM in 1808 and soon became his friend, neighbour and main publicist and popularizer of his Utilitarian philosophy.

Utilitarianism was largely a middle-class creed and one aspect of Mill's position was opposition to the aristocracy. He recommended reducing the power of the House of Lords, believing that aristocratic privilege gave power to a narrow class to treat the rest of society as they please. Mill took it as a postulate of human nature that both individuals and groups seek to augment their own happiness and advantage irrespective of the cost to

others. This position obviously denies any notion of benevolent monarchy or aristocracy for no advantaged minority could be relied upon to act in the interests of all. In his best-known essay, on 'Government' (1820), Mill argued that good government has to be representative and that the representative body must have an identity of interest with the whole society. Otherwise it would misuse its power. The logic of this position clearly points in a democratic direction yet in considering the extent of the franchise Mill argued for the exclusion not only of children but also of women, whose interests he considered already sufficiently covered by their fathers or husbands. Mill decided that the male population, of an age to be determined by the law, could be regarded as the natural representatives of the whole society. On this basis it remains unclear whether Mill was recommending universal male suffrage, which would have been a highly radical position still twelve years prior to Britain's first Reform Act. At the end of the essay he described 'the middle rank' as the source of all that is best in human nature and believed that their guidance and advice would be overwhelmingly accepted by those beneath them.

The right to vote was one thing; the free use of it quite another. Before 1872 voting was a public act and James Mill was one of the main campaigners against this situation. He noted that votes were effectively bought – what he called 'prostitute votes' – for the tenant was bound to vote the way his landlord advised rather than risk being turned out of his property. In this way the immoral influence of property took its effect and this corruption in voting served to undermine morals in the wider society.

Among the other topics Mill studied were economics, psychology, jurisprudence, liberty of the press, prisons and education. His last major piece was an extraordinary article on the Church of England, in which his suggested reforms would have transformed it from a religious into an educational institution. Mill, then, was a significant advocate of thorough but peaceful reform for various social institutions, yet now he remains less famous for his own writings than for the people with whom he was associated. As well as being the main popularizer of Bentham's ideas he also became friendly with DAVID RICARDO and did much to stimulate the latter's *Principles of Political Economy* (1817). The next association is less complimentary for Mill's article on 'Government' was famously savaged by LORD MACAULAY who replaced Mill's focus on an acquisitive human nature with emphasis on the particular social and cultural characteristics of separate societies. But perhaps Mill is now best known for the rigorous education he imposed on his eldest son, the philosopher and economist John Stuart Mill. If J.S. Mill's achievements relatively diminished those of his father they at least simultaneously vindicated his father's educational methods.

Further reading

Bain, A. (1967 [1882]) *James Mill. A Biography*, New York: Augustus M. Kelly.
Haakonssen, K. (1985) 'James Mill and Scottish Moral Philosophy', *Political Studies* 33, 4: 628–41.
Mill, J. (1992) *Political Writings*, ed. and intro. T.Ball, Cambridge:Cambridge University Press.
Thomas, W. (1979) *The Philosophic Radicals. Nine Studies in Theory and Practice 1817–1841*, ch. 3, Oxford: Clarendon Press.

SEE ALSO: Bentham, Jeremy; Macaulay, T.B.; Mill, J.S.; political economy; Ricardo, David

MICHAEL LEVIN

MILL, JOHN STUART (1806–73)

In the fields of philosophy, political economy and political thought, Mill is usually recognized as the most influential writer of the mid-Victorian period, some of whose texts, notably *On Liberty* (1859), continued to be important in twentieth-century LIBERALISM. The son of an *émigré* Scot, the historian of British India, JAMES MILL, J.S. Mill was born in London on 20 May 1806. Subjected to a famously intensive, overly intellectual education by his father, the foremost disciple of JEREMY BENTHAM, Mill fils in adolescence also embraced the latter's principles wholeheartedly, claiming they gave 'unity to my conception of things. I now had opinions; a creed, a doctrine, a philosophy: in one among the best senses of the word, a religion'. In 1823 he joined the East India Office serving as a clerk under his father, and he founded a Utilitarian Society to debate Benthamite principles. But in 1826 came a 'mental crisis', as he described it in his *Autobiography*, provoked in part by asking himself the question, if 'all your objects in life were realised... would this be a great joy and happiness to you', and answering 'no'. The crisis passed, but

Mill concluded from it that the Benthamite system was deeply, though not essentially, flawed, and that 'the only chance is to treat, not happiness, but some end external to it, as the purpose of life'. The clearest early statement of Mill's distancing himself from Benthamism is evident in essays on Bentham (1838) and COLERIDGE (1840). MACAULAY's attack on his father forced Mill to rethink certain other issues, such as the vote for women, for which he would become a leading advocate thereafter. During the 1830s he came under the influence also of Saint-Simonism (see SAINT-SIMON, HENRI DE), and, through personal acquaintance, THOMAS CARLYLE, the leading critic of Benthamism. Though his reputation stemmed chiefly from his writings, Mill did enter Parliament in 1865, where he introduced the first motion to extend the franchise to women. He was defeated in 1868.

Some of Mill's early writings, notably the essay 'On Genius' (1832), with its plea for intellectual originality and anxiety over conformity, foreshadow the main themes of his mature liberalism. These themes were reinforced in particular by his reading of ALEXIS DE TOCQUEVILLE's *Democracy in America* (2 vols, 1835, 1840), which stressed the tendency of modern democracy towards 'tyranny of the majority'. Mill's initial reputation, however, was established first by the *System of Logic* (1843), and the *Principles of Political Economy* (1848). Amongst its other achievements, the *Logic* raised the question as to whether a comparative analysis of national character, which Mill termed 'ethology', could be meaningfully attempted. The *Principles* were intended as an exposition of orthodox Ricardianism, but successive editions became increasingly radical. In the wake of the revolutions of 1848, Mill became increasingly sympathetic to the notion that certain forms of voluntary, non-violent socialist experimentation (notably those of CHARLES FOURIER's followers) might point the way to a higher form of 'character' than the soulless, money-grubbing ideal of which he became increasingly contemptuous. When he termed himself a 'socialist' in his *Autobiography*, it was his enthusiasm for such experiments that was principally being described. But Mill nonetheless continued to praise the assertive, go-ahead entrepreneurial ideal (associated with England and the USA in particular) as most likely to assure national progress in the foreseeable future. The *Principles* also asserted, moreover, that a period might be reached, which Mill called the 'stationary

State', when population, production and consumption would have reached their natural limits, but moreover when society might concentrate its efforts upon intellectual and moral progress. In the latter decades of his life Mill came increasingly to argue against both the right of inheritance and against the right of private property in land, and in favour of industrial co-partnership, or co-operation, rather than competition between capitalists and workers. These ideals, again, modify his 'liberalism' substantially.

The chief writings of Mill's maturity are *On Liberty* (1859), *Considerations on Representative Government* (1861), *Utilitarianism* (1863) and *The Subjection of Women* (1869), the latter in particular being co-authored by his wife, Harriet Taylor Mill. His *Autobiography* was published in 1873, and an incomplete study entitled *Chapters on Socialism* was published after his death at Avignon in 1873. Though *The Subjection of Women* aroused the greatest antagonism from contemporary readers, Mill's later reputation is much more indebted to *On Liberty*, now often described as the classic modern treatment of the topic.

On Liberty's starting-point is 'the nature and limits of the power which can legitimately be exercised by society over the individual'. Liberty has been historically threatened by tyrants or oligarchies. It now faces the pressure of majoritarian demands for conformity of opinion, which must be resisted by an intellectual elite that, for Mill, is alone capable of leading society progressively forward through innovation, the generation of new ideas and the challenge of customary mores that threaten perpetually to retard social development and eventually halt it entirely. *On Liberty* aims chiefly to defend what Mill famously terms one 'very simple' principle – it is anything but – 'that the sole end for which mankind are warranted, individually or collectively, in interfering with the liberty of action of any of their number, is self-protection', or the prevention of harm to others. In a 'civilised community', Mill asserts, individuals have an absolute right of their own independence, and no paternal interference to improve or correct their morals or behaviour is justified. In 'uncivilised' or 'backward' communities, however, – such as India, from the governance of which Mill derived his livelihood – 'despotism' was a 'legitimate mode of rule... provided the end be their improvement and the means justified by actually effecting that end'. Most modern readers condemn

this as overtly self-justificatory: 'liberty' as such is not the primary or first principle being defended here, but is trumped by 'progress'. Moreover, Mill also claims that utility remains 'the ultimate appeal on all ethical questions', though defines this as 'utility in the largest sense, grounded on the permanent interests of man as a progressive being'. Thus there are several competing first principles here: liberty, utility, progress and, we will see, individuality as well, whose ranking is unclear.

Chapter Two of *On Liberty* defends freedom of speech and thought, chiefly on the grounds that we cannot presume infallibility of opinion, and that, empirically and sociologically, most people's opinions are derived from their immediate environment, rather than well-reasoned thought or acute penetration. Thus if we live in London, we will tend to be Anglicans, and in Peking, Confucians. The religious example is important: religious intolerance is a key target throughout the text. Persecution hinders mental growth, and the displacement of false by true opinions. In Chapter Three, 'Of Individuality, as One of the Elements of Well-Being', Mill defines individuality as the self-creation of character, and describes this as commonly involving asserting oneself against 'the traditions or customs of other people', this being indeed both 'the chief ingredient of individual and social progress' as well as 'one of the principal ingredients of human happiness', though the latter assertion blithely disregards what Mill elsewhere recognizes as a powerful tendency, based in natural sociability, towards conformity of opinion. Here, however, it is diversity, originality, genius, creativity and the forging of one's own desires and impulses that combine to define 'character', whose antithesis is both a 'mean, slavish' character constantly engendered by the focus on money-getting endemic in commercial society, and a world-denying passivity that Mill associates with Christianity, and contrasts to 'pagan self-assertion'. Mill is here again insistent that his concern is with both individual and national character: like individuals, nations – indeed 'the whole East' – may fall under the despotism of custom, and thus cease to be progressive.

Mill's central discussion of the 'harm' principle with respect to freedom of action comes in Chapter Four of *On Liberty*, in which he attempts a closer conceptualization of the distinction between 'other-regarding' and 'self-regarding' actions, or those which harm others and those which do not.

The former may, Mill contends, include the encroachment on the rights of others, or inflicting loss or damage upon them. But while setting a bad example to others through drunkenness, incontinence or gambling may 'seriously affect' others, it is only when a 'distinct and assignable obligation' is violated that an action becomes other-regarding. Thus, asserts Mill, drunkenness that results in inability to support one's family or pay one's debts is culpable and other-regarding, while drunkenness as such is not. We now see how crucial economic context is to Mill's key conceptual distinction. Any debilitating act, such as drug addiction, which affects our capacity to support ourselves and our family, is other-regarding, but the rich may indulge to their heart's content, in the knowledge that they can still meet their obligations, while far greater stringency and restraint is called for on the part of the poor. In Chapter Five, 'Applications', Mill introduces a number of examples to test the distinction, but some appear self-interested (the sale of opium to China is condoned; the East India Company derived considerable revenue therefrom), while others – the enforcement of compulsory labour on those unwilling to support their own children through work – seem quaintly illiberal today. Indeed, Mill even suggests that proof of one's ability to support children might be supplied before any licence to produce them might be issued. Despite such difficulties, however, most modern readers concede that some such distinction as the harm principle indicates is basic to any rational approach to jurisprudence and legislation.

Like *On Liberty*, *Considerations on Representative Government* centrally defends the role played by the intellectual elite in social progress, the chief dangers of modern democracy being ignorance and incapacity in the governing body, and a propensity to succumb to influences other than those dedicated to the general welfare of the community. Mill's solution is to propose a system of proportional representation, previously described by Thomas Hare, in which parliamentary candidates gaining a certain percentage of the vote but less than a majority could have such votes credited to a national list of candidates, with the net effect being that elected representatives would much more nearly reflect the actual division of opinion in the nation. Beyond this, Mill also proposes literacy and numeracy tests for voters, giving more votes to educated voters, and disfranchising those in receipt of poor relief, or public welfare

funds. Such proposals, again, seem preposterously illiberal by later standards, as does Mill's continued defence of despotic rule over 'less advanced' nations, though these are partly offset by Mill's insistence on the extension of the franchise to women. There are also notable discussions in the text about the relationship between nationality, or a sense of common identity shared by a people, and the right of self-rule; and of the importance of local government in fostering a sense of commitment to the democratic process, and resisting the persistence trends towards both centralization and what Tocqueville had described as a negative form of 'individualism', the propensity in democracies for people to withdraw into their private circles of family and friends, and to abandon the duties of citizenship, resulting in greater concentration of power at the centre.

The brief essay *Utilitarianism*, too, while notionally a restatement of the Benthamite inheritance, centrally defends the intellectual elite from a more philosophical viewpoint. Here Mill's chief contention is that the 'higher' pleasures of the intellect, feeling and imagination are more valuable than the 'lower' or bodily pleasures, such that utilitarianism as such does not command or sanction a shallow hedonism, as Carlyle and others insisted. Instead, not only did those with experience of both prefer the higher; a 'sense of dignity' also inhibited indulgence in the lower. It is, Mill famously insists, 'better to be a human being dissatisfied than a pig satisfied; better to be Socrates dissatisfied than a fool satisfied', though Socrates' fate is not one most willingly embrace. More importantly, Mill insists that utilitarianism can only gain its ends by 'the general cultivation of nobleness of character', which entails the recognition that a readiness to sacrifice our own happiness to that of others 'is the highest virtue that can be found in man'. This resolves the central utilitarian dilemma or conflict between a presumed psychological egoism, or propensity to pursue happiness and avoid pain, and the moral command to promote the greatest happiness of the greatest number, though Mill concedes that 'the present wretched education and wretched social arrangements' will make such Stoic sacrifices less common than would be ideal. Promoting such a sense of duty is however based in part on natural sentiment, 'the social feelings of mankind, the desire to be in unity with our fellow creatures', which is given greater prominence than in *On Liberty*, and which

Mill concedes tends to conflict with the propensity of commercial society to promote a sense of conflict and competition with others. Citizenship and morality, evidently, are underpinned by principles at variance with the promotion of economic man.

Finally, Mill's *The Subjection of Women* (1869), written with his wife, is the foremost feminist tract of its epoch. Besides offering a lengthy description of the legal subordination of women, and the general advantages to social progress that the incorporation of their abilities into public life would entail, Mill/Taylor combat a number of key prejudices against such developments, notably based on a theory of innate female inferiority. The existing system of marriage is condemned as depriving women of property rights, rights of inheritance, rights over their children, the right of separation and the right to resist an oppressive husband. The existing exclusion of women from most branches of employment is contrasted to the advantages that would result from a system of free competition, where women had adequate training and education to unfold their capabilities. The advantages to society of greater equality between the sexes, then, would be threefold: social relations would be governed by a stronger principle of justice, the family forming a partnership rather than being governed by the despotic rule of the husband and father, with obvious advantages for the more democratic education of children; the mass of mental faculties available to society would be doubled, with women likely to exert a softening influence on public opinion (whether through primary or secondary nature is not stated); and, most important of all, women would themselves gain immeasurably in happiness.

Further reading

Cowling, Maurice (1963) *Mill and Liberalism*, Cambridge: Cambridge University Press.

Cranston, Maurice (1958) *J.S. Mill*, London: Longmans, Green.

Gray, John (1983) *Mill on Liberty – A Defence*, London: Routledge and Kegan Paul.

Hamburger, Joseph (1965) *Intellectuals in Politics: John Stuart Mill and the Philosophic Radicals*, New Haven, CT: Yale University Press.

Himmelfarb, Gertrude (1974) *On Liberty and Liberalism. The Case of John Stuart Mill*, New York: Knopf.

Packe, Michael (1974) *The Life of John Stuart Mill*, London: Secker and Warburg.

Rees, J.C. (1985) *John Stuart Mill's On Liberty*, Oxford: Clarendon Press.

Ryan, Alan (1974) *J.S. Mill*, London: Routledge and Kegan Paul.

Semmel, Bernard (1984) *John Stuart Mill and the Pursuit of Virtue*, New Haven, CT: Yale University Press.

Ten, C.L. (1980) *Mill on Liberty*, Oxford: Oxford University Press.

Thomas, William (1985) *Mill*, Oxford: Oxford University Press.

Thompson, Dennis (1980) *John Stuart Mill and Representative Government*, Princeton, NJ: Princeton University Press.

Tulloch, Gail (1989) *Mill and Sexual Equality*, Hemel Hempstead: Harvester.

SEE ALSO: feminism and the female franchise movement; intellectuals, elites and meritocracy; liberalism; political economy; theories of the state and society: the science of politics

GREGORY CLAEYS

MOMMSEN, THEODOR (1817–1903)

The historian Theodor Mommsen was born in Garding, Schleswig, the son of a Protestant minister. Mommsen studied Law and Classics at Kiel, and then spent three years in Italy, where he worked on Latin inscriptions. When he returned he was appointed to a chair of Civil Law at Leipzig in 1848, but lost his post after taking part in revolutionary activities in Saxony. He was subsequently professor at Zurich and at Breslau (now Wrocław in Poland), and in 1858 he took up the chair of Ancient History at Berlin. In addition he was president of the Prussian Academy of Arts and Sciences. He won the Nobel Prize for literature in 1902.

Mommsen is widely recognized as the most significant German historian of the nineteenth century. He was a prolific publisher, with over a thousand titles to his name by the time of his death. Among his major achievements was his work on the *Corpus Inscriptionum Latinarum*, a massive collection of Roman inscriptions preserved since antiquity on various enduring materials. He conceived the project as a young man in Italy and worked on it as editor and principal contributor for a number of years under the auspices of the Berlin Academy. The collection became an indispensable source for Roman history, complementing existing literary sources with the new historical methodology of the day, and transforming the way in which historians approached the history of the ancient world. In addition he was an adviser on the

Monumenta Germaniae Historica, and on the *limes* research on Roman border fortifications. He is best known, however, for his own historical writing on Roman history. Three volumes dealing with the history of Rome up to the end of the Republic and the reign of Julius Caesar were published between 1854 and 1856 as *Römische Geschichte*. He clearly drew parallels between the politics of the Republic and political developments in contemporary Germany, and many contemporaries found that his clear admiration for the strong leadership of Julius Caesar sat ill with his own liberal political views. A fifth volume of the work – on the provinces during the imperial period – was published in 1885. (The fourth volume was to have been on the emperors, but he abandoned it.) Perhaps his most significant work, however, was that on Roman constitutional law, published in three volumes as *Römisches Staatsrecht* between 1871 and 1888. In this work Mommsen codified Roman public law as the Romans themselves had never done, bringing together the countless instances of public laws to show the historical development of Roman constitutional arrangements. This was followed by a work on Roman criminal law (*Römisches Strafrecht*, 1899).

In addition to his academic career Mommsen also pursued a career in politics as a committed liberal. He sat in the Prussian diet for the Progressive Party from 1863 to 1866, and then from 1873 to 1879 as a National Liberal. He was a member of the Secession group (a splinter party from the National Liberals) from 1881 to 1884. Outside Parliament he engaged actively in contemporary political issues, as in 1880 when – along with some seventy other leading figures – he challenged HEINRICH VON TREITSCHKE's attribution of the negative effects of modernization to the influence of Jews.

SEE ALSO: historiography and the idea of progress

TIM KIRK

MORRIS, WILLIAM (1834–96)

The most inspirational of the late nineteenth-century British socialists, Morris was born at Walthamstow near London, on 24 March 1834, the son of a wealthy discount broker. In 1840 the family acquired a 100 acre estate, where Morris hunted, fished and gardened; the family brewed its own beer, and made its own bread and butter. Sent to Marlborough College in 1849, Morris seemed bent on the priesthood, though he had a penchant for Gothic architecture and myth. Expelled for unruliness (he recalled he had chiefly learned 'rebellion' at school) Morris nonetheless went on to Exeter College, Oxford, in 1853, where he fell under the spell of JOHN RUSKIN's aesthetic and social theory, and shared the pre-Raphaelite interests of Burne-Jones, Millais and Rossetti. In the 1850s Morris dabbled in architecture, painting, furniture design, stained glass and other crafts, besides publishing poetry. His firm, Morris & Co., founded in 1861, did much to found the Arts and Crafts Movement. By the late 1870s Morris found himself increasingly interested in politics, and after reading J.S. MILL's 'Chapters on Socialism' (*Fortnightly Review*, 1879) proclaimed himself a convert to socialism. For the next 17 years, until his death on 3 October 1896, he laboured tirelessly for the cause.

There are several elements that are distinctive in Morris's socialism, though in combination they defy easy categorization. The first is that, in keeping with the injunctions of John Ruskin's famous chapter on 'The Nature of Gothic' in *The Stones of Venice*, Morris wished to combine social justice with aesthetic creativity, with making the world beautiful, and treating as fit objects of beauty not only painting, sculpture and architecture but also equally all household goods. The modern excessive division of labour and production for production's sake he rejected in favour of allowing workmen a maximum of creative input into the production process. Second, he rejected not only the ugliness but also the ecological damage created by industrialization, pleading for a more decentralized, cleaner society and system of production. Third, he imagined socialism in terms, at least in part, of medieval ideals as contrasted to the vulgar competitiveness and drabness of commercial society. This view was popularly presented in his famous utopia, *News from Nowhere* (1890), which was aimed at refuting EDWARD BELLAMY's *Looking Backward* (1889), and is set in the mid-twentieth century. A revolutionary socialist like Marx (see MARX AND MARXISM), Morris nonetheless here envisioned a very different society from what Marx had described in the *Manifesto of the Communist Party*. Exchange would be abolished, production geared to need, industry decentralized, individuals encouraged to maximum creativity, population reduced, centralized executive government replaced by local 'mote' meetings in which minority opinions were respected. Read in conjunction with his social and political lectures, this presents a compelling vision of an alternative future for British society.

Further reading

Arnot, R. (1964) *William Morris, the Man and the Myth*, London: Lawrence & Wishart.
Glasier, J. (1921) *William Morris and the Early Days of the Socialist Movement*, London: Longmans.
Lindsay, Jack (1975) *William Morris. His Life and Work*, London: Constable.
Meier, Paul (1978) *William Morris. The Marxist Dreamer*, 2 vols, Sussex: Humanities Press.
Morris, William.*Collected Writings*, ed. May Morris, London: Longmans, Green & Co.
—— (1994) *Journalism* and *Political Writings*, Bristol: Thoemmes Press.
Stansky, Peter (1983) *William Morris*, Oxford: Oxford University Press.
Thompson, E.P. (1955) *William Morris. Romantic to Revolutionary*, London: Lawrence & Wishart.

SEE ALSO: aesthetics, painting and architecture; early socialism; Marx and Marxism; utopianism

GREGORY CLAEYS

MOSCA, GAETANO (1858–1941)

Italian political scientist and jurist, and pioneer of elite theory, Gaetano Mosca was born in Palermo, Sicily, in 1858 and educated at Palermo University. He combined an academic with a political career, teaching constitutional law, public law and political science in Palermo, Turin and Rome, and serving from 1908 as a conservative-liberal deputy in Parliament. From 1914–16 he was under-secretary of state for the colonies, and in 1918 he was appointed a life senator. Mosca was also a regular contributor to newspapers, until increasing governmental censorship in the later 1920s induced him to stop. Although he was highly critical of democratic institutions in his early writings, Mosca came to regard parliamentary government as the least defective of political systems. However, he refused to take any public stance against fascism, simply confining himself to a few incidental remarks on the virtues of representative government in his writings on the history of political ideas, which constituted his only significant output

in the fascist period. He remained a senator until his death in 1941.

Mosca's two most important works were the *Teoria dei governi e governo parlamentare* (1884) and the *Elementi di scienza politica* (1896). In these he explored a similar line of thought to Pareto (whose views on the distinction between elites and masses appear to have been arrived at independently and more or less simultaneously) arguing that all societies, in every age, irrespective of their character (whether it was bureaucratic, plutocratic, military or religious) and of the myth that underpinned them (the will of God, or the will of the majority, or the dictatorship of the proletariat) were ruled by organized minorities. Pareto disliked the term 'elite', on the grounds that it implied an often unwarranted moral superiority, and preferred instead the more neutral concept of the 'political class'. He accepted Marx's idea about the ubiquity of class divisions and conflicts, but rejected the notion that these might be eliminated: a ruling class could be overthrown, but it would necessarily, he maintained, be replaced by another.

Mosca saw the composition and the manner of ruling of political systems as oscillating between alternative poles or 'principles'. A ruling class could be based on inheritance (the 'aristocratic principle') or be open to talented individuals from the lower classes (the 'democratic principle'); rulers might heed the wishes of the ruled (the 'liberal principle') or disregard them (the 'authoritarian principle'). In common with classical writers such as Aristotle, Mosca – who considered himself a liberal – was inclined to see the best political system as one in which none of these principles was pushed to an extreme. The liberal and authoritarian principles should be balanced; and while the hereditary principle could result in the ossification of the ruling class, a degree of closure might be beneficial, in that it could reduce the intensity of the struggle for power and allow for the transmission of valuable skills and traditions.

Mosca had no interest in methodology or philosophy, and did not subject many of his generalizations to serious empirical scrutiny. Nevertheless his main work, the *Elementi di scienza politica*, remains unsurpassed as a general treatise on politics.

Further reading

Nye, Robert (1977) *The Anti-Democratic Sources of Elite Theory. Pareto, Mosca, Michels*, London: Sage.

Albertoni, E. (1987) *Mosca and the Theory of Elitism*, Oxford: Basil Blackwell.

SEE ALSO: democracy, populism and rights; intellectuals, elites and meritocracy; Pareto, Wilfred; social theory and sociology in the nineteenth century; theories of the state and society: the science of politics

CHRISTOPHER DUGGAN

MYTHOLOGY, CLASSICISM AND ANTIQUARIANISM

The nineteenth century was fascinated by the past. Its flourishing interest in history is paralleled by an enthusiasm for myth, for the culture of the classical world and for antiquarian activities of all types.

Mythology

Myths here are treated loosely as ancient 'stories' of gods and heroes. The nature of the relationship between myth and religion, and myth and history, which this loose 'definition' raises, was precisely what was at issue for nineteenth-century thinkers in much of what follows.

Exploration and cultural penetration had led to a mythographic revolution in Europe in the eighteenth century. This added Asian and American myths and deities to the more familiar Latin and Greek pantheons. European antiquarianism also encouraged interest in Norse, Icelandic and Celtic mythologies. A number of different approaches to myth in this period need to be distinguished in order to understand the inheritance bequeathed to the nineteenth century.

Some responses to myth that we will associate with the nineteenth and twentieth centuries were in fact prefigured remarkably early. Bernard de Fontenelle, for example, in his *De l'origine des fables* (1724), pointed to similarities between Greek and Amer-Indian myths, and proposed a theory of world-wide polygenesis of motifs. Charles de Brosses's *Du culte des dieux fétiches* (1760) pointed out 'primitive' traits in Greek religion and dismissed both allegory and euhemerism as viable explanations. Giambattista Vico's *Scienza nuova* (1744) also showed an understanding of something of the complexity of myth. It listed creative imagination, religious inspiration, impressions created by natural phenomena and reflections of social institutions as alternative and coexistent ingredients of mythogenesis. However, these anticipations of later attitudes are the exceptions rather than the rule.

More typical of early readings was Enlightenment rationalism and the syncretic readings of myth that it encouraged. French infidelism and the Enlightenment tradition of Pierre Bayle (1647–1706) and Voltaire (1694–1778) influenced the sceptical, allegorical traditions in which all 'myth' – including Christianity – was reduced to natural, erotic and astronomical meanings. Key figures in this tradition include Charles Dupuis (1749–1802) and Constantin Volney (1757–1820) on the Continent, and Sir William Hamilton (1730–1803), Erasmus Darwin (1731–1802) and Richard Payne Knight (1751–1824) in Britain.

A second type of syncretism is represented by the conservative response to the sceptics. This emanated largely from Christian apologetics who assimilated the new mythological materials to a narrative of Christian pre-eminence, usually by arguing that all mythology emanated from the Flood.

Jacob Bryant's (1715–1804) work followed this line of attack. Sir William Jones (1746–94) offered more scholarly arguments for accepting essentially the same biblical narrative, with a Cushite diffusion after the Flood into India, China, America, Egypt, the Mediterranean and Scandinavia. He based his assertions on his discovery of the affinity of Sanskrit, Greek and Latin, which pointed to the languages having 'sprung from some common source'. This laid the foundations for historical and comparative linguistics, and the notion was applied, by extension, to their myths.

Jones's theory was developed, sometimes in extravagant fashion (such as by Capt Francis Wilford), sometimes more temperately (by the Anglicans Thomas Maurice and G.S. Faber, for example). The sense of urgency with which these mythographers tried to defend the biblical narrative is particularly clear in the revolutionary decade of the 1790s. By the 1810s, however. mythography and Indology, and this 'apologetic' approach to them, were drawing less interest.

At the same time, Romanticism was embracing myth emotionally. While Voltaire was denigrating myth and all 'priestly deceit' in religion, Johann Gottfried Herder (1744–1803) venerated it. By studying myth alongside poetry and language, he attempted to understand the spiritual development of mankind. The effect was to confirm the religious significance and intrinsic worth of myth. Herder's influence can be seen in Schiller's and Goethe's treatment of myth, and in the Romantic idealization of Greek myth generally.

These approaches to myth constitute the inheritance that the nineteenth-century would build on and transform. The vitality of the Romantic reception of myth, and its link with poetic imagination, can be seen lingering in a number of nineteenth-century minds, although the turn to scientific rationalism and empirical enquiry tended largely against this. Rationalism and syncretism of the eighteenth-century type were transformed, but the interest in relating the various mythologies of the world remained a guiding interest (parodied in *Middlemarch*'s Mr Casaubon). Another broad similarity between these earlier readings of myth and those of the nineteenth century lies in the way in which contemporary religion so clearly informs them.

Poets including Coleridge (1772–1834), Landor (1775–1864), Keats (1795–1821), Peacock (1785–1866), Southey (1744–1843) and Shelley (1792–1822) were influenced by the readings of myth outlined above. Solar symbolism and the libertine interpretation of religion clearly found appeal. In particular, it is noteworthy that the pagan myths of European antiquity assumed a new immediacy and universality as they were identified with the cults of the contemporary 'primitive' or oriental world. This contributed to the Hellenism of contemporary poets. Shelley's admiration for classical Greece in *Hellas* (1822), for example, was closely linked to the search for the Asiatic roots of Greek myth, which he explored in *Prometheus Unbound* (1820). His poetic use of primitive and oriental 'Bacchic' elements in Hellenic myth challenged the norms of polite classicism. He drew instead on the sceptical tradition that highlighted the irrationalism and psychopathology of the religious impulse throughout history.

Developments in the scholarly study of myth also show clear affinities with the work discussed above. The awareness of oriental culture in the later seventeenth and eighteenth centuries led to the development of comparative philology and the realization that the languages of Europe, Iran and India were related. This stemmed from Jones's work and occupied scholars into the 1840s. This work matured, in the mid- to late century, in the efforts to reconstruct the protolanguage (now known as 'Proto-Indo-European') from which these several ancient languages were descended. In all this the work of German scholars was particularly prominent (Schlegel, Rask, Grimm, Bopp, Rapp, Schleicher, Curtius).

When the new comparative method was applied to mythology, practitioners took their cue not from the sophisticated works of Fontenelle, De Brosses, Vico or Herder, but from Christian Gottlob Heyne (1729–1812) and Gottfried Hermann (1772–1848). They were distinguished linguistic scholars, but they were not methodologically sophisticated in terms of their approach to myth. The result was that allegory remained the dominant mode of explanation, in particular nature allegory reduced to a single type. The storm gods of Adalbert Kuhn, the animal allegories of Angelo de Gubernatis, the fire mythology of Johannes Hertel and the moon myths of Georg Husing all fit in this tradition.

The solarism of Friedrich Max Müller (1823–1900) was by far the most influential of these allegorical accounts. Müller came to Britain at the age of 25 and enjoyed a prestigious academic career. In 'Comparative Mythology' published in *Oxford Essays* in 1856, he outlined the essential elements of his theory – that the languages and myths of India and Greece were related; that, as Heyne had suggested, a mythopoeic age must have existed during which the race from whom all later Aryan peoples sprang had occupied a single area and spoken a single language; and that almost all Aryan myths were related to the functions of the sun.

He allied this with a theory of language prefigured by Heyne and Hermann. According to this, human language is a 'disease' that hides the purity of thought and is in constant danger of disintegration through the decay of metaphors. The creation of myth is a kind of defence mechanism against this evanescence of metaphors.

Müller's view was that the early names given to natural objects had arisen from an innate religious faculty, and the later myths represented the decay of that early religious intuition of humankind. This acted as a bulwark against Darwinism: the original Aryans had been a noble, 'civilized' race, and contemporaries were not descended from savages.

Müller's academic reputation and the mid-century interest in Aryan culture ensured a widespread influence for solar theory. Paintings of mythical themes, such as those by G.F. Watts and Lord Leighton, portrayed childlike, innocent deities with a fascination for the sun. Matthew Arnold in his *Pagan and Mediaeval Religious Sentiment* (1864) and John Ruskin in *The Queen of the Air* (1869) both had reference to solar theory in their readings of myth in ways that enabled them to avoid the moral problems of Greek myths. (Furthermore, the concept of development from a common, primitive origin was taken up eagerly in other disciplines, inspiring the comparative study of law, institutions, politics, customs.)

The theory had its propagators, but even Müller himself criticized the extremes to which some of his disciples took his ideas – notably the popularizations of his work in the 1860s and 1870s by George Cox. He abandoned the attempt to find genuine etymological derivations between Indian and Greek myths, and simply assumed that all myths that were similar were necessarily derived from a single source.

However, naturism drew many criticisms, too, particularly because it tended to degrade myth, focusing on origins to the exclusion of development, and on linguistic issues to the detriment of social questions. Andrew Lang had a running debate with Müller along these lines in the late 1880s and 1890s. Nor should we forget that Friedrich Schelling's *Philosophie der Mythologie* (published posthumously in 1857) rejected all attempts to impose on myth a secondary 'meaning' – myth must be understood as myth, on its own terms, not as metaphor or history or any other substitute. In this he was followed by Ernst Cassirer (1874–1945) in the second volume of his *Philosophy of Symbolic Forms*.

John Addington Symonds (1840–1893) also regarded the theory as a device that squeezed the essential vitality from ancient Greek life (*Studies of the Greek Poets*, 1873). He adhered instead to the major alternative to Müller's theory of Greek myth that was available in mid-century Britain, that of George Grote (1794–1871).

Grote was the first British historian of Greece to draw a firm line between the prehistoric period and the 'historic', which could only be said to have started when records began (*History of Greece*, 12 vols, 1846–56). The creation of myth belonged firmly in the former period, and as such could not be treated as evidence of historical fact. Rather, it was simply evidence of what the Greeks had once believed.

Thus myth, and the mythical imagination, were the product of a specific time in history. Using a concept of development indebted to the Scottish Enlightenment and to Comte, Grote depicted the developing 'rationalism' of the Greeks in the sixth and fifth centuries BCE as a manifest progression beyond this mythopoeic stage. He frequently described this as the transition from 'Hellenic youth' to 'Hellenic manhood'.

However, he undermined any simple, unilinear reading of his theory by showing that, philosophers and poets notwithstanding, many people in fifth-century Athens had continued to believe in their myths (a fact that he thought helped to undermine the democracy). He also made an extended comparison between the mythopoeic mindset of Greece and that of Europe in the Middle Ages. His point is thus a clear lesson to his contemporaries: that man *can* develop beyond 'superstition', and progress to a rationalism that would be supportive of democracy – but, on historical evidence, he frequently fails to do this.

One can see Grote's influence in Ruskin (1819–1900), Symonds and Walter Pater (1839–94). Although the point that Grote wished to emphasize from his conception of myth was that man can progress beyond the mythopoeic to a more 'advanced' rationalism, for these critics there was another, more important point. This was that, if the myths were not to be regarded as 'historical' evidence, they were instead the product of an imagination with its wellspring in the human (rather than in God or in transcendental knowledge). This in turn suggested – for Pater in particular – that the myths were existential images of perennial human needs and aspirations, created by an imaginative faculty that was capable of functioning in any age, including the modern. Myths and the mythic imagination thus became, in contrast to Grote, a possible route out of present difficulties.

A major turning point in approaches to myth – and in particular Greek myth – came towards the end of the century. The so-called 'ritualists' used the insights of archaeology and anthropology to press a radically new vision of the Greeks. For them, myths *were* the product of historical events – of ritual practices that had predated the myths. They were 'the spoken correlative of the acted rite', and arose from the collective thought of the social group. The irrationality and sexuality inherent in the myths could not be written away but were rather signs that these were fundamental aspects of Greek life.

The ritualists were indebted to E.B. Tylor's *Primitive Culture* (1871) and James G. Frazer's *The Golden Bough* (12 vols, 1890–1915; abridged edition 1922). Frazer (1854–1941) argued that savagery, cruelty and irrationality had survived well into the classical age of Greece, not only in myth but also in rituals. His relation of primitive religion to anxiety over the food supply, and his concept of the dying and reborn deity, particularly influenced the ritualists. More generally, his approach signalled an important switch in focus to the social rather than the intellectual origins of myth.

Jane Ellen Harrison's (1850–1928) study of the non-literary evidence for Greek religion led her to argue against a religion of 'serene' Olympians in favour of a world that was as much preoccupied with chthonic worship and the fending off of daimons, spirits and ghosts as with the traditional Olympian gods. Indeed, she saw the Olympians' dominance in religion as a reflection of the dissolution of group identity and the imposing of patrilinear society on a previously matrilinear model. Hers was a Hellenism that emphasized and admired the mysterious, mystical, untamed, ecstatic (influencing Yeats and Lawrence, among others), in opposition to a humanistic Hellenism that saw Greeks as the ideal image of rational humanity.

Francis Cornford's (1874–1943) *Thucydides Mythistoricus* (1907) followed Harrison's lead in examining the non-rational parts of enlightened Greek thought, presenting a Thucydides markedly less 'rational' than the Victorians had seen. *From Religion to Philosophy* (1912) saw modes of thought in Greek philosophy prefigured in myth, and *The Origins of Attic Comedy* (1914) considered the ritual origins of comedy.

The Olympians and Greek rationality had their supporters too, however, including Edward Caird (1835–1908) and Lewis Farnell (1856–1934). Gilbert Murray (1866–1957), although also influenced by anthropology and a friend of Harrison's, offered a less positive account of chthonism, polygamy, polyandry and fertility goddesses, seeing in 'Olympian religion' a striving of the human spirit towards a more nearly perfect fulfilment.

Although classical mythology, and Greek in particular, was the dominant interest for Victorians, other myths were also important. James MacPherson's (1736–96) 'Ossian' collections had kindled wide interest across Europe in the old Celtic myths of Scotland and Ireland (*The Poems of Ossian*, 1760–3). They were also an influence on Blake, Goethe and Byron. However, their status as forgeries helped to sideline them. The Scottish romances of Sir Walter Scott (1771–1832) also attracted much popular interest in the myths. An important later poetic use of the myths was Tennyson's *The Voyage of Maeldune* (1892).

During the nineteenth century, the numbers of people speaking Celtic languages continued to decline. Scholars, meanwhile, followed the lead of German philologists and compiled grammars and dictionaries of the Celtic languages. In both Ireland and Wales the great medieval codices, like the *Book of the Dun Cow* and the *Black Book of Carmarthen,* were edited and translated. In all Celtic countries, folklorists recorded and translated huge volumes of oral tradition.

Popular versions of the myths appeared. Lady Charlotte Guest offered translations of early Welsh mythology as *The Mabinogion* (1838). In addition, there were William Carleton's *Traits and Stories of the Irish Peasantry* (1830) and *Tales of Ireland* (1834), and T. Crafton Croker's *The Fain, Legend and Tradition of the South of Ireland* (1825) and *Legends of the Lakes* (1829). Later popular collections of note include Lady Jane Francesca Wilde's *Ancient Legends, Mystic Charms and Superstitions of Ireland* (1888) and Lady Isabella Gregory's retellings of ancient stories in *Cuchulain of Muirthemne* (1902) and *Gods and Fighting Men* (1904).

By mid-century, there was an awareness among the educated that the Celtic-speaking peoples were the inheritors of a rich ancient heritage. Critical attitudes were selective and subjective, however. Many saw the Celts as the exemplars of the type of medieval heroism that Scott had depicted in his popular historical novels earlier in the century. On the other hand, in his study of newly emerging Celtic texts, *Essai sur la poésie des races celtiques* (1854), ERNEST RENAN found the Celts reserved, lacking in political aptitude and fatalistic. Similarly, Matthew Arnold's *On the Study of Celtic Literature* (1867) reduced characteristic Celtic traits to their sense of magic and of melancholy, and their gift for style.

Standish James O'Grady (1846–1928) is regarded as the Father of the 'Irish Literary Revival' of the late century (that is, the creation of a literature written in English). His *History of Ireland* (1881) and subsequent historical novels (including *Finn and his Companions* (1892) and *The Coming of Cuchulain* (1894)) posit Celtic warriors that seem to have much in common with model Tory Victorian gentlemen. The most influential figure in the 'Revival' was W.B. Yeats (1865–1935). Inspired by O'Grady and the Fenian leader and journalist John O'Leary (1830–1907), he founded the National Literary Society in Dublin in 1891 and published numerous plays and poems based on characters and themes from Celtic mythology.

Traditionally linked to Celtic tales, the story of King Arthur deserves mention. Here we move in to a slightly different aspect of the function of myth – the 'mythologizing' of the past. In the period of the French Revolution and the Revolutionary and Napoleonic Wars, his position as a national hero was cemented, associated with nobility, order, authority and, crucially at this time, military prowess. Throughout the century he is manipulated according to need, and one can read in his treatment something of nineteenth-century concerns about identity in Britain. For example, Thomas Love Peacock's novel *The Misfortunes of Elphin* (1834), written in the context of the crisis over parliamentary reform, turned to the Arthurian legend to supply a model of benevolent aristocratic leadership. Edward Bulwer Lytton's epic *King Arthur*, written in the years leading up to 1848 (and published in 1849), invoked Arthur as a strong leader who listened to and cared for his people, making clear that this was a better solution to popular distress than revolution. Strikingly, new developments in racialist theory in the second half of the century are captured in the way in which Arthur was reconfigured as a Saxon hero. Tennyson's *Idylls of the King* (1859) was the most influential promoter of Arthur's Saxon origins. Although critics noted the difficulty in transforming the Celtic legend into English national epic, Arthur had become definitively a Saxon rather than a Celt by the end of the century.

Finally, Bishop Percy's translation of Mallet's *Northern Antiquities* (1770) had given currency to the Norse myths, the second volume including a translation of the Icelandic saga *Edda*. THOMAS CARLYLE pursued this interest, and his search for heroes, in *The Early Kings of Norway* (1875). WILLIAM MORRIS turned to the Norse cycles in *Sigurd the Volsung* (1877).

Classicism

In the treatment of myth, it was clear that nineteenth-century Britain was predominantly concerned with the mythology of the Greek world. 'Classicism', however, is a rather different phenomenon, encompassing a broad range of activities, whose common theme is reference to the classical period. 'Classical' here implies a stylistic value judgement, referring quite strictly to fifth- and fourth-century BCE Athens and late Republican and Augustan Rome.

In art and architecture, classicism involves adherence to, or imitation of, classical style, principally that of fifth-century Greece. The idea that the art of ancient Greece set a standard for future achievement had been a touchstone of the Renaissance and was elevated to dogma by Winckelmann (1717–68) and the neoclassical critics who followed him. Frequently opposed to Romanticism, naturalism and medievalism, the term became very elastic indeed, and varied according to the concept to which it was opposed. As a result it could sometimes be used with the connotation of 'conservative' or 'bound by rules' in contrast to 'revolutionary' or 'inspirationally creative'. Conflicts over notions of 'classicism' were thus at the heart of many aspects of 'modern' style.

Literary classicism means the use or imitation of classical models and motifs. The Hellenism of nineteenth-century poets is a complex phenomenon and cannot be treated adequately here. In brief, a variety of poets were inspired by the beauty of Greek literature and of Greece as a place (regardless of whether they had actually visited the country), and by a sense of its 'primitivism' that could easily elide into a notion of 'childlike' innocence.

In the early period, Keats was inspired by a sense of the profound beauty of Greek poetry and art. For Shelley and Byron (1788–1824), sensuous beauty was set alongside the glory of (a highly romanticized conception of) Greek freedom. We have also already mentioned their absorption in myth. Later in the century, Hellenism in poetry is particularly associated with the work of Matthew Arnold (1822–88), Arthur Hugh Clough (1819–61), Algernon Charles Swinburne (1837–1909), Alfred (Lord) Tennyson (1809–92) and Robert Browning (1812–89).

The Greek and Latin classics formed the dominant element in school curricula in Britain, and a knowledge of both languages was required for university entrance throughout the century. Classics thus functioned as a common frame of reference among the educated classes broadly speaking, not just among a small community of classical scholars.

This meant that, when writing about aspects of the classical history, a wide audience could be expected that, furthermore, was used to discussing contemporary problems through the lens of, or with reference to, the classical world. Nineteenth-century society, religion and politics were the touch-stones of British discussions of the ancient world.

We have already seen this in action in readings of Greek mythology. In addition, the study of Homer was constrained by its perceived implications for biblical scholarship, which can be seen clearly in the reception to Wolf's *Prolegomena ad Homerum* (1795) and the many works that Gladstone devoted to the bard, published from mid- to late century. Discussions of the Athenian democracy were fre-quently couched in terms of British constitutional development, ranging from William Mitford's conservative polemic (*History of Greece,* 10 vols, *1784–1810*) which was firmly countered by Grote's highly influential pro-democratic riposte (see above). Further, the study of Socrates in the early and mid-century was influenced by liberal Anglican concerns to combine rationality, reverence and moderation in religious and social life. Similarly, the study of Aristotle and Plato was informed by the belief that their works provided intellectual support in a secular society for values that had previously been thought of as 'Christian'.

Here as elsewhere we see a far greater pre-occupation with the Greek than with the Roman world. This is associated with the broader turn away from the values, ideas and institutions asso-ciated with the Roman and Christian past from the second half of the eighteenth century onwards. This move was fuelled by the example of 'democracy' offered by ancient Athens to a world coming to terms with what modern 'democracy' would mean. However, Rome was far from neglected. A great deal of scholarly attention was paid to the trans-lation of Niebuhr's *History of Rome* (translated by J.C. Hare and Connop Thirlwall, 8 vols, 1828–32), and Macaulay's *Lays of Ancient of Rome* (1842) achieved a wide popular readership. Moreover, the example of imperial Rome was used increasingly, towards the end of the century, as a warning to the British of the dangers of 'luxury' and 'decline'.

Antiquarianism

Elements of the Victorian engagement with the past that we have been discussing were supported by antiquarian activities. Antiquarianism *per se* is a broader phenomenon, however, embracing archaeology, architecture and art history, con-servation, heraldry, ecclesiastical, documentary, musical and literary study – the common link being that all these subjects are based on the *material* remains of the past.

Victorian antiquarians formed a socially homogeneous group in Britain, on friendly terms with each another – typically middle class and male, they were largely university-educated pro-fessionals (architects, surgeons, engineers) who were self-taught, enthusiastic and committed amateurs in the field of antiquarianism. There were many local societies, and at national level there was the Society of Antiquaries (inaugurated in 1707) as well as the two rivals, the British Archaeological Association and the Archaeological Institute, each with their own publications.

What separated antiquarians from historians was the antiquarians' focus on *artefacts,* their collection and descriptive classification. The gap widened between historians, antiquarians and archaeologists as the century wore on, with the onset of professionalization and specialization. Within antiquarian studies itself, amateurs were further sidelined by governmental activities in the field of record and manuscript activity that created a nascent class of professional record scholars in employment at the new Public Records Office.

Further reading

Barczewski, S.L. (2000) *Myth and National Identity in Nineteenth-Century Britain. The Legends of King Arthur and Robin Hood*, Oxford: Oxford University Press.

Bullen, J.B. (ed.) (1989) *The Sun is God: Painting, Lit-erature and Mythology in the Nineteenth Century*, Oxford: Oxford University Press.

Feldman, B. and Richardson, R.D. (1972) *The Rise of Modern Mythology 1680–1860*, Bloomington, London: Indiana University Press.

Jenkyns, R. (1980) *The Victorians and Ancient Greece*, Oxford: Blackwell.

Levine, P. (1986) *The Amateur and the Professional: Antiquarians, Historians and Archaeologists in Vic-torian England 1838–86*, Cambridge: Cambridge University Press.

Puhvel, J. (1987) *Comparative Mythology*, Baltimore, London: Johns Hopkins University Press.

Spencer, T. (1954) *Fair Greece, Sad Relic: Literary Philhellenism from Shakespeare to Byron*, London: Weidenfeld & Nicolson.

Turner, F.M. (1981) *The Greek Heritage in Victorian Britain*, New Haven, London: Yale University Press.

Vance, N. (1997) *The Victorians and Ancient Rome*, Oxford: Blackwell.

SEE ALSO: anthropology and race; historiography and the idea of progress; religion, secularization and the crisis of faith

LIZ POTTER

N

THE NATION, NATIONALISM AND THE NATIONAL PRINCIPLE

The 'principle of nationality' – the belief that each nation had a right of self-determination and should find expression in its own distinct state – was the most subversive and arguably the most potent political idea of the nineteenth century. It inspired a succession of revolutions and wars; it broke up empires and overthrew dynasties; and it left the map of Europe and North and South America (and soon Asia and Africa too) changed beyond recognition between the 1770s and the Treaty of Versailles in 1919. Quite why nationalism should have become the force it did in this century is a subject of much debate among historians, sociologists and anthropologists. Some have pointed to the corrosive effects of economic modernization, with the break-up of old rural hierarchies and the need for fresh integrative structures and systems of communication; others have highlighted such factors as the development of 'print capitalism' and its role in producing emotionally charged 'imagined communities'; still others have focused on the intellectual revolution occasioned by the Enlightenment, with the discrediting of traditional epistemologies, and the search by the educated classes for new secular cosmologies.

The genesis in the second half of the eighteenth century of 'nationalism' – the idea that individuals derive their essential identity from a nation, whose interests they should seek to promote and defend – has more often been assumed than demonstrated, and in recent years a number of historians have rightly pointed to the existence of well-defined currents of nationalist thought in some of the older Western states, above all England, from the Middle Ages onwards. Wars, they have shown, were

a particular catalyst to such thinking – in the fourteenth, fifteenth and sixteenth centuries, as in the nineteenth and twentieth. Nor did the term 'nation' undergo any radical shift in meaning, as has frequently been suggested: writers such as Milton, Shakespeare and Bacon used the term in much the same way as it would be today. Even the desirability of some degree of congruence between nation and state appears to have been quite widely accepted. Machiavelli's famous call in *The Prince* (1513) for Italians to liberate their land from 'barbarians' was echoed in more general terms by his French contemporary Claude Seyssel: 'All nations and reasonable men,' he wrote, 'prefer to be governed by men of their own country and nation – who know their habits, laws and customs and share the same language and lifestyle as them – rather than by strangers.'

What gave nationalism particular potency from the later eighteenth century was the emergence of the doctrine of popular sovereignty. This doctrine – most clearly enunciated by Jean-Jacques Rousseau in *Du Contrat social* – derived sustenance from extensive discussions among intellectuals of the Enlightenment about 'national genius' and 'national character', and the growing interest in historical study as a tool for the understanding of societies and furtherance of civil progress. Rousseau did not spell out exactly what it was that defined a 'people', but it was in 'the people' that sovereignty lay. Moreover, as he suggested in his *Considérations sur le gouvernement de Pologne* and *Projet Corse* states should seek to protect and nurture the particular character and customs of their people – through, for example, education and patriotic festivals – so as to foster patriotism (which he saw as crucial to the liberty of the ancient city states that he so admired). 'A child, on opening its eyes,' he wrote, 'ought to see *la patrie*'; and everyone should be taught 'love of their country, that is to say, love of liberty and the laws'.

The binomial of popular sovereignty and the nation found its first clear expression in the American Revolution of the 1770s; but it was with the French Revolution, and the ensuing cataclysm of the Napoleonic Wars, that nationalism erupted onto the stage as an active political principle, sweeping east and south across Europe, westwards into South America, and then later moving on into Asia and Africa. For the French revolutionaries the nation was represented by the Third Estate, and it was this Estate, 'the people', that should determine what the nation was and how it should be governed. This was liberal, but also profoundly subversive. In theory at least now, any group that identified with the new dispensation in Paris could elect to become part of the French nation: as happened in 1791 with the annexation of the papal enclave of Avignon to France following a popular plebiscite.

A far less liberal dimension to the new nationalism – and one that was to have devastating implications for much of nineteenth- and twentieth-century history – was its aggressive rationalism. In part this was the result of Enlightenment universalism, which was at root humane and irenical. But the assertion that the French nation was 'one and indivisible', and the ensuing pursuit of legal, administrative and cultural standardization and uniformity, derived also from other more practical, less idealistic preoccupations: fears that the revolution might be subverted from within and from without. The often quite extraordinary initiatives to make '*la patrie*' the object of mass veneration – the populist rhetoric, the theatrical ceremonies and festivals, the new appellations and symbols, the cult of the flag, the Marseillaise – served to mobilize a nation that by 1792 had more than a million men under arms and was about to embark on nearly a quarter of a century of war.

The rationalism of the French Revolution, and the idea that nations could be constructed on universal principles, irrespective of history and traditions, was to receive a prompt challenge from several quarters. The most eloquent (and influential) riposte came from EDMUND BURKE, in England. Burke, in his *Reflections on the Revolution in France* (1790) argued that nations were discrete, divinely ordained entities, whose distinctiveness was the felicitous product of slow, providentially guided, development. Change, if change were needed, should be evolutionary, not revolutionary, and should build on the accretions of the centuries. Burke's views were to be echoed by a number of Continental European writers (notably such aristocratic French opponents of the revolution as BONALD and CHATEAUBRIAND), and were to provide the theoretical underpinning of the post-1815 Restoration order in Europe, with its conservative alliance of Throne and Altar, and uncompromising rejection of popular sovereignty and the principle of nationality. In the later nineteenth century they were to receive a radical and aggressive reworking in 'integral nationalism'.

In Central Europe, the impact of the French Revolution, and the traumatic experience in particular of invasion by the Napoleonic armies, stimulated some very different thinking about the nation. While France and England had enjoyed several centuries of continuous existence as nation-states, and developed a fairly strong sense of national consciousness (albeit rudimentary still in many rural areas, especially in southern and western France), so making appeals to history or voluntarism appear quite logical, in those regions where there was no historical congruence between nation and state a more metaphysical and abstract basis for nationalism was needed. The principal source for this alternative version of nationalism – often referred to as 'organic' or 'eastern' – was Germany.

In the years immediately before the French Revolution the German philosopher, critic and ardent collector of folk songs, Johann Gottfried von Herder, had elaborated a theory according to which humanity was characterized not by a universal rationality, but by difference. Nations, he argued, were the natural building blocks of mankind, and had a primordial, God-given existence. Each was endowed with a distinctive character, which over time had become etched deep into the soul of the common people. Through scholarly study, above all of language (the principal manifestation of a nation's soul), he believed that it should be possible to uncover the primal 'folk character' of each nation and remove the alien and unnatural incrustations with which it had become overlaid. Herder was very much a man of the Enlightenment, and his instincts were humanitarian. He aspired to a multifarious world, tolerant of the diversity of nations. In the hands of a younger generation of German intellectuals, however, angry at the defeats inflicted on their fellow countrymen by Napoleon, his ideas on the nation assumed a more menacing character.

For these intellectuals – men such as Friedrich Schleiermacher, Friedrich Jahn and Johann Gottlieb Fichte – Herder's idea of the nation as a natural, organic entity, existing over and above individuals, was grafted on to Kantian notions of autonomy, to produce a doctrine of nationalism in which will, struggle and self-determination were central tenets. For these post-Kantians freedom was no longer, as in the US, French or British models, something extraneous to the nation, which the state should seek to safeguard. Rather, freedom was a matter of self-realization, to be achieved through the total absorption of the individual in the collective life of the nation, outside of which, they argued, he had no meaning or purpose. In the case of suppressed nationalities – like that of Germany – this meant 'awakening' the national soul. As Fichte argued in his famous *Addresses to the German Nation*, delivered in the wake of the Prussian defeat at Jena in 1806, Germany would have to generate the same extraordinary collective spiritual energy as the French had shown, if it wanted to be free, and that could only come through a programme of education designed to fuse the will of the individual totally with that of the nation-state.

This German version of nationalism was to prove highly influential, particularly in Eastern Europe and the Middle East. It helped to generate a huge scholarly industry of cultural, linguistic and historical research in the first half of the nineteenth century. Across Europe, members of the educated classes gathered folk songs, unearthed and reconstructed (or in some cases, as with Romanian, effectively invented) submerged languages, collected sagas and myths, assembled vast tomes of historical documents, and made patriotic episodes from the past the subjects of novels and paintings. Though the practitioners of this research were often motivated more by academic and aesthetic concerns than political ones, these attempts to uncover the folkloric 'soul' of peoples provided the platform for many of the nationalist movements in the later nineteenth century, especially in Eastern Europe (but also in Ireland, to mention a 'Western' anomaly).

In the period between the Vienna settlement of 1815 and the revolutions of 1848–9, it was the 'Western' or liberal version of nationalism that was to be most in evidence in European politics. The re-establishment of absolutism, the rejection of the principles of 1789, and the alliance of Throne and Altar, ensured that the national resistance movements that had begun to appear in Italy, Germany, Holland and other parts of Europe under French occupation continued to exist and operate after 1815 – typically through the medium of secret societies such as the Carbonari or GIUSEPPE MAZZINI's Young Italy – and to link the pursuit of national self-determination to constitutionalism and a measure of secularization and democracy (though quite how much democracy proved a source of perennial contention among liberals). Revolution was the main instrument of change: Greece, Poland, Belgium and Italy all witnessed liberal national risings in this period. So too did South America, where in the 1820s, under the leadership of SIMON BOLIVAR and José de San Martin, Spanish imperial rule was brought to an end and independence secured.

In theory the liberal nationalism of these years was strongly humanitarian in its outlook. Self-determination, freedom from foreign rule, representative government and guarantees of personal liberty would, it was felt, usher in a new world order. As states became coterminous with nations, and the *ancien régime* elites were dislodged from power under the impact of the rising tide of democracy, so governments would come to rest on more stable foundations and the causes of international conflict disappear: for were not 'the people' instinctively more inclined to peace and the pursuit of material prosperity than bellicose kings and aristocrats? Free trade would help to cement this new order. And where disputes did arise, international arbitration, of the kind that JEREMY BENTHAM had advocated back in 1789 in his influential *Plan for a Universal and Perpetual Peace*, would prevail. Tennyson summed up the optimism of the age in his poem *Locksley Hall* (1842), when he envisioned a time when 'the war-drum throbb'd no longer and the battle flags were furl'd/ In the Parliament of man, the Federation of the world'.

In practice, though, the liberal nationalism of 1815–48 was far from being wholly irenic and tolerant. To begin with, the idea of self-determination was intertwined with a romanticist glorification of suffering and struggle – 'through blood and darkness to light', as German liberals explained the red, black and gold of their tricolour. 'Holy' wars of liberation were accordingly necessary, desirable even, to give nations – in the words of a leading Italian follower of Mazzini – 'a baptism of blood'.

Second, liberal nationalism was extremely vague about who or what exactly constituted a nation, and linguistic, territorial and historical claims were invoked or discounted in an almost arbitrary fashion according to the standpoint and interests of the observer. Thus English liberals (including JOHN STUART MILL) tended to dismiss Irish nationalism on the grounds that the 'principle of nationality' should further, not retard, the cause of human progress; and how could a small, economically backward, Catholic state be regarded as a step forward? German liberals in 1848 looked to scotch Polish claims for independence by invoking Fichtean voluntarism. As a prominent deputy of the left put it: 'Mere existence does not entitle a people to political independence: only the force to assert itself as a state among the others.'

Nor, when they were examined closely, did the ideas of those liberal nationalists such as Giuseppe Mazzini, who volunteered some theoretical justification for their beliefs, augur well for freedom and peace. In the absence of any widespread national sentiment in the peninsula, Mazzini based his conviction that Italy was a nation (and a great one at that) ultimately upon a religious intuition, namely that it had been ordained by God. This, more than any alleged oppression of the people, provided the moral basis for the struggle against the 'foreigner', just as after Italy's unification in 1860 it was used by some of Mazzini's intellectual heirs to support the government's suppression of 'anti-national' internal dissent. No less perilous was Mazzini's use of Herder's idea of 'mission'. In theory, Mazzini (like Herder) envisaged a harmonious world of free, self-confident nations, each contributing its unique qualities to the enrichment of humanity. In practice, though, it was hard for 'mission' to avoid a strong impulse towards competitiveness, even expansion.

Indeed, the dividing line between distinctiveness and assertions of superiority was a thin one, especially when past glories – real or imagined – were resurrected and used as a spur to national revival. Moreover, the scholarly passion for 'national' histories stirred up a hornets' nest of memories of wars, conquests and persecutions that contributed, especially in the later nineteenth century, to an atmosphere of growing international mistrust. The movement for German unification fed on deep strands of Francophobia, a belief that the French harboured inveterate, perhaps incorrigible, hegemonic ambitions, cultural and political, that

would have to be defeated if Germany were ever to be truly herself. Similar sentiments could be found among the followers of Mazzini in Italy, while further east, in the Balkans, centuries of ethnic and religious conflict ensured that nationalism here was to be riddled with mistrust and hatred, and claims and counter-claims of superiority and inferiority. The hopes of Romantic nationalists like JULES MICHELET in the 1840s that by 'being themselves' the peoples of the world would come together 'with open hearts' were unrealistic.

It was in part an awareness of the dangers inherent in nationalism that led many liberals, especially in Britain, but also in France and the USA, to be sceptical about the application of the national principle in politics. Byron and DISRAELI – both of whom shared a Romantic identification with the underdog, and voiced strong sympathy for the struggles of oppressed peoples – were less typical than CARLYLE, COLERIDGE and LORD ACTON. In his well-known 1862 essay, *Nationality*, Lord Acton described the 'theory of nationality' as 'a retrograde step in history'. He argued that a state that contained a diversity of peoples, and that guaranteed their rights and peaceful coexistence, was 'one of the chief instruments of civilisation'. By contrast a state that sought to 'neutralise, to absorb, or to expel' other nations, risked destroying 'its own vitality'. He concluded that the most perfect dispensations were multi-national ones, like the British and Austrian Empires.

John Stuart Mill was also well aware of the dangers posed by nationalism. He had been appalled at the bloody denouement of the revolutions of 1848–9, and at how:

> in the backward parts of Europe... the sentiment of nationality so far outweighs the love of liberty, that the people are willing to abet their rulers in crushing the liberty and independence of any people not of their own race and language.

But he also conceded that the principle of nationality could be politically beneficial. In general, he argued, in the chapter on nationality in his *Representative Government* (1861), it was desirable for free government that a state and a nation should coincide: people liked to be represented by their own kind. But the national principle should certainly not be binding. There was a practicality threshold to be crossed: Hungary was ethnically too much of a hotchpotch to be unscrambled.

More importantly there was a moral threshold to be considered. It was manifestly to the advantage of the Bretons and Basques to be part of the French nation, just as it was for the Welsh and Scots to be part of Britain. Secession would condemn them 'to sulk on [their] own rocks, the half savage relic of past times, revolving in [their] own little mental orbit, without participation or interest in the general movement of the world'.

Although there was an implicit economic dimension to Mill's dismissal of smaller nationalities, in general liberals found it difficult to articulate a clear connection between nations and economies. This was mainly because the liberal anti-mercantilist orthodoxies envisaged no theoretical role for national governments: the main unit of wealth creation was the individual or the company. Indeed prior to the widespread adoption of protectionism in the 1870s and 1880s, the only important discussions of economic nationalism were in Germany. Here in 1840 FRIEDRICH LIST – who had been an influential advocate of the *Zollverein* – published his celebrated *The National System of Political Economy*, which argued that free trade was appropriate only to the most advanced economies, such as the British, and that if other countries were to catch up and compete, their governments needed to adopt national policies to foster their commercial, industrial and agricultural sectors.

Such ideas, however, found little support at a time when liberal Britain was widely regarded as the paragon of the successful state. But the devastating victories of less than liberal Prussia over France in 1870, and the ensuing emergence of *realpolitik*, weakened faith in the claims of classical liberalism. So, too, did the onset of industrial and agricultural recession. Social Darwinism also took its toll: if, as Darwin had shown, species flourished according to their capacity to adapt to circumstances, why should the same not be true of peoples, races or nations? And if states were to be successful, or simply survive, was it not incumbent upon governments to intervene – if need be at the expense of individual freedoms – and ensure that their societies were strong and that their citizens or subjects were educated and trained in a way that best enabled them to compete?

Already in the Far East in the 1850s, the arrival of Commodore Perry and his warships persuaded Japan to embark on a process of state-promoted modernization that would enable the country to catch up economically and militarily with the Western world. The reforms – focused on the person of the Emperor – had spectacular results, enabling Japan to take on and defeat both China (1894–5) and Russia (1905). Japan was the most remarkable instance of what has been described as 'reform nationalism' (in which Western models and practices were embraced in order to 'defend' existing traditions against foreign intrusion or rule), but varieties of it emerged in a number of Asian and African countries in the late nineteenth and early twentieth centuries, especially within the Ottoman Empire.

However, the underlying impulses of 'reform nationalism' – a perceived threat from outside, and the need to mobilize the people in order to meet it – also informed the extraordinary growth of nationalist rhetoric in most European countries in the last quarter of the nineteenth century. Prussia had shown on the battlefields of Spicheren and Sedan what a disciplined and patriotic 'nation in arms' could achieve; and if, as was coming to be widely accepted, war was the expression of deep biological urges, and not as many liberals had fondly believed, merely the sport of irresponsible kings and aristocrats, then states needed to ensure they were strong enough to deal with the predatory instincts of neighbours. That meant internal cohesion and unity, and the suppression of those groups (ethnic or racial) that were felt to threaten the organic purity and vitality of the national body.

The idea of 'race' (see ANTHROPOLOGY AND RACE) became increasingly entangled with nationalism in the later nineteenth century. The COMTE DE GOBINEAU, had launched this particularly insidious bandwagon with his *Essai sur l'inégalité des races humaines* (1853–5),which had argued for the superiority of a so-called white 'Aryan' race, and for the degenerative consequences of miscegenation. Though Gobineau's ideas met with considerable opposition in his native France – RENAN, for example, in his famous Sorbonne lecture of 1882 pointed out that historians, anthropologists and philologists all used the term 'race' in very different ways, and that it was a far too crude a category to have any serious political validity – in the USA and Britain the idea of Anglo-Saxon superiority attracted a number of influential apologists. In Germany, where the concept of the nation had from the outset been linked to concerns to recover and defend a primordial '*volk* character', the idea of race struck a particular chord with sections of the insecure middle classes, and spawned from the 1880s increasingly xenophobic currents. Anti-Semitism, which until then had been to a large extent religio-cultural in character, now began to take on a strongly racial hue.

Racial ideas, and the growing concerns of states to promote national cohesion, were fuelled by the widespread socio-economic dislocation of the late nineteenth century, by the rise of revolutionary Marxist socialism, by persistent international rivalries (in Europe, and increasingly from the 1880s in Africa and Asia) and by the omnipresent shadow of war. Fear, and its reflex emotion of aggression, became central to the politics of many countries. As Hobsbawm has noted, the key term in the lexicon of the French right in the 1880s was not 'family', 'order' or 'tradition', but 'menace'. Almost everywhere, minority ethnic groups found themselves the target of suspicion or persecution, above all in Eastern Europe and the Balkans, where civic traditions were relatively weak and political instability pronounced. But in the West, too – in Britain, Spain and France – governments showed themselves increasingly intolerant of minority claims (Irish, Basque, Catalan, Breton, Provencal), and thereby often fuelled the very nationalism they had wanted to suppress.

The militant, or as it is sometimes generically called, 'integral', nationalism of the late nineteenth and early twentieth centuries had its spokesmen in many countries, but it was probably at its most strident in those countries such as Germany and Italy where strong feelings of internal and external 'menace' were combined with frustrations at unfulfilled national ambitions. Its most elaborate philosophical formulations occurred in France. Here, stung by the defeat of 1870, writers such as HIPPOLYTE TAINE and MAURICE BARRÈS identified the cause of their country's misfortunes in the disjuncture arising from the imposition of doctrinaire liberalism on the 'real' French nation at the time of the revolution. Like Bonald and Chateaubriand nearly a century before, they saw this 'real' nation as the product of historical evolution, and thus as in essence still Catholic and monarchist; and in a manner reminiscent of the German Romantics of the early nineteenth century, they regarded it as a spiritual community, with claims prior to the individual, which through race, environment and collective memories mystically informed and shaped the soul of the French people. According to Barrès's disciple, CHARLES MAURRAS (the founder of Action Française who coined the phrase 'integral nationalism'), only a Frenchman born and bred could ever fully appreciate the beauties of Racine's line: '*Dans l'orient désert quel dévint mon ennui.*'

By 1914 militant nationalism, now generally associated with the political right, had pervaded most of Europe and parts of Asia, and was beginning to make inroads into Africa, too. For most on the left, this was a source of deep concern. While some socialists, especially in Central and Eastern Europe, were inclined to take a pragmatic view of the national principle and were willing to back independence movements in places such as Ireland and Poland in so far as they might hasten the demise of the old capitalist or feudal order, most shared the views of Marx and Engels that nationalism was at root an instrument of bourgeois hegemony that threatened international proletarian solidarity and encouraged exploitative imperialism. The surge of popular enthusiasm that greeted the outbreak of the Great War proved profoundly disappointing to them. The nation had clearly become for many workers, as well as the middle classes, a fundamental locus of identity. Four years of slaughter did little to change this, and the twentieth century, like the nineteenth, was to remain heavily in thrall to the idea of the nation and national self-determination.

Further reading

Anderson, B. (1983) *Imagined Communities: Reflections on the Origin and Spread of Nationalism*, London: Verso.

Gellner, E. (1983) *Nations and Nationalism*, Oxford: Blackwell.

Greenfeld, L. (1992) *Nationalism. Five Roads to Modernity*, Cambridge, MA: Harvard University Press.

Hastings, A. (1997) *The Construction of Nationhood. Ethnicity, Religion and Nationalism*, Cambridge: Cambridge University Press.

Hobsbawm, E.J. (1990) *Nations and Nationalism since 1780: Programme, Myth, Reality*, Cambridge: Cambridge University Press.

Hutchinson, J. and Smith, A.D. (eds) (1994) *Nationalism*, Oxford, Oxford University Press.

Kedourie, E. (1960) *Nationalism*, London: Hutchinson.

SEE ALSO: anthropology and race; democracy, populism and rights; social theory and sociology in the nineteenth century; theories of the state and society: the science of politics

CHRISTOPHER DUGGAN

NIETZSCHE, FRIEDRICH (1844–1900)

'Nietzsche,' wrote Eric Voegelin, 'has the distinction of being the only philosopher who ever has been considered the major cause of a world war.' In fact, he has been blamed for two, since his ideas supposedly provided a justification for the Prussian militarism that inspired the First World War as well as being one of the major intellectual sources of Nazism. The passionate wars of words that still rage over the meaning of Nietzsche's ideas have seen them (or rather, some of them) being used to justify fascism, anti-fascism, eugenics, libertarianism, feminism, anti-feminism, liberalism, post-liberalism, environmentalism and cyborg theory; that is to say, just about anything and everything. The literature on Nietzsche is enormous and grows apace. But then one would expect nothing less from a philosopher who has coined so many familiar phrases: 'God is dead', 'become what you are', 'the will to power', the '*übermensch*' (superman), 'slave morality', the 'eternal return', the 'blond beast', the 'free spirit', the 'good European', the 'Anti-Christ' and the 'revaluation of all values' have all passed into the vernacular. What these slogans mean is of course the source of the confusion.

Nietzsche was born in Röcken in Saxony in 1844, the son of a pastor. Educated at the famous school at Pforta, he excelled in Classical Studies, and went on to study Theology and Philology at the universities of Bonn and Leipzig. In 1868 he became an ardent follower of the musician Richard Wagner, and in the following year was appointed to the chair of Classical Philology at the University of Basel. From 1871 he began to suffer from exhaustion; in 1876 he was granted extended leave from his duties and in 1879 retired on a pension on the grounds of ill health. Thereafter he spent much time in Italy, Nice and Sils-Maria in Switzerland, until collapsing in Turin in 1889 and losing his sanity. The last 11 years of his life were spent in the care of his mother and, after her death in 1897, in care in the Villa Silberblick in Weimar. He died in 1900.

Commentators have from the beginning of his reception divided Nietzsche's corpus into two periods: an early period before 1880 when his radical ideas were starting to emerge based on his consideration of philological and pedagogical questions (*The Birth of Tragedy*; *Untimely Meditations*; *Human, All too Human*); and the later period, following his break with Wagner and before his collapse into madness, when the 'visionary' works were written (*The Gay Science*; *Thus Spake Zarathustra*; *Beyond Good and Evil*; *On the Genealogy of Morals*; *The Case of Wagner*; *The Anti-Christ*; *Ecce Homo*; *Nietzsche contra Wagner*; *Twilight of the Idols*). The *Nachlass* (unpublished writings) included numerous fragments and notebooks, many of which were subsequently compiled by Nietzsche's editors, among them his sister, into what is probably his most famous book, whose title, *The Will to Power*, has passed into legend.

Several principal themes emerge from this work: the genealogical method; the theory of Judeo-Christianity and the 'slave revolt in morals'; the notion of the Superman and the 'eternal return'. The first, the so-called 'genealogical method' has since Nietzsche been put to use most famously by the French philosopher Michel Foucault in his studies of the emergence of hospitals, asylums and prisons. It is based on the careful, detailed analysis of the histories of different words and concepts, finally drawing these separate analyses together, showing how they interact. The concepts do not need to be opposites, nor are they impersonal historical forces, hence the method is not dialectical. It seeks to show how the historical connections between ostensibly unrelated subjects comprise the substratum of the ideas and conditions that created the modern world, the substratum that is usually taken as given and hence left unanalysed. For Nietzsche, this meant bringing together the history of good and evil, and the history of morality and law, showing how both are the products of thought that shaped society, not aspects of an inexorable law of history. And he concludes that both have contributed to the parlous condition of Western civilization that he describes throughout his later writings.

The second major theme is the concept of 'slave morality'. Nietzsche's attack on the morality of Western civilization has often been construed as a form of nihilism, though in Nietzsche's eyes it was precisely modern nihilism that he felt he was combating. Nietzsche hailed ancient societies, especially Sparta, as societies that valued the strong, and promoted excellence in all spheres: physical, intellectual, moral, sexual and religious. But with the development of Judaism, and especially with the emergence of Christianity (which he saw as a kind of Judaism for the masses), there grew up a way of thinking that promoted the weak at the expense of the strong, encouraged philanthropy and led inextricably to the feminization and degeneration of the concept of aristocratic will to power. This decadence brought about by the rise of the masses to prominence Nietzsche called the 'slave revolt in morality'. Modern society, based upon the values of Judeo-Christianity, Nietzsche called 'nihilistic' because he believed that unless its values were reversed, they would lead to the eventual demise of that civilization under the weight of the 'rabble' and its homogeneous drabness.

In other words, Nietzsche subjected common assumptions to close historical scrutiny. That is not to say that most historians would find much to agree with in Nietzsche, but nevertheless the genealogical method permitted Nietzsche to make insights into the make-up of society that other fields of study would not. For example, on the question of sin, Nietzsche argued (in *The Gay Science*) that it held sway wherever Christianity was dominant, but that it was in fact a Jewish invention. This claim was another arrow in his quiver that was used not merely to show the connections between Judaism and Christianity, but to argue that Christianity aimed to 'Judaize' the world, that is, to make its values the dominant values in Western society.

To combat this decadent system of morality Nietzsche turned to several related themes. The prophetic figure of Zarathustra, though superficially similar to the Zoroaster of the Persian religion that bears his name and that – like Nietzsche – conceives of the world as a struggle between good and evil, is an allegory for the concept of the Superman. No concept in the Nietzschean corpus has received so much attention. The Superman ('Overman' would be a better translation of *Übermensch*, since 'Superman' has obviously Darwinian and mythical connotations) has been variously seen as a Golem-like homunculus, as the embodiment of the eugenic dream of breeding a superior race of human beings and as a metaphor for man's overcoming of himself and his received values. Whether Nietzsche meant the Superman to be a real or an allegorical figure (naturally, it is possible to find textual evidence to defend both points of view), he is clearly intended as a counter to the degenerate, stultified morality of Western nihilism. Thus, when Zarathustra comes down from the mountains to proclaim 'God is dead. God remains dead. And we have killed him', it is clear that only by the production of men like the Superman can this death of God, this demise of previously guiding values, adequately be dealt with. In God's place, Zarathustra proclaims the 'will to power', the will to risk one's life in quest of one's self-chosen values.

Apart from these three major themes, Nietzsche's contribution to philosophy lies in his challenge to epistemology (the theory of knowledge). His claims make him key to the development of both modernism and post-modernism, since he argues that there is no objective viewpoint from which to make judgements about the world; that there is no coherent, stable self; and that there is no temporal continuity between events. These claims have led to him being labelled a nihilist or relativist. But whilst he recognized that it was hard (thanks to the 'old habit' of associating every event with the guiding hand of a God) not to think that even aimlessness must be intended, Nietzsche does not make this argument in order to promote anarchy or randomness. Rather he explicitly says that the lack of objectivity is what allows us really to 'become what we are', because it means that each person must face up to the challenge of life, and must learn to judge for himself. 'Once you know that there are no purposes,' he wrote in *The Gay Science* (§109), 'you also know that there is no accident; for it is only beside a world of purposes that that the word "accident" has meaning.' The principle of the 'eternal return' – the claim that everything that happens has happened before and will happen again, in exactly the same way – was Nietzsche's way of removing the notion of purpose or ends from the world, and replacing it with an emphasis on states of becoming. Hence his new maxim: 'so live that you must wish to live again'. Should one not do so, one is faced with the terrifying prospect of making the same mistakes again and again in endless replay. Nietzsche's philosophy, therefore, far from being a rejection of morality and an explosive transgression of the law, is in fact a frantic attempt to fill the void left by the death of earlier certainties (admittedly, ones whose death he has himself proclaimed); it is a search for human values in a purely human world.

Nietzsche has been accused of promoting amorality and nihilism, of glorifying warfare and advocating the murder of the weak, of hatred for women and scorn for Christianity, if not religion *per se*. Whilst there is some truth to all of these claims, to focus on any one of them is fundamentally to miss the point of Nietzsche's call for an '*Umwertung aller Werte*' (a revaluation of all values).

This may have been, following Schopenhauer, based on a pessimistic diagnosis, but it was by no means a call for amorality, which would be a form of radical relativism where the value of nothing could be judged, and Nietzsche was quite clear about his likes and dislikes. Even Schopenhauer's theory of the will to live he eventually found too emotionally deadening, and replaced it with the 'will to power'.

An example of what happens when one picks up on only one aspect of Nietzsche's rich, complex and even self-contradictory thought is provided by the history of his association with Nazism. It is this association more than any other that has given rise to much heated debate. As well as being blamed for the outbreak of the Great War (he was mistakenly held to form with HEINRICH VON TREITSCHKE a kind of warmongering duumvirate) a rather selective sample of his ideas was promoted around the world by the eugenics movement, which saw in the notion of the Superman a philosophical counterpart to the science of the 'well born' race inspired by the Englishman FRANCIS GALTON and his protégé Karl Pearson. This science aimed to promote 'consciousness in evolution' and is indeed superficially akin to Nietzsche's call for the strong to become masters of the world (if one does not stop for too long to consider who Nietzsche means by 'the strong') and his advocacy in *Ecce Homo* of the 'merciless annihilation of all degenerate and parasitic elements' ('*schonungslose Vernichtung alles Entartenden und Parasitischen*'). The fact that Nietzsche himself rarely used the word 'race' did not prevent his early English (mis)translators making free with the word. Later these same ideas were picked up in Germany by the Nazis themselves, who pounced on the concept of promoting the strong at the expense of the weak, and saw Nietzsche's attack on Christianity as a history of moral evolution to set alongside DARWIN's and HUXLEY's explanations for biological evolution.

Long before the Nazis came to power, foremost in the efforts to 'Nazify' Nietzsche in Germany was Nietzsche's sister, Elisabeth Förster-Nietzsche, a violent anti-Semite who, together with her husband, the Wagnerite Bernard Förster, set up a human breeding colony in Paraguay that aspired to create racially pure Aryan children. Like her, the Nazis were able to promote Nietzsche's thought only by hiding substantial parts of it. Nietzsche's swingeing attacks on the narrow-minded Romanticism of German nationalism, his scoffing at the boringly uniform, self-satisfied, 'homesick' state of German culture and his belief in the gifts of the Jews (this philo-Semitism relying on remarkably similar stereotypes as the anti-Semites) were all rather inconvenient for the Nazis. Under the 'guidance' of Professor Alfred Bäumler, carefully manipulated editions of Nietzsche's writings were produced in the Third Reich, in which the guilt of the Jews for introducing monotheism and the 'slave morality' into ancient civilization were present, but the claims that only the Jews had the ability to overcome the problems facing Western civilization were not. These mendacious publications were to blame for the long-held belief that Nietzsche was a direct forerunner of Nazism. Only the efforts of scholars such as Walter Kaufmann after the Second World War slowly managed to get the facts straight, so that now, whilst the meaning of Nietzsche is open to debate, we at least have reliable texts. Even so, not only the Nazis have engaged in the systematic manipulation of Nietzsche's words; nor have they alone tried to claim that the books published during his lifetime did not represent his real opinions. Contemporary philosophers and politicians regularly engage in attempts to tell us 'what Nietzsche really meant'.

Nietzsche was described by one of his first exegetes, the Danish critic George Brandes, as an 'aristocratic radical'. Whilst reading his coruscating books is an exhilarating experience, it is well to remember that Nietzsche was not the Superman he wanted to promote. After the Holocaust, appealing to Nietzsche to 'live dangerously' or to advocate 'daring' forms of transgressive behaviour can only seem puerile at best and scandalous at worst. Nietzsche was no fascist; indeed his scorn for political anti-Semitism and German nationalism was explicit. Yet he was fiercely anti-democratic, anti-Christian, misogynist and attracted by the rhetoric of eugenics, at least metaphorically. Hence his thought – philosophizing with a hammer, as he put it – remains dangerous, as the continuing fight to lay claim to it illustrates. In this dangerous, because indeterminate, aspect of Nietzsche's thought lies the frisson of its appeal and its repellent fascination.

References

Brandes, George (1914) *Friedrich Nietzsche*, trans. A.G. Chater, London: William Heinemann.

Voegelin, Eric (1944) 'Nietzsche, the Crisis and the War', *The Journal of Politics*, 6, 2: 177–212.

Further reading

Ansell-Pearson, Keith (1994) *An Introduction to Nietzsche as Political Thinker*, Cambridge: Cambridge University Press.
Appel, Fredrick (1999) *Nietzsche contra Democracy*, Ithaca, NY: Cornell University Press.
Santaniello, Weaver (1994) *Nietzsche, God and the Jews: His Critique of Judeo-Christianity in Relation to the Nazi Myth*, Albany, NY: State University of New York Press.
Stone, Dan (2002) *Breeding Superman: Nietzsche, Race and Eugenics in Edwardian and Interwar Britain*, Liverpool: Liverpool University Press.

SEE ALSO: Darwin, Charles; Galton, Francis; religion, secularization and the crisis of faith; Social Darwinism; Stirner, Max; Strauss, David Friedrich; Treitschke, Heinrich von

DAN STONE

NOVELS, POETRY AND DRAMA

The nineteenth century witnessed a very substantial growth in the production of the three major literary modes: the novel, poetry and drama. The novel developed to become one of the characteristic forms of nineteenth-century thought, capable of wide-ranging and inclusive representations of society, social change and individual psychology. Indeed, the simultaneous range and depth of the novel's representation of social and individual life make it one of the outstanding achievements of nineteenth-century European and US culture. Poetry, more tied to differing national traditions, nevertheless prospered in the period, though its earlier situation of cultural centrality was generally displaced by the novel. Drama, meanwhile, developed in several directions, assimilating a range of popular forms such as melodrama and burlesque, but also diversifying at the end of the century into broadly differentiated elite and popular forms.

The growth in all three modes was linked to strongly rising rates of literacy in Europe and North America; to the establishment of national systems of education, occurring at different rates in different national contexts; to the assimilation and in some cases the displacement of traditional popular-cultural forms (such as the ballad, the chap-book and oral poetry) by literate and metropolitan ones; and to the success of capital-intensive publishing and theatre-building in catering for the large urban populations in place at the end of the century.

The novel is a highly flexible and inclusive form, with a capacity to assimilate many differing modes of life and experience, told in equally diverse ways. This remarkable flexibility enabled the novel to address, and articulate in powerful ways, many of the most important social and historical issues of the nineteenth century: of gender, social class, national and even imperial histories, and provincial and metropolitan relations. The form's inclusiveness also meant that the novel assimilated, to varying degrees, popular narrative forms such as the romance and the fairy story; throughout the century the novel would retain both elite and popular readerships, and only in the last decades of the period did the distinction between 'high' and 'mass' versions of the form become more rigid.

It was the realist novel in particular that became the form in which the most ambitious attempts were made to write social and personal histories in large and inclusive ways. But realism only developed during the course of the century, and throughout the period it coexisted with a range of other kinds of novel: romance, Gothic, adventure story, social-problem novel and, towards the end of the century, science fiction and utopian romance. In all of these forms the presence or absence of formal realism varied, so realism is best thought of as an aspiration or formal possibility rather than a fixed characteristic. Towards the end of the century, especially in France but to a lesser degree in Britain and the USA, the realist social novel was transformed into the more strictly naturalist mode, in which the role of the novelist was conceived as comparable to that of the scientist or naturalist studying his human specimens; the work of Émile Zola (1840–1902) is pre-eminent in this trend.

At its most complex and sustained, the realist novel combined minute and psychologically compelling accounts of individual lives with a wider sense of society and social change. In ways that are cognate with the growth of contemporary disciplines such as sociology, psychology and anthropology, the novel, drawing upon various formal means, could simultaneously provide strikingly individual characters, yet also show how these people emerged from a whole way of life. The novel's capacity in this respect represented as much a stage of national and social development as it did the individual capacities of the novelists. Walter Scott (1771–1832), Charles Dickens (1812–70), W.M. Thackeray (1811–63) and George Eliot (1819–80); Honoré de Balzac (1799–1850), Stendhal (1783–1842), Victor Hugo (1802–85), Gustave Flaubert (1821–80) and Émile Zola; FEODOR DOSTOEVSKY (1821–81) and LEO TOLSTOY (1828–1910); all, in their different ways, managed to produce strikingly ambitious novels that mediated between the individual and the social, or between the 'private' and the 'public'. That is, their novels held together these two poles: panoramic overviews of whole societies, often undergoing profound transformations; and psychologically complex individuals, produced by the contradictory forces at work within society, yet also agents in its movement.

If the novel in this respect was cognate with other emergent disciplines, it was also closely related to another predominant nineteenth-century mode of thought: the capacity to understand human affairs as subject to historical change and development. In fact the novel was one of the principal means by which the nineteenth century imagined both its own immediate past, and the longer historical vistas that preceded it. Walter Scott was the European pioneer of the historical novel, laying down patterns for understanding the pre-modern world that were remarkably influential throughout the century both in European and US fiction; but his importance is not only in the development of the novel, but also in establishing structures of feeling and perception that were sustained outside the novel also. The historical fictions of Balzac, Nathaniel Hawthorne (1804–64), Alessandro Manzoni (1785–1873) and Leo Tolstoy testify to Scott's influence; the last-named writer's *War and Peace* (1865–72) is perhaps the century's most sustained effort at imaginative engagement with the dramatic and transformative process of world-historical change.

Scott's novels also provided imaginative models for the ways in which pre-modern peoples had been, or were to be, assimilated into the modernity of the nineteenth-century nation-state. His portrayal of the clan or tribal society of the Highlands was to be replicated, obviously with different emphases, by Fennimore Cooper (1789–1851) in the USA, by Tolstoy in Russia and later still by the novelists of empire at the end of the century such as Rider Haggard (1856–1925). The structure of feeling that Scott established, by which the transition to modernity simultaneously meant the loss of affect and glamour, was one that was not confined to the novel but which received its first and most powerful articulation there.

The novel was thus one of the principal sites in which the national imaginary was developed, both with respect to the historic and developing nation-states of Europe and the emergent USA. The relation of province to metropolis was also extensively figured in the nineteenth-century novel; the charged movement from one to the other is one of its staple narrative motifs, and in telling this story the novel provided an imaginative map of the nation-state. London, Paris and St Petersburg all figure both as narrative destinations and socio-culturally advanced centres in the novels of Dickens, Balzac, Flaubert and Dostoevsky. The novel also provided maps of these cities themselves, with their distinctive social geographies of West and East Ends (or their equivalents), and the striking juxtapositions of wealth and poverty that characterized them.

The novel could thus give narrative and imaginative shape to the lives that people led, both their own and their countries'. An important imaginative pattern of this kind, throughout the nineteenth century, was the novel of personal development or education, of which the prototype was Goethe's novel *Wilhelm Meister* (1777–1829). This kind of novel, known as a *Bildungsroman*, traces the individual's development from childhood to maturity, and explores the possibilities for personal fulfilment made available by society. This story is evidently capable of being told with very different emphases and with widely varying outcomes: of successful assimilation, of resigned acceptance of failure, of outright disaster and despair. Versions of the *Bildungsroman*, whether or not in conscious imitation of Goethe's novel, are especially significant in both France and Britain; important examples include Honoré de Balzac, *Illusions perdues* (*Lost Illusions*) (1837–43), Gustave Flaubert, *L'éducation sentimentale* (*Sentimental Education*) (1869), Charles Dickens, *David Copperfield* (1849–50), and W.M. Thackeray, *Pendennis* (1848–50).

It is arguable whether the *Bildungsroman* can be unproblematically adapted as a narrative of a woman's life; certainly Charlotte Brontë, *Jane Eyre* (1847), and George Eliot, *The Mill on the Floss* (1860), dramatize in very different ways the blockages that prevent their female protagonists from assuming the career paths of their male counterparts. Women writers nevertheless were able to use the novel to explore the contours defining women's lives; at times the form could be used to articulate an explicit feminism, though it could equally be used for more politically neutral explorations of domestic life. Thus at the beginning of the century Jane Austen (1775–1817) could write novels focused on small groups of gentry families in rural England; at the end of the century a group of women novelists could use the form to articulate the politics of the new feminism. In between novelists as various as George Sand (1804–76), Elizabeth Gaskell (1810–65), Harriet Beecher Stowe (1811–96), Charlotte Brontë (1816–55), Emily Brontë (1818–48), George Eliot (1819–80) and Margaret Oliphant (1828–97), as well as innumerable other writers, wrote novels that represented the whole range of the social and personal life of the age.

The novel is such a pervasive and even dominant form in the nineteenth century that it is possible to speak of the period as being 'novelized'. That is, the way the nineteenth century represented itself to itself took shape most readily through the novel; many of the most important stories that the century wished to tell about itself were naturally cast into this medium. Novels were therefore written that presented, in innumerable conflicting narratives, crises of class relationships, reconfigurations of gender, agonies of religious doubt and the various social 'problems' of the age. But it was also the form that was most hospitable to stories of everyday life, whatever the extent to which these were formed by those larger social issues. The novel therefore performed functions that in the late twentieth century would be taken on by television: it became a space in which all the anxieties and fantasies of the age could be cast into narrative form and be resolved, or otherwise brought to a conclusion, often wish-fulfilling but occasionally tragic. The history of the novel in the nineteenth century is not therefore just the history of its outstanding achievements, but also of its place, in all its multiple popular forms, in the imaginative life of nineteenth-century people.

The formal variety of the novel was matched by its linguistic variety; just as the form could assimilate many other kinds of writing, so too it could draw life from the multiple varieties of national languages that, in the nineteenth century, were still in many instances in the process of development. While the practice of individual novelists obviously varied widely, all reproduce the complex national-linguistic situations that surrounded them, and thus the novel

was a form that could both exploit and contain the linguistic variety represented by dialect, slang, jargon and demotic speech. The comic energy of writers as various as Charles Dickens and Gustave Flaubert can be traced to this capacity to draw upon the linguistic creativity and energy of their surrounding social world.

The history of poetry in the nineteenth century can be understood as differing national developments of, and reactions to, Romanticism. Though any definition of Romanticism is necessarily controversial, it can certainly be understood as a reaction against the neoclassicism and the rationalism of the eighteenth century; in all its manifestations, Romanticism stressed creative freedom and spontaneity, and sought to found poetic expression on the absolute authenticity of the creative subject. In differing national contexts it found inspiration in the Christian Middle Ages and in newly rediscovered popular poetic traditions. Its geographical and historical heartlands are Germany and Britain in the late eighteenth and early nineteenth centuries; 'Romantic' poetry however became widely written in France in the 1820s, and, according to the particularities of national poetic traditions, at different periods of the nineteenth century elsewhere in Europe and the USA. Throughout the century, new movements in poetry either developed aspects of Romanticism (as in symbolist and decadent poetry at the end of the period), or reacted against it in ways that sought some 'return' to older classical values. Romanticism in its various poetic incarnations thus represents a major shift in mentality or sensibility, and can therefore be seen as a significant characteristic of nineteenth-century thought.

Although in general terms poetry lost its position of cultural centrality in the course of the nineteenth century, it was still capable of attracting a wide readership. At the beginning of the period the British poet Byron (1788–1824) developed a European-wide fame that was indeed one of the means by which Romanticism was transmitted; Byron's influence upon the Russian poet Alexander Pushkin (1799–1837), for example, was profound, and by this means he was influential on the course of Russian poetry throughout the century. Later in the century also the poetry of Alfred Tennyson (1809–92) could become a bestseller. However, if it is true that literary history represents a secular competition between the genres, then the nineteenth century witnessed the triumph of the novel, and the poetic genres were relegated to a minority status from which they have never recovered. It is also the case that the means by which poetry was to renew itself in the twentieth century were prepared in the nineteenth: the poetry of the decadents in the 1890s, and the demotic idiom of writers such as Jules Laforgue (1860–87) and William Henley (1849–1903) contributed to the dramatic shifts in poetic sensibility of the early twentieth century. But like the comparable late nineteenth-century developments in the drama and the novel, these shifts also reinforced distinctions between avant-garde and popular art that had not been so apparent earlier in the century.

One of the features of the Romantic shift in sensibility was a renewed interest in popular and 'folk' forms of poetry, especially the ballad. This resulted in widespread imitation of traditional forms, greatly increasing the range of available modes in the course of the nineteenth century. A seminal moment in this respect for English poetry was the publication of *Lyrical Ballads* (1798–1802) by William Wordsworth (1770–1850) and SAMUEL TAYLOR COLERIDGE (1772–1834); comparable reuses of traditional and dialect forms can be found in most European traditions. Cognate with this interest was the rediscovery, in many national contexts, of previously neglected primary epics: The *Kalevala* in Finland, the *Cid* in Spain, the *Chanson de Roland* in France and the *Nibelungen Lied* in Germany were all rediscovered or rewritten at the beginning of the nineteenth century and were important episodes in the development of a national consciousness in those countries. More importantly for the writing of original poetry, these ancient poems formed the basis for repeated attempts, in the course of the century, for poets to forge a distinctive national idiom; the work of Tennyson and WILLIAM MORRIS (1834–96) in Britain, W.B. Yeats in Ireland (1865–1939) and Henry Wadsworth Longfellow (1807–82) in the USA can all be partly understood in this context.

The beginning of the century thus saw a considerable extension to the repertoire of available poetic forms in most European countries; and all poetic traditions were marked, during the course of the century, by widespread formal experimentation. The Romantic ode, the ballad, the comic epic and the expressive lyric all developed alongside or in opposition to poetry written in the traditional neoclassical forms. Evidently,

differing constituencies were drawn to varying parts of this repertoire. British working-class poets, for example, generally found the older more public forms of a broadly neoclassical idiom more congenial than the romantic sublime. Equally, while in Britain at least there were numerous women poets of Romanticism, later nineteenth-century women poets such as Christina Rossetti (1830–94) and Elizabeth Barrett Browning (1806–61) could use forms as varied as the ballad, the fairy story and even the epic (*Aurora Leigh*, 1857) to articulate their particular religious and feminist concerns.

A roll-call of only the most famous nineteenth-century poets would include many, perhaps even a majority, of writers who became or have become canonical in both their own national literatures and in world literary history: Goethe (1749–1832); Hölderlin (1770–1843); Heine (1797–1856); LAMARTINE (1790–1869); HUGO (1802–85); Baudelaire (1821–67); Mallarmé (1842–98); Verlaine (1844–96); Rimbaud (1854–91); Leopardi (1798–1837); Pushkin (1799–1837); Lermontov (1814–41); Shelley (1792–1822); Keats (1795–1821); Browning (1812–89); Clough (1819–61); Arnold (1822–87); Longfellow (1807–82); Whitman (1819–92) – in addition to those already mentioned. Clearly all these distinctive contributions, and those of the innumerable poets whose work surrounds theirs, cannot be simply summarized. Nevertheless, their place in the various national canons is partly a matter of the intersection of their personal trajectories with national and linguistic histories. Thus the absolutely central place of Goethe in the literature of Germany is partly a function of the intersection of his multiple and extraordinary talent with a historical moment of national awakening. In a different but related way, the distinctive and idiosyncratic poetry of Walt Whitman became canonical in part because of the peculiarly US and democratic idiom that he sought to forge. And in all cases the creation of a national poetic canon was partly a function of maturing national education systems that, in differing ways and at different times, sought to use poetry as a locus of national consciousness.

The history of the drama in the nineteenth century depended upon a wide range of factors beyond the individual creativity of its writers, actors and producers. Above all it depended upon substantial capital investment in theatres; throughout the course of the century the number of cities with theatres, and the range of theatres within the larger cities, increased greatly, so that at the end of the century most European and US cities had their own theatres providing both high-cultural and popular forms of drama. At the beginning of the century, by contrast, the outlines of this situation were only visible in London and Paris.

European theatre in the early nineteenth century inherited from the previous century traditions of prestigious theatrical performance (with an accompanying established classical repertoire) that depended to a greater or lesser degree on court or aristocratic patronage. In London and Paris, where theatres were large-scale commercial enterprises, this element of patronage had already greatly diminished at the beginning of the century; elsewhere in Europe, especially in Germany and Russia, such patronage was crucial to the development of the form. But accompanying such theatres, devoted to a classical repertoire, were new and predominantly popular theatrical spaces in which developing and demotic forms of drama were performed. The mode of this new drama was overwhelmingly that of melodrama; the story of the nineteenth-century drama is above all one in which this popular mode made its way up the escalator of cultural prestige to become the predominant mode in nineteenth-century theatre of all kinds. And alongside this story, which is that of dramatic representation properly understood, the nineteenth century witnessed the development of various modes of mass popular entertainment, known variously as music hall, vaudeville, burlesque and *boulevard*. By the end of the century, therefore, most major European and US cities afforded a range of dramatic performance from popular-cultural and demotic entertainment, small-scale popular melodrama, lavish and capital-intensive burlesque performance, more prestigious drama in a broadly melodramatic mode, performances of the classical repertoire, and new and experimental forms of naturalist and expressionist drama.

The nineteenth century therefore witnessed an unprecedented programme of theatre building. This took the form of new or wholly refurbished national theatres such as Drury Lane and Covent Garden (London 1815), the Comédie-Française (Paris 1808) or the Bolshoi Theatre (Moscow 1856). But equally significant was the building of numerous suburban and working-class theatres

for the performance of melodrama and other forms of popular-cultural theatrical entertainment (such as the Surrey Theatre [London 1814]). The century also witnessed a number of technical advances that enabled theatre to provide some spectacular effects; gas-lighting and technically complex and illusionistic stage-settings came to be features of most forms of theatre, but melodrama attracted audiences partly by its impressive and overwhelming recreations of explosions, ship-wrecks, waterfalls, horse-races and other tremendous occurrences. The mid-century onwards saw attempts, in many European and US theatres, to provide historically authentic productions of historical plays, and naturalistically accurate recreations of the contemporary social world; these fed into the various European attempts to renew the drama in the last two decades of the century in the name of greater realism and naturalism.

The predominant theatrical mode of the nineteenth-century drama was therefore melodrama; it was partly against this that these emergent late nineteenth-century forms measured themselves. Melodrama was by no means confined to the theatre; it was a characteristic mode in nineteenth-century painting and the novel also. However the theatre provided its most visible setting; it is indeed a mode of theatre that seeks to dispose its actors into legible symbolic configurations, in which a highly marked language of gesture and movement indicates the now-visible moral and social relationships that are being enacted. It is moreover a mode that draws upon all the resources of the theatre: music, costume and spectacular effects are all deployed to emphasize the symbolic configurations that melodrama dramatizes. It is therefore a mode that is especially well placed to dramatize oppressive familial, class and gender relations; equally it tends to resolve the conflicts that it dramatizes by acts of simplifying heroism. Its greatest nineteenth-century writer was Guilbert de Pixérécourt (1773–1844), whose plays were produced not only in his native France but also widely translated and otherwise plagiarized in British, US and European theatres; Douglas Jerrold (1803–57) and Dion Boucicault (1820–90) also wrote widely produced melodramas – the relative unfamiliarity of these names compared to those of their contemporary novelists and poets bearing testimony to the disrepute into which melodrama fell in the twentieth century. But the real vitality of the mode is to be seen in the innumerable stage adaptations of famous novels, such as those of Dickens or *Uncle Tom's Cabin* (1853), and in the widely disseminated and more anonymous popular productions that were the staple of the cheaper theatres throughout the century.

In the last quarter of the century, in most centres of theatrical production, attempts were made to renew the drama by means of a greater realism, understood as a repudiation of conventional theatrical gestures and language; by the establishment of greater historical accuracy in costume and setting; and by the introduction of the radical genre of naturalism, paralleling developments in the novel. These different developments can be seen, in varying ways, in the work of Henrik Ibsen (1828–1906), August Strindberg (1849–1912), Anton Chekhov (1860–1904) and George Bernard Shaw (1856–1950). These playwrights, and the producers, critics and impresarios who championed them, undoubtedly revitalized the theatre in the sense of making it capable of addressing, in intellectually and artistically compelling ways, some of the great issues of the day; but they also reinforced an increasing division between elite and popular forms of theatre that had not characterized the older melodramatic modes. Furthermore, the increasing social segregation of nineteenth-century cities reproduced itself especially visibly in this most public and social art form; these social divisions were reproduced not only in the seating arrangements within the theatres ('Dress Circle' means precisely those seats in which the audience were expected to wear evening dress), but also in the gulf that divided the major 'West End' theatres and their more 'artistic' counterparts on the one hand, and the myriad forms of cheap theatrical entertainment to be found elsewhere in the city. These divisions long survived the nineteenth century in which they first became entrenched.

Further reading

Armstrong, I. (1993) *Victorian Poetry: Poetry, Poetics and Politics*, London: Routledge.
Bakhtin, M. (1981) *The Dialogic Imagination*, trans. C. Emerson and M. Holquist, Austin: University of Texas Press.
Meisel, M. (1983) *Realizations: Narrative, Pictorial, and Theatrical Arts in Nineteenth-Century England*, Princeton: Princeton University Press.
Moretti, F. (1998) *Atlas of the European Novel 1800–1900*, London: Verso.

SEE ALSO: religion, secularization and the crisis of faith; Romanticism, individualism and ideas of the self

SIMON DENTITH

NOYES, JOHN HUMPHREY (1811–86)

John Humphrey Noyes was a radical US theologian and social activist who founded the Oneida Community in New York State. Noyes taught that the Second Coming of Christ had occurred in 70 CE, and, as a result, the human race was capable of something approaching perfection. He believed that a group of enlightened Christians living in community and practising community of goods (which he called Bible Communism) should be able to improve most aspects of their lives.

In 1841, a group of his followers formed the Putney Society in Vermont. As a result of a prosecution brought for adultery based on the practices of the community, Noyes fled to New York in 1847. In 1848, he and his followers established a community at Oneida Creek, New York. This community, which had a number of relatively short-lived offshoots, lasted until 1881.

The charge of adultery was based on the earliest practice of what came to be called 'complex marriage', a system in which all members of the community were assumed to be married to each other. 'Complex marriage' included at least the possibility of sexual relations between any men and women of the community. Any man or woman could approach any other member of the community of the opposite sex; multiple relationships were encouraged, and exclusive relationships were prohibited.

Such a regime could easily have produced more children than the community could support, but it did not because Noyes developed a distinction between 'propagative love' (sexual intercourse to produce children) and 'amative love' (sexual intercourse to express love). The means by which the distinction worked was what Noyes called 'male continence' (*coitus reservatus*), in which the man avoided ejaculation.

When the community could afford children, they undertook a eugenic experiment, which they called stirpiculture. Now that they were to have children, they wanted to have the best children possible, which meant children from the spiritually most advanced members of the community. Although a board of the community chose those to have children, as the obviously most spiritual advanced member of the community, Noyes fathered many of the children. The system worked well and was successful on almost any measure including the physical and intellectual quality of the children.

To avoid or at least reduce the tensions that inevitably develop in a close-knit community, Noyes instituted a system of 'Mutual Criticism'. Each individual was criticized in an open meeting and his or her faults of conduct and character were identified and discussed. To reduce bad feelings, at the next meeting positive statements were made about the individual. All members of the community were criticized, and members reported that the system produced positive results.

The Oneida Community also experimented with a number of other ways of improving the lives of its members, including dress reform and communal childcare. The community was very successful, but, as Noyes aged, tensions over the future of the community, among other issues, were not defused by mutual criticism. Noyes left the community and died shortly thereafter, and the community broke up.

Further reading

Noyes, J.H. (1875) *Essay on Scientific Propagation*, Oneida, NY: Oneida Community.
——(1875) *History of American Socialisms*, Philadelphia: Lippincott.
Parker, R.A. (1935) *A Yankee Saint: John Humphrey Noyes and the Oneida Community*, New York: Putnam.
Thomas, R.D. (1977) *The Man who would be Perfect: John Humphrey Noyes and the Utopian Impulse*, Philadelphia: University of Pennsylvania Press.

SEE ALSO: early socialism; utopianism

LYMAN TOWER SARGENT

O

O'CONNELL, DANIEL (1775–1847)

Born near Cahirciveen, Co. Kerry on 6 August 1775, O'Connell attended schools at St Omer and Douai until he had to flee before the French revolutionaries. In London, where he was enrolled in Lincoln's Inn, he was profoundly affected by GODWIN's *Political Justice* and PAINE's *Age of Reason*. The rights of the individual, social justice, political rationality and non-violence became cornerstones of his philosophy. Finishing his law studies in Dublin, he was attracted by the reform policies of the United Irishmen but condemned their 1798 rebellion and their attempts to promote a French invasion. He also criticized the Government's repressive measures and its corrupt and oligarchic regime. Opposing the Union between Ireland and Britain, the restoration of the Irish Parliament was to remain his prime objective.

In the decades following the Union he concentrated on winning civil and religious liberty for his fellow Catholics. The agitation that O'Connell now organized differed from other contemporary movements only in size and achievement. Although as a conscientious Catholic he could not take the oaths prescribed to enter Parliament, his famous election victory in 1828 forced the Government to concede Catholic emancipation.

In Parliament O'Connell formed a natural alliance with the English radicals. He supported the Reform Bill, manhood suffrage, triennial parliaments, the secret ballot and an elective House of Lords. He advocated the abolition of slavery, capital punishment and flogging in the army. He condemned discrimination against the Jews, and urged various reforms in the legal system. Proclaiming himself a Benthamite (see BENTHAM, JEREMY), he supported free trade and opposed Government intervention. He championed the moral-force Chartists against the physical-force wing. Leading a party of between thirty and forty Irish MPs during the 1830s, O'Connell made a formidable contribution to British politics.

In 1835 he formed an alliance with Melbourne's Government, the result of which gave Ireland a number of reforms and an equitable administration. When Peel returned as prime minister in 1841, O'Connell relaunched his campaign for Repeal, the most notable characteristic of which was the 'monster meeting' held at various historic sites all over Ireland. Although he failed to get an Irish Parliament through the moral force of public opinion, O'Connell had introduced his people to the ways of democracy, liberalism and moderate nationalism. His organizing genius captured world-wide attention; and his advocacy of the separation of Church and state, of liberty of conscience, freedom of education, of the press and of assembly appealed to liberal Catholic intellectuals on the Continent.

Radical in politics, his social philosophy remained conservative, and he had little to contribute to the solution of the Irish land question. Emphasis on individual rather than national rights, on reform rather than revolution, on the link with Britain rather than republican separatism, made O'Connell appear in the eyes of Young Ireland a man of the past. He died on 15 May 1847.

Further reading

MacDonagh, Oliver (1991) *O'Connell: The Life of Daniel O'Connell 1775–1847*, London: Weidenfeld & Nicolson.

SEE ALSO: anti-colonial movements and ideas; the nation, nationalism and the national principle

DONAL McCARTNEY

OWEN, ROBERT (1771–1858)

The founder of British socialism, Robert Owen was born to humble parents in Newtown, Wales, on 14 May 1771, and returned there to die on 17 November 1858. An intellectually precocious youth, he read widely, and by the age of 10 experienced a religious crisis, the implications of which would prove crucial for his life's work and ideas. After being apprenticed to a Stamford cloth-merchant, he moved to London. In the early 1790s he commenced a partnership in Manchester manufacturing 'mules' to produce thread by steam-power, and soon became manager of a mill employing 500. Displaying enormous talent as a manager, he moved on 1 January 1800 to assume supervision of a mill constructed by David Dale at New Lanark, on the banks of the Clyde south of Glasgow. At New Lanark Owen's profits were considerable, but he regarded the mill's population, prone of drunkenness, pilfering and petty vice, as capable of significant moral improvement. He thus began to apply principles described in his first substantial publication, *A New View of Society; or, Essays on the Principle of the Formation of the Human Character* (1813–14), which centred on one leading idea, that 'the character of man is formed for, and not by, him'. This form of philosophical necessitarianism, or environmentalism, was later modified to acknowledge certain evident tendencies or propensities in behaviour, but remained the foundation of Owen's entire system of thought. He used it to assert that punishment was illogical, since crime was not a function of free will, but resulted from poor upbringing. It remained the optimistic core of Owen's assumptions about the socialist future, where war, social conflict and crime would be supplanted by peace, harmony and prosperity.

At New Lanark real wages improved, working hours were reduced, education for children was introduced, and moral improvements did indeed result. The key to this programme was undoubtedly education, and Owen in this period was associated with reformers like Joseph Lancaster. New Lanark was not, however, a 'socialist' experiment; profits were divided amongst the partners according to their investment. But Owen did plan upon extending the public aspects of community reorganization, notably by the construction of a common kitchen and dining facilities.

Dedicated to William Wilberforce, whose evangelical approach to moral renewal was attracting considerable attention, *A New View of Society* urged the extension of such reforms to the nation at large by reducing gambling, drunkenness and illegitimacy as well as introducing penal and factory reforms, and disestablishing the Church of England. There was nothing particularly socialistic about these proposals, however; indeed Owen denied that the Government should directly employ the poor, suggesting instead that public works schemes on roads, docks and the like be paid less than the average rate of wages, and insisting that the norm should be that the adequately educated poor would seek and find employment for themselves, except in periods of exceptional crisis. Leslie Stephen was thus quite wrong to suggest that Owen's 'essential views' were presented here. A few acute observers, however, notably William Hazlitt, recognized after 1815 a clear affinity between Owen's ideas and those of WILLIAM GODWIN, whose *Enquiry concerning Political Justice* (1793) had been so influential a generation earlier. (In fact Owen had met with Godwin in London some fifty times between 1813–18.)

By 1815 Owen had moved markedly in the direction of a more comprehensive and radical reform scheme. In the *Observations on the Effects of the Manufacturing System* (1815) he first focused upon the quest for 'immediate pecuniary gain' as the driving spirit behind the existing commercial system, operating according to the principle of 'buying cheap and selling dear'. The new manufacturing system, he insisted, was creating a new type of character in the labour force, and greed for profit promoted their ever greater degradation by their employers. Machinery was rapidly displacing manual labour in an increasing number of trades, and threatened to produce an increasingly impoverished working class.

Frustrated by his inability to convince fellow-manufacturers to agree to similar measures, Owen in 1816–17, amidst rising post-war economic dislocation, widened his efforts to providing a solution to poverty as such. By the summer of 1817 he had refined 'the Plan' to comprise the resettlement of the unemployed poor in 'Villages of Union' of some 500 to 1,500 in the countryside, constructed in the form of a large quadrangle, with public buildings at the centre, and heavy industry at the peripheries. Here labour would alternate between agriculture and manufacturing, and, crucially, the results would be shared in common and distributed and organized according to the principle of 'mutual and combined interest'. Self-sufficiency was the initial goal; later communities could trade with one another upon equitable principles. At a crucial meeting at the City of London Tavern in August, Owen assailed the clergy as the principal opponents of all social change, principally because of the idea of 'original sin', which was being given increasing prominence by evangelicals. He now began to speak in terms of the 'millennium', and to assume that not only the poor, but also the entire population, would eventually inhabit the new co-operative villages.

His principal goal now became the overcoming of separate, divided, antagonistic social interests, and their replacement by a harmony of interests. In his seminal *Report to the County of Lanark* he also proposed abolishing the existing money system and replacing it by a currency based on labour-time, and aimed at superseding both competition and the problem of underconsumption, or finding a market to match existing productive capacity. By 1820 Owen called this 'the social system', which was designed to promote common aims and co-operative economic benefits, as opposed to 'the individual system' of competition and 'buying cheap and selling dear', which promoted selfishness, economic waste and the excessively concentrated accumulation of wealth. The principal error of the modern economic system he now identified as the idea:

> that man can provide better for himself, and more advantageously for the public, when left to his own individual exertions, opposed to and in competition with his fellows, than when aided by any social arrangement which shall unite his interests individually and generally with society.

From 1815, in *Observations on the Effects of the Manufacturing System*, he identified the growth of factories as a chief threat to working-class moral and economic health, though he did not reject industrialization as such, but rather viewed machinery as capable of lightening the burden of human labour when not introduced to displace it. Practically, the remainder of Owen's life was devoted to the construction of a successful community, intended to serve as a model of the superiority of 'socialism' (the term gained increasing acceptance in the late 1820s to describe Owen's system) to any system based on competition of interests. About £40,000, or four-fifths

of Owen's fortune, was expended on the acquisition of the New Harmony community in Indiana in the mid-1820s, but owing to lack of supervision, poor choice of members and insufficient unity, this lasted only a few years. (A few smaller communities were also attempted at Orbiston near Motherwell, and elsewhere.) After flirting with trade unionism and the formation of 'labour exchanges' where artisans could exchange goods on the basis of cost price, Owen raised funds for a final great communitarian effort, on 533 acres at Queenwood or Harmony, in Hampshire, which commenced in 1839. He created a powerful new organization, the Association of All Classes of All Nations, which at its peak had some fifty branches throughout Britain, concentrated in the industrial Midlands. These helped to raise funds, and to provide a labour force, for the Queenwood experiment. When this finally failed in 1845, after the expenditure of over £40,000, owing to poor agricultural land, overinvestment in building and insufficient capital, the Owenite movement, which had attracted as many as 50,000 to weekly meetings in the early 1840s, collapsed with it. Though he agitated for reform in Paris during the 1848 revolutions, Owen embraced spiritualism in the early 1850s, thereby undermining the materialism of his earlier philosophy. Owen's ideas nonetheless remained of some importance after the revival of socialism in the 1880s, through William Morris and others, and through the secularist agitation of George Jacob Holyoake, an Owenite lecturer who had served six months in prison for blasphemy, in particular, and through the Fabian socialists, many of whom, notably Frank Podmore, wrote on him.

The development of Owen's thought after 1820

Two false assumptions have often served to deflect serious examination of Owen's ideas: that his thought was fully formed by 1820, and that, as HARRIET MARTINEAU and LESLIE STEPHEN were wont to insist, he was a man of 'one idea', namely the environmental determination of character. In fact, while his essential commitment to socialism, social equality and co-operative economics, and opposition to individual competition, was fixed by 1820, Owen's ideas continued to develop through the mid-1840s.

In his political economy, he refined his analysis of the workings of the competitive system (partly under the influence of two early co-operative economists, William Thompson and John Gray). By the early 1830s he had begun to argue that a series of cyclical economic crises would produce increased concentration and centralization of capital, but also eventually the confrontation of a small class of wealthy capitalists and bankers by an immiserated majority of workers. Soon 'the wholesale and retail trade of the kingdom' would 'be absorbed by a few great houses' until 'the whole business shall be taken up by banking bazaars, which will supersede banking, and every more expensive and hazardous mode of representing and distributing throughout society the wealth of the producers'. Expanding free trade at present, Owen insisted, would only:

> extend individual competition to such a degree, that the wealth of society would accumulate among a few favoured individuals in two or three favoured countries . . . in the same manner that wealth now accumulates in this country in the hands of a few accidentally favoured individuals, to the great injury of the mass of the people.

This clearly anticipated in its outlines the theory of crisis later associated with Karl Marx and Friedrich Engels (see MARX AND MARXISM); the latter in fact began his first serious study of political economy at Manchester in 1843 under the tutelage of a local Owenite lecturer, John Watts. Owen also continued to insist that the only just system of exchange consisted of a reciprocity of benefits, or more specifically the exchange of produce based upon an equal amount of labour and equivalent cost of raw materials. This he thought could be effected by a system of labour notes, which would obviate the need for any currency based upon a gold or silver standard and thus subject to independent fluctuation in value.

In both his economic and social theory, Owen paid considerable attention to the division of labour, regarding the process of increasing specialization (as Adam Smith and even more Adam Ferguson had done) as posing a potentially severe threat to working-class well-being. While the early French socialist CHARLES FOURIER was most detailed in his proposals for alternation of task in his communities, Owen was insistent that none should engage exclusively in either agriculture

or manufactures. By the late 1820s he had begun to propose a scheme for the reorganization of society according to the principle of age, which was presented in full in *The Book of the New Moral World* (1836–44). This was based upon the principle that all should pass through the same general scheme of education, employment, and the management and supervision of others. Society was to be classified into eight age groups, each of which would function as one section of the division of labour did in the existing society. The first 'class' (in Owen's term), from birth to age 5, would be educated. The second, ages 5–10, would assist with domestic labour. Those 10–15 would help to supervise this group, while learning practical skills in industry and agriculture. Those aged 15–20 would supervise the group younger than them, while engaging in production. The 20–25 year old group would supervise the production process, while those 25–30 would distribute the wealth produced. The 30–40-year-old group would have the responsibility of governing the community. The eldest formal group, aged 40–60, would oversee 'foreign affairs', or the relations between communities. This system alone, he insisted, was capable of generating a full equality of rights, and the full supersession of the division of labour, and its replacement with an ideal that would unite:

> in the same individual the producer, and the possessor of wealth, the communicator and the recipient of knowledge, the governor and the governed, to destroy the invidious distinctions that have split up the one great family of man into sections and classes.

This scheme also entailed the abolition of the traditional family, not only because of the necessity of educating all of the children of the community in common, apart from their parents, in order to prevent a 'family interest' developing in opposition to the community. Though his own marriage was quite traditional, Owen from the mid-1820s onwards also began to give greater stress to equality for women, and to proposals for greater freedom of divorce. These were most fully developed in his *The Marriage System of the New Moral World* (4th edn, 1840), which assailed the existing system as productive of prostitution, duplicity and misery for the female sex.

Politically, Owen's ideas can be divided into two categories: his analysis of the existing political system, and his positive ideal of social organization.

In both he was strikingly distant from the plebeian political radicals, his chief competitors for working-class support. These, in keeping with the view of THOMAS PAINE, and reiterated against Owen by reformers like W.T. Sherwin, insisted that working-class distress emanated from heavy taxation imposed by a corrupt and oppressive government keen to pay inflated salaries to the aristocracy and its dependants. Owen by contrast insisted that taxation was not the cause of distress, and that, even if the national debt and all taxation were abolished, the competitive system and industrialization would still engender distress. Poverty thus resulted from injustices in the wage relationship and from the consequences of the competitive system. This forced a shift of focus, accordingly, from the political to the economic sphere. The most important example that lent validity to this view was the USA, the beacon of republican hope since the late eighteenth century, which by the late 1830s had begun to enter the international economy, commenced industrialization and urbanization, and witnessed both the centralization of wealth and growth of a class of urban poor. This was the clearest argument against political reform as such: poverty knew no distinction between forms of government, republican or monarchical. This argument would remain an essential dividing point between socialists and radical reformers throughout Europe and elsewhere through the nineteenth century and beyond.

In the same vein Owen regarded the existing political process as mirroring the class antagonisms that were generated by the competitive system. If the latter were regarded, partisanship, elections (to which he remained resolutely opposed) and all forms of existing political organization, from autocracy to democracy, might be abolished. These would be replaced, in turn, by the scheme of social organization already described, whereby the principle of age would ensure that all members of any community would eventually become members of its ruling group, with no contest for leadership or election being necessary in the future.

In his personal style Owen was often irritatingly dogmatic and prone to paternalism. During the years 1838–45, when his organization competed chiefly with the radical democratic movement called Chartism, this paternalism often harmed the image of the Owenite movement, though writers like John Francis Bray and even leaders like James Bronterre O'Brien acknowledged the importance of his economic analysis, and even the potential validity of co-operative economics.

Although Owen's thought is often described as 'utopian', he denied that the label applied to his essentially practical reform programme. The essentially derisory category of 'utopian socialist' imposed on Owen by Marx and Engels, and often reiterated in the subsequent historiography, relies on the insistence on three assumptions: (1) that all forms of early socialism assumed that the proletariat was only as 'suffering mass': many of Owen's followers accepted a transformatory role for the working class; (2) that society could only be transformed by propaganda and experiments: many of Owen's followers urged parliamentary reform and agreed with the Chartist agenda; (3) that the early socialists did not believe that seeds of new society lay in the economic development of the old: most Owenites accepted some variation of an economic interpretation of history (often based on a Scottish 'conjectural' four-stages theory), and moreover insisted that socialism could only be founded in the industrial age, not at any preceding period. It is thus more sensible to classify Owen as an 'early' rather than a 'utopian' socialist.

Further reading

Claeys, Gregory (1987) *Machinery, Money and the Millennium: From Moral Economy to Socialism, 1815–1860*, Princeton, NJ: Princeton University Press.
—— (1989) *Citizens and Saints: Politics and Anti-Politics in Early British Socialism*, Cambridge: Cambridge University Press.
Harrison, J.F.C. (1969) *Robert Owen and the Owenites*, London: Routledge & Kegan Paul.
Owen, Robert (1993) *Selected Works of Robert Owen*, ed. G. Claeys, 4 vols, London: Pickering & Chatto.
Podmore, Frank (1906) *Robert Owen: A Biography*, 2 vols, London: George Allen & Unwin.
Taylor, Barbara (1983) *Eve and the New Jerusalem. Socialism and Feminism in the Nineteenth Century*, London: Virago Books.
Thompson, Noel (1984) *The People's Science. The Popular Political Economy of Exploitation and Crisis, 1816–34*, Cambridge, Cambridge University Press.

SEE ALSO: early socialism; political economy; theories of education and character formation

GREGORY CLAEYS

P

PAINE, THOMAS (1737–1809)

The most influential Anglo-American theorist of
natural-rights doctrines during the period span-
ning the American and French Revolutions,
Thomas Paine was born at Thetford, England, on
29 January 1737, the son of a Quaker stay (corset)
maker. Having run away to sea, he followed the
family trade, then worked as an excise officer, and
later a shopkeeper. Emigrating to the American
colonies in 1774, he befriended Benjamin Franklin,
with whom he had a common interest in scientific
matters. Soon after the colonists' revolt began in
mid-1775, Paine published *Common Sense* (1776),
the first tract to argue for complete independence
from Britain. It was enormously important in
shifting colonial opinion away from compromise,
and gained the attention of Washington, JEFFERSON
and others. During the War of Independence Paine
joined the army, but his chief contribution came
again from his pen, in the form of sixteen pamphlets
entitled *The American Crisis* (1776–83), which did
much to aid morale during the most difficult
phase of the war. Afterwards he concentrated upon
the construction of a single-arch iron bridge, a
substantial model of which was built.

After the outbreak of the French Revolution
Paine returned to Britain, where he was outraged
by the ferocious assault on the revolutionaries'
aims and principles by EDMUND BURKE, in *Reflections on the Revolution in France* (1790). This
occasioned Paine's most important book, *Rights of
Man*, which appeared in two parts in February
1791 and February 1792. Its enormous success – it
was the bestselling tract over a single decade ever
printed, with at least 200,000 copies (and possibly
500,000) printed – generated a vicious controversy
that was finally curtailed only by the outbreak of
war with France in 1793, and then severe
Government repression in 1795. Paine himself fled
to France, where his pleading for leniency in the
case of Louis XVI and friendship with the moderate Girondins nearly cost him his head during
the Robespierrian Terror. In prison he wrote *The
Age of Reason* (1794), a passionate defence of
deism but declamation against the literal truth of
the Bible. When Paine was finally able to return to
the USA in 1802, he found his religious opinions
had rendered him deeply unpopular, and he
remained isolated until his death at New Rochelle,
New York, on 8 June 1809.

The development of Paine's thought

Many of the leading themes in Paine's thought
were introduced in cursory form in *Common Sense*.
Here he drew a sharp distinction between society
and Government, arguing that the former was
produced by our wants, the latter our wickedness,
with Government being thus merely a necessary
evil. More important, however, was his attack
upon both monarchical Government in general,
and the British constitution in particular. He dismissed the claim that the tripartite British model of
monarch–lords–commons 'balanced' itself successfully because of the checking tendency of each
component, insisting instead that British liberty
rested solely on the virtues of the Commons,
although the monarchy remained the most powerful branch of Government. (In anther tract
published in 1776 but only recently identified as
Paine's, *Four Letters on Interesting Subjects*, Paine
made a stronger case for seeing Britain as possessing 'no fixed constitution' as such, and as being
essentially absolutist because there were no written
restrictions on the power of the legislature.)

Hereditary kingship Paine assailed in *Common Sense* as intrinsically unjust, because no family had a perpetual right to give preference to itself above all others. Kings were too fond of waging war and bestowing patronage, and could ascend to the throne in the ignorance of youth and remain until the bewilderment of old age. Proclaiming the colonists' cause to be that of all mankind, Paine portrayed a glorious epoch of prosperity that would succeed the breach from Britain, in which commerce and foreign trade, freed from mercantilist restrictions, would enrich Americans rather than Britons. The most important argument in *Common Sense*, thus, was the direct assault upon monarchical Government, and the suggestion that a pure republican form of Government could survive amidst conditions less primitive than those described by, notably, Jean-Jacques Rousseau in the *Social Contract* (1762). Equally impressive, however, was Paine's lack of deference to traditional political authority: *Common Sense* inaugurated the democratic age by first rendering contemptible and ridiculous the ruling elites of monarchy and aristocracy, and then proclaiming a modern form of republicanism capable of embracing both a substantial population and one engaged in, and enriched by, trade as well as agriculture. Though Paine did warn that commerce had eroded British patriotism, there was here no suggestion of any necessary contradiction between public virtue and commerce, or of the threat of luxury goods to social equality or selfless patriotism. With one blow the pretence to have founded a uniquely free constitution with the 'Glorious Revolution' of 1688 had been pierced. The classical republican tradition was here laid to rest; from its ashes arose modern republicanism.

Of Paine's other writings during the period between the American and French Revolutions, his *Letter to the Abbé Raynal* (1782) is of interest for its claim that commerce could create 'universal civilization' by basing the international system upon the fulfilment of mutual need rather than national or dynastic rivalry. Both *Dissertations on Government; the Affairs of the Bank; and Paper Money* (1786) and *Prospects on the Rubicon* (1787) addressed the relationships between states, banks and systems of public funding, with the latter warning of the deleterious influence of a burgeoning national debt.

Despite superficial similarities, *Rights of Man* addressed a vastly dissimilar problem in its effort to defend the French revolutionaries against Burke, and to vindicate their principles and promise. For the French Revolution had occurred in an old nation, lacking the essential social equality, easy availability of land, and absence of a resident monarch or territorial aristocracy that characterized the American colonies. The central argument of *Rights of Man* is popular sovereignty, or the right of any people to manage its own affairs, and to overturn the decisions, and even reject the constitution, established by preceding generations. This gave the French the right to limit, or entirely overthrow, the monarchy, as it did Britons the right to alter the settlement of 1688 if they so chose. (Burke had insisted that this remained unalterable.) The right of self-government in turn was based upon pre-existing natural rights held by all and granted by the Creator as described in the book of Genesis, 'whether taken as divine authority or merely historical', and were continued in perpetuity as if God created each person uniquely. The Bible thus crucially established what Paine called the unity of man, 'by which I mean that men are all of one degree, and consequently that all men are born equal, and with equal natural rights'. In keeping with the tradition popularized by Locke in particular, Burke had argued that certain natural rights had existed at the beginning of society, but that these had been superseded by civil rights, which could alone be discussed meaningfully in an advanced state. Paine, however, contended that all civil rights depended on and could be assessed in terms of pre-existing natural rights. Such rights were therefore possessed universally; if one nation were freer than others, it set an example of God's intentions, not historical *fortuna*.

The aim and end of all governments was thus to uphold natural rights. Paine distinguishes in *Rights of Man* between three forms of Government: those based on priestly rule, those based on monarchy or aristocracy, and those founded on popular sovereignty. Only the latter fully recognized the necessity of upholding natural rights by an agreement made amongst the whole people. Here Paine again forcefully contended that Britain had no written 'constitution' as such. Instead, free nations required their peoples to delegate authority to a constitutional convention to decide in outline upon constitutional arrangements, and then to seek popular approval thereof before enshrining any decisions in written form. *Rights of Man* contains a frontal assault on the existing British system of Government, which restricted the franchise to a tiny minority, ensured that the legal system protected the privileges of the propertied elite, defended a monopolistic Anglican Church and rested on an oppressive and grossly unfair system of taxation. Various commercial monopolies interfered with freedom of trade, whilst game laws prevented small farmers from hunting even on their own land. Primogeniture and entail ensured the concentration of landed property in the hands of the aristocracy.

These were the central contentions of *Rights of Man*, Part One. During the year preceding the appearance of Part Two, a pamphlet war of epic proportions had broken out in Britain that appeared to fuel a growing sympathy for parliamentary reform, or even more substantial innovations. In Part Two Paine restated his case, but with some important modifications and additions to his general principles. He again laid great stress on the applicability of popular democratic institutions of the American type to Europe, and the economic advantages of abolishing expensive monarchies and courts, large standing armies and exorbitantly paid governments. All hereditary Government, he now reiterated, was 'in its nature tyranny'. Democracy was cheap: it would reduce taxes greatly as a result, and the money released would promote universal opulence among the lower orders. Democracy was pacific: it would abolish the universal propensity to warfare endemic among monarchies, which Paine thought was one of the chief causes of poverty in Europe, 'and produce a revolution in the uncivilized state of governments'. The savings, again, would be enormously beneficial to the poorer classes in particular. Democracy wished to promote trade, which was based on the universal satisfaction of needs. As in Part One, Paine insisted that such reforms required a constitutional convention that laid down first principles and invited popular ratification thereof. He again trumpeted the virtues of representative institutions, which permitted the extension of democracy over a vast extent of territory. Government must learn to become 'nothing more than a national association acting on the principles of society', in other words, an association for promoting universal prosperity, not a machine for grinding taxes from the poor.

Yet Part Two was in one notable respect less optimistic than Part One, especially where commerce was concerned. For Paine now seemed to acknowledge that however much prosperity might be unleashed by democratic republicanism, poverty might still exist. To combat this possibility, he suggested a remarkable programme of social reforms that has been seen as providing the first set of proposals to underpin the welfare states of the late nineteenth and twentieth centuries. He now announced that the goal of Government was providing 'for the instruction of youth, and the support of age, so as to exclude, as much as possible, profligacy from the one, and despair from the other'. Funds were to be dedicated to educating the children of the poor, providing subsistence for those unable to work after the age of 50, and for all after age 60, for helping poor mothers and demobilized soldiers and sailors, assisting the funeral costs of the poor, and even constructing two workhouses to employ some of the poor of London. These measures were to be paid for by a progressive tax on inheritance. At the same time the poor's rate, or tax on landed property, could be abolished completely. But most importantly, they indicate that Paine had altered his view of Government substantially by early 1792: far from being merely a necessary evil, it could play a powerful redistributive role in assisting the poor and ensuring the maintenance of social equality.

The reputation of *Rights of Man* thus rests on six key themes: (1) *republicanism*: Paine broke clearly from the Whig and even radical interpretation of the British constitution, by which the settlement of 1688 had established the best possible form of Government; his rejection of the notion that the British constitution was balanced, his support for a pure democracy defined by a written constitution formed by a constitutional convention and approved by the people; and his rejection of monarchy as such in favour of an elected executive, and a unicameral elected representative body, constituted a dramatic redefinition of the boundaries of political understanding; (2) *natural rights*: Paine's insistence on the universal possession of equal natural rights (with corresponding duties to uphold the rights of others) transcended existing debates about historically grounded liberties, and the precedence of civil over natural rights in modern societies; despite later assaults on rights doctrines by utilitarians and Marxists in particular, the language of rights retains enormous importance in modern politics; (3) *commerce and equality*: Paine's approach to commerce was more than 'liberal': far more than David Hume or Adam Smith, for instance, he ambitiously assumed universal commerce would, in conjunction with republicanism, promote the abolition of war; nor was he seriously concerned with the threat to republican virtue of such a widespread and opulent commercial system; Paine's willingness to provide a safety net for the poor, however, established the limits of his commercial optimism; (4) *style and language*: the language of *Rights of Man* is in keeping with its democratic sentiments: Paine aimed to demystify government by satire and ridicule as well as sustained argument, and to empower his readers with a sense of their rights and duties; he also made a virtue of his own humble origins, and appealed constantly to simple moral precepts susceptible of a universal application, famously claiming that 'Independence is my happiness, and I view things as they are, without regard to place or person; my country is the world, and my religion is to do good.' We know from reports by readers how cathartic their reaction sometimes was, and how widespread was the sentiment that *Rights of Man* had established, as one Scot put it, that 'Politics is no longer a Mysterious System but Common Sence.'

Two other more brief political works extended these themes in the 1790s: the *Letter Addressed to the Addressers* (1792), which is a pithy restatement of his republicanism, and the longer *Dissertation on First Principles of Government* (1795), which analysed the French constitution of that year. By far the most influential of Paine's later works, however, was *The Age of Reason* (1794), which was motivated by the belief that the atheism widely associated with the revolution and republicanism – which Paine opposed – was not their inevitable consequence, and by the belief that orthodox Christianity was not the sole or best means of establishing a Christian system of morality. The sum of Paine's religious beliefs, as he announced at the beginning of the text, consisted of a belief in one God, the hope for 'happiness beyond this life' and devotion to 'the equality of man'. From these ideals flowed religious duties, which Paine defined as consisting of 'doing justice, loving mercy, and endeavouring to make our fellow-creatures happy'. This was Paine's statement of the 'true religion' he sought to assist. Much more controversial, however, was his insistence that the sole proof required for belief in God lay in nature itself, and his concomitant attack on the Bible as a tissue of

invention, poetry, history and myth. Part Two of the *Age of Reason* (1795) examines the Old and New Testaments in detail, and attacks, amongst other things, the book of Genesis as 'an anonymous book of stories, fables and traditionary or invented absurdities, or of downright lies', which had interesting repercussions for Paine's theory of rights. Though he reaffirmed his deism, defined as 'the belief in one God, and an imitation of His moral character, or the practise of what are called the moral virtues', Paine again reiterated that the Bible was 'a dead letter' and 'fit only to excite contempt'. Thereafter the Paineite tradition of radicalism in Britain and the USA in particular found that its promotion of secularism was often an uphill battle. Paine himself, however, helped to found the Church of Theophilanthropy in Paris in 1797, with the aim of proving that the love of man and God alike could be based on no other revelation than nature.

Paine's final work of importance is the little-read but interesting *Agrarian Justice* (1797). In this book he extended his reservations about the prospects of *laissez-faire* to curtail poverty, and indicated that poverty resulted in part at least from low wages and economic exploitation. Central to his argument here was a distinction between natural property, principally in the earth, and artificial property, created by people. The former, he contended, remained in principle the property of the human race, but since periodic redivision of land was impracticable (a contemporary critic, Thomas Spence, disagreed) landlords owed the dispossessed both a lump sum and an annuity in compensation. Given Paine's deism and ridicule of the Bible there are similar difficulties here about the origin of this common right, which Paine derived, via the natural jurisprudence tradition, again from Genesis, from which he argued that land was 'the free gift of the Creator in common to the human race'. What is more important to stress, perhaps, is that Paine in *Agrarian Justice* conceded that poverty tended to increase with the process of civilization, rather than receding before the gains of free trade. He also introduced a new argument about the social context of the creation of wealth, insisting that:

All accumulation, therefore, of personal property, beyond what a man's own hands produce, is derived to him by living in society; and he owes on every principle of justice, of gratitude, and of civilization, a part of that accumulation back again to society from whence the whole came.

This led him to reinforce his commitment to guaranteeing a substantial measure of social equality (though without moving in the direction of communism) through redistributive taxation, for which *Agrarian Justice* in essence presents an elaborate argument.

Further reading

Aldridge, A.O. (1960) *Man of Reason. The Life of Thomas Paine*, London: The Cresset Press.
—— (1984) *Thomas Paine's American Ideology*, Newark: Associated University Presses.
Ayer, A.J. (1988) *Thomas Paine*, London: Secker & Warburg.
Claeys, Gregory (1989) *Thomas Paine: Social and Political Thought*, Boston: Unwin Hyman.
Conway, Moncure (1892) *The Life of Thomas Paine*, 2 vols, New York: The Knickerbocker Press.
Fennessy, R.R. (1963) *Burke, Paine and the Rights of Man*, The Hague: Martinus Nijhoff.
Keane, John (1995) *Tom Paine: A Political Life*, London: Bloomsbury.
Philp, Mark (1989) *Paine*, Oxford: Oxford University Press.

SEE ALSO: Theories of the state and society: the science of politics; Democracy, populism and rights; Liberalism Ideas of War and Peace

GREGORY CLAEYS

PANKHURST, EMMELINE (1858–1928)

The well-known militant suffragette was born in Manchester – a leading centre of the women's enfranchisement movement – into a family with radical political beliefs. She attended her first suffrage meeting at the age of 14, and in 1879 married Richard Pankhurst, a radical lawyer and strong advocate of women's suffrage. Of their four children Christabel (b. 1880) and Sylvia (b. 1882) were the most actively involved in their mother's campaign, though Sylvia and her mother later clashed, especially on the latter's support of the First World War and her movement to the political right.

In the late 1880s Emmeline was one of the co-founders of the Women's Franchise League that campaigned to include married women in suffrage legislation rather than restrict it to single and widowed women. But her principal claim to fame is as the founder in 1903 of the Women's Social and Political Union (WSPU), with the specific aim of recruiting working-class women into the campaign for the vote.

Both Richard (who died in 1898) and Emmeline had allied themselves with the Independent Labour Party during the 1890s, and initially the WSPU concentrated its activities on promoting support for women's suffrage within socialist and trade union branches in the Manchester area. But within a few years of its foundation, three significant changes had occurred. First, its geographical base was transferred to London and its financial security was underwritten by the Pethwick-Lawrences. Second, by 1907 it had broken its connection with its earlier socialist and labour movement associations. Third, the WSPU became more militant in its campaign to achieve female suffrage. The heckling of politicians, hunger strikes and attacks on private property became part of its strategy. Emmeline Pankhurst herself was imprisoned on numerous occasions, and her example inspired many other women to commit acts of civil disobedience.

It was such tactics as well as its sole objective of Votes for Women that differentiated the WSPU from the National Union of Women's Suffrage Societies led by Millicent Garrett Fawcett. Both sections of the women's suffrage movement ceased their campaigning on the outbreak of the First World War in 1914. Mrs Pankhurst herself was intensely patriotic and 'a fight to the finish against Germany' was among the objectives of the Women's Party that she founded together with her daughter Christabel in 1917. It also supported a variety of equality measures between women and men, including equal pay for equal work and equal marriage and divorce laws.

After the First World War she spent several years in Canada, concentrating her efforts on social and moral issues rather than women's suffrage. By then however significant alterations to the parliamentary franchise were already in train in Britain. Legislation in 1918 extended the vote to women over 30 with a basic property qualification, while in 1928, the year of Emmeline's death, men and women achieved equality before the law at the same age of 21.

Further reading

Pankhurst, Emmeline (1914) *My Own Story*, London: Eveleigh & Nash.

Pugh, Martin (2001) *The Pankhursts*, London: Allen Lane.

Purvis, June (2002) *Emmeline Pankhurst: A Biography*, London: Routledge.

SEE ALSO: feminism and the female franchise movement

DAVID GLADSTONE

PARETO, WILFREDO (1848–1923)

Influential sociologist, economist and engineer, and leading proponent of elite theory, Wilfredo Pareto was born in Paris in 1848, to an Italian father of noble extraction – who had allegedly fled Italy on account of his republican beliefs – and a French mother of humble origins. The family moved to Piedmont in the mid-1850s, and after being educated in technical schools, Pareto entered the prestigious Turin Polytechnic, seeking to follow in his father's footsteps and become an engineer. The five-year course in civil engineering paved the way for much of Pareto's subsequent intellectual development. The first two years were devoted to mathematics, a subject in which he excelled. His proficiency as mathematician underpinned his later work as an economist. His graduation thesis on *The Fundamental Principles of Equilibrium in Solid Bodies* afforded a paradigm for his subsequent vision of both economics and sociology.

After graduating in 1870, Pareto entered business, and became the managing director of an iron-mining company based in Florence. He moved in wealthy circles, but espoused progressive republican and democratic ideas. He denounced militarism and religion as 'the greatest scourges afflicting mankind', and became a staunch defender of free trade. With the advent of the left to power in Italy in 1876, the drift towards protectionism and what seemed the increasingly corrupt character of parliamentary politics turned Pareto into a vehement critic of the Government and its policies. In 1882 he stood unsuccessfully as an opposition candidate. More and more he found his business activities being hampered by the need to broker deals with Members of Parliament and ministries, and he longed to retire. It was around this time that his views on the ruling class in Italy began to crystallize: he saw it as a nexus of influence and pressure, using power to win economic favours and buy votes, and whose activities were hidden behind a smokescreen of elections and representative Government.

In 1891 Pareto retired to Fiesole with his young and penniless Russian wife, Dina Bakunin. He threw himself into a crusade against the protectionist and militarist policies of the Government and produced dozens of brilliantly polemical articles. His journalistic forays brought him into close contact with other Italian free-trade publicists, and it was through one of these, Maffeo Pantaleoni, that he was introduced to the new economic theories of Léon Walras. Pareto's skilful exposition and elaboration of Walras's mathematically expressed equilibrium system in the *Giornale degli economisti* rapidly gained him international recognition, and in 1893 he succeeded Walras as Professor of Political Economy in Lausanne. Three years later his first major publication appeared, the two-volume *Cours d'economie politique* (1896–7), a work that highlighted the interdependence of society and the economy, and which proposed a situation of efficiency or optimality (the so-called 'Pareto optimum') in which nobody could be made better off without making someone else correspondingly worse off. This concept was to be fundamental to modern welfare economics.

Implicit in the *Cours* was a mechanistic and essentially illiberal vision of history. Human nature, according to Pareto, was constant, and the social divisions that stemmed from the distribution of wealth were more or less unchanging. Any idea of progress or evolution was accordingly illusory. 'We must learn to accept that the optimistic belief...according to which the structures of society can be radically changed, is a myth', he told the Italian socialist leader Filippo Turati. 'Man is an ugly beast, and an ugly beast he will remain for many, many centuries to come.' Mounting socioeconomic unrest, and the Government's brutal response to episodes such as the workers' riots in Milan in May 1898, intensified Pareto's pessimism. So, too, did a growing disenchantment with politics in general and with socialism in particular. He came to see the rise of trade unions as simply heralding the replacement of bourgeois privileges with workers' privileges, and one form of oppression – that of the middle classes – with another – that of the proletariat. His earlier faith in democracy waned, and during the last two decades of his life he became increasingly anti-democratic in outlook.

This shift in Pareto's outlook was further intensified by a new intuition, one that was to inspire his major sociological writings from the turn of the century. This was the idea (which came to him as a result of reflecting on the astonishing – since in his view so wrong-headed – popularity of what he called the 'new gospel' of Marxism in Italy in the 1890s) that much of human activity was the product not of reason but of feeling. He set out his new views in *Les Systèmes socialistes* (1901–2), a work that examined the history of socialist ideas from ancient times to the present, and which argued that the power of these ideas lay not in their capacity to produce a better world, but in their ability, through myths, to foster hopes that could galvanize the masses into action. Socialism, he suggested, was politically more powerful than liberalism because it appealed to emotion rather than reason; but in practical terms there was little to choose between them: both simply enabled 'elites' to capture and keep power.

Pareto developed his sociological ideas further in the *Manuale d'economia politica* (1906) and the monumental *Trattato di sociologia generale* (1916). In this latter work he explored the relationship between human behaviour and society, and drew a distinction between logical actions – those, and they were relatively rare in his view, where the means were appropriate to the ends – and non-logical ones. Non-logical actions were frequently just a 'bundle of idiocies', but they could be 'socially useful'. They were often kitted out in justificatory rational terms (what he called 'derivations'), but were in reality just instruments for the satisfaction of basic human emotions and instincts (what he called 'residues'). He regarded all political doctrines as abstractions that could not change the fundamental opposition between elites and masses that was to be found in every society. All elites governed using force and cunning, and were replaced in due course by other elites claiming to speak for the oppressed or disadvantaged. History was thus little more than 'a graveyard of aristocracies'.

Despite serious ill health, Pareto continued to write until the end of his life. He died in 1923.

Further reading

Nye, Robert (1977) *The Anti-Democratic Sources of Elite Theory. Pareto, Mosca, Michels*, London: Sage.
Powers, C.H. (1987) *Wilfredo Pareto*, London: Sage.
Wood, J.C. and McLure, M. (eds) (1999) *Wilfredo Pareto. Critical Assessments of Leading Economists*, London: Routledge.

SEE ALSO: democracy, populism and rights; intellectuals, elites and meritocracy; Mosca, Gaetano; social theory and sociology in the nineteenth century; theories of the state and society: the science of politics

CHRISTOPHER DUGGAN

PARNELL, CHARLES STEWART (1846–91)

Born on 27 June 1846 at Avondale, County Wicklow, Charles Stewart Parnell was educated in schools in England but left Cambridge without taking his degree. He was elected to Parliament in 1875 as a Home Rule candidate for Meath. In Westminster his obstructionist tactics won him support at home from the extreme nationalists and their allies among the Irish-Americans. An agricultural crisis led to the foundation of the Land League in 1879 to protect the tenantry from eviction and exorbitant rents. Parnell became its president. Elected chairman of the Irish Parliamentary Party in 1880, he was now in control of both the constitutional and agrarian agitations with support from the more extreme revolutionaries. This balancing of moral and physical force gave him a unity of strength never before enjoyed by an Irish political leader, and provided a 'New Departure' in Irish politics. A Protestant landlord leading a Catholic peasantry in an agitation to overthrow landlordism became the charismatic 'Uncrowned King of Ireland'. His social philosophy, however, was to reform the system, not to eliminate the landlords. He hoped that landlords would play a responsible role in Irish society. When this failed he became convinced that the remedy lay in the creation of a peasant proprietorship and not in land nationalization urged by more radical colleagues.

The Government's response was two-fold: Parnell and fellow agitators were imprisoned; and Gladstone's Land Act (1881) established a commission to regulate rents. The Kilmainham 'treaty' was an arrangement whereby Parnell was released from prison to use his influence to end the land war and the Government agreed to amend the Land Act in favour of the tenants. The 1881 Act initiated the series of measures that eventually transferred ownership of the land to the tenants.

The Irish National League with Parnell as president replaced the Land League. The new organization concentrated on the struggle for Home Rule. In the general election of 1885 Home Rule candidates won eighty-six seats, which was the exact difference between Tories and Liberals. Gladstone committed the Liberals to Home Rule. The principle behind Parnell's political philosophy was clear: the re-establishment of an Irish Parliament. On the constitutional details, or the continuation of the link with Britain, he remained ambivalent. His political achievements and legacy were not to be found in abstract ideas but rather in the inspiration and leadership that he provided in the drive towards national independence.

The O'Shea divorce scandal in which Parnell was named as co-respondent brought about his downfall. Gladstone declared he would be unable to carry Home Rule if Parnell remained leader. The once powerful Irish Parliamentary Party split into Parnellites and anti-Parnellites. The Irish bishops declared him morally unfit for leadership. And a majority of the electorate supported the anti-Parnellites. In the struggle for political survival Parnell overtaxed his energies and died at Brighton on 6 October 1891.

Further reading

Bew, Paul (1980) *C.S. Parnell*, Dublin: Gill & Macmillan.
Lyons, F.S.L. (1977) *Charles Stewart Parnell*, London: Collins.

DONAL McCARTNEY

PÉGUY, CHARLES (1873–1914)

Charles Péguy was born on 7 January 1873 in Orléans, and was killed in action on the Marne on 5 September 1914. A poet and journalist, his political views evolved from socialism to nationalism and Catholicism. He came to symbolize the patriotism of his generation.

Having lost his father at an early age, Péguy was raised in a peasant environment, in a country dominated by memories of its defeat and humiliation in the Franco-Prussian War. Educated at the Lycée d'Orléans and the Ecole Normale Supérieure, his later student life was spent campaigning for socialism and analysing the life of Joan of Arc.

Péguy articulated his anti-militarist and internationalist political views in a series of articles for the *Revue blanche* in 1899. The following year, however, he was moved to establish his own journal in order to escape socialist party control over its press. He acted as reporter and editor of the *Cahiers des Quinzaine* from 1900 until his death in 1914.

In the early 1900s, Péguy shared many of the views of the Dreyfusard political left, namely virulent opposition to the Catholic Church, nationalism and *revanche*. Yet he also developed an independent socialist analysis, strongly opposed to the Marxism of the socialist leader JULES GUESDE.

The Moroccan crisis of 1905 was a turning point in Péguy's political thinking. Having rejected the chauvinistic patriotism of the right and espoused the principle of internationalism, he suddenly awakened to the threat of imminent German attack. While the rest of France underwent a patriotic national revival, Péguy turned his attention to likening the present danger to the ancient menace of barbarian invasion in *Notre patrie* (Our Fatherland), published in 1905. While he continued to associate himself with the socialist left, Péguy reversed his earlier position to argue that France's failure to launch a war of revenge had compromised its destiny to lead the world towards liberty. His new political views were now more aligned with the nationalist position, and he reaffirmed his commitment to *revanche* in *À nos amis, à nos abonnés* (To our Friends, to our Subscribers) (1909) and *Notre jeunesse* (Our Youth) (1910). Yet unlike the nationalists, he also condemned German anti-socialism for betokening opposition to all things French: the revolution, the Catholic Church and the nation's civilizing mission. It was only on the eve of the First World War that Péguy finally renounced his socialist ideals and acknowledged the legitimacy of war.

With his Catholic faith restored by 1910, Péguy revived his old interest in Joan of Arc. In *Le mystère de la charité de Jeanne d'Arc* (*The Mystery of the Charity of Joan of Arc*) (1897), he had described Joan as the inspiration for resolving the troubles of France. Just as she had repelled the English from French soil in the fifteenth century, so the people of France, following her inspiration, could expel the German occupiers in the late nineteenth century. In 1912, he published sonnets which were later collected under the title *La Tapisserie de sainte Geniève et de Jeanne d'Arc* (The Tapestry of Saint Geniève and Joan of Arc).

Péguy's life was cut tragically short in the early days of the First World War. In the 1930s and 1940s, however, he came to be revered at once as a patriot, revolutionary and conservative.

Further reading

Sussex, R.T. (1980) *The Sacrificed Generation: Studies of Charles Péguy, Ernest Psichari and Alain-Fournier*, Capricornia No. 2. Townsville: James Cook University of North Queensland.

SEE ALSO: Marx and Marxism; religion, secularization and the crisis of faith

KARINE VARLEY

POLITICAL ECONOMY

Nineteenth-century political economy (or economics, as it came increasingly to be called) had its roots in the eighteenth-century writings of David Hume and Adam Smith. What is now called classical economics, based on Smith, restated and developed by DAVID RICARDO in 1817, and systematized by JOHN STUART MILL in 1848, dominated for the larger part of the century. From the 1870s on there were major changes in the intellectual foundations of the subject, introduced by WILLIAM STANLEY JEVONS in England, Léon Walras in Switzerland and Carl Menger in Austria, but the main policy conclusions were less affected. Broadly speaking, nineteenth-century economists favoured stable money, free trade and *laissez-faire*, with a variety of qualifications, though there were always dissenting voices. In the later years of the century, too, the social foundations of the subject changed as what had previously been a hobby of gentlemen or of writers who had made their reputations elsewhere became professionalized, with university chairs, learned societies and specialist journals.

The economic world changed almost beyond recognition during the nineteenth century, from what was still an essentially pre-industrial world of agriculture and handicrafts, horses and sailing ships, to a world dominated by industrial capitalism, railways and steamships. In another and perhaps more fundamental sense, though, one could say that nothing had changed. At the start of the century, the European economy was already dominated by private property and market exchange. By the end of the century the market had spread its influence further, but the same economic principles applied. In some areas, such as monetary theory, there was little change at the most basic level, though the theory had to be applied to changing monetary institutions.

Money and Say's law

David Hume had argued, as early as 1752, that a change in the quantity of money in circulation must lead to a corresponding change in prices. This is the quantity theory of money. It followed that a shortage of money in circulation could not be a problem in itself because prices would adjust, while an increase in the stock of money would bring no lasting benefits because increased prices would leave the real situation unchanged. He admitted that activity might be stimulated temporarily while prices rose, but in the long run the only result would be inflation. Nineteenth-century economists took this to heart. Governments might be tempted to take a short-term view and stimulate the economy by creating money, but they should be prevented from doing so. Sound money became a quasi-moral imperative.

The natural complement to Hume's monetary theory was Say's law (so named much later), which was implicit in Smith but was developed and stated more clearly by JEAN-BAPTISTE SAY and James Mill at the beginning of the nineteenth century. According to Say's law there can never be a general shortage of demand, or general overproduction, though there can be overproduction of particular things. The basic idea is simple and, up to a point, correct. People do not aim to earn money for its own sake, but to be able to buy things with it. An increase in production would normally generate a corresponding increase in incomes and in demand. The corollary is that there is no need to stimulate demand, say by an expansionary monetary policy. No one doubted that there were occasional crises and depressions, but they were mere blips caused by wars or other shocks. John Stuart Mill explained how demand might fall if people delayed spending, but argued that accumulated money holdings would be released after a while, restoring demand.

Hume's theory dealt with the international dimension as well. In his time, money consisted of gold and silver. A deficit in trade with other countries would lead to an outflow of monetary metals, hence to a reduction in the money stock and a fall in prices, restoring competitiveness, righting the balance of trade and inducing a return flow of money. The world's money stock would flow between countries until an equilibrium was reached. It followed that there was no need to worry about the balance of trade. The system would look after itself.

Hume's monetary theory dominated throughout the nineteenth century but monetary debates flared up from time to time because the monetary and financial system was changing and developing. As banknotes came to be used more extensively in place of gold and silver coins, an outflow of precious metals (still the international standard) no longer automatically cut the supply of money in circulation. New legislation was required to control the issue of notes by (privately owned) banks. In Britain, for example, the right to issue notes was progressively confined to the Bank of England and the Bank's note issue was linked to its gold reserves, to make a predominantly paper money behave as if it were metallic money.

Classical political economy

In the years around 1800, the sciences and humanities were slowly disentangling themselves from philosophy and establishing an independent existence. Political economy was no exception. The Enlightenment philosophers had ranged across many disciplines without drawing any sharp boundaries. The school of political economists that emerged in Britain immediately after the Napoleonic Wars based itself squarely on Adam Smith, but on Smith's *Wealth of Nations* and not on his work as a moral philosopher. Their work was prompted by immediate political issues like the Corn Laws and the Poor Laws, it influenced current political debates and was popularized by a variety of writers who set out to educate and influence the general public, but the classical school always thought of political economy itself as an objective science. These writers, including THOMAS ROBERT MALTHUS, Ricardo and John Stuart Mill, are now called the classical economists.

Malthus's *Essay on Population*, published in 1798, exemplifies a view of population and living standards that went back much earlier and that continued to dominate thinking through much of the nineteenth century. If incomes were high, it was thought, population would grow until it outstripped food supplies. An increased population would mean increased competition for jobs driving wages down to subsistence, with population limited to the number the economy could support. This was not an unreasonable view. Wages really were pretty low. We now know from the experience of modern developing economies that population can grow at up to 3 per cent a year, while even in the Britain of the Industrial Revolution the economy was growing at less than half a per cent per year. Population clearly could outrun economic growth. The Malthusian view was not quite as bleak as it might seem. Food prices fluctuated with the harvest and skilled workers typically earned twice the unskilled wage, so a wage that allowed an unskilled worker's family to survive a bad year would allow most people, most of the time, to live well above bare subsistence. In a growing economy, moreover, wages could remain some way above the subsistence minimum for as long as growth continued.

The Malthusian view, however, meant that economic growth would be matched by population growth, putting more and more pressure on food and on limited agricultural land. Eventually, the system must reach a stationary state, with wages forced down enough for population growth to be choked off by starvation and infant mortality. The Napoleonic Wars gave Britain a rather nasty shock, when a growing population and a series of bad harvests coincided with Napoleon's blockade. Food prices shot up, and the limits seemed frighteningly close.

The Corn Laws of 1815, designed to protect British agriculture from foreign competition after the war, prompted furious debates and remained a key political issue until they were repealed in 1846. A by-product of the 1815 debate was a new theory of rent and profit, proposed by Malthus, Edward West, Robert Torrens and David Ricardo within weeks of each other during 1815. Ricardo's *Principles of Political Economy* of 1817 developed the argument more fully. The basic idea is that the best land will always be preferred for cultivation but, as the economy and the population grow, worse and worse land will have to be brought into use. Returns in agriculture fall, squeezing profits. As demand for food grows, the price rises, making it worth cultivating poorer land, but wages have to rise in line with food prices to allow workers to survive (the Malthusian wage theory). Good land still produces as much as before, but as it grows scarcer, the owners can demand more rent. Profits are squeezed between the two, progressively falling as the economy grows until the stationary state is reached. The policy implications followed directly. Corn imports relieve the pressure on the land and keep profits and growth up, allowing the manufacturing sector to continue growing. By restricting imports the Corn Laws served the interests of the landlords but of no one else. Ricardian economics was an analytical advance but it was also a weapon in the struggle against agricultural protection.

Ricardo's main emphasis was on the special case of agriculture and the corn trade, but he also developed a new, more general, theory of the gains from trade. Trade, he argued, depended on comparative, not absolute, advantage. Even if one country is less efficient at producing everything than its trading partners, it can still gain from trade. Ricardo's example was trade in cloth and wine between Britain and Portugal. Suppose Portugal has lower real costs than Britain in both industries, but with a much greater advantage in the production of wine. Then it will still pay both countries if British cloth is traded for Portuguese wine, because what matters is the relative price at which the products are traded. Ricardo's theory of growth and profit went out of fashion later in the century because it involved too many special assumptions and ignored technical change, but his theory of comparative advantage remained. Free trade became an article of faith for most nineteenth-century economists.

Adam Smith's price theory was based on a distinction between 'market' and 'natural' prices. Market prices, the actual prices at which goods are sold, can vary from day to day or from hour to hour as supply and demand vary, but if prices get out of line with costs corrective forces come into play. Capital will flow out of activities yielding low profits, reducing supply and raising prices, towards those where profits are higher. After a disturbance, therefore, market prices will tend to return towards 'natural' cost-based prices that equalize returns between different activities. This account explains the general movement of prices and also shows how the system responds to changing circumstances. An increase in demand for a particular product, for example, will raise its market price, inducing increased production in response to demand.

As a description of the pricing process Smith's analysis was generally accepted, but Ricardo was unhappy with the apparent implication that prices could be derived by adding up costs. If (real) wages increase, for example, it looks as though all prices would rise (because wages are a major element in costs) but Ricardo pointed out that profits would have to fall, counteracting the effect on prices. In his *Principles* of 1817, he suggested a drastic simplification: the price of each good should be proportional to the labour required to produce it. This is not quite as silly as it might seem, since the labour required was to include all labour required to produce materials, equipment and so on. Even so, it cannot be exactly true, as Ricardo himself knew. If capital–labour ratios vary (as they do), two goods produced by the same amount of labour but with different amounts of capital investment will have different prices. He argued, rather weakly, that the labour theory of value was a reasonably good approximation and his prestige and the lack of good alternatives was such that it continued to be taken seriously for a long time.

'Classical' political economy was given a new lease of life in 1848 by John Stuart Mill's *Principles of Political Economy*. He developed the Ricardian framework, for example by adding a new emphasis on the role of demand in international trade and elsewhere, and added a quite different political slant. Adam Smith's critique of special interests and Ricardo's opposition to the Corn Laws had been radical in their day, but no longer seemed relevant. Mill saw real possibilities of improving the lot of working people. He favoured producers' co-operatives and profit-sharing, with an enlarged role for the state, arguing that the laws governing the production of wealth were timeless, but that the distribution of wealth depended on human institutions that could, and perhaps should, be changed.

Alternatives to classical economics

Mill's slightly younger contemporary, Karl Marx (see MARX AND MARXISM), was without question one of the most important writers of the nineteenth century. He spent many years working on economics but, paradoxically, had much less impact on thinking about economics than (say) politics or history. He emphasized the massive transformation that had been brought about by industrial capitalism, but the analytical framework of his economics looked back to Ricardo at a time when even Mill's updated version of the classics was beginning to crumble.

Marx put the labour theory of value at the heart of his analysis, treating it not as a theory of price but as a method of calculation independent of market prices. Value, to him, was defined by the labour required in production, while prices were a converted or distorted reflection of values. This allowed him to argue that labour, and labour alone, is (by definition) the source of value, so if wages fall short of the value produced (as they must) this represents 'exploitation' of labour to produce 'surplus value'. All non-wage incomes have to come out of the surplus value generated by productive workers. Marx played down the role of rent and rejected the Malthusian population mechanism but he retained the subsistence wage of the classics, so his theory of surplus value was essentially the same as Ricardo's, with a different terminology and a new political slant. He too predicted a falling rate of profit, but gave a different (and, it is now clear, invalid) explanation. Where the classics thought declining profits would lead to a stationary state, Marx foresaw the revolutionary overthrow of the system.

The first volume of Marx's *Capital* appeared in 1867. Taken on its own it seemed to rely on a wholly dogmatic labour theory of value. The third and final volume, which could be seen as meeting some of the obvious objections by linking labour values to 'prices of production' (Smith's natural prices), was never finished and was assembled by Engels for publication in 1894. By that time economics had moved on, and Marx's economics had little impact outside what was, at that date, a very small coterie of dedicated Marxists. Marxism came to have a huge political and intellectual impact in the twentieth century, but Marx's economic analysis only played a very minor role.

A quite different and ultimately more successful approach emerged in the middle years of the century in the work of a succession of French engineers, or scientists with an engineering training. The most important were Antoine Augustin Cournot and Jules Dupuit. Starting in 1838, Cournot developed a mathematical analysis of supply and demand in competitive industries, together with a theory of monopoly (one supplier) and of oligopoly (a few sellers). The last of these is still the dominant theory today, and is universally known by his name. A little later Dupuit put forward an analysis of the gains from public projects, such as the building of a bridge, and developed many key ideas of modern welfare economics in the process. In retrospect, these writers, with others such as the German Heinrich von Thünen, pointed the way to later developments, but they had little impact at the time, perhaps because they were isolated individuals who made little attempt to convert others and because their work was difficult and mathematical. One might say that they adopted a style appropriate to the professionalized academic economics of the twentieth century but before there was a professional audience to address.

Utilitarianism and the marginal revolution

Utilitarianism in some form or other goes back a long way, but it took its definitive form in the writings of JEREMY BENTHAM at the beginning of the nineteenth century. Utility is a measure of the happiness or well-being of an individual, pleasure minus pain. The principle of utility says that policies should be judged by their effect on the sum total of utility in the community, the 'greatest good of the greatest number'. This embodies a number of tenets: that policies should be judged by their effect on individuals, that all individuals should count equally, and so on. Bentham was closely associated with the classical economists in a wider grouping known as the philosophical radicals. James Mill, in particular, was a substantial economist in his own right and a close friend both of Bentham and of Ricardo. At that stage, utilitarianism was not seen as part of political economy but as complementary to it – political economy would establish what was possible, while the principle of utility would guide policy choices.

Despite their utilitarian connections, the classical economists denied any direct connection between prices and utility. Earlier writers had commonly, if vaguely, explained the value of goods in terms of their utility and scarcity. Classical writers rejected this connection, citing what is called the water–diamonds paradox: water is essential but often free, while diamonds are of trivial use but have a high price. Utility, it was said, could not determine price. The resolution of this paradox depends on the distinction between total and marginal utility. It makes little sense to talk of the overall contribution of water to my utility because I could not live without it, but it makes perfect sense to talk about the marginal contribution of an extra litre of water. If water is available without charge I will use as much as I want, to the point where an extra litre has no value to me. The marginal utility of water, like its price, will be zero. Note that this is not a statement about the value of water, but about the amount I choose to use. Diamonds, however, are expensive so I will only buy a diamond if its (marginal) contribution to my utility at least matches that of other things I could buy with the money. If I maximize my utility, it follows that the marginal utilities of things I buy are proportional to their prices. The elements of this line of argument had been available for a long time, but it did not fully penetrate the mainstream of economics until the later years of the nineteenth century, in what has been called the 'marginal revolution'.

By the 1860s there was growing dissatisfaction with the state of economic theory. Ricardo offered clear-cut answers to a limited range of questions but only on implausible assumptions, while dropping his strong assumptions left the results inconclusive. Malthusian wage theory seemed largely irrelevant, and there was no adequate theory of demand or of substitution between different methods of production.

In the final decades of the century, a new 'neoclassical' economics took over, based on demand and supply analysis with both demand and supply explained in terms of rational maximizing behaviour. Demand for consumer goods from utility-maximizing consumers depends on marginal utility. Profit-maximizing competitive firms set supply so that marginal cost, that is, the cost of an extra unit of output, equals the net selling price. If price exceeds marginal cost it pays to expand, and if marginal cost exceeds price it pays to cut back. Similarly, firms' demand for labour and other inputs depends on their marginal contribution to output and hence to revenue. With hindsight, we can pick out a number of elements of the new direction earlier in the century, but they did not come together into a successful and widely accepted alternative to classical economics until the 1870s.

The pioneers of the new economics, Jevons in England, Walras in Switzerland and Menger in Austria, arrived at their conclusions independently and developed their conclusions in different ways. Jevons saw the marginal approach as directly opposed to that of the classics, though ALFRED MARSHALL was later to synthesize the two, arguing that long-run equilibrium prices will satisfy both Jevons's marginal conditions and the classical condition of equalization of returns. Walras aimed to describe the general equilibrium of a system of interdependent markets through a system of simultaneous equations. Menger rejected the mathematical approach and emphasized the subjective element in valuation. He and his Austrian successors emphasized that input demands, and hence prices, are derived from the (subjective) value of the goods they are used to produce, reversing the classical idea that the prices of final goods derive from input costs.

Historical economics

The rise of neoclassical economics was paralleled by the emergence of a rival, historical school, in Germany and Britain, which rejected the implicit claim, common to classical and neoclassical economics, that economic theory was timeless and universal. Different societies and periods, it was argued, were characterized by different institutions and patterns of behaviour, and hence had to be analysed differently. Beyond that, the historical school was very varied, including some who thought that standard economic theory applied to developed market economies but not to other societies, and some who rejected deductive economic theory as a whole. Towards the end of the century the historical approach within economics faded from view, not because its adherents gave up but because they created new disciplinary homes for themselves. The second generation of British historical economists turned to more detailed historical work and effectively founded economic history as a discipline in its own right, with its own place in universities, its own journals, and so on. In much the same way, the historical critics of orthodox economics in Germany, most notably MAX WEBER, came to be regarded not as economists but as pioneers of sociology.

The professionalisation of economics

Political economy had a massive influence on thinking and policy in Britain and elsewhere during the early and middle years of the nineteenth century. The ideas of Smith, Ricardo and others were successfully popularized by journalists and political pressure groups (like the Anti-Corn Law League). Sound money and free trade became axioms of British policy. Despite its success, however, economics had almost no settled institutional base during the first half of the century, and what little teaching of economic principles there was in universities was still squeezed into courses on other subjects such as jurisprudence or moral philosophy.

By 1900, and still more by 1914, things had changed beyond recognition. Political economy had renamed itself as economics, a change that was itself significant – the practitioners of the new economics saw themselves as above politics. Mathematics played an increasing role, though some, like Alfred Marshall, preferred to hide the mathematics in footnotes and appendices, and translate the results into words. The marginal principle, after all, is simply the calculus of maximization translated into words. The USA was starting to become an important centre of economic thinking, foreshadowing its twentieth-century dominance. Professional societies like the American Economic Association and the (British) Royal Economic Society were established. The focus of publication was shifting to academic journals, like the *Quarterly Journal of Economics* (USA, 1886) and the *Economic Journal* (UK, 1890), though books continued to play a significant role in the dissemination of ideas until about the mid-twentieth century. Economics was now a regular part of university life, with the full apparatus of professors, lecturers, faculties or departments of economics, degrees and degree examinations, and so on. Economists could aim at an academic career or, increasingly, a role in Government departments, banks, and so on. Economics could be a professional identity and a sensible career choice, not a hobby.

Further reading

Backhouse, R.E. (2002) *The Penguin History of Economics*, Harmondsworth: Penguin.
Blaug, M. (1996) *Economic Theory in Retrospect*, Cambridge: Cambridge University Press.

SEE ALSO: Marx and Marxism

ANTHONY BREWER

PROUDHON, PIERRE-JOSEPH (1809–65)

Pierre-Joseph Proudhon, who became an anarchist hero, was often reviled by other early socialists as a conservative. Unlike most early socialists, he came from a poor background. His mother's family were peasants, while his father was a cooper in the Franche-Comté. However, education was important to the family and his father's cousin was Professor of Law at the University of Besançon, a Jacobin leader and a freemason. Proudhon's mother encouraged him to attend the *collège* in Besançon, which he did until he was 17, although the family never had the money to buy the necessary textbooks. He was apprenticed to a printer and typeset FOURIER's *Le Nouveau Monde industriel et sociétaire*, met the author and was influenced by his ideas. In 1839 Proudhon was awarded the Suard prize by the Besançon Academy, 1,500 francs a year for 3 years, which gave him the economic opportunity to move to Paris. He wrote first on grammar, then on the economy and politics. In 1840 he brought out *Qu'est-ce que la propriété?*, the first and best-known of a large number of publications. The Academicians were appalled. Proudhon was charged with undermining private property, but the jury in Besançon threw out the charge.

Qu'est-ce que la propriété is easy to read, but even on first glance the reader is aware of gross and perhaps deliberate contradictions. Proudhon liked to shock by his manipulation of language; the phrase 'property is theft' guaranteed him an audience. The 'property' of the title was 'private' property. It is never entirely clear what degree of private ownership he found tolerable. His criticisms were aimed at those who owned an excessive amount and used their wealth to exploit others. 'Surplus' property was, in his view, the enemy of equality and social harmony. But he was critical of communists who attacked the actual notion of private property. He claimed to believe in liberty, but he was not a democrat. He was an anarchist, but did not believe in chaos. For him, anarchy was simply the absence of a sovereign; society should be based on co-operation, not coercion. His ideal society was one of small landowners. Whenever he spoke of industry, it was always small-scale and artisanal.

Proudhon's prime objective in this, as in most of his works, was to define a just society and persuade his reader of its equity. He was opposed to privilege and slavery, and stood for, he claimed, equality of rights, the rule of law and justice. All would agree, he asserted, that equality of conditions and equality of rights were identical and that therefore property rights were synonymous with robbery. Presumably the author was aware that almost none of his readers would agree! He claimed that developments in modern times exacerbated this situation. The revolutions of 1789 and 1830 grounded modern society on three principles: the sovereignty of human will, which he equated with despotism; inequalities of wealth and rank; rights of private ownership of property. Are these, he asks, in harmony with justice? The first self-evidently was not. Neither was the second; but it could easily be changed by eliminating the third. The Declaration of Rights stipulated that the right to property was inalienable, but Proudhon asserted that property and society were utterly irreconcilable institutions. Property was incompatible with civil and political equality. He unequivocally stated 'the right of property was the origin of evil on the earth'. If, he argued, the right of property was based on labour, then permanent ownership could not follow. It was a delusion, he claimed, to talk about the organization of labour while private property existed. Proudhon took issue with Fourier who argued that everyone should be rewarded according to their capital, labour and skill on the grounds that such a division was essentially unequal. Inequality of talent should not, he claimed, mean inequality of reward. Society could survive without its great artists, but not without its food producers.

Private property and communism were habitually depicted as the only choices for society. Proudhon disliked both. While denying the right of an individual to have exclusive control over a piece of property, Proudhon was convinced that communism was as unfair and as riddled with inequalities. It was mere oppression and slavery. Society should be based on equality, law, independence and proportionality; this would be liberty. What did Proudhon mean by proportionality? So far, he had roundly condemned exclusive rights of personal ownership, but had been equally critical of communism. It appears that what he was proposing was an equalizing process, but not egalitarianism. He then drew a distinction between property and possession. Law, Government, the economy and all institutions could be revolutionized if the right of possession was preserved and property rights abolished. He was not opposed to moderate levels of private use of the land. Did this seal of approval stop short of outright ownership? Or is the difference between property and possession quantitative rather than

qualitative? What Proudhon said was ambiguous, although his conclusion seemed to lead towards the former definition.

Thus, after 300 pages of invective and some of the most quotable phrases on the iniquity of private property, Proudhon's conclusion was a damp squib.

After one of the most uncompromisingly radical statements made by any of the early socialists, Proudhon seemed to take fright from the logical conclusion of his criticisms. All he asked for was the reduction and eventual elimination of interest rates and a tax on profit. Having slated the Orleanist regime, he declared that he would retain the monarchy, asking only for less elitist attitudes from the King and more efficient Government. Why? He realized that there were few democrats in France and those who went by that name had themselves ambitions to become kings. He wanted change, but did not believe that the existing regime had to be overturned to achieve it. His delightful conclusion summarized his actual approach. 'Property is like the dragon which Hercules killed: to destroy it, it must be taken, not by the head, but by the tail, – that is, by profit and interest.'

In Paris Proudhon met MARX, BAKUNIN and HERZEN, the start of lasting friendships with the last two. Marx liked Proudhon's first book, but subsequently they could not agree. Proudhon thought Marx too doctrinaire. Marx dismissed him as a '*petit bourgeois*' thinker. Proudhon did not become a full-time writer; when his scholarship ran out he went to work for a shipping company in Lyon; his employers were friends and left him time to write.

Proudhon had set the tone of his philosophy, which he continued to develop while working for the Gauthier brothers in Lyon. In 1846 came *Système des contradictions économiques ou philosophie de la misère*, to which Marx replied with *Misère de la philosophie*. Proudhon criticized communists like CABET, who dreamt of the disappearance of individual ownership. Proudhon was convinced that neither revolution nor the centralized state would solve the social problems of the day. He opposed Louis Blanc's socialism from above; socialism had to come from the people. His ideal was a community in which as many people as possible owned modest quantities of land, enough to sustain a family, in which industry was small-scale and artisanal, and in which economic competition and profit were absent. On the eve of the 1848 revolution, Proudhon was planning the launch of a newspaper, *Le Peuple*. He was convinced that he was one of the few who understood 'the people' and in return expressed faith in the collective wisdom of the same. Proudhon began to define his solution to economic problems as mutualism, or a harmonizing equilibrium. The term must have been suggested to him by the name of the Lyon silk workers' mutual aid association, the *Society of Mutual Duty*.

After the February revolution in which he had no role, other than to help Flocon his printer employer produce posters and placards, Proudhon became a vigorous publicist. He used his new paper, *Le Représentant du peuple* to offer practical advice on the economic crisis of the day. He was convinced that the economy would recover if interest rates were substantially reduced, if not actually eliminated. Investors were less than charmed. Because the provisional Government did not seem to be doing too well sorting out the economy, Proudhon's solutions quickly became well known and popular. Up to 40,000 copies of his paper were sold on days when Proudhon had written the leading article. Many were reprinted as short, cheap pamphlets with a particular emphasis on unemployment and poverty, including 'The Solution to the Social Problem' and 'The Malthusians', in which he attacked *laissez-faire* capitalism.

Proudhon was so rude about the ambitious republicans who grabbed control that they left him off their list of candidates for the National Assembly and he was only elected in the June by-elections. He had long since dismissed BLANC's plans for state intervention as a fraud on artisans and now he unfairly blamed Blanc for the creation of the national workshops. Blanc returned the compliment and ignored Proudhon's project for reorganizing credit. Proudhon was also at odds with CONSIDÉRANT and Leroux. Subsequently Leroux commented that in 1848 Proudhon, Cabet and Louis Blanc were a revolutionary triad, Proudhon representing liberty, Cabet fraternity and Blanc equality. If so, they were a very divided trio.

Proudhon's main mission was to promote financial reform, but his proposals were greeted by his fellow deputies as a one-man attack on private property. On 8 July he proposed to the Assembly's Finance Committee, of which he was a member, a 33 per cent reduction of all rents for 3 years to alleviate the impact of the economic crisis on the poor. Most deputies were property owners and, scandalized, passed a motion of censure on him.

Only the Lyon silk-worker, Greppo, voted for him, the remaining 691 voting against. The Assembly condemned his proposal as 'an affront to the moral order, an attack on private property'.

Disillusioned with Parliament, Proudhon focused his attention on his bank project and his journalism. He promoted a People's Bank as a solution to constant economic crises and unemployment. It was to be a producer and consumer co-operative, resembling Flora Tristan's plan for a union of all workers and Cabet's Icarie. Unlike Blanc's social workshops, Proudhon's co-operative would consist of individual, one-off agreements between autonomous workers. Like Tristan, Proudhon realized that the strength of the poor lay in numbers. He calculated that 250,000 workers in the capital alone, earning 2 francs a day each for about 300 days a year, meant a total earning power of 150 million francs a year. This potential power could be released and workers emancipated from uncertainty and poverty by the creation of a system of direct exchange of the goods they produced. In his bank workers would combine to get orders and to make goods and co-operate in the exchange of the items produced. The bank would offer cheap or even interest-free credit. There would be warehouses in which finished goods could be stored preparatory to being traded for goods of equal value or in exchange for notes issued by the bank. Thus the bank would consist of two sections, one for production and a syndicate to organize distribution. In September a committee for the bank in the Seine department was set up, consisting of twenty-two artisans, including masons, metal workers and a doctor. The scheme attracted 27,000 subscribers. Proudhon frequently referred to the unimpeachable merits of the bank in his new paper, *Le Peuple*, but it never left the drawing board. Despite its practical failure Proudhon was regarded as an inspiration for the numerous producer and retail co-operatives and mutual-aid societies that were set up during the republic.

When he wrote *Idée générale de la révolution* (1851), which sold 3,000 copies and was instantly reprinted, he still hoped that a democratic, self-governing Bank of Exchange could be created to replace the Bank of France. He remained convinced that if his bank were established, the fairness and harmony of the new, equitable economic structures would eliminate the need for legal and political systems and armies.

Proudhon wanted an economic, not a political, revolution, which he explained in *Confessions d'un révolutionnaire pour servir à l'histoire de la révolution de février* (Brussels, 1849). His was no class war to bring the proletariat to political power, but a new equilibrium, a just society, in which no one would suffer from extremes of deprivation and no one indulge in excess wealth. He assumed that the basis of this change would be moral and that man, a fairly rational being, would see its benefits. The state had no role to play. When prince Napoleon, son of Jérôme Bonaparte, asked Proudhon what would be his ideal society, he answered, 'I dream of a society in which I would be guillotined as a conservative.'

During the early decades of the Third Republic Proudhon was seen as an example for anarchist, federalist and trade union groups. He is often excluded from accounts of socialism, but he had a substantial impact on its development. He condemned socialists as unrealistic utopians, yet his solutions were as idealistic as those of Fourier and Cabet. He rejected state-led socialism; socialism had to come from the people. Like many early socialists, Proudhon thought political institutions far less important than economic to the reform of society. His views were sometimes conflicting, ambivalent or unpopular. He proclaimed himself both a republican and an anarchist, the former signifying no specific system, the latter simply meaning an opponent of a centralized regime dominated by one man or a small group. He was, like all early socialists, primarily a moralist. He rejected violent revolution. He had little faith in the embryonic democratic system introduced in 1848 and changed his mind several times about Louis Napoleon. Early socialists were sometimes suspicious of him because his views on politics sounded similar to those of conservatives and his hostility to women's rights exceeded anything a conservative would have dared to say.

Further reading

Two editions of Proudhon's prolific complete works were published in France, the first in twenty-six volumes (1867–70) and the second between 1923 and 1961. *Qu'est-ce-que la propriété?* is his best known and most translated work, the most recent edition being that edited by D.R. Kelly and B.G. Smith (Cambridge Texts in the History of Political Thought, 1994). The first English edition of his *Idée générale de la révolution* (1851) brought out by Freedom Press dates from 1923; the most recent (1989) is the work of R. Graham. S. Edwards edited and translated

excerpts from his huge number of books in *Selected Writings* in 1969. More has been written about Proudhon in English than about any other early French socialist.

Copley A. (1989) 'Pierre-Joseph Proudhon: A Reassessment of His Role as a Moralist', *French History* 3, 2: 194–221.
Fitzpatrick M. (1985) 'Proudhon and the French Labour Movement', *European History Quarterly* 15: 407–30.
Hoffman, R.L. (1972) *Revolutionary Justice: The Social and Political Theory of P.J.Proudhon*, Chicago: University of Illinois Press.
Pilbeam, P. (2000) *French Socialists before Marx. Workers, Women and the Social Question in France*, Teddington: Acumen.
Vincent K.S. (1984) *Pierre-Joseph Proudhon and the Rise of French Republican Socialism*, Oxford: Oxford University Press.
Woodcock G. (1987) *P.J. Proudhon: A Biography*, 3rd edn, Montreal: Black Rose Books.

SEE ALSO: Bakunin, Mikhail; Deroin, Jeanne; early socialism; Godwin, William; Kropotkin, Pietr

PAMELA PILBEAM

PSYCHOLOGY, THE EMERGENCE OF

'Psychology has a long past but a short history'

An essay about the development of nineteenth-century psychology can be appropriately prefaced by that most clichéd of quotations about the subject's past. Although the words are claimed by many, it is most often attributed to the German experimental psychologist Herman Ebbinghaus whose longstanding self-absorption with learning three-letter nonsense syllables, and the propagation of similar work, epitomized much of the novelty of nineteenth-century psychology. Thus we had a growing attachment to exuberant empiricism, which increasingly meant the explicit and self-conscious selection and manipulation of fragments of the external world, coupled with a gathering restriction on what the organism could think, or say, or do about such selections and manipulations. A major inspiration for this increasingly controlled set of practices was physiology, particularly the early experimental exploration of the nervous system and the senses. It should not, however, be assumed that such efforts lacked an intellectual context; as we will see here, 'Psychology is philosophy pursued by other means.' This philosophical move also took the form, in some writers' hands, of a kind of moral discourse, that is to say that what was judged to be the case as far as human action and belief were concerned was often mixed up with what should be the case (see Richards 1995 on the moral project that formed much nineteenth-century US psychology). Such a tendency was compounded even more by descriptions of the person that allowed for the possibility of moral improvement; thus in Alexander Bain's psychology of the 1850s the intellect and the will could control or direct the unruly emotions (Bain 1855, 1859). Thus, nineteenth-century psychology is characterized by the growth of a physiology-inspired experimentation, nurtured within pre-existing, but also evolving, philosophical, conceptual and moral frameworks, with the whole enterprise devoted to the study of human (and animal!) consciousness.

One other point to make is that the bulk of nineteenth-century psychology seemed to be concerned almost exclusively with the individual and with the self. There were no strong collectivist traditions as we understand them today; no ready use of Marx (see MARX AND MARXISM) or Engels, even though both had much to say about psychology and consciousness as the product of social and economic forces (for a useful introduction to their psychological views, see Smith 1997: 433–51). Indeed the nearest that, say, JOHN STUART MILL or Bain in the middle of the century came to a social accounting was when they talked about the individual's moral responsibility to the group, since for them society was no more than a collection of individuals (see Charpentier 2002 for a recent coverage of this neglected aspect of their joint work). Even as late as the early twentieth century, the British psychologist Stout was only able to invoke the social as a kind of moral and reciprocal mirror where the *other* acted as the reflective surface for the self. Here the major role accorded the other was as the judge of one's own actions and beliefs, whose expression could be altered depending on the reactions to them of the other, with the other presumably being similarly shaped by *one's* reactions to them (Stout 1907: 538–45). This notion of Stout's, which draws heavily on the work of the US Pragmatic philosopher Royce, seems to parallel William James's notion of the social self where

'a man has as many social selves as there are individuals who recognise him' (1890: 281).

'Time present and time past': James's *Principles*

The most influential nineteenth-century textbook in the English language on the nature, content and practices of psychology was William James's *The Principles of Psychology,* which first appeared in 1890 and was then reprinted 'innumerable times' (to quote the publishers of the authoritative version of 1981). Given that any major textbook both recapitulates the past as well as telling it as it is, so James's *Principles* says something about the past and the present of the subject, while even the future of psychology is not excluded since the book has had a serious influence long after its initial publication.

William James was trained both as doctor and as a philosopher (see Fancher 1990 and Richards 1996 for short and lively accounts of his life and work, including his attachment to Pragmatism, that most American of philosophies and rules for the moral life). Both interests are present in the extensive chapters in the *Principles* on neurophysiology as the materialistic basis for any modern psychology (including the study of movement), as well as in the speculative neuromuscular networks outlined in the chapter on the will. Further, the coverage of what he termed the Mind–Stuff Theory (which contained a sturdy refutation of the role of the unconscious), the treatment of epistemology and the nature of reality, and the systematic laying out of the material in all the chapters shows his commitment to the intellectualized nature of psychology, and how it should be pursued as argumentation. There is also James's utilization of the outcomes of experimental psychology, from the extensive descriptions of the physical stimuli to investigate spatial perception and the findings from their employment, to the quantitative outcomes of experiments on attention by Wundt and his students. (This was in spite of his assertion that Wundt's notoriously lengthy experimental investigations 'could hardly have arisen in a country whose natives could be *bored*' – 1890: 192, James's emphasis). Furthermore, James's early declaration that psychology is a natural science would not look out of place in a modern introductory text, while the bulk of the chapter headings would seem equally familiar. Thus we have Functions of the

Brain, Attention, Memory, Perception of Time and Space, the Stream of Thought, Reasoning, etc., but with the odd exceptions such as Instincts, Hypnotism and the more obviously philosophical chapters listed earlier. None of this is surprising since James was the critical, immensely well-read and entirely non-parochial heir to what was current and what had gone before in Britain and Europe.

There is one area, however, in which James shows both his acute sense of the danger lying in this past material and an overwhelming need to draw its fangs: this is in the psychologist's treatment of the self as an experimental object. There are at least two places where he lays out the possibility, if not the actuality, of what psychologists can and must do in treating minds as objects in exactly the same way as chemists or biologists treat their subject matter, thus ensuring that psychology can adopt a natural-science approach. The first is contained on pp. 183 to 185 of Chapter 7, *The Methods and Snares of Psychology*, where the psychologist, by virtue of their skills and training, can become 'a reporter of subjective as well as objective facts' (1890: 184–5). To help achieve this, James both differentiates between several 'realities' (*The Psychologist*; *The Thought Studied*; *The Thought's Object*; *The Psychologist's Reality*) that combine to form the 'irreducible data of psychology' and, in his critical sections on Introspection, shows how the psychologist can avoid the fallacies of using this key experimental technique in reporting on the thought studied and its various contexts. For James, embodied minds form the stuff of psychology, not the detached ones posited by his bugaboo IMMANUEL KANT, whose anti-psychology views are robustly savaged. Thus, when James considers the *Transcendental Self*, whose prime mover he takes to be Kant, the knives are out: 'Kant's own statements are too lengthy and too obscure for verbatim quotation here' (1890: 341), and 'Kant's way of describing the facts is mythological' (1890: 344), and 'With Kant, complication of both thought and statement was an inborn infirmity, enhanced by the musty academicism of his Königsberg existence' (1890: 346). Although such *ad hominem* outbursts are matched by more considered argument, one eventually finds James reasserting his earlier diagram of the four psychological realities, but now supplemented by what he argued were the calamitous confoundings forced onto psychology by Kant and his followers,

with the *Psychologist* and *Thought* becoming the *Transcendental Ego*, *Thought's Object* and the *Psychologist's Reality* telescoped into the *World*, with all of them subsumed under the *Absolute Self-Consciousness* (1890: 346). For James to have given in to so drastic a challenge to the '*irreducible* data of psychological science' (1890: 346, my emphasis) would have meant that the century-long attempt to establish psychology as a natural science had have been set at nought. So how was psychology-as-science actually achieved?

One upon a time in the West

The start of the nineteenth century was not propitious for any form of empirical psychology since Kant, the most influential philosopher of the period, had ruled that the self which was the origin of all our beliefs and actions was entirely inaccessible to either the person themselves or by extension to anyone else. This was quite simply because the self, which was taken by Kant to be 'pure self-consciousness', was unable to reflect on itself, since this form of the self was 'not ... an object of experience', but was a 'necessary condition of experience' (all quotations from Körner 1955: 112). Thus neither experimentation as practised by the scientist nor systematic introspection (the empirical tool of the theoretician and philosopher) would be able to uncover this foundational self. All that one could do was to list and describe the nature of the given or *a priori* categories of knowledge about the world as ways of accounting for our knowledge about the world, and to treat the outward expression of the foundational self as a mere presentation rather than the thing itself. It is not too much to argue that attempts to overthrow this doctrine were one of the major driving forces behind much of nineteenth-century psychology, as we saw earlier in James's treatment of the self.

The only form of psychology allowed by Herbart, who was Kant's material and philosophical successor at Königsberg, was what he termed the 'statics and Dynamics of the Soul', an interesting if, in its historical context, somewhat bizarre attempt to model the collision of hard and soft ideas in the mind using contemporary mathematical methods (see Boring 1950 for the most complete account extant of Herbart's formal system). What is more significant about Herbart for later German psychology, however, is his continuing use of an idea first suggested by Leibniz, then reinterpreted by Kant and incorporated into his own system of the *a priori*, that is, the notion of *apperception*. For Leibniz, apperception was the reflected-on version of the percept or the original sensation. In Kant's hands, apperception became the permanent and omnipresent link between the inaccessible self (and hence its unobservable operations) and its external presentations or expressions. Thus reflection on a percept was, in principle, possible by the self, but the nature of its activity could only be inferred at best from the resulting and external presentations. The problem for the start of the century, therefore, became whether one could have a psychology consisting of the study of the pure self or ego, or one that merely investigated its products.

An important starting-point here is the work of the Scottish School, which is often linked to the earlier intellectual movement of the Scottish Enlightenment, including the School's fundamental rejection of the views of David Hume, often cited as the movement's *crème de la crème*. Hume is best known for his thoroughgoing empiricism and associationism, and its more radical extensions (in his case to account for causality), where associationism argues that human ideas are formed from the simple conjunction of external events in time and space. The Scottish School rejected such a foundationless approach to moral belief and action, and instead invoked the notion of a Common Sense, that is, a source of built-in and collective truths about the world which allowed one access to the 'the commonsense of mankind', whose 'original and natural judgements' were the 'inspiration of the Almighty' (Thomas Reid 1764; cited in Leahey 2000: 178–80). Although Reid's student DUGALD STEWART was more favourably inclined to Hume, the School nevertheless assumed certain innate *powers* or *faculties* of the mind, which could be explored by informal empirical means (Stewart, for instance, pointed to the limits of human attention by noting that it was impossible to look simultaneously at both eyes of another person). Stewart's topics in his *Elements of the Philosophy of the Human Mind* (1792) are, moreover, the standard ones of the emerging psychology, with chapters covering perception, memory, attention, learning and imagination. These were not, however, treated as the products of Kantian metaphysical or transcendental phenomena, but as accessible immediate truths

underwritten by God. Such a lower-level, *a priori* argument makes for a better and more empirical psychology, but there is still the stumbling block of the guarantor! The Scottish School is also of considerable international importance in that it helped launch a morally toned psychology in the USA. This was brought about in no small manner through the European peregrinations of the US physician Benjamin Rush. His time in Edinburgh brought him into contact with the Common Sense school whose Christian basis found favour with the increasing number of American colleges teaching 'moral philosophy' to their students (see Richards 1995; also Goodwin 1999, for a short section on Rush as a pioneer of physical psychiatry). The key players in the next part of our story, however, eschewed the Christian for the strongly material (and physiological). In effect this endorsed the view, contra Kant, Herbart and their followers, that psychology was actually all about the presentations and products of the self. And that the self was really to be found in its products, and that these material phenomena could be systematically related back to what was, by inference, an essentially material self.

To the Principles

Let us next consider the physiologist Weber and the astronomer Bessel, whose experimental work jointly cut the Gordian knot around psychology's throat formed from Kant's unknowable ego and the God-given moral realities of the Scottish School. Weber and Bessel's efforts indicated both the actuality of a systematic investigation of the senses and behaviour, and the essential role played by measurements such as reaction time and judgements of differences between stimuli in distinguishing between conditions. In 1834 and 1846, Weber published his experimental studies of two-point touch sensitivity and the discrimination of lifted weights (see Boring 1950). The work was systematic in that Weber tested various parts of the body and then made comparisons between the body's differential ability to distinguish between one and two points. He also noted that lifted weights were more finely discriminated if the person was actively involved in lifting the weight rather than having it placed on their outstretched palm. The lifted weight studies seemed further to suggest a simple rule linking the increase in the weight needed to make it seem heavier than a comparison weight, and the comparison weight itself, the so-called *Weber fraction*. Bessel in 1822 built on the observation that the astronomer Maskelyne had in 1796 dismissed an assistant for systematically 'mistaking' the times of stellar transits by a second. This suggested to Bessel both the existence of consistent individual differences in the timing of actions (referred to as the *personal equation*), and the possibility of using latency for differentiating between astronomical judgements. Thus a psychology beckoned that was more physiological, systematic, empirical and secular.

Gustav Fechner, the creator of psychophysics (the study of thresholds and psychological scales), drew heavily upon Weber, with the so-called *Weber–Fechner* law being only one of the results. Fechner also used Weber's approach to empirically demonstrate the truth of the holistic philosophy of panpsychism to which he was heavily committed. His *Elements of Psychophysics* was finally published in 1860, but in such a form that the philosophical components could be easily stripped out, leaving Fechner's revolutionary methodology, and his results and theories, to be plundered. This was quickly done by the most famous figure in nineteenth-century experimental psychology Wilhelm Wundt, whose laboratory in Leipzig (founded in 1879) had both helped to institutionalize the subject and had acted as a magnet for psychologists from both Europe and the USA. But Fechner was by no means the only influence on Wundt, the associationistic philosophy of John Stuart Mill, for instance, was cited by him for its experimental inspiration, while both Kant and Herbart had contributed to his structural notion of the mind through, for example, their notion of apperception. Equally important was the grounding of psychology in physiology: it should be noted, for example, that Wundt's major textbook on psychology was entitled *Principles of Physiological Psychology* (1874/1904), while his long-term association with Helmholtz at Heidelberg had impressed him with the power of a mechanistic biology. Although Wundt's principle methodology was systematic introspection, whose philosophical roots start at least as early as Kant, he was also happy to collaborate with the Dutch researcher Donders in using reaction times *à la* Bessel and Helmholtz (who had used it to measure the speed of the nervous impulse) in order to tease apart mental operations, while the continuing work on psychophysics used error counts as their basic measures.

As far as Britain was concerned, the doctrine of associationism was reasserted by J.S. Mill and Alexander Bain during the early and middle parts of the century contra the *a priori* of the Scottish School and Kant, although Bain added the structuring elements of the Emotions, the Intellect and the Will to the associationistic dynamic. He also pioneered what became the standard order of appearance in all introductory psychology textbooks in his two volumes from 1855 and 1859, that is, starting with neurophysiology and the brain, and then moving on to topics in psychology such as memory, perception, the will, etc., familiar from Dugald Stewart's *Philosophy of Mind*. Bain is also famous for founding *Mind* in 1876, the first psychology journal in English, although after the turn of the century it became the philosophical journal that it is today (see Neary 2001 on the early years of *Mind*). Although Bain strove to provide a physiological grounding for psychology where possible, the psychology of the mid-nineteenth century was too extended and too philosophical to be so easily captured. Consequently, Bain's work is as much speculative as empirical and, in this respect, not dissimilar from James's *Principles of Psychology*.

The other strand of importance in British and then US psychology is that of adaptation or meaningful change. Since this is often associated with evolutionary doctrines, it is also thought to be exclusively concerned with the impact of Darwinian thinking on psychology, particularly after the publication of the most obviously psychological of his works, *The Expression of the Emotions in Man and Animals* (1872). But just as there were several competing evolutionary accounts in the nineteenth century, so there was at least one major alternative to Darwinian adaptation in psychology; this was developed by HERBERT SPENCER who drew on the more (psychologically) congenial doctrine of Jean-Baptiste Lamarck, that is, the direct inheritance of acquired characteristics, or how the giraffe obtained (*and kept*) its long neck from generation to generation. Spencer's 1855 *Principles of Psychology* set out to synthesize the whole of psychology around an evolutionary framework, where associationism provided the mechanism for laying down psychological phenomena such as habits and instincts, with Lamarck's doctrine assuring their direct transmission to the next generation. Given such intra- and inter-generational plasticity, so the acquired actions etc. could be altered to improve one's chances of survival in the face of changing circumstances. This proved to be so potent an approach to the psychology of adaptation that William James felt obliged to take on Spencer and the Lamarckians in order to defend his hero Darwin from their attacks (1890: 1,270–80), but it was still, in 1890, a close run thing!

Crossing the frontier

All dates are collectively constructed to give order to events, but at what a cost! Thus there are people and movements who straddle the nineteenth and twentieth centuries whose contributions are often thought to belong to the latter epoch, but whose cultural and intellectual groundings are most definitely in the former. Take for example SIGMUND FREUD who, in 1900, was hardly known even in his native Vienna, but was on the verge of eventual immortality with *The Interpretation of Dreams*, and *The Psychopathology of Everyday Life* (published in 1900 and 1901 respectively). Historians have rightly taken him to be a product of the nineteenth century (see Sulloway 1979 for the rigorous application of such a thesis), but few view him culturally as anything other than a modern. Even Darwin, whose contribution to nineteenth-century work has been mentioned above, can, in some ways, be seen as exerting an even more powerful effect on twentieth-century psychology than earlier. There are similar if rather more minor figures who illustrate this problem of the arbitrariness of dates, people such as Hugo Munsterberg who, although a nineteenth-century Wundtian, made his major contribution, particularly in the USA from 1900 onwards, in industrial psychology, an area that was antithetical to Wundt's notion of a scientific psychology. Equally problematic is James Broadus Watson whose Behaviourism is properly seen as belonging to the twentieth century, but whose education crossed the two centuries, and some of whose direct influences were distinctly nineteenth century, for example the reductive and mechanistic biologist Jacques Loeb; while Stout (1907) and James Ward (1885) in Britain seemed to point both backwards to Fechner and forwards to twentieth-century Gestalt psychology with their adherence to a holistic and top-down account of the mind in opposition to Bain's associationism.

References

Bain, A. (1855) *The Senses and the Intellect*, London: Longmans.
—— (1859) *The Emotions and the Will*, London: Longmans.
Boring, E.G. (1950) *A History of Experimental Psychology*, second edn, New York: Appleton-Century-Crofts.
Charpentier, L. (2002) 'Clarifying the Utilitarian Meaning in Alexander Bain's Association Psychology', unpublished PhD thesis, University of Edinburgh, UK.
Darwin, C. (1872) *The Expression of the Emotions in Man and Animals*, London: Murray.
Fancher, R.E. (1990) *Pioneers of Psychology*, second edn, New York: Norton.
Fechner, G. (1860) *Elements of Psychophysics*, New York: Holt, Rinehart & Winston [translation dated 1966 by H.E. Adler of *Elemente der Psychophysik*, Volume 1, Breitkopf & Härtel].
Goodwin, C.J. (1999) *A History of Modern Psychology*, New York: Wiley.
James, W. (1890) *The Principles of Psychology*, Cambridge, MA: Harvard University Press [Harvard Approved Edition, 1981; originally published by Holt in two volumes].
Körner, S. (1955) *Kant*, Harmondsworth: Penguin.
Leahey, T.H. (2000) *A History of Psychology*, fifth edn, New Jersey: Prentice Hall.
Neary, F. (2001) 'A Question of "Peculiar Importance": George Croom Robertson, Mind and the Changing Relationship between British Psychology and Philosophy', in G. Bunn, A.D. Lovie and G.D. Richards (eds) *Psychology in Britain*, London: BPS Books and Science Museum, pp. 54–71.
Richards, G. D. (1995) 'To Know our Fellow Men to do Them Good': American Psychology's Continuing Moral Project', *History of the Human Sciences*, 8, 3: 1–24.
—— (1996) *Putting Psychology in its Place*, London: Routledge.
Smith, R. (1997) *The Fontana History of the Human Sciences*, London: Fontana Press.
Spencer, H. (1855) *Principles of Psychology*, London: Longman.
Stewart, D. (1797) *Elements of the Philosophy of the Human Mind*, London: Straham & Caddell.
Stout, G. F. (1907) *A Manual of Psychology*, fourth edn, London: University Tutorial Press.
Sulloway, F.J. (1979) *Freud, Biologist of the Mind: Beyond the Psychoanalytic Legend*, New York: Basic Books.
Ward, J. (1885) 'Psychology', in *Encyclopaedia Britannica*, ninth edn, Edinburgh: Black.
Wundt, W. (1874) *Principles of Physiological Psychology*, New York: Macmillan [translation dated 1904 by E.B. Titchener of *Physiologische Psychologie*, Leipzig: Engelman].

SEE ALSO: main currents in scientific thought; theories of education and character formation; theories of law, criminology and penal reform

SANDY LOVIE

R

RANKE, LEOPOLD VON (1795–1886)

Leopold von Ranke (ennobled in 1865) was a German historian who is sometimes referred to as the 'father of modern history'. He not only had a major impact on the style of German historiography right up to the mid-twentieth century but he also influenced the set-up of the academic discipline of history in Britain and the USA, in so far as he developed a methodology of historical source research and source critique.

Born a lawyer's son, he studied in the university town of Leipzig Philosophy and Protestant Theology, whereupon he started work as a grammar school teacher. In 1824, he published his first great work, *History of the Latin and Teutonic Nations from 1494 to 1514* (*Geschichte der romanischen und germanischen Völker von 1494–1535*, trans. 1887), a book that reflected his life-long desire to come to an understanding of the culture and history of the Occident and which made him instantly famous and earned him a professorship at Berlin University where he stayed from 1825 until his retirement in 1871. From 1832 to 1836 he edited the conservative journal *Historisch-politische Zeitschrift*. His conservative stance brought him close to the Prussian king Frederick William IV: in 1841 he became historiographer of the Prussian state. He was equally close to the Bavarian king Maximilian II who had been Ranke's student, and in 1858 he was appointed director of the Historical Committee of the Bavarian Academy of Sciences in Munich.

His most well-known other works are: *The Ecclesiastical and Political History of the Popes of Rome during the Sixteenth and Seventeenth Centuries* (*Die römischen Päpste, ihre Kirche und ihr Staat im 16. und 17. Jahrhundert*, 1834–6, trans. 1840); *History of the Reformation* (*Deutsche Geschichte im Zeitalter der Reformation*, 1839–47, trans. 1845–7); *Memoirs of the House of Brandenburg and History of Prussia during the Seventeenth and Eighteenth centuries* (*Neun Bücher preussischer Geschichte*, 1847–8, trans. 1849; new extended German edition entitled *Zwölf Bücher preussischer Geschichte*, 1874); *Civil Wars and Monarchy in France, in the Sixteenth and Seventeenth Centuries* (*Französische Geschichte, vornehmlich im 16. und 17. Jahrhundert*, 1852–61, books 1–6 trans. 1852); *A History of England, Principally in the Seventeenth Century* (*Englische Geschichte, vornehmlich im 16. und 17. Jahrhundert*, 1859–68, trans. 1875).

Ranke stood for a narrative history with a claim to portray history 'as it actually was' – '*wie es eigentlich gewesen*' – a famous and often cited dictum found in the preface to his *History of the Latin and Teutonic Nations*. He demanded to study history without any preconceived ideas induced by some dogmatic superstructure: he broke with the Enlightenment model of history as a 'teacher' with 'teaching goals'. It was not the task of the historian to judge the past and preach to the present; history should be understood out of itself, not out of the present and with the questionable benefit of hindsight. Ranke rejected the Hegelian notion of seeing in each epoch only the early stage for the following ones (see HEGEL AND HEGELIANISM); he repudiated any kind of teleological constructions of a philosophy of history that would already know its ending. On the other hand, Ranke did not approve of the Romantics' tendency to see certain historical epochs as being closer to God's heart than others: instead, every epoch showed other aspects of the God-given human spirit and was thus equally valuable. So, in Ranke's eyes, each generation, each historical epoch was 'immediate to God' – never a mere transitory station in the development towards some, however defined, goal in history. It was not progress in history he was looking for, but history's truth. Individuals determining the course of history were both free in their decisions and dependent on the historical circumstances of their respective epoch. Ranke was interested in the histories of states and peoples as original creations of the spirit of man and thus as 'thoughts of God', each one of them being unique. Searching for the prevailing ideas in history, he was ultimately looking for God in history whilst stressing that one could not discern from the historical events as such God's ultimate design for the world. Although deeply religious, he always remained a secular historian.

The method he advised historians to adopt was to 'understand' historical facts and developments in their genesis and to refrain from 'explaining' them by means of mechanistic cause–effect models and historical 'laws'. Such an 'understanding' of history was at the heart of 'historicism' – the prevailing philosophy of history in the nineteenth century. Ranke saw the historian's task in comprehending history's individual phenomena embedded in an understanding of the general principles weaving through them.

Ranke demanded to go 'back to the sources': not relying on historians' accounts but writing history solely based on the detailed study and philological-textual analysis of documents such as diaries, private letters, public reports or diplomatic dispatches. He did himself what he preached, extensively touring during his life archives in Germany, Austria, Italy, France and England. His methodology of historical source research and source critique became instrumental world-wide in setting up history as an academic-scientific discipline.

Ranke was convinced that his conception of history and his historical method were objective and free from the value judgements of the historian investigating historical facts. In the twentieth century such presuppositions were increasingly being questioned, stressing the notion that every question asked by a historian relates to the respective present and its value systems and perceptions of the world. Still, until the 1950s, the historical discipline in Germany remained strongly attached to the principles of historicism and to Ranke's 'primacy of foreign policy' and his focus on political history, embarking at a much later stage on the course initiated by Western European historiography in the realm of social history. Ranke's most enduring legacy is his admonition to 'go back to the archives' and to subject original sources to a methodical analysis and critique.

Further reading

Krieger, L. (1977) *Ranke: The Meaning of History*, Chicago: University of Chicago Press.

Laue, T.H. von (1950) *Leopold von Ranke: The Formative Years*, Princeton: Princeton University Press.

Mommsen, W.J. (ed.) (1988) *Leopold von Ranke und die moderne Geschichtswissenschaft*, Stuttgart: Klett Cotta.

Powell, J.M. and Iggers, G.G. (1990) *Leopold von Ranke and the Shaping of the Historical Discipline*, Syracuse, NY: Syracuse University Press.

SEE ALSO: historiography and the idea of progress

DETMAR KLEIN

RELIGION, SECULARIZATION AND THE CRISIS OF FAITH

Secularization is a process whereby religion becomes less and less significant in a society. Usually the term also carries the added connotation that this process is an inevitable by-product of modern social changes or modern thought. While it has been traditional to view the West in the nineteenth century as having been marked by secularization, since the 1980s this judgement has been increasingly challenged. Historians have disagreed sharply about when secularization happened, where it happened, why it happened and even whether or not it happened. De-Christianisation, anti-clericalism, the rise of religious pluralism, the decrease of institutional patterns of behaviour and what might be termed the decline of Christendom are all trends that arguably have often been confused with secularization in past discussions. What is clear is that the separation of Church and state was a strong trend in the nineteenth century, and that European church attendance declined in the late nineteenth and early twentieth centuries. It is also apparent that in nineteenth-century Europe and North America there was a much more vocal, visible and influential group of people articulating a thoroughgoing denial of religious beliefs than had been the case in the past. In addition to numerous popular radicals, these unbelievers included a significant number of leading intellectuals – philosophers, writers, scientists and others – whose opinions carried considerable weight and aroused much interest. When many of these figures retold the story of their personal development, they included as a central, formative event the time when they came to the point where they could no longer give their adherence to the faith of their forebears. The primary intellectual factors that triggered these crises of faith were the challenge of biblical criticism, the clash between religion and various scientific ideas – most obviously Darwinism – and a moral critique of Christian doctrine. Political commitments and new professional identities were strong prompts towards unbelief that were less directly an intellectual challenge. Any theory that assumes that such changes were inevitable or irreversible, however, is brought into question by countervailing patterns in which erstwhile sceptics or subsequent generations returned to faith. Some scholars have also attributed secularization to more impersonal as well as non-intellectual factors such as industrialization and urbanization.

Secularization

Those who maintain that secularization has occurred have supported their claims by pointing towards a variety of different factors, most notably Church–state relations, religious practice and religious belief. Changes in Church–state relations during the nineteenth century can be easily demonstrated, but it is problematic to enlist this evidence as proof of secularization. There is no doubt that the separation of Church and state was accelerating during this period. The campaign for Italian unification brought the papal states to an end. In 1870 Rome was made the capital of the Italian state and the temporal authority of the papacy effectively ceased. France saw the aggressive implementation of purely secular state education in the latter decades of the nineteenth century, and the formal separation of Church and state in 1905. The British Isles saw the steady erosion of Church establishments as well, including disestablishment in Ireland in 1869. In the 1850s the Canadian colonial legislature appropriated for secular use land that had been hitherto reserved in order to generate income

for clergymen of the established churches of England and Scotland. Nevertheless, while this trend is indisputable, it is less clear that it carries the weight that is usually given to the term 'secularization'. The USA, after all, is often viewed as both the Western nation that is most vigilant about the absolute separation of Church and state and the least secularized one. Some critics of secularization theory have argued that religious changes in the modern West are better viewed in terms of a market model or religious economies. From this perspective, established churches are often seen as complacent monopolies that induce popular alienation from religious participation, perhaps leading on to an erosion of religious belief, while removing them might create religious vitality in a society through an energized religious market. An interesting case study for an examination of the relationship between Church–state issues and secularization is nineteenth-century England. The steady removal of the privileges of the Church of England, for example the ending in 1868 of compulsory Church rates (taxes in order to support Anglican worship), came about not through a general weakening of the importance of faith in society, but rather as the result of a forceful political campaign by Nonconformists who were typically deeply devout Christians with an alternative theological vision that prompted a rejection of Church establishments. In order to avoid the jarring conclusion that secularization happened because loyal people of faith tenaciously demanded it, it might be better to refer to this change as the death of Christendom, or de-Christendomization, a process whereby the Church using or benefiting from the power of the state is curtailed or ended.

It also seems apparent that religious practice as measured by church attendance generally declined in Western Europe in the late nineteenth and early twentieth centuries. Once again, however, questions need to be asked regarding the extent to which this change might fittingly be labelled 'secularization'. There is evidence to indicate that church attendance was even lower, for example in the medieval period, and yet it would empty secularization of its import to apply it to that situation. It has been argued that factors unrelated to the abandonment of religious beliefs such as the increased availability of leisure and recreational opportunities may account for modern decreases in church attendance. One line of thought in this regard is that perhaps many of those who moved closer to unbelief did not stop attending because they stopped believing, but rather stopped believing because they stopped attending. Moreover, the vast majority continued to affirm religious ideas such as belief in God; a significant pattern of people 'believing without belonging' has been identified. Whatever the reason, a weakening of ties with organized religion was a noticeable trend. In the Netherlands, only 1,000 people reported that they had no religious affiliation in the 1859 census; by the 1899 census, however, their ranks had swelled to 115,000.

Arguably, the clearest evidence for secularization would be a steady decline in religious belief. It is beyond question that the nineteenth-century West witnessed the rise of articulate unbelievers – including those who forcefully denied all religious beliefs – in a way without precedent. Nevertheless, the assumption sometimes implicit in secularization theory that such people were the vanguard of the future is less certain. A strong case can be made that the dominant trend is not actually secularization but rather the rise of religious pluralism (perhaps as a by-product of de-Christendomization), with atheism and other unbelieving or sceptical traditions being amongst the options in the religious market. It is also necessary to make a distinction between secularization and de-Christianization. For example, a significant trend amongst nineteenth-century 'secularists' was a move into spiritualism. In England, ROBERT OWEN, who had led an attack on Christianity in the name of rationalism, is a prime example of this trend. Influential figures in other areas of supposed secular advance who also became enamored with spiritualism were ALFRED RUSSEL WALLACE, the co-discoverer of what came to be known as 'Darwinism', and Sir Arthur Conan Doyle (the hyper-rationalism of his fictional creation, Sherlock Holmes, notwithstanding). VICTOR HUGO is an example of a French freethinker who developed an interest in spiritualism. It would seem more appropriate to view embracing spiritualism as opting for an alternative spirituality than as evidence for secularization. Another example would be US intellectuals such as RALPH WALDO EMERSON and HENRY DAVID THOREAU who replaced traditional Christian beliefs with Transcendentalism, a movement that also may justly be viewed as an alternative spiritual tradition. At the start of the twenty-first century, it became increasingly popular for

scholars to argue that the secularization of the West took place during the 1960s, a view that retains a commitment to secularization theory while simultaneously conceding that it is not relevant to nineteenth-century studies. Nevertheless, whether or not it is helpful to think of the nineteenth-century West in terms of 'secularization', the very real intellectual challenges to faith that arose at that time are certainly an important aspect of the contours of the thought of the period.

Biblical criticism and moral critiques

The nineteenth century produced a harvest of writings in a discipline that was just then emerging: modern biblical criticism. Such studies questioned traditional readings, especially regarding the historical nature and accuracy of biblical narratives, as well as the authorship of various biblical documents, their date of composition and their unity as single-authored works emanating from a particular person with a particular purpose in mind at a particular time. Germans led the way in this field. F.C. Baur was the scholar at the centre of the radical Tübingen school of New Testament studies. The most explosive work of German biblical criticism, however, was unquestionably D.F. STRAUSS's *Life of Jesus* (1835). It is probable that no single work written in the nineteenth century – not even Charles Darwin's *On the Origin of the Species* – provoked more crises of faith in the West than this one. Strauss argued for a mythical view of the accounts in the gospels. In other words, these stories could not be credibly explained in either supernatural or naturalist ways and should instead be viewed as unhistorical tales that evolved over time as a result of religious assumptions or expectations. Ultimately, Strauss admitted that he no longer could consider himself a Christian. Strauss's *Life of Jesus* provoked innumerable crises of faith. Among those influenced by Strauss was the German communist Friedrich Engels, who was set on his road to unbelief by reading this work. The English novelist George Eliot (Marian Evans), who had been raised as an evangelical, was led to abandon orthodox Christianity through her encounter with this text. Moreover, her translation of it into English, published in 1846, led to many more such encounters, including a significant impact amongst popular radicals, with the loss of faith of the Chartist leader Thomas Cooper being perhaps the most prominent example. Cooper, in turn, recapitulated Strauss's ideas in his popular *Cooper's Journal*, and thus the process of dissemination continued.

Biblical criticism was so unsettling in Protestant countries because the Bible had come to be viewed as the foundational authority for all true religion by so many of their inhabitants. Criticism of the gospels, as Strauss had done, was particularly undermining because it also simultaneously challenged traditional views of Christ. Moreover, Roman Catholic countries were not immune either. ERNEST RENAN's *Life of Jesus* (1863), which had a substantial impact in his native France and beyond, offered a portrait of Christ that was devoid of miracles. For popular radicals in the English-speaking world, the somewhat crude anti-Bible polemic offered in THOMAS PAINE's *The Age of Reason* (1793) was another influential trigger for crises of faith.

It is also clear that moral critiques of the contents of the Bible, Christian theology and the behaviour of the Church, and of Christian leaders and Christians generally, induced numerous crises of faith. Christian doctrines such as endless punishment in hell, predestination and substitutionary atonement struck many as morally offensive, thus making Christianity as a whole seem untenable for some. Romanticist intellectual currents helped to reposition these once widely accepted doctrines in this more unfavourable light in the eyes of many (see ROMANTICISM, INDIVIDUALISM AND IDEAS OF THE SELF). The English philosopher HERBERT SPENCER attributed his loss of faith to his growing moral objections to Christian teaching, and a study of plebeian radicals has argued that moral objections to religion loomed largest in their accounts of their moves into unbelief.

Science and Darwinism

As the nineteenth century progressed, scientific thought was often viewed as undermining faith, and was repeatedly employed with that intent. In Germany, materialist scientific ideas often assailed religious belief. Carl Vogt's *Blind Faith and Science* (1854) was followed the next year by Ludwig Büchner's *Force and Matter* (1855), both highly influential books, and their authors were both prominent models of men of science who opposed religion. The scientific work with by far the most ripple effects, however, was undoubtedly Charles Darwin's *On the Origin of the Species* (1859). Darwinism was considered by many to

be a challenge to faith because it appeared to undermine the notion that human beings were unique creatures made in the image of God and possessing an immortal soul and a moral nature that set them apart from animals. It also did not seem reconcilable with a more literal interpretation of the accounts in the book of Genesis of the origin of the species. Furthermore, it assumed that cruelty, violence and death on a massive scale were written into the very pattern of life, a notion that seemed incompatible with belief in a good, loving and all-powerful divine creator. Losses of faith ensued. Darwin himself quietly became an agnostic. The English mathematician and philosopher W.K. Clifford had his crisis of faith due to his encounter with Darwinism, and then proceeded to add to the sceptical tradition by arguing that it was immoral to believe something without sufficient evidence (something that he thought religious claims lacked). The German scientist Ernst Haeckel also lost his faith through imbibing Darwin's work. He went on to unsettle the faith of many others by disseminating Darwinism, notably in his *History of Creation* (1868) and *The Riddle of the Universe* (1899).

It must be borne in mind, however, that many Christians did not believe that Darwinism was incompatible with faith and readily harmonized it. For example, the leading champion of Darwinism in the USA, the Harvard professor Asa Gray, was a theologically conservative Christian. The so-called 'battle between science and religion' was, to a certain extent, manufactured by scientists who personally disliked religion, who opposed it for political reasons or who felt that it was necessary to curb the authority of religion in order to develop a new profession for themselves (being scientists) that would be recognized as having its own sphere of authority in which it was the final arbiter of what is true. T.H. HUXLEY, the scientist who championed Darwinism in England, is an example of someone who took this combative approach. Huxley also made an enduring contribution to the conceptualization of unbelief by coining the word 'agnosticism' in 1869. In the USA, the war metaphor of the relationship between scientific and religious thought was advanced through J.W. Draper's *History of the Conflict between Religion and Science* (1874) and A.D. White's *History of the Warfare of Science with Theology in Christendom* (1896). Darwinism was also unsettling because it undermined the argument from design, the notion that the evidence of order, design and intentionality in creation proved that there must have been a divine creator. Christians had employed this argument so prominently that it almost came to be viewed as a kind of tenet of faith. By giving a cogent alternative explanation for the evidence for design in nature, Darwinism dislodged a prominent plank of Christian apologetics and gave numerous people confidence that it was possible to have a credible world-view without recourse to religious ideas. Although Darwinism sometimes prompted crises of faith, more often people who were already alienated from religion latched onto it as an alternative way to understand the world, and these individuals sometimes enlisted Darwinism as a powerful weapon in campaigns to undermine faith.

Scientific work in other disciplines also contributed to crises of faith, the fields of anthropology and comparative religion being prime examples. Studies of more 'primitive' societies in remote parts of the world undercut the notion that one's own religion was the result of divine revelation and instead fostered the suspicion that it was simply the product of culture. Christian beliefs regarding atonement and baptism, for example, could lose their unique import once one perceived analogies to tribal sacrificial and purification rituals elsewhere. A Canadian sea captain, Robert C. Adams, who came to such conclusions through his travels, went on to be a vocal unbeliever. Sir John Lubbock's *Pre-Historic Times* (1865) and *The Origins of Civilization* (1870) triggered crises of faith along these lines. The work of the anthropologist Edward Burnett Tylor further served to unsettle believers.

Secular prophets

The nineteenth century also produced figures who predicted that humanity would leave religion behind as it progressed toward maturity. To a certain extent, these became self-fulfilling prophesies as some people were convinced by these ideas and then abandoned their religion in order to keep in step with the proclaimed march of progress. One of the most influential of such figures was the French philosopher AUGUSTE COMTE. In his Positivism, Comte argued that human knowledge advanced through three stages: the theological, the metaphysical and the positive (scientific). Therefore, appeals to the supernatural or the divine reflected the most primitive attempts to grasp reality and were destined to be replaced by higher lines of thought. Comte also developed a 'Religion of

Humanity' that was intended to fulfil some of the social and cultural functions of religion, although T.H. Huxley waggishly dismissed it as 'Catholicism minus Christianity'. Even so, Comte had a significant impact in Europe and beyond.

The greatest of the nineteenth-century secular prophets, however, was Karl Marx (see MARX AND MARXISM). Marx, a German, was the leading theorist of communism and critic of capitalism. He was convinced that the existing political and economic structures were inherently and profoundly unjust, and he heralded a better world that would be achieved through class struggle. He opposed religion as an illusory distraction from these realities, famously terming it 'the opium of the people'. Since religious and economic injustice mutually reinforce each other, overcoming the one implied overcoming the other. Marx, like Comte, proclaimed that humanity would move beyond religion and that the future would ultimately be a totally secular one. Linking an anti-religious message with radical politics proved particularly compelling, inducing many European popular radicals to make a break with religion.

Attention should also be drawn to those intellectuals who attacked Christianity directly and vehemently in ways that were particularly lucid and penetrating. The two most important of such figures were German: FEUERBACH and NIETZSCHE. Ludwig Feuerbach's most famous work was *The Essence of Christianity* (1841). In it, he argued that we recognize our own ideal and potential selves in the mirror of our notions about God, the optical illusion of which spells spiritual alienation. Overcoming such alienation, in effect, secularizes religious doctrines to the degree that they are reducible to human ideals that unfold from within our own nature. For many, this was a conclusive admission that theology was just anthropology. Friedrich Nietzsche, the originator of the notion that God is dead, uncompromisingly attacked Christianity in such provocatively entitled works as *Beyond Good and Evil* (1886) and *The Anti-Christ* (1889). In his *On the Genealogy of Morals* (1887), Nietzsche analysed the sacrificial and ascetic values of Christianity, finding them resentful and self-destructive.

Politics and professions

Intellectual ideas are always received in a concrete context that also exerts its own influence. Political commitments proved one of the most important factors influencing people to abandon religion in the nineteenth century. Religion was frequently viewed as aligned with ruling elites and conservative politics, and therefore, conversely, irreligion became a political weapon, a way of furthering radical politics. Radicals, of course, often had good evidence from which to deduce that the Church was one of their main opponents. In 1864, for example, Pope Pius IX had issued the Syllabus of Errors, making it quite explicit that the papacy would not bend to accommodate liberal political trends. An Italian nationalist such as GIUSEPPE MAZZINI knew that anti-clericalism was essential to his struggle. Political antagonisms polarized France and Germany into conservative factions who championed the cause of the Church and radical factions who made a point of repudiating religion. In the last third of the nineteenth century, French republicans and German Social Democrats both created political cultures that exerted pressure on adherents to dispense with their religion. Many socialists came to view religious commitments as unwelcome because they produced divided loyalties.

It has already been noted that some scientists attacked religion as a way of establishing the legitimacy of their own emerging profession and its claims to speak authoritatively. Other professional identities, however, also were sometimes particularly apt to produce unbelievers – less as an occupational hazard then as a badge of membership. For example, in France both the teaching and the medical profession had high numbers of unbelievers due to efforts to carve out their professional domain in the face of opposition from the Roman Catholic Church. Being a freethinker also became a possible profession in its own right in the nineteenth century, with most countries having figures who made a vocation of speaking, writing and editing in a sceptical vein. CHARLES BRADLAUGH in England, Robert G. Ingersoll in the USA, Viktor Lennstrand in Sweden and Fernando Lozano in Spain are prominent examples of such figures. Many secularist or freethinking societies were founded in the nineteenth century. In retrospect, these often look remarkably similar to small religious denominations or sects, although in France a mass freethinking movement did flourish.

In conclusion, it is important to keep nineteenth-century trends toward unbelief in perspective. A crisis of faith, after all, could be resolved by a reaffirmation of religious belief as well as abandonment of it, and a lost faith might later

be regained. In mid-Victorian England, for example, a significant number of popular radicals who championed unbelief later came back to faith and actively and publicly defended it, including Thomas Cooper, the disseminator of Strauss's ideas. The intellectual climate in France in the late nineteenth and early twentieth centuries was also marked by a wave of erstwhile sceptics rediscovering the Church including, most symbolically, the writer Ernest Psichari, a grandson of Ernest Renan. In many ways, the nineteenth century must be recognized as a remarkably religious age, especially in the British Isles and North America. Even the crises of faith themselves may be viewed as a perverse tribute to the religious intensity of the period. Nevertheless, it is beyond doubt that in the nineteenth-century West unbelief was being publicly and forcefully championed to a hitherto unprecedented extent.

Further reading

Chadwick, O. (1975) *The Secularization of the European Mind in the Nineteenth Century*, Cambridge: Cambridge University Press.

Larsen, T. (2001) 'The Regaining of Faith: Reconversions among Popular Radicals in Mid-Victorian England', *Church History* 70, 3: 527–43.

McLeod, H. (2000) *Secularisation in Western Europe, 1848–1914*, London: Macmillan.

Turner, J. (1985) *Without God, without Creed: The Origins of Unbelief in America*, Baltimore: Johns Hopkins University Press.

SEE ALSO: conservatism, authority and tradition; historiography and the idea of progress; Romanticism, individualism and ideas of the self

TIMOTHY LARSEN

RENAN, JOSEPH-ERNEST (1823–1892)

Renan served several genres (history, Semitic philology, philosophy) but he made his name – and many an enemy – primarily due to his biblical scholarship and his attempt to apply 'scientific' rigour and methods in the study of biblical tradition and the life of Jesus Christ himself. Faith in science was Renan's major animating spring. He was born in Brittany on 28 February 1823 (Renan, author of *La Poesie des Races Celtiques*, believed that his Celtic (Breton) origins balanced his rationalism with a poetic quality – a self-perception shared by his greatest British admirer Matthew Arnold, who had partly Cornish origins). Renan was educated to become a priest, completing his education in the prestigious Saint-Sulpice seminary. Yet, he did not take vows in the end. He renounced his vocation in 1849, as his historical researches and his philological study of Semitic languages led him to question the shibboleths of revealed Christianity. Subsequently to his departure from Saint-Sulpice, Renan continued to study, securing the *agrégation* in 1849 and a doctorate at the Sorbonne in 1852.

His first book, *L'Avenir de la science* (written in 1848–9, and published in 1890) showed clearly his belief in science, which would permeate his entire life and work. Renan began in the early 1850s his life-long co-operation with the *Revue des deux mondes* and the *Journal des débats*. In 1856 he married Cornelie Scheffer, with whom he had three children (two of which survived). In 1856 he was elected to the Académie des Inscriptions et Belles Lettres. And major recognition came when, in 1859, Napoleon III's education minister appointed Renan Professor of the chair of Hebraic, Chaldean and Syrian languages at the Collège de France.

At his inaugural lecture at the Collège de France (23 February 1862) Renan claimed that Jesus was such an 'incomparable man, so great [a man]', that it was understandable why so many people came to be so struck by his character and teachings as to take him for a God. This would not do for Renan though, as he thought that everything had to be judged from the point of view of positive science. Within days from the inaugural lecture, his course was suspended. When, undeterred, Renan published in 1863 his *Vie de Jésus*, where he explicitly rejected the divinity of Christ, Renan was dismissed from the Collège de France – he was to be reinstated after the republican 1870 revolution against the defeated Second Empire, in 1871, and even to become the director of the Collège from 1883 until his death in 1892.

Meanwhile, Renan published the series of books entitled *Les Origines du Christianisme*. The *Vie de Jésus* (1863) was the first in the series, to be followed by *Les Apôtres* (1866), then *Saint Paul et sa mission* (1869), until the eighth and final volume appeared in 1883.

Following France's humiliating defeat in the Franco-Prussian War, Renan published *La Réforme intellectuelle et morale de la France* (1871), where he attributed the outcome of the war to the superiority of Prussian education and exhorted France to turn to science education.

His autobiographical *Souvenirs d'enfance et de jeunesse* (1883), of which the most famous part is the *Prière sur l'Acropole,* relate the circumstances that led him to lose his faith (Fraisse 1979; Pommier 1972).

Despite his significance during his time due both to his biblical scholarship and to his standing as an inspiration for freedom-of-enquiry liberals, and despite the voluminousness of his scholarly and critical work, Renan is most remembered for his famous Sorbonne lecture *Qu'est-ce qu'une nation?* (11 March 1882), which acquired canonical status in the literature on nationalism and nationhood in the late twentieth century and since. The lecture has to be seen in the context in which it was contributed: 12 years after the Franco-Prussian War and the annexation of Alsace and much of Lorraine by the newly formed German Empire. German historians had stepped into the fray of political debate arguing that Alsace and Lorraine were German by right, because the population of the two provinces spoke German and shared a German culture more generally. Renan begged to differ. Language, culture or race were not enough to define a nation, according to him. What Renan offered instead is what is still considered to be the best known articulation of the theory that nationality is primarily a matter of will, of the desire of a group of people to live together, and an eloquent exposition of how such a desire comes about. Some of his statements in the lecture have been quoted innumerable times. The significance of some of his statements in that text has been highlighted in one of the most successful late twentieth-century books on the origins of nationalism, Benedict Anderson's *Imagined Communities* (1991). Some of his statements in that lecture have become very well known and oft-quoted:

A nation is a soul, a spiritual principle. Two things, which are really only one, go to make up this soul or spiritual principle. One of these things lies in the past, the other in the present. The one is the possession in common of a rich heritage of memories; and the other is actual agreement, the desire to live together, and the will to continue to make the most of the joint inheritance.

(Renan 1995: 153)

And, as he put it in the most quoted sentence in the lecture:

> The existence of a nation is (if you will forgive me the metaphor) a daily plebiscite, just as that of the individual is a continual affirmation of life [emphasis added].... A province means to us its inhabitants; and if anyone has a right to be consulted in the matter, it is the inhabitant. It is never to the true interest of a nation to annex or keep a country against its will. The people's wish is after all the only justifiable criterion, to which we must always come back.
> (Renan 1995: 154)

Reference

Anderson, Benedict (1991) *Imagined Communities: Reflections on the Origin and Spread of Nationalism*, London: Verso.

Fraisse, Simon (1979) Renan occupied de l'Acropole. Paris: A.G. Nizef Pommier, Jean (1972) Un itinéraire spirituelle: du séminaire à la "Prière sut l'Acropole". Paris: Zizef.

Renan, Ernst (1996). Qu'est-ce q'une Nation? Et autres éctifs politiques. Ed. Raow Girarder. Paris: Imprimerienationale.

SEE ALSO: the nation, nationalism and the national principle; religion, secularization and the crisis of faith

GEORGIOS VAROUXAKIS

RICARDO, DAVID (1772–1823)

David Ricardo's *Principles of Political Economy* (1817) played a decisive role in setting the argumentative style of modern economics. The work was a systematic critique of central theoretical propositions established in Adam Smith's *Inquiry into the Nature and Causes of the Wealth of Nations (1776)*, chiefly concerning price formation and the distribution of income. Ricardo's focus on questions of value and distribution, and his analytical style of exposition, shaped the literature of English political economy, and can be seen at work both in JOHN STUART MILL's own *Principles* of 1848, and Karl Marx's *Capital* Vol. I of 1867 (see MARX AND MARXISM), a work whose chief economic inspiration can be traced back to Ricardo. The formal clarity of Ricardo's work is however achieved by abandoning the Smithian application of economic analysis to debate on the compatibility of commerce and civic virtue, and the consequences for the civilizing process of commercial values. Moreover, recent scholarship has shown that the logical framework developed by Ricardo is not as consistent and clear-cut as it appears. While both of these properties are naturally suggestive of the limitations of modern economics, the influence of Ricardian economics is indirect, there being no lineal descent from the classical economics of Ricardo to the neoclassical economics of the twentieth century. Ricardo's direct influence was confined chiefly to Britain, and had waned greatly by the 1830s. WILLIAM STANLEY JEVONS famously observed that Ricardo represented a false start for modern economics, and the writings of British economists of the late nineteenth and early twentieth centuries were informed by a social and ethical stance quite foreign to Ricardo. Nonetheless, Ricardo was intellectually liberal and a supporter of reform, qualities that set him apart from his friend and critic ROBERT MALTHUS.

Ricardo was born on 18 April 1772, third son of an Amsterdam Sephardic Jew who had settled in London around 1760, become a leading figure in the local Spanish and Portuguese Jewish community, and subsequently made his fortune on the Stock Exchange. At the age of 11 David Ricardo was sent to Amsterdam to be educated at the Talmud Tora, remaining there for two years, completing his education on his return in Britain and then entering his father's business at the age of 14. David Ricardo's independent spirit was demonstrated by his courtship and marriage, at the age of 21, of Priscilla Wilkinson, daughter of a Quaker surgeon. Although the resulting breach with his family was later healed, his renunciation of the Jewish faith was permanent, adopting a commitment to Unitarianism in common with many contemporary progressive rationalists. Although he left his father's employment, his already solid reputation ensured the continuing support of friends in the City, by 1801 being a member of the Committee for General Purposes of the Stock Exchange during its reorganization. He continued to deal on his own account as a jobber until 1819, although he diversified considerably into the acquisition of landed property in the later years of the Napoleonic Wars, acquiring the manor of Minchinhampton, near Stroud, Gloucestershire, in 1814, including the property Gatcombe Park, which later in the early 1970s became the residence of the Princess Royal. Other purchases followed, including in 1816 the Manors of Bromesberrow and of Bury Court, at the southern end of the Malvern Hills. In 1819 he gave Bromesberrow Place to his eldest son, and it was here that the Ricardo Papers were later discovered. In 1799, during a visit to Bath, Ricardo came across a copy of Smith's *Wealth of Nations*, and this chance encounter sparked his interest in political economy, although it was to be 10 years before he began writing on the subject. During his forties he increasingly adopted the lifestyle of a country gentleman, dividing his time between Gatcombe Park and his house in Upper Brook Street, which now forms part of the site of the American Embassy. At his London house he hosted breakfasts to promote political and economic discussion, which institution contributed to the formation of the Political Economy Club in 1821. In 1819 he became Member of Parliament for the rotten borough (there were twelve electors) of Portarlington in Ireland, a constituency that he never visited. He became an active, but independent, contributor to debates both within the chamber and without, his last contribution being a plan for a national bank, continuous with issues raised in his first economic writings. He died following an ear infection on 11 September 1823 at home in Gatcombe.

Ricardo's first foray into economic argument concerned the manner in which bank notes depreciated in relation to gold, while coin did not; from newspaper articles of 1809 he went on to compose the pamphlet *The High Price of Bullion, a Proof of the Depreciation of Bank Notes* (1810), in which he argued that the reason for the depreciation was the lack of restriction in the issue of bank notes on the part of the Bank of England. What is however immediately striking in this essay is the manner in which the question of the value of a circulating medium is placed in the context of the progress of wealth in different nations, and the effects on commercial relations of differential rates of depreciation between countries – or as we would say today, the relation of domestic inflation to exchange rates and international competitiveness. Shortly after the appearance of the pamphlet a parliamentary committee was established to examine the issue, leading to the 'Bullion Report' of August 1810 that endorsed the substance of Ricardo's analysis. In the ensuing controversy Ricardo defended the Report, and in this way established his reputation as a leading political economist. He had made the acquaintance of JAMES MILL two or three years before, which acquaintance now deepened into a major influence

upon Ricardo's intellectual development. Robert Malthus's review of Ricardo's pamphlet in the *Edinburgh Review* also brought a contact who was to be important in discussion of the economic issues with which Ricardo was increasingly concerned.

Although Ricardo first came to public attention with this and related publications on the currency question, he is chiefly known to later generations of economists for his *Essay on the Influence of a Low Price of Corn on the Profits of Stock* (1815), and the development of its arguments two years later in his *Principles*. The domestic grain market was at this time protected by the 1804 Corn Law that prohibited exports above 54s. a quarter, and imposed a sliding scale of duties on imports, the duty liable falling with the domestic price. Population growth and the impact of the Napoleonic Wars had combined to raise the domestic price of grain, the actual expansion of output feeding through into increased costs and, therefore, rents. The high price of grain came to symbolize a clash between the interest of landlords in high prices, and that of manufacturers in low prices – for grain was a staple foodstuff, and any rise in the price of bread triggered a demand for higher wages. Ricardo's pamphlet was prompted by parliamentary debate in the February of that year, a new Corn Law being passed in March that abolished the sliding scale and set a level of 80s. a quarter above which imports were free, and below which they were prohibited. This was widely perceived as support for the landed interest, and Ricardo's analysis sought to demonstrate the connection between wages, profits and rent in the distribution of income. His contribution coincided with the appearance of three other major pamphlets on the question, one of them by Robert Malthus; and their joint significance lies in part at least in the manner in which all four writers shared a new approach to the general question of the production and distribution of wealth. The importance of Ricardo's essay lies however in the identification of the existence of agricultural rent as a means of regulating the rate of profit between different investments; and in developing this he laid the basis for a systematic treatment of diminishing returns to capital and labour in agriculture. His general conclusion was that profits and wages were fixed in an inverse relationship, so that the higher wages were, the lower profits became. High wages therefore not only posed a short-term threat to manufacturing profit, in the long run the consequent depression of the rate of profit would bring about a decline of investment.

This argument was expanded in his *Principles of Political Economy and Taxation* into a more general treatment of value, capital and profit, developing at the same time a theoretical treatment of the comparative advantages of international trade that has survived in the textbooks of international economics up to this day. Ricardo ignored Smith's general argument concerning commercial progress, government and civil society, and focused on aspects of his work relating to the level of prices and wages, and returns to investment and the distribution of income. The outcome was a theoretical system that rationalized Smith's own unsystematic treatment of value, capital, wages, price and profits, presupposing a primarily agricultural economy, in which there was an inherent conflict of interest between manufacturers and landholders, and between landholders and their tenant farmers. The manufacturers wanted cheap bread for their workers; the landholders wanted protection for the high level of rents they were charging their tenants; and the tenant farmers wanted low rents, since there was an inverse relationship between rents and profits. Given Ricardo's simple assumption that the profits on agricultural investment set the rate of return on capital for the economy as a whole, this meant that protection for the landlord ultimately depressed the rate of profit in the economy as a whole, potentially bringing new investment to an end in a form of stationary state. The original schema of the 1815 *Essay* thus led to an economic demolition of protectionist policy, arguing that free trade was the most certain way to secure the future prosperity of the nation – a conclusion that he certainly shared with Smith, but which he arrived at by a different analytical route.

There is much common ground between Ricardo's pamphlet and Malthus's *Inquiry into the Nature and Progress of Rent*, but an important point of difference emerged in their treatment of the landed interest. Malthus supported the existence of the Corn Laws on the grounds that they offered protection to agriculture; and in developing this line of argument his sceptical attitude to economic growth based upon an expansion of manufacturing production once more becomes apparent. Malthus, while operating very much in the same kind of Smithian framework as Ricardo, considered that Government intervention was necessary to regulate the growth of manufacturing, in the general interests of social and political stability. This was not however inconsistent with Smith's arguments concerning a regime of liberty, since, unlike some of his later exponents, Smith had always recognized the impossibility, or even undesirability, of a truly minimalist state – the chief thrust of Smith's arguments involved a reduction of Government activity as much as was practicable, and not a utopian dismantling of Government's capacity to regulate the maintenance and growth of national wealth.

Ricardo's reputation in the years following his death in 1823 emphasized the axiomatic and deductive nature of his political economy, as opposed to the more applied and inductive tendencies of Malthus. This was something of a disservice to Ricardo, in that as an MP from 1819 to his death he actively engaged in parliamentary debate, and was a member of the Select Committee on Agriculture that reported first in 1821 and then again the following year. By now, the problem was the low, rather than the high, price of corn, the 1822 average price of wheat moving towards half the 1815 level. Given the relation of supply and demand for foodstuffs, low grain prices benefit the consumer and sharply reduce farm incomes, so that the historically low prices of 1822 led to agricultural distress. The agricultural interest blamed the low price on deflationary monetary policy, associated with a return to gold, linked of course to the issues with which Ricardo had begun his career as a political economist. He steadfastly opposed the protectionist recommendations of the Committee and argued against them in the House, publishing in April 1822 a new pamphlet *On Protection to Agriculture*, which within two months of its first appearance had to be reprinted three times. His arguments for free trade in grain, and by extension free trade as a general policy, provided systematic support to the free-trade movement in Britain that eventually succeeded in its aims in the 1840s.

Further reading

Blaug, M. (1958) *Ricardian Economics. A Historical Study*, New Haven: Yale University Press.

Hollaner, S. (1979) *The Economics of David Ricardo*, London: Heinemann.

Peach, T. (1993) *Interpreting Ricardo*, Cambridge: Cambridge University Press.

Sraffa, P. and Dobb, M.H. (eds) (1951–5) *The Works and Correspondence of David Ricardo*, 10 vols, Cambridge: Cambridge University Press.

KEITH TRIBE

ROMANTICISM, INDIVIDUALISM AND IDEAS OF THE SELF

While critics suggest various dates for the age of Romanticism and some reject the notion of Romanticism as a period altogether, most describe the Romantic condition as intimately tied to individuality and notions of selfhood. This seems to fit the phenomena of Romanticism, ranging from the celebration of fantasy and irrationality to inwardness and Romantic love, and from political disinterest to the solitude in Caspar David Friedrich's paintings. However, this emphasis on individuality is only half of the story of a condition at whose core can be seen, rather than an actual self, the mere compulsion to have a self. No preceding age had placed such pressure on the individual to have, experience, exhibit, prove, live and perform his or her selfhood. For the Romantics, the self is not simply there, but is yet to be brought about by the individual, each individual facing the task of institutionalizing his own self. While Romanticism is certainly not a united front, the overall Romantic element in this response is the conceptualization of a spectral self – a self that, at least to some degree, is understood to be comprehensible by means of perception. As the optical metaphor of reflection indicates, the Romantic self is, in its essence, a matter of appearance. Thus, proving the existence of the self (even to oneself) requires some externalization and phenomenalization of the self that allows an observatory, perhaps even visual, relationship to it. While this emphasis on the visual and modes of appearance explains the underlying connection between Romanticism, the arts and aesthetics, it also has distinct implications for political, legal and economic thought, ranging from discussions surrounding political representation and equal rights to the legal assurance of individual property rights.

Especially in the early Romantic period, the intellectual centres can be localized in time and space. In both of the key sites, namely in the German states and England, but also in France, the years between 1797 and 1800 were decisive. These years mark the flourish of the philosophically attuned Jena Romanticism or German Early Romanticism (*Deutsche Frühromantik*) (the Schlegel brothers, Novalis, Tieck and, along with them, Schleiermacher), fuelled also by the atheism accusation against Fichte, which led to the 1797 suspension of his professorship in Jena. Geographically close to

Jena, the Weimar classicism of Goethe and Schiller was seen for a long time as standing in opposition to Romanticism, although many scholars have doubted the heuristic value of a rigid border between classicism and Romanticism. German Idealism (SCHELLING, Hegel [see HEGEL AND HEGELIANISM]) was also a close relative of Romanticism. In 1798, Wordsworth and COLERIDGE – referred to, along with SOUTHEY, as the Lake Poets due to their later residence in the Lake District – travelled to Germany, where they were exposed to Kantian philosophy. It was here that Wordsworth began work on the *Prelude*. Romanticism also reached some writers of the previous generation: for example GODWIN's *Enquirer* (1797) marked the radical anarchist's move to the aesthetic. Curiously, all of the key earlier Romantics (CHATEAUBRIAND, Coleridge, CONSTANT, Hölderlin, Wilhelm von Humboldt, Novalis, FRIEDRICH SCHLEGEL, Schleiermacher, DE STAËL, Tieck and Wordsworth) were born in the years around 1770. Other centres of Romantic thought include London, Berlin (E.T.A. Hoffmann and Varnhagen von Ense's circle, including the Humboldts), Paris and Bayreuth (Jean Paul [Richter]), while some Romantics such as Walter Scott favored the countryside ('Abbotsford', Scotland). In France, the notion of Romanticism marks less of a distinct period, although several key writers have been considered Romantics (in addition to Chateaubriand and de Stael: Baudelaire, Hugo and George Sand). In Italy, Romanticism arrived delayed by means of an essay by Madame de Staël in 1816, an essay urging the Italians to follow emerging German ideas at a time when parts of Italy were occupied by a German-speaking power. It should not come as a surprise that key thinkers (Manzoni, Leopardi) remained at a distance to what they perceived as Romanticism. Romanticism also came a little later to Russia and Poland, but became a major movement often tied to national ideals (Lermentov, Pushkin; Mickiewiz, Slowacki). In the USA, Charles Brockden Brown, followed by Melville and Poe, discovered the mental space in correlation with the geographical open space of the Americas.

Individualism, individuality, the self and psyche

In order to discuss the ideas of individuality in Romanticism, it is useful to distinguish between the concepts of individualism, individuality, the self and the psyche. Whereas individualism demarks a sphere of relative freedom of action for the individual, it does not require a qualitative difference between individuals, nor does it involve a conscious notion of selfhood. Individuality, on the other hand, characterizes an essential feature that makes the individual unique (and not just different from others). This uniqueness – be it a singularity, an infinity or the autonomy of the individual – prohibits a complete subsumption of the individual under some entity or group without an annihilation of that very individuality. The self (*le moi, das Ich*) is fashioned through the transformation of the unique, and thus unrepresentable, individuality into a presentable totality. The prerequisite for the self is self-reflection, that is, a relationship to its own uniqueness that by virtue of this reflection becomes externalized, thereby becoming a subject of presentation and aesthetics. The psyche, on the other hand, does not rely on outward presentation, but instead opens up the inward being as a site for a multiplicity of forces. Using this terminology, the Romantic endeavour can be described as turning individuality into a self, an endeavour that in more than one case led to the formation of the psyche.

For the German Romantics, the demand for a self had two main sources in the ideas of the preceding centuries: Pietism and Kantian philosophy. From Pietism, the Romantics inherited the search for the self and a permanent self-questioning, but in contrast to the Pietists, they did not merely attempt to locate an existing agent, but rather understood the degrees to which the search itself influences the actual nature (and perception) of the self. From Kant, they assumed the idea that all experience and cognition can only be a balance between conceptual processes and sensual perception, thus ruling out a metaphysical perspective for human beings. However, many Romantics attempted to rehabilitate an absolute perception of the individual in its totality by and for human beings.

Beyond mere theory, the ideal of transforming individuality into a conscious self was one of the strongest forces in the development of ideas and of culture as a whole in the period around 1800. The absence of a clear notion of the self led to various forms of behaviour that aimed to prove or compensate for the existence of the self. Specifically, the new self had to respond to two aspects of individuality. First, the self must exist independently and autonomously. Second, the self could only be understood as a radically individual

quantity, that is, as the consciousness, history and position of a single person. These two determinations appear to have amalgamated in Romanticism.

One's own autonomy must be immediately seen and experienced, that is, the independence of the self had to become itself the object of a sensual experience by the individual. Autonomy must be displayed and lived (and not just abstractly, juridically possessed). Emerging genres and cultural trends such as the *Bildungsroman*, art dilettantism, Romantic love, the rehabilitation of suicide and extreme tourism in the Alps can be seen as examples of responses to these dual demands on the self. Echoes of compulsive demands for the self can also be seen in the invention of 'addiction' around 1800 (the medical discourse of addiction begins with Benjamin Rush and Thomas Trotter). What was once tolerated, even celebrated, and, in the worst cases, overlooked as a minor vice, came to be sanctioned and pathologized in the name of a free and self-controlled self. Thus, when de Quincey discovered opium-induced dream states as a vehicle for reaching what he understood as the deeper layers of memory (*Confessions of an English Opium-Eater*, 1821–2), he vehemently denied the intoxicating and addictive aspects of the drug.

From alienation to Romantic love

Many Romantics portrayed their contemporary age in terms of fragmentation and alienation, and saw this fragmentation further duplicated within the individual. In response to this perceived disconnectedness, they described their work as a search for a new transcendence and unity of separate spheres, modelled after remote historical periods, particularly the Middle Ages (Schlegel, Scott), or notions of religious unity (Chateaubriand, Novalis) or unity within the realm of nature (Coleridge, Hölderlin, Wordsworth). This Romantic self-description has led many later critics to see Romanticism as a conservative nostalgic by-product of the decline of the feudal order and the rise of industrialism. Whereas, within feudal society, each individual had a designated place according to religion, profession, family, age and sex, the eighteenth century uprooted the individual from these predetermined positions, thus both necessitating and allowing for self-definitions. However, as other critics have pointed out, the claim for a state of disconnection turned out to be quite productive for the Romantics. The greater the distance between fragmented individuals is believed to be, the greater the intensity of perception, vision and feeling could be in compensating for this distance. Indeed, emphasizing distance and fragmentation allowed the Romantics to focus productively on those techniques that simultaneously unite and separate the individual spheres. Thus, the key tension at work within Romanticism, namely that between the radical uniqueness of the individual on the one hand and the desired self-annihilation and mystic fusion in a universal order on the other, opened the way for new modes of perception and communication.

One of the key 'media' – to use a term coined by the sociologist Niklas Luhmann – of Romanticism was love. Precisely because each individual is increasingly understood as a world in himself or herself, a strong medium was required that nevertheless bridges the gap between individuals, thus establishing, for example, family units in a society that rejected arranged marriage. Love accomplished this by making the singularity of the loved one the magnifying glass through which one experienced the world and oneself (see de Staël, *On the Influence of the Passions on the Well-Being of Individuals and of Nations*, [*De l'influence des passionssur le bonheur des individus et des nations*] 1796).

The totality of perception made possible by Romantic love also allowed for an appreciation of sexuality as one legitimate aspect of love. To love meant to love relationality. The price of this love was the preservation of the very distances that love set out to overcome.

Still, Romantic love preserved the asymmetry between the sexes, with the man's love reflecting the nature of relation (as Luhmann puts it: the man loves loving), and the woman simply loving the man. Whereas this imbalance ensured a more direct emotional involvement of the woman, it bared her from reflection and thereby also from gaining a self. In his *Philosophical Studies* (*Philosophische Studien*, 1800), Novalis made explicit that which seems to underlie most thought around 1800: 'The man has to master his nature and to accomplish law and control for the Individuo.... The woman has to obey nature – and to master her individual.'

Romantic aesthetics

The dynamic processes of visualization and coming to appearance lay at the core of the Romantic aesthetic debates. One of these key aesthetic debates centred on the status of the symbol. On the one hand, authors such as Goethe, Schelling, Hegel, Coleridge, Novalis and later CARLYLE, despite their many differences, all described the aesthetic in response to Kant as connected to the production of symbols that present the infinite in finite manner, and, by extension, the invisible as visible. For these authors, aesthetics served as a correction or compensation for the extreme complexity of the world. Symbols also became the mode of appearance for the self. For Schelling, elaborating on Kant, the aesthetic process was necessary because it alone could manifest the infinite subject in finite form. Coleridge understands aesthetic perception in similar terms: 'The primary IMAGINATION I hold to be the living Power and prime Agent of all human Perception, and as a repetition in the finite mind of the eternal act of creation in the infinite I AM' (Coleridge, *Biographia Literaria*, 1817). On the other hand, authors such as Schlegel, Novalis, Shelley and Baudelaire instead rehabilitated allegory as the key mode of aesthetics, and focused on the opposing tendency to bring about effects of temporal and spatial infinity from the spirit of finitude. Instead of presupposing an infinite self that faced the problem of adequate finite representation, these authors concerned themselves with certain modes of presentation that project an infinite selfhood that was beyond re-presentability (*Darstellbarkeit*). These authors employed rhetorical figures other than the symbol, such as allegory, irony, wit, fragmentation and paradox, and they conceived of aesthetics as a mode of production and generation, which included the production of the self.

Such aesthetics of production were the foundation for the conception of the fragment as a projected totality in Early German Romanticism. Friedrich Schlegel, his brother A.W. Schlegel, Novalis, Schleiermacher and Tieck published several collections each containing hundreds of 'fragments' in journals like the *Athenaeum* (1798–1800, eds. F. Schlegel and A.W. Schlegel). It has been argued by critics such as Philippe Lacoue-Labarthe and Jean-Luc Nancy that these fragments exemplify the essence of modern literature and perhaps modernity in general through their call for completion. Rather then being conceived of as incomplete parts of a previously existing whole, these fragments project a whole that is yet to come. More than a mere construction plan, the fragment reflects upon itself in such a way that this reflection opens up a space beyond that which is stated in the fragment itself, thus enlarging it beyond its contours. Simultaneously with the genre of the fragment, the discipline of hermeneutics developed rapidly (Schleiermacher). Hermeneutical thought sought to understand a text by means of executing the text's own movements and reflections, thus adding to the complexity of the text, rather than reducing it to a single meaning. This hermeneutical approach resulted in incomprehensibility, which is the *modus operandi* of the fragment and the fragmented self, as they do not represent a whole but rather present and enact it.

For Schlegel and Novalis, the self is such a fragment. The self strives to complete itself through self-observation, reflecting upon itself from a higher level. The self is a perpetual work-in-progress. However, these self-reflections produce an image of the self that is still incomplete, as it lacks a depiction of the self's ability to observe itself. Thus, each self-observation has the very act of the observation as its blind spot, opening up a infinite process of reflection, including reflections on reflections, and observations of observations.

The era of Jena Romanticism ended abruptly with the death of Novalis (1801) and Friedrich Schlegel's conversion to Catholicism (1808). Nevertheless, notions of infinite reflection continued to haunt many thinkers of the age, including Kierkegaard and Hegel. Hegel especially vehemently rejected Schlegel's thoughts in his introduction to *Lectures on Aesthetics* (*Vorlesungen über die Ästhetik*, 1823, 1826, 1828–9). Still, it has been argued that Hegel's condemnation of Schlegel is less an indication of the differences between the two men than of their structural proximity. Indeed, Schlegel's infinite reflection poses a threat for Hegel's teleology, in which a negation of the negation would bring the endlessness of reflection to a halt.

Bildung – formation

A key Romantic strategy for dealing with the pressure to demonstrate the existence of the self is present in the attempts to historicize the self. After Rousseau's *Confessions* and *Émile ou de la éducation*, many writers turned their attention to constructions of selfhood by means of memory and (auto)biography. By organizing a life in such a way that earlier phases and events were understood as the preconditions for later stages, the complexity of the individual is reduced to a diachronic scheme. The goal of this historicization was not simply the resulting form, but formation (*Bildung*) as such. The most influential result of this new focus on the changeable self was the *Bildungsroman*, with Goethe's *Wilhelm Meister's Apprenticeship* (*Wilhelm Meisters Lehrjahre*, 1795/96) serving as a model for several dozens of novels within a decade after its publication. Schlegel famously summarized the three tendencies of his age as Goethe's *Wilhelm Meisters Lehrjahre*, the French Revolution and Fichte's philosophy (see *Fragments* in: *Athenaeum*). The 'novel of formation' narrates the development of a typically male protagonist who undergoes maturation without clear guidance from an authority figure. His curriculum vitae results from the tensions between his actions and events on the one hand and his emerging awareness of his development on the other, a tension that seems to drive many developments in the novel. The term *Bildungsroman* has also often been used to describe Hegel's *Phenomenology of the Spirit* (*Phänomenologie des Geistes*, 1806). In this text, self-formation begins when that which will become 'spirit' leaves its undifferentiated origin to perfect itself through a dialectical process of both finding itself in an external entity and negating the very externality of this entity in a return to itself.

One of the key problems posed by Goethe's novel is that Wilhelm does not learn anything until the very end of the novel, when suddenly all elements of his chaotic life reappear and it turns out that many of the seemingly disconnected protagonists are part of one family, a family Wilhelm soon enters by means of marriage. This has led some critics to argue that the task of *Bildung* is to tell one's life retrospectively in such a way that each individual step 'makes sense' as a necessary component of the subsequent self-knowledge. Seen in this light, the self is the product of a later composite of disparate memories into a complete narrative. Novalis and Tieck radicalized this scheme of the reflexive self. In *Apprentice to Sais* (*Lehrlinge zu Sais*) (1799), Novalis described the self as a riddle in the form of a hieroglyph. This hieroglyph, it turns out, is a map of the protagonist's life that transposes the diachronic path into a synchronic image. That is, the self turned out to be the image of the process of searching for the self.

Unity with nature

Another Romantic answer to the demand to prove the existence of the self was staged in encounters with 'nature'. The basic idea was that all beings are united by a universal and natural self that underlies all seemingly coincidental aspects of life. Striving to transcendence and absolute unity seems to contradict the Romantic focus on individuality. However, several Romantics stress that radical individuality is the condition of possibility for speaking in someone else's name, loving, and thus reaching out to universal categories, that is, to nature. The task was to unearth a basic and natural likeness of man, a task expressed as a political project in Schiller's 'Ode to Joy' (*An die Freude*), which Beethoven employed in his Ninth Symphony.

Unlike earlier writers, these Romantics did not simply use images of landscapes as conventional allegories of the inner condition of man. Rather, the encounters between the individual and nature marked the beginning of a complex dialogue that allows exchange between concepts of subject and object, speaker and listener, observer and observed, and inside and outside (Coleridge, Hölderlin, Wordsworth). Such encounters were considered to engage the human faculties of imagination and intuition, that is, the realm of inner sentiments that was deemed to be natural and true. The goal was to catch these faculties in the act, to manifest them, and thereby to prove the existence of the free inward self, the innermost nature that connects all beings. This form of selfhood has been called 'expressive selfhood' by Charles Taylor. Expressing and articulating the inner voice was considered the proper access to 'nature', a nature that did not operate along the lines of an inside–outside dichotomy, since the inward self was in essence natural.

Wordsworth in particular dedicated many of his major works to transcending singular experiences, in an attempt to arrive at the natural self. Reaching this universal selfhood was essentially connected to acquiring a double vision that used images of nature as a means of entry into the world beyond the visible realm. Therefore, the ability to see beyond the visible world was the key faculty that unites mankind. Wordsworth considered individually acquired imagination to be this faculty. The most individualistic faculty is thus the very door to universality: the better one understands that which makes the individual an individual, namely imagination, the better one understands mankind in general. Wordsworth considered recollection to be the means of accessing an individual's formation of imagination – the topic of the *Prelude*. The work of recollection is therefore the key to understanding not just the individualistic, but also the universal self. In the ode 'Intimations of Immortality from Recollections of Early Childhood' (1802–4), Wordsworth wrote:

> Those first affections,
> Those shadowy reflections,
> Which, be they what they may,
> Are yet the fountain-light of all our day,
> Are yet a master-light of all our seeing.

The recollections from early childhood colour all later perceptions in such a way as to make possible their unity, a unity that becomes the condition for transcendence, as the ode makes clear later on:

> Though inland far we may be,
> Our Souls have sight of that immortal sea.

Critics in the 1990s stressed the degree to which the telling of early recollections in Wordsworth is a project of conscious constructivism that finds or invents those primal scenes that seem necessary for explaining later visions, thus delineating Wordsworth's project as a *Bildungsroman* of the imagination.

The rise of the psyche

Romanticism was the age in which psychological explanations for human behaviours emerged as a powerful paradigm. Building upon the English sentimental novel of the eighteenth century and the new discipline of empirical psychology (Karl Philipp Moritz), the inward being became a site for the staging of events. Ranging from Schlegel, who described the individual as a 'stage' (*On Goethe's 'Meister'*, *Über Goethes Meister*), to Byron's 'mental theatre' (see Manfred 1817), the attention to inner processes no longer ended in an outward phenomenalization of the self, but rather remained entrapped within the individual. Even though the concept of psychology originally served to strengthen the individual in its perfectibility and morality, it became more and more of a prison. The thought of psychology culminated in the invention of 'trauma' in Romanticism. Before the medical-psychological discourse considered trauma during the later nineteenth century, several Romantic writers conceptualized trauma within a narrative of certain wounding events of one's life that determine the life as a whole by unconsciously forcing the individual to repeat the wounding situation in dreams, fantasies and actual behaviour. This new idea of trauma lent urgency to the project of (auto)biography, since hidden childhood events might conceal the key to one's personality. Unlike older models of personality such as the character studies of physiognomy, the idea of trauma also held the possibility of therapy, of undoing the harmful event of the past (see Balzac's *Adieu* (1830), in which a dangerous trauma therapy is undertaken). One of the first major texts that presented trauma as the cause of that which Freud called the repetition compulsion (*Wiederholungszwang*) is E.T.A. Hoffmann's 'Madame de Scudery' (*Das Fräulein von Scuderi*) (1827). In this text, a jeweller is forced to replay a deadly scene that occurred during his mother's pregnancy and is unable to free himself from the paradigm of his traumatic congenital impression. In Hoffmann's texts, the individual cannot free itself from the self and becomes subjected to it. Instead of responding to the demand to have a self by creating some positive notion of the self as most earlier Romantics did, Hoffmann presented the self-compulsion as such as the (only) essence of selfhood.

The absence of selfhood is also a central idea in several Gothic novels and, most famously, Shelley-Wollstonecraft's *Frankenstein: or the Modern Prometheus* (1818, 1831). The monster's search for his identity, origin and master, as well as his hope for a partner, reveals the futility of the self-compulsion. That is, the monster is a monster only because he keeps hoping to find the self that he cannot have. The monster is pure life, unrestricted by self-knowledge or consciousness. Many texts of the era present the absence of a self as a state of an excess of life and of unlimited expansion, ranging from Goethe's *Elective Affinities* (*Wahlverwandtschaften*) (1809), Keats's 'Lamia' (1818) and Shelley's 'Prometheus Unbound' (1820).

Politics and economics

It has often been argued that Romanticism replaced social responsibilities and traditions with the inward formation of imagination. Nonetheless, significant political thought arises from Romanticism and Romantic individuality. Wilhelm von Humboldt's *Limits of the State* (*Ideen zu einem Versuch die Gränzen der Wirksamkeit des Staats zu bestimmen*) (1792, 1797) became a key source for liberalism, in particular JOHN STUART MILL's *On Liberty*. In addition to the explicit political ideas of the Romantics (including those of Chateaubriand), Romanticism is crucial in its appreciation of unique individuality. In so far as unique individuality was understood as means of access to universality and nature, its appreciation fuelled the various equal-rights movements as well as the foundation of theories of natural right.

In economic thought, Romanticism was the period when a shift from models of balance (Adam Smith) to models of expansion took place. Instead of counting on a self-regulated balance by means of supply and demand, the Romantic theorists foresaw the possibility of radical imbalances in which a small number of people would take in the majority of the capital (RICARDO, J. B-. Say, Adam Müller). Even though most thinkers warned of this possibility, their economic theories can be seen as a reaction to the probability of imbalance. This shift is paralleled by a conceptual turn from the gold standard of money to a standard of credit (paper money). Whereas the French paper money experiment ended disastrously in hyperinflation (1797), notions of ghostly money and capital now appeared everywhere in Romantic thought and fiction (notably in Chamisso's *Peter Schlemihl* (1814) and Goethe's *Faust II* [1832]). Curiously, this money is closely connected to questions of selfhood: like the self, paper money also needs to constantly prove its value.

References

Luhmann, N. (1986) *Love as a Passion: The Codification of Intimacy*, trans. J. Gaines and D.L. Jones, Cambridge, MA: Harvard University Press.

Taylor, C. (1989), *Sources of the Self. The Making of the Modern Identity*, Cambridge, MA: Harvard University Press.

Further reading

Izenberg, G.N. (1992) *Impossible Individuality: Romanticism, Revolution, and the Origins of Modern Selfhood, 1787–1802*, Princeton: Princeton University Press.

Lacoue-Labarthe, P. and Nancy, J.-L. (1988) *The Literary Absolute: The Theory of Literature in German Romanticism*, trans. P. Barnard and C. Lester, Albany: State University of New York Press.

Man, P. de (1984) *Rhetoric of Romanticism*, New York: Columbia University Press.

SEE ALSO: anthropology and race; intellectuals, elites and meritocracy; novels, poetry and drama;

religion, secularization and the crisis of faith; theories of education and character formation

FRITZ BREITHAUPT

ROYER-COLLARD, PIERRE PAUL (1763–1845)

The French political thinker, lawyer, philosopher and deputy (between 1815 and 1842) Pierre Paul Royer-Collard was leader of the group of the so-called *Doctrinaires* under the Restoration (1815–30). He was born to a Jansenist family in the Marne. As a Paris-based lawyer from 1787, Royer-Collard witnessed the first years of the French Revolution at first hand and was elected to the Paris Commune. During much of the reign of the Directory he was a representative of Marne in the Council of 500. He displayed staunch monarchist preferences already then. With the first Restoration, Louis XVIII appointed him supervisor of the press.

His intellectual power, scholarship and erudition, and, not least, his notorious oratorical powers made Royer-Collard 'the most respected statesman of the Restoration' (Artz 1931: 58). He is also credited with having initiated the revived interest in philosophic studies that characterized the Restoration, which most historians think dates from his lectures on the history of philosophy at the Sorbonne shortly before the fall of the Empire, in the years 1812–14. He had opposed a philosophy of perception inspired by Scottish thinkers, particularly Thomas Reid, to the dominant sensualist views (influenced by the scepticism of Condillac, who had argued that all knowledge was mere sensation).

In 1815, Royer-Collard was elected to the Chamber of Deputies. Although initially he was not completely innocent of support for some repressive measures, he shortly afterwards distanced himself forcefully from the 'Ultras' and became identified as a leading figure of moderate constitutional monarchists. He soon found himself the leader of an extremely influential small group of constitutional monarchists that emerged in early 1816 and was dubbed by a newspaper the '*Doctrinaires*'. Composed of such liberal thinkers as Royer-Collard, GUIZOT, de Broglie, Barante, Rémusat, the group of the *Doctrinaires* soon emerged as the left centre of French politics of the Restoration. They sought to achieve a compromise between the 'Principles of 1789' and the 'Principle of Legitimacy', and regarded the Charter of 1814 as the '*juste milieu*' (Starzinger 1991).

Royer-Collard believed in the maintenance of an equilibrium among three powers: a hereditary monarchy, a hereditary peerage and a representative assembly to be recruited from the middle class. When any of these three powers became too strong, the equilibrium was upset (Artz 1931: 56–8). In the Chamber he was a staunch defender of the Charter of 1814, as the contract between legitimate power and the nation. This, however, did not mean that he accepted, even by implication, the idea of popular sovereignty. For Royer-Collard was in fact one of the two major exponents (the other being fellow-*Doctrinaire* Guizot) of the idea that only reason is sovereign (the sovereignty of reason).

References

Artz, F.B. (1931) *France under the Bourbon Restoration, 1814–1830*, Cambridge, MA: Harvard University Press.
Starzinger, V.E. (1991) *The Politics of the Center: The Juste Milieu in Theory and Practice, France and England, 1815–1848*, New Brunswick, Transaction Publishers.

Further reading

Craiutu, A. (1998) 'Between Scylla and Charybdis: The "Strange" Liberalism of the French Doctrinaires', *History of European Ideas*, 24, 4–5: 243–65.
—— (1999) 'Tocqueville and the Political Thought of the French Doctrinaires (Guizot, Royer-Collard, Rémusat)', *History of Political Thought*, 20, 3: 456–93.
Jardin, A. and Tudesq, A.-J. (1983) *Restoration and Reaction, 1815–1848*, Cambridge: Cambridge University Press.
Kelly, G.A. (1992) *The Humane Comedy: Constant, Tocqueville and French Liberalism*, Cambridge: Cambridge University Press.

SEE ALSO: liberalism

GEORGIOS VAROUXAKIS

RUSKIN, JOHN (1819–1900)

John Ruskin was a British art critic and social theorist. In mid-life Ruskin shifted his emphasis from art and architecture to social and economic issues. He criticized the division of labour and delivered a scathing attack on the practice of *laissez-faire* that underpinned the liberal interpretation of classical economics. Ruskin was eclectic, often contradicted himself and did not identify with any particular political party. In one thing, however, he was completely consistent: throughout his adult life he stressed the basic Christian ethic of co-operation and brotherhood as being in direct contradistinction to the values of industrial capitalism. For this reason, Ruskin gained many distinguished disciples, and despite his anti-democratic stance, became a key influence in the socialist revival in the last quarter of the nineteenth century.

Early biographical details

Ruskin was born in London, the only child of John James and Margaret Ruskin. His father was a founding partner in the company Pedro Domecq sherries. His mother was kindly, but rigorous in her pursuit of the Protestant evangelical tradition, her most earnest wish being that her son should become an Anglican bishop. Under his parent's close supervision, Ruskin's primary education was confined to a combination of the daily Bible reading enforced by his mother and the more secular, although nonetheless erudite, taste of his father for Scott, Byron, Shakespeare and the visual arts.

This early period in Ruskin's development was punctuated by annual tours to the Continent with his parents that left him free to write and sketch, and to indulge his love of the natural world. He had minimal contact with his own peer group, and from the age of 12 he was exposed to a period of indifferent ecclesiastical tutelage until he left home for Christ Church, Oxford, in 1837. Once there, Ruskin began to realize he was not destined for the Church, although he gave little indication at this time of questioning his evangelical inheritance. Instead, he showed a propensity for the visual arts and for future literary brilliance. He published poetry and criticism, and won the Oxford Newdigate Prize for poetry in 1839. His studies were, however, interrupted by ill-health, and he did not receive his degree until 1842. That year also saw the beginning of the first volume of *Modern Painters.* This was followed by a second volume, published in 1846, and in 1849 by the publication of *The Seven Lamps of Architecture*, which emphasized the religious significance of architecture and the desirability of the Gothic form.

Art and society

There was no cataclysmic watershed in Ruskin's transition from art to social critic; it was a continuous thematic development where the moral centrality evident in his early works of art criticism began to take on a more immediate social significance. In his writings and lectures in the 1850s Ruskin continued to function in his primary role as an art critic, but as his intolerance of economic inequality and exploitation increased, he became a deliberate and conscious social moralist. His critique of the nineteenth-century POLITICAL ECONOMY remained inextricably inter-related with his role as an aesthete (see AESTHETICS, PAINTING AND ARCHITECTURE) and his conviction that the inherent moral dimension of art and architecture was a reflection of the nation's values. Following the example of CARLYLE, he did not locate social ills in class inequality, but in the kind of work men were forced to do and in the conditions under which they laboured. In vol. two of *The Stones of Venice* (1853), he used a romantic (see ROMANTICISM, INDIVIDUALISM AND IDEAS OF THE SELF)/organicist metaphor for his critique of contemporary production methods, translating his admiration for the natural forms of Gothic architecture into a social principle that opposed competition and alienation with co-operation and unity. He criticized the crude nineteenth-century interpretation of Adam Smith's division of labour, which he claimed was destroying creative freedom, and placed his emphasis on the method of production, the intrinsic value of the end product and its effects on the quality of life. He thought that only by moving these ethical considerations from the periphery to the centre of production would a proper sense of values be restored.

In pursuit of this aspiration Ruskin taught drawing for a time at the Working Men's College, established in London in 1854, by a group of Christian Socialists under the leadership of F.D. MAURICE. They were not socialists in the later political interpretation of the movement, and proved too moderate to satisfy Ruskin, who was well aware of the growing unrest of the workforce. They did, however, in their emphasis on co-operation, provide a radical alternative to the prevalent orthodox Christian acceptance of social and economic injustice. Even after Ruskin's evangelical 'unconversion' in the late 1850s, he continued to adhere to the fundamental Christian ethics that underpinned his constant push for moral regeneration. Up to 1859 he continued to hope that this regeneration could be achieved through art, and his conscious moralizing was still contained within the esoteric but recognizable framework of art and architecture.

By 1860, at the age of 41, Ruskin had accepted that society was not going to be saved by art, and that he needed to direct his all-pervading sense of justice at the political economy and a system of values that, he considered, were little more than respect for convention. What he proposed was an alternative set of values, derived from Christian principles, but devoid of evangelical hypocrisy, which were to be the salvation of a sick capitalist society. The lectures he gave in the industrial Midlands in the late 1850s – *The Political Economy of Art* (1857) and *The Two Paths* (1859) – were a positive statement of Ruskin's continuity of purpose and conviction. The ethic these lectures located had developed out of the aesthetic realism of *The Stones of Venice,* and anticipated the more overt critique of classical economics in *Unto this Last* (1862).

Critique of Political Economy

Unto this Last was comprised of four essays first published in serial form in 1860, in the *Cornhill Magazine.* These essays generated such hostility that the editor, Thackeray, informed Ruskin that publication would have to cease after the fourth instalment. Ruskin, however, never lost faith in the 'rightness' of his convictions, and remained hostile to the social implications of *laissez-faire* economics for the rest of his life. The central ideas of *Unto this Last* were further developed in *Munera Pulveris* (1862–3, published in book form in 1872), *The Crown of Wild Olive* (1866), *Time and Tide* (1867) and *Fors Clavigera* (1871–84).

The initial hostile reception of *Unto this Last* merits comment. Some critics viewed it as an affirmation of Ruskin's 'socialism', but it was more likely his implicit attack on liberalism that caused offence, if not fear, among middle-class entrepreneurs. For the greater part of the nineteenth century 'economics' meant *laissez-faire*: the liberal interpretation of the classical system established in the previous century by Adam Smith, and subsequently amended by DAVID RICARDO. This system was condemned by many reformers as promoting a self-seeking 'economic man', devoid of human sentiment and unencumbered by state interference.

Ruskin considered the *laissez-faire* system to be totally immoral as it enshrined a very negative form of liberty, which exploited the labour force, wrongly divorced economics from everyday life and, in fact, left people 'free' to starve. In response, he wrote *Unto this Last* in which he stressed an abundance of resources, opposed competition with co-operation and advocated a consumer ethic summed up in his now famous aphorism: THERE IS NO WEALTH BUT LIFE. In this small book, Ruskin attacked the whole language of the '*soi-disant*' science of economics as obscure, and, in effect, dismissed the a priori notions of MALTHUS, Ricardo and MILL as irrelevant.

The effect of Ruskin's attack on a hitherto sacrosanct system was further exacerbated by his practical suggestions for reform. These conditions transgressed all the rules of the non-interventionist British economic system: fixed wages, Government-subsidized industries, state care for the poor, elderly and infirm, quality control of goods and state education were all recommendations that went against dogmatic utilitarian presumptions and earned him both derision and allegations of socialism. There was obviously some justification for these allegations in terms of economic reform, but in fact there were no socialistic ideals of equality in Ruskin's utopia (see UTOPIANISM). He thought equality not only undesirable but also unobtainable, because leaders would always be required to initiate democratic programmes of action. Neither did he advocate the nationalization of land, insisting instead that landlords should retain ownership but should be induced to use their land wisely in the interest of a better quality of communal welfare. Despite these anti-democratic trends, however, Ruskin, and in particular, *Unto this Last*, was to become the inspiration of many socialist leaders.

In 1878 Ruskin reinforced the communitarian message of *Unto this Last* with the foundation of the Guild of St George, a scheme to which he gave a great deal in terms of both energy and finance. He set out the details in *Fors Clavigera*, a series of letters addressed to 'The Workmen and Labourers of Great Britain'. The society he envisaged was to have Ruskin as its master, presiding over a small community, which, in return for spiritually rewarding labour, would enjoy fixed rents and favourable working conditions. This scheme, like most of Ruskin's practical experiments, was doomed to failure, but its philanthropic legacy persists today.

Ruskin's influence

It was not for his practical experiments, however, but as an ethical theorist, that Ruskin's influence was most keenly felt. Many of his disciples were themselves very influential, with the effect that much Ruskinian thought was absorbed but often unacknowledged. This situation was exacerbated by Ruskin's refusal to identify with any political party, although many of his adherents were anxious to annexe him to their cause.

One such, was FREDERIC HARRISON (1831–1923), who was a prolific writer and philosopher, and an enthusiastic disciple of Ruskin (*John Ruskin* [1902]). Harrison was influential in many areas of reform, and from an early age a follower of the Positivism of AUGUSTE COMTE. Throughout his life Harrison was keen to establish an intellectual synthesis between Ruskin and Comte, and, indeed, in their emphasis on co-operation and moral paternalism there were obvious similarities. Positivism was influential for a time within the socialist movement, but, ultimately, it was Ruskin whose thinking had the greater impact.

WILLIAM MORRIS (1834–96) was also a disciple whose considerable debt to Ruskin Morris was always careful to acknowledge. Following Ruskin's example, Morris drew his social inspiration from his aesthetic studies and his own experiences of craftsmanship. As with Ruskin, the nature of creative activity in a medieval society provided Morris with the metaphor for his critique of capitalism and also, as with Ruskin, the division of labour was a focal point of his attack. Morris's association with revolutionary Marxism later distanced him from Ruskinian thinking, but if Morris's greatest contribution to socialism is considered to be his account of work, then it should be acknowledged that this ethic came largely from Ruskin.

J.A. HOBSON (1858–1940) was another very important figure who professed his enormous debt to Ruskin, (*John Ruskin Social Reformer* [1898]). As the leading intellectual force behind new liberalism, and one who sought fundamentally an accommodation of socialism and liberalism, Hobson's reputation is central in any assessment of Ruskin's influence. Although there were some points of departure, Hobson was indebted to Ruskin for two basic principles. First was the principle of humanism, which underpinned Ruskin's economic critique and from which

Hobson came to believe that all scientific principles should be subservient to ethical ones. And, second, he was also heavily influenced by Ruskin's organicist vision of society, which prompted Hobson to redefine his own concepts away from individualism towards a more collectivist ideal of communal welfare. Through Hobson, Ruskin unwittingly helped facilitate a liberal-socialist synthesis, a compromise in which competition was minimized but still retained, in which a level of subsistence was guaranteed and a national health and employment scheme was ultimately initiated. If Hobson is rightly seen as the bridge between nineteenth- and twentieth-century social thought, Ruskin must be recognized as the inspirational factor.

Ruskin's political ambiguity

The last quarter of nineteenth-century Britain was marked by economic depression. There was a revival of socialism and there was also a concomitant change in the readership and reception of Ruskin's social writings. The publication of cheap pamphlets and pocket editions, and the advent of circulating libraries, made Ruskin's works more readily available to the newly literate working classes. *Unto this Last*, republished in 1877, became essential reading for trade unionists and socialists, and tracts from Ruskin's writings were quoted in many speeches made by prominent individuals. One of these was Keir Hardie, who, along with most of the twenty-nine labour MPs elected to Parliament in 1906, quoted Ruskin's writings as inspirational. Despite his anti-democratic stance, Ruskin's central issues could be accepted as pivotal to the utopian, ethical socialism that became the dominant form. As OWEN was largely forgotten, and Marx was generally dismissed (see MARX AND MARXISM), the Christian socialist revival resonated with Ruskinian thinking and attracted a large working-class following. Some 20 years after its original rejection, *Unto this Last*, with its quasi-religious combination of moral and practical economic reform, suddenly appeared infinitely appealing.

This left-wing reverence for Ruskin's writings does not, however, confirm him as a socialist. His elements of utopianism, his insistence on co-operation and his call for greater state intervention predisposed him to socialism, but he had no sense of evolution and was anti-collectivist in his insistence on moral paternalism. Always visual in approach, Ruskin saw his perfect society mirrored in the construction of a Gothic cathedral; this process was integrated but hierarchical, and ultimately produced something greater than the sum of its parts.

By the end of the nineteenth century sales of Ruskin's books escalated in the industrial cities and his influence was further disseminated through numerous small societies. Ruskin's work also sold well overseas. He was widely published in the USA, and *Unto this Last* was translated into French, German and Italian. Through the influence of TOLSTOY, it was also published in Russian. Another great admirer, GANDHI, claimed that reading *Unto this Last* had changed his life and he had the book published in Gujerati. As an economist, Ruskin was not without his critics, but his allies especially appreciated his analysis of 'wealth' and 'value', and his emphasis on producing only goods that were life-enhancing.

Further reading

Anthony, P.D. (1983) *John Ruskin's Labour*, Cambridge: Cambridge University Press.

Cook, E.T. and Wedderburn, A. (eds) (1903–12) *The Library Edition of the Works of John Ruskin*, London: George Allen.

Hobson, J.A. (1898) *John Ruskin Social Reformer*, London: James Nesbit & Co., Ltd.

Sherburne, J.C. (1972) *John Ruskin or the Ambiguities of Abundance*, Cambridge, MA: Harvard University Press.

SEE ALSO: aesthetics, painting and architecture; early socialism; Harrison, Frederic; Morris, William

GILL COCKRAM

RUSSIAN THOUGHT IN THE NINETEENTH CENTURY

The nineteenth century in Russia was an epoch of instigation and rapid growth of extremely diverse philosophical ideas and movements. On the one hand, Russian thought comprises multiple attempts to understand, interpret and radicalize the intellectual and socio-political traditions of the West, reconciling them with native Russian culture and bringing East and West together. On the other hand, Russian thought includes sweeping rejections of the Western intellectual legacy, as well as devastating criticism of Russian culture as inferior, backward and, in some cases, non-existent. But whether it defined itself through the lens of the Western world, searched for its identity in the depths of 'the Russian soul' or tried to synthesize these two approaches, nineteenth-century philosophical discourse in Russia was characterized by deep self-reflection and critical re-examination of values and traditions.

The main philosophical thrust of the epoch was to oppose authoritarian tendencies both in thought and in political practice, to champion the right of the individual to choose his own destiny and to explain the nature of freedom and the relation of the individual to the greater social world in which he finds himself. The ways in which nineteenth-century Russian thinkers approached these questions ranged from religious-philosophical visions to socialist utopias; from extreme idealism to 'scientific' materialism; from models of unconditional ethics to theories of 'rational egoism'; from radical individualism to varying conceptions of universality and communality; from moderate conceptions of history and progress to extreme revolutionary and anarchist programmes; from mysticism to Marxism (see MARX AND MARXISM).

General considerations and methodology

The overall intellectual atmosphere of nineteenth-century Russia was characterized by passionate engagement with European philosophy – predominantly German Idealism and French social-political thought – and its creative (often quite radical) interpretation. The prevailing attitude of intellectuals was profound dissatisfaction with their country's socio-economic conditions, which often drove them to put new ideas into practice in order to overcome 'oppressive reality'. Long before Russian thinkers had heard of FEUERBACH or Marx, they were determined to forgo disinterested speculations about the world in favour of changing it.

Indeed, in its purely theoretical form, philosophy scarcely existed in Russia at the time. While there were some objective reasons for that, such as the repressive acts of Tsar Nicolas I who ordered philosophy departments closed at all universities in the first half of the century, there was also a subjective sentiment shared by the majority of learned Russians – their extreme suspicion of any speculation detached from urgent ethical and social pressures. Very few of the significant philosophical writings of the time were concerned with pure theory; in one way or another, all brought together philosophy, history, politics and some elements of cultural critique.

Philosophical studies and exchange of ideas commonly took place in informal settings – private conversations, literary salons and *kruzhki* (circles or discussion groups). Having emerged from heated debates, ideas and theories found their written expressions in popular essays, novels, socio-political commentaries, literary criticism and philosophical correspondence. Philosophy in Russia was viewed and practised primarily as a literary, rather than a theoretical, endeavour. The writings of DOS-TOEVSKY and TOLSTOY present vivid examples of such philosophical literature.

It is important to note that the exchange of ideas in Russia was almost always a dangerous enterprise and the nineteenth century was no exception; many writers and participants in semi-private discussions were severely punished by the tsarist authorities. For better or worse, the risk-taking nature of Russian philosophy, its favouring of ideas for which one could live or die, was a powerful symptom of that epoch. The pathos of ultimate sacrifice for ideals so skilfully used and abused by the twentieth-century Soviet ideologues was first proclaimed and lovingly fostered by their nineteenth-century predecessors.

The beginning

The beginning of the nineteenth century in Russia was marked by the assassination of the despotic Paul I (1801) and the ascent to the throne of a more progressive emperor, Alexander I. Russia's exhausting yet victorious campaign against Napoleon's invasion of 1812–14 intensified patriotic sentiment in the country while the new emperor's liberal gestures raised hopes for social reform among a new generation of educated gentry.

The aftermath of the war, as well as the Tsar's failure to live up to his promises, enhanced the liberals' discontent with the autocratic system and eventually led to the Decembrist uprising in 1825 (a military coup organized by young officers who favoured constitutional monarchy, increase of civil and political rights, and abolition of serfdom). Quickly and violently suppressed by Alexander's successor, Nicolas I, the uprising provoked a new

wave of repression and persecution of freethinking. However, it also provided a crucial political precedent for later democratic movements.

The Decembrists' ideas and actions as well as their tragic fate produced various responses in their contemporaries. In 1829 Peter Chaadaev (1794–1856), one of Russia's most radical cultural critics, wrote his famous *Philosophical Letter*. Originally written in French, this letter was the first of eight and the only one to appear in print in Russian translation (1836) during Chaadaev's lifetime. The letter spoke in no obscure terms of Russia's extraordinary social apathy, intellectual indolence and cultural backwardness, its mindless imitation of Western ideas, its lack of originality in thought and artistic expression. According to Chaadaev, Russians lived, as it were, 'outside history', for their collective consciousness exhibited no signs of historical continuity or deeply rooted tradition. His final diagnosis of his country was merciless: Russia never composed an integral part of the human race, but existed only in order 'to teach the world some great lesson'. This pessimistic picture was somewhat tempered by Chaadaev's later claim that perhaps because of its exclusion from the family of European nations Russia managed to avoid their ailments. This lack of heritage, Chaadaev predicted, could be transformed into a great opportunity.

Chaadaev's writings sparked incessant discussions concerning the nature and meaning of history, the place of Russia among other nations, its future and historical mission. It provided a rich context for the intense debates of the 1840s concerning Hegel's philosophy of history (see HEGEL AND HEGELIANISM) and initiated the split between the two philosophical movements in Russia: that of the Slavophiles and Westernizers.

Slavophiles

The main representatives of the Slavophile movement were Ivan Kireevsky (1806–56), the founder of the movement; Alexei Khomyakov (1804–60), historian, lay theologian, poet and innovator; Konstantin Aksakov (1817–60) and Yury Samarin (1819–76), social critics who later became active politicians. At the core of Slavophilism lies the idea of the fundamental difference between Russian and European civilization, and the belief in the uniqueness of Russia's spiritual and historic destiny. Although Slavophiles shared Chaadaev's vision of Russia's messianic future, they strongly disagreed with his basic assumptions. While for Chaadaev the exemplary connection between religion, philosophy and social progress was found in Roman Catholicism, for the Slavophiles it lay in the depths of Eastern Orthodoxy and in the semi-democratic social models adopted by the ancient Russian cities. Unlike Chaadaev, the Slavophiles did not see pre-Petrine Russia as a 'blank sheet of paper' with no values and traditions of its own; to the contrary, in Russia's past they saw inexhaustible spiritual resources, cut off by Peter the Great's opening to the West. They took it upon themselves to uncover, revive and once again make these resources philosophically and socially relevant.

Some Slavophiles, particularly Khomyakov and later Kireevsky, drew inspiration from the Eastern patristic tradition and from the teachings of the Orthodox *startsy* – religious elders and followers of a 1,000-year-old Orthodox monastic practice, whose task was to study and communicate the teachings of the Church Fathers in order to provide spiritual guidance. Not only were *startsy's* writings widely read by learned Russians in the nineteenth century, but also personal relationships with these wise men were crucial for many prominent thinkers and writers. Thus, among *startsy's* famous interlocutors were novelists and thinkers Dostoevsky, Tolstoy, Kireevsky, Soloviev and Leontiev.

The Slavophiles embraced the Orthodox ideal of spiritual wholeness of a person promoted by the *startsy* and transformed it into the philosophical concept of *sobornost'* (unanimity). Introduced by Khomiakov, *sobornost'* (which denotes the state of being together and has also been interpreted as 'harmony' or 'organic community') quickly became and still remains one of the most popular terms in Russian philosophico-religious discourse. In their vehement opposition to both authoritarianism and individualism, the Slavophiles praised *sobornost'* as the authentic expression of reciprocity, mutual responsibility and freedom in faith and love. Their social models were based on the ideal of Russian *obshchina* (village-commune) that, according to the Slavophiles, managed to preserve an intricate equilibrium of commonality and inner freedom of its members.

Like their ideological opponents the Westernizers, the Slavophiles were trained in Western ideas. As young men, some of them were profoundly influenced by Schelling and all of them were Hegelians at various stages of their intellectual career. As a result of their meditations on the philosophical systems of Aristotle and Hegel both Kireevsky and Khomyakov came to believe that the mainstream European philosophical tradition placed a disproportionate emphasis on reason, which destroyed the primordial spiritual wholeness of a person and transferred the root of a person's inner life from the moral and aesthetic sphere to the sphere of abstract reasoning.

Despite certain conservative drawbacks, Slavophile philosophy represents an important attempt of Russian thought to engage in a philosophical dialogue with the Western intellectual tradition. The Slavophiles' concern with the tragic, self-destructive disintegration of human nature, their idea of 'integral knowledge' (which united rationality, intuition and revelation) and their ideal of *sobornost'* were later developed by such thinkers as Dostoevsky and Soloviev.

Westernizers

The Westernizing movement developed in parallel and opposition to that of the Slavophiles. While Slavophiles saw Russia's separation from the West as a virtue and source of spiritual potential, Westernizers were eager to educate and modernize Russia by using European intellectual and cultural models. Also, whereas Slavophiles valued the traditions of Russian society (although they were not altogether uncritical of autocracy and sharply criticized the institution of serfdom), the majority of Westernizers advocated radical social and political transformation.

Originally followers of Schelling's *Naturphilosophie* and FICHTE's voluntaristic ideas, in the 1840s Westernizers single-mindedly turned to Hegel. Hegel's dialectics and his vision of world history as a rational process captured the minds of Russian intellectuals to the extent that some of them would stop speaking to each other if they disagreed over some key passage in Hegel's work. Ironically, Hegel's philosophy was later just as avidly rejected by Westernizers. Tested against gloomy and repressive Russian reality, Hegel's ideas inevitably lost their appeal. For example, Vissarion Belinsky (1811–48), a famous literary critic and socialist ideologue, at first promoted Hegel's dialectic as a powerful means to make sense of reality, or reconcile with it. However, as much as Belinsky tried to see the triumphant march of Reason in history, he only saw the triumph of contingency, irrationality and animal forces. He came to believe, like the existentialist philosophers some years later, that in the face of absurdity and death, no thinking and feeling person can afford any 'odious reconciliation with an odious reality'; one has to forfeit such reconciliations in the name of individual freedom and dignity.

Anti-Hegelian conversion coloured the writings of another prominent Westernizer – ALEXANDER HERZEN (1812–70) who, under the impact of personal tragedies and social catastrophes he witnessed in 1848 in France, developed an elaborate 'philosophy of contingency' that celebrated possibility and chance. Herzen attacked determinism and advocated active involvement in the making of history. Influenced by FOURIER, he became an ardent supporter of socialism and argued that Russia was predisposed to socialism because of its communal spirit and lack of bourgeois culture – an idea later elaborated by Chernyshevsky and in the 1870s enthusiastically embraced by the populists (narodniks).

Although Herzen emphasized social reform, he strongly disapproved of violence and terror as a means to achieve it, and opposed the contagious rhetoric of sacrificing the lives and resources of today in the name of future justice, happiness and prosperity. This sets him apart from the majority of contemporary socialists and especially from the younger radicals. For example, Belinsky declared that bloodshed might be necessary on the way to freedom from humiliation and suffering. The nihilists' and the anarchists' preaching of the destruction of the oppressive past and their justification of revolutionary terror was supplemented in the twentieth century by the Bolsheviks' programme to exterminate the oppressors and establish proletariat dictatorship. Herzen saw the danger of such 'social development' already in the 1850s when he expressed his disgust for bloody revolutions and predicted that socialism without political freedom would degenerate into an autocratic communism.

Regardless of Herzen's caution, in the second half of the nineteenth century, several powerful waves of revolutionary activity struck Russian society. By the early 1860s, Westernism diffused and gave way to various versions of political radicalism – nihilism, populism (narodnichestvo, derived from the Russian word narod, which means 'common people'), anarchism and, finally, Marxism.

Nihilism, populism, anarchism and early Marxism

The reign of Nicolas I (1825–55) was marked by increasing conflict between his autocratic power and the intellectuals who yearned for educational reforms, freedoms and political rights. The educated Russians were appalled at the state control over universities, an institution of ubiquitous censorship and the establishment of the secret police whose purpose was to inform the officials of anti-Government sentiments. Constant persecution of freethinking paralysed public intellectual life. Virtually all social thinkers of the time endured official persecution, imprisonment or exile and many, like Herzen, chose to leave Russia and publish abroad.

The situation changed somewhat in the 1860s and 1870s when Nicolas's successor Alexander II abolished serfdom (1861), introduced elements of Western legal systems and eased censorship. Many upper- and middle-class Russians, however, believed that the reforms had not gone far enough and continued to demand radical democratization. The organized terrorism that emerged in the late 1860s had serious consequences: in 1866 an unsuccessful attempt on the life of Alexander II provoked a strong conservative reaction and Alexander's assassination in 1881 put an end to all liberal hopes. Under Alexander III (1881–94) civil freedoms were severely infringed upon by special decrees that gave officials licence to punish political suspects without recourse to the courts.

The inter-related movements of nihilism (1860s), populism (1870–80s) and anarchism constituted an integral part of this explosive sociopolitical situation. The nihilists, impressed by Feuerbach's critique of Christianity on the one hand and advances in the natural sciences on the other, urged socialist and materialist views, and the annihilation of all religious and moral values of the past. The two philosophical cornerstones of nihilistic ideology – anthropological realism and rational egoism – were developed by Nikolai Chernyshevsky (1828–89) and defended by his adherents. The nihilists' doctrine deliberately excluded any vestige of Idealism and was based on truncated versions of Feuerbach's historical anthropologism, COMTE's Positivism and J.S. MILL's utilitarianism. By reducing human nature to a sum of psychological and physiological factors, and the human condition to a mixture of external circumstances, they efficiently eliminated the problem of individual responsibility. People were considered good or evil depending on their circumstances and the key to moral development lay in the improvement of social and material conditions. The nihilists also espoused a strictly utilitarian view of the arts and intellectual pursuits (popularized earlier by Belinsky), and considered any human endeavour indifferent to immediate human needs not only frivolous, but immoral.

The doctrine of rational egoism grew from the alleged psychological fact that people invariably act in accordance with their idea of what is beneficial for them. In his fiction Chernyshevsky portrayed a Pleiad of 'new people' – rational egoists with a socialist vision – determined to build a harmonious society of rational agents who, while seeking their own benefit, would benefit society as a whole. Chernyshevsky's work stirred up a whole generation of revolutionaries and provoked immense ideological debates. For example, his ideas were highly praised by Marx, Plekhanov and LENIN, but were severely attacked by Dostoevsky in his post-Siberian novels.

While the nihilists' rebellion was chiefly an intellectual one, the populists were ready to take action: they were associated with a peasant uprising in the 1870s, and as a part of the People's Will society they were involved in the assassination of Alexander II in 1881. The populists romanticized the virtues of common people, believed in their egalitarian and socialist instincts, and felt that intellectuals must devote themselves to 'going to the people', learning from them and helping to deliver them out of the bondage of economic and social injustice. Struck by Marx's depiction of the inhumanity of capitalist production, populists were eager to prove that Russia could reach socialism without going through the pain and humiliation of capitalism. Their ethical views found vivid expression in the teaching of Petr Lavrov (1823–1900) who emphasized the debt that the educated class owed to the people. Inspired by Lavrov, many young populist devotees left the universities and went to work among the people and popularize revolutionary ideas. Although they were eventually disillusioned about the real nature of Russian village life, the ideology of indebtedness became firmly rooted in Russian intelligentsia and was later effectively exploited by the Soviet regime.

Russian anarchism shifted its focus from the populist's general concern for common people to claims of individual liberty. MIKHAIL BAKUNIN (1814–76), a relentless political activist and founder of Russian anarchism, took part in European revolutionary movements in 1848–9, collaborated with Herzen on developing the democratic socialist doctrine, intermittently supported the populist movement and vehemently opposed Marx's version of state socialism, both in writing and personally. A fanatical lover of liberty, as he called himself, Bakunin stressed human instinct for freedom and advocated the rights of the individual to rebel against all forms of authority – political, cultural, religious and intellectual.

In 1883 in Switzerland, a group of former populists led by Georgii Plekhanov (1856–1918) founded the organization for 'Emancipation of Labour', dedicated to popularization of Marxism in Russia. The socialist-oriented Russian public enthusiastically supported their cause and by the late 1880s Marxism and its various versions and adaptations claimed their prominent place in Russia. 'Emancipation of Labour' later became known as the Russian Social Democratic Workers' Party from which the Bolshevik bloc fractured in 1903 under Lenin's leadership.

Religious and moral developments in Russian literature and philosophy

Although literary giants Tolstoy and Dostoevsky, and religious philosophers Soloviev and Leontiev, shared no unified ideological platform, they all belonged to a group of intellectuals who opposed political radicalism and sharply criticized the inadequacies and shortcomings of materialism and positivism.

The revival of metaphysical Idealism in the 1880s is associated primarily with the name of Vladimir Soloviev (1853–1900), poet, theologian and mystic as well as the most systematic Russian philosopher. The Orthodox quest for wholeness, reflected in the Slavophile teaching, culminated in Soloviev's work that attempted to demonstrate how faith and reason, religious belief and speculative philosophy all contribute to the inner unity of the intellectual world. Drawing extensively from both Eastern and Western intellectual and spiritual traditions, Soloviev managed to offer a truly remarkable philosophico-mystical synthesis of religion, philosophy and science. His aesthetics and theory of knowledge were inspired by Schelling, while his metaphysics and philosophy of history exhibited strong influence of Spinoza and Hegel. In his writings on Russia's national destiny Soloviev spoke of the integration of the human spirit with God in history, but at the end of his life he abandoned this relatively optimistic view of historical process and formulated an apocalyptic vision of a historical disaster of cosmic proportions. Soloviev's idea of 'Godmanhood' and his mystical visions of *Sophia* ('divine wisdom', or the World Soul), through which he attempted to articulate the common metaphysical ground of divine and created existence, laid foundation for the future development of Russian religious philosophy and gave rise to the school of Russian symbolist poets and thinkers of the early twentieth century. In contrast with contemporary revolutionaries, Soloviev believed in a liberal theocracy that would unite people under the spiritual rule of the Pope and the secular rule of the Russian Tsar.

The great Russian novelist, Leo Tolstoy (1828–1910), opposed political radicalism from a perspective of what he saw as true Christianity, that is, the ideal of universal love, brotherhood and non-violent resistance to evil. The profound influence of Rousseau is evident in Tolstoy's overall anti-intellectualist and anti-aristocratic world-view and his belief in the redeeming power of natural simplicity. He based his ethics on the idea of rational apprehension of duty combined with semi-religious partaking in the high moral order of life. Paradoxically, one of the world's greatest masters of fiction, Tolstoy in his late writings insistently placed his moral code over aesthetic values and even tried to modify his own creative activity in accordance with his rigid morality.

While Tolstoy tried to deprive religion of its mystical element and subordinate it to morality, the ethics and metaphysics of Feodor Dostoevsky (1821–81) remained firmly rooted in the tradition of Orthodox mysticism. Dostoevsky's legendary novels explored tragedies and paradoxes of the human condition from various, often incommensurable, perspectives. He was also an active polemicist and, like Tolstoy, published numerous essays on the current social and political questions. His post-Siberian novels offered passionate and quite elaborate critique of the contemporary versions of utilitarianism, nihilism, revolutionary utopianism and scientific materialism. The origin of the existentialist philosophy is commonly traced back to Dostoevsky's approach to the paradoxical nature of freedom and his penetrating critique of rationalism.

Konstantin Leontiev (1831–91), one of the most provocative nineteenth-century Russian thinkers, sharply criticized liberal egalitarianism as detrimental to culture and individuality, and detested the socialist and utilitarian preoccupation with the welfare of future generations that had to be achieved at the expense of concrete living individuals. Passionate aesthete and proponent of elitist culture, Leontiev viewed the processes of modernization and industrialization with great suspicion, a sentiment that both Dostoevsky and Tolstoy shared for quite different reasons. As a religious thinker, Leontiev rejected European 'pseudo-Christianity' and praised instead a Byzantine version of Christianity. Based on Leontiev's wide-ranging critique of bourgeois complacency, anti-aestheticism and conformity, his views were often compared to those of NIETZSCHE (although his books were written two decades earlier than any of Nietzsche's writings became known in Russia). Leontiev's work also anticipated the twentieth-century critique of mass culture.

Not all religious Russian thinkers viewed modernization and advances of the natural sciences in a negative light. For example, in the writings of Nikolai Fedorov (1828–1903) one finds the curious mixture of a deeply religious world-view and enthusiastic belief in the unlimited future possibilities of technological progress. Prominent themes of Fedorov's philosophy included the issues of human mortality and the possibility of universal salvation that he approached from a characteristically utopian perspective.

Conclusion

Russian thought in the nineteenth century exhibits great complexity in inter-relatedness of ideas and movements, which is why the boundaries between them are largely fictitious. The intellectual world of nineteenth-century Russia was quite small and representatives of various movements often had strong personal and ideological influence on each other. Ideas and theories were conceived, tested and revised in the process of long and impassioned debates. The greatly polemical nature of Russian thought is apparent in the texts of all thinkers described here. The energy and insight with which these thinkers examined and questioned traditions and values would continue to inform Russian intellectual history through the next century.

Further reading

Berlin, I. (1978) *Russian Thinkers*, London: The Hogarth Press.

Edie, J.M., Scanlan, J.P. and Zeldin, M.B. (eds) (1976, 1984 [1965]) *Russian Philosophy*, Chicago, IL: Quadrangle Books, 3 vols, rpt. Knoxville, TN: University of Tennessee Press.

Masaryk, T.G. (1955) *The Spirit of Russia. Studies in History, Literature and Philosophy*, trans. E. and C. Paul, with additional chapters and bibliographies by J. Slavik, 3 vols, London: Allen & Unwin.

Walicki, A. (1980) *Russian Thought from the Enlightenment to Marxism*, trans. H. Andrews-Rusiecka, Oxford: Clarendon Press.

Zenkovsky, V. (1953) *A History of Russian Philosophy*, trans. George L. Kline, 2 vols, London: Routledge & Kegan Paul.

SEE ALSO: Bakunin, Mikhail; Dostoevsky, Feodor; early socialism; Hegel and Hegelianism; Herzen, Alexander; Lenin, V.I.; Marx and Marxism; the nation, nationalism and the national principle; Tolstoy, Leo; utopianism

EVGENIA V. CHERKASOVA

S

SAINT-SIMON, HENRI DE (1760–1825)

Claude-Henri de Rouvroy, Comte de Saint-Simon was acknowledged as a precursor of socialism, partly because of his ideas on social reform, partly through the movement that took his name.

Despite his impeccable noble pedigree, Saint-Simon was one of the more spectacular class renegades of the 1790s. He supported the revolution and initially did well from speculating in property confiscated from the Church and the new paper money. After a spell of wild debauchery and extravagance during the Directory, he lost the lot. He worked as a clerk and asserted his claim to be heard as a philosopher, although most of the material he wrote during the Empire was not published in his lifetime and he was regarded as a somewhat eccentric ex-libertine. Saint-Simon acknowledged a philosophical debt to Condorcet. His plans for socio-political reform were also related to the ideas of Turgot and SIEYÈS. Saint-Simon's first draft for the society of the future, in which its productive and competent elements would govern rationally, was published in 1802. He developed his ideas with a variety of glosses during the Empire, but failed to attract publishers.

At the Restoration Saint-Simon quickly insinuated himself as a spokesman for those assorted politicians and businessmen who came to be called liberals, including the banker, Jacques Laffitte, men who previously would have considered him a reprobate and raffish outsider. They welcomed his various proposals that industrialists and businessmen should take a leading role in the state and that economic development should be a priority. He linked his ideas to those of liberal economists like J.-B. SAY. He claimed to have coined the words 'industriel' and 'industrialisme'. He increased his standing among the liberals by joining Say and others in founding the Société de Paris pour l'Instruction Élementaire in June 1815. They were concerned to define how to educate the poor in obedience and usefulness at the lowest possible cost and investigated the Bell and Lancaster system in England. Saint-Simon was commissioned to write a report on the society's experimental school at Popincourt. He concluded that they would do better to practise on biddable middle-class children instead of the Popincourt poor.

During 1816 Saint-Simon published four issues of a journal, *L'Industrie,* financed by industrialists and scientists, to publicize developments in science. He acquired AUGUSTE COMTE as secretary. The journal appeared irregularly between 1816 and 1818. The first issue contained a fairly routine financial study, but in the second Saint-Simon attacked the thieves and parasites in society who made no productive contribution to society. He contrasted them with the industrious Americans. Although the feathers of the cautious subscribers may have been ruffled by this article, the volume also contained the first thorough survey of the previous 30 years of economic development written by a leading expert, Chaptal. The third volume was more provocative. Saint-Simon's claim that politics stemmed from morals that were based on relative, not absolute, values shocked his readers, especially when he asserted that the Christian moral code was out-of-date and needed rethinking; this at a time when France was just beginning to emerge from the White Terror into an age of Catholic religious revival. Some of his subscribers denounced him to the prefect of police.

In 1819 Saint-Simon paid most of the cost of his new periodical, *Le Politique*. Twelve issues appeared, mostly cautious in tone, although the distinction between idlers and the industrious continued to be stressed. When this journal folded Saint-Simon put up the money for *L'Organisateur*. He began with a parable in which he asked his readers to consider the contrasting consequences of the loss to France of all its royals and senior clerics, whom he thought would be eminently and immediately replaceable, compared with the loss of its major businessmen and industrialists, whose loss would be very damaging. Not entirely surprisingly, Saint-Simon was charged with insulting the royal family. His jury trial, in February 1820, coincided with the actual, rather than the literary, assassination of the heir to the throne, the duc de Berri. Saint-Simon was acquitted and the juxtaposition of the imagined and real murder gave him the publicity he had been seeking for many years. Saint-Simon, encouraged, combined some of his torrent of brochures exhorting rapid economic growth into a two-volume *Système industriel*. This was swiftly followed a year later by a further collection of pamphlets, *Catéchisme des industriels*.

Like other contemporary theorists, Saint-Simon addressed the combined problems of the repercussions of the French Revolution and the impact of economic change in the context of social evolution over a long time-span. He was not alone in identifying class conflict as a problem aggravated by 1789. He argued for a complete rethinking of the basis of Government and society that took into account that the sources of wealth were varied, including industry and commerce as well as land. All of those with an active stake in the country should be involved in Government. There was nothing particularly new in this thesis; it had been the basis of the 1791 constitution and also that of 1814. Lawyers should be excluded; he judged them parasites, part of the bourgeoisie who had played a dominant and destructive role in the revolution. 'Industriels' on the other hand had had no impact in 1789. Economic growth would change their role.

Saint-Simon turned against the liberals in his latter years, realizing that they did not correspond to his 'industriels', but that many were the lawyers and other idlers he detested. He also lost faith in the power of liberal economics to generate the industrial growth he considered vital. In place of liberalism he began to put large-scale public works

and international ventures. Saint-Simon argued that although the revolution had begun the modernization of France, and that the middle class had begun to share power with the nobles, more changes were needed if further revolution and upheaval were to be averted. They should be based on a rational analysis of society. His analysis and the language he used were to be vital building bricks for the early socialists, leading to the construction of theories of class conflict. Saint-Simon divided society into 'industriels' and 'oisifs', terms he used in varying ways and whose ambiguity offered ample scope for confusion. For him 'oisifs' were those who did not work for their crust, primarily landowners and investors at the top of the ladder. The 'industriels' were the productive sector, including everyone who had to do some work to survive, as farmer, artisan, doctor, journalist and so on. In some ways his 'industriels' correspond to the electorate based on tax contributions set up in 1814, although he may have planned to include a wider cross-section of income in his politically active group. Saint-Simon called for a radical reworking of the social framework to address the urgent problems of poverty and social inequality. In his last book, *Nouveau Christianisme*, Saint-Simon observed the need to work for improvement in man's moral and physical condition through religion. He urged the development of a new form of purified Christianity, returning to the basic principles of the original disciples. His emphasis on non-traditional simple faith was not unlike that of a number of small sects that sprang up for a time throughout Europe.

Saint-Simon wrote fast and frequently changed his mind; it is easy to point to contradictions in his thought. He did not develop a single, coherent blueprint for the future. In his last book he argued that society should no longer be based on war but on industry and the love of Christ. He recommended large-scale public works and the return to religious faith as the way to reform society and the economy. This solution attracted young graduates of the École Polytechnique and the School of Medicine, engineers, doctors and their sisters and wives. This new band of reverent followers created what they called a Saint-Simonian 'school'. After Saint-Simon's death in 1825, the group, several of whom were young Jews, dispossessed from university and other careers by the intolerance of the Restoration, including Halévy and Rodrigues, also Duvergier and Bailly, agreed to publicize his ideas and worked to turn them into a coherent creed for social reform. Rodrigues, formerly a lecturer at the École Polytechnqiue and Enfantin, a graduate of the school, embarked on *Le Producteur,* a journal that Saint-Simon had been planning at the time of his death. It survived until September 1826. The founding group were young men who had been active in the *charbonnerie,* including Bazard, Carnot, Chevalier, Adolphe Blanqui, Leroux and Buchez; men whose subsequent careers were very divergent. A series of public lectures given by Bazard in 1828 stating their theories were published, *Doctrines de Saint-Simon. Exposition* (1828–30). They provided a clear account of Saint-Simon's demands for a rationally ordered society and described the present 'class' system in the country. In 1830 Leroux dedicated his paper *Le Globe* to Saint-Simonian ideas.

Although they called themselves Saint-Simonians, their ideas seemed much nearer, initially, to those of FOURIER. Like Fourier they argued that the worst faults of their own society were the repression of women and workers, and they dedicated themselves to reforming these iniquities. At the outset the group took decisions by majority vote and men and women shared the leadership. Like Fourier, they emphasized the very practical nature of their solutions. They embarked on small-scale projects to promote self-help among workers. Saint-Simon, on the other hand, had looked to a more cosmic statement of the problem, to be addressed by changing the state. The affinity of Saint-Simonians to Saint-Simon was closest in the increasing importance they all placed in a revivalist 'new' Christianity. Saint-Simonians addressed the social question from a spiritual base, turning their organization into a sect.

Saint-Simonian women constituted a separate section from 1829. They organized their own meetings, which by October 1830 had a regular attendance of around 200. Their leader was Claire Bazard, wife of one of the main theoreticians. The women's section lacked the discipline and hierarchy of the men, but was more active in its social work, particularly in educational classes for working people. Cécile Fournel, whose engineer husband devoted his fortune to the cause, and Eugénie Niboyet, also took a leading role.

Uniquely for their time they sought artisan members, including women. Following the 1830 revolution they held large public recruitment meetings, ran evening literacy classes, and members with medical training offered their services free to bring in converts. By the summer of 1831 the Parisian group had 220 worker members, 100 of them women, who had taken the Saint-Simonian membership oath. Saint-Simonians became enthusiastic believers in the 'new woman' (their own phrase). According to ENFANTIN, on his deathbed Saint-Simon had declared, 'Man and woman together constitute the social individual.' Saint-Simon himself however had little input into this feminism. His only links with women's rights were his fleeting aspiration to marry MME DE STAËL and his suggestion in 1802 that women should be represented in his proposed Conseil de Newton, a sort of European brains trust.

The most ambitious Saint-Simonian project was hostels for worker members, whose structure is reminiscent, in some aspects, of Fourier's *phalange*, and theoretically would have offered women freedom from domestic and family responsibilities. Working in the poorest and most deprived parts of Paris, two directors in each section, one male, one female, tried to acquire a building where the members could live and eat, and hold meetings together. These 'communal houses' were supposed to be self-supporting, run on the wages contributed by their worker residents. The directors actively sought worker, particularly family, membership. Unsurprisingly they were often regarded as a soft touch, a charitable foundation, and the artisans who joined were frequently in financial difficulties. The directors then helped to pay off members' debts and redeem their property if it was in pawn. Funds did not always stretch so far. Only two hostels were actually created, housing twenty-five families and 1,200 non-resident worker members, one run by Prévost in rue Popincourt and one run by Botiau and Niboyet in rue Tour d'Auvergne. The hostel project had to be abandoned when money ran out. During 1831 the movement became dominated by Prosper Enfantin whose influence caused it to fragment. Many Saint-Simonians became Fourierists. Although the movement disappeared, Saint-Simonians tended to maintain links with each other. The Saint-Simonians attracted members who were to play leading roles in France long after the movement had collapsed, including Hippolyte Carnot and Michel Chevalier.

Further reading

Baker, K. (1989) 'The Closing of the French Revolution. Saint-Simon and Comte', in F. Furet and M. Ozouf (eds) *The Transformation of Political Culture 1789–1848*, Vol. 3 of *The French Revolution and the Creation of Modern Political Culture*, 323–50, Oxford: Pergamon.

Carlisle, R.B. (1987) *The Proffered Crown. Saint-Simonianism and the Doctrine of Hope*, Baltimore, London: Johns Hopkins University Press.

Manuel, F.E. (1956) *The New World of Henri Saint-Simon*, Cambridge, MA: Harvard University Press.

Moses, C.G. (1982) 'Saint-Simonian Men/Saint-Simonian Women: The Transformation of Feminist Thought in 1830s France', *Journal of Modern History* 54: 240–67.

Saint-Simon, H. de [pub. anonymously] (1802) *Lettre d'un habitant de Genève à ses concitoyens*.

—— (1821) *Du système industriel*, Paris, A.-A. Renouard.

—— (1823–4) *Catéchisme des industriels*, Paris. Impr. de Sénier.

—— (1969 [1825]) *Le nouveau Christianisme*, ed. H. Desroche, Paris: Bosange pére.

Pilbeam P.M. (1999) 'Un aristocrate précurseur des socialistes: Henri de Saint-Simon', in English in C. Grell and A. Ramières, *Le Second Ordre: l'idéal nobiliaire*, Paris.

—— (2000) *French Socialists before Marx: Women, Workers and the Social Question in France*, Teddington: Acumen.

SEE ALSO: Deroin, Jeanne; early socialism; Enfantin, Barthélemy-Prosper; Fourier, Charles

PAMELA PILBEAM

SAY, JEAN-BAPTISTE (1767–1832)

Jean-Baptiste Say was a French political economist. Having been active in revolutionary politics for a decade, Say's first work of political economy was published in 1800, entitled *Olbie, ou essai sur les moyens d'améliorer les mœurs d'une nation* (Olbie, or Essay on the Means of Improving the Morals of a Nation). After this work was heavily criticized, Say embarked on the writing of the *Treatise on Political Economy* (*Traité d'économie politique*), published in Paris in 1803. Say's writing was censored on refusing to rewrite the book as a justification of Bonaparte's Empire. He was forced to wait until 1814 to publish a second edition; this received far more attention than the first, and three further editions followed. A third edition followed in 1817 and two further editions appeared before Say's death. Fame as a political economist was established across Europe by the time of Say's appointment to the Chair of 'Économie industrielle' at the Conservatoire des Arts et Métiers in 1819. It continued to grow throughout the 1820s, as the revolutionaries of 1830 acknowledged in granting him a Chair in 'Économie politique' at the Collège de France. Say published what he believed to be his most important work in 1828–9, the *Cours complet d'économie politique pratique* (Complete Course of Practical Political Economy). The subtitle of the work indicated Say's main aim: to make political economy 'everybody's business'. Say believed that it was vital to combat the mercantile systems that had perverted the commerce of Britain, France and the wider world. In their place it was possible to create a society that was both more just towards the poor and more productive.

Throughout his life Say remained a revolutionary in his hatred of aristocracy and luxury-based commerce. Politically he always described himself as a republican, embracing fully the austere moral code this entailed. Although he described his own work as continuing that of Smith in separating political economy from morals and politics, he was in fact Smith's disciple only in the general sense that he borrowed many of the arguments of the *Wealth of Nations*. Marx called Say 'insipid' in *Capital* (see MARX AND MARXISM). Rather than being seen as the weakest of the classical economists, Say's ideas are best understood in the context of the failure of republican constitutionalism in France, and the ongoing search for a state that was popular, stable, egalitarian in social structure, and commercially advanced.

Of Genevan and Calvinist merchant stock, both branches of Say's family were prominent in commerce at Lyon. At the age of 9 he attended a Catholic boarding school, the *philosophe*-orientated curriculum of which caused the school to be persecuted by the Bishop of Lyon. Looking back in his *Memoirs*, Say identified this as the source of an opposition to religion that continued until the end of his life. During the Restoration he planned to write a book showing the damage done to humanity by religious belief. The business problems of Say's father Jean-Étienne put an end to Say's education. In 1787 Etienne Clavière employed him in his Paris-based life assurance company. At some point before the revolution Say became Clavière's secretary. He remained in this position until he volunteered for the revolutionary army in August 1792.

Serving Clavière was the defining moment in Say's early intellectual life. Before the age of 25 Say enjoyed access to one of the most radical intellectual coteries in Paris. Numerous figures who rose to prominence in the 1790s were well known to Clavière, including Mirabeau, Brissot, SIEYÈS and Condorcet. Say found himself in a circle of men who were committed to justifying large-state republicanism against the accusation, shared by such luminaries as Montesquieu, Voltaire and Smith, that such forms of Government were only possible in small states. Clavière's group was also intent on justifying a form of republicanism that was modern, in that it was fully compatible with the commercialization of French society, against which Rousseau had so vehemently argued. Through working on Mirabeau's letters to his Aix constituents, entitled *Le Courrier de Provence*, Say became converted to these points of view. After the Terror, Say was a founder member of the journal *La Décade philosophique*, which sought to promote modern republicanism in France.

The ethics of a stable republican life that Say drew from such sources entailed an absolute probity in public and private life, and the value of industry, economy, propriety and moderation. A willingness to sacrifice self for the good of the republic was essential. In order to establish this morality only the productive groups of society were to be citizens. A greater equality of wealth had to be sought, the ideal of which Say described as a 'comfortable medium'. In the *Treatise* Say aimed to show that moderate wealth could be established in modern societies without political or social upheaval. Once laws such as primogeniture had been abolished, Say believed that industrious activity would generate enough wealth to ensure that the lowly labourer could enjoy the benefits of modern productivity. Government involvement in the economy had to be limited because of the temptation to corruption that no political officer could resist in the existing moral climate. But this did not mean that markets could be relied upon to be a force for morality by their independent action alone. Say had no faith in the 'hidden hand'. People from all of the productive groups of society had to be taught that self-interest corresponded with a life lived according to the precepts of virtue.

The role of political economy was to provide the education that would direct individuals in the economic realm. The French had to be taught to avoid the British example of inequality and social hierarchy favoured by CONSTANT. Say developed friendships with those whose view of politics and morals he believed he shared, and described those of BENTHAM as being superior to any other writer of the post-revolutionary era. The 'Law' associated with his name, that supply creates its own demand, was intended to prove the stability of an industrious and frugal culture, the foundation of a commercial society characterized by equality and independence.

Further reading

Forget, E.L. (1999) *The Social Economics of Jean-Baptiste Say: Markets and Virtue*, London: Routledge.

Sowell, T. (1972) *Say's Law: An Historical Analysis*, New Jersey: Princeton University Press.

Steiner, P. (1998) *Sociologie de la connaissance économique: essai sur les rationalisations de la connaissance économique (1750–1850)*, Paris: Presses Universitaires de France.

Whatmore, R. (2000) *Republicanism and the French Revolution: An Intellectual History of Jean-Baptiste Say's Political Economy*, Oxford: Oxford University Press.

SEE ALSO: industrialism, poverty and the working classes; liberalism; political economy

RICHARD WHATMORE

SCHELLING, F.W.J. (1775–1854)

F.W.J. Schelling's philosophy stands between Fichte and Hegel, as a struggle against both. Fichte had renewed critical philosophy by doing away with the thing-in-itself and by asserting the primacy of the free 'I am'. In the writings of his early youth, Schelling used Fichte's theory of science to interpret and criticize Spinoza: Spinoza's absolute substance is nothing other than the I. But a tension was visible right from the outset: the absolute I is mine, but it is also the Absolute as such, with all the characters of divinity. Hence the wavering between metaphysics and transcendental philosophy, a mark of Schelling's entire intellectual journey. In the first phase of his philosophy (*philosophy of nature*), Schelling sought to legitimize the path from nature to spirit, in opposition to Fichte's path from the I to nature, regarded as a mere object of representation. He used analogy as a tool for the extrapolation of empirical data borrowed from experience, arguing for the unity of all phenomena beyond the point where the power of mathematics gives out. Whereas physical science proceeds by general laws allowing for progress from one area of the real to another, this philosophy of nature considers nature as a dynamical, living totality that governs the action of opposite, mutually destructive forces. In the *System of Transcendental Idealism* (1800), Schelling went on to show the correspondence between the acts of intelligence and the moments of construction of matter. Furthermore, the ideal penetrates the real in two ways: in nature through the living organism, in spirit through the work of art. From 1801 Schelling developed the *philosophy of identity*. The Absolute is neither subject nor object, neither spirit nor nature, but the identity or indifference of both. The 'potencies' of the Absolute are defined by the excess of objectivity in nature, the excess of subjectivity in spirit, yet both nature and spirit are to be understood as a 'subject-object.' The philosophy of identity, which never leaves the Absolute (or Reason), tries to solve the problem (unsolved by Aristotle and abandoned by modern natural science) of the specific determination of beings via the idea of the continuity of forms. Art is now the expression of the infinite in the finite; Schelling believed in the forthcoming birth of a new mythology, source of inspiration for the renewal of art. *Of Human Freedom* (1809) marks the break with the philosophy of identity. In it, Schelling abandoned the deductive method in favour of systematic narrative. A finite being cannot arise from the Absolute, and therefore it comes into being by means of an entirely free act. The will proper to human being aims at existing for itself, as a universe to itself: this is the origin of evil, which does not arise from the ground (*Grund*) of nature but from an enlightened will alien to universal love. The fall of human being is also the beginning of history, which is essentially a return to God (ground and existence coincide in God only). In the *Ages of the World* (1815) Schelling expanded from the becoming of nature and man to the becoming of God. In order for God to be, it must come from non-being (first potency); in opposition to this, God is the being who is, *das Seyende* (second potency); finally God is the union of being and non-being (third potency). Each of these potencies aims at being by rejecting the other two. This creates a cycle, which will end only by sacrifice in favour of a higher will, a will that wills nothing and that belongs to no

being – *Übergottheit*. God is thus absolute freedom, free from all form of being. The matter of successive creative processes (nature, spirit, soul of the world) finds its origin in the renunciation of the three potencies. In his so-called *Later Philosophy* (1821–54), Schelling found in mythology and religion a confirmation of this theosophy. Interpreting mythology in terms of the history of human consciousness, he showed that while natural religion conceives God in its diverse potencies, Christianity is the revelation of the unity that overcomes them. Finally, philosophy leads to a fully spiritual religion. At the end of his career, Schelling distinguished between rational philosophy, or construction of what is possible, from 'positive philosophy', which starts from the pure fact of absolute freedom.

Further reading

Beach, Edward Allen (1994) *The Potencies of Gods*, Albany: State University Press of New York.
Bowie, Andrew (1993) *Schelling and Modern European Philosophy*, London: Routledge.
Brown, Robert (1977) *The Later Philosophy of Schelling*, Lewisburg: Bucknell University Press.
Esposito, Joseph (1977) *Schelling's Idealism and Philosophy of Nature*, Lewisburg: Bucknell University Press.
White, Alan (1983) *An Introduction to the System of Freedom*, New Haven, Yale University Press.

SEE ALSO: main currents in philosophy

PIERRE KERSZBERG

SCHLEGEL, CARL WILHELM FRIEDRICH VON (1772–1829)

Friedrich Schlegel was a leading representative of German Romanticism, philosopher, writer and critic. His great creativity and brilliant classical education allowed him to contribute – notably and importantly – to various fields of human science. A bright literary critic, he also wrote on the theory of language and poetry, philosophy of history and hermeneutics. Schlegel's works have had profound influence not only on the German Romantic movement but also on the next generations of philosophers, historians, writers, linguists and historians of literature.

Born in Hanover (Saxony) on 10 March 1772 Friedrich Schlegel showed an early interest to the

Ancient Greek and Roman culture, languages and philosophy. However, following the advice of his family, he started studying Law at Göttingen University in 1790. It was May 1793 when Schlegel abruptly decided to break away from his legal studies and devote his entire life to the study of the nature of the literary. Schlegel was very active in self-educating. He was well aware of every important stream of German thought. Particularly, he was influenced by KANT's *Critique of Judgment* and Fichte's doctrine of the world-creating ego, SCHELLING's natural philosophy and Schleiermacher's mysticism.

In 1794 Schlegel moved to Dresden where he betook himself to the study of Greek and Roman literature. His work resulted in a series of publications in German literary journals. In his articles, Schlegel argued that Greek civilization had reached harmony and perfection in its art and culture. According to Schlegel, Greek art is bound to nature. By contrast to its antique antecedents, modern arts abandoned its natural origin and took the path of the infinite progress that allows for multiple achievements but hinders the way to true perfection and balance.

In 1798 Friedrich and his elder brother August Wilhelm von Schlegel (translator and critic) set up a quarterly *Athenaeum* (*Athenäum*) that laid down the theoretical basis for German Romanticism. Friedrich Schlegel both edited this journal and contributed his theoretical articles. *Dialogue on Poetry* (*Gespräch über die Poesie*, 1800) is the most significant of his works published in *Athenaeum*. The four parts of this work provide a brief outline of the history of Western poetry, describe the distinctive features of the Romantic style in literature and analyse the style of Goethe's early and later works. *Dialogue* also puts forward a new interpretation of mythology as a product of human mind.

During his work at *Athenaeum*, Schlegel paid particular attention to the theoretical issues of Romanticism. He developed his conception of Romantic poetry as the only authentic type of literature. Schlegel insisted that it should be at once philosophical and religious, rhetorical and prosaic – in effect, it should embody the life itself. Also Schlegel developed a new conception of irony based on the notion of Socratic irony and Fichte's doctrine of the self-induction of thought by means of self-affirmation and self-negation. Romantic irony results from the discrepancies between the real and the ideal; it is rooted in the disagreement between the finite and the infinite.

At this time, Schlegel mostly writes short and self-contained passages that he calls 'fragments'. He praises this form of expression as the best way of literary communion: it unites the genres and amalgamates philosophy, religion, poetry and rhetoric.

Schlegel's Romantic speculations found their imaginative expression in his novel *Lucinde* (1799). Experimental in its form and contents, this novel reveals the essence of love between man and woman. Described as the harmony between feelings and mind, and the synthesis of the masculine and the feminine, love requires education and culture from a woman. This semi-biographical novel refers to Schlegel's relationship with Dorothea Veit, whom he married in 1804.

In 1802 Schlegel moved to Paris. This opened a new stage of his intellectual development. From now on, he focused on linguistics and comparative studies of languages and literatures. In Paris Schlegel studied Sanskrit and Indian culture and published his *On the Language and Wisdom of the Indians* (*Über die Sprache und Weisheit der Indier*, 1808). In this work, he examined India's culture and philosophy, and analysed the inter-relation between Sanskrit and modern Indo-European languages. For the first time in the history of science he clearly demonstrated that it is grammatical structure of languages – rather than their vocabulary – that constitutes the primary subject matter of comparative linguistics. In 1808 Schlegel and his wife became Roman Catholics. Schlegel had prepared himself for this event beforehand by studying patristic and scholastic texts.

In 1809 in Vienna Schlegel started his political career as an Imperial Court Secretary. At the same time, he continued his research work and gave two series of lectures, namely *A Course of Lectures on Modern History* (*Über die neuere Geschichte*, 1810; first published in 1811) and *Lectures on the History of Literature* (*Geschichte der alten und neueren Literatur*, 1812; first published in 1815). Here, Schlegel's general attention shifted from the theory of literature to the consideration of its patriotic function and its conformity to Christian world outlook. He also considered the types of tragic conclusion and other particular issues. In the period between 1820 and 1823 Schlegel co-edited the Catholic magazine *Concordia*.

Schlegel died on 11 January 1829. His intellectually turbulent life that had led him from his early Romanticism to Catholic conservatism resulted in a number of important contributions to the human sciences.

Further reading

Eichner H. (1970) *Friedrich Schlegel*, New York: Twayne.

Schlegel, F. (1849) *A Course of Lectures on Modern History...*, trans. L. Purcell and R.H. Whitelock, London: H.G. Bohn.

—— (1859) *Lectures on the History of Literature, Ancient and Modern...*, trans. H.G. Bohn, London: H.G. Bohn.

—— (1968) *Dialogue on Poetry and Literary Aphorism*, trans. E. Behler and R. Struc, University Park: The Pennsylvania State University Press.

—— (1971) *Lucinde and the Fragments*, trans P. Firchow, Minneapolis: University of Minnesota Press.

—— (2001) *On the Language and Wisdom of the Indians*, trans. E.J. Millington, London: Ganesha Publishing; Tokyo: Edition Synapse.

SEE ALSO: Kant, Immanuel; Romanticism, individualism and ideas of the self; Schelling F.W.J.

EVELINA BARBASHINA

SHAW, GEORGE BERNARD (1856–1950)

Born in Dublin in 1856, Bernard Shaw was a largely self-educated man. His Protestant, lower middle-class family moved to London (1873) and he followed, in 1876, to seek his fortune as a writer. Subsequently, he became a leading spokesman of the newly founded Fabian Society (1884), advocating a distinctive, reformist socialism. Shaw's artistic career developed more slowly, but, during the 1890s, he achieved success as a playwright, promoting an 'Ibsenite' agenda of social reform. In the Edwardian period, *Man and Superman* (1903), *John Bull's Other Island* (1904) and *Major Barbara* (1905) cemented an international reputation as a master of the 'intellectual comedy of manners' and explored the contemporary issues of eugenics, imperialism and philanthropy. Having resigned from the Fabian Executive in 1911, Shaw's contribution to twentieth-century debate – e.g. *The Intelligent Woman's Guide to Socialism and Capitalism* (1928) and *Everybody's Political What's What* (1944) – emphasized the technocratic, at the expense of the democratic, aspect of socialism. Visually distinctive and personally eccentric, Shaw died in Hertfordshire in 1950, having enjoyed further artistic success with plays such as *Heartbreak House* (1920) and *Saint Joan* (1923).

In the early 1880s, Shaw adopted a secular radicalism, then abandoned it for an eclectic, libertarian socialism that synthesized concepts drawn from PROUDHON, RUSKIN and Marx (see MARX AND MARXISM). However, by the late 1880s, the ideas of HENRY GEORGE, LASSALLE, JEVONS and Sidney Webb were far more important to the *statist* municipal collectivism that Shaw had come to advocate. Building on two essays on political tactics and economics that he contributed to the *Fabian Essays in Socialism* (1889), Shaw sought to accommodate both 'labourists' and 'permeators' (see SIDNEY AND BEATRICE WEBB) in texts such as the *Fabian Election Manifesto* of 1892, and argued for the 'subordination of commercial enterprise to national ends' in *Fabianism and the Fiscal Question* (1904). A Fabian lecture on 'Equality' in 1910 introduced the distinctively Shavian idea (later popularized by *The Intelligent Woman's Guide*) that a fully socialist society would distribute income according to a principle of exact arithmetical equality.

Always fond of paradox, between 1890 and 1914 Shaw sought to develop an artistic philosophy that sat uneasily with the humdrum moderation of Fabianism. Many vitalist and evolutionist arguments were published as prefaces to Shaw's plays, but he also wrote two notable books of criticism: *The Quintessence of Ibsenism* (1891) – which drew attention to the merits of Ibsen's *feminism* – and *The Perfect Wagnerite* (1898). The latter drew on Nietzschean themes and introduced the 'life-force' philosophy made far more explicit in *Man and Superman*, a play that debunked socialism, democracy and progress ('the illusion of illusions'). Strictly speaking, Shaw's infamous apologies for Stalinism and fascism (as necessary gateways to collectivism) fall outside our period; but it is plausible to argue that they were logical extensions of nineteenth-century concepts of the 'artist-legislator', of 'clerisy' and of '*realpolitik*', once the events of 1914–22 had seemed to demonstrate the efficacy of political violence and the inefficacy of liberalism.

Further reading

Griffith, G. (1993) *Socialism and Superior Brains: The Political Thought of Bernard Shaw*, London, New York: Routledge.

Innes, C. (ed.) (1998) *The Cambridge Companion to George Bernard Shaw*, Cambridge: Cambridge University Press.

Shaw, G.B. (ed.) (1996) *Fabian Essays in Socialism*, London: Pickering & Chatto, Democratic Socialism in Britain series (first published 1889).

SEE ALSO: intellectuals, elites and meritocracy; Marx and Marxism; Social Darwinism; novels, poetry and drama

CLIVE E. HILL

SIDGWICK, HENRY (1838–1900)

The British academic, Henry Sidgwick, was a prolific author on philosophical, political and economic issues throughout his adult life. His main contributions to nineteenth-century thought were challenging, but ultimately conservative, arguments on the controversial subjects of hedonism, individualism, democracy and collectivism.

In May 1838, Sidgwick was born in Skipton, Yorkshire; a member of a prosperous cotton-spinning family that also enjoyed a strong Anglican sacerdotal tradition. Thus, the death of his father in 1841 did not preclude a 'middle-class' education for Henry, culminating in successful studies at Rugby School and Cambridge University. In 1859 he was elected a fellow of Trinity College, Cambridge, and – despite his subsequently controversial support for the admission of women to the university – after a series of promotions, he became Knightsbridge Professor of Moral Philosophy in 1883. In 1876 Henry married Eleanor Balfour (1845–1931), an industrious scholar, a campaigner for female education and Principal of Newnham College from 1892 to 1910. As well as producing a substantial *œuvre* in philosophy, politics and economics (which included several posthumous works), Sidgwick shared his wife's interest in the supernatural. As prominent members of the Society for Psychic Research, they toured the British Isles frequently during the 1880s and 1890s seeking evidence for a variety of psychic phenomena (cf. Blanshard 1984: 213–18). Sidgwick's four most significant publications were *The Methods of Ethics* (1874), *Principles of Political Economy* (1883), *The Elements of Politics* (1891) and The *Development of European Polity* (1903).

A correspondent of JOHN STUART MILL, Sidgwick lacked the direct personal connection with JEREMY BENTHAM necessary to be considered a 'Philosophic Radical'. Nevertheless, the detailed and sympathetic discussion of the theories of Hume, Bentham and the younger Mill in *The Methods of Ethics* has led to the common assumption that Sidgwick represented the 'next generation' of British utilitarian thinkers. Against this, however, the leading twentieth-century commentator on Sidgwick has argued that 'it is a mistake to view the book [*Methods*] as primarily a defence of utilitarianism' (Schneewind 1977: 192) and has emphasized its engagement with common-sense morality. Moreover, the frequent references to Aristotle, Plato, Butler, KANT and GREEN also seem irreconcilable with the view of *Methods* as a late-utilitarian manifesto.

Sidgwick expanded the idea of 'rule-utilitarianism' beyond the jurisprudential framework established by Bentham and Austin, and sought to show that moral intuitions (rules of common-sense morality) are an essential foundation for ethical calculation in everyday life. He argued that the role of a utilitarian philosopher should be limited to using the utility principle to develop criticisms of already existing rules – but in a manner that did not subvert society's current consensus of moral belief (cf. Schneewind 1977: 340–51). The same concern to promote consensus can be seen in his attempt to reconcile egoism (any theory that justifies actions in terms of an agent's own happiness) and utilitarianism ('the ethical doctrine that takes universal happiness as the ultimate end and standard of right conduct') through a system of 'universalistic hedonism' that had certain Kantian features. However, Sidgwick's academic approach led him to conclude that no complete reconciliation of these perspectives was possible – not even through reference to the 'third position' of common-sense morality.

In the years after 1886, Henry Sidgwick was associated politically with the Liberal Unionist party (which worked in alliance with the Conservatives). He shared with HERBERT SPENCER, ALBERT VENN DICEY and a variety of other late-Victorian 'Individualists' serious reservations about a fully universal suffrage and this helps us to understand his movement away from 'Gladstonism'. Sidgwick seems to have originally favoured an ungendered household suffrage, but to have subsequently concluded (during the 1880s) that only single, propertied women should be entrusted with the vote, thereby reducing even further the proportion of the population that would enjoy political influence in his favoured form of polity. Democracy was both an unreliable philosophy of Government and a potential gateway to state collectivism.

The liberal component of Sidgwick's empirical utilitarianism seemed radical in the third quarter of the nineteenth century, but by the 1880s he was unwilling to follow Mill in the direction of even a 'qualified' socialism. Sidgwick's *Principles of Political Economy* (1883) was notable for its assertion that a strictly utilitarian view of economic efficiency could identify a number of 'market failures' that appeared to validate the case for increased state intervention in the economy, but Sidgwick qualified this collectivism by arguing that a democracy was barely competent to engage in national economic management. Moreover, his popular essay on 'Economic Socialism' (1886) reasserted the Smithite argument that wealth is produced most efficiently in a society where Government leaves private industry to its own devices.

Critical debate about Sidgwick has been conspicuously absent from recent literature on liberalism. Although there are clear discrepancies between the views of Sidgwick taken by scholars such as Schneewind and Rawls regarding the classification of Sidgwick as a utilitarian philosopher, there was no direct engagement between the two commentators. (Moreover, Rawls's two-page introduction to the 1981 Hackett edition of *Methods* hardly constitutes a major piece of research.) Only Taylor (cf. Taylor 1992: 221) can be said to have taken a 'revisionist view' – he criticized the common assumption that Sidgwick sought to reconcile collectivism and individualism, and to place him firmly in the 'Individualist' camp – and Taylor's work is completely ignored in the collection of essays edited by Harrison (cf. Harrison 2001). At the present time, a fully fledged Sidgwick revival seems possible, but unlikely.

References

Blanshard, B. (1984) *Four Reasonable Men: Marcus Aurelius, John Stuart Mill, Ernest Renan, Henry Sidgwick*, Connecticut: Wesleyan University Press.

Harrison, R. (ed.) (2001) *Henry Sidgwick*, Oxford: British Academy/Oxford University Press.

Schneewind, J. (1977) *Sidgwick's Ethics and Victorian Moral Philosophy*, Oxford: Clarendon Press.

Taylor, M. (1992) *Men versus the State: Herbert Spencer and Late Victorian Individualism*, Oxford: Clarendon Press.

SEE ALSO: liberalism; main currents in philosophy; political economy; theories of the state and society: the science of politics

CLIVE E. HILL

SIEYÈS, EMMANUEL-JOSEPH (1748–1836)

The French political theorist, political economist, and statesman Emmanuel-Joseph Sieyès's main contribution to political and economic thought was his justification of what is often termed the modern republic: the constitutional order combining the rule of law, limited Government and law-making by representatives of the people within a commercial society. His most famous act was to persuade the members of the Third Estate in the Estates General of 1789, and members elected from the other two orders who would join them, to declare themselves representatives of the sovereign nation. The constitutional revolution thereby defined had been justified by Sieyès in three pamphlets written concurrently and published between the end of 1788 and the spring of 1789. The most influential, *What is the Third Estate?* (*Qu'est-ce que le Tiers État?*), appeared in January 1789. The two others are especially important in working out what Sieyès actually envisaged in proposing rapid and varied constitutional innovation: *Essai sur les privilèges* (Essay on privileges) and *Vues sur les moyens d'exécution don't les représentants de la France pourront disposer en 1789* (*Views on the Means of Execution that the Representatives of France will Have at their Disposal in 1789*). Sieyès subsequently published numerous commentaries on the course of the revolution, which he retained some hopes of redirecting. The most notable include: *Préliminaire de la constitution: reconnaissance et exposition raisonnée des droits de l'homme et du citoyen* (*Prologue to the Constitution: Recognition and Reasoned Exposition of the Rights of Man and Citizen*) (July 1789); *Dire de l'abbé Sieyès sur la question du veto royal à la séance du 7 septembre 1789* (*Speech by the Abbé Sieyès on the Question of the Royal Veto*); Letters to the *Moniteur* rebutting Thomas Paine's view of republicanism (6 and 16 July 1791); *Des intérêts de la liberté dans l'état social et dans le système représentatif* (*The Benefits of Liberty in the Social State and the Representative System*), published in the *Journal d'instruction sociale*, 8 June 1793; *Du nouvel établissement public de l'instruction en France* (*Concerning the New Public Establishment of Instruction in France*), published in the *Journal d'instruction sociale*, 22 June–6 July 1793; *Opinion de Sieyès sur les attributions et l'organisation du constitutionnaire proposé le 2 thermidor* (*Sieyès's Opinion on the Organization and Attributes of the Proposed Constitutional Jury*), speech in the Convention, 5 August 1795.

In 1789 Sieyès made national sovereignty the watchword of the new revolutionary order. Shifting political language to his sense of this term was an enormous achievement. In the recent past national sovereignty had been used to justify possible divisions of political authority between kings and *parlements*, kings and estates, and between the king and the people. Sieyès severed the link with these corporatist perspectives on the body politic. National sovereignty now signified a unified but abstract being, the nation, as represented by a political body, the members of the self-proclaimed 'national assembly'. The first aspect of national sovereignty highlighted by Sieyès was the representative system it entailed. The second was civil equality, because the nation could never maintain itself in the midst of privileged classes or castes. It became essential to reorganize France into equal administrative units under a central government and legislature. The nation thus became a homogeneous political entity standing above other political actors. Following Hobbes, Sieyès argued that a free and stable society could only be established if the sovereign reigned over all of the component parts of the political realm. Neither the people acting as a body, the landed proprietors, the monarch, merchants or capitalists, could be entrusted with ultimate political authority. National sovereignty did not, evidently, mean popular sovereignty. Sieyès was as implacably opposed to democracy as he was to the sovereignty of a hereditary monarch. He continued to try to establish what he called a 'republican monarchy' or 'monarchical republic' despite his belief that the national assembly had betrayed him, between the autumn of 1789 and the spring of 1790, by nationalizing the property of the Church, and by giving the King a suspensive veto over acts of law. It was ever more apparent as the decade progressed that there was a large gap between what Sieyès intended for France and the more popular philosophy

imputed to him by many leading revolutionaries. Uncertainty about his actual beliefs came to a head after his involvement with Bonaparte in the creation of the Consulate in 1799. Although it is now clear that Sieyès was seeking to justify the kind of modern republic we would recognize today, what he meant by this has remained unclear. As a consequence, his influence over leading figures in nineteenth-century thought, such as BENJAMIN CONSTANT, has been understated. The miraculous recovery of Sieyès's papers in the 1960s, now available for scrutiny in the Archives nationales de France, has enabled scholars to reassess his work. In the process they have restored him to the kind of prominence he enjoyed among contemporary political writers in the 1790s.

Sieyès was born in the small Provençal town of Fréjus, the son of an administrator in the service of the King. Although he felt no calling, Sieyès accepted his father's demand that he enter the Church, arriving at the seminary of Saint-Sulpice at Paris in 1765. Ordained as a priest in 1772, Sieyès became, through paternal patronage, secretary to Lubersac, appointed in 1775 Bishop of Tréguier in Brittany. Five years later he followed Lubersac to a new diocese, Chartres, and became the Bishop's vicar-general. In 1783 he was made a canon and in 1786 councillor to the assembly of the French clergy. In 1787 he was appointed representative of the clergy in the Provincial Assembly of Orléans, and in 1788 chancellor of the chapter at Chartres. His moderate clerical ascent ended in the autumn of 1788, when he began to outline the proposals for the Estates General that were to bring him national renown.

Sieyès was elected to the Estates General by the Third Estate of Paris, taking his seat on 25 May. On 10 and 15 June he presented two motions that led to the transformation of the Estates General into a National Assembly. On 14 July he was elected to the Committee charged with drafting a new constitution and was assigned the task of drawing up a declaration of rights. Despite becoming disillusioned with the Assembly, Sieyès was largely responsible for the territorial redivision of France into departments. As a member of the Directory of the Departement of Paris he was involved, in April 1791, in defending liberty of worship, and surfaced again in the National Convention, in which he voted for the death of the King. When the Terror began, until July 1794, he disappeared from active politics. During 1795,

Sieyès served in foreign affairs, negotiating the Franco-Dutch Treaty in May of that year. Under the Directory he was elected to the Council of 500 but refused to serve as a minister. He did, however, agree to act as special envoy to the court of Berlin, where he remained for almost a year from May 1798. In the spring of 1799 he returned to the political stage once more, acting first as Executive Director and subsequently as president of the Directory from 18 June 1799. Acknowledging the need for a new constitution, and for the involvement of a leading military figure, he agreed to work with Bonaparte in planning what became the *coup d'état* of 9–10 November 1799. Having become one of three consuls, he was out-manœuvred by the more populist Bonaparte in the formation of the Consular constitution. Again he retreated into obscurity. In name he was made first president of the Senate, maintained his senatorial status throughout the Empire, and became a count in 1808. In reality he had retired to the comfortable estate granted to him for public service. After Waterloo he was exiled as a Bonapartist and regicide, and lived in Brussels until 1830. The revolution in France of that year allowed him to return to Paris, where he lived hand-to-mouth and largely in isolation until his death.

The seeds of Sieyès's later ideas can be found in his first work, completed in 1775, the *Lettres aux économistes sur leur système de politique et de morale* (*Letters to the Physiocrats concerning their Political and Moral System*). Despite being approved by the censor, for an unknown reason it was never published, although the most likely is Turgot's fall from power. Sieyès continued to add notes to the manuscript for at least the next decade. As the title implies, it was an examination of the physiocratic diagnosis of the ills of the French state, as expounded by François Quesnay and Victor Riquetti de Mirabeau. Sieyès shared the view of the physiocrats that human society was best conceived as a means of better satisfying the subsistence needs shared by all of its members. Like them he recognized the importance of combating the tendency of modern commercial societies to become amoral arenas dominated by merchants, aristocrats or despots. Neither party had any faith in remedies associated with the restoration of classical republicanism, Christian charity or the community of goods. But Sieyès rejected the physiocratic claim that agriculture was the exclusive source of the net product, the

measure of wealth creation. Accordingly, he opposed the social order they favoured for modern France. In associating the rational exercise of authority with the landed class, the physiocrats were establishing what Sieyès called a '*ré-privée*' rather than a legitimate society, which he called a '*ré-publique*'. They were creating an aristocracy from a contingent group in society, which had no natural right to exercise sovereignty. The physiocratic division of society into productive agricultural and sterile commercial and manufacturing classes was condemned as a vestige of feudalism. They were mistaken, he argued, because of the necessity of establishing a commercial society founded on the productive power of labour if modern states were to maintain order and defend. Sieyès claimed that the most important movement in modern history was 'the conversion of the largest part of the toiling class, who were forced to provide personal services, into free artisans who produce tangible wealth'. This had been responsible for 'the prosperity of modern nations' and was in opposition to 'all the different kinds of idleness' epitomized by aristocracy. Sieyès outlined a conjectural history describing how a multitude became a democratically governed society before the progress of commerce and increasing size of the state made it necessary to establish a modern nation: a single body with a will, governed by 'indirect democracy' or the system of representation. Smith's description of the natural progress of opulence, in Books III and IV of the *Wealth of Nations*, clearly played a large role in Sieyès work. At the same time he rejected Smith's cautious approach to politics founded on the claim that the British constitution was on the whole suited to commerce. Sieyès held this to be insufficient, arguing that Britain's was as aristocratic as France and consequently had as corrupt a constitution. Political procedures and constitutional mechanisms could be found that would genuinely increase the liberty and happiness experienced in society, while combating 'the unfortunate descent into commercial greed'.

Sieyès claimed that he had 'gone beyond Smith' in 'recognising the distribution of large professions or trades as the true principle of the progress of the social state'. What Sieyès meant by this was that the division of labour had altered the social structure of modern society and made imperative political change in accordance with this movement. Smith, because of his British prejudices, had failed to acknowledge that modern constitutions had to ensure 'the representation of labour'. Sieyès explained that the division of labour was a representative system. Those who served the individual by producing goods were akin to those who made political decisions. Applying the division of labour to political life required the separation of powers, and an absolute distinction between the making of law and its execution. Law was to be made by legislators indirectly elected from the body of the people. The execution of law was to be overseen by a single representative, the Bourbon king. All of those involved in politics, as representatives, could lose their position if the national will asserted itself and judged them to be failing in carrying out their duties. Such a view of politics had two important consequences. The first was that the popular element of the constitution had to be limited to association with the abstract sovereign body or nation. Democracy was a flawed system of government because it was backward looking, and incompatible with the division of labour as it had developed in all walks of life. The second was that political stability was fostered by Sieyès's representative system because of the division of labour. Commercial ties between individuals created groups with interests that were expressed through the representative system. In this way what Montesquieu had called 'intermediary powers' were established between the government and the people; they were conducive to a culture of peace and moderation. In an argument reminiscent of Madison's tenth *Federalist*, Sieyès argued that his republic was most suited to large states in which expansive commerce would be coupled with greater means of self-defence.

In all of his writings Sieyès argued that citizens had to become independent, but at the same time persuaded to recognize their need for social ties and the duties that accompanied them. One of the first roles he identified for national legislators was to enlighten men about their 'happiness'. This entailed fixing the meaning of the term 'industry' to make apparent the difference between productive industry and 'false riches, those of secondary importance, and especially wasteful, destructive, or ruinous wealth'. When the revolution became more violent and unstable, he began to concentrate on protecting constitutional laws from the irrational acts of overpowerful legislators by means of a constitutional jury. Civic instruction also became the essential bedfellow of constitutional reform. While

he shared the view of Condorcet, his fellow editor of the *Journal d'instruction sociale*, that the state ought to direct the intellectual, moral and physical education of its citizens, he was less optimistic about the individual's capacity to reason independently and enlighten their own self-interest. Accordingly, it was necessary to establish institutions that would make the practice of certain social virtues habitual by instilling them in the general populace. The most important was a series of local and national fêtes to commemorate 'the work of nature, human society, and the French Revolution'. Through these measures a more justly governed and egalitarian commercial society would develop.

Further reading

Forsyth, M. (1987) *Reason and Revolution: The Political Thought of the Abbé Sieyès*, Leicester: Leicester University Press.
Hont, I. (1994) 'The Permanent Crisis of a Divided Mankind: The Contemporary Crisis of the Nation State in Historical Perspective', *Political Studies* 42, 1: 166–231.
Pasquino, P. (1998) *Sieyès et l'invention de la constitution en France*, Paris: Editions Odile Jacob.
Sieyès, E.-J. (2002) *The Political Writings of the Abbé Sieyès*, ed. and trans. M. Sonenscher, Cambridge, MA: Hackett.

SEE ALSO: liberalism; the nation, nationalism and the national principle; theories of the state and society: the science of politics

RICHARD WHATMORE

SIMMEL, GEORG (1858–1918)

Georg Simmel's reputation has long suffered by being under the shadow of WEBER. Certainly one cannot find a rigorous, systematic sociology in Simmel's work, as one can in Weber's. Yet what is so striking about Simmel is precisely his lack of system, his eclectic range of interests, and wide-ranging subjects of research. From an early period (1890–1908), whose high point was the publication of the *Philosophie des Geldes* (*Philosophy of Money*), in 1900, Simmel devoted himself to trying to establish sociology as an independent discipline. But he devoted just as much effort to philosophical studies (*Kant* (1904), *Die Probleme der Geschichtsphilosophie* (*Problems of the Philosophy of History*) (1892), *Schopenhauer und Nietzsche* (1907)) and to studies of art and aesthetics (*Rembrandt* [1916]), metaphysics (*Lebensanschauung* [*Philosophy of Life*, 1918]) and contemporary civilization, including numerous articles on the position of women, sexuality, religion, the city, aristocracy, friendship and love, marriage, pessimism and his famous piece on 'The Stranger'.

In his attempt to promote sociology, stated most clearly in his article 'The Problem of Sociology' (*Annals of the American Academy of Political Science*, vol. 6, 1895), Simmel did not set out to define 'society'. Rather than hypostatize society, Simmel insisted that society was no more than the interactions or reciprocal effects (*Wechselwirkungen*) and 'essential interrelatedness' (*Wesenszusammengehörigkeit*) that comprise it. Since society is no more than the sum total of reciprocal relations, all areas of human interaction come into Simmel's purview, as examples of what he terms 'sociation' (*Vergesellschaftung*). For Simmel, sociology must study not society as a totality, must not concern itself with the relation between the parts and the whole, since this notion of 'the whole' already presupposes the thing that is to be understood; rather, sociology must seek to comprehend the various forms of 'sociation', and thus understand society as a form of becoming, as experience and as never-completed aesthetic object.

The clearest example of this approach is provided by Simmel's *Philosophy of Money*, in which the necessary inter-relatedness of the mature money economy and the cosmopolitan, intellectual world of the metropolis is shown to be the focal point of modernity. Simmel was born in the heart of Berlin, and his sociology, with its aestheticization of reality, its relativism and stress on the fragmentary, chaotic and discontinuous experience of modernity, was largely a description of that city; as one commentator put it in 1901, the *Philosophy of Money* 'could only be written in these times and in Berlin'. Like Walter Benjamin and Siegfried Kracauer (the latter a student of Simmel's), Simmel captured the alienating, transitory feel of the modern city, but insisted also on the excitement gained through 'the unexpectedness of onrushing impressions' and the 'heightened awareness and predominance of intelligence' that underpins metropolitan life. Like BERGSON, Simmel saw life as a creative energy, and nowhere is this more clear than in his description of the modern city.

Although Simmel, as a result of anti-Semitism, was not promoted to a professorship until 1914 – and then in Strasburg rather than Berlin – his lectures were enormously popular. Despite the curmudgeonly attitude of the Prussian authorities, he occupied a stellar place in Berlin's intellectual life and, until the watershed of the Great War, was at the forefront of the analysis of metropolitan modernity. His strength as a philosopher lies precisely in his rejection of system and his wide-ranging and engaging illustrations of what he meant by sociation. As one of his favourite students, George Lukács, put it, Simmel was 'the true philosopher of impressionism', 'a philosophical Monet'.

References

Simmel, George (1950) 'The Metropolis and Mental Life', in Kurt H. Wolff (ed.) *The Sociology of Georg Simmel*, 409–24, here p. 410, New York: The Free Press of Glencoe.

Further reading

Frisby, David (1992) *Simmel and Since: Essays on Georg Simmel's Social Theory*, London: Routledge.
—— (1992) *Sociological Impressionism: A Reassessment of Georg Simmel's Social Theory*, 2nd edn, London: Routledge.
Frisby, David and Featherstone, Mike (eds) (1997) *Simmel on Culture: Selected Writings*, London: Sage.

SEE ALSO: Bergson, Henri; Durkheim, Emile; Mosca, Gaetano; Nietzsche, Friedrich; Pareto, Wilfredo; social theory and sociology in the nineteenth century; Tönnies, Ferdinand; Weber, Max

DAN STONE

SISMONDI, JEAN-CHARLES-LÉONARD SIMONDE DE (1773–1842)

Jean-Charles-Léonard was a Genevan political economist and historian. In political economy Sismondi came to prominence as the leading liberal critic of *laissez-faire* in the first half of the nineteenth century. As a historian, he was a dedicated student of Gibbon, and sought to chart the uneven development of modern forms of liberty as independence in Italy and in France.

Sismondi's first work of political economy, completed at the end of the eighteenth century, analysed the economic situation of two newly annexed branches of France's Empire; first

Geneva, in the *Statistique du département du Léman* (Analysis of the Leman department), and second Tuscany, in the *Tableau de l'agriculture toscane* (Outline of Tuscan Agriculture). In 1803 he published a more general work of political economy that received favourable attention: *De la richesse commerciale, ou principes d'économie politique, appliqué à la législation et du commerce* (Of Commercial Wealth, or the Principles of Political Economy, Applied to Law and to Trade). Sismondi here claimed to be to applying Adam Smith's 'science of the statesman or legislator' to the post-revolutionary world. Like SAY's *Treatise on Political Economy*, which appeared in the same year, Sismondi sought to restrict the involvement of the state in the production of wealth. At the same time he aimed to foster forms of commerce compatible with an austere code of morality, and accordingly attacked luxury, ostentation and prodigality.

During the Restoration he became more pessimistic about the prospects for commercial reform, having seen at first hand the squalor and misery that accompanied mechanization and the growth of the factory. Sismondi continued to blame the dominant mercantile system that governed public policy in the major states of Europe. But he ceased to have faith in solutions founded on the liberty of trade, and rejected the optimistic assessments for future growth and long-term stability epitomized, he believed, by the work of Say and RICARDO. His attack on their ideas, rejecting the free market as a means of guaranteeing stability in commercial society, was published in the article 'Political Economy', written for the *Edinburgh Encyclopaedia* in 1816, and in book form in 1819 as *New Principles of Political Economy* (*Nouveaux principes d'économie politique*). The latter work identified large farms and factories, the extension of the division of labour and the increased use of machinery in place of labour as signs of contemporary economic malaise. Their root cause, Sismondi claimed, was a disjunction between the production of wealth and its consumption. He argued that the Say–Ricardo doctrine of expanding demand without regard to the capacity of the market to supply goods risked the creation of a 'general glut': when goods were sold at less than their cost of production, with dire consequences for employment. His great fear was that governments would 'excite production' during periods of distress, leading to a short-term rise in wages,

a consequent rise in population and the ultimate unemployment of this population when returns on capital fell. Such problems could only be addressed indirectly. In the short term he advocated guaranteed wages to sever the link between income level and population growth. He also supported Poor Law Relief and restrictions on the right to marry unless adequate prospects could be proven. In the longer term it was essential that governments encouraged laws to protect the worker from abuse by aristocrats and capitalists.

In his day Sismondi was best known outside Britain as a historian. Between 1807 and 1818 he published his celebrated *History of the Italian Republics* (*Histoire des républiques italiennes*) in sixteen volumes. This was followed in 1813 by *De la littérature du midi de l'Europe* (Historical View of the Literature of the South of Europe) and *Julia Sévéra*, a description of the manners and customs of the Gauls under Clovis. Between 1818 and the end of his life he laboured on what he considered his greatest work, the *Histoire des Français* (History of the French), which, although voluminous, was never completed. MICHELET claimed that in these works he could discern the prejudices of Genevan and Italian republicanism. At the same time he called Sismondi the founder of the historical discipline in France, and his work monuments to the nations whose history they described.

Although he was born and died in Geneva, Sismondi's life was one of continuous exile and adventure. From a prosperous bourgeois family, Sismondi was educated in Philosophy and in Law at the Geneva Academy. His family abandoned Geneva in 1794 when the French Terror was beginning to infect the city, resulting in the short-term imprisonment of Sismondi and his father. Initially they wanted to return to Peasmarsh in Sussex, where they had spent time in 1793, but lack of funds caused them to move to Pescia in Tuscany, where they remained until 1800. On returning to Geneva, Sismondi became involved with the circle of friends, headed by the Pictet brothers, who wrote for the journal *Bibliothèque Britannique*. This led to wider intellectual friendships, particularly with CONSTANT. Both men were then working at resolving the problem of establishing free constitutions in large republics. Constant caused Sismondi to become a member of GERMAINE DE STAËL's Coppet Circle. With respect to politics Sismondi shared the Circle's Anglophilia. Democracy, he stated, was among the worst forms of Government. He admired the British constitution because, in his eyes, it guaranteed limited Government through a balance between monarch, aristocracy and people. Sismondi was well known to correspondents and readers of his books across the globe as the most cosmopolitan of men, and an arch-opponent of slavery, empire and 'pointless wars'. The irony is that he has been largely neglected by historians in the Anglophone world.

Further reading

Salis, J.-R. de (1932) *Sismondi, 1773–1842. La vie et l'œuvre d'un cosmopolite philosophe*, Paris: Librairie Ancienne Honoré Champion.
Sismondi, J.-C.-L. Simonde de. (1847) *Political Economy, and the Philosophy of Government. With an Historical Notice of his Life and Writings, by Mignet*, London: Chapman.
Stedman-Jones, G. (2002) 'National Bankruptcy and Social Revolution: European Observers on Britain, 1813–1844', in D. Winch and P.K. O'Brien (eds) *The Political Economy of British Economic Experience 1688–1914*, 61–92, Oxford: Oxford University Press.
Sowell, T. (1974) *Classical Economics Reconsidered*, New Jersey: Princeton University Press.

SEE ALSO: industrialism, poverty and the working classes; liberalism

RICHARD WHATMORE

SMITH, SYDNEY (1771–1845)

Sydney Smith, satirist, social critic, society wit and Anglican clergyman, was born in Woodford, Essex, England in 1771. The second of five children, Sydney was the son of a difficult and authoritarian business speculator and an epileptic but loving mother. Sydney was educated at Winchester School and New College, Oxford, and in consequence became a life-long advocate of university reform. His father refusing to finance him for a career in law, Smith accepted ordination in 1794 in the Church of England, and was given a country parish. Its squire took him as tutor to his son and in 1798 sent them both to live in Edinburgh for its educational advantages.

Smith's intellectual abilities and attractive personality made him welcome in literary and academic circles, and also a friend of Francis Horner, DUGALD STEWART, HENRY BROUGHAM and FRANCIS JEFFREY.

In 1801 Smith suggested to Horner and Jeffrey that they start what shortly became the *Edinburgh Review*, a politically liberal journal of serious book reviews and articles. It became an immediate success, and for decades afterwards greatly enhanced the intellectual life of Scotland and England. Smith, Horner and Jeffrey edited the first four issues, and Jeffrey then became its editor until 1829. During this period Smith contributed seventy-seven anonymous reviews, in addition to his clerical duties in country parishes far from London to which the Smith family had moved in 1803.

Politically, Smith was a Whig sympathizer, and his social and political views were those of liberal reform. He wrote at length in support of Catholics' emancipation from the many disabilities English law laid upon them, criticizing especially Catholics' inability to become members of the British Parliament and to occupy the higher ranks of Government. Although he thought Catholic and dissenting Protestant religious creeds badly mistaken, he was strongly in favour of their believers' right to practise them. He was equally in favour of advanced education for women and argued that in many important ways they were superior to men. The improvement of prison conditions, of the working conditions of children and the abolition of the game laws that so heavily penalised working-class poachers were among his favourite causes. He sympathized with the early efforts of the Americans to govern themselves and spoke well of the political and economic development of Australia.

Smith was a natural and rapid writer of lucid, often entertaining, prose but he also paid much attention to achieving clarity of thought accurately expressed. Although a benevolent and merry man he could be a severe enemy of nonsense. His career was hampered by his superiors' belief that he was a sceptical critic in clerical clothing. Nevertheless, his social connections with such Whig leaders as Lord Holland eventually made him a canon of St Paul's London. He died in that city on 22 February 1845.

Further reading

Smith, Sydney (1869) *Works*, London: Longmans, Brown & Green.
Virgin, Peter (1994) *Sydney Smith*, London: Harper Collins.

SEE ALSO: Brougham, Henry; Jeffrey, Francis; liberalism; main currents in philosophy; political economy; Stewart, Dugald

ROBERT BROWN

SOCIAL DARWINISM

'Social Darwinism' is the much-contested, loose and in some respects inaccurate term widely used to describe the application of evolutionary theory, and of biological or other models drawn from the natural sciences, to social issues, and especially to attitudes towards the poor and towards non-European peoples, in the second half of the nineteenth century. The term implies that the discovery of the theory of natural selection by the British naturalist CHARLES DARWIN (1809–82), as announced in *Origin of Species* (1859), produced a new set of attitudes, focused on the notion of the 'survival of the fittest'. Darwin's account of the survival of 'favourable' over 'unfavourable' variants in species, and of the inheritance of favourable characteristics and their role in sexual selection and the attainment of subsistence, and his argument that species were mutable, was indeed a breakthrough in evolutionary thought. But while contemporaries were quick to apply evolutionism to humanity, many recognized that the social model often associated with the phrase, 'the survival of the fittest' in fact preceded the work of Darwin and ALFRED RUSSEL WALLACE (1823–1913) (the co-discoverer of the theory). Most agreed that it had been first popularized by T.R. MALTHUS, whose *Essay on Population* (1798) had argued that population growth tended naturally to outstrip the provision of the means of subsistence, and that 'positive' checks, such as disease, warfare and poverty, were a natural means of limiting the growth of numbers. As HENRY MAINE put it:

> The central seat in all Political Economy was from the first occupied by the theory of Population. This theory has now been generalised by Mr. Darwin and his followers, and, stated as the principle of the survival of the fittest, it has become the central truth of all biological science
> (*Popular Government*, 1886: 37)

These assumptions, integrated by 1820 into the work of the leading liberal political economists, notably DAVID RICARDO (*Principles of Political Economy and Taxation*, 1817), had given political economy the reputation of 'the dismal science' for the presumption that wages would not naturally rise above the subsistence level. The model of an intensely competitive society in which individual virtues such as thrift and abstinence might be the sole means of guaranteeing 'survival' was cemented by the passage of the Poor Law Amendment Act of 1834, or 'New Poor Law', which made the receipt of poor relief much more difficult and punitive, with the aim of reducing the costs of relief. Here a distinction between the 'deserving' and 'undeserving' poor is evident, which facilitates the later development of the language of 'fit' and 'unfit'.

If 'Social Darwinism' is thus often a variation on Malthusianism, it remains to be seen more precisely what contribution Darwin made to these strands of thought through *Origin of Species* and *Descent of Man* (1871), and how the ensuing debate developed ideas not previously conceived or thought through.

To complicate matters, it is also widely conceded that HERBERT SPENCER (1820–1903) had applied evolutionary theory drawn from natural science, rather than, for example, a stadial or 'conjectural' notion of historical progress, well before *Origin of Species*, and had indeed begun the construction of a complex philosophic system based on these assumptions. Not only did Spencer coin the term 'survival of the fittest' (in 1852), he described a 'law of progress' carrying society forward to greater perfection in terms of the advancement towards differentiation, individuation and complexity, and asserted that the struggle for existence produced an improvement in 'type'. Spencer's starting-point was thus, like Darwin's and Wallace's, Malthusian: the pressure of population was the chief cause of human progress. Biological evolution was thus from lower organisms to the more complex, and human social evolution moved from tribal society to an industrial, liberal, individualistic state. Any threat to freedom potentially interfered with the evolutionary process, and Spencer came adamantly to oppose 'the coming slavery' of the state, including factory legislation, sanitary inspection by Government officials and public management of the Post Office. Because these views became extremely influential in Europe and the USA in particular, 'Social Darwinism' is often associated with the promotion of extreme *laissez-faire* ideas of the sort that Spencer popularized in *The Man versus the State* (1881) and other works. As we will see, this is also highly contentious. But Spencer was widely influential, and was a key source for the ideas of the leading US Social Darwinist, WILLIAM GRAHAM SUMNER (1840–1910), among others. A similarly individualist conclusion was drawn from Darwinist premises in France by Clémence-Auguste Royer (1830–1902).

A recent study of the subject (Mike Hawkins, *Social Darwinism and European and American Thought 1860–1945*, 1997) argues that four main assumptions compose the Social Darwinist world-view: (1) biological laws govern the whole of organic nature, including humans; (2) the pressure of population growth on resources generates a struggle for existence among organisms; (3) physical and mental traits confer an advantage on their possessors in this struggle, or in sexual competition; which advantages can, through inheritance, spread through the population; (4) the cumulative effects of selection and inheritance over time account for the emergence of new species and the elimination of others. In order to ascertain how distinctive lines of Social Darwinism thought emerge after 1859, we need to see how these notions developed after *Origin of Species*.

The most important single development lay in the consequences of Darwin's own focus upon mankind in *Descent of Man*. *Origin of Species* had not contended that the 'best' types survived as a result of evolutionary struggle, only that members of species who left the largest number of offspring would promote the characteristics of that group in the species as a whole. Between 1859 and 1871, and while *Descent of Man* was being composed, Darwin responded to a variety of proposed applications of natural selection to human society. The most influential on his own thinking appear to have been A.R. Wallace's 1864 research on the tendency of natural selection to promote human intelligence, Darwin's cousin, FRANCIS GALTON's (1822–1911) pioneering 1865 article on 'Hereditary Talent and Character', which lamented that 'we are living in a sort of intellectual anarchy, for the want of master minds', and an article by W.R. Greg 'On the Failure of "Natural Selection" in the Case of Man' (1868). Collectively these arguments presented the case for seeing 'intelligence' as the quality most suitable for defining what 'fitness' was in the human species, and this view Darwin conceded in *Descent of Man*. Darwin was willing to give environmental factors an important role to play in moral and intellectual evolution, and was thus less insistent on hereditary factors than Lamarck or Spencer. But increasingly after 1871 he came to argue that the optimal outcome of human natural selection would be the triumph of 'the intellectual and moral' races over the 'lower and more degraded ones', even writing in 1881 that 'at no very distant date, what an endless number of

the lower races will have been eliminated by the higher civilised races of the world'.

While assumptions about the inevitable displacement of native peoples by colonizing and imperial Europeans are common in this period (e.g. in Charles Dilke's *Greater Britain*, 1869), and become increasingly widespread during the great imperial scramble of the 1880s and 1890s, the idea of race thus plays a crucial role in the creation of Social Darwinism in the early 1870s. It is not merely the introduction of the language of race as such, however, but a particular approach to racial categorization and classification, which was crucial to making Social Darwinism essentially racist or racialist. Darwin himself had used the notion of 'race' very loosely in *Origin of Species* to denote species generally, but by *Descent of Man* he argued that 'civilised races' 'encroach on and replace' the savage, with the 'lower races' being displaced through the accumulation of capital and growth of the arts. This is, as such, a discourse on civilization rather than an assessment of the necessarily different developments of lighter- and darker-skinned peoples. But the two concepts are, of course, virtually coterminous: the brahman priest, master of a 3,000-year-old civilization, is placed on the same level as the most primitive jungle tribesman. Social theorists from the 1870s onwards placed increasing stress on utilizing anthropology, philology and history to establish a common origin and lineage for lighter-skinned European peoples, and especially their derivation from a common 'Aryan' stock. Writers like Dilke developed the idea of the civilizing racial destiny of 'saxondom', while the nascent study of comparative Government commenced, in Edward Freeman's famous exposition (*Comparative Politics*, 1873) with the assumption of an essential affinity between Greeks, Romans and Teutons. Where the preceding century had explained differences in levels of civilization chiefly in terms of climate (in Montesquieu's *Spirit of the Laws*, 1748, notably), such differences were now increasingly ascribed to ontological variations in outlook and potential defined by race as skin pigmentation. A variety of sciences and pseudo-sciences, such as anthropometry (the measurement of skull size), promoted a much more rigid, ontological and determinist notion of racial hierarchy, and of Saxon, Teutonic or Caucasian superiority. The idea that race was a central explanatory category in human life, and that some races, and specifically the 'Aryan' or 'Teutonic', would naturally dominate over others, contended for, for instance, in Robert Knox's *The Races of Men* (1850), and in JOSEPH GOBINEAU's *Inequality of the Human Races* (1854), predates Darwin. What evolutionism did was to add a supposedly scientific account of racial differentiation, and to define human destiny generally in terms of an inevitable struggle of contending groups, which now were often primarily construed in racial terms. Such trends were developed in Germany by Ernst Haeckel in particular. In the USA racial inequality was justified on Darwinian grounds by Joseph Le Conte (1823–1901), among others (see *The Race Problem in the South*, 1892). Nor was this solely from a 'conservative' or reactionary viewpoint; Darwin's radical disciple T.H. HUXLEY published an essay entitled 'On the Natural Inequality of Men' (1865), which argued that blacks were inferior, while the socialist H.G. WELLS assumed in his *Anticipations* (1902) that if:

> those swarms of black, & brown, and dirty-white, and yellow people . . . do not come into the new needs of efficiency . . . they will have to go. So far as they fail to develop sane, vigorous and distinctive personalities for the great world of the future, it is their portion to die out and disappear.

A.R. Wallace, too, apparently believed that racial differences were ineradicable, though crucially he did not view primitive peoples as intellectually inferior to those more advanced. The Italian criminologist Enrico Ferri also attempted an ambitious synthesis of Darwin, Spencer and Marx in *Socialism and Positive Science* (1894).

Racialism was the chief external application of Social Darwinism precepts in the imperial age. Internal to European nations, there were two main areas in which such ideas were applied: to ideas of the poor; and to theories of the state and moral philosophy. Respecting the poor, the notion of a 'domestic race' (as Darwin termed it) also developed in the 1870s, usually in conjunction with a perceived threat of the degeneration of the species through the greater fecundity of its poorest members. This led to frequent debates about whether sterilization in particular was an appropriate method for dealing with mental incapacity, and a range of other diseases that might qualify one as 'unfit'.

Social Darwinism and politics

The application of evolutionary theory to political thought produced a surprisingly wide range of responses, which undermines the assumption that an extreme form of *laissez-faire* liberalism was the natural social concomitant to Darwinism. What unites the various political strands of this type of Social Darwinism is not the specific political stance assumed, but the application of the idea of social evolution to a higher societal type on the basis of competition between 'fit' and 'unfit' groups and individuals, whose 'fitness' or 'value' to society could be defined in various ways.

Liberals adapted evolutionism in a variety of ways, often following the recommendation offered by Darwin himself in the *Descent of Man*, that a society which promoted 'open competition for all men' and enabled 'the most able' to rear the largest number of offspring was the natural social and political concomitant to the principles of natural selection. One of the first liberals to apply evolution was WALTER BAGEHOT (1826–77), whose *Physics and Politics* (1869) tried to prove that liberal democracy guaranteed evolutionary progress and suited higher forms of social growth. To Bagehot constitutional Government permitted looser social bonds than military despotism, while only those societies that permitted political freedom could in his view promote those evolutionary variations which were necessary for the higher progression of the species. Analogously, competition in the world of ideas would also promote the development of better ideas (as J.S. MILL had suggested in *On Liberty*, 1859, ch. 1). Because the notion of 'fitness' in Social Darwinism was frequently linked to ideas of economic competition and efficiency, it was easily adaptable as a radical critique of the existing aristocracy (as W.R. Greg suggested), a class deriving its wealth from privilege rather than merit, and idleness rather than effort (as classical political economy had also sometimes suggested). By the early 1880s such discussions became much more acute, as poverty deepened in Britain and elsewhere. Although Herbert Spencer continued to argue, in a series of influential articles in the *Contemporary Review* written against Beatrice Webb in particular, that state intervention to limit poverty would end social progress, since no mechanism would exist to weed out the 'unfit', the tide of thought had begun to move in a much more collectivist direction. In the USA similar themes were pursued by J.D. Rockefeller and W.G. Sumner, while in Belgium liberal political economy was assimilated to Darwinism by Gustave de Molinari. In Britain, however, there now began a substantial turning away from the association of evolution with *laissez-faire* liberalism that Darwin himself, among others, had assumed to be normal in the 1870s.

Typical of 'New Liberal' arguments in this period was the work of David Ritchie (1853–1903), notably *Darwinism and Politics* (1889), whose central contention was that evolutionary theory 'lends no support to the political dogma of Laissez faire'. Instead, for Ritchie, it was the duty of the state to act as a benevolent institution, raising individuals above the mere necessity of a 'struggle for life' to a higher social and cultural level. In *The Principles of State Interference* (1891), Ritchie confronted Spencer directly, contending that if the history of progress was 'the record of a gradual diminution of waste . . . the State is the chief instrument by which waste is prevented'. Like Greg, Ritchie supported the view that aristocracy functioned as an anti-evolutionary institution. A similar ideal with respect to morality was upheld by T.H. Huxley (1825–95), who agreed that while a crude struggle for existence characterized the early stages of society, the emergence of moral feeling altered evolution. The state had a particular duty to educate the poor, since overpopulation might lead to reversion to an earlier stage (see *Evolution and Ethics*, 1893). Writers like Patrick Geddes, similarly, were to argue that moral evolution was towards 'the golden rule of sympathy and synergy', while BENJAMIN KIDD's *Social Evolution* (1894) adopted the German naturalist August Weissmann's arguments against the inheritance of acquired characteristics to argue for an altruistic basis for human social behaviour, and thus the ultimate value of various social reforms. Kidd was also notable for the stress he gave to non-rational factors in human evolution, especially religion, which he believed increased solidarity and efficiency by promoting the sacrifice of self-interest to that of the community.

A similar line of argument was followed by those anarchist thinkers who treated evolutionism, notably PIETR KROPOTKIN (1842–1921), whose assumption of a natural human sociability is developed in *Mutual Aid* (1902). This argued that groups which had been most successful from the evolutionary standpoint had developed practices of mutual assistance, in the form of clans, village communities and medieval cities. Such forms of solidarity for Kropotkin were destroyed by the modern centralized state, which needed to be replaced by a commune of freely associated producers. A similar line of argument was

developed by the French anarchist Emile Gautier in *Le Darwinisme social* (1880).

Once it could be demonstrated that evolutionism could be bent in a collectivist direction, socialists were bound to take up its postulates. This happened earlier in Germany than elsewhere, somewhat to Darwin's dismay. Marx famously wanted to dedicate the first volume of *Capital* (1867) to Darwin, and his son-in-law, Paul Lafargue, became a zealous interpreter of Darwinian ideas (see MARX AND MARXISM). Many socialists applauded what they saw as the secularist implications of the Darwinian system. Like some liberals, socialists contended that the inheritance of wealth and prestige inhibited the promotion of 'fitness' (e.g. Enrico Ferri, *Socialism and Positive Science*, 1894). The most famous socialist to adapt evolutionism was of course its co-discoverer, A.R. Wallace, who promoted plans for land nationalisation and co-operative industry. (It might be added, however, that Herbert Spencer in fact applauded the aims of Wallace's Land Nationalization Society, and agreed that the land ought to become public property and the landlord merely a tenant upon it.) Another writer, Karl Pearson (1857–1936), who became professor of eugenics in 1911, interpreted Darwinism from a socialist viewpoint in *The Ethic of Freethought* (1887) and *The Chances of Death, and Other Studies in Evolution* (1897). His principal argument for socialism, which included the collectivization of production and universal moral duty to work for the community, was again its probable greater efficiency in the production and distribution of resources, and its greater capability to limit the struggle for existence. Pearson's emphasis on 'efficiency' matched similar proposals elsewhere round the turn of the century, when an 'efficiency movement' began to develop (see, e.g., Arnold White, *Efficiency and Empire*, London, 1901, which links eugenics to efficiency). The general arguments respecting the application of evolution to socialism are summarized in F.W. Headley, *Darwinism and Modern Socialism* (1909).

Eugenics

The most important practical development in Social Darwinism after 1870 resulted from the research of Francis Galton into heredity, and the founding of eugenics. Commencing with *Hereditary Genius* (1869), Galton attempted to prove that intelligence, in particular, was transmitted hereditarily. 'Eugenics', after the Greek, 'good in stock', or 'heartily endowed with noble qualities', was intended to described 'the science which deals with all influences that improve the inborn qualities of a race; also with those that develop them to the utmost advantage'. This Galton also construed in terms of making 'every individual efficient, both through nature and by nurture'. From a moral viewpoint, Galton hoped that a 'sentiment of caste' would develop by which the intellectually endowed would naturally be led to breed only amongst themselves, perhaps even settling in small co-operative communities in the countryside. Practically, Galton pursued a plan not only of eugenic research, which resulted in the foundation of a laboratory at University College London, as well as a society and journal. He also promoted the notion of limiting the right of marriage to those qualified by the absence of any debilitating hereditary tendencies, especially feeblemindedness. He also proposed separation of 'habitual' criminals, and the curtailing of 'indiscriminate charity'. The growing risk of the physical degeneracy of the species Galton associated with the loss of strength, of will-power, of the willingness to labour, and an increasing proneness to bohemianism, dissoluteness and complacency. 'Rural vigour' was in particular sapped by the industrial life of the great towns: we witness here a revival of an idea common to various forms of radicalism and republicanism from the sixteenth century to the late nineteenth. Galton's politics were collectivist, communitarian and utopian, but not socialist as such. Eugenics achieved a considerable popularity late in the century in part because it lent scientific legitimacy to discussions of marriage, sex and birth control, which corresponded to the growing demands for female political emancipation by the Suffragettes. Its intellectual elitism found favour with groups like the Fabian socialists, while other types of radicals applauded its interventionist tendencies. Disagreements, however, occurred over allegations by leading eugenicists that pauperism resulted from the transmission of inherited characteristics, such as theft, drunkenness and laziness.

Social Darwinism, secularism and religion

Though Darwinism excited a fierce, often bitter debate between scientists and theologicans, 'Social Darwinism' is not synonymous with 'secularism' as such. Not only did Social Darwinism, or even more broadly science as such, not 'cause' the widespread late nineteenth-century crisis of religious faith. A lengthy period of biblical criticism preceded *Origin of Species*, in which works like D.F. STRAUSS's *Das Leben Jesu* (1835) and, later, ERNEST RENAN's *La Vie de Jésus* (1860) or John Seeley's *Ecce Homo* (1865) stressed the human character of Christ. The growth of materialist philosophy, for example in the works of LUDWIG FEUERBACH (*Das Wesen des Christentums*, 1840), also sapped religious belief. The discovery of primitive human remains from the 1840s onwards cast serious doubts upon the validity of sacred chronology. Geological discoveries assisted in this process, and promoted an ideal of the struggle for existence as well (which Darwin noted in Charles Lyell's *Principles of Geology*, 1833). Darwin did, however, indisputably weaken religious belief, notably by casting strong doubts upon the biblical account of the Creation, the accepted 4,000-year chronology of human development and the story of the Flood, putting in their place instead a notion of the linear progress of species towards an eventual perfection. The providentialist account of human history, thus, notably associated with works like William Paley's *Natural Theology* (1802), was badly dented. And, of course, the suggestion that humanity was descended from remote pre-human beings, developed after *Origin of Species* by T.H. Huxley's *Man's Place in Nature* (1863) in particular, fatally undermined the notion of a special creation of mankind by God. (Huxley coined the term 'agnostic' to define the lack of scientific evidence for God). Evolutionary writers, in addition, often proclaimed the reconciliation of Darwinism and religion, or that there was no necessary antagonism between them; Spencer, for instance, took up an argument from Henry Mansel's *The Limits of Religious Thought* (1858), and asserted that there was an 'unknowable' realm beyond the limits of scientific knowledge. Science and religion as such, therefore, could not conflict. A variety of writers, however, attempted to use evolutionary arguments in order to construct a metaphysic that would serve as a substitute for religion. Darwin's leading German follower, Ernst Haeckel (1834–1919), expounded a theory of evolutionary laws linking everything from human consciousness to planetary movements (cf. *The Riddle of the Universe*, 1899). FRIEDRICH NIETZSCHE (1844–1900) developed a highly influential account of one central instinctive principle, 'the will to power', which lay beyond morality, and which he associated with the need to create a 'master race' capable of resisting the dominant egalitarian slave morality of the modern epoch. In his assertion that human destiny relied on the production of mankind's 'highest types' or specimens, Nietzsche clearly echoes prominent Social Darwinist themes. In the 1930s and 1940s his ideas were perverted by Hitler and other National Socialists, who presumed their own elevation, and the degradation and destruction of the Jews, was in keeping with Nietzschean ideals, though Nietzsche was himself no anti-Semite. A later interpreter of Darwin in a metaphysical direction was HENRI BERGSON (1859–1941), whose *Creative Evolution* (1907) described a vital principle that underlay both organic and inorganic matter, and gave them a capacity of adapting to their environments. In human beings this chiefly assumed the form of intelligence, which did not develop towards any particular end, but which facilitated human adaptation to increasingly complex and swiftly evolving structures. A similar conception of 'life-force' was developed by GEORGE BERNARD SHAW (1856–1950) as a form of evolutionary theology, in which mankind was construed as an important, but flawed, experiment on God's part. Like Nietzsche, however, Shaw thought Darwin had paid too much heed to the role of the environment in evolution, and emphasized the active and creative elements in human development.

Social Darwinism and war

Finally, it should be noted that as social theory evolutionism also had a powerful impact on notions of international conflict, notably by popularizing the doctrine that 'might is right', which is often associated with Nietzsche, and which was developed in Germany by TREITSCHKE, among others. As Benjamin Kidd put it, 'Within half a century the *Origin of Species* had become the bible of the doctrine of the omnipotence of force' (*The Science of Power*, p. 45). Bagehot and LEONARD HOBHOUSE, among others, developed this application of the theory in Britain, while GUSTAVE LEBON (1841–1931) and Vachet de Lapouge (1854–1936) gave stress to the inevitability of racial conflict in France, and Ludwig Gumplowicz (1838–1909) echoed similar themes in Austria.

Further reading

Blacker, C.P. (1932) *Eugenics: Galton and After*, London: Duckworth.

Burrow, J.W. (1966) *Evolution and Society. A Study in Victorian Social Theory*, Cambridge: Cambridge University Press.

Clark, Linda L. (1984) *Social Darwinism in France*, Tuscaloosa: University of Alabama Press.

Crook, D.P. (1984) *Benjamin Kidd. Portrait of a Social Darwinism*, Cambridge: Cambridge University Press.

—— (1994) *Darwinism, War and History*, Cambridge: Cambridge University Press.

Haller, John S., Jr (1971) *Outcasts from Evolution: Scientific Attitudes of Racial Inferiority, 1859–1900*, Urbana: University of Illinois Press.

Hawkins, Mike (1997) *Social Darwinism in European and American Thought 1860–1945*, Cambridge: Cambridge University Press.

Himmelfarb, Gertrude (1962) *Darwin and the Darwinian Revolution*, New York: Norton Books.

Hofstadter, Richard (1955) *Social Darwinism in American Thought*, Boston: Beacon Press.

Jones, Greta (1980) *Social Darwinism and English Thought*, Brighton: Harvester.

Pick, Daniel (1989) *Faces of Degeneration. A European Disorder, c. 1848–c. 1918*, Cambridge: Cambridge University Press.

GREGORY CLAEYS

SOCIAL THEORY AND SOCIOLOGY IN THE NINETEENTH CENTURY

Sociology and modernity

The term sociology did not exist at the beginning of the nineteenth century; by the end its early major thinkers – AUGUSTE COMTE, Karl Marx (see MARX AND MARXISM), ALEXIS DE TOCQUEVILLE, HERBERT SPENCER and EMILE DURKHEIM – had produced the classic writings of the discipline, many of which are still read today. There is, then, one sense in which sociology began in the nineteenth century as a series of reflections on the nature and destiny of industrial Europe. However, in another sense sociology is as old as the Western intellectual tradition. If one defines the subject as the study of the structure and nature of society, then there has been sociology for as long as there has been reflection upon the human condition. Indeed Comte, who in 1830 invented the term, declared that Aristotle was the real founder of sociology.

Nevertheless the immediate background may be traced to a few inter-related factors: the eighteenth-century Enlightenment and the Romantic reaction to it, the great French Revolution of 1789 and the process of industrialization. Together they cover the greatest transformation in recorded history; that marked by the twin revolutions that produced industrial society and democratic politics. From the Enlightenment we derive the belief that society could be understood in a rational and objective manner. The very term 'social science' was coined by one of its key figures, JEREMY BENTHAM, who was acknowledged by Comte as a direct precursor. From the political and industrial revolutions came the awareness that the old regimes were crumbling; that a seemingly static and eternal order had come to an end; that agriculture was gradually losing predominance to industry; the countryside to the towns; the old, organic society to atomization and individualism. The once settled order of court society was being replaced by the intrusiveness of the mass, and aristocracy was being forced to compromise with democracy.

Well might such changes invoke serious reflection. Intelligent observers pondered what was happening. What would hold society together once hereditary monarchs and established estates were destroyed? What would be the dynamic and destination of societies where new classes, devoid of experience and education, had forced themselves onto the political stage? The apposite model, to defenders of the old order, derived from Greek history and suggested that democracy rapidly collapses into tyranny. To the radicals, however, the new society would be one of advancing knowledge and education, the removal of ancient superstitions and encrusted hierarchies, and, consequently, progress towards a rational, efficient and peaceful condition. Opportunity would be open to all and superior positions attained only by genuine achievement and merit. It was as part of this debate that sociology arose. Sociology, then, emerged as the attempt to understand and influence modernity.

Social change

Already in the eighteenth century the main writers of the Scottish Enlightenment (Adam Smith, Adam Ferguson, John Millar) had asked how society developed; how the modern West had ascended from savagery through barbarism and up to its current civilized condition. In an attempt at a unified social science they had outlined the pattern of social progression from hunting, pastoral and farming through to modern commercial society. Meanwhile in France the Marquis de Condorcet had produced a seven-step theory of social progress that went one stage further. He believed that if you grasped the logic of development, then you could deduce where it was heading. You could predict the future. In this way Condorcet helped set the agenda for much nineteenth-century social theory.

In his *System of Logic* (1843) JOHN STUART MILL outlined the task of the social sciences as being to discover the laws by which one stage of society produces its successor. Mill himself was convinced that human history exhibited a certain order of development. However, unlike some of his major contemporaries, Mill did not suggest clearly delineated stages nor did he feel confident in forecasting the future. This was in stark contrast to Auguste Comte, with whom he had an intense but fairly short-lived correspondence in the 1840s.

For Comte the advance of humanity was determined by the progress of the human mind. He claimed to have discovered the fundamental law by which each branch of knowledge passes through the consecutive stages that he labelled theological, metaphysical and positive. Whereas for Comte, as with Hegel (see HEGEL AND HEGELIANISM), intellectual development was primary, Marx gave significance to what he termed the mode of production. He outlined the sequence whereby feudalism generated capitalism that, in its turn, was destined to produce its own grave-digger, communism. Spencer also followed what was becoming almost a norm and produced a three-stage sequence of development. In his scheme primitive anarchy gave way to militant societies that, in their turn, were replaced by industrial societies. This inevitable development was simultaneously a long-term progression from homogeneity to heterogeneity, that is, from a very simple to a highly complex social structure.

This emphasis is now more associated with Emile Durkheim. His concern was with social solidarity and he explained how the gradually developing division of labour had moved society from primitive and fundamental mechanical solidarity to the organic solidarity typical of modern industrial societies. Whereas originally society had been united by its similarities of beliefs and practices, Durkheim believed that it was now held together by its differences; greater specialization had facilitated the economic survival of larger numbers but had simultaneously increased mutual dependence. We thus have a model of development that has only two fundamental stages, the origin and the destination, with a rather hazier picture of anything in-between, which is seen less in its own terms than as part of the process of transition between the beginning and the end. This was also true of Alexis de Tocqueville whose writings were intended to illustrate the inevitable process that led from the aristocracy of his French ancestors to the democracy that he observed in North America. Summing up the cumulative changes in France since the eleventh century, he concluded that the nobility had gradually declined as the commoners had risen. It seemed that they were getting nearer to each other and would eventually meet.

Of all these theories one can ask: What moved some societies forward and what held others back? Nineteenth-century social science emerged, in large part, as an attempt to answer this important question. For Marx social change was facilitated by class conflict; for Mill from the free development of ideas; for Durkheim from an increasing division of labour. For Tocqueville providence, the guiding hand of God, lay behind the visible social processes, and the God who set this process in motion, who watches and guides it, is the God of Christianity. God had apparently chosen to advance only the Christian nations. They were favoured with social progress denied to the heathen. Tocqueville's theological explanation, though far from ubiquitous in social theory, shared the normal tendency of presuming European superiority. All these theories outlined how societies developed along a monolinear trail that led upward from barbarism to civilization. Non-European societies were thus categorized as backward; as occupying a lower step on a ladder that ascended to the place where 'we' in the West now were. In this way they formed part of the culture of the European imperialism that was such a significant feature of the century (see IMPERIALISM AND EMPIRE).

Social cohesion

Western society, then, was visibly moving forward. This was precisely what those in the Enlightenment tradition had recommended. Their critics, however, asked how society might still hold together. The more stable pre-modern order was held together by bonds of class or estate that were legitimated by traditional usage. People knew where they stood, what they could do, how they should behave and on whom they could rely. Society appeared as an organic, cohesive totality in which certainty provided security and everyone knew their place.

How different was the condition of modernity! To its critics tradition suddenly appeared to count for little. It had been replaced either by a spurious and shallow rationality or, possibly worse, by momentary fashion. In modern society each individual stood alone, privatized, cut-off from wider supports and devoted increasingly to personal selfishness and material well-being. The social aggregate seemed to have been broken down into its particular components. THOMAS CARLYLE doubted whether the very term 'society' could properly be applied to such an aggressively individualist condition. Tocqueville pointed out that the word 'individualism' was unknown to our ancestors.

It was, on the whole, the conservatives who feared that individualism had cut away the ties that bound one person to another. This view had been significantly developed by the German Romantics (see ROMANTICISM, INDIVIDUALISM AND IDEAS OF THE SELF), notably by Novalis, Schleiermacher and Müller, and by JOSEPH DE MAISTRE in France, as a counter to the particularistic analysis of individualist theory. Such an approach lies behind the Romantics' development of an organic theory of society, and is also, of course, particularly pronounced in the writings of Hegel. The emphasis on all parts of society as integral components of a social totality ran directly counter to a philosophical trend that in England and France had a few centuries of development behind it. The attempt to create an individual/society dichotomy had served anti-feudal ideology as it appeared to free the individual from traditional social bonds.

Yet to the counter-revolutionaries a philosophy of consent and natural rights seemed socially dangerous, while the abstraction of the individual from his or her social context appeared totally unrealistic. BURKE and the Romantics viewed man as primarily social and only secondarily individual. They could visualize people only in a context; in the actual environment in which they lived. Thus they put the individual back into the group, and on these grounds have sometimes been claimed as the real founders of sociology. This view is associated in our own time with R.A. Nisbet, who has embarrassed other sociologists with the assertion that the concepts and perspectives of their subject link it to both medievalism and philosophical conservatism.

In *The Positive Philosophy* Auguste Comte emphasized that the scientific study of society combined two aspects: social dynamics examines the laws of development while social statics considers those of coexistence. In this way sociology is heir to both Enlightenment optimism and Romantic pessimism. This concern with both progress and social cohesion is the hallmark not just of Comte's theories but also of those of such otherwise divergent figures as Tocqueville, Marx and Durkheim.

Scientism

Sociology, then, had investigated how society moves and how it holds together. Its next task was to define its relationship both to ordinary ideas and to the academic disciplines. As a distinctive and specialist form of knowledge sociology had to demonstrate that it was not reducible to ordinary mass opinion. Both Mill and Comte believed that the opinions of the many should be formed by the better-educated few. Durkheim commenced *The Rules of Sociological Method* with a clear and determined attempt to differentiate sociology from ordinary common-sense views. Sociologists, he believed, should free themselves from the false ideas of untrained people. They should become scientists.

Jeremy Bentham had recommended himself as the Newton of the moral world. His 'felicific calculus', in outlining seven dimensions of pleasure and pain, was an attempt to attain precision in tabulating human actions. In France, Condorcet and SAINT-SIMON had, in their different ways, also advocated the application of scientific methods to human society.

Here, once more, social theory followed where the Enlightenment had led. Comte had first referred to his work as social physics before renaming it sociology and Spencer wished to fulfil Bentham's aim by himself becoming 'the moral Euclid'. Yet more than physics and mathematics, it was biology that seemed to provide the appropriate model. For Comte the influence of biology should serve to direct sociology along the right path. Already prior to Darwin, social theory had tried to combine a law of progress with biological method, so later in the century adaptation to evolutionary theory was not hard to achieve. This attempt has been most associated with Herbert Spencer, for whom 'the survival of the fittest' furnished the fundamental law of social growth, though now it is better known in the case of Durkheim. In one of the greatest works of nineteenth-century social theory, *The Division of Labour in Society*, Durkheim outlined how the struggle for existence led to greater division of labour for human society through exactly the same laws that operated when 200 species of insects occupied the same oak tree. Furthermore, Durkheim's important distinction between normal and pathological moral facts was quite explicitly derived from the methods used by naturalists.

Though sociology wished for the status that attached to the scientific label, its advocates did not want it too closely identified with any of the other scientific disciplines. That would have threatened its claims to autonomy and distinctiveness. Comte and Durkheim both wanted the various sciences clearly differentiated, with sociology seen as a science in its own right. Psychology was already established as a science of human behaviour so it had to be made clear that sociology had its own different subject matter. Comte declared that he could not regard society as primarily composed of individuals, for the basic social unit was the family. Furthermore society could not be studied scientifically if it was separated into portions that were then examined in isolation. According to Mill, Comte always spoke of psychology with contempt. Durkheim was likewise concerned to resist suggestions that sociology was reducible to psychology. For him sociology was not a section of any other science. It was itself a separate and independent science. In Germany his contemporary FERDINAND TÖNNIES carefully distinguished the sociological view from the biological and psychological ones.

Having established its own terrain, sociology had to place itself in relation to the other disciplines. How was its position to be understood? Was it, in ascending order, one science among many; or the ultimate and leading science; or the harbinger of one complete and overall science? For Comte there were 'Five fundamental Sciences in successive dependence'. These were astronomy, physics, chemistry, physiology and what he originally termed social physics. Each science presupposed the advances made by its predecessors and so sociology, as social physics came to be called, was placed at the summit, ahead of all the other sciences but simultaneously dependent on them. On this notion, sociology, the greatest of the sciences, was also the latest of them. A similar view was held by Durkheim, but less to celebrate sociology than to explain its still underdeveloped condition. He pointed out that the study of society was the last discipline to achieve scientific status, but through its advance all science would eventually be unified. For Spencer the principle of evolution would lead to the unification of all knowledge. Though their political views were fundamentally different, Marx shared this same aspiration, believing that the natural and social sciences would become incorporated: there will be one science.

'Our method is objective' declared Durkheim in the conclusion to his *Rules of Sociological Method*. How, then, was the emerging discipline of sociology to understand its relationship to its subject matter? Was the sociologist an outside, aloof observer or a practical participant in policy debates? In practice social theory in general, and often its leading individuals in particular, have tried to have the best of both worlds, that is, to claim an elevated status for a particular viewpoint. This is both less surprising and less discreditable than might initially appear. First, it is highly unlikely that anyone would even come to the study of society unless they had particular commitments; and, second, the actual study itself can plausibly strengthen the claims of the policy proposals that result. Social theory and social policy have sometimes appeared as distant extremes of the sociological spectrum, whereas in fact social theory has quite normally had a practical intent, just as social policy has been based on theoretical presuppositions, however inexplicit. Thus it is doubtful whether anyone ever sat down to write a detailed and sophisticated work of social theory simply out of intellectual curiosity.

One of Comte's early writings was called *Plan of the Scientific Researches Necessary for the Reorganization of Society* (1822). In its very title we find the joint endeavour of science and policy, the supposition that the investigation of society has the purpose of eventually improving it. This was all the more necessary in that much nineteenth-century social theory, in its quite various ways, echoed Burke's view that a society that casts off its ancient moorings is in mid-ocean without a compass. A sense of crisis combined with one of purpose, then, is a normal feature. Comte believed that his society was in a political and moral crisis that had been caused by intellectual anarchy. The most vivid image of a society out of control remains Marx's identification of modern capitalism with Goethe's sorcerer's apprentice: 'no longer able to control the powers of the nether world whom he has called up by his spells'. Durkheim concluded *The Division of Labour* by pointing out that morality was going through a deep crisis. Tradition has lost its authority and individual judgements have been freed from collective constraints. Each of these thinkers faced the problem of how the crisis might be resolved. Comte presumed that scientific ideas would lead to the reorganization of society; Marx that communism would combine industrialization with classlessness, while Durkheim hoped to combine the division of labour with social cohesion. Likewise Tocqueville, for whom the rise of democracy was inevitable, hoped it could be combined with freedom rather than with servitude.

However, the more the pattern of social change and integration seemed scientifically fixed, inexorable and pre-determined the less scope this seemed to allow for free human action. While trying to be a science, sociology was simultaneously always associated with a project of reform, just as for the Enlightenment understanding was a prelude to liberation. Social science, so hard won, seemed to have been achieved at the cost of freedom. How far, then, had social determinism compromised individual choice? On the whole our major theorists were unwilling to leave mankind as the completely controlled puppets of objective forces. We can see this aspect in a number of thinkers usually associated with strongly determinist theories of history. Auguste Comte, for example, believed that the laws of social movement are subject to considerable variation and so could be influenced by purposive human action. Karl Marx acknowledged that in the move towards a new social order it was possible for determined action to 'shorten and lessen the birth-pangs'. Tocqueville believed that within the constraints of the providential plan each person and each society had an area within which they were free. And, last, Durkheim explained that even though societies developed in accord with certain laws there was still an area open to individual effort and direction.

The issue of how science might combine with politics and policy, and determinism with freedom, brings us to the problematic relationship of Marxism and sociology. Marx himself did not use the concept 'sociology' and cared little for Comte, the inventor of the term. For many of Marx's followers sociology was a bourgeois ideology. This distancing was often reciprocated from the other side. From one perspective, common in the late nineteenth century, sociology and socialism were in opposition. The former aimed to provide an alternative explanation to the latter; it was a means of holding socialism at bay. With hindsight that part of socialism that sought merely to explain society was part of the same enterprise as sociology. Certainly we find in the writings of Marx and Engels many of the normal characteristics of nineteenth-century social theory. There is the insistence that society be seen as a whole, as one unit; there is a theory of how the parts of society fit together and of how societies as a whole change and develop. In the effort to distinguish itself from so-called 'utopian socialism' there is also the assertion that the method is scientific. So whatever Marx himself thought of the term it is clear that he was involved in the sociological project to understand objectively the structure and dynamics of modern societies. For that reason he has, post-humously, been granted his place as one of the founding influences on the discipline.

Conclusion

At the beginning of the nineteenth century the term 'sociology' did not exist; by the end it not only existed but also was forming into a self-conscious academic discipline. Sociology made its first inroads into the universities in the USA when a department was set up at the University of Chicago in 1892. In France Durkheim was awarded a Chair in Social Science in 1895. The first sociology professorship in Britain was that of Leonard Hobhouse at London University in 1907. No such post was created in Germany until 1925.

Durkheim's *Division of Labour in Society* was published in 1893 and his *The Rules of Sociological Method* in 1895. He thus provides convenient markers as to where sociology had arrived by the end of the nineteenth century. It had been the century of the great systematizers and also the great optimists concerning the discipline's scientific credentials. They were to have few successors. The next great figure, who did much to set sociology upon a different path, was MAX WEBER. His *The Protestant Ethic and the Spirit of Capitalism* (1905), though clearly and intentionally anti-Marxist, simultaneously signifies a basic shift from the self-confident pioneers of the nineteenth century to the piecemeal investigators of the twentieth. Weber sought to investigate specific causes without providing universal laws. For him there was no basic law of social development. Instead it seemed a fortuitous coincidence that modern capitalism had emerged. Furthermore, Weber did not share the positivism of Comte, Marx and Durkheim. His emphasis upon the subjective aspects of sociological analysis implied a distancing from the methods of the natural sciences. Last, rather than putting sociology at the apex of the academic disciplines, Weber saw it as secondary to history.

Looking back from a century and more later, we see how fundamentally the optimism of the pioneers has evaporated; but that story would belong to a successor volume, a *Dictionary of Twentieth Century Thought*.

Further reading

Aron, R. (1979) *Main Currents in Sociological Thought*, 2 vols, Harmondsworth: Penguin Books.

Giddens, A. (1997) *Capitalism and Modern Social Theory*, Cambridge: Cambridge University Press.

Hawthorn, G. (1992) *Enlightenment and Despair. A History of Social Theory*, Cambridge: Cambridge University Press.

Nisbet, R. (1972) *The Sociological Tradition*, London: Heinemann.

SEE ALSO: Bentham, Jeremy; Comte, Auguste; Durkheim, Emile; historiography and the idea of progress; Marx and Marxism; Mill, J.S.; Saint-Simon, Henri de; Spencer, Herbert; Tocqueville, Alexis de; Weber, Max

MICHAEL LEVIN

SOREL, GEORGES (1847–1922)

Georges Sorel was a French highway engineer who in middle age turned himself into a social theorist of considerable originality and learning, but also great idiosyncrasy. He is notable as the foremost intellectual interpreter of the syndicalist movement, a student and critic of Marxism, and as an intransigent critic of the Third Republic who had much in common with extremes of left and right, and whose venom was directed against the politicians of the centre. He is best understood, however, as a moralist who saw in violence not mere destruction but the potential for regeneration of a decadent bourgeois society.

Sorel was born in Cherbourg in 1847 and educated at the elite Ecole Polytechnique in Paris. He joined the Bridges and Roads Department (Corps des Ponts et Chaussées) and from 1870 to 1892 he was employed as an engineer both in metropolitan France (chiefly in Perpignan) and in Corsica and Algeria. On receipt of a small legacy he was able to retire to the suburbs of Paris and devote himself to writing. He was the author, notably, of three key works published in 1908: *La Décomposition du marxisme* (The Decomposition of Marxism); *Reflections on Violence* (*Réflexions sur la violence*); and *The Illusions of Progress* (*Les Illusions du progrès*). He died in Boulogne-sur-Seine in 1922. A thinker of genuinely European interests, he was particularly well read in Italian social and political theory. Much of his work was first published in Italian, including *Reflections on Violence*, which first appeared as a series of articles in *Il devenire sociale* in 1905–6.

Sorel's name is commonly coupled with syndicalism, the revolutionary brand of trade unionism that flourished briefly on the eve of the First World War, chiefly in Mediterranean Europe. In his best-known work, *Reflections on Violence*, he espoused the doctrine of the 'general strike' as the instrument for the overthrow of the state apparatus. But he had no real connection with the syndicalist movement and is better understood as the interpreter of syndicalism rather than its theorist. His syndicalist phase was in fact short-lived, and formed part of a bewildering political odyssey. He was a Marxist at the outset of his literary career in the 1890s, though he felt the attraction of BERNSTEIN's revisionism. The Dreyfus Affair, which had a deep impact on his thinking, made him first into a reformist socialist who backed 'Millerandism', or the participation of socialist ministers in Government; it was his disillusionment with the failure of the 'Dreyfusard revolution' that precipitated his syndicalist phase, in which he bitterly denounced Millerandism. Thereafter he flirted briefly with the royalist nationalism of the Action Française. In 1919 he hailed LENIN as the new champion of his values. The same year saw the foundation of the Italian Fascist movement, whose leader, Mussolini, claimed Sorel – not wholly without reason – as the forerunner of Fascism. Nevertheless we can try and make sense of his intellectual journey by identifying certain continuing threads in his outlook.

Sorel was perhaps the quintessential representative of the pre-war attack on rationalism. Like BERGSON and other critics of rationalism, he deprecated the 'spirit of system' that his generation associated with thinkers such as TAINE, whose outlook was shaped by Darwinism (see DARWIN, CHARLES) and by faith in science: in a word, by Positivism. Sorel explicitly proclaimed that inconsistency was a virtue: an aid in achieving a more rounded understanding of society, precisely because of the fluid character of social reality. It would be a mistake, therefore, to look for the kind of consistency in Sorel that we seek in systematizers such as Hegel or Marx.

Sorel was essentially a moralist, concerned at the degeneration of the bourgeois society in which he lived. Whether on the far left or the far right in politics, he was consistently and vehemently anti-bourgeois. History, for Sorel, was an endless struggle against decadence. He followed Vico in seeing historical change as a cyclical process, a recurrent process of rise and decline. The practical problem was therefore how to stave off the onset of decline. In his political writings Sorel did not aim at the creation of a systematic social theory, but at the identification of a political force that might act as the agent of the regeneration of society. This political force might be socialism or syndicalism or royalism or Bolshevism or Fascism. The precise political doctrine did not matter: the point was that he invested it with the capacity to reverse the process of decay.

There was a strong puritan strain in Sorel, as in many socialist thinkers of the nineteenth century, such as PROUDHON, with whom he had a great deal in common. So he praised the virtues of chastity, loyalty, duty, discipline, family life and pride in work. For a thinker who was so vociferously anti-bourgeois these sound like bourgeois values, but this somewhat ascetic morality coexisted in Sorel's mind with a heroic ethic. The bourgeoisie, he thought, had become a symbol of degeneration, devoted to comfort and ordinary pleasures. Sorel sought another class, a more vigorous and uncorrupted class, to overturn existing society. This was the role he attributed to the proletariat in his Marxist and syndicalist phases. The prospect of a victory for the working class over the bourgeoisie would depend, he thought, on the austerity of its sexual morals.

There is an interesting comparison to be drawn with NIETZSCHE here. Nietzsche thought that socialism, like Christianity, constituted a slaves' revolt against the creative forces in society. Sorel responded by distinguishing between the eternal rebellion of the working class proper, of which he disapproved, and true socialism, which he saw as a battle waged by a dedicated elite of skilled producers capable of forging a new civilization. He saw in these skilled producers the embodiments of a new morality grounded in the virtues of medieval craftsmen; and there is a striking affinity here with English social critics and moralists such as RUSKIN and MORRIS. Revealingly, Sorel opposed many of the workers' demands, such as the demand for the 8-hour day, which he thought was a symptom of decadence.

But it was the relationship with Marxism that was crucial to Sorel's work. He engaged with Marx much more seriously than other French thinkers of his generation: significantly, whereas his contemporary, DURKHEIM, mentions Marx only once in *The Division of Labour in Society*, Sorel mentions him more than any other writer. Influenced by Bernstein, he remained in an important sense a revisionist, although he came to see that revisionism must take a different direction from that sketched by Bernstein. Sorel accepted most of Bernstein's empirical critique of Marxism, but argued that the idea of the class struggle could still be salvaged. Like Bernstein, he believed that it was the movement that mattered, not the end; he did not believe in historical absolutes. The class struggle should therefore not be seen as an objective necessity, a law of history, but should instead be reinterpreted in subjective terms, as a sort of social poetry. In other words, the idea of the class war is a myth.

The concept of the myth is of pivotal importance in Sorel's thought. He defined a myth as any idea capable of moving people to action. The Pragmatism of WILLIAM JAMES was an important influence here. But we can also detect a Darwinian influence in the notion – which goes back before Darwin to Schopenhauer – that ideas survive not because of their truth but because they are useful, in other words adapted to the environment.

For Sorel the idea of the general strike was a myth: indeed, it was the central myth of the syndicalist movement. It conjured up the image of a heroic working class defying the capitalist order, for the general strike would precipitate the overthrow of the capitalist system and inaugurate a new socialist era. The idea that heroic myths could generate new morality was central to Sorel's thinking. He saw myths as 'systems of images' that enable participants in social movements to see their next action as a decisive part of the battle leading to the triumph of their cause. But for Sorel it was not the cause itself that mattered, but the struggle, for the struggle itself would prove invigorating.

Sorel was sceptical of the concept of 'progress' and denounced those who believed in harmony. He denounced 'peacemakers' who advocated, for instance, compulsory arbitration in industrial disputes. It was not that he thought peacemaking futile; rather, he disapproved of peace as an ideal, because it would sap any remaining virtues. In *Reflections on Violence* he argued that the process of degeneration could be stopped only by one of two 'accidents': either by a great European war or by a great extension of proletarian violence. The two were, so to speak, functional equivalents. Significantly, Sorel recognized that the point of proletarian violence might be the reinvigoration of the bourgeoisie rather than its overthrow: it might restore to capitalism the warlike qualities it had once possessed. He despised the French bourgeoisie not so much because they were bourgeois as because they were weak-kneed compromisers who were obsessed with the feeble and chimerical notion of social duty. American capitalists, by contrast, still displayed warrior-like qualities and therefore retained Sorel's admiration.

Further reading

Jennings, J. (1985) *Georges Sorel: The Character and Development of his Thought*, London: Macmillan.

Sorel, G. (1999) *Reflections on Violence*, ed. J. Jennings, Cambridge: Cambridge University Press.

Stanley, J.L. (1982) *The Sociology of Virtue: The Political and Social Theories of Georges Sorel*, Berkeley, Los Angeles: University of California Press.

Vincent, K.S. (1990) 'Interpreting Georges Sorel: Defender of Virtue or Apostle of Violence', *History of European Ideas* 12: 239–57.

SEE ALSO: ideas of war and peace; Marx and Marxism; social theory and sociology in the nineteenth century; theories of the state and society: the science of politics

H.S. JONES

SOUTHEY, ROBERT (1774–1843)

One of the most important of the early nineteenth-century British conservative critics of commercial society and industrialization, Southey was born in Bristol on 12 August 1774, the son of a linen-draper. Educated at Westminster School and Balliol College, Oxford, he fell under the spell of WILLIAM GODWIN's philosophical anarchism in the mid-1790s, and planned with COLERIDGE and Robert Lovell to found a utopian community or 'Pantisocracy' in the USA. A republican poem, 'Wat Tyler', was written in 1794, though not published until 1817, by which time Southey's ardour had cooled considerably. Famous as a poet following the publication of *Thalaba* (1801), *Madoc* (1805) and *The Curse of Kehama* (1810), Southey also wrote a number of histories, including *The History of Brazil* (1810–19), was a regular contributor to the *Quarterly Review* from 1808–39, and wrote a noted *Life of Nelson* (1813), the year he became Poet Laureate, and a *Life of Wesley* (1820).

Southey's social and political thinking is revealed chiefly in his reprinted articles, *Essays Moral and Political* (1831), and in *Sir Thomas More; or, Colloquies on the Progress and Prospects of Society* (2 vols, 1829). Though his transformation from revolutionism to Toryism was abrupt, what connects these phases of his thought was, as Hazlitt stressed, philanthropism, or a concern for the poor. Resolutely opposed to democracy and political radicalism, and supportive of repressive measures like the suspension of Habeas Corpus in 1817, Southey nonetheless remained a consistent critic of Malthusianism, and adherent to a paternalist view of the poor. His *Colloquies* outlines the effects on pauperism of the decay of the feudal system in a manner later popularized by CARLYLE and RUSKIN. More dramatic was its applause for the experimental factory reforms introduced by ROBERT OWEN at New Lanark, which he had visited in 1819. While critical of Owen's propensity to create a uniformity of character, and his failure to utilize Christianity as the basis of his organization, Southey nonetheless offered a substantial description of Owen's planned socialist communities, which, without going as far as supporting community of goods, anticipated 'the great and unequivocal good of exalting one whole class, and that a numerous one... bettering their condition in every way, moral and physical... increasing their respectability, their comforts, their means and their expenditure'. Like Owen, Carlyle, Richard Oastler, John Fielden and others, he scathingly attacked the effects of the manufacturing system upon factory workers, describing it as 'a system which in its direct consequences debases all who are engaged in it'. Southey thus helped to create that climate of opinion by which Lord Shaftesbury was able to introduce reforms that would eventually introduce large-scale Government intervention in the name of paternal responsibility for the working classes as a whole. He died on 21 March 1843.

Further reading

Southey, Charles Cuthbert (1849) *The Life and Correspondence of Robert Southey*, 6 vols, London: Longmans, Brown, Green & Longman.
Southey, Robert (1814) *Letters from England*, 3 vols, London: Longman, Hursy, Rees, Orme & Brown.
—— (1824) *The Book of the Church*, 2 vols. London: John Murray.
Warter, John Wood (ed.) (1856) *Selections from the Letters of Robert Southey*, 4 vols. London: Longmans, Brown, Green & Longman.

SEE ALSO: conservatism, authority and tradition; religion, secularization and the crisis of faith

GREGORY CLAEYS

SPENCER, HERBERT (1820–1903)

The Victorian polymath, Herbert Spencer, is commonly esteemed for his contribution to the development of nineteenth-century sociology. Also famous for coining the phrase 'the survival of the fittest' (1864) and supporting an ultra-individualist liberalism in politics, Spencer saw himself as the author of a complete world-view (his 'synthetic Philosophy') that universalized a theory of progress through evolution. This purported to describe the interconnections of physics, biology, philosophy, psychology and sociology, as well as all the other natural and social sciences, by making extended use of the philosophical intuition of SCHELLING (later adopted by COLERIDGE) that all existing things tend to distinguish themselves from their environment – 'individuation' or 'differentiation'. Although Spencer's system has frequently been interpreted as a mere apology for the social order of Victorian Britain, his relationship with 'the establishment' was ambiguous, given his relatively humble social origins and his views on issues such as evolution, religion, land ownership and imperialism: his final public action was a denunciation of the Boer War.

Born into a lower middle-class Derbyshire family in 1820 and privately educated by his schoolmaster father and his uncles, Spencer was raised in the English tradition of individualistic and evangelical Christianity. Despite a well-recorded liaison with Mary Ann Evans (a.k.a. George Eliot) in the early 1850s, and a wide-ranging social life, he was a life-long bachelor. He worked as a railway engineer from 1837 to 1848, with only occasional forays into journalism, although recent historical scholarship has revived interest in an early political publication, a series of letters on *The Proper Sphere of Government* (also issued as a pamphlet) in 1843. Spencer's workplace experiences stimulated a life-long interest in both mathematics and the natural sciences, but, in the mid-1840s, various attempts to make his fortune through industrial and medical inventions all failed. In 1848 he became a full-time professional writer in London. From 1864 to 1893, he was a member of the elite scientific association, 'The X Club', whose other members were Busk, Frankland, Hirst, Hooker, HUXLEY, Lubbock, Spotiswoode and Tyndall: DARWIN and GALTON were occasional guests. It was from this association that he acquired the entirely appropriate nickname of 'Xhaustive' Spencer!

The first of Spencer's works to receive significant attention from his contemporaries was a heterodox book on individualistic ethics and politics (*Social Statics*, 1850/1) in which he sought to apply his 'equal freedom principle' to a variety of practical issues, while in 1855 he published the less well-received *Principles of Psychology* that attempted to explain human intelligence in terms of the Lamarckian evolution of the species. This relative failure encouraged Spencer to undertake the grand project of a 10-volume 'system of synthetic Philosophy' in order to disseminate his general conception of evolution and rebut his critics. The 'system' took up most of the rest of his adult life, partly because several volumes were amended and republished several times before his death in 1903, although the final volume (part of the enlarged *Principles of Sociology*) was completed in 1896. The major components of the 'system' were *First Principles of a New System of Philosophy* (1862; with five subsequent editions), *The Principles of Biology* (1864–7; with a revised edition in 1898–9), *The Principles of Psychology* (1855; with three subsequent editions), *The Principles of Sociology* (1876; with two subsequent and enlarged editions) and *The Principles of Ethics* (1879; with two subsequent, enlarged editions). Other major works were *Education: Intellectual, Moral, Physical* (1860), *Descriptive Sociology* (1867–81; and posthumously 1910–34), *The Study of Sociology* (1873; with twenty (!) subsequent editions), *The Man Versus the State* (1883), *Various Fragments* (1897; with a subsequent edition) and *Facts and Comments* (1902; with a subsequent edition), and the posthumous *An Autobiography* (1904) – which was largely written in the 1880s.

Spencer's evolutionary philosophy was open to (and often received) the charge of atheistic materialism for, despite seeking to appear agnostic rather than deliberately irreligious, it set aside the question of the ultimate causes of things (in themselves) as 'The Unknowable'. The initial assumption of the 'synthetic Philosophy' was that force is universally persistent and matter is indestructible, although motion and matter are periodically absorbed and dissipated ('dissolution') into simpler forms when systems become over-complex and unsustainable. Nevertheless, the 'multiplication of effects' over time favours the development of complex bodies in both the inorganic and the organic portions of the universe. The most famous expression of this 'induction' as a 'rational generalization' was Spencer's 1857 statement that 'Every active force produces more than one change – every cause produces more than one effect' and his further observation from the same year that (as 'an inevitable corollary' of the former) 'throughout creation there must have gone on, and must still go on, a never-ceasing transformation of the homogenous into the heterogeneous'.

At much the same time, he concluded that (at least in principle) it should be possible to order the whole of human knowledge on the basis of the concepts just outlined, the last of which had originally formulated by the German embryologist, Karl Ernst Von Baer (1792–1876).

In his *Autobiography*, Spencer claimed that studying Lyell's *Principles of Geology* led him to reject the Lyellian critique of Lamarck in 1840, and to accept that 'all organic forms' had 'arisen by progressive modifications, physically caused and inherited'. This idea later appeared in Spencer's early publications and by the 1860s (when writing *The Principles of Biology*) he concluded that simple forms of life were inherently unstable and prone to modification, because they were unequally exposed to the primeval forces posited by his philosophy as a whole. As well as noting the effects of heat and light, Spencer speculated that '[c]ontinued pressure on living tissue, by modifying the processes going on ... [within] it ... gradually diminishes and finally destroys its power of resuming the outline it had at first' (1864) and that, as a consequence, all organisms sought to re-establish equilibrium with their environment through adaptation, which led to the observable phenomenon of organic evolution. Furthermore, complex beings could be said to be 'superior' to (or more 'efficient' than) their primitive ancestors because they embodied more completely the principle of 'the physiological division of labour' as expounded by a French zoologist, Henri Milne-Edwards (1800–65) – a principle that Spencer himself came to agree with during the 1850s.

Spencer's mature theory described the Lamarckian form of adaptation as '*direct equilibration*', but he acknowledged that this could not explain all known examples of biological development and he drew upon the recently published Darwinian concept of 'natural selection' to complete the argument. Where only part of a species survived exposure to a selective environmental pressure, an inherited (but static) characteristic that allowed the remnant to continue and procreate could be preserved and become dominant. Here, Spencer spoke of the '*indirect equilibration*' of a species and its environment. Moreover, when a whole species failed to adapt successfully and became extinct – thereby failing the test of 'fitness' provided by its environment – the biosphere as a whole could be said to have returned to equilibrium, despite the temporary loss of diversity. In the latter years of his life, Spencer wrote several articles defending this theory against the neo-Darwinian ideas of Auguste Weismann (1834–1914).

In the early part of his career, Spencer was a believer in phrenology and, in 1852, he attempted to synthesize phrenological and associationist ideas in a literary essay on 'The Philosophy of Style'. However, when it came to developing his 'synthetic Philosophy', Spencer did not seek to defend phrenology. Instead, he contended that human consciousness had evolved as a result of general physical evolution, rather than arising from the state of one particular organ (i.e. the skull). Spencer argued that the sophistication of human consciousness reflected, and corresponded to, the sophistication of the structure and functions of the human nervous system, even if the 'substance of Mind' itself could not be known. All of the higher animals (and not just humans) made use of mental processes to adjust to their environments and the nervous system changed slowly over time, so that both the physical adaptation and the corresponding association of ideas could be transmitted across the generations. Instinct, emotion, will and reason were all, in effect, Lamarckian adaptations. For example, the association of pleasure with experiences that were useful in the struggle for survival was a 'naturalization' of the psychological theories of Locke, Hartley and JAMES MILL, although Spencer believed that the psychological and instinctual inheritance of each individual prevented children from being '*tabula rasa*'.

Another important consequence of Spencer's presupposition that individual human psychologies (and consequently the social life of human groups) were determined by a combination of their evolutionary origins and the physiological qualities of the species was the further assumption that the bodily differences between the sexes were sociologically important. In *Social Statics*, Spencer had argued that 'differences of bodily organization' and 'trifling mental variations' between the sexes should not disqualify women from enjoying equal political and civil rights, but in *The Principles of Sociology* he abandoned this position and took a more conservative view. There, he argued that women's intellectual and emotional growth was retarded by the physiological process of childbearing, and that the traditional combination of male aggression and female submission had been socially selected in the earliest stages of human evolution. Hence, Spencer became a firm opponent of female emancipation and argued that modern women retained a sufficient measure of 'social power' to defend their own interests and to contribute to the education of *all* children within the family. The latter function was particularly important because it ensured the maintenance and development of the ethic of 'private beneficence' necessary for the effective operation of Spencer's *laissez-faire* utopia (see below).

Spencer's ethical theory was certainly characterized by a stronger measure of continuity than his views on psychology and gender, for he consistently defended the equal-freedom principle that he first expounded in *Social Statics*: 'Every man has freedom to do all that he wills, provided he infringes not the equal freedom of any other man' (1850/1). Moreover, his later works clarified the benefits of utilitarian and liberal actions on the same grounds established by his evolutionary psychology, at least to his own satisfaction. Pleasure improves function while negative freedom, as opposed to paternalistic dependence, establishes the necessary adaptive connection between actions and consequences, even if the interdependence associated with voluntary co-operation and restraint based on contract is an inevitable feature of 'higher' societies. Good conduct was defined as action that maximized 'rational' utility (for everyone) in a society arranged in accordance with the 'law of equal freedom'. At the same time, Spencer was eventually forced to admit that his evolutionary principles could not act as a substitute for moral judgement and calculation of a more traditional kind: 'The Doctrine of Evolution has not furnished guidance to the extent I had hoped. Most of the conclusions drawn empirically, are such as right feelings, enlightened by cultivated intelligence, have already sufficed to establish' (1893).

A similar criticism might be directed at Spencer's sociological system as well, given the tension between the positivist assumption of the possibility of an objective, evolutionary science of society and a periodic recognition that social action must be interpreted sympathetically, with reference to the subjective beliefs of individual human agents. Nevertheless, Spencer's more typical approach to the subject was objectivist, materialist and functionalist. The physical, biological and economic conditions of a society's existence and the interdependent arrangement of its parts (each of which was assumed to have self-regulated functions) were far more important to Spencerian social analysis than the 'independent' role of social ideologies or personal beliefs. 'Public Opinion', while important to the theory of social evolution as a whole, was conditioned by social and economic factors, which operated in a reasonably regular and 'law-like' fashion. It was therefore possible for Spencer to present his sociological theory as one of 'super-organic Evolution', consistent with both the overarching themes of the 'synthetic Philosophy' and

the encyclopedic tables of 'sociological Facts' (collated on both contemporary and historical subjects) found in the *Descriptive Sociology*.

Herbert Spencer frequently described human society as an 'organism' and drew attention to common features shared with biological entities, such as regulative systems (e.g. governments and nerve systems), sustaining systems (e.g. productive industries and nutritional organs) and distributive systems (e.g. roads, railways, veins and arteries). Yet, while an animal organism had a single consciousness that ordered its whole being, a 'social organism' enjoyed a heterogeneous and plural consciousness in each and every 'cell'. Hence, according to Spencer, society had no moral personality that could justify claims against the interests of its members; it could only progress when enough of those members agreed upon the justice of certain practices in a coalition known as 'Public Opinion'. Such changes, moreover, were deemed to parallel the zoological process of evolution, which – as we have seen – Spencer understood primarily, but not exclusively, as one of Lamarckian 'functional adaptation'. Thus, according to the principles of Spencerian philosophy, liberal politics and utilitarian ethics could be seen as 'acquired characteristics' that benefited the whole 'social organism'. Yet, in practice, these theories were contested by conservative and socialist thinkers of a variety of hues, whose ideas Spencer felt obliged to rebut in more polemical works, such as *The Man versus the State*.

In Spencerian sociology, the two great epochs of human history were 'militant society' (feudalism) and 'industrial society' (capitalism), following as they did upon the original evolution of the organizing structure of our individual lives from family to tribe to nation. Thanks to its systematic emphasis upon warfare, 'militant society' had been superseded because it was unable to allow civilization to progress by 'individuation', that is, by the more and more complex versions of the division of labour that characterized 'industrial society'. In keeping with the general concept of the 'social organism', this liberal, market community was presented as a complex, heterogeneous and individuated system whose development paralleled that of the 'higher' animal organisms, because its regulative system – the state – played a restrictive and specialized role.

However, Spencer did not simply describe the 'night-watchman state' metaphorically; he also recommended it in no uncertain terms. As early as 1852, in the essay 'A Theory of Population', he had concluded that the Malthusian trap was illusory and that the minimal state was best adapted to preside over a scenario where 'population pressure' would generate the reduced species fertility, the increased economic productivity and the co-operative culture of 'social sentiments' that would sustain and develop liberalism and capitalism into ever more desirable and eventually even 'anarchistic' forms. In later life, he remained attached to these ideals, but became increasingly disenchanted with the populist element of Gladstonian liberalism – although, as late as 1881, he was a supporter of the 'Anti-Aggression League' – and with the collectivism of Chamberlain and the 'New Liberals'. Instead, Spencer became closely associated with the conservatism of the so-called 'late-Victorian Individualists', notably through his contribution to the volume of essays *A Plea For Liberty* (1891), as edited by Thomas Mackay of 'The Liberty and Property Defence League', an anti-collectivist pressure group.

At the same time, it should be noted that Spencer *seemed* more conservative as he grew older, partly because his critics had moved 'to the left' and partly because the apparently utopian argument of his most famous early work, *Social Statics*, was actually qualified in a number of respects. For example, a chapter on 'The Right to Ignore the State' acknowledged the right of civil disobedience to unjust laws in principle – as a corollary of the equal-freedom principle – but insisted that its applicability varied 'directly as the social morality' was 'vicious' (the present) or 'virtuous' (the future). Moreover, while a chapter on the land question – 'The Right to the Use of the Earth' – contended that in the ideal 'industrial society' everyone would have an equal right to use of the earth's resources, which could be ensured through common ownership of land, important conditions were applied to this normative recommendation. In particular, Spencer argued that the expropriation of much the greater part of privately owned land (when it was honestly acquired and improved by good management) would involve significant, and probably unaffordable, measures of financial compensation. Hence, questions of practicality and the distinction between 'relative' and 'absolute' (that is ideal) ethical principles, as made explicit in Spencer's later works on *Ethics*, seem to explain the apparent contradiction

between Spencer's early and late politics, plus the recognition on his part that a 'land nationalization' argument could be used to justify other socialistic measures that were quite incompatible with his lionization of the private entrepreneur. Nevertheless, Spencer's original formulations were indicative of an iconoclastic tendency, given the centrality of land to certain Victorian ideals of 'home' and 'nobility', and there was indubitably an element of inconsistency over time in his attitudes.

After the First World War, Spencer's reputation went into a long decline but later, in the 1970s, interest revived. A major dispute arose among scholars when David Wiltshire argued that Spencer's evolutionism, organicism and functionalism were not compatible with his advocacy of *laissez-faire* and methodological individualism, and John Peel contended that they were. Wiltshire's critical observation was that liberalism 'posits the harmonization of the interests of free individuals' while '[s]ocial evolution tends inexorably towards the hegemony of the centralized state, and perpetuates aggression' and that in 'this irreconcilable contradiction lies the main flaw of Spencerian social and political theory' (Wiltshire 1978: 256.). On the other hand, another objection might be made to the effect that the slightly later 'new biology' of KROPOTKIN (and others) suggested that human social evolution can also be understood in terms of decentralization and peaceful mutual aid. On this second view, Spencer's fault would not be that of seeking a model for human behaviour in the non-human world, but in positing a *capitalist* 'natural order' (or 'naturalizing' capitalism). Nevertheless, Spencer's ideas seem to have become part of the warp and weft of liberal debate during his lifetime; his work had a significant impact on a number of other nineteenth-century social theorists such as BENJAMIN KIDD, BEATRICE POTTER (WEBB), Lester Frank Ward, SIDNEY WEBB and Edward Youmans, and some of his ideas influenced important figures in the arts, such as the composer Hubert Parry and the novelist Jack London.

References

Peel, J.D.Y. (1971) *Herbert Spencer: The Evolution of a Sociologist*, London: Heinemann.

Wiltshire, D. (1978) *The Social and Political Thought of Herbert Spencer*, Oxford: University Press.

Further reading

Perrin, R. (1993) *Herbert Spencer: A Primary and Secondary Bibliography*, New York, London: Garland.

Taylor, M. (1992) *Men versus the State: Herbert Spencer and Late Victorian Individualism*, Oxford: Clarendon Press.

CLIVE E. HILL

STAËL, MME DE (1766–1817)

Anne-Louise-Germaine Necker, Baronness de Staël-Holstein was born in Paris to Swiss Calvinist parents, Jacques and Susan Necker. Her father was the finance minister of Louis XVI in 1789. Her mother opened one of the most flourishing literary salons in Paris during the last decades of the old regime. The sole daughter of the family, she married the Swedish ambassador to France, Baron Erik de Staël-Holstein, in 1786 and joined European court life.

Thanks to her privileged social background and excellence in conversation, Mme de Staël became the most famous *salonnière* of the revolutionary period. She is also known as an eminent woman author of the revolutionary period, whose seventeen volumes of collected works cover a wide variety of genres, including novels, plays, moral and political essays, literary criticism, history, biography and poems. She was also and above all a political thinker, and among the founders of LIB-ERALISM in France.

While her gender has obscured her due place in male-centred historical traditions, it certainly contributed to de Staël's concept of public opinion. As an heir to the salon culture of the old regime, de Staël placed women at the centre of the formation of public opinion. Historically, salons started during the religious wars at the end of the seventeenth century. Initial *salonnières* perceived salon activities as a social movement that could pacify society by transforming the belligerent mentality of men through literature and polite conversation. By 1750, salons were at their apogee. French *philosophes* believed that *salonnières* embodied modern civilization, defined as peaceful, tender, sociable and enlightened. As Montesquieu remarked, their mission was to co-ordinate different and egotistic opinions expressed by their male participants into a moral consensus in the name of public opinion.

Mme de Staël adapted this salon culture of the old regime to the revolutionary period. In *Lettres sur Rousseau*, she suggested that women should shape public opinion by transmitting the civilizing and prescriptive force of salon culture to print culture, and that a modern *salonnière* should be simultaneously an author. In this light, her principal literary works, such as *De l'influence des passions*, *De la littérature* and *De l'Allemagne* had an eminently political function of creating a common moral and cultural disposition among mutually opposing monarchists and republicans as a pragmatic means of ending the social dissension engendered by the French Revolution.

A keen concern for the moral regeneration of the ruling elite nourished her reflections on liberty as well. In *Lettres sur Rousseau*, de Staël combined the spiritual liberty of Rousseau and the theory of natural sociability of sensationalist philosophers, and defined moral liberty at the crossroad of liberty and order. She assumed that the freedom of judgement, a crucial component of individual liberty, derived from a delicate balance between the ethical independence of individuals from society and the social influence upon individuals of state action and education. She considered that religious feeling guided reason towards conscientious acts. This is where she sympathised with Rousseau's 'religion of the heart' and her Genevian Calvinism influenced her political posture. This synthesis of two mutually opposing discourses was another major characteristic of de Staël's thought.

Although de Staël held her salon continuously between 1786 and 1817, her direct political influence as a *salonnière* reached a peak in 1791, when she collaborated with Narbonne, her then companion and the minister of war, to assist in stabilizing the constitutional monarchy. However, by the time she returned to Paris in 1795 as a newly converted republican, after a short exile to Switzerland and England during the Terror, her salon became an important laboratory for developing political and philosophical reflections on liberty rather than an arena of direct political influence.

De Staël's republicanism between 1795 and 1799 went hand in hand with her inclination towards the ideas of the *idéologues*, the politically influential intellectuals of the Directory who were frequent guests at her salon. During this period, she laid emphasis upon some of their ideas, including the assumption that ideas were shaped by external influences via sensation, as well as a faith in applying an analytic method and calculation in the social and moral sciences. She even asserted that state actions and the role of writers were indispensable to familiarize the French with liberty, though she was strongly opposed to the idéologues' atheistic and materialistic tendency.

However, by 1803, de Staël parted from the *idéologues* and mockingly called their ideas 'the moral founded upon interest'. Her antipathy was crystallized after the *idéologues* assisted in bringing Napoleon to power on the 18 Brumaire. Indeed, representative *idéologues* such as Destutt de Tracy and Volney became senators of the empire although they were soon disappointed by Napoleon's neglect of liberty. De Staël considered that a lack of a spiritual and metaphysical dimension among the *idéologues* made them obedient to the unjust temporary sovereign in exchange for material rewards, and that the utilitarian and atheistic aspects of their sensationalist philosophy had laid a moral foundation for Napoleon's political despotism.

Instead, de Staël reasserted that the metaphysical independence of individuals from social influence was essential to moral judgement, an idea fully expressed in *De l'Allemagne*. This was a sphere where rational calculations were useless, and included writers' moral independence from state authority and the citizens' judgement on the moral legitimacy of political institutions and the political conduct of policy-makers. Her alienation from republicanism therefore commenced with a rejection of its moral implication on liberty at the turn of the century.

A head-on political confrontation with Napoleon eventually led to her expulsion from the French territory in 1803. During a decade of painful exile in Coppet in Switzerland, de Staël gained further intellectual maturity in contact with B. CONSTANT, SISMONDI and SCHLEGEL. She inaugurated a new intellectual current characterized by respect for individual liberty and a high regard for different national cultures. Finally, her ideological opposition to the Corsican reached a climax in 1813 when Napoleon suddenly banned the publication of *De l'Allemagne* in France. However, the success of the book across the whole of Europe was such that, by the time of Napoleon's fall, Mme de Staël had become a cosmopolitan woman author of unprecedented popularity.

As a political thinker, de Staël's central concern was the division of powers. While French revolutionaries considered this in terms of a juridical division of tasks based upon the superiority of the National Assembly over the Executive, she affirmed that the most difficult problem consisted of how to unite these institutions instead of dividing them. Her master in this regard was Montesquieu, with his famous principle of checks and balances. However, she adopted two different attitudes towards this concept before and after 1793.

Between 1789 and 1793, de Staël espoused a principle of national sovereignty that considered the single National Assembly sovereign, sanctioning its pre-eminence over the Executive. She rallied to La Fayettists until the collapse of the constitutional monarchy in 1792. She also supported the constitution of 1791 that abolished nobility by rejecting the second chamber. In this context, she introduced into France some elements of the British parliamentary system, writing articles with the aim of ensuring a harmonious junction between the single legislature and the constitutional monarch. She thus promoted such notions as a distinction between the political and penal responsibility of ministers, the formation of a cabinet of ministers and the inviolability of the chief of the executive. While in Britain the establishment of the parliamentary system had dispensed with the monarchical veto in practice, de Staël assumed that the initiative of legislation and the veto were indispensable prerogatives of the French head of state, in order to guarantee the political unity of France.

During the Terror, she decisively parted from a juridical way of conceiving a new social and political order, and introduced sociological reflections to establish liberty in post-revolutionary France. It seems that her stay in England in 1793 and the British debate upon the French Revolution and Whig ideas in particular modified her views of the revolution. Whigs like Sir James Mackintosh had concluded that the principle of national sovereignty and an absence of the middle class in society had made the Terror possible. De Staël had introduced these British ideas of liberty into the political debates of the Directory after 1795.

De Staël followed Mackintoch in rejecting the notion of national sovereignty when she converted to republicanism in 1795. At the same time, her principal concern between 1795 and 1799 consisted of applying to the Republic two axioms of the constitutional monarchy, liberty and order. It was during the Directory that she produced her most important works as a political thinker: *Réflexions sur la paix* and *Circonstances actuelles qui peuvent terminer la révolution française.*

According to these essays, de Staël's political liberalism can be defined as a constitutional equilibrium between legitimate state authority and the liberty of the nation characterized by the division of legislative powers. One of the objectives of her political liberalism, guaranteed by the existence of the second chamber and its sociological composition, was to preserve the economic and social status quo, and to protect the interests of big landowners, most of whom were nobles. This is why, after 1795, she admired the English House of Lords as a tangible example of the guarantee of liberty. She considered that either the monarchy or the Republic would be legitimate as far as these conditions were met, and she sanctioned the constitution of the year III (1795) that institutionalized the second chamber for the first time since 1789.

Against a large majority of revolutionaries who tried to fuse the elite of the old regime and the revolution, de Staël tried to preserve a distinct social status for big landowners of the old regime in post-revolutionary social order:

> si les deux chambres en France étaient parfaitement distinctes; si le pouvoir de l'une était prolongé par delà celui de l'autre, si la condition d'âge, de propriété était beaucoup plus forte, il s'établirait naturellement la balance des deux pouvoirs qui sont dans la nature des choses, de l'action qui renouvelle, et de la réflexion qui conserve.

Her unique definition of the second chamber reflected her efforts to rally *émigrés* to the French Revolution. If republicans protected property, the Republic would be loved by property owners, including *émigrés*, and such measures could help to terminate the revolution. Her opinion, in this regard, contradicted that of many republicans, but found some echo among *émigrés* at the turn of the century.

Les Considérations sur les principaux événements de la révolution française, posthumously published in 1818, was de Staël's most influential work in terms of its impact on public opinion. It was also the first historical account of the French Revolution written by a contemporary. In this book, de Staël resurrected a widespread counter-revolutionary historical myth according to which the Frankish lords' political power had gradually eroded as a result of the concomitant rise in power of the French absolute monarch and the common people during the process of state centralization. She emphasised that this historical memory led to the division between nobility and common people during the revolutionary years.

De Staël defined the objective of the French Revolution as a resurrection of aristocratic liberty linked with the notion of social inequality in a modern context, through the institutionalization of the chamber of peers. Thus, she attributed the ultimate mistake of the French Revolution to the unicameral legislature in 1789. She compared the Charter of 1814 with the political reforms of Necker between 1788 and 1789, and suggested that the Restoration could finally institutionalize liberty, thanks to the newly institutionalized hereditary chamber of peers. In fact, her historical interpretation of the French Revolution primarily reflected her political vision of the second Restoration, and her book immediately prompted the emergence of two distinct groups of liberals.

On the one hand, the *Doctrinaires* applauded de Staël's notion of the moral influence of the governing elite, and considered that a key element in the liberal political institutions lay in the existence of a hereditary second chamber. However, a lack of political cohesion in the group was demonstrated by the negative reactions of some *Doctrinaires,* when the duc de Broglie, influenced by the ideas of de Staël, prepared the reform of the electoral law in 1819–20.

On the other hand, liberals of a more democratic tendency accepted the liberal principles of *Considérations* but refused de Staël's sociological application of these principles. They gradually came to constitute a group of *indépendents* headed by B. Constant, who objected to her notion of hereditary magistracy. Instead, they suggested that the second chamber should be selective in terms of wealth, not restricted to landownership. It indicates that their vision of social and political change contradicted that of de Staël. While she believed in a social status quo characterized by the preservation of feudal agriculture and political domination over the peasantry, the *indépendents* accepted further social and economic change through the introduction of the free market in French society.

Consequently, their more bourgeois perspective led to a historical interpretation of the French Revolution different from that of Mme de Staël. In particular, Bailleul, a former republican, distinguished the French Revolution from the British Glorious Revolution of 1688, contrary to de Staël, and affirmed that the former represented a distinct historical phase marking the emergence of common people in the political sphere. By the middle of the 1820s, this democratic current became predominant among left-wing liberals, and the second-generation historians of the French Revolution, such as THIERS and Mignet, began writing the history of the French Revolution by refuting Mme de Staël and following Bailleul.

As an Enlightenment woman *philosophe*, Mme de Staël passed the ideological legacy of the Enlightenment on to the revolutionary period and transformed an abstract concept of liberty into a series of political and constitutional principles. While the British influence was prominent in terms of her emphasis upon the modern parliamentary system, she nonetheless conceived moral liberty under the influence of thinkers such as Rousseau, and rejected the exclusively materialistic and utilitarian vision of individuals inherent in eighteenth-century sensationalist philosophy.

Although her political liberalism had little effective political influence upon contemporary French politics, de Staël's political ideas and vision of the modern individual made a firm imprint upon the subsequent generation of liberals, such as Constant, Rémusat, GUIZOT and TOCQUEVILLE. It is on this account that she might be called the mother of French liberalism.

References

Goodman, D. (1995) *The Republic of Letters, a Cultural History of the French Enlightenment*, Ithaca, London: Cornell University Press.

Staël, Mme de (1820–1) 'Réflexions sur la paix intérieure', *Oeuvres complètes*, vol. III, 25, Paris: Slatkine.

Takeda, C. (2001) 'Mme de Staël's Contribution to Liberalism in France (1788–1826)', PhD dissertation to Royal Holloway College, University of London.

Further reading

Staël-Holstein, Germaine de (1967) *Oeuvres complètes*, 3 vols, Genève: Slatkine.

—— (1987) *An Extraordinary Woman. Selected Writings of Germaine de Staël*, trans. and intro. V. Folkenflik, New York: Columbia University Press.

—— (2000) *Madame de Staël on Politics, Literature, and National Character*, ed. Morroe Berger, New Brunswick, London: Transaction.

Herold, J. Christopher (1959) *Mistress to an Age; a Life of Madame de Staël*, London: Hamish Hamilton.

Winegarten, Renee (1985) *Mme de Staël*, Leamington Spa: Berg.

SEE ALSO: liberalism

C. TAKEDA

STEPHEN, LESLIE (1832–1904)

Often portrayed as an 'archetypal Victorian', Leslie Stephen is associated with the development of a liberalism that took account of both sociology and Darwinism. His contributions to British political thought, intellectual history, literary criticism and biography have all received significant acclaim, although he has also been seen as an inflexible dogmatist.

As members of the 'Clapham sect' (see MACAULAY), Stephen's family was politically well connected and he began an academic and sacerdotal career at Cambridge University in the 1850s. However, the avid reading of J.S. MILL, German biblical criticism, COMTE, SPENCER and DARWIN (plus knowledge of Lyellian geology acquired through discussing his hobby of rock climbing) informed a loss of Christian faith, subsequent clerical resignation (1862) and a final departure from his Trinity Hall Fellowship (1865). Although Stephen published some 'juvenilia', his career as a 'Victorian man of letters' is normally taken to have begun at the latter date, when he returned to London. His personal life was generally unhappy, for although he fathered five children – including the artist Vanessa Bell and the novelist Virginia Woolf – both his wives predeceased him. Moreover, Stephen's biographers have usually confirmed the unsympathetic description of his domestic persona in Woolf's *To the Lighthouse* (1927).

Throughout his whole career, Stephen wrote or edited thirty books, composed nearly 250 essays, contributed almost 400 entries to *The Dictionary of National Biography* (he acted as an editor from 1885 to 1891) and was a regular contributor to weekly magazines and the daily press. Stephen's early books, such as *The Playground of Europe* (1871) and *Freethinking and Plainspeaking* (1873) reflected a personal interest in Alpine mountaineering (*Playground*) and a need to justify his breach with Christianity using 'science' (*Freethinking*). Three volumes entitled *Hours in a Library* (1874/6/9) collected together many of his literary essays and emphasized his early concern with authorial psychology plus a developing interest in the Enlightenment.

The History of English Thought in the Eighteenth Century (1876) was a pioneering work of intellectual history, which aspired to explain the Deist controversy of that period in terms of 'social development', but which – in practice – concentrated on reconstructing the logical arguments of philosophers and theologians. Stephen's last major book, *English Literature and Society in the Eighteenth Century* (1904), was more successful in applying this 'externalist' methodology to the 'rise of the novel', by referring to such developments as the Industrial Revolution and the growth of a leisured middle class. *The Science of Ethics* (1882) was an earlier attempt to 'sociologize' a discipline – Stephen's achievement here was to fuse a Spencerian view of the function of morality with a Humean descriptive ethics. *The English Utilitarians* (1900) also defended an organicist and evolutionary perspective in history against utilitarian individualism, but recognized the significant contribution of BENTHAM and the Mills to liberal theory, representative democracy and 'progressive' social legislation.

Further reading

Annan, N. (1984) *Leslie Stephen: The Godless Victorian*, London: Weidenfeld & Nicolson.
Zink, D. (1972) *Leslie Stephen*, New York: Twayne Publishers.

SEE ALSO: intellectuals, elites and meritocracy; liberalism; religion, secularization and the crisis of faith; Social Darwinism

CLIVE E. HILL

STEWART, DUGALD (1753–1828)

Dugald Stewart was the pupil of Adam Ferguson and Thomas Reid, an influential Scottish Enlightenment philosopher and lecturer, and the foremost early interpreter of the work of Adam Smith. Stewart was born, largely educated and died in Edinburgh. A student of the Mathematical Sciences and Philosophy, and son of an Edinburgh Professor of Mathematics, Stewart was called to act as a substitute lecturer for his ailing father at the age of 19, and later (1778–9) to substitute for his former teacher Adam Ferguson in delivering an original set of lectures in Moral Philosophy. He was elected Professor of Mathematics in the University of Edinburgh in 1775 at the age of 21, and when Ferguson resigned the chair of Moral Philosophy at Edinburgh in 1785, Stewart succeeded him and continued in that post until his retirement in 1810. In this position, Stewart presented lectures on Moral Philosophy, Principles of Government and, from 1800 onward, Political Economy to a generation of influential thinkers within both Whig and Tory circles. Among an influential coterie of former students, those lectures became legendary.

Dugald Stewart's classes in Moral Philosophy were attended by many who would go on to become important figures in their own right in nineteenth-century economics and politics, indeed sometimes more important than their instructor himself. Their number included Walter Scott, Francis Horner and FRANCIS JEFFREY, although in his *Life of Francis Jeffrey*, Henry Cockburn claimed that he could find no direct evidence that Jeffrey was actually enrolled as a student in the Moral Philosophy lectures – a fact Cockburn attributed to the power exercised over the education of the young Jeffrey by his fiercely anti-Whig father. JAMES MILL and James Mackintosh, however, were frequently in attendance. Stewart's separate series of political economy lectures, beginning in the winter of 1800, were attended over their succeeding eight sessions by approximately 500 students, including SYDNEY SMITH, Henry Cockburn, Francis Horner, Lauderdale, Palmerston, Lord John Russell, HENRY BROUGHAM, Henry Petty-Fitzmaurice (3rd Marquis of Lansdowne and grandson of Sir William Petty), Macvey Napier and Francis Jeffrey. James Mackintosh would later seek to immortalize Stewart's intellectual leadership with the observation that his students 'were among his best works.' The impact of Stewart's thinking on the *Edinburgh Review*, launched in 1802 by Smith, Jeffrey and Horner, has been recognized also to have been direct and powerful. Indeed, comparing the available record of those who attended Stewart's lectures in Edinburgh and the authors of the articles in the *Edinburgh Review* during its first decade of publication reveals that 412 of the 623 articles were written by one or other of them.

While it may be largely unquestioned that Stewart's lasting reputation lies fundamentally in the transmission of Adam Smith's economics to the next generation, the direct influence of Stewart's lectures on Smith's *Wealth of Nations* (which were not to be published until mid-century) is more difficult to establish. Certainly he transformed the Smithian legacy even as he transmitted it, both by concentrating on the issue of free trade and by narrowing the focus Smith's 'science of the legislator' to exclude the consideration of the forms of Government from the domain of political economy. This separation of the study of political economy from the study of the theory of Government or new constitutions was an innovative and significant step in the direction of establishing the province of economic science. For Stewart, political economy involved the production of 'general principles', which, when carefully applied to particular circumstances, could 'enlighten and direct the policies of future legislators' (*Life and Writings of Adam Smith*, 10: 53). He supported this revision of the political economist's brief in clear and unequivocally political terminology:

> Smith, Quesnay, Turgot, Campomanes, Beccaria, and others, have aimed at the improvement of society, – not by delineating plans of new constitutions, but by enlightening the policy of actual legislators. Such speculations, while they are more essentially and more extensively useful than any others, have no tendency to unhinge established institutions, or to inflame the passions of the multitude.
>
> (*Life and Writings of Adam Smith*, 10: 55–6)

Such tendencies to unhinge and inflame were in Stewart's view more the product of 'the mistaken notions concerning Political Liberty which have been so widely disseminated in Europe by the writings of Mr. Locke' (*Collected Works*, 8: 23) In emphasizing the greater value to political progress and stability of an *expedient* political economy, Stewart effectively left behind one important version of the natural law and jurisprudence tradition in the Scottish Enlightenment (with its emphasis on confounding patriarchialism and indefeasible hereditary right), and embraced another vision of the constitution as something at once progressive, organic and mechanical.

In his own time, Stewart was recognized as far more than the reformulater of Adam Smith. The influence of his own writings, including the first and second volumes of his *Elements of the Philosophy of the Human Mind* (I: 1792; II: 1815) and his *Outlines of Moral Philosophy* (1793) have been linked to the approach or methodology in matters theological, scientific and political economic of the Oxford Noetics – a group of Oxford intellectuals whose membership included Edward Copleston (1776–1849), Richard Whately (1787–1863) and Nassau Senior (1790–1864). Widely read in both Britain and the USA, the *Elements* conveyed the principles of Common Sense philosophy to a transatlantic audience, and provided what one commentator has called 'the only systematic epistemological survey of contemporary scientific debates available in Britain before 1830' (Corsi 1987: 97). As such, Stewart's epistemology, with its rejection of both associationalist psychology and physiological materialism, was taken up in development of JOHN STUART MILL's writings on the method proper to the conduct of political economy.

References

Corsi, P. (1987) 'The Heritage of Dugald Steward: Oxford Philosophy and the Method of Political Economy', *Nuncius: annali di storia della scienza* 2, 2: 89–144.

Stewart, D. (1854–60) *The Collected Works of Dugald Stewart*, ed. W. Hamilton, 11 vols, Edinburgh: Thomas Constable, Vols 2–4, *Elements of the Philosophy of the Human Mind*, Vol. 1: 1792; Vol. 2: 1814; Vol. 3: 1827; Vol. 5, *Philosophical Essays*, 1810; Vols 8–9, *Lectures on Political Economy*, 1855–6; Vol. 10, 5–98, *An Account of the Life and Writings of Adam Smith LL.D*, 1793.

Further reading

Haakonssen, K. (1984) 'From Moral Philosophy to Political Economy: The Contribution of Dugald Stewart', in V. Hope (ed.) *Philosophers of the Scottish Enlightenment*, 211–32, Edinburgh: Edinburgh University Press.

Milgate, M. and Stimson, S. (1996) 'The Figure of Smith: Dugald Stewart and the Propagation of Smithian Economics', *The European Journal of the History of Economic Thought* 3, 2: 225–53.

Skinner, A.S. (1992) 'Political Economy: Adam Smith and his Scottish Predecessors', in P. Jones and A.S. Skinner (eds) *Adam Smith Reviewed*, 217–43, Edinburgh: Edinburgh University Press.

Winch, D. (1983) 'The System of the North: Dugald Stewart and His Pupils', in S. Collini, D. Winch and J. Burrow (eds) *That Noble Science of Politics*, 23–63, Cambridge: Cambridge University Press.

SEE ALSO: Brougham, Henry; Jeffrey, Francis; main currents in philosophy; political economy

SHANNON STIMSON

STIRNER, MAX (1806–56)

The philosopher Max [Johann Kaspar Schmidt] Stirner was born in Bayreuth and studied at Berlin (where he attended Hegel's lectures), Erlangen and Königsberg. While teaching at a private girls' school in Berlin he became associated with the left Hegelians around BRUNO BAUER (1839–44), and in 1845 he published the book for which he is chiefly remembered, *Der Einzige und sein Eigentum* (*The Ego and his Own*). Although the book elicited a prompt critical response it was not a financial success. Stirner had given up his job, spent the rest of his life in poverty, and without writing anything more of interest.

The impact of *The Ego and his Own*, however, was extraordinary. Stirner took issue with all his revolutionary contemporaries, arguing that their radicalisms amounted to little more than a humanistic restatement of the values of the old religions. Real radicalism lay in recognizing that only the individual mattered, and that all apparent social formations and institutions, such as classes or nations – all semblances of order – were illusory. He charged his contemporaries, particularly FEUERBACH, with separating human nature from God, but retaining the notion that the essence of human nature remains something above humanity, to be striven for, so that Christian ethics are merely secularized rather than superseded. For Stirner, however, there are no absolute values to be striven for, so there can be no prescriptive moral code: all that matters is individual self-realization. 'Egoism' is the expression of a more sophisticated form of civilization, while adherence to the claims of society is the true 'state of nature', from which individuals must free themselves just as children outgrow their mothers. This is not to confuse egoism with selfishness, greed or narrow self-interest, however, and individuals who, for example, subordinate everything to their own material self-enrichment are slaves to their compulsions rather than true egoists. Although he denied the existence of any social reality beyond the individual, Stirner's work did consider the implications for existing social institutions, and in particular the state, which embodied all that he rejected; on the other hand there is little indication of the ways in which individual egos might interact in the absence of social institutions and ideologies. Even more personal-level relationships with others, especially those involving commitment, are seen as illegitimate constraints.

Locating Stirner's thought has been a problematic matter for intellectual historians, not least because apart from the one book there is very little other material from which to derive a sense of intellectual profile, still less development. It has been suggested that writing the book was in a sense his own path to self-realization, endowing him as it did with an identity other than that of an unremarkable schoolteacher with intellectual friends. Its immediate impact was on the contemporaries in his circle, including Karl Marx and Engels, who devoted a substantial part of *The German Ideology* solely to a scathing attack on 'saint Max'. Feuerbach and Moses Hess also responded to his criticisms. For later generations many of Stirner's themes seemed to anticipate NIETZSCHE's preoccupations, and beyond that both fascist thinkers such as Mussolini and post-war existentialists have referred directly to Stirner's influence. Stirner's greatest influence, however, has, arguably, been on the development of anarchist thought.

Further reading

Carrol, John (1971) *Max Stirner: The Ego and his Own*, London: Jonathan Cape.
Stirner, Max (1963) *The Ego and his Own*, New York: Libertarian Book Club.

SEE ALSO: Hegel and Hegelianism

TIM KIRK

STRAUSS, DAVID FRIEDRICH (1808–74)

David Friedrich Strauss was a Protestant theologian from the Swabian region of Southwest Germany, who shook the world of Church and theology in 1835–6 with his work on *The Life of*

Jesus (*Das Leben Jesu*, trans. 1842–4) – a work often referred to as the most important theological milestone in the nineteenth century. It was soon translated into various languages, saw several editions and triggered off the publication of some fifty theological counter-polemics. Strauss thus became famous beyond the borders of Germany. He is regarded as a major influence on both the development of Protestant theology and the atheistic critique of religion.

Son of a merchant and a Protestant minister's daughter, he studied theology with the aim of becoming a minister. His studies led him to Hegel whose dialectical thinking had a profound impact on him (see HEGEL AND HEGELIANISM). In 1832, Strauss was offered a position in the famous Protestant Seminary in the Swabian university town of Tübingen. The publication of *Das Leben Jesu* triggered off a furious debate about his contention that the gospels had to be seen as myths and not as historical accounts of the life of Jesus. Not surprisingly, such a public assault on the bastions of traditional Christian faith put an end to any hopes of him ever becoming a minister. Due to his radical theological ideas even a university career subsequently proved to be elusive, forcing him to work as a private scholar and writer. In the revolutionary year of 1848 he failed to secure a mandate to the German parliamentary assembly in Frankfurt but managed to be elected as a moderate liberal to the Diet of his home state of Württemberg.

During his life he published several successful works, amongst which biographies of historical personalities who had been 'dissenters' like himself, for example the biography of *Ulrich von Hutten* (1858, trans. 1874). His *Christliche Glaubenslehre* (Christian Dogma, 1840–1) portrayed the traditional Christian belief system as being inferior to science. In 1864 he wrote a popularized version of his early masterpiece – *The Life of Jesus for the People* (*Das Leben Jesu für das deutsche Volk bearbeitet*, trans. 1879). In his last work *The Old Faith and the New: A Confession* (*Der alte und der neue Glaube*, 1872, trans. 1873) he explained his concept of a humanistic religion based on science and materialism.

Strauss's goal was to develop Christianity into a humanistic religion by means of interpreting the gospels as myths and stressing the identity of Christ with humanity. Strauss did not deny the historical existence of Jesus; he viewed Jesus as a historical person, as a Jewish prophet who grew up in Nazareth, was baptized by John, had disciples, opposed the Pharisees, was an exceptional man giving the impression to be the Messiah and was crucified. But the crucial point in Strauss's argument was that Jesus was only human and not divine. From a historical perspective there were no divine incarnation, miracles or resurrection – a contention that was diametrically opposed to the Church teachings, which saw the gospels as 'supernatural history' based on the direct intervention of God. Strauss was not the first and only one of contemporary theologians to question certain elements of the historical veracity of the gospels, in particular the virgin birth: his theology needs to be seen in the context of the so-called 'life of Jesus-research'. This research had been inspired by the Enlightenment and was conducted by Protestant theologians from the late eighteenth century onwards as a scientific enquiry into the life of Jesus by means of biblical and non-biblical sources. They asked themselves to what extent the gospels could be considered a reliable source for the reconstruction of the life of the historical Jesus, and they tried to distinguish between the teachings of Jesus and those of the Apostles. What they struggled with most in their efforts to come close to the historical Jesus were supernatural events such as the miracles. But Strauss went further: he was the first to de-mask the gospels in their totality as myths. By doing so, he denied the centrality of the historicity of Jesus as God's son for Christianity – a tenet that was held inalienable by his theological opponent Schleiermacher. Strauss regarded the authors of the gospels not as frauds but as propagandists of a 'truth' that they had come to believe in as the fulfilment of messianic prophecies: since Jesus was believed to be the prophesied Messiah all the other prophesies, such as the virgin birth, were projected as real historical events onto his life, with the miracles serving as confirmations of his divine power.

Strauss deemed the idea of a 'Christ' to be a valid one, but its realization would not be enacted in a historical individuality, in a single person, but rather in the whole of mankind. His logical conclusion was to see the gospels merely as myths containing excellent maxims of life conduct and portraying the idea of the '*Gottmensch*' (God-man). God was an impersonal, infinite spirit manifesting itself in the finite forms of the natural world and the human spirit. This infinite spirit was neither God by himself nor man by himself, but the God-man, neither the infinite alone nor the finite alone. Unity of man and the divine could never be reached in one individual but only in the whole of humanity.

Strauss thus attacked the very core of traditional Christology, substituting an individual, Jesus, with the idea of a 'Christ' manifesting itself in humanity. It can be argued that such an idea is basically un-Christian and even a-theistic. His peculiar fusion of theology and philosophy was certainly un-Christian in the orthodox sense. He laid the theoretical groundwork of a critique of religion that was elaborated upon by philosophers such as FEUERBACH and Marx (see MARX AND MARXISM), and which in connection with the theories of DARWIN was a powerful tool to question religious belief as such.

Further reading

Harris, H. (1973) *David Friedrich Strauss and his Theology*, Cambridge: Cambridge University Press.
Lawler, E.G. (1986) *David Friedrich Strauss and his Critics: The* Life of Jesus *Debate in Early Nineteenth-Century German Journals*, New York: Peter Lang.
Madges, W. (1987) *The Core of Christian Faith: D.F. Strauss and his Catholic Critics*, New York: Peter Lang.

SEE ALSO: Darwin, Charles; religion, secularization and the crisis of faith; Social Darwinism

DETMAR KLEIN

SUMNER, WILLIAM GRAHAM (1840–1910)

The child of first-generation, English artisan migrants, the US sociologist William Graham Sumner was born in New Jersey in 1840. His formal education was undertaken at the public schools of Hartford, Connecticut, and Yale College (1859–63). Having spent 3 years in Europe, during the Civil War, Sumner became a tutor at Yale in 1866, a professor in 1872 and was associated with the college until his death in 1910.

From 1866 to 1872, Sumner sought to combine his scholarly life with the vocation of an Episcopalian clergyman, but his reading of German biblical scholarship, DARWIN and SPENCER undermined his faith. The political science that he subsequently developed was robustly secular and involved the forcible recommendation of both *laissez-faire* economics and 'rugged individualism', rather than state collectivism or sentimental philanthropy. In his final, anthropological works – *Folkways* (1906) and the posthumously published *The Science of Society* (with A. Keller and M. Davie, 1927) – Sumner argued that unconscious adaptation to the environment ('the struggle for existence') was the mainstay of human culture in all 'primitive' societies.

Sumner rarely courted easy popularity. One of his first books, *A History of American Currency* (1874), polemicized for the gold standard (and against paper money) at a time when bimetallism was being hotly debated in Reconstruction America. An 1883 pamphlet, *What Social Classes Owe to Each Other*, criticized the socio-political principle known today as 'equality of outcome' and argued against the view the state 'owes anything to anybody except peace, order, and...guarantees of rights'. In the wake of the Spanish-American War, his ironically titled essay, 'The Conquest of the United States by Spain' (1899), argued that a centralized, imperialist USA would impose more 'burdens than benefits' on its citizens.

Sumner's pacifism indicates the closeness of his position to that of Spencer. He viewed industrialism as constructive and militarism as wasteful, but he was not convinced that the industrial model of social life would *always* succeed at the expense of the military; he did not share Spencer's 'cosmic optimism'. The term 'Social Darwinist' should be applied to Sumner with caution, because he made infrequent use of analogies between human societies and the animal kingdom, and he was sceptical regarding the hypothesis that human instincts are inherited characteristics, ultimately transmitted to modern mankind from distant animal ancestors. He does seem to have used 'Darwinist' arguments as a rhetorical device, however, in order to stigmatize the 'undeserving poor' as evolutionary failures, although the main basis of his judgement was a moral standard of self-sufficiency. It should also be noted that Sumner's contemporaries, Lester Frank Ward (1841–1913) and Charlotte Perkins Gilman (1860–1935), demonstrated that it was equally possible for US sociologists to use evolutionary and organicist arguments to justify the opposing political positions of collectivism, feminism and even socialism.

Further reading

Bannister, R.C. (1973) 'William Graham Sumner's Social Darwinism: A Reconsideration', *History of Political Economy*, 5, 1: 85–109.

Starr, H.E. (1925) *William Graham Sumner*, New York: Henry Holt.

SEE ALSO: Darwin, Charles; Social Darwinism

CLIVE E. HILL

SUN YAT-SEN (1866–1925)

Sun Yat-Sen was born in 1866, in a peasant family in Kwangtung Province, and spent his boyhood without receiving formal education. At the age of 13, his elder brother – a wealthy farmer in Hawaii – called him to Hawaii where he received a modern education in a mission school for 4 years. There he became acutely conscious of China's necessity for reform. When he returned to his home country, he obtained a medical qualification in Hong Kong, and started to practice in Macao. But he then decided to fight for the cause of modernizing China, and founded a revolutionary association in 1894, based on Chinese merchants abroad and the secret societies called 'Heaven and Earth'. In 1895, he planned the first insurgency in Kwangtung that, however, ended in failure. He escaped from the country and wandered to Japan, the USA and England, living an exile's life, while trying to master modern political thought. After this, until the Revolution of 1911, Sun's revolution movement aimed by insurrection to overthrow the despotic rule of the Q'ing dynasty, and replace it with a republican system. During this time, Sun stayed mostly in foreign countries, seeking to extend his influence and gain further support. In 1905, he gathered Chinese revolutionary factions from various parts of China in Tokyo, and established the Chinese Revolutionary League. Even after he served as the premier of the league, he was severely criticized by the members of the league as well as by Zhang Binglin, Song Jiaoren and other nationalists for his reliance on foreign assistance. The general principles of Sun's revolutionary movement comprised 'The Three People's Principles' – that is to say: (1) Nationalism (removing the Q'ing dynasty); (2) People's Rights (establishing a republican system of government); (3) People's Livelihood (limiting the influence of capitalism and concentrating on land). Even after the last emperor of the Q'ing dynasty was deposed from the throne by the Revolution of 1911, Sun continued to struggle against the old influence of Beijing like Yuan Shi-kai and others. In the process, he was disappointed with the lack of support from Japan and European countries. On the other hand, he attached great importance to the relationship with the Soviet Union, which expressed its willingness to support the People's Liberation Movement. Therefore, in 1924, China accepted assistance from the Comintern and absorbed the party members of the Chinese Communist Party into the National Party. The Three People's Principles were changed to alliance with the Soviet Union, gaining the approval of the Communist Party and helping workers and peasants. And then he started the People's Revolution to overthrow imperialism and the Beijing warlord government. His last words before his death in 1925 were 'The Revolution is not yet successful.'

Further reading

Schiffrin, Harold Z. (1968) *Sun Yat-Sen and the Origin of the Chinese Revolution*, Berkeley: University of California Press.

SEE ALSO: anti-colonial movements and ideas

TAKASHI MITANI

T

TAGORE, RABINDRANATH (1861–1941)

Where the mind is without fear and the head is
   held high;
Where knowledge is free;
Where the world has not been broken up into
   fragments by narrow domestic walls; . . .
Where the clear stream of reason has not lost its way
   into the dreary desert sand of dead habit; . . .
Into that heaven of freedom, my Father, let my
   country awake.

The above poem from Tagore's *Gitanjali* collection (1913) in several ways epitomizes his thought. The paramount importance for people to 'live and reason in freedom' (Sen 1997: 57); the importance of openness, as opposed to a world 'broken up into fragments by narrow domestic walls' – be the walls national, colonial, religious, cultural; the importance of rationality and the need for reason to be left to do its work free from the paralysing effects of 'dead habit'; and the evocation of a heavenly Father, indicative of his (far from easily classifiable, yet strong) religiosity. Finally, all these ideas are evoked in the form of a poem: reminding us that Tagore served many genres. He published some 200 books, including poetry, songs, plays, short stories, novels, and essays, and his letters were to some of the greatest figures of his time as well as to less eponymous recipients. He was also a quite idiosyncratic and talented painter.

He came from a very wealthy and influential Bengali family. His grandfather, Dwarkanath (1794–1846), was a successful businessman as well as a generous philanthropist. Rabindranath seems to have rejected his legacy, probably due to his business-mindedness and worldliness (Dutta and Robinson 1997: 8–9). In this, Rabindranath was closer to his father, Debendranath (1817–1905), who had no interest in the family firm and occupied himself instead with a spiritual and religious search for true Hinduism. He rejected many contemporary Hindu practices (like what he saw as idolatry and the practice of suttee) and joined a reformist religious group, the Brahmo Samaj. In his footsteps, his youngest son, Rabindranath, was deeply religious, yet his beliefs were quite unorthodox and nondenominational.

In 1901, Rabindranath founded a school, Santiniketan (Abode of Peace). He used innovative educational methods that seem to have been particularly appreciated by those who were exposed to them. His influence from there on generations of Indian elites can hardly be overestimated. He is probably the only person ever to have created the national anthems of two different nations: India after independence chose his 'Jana Gana Mana Adhinayaka'; and Muslim Bangladesh has also chosen one of his songs ('*Amar Sonar Bangla*') to be its national anthem. This is only fair, given how conspicuously nonsectarian and syncretic Tagore showed himself throughout his life, acknowledging and celebrating all the diverse traditions that made up India's rich inheritance, including, besides Hindu tradition, the Muslim and the English.

For some time in the early twentieth century Tagore received astonishing acclaim in Europe and the USA. Characteristically, his selection of poetry *Gitanjali*, published in English translation in March 1913, ended up being reprinted ten times by November that same year, when the award of the Nobel Prize in Literature to Tagore for that book was announced. W.B. Yeats, Ezra Pound, Romain Rolland and many other major figures were among his staunchest admirers in the West. He was also translated into Russian by no less than Anna Akhmatova.

He was the first person to call his great contemporary, MOHANDAS GANDHI, 'Mahatma' (Great Soul), generously acknowledging Gandhi's contributions to India, despite their many and major differences on subjects such as nationalism/patriotism (with Tagore being critical and suspicious of nationalism), the advisability or otherwise of cultural cross-fertilization and interchanges (with Tagore celebrating and recommending it as long as it did not do away with the indigenous stem on which the foreign influences would be engrafted), the role of rationality (Tagore defending reasoning valiantly against the pitfalls of traditionalism), the importance of science (Tagore being in favour, Gandhi at best sceptical), the significance and presuppositions of economic and social development (with Tagore showing himself a staunch realist about the necessity for India to become powerful through economic and social development in order for her to be able to emancipate herself and interact with the English and the rest of the world on equal terms) (Sen 1997).

His position on British colonialism and the Raj is subtle and often misunderstood. He was very critical of the British administration of India, but, at the same time, he was always at pains 'to dissociate his criticism of the Raj from any denigration of British – or Western – people or culture. . . . unlike Gandhi, Tagore could not, even in jest, be dismissive of Western civilization' (Sen 1997: 60). Tagore believed that there were some extremely valuable things about British culture and influences, and that it was fortunate for his countrymen that they were able to access them in English. At the same time he was against aping the West and rejecting India's own heritage. He had confidence in Indian culture and believed that it could only be enriched by contact with the West as well as other cultures. It is not surprising therefore that Tagore was all his life deeply suspicious of nationalism (Berlin 1997; Sen 1997). In his novel *The Home and the World* he offers a subtle allegory about the impasses of narrow, exclusive patriotism (See Nussbaum 1996: 3–4).

References

Berlin, I. (1997) 'Rabindranath Tagore and the Consciousness of Nationality', in I. Berlin, *The Sense of Reality: Studies in Ideas and their History*, ed. Henry Hardy, 249–66, London: Pimlico.
Dutta, K. and Robinson, A. (eds) (1997) *Rabindranath Tagore: An Anthology*, London and Basingstoke: Picador.
Nussbaum, M.C. (1996) 'Patriotism and Cosmopolitanism', in M. C. Nussbaum *et al.*, *For Love of Country: Debating the Limits of Patriotism*, ed. Joshua Cohen, Boston: Beacon Press.
Sen, A. (1997) 'Tagore and His India', *The New York Review of Books*, 26 June: 55–63.

Further reading

Dutta, K. and Robinson, A. (1995) *Rabindranath Tagore: The Myriad-Minded Man*, London, New York: St Martin's Press.
——(eds) (1997) *Selected Letters of Rabindranath Tagore*, Cambridge: Cambridge University Press.
Tagore, R. (1961) *Towards Universal Man*, London: Asia Publishing House.

SEE ALSO: anti-colonial movements and ideas; the nation, nationalism and the national principle

GEORGIOS VAROUXAKIS

TAINE, HIPPOLYTE (1828–93)

Hippolyte Taine was a French philosopher of materialist and determinist tendencies who turned his attention successively to literary criticism, art history and finally to political history. He was the author notably of *Les Philosophes français du XIX siècle* (The French Philosophers of the Nineteenth Century, 1857), of a *History of English Literature* (*Histoire de la littérature anglaise*, 1863–4), and of *On Intelligence* (*De l'intelligence*, 1870), but he won his lasting renown as the author of a six-volume and incomplete history of the French Revolution, *Origins of Contemporary France* (*Origines de la France contemporaine*, 1875–94) which took issue with the revolutionary mythology that underpinned the emergent Third Republic.

Taine was born in 1828, the son of a country lawyer in the Ardennes, and received an elite Parisian education at the Collège Bourbon and the Ecole Normale Supérieure. His heterodox religious opinions hampered the development of his academic career, and after a spell as a provincial secondary school teacher he settled in Paris and made his living chiefly from his pen. He was Professor of Aesthetics and the History of Art at the Ecole des Beaux Arts in Paris from 1864 to 1883, with one brief interruption. In 1863 he was denounced as an enemy of religion by the Bishop of Orléans, Mgr Dupanloup, who subsequently on four occasions helped block his election to the Académie Française. He was finally elected in 1878, shortly after Dupanloup's death and when the early volumes of the *Origins of Contemporary France* had helped win over conservative opinion to his cause.

As a philosopher Taine is difficult to classify, except negatively: he never ceased to proclaim his opposition to the spiritualist school descended from Victor Cousin. He is sometimes identified as a Positivist, but he was unhappy with the Positivists' limitation of science to the search for laws governing the observable relations of phenomena: he never abandoned the quest for ultimate causes. He was something of an empiricist, devoted to the collection of 'facts', and for this reason was attracted by English thought; yet he was also a rationalist, who sought to derive phenomena from some ultimate cause. He remained a determinist, but one who was convinced – as he told LOMBROSO in 1887 – that determinism did not deny but underpinned the idea of moral responsibility.

Taine had a solid grounding in English culture from his boyhood, and both at the Collège Bourbon and at the École Normale he read widely in English literature of the seventeenth and eighteenth centuries. England was one of the case studies he used for his interest in the relationship between national character and literature, and he articulated this interest in a series of articles he published on CARLYLE, Tennyson and MILL in 1860–1, which subsequently formed the basis of his *History of English Literature*. He also published an influential volume of *Notes on England* (*Notes sur l'Angleterre*) (1872). This continues to be widely cited by historians of Victorian England, especially those interested in the history of the family, of education and of religion. What is less often realized is just how slender a first-hand knowledge his observations rested on: when they were published Taine had visited England only three times, for a total of about 11 weeks, and his impressions were clearly influenced by the predominantly Liberal Anglican circles in which he moved in England. While he had a strong sense of the philistinism that pervaded Victorian culture, he focused on those aspects of British society that gave it a stability that post-revolutionary France lacked: a habit of voluntary association that acted as a counterweight to state power; a system of political representation that worked with the grain of social hierarchy; an educational system that emphasized moral as well as intellectual instruction; and a national Church that eschewed dogma, exercised moral leadership and was in tune with the intellectual currents of the day.

It was France's defeat at the hands of Prussia, combined with the experience of the Paris Commune, that prompted Taine to publish his observations on Britain. They were also the chief cause of the redirection of his interests after 1871 towards the political history of contemporary France, and in particular to the origins and course of the French Revolution. He told a friend in 1878 that his book would be a 'medical consultation': it would diagnose the sicknesses in the French body politic that had let to defeat and civil war. But the idea that Taine's turning to political history was a radical break with his previous career is a half-truth. In fact it would be appropriate to read the *Origins of Contemporary France* alongside his *History of English Literature* and his *Notes on England*: all three works aimed to identify a 'national spirit' that gave their peculiar character to the literary and political lives of France and Britain. Whereas the English national spirit, shaped by Protestantism and a tradition of civic activity, was practical, empirical and reformist, the French suffered from a 'classical spirit', born of the *ancien régime*, which was abstract, rationalistic and in the end revolutionary. Following BURKE, he depicted the French revolutionaries as addicted to the application of a 'geometrical' mode of reasoning to politics.

The appeal to the influence of 'race', or national character, gave Taine's history an unmistakeably deterministic character: indeed, he explicitly declared that from the moment of the calling of the Estates-General the course of the revolution was set. The volumes had an inexorable character that did not, however, get in the way of a resounding public success. Curiously, this success was achieved in spite of the lack of an obvious partisan readership. The book was certainly not written to appeal to republicans, for it launched a frontal assault on the principles of 1789, which Jules Ferry declared to be 'the gospel of the republic'. On the other hand it offered only limited comfort to Catholic and royalist opponents of the Third Republic, for far from lamenting the demise of the *ancien régime* he saw it as bearing chief responsibility for the birth of the classical spirit and hence for the outbreak and course of the revolution.

Further reading

Biddiss, M. (1998) 'Hippolyte Taine and the Making of History', in N. Atkin and F. Tallett (eds) *The Right in France, 1789–1997*, 71–87, London: Tauris.

Jones, H.S. (1999) 'Taine and the Nation-State', in S. Berger, M. Donovan and K. Passmore (eds) *Writing National Histories: Western Europe since 1800*, 85–96, London: Routledge.

Ozouf, M. (1989) 'Taine', in F. Furet and M. Ozouf (eds) *Critical Dictionary of the French Revolution*, 1,011–20, Cambridge, MA, London: Harvard University Press.

Pitt, A. (1998) 'The Irrationalist Liberalism of Hippolyte Taine', *Historical Journal* 41, 4: 1,035–53.

SEE ALSO: historiography and the idea of progress; intellectuals, elites and meritocracy; theories of the state and society: the science of politics

H.S. JONES

THEORIES OF EDUCATION AND CHARACTER FORMATION

Resonances from both the French Enlightenment and Revolution, and the burgeoning consequences of industrialization and urbanization, ensured that nineteenth-century Western European society experienced changes to almost every facet of its fabric. The 'set of assumptions about society, man, character and education' contained in the ideas of French Enlightenment philosophers were radical, not least those about education. They encompassed Helvétius's fundamental belief that '*l'éducation peut tout*', those in Jean-Jacques Rousseau's *Émile* (1762) and Condorcet's view that maintenance of a democratic society necessitated a free, compulsory, secular and universal education system (see Silver 1977: 59–66; Vaughan and Archer 1971: 160–71). Not only were Helvétius's views seminal for the development of the concept of egalitarianism but, together with those of Rousseau and Condorcet, they indicated that education was not only synonymous with social reform but also a vital precursor. Rousseau uniquely perceived education as the 'new form of a world that had embarked upon a historical process of dislocation'. For him education became 'the art of managing opposites with an eye to the development of a truly autonomous or self-reliant freedom' necessitated by the changing world (see Soëtard 1994a). It was not surprising, then, that

the nineteenth century, especially the first half, witnessed a flowering of education theories. Inevitably, the aim and content of education came under considerable scrutiny: the former because the development of character is pertinent to the development of man while the latter embodies those aspects of a society's knowledge, culture and values deemed significant.

Rousseau stated in *Émile* 'all that we lack at birth, all that we need when we come to man's estate, is the gift of education', which is derived from nature, from men, or from things. He added that since 'we know nothing of childhood', that educators had failed to ascertain 'what a child is capable of learning', the aim of successful education had to be the 'goal of nature' (Rousseau 1911: 1, 6). These concepts and their ramifications were influential in the development of the education theory of the Swiss Johann Pestalozzi (1746–1827). Its basis rested on his attempt to reconcile the Rousseauian paradox of education of the (free) individual with that of the (useful) citizen, and he believed the answer lay in the school. As an intermediary, yet separate, structure between the demands of the home and society the education process would not only ensure the transmission of the knowledge deemed worthwhile by society but also enable children to acquire their freedom as autonomous individuals through the natural development of their innate abilities (see Soëtard 1994b). He was aware that to achieve this latter aim, a child had to become aware of the essential nature of things in order to be able to gain a clearer understanding of the world. How a child perceives and understands external reality was crucial to his educational theory, and sense perception was for Pestalozzi the underlying basis of knowledge. Training for the senses consequently dominated much of his method but he also insisted on the need for spontaneous activity in children: they were not to receive passively and reproduce the opinions of others, but to be 'a free and living agent' (Fitch 1900: 362). The practical success of this approach in his schools, especially at Yverdon, and his publications, attracted considerable interest, not least in Germany.

Friedrich Froebel (1782–1852) is best known for his concept of the kindergarten although most of his life was concerned with the education of a wider age range of children. In his search for greater organic cohesion to Pestalozzi's subjects of instruction, being concerned by the vagueness of the concept *Anschauung* Pestalozzi had used, and inspired by *Naturphilosophie*, Froebel conceived a concept of education based on unity in the natural world. Mankind should be taught to see nature as a fully interlocking system, with itself an integral component, and good schools would be those offering a natural education, teaching pupils 'the relationships which exist within the material world and which link that world and himself to the ground of all being' (Froebel 1826: 338). In the curriculum, which he wanted split into the Pestalozzian components of language, nature and mathematics, nature was to be 'studied in its manifold variety, as directly as possible through activity methods and play' (Froebel 1826: 338). Thus, children's play and their active involvement with the environment would constitute the content of the curriculum as well as the means of implementing it. Like Pestalozzi, he maintained that proper education would enable 'the child's powers and aptitudes and his physical and mental activities [to] be developed in the order of succession in which they emerge in his life' (Froebel 1826: 337). Unlike him, Froebel was concerned solely with the education of the autonomous human being and not with the training and development of a 'viable' citizen (see Heiland 1993).

Utilizing some Pestalozzian ideas, the education theory of Johann Herbart (1776–1841) was, nonetheless, based firmly on his own distinct philosophy and psychology of the mind. The crux of his theory was the concept of educational teaching in which teaching was to be subordinated to education, i.e. only appropriate teaching would be a successful means of promoting education, the ultimate goal of which was character formation. Educational teaching recognized the child's natural liveliness and focused on the 'practice and skills of the pupil': at all times, therefore, teaching was not to 'encroach upon the individuality of the pupil' (see Holinger 1993). Equally important was Herbart's insistence that teaching must be structured to encourage the development of pupils' interests into a 'multi-centred interest': 'Learning must serve the purpose of creating interest. Learning is transient but interest must be lifelong' (J.H. Herbart, *Paedogogische Schriften,* cited in Holinger 1993). Such an interest would enable pupils to be able to continuously expand their circle of thought, acquire a deeper understanding of the world and participate in the development of society. He was careful to point out, however, that

this development process was not solely for the acquisition of knowledge, the shaping of attitudes and skills but primarily to develop the pupils' moral insight and character. By the time Herbart had achieved a definitive, practical form of his theory for employment in the Prussian education system, there was no longer an interest in implementing it. It was only through the proselytizing work of Ziller (1812–82), Stoy (1815–85) and Rein (1847–1929) that his theory exerted any influence on education practice in Europe and the USA.

Committed to the rights of individuals, WILHELM VON HUMBOLDT (1767–1835) believed that not only should they be allowed to develop in accordance with their innate personalities but also, in the case of children, parental rights should be regulated, if necessary, to ensure that they did not 'exceed normal bounds'. He shared Plato's view that education should play the key role in the development of society and argued, as a consequence of his belief in French revolutionary ideals as well as being aware of the need for the liberalization of Prussian society, that education should be made universally available. Furthermore, its role was 'to shape man himself' to ensure 'the complete training of the human personality', by which he meant 'the highest and best proportioned development of his [man's] abilities into a harmonious entity' (W. Humboldt, *Gesammelte Schriften,* I, p. 106, 145, cited in Hohendorf 1993: 617). This notwithstanding, he was aware of the social nature of man's existence and the necessity of the individual contributing to society's development: 'self-education can only be continued ... in the wider context of development of the world' (W. Humboldt, *Gesammelte Schriften,* VII, p. 33, cited in Hohendorf 1993: 622). Although he attempted to implement these views while he was charged with reforming Prussian education, his short tenure of office, a distaste for conflict and the volatile political climate of the time ruled out any truly effective implementation of his views: a tragedy for the subsequent development of German education.

While Rousseauian and French revolutionary ideals became integral components of German education theories, ironically this was not the case in France in the first half of the century, the exception being the theory of CHARLES FOURIER (1772–1837). Convinced of the existence of an underlying design in the world, Fourier's education theory was designed to provide individuals with an understanding of it in conjunction with the natural development of their innate instincts, thereby creating autonomous beings. Disparaging current public education methods as disastrous, Fourier postulated that a child's educational activities were to be such that there would be 'an integral play of the faculties and attractions of the soul, combined with the integral exercise of the faculties of the body by means of proportional gymnastics' (Bowen 1981: 384). A diametrically opposed approach lay behind Napoleon Bonaparte's concept of education for the majority of French children, whereby the state, and not the individual, was to be the beneficiary as well as the determinant of educational aims, content and provision. The implication of this approach for character formation was clear: 'God and the Emperor, these are the two names that one must engrave in the heart of children. It is to this double thought that all the system of national education must address itself' (Fontanes, quoted A. Rendu, *Essai sur l'instruction publique*, 1819, 3, p. 4, cited in Vaughan and Archer 1971: 184). His institution and staffing of the Imperial University, however, ensured that secondary education in the *lycées* remained general and non-vocational, and in which the preservation of the teaching of classics ensured, *inter alia,* character formation by cultivating the pupils' 'imagination, sensibility, a moral sense as well as ... reason and judgement' (Anderson 1975: 27).

Rejecting the emphasis upon virtue and morality characteristic of Rousseau and Fichte's social reform theories, the British socialist ROBERT OWEN (1771–1858) and the utilitarians, including JEREMY BENTHAM (1748–1832), espoused instead the concept of the greatest good for the greatest number as their criterion for social progress. Accepting Helvétius's view that all individuals are blank at birth, so that 'education is everything' in their subsequent development, Owen believed children could 'be formed collectively to have any human character. And ... ultimately moulded into the very image of rational wishes and desires' by careful teaching (Owen 1813: 22). The corollary, that almost all the evils of life were the result of educational errors, meant that for a state to be well governed it 'ought to direct its chief attention to the formation of character' (Owen 1814: 73). While this view had as its ultimate goal the benefit of society, Owen's ideas gained wider recognition,

partly from their successful implementation in the Institute for the Formation of Character at New Lanark in Scotland, but also for their insight into the significance of early childhood in human development. His approach ensured that the children were active participants in a learning process that focused on understanding, training children to think and act rationally as well as developing an awareness of the needs of others. His emphasis upon character formation and the nexus between education and the environment succeeded, as Silver observes, in making education a mass issue as well as showing 'that it was possible to educate humanely' (1977: 234).

Bentham's education theory, published in *Chrestomathia* (1815–17), contained an innovative approach to the curriculum whereby only socially useful knowledge, or that which would enable children to be prepared for their future careers, was deemed acceptable. This vocational approach, with science and technology as its key components, meant that other knowledge was deemed unacceptable for the education of middle-class children for whom *Chrestomathia* was intended. The pedagogy advocated was based on a systematic approach, proceeding from the particular to the general, from simple ideas and examples to more complex and abstract ones. To ensure that the children's learning was based on understanding, Bentham stipulated that their knowledge should be tested consistently and, as an incentive to learning, he emphasized the need for individual competition. The stress on efficiency and productivity was tempered by other proposals. Thus reward and punishment were to be minimized, corporal punishment was abolished, peer help was advocated, lessons were to be short and varied in content and methodology, while, most significantly, the pupils were to be self-governing. Bentham's theory emphasized education's role in increasing productivity, thereby benefiting the general economic good and morality through its contribution to the achievement of the greatest happiness of the greatest number. *Chrestomathia* was an undeniable challenge to the existing education order for it breathed, in Simon's view, 'a positive optimism, and advocates a coherent educational policy .... with its clear purpose, its efficiency, its close links with the widest spheres of social activity' (1974: 84).

A very different perspective shaped the educational views of Thomas Arnold (1795–1842), the reforming headmaster of Rugby School. A leading member of the Broad Church Party, Arnold subscribed to the belief that education's role in forming good character was justified only by its religious content. Its presence, furthermore, would ensure that the development of morality in individuals would be synonymous with the promotion of social order. He remained opposed to the division of secular and spiritual affairs, believing that Church and state should be a unity, initiating reform of social institutions as well as promoting the concepts of state and citizenship. Although he envisaged a complete extension of the franchise, Arnold was pessimistic about the roles to be played by both the middle and working classes given the limitations of their current schooling. This reflected his belief that education had two components, professional and liberal. The first, encompassing the basics relevant to future employment, currently formed the major component of most middle-class children's education due to their limited time at school. Consequently, a liberal education, fundamental for training in citizenship, was usually ignored, because 'people are accustomed to think that it is learnt more easily', and its absence made him sceptical about any future political control likely to be exercised by this class. Similarly, he felt that the schooling given to the working class did not constitute an education, being merely the preparatory steps to it, and to expect any significant moral or religious improvements from it was 'to look for a crop of corn after sowing a single handful of seed' (T. Arnold, *Sermons*, 2, pp. 264–6, cited in Bamford 1970: 59). It is not surprising, then, that Arnold stressed character formation, grounded in a liberal education, as the key role of a school. By liberal education, Arnold meant, but only in relation to able pupils, a thorough study of the classics, occupying more than half of the curriculum, and in which religious studies were given as much weighting as the remaining components. His emphasis upon the development of reasoning skills by pupils, together with the acquisition of leadership skills gained from the structure and life of a school, was intended to ensure that education would provide them with a sound foundation in citizenship. Like their author, Arnold's education views represent something of a paradox. In many respects, his views were not innovative, especially with respect to the curriculum, and ignored the developments in society that would affect the lives and careers of the majority

of pupils. Nonetheless, Arnold's legacy was the indelible linking of character formation with the educational role of the English public school.

Apart from those of Froebel and Arnold, the education theories cited above had little widespread impact on mass-education provision during most of the nineteenth century, for the state education systems of Britain, France, Germany and elsewhere developed a limited and conservative approach to educational content and teaching methodologies. It was in reaction to the stultifying effects of these systems, and mounting economic and social problems, that new education theories were formulated during the last two decades of the century. In general the theories may be considered as being representative of one of two distinct approaches to education. One was the 'New Education' whose advocates, predominantly British theorist-practitioners, included Edmond Holmes (1850–1936), J.H. Badley (1865–1967), Norman MacMunn (1877–1925) and A.S. Neill (1883–1973), and whose ideas and practices laid the foundation for what became known as 'progressive' education. The other approach, derived from the idealist philosophy of Hegel, had its most eminent exponent in the USA with the philosopher JOHN DEWEY (1859–1952).

The importance of the New Education movement rested not only on its advocacy of significant changes to the curriculum but also its pioneering of important changes in teaching methods, especially for young children. Returning to a Rousseauian approach, memorization and rote learning were rejected in favour of an emphasis upon participation and activity, reflecting a belief that the child was 'a self-educating organism, not a passive recipient of information' (see Skidelsky 1969; Selleck 1968). Probably the most influential advocate of this view was Edmond Holmes, an inspector of elementary schools for 30 years who ultimately became the chief inspector for elementary schools in England and Wales. He observed that what was required of the pupils by the state system was 'blind, passive, literal, unintelligent obedience', for the real aim of the system was to teach them how to behave. This went against the Pestalozzian concept of child development, espoused by the movement, and Holmes argued that if 'self-realization is the first and last duty of Man', then a child-centred approach to learning, in which the child's interests were to predominate, was a prerequisite. Such an approach would place heavy demands upon teachers, for it required 'a blend of imagination, intelligence, and patience, which we call genius'. While acknowledging that many teachers lacked this quality Holmes believed they could be trained to develop it but would not provide any prescriptions, beyond advocating the need for child studies in the training, fearing that if he did they would become dogma. Instead, he contented himself by saying that if a spirit of freedom could be developed among teachers, the self-realization of pupils would occur. The considerable criticism these ideas generated when published in *What is and what Might be* (1911), despite the fact that many had appeared in his published annual inspector's reports of the previous two decades, was indicative both of the lack of success of the century's earlier education theories and of the conservatism of national education systems.

An opponent of the extreme aspects of Holmes's view was John Dewey. In his earliest education tract, *My Pedagogic Creed* (1896), Dewey emphasized the inter-relationship between individuals and society, observing that for the latter to develop, individuals had to possess the potential to progress beyond the levels reached by their predecessors. Education thus had to 'begin with a psychological insight into the child's capacities, interests and habits. It must be controlled at every point by reference to these same considerations' (1897: 86). He added that every pupil had to develop 'complete possession of all his powers' for it was only by this approach that children would be prepared for their life in society. Dewey equated the formation of character and self-realization as being the 'only genuine basis of right living', where right living was synonymous with democratic practices. Reiterating one of Hegel's key maxims, that for individuals to achieve self-realization they had to employ their individual talents for the well-being of society, Dewey envisaged the role of education as being to help children achieve self-realization through the development of character, habits and virtue. While he recognized the importance of a child's interests in achieving this aim, he was unwilling to allow these to determine solely what should be taught. In this sense, Dewey was teacher-centred in his approach although he did share a belief with Holmes that children gained understanding through experience, and that a pragmatic approach should be a component of education rather than a purely passive, theoretical

one. Dewey was sceptical about education systems that made the formation of character their main aim for he felt that the major work of their schools had nothing to do with it. Moral education had to be an integral component of education and he was convinced that a balanced curriculum, reflecting the 'standard factors of social life', would provide the necessary moral insight for pupils. Similarly, the school was not to be viewed as an institution in itself but rather as a reflection of society. Consequently, society was seen as playing an educative role by providing resources for certain studies and, in this respect, Dewey's views represented something of a precursor to the concept of polytechnical education developed by Nadezhda Krupskaya (1869–1939) in the Soviet Union in the 1920s.

While Dewey was an education theorist influenced by Hegelian Idealism, by the end of the nineteenth century other concepts of Idealist theory had developed, influenced more by Ancient Greek philosophy, especially that of Plato, than Hegel. With its concerns for 'society as an organic spiritual community' and the 'ethical nature of citizenship', whereby the individual 'found happiness and fulfilment ... in the development of "mind" and "character" and in service to a larger whole', one willing advocate was Robert Morant (1863–1920) (Harris 1992: 126–8). Educated in the Arnoldian tradition but not an education theorist in the usual sense, being *par excellence* an administrator in the English education system, Morant had, nonetheless, certain, strong views about education that were conveyed in his numerous, and sometimes lengthy, memoranda and circulars. More importantly, his views cannot be overlooked, for by becoming embodied in national education policy for the best part of a decade at the turn of the century, they effectively shaped the education experienced in state schools by many more children than most education theorists ever achieved. Nowhere was this seen more clearly than in his prefatory memorandum to the 1904 Education Code. Morant's memorandum outlined the aims for all elementary schools and, headed by the Wykehamist motto 'Manners makyth Man', the emphasis was upon character formation. Thus the main aim of elementary education was:

to form and strengthen the character and to develop the intelligence of the children entrusted to it, and to make the best use of the school years available, in assisting both girls and boys, according to their different needs, to fit themselves, practically as well as intellectually, for the work of life.

(Board of Education 1904: vii)

Morant's aims reflected some aspects of both Idealist and progressive theories for the curriculum took into account the nature and capabilities of children, instead of making education conform to the views of the educator, and also provided an 'ordered freedom' for both pupils and teachers. Henceforward, an elementary school was to be seen as 'living organism', in relation to pupils and society's needs.

In some respects, education theory at the onset on the twentieth century remained preoccupied with the same essential concerns as in previous centuries, not least being the formation of character. But there were significant differences, the main ones being that education theory was now much more concerned with the education of all children, rich or poor, male or female, and in which their ideas and interests were to be identified and acted upon. Unfortunately, as the new century progressed it was to reveal in many instances, as the past had done, the continuance of the gap between theory and practice.

References

Anderson, R.D. (1975) *Education in France 1848–1870*, Oxford: Clarendon Press.

Board of Education (1904) *Code of Regulations for Public Elementary Schools, Parliamentary Papers*, LXXV [Cd.2074].

Bowen, J. (1981) *A History of Western Education*, London: Methuen.

Dewey, J. (1897) *My Pedagogic Creed*, New York: E.L. Kellog & Co.

Fitch, J.G. (1900) *Educational Aims and Methods*, Cambridge: Cambridge University Press.

Froebel, F. (1981 [1826]) *The Education of Man*, cited in J. Bowen, *A History of Western Education*, Vol. 3, 338, London: Methuen.

Harris, J. (1992) 'Political Thought and the Welfare State 1870–1940: An Intellectual Framework for British Social Policy', *Past and Present* 135 (May): 126–8.

Heiland, H. (1993) 'Friedrich Fröbel (1782–1852)', *Prospects* 23, 3–4: 473–91.

Hohendorf (1993) 'Wilhelm von Humboldt (1767–1835)', *Prospects* 23, 3–4.

Holinger, N. (1993) 'Johann Friedrich Herbart (1776–1841)', *Prospects* 23, 3–4: 649–64.

Owen, R. (1813) 'Second Essay', *A New View of Society*, London: Cadell & Davies.

——(1814) 'Fourth Essay', *A New View of Society*, London: Cadell & Davies.

Rousseau, J.J. (1911) *Émile*, London: Dent.

Selleck, R.J.W. (1968) *The New Education: The English Background 1870–1914*, Melbourne: Sir Isaac Pitman & Sons.

Silver, H. (1977) *The Concept of Popular Education*, London: Methuen.

Simon, B. (1974) *The Two Nations and the Educational Struggle 1780–1870*, London: Lawrence & Wishart.

Skidelsky, R. (1969) *English Progressive Schools*, Harmondswoth: Penguin.

Soëtard, M. (1994a) 'Jean-Jacques Rousseau (1712–78)', *Prospects* 24, 3–4: 423–38.

——(1994b) 'Johann Heinrich Pestalozzi (1746–1827)', *Prospects* 24, 3–4: 297–310.

Vaughan, M. and Archer, M. (1971) *Social Conflict and Educational Change in England and France 1789–1848*, Cambridge: Cambridge University Press.

N.D. DAGLISH

THEORIES OF LAW, CRIMINOLOGY AND PENAL REFORM

At the beginning of the nineteenth century, legal theory, criminology (in so far as this discipline then had an existence) and penal reform all wore the effects of post-Enlightenment classical thinking. While this had brought about dramatic changes from pre-modern thinking in these areas, the concepts and ideas were still very different from our understandings of such matters today. Nonetheless, subsequent changes in thought provided, at the end of it, the foundation stones for many of the twentieth-century developments in these areas. By the end of the nineteenth century, how it was possible to think about law, criminology and penal reform had become identifiably modern.

At the start of this period, legal theorists had inherited the natural law tradition of their immediate predecessors such as Locke, Rousseau and KANT. Through the work of these scholars and philosophers, legal theory had been able to disengage itself from any links with God and the idea of Divine Law, previously embodied in the absolute monarchs who ruled the pre-modern world. Now, however, reason and rationality were seen as the driving force of law. From being some mysterious, incalculable and unpredictable force, decipherable only by those who ruled, law had become, as it were, man made. It now prescribed certain fundamental rights for all the citizens of a given society (although there were very wide differences between writers such as Locke and Rousseau as to the *extent* of these rights), who could then call upon the law in protection of them. In such a world law should provide security and order, by reference to some inviolable ideas of justice. Essentially then, legal theory, in the manner of Kant, had become consumed with the idea of what law *ought* to be. As such, there was no distinction between law and morality, since 'moral truth was an absolute which could be directly understood *a priori* by reason, and which could be expressed in the form of a categorical imperative or understandable natural law' (Lloyd 1971: 187). Natural law was pursued to its apotheosis in the nineteenth century by Hegel (see HEGEL AND HEGELIANISM). In his work, it was as if the modern state had simply replaced the absolute monarchs of the old regime as the font and embodiment of law and authority. He saw this teleologically as a binding historical law, wherein the consciousness and will of its people would only attain full realization in this form.

However, during the first half of the nineteenth century, growing importance was given to the need for law not to be seen as obeying abstract principles but instead to meet the demands of increasingly complex industrial societies. There were growing demands on the need for law to represent the interests of the new middle-class power-brokers of modern society. At the same time the consequences of the French Revolution had made clear the dangers of natural law *in extremis* and led to a retreat from such theories. As a result, we see the emergence of a school of thought which demanded that the law should lay down clear and reliable rules of behaviour upon which individuals, as freethinking rational citizens, could act accordingly. Again, in these respects, we see crucial importance of the work of JEREMY BENTHAM as a nineteenth-century legal theorist. Instead of law corresponding to universal natural principles, for him it should follow the rules of utilitarianism. Here, human action was seen in terms of pleasures and pains, and human needs reduced to a calculus of felicity, against which ideas that would produce the greatest happiness for the greatest number would be weighed and tested. As such, law would be objectively judged against human values, pleasures and pains (it did not have some pre-given 'natural' qualities). The aim of law was thus to make possible the maximum freedom of each individual to pursue what was good for them. Ideally suited to early nineteenth-century industrialization, there were no longer natural rights that all could ascribe to. Instead, while anti-egalitarian

elements must be removed by law to ensure the greatest happiness of the greatest number, the free play of forces (in accordance with *laissez-faire* economics) would best serve the general interest. Law, as it were, had a peripheral role to play, merely helping to set the ground rules for these forces to take effect.

Yet, notwithstanding his own commit to individualism, Bentham can also be seen as one of the first of the nineteenth-century collectivists: the pursuit of individual happiness was dependent, a priori, on an *enhanced* role for the state, which would continually have to readjust its legal framework to ensure conditions were possible to bring about Bentham's continually shifting maxim. Indeed, Bentham himself was a very active social and legal reformer, and there is a unity between his philosophical first principles and his reform plans: most notably, in the area of penal reform, his blueprint for a model prison, the Panopticon. This institution would adhere rigorously to his utilitarian principles in terms of the management of its inmates (its purpose would be to 'grind rogues honest', by providing them with productive labour and keeping them under constant surveillance). At the same time, it was to be built by the state but then leased out to a private contractor. Only a handful of such institutions were ever actually built. However, the ideas underpinning it had significant influence on subsequent prison development during the nineteenth century and beyond.

However, a much narrower role for the law was envisaged in the analytical positivism of John Austin and his successors in legal theory. Influenced by the empiricism of AUGUSTE COMTE, whereby understanding of the world was based on observation and experience, rather than a priori ideas and concepts, law was effectively denuded of the social purposes attributed to it by Bentham. In what amounted to a closed logical system, there was a strict separation between the law as it is and the law as it ought to be. The task of analytical positivists such as Austin were to try and identify 'the law as it is'. Law was divorced entirely from the realm of metaphysics and high ideals, and instead was defined by Austin as 'a rule laid down for the guidance of an intelligent being by an intelligent being having power over him' (1876: 86). Law, then, was 'the command of the sovereign'. Laws 'properly so called', as opposed to custom, morals and so on, are those set by political superiors to their subordinates, or laws set by private subjects in pursuance of legal rights granted to them, and contain enforceable obligations and sanctions for their breach. At the same time, this ensured that the law was seen as a set of rules existing separately and in its own right, containing within itself (rather than being shaped by reference to any exterior social forces and influences) the seeds of its own development. This very narrow, restricted role was reflected in developments in criminal law, tort and contract. Instead of the elementary forms of protection, care and responsibilities that utilitarianism prescribed, it now cleared the way for nineteenth-century entrepreneurs, providing minimal encumbrances to them, while at the same time assuming that all these were free to make rational choices about the course of business activity they set out on. If they made the wrong choice, there would be nothing the state could do to assist them. In each of these areas of law, there were attempts to develop it on a consistent and reliable basis, since, in another aspect of nineteenth-century legal theory, without these parameters, the very existence of what was thought to be law was absent: only custom prevailed. Indeed, in the colonizing thrusts of the nineteenth century, such customs could be ignored or repressed and, instead, 'law' could be imposed by the colonizing power.

As it was, the administration of criminal law was based around ideas of reason and rationality, with only a very small and reluctant space made available for any departures from this standard, as with the very narrowly prescribed insanity laws in Britain, set out by the M'Naghten Rules in 1843. Similarly, the courts were at pains to keep firmly in check any other defences in criminal law that might undermine implied rationality and responsibility for one's actions. As regards contract and tort, promises and intentions – expressions of the will – were held to create liability. The growing inclination of judges in the early nineteenth century to award damages for loss of expectation in business dealings was often a reward for diligence and foresight, and a penalty for their lack. At the same time, beyond contractually established relationships, the duties of care owed between individuals and between individuals and the state was kept to a minimum. In effect, rights and responsibilities were contractually rather than normatively based. As such, the *Gesellschaft* type of law in which these found expression during the first half of the nineteenth century ensured that a whole range of duties towards others, particularly those in relationships of dependency, and taken for granted today, were lacking at that time.

As regards penal reform and criminology, then, in England, Beccaria (1764) had a significant influence on the thinking of such early modern penal reformers as Blackstone, Eden, Romilly and Bentham himself. Notwithstanding the existence of a penal system known as 'the bloody code' in England around 1800 (and whose dramatic effects were actually enhanced by a frightened ruling class that held on to power in that country, unlike elsewhere at this time) it began to be challenged by appeals to reason and rationality. The first main target of penal reformers in the early nineteenth century was the death penalty. Its use was significantly curtailed. There were between 6,000 and 7,000 executions in England between 1770 and 1830; but between 1837 and 1868 (when public executions were abolished) there were just 347 (Gatrell 1994). By this point, the death penalty had been abolished for offences such as forgery, coining, sheep and horse stealing, and sacrilege, to name just a few. For all intents and purposes, it was available only for murder after the Offences against the Person Act 1861. At the same time, the administration of punishment began to shift away from reflecting community mores and ritualistic ceremonies towards a more anonymous, routinized, standard form, conducted through the offices of central Government bureaucracy.

In these respects, reform of the prisons was a central component in these new ways of thinking about punishment. From the chaotic, unregulated, disorderly places of detention that they had become in the pre-modern era, by the 1840s they were being turned into more recognizably modern institutions, systematic and purposeful. They were needed not only to replace pre-modern punishments directed primarily at the human body, but, in addition, the increasingly restricted opportunities for transportation. From being mere holding places preliminary to those other forms of punishment, they were now constructed around attempts to deter and reform (often reform through deterrence) those who were sent to them, with a combination of labour, penance and reflective solitude. Here, the USA led the way in prison development. There was the separate system (practised at Auburn), where one's entire prison sentence would be spent in the solitude of one's cell; and the silent system, originating at

Philadelphia, which allowed the prisoners to work together, but in strict silence. A modified version of the two was introduced to the English prisons system in 1843. During the course of the nineteenth century, prisons' conditions became uniform and unremittingly severe, ensuring adherence to the less-eligibility principle.

As regards criminology, it became something more than an extension of jurisprudence, providing, as it were, a prescription of appropriate responses to breaches of the criminal law. Instead, it became a science wherein those who broke the law were understood as having a fundamental character defect. Initially, it was thought this might stem from the criminal's refusal or inability to deny wayward impulses, or as a rational citizen their incorrect calculations about developing their self-interest. As such, criminology begins to develop an understanding of both crimes and criminals. First, we see the development of a criminal cartology: maps of crime (most notably in the work of Guerry and Quetelet in France and Belgium respectively), whereby, in conjunction with the recording of crime and the production of criminal statistics (which became more systematic in Britain from 1857), it became possible to chart the distribution and demography of crime, and to then match up crime rates with other social indices. Thus, in England, Henry Mayhew (1862) offered a series of empirically supported claims about the pattern and concentration of urban crime: which also seemed to point towards the presence of a distinct criminal class, an acute worry in the mid-nineteenth century. In these respects, criminology embarked on a search to explain the differences between these concentrations of criminals and the rest of the population, the danger and threat they posed, and their deficiencies in rationality and reasoning (which, it was thought, lay at the heart of their difference). Thus, having identified their locations and social characteristics, it now began to search for their individual features that were likely to propel them towards crime. Hence is the work of the phrenologists Gall and Spurzheim in the first half of the nineteenth century which argued that the shape and contours of the human skull were an external index of character. Here, it would be possible to identify criminals or potential criminals on the basis of their physical appearance. Increasingly, criminality was seen as pathological, in the sense that criminal acts were not the result of reasoned thought but, instead, were the product of physical causes that lay beyond the control of the particular individuals concerned.

This particular phase in the development of criminological thought reached a famous peak in the dramatic findings of CESARE LOMBROSO's (1876) L'uomo delinquente. Inspired by DARWIN's theory of evolution and Comte's empiricism, he produced the concept of 'the born criminal'. Based on his observations of Italian soldiers and prisoners, he claimed that criminality was an inherited trait, characterized by physical degeneracy and disease, with criminals possessing the anatomical characteristics of primitive throwbacks – low, receding foreheads, facial protuberance, strong jaws and cheek bones, small brains and so on (although he was prepared to modify his views in subsequent editions of his book, placing a less rigid insistence on determinism). While Lombroso's work on criminal anthropology was particularly influential in Continental Europe, in Britain (and its white colonies) and the USA, the eugenics movement made a more significant impact on criminological thought during the second half of the nineteenth century. Here, the issue of crime and criminality moved to broader social concerns about racial degeneracy, which were beginning to be brought to light in a series of social surveys, official reports and investigative journalism. There were fears that crime, as an inherited trait, would be passed down from one generation to the next and ultimately create an entire race of criminals. Through the development in the work of important members of the eugenics movement (FRANCIS GALTON, Karl Pearson and W.F.R. Weldon) of such statistical concepts as standard deviation and multiple correlation, it was claimed that human qualities, including intellectual ability, were distributed according to the law of ancestral heredity: just as in plant or animal life, there would be a distribution in the racial stock of both good and bad (paupers, the disabled, criminals, lunatics and so on) specimens. However, this distribution would be influenced by the rate of breeding. And, at that time, it seemed that the reproduction rate of the various bad specimens was dramatically exceeding that of the good. What was thus needed to prevent crime was state action – the modern state had to become more interventionist – directed at its biological causes, in the form of sterilization and castration.

We do see the emergence of a more interventionist state, but one that was now prepared to address some of the social causes of crime. Enrico

Ferri, a student of Lombroso, emphasized that crime, like other forms of human behaviour, was the product of three interconnected causes: anthropological, physical and social. Once the social causes of crime began to influence the development of criminological thought, then it became clear that (most) crime itself was not the product of some inherited disposition – and that criminals themselves were not constitutionally different from the general population but might be responsible and suitable objects of penal discipline and reform. Instead, there was growing recognition not just that individual criminals were reformable, but, by controlling the conditions of the environment, the state had a role to play both in relation to the causes of crime and more general social conditions indissolubly linked to degeneracy and unfitness. As the English prison chaplain and penal reformer William Morrison wrote:

> causes [of crime] . . . must be examined and dealt with by the statesman and anthropologist. It is the task of the former, aided by the philanthropist, to so ameliorate the social conditions of existence as to deprive crime of its roots; it is the duty of the second to thoroughly investigate the physical and mental causes of crime, and to *inquire how far they admit to remedy* [my italics].
> (1889: 22)

We are now moving into a new realm of thinking about crime and criminality: one that involves a shift away from reliance on the criminal law and harsh penal sanctions to deter rational citizens from crime; and a shift from the rigidly deterministic insistence that those who did break the law were ultimately 'different' from the rest of the population and irredeemably determined to their fate. Now, what we find taking place is a shift towards concepts of medicalized treatment and training to bring about the reform (or 'cure') of criminals. As such, there were increasing demands for the individualization of punishment – punishment that would now match the criminal rather than the crime; and suggestions that criminological experts rather than judges should determine what might be the most appropriate sanction to cure a particular case of 'crime illness'. These ideas became particularly prominent in Continental Europe towards the end of the nineteenth century, and led to an emphasis on indeterminate sentencing at the expense of fixed penalties associated with the early modern period.

One of the first areas in which these ideas took root was in relation to the punishment of juvenile offenders. During the course of the nineteenth century, there had been growing recognition that juvenile, or child, offenders constituted a different segment of the criminal class; the principles of rationality and responsibility could not be rigidly applied to them, just as they could to adults. Individual penal reformers and philanthropists such as Mary Carpenter in England had campaigned (successfully) for the introduction of separate institutions for juvenile offenders. This then became a matter of state responsibility with the introduction of industrial and reform schools for 'wayward juveniles' in 1854; although, for the most part, their regimes were still built largely around the idea of harsh penal discipline. However, the Elmira Reformatory, opened in 1876 in New York State, pointed the way towards new possibilities in the institutional treatment of offenders. It was designed as a 'moral sanitarium' (for 16- to 20-year-old male first offenders) rather than a penitentiary or prison. In contrast to the uniform, unremittingly severe conditions and segregative individualization associated with Victorian adult prisons, at Elmira there were individualized programmes for the prisoners, designed to bring out the propensities to crime that lay hidden in their backgrounds; and education and instruction designed to assist in their post-institutional readjustment.

In this way, it was anticipated that Elmira's end product would be different from that of the adult prisons. Whereas the latter hoped to release an ex-convict who had now made the choice to be a good citizen, Elmira had in mind the rehabilitated former criminal, now restored to normality. Nonetheless, in England, penal reform only cautiously followed the route more eagerly followed in Europe by the new criminologists of the late nineteenth century. In that country, at least, crime problems, it seemed, were being held in check; statistics showed a declining crime rate. There were still concerns about crime, but these were now concentrated around particular groups of offenders rather than the criminal class as a whole – in particular, habitual, recidivist criminals (for the most part, petty property offenders) now became the focus of criminological discourse and penal reform strategies. This group seemed to be beyond the existing legal and penal framework. They were not insane, according to the very narrow precepts allowed this concept in criminal law; and they were clearly not deterred by the existing penal sanctions, as their propensity to commit more crime on release from their latest prison sentence was thought to clearly demonstrate. It was only in this small space that indeterminate prison sentences began to be introduced in England and similar societies towards the end of the nineteenth century.

Other than this, penal reform in these countries began to move away from the insistence on deterrence in a way that constructed alternative sentences for those either not fully responsible for their actions or not so steeped in criminality that they did not warrant the dramatic step of a prison sentence. During the second half of the nineteenth century we thus see the emergence of separate procedures for juveniles, the introduction of probation for first offenders, recognition that some forms of criminality (such as habitual drunkenness) were more appropriately dealt with through medical rather than penal responses, and the avoidance of prison for potential fine defaulters by giving them time to pay. Meanwhile, prison conditions were steadily alleviated, with some improvement in conditions. As the *Report of the Gladstone Committee* stipulated, the purpose of prisons was to make criminals 'better men and women, both physically and morally, than when they came in' (1895: 12–13). At the formal level at least, the new purposes of prison, alongside the other penal reforms of the period, and the commitment to rehabilitation rather than repression, became the emblems of a modern, rational penal system – and were to provide the framework for most subsequent penal developments for the best part of the twentieth century.

These changes in criminological thought – about the role of the modern state, about free will and responsibility, about remedying social problems and individual deficiencies – were also being reflected in legal theory. As it was, nineteenth-century *Gesellschaft* law might protect individual rights but it seemed that it was not fulfilling its duties and obligations towards protecting society as legal theorists Geny and Ihering were now beginning to argue it should: the scope of the criminal law should be extended and serve the interests of social defence rather than just adjudicate on matters of guilt and innocence. If penal sanctions could thus incorporate the indeterminate prison sentence to this effect, the criminal law itself was prepared to lessen its insistence on responsibility, with an extension of the defences to it (under certain circumstances), including diminished responsibility, provocation and necessity. In the areas of contract and tort, responsibilities were extended between citizens.

At the same time, the state was beginning to take a greater role in reducing the variety of everyday risks its citizens faced: risks against poverty in old age, against the consequences of unemployment, of poor working conditions. All such risks, around the end of the nineteenth century, could now be reduced through programmes and legislation that provided for compulsory social insurance. Legal theory characterized this emerging pattern of law and social and penal reform as 'collectivism'. This saw 'the school of opinion … which favours the intervention of the state, even at some sacrifice of individual freedom, for the purpose of conferring benefits upon the mass of the people' (Dicey 1906: 119). We do not necessarily have to share these Whig assumptions to recognize the importance of the changes in the areas of law, criminology and penal reform that had taken place over the course of the nineteenth century, exemplifying the shift from pre-modern to modern social arrangements.

References

Austin, J. (1876) *Lectures on Jurisprudence*, London: Murray.

Beccaria, C. (1764) *On Crimes and Punishments*, Indianapolis: Hackett.

Dicey, A. (1906) *Law and Public Opinion in England during the Nineteenth Century*, London: Macmillan.

Gatrell, V. (1994) *The Hanging Tree*, Oxford: Oxford University Press.

Lloyd, D. (1971) *Introduction to Jurisprudence*, London: Stevens.

Lombroso, C. (1876) *L'uomo delinquente*, Milan: Hoepli.

Mayhew, H. (1862) *London Labour and the London Poor*, London: Griffith, Bohn & Co.

Morrison, W. (1889) 'Reflections on the Theory of Criminality', *Journal of Mental Science* 37: 14–23.

Report of the Gladstone Committee (1895), London: HMSO.

Further reading

Atiyah, P. (1979) *The Rise and Fall of Freedom of Contract*, Oxford: Clarendon Press.

Beirne, P. (1993) *Inventing Criminology*, Albany: State University of New York Press.

Wiener, M. (1990) *Reconstructing the Criminal*, Cambridge: Cambridge University Press.

SEE ALSO: Darwin, Charles; democracy, populism and rights; Social Darwinism

JOHN PRATT

THEORIES OF THE STATE AND SOCIETY: THE SCIENCE OF POLITICS

An old and familiar narrative of nineteenth-century social and political thought holds that the classical tradition of political theory was extinguished with the rise of the social sciences. Henceforth a 'science' of politics, excluding normative concerns, would be strictly subordinate to the overarching science of sociology. Politics would be epiphenomenal, the product of laws of social science. This narrative works better for France, and perhaps Germany, than for Britain, where theoretical sociology was weak; and in the British case an alternative version of the narrative might assert that political economy posed the most fundamental threat to classical political thought. But intellectual historians have become more sceptical of the claim that the 'dual revolution' in politics and economy at the end of the eighteenth and beginning of the nineteenth centuries brought about a total transformation of the intellectual landscape and eliminated older intellectual traditions. They have become more aware of the resilience of a prudential approach to political thought that, refusing to accept the inevitable triumph of a sociological view of the world, instead presented itself in novel form as a 'science of politics', 'science politique' or 'Staatswissenschaft'.

The idea of a political science was by no means new in the nineteenth century. The term itself can be traced back to the sixteenth century, when Bodin and his jurisprudential contemporaries aspired to create a 'civil science'. In the following century Hobbes, notably, conceived of the state as a mechanism that could be understood scientifically. In the Enlightenment these traditions were carried on by philosophers such as Montesquieu on the one hand and by the more practically minded Cameralists on the other. But it was in the nineteenth century that the concept really came into vogue. In France, the class of moral and political sciences at the Institut de France, created by the Idéologues in 1795 but abolished by

Napoleon in 1803, was refounded by GUIZOT in 1832 as the Académie des Sciences Morales et Politiques; and TOCQUEVILLE prefaced his study of Democracy in America (De la démocratie en Amérique) in 1835 with the proposition that 'a new political science is needed for a new world'. In Britain, MACAULAY declared in 1829 that 'that noble Science of Politics' was, of all sciences, 'the most important to the welfare of nations'. And in Germany, Restoration liberals compiled a massive Staatslexikon (State Lexicon), an 'encyclopedia of the political sciences' ('Staatswissenschaften') with the aim of providing an authoritative exposition of liberal principles as the realization of a truly scientific understanding of politics.

Undoubtedly the French Revolution played an important part in the emergence of this new kind of political discourse. Post-revolutionary liberals were newly conscious of the fragility of political and social order, and sought to detach the valid principles of 1789, such as constitutional Government and the rule of law, from the political extremism that had produced the Terror. They typically deployed the science of politics as a remedy for the excesses of political voluntarism, summoning reason and empirical knowledge as counterweights to will and passion. Moreover, since the derailment of the French Revolution was commonly attributed to the abstract rationalism of the Enlightenment, the science of politics had to be an empirical science grounded in the facts. The German Liberal Carl von Rotteck – co-editor, with Welcker, of the Staatslexikon – described in the preface the conflict between revolution and reaction in Restoration Europe, and depicted the purpose of the encyclopedia as the foundation of a new, rational political creed rooted in political reality and capable of rallying the moderates on both sides. Political science was an antidote to political extremism.

Rotteck, Professor of State Sciences at Freiburg and a deputy in the Baden lower house, was already the author of a four-volume Textbook on Rational Law and the Sciences of State (Lehrbuch des Vernunftsrecht und der Staatswissenschaften, 4 vos, 1829–35), but the Staatslexikon reached a much wider readership. It was published in the wake of its editors' dismissal from their chairs on political grounds in the backlash against the 1830 revolutions, and was marketed both as a handbook for civil servants and as a volume aimed at the educated of all classes. Its main counterpart in north Germany was Friedrich Christoph

Dahlmann's *Die Politik auf den Grund und das Maß der gegebenen Zustände zurückgeführt* (Politics Explained on the Basis of and in Relation to Prevailing Circumstances, 1835), based on his lectures at Göttingen. This volume quite explicitly aimed to provide a political education for the middle class, which Dahlmann identified as the centre of gravity of the state. Like the editors of the *Staatslexikon*, he set out to resolve the problem of how to reconcile order and change. Their closest analogues in France were the group known as the *Doctrinaires*, the most notable of whom, ROYER-COLLARD and Guizot, both had a deep influence on Tocqueville. They saw the rise of the middle class and the concomitant development of a democratic social state as inevitable processes: the point was to understand them and to seek to moderate and channel them.

This science of politics became the most important idiom in which to couch reflections on the relationship between state and society. Thinkers such as Macaulay, Guizot and Tocqueville were all conscious of the idea that the progress of society was governed by an autonomous law, and that, moreover, social change shaped political institutions. All shared the broadly historicist approach to political thought that was so characteristic of the nineteenth century and held that the transition to commercial society (Macaulay) or to a democratic society founded on equality of conditions (Tocqueville) demanded a new kind of political system. This approach had its origins in the distinctive ideas of the Scottish Enlightenment, and in particular in the idea of autonomous social change as the motor of history. Moreover, it was because there were objective constraints on political action and political will that a political science had to be empirical rather than deductive. Macaulay's crushing review of JAMES MILL's 'Essay on Government' was a classic exposition of the inductivist critique of the attempt to deduce what is the best form of Government from universal axioms about human nature. No historicist could accept the possibility of universal axioms about human nature, since human beings are the creatures of time and place.

The emergence of the science of politics should be seen as an aspect of a movement away from deductive political theory in the aftermath of the French Revolution. Whereas KANT had taken the view – shared by many philosophers before him – that forms of Government actually experienced by

states were mere historical accidents that offered little guidance in determining the proper purpose of the state, nineteenth-century writers almost universally took it for granted that a science of politics must be empirical and historical. Hegel was in the vanguard here: the essentially historical character of political philosophy (see HEGEL AND HEGELIANISM), and indeed of all philosophy, was one of his fundamental insights, and it had a profound impact on German political thought, which under Hegel's influence recognized that it must take existing state forms as the starting-point of its enquiries. The Heidelberg jurist and academic liberal Robert von Mohl was quite clear that human nature was diverse and historically determined, so that it was impossible to pin down *the* purpose of the state without reference to historical circumstances or public opinion. This was a widely accepted view in the nineteenth century. J.S. MILL, for instance, accepted that human nature was historically determined. His abortive science of 'ethology', sketched in Book VI of his *System of Logic* (1843), was intended to demonstrate how national character could be traced to the action of the universal laws of mind in time and place, and thus to show that the absence of a universal human nature did not prevent the formation of a genuinely scientific moral or social science.

A central tenet of nineteenth-century LIBERALISM was the belief that, in modern society, public opinion must in the long run prevail. This was fundamentally what distinguished representative Government from despotism. An early exposition of this doctrine came with MME DE STAËL's attempt to confront the question of how to 'close' the French Revolution in her posthumous work, *Des circonstances actuelles qui peuvent terminer la révolution et des principes qui doivent fonder la république en France* (The Present Circumstances that Might Close the Revolution in France and the Principles that Should Underpin the Republic in France), which was composed in 1798–9 but published only a century or so later. A crucial chapter on public opinion came, significantly, in the wake of chapters on royalists and republicans, and here Staël argued that the reign of public opinion represented the only hope of transcending the partisan conflict that had riven France for a decade. One of the most important spokesmen of this tradition in the early nineteenth century was Staël's friend and one-time lover BENJAMIN CONSTANT, a vocal and unreserved exponent of the idea of the

Government of opinion. For Constant modern Government must rest on spontaneously expressed popular opinion, and consequently the free press was the cornerstone of constitutional Government.

Most liberals, however, took a more complex view than Constant, arguing that opinion had to be guided by informed and educated leadership. This was indeed Staël's point of view. In *De la littérature considérée dans ses rapports avec les institutions sociales* (Literature Considered in its Relations with Social Institutions, 1800) she articulated the hope that men of letters might assume a ministry of secular spiritual leadership, and that the formation of that ministry might be advanced by the creation of moral and political sciences based on the model of the positive sciences. This view almost certainly shaped SAINT-SIMON's thinking, and through him that of COMTE, although both these writers took it in a more authoritarian direction than Staël envisaged. But the idea that the purpose of political science was in large measure to ensure that opinion could be guided was characteristic of many nineteenth-century liberals. BAGEHOT and Gladstone, Guizot and RENAN, all supposed that a science of politics must be a practical rather than a theoretical science, grounded in inductive knowledge of politics derived chiefly from history, and serving to underpin the art of political leadership.

The distinctive concern of the practitioners of the science of politics was with the dialectic of state and society: they sought to nourish a political prudence that knew when institutions had to be reformed if they were to continue to exert any legitimate authority over civil society. Characteristically this was a liberal – or, in Britain, a Whig-liberal – project, and was classically articulated in Macaulay's speeches on the parliamentary debates preceding the passing of the Great Reform Act in 1832. The science of politics was intimately associated with key liberal ideas such as constitutionalism and representative Government. Representative Government was important because it institutionalized the interdependence of state and society. Parliament would serve as a vital ligament between state and society. Because society was potentially a self-regulating mechanism tending towards equilibrium it did not require external regulation: instead, law must emerge from social interests as articulated in Parliament, and must therefore support society's self-regulation instead of replacing it.

In Britain, one of the most notable analysts of the dialectic of state and society was the economic and political commentator Walter Bagehot. He drew heavily on Burke, from whom he learnt that political institutions must depend on time and place, and that politics must therefore be a practical art. He was critical of those cultural elitists – he singled out MATTHEW ARNOLD – who he thought risked stifling the seeds of progress: for Bagehot the whole problem was to find forms of Government compatible with a rapidly changing society. He found the solution in what he called 'Government by discussion', a distinctively modern form of Government; and in particular in the English system of parliamentary Government. In the English system, characterized by the fusion rather than the separation of powers, Parliament exercised real power and hence could play a key role in not merely reflecting but shaping and leading public opinion.

What was 'scientific' about this science of politics? What distinguished it from a purely prudential art of Government? J.S. Mill objected to a merely empirical political science on the ground that it would tend to sanctify the status quo: what is, has to be. Hegel objected to Haller's Restoration conservatism on similar grounds. The chief answers to this line of objection lay in the development of the comparative method and the historical method as the keys to the creation of what the historian Sir John Seeley termed 'the impartial study of politics', which would be capable of identifying the direction of historical change and so enabling statesmen to adjust to it as well as to channel it. Both methods enjoyed enormous prestige. In Britain, HENRY MAINE's *Ancient Law* (1861) was a crucial influence, but in Continental Europe a key role was played, a generation or more previously, by the jurist and proponent of the historical school of law, Carl von Savigny. Prominent exponents of the comparative method included E.A. Freeman and HENRY SIDGWICK in Britain, Emile Boutmy in France and Rudolf von Gneist in Germany. History supplied the data for an inductive science of politics, while the comparative method bolstered the rhetorically important claim to impartiality and also enabled law-like generalizations to be formulated.

It is important to stress two points about the 'science of politics'. The first is that there was no radical gulf between 'political science' and 'social science': in fact, for most of the nineteenth century the terms were uses more or less interchangeably, at least in Britain and France. The second is that in the nineteenth century these were not purely academic projects but instead aimed at shaping public opinion. The *Staatslexikon*'s editors proclaimed that their aim was to educate active citizens, and this was an aim they shared with the Social Science Association, that 'outdoor parliament' which did so much to shape and articulate a liberal public opinion in mid-Victorian Britain. Likewise in France the École Libre des Sciences Politiques, although it eventually became best known as an institution that provided a specialist training for aspiring higher civil servants, in the first instance emerged from a belief that the disaster of the Second Empire had been due to the absence of an educated and self-reliant middle-class opinion. Under the influence of thinkers such as TAINE it set about shaping a politically informed public opinion.

While the science of politics was predominantly understood as an inductive science, there was a different, deductive, tradition that can be identified with Comte and his followers in France and with J.S. Mill in Britain. They both questioned the scientific standing of a purely empirical science of politics, arguing that to count as a science it must have some logical dependence on the higher-level generalizations of a broader science of society. Significantly, perhaps, Comte abandoned the term 'political science', which he had deployed as a synonym for 'social science' and 'social physics' in the 1820s, and replaced them all with his own neologism, 'sociology' (see SOCIAL THEORY AND SOCIOLOGY IN THE NINETEENTH CENTURY). In his influential *System of Logic* Mill argued that the most that the autonomous study of politics could do was to formulate empirical generalizations: if these were to count as scientific laws, it had to be possible to 'verify' them by showing *post hoc* how these generalizations might be deduced from psychological laws. That said, Mill himself made a significant and influential contribution to the inductive study of politics in his *Considerations on Representative Government* (1861).

The inductive science of politics should also be distinguished from traditions of social theory, associated with thinkers such as Saint-Simon and Comte, Marx and Engels (see MARX AND MARX-ISM), which sought to found a science of society upon long-run laws of historical development that would provide certain knowledge of the future development of society. Comte argued that to aspire to scientific status a branch of study must have its own distinctive method and its own distinctive subject matter; and he maintained that what was distinctive about sociology was that it dealt with a subject matter that changed over time, and that its method must therefore be historical. This view was echoed by both Hegel and Mill. But here the historical method was deployed in the search for certain laws of historical development, rather than to furnish the data for an empirical science of politics. In the one case, social science closed off the possibility of political life as an autonomous arena; in the other, it underpinned it.

It was Marx and Engels who were the chief exponents of the view that the state was epiphenomenal and that the struggles in civil society drove the course of history. They claimed their socialism to be scientific rather than utopian because it did not so much hold out communism as a goal as demonstrate its necessity. To that extent it seemed to erode the autonomy of the political. As with all propositions about Marxism as a system, however, this has to be subjected to a number of qualifications. In his journalistic and historical writings, such as *The Eighteenth Brumaire of Louis Bonaparte*, Marx seems to have assumed a more complex relationship between the economic base and the superstructure than he elsewhere implied. Since the point of Marxism was to provide a scientific foundation for a revolutionary movement it had to allow some room for political agency.

Evolutionary social theory, which flourished in the second half of the nineteenth century, tended to reinforce the quest for grand laws of history as the basis for social theory. Thinkers in this tradition treated society as an organism, and set out to determine the laws that governed the course of its evolution. It is now well known that evolutionary social theory predated DARWIN's *Origin of Species*, and even after Darwin wrote it continued to be influenced by Lamarckian assumptions about the mechanism by which societies evolved: Bagehot's *Physics and Politics* (1872), though purportedly concerned with the relevance of the concept of natural selection to the understanding of society, is a good example of this (see DARWIN, CHARLES and SOCIAL DARWINISM). More strictly Social Darwinist doctrines that saw the struggle for existence and the extinction of nations or races through warfare as the mechanism of social evolution really came into their own only in the era of the 'New

Imperialism' after about 1890; and they were less influential in Britain and France, the major imperial powers, than in Germany, whose colonial empire was small. Even then their importance was tempered by the widespread belief that rationality and altruism – themselves products of the evolutionary process – equipped man to rise above and conquer the determinism of biology.

While the science of politics was an international project that attracted liberals, in particular, in many different countries, it is possible to identify some distinctive national traditions. In Germany, the political or 'state sciences' emerged organically from the older tradition of Cameralism, an early modern tradition of administrative science closely linked to the training of public officials. In comparative perspective the most distinctive characteristic of the political sciences in Germany was that they retained close associations with the education of servants of the state. This tradition had no counterpart in Britain, where the Trevelyan report had insisted on the superior value of a liberal as opposed to a practical education for civil servants. Neither did it have an analogue in France until the creation in 1872 of the École Libre des Sciences Politiques, which soon acquired a virtual monopoly over the education of higher civil servants. But that School was a private foundation, its intellectual influences were Anglophile rather than Germanophile, and the concept of the political sciences it espoused owed more to British than to German models.

Another key variable was that the academic study of law, and especially of public law, was of much greater importance in Germany and, to an extent, in France. In Britain, by contrast, the idea of public law and with it the legal concept of the state were weakly articulated, and with the exception of isolated figures such as Maine, Pollock and DICEY, the British model of political science owed more to political economy and history than to law. This divergence has had an enduring significance: in Germany and France, the academic study of political science emerged under the umbrella of the law faculties, whereas in Britain it was nurtured in departments or faculties of history.

The mode of thought described here is far removed from academic political science as it emerged in the twentieth century and flourished after the Second World War. A full account of the origins of this political science lies beyond the scope of this volume, but an important transitional stage was the flowering of elite theory in the writings of Michels and Ostrogorski, PARETO and MOSCA (see INTELLECTUALS, ELITES AND MERITOCRACY). Drawing on crowd theorists such as Taine, LEBON and Sighele, these writers maintained that the fundamental difference in all societies was between the class that rules and the class that is ruled. All societies – democratic or authoritarian, republican or monarchical – were ruled by elites, and the point was to classify elites and to understand how they compete. Earlier liberals, much as they might attend to the role of the political leader in guiding opinion, nevertheless saw opinion as a potentially positive and progressive force. Public debate, whether in Parliament or in the press or in public meetings, helped generate rational opinion. What made elite theory different was that it depicted opinion as a fundamentally irrational force, but also as something capable of being understood scientifically and manipulated. This understanding of leadership was borrowed from crowd theory's 'hypnotic' model of the relations between leader and crowd. The emphasis on educating public opinion thus disappeared, and in the hands of this school 'political science' acquired a neo-Machiavellian style. Its focus was now on advising political leaders how they might best direct mass politics.

Further reading

Collini, S., Winch, D. and Burrow, J. (1983) *That Noble Science of Politics: A Study in Nineteenth-Century Intellectual History*, Cambridge: Cambridge University Press.

Lindenfeld, D.F. (1997) *The Practical Imagination. The German Sciences of State in the Nineteenth Century*, Chicago, Illinois, London: University of Chicago Press.

Smith, W.D. (1991) *Politics and the Sciences of Culture in Germany, 1840–1920*, ch. 1, New York: Cambridge University Press.

SEE ALSO: conservatism, authority and tradition; democracy, populism and rights; intellectuals, elites and meritocracy; liberalism; the nation, nationalism and the national principle; political economy; social theory and sociology in the nineteenth century

H.S. JONES

THIERS, LOUIS-ADOLPHE (1797–1877)

The French historian, political thinker and politician Louis-Adolphe Thiers played a protagonist's role during some of the most crucial moments of nineteenth-century French politics, not least the outbreak of the July Revolution of 1830 and the founding and the survival of the Third Republic in the early 1870s. Born in Marseilles and educated there as well as in nearby Aix-en-Provence, Thiers was always described as possessed of a 'southern' temperament. Being the son of a locksmith, he was the quintessential self-made man, the parvenu who was determined to succeed through his intelligence, talents and will-power. He was physically unprepossessing, but his talents and energy won over many influential men who were to help the young provincial rise in the Parisian scene that he entered in 1821.

Thiers worked during the 1820s as a journalist in the important opposition newspaper *Le Constitutionnel,* and as a historian. His greatest achievement in the latter capacity was a ten-volume history of the French Revolution, published between 1823 and 1827.

In the end of 1829, being staunchly opposed to the reactionary Polignac ministry (which had recently replaced the moderate Martignac ministry), Thiers founded, along with his friend and fellow historian, François Mignet (1796–1884) and Armand Carrel (1800–36), the newspaper *Le National,* which immediately emerged, in the first half of 1830, as the foremost forum of opposition to the regime. It was in a leading article in *Le National* (4 February 1830, pp. 1–2) that Thiers formulated his famous definition of the role of the monarch in a constitutional monarchy: '*le roi règne et ne gouverne pas*' (Laquièze 1997) – the notion probably did not originate with Thiers; it is attributed to Jan Zamoyski. But it was Thiers who made it an effective instrument of opposition to King Charles X during the last months of the Restoration in France. Besides having contributed very significantly towards preparing the country for what turned out to be the revolution of July 1830 through *Le National,* Thiers proved also instrumental in resolving the crisis once the Paris crowds had overthrown Charles X at the end of July 1830. It was Thiers who had earlier proposed, in the pages of *Le National,* that Charles X be replaced by the duc d'Orléans after the model of the Glorious Revolution of 1688 in England. It was Thiers who, during the crucial days of late July 1830, convinced the opposition journalists and then the deputies to opt for the Orléans solution. And it was Thiers who was sent to gauge the intentions of the duc d'Orléans, met with the duc's sister and returned offering the deputies a response calculated to convince them to offer the throne to Louis-Philippe d'Orléans.

During the reign of Louis-Philippe – the July Monarchy (1830–48) – besides being a deputy throughout the reign, Thiers became a minister several times, and twice served as President of the Council of Ministers (the equivalent of Prime Minister) – in 1836 and 1840 respectively, both times for a few months only, falling mainly due to disagreements with the King on foreign policy. His second ministry (March–October 1840) was marked by a very serious crisis in the Middle East. France's support for her *protégé,* the Pasha of Egypt, Mehemet Ali, in his attempt to conquer Syria and threaten the Ottoman Empire's integrity more and more resulted in a confrontation between France and the other great powers that almost led to war between France and Britain, not least because of the populist nationalism adopted by Thiers and matched fully on the British side by Lord Palmerston. King Louis-Philippe sacked Thiers and replaced him with FRANÇOIS GUIZOT. During the rest of the July Monarchy Thiers remained out of ministerial office and was the leader of the left-centre opposition to Guizot's ministry. In the late 1840s he formed an alliance with Odilon Barrot, leader of the so-called dynastic left; they supported the Banquet Campaign of the republicans in 1847. After the Revolution of 1848 Thiers gradually shifted to more and more conservative positions and he came to support Louis Napoleon Bonaparte for the presidency in December 1848. He supported the President's policies in 1849–50, but, by the beginning of 1851, he had started warning against Louis Napoleon's bid to increase his powers. He was therefore forced to two years' exile after Louis Napoleon's *coup d'état* of December 1851.

Thiers re-entered political life in 1863 as a deputy for Paris and spent the next seven years being the leader of the opposition to the Empire in the representative body. In the crucial period before the disastrous Franco-Prussian War Thiers had warned against such a war (being one of the very few to do so).

Thiers's real moment of glory came after the fall of the Second Empire, following France's humiliating defeat in the Franco-Prussian War. He emerged for some time as the reliable, veteran politician who steered the vessel of the state at its most crucial moments. He played a decisive – if also highly controversial – role in the choice of the republican regime and then in its consolidation. It was he, the former constitutional monarchist, who proved most influential in convincing the French masses to accept what he called a 'conservative republic' ('the republic will be conservative or it will not be at all' he argued) and who most forcefully insisted on the necessity of establishing a republic as 'the regime that divides us least' ('*le régime qui nous divise le moins*') – part of the explanation for Thiers's successes was arguably attributable to his capacity to formulate ideas in the form of such watchwords or slogans, what his British contemporary, Walter Bagehot, called 'his brilliant epigrams', which 'sounded like statesmanship', and yet were 'not a policy, but only a political epigram' (Bagehot 1968: 438–9). But no matter how appealing his epigrammatic statements might have been, his major contribution to the consolidation of the republican regime that he helped establish was his brutal suppression of the Paris Commune in 1871, when, as chief of the provisional executive in Versailles, he ordered the troops to attack the Paris Communards. The price in blood and class bitterness was very high, but after this the republic of M. Thiers was not seen as dangerous by the friends of order in the French provinces or among the Parisian bourgeoisie. Thiers became the first President of the Third Republic between 1871 and 1873.

References

Bagehot, W. (1968 [1872]) 'M. Thiers', in *The Collected Works of Walter Bagehot*, ed. N. St John-Stevas, Vol. IV, 437–9, London: The Economist.
Laquièze, A. (1997) 'Adolphe Thiers théoricien du régime parlementaire: ses articles dans *Le National* en 1830', *Revue Française d'Histoire des Idées Politiques* 5, 1: 59–88.

Further reading

Bury, J.P.T. and Tombs, R.P. (1986) *Thiers 1797–1877: A Political Life*, London: Allen & Unwin.
Malo, H. (1932) *Thiers, 1797–1877*, Paris: Payot.

SEE ALSO: historiography and the idea of progress; liberalism

GEORGIOS VAROUXAKIS

THOREAU, HENRY DAVID (1817–62)

US cultural icon, unsparing social critic, proto-environmentalist and nature writer, Henry David Thoreau holds a key place in the traditions of US and world literature. Although considered primarily a man of letters, Thoreau contributed significantly to nineteenth-century political and social thought, as well as the natural history of New England and US Romantic religion. His writings also announced a new environmental ethic and inaugurated the tradition of US nature writing.

Thoreau was born in the small town of Concord, Massachusetts, 16 miles west of Boston, the old colonial capital. Like many other farming communities of the region, Concord would undergo rapid transformation during the middle decades of the nineteenth century as traditional agrarian patterns of life gave way to industrialization and a mixed manufacturing economy. Thoreau's father, John, worked variously as a grocer and pencil-maker, while his mother, Cynthia, took in boarders to supplement the family income. Despite changing economic circumstances, however, throughout most of Thoreau's life Concord remained a rural community surrounded by extensive tracts of pasturage, swamps and woodlands. Not far from the centre of town were several lakes, including Walden Pond itself, which Thoreau later celebrated for its pristine natural beauty.

At the age of 16, Thoreau matriculated at Harvard College. When he arrived in Cambridge in the autumn of 1833, Harvard was not the cosmopolitan seat of liberal learning it was to become later in the century, but a small, provincial, highly regimented academy whose curriculum still adhered to a classical programme of studies emphasizing rote learning and memorization. Instructors drilled their charges in a pre-set curriculum of Greek, Latin, history, English, maths and a modern language. Despite his love for the classics, Thoreau found the Harvard curriculum bleak and stultifying. His tutelage under Edward Tyrrel Channing, Harvard's Professor of Rhetoric, did, however, yield some important dividends for his development as a writer. Thoreau also took advantage of his time at college to extend his knowledge of foreign languages beyond the required course format: to his mastery of Greek and Latin, he added a competency in French, Italian, German and Spanish. Later on in life, he even undertook the study of Algonquian dialects. Language, indeed, was an object of perpetual fascination to him, evident later, throughout his published writings, in his flair for etymological puns and word-play, as well as in his more sustained inquiries into the natural origins of words.

On his return to Concord after his graduation in the autumn of 1837, Thoreau became better acquainted with RALPH WALDO EMERSON, a neighbour and sometime Harvard tutor who had delivered the Phi Beta Kappa address at the Harvard commencement earlier that summer. The previous year Emerson had published his first book, a little volume entitled *Nature,* which quickly acquired the status of a manifesto for the new movement of young Unitarian reformers from the greater Boston area who would come to be known as Transcendentalists. Ostensibly a philosophical meditation on nature, Emerson's book actually offered to its readers a radical new philosophical, religious and literary vision that tended to subvert the primacy of received tradition, the Christian Bible and the authority of revealed religion. Despite its New England trappings, *Nature* also served its US readers as an important early conduit for the ideas and values associated with European Romanticism; indeed, the Transcendentalist movement that Emerson helped to foster represented the first wholesale expression of Romantic ideology in the USA. Apparently, *Nature* found a warmly sympathetic reader in Thoreau, as it did many young Unitarians of his generation, and he discovered in Emerson a literary mentor and model of enormous appeal. The friendship that grew from this early acquaintance, despite a difference in age of 14 years, became the most formative of the two men's respective careers. Henceforth Thoreau also came to conceive his own writing as an expression of the new Transcendentalist ethos.

From the time of his Harvard graduation in 1837 till his early death from tuberculosis in 1862, Thoreau supported himself through an assortment of odd jobs, most notably surveying, carpentry and running his father's pencil-making business. At the same time, he made it a point of honour not to work at such jobs more than a portion of each day or year, in order to save himself for his literary labours and the more exacting contemplative experience of his daily excursions in the countryside around Concord. In the spring of 1845, Thoreau borrowed an axe and set about building a small house on the shores of Walden Pond where he lived in semi-seclusion for over two years, free of the domestic cares of the town, in order, as he wrote, 'to transact some private business with the fewest obstacles'. Thoreau conceived this episode in his life in part as an economic experiment – how to make do with less – and in part as a demonstration of the practical and spiritual benefits of simplicity in life. Out of this experience emerged Thoreau's most famous book, *Walden*, which he worked on almost continuously for the better part of ten years. To keep track of his daily and seasonal observations in nature, Thoreau also kept a journal, which by the end of his life amounted to a record of some two million words. This voluminous record might well be termed his master-work since it not only served as the principal repository for material used in the composition of his various books, lectures and essays, but it also constituted a massive literary enterprise in its own right. As this devotion to journal-keeping indicates, however various his outward modes of employment, Thoreau considered himself first and foremost a writer. His literary reputation rests principally on the two books published in his lifetime: *A Week on the Concord and Merrimack Rivers* (1849) and, more famously, *Walden* (1854), a work eventually welcomed into the company of world classics. In addition, Thoreau produced several other works published in book form posthumously, notably *Maine Woods* (1864) and *Cape Cod* (1865), as well as a host of occasional essays and poems. Among his several political essays, the most influential has been 'Resistance to Civil Government', popularly known as 'Civil Disobedience,' first published in 1849.

To characterize Thoreau as a Transcendentalist serves as a useful preliminary designation if only because it correctly situates his thought in the larger context of nineteenth-century Romanticism. Like other Transcendentalists, Thoreau generally found himself most at home in the intellectual company of philosophical idealists, beginning with Plato and the Neoplatonists, rather than philosophers of the rationalist school; he thought that intuition and the human imagination provided a more direct access to truth than the rational understanding; he conceived nature itself as the perfect embodiment and expression of spiritual reality, far exceeding any humanly mediated scriptures or revelations; he believed in what Emerson called the infinitude of the private man, that divinity dwells in the human heart, and that the individual conscience, not the dictates of the state or the impulses of the mob, was the final arbiter of the moral law; he was convinced that great art was the spontaneous free expression of the artist's natural inspiration and genius, and not the result of a slavish conformity to artificial aesthetic conventions or criteria; and he held that nature's own organic process and forms provided the best models for artistic creation. At the same time, even more than for some of his like-minded Transcendentalist friends, Thoreau's thought resists easy categorization. He was not a systematic thinker, and efforts to pin him down to a few philosophical rubrics are bound to distort the dynamic nature of his thinking and the rhetorical character of his most representative writing.

Any assessment of Thoreau's political and social thought must reckon first of all with his fierce individualism. He was not the misanthrope he has sometimes been made out to be – in fact he was a devoted friend and trusted neighbour – but he was temperamentally suspicious of organizations and commonly avoided humanitarian societies, churches and social reform movements of all kinds. Consequently, it is not surprising that much of his thinking about politics and society took the form of social criticism, and in this he could be both stinging and censorious. The famous opening chapter of *Walden*, for example, consists essentially of a thoroughgoing critique of the norms and mores of rural New England life. 'The mass of men lead lives of quiet desperation,' he famously pontificated; they have become the tools of their tools, the slaves of their possessions. His contemporaries had gotten their lives upside down, misconstruing material means for life's ultimate ends. Writing here like an indignant Hebrew prophet, Thoreau upbraided his Yankee neighbours for their thoughtless materialism and implored them to remake their lives according to a vision of life's higher spiritual purpose. The situation, he insisted, required radical revaluation. But the solution was not to be found in humane societies or charitable associations. On the contrary, the reform of society must always begin with the reform of the individual. To Thoreau, reformers and philanthropists evoked particular scorn since dubious personal motives so often vitiated even their loftiest undertakings. Overtures to join this or that communal society of the day – Brook Farm and Fruitlands were notable examples – left him profoundly unmoved.

Thoreau's habitual distrust of social reform movements extended to political structures as well. He begins his famous essay on civil disobedience polemically with this motto: 'That government is best which governs least.' Yet despite his suspicion of Government and politics, Thoreau was no anarchist: he firmly believed that Government had a constructive, if limited, role to play in enhancing the quality of human life. The problem was that, left to its own political and bureaucratic devices, Government was as likely to multiply human error as to mitigate it. Thoreau's general attitude to the social and political upheavals of his time could thus be described as one of principled aloofness. There were, however, a couple of major exceptions to this usual policy of reserve. One came in response to US aggression against Mexico in 1846 when Thoreau famously chose to spend a night in jail rather than pay a tax levied to support the war. He used this episode to give dramatic form to his essay on nonviolent civil disobedience, which had such important repercussions in the thought of the modern freedom fighters Mohandas ('Mahatma') Gandhi and Martin Luther King, Jr. In this essay, consistent with his faith in a divinely sanctioned moral law, Thoreau appeals to a higher tribunal of human conscience to counteract the laws of a corrupt state. The institution of slavery in North America represented another set of evils that Thoreau was constitutionally unable to ignore. Nothing inspired more abhorrence in him than the slave trade, and few spoke out on the issue with more vehemence. Though he never formally joined any anti-slavery society, he agitated vigorously on behalf of abolitionism and served as a local agent in the Underground Railroad, helping smuggle run-away slaves through Concord on their way to Canada. Despite his rejection of violence earlier in life, the continuing horror of the slave trade forced him to conclude that forcible resistance might sometimes be necessary. His controversial defence of John Brown after the unsuccessful raid on Harper's Ferry in 1859 represents the height of his political radicalism and presages his later support of northern military action in the Civil War.

Thoreau's attitudes to organized religion were hardly less critical than his attitudes to politics and society, and in certain respects much more so. To the charges of corruption and greed that he sometimes levelled at unjust Government, he added arrogance and hypocrisy in the case of religion. He had little good to say about the clergy, even though he counted some clergymen as his friends, or about institutional worship, or about religious dogma and creeds, or about pious expressions of faith, because all of these seemed inauthentic to him. On the other hand, Thoreau expressed passionate support for the ideals of religious life and the sources of religious inspiration, particularly the ethical teachings and prophetic traditions of the Christian Bible. He also found important inspiration in the scriptures, mythologies and wisdom traditions of several other religions, in particular the classical texts of India and China. What complicates matters here is that, by nature and temperament, Thoreau was himself a deeply spiritual and devout individual; it was simply that the focus of his devotion had shifted from the Christian Church to the natural world outdoors. Thoreau's own religious life may thus be characterized as committedly nonsectarian, anti-institutional, personal, nature-centred and, perhaps above all, experiential. Like the mystics and contemplatives of orthodox traditions, he sought divine contact at the level of direct experience and not at the level of faith alone.

The prevailing empiricist cast of Thoreau's religious thought clearly shaped his attitudes to nature as well and favoured his interest in natural science. Despite his admiration for the cultivated Emerson, Thoreau was never entirely comfortable with the sort of armchair philosophizing his friend sometimes practised nor the easy generalizations to which he sometimes subjected the natural world. For Thoreau nature was not just a 'symbol' of the spiritual world, as Emerson had conceived of it in *Nature,* but the very substance and life of reality itself. To understand nature properly one had to approach the natural world on its own terms and be prepared to forgo all of one's prior assumptions. Consistent with this belief, Thoreau spent long hours of each day observing natural forms and phenomena in the countryside around his home, and meticulously recording his findings in his journals. In doing so, he contributed importantly to the growing body of knowledge about the natural history of Massachusetts. Additionally, Thoreau's published writings provided the first compelling formulation of an environmentalist ethic in the USA, and served as the foundation for the subsequent tradition of US nature writing. Yet, despite his keen interest in natural science, Thoreau also considered the scientific method somewhat limited, its results often barren of essential human meaning. The facts of nature only acquired their true significance, he believed, when brought into relationship with the human mind. Thoreau's mature treatment of nature thus fused the Transcendentalist Idealism exemplified by Emerson with an empiricism shaped by his own contemplative experience and precise field observations.

Further reading

Hodder, Alan D. (2001) *Thoreau's Ecstatic Witness*, New Haven: Yale University Press.

Peck, H. Daniel (1990) *Thoreau's Morning Work: Memory and Perception in* A Week on the Concord and Merrimack Rivers, *the* Journal, *and* Walden, New Haven: Yale University Press.

Richardson, Robert D. (1986) *Henry Thoreau: A Life of the Mind*, Berkeley: University of California Press.

Thoreau, Henry David (1971–) *The Writings of Henry David Thoreau,* ed. William L. Howarth *et al.*, Princeton: Princeton University Press.

SEE ALSO: mythology, classicism and antiquarianism; novels, poetry and drama; religion, secularization and the crisis of faith

ALAN D. HODDER

TOCQUEVILLE, ALEXIS DE (1805–59)

Alexis de Tocqueville, politician, historian and sociologist, could trace his ancestors back to the time of William the Conqueror. The ancestral home was Tocqueville in Normandy though Alexis was born in Paris, the centre of the revolution that had broken out 16 years earlier. Though very much an aristocrat, Tocqueville was fated to live in the country where aristocracy had suffered its most spectacular defeat. Here, then, in the contrast between aristocracy and democracy we find the polarity that informs all his major writings.

The French Revolution of 1789 had culminated in the great terror of 1793–4 when, among many others, half a dozen of Tocqueville's immediate relatives had been guillotined. His mother had watched her parents and grandfather being led to their deaths. Both Tocqueville's parents had been imprisoned but were saved by the fall of Robespierre in July 1794. The next French revolution, that of July 1830, replaced the restoration monarchy of Charles X with the constitutional one of Louis-Philippe. It was less significant and violent than its predecessor yet still met with Tocqueville's disapproval. He reluctantly swore allegiance to the new regime but took the opportunity to leave France for the USA. His nominal purpose was to inspect US penal institutions and, with his friend Gustave de Beaumont, a report was produced in 1833. His real concern, however, was to investigate democracy in its most advanced form and thereby understand a trend already influential in Europe. Tocqueville was in the USA for less than a year, from May 1831 to February 1832. It was a short visit but one put to distinctly good effect. His report, *Democracy in America,* appeared in two volumes in 1835 and 1840. It won him instant celebrity and remains his most influential work.

France was now experiencing revolution almost in each generation and, more explicitly than anyone else, Tocqueville saw the 1848 outbreak approaching. By then he had been closely involved in political affairs, having been a member of the Chamber of Deputies since 1839. The February 1848 revolution rid France of monarchy for the last time. In May Tocqueville was elected to the new legislative assembly and in June he became Minister of Foreign Affairs. Of those granted a personal entry in this Encyclopedia only BOLIVAR, DISRAELI, GUIZOT, LENIN and LINCOLN attained higher political office. Tocqueville's elevation, however, was followed by rapid and self-induced decline. He resigned from ministerial office after just five months. Then, three years later he opposed Louis Napoleon's coup of December 1851, was arrested and held for one day, and left public life for the tranquillity of his study.

Tocqueville, clearly, lived through a time of important political events and the revolutions in France were stark indicators of the wider egalitarian trend. Yet the most egalitarian society was the USA. It had emerged with a weaker and less historically entrenched aristocracy than those of Europe and so had advanced without generating formidable counter-movements. Though the USA might display the foremost egalitarian condition, a young society, necessarily, could not furnish evidence of long-term historical trends. For this Tocqueville looked to France. Contemplation of 700 years of French history confirmed its direction of social change. In France the importance of aristocracy had gradually declined. At one time nobility could only be inherited; by the thirteenth

century it could be purchased or conferred. In the conflicts of attrition between the crown and the nobility either side might grant the common people influence in order to tip the scales of power in a desired direction. In this way even the kings had unwittingly become constant levellers. Gradually printing and the spread of education created opportunities for all classes. It seemed to Tocqueville that from the Crusades through to the introduction of municipal corporations, firearms, Protestantism, commerce, manufacture and the discovery of America, the egalitarian trend had been consistently advanced. He presumed that in time inherited class distinctions would disappear.

It was this process that Tocqueville termed 'democracy'. We must emphasize that for him democracy was much more than what it is today, the name for a political system. Indeed the system itself, democratic politics, seemed to Tocqueville merely one aspect of the wider egalitarian trend. Democracy, then, was the movement that challenged the aristocratic society enjoyed by his forebears. This long-term development was far too deeply rooted in the character of society for any politicians or statesmen to alter it. The movement was all-powerful and inevitable. The only rational response was to accept it. Those of his class who still resisted were labouring in vain.

Like Marx (see MARX AND MARXISM) and COMTE, Tocqueville decided that society was advancing in an ascertainable direction, thought quite unlike them he believed that the moving force was God's providential plan. Furthermore the God of Christianity favoured only the Christian nations. They alone were advancing in a democratic direction. They would thus increasingly come to resemble each other while simultaneously becoming more distinct from the rest. Here again Tocqueville was a man of his time in the belief that only Western nations contained any social dynamism. From one perspective his notion of providence suffers the disadvantage of not being open to proof. However, it eminently suited Tocqueville's purpose of winning over his own class of Catholic aristocrats to the new social order. The Church itself might have been closely linked to the *ancien régime* and the revolution to anti-clericalism, yet Tocqueville was reassuring his countrymen that God had not abandoned them. Modern society was part of God's design and, therefore, Christians should reconcile themselves to the democratic order.

Conciliation, however, as Tocqueville wanted it, was far from resigned acceptance of all democracy's tendencies. As a historian and aristocrat he saw modern society from a comparative perspective. Unlike today's political science, where comparative politics usually indicates comparison between different contemporary states, Tocqueville chose to compare his own society's past with its present. Though he accepted the latter, he was well aware of its dangers. In modern society equality of opportunity had removed many barriers to ability and effort, but the chance to rise also produced an equal chance to fall. Society, then, was more fluid and mobile. It became more restless and individualist, marked by what Tocqueville termed 'unquiet passions'. The class solidarities that derived from a fixed position were in decline. Now no one knew their place nor on whom they could rely. In this situation the individual was weaker than before and more vulnerable to the social and political pressures that modern society created. Class implied a stratified hierarchy and this democracy seemed to destroy. Indeed it was definitional for Tocqueville that democracy was the broad egalitarian process. It seemed possible that a counter tendency might develop in the new 'manufacturing aristocracy'. Its advantage was that talent from any source might ascend to great heights. This benefit scarcely compensated for what had been lost. Former classes had given their members a sentiment of solidarity. The highest class, the landed aristocracy, had also, at their best, felt a sense of responsibility for their social inferiors. It seemed unlikely that any new commercial class would match them in this respect.

We see intimations in Tocqueville of what were later termed 'anomie', 'the lonely crowd' and 'the fear of freedom'. It seemed to him that democracy left individuals isolated while simultaneously exposing them to awesome new dangers. These were constituted by an old institution, the state, and a new sociological phenomenon, mass society. When protected from one, freedom could easily be lost to the other. Its survival was the greatest danger that modern societies faced. By the nineteenth century the state as such was not a new institution. What was novel was its current situation. In aristocratic societies a whole range of regional, occupational and religious organizations stood between the individual and the state. Tocqueville referred to these as 'secondary powers' or 'intermediate associations'. Their own powers curtailed, filtered and distanced those of the state. In providing countervailing institutions of power, wealth, influence, privilege, expertise and control they furnished the space within which a modest but vital amount of liberty had been attained. Their number and diversity meant that general liberty benefited greatly from the impossibility of any one group achieving predominance.

Modern society provided a marked contrast. The secondary powers were getting weaker. The nobility was losing its privileges, the cities their independence and the various provincial bodies had lost out to the increasingly centralized state. The danger now was that the type of participatory citizenship that Tocqueville so admired in New England might eventually fall under the sway of a centralized class of public officials. In this situation the scrutiny of public officials, the watchful suspicion and vigilance that was so central to the preservation of liberty, would be sacrificed. Public needs would no longer be met by the public themselves but by a growing band of officials upon whose shoulders tasks were willingly transferred and gratefully accepted. The power of the state might thus be fatally augmented by the complicity of both sides – an apathetic public happy to spare themselves the burden of participation and a Government intoxicated with the delights of unlimited control.

Such a society was one in which individual freedom finds no refuge. Democracy had so flattened out personal differences and peculiarities that anyone distinctive was endangered by the pressures of the conformist mass. Here, then, was democracy in its worst incarnation. The decline of intermediate powers that facilitates the emergence of an irresponsible, all-powerful state simultaneously results in the creation of what Tocqueville termed 'mass society'. Now individual liberty is assailed on both sides, from the state above and the mass below, for where all are the same the majority is dominant and each is bound by its will. Democracy, then, threatens the very liberties it sought to secure. If the people are passive they become subservient to an all-powerful state; if they are collectively active they produce the 'tyranny of the majority' that crushes individual freedom. The US experience already exhibited these dangers, but it was in his own country that Tocqueville found still greater cause for concern.

Tocqueville had gone to the USA to see the future faced by France, for both were subject to the same overall plan. Yet frequently the particular seemed to disrupt Tocqueville's general outline and nowhere more poignantly and depressingly than in the peculiarities of the French. In France it had not required modern democracy to produce centralized Government; that had already come about through Louis XIV. Furthermore France had moved to democracy through revolution while the USA had achieved it peacefully. In 1847 Tocqueville noted that the French Revolution of 1789 had destroyed all privileges except that of property. This it left as an isolated and exposed advantage in an otherwise egalitarian society. Tocqueville thus predicted the political battle between 'haves and have-nots' that resumed in the following year. He took socialism to be the essential feature of the revolution of 1848 and the one he disliked most. Tocqueville viewed socialism as the worst aspect of democracy. It set one class against another, glamorized violence, exalted materialism and confirmed state centralization. It thus seemed basically incompatible with the preservation of freedom. Democracy gave power to the lower classes but could not guarantee how they would be used. All it ensured was an equal society. It remained a fundamental yet still open question as to whether the people would be equal in liberty or equal under tyranny.

John Stuart Mill wrote long reviews of both volumes of *Democracy in America,* which did much to make Tocqueville known in Great Britain. Both writers shared a sense that their own commitment to liberty was insufficiently matched by others. Tocqueville's analysis fundamentally influenced the important Chapter 3 of *On Liberty,* where Mill argued that the growth of mass society threatened to bring Western progress to a halt. *On Liberty* was published in 1859, the year of Tocqueville's death. Tocqueville's last major publication, *The Old Regime and the French Revolution,* had been published three years earlier and was intended as the first volume of a more extended study of the revolution. Some of its themes, such as the slow decline of inequality, are already familiar to us, but here Tocqueville was concerned to show how a trend common to all countries had in France produced a revolution of unparalleled rapidity and violence. He noted how over the previous three centuries the French kings had detached the nobility from the people by drawing them into the court at Versailles. Gradually the local functions of the nobility ceased while their privileges continued, a disparity that

created particularly strong resentment. Meanwhile the peasantry were being released from serfdom and many other antiquated restrictions. What the revolution destroyed, therefore, were merely the remnants of feudalism. Serfdom in Germany had survived much longer than in France, yet the revolution occurred not where oppression was greatest but, rather, where conditions were rapidly improving. This is Tocqueville's famous and counter-intuitive revolution of rising expectations. He believed that 'it is not always when things are going from bad to worse that revolutions break out. On the contrary' the most dangerous moment for an oppressive government is when it relaxes the pressure. It is then that popular protest is likely to begin. Consequently 'the most perilous moment for a bad government is one when it seeks to mend its ways'. This analysis was made in respect of the fall of the Bourbons but has recently been applied to the fall of communism. Thus in his analysis of democratic tyranny Tocqueville has sometimes been regarded as an analyst of modern totalitarianism. In a strict sense this is obviously impossible. It's better to say that Tocqueville's analysis of the social basis of freedom later provided the basis for an analysis of totalitarianism, particularly through an understanding of the significance of 'intermediate powers'. Without such institutions a society is in danger of totalitarianism; with them it fortifies freedom by creating a strong 'civil society'. This latter term, much in vogue in respect of post-communist societies, is usually associated with Hegel, but the way it is now used exactly captures Tocqueville's sense of the importance of having powerful, independent social institutions through which the strength of the state can be countered.

We end here with Tocqueville as sociologist, though he is hard to place under modern classificatory labels, whether as between the academic disciplines of sociology and politics or between the ideological movements of liberalism and conservatism. In the French Chamber of Deputies he sat as an independent between Government and opposition. He thus remained his own man, an example of the very independence and individuality that it was his life's work to preserve.

Further reading

Lamberti, J.C. (1989) *Tocqueville and the Two Democracies,* Cambridge, MA: Harvard University Press.
Lively, J. (1965) *The Social and Political Thought of Alexis de Tocqueville,* Oxford: Clarendon Press.

Stone, J. and Mennell, S. (eds) (1980) *Alexis de Tocqueville. On Democracy, Revolution, and Society. Selected Writings*, Chicago: University of Chicago Press.
Tocqueville, A. de (1994) *Democracy in America*, 2. vols, London: David Campbell.

SEE ALSO: democracy, populism and rights; historiography and the idea of progress; Mill, John Stuart; social theory and sociology in the nineteenth century

MICHAEL LEVIN

TOLSTOY, LEO NIKOLAEVICH (1828–1910)

Count Leo Nikolaevich Tolstoy was a master of Russian realistic fiction. Already in his lifetime he had also achieved world renown as a moral thinker and religious anarchist. His views on pedagogics, history, religion and a moral way of living, as well as his personal persistence and courage in the advocating of his ideals, attracted a large number of followers both in Russia and outside the country. Tolstoy's novels and essays have been translated into most languages.

Leo Tolstoy was born into the family of prominent aristocrats on 9 September 1828 in the family estate Yasnaya Polyana in central Russia. For three years Tolstoy studied Oriental Languages and Law at the University of Kazan. After leaving the university in 1847 without a degree, Tolstoy entered the army and took part in the Crimean war (1853–5).

Tolstoy began his literary career by publishing the autobiographical trilogy *Childhood* (*Detstvo*, 1852), *Boyhood* (*Otrotchestvo*, 1854) and *Youth* (*Iunost*, 1857). In his *Sevastopol Stories* (*Sevastopolskiye rasskazy*, 1853–5) Tolstoy pictures the courage of simple soldiers and shows the true meaning of heroism. The theme of war was pursued in his novel *War and Peace* (*Voyna I Mir*, 1865–9) that was to become the Russian national epic. Tolstoy represents a gallery of Russian characters of various social classes and thus shows that it is not great personalities that determine historical events. In his novel *Anna Karenina* (1873–7), Tolstoy created a realistic story of an extramarital affair.

In 1862 Tolstoy married the 18-year-old Sophia Berg. At the peak of his literary glory and family happiness, Tolstoy underwent a profound crisis of world-outlook that he later described in *My Confession* (*Ispoved*, 1879–82). Searching for the meaning of his life, he turned to the Bible. He formulated his own rationalistic version of Christianity in *What I Believe?* (*V Chyom moya vera*, 1884) and *The Kingdom of God is within You* (*Tsarstvo Boziee vnytri Vas*, 1893).

For the rest of his life Tolstoy tried to live in accordance with the principles he formulated in his religious writings, namely moderation and simplicity in each and every sphere of life, obligation to work and nonresistance to evil. He wrote a number of articles on pedagogics and opened schools for peasant children on his estate. Tolstoy argued for the importance of the author's moral position and the domination of morality over beauty and harmony. Tolstoy's later fiction written after his conversion remains preoccupied with moral questions.

Leo Tolstoy died at the age of 83 in 1910 from acute pneumonia in a small railway station of Astapovo that was later renamed after him. He left ninety volumes of writings and thousands of followers all over the world.

Further reading

Redpath T. (1960) *Tolstoy*, London: Bowes & Bowes.
Simmons E. (1946) *Leo Tolstoy*, Boston: Little, Brown & Company.
Tolstoy L. (1928–37) *The Works of Leo Tolstoy*, trans. L. Maude, A. Maude, J. Duff, 21 vols, Oxford: Oxford University Press.
Troyat H. (1967) *Tolstoy,* Garden City, New York: Doubleday.

SEE ALSO: novels, poetry and drama; Russian thought in the nineteenth century

EVELINA BARBASHINA

TÖNNIES, FERDINAND (1855–1936)

Ferdinand Julius Tönnies, the erstwhile Professor of Economics and Political Science in Kiel, Germany, is also regarded as the 'first German sociologist'. Tönnies, who was born in the small farming community of Riep near Oldenswort on 26 July 1855, ranks with thinkers like AUGUSTE COMTE, HERBERT SPENCER, EMILE DURKHEIM, MAX WEBER and GEORG SIMMEL among the 'founding fathers' of modern sociology. His writings offer a wide-ranging perspective on the social, cultural and philosophical concerns that characterized the final third of the nineteenth as well as the first three decades of the twentieth century. But many of his theoretical concerns, which cover an exceptionally broad thematic spectrum, have lost nothing of their validity today. Particularly his writings on Thomas Hobbes (Tönnies was president of the British Thomas Hobbes Society and one of the foremost Hobbes scholars of his times) are exceptionally fruitful scholarly expositions, but so are many of his smaller writings, like his famous book on the *Kritik der öffentlichen Meinung* (1922) or his numerous writings on education.

For various reasons though, Tönnies is mostly identified with his distinction between the antagonistic pair of *Gemeinschaft* ('community') and *Gesellschaft* ('society'), which he most famously developed in his book *Gemeinschaft and Gesellschaft: Abhandlung des Komunismus and des Sozialismus als empirischer Kulturformen* (1887), as well as in several smaller articles and expositions published in consecutive years.

In his book *Gemeinschaft and Gesellschaft* Tönnies argued that the socio-cultural development of 'modernity' (Tönnies actually never uses this term, as he clearly preferred to use the term *Neuzeit*, which seemed more 'neutral' to him) can be explained by the historically traceable differences in the ways and common features of human social life, which characterize pre-modern organic 'communities' and modern mechanistic 'societies' respectively. In short, therefore, Tönnies's distinction relies on a conception of 'modernity' (i.e. industrial 'societies', capitalism, democracy, etc.) as simply being something distinctly different from what is taken to precede it (i.e. pre-modern agricultural 'communities', bartering, feudalism, etc.) or to coexist with it outside Europe and in the Europeanized societies of North America.

In his study Tönnies primarily summarizes the relationship between the individuals who make up a *Gemeinschaft* and a *Gesellschaft* respectively, as well as their corresponding 'social' (and to some degrees at least also 'cultural') identities by stressing that they can either be grasped as 'organic' and 'real', which he regards as the quintessential 'essence' of *Gemeinschaft*, or they can be grasped as an 'ideational' and 'mechanical' construct, which Tönnies regards as the quintessential 'essence' of *Gesellschaft*. Consequently Tönnies

refers to *Gesellschaft* as the realm of the 'public sphere' or *Öffentlichkeit*, and in distinction argues that one finds oneself in the realm of *Gemeinschaft* from the beginning of one's life onwards, and that one is, therefore, also bound to this realm with all possible consequences – negative or positive. Yet in contrast one enters the realm of *Gesellschaft*, as if one entered 'unknown territories' or, as Tönnies calls it, *die Fremde*. *Gemeinschaft*, therefore, represents a 'lasting' and 'authentic' form of 'social life' (*Zusammenleben*), while *Gesellschaft* only represents a 'passing' and 'superficially structured' form of 'social life'. In consequence, Tönnies defines *Gemeinschaft* as a 'living organism', while he defines *Gesellschaft* as a 'mechanical aggregate and inorganic artefact'.

In the social realm of *Gemeinschaft*, people are, therefore, 'essentially connected' (*wesentlich verbunden*) with each other, while they are 'essentially separated' (*wesentlich getrennt*) from each other in the social realm of *Gesellschaft*. The result of this is, that while people are 'essentially connected' with each other in the social realm of *Gemeinschaft*, despite what might separate them individually, they are 'essentially separated' from each other in the social realm of *Gesellschaft*, despite what might connect them individually.

This decisive difference in the relationship between the individuals who make up a 'community' and a 'society' respectively, as well as their different corresponding social identities, are also reflected in the two forms of 'will'. Tönnies associates with the terms *Gemeinschaft* and *Gesellschaft* respectively. Tönnies argues that on a 'psychological level' the antagonistic pair of *Gemeinschaft* and *Gesellschaft* coincides with the chasm between what he calls *Wesenwille* and *Kürwille*, where *Wesenwille* is the form of 'will' characteristic of 'community', and where *Kürwille* is the form of 'will' characteristic of 'society'. The theory of 'community', therefore, asserts a total and organic 'unity' of collective communal 'wills', while the theory of 'society' asserts a total and inorganic (or even mechanistic) 'separation' of individual 'wills'. In his book *Philosophische Terminologie in psychologisch-soziologischer Ansicht*, first published in 1906, Tonnies explains the nature of the two different forms of will as 'natural' on the one hand, and as 'artificial' on the other: 'We refer to a form of will as "natural", if it mainly consists of emotions (*Gefühle*), while we refer to a form of will as "artificial", if it mainly consists of thoughts (*Gedanken*).'

Wesenwille is consequently understood as a real and natural unity of emotions, drives and desires that influence the thoughts and actions of the individuals who comprise a *Gemeinschaft* (*qualitatively* their actions are, therefore, characterized by virtue, honesty, kindness and loyalty). *Wesenwille* is thus best described as a 'unity of life'. Consequently *Wesenwille* is the psychological equivalent of the human body or the principle of the 'unity of life', particularly if this principle is thought of as a vital part of *that* form of reality which involves the process of thinking, as Tönnies argues. As a result, *Wesenwille* clearly involves this process of thinking for Tönnies, and it also means that the strong desire to *will* one's own *Ursprung* or 'origin' determines the social identities of the individuals who make up a 'community'. It is a vital part of their social identities to *will* this origin, and to be aware of and know this origin at the same time. In clear contrast to the animal (and plant) world, the continued preservation of mankind, therefore, clearly depends on knowledge, but as far as Tönnies is concerned this knowledge is mainly related to the knowledge and awareness of one's own *Ursprung* or 'origin'.

Kürwille, however, is defined as an artificial construct of the process of thinking, which is originally conditioned by the communal features of *Wesenwille*, but is mainly shaped by an egoistic element of 'striving' or *Bestreben* as well as by an egoistic element of 'cunning' or *Berechnung*, which outweigh the communal and altruistic features of the original condition. *Kürwille* is thus best defined as an artificial construct of the process of thinking as such, which only gains an independent reality with reference and relation to its *originator* or the subject of thought, even if this independent reality can also be both realized and acknowledged by other subjects as well. In consequence *Kürwille*, therefore, essentially means that a definite degree of *Willkür* (Tönnies actually used this term to describe the form of 'will' characteristic of society until the third edition of his book when he changed it to *Kürwille*) or a 'will at random', i.e. an 'arbitrary will', determines the social identities of the individuals who make up a 'society', which thus gives rise to a meaningless 'uniformity of life'. Thus *Kürwille* results from the abstraction of everything real, concrete and original, and constantly looks for their transformation into the meaningless 'uniformity of life', which basically consists of everything that has become similar and is, therefore, no longer individually differentiable.

Tönnies's book and the various perspectives it offered gained a considerable influence on mainstream sociology. Even though the convinced social democrat Tönnies just wanted to define fundamental sociological categories and explicitly warned of 'false interpretations and seemingly clever attempts at their concrete utilisation' his critical analysis of *Gesellschaft* and his seemingly implicit preference for and appraisal of *Gemeinschaft* gained a strong ideological momentum in openly nationalist movements in Germany, which were keen to show the dangers of modern 'society' and wanted to re-establish the values inherent in and associated with the concept of 'community'. Against his own will, Tonnies's concept of *Gemeinschaft* was misinterpreted by the national socialist ideologues, who applied a völkisch reading to it and coined the dangerous phrase of a *Volksgemeinschaft*. How mistaken, yet fateful this interpretation actually was, is well known, but many of the ambiguities of Tönnies's book are at least in part due to the fundamental flaws inherent in oversimplifying binary antitheses like *Gemeinschaft* and *Gesellschaft*. Banned from teaching and stripped of his state pension by the National Socialist government, Tönnies died increasingly isolated and impoverished on 9 April 1936 in Kiel.

Further reading

Mitzman, Arthur (1973) *Sociology and Estrangement: Three Sociologists in Imperial Germany*, New York: Knopf.

A 24-volume German-language edition of the complete works of Ferdinand Tönnies is currently being prepared by the German publisher *de Gruyter* (4 volumes of which have been published already by the end of 2002).

The most commonly referred to editions of his main book *Gemeinschaft und Gesellschaft* are: Ferdinand Tönnies: *Community and Association* (London: Routledge, 1974). And: Ferdinand Tönnies: *Gemeinschaft und Gesellschaft* (Darmstadt: Wissenschaftliche Buchgesellschaft, 1991).

FRANZ SOLMS-LAUBACH

TREITSCHKE, HEINRICH VON (1834–96)

Heinrich von Treitschke, German nationalist historian, journalist and politician, was born in Dresden. He was appointed Professor of Government at Freiburg University in 1863, and Professor of History at Kiel (1866), then at Heidelberg (1867) and Berlin (1874), where he was successor to LEOPOLD VON RANKE (a chair turned down by BURCKHARDT). He was a member of the Reichstag for the National Liberal Party from 1871 and 1879, and then as an independent until 1884. From 1866 to 1889 he was editor of the *Preussische Jahrbücher*, which he used as a platform for his political polemics. In 1886 he became official historian of Prussia, and in 1895 he became editor of the *Historische Zeitschrift*.

Treitschke was one of the most influential historians of his time, but is remembered as much for his stridently nationalistic political views and his anti-Semitic prejudices – including the slogan 'the Jews are our misfortune' – as for his historical writing. Although his earlier work, particularly his *Habilitationsschrift* of 1858, anticipated some of his later positions, he also wrote about constitutional history in a conventionally liberal mode, and even expressed admiration for British parliamentary institutions. His major work was an unfinished history of Germany in the nineteenth century, covering the period up to the 1848 revolutions in five volumes. It was an uncomplicated, triumphalist account that reflected his admiration for Prussia – although he was a Saxon – and his satisfaction at the outcome of German history as he understood it: the crowning achievement that was the second Reich. Treitschke was a popular success. His lectures were popular with students in Berlin, and he exercised enormous influence on the elite of the next generation. His *History of Germany* was famously to be found in the homes of most educated Germans, and did much to shape the German middle classes' understanding of their recent history. Treitschke's popular appeal rested to a large extent on the rhetorical nature of his exposition, particularly in his lectures, which were characterized by polemics against the enemies of the Reich, and apt to be punctuated by intemperate slogans. (He is reported to have called out on one occasion 'mulattos are inferior'.) He was dismissive of the new approaches to historical methodology based on the close critical examination of sources, and organized his *History of Germany* around biographies, arguing that history is made by men. Treitschke's reputation has been dominated by his racist nationalism, and nothing locates him more accurately than the public rebuke delivered in 1880 by Theodor Mommsen (with the support of many others) in response to his assertion of the previous year that Jews were responsible for the ills of modernity.

Further reading

Davis, Henry William Carless (1914) *The Political Thought of Heinrich von Treitschke*, London: Constable.
Dorpalen, Andreas (1957) *Heinrich von Treitschke*, New Haven: Yale University Press.

SEE ALSO: historiography and the idea of progress

TIM KIRK

TUCKER, BENJAMIN R. (1854–1939)

Benjamin R[icketson] Tucker, who was born into a Quaker family in Massachusetts, was the foremost US anarchist thinker and publicist before EMMA GOLDMAN (1869–1940). He rejected religion at age 12, refused to attend Harvard at age 16 and dropped out of the Massachusetts Institute of Technology after a few years. He worked as a tour manager for Victoria Woodhull (1838–1927) and became, while still a teenager, one of her many lovers.

Tucker was converted to anarchism after a meeting in 1872 with Josiah Warren (1798–1874), author of *Equitable Commerce* (1852). He then read the works of PIERRE-JOSEPH PROUDHON (1809–65), and translated some of them into English, and MAX STIRNER (1806–50).

Tucker published *The Radical Review* (four issues from May 1877 to February 1878) and, his most important contribution, *Liberty* (1881–1908), and a compilation of his writings, mostly drawn from *Liberty*, was published as *Instead of a Book* (1893). Probably his best-known feat as an editor was asking GEORGE BERNARD SHAW (1856–1950) to write a critique of *Degeneration* (1892–93) by Max Nordau (1849–1923), devoting an entire issue of *Liberty* to it, and then mailing free copies to editors of journals and newspapers all over the USA. He was also instrumental in distributing *Leaves of Grass* by Walt Whitman (1819–92) when it was banned from the mails. Tucker openly sold the book and informed the Government that he was doing so. Others followed his lead, and Whitman spoke of Tucker with gratitude for the rest of his life.

Tucker called his position 'scientific anarchism' and described himself as an individualist anarchism, following Warren. For Tucker the state was based on force and fraud, and was the cause of human exploitation. As with most anarchists, Tucker made a clear distinction between society, which was natural and based on human social needs and desires, and the state, which supports the privileged.

Without the state people are capable of adjusting their claims equitably among themselves. The state imposed solutions for the benefit of some people and at the cost of others. Tucker condemned both the capitalist state, which benefited the rich, and all forms of state socialism, which he contended would always end up restricting human freedom.

In 1908, the building housing *Liberty* burned down and ended Tucker's publishing business. After this tragedy, Tucker generally withdrew from political activity, and he moved his family to France, where he lived until his death. While in France, he wrote a few articles on specific issues for US newspapers but mostly simply lived quietly in Le Vésinet and later, after spending the war years in England, in Nice, and when he could no longer afford French taxes, in Monaco.

Further reading

Coughlin, M.E., Hamilton, C.H. and Sullivan, M.A. (eds) (1986) *Benjamin R. Tucker and the Champions of Liberty: A Centenary Anthology*, St Paul, MN: Michael E. Coughlin and Mark Sullivan.

Tucker, B.R. (1881–1908), *Liberty (not the Daughter but the Mother of Order)*, Boston, MA: B.R. Tucker.

—— (1893) *Instead of a Book by a Man too Busy to Write One. A Fragmentary Exposition of Philosophical Anarchism*, New York: B.R. Tucker.

LYMAN TOWER SARGENT

U

UTOPIANISM

'Utopianism' can be construed in a narrow sense, to entail the imagining, often in fictional form, of ideal societies inspired by the tradition founded by Thomas More's *Utopia* (1516), which described a country containing much greater social order and equality, largely underpinned by community of goods; or in the wider sense of a desire for fundamental social improvement, and the creation of a society markedly better for the majority (without necessarily being perfect) than whatever society serves as a frame of reference. In addition, the broader definition of 'utopianism' encompasses descriptions of negative or 'anti-utopias' or 'dystopias', some of which appear in satirical form. In terms of their response to two major problems, that of evolution or historical change, and that of needs or wants, most utopias fall broadly into two categories: (1) they are either static or dynamic utopias, in other words they recognize a limitation of resources and respond by simplifying needs ascetically, and often appeal to a past 'golden age' as their ideal; or, by contrast, they describe a regime of plenty, with the virtually unlimited satisfaction of wants, and seek the future creation of an ideal society; and (2) they are either hierarchical or egalitarian. Pre-modern utopias tend to be both static and hierarchical, and aiming to recapture the idealized past; modern utopias tend to be dynamic and egalitarian, and to be set in an improved future. (One of the first to do so is Louis-Sebastien Mercier's *L'An 2440*, 1771). There are utopian *elements*, too numerous to indicate here, in mainstream nineteenth-century European liberalism and conservatism, and particularly in idealized notions of the monarchy, of empire, or of particularly glorious epochs in national histories, and

in images of classical antiquity, including the Athenian *polis*, Sparta, and the Roman Republic and Empire. Romanticism in art and literature, too, from Rousseau to Gauguin and beyond, tended to idealize the primitive while lambasting the fundamental degeneracy of civilization.

The French Revolution and its aftermath

The crucial moment of transformation in this trend is the period 1790–1830, defined by the coincidence of the French and Industrial revolutions. Many eighteenth-century utopias had been linked to voyages of exploration, and the discovery of ideally virtuous, and usually more primitive, societies, and are linked to the notion of the 'noble savage'. Some utopian works at the end of this period of this development – for instance Condorcet's *Sketch for a Historical Picture of the Progress of the Human Mind* (1794) include the perfection of the sciences as an important quality in the future egalitarian society; others, like WILLIAM GODWIN's *Enquiry concerning Political Justice* (1793) or Thomas Northmore's *Memoirs of Planetes; or, a Sketch of the Laws and Manners of Makar* (1795), opt for a more Spartan, Stoic or Rousseauist self-sufficiency and declaim against luxury in diet, dress and accommodation as effeminate and corrupting. Most utopias of the revolutionary period tend therefore to be inspired by republicanism, and thus to emphasize the need for civic virtue, political participation and a citizens' militia, and to be anti-commercial and, in keeping with a tradition of the association of virtue with simplicity, the state of nature or 'natural society', even primitivist. A few are communistical, such as John Lithgow's *Equality. A Political Romance* (1802), one of the first US utopias, in which all property is held in common, four hours of labour suffice and money is described as the root of all evil. Some utopias of the period also describe considerable economic intervention and regulation, such as William Hodgson's *The Commonwealth of Reason* (1795), in which committees regulate agriculture, trade and food supplies, and national manufactories offer employment. This primitivist strain, however, is already in retreat in the 1790s: Godwin in later editions of *Political Justice* concedes that 'luxury' is vicious when it entails an additional burden of labour on others, but harmless when it merely means procuring goods beyond necessaries. The most famous communistical proposal in France, GRACCHUS BABEUF's 'Manifesto of the Equals' (*c*.1796), was similarly inspired by the notion of a return to nature, here inspired by Morelly's communistical *Code de la nature* (1755).

Socialism and utopia

Most nineteenth-century utopianism is of the egalitarian and socialistic type, but rejects a more primitive form of agrarian republicanism in favour of an ideal of expanding needs that can be satisfied with some assistance from technology. By the late nineteenth century a rural ideal tends to give way to an urban image, though egalitarianism, usually guaranteed by community of property, remains the central theme throughout. In the USA, particularly, a tradition of radical Protestant communalism continues throughout this period, with groups of Shakers, Rappites, Moravians, the Separatists of Zoar, the True Inspirationists of Amana, Mormons and others being succeeded by Fourierist colonies encouraged by Albert Brisbane and Horace Greeley in particular, experiments like Brook Farm, and the more long-lived community founded by JOHN HUMPHREY NOYES at Oneida, New York, in 1847. Though most disappeared or became secularized by 1900, the longevity of many of these religious communities indicated for many commentators, notably Noyes in his *History of American Socialisms* (1870), that no community not founded on religion could long survive. (Many European socialists, however, either opposed religion or attempted to build upon a secularized version of Christianity like COMTE's Positivism.) Nonetheless communitarianism played a vibrant role in the expansion of the frontier westwards, and in experimentation in lifestyle that departed markedly from the US norm, whether because of

their liberal attitudes respecting race, for instance in Frances Wright's Nashoba community (1825–8); sexuality and marriage (amongst the Mormons, or at Oneida); authority (in Josiah Warren's anarchical experiments); or, more commonly, forms of property ownership and management.

The leading socialist writers of the period were ROBERT OWEN, who was active in both Britain and the USA; CHARLES FOURIER and his followers; the followers of HENRI DE SAINT-SIMON, and ETIENNE CABET; in Germany, Moses Hess, Wilhelm Weitling and later Karl Marx (see MARX AND MARXISM), Friedrich Engels and their disciples. Robert Owen (1771–1858) achieved fame as a cotton-spinner at New Lanark near Glasgow, but became severely critical of the effects of industrialization on the working classes, and from 1817 promoted instead co-operative communities of some 2,000 persons working and living in common as the model to be achieved. The Owenite movement, which reached its peak between 1837–45, produced some literary utopias, notably John Minter Morgan's *Hampden in the Nineteenth Century* (1834) and John Francis Bray's *A Voyage from Utopia*, (1842; first printed in 1957), but concentrated on communitarian planning, and produced an important literature, notably by William Thompson and John Gray, analysing the workings and necessary failings of the capitalist system. Owen's communitarian plan was first tested on a large scale at New Harmony, Indiana, which experiment lasted some five years, and then at Harmony or Queenwood, Hampshire, of a similar duration. Besides the notion of a model community with property shared in common, the utopian components in Owen's thought include an opposition to specialization or a narrow division of labour, the hope of the development of substantially more benevolence, selflessness or community spirit in the future, the abolition of economic competition and the expectation that a successful demonstration of his principles would lead competitive individualist capitalism to be abandoned in favour of his scheme. In his ultimate vision of social organization, described in *The New Moral World* (1836–44), Owen proposed the reorganization of society according to age groups, with government of communities devolving upon the group aged between 30 and 40. At its peak the Owenite movement attracted as many as 10,000 adherents to weekly lectures at some fifty local branches called 'Halls of Science'.

The son of a Besançon merchant, Charles Fourier (1772–1837) was like Owen a critic of the anarchy and greed promoted by the existing system of commerce, and keen to demonstrate the savings that shared activities such as cooking would achieve in his ideal community, the Phalanx. Unlike Owen, he did not seek communism, but rather a division of goods between capital (four-twelfths), labour (five-twelfths) and talent (three-twelfths). Agreeing with Owen that stultifying and repetitive labour was a key problem in modern society, Fourier extended the idea of rotation of task much further, arguing that individuals might have as many as eight jobs per day, with manufacturing occupying no more than a quarter of the labouring day, and appealing to the idea that labour should be as 'free' and 'attractive' as possible. Fourier's theory of 'passionate attraction', first outlined in the *Theory of the Four Movements* (1808), also described the ideal future in terms of an unleashing of repressed desires, and the governance of life through the maximum gratification of the passions rather than the more traditional approach of their restriction by reason. Fourier proposed, accordingly, the guarantee of a 'sexual minimum' in the Phalanx akin to a minimum wage, and has often been linked to FREUD. As with Owen, 'harmony' is a crucial Fourierist theme. Fourierist communities were established in France (Godin's Familistère, founded in 1859, being the best-known example), Britain and the USA. A leading interpreter of these ideas in France was VICTOR CONSIDÉRANT.

The followers of the French nobleman Henri de Saint-Simon (1760–1825), who turned his ideas on modern industry in a socialist direction, included Olinde Rodrigues, BARTHÉLEMY-PROSPER ENFANTIN, Gustave d'Eichthal, Michel Chevalier, Saint-Armand Bazard, and Philippe Buchez. Saint-Simon himself had engaged in an extensive analysis of the emergence and significance of industrial society, in which he concluded that the 'industrialist' (labourers, scientists and managers) should assume the management of society, which would be reorganized meritocratically, with scientific power supplanting earlier forms of religious and spiritual authority. The management of the industrial system would thereafter replace 'politics', which were based upon class conflict, while European nationalism would give way to a European Parliament. Like Owen, the Saint-Simonians cast their scheme in the form of a 'new

religion' designed to provide a spiritual basis for the scientific understanding of nature that underpinned the new industrial order.

The revolutions of 1848 popularized a variety of other French socialist schemes, notably LOUIS BLANC's proposals for the organization of labour. The most impressive socialist vision of the 1840s to be cast in utopian form, however, was Etienne Cabet's *Voyage en Icarie* (1840), which portrays an ideal nation symmetrically organized into one hundred provinces, each subdivided into ten communes of one town, eight villages and numerous farms. The capital, Icaria, is similarly symmetrically organized, with straight streets separated by squares. Every aspect of public life is carefully planned, all property is owned in common and utilized with the view of promoting equality. Education is universal, political organization democratic, with universal suffrage. Religion is a simple system of morals without ceremonies. The inhabitants of each street dine communally once a day, and, though there is some variety, all dress alike in garments that are chiefly elastic, and thus designed to fit all sizes. Distribution is according to the principle 'from each according to their needs, to each according to their ability'. Production is centralized in large factories, and work is organized with military discipline, though harsh labour has been eliminated by the invention of useful machinery. Houses are as similar as possible, furniture being placed in the same location, and its type fixed by decree. Social mores are similarly routinized; there is no adultery or prostitution. The production of works of art and literature is overseen by a censor, harmful past works having been destroyed, and there is apparently little scope for individuality. Cabet did however actually attempt to implement the Icarian programme, establishing a community of 500 at Nauvoo, Illinois, in 1848, which eventually relocated to Icaria Speranza, California, where it finally disintegrated in 1898.

The early German socialists attracted a much smaller following. Amongst them may be mentioned, however, Moses Hess (1812–75), who converted Friedrich Engels to communism; Wilhelm Weitling (1808–71), author of *Guarantees of Harmony and Freedom* (1842) and others work, who later attempted a US experiment at Communia (1847–56); and the technological utopian and inventor John Adolphus Etzler.

The German socialists Karl Marx (1818–83) and Friedrich Engels (1820–95) denied that their socialism was 'utopian', and proclaimed instead its 'scientific' status, as based on actual historical development, and upon the necessity of proletarian class struggle to overthrow the existing system. Nonetheless there are clear utopian elements in Marx and Engels's writings, notably in their Fourierist comments about rotation of task in the 'German Ideology' (1845–6), which emphasize a romantic ideal of creativity as essential to the definition of humanity; in the universalization of communal property following the revolution, as described in *The Communist Manifesto* (1848); in the evident expectation of a substantial improvement in human behaviour in the post-revolutionary society, with a corresponding decline in coercive institutions like the police and ultimate 'withering away' of the state; and in the presumption of the viability of completely centralized management of the economy. Given the assumption that communism was practicable on a national, as opposed to a merely communal, level, such assumptions might even be seen as more 'utopian' than those of Marx and Engels's socialist predecessors.

Middle and late nineteenth-century utopianism

LIBERALISM, CONSERVATISM AND UTOPIANISM

Though Adam Smith had acknowledged the unlikelihood of a universal system of 'natural liberty' or freedom of trade ever being achieved, which cast his own project in a utopian light, most nineteenth-century liberals saw themselves as explicitly anti-utopian, in the sense of relying on a system of private property to promote wealth, and upon gradual social and political reforms to create a liberal and more democratic society. One exception, however, was JOHN STUART MILL, who in his *Principles of Political Economy* (1848) suggested that a 'stationary state' might one day be reached in which the growth of population and accumulation of capital and expansion of production and consumption might be relinquished in favour of an emphasis on the qualitative, cultural, moral and intellectual improvement of social life. Some forms of late nineteenth-century liberalism, notably New Liberalism in Britain, assumed a much more collectivist approach to social issues, and writers like JOHN HOBSON accordingly moved much closer to contemporary socialism. Liberal and radical reformers also occasionally adopted the utopian genre to popularize their schemes: Henry Forest's

A Dream of Reform (1848), for instance, imagines a reduction of the working day and reform of the factory system, the election of the monarch and construction of healthy, well-organized cities, without being socialist. Conservatives occasionally also adopt the genre, though mostly satirically, as does BENJAMIN DISRAELI in *The Voyage of Captain Popanilla* (1827), an attack on Whiggism and utilitarianism. Some conservative (but also some radical) thought also assumes a utopian direction in its portrayal of an idealized past, notably in the medievalism, in Britain, of ROBERT SOUTHEY, THOMAS CARLYLE and JOHN RUSKIN, and the ideal of an essentially rural, pre-commercial 'Merrie England'. Pastoral themes also predominate in the thought of RALPH WALDO EMERSON, in HENRY DAVID THOREAU's *Walden* (1845), and in the Fourierist enthusiasms of the New England Transcendentalists in the USA, while, at the popular level, and especially for would-be emigrants, the USA itself figures as a crucial symbol of utopia throughout the period, continuing an ideal evident from the sixteenth-century Spanish conquest.

UTOPIAN FICTION

Between 1870 and 1900 there was a sudden and widespread surge of interest in the utopian genre, the result both of substantial economic and social upheaval, and of the intellectual impact of Darwinism and socialism. Literary utopianism in the mid- and late nineteenth century assumed a wide variety of forms. Besides the leading works inspired by the socialist movements in the USA, Britain, France, Germany and elsewhere, the advent of Darwinism was a crucial source of utopian inspiration from the 1870s onwards. Amongst the chief fictional utopias published in English in this period is Samuel Butler's *Erewhon, or Over the Range* (1872), which uses the device of a discovery of an unknown society to explore a *mélange* of ideas, including hostility to technology, Darwinian approaches to the regulation of population and advancement of science, to which Butler was largely hostile, cast principally in dystopian form, and as a satire of Victorian manners. This was followed by a sequel, *Erewhon Revisited* (1901), which focuses on the degeneration of religious belief into superstition. In France, works like Samuel Berthoud's *L'Homme depuis Cinq Mille Ans* (1865) popularized scientific optimism, while socialist utopias included Alain Le Drimeur's *La Cité future* (1890) and Emile Zola's *Travail* (1901).

One of the most popular works published in the period was Edward Bulwer-Lytton's *The Coming Race* (1871), which explores a society of highly evolved subterranean beings who possess a great natural power called 'vril'. Their society is largely decentralized and family-centred. More a satire on evolutionary thinking, the novel is not meant to function as a positive utopian ideal suitable for imitation, but like Swift's *Gulliver's Travels* is chiefly satirical. Many lesser-known late nineteenth-century texts do provide such an image, however. Amongst these can be mentioned W.H. Hudson's *A Crystal Age* (1887), which applauds the virtues of simplicity; *Etymonia* (1875), which describes a communal society in which labour and exchange are strictly regulated; *In the Future: A Sketch in Ten Chapters* (1875), which accounts for the abolition of poverty; E.J. Davis's *Pyrna: A Commune; or, Under the Ice* (1875), which discusses a community founded on the principle of brotherly love and sexual equality where 'unhealthy' procreation has been eliminated; and Joseph Carne-Ross's *Quintura. Its Singular People and Remarkable Customs* (1886), another egalitarian utopia. From the 1880s onwards anti-utopian satires also become increasingly common; those of note include *James Ingleton. The History of a Social State A.D. 2000* (1893), in which individualism has first been abolished by a collectivist revolution, then restored under a monarchy. Two themes thus become more prominent in literary utopias from 1880–1900: the growing role of science and technology, and its uses both in prolonging life, eliminating waste and disease, and, by eugenic techniques, improving the human race; and the emergence of revolutionary socialism as a significant challenge to the established order, which popularized utopian ideas on a much wider scale than previously.

The most prolific and influential author of utopian works of the period was H.G. WELLS (1866–1946), who produced in quick succession *The Time Machine* (1895), *The Island of Doctor Moreau* (1896), *The Invisible Man* (1897), *When the Sleeper Awakes* (1899) and *The First Men in the Moon* (1901). *Anticipations of the Reaction of Mechanical and Scientific Progress upon Human Life* (1902) was a non-fictional excursus into future forecasting in which Wells predicted the further growth of the middle classes, a decline in family size, the extension of 'machine' politics in democratic regimes, the gradual emergence of a world state and the use of eugenic ideals to discriminate against the 'people of the abyss'. The theme that the purpose of life was the deliberate evolutionary creation of higher types, possessed of a passion for order and efficiency, is continued in Wells's most famous, and also last, fictionalized model society, *A Modern Utopia* (1905). This describes a collectivist society that provides universal welfare, though population expansion is strictly regulated. Political dominance, and the task of social improvement, are entrusted to the samurai class, loosely modelled on Plato's Guardians, though they are not an entirely hereditary caste.

LATER NINETEENTH-CENTURY SOCIALISM

The most important later British socialist writer explicitly to adopt the utopian form was WILLIAM MORRIS (1834–96), whose *News from Nowhere* (1890) describes a post-revolutionary, twentieth-century London reduced in size and population, cleansed of pollution and heavy industry, and united by a system of voluntary exchange and rotation of work. There is no coercive or centralized state apparatus, but a consummate dedication to artistic creativity, individual variation in taste and social equality. Medieval styles prevail, crime is greatly reduced and politics, conducted almost entirely at the local level, includes a substantial toleration of minority opinion. This is, to an important degree, an aesthetically based utopia, much influenced by the writings of John Ruskin (and notably the famous discussion of the role of the worker in the process of production in the chapter entitled 'The Nature of Gothic' in *The Stones of Venice*). This linkage of art to socialism was supported by writers like Oscar Wilde in 'The Soul of Man under Socialism' (1891). Morris's chief target is the American EDWARD BELLAMY (1850–98), whose *Looking Backward 2000–1887* (1889) instigated widespread interest in socialism in North America, Europe and elsewhere, and spawned a movement known as 'Nationalism'. Bellamy envisaged a highly structured, centralized, industrialized society in which a comprehensive welfare system, universally-mandated labour and relatively equal distribution ensure a high standard of living. Crime has virtually disappeared, lawyers and juries are no longer necessary, and education is universal. Women play a substantial (though not equal) role in industrial and social organization, and promote the improvement of the species by mating with the most superior men. A sequel was published entitled *Equality* (1897), which attempts to respond to issues raised by the public reception of *Looking Backward*.

Here there is greater equality between the sexes, but not much between different races. *Looking Backward* spawned an astonishing interest in the utopian genre in the USA in particular. Dozens of US imitations appeared, (and over sixty world-wide) like Bradford Peck's *The World a Department Store* (1900) and W.D. Howells's *A Traveller from Altruria* (1894), as well as anti-Bellamy dystopias, while writers such as A.R. WALLACE, the British evolutionist and land nationalisation advocate, and Ebenezer Howard, founder of the British Garden City movement, acknowledged a debt to Bellamy. In Russia alone there were seven translations before 1917, and Maxim Gorky declared the book was widely read by Russian youth; in 1889 it was banned from public libraries as a result. Less influential but also notable in this period are Theodor Hertzka's *Freeland* (1890) and Laurence Gronlund's *The Co-operative Commonwealth* (1886).

Following Marx and Engels's dictum that the communist future could not be described in detail, but must unfold historically, the large late nineteenth-century Social Democratic movement in Germany inspired few literary utopias. An exception was the immensely popular *Woman under Socialism* (1883) by the Social Democratic leader Auguste Bebel, which gave a detailed image of future social organization, including the minutiae of everyday life, and doubtless inspired John Petzler's *Life in Utopia* (1890). Eugene Richter's *Picture of a Socialistic Future* (1893) was a bestselling liberal satire on the notion of a ubiquitous, all-controlling state that would eventually eliminate all forms of liberal freedom. But a reluctance to embrace the utopian genre was also shared by moderate socialist reformers, such as the Fabian SIDNEY WEBB, who emphasized that socialism was not a utopia, but a concrete principle of social organization.

Conclusion

At the turn of the twentieth century utopianism was more popular than ever before. Driven by the astonishing inventions and discoveries of the past half-century, it was easy to imagine a world steadily and indefinitely improved by science and technology, and human mastery expanding to include air and even space travel. But as utopia moved towards science fiction, it also acknowledged a gloomy *fin de siècle* malaise rooted in a post-Darwinian sense of degeneration and decline, and reflected both the hopes and threats of the growing socialist movement, which heralded a regime of universal peace, prosperity and social justice. This would merge into the scientific, moral and political pessimism of the most influential twentieth-century dystopias, by Zamiatin, Huxley and Orwell, which would, in turn, take up apocalyptic themes expressed by writers like Richard Jefferies (*After London*, 1885), in which an inversion of Baconian optimism respecting science and technology, or a political degradation into dictatorship of the socialist revolution (in Jack London's *The Iron Heel*, 1907, for instance), would illustrate the increasingly bleak face of utopianism.

Further reading

Armytage, W.H.G. (1960) *Heavens below. Utopian Experiments in England, 1560–1960*, London: Routledge Kegan Paul.

Claeys, Gregory (ed.) (1994) *Utopias of the British Enlightenment*, Cambridge: Cambridge University Press.

—— (ed.) (1997) *Modern British Utopias. c. 1700–1850*, 8 vols, London: Pickering & Chatto.

—— (ed.) (2005) *Late Victorian Utopias*, 6 vols, London: Pickering & Chatto.

Claeys, Gregory and Sargent, Lyman Tower (eds) (1999) *The Utopia Reader*, New York: New York University Press.

Geoghegan, Vincent (1987) *Utopianism and Marxism*, London: Methuen.

Goodwin, Barbara (1978) *Social Science and Utopia. Nineteenth Century Models of Social Harmony*, Atlantic Highlands, NJ: Humanities.

Goodwin, Barbara and Taylor, Keith (1983) *The Politics of Utopia*, New York: St Martin's Press.

Kumar, Krishan (1987) *Utopia and Anti-Utopia in Modern Times*, Oxford: Basil Blackwell.

Levitas, Ruth (1990) *The Concept of Utopia*, Syracuse, NY: Syracuse University Press.

Manuel, Frank and Fritzie (1979) *Utopian Thought in the Western World*, Cambridge, MA: Belknap.

SEE ALSO: anthropology and race; early socialism; Marx and Marxism

GREGORY CLAEYS

W

WALLACE, A.R. (1823–1913)

The co-discoverer, with CHARLES DARWIN, of the theory of natural selection, Wallace was born at Usk, Monmouthshire, on 8 January 1823. After articling with an elder brother as a land surveyor and architect, he decided to travel and to become a naturalist. *Travels on the Amazon and Rio Negro* was published in 1852, and some twenty-five books would follow on a wide range of subjects, including Darwinism, vaccination, the habitability of Mars and land nationalization. Early exposure to the writings of Paine and Owen weakened his religious faith and enhanced his sense of social justice. Eventually he would conclude that much of modern science, including geology, could not be reconciled with the Scriptures, and would condemn the uses made by religion to mask poverty and exploitation. Besides his work as a naturalist, which included *The Malay Archipelago* (1869), *Tropical Nature* (1878) and *Island Life* (1880), Wallace achieved fame following the publication of his essay, 'On the Law which has Regulated the Introduction of New Species', *Annals and Magazine of Natural History* (September 1855), which argued that every species emerged as a mutation from a previously existing species. He communicated these views to Charles Darwin, and their joint presentation of a paper at the Linnaean Society in 1858 acknowledged that both, jointly also under the influence of MALTHUS, had reached similar conclusions at the same time.

Wallace, however, was unwilling to accept that natural selection was applicable to humanity, contending that human reasoning, and the capacity for morality and tool-making, lifted mankind above the animals. Nor did he follow many post-Darwinians into a racial classification in which non-whites were condemned as savages or primitives incapable of civilization, his own experience in Borneo and Malaya having convinced him that native capabilities were approximately similar to those of Englishmen. By the 1860s, moreover, he had come to believe that the civilization being exported by Europeans bred only increased misery, poverty and social inequality, and he became an increasingly prominent critic of imperialism.

Like ROBERT OWEN, Wallace also embraced spiritualism, which he felt demonstrated that a superior and guiding intelligence was present in the world. Much of his enthusiasm for social reform from the 1880s was channelled into the cause of land nationalization. Becoming president of the Land Nationalization Society in 1882, he published an important defence of its aims, contending that ownership was never absolute, and was justified only when individuals actually occupied their land. Condemning the exclusion of the poor from common land by successive enclosures, Wallace became increasingly egalitarian, and argued for equality of opportunity for women. Under the impact of Edward Bellamy and Henry George, he converted to socialism in 1890, and proposed nationalization of the railways, a national health system, universal education, a co-operative system of production and the relinquishment of the empire and militarism. He died on 7 November 1913.

Further reading

Marchant, James (1916) *Alfred Russel Wallace: Letters and Reminiscences*, 2 vols, London: Cassell.
Wallace, Alfred Russel (1882) *Land Nationalization, its Necessity and its Aims*, London: Trubner & Co.
—— (1908 [1905]) *My Life. A Record of Events and Opinions*, 2nd edn, London: Chapman & Hall.
—— (1898) *The Wonderful Century. Its Successes and its Failures*, London: Swan Sonnenschein.

Raby, Peter (2001) *Alfred Russel Wallace. A Life*, London: Chatto & Windus.

GREGORY CLAEYS

WASHINGTON, BOOKER T. (1856–1915)

Booker T. Washington came to be the foremost political leader of the African American people in the late nineteenth century. He followed in the footsteps of such major figures as Henry Highland Garnet (1815–82) and Frederick Douglass (1818–95), former slaves who rose to prominence in the abolitionist movement prior to the Civil War (1861–5). Douglass dominated the political scene during Reconstruction (1865–77), agitating for civil rights for freed blacks and supporting suffrage for all US women (which occurred with the Nineteenth Amendment to the US Constitution in 1920; see FEMINISM AND THE FEMALE FRANCHISE MOVEMENT). Washington's political platform differed from Douglass's, which emerged from his abolitionism and called for immediate assimilation of African Americans into all walks of life. Washington conceded at points to racism and segregationism, the legal division of races; later Washington's popularity with whites would grow and black resistance to his accommodation of segregationism would increase.

Washington was born in the last decade of US slavery on a plantation in Franklin County, Virginia, where his mother, Jane, was the cook. He detailed his slave experiences, with the help of a ghost writer, in his autobiography, *Up from Slavery*, published in serial form in the popular magazine, *Outlook*, during 1900–1, subsequently publishing it later that year as a complete text. Following the conventions of the popular slave narrative, widely published in *ante bellum* USA in support of abolitionism, he begins his narrative with the traditional 'I was born', noting the location of his birth and revealing his uncertainty of the date of his birth and his parentage, though he alluded to the plantation rumours that named a prominent, local white man. He vividly described his years under slavery, detailing the meanness of the system of slavery and the want of adequate food, housing and clothing. Despite this revelation of oppression, Washington chose to characterize slavery as a 'school' for blacks, not to justify slavery, but to clarify to racist whites that slavery left a people prepared for freedom instead of the nation of potential loafers and criminals white southerners feared. *Up from Slavery* was designed as an argument for the political, social and economic future course of policy treating freed African Americans using Washington's individual life as an example.

The most important theme in Washington's narrative was the want of a formal education for himself and for other blacks. Longing to attend school even as a very young boy, Washington attended a school for blacks after his stepfather moved the family to Malden, West Virginia, following Emancipation. With his stepfather and brother, Washington worked in the salt mines, but was fortunate enough to attend a night school. In the fall of 1872, he left Malden to travel nearly 500 miles to attend the Hampton Institute, in Hampton, Virginia, the school for African Americans and Native Americans founded by General Samuel C. Armstrong (1839–93), a white philanthropist dedicated to the education of people of colour. Washington uses this lengthy portion of his narrative to appeal to potential white patrons in securing additional funding for Negro education.

Washington paid his way through college working full time as a janitor, graduating with honours in 1875, serving as faculty for the next five years. In 1881, the Alabama legislature granted Washington funding to begin his own school for African American technical education. On 4 July 1881, the Tuskegee Normal and Industrial Institute opened its doors. The deep success of the Tuskegee Institute added to Washington's power and renown, and added strength to his argument that to succeed, freed Blacks required technical skills rather than lofty education.

His rise as a national black leader is marked by a speech given at the Cotton States and International Exposition, which opened on 18 September 1895 in Atlanta, Georgia, seven months after the death of Douglass. This was a crucial political period: the death of Douglass; the failure of Reconstruction; 'Jim Crow' legislation legalized by Supreme Court cases such as *Plessy v. Ferguson* (1896) that established the notion of 'separate but equal' as the defining national philosophy of racial and social interactions and restriction; and a marked rise in the lynching of black men all foretold of a white backlash to any gains made by African Americans following the end of the Civil War. Washington's 'Atlanta Exposition Speech' is indicative of his conciliatory approach to southern racist ideology and northern economic interests while simultaneously promoting education and economic uplift for nearly 70 million African Americans. The phrase most closely associated with Washington's accommodationist ideology, which critics at the time and for the next 100 years would use to pinpoint his potential betrayal of his people, emerged from this oration. Washington clarified to his white audience that blacks were willing to accept that 'In all things that are purely social we can be as separate as the fingers, yet one as the hand in all things essential to mutual progress.' This speech was reproduced nationally and praised from then-president Grover Cleveland as well as the white sponsors of the Exposition and white philanthropists eager to finance Negro education.

Referred to as both the 'sage of Tuskegee' and as the 'Wizard of the Tuskegee Machine', Washington spent the next 20 years of his life working to achieve a balance between conflicting forces and discrepant ideas about the future of the race he purportedly led. In order to gain sufficient financial backing, Washington continued to promote the idea of individual uplift and self-help that he had come to use effectively at Tuskegee. Over time, more African Americans came to criticize his approach. Although initially W.E.B. DU BOIS (1868–1963) sent a letter of praise following the Atlanta Exposition and supported Washington's leadership, the two came to vie publicly and privately for political power and the unofficial position of leader of the black race, particularly over the key issue of segregation versus integration of the races. Ultimately, Washington came to recognize and support Du Bois's efforts at advocating integrationism.

Further reading

Baker, Houston A. Jr (2001) *Turning South Again: Re-Thinking Modernism: Re-Reading Booker T.*, Durham: Duke University Press.

Wallace, Maurice (2002) 'Constructing the Black Masculine: Frederick Douglass, Booker T. Washington, and the Sublimits of African American Autobiography' in Cathy Davidson and Jessamyn Hatcher (eds) *No More Separate Spheres! A Next Wave American Studies Reader*, Durham: Duke University Press.

Wintz, Cary D. (ed.) (1996) *African American Political Thought, 1890–1930: Washington, Du Bois, Garvey, and Randolph*, New York: M.E. Sharpe.

SEE ALSO: anthropology and race; anti-colonial movements and ideas

PAMELA RALSTON

WEBB, BEATRICE (1858–1943) AND SIDNEY (1859–1947)

Perhaps the most famous example of a married couple who were also 'intellectual partners', Sidney Webb and Beatrice Potter Webb made a significant contribution to both reformist socialism and British social historiography. Sidney's formal education (begun in London, Switzerland and Germany) culminated in an external (part-time) University of London degree in Law (1886); from 1878 to 1891, he was a civil servant. Beatrice was largely self-educated and, as a daughter of a prosperous businessman, she achieved financial independence through inheritance in 1892. Following their marriage (also in 1892), the Webbs supplemented this income with authorial earnings, and cultivated 'high society'. Beatrice is generally taken to have 'led' the partnership, but Sidney served as a Labour MP, peer (Baron Passfield) and Government Minister in the 1920s and 1930s, as well as producing a significant independent *œuvre*. Beatrice's early writings on poverty and her first book, *The Co-operative Movement in Britain* (1891), are also classics in their own right.

Sidney was already established as a political essayist prior to meeting Beatrice in 1890. Having concluded that the moral goals of Positivism were better expressed through limited collectivism, rather than the original Comtean utopia, he became a leading member of the Fabian Society (at the invitation of GEORGE BERNARD SHAW), writing the most successful early Fabian tract, *Facts for Socialists* (1887). Sidney led the Fabian faction known as 'permeators', who sought to convert the Liberal Party (and other non-socialists) to collectivist policies on 'practical grounds', and worked in uneasy tension with 'labourists' (e.g. Hubert Bland) who favoured closer links between the Society and the organized labour movement. 'Permeation' relied upon a version of 'Zeitgeist' theory, but the subsequent failure of the Webbs' campaign to reform the Poor Law (1909–13) led them to reassess the strength of established capitalist interests and to look more sympathetically on the 'sectionalism' of trade unions. They joined the Labour Party in 1914.

The thoroughness of the empirical investigations found in works such as *The History of Trade Unionism* (1894), *Industrial Democracy* (1897) and *English Local Government* (eleven volumes, 1906–29) is well known, but Webbian history also exhibited a sophisticated concern with sociological functions, originally derived from a common knowledge of the synthetic philosophy of SPENCER. *English Local Government* was connected with the political project of Fabian socialism (which sought to devolve welfare functions to municipalities wherever possible) and Sidney's service as a London County Councillor (1892–1910), where his interest in secondary and technical education indicated a concern for 'culture', as part of 'the good life', which was sometimes lost on his critics. After 1914, the Webbs continued to influence socialist debate through works such as their 'corporatist utopia', *A Constitution for the Socialist Commonwealth of Great Britain* (1920), and the classic text of 'fellow-travelling': *Soviet Communism* (1935).

Further reading

Cole, M. (ed.) (1949) *The Webbs and Their Work*, London: Frederick Muller.
Harrison, R. (1999) *The Life and Times of Sidney and Beatrice Webb, 1858–1905, The Formative Years*, Basingstoke: Macmillan.

SEE ALSO: intellectuals, elites and meritocracy; Marx and Marxism; social theory and sociology in the nineteenth century; theories of the state and society: the science of politics

CLIVE E. HILL

WEBER, MAX (1864–1920)

Traditionally, Weber's writings have been divided into two: his sociological writings and his political writings. The former are supposedly concerned with the purely formal procedure of constructing broad typologies of legitimacy, administration and authority, while the latter ostensibly deal more expressly with coercion, conflict, power and violence in particular societies, and in concrete, historical situations. In fact, the two themes are inseparable and run through all of Weber's disparate and remarkably wide-ranging works.

From the famous essay on *The Protestant Ethic and the Spirit of Capitalism* to the writings on the world's religions, to the lectures on *Politics as a Vocation* and *Science as a Vocation* to the attempts in his *magnum opus*, *Economy and Society* (*Wirtschaft und Gesellschaft*) to identify different types of authority, Weber's works are the working-through of one fundamental problem: how to deal with the problem of violence and legitimate domination in a modern world where traditional forms of authority have lost their way.

In this massive project of historically understanding the systematic rationalization and regulation of modern life, Weber took his lead from Karl Marx (see MARX AND MARXISM) and FRIEDRICH NIETZSCHE, among others (SØREN KIERKEGAARD, for example). As Weber's wife Marianne famously reported her husband as saying, one can judge 'the honesty of a contemporary scholar' by his intellectual 'posture towards Nietzsche and Marx'. Weber's project, in other words, took up Nietzsche's claim that God was dead and Marx's claim that economic laws conditioned the structures of power. Where Weber was long regarded, by those coming from the Parsonian school of sociology (the basically optimistic functionalist school of social theory that developed in the USA in the 1950s under the lead of Talcott Parsons), as a theorist of legitimacy and stability, or as a theorist of the origins of capitalism, he is now more likely to be seen as the sociological counterpart to Nietzsche. Indeed, his writings are characterized far more by melancholy than a belief in progress, and it is hard to escape the conclusion that Weber's theories of legitimacy and stability rest ultimately on nothing more than the threat of violence. Naked power, in other words, is the basis of 'legitimacy' in secular modernity. When combined with Weber's famous notion of the 'iron cage' (*Gehäuse der Hörigkeit*), his definition of the state as 'a human community that (successfully) claims the *monopoly of the legitimate use of physical force* within a given territory', and his claim that modernity meant the 'disenchantment of the world' (*Entzauberung der Welt*) this is a bleak picture indeed. Nevertheless, Weber set out to analyse the possibilities of ethical life under these conditions of rationalization.

How did Weber arrive at such a bleak pass? The answer lies in the fact that his methodology was by no means the synchronic one often associated with mid-twentieth-century sociology, but was strictly diachronic, or historical. And because of his integration (a rather ambivalent one, to be sure) of thought-processes and economic and social structures he neatly sidestepped the Idealism–materialism debate that so dominated much of German philosophy, and produced a broad theory that nevertheless provided for explanation on a human scale.

This kind of explanation is most clearly set out in *The Protestant Ethic*. That essay has most often been regarded as a rather simplistic explanation for the rise of capitalism in the West, which sees it as a direct outcome of the call of the Protestant sects to create wealth. Yet a careful reading reveals something quite different. Weber, to be sure, cites Calvin and other spiritual leaders among the Baptists and Quakers to the effect that one should make oneself rich; yet he also notes the paradox that these sects are characterized primarily by their 'inner-worldly asceticism'. Far from being an Idealist argument – one that claims that the ideas promoted by Protestantism resulted in the development of economic realities – or a materialist argument – one that claims that economic reality dictates the dominant ideas of an age, including religious ones – Weber instead puts forward the notion of 'elective affinities' (*Wahlverwandtschaften*). That means that, far from there being a direct line between Protestantism and capitalism (an argument that hardly helps to explain the rise of Japanese capitalism, for example), there existed rather certain strands within that religious outlook that, *unintentionally*, sowed the seeds of a way of life that allowed primitive forms of market-oriented activity (such as also existed in China or India) to develop into the fully fledged capitalism that characterized the modern West. It is the claim that such an outcome was unintended that is really key here. Weber was by no means so thoughtless as to put forward monocausal, least of all determinist, arguments. Although some commentators have seen this caution as a weakness, as a reflection of Weber's reluctance to put his cards on the table, it is better regarded as a sign of his deep insight into the complexity of causation and historical change.

Given the role of unintended consequences in history, and given Weber's diagnosis of the threat of violence that underpinned modern society with its loss of cosmic certainties, Weber turned to the notion of scientific research as a way of finding meaning. Hence, in his two famous lectures delivered in 1918 shortly before his death, Weber set out the notion of value-freedom (*Wertfreiheit*). Weber knew that meaning in society is created intersubjectively, and that therefore the study of 'pure facts' was a chimera. Nevertheless, he argued that, in contrast to political activity (which he knew something about, being an active supporter of the National Liberals, and speaking in the period of the demise of the German empire and the chaos of the early years of the Weimar Republic), in which it was necessary to make judgements and to promote them, in science (by which is meant all forms of academic study) one should not have to make practical value judgements. The context of this claim was Weber's diagnosis of modernity's disenchantment, its absence of 'eternal' guides to behaviour. Hence, rather than being a naïve call to objectivity, Weber's idea of value-freedom was designed to make science not only possible under disenchanted conditions, but also to make it desirable as a way of creating meaning. The lecture hall was conceived as a place where market forces and the clash of values that characterized modern politics should and could be resisted. The teaching of an 'ethic of responsibility' too would help overcome the overbearing rule of technocracy. This too was part of his response to Nietzsche's godless world.

His attempt in *Economy and Society* to build a typology of authority also needs to be seen in this light, rather than as a formal exercise in a historical description. Early societies were founded on a kind of legitimate domination derived from a belief in the innate right of the monarch or other traditional leader. Modern societies had no such legitimacy, being characterized more by the Marxist notion of 'alienation', and Weber's typology was a way of trying to find one. It is worth noting that even when discussing the earlier types of rule – traditional or charismatic – Weber still sees their legitimacy as resting on an 'authoritarian power of command'. But that does not make the task for the modern, rational type of authority, existing in an age without natural rights, any easier to solve. Since, however, it is unlikely that any modern, rational authority can exist purely on the basis of an inner conviction of 'validity' held by its subjects, Weber has to conclude that such authority ultimately rests on coercion. It remains only to find a way of bringing together the different classes and interest groups; but coercion underpins that cohesion. The state is lawful if it can enforce its commands. Hence in his 1895 Freiburg address, Weber advocated an emotional commitment to the nation channelled through the political institutions of plebiscitary leadership. Although in normal times these affective ties to the nation go unrecognized, at times of crisis they are made manifest, and Weber believed that encouraging these kind of 'deep and elemental psychological foundations' would not only resist the domination of the bureaucracy (*Beamtenherrschaft*) but would also prevent such crises from breaking out. It is only fair to point out that this charismatic use of the plebiscite, though it sounds superficially like the kind of irrational aestheticization of politics on which fascism relied, was conceived of by Weber as a way of steering a technocratic, managed society in a democratic direction by encouraging mass participation. Yet, since in a capitalist society, such emotional ties depend on the vagaries of the business-cycle, the risks are clearly great. But Weber believed there was no alternative, since it was not possible to reinstate some kind of traditional rule based on substantive justice, legal legitimacy or supernatural values.

It was therefore Weber's fundamental agreement with Nietzsche's diagnosis of the modern world that led him to advocate value-neutral science, even though he knew full well that such a thing was impossible. In other words, rather than resort to fantastical solutions such as Nietzsche's Superman, Weber sought to find a way of reconciling mankind to the melancholy condition in which it found itself in rationalized, bourgeois capitalism, though without abandoning its aspirations for an ethical life. And it was largely as a result of the inspiration he received from Nietzsche that Weber's view of history was such a tragic one. As the *Protestant Ethic* reveals, Weber saw large-scale historical change as resulting from the unintended consequences of human thought and actions. Thus, for all the leanings towards economic sociology and structural analysis, Weber's view of history rested on a notion of contingency that was fundamentally different from the speculative philosophies of history of the eighteenth and nineteenth centuries (such as that of Hegel (see HEGEL AND HEGELIANISM)), and in particular from Marx's belief in the relationship between the classes and the means of production as the motor of history.

The breadth of his work also goes some way to telling us why his ideas are still so hotly debated and why he is regarded (along with Durkheim and Marx) as a 'father of sociology'. His various studies, for example on the agrarian conditions of ancient societies, of Chinese or Indian religions, or on the sociology of law, were not randomly acquired interests; rather they formed a historical study of such proportions that very few scholars have had the ability to question his conclusions with a comparable knowledge-base. Just one illustration of these debates is also the most famous: the *Protestant Ethic* debates. Following numerous attacks from contemporaries, especially the historian Felix Rachfahl, Weber set out his thesis in fine in his 'Anticritical Last Word on *The Spirit of Capitalism*' in 1910. Like many later critics, Rachfahl argued that the distinction between traditional and capitalistic economies was dubious; that the notion of inner-worldly asceticism was just as characteristic of Catholicism as of the Protestant sects; that there were no clear factual links between the sects and the rise of capitalism; that capitalism was carried by a few great entrepreneurs rather than by the *petit bourgeois*; and that the Reformation's contribution to the rise of capitalism lay not in the idea of a 'calling' but in a general tolerance of different modes of living. In other words, the identification of religious causes at the expense of all others was Rachfahl's main complaint. It was left to Weber only to point out that this was not in fact his thesis, though this has not prevented scholars ever since from continuing to read too much into his essay. Yet the study of the Protestant sects and the religion-inspired 'style of life' that unintentionally became the 'spiritually adequate' basis for the development of modern capitalism represents just one corner of one aspect of Weber's field of study.

There have of course been many challenges to Weber's world-view. In particular, it is possible to point to 'paradoxes of modernity' that mitigate Weber's bleak vision. Some commentators feel that, as a vision of modernity, Weber's description of the social is no longer appropriate to a post-industrial, globalized, electronic age. But violence, domination and surveillance proceed apace, even in the age of post-modernism when blueprints for organizing the world have (supposedly) been abandoned.

Finally, it is tempting to argue that Weber has the last laugh anyway. He was far from blind to the fact that the rationalized structures of modernity can themselves become the focus of the affective life (a love of rationality for its own sake), as the studies of the Frankfurt School prove. These, most famously Adorno and Horkheimer's *Dialectic of Enlightenment* (*Dialektik der Aufklärung*, 1944), merged Weberian definitions of modernity with Marxist notions of coercion and discipline in order to arrive at a stark vision of the total domination over nature leading to totalitarianism, in a searing critique of the rational, Enlightenment project.

But beyond this, one may find in Weber a definition of the modern that actually goes against what is generally held to be 'Weberian' in social theory. Weber himself was not so naïve as to hold to the rigid vision of rationalization, bureaucratisation and secularization with which his name is associated, as one small example reveals. In the standard translation of *Science as a Vocation* in the selection of Weber's essay edited by Gerth and Mills, the following passage appears:

> Today the routines of everyday life challenge religion. Many old gods ascend from their graves; they are disenchanted and hence take the form of impersonal forces. They strive to gain power over our lives and again they resume their eternal struggle with one another.

In the original German, the first sentence reads '*Heute ist es religiöser Alltag*', which might better be translated as 'today the everyday is religious'. Despite the best efforts of Gerth and Mills to present Weber as a theorist of secular, rational modernity, Weber himself saw that there was no disappearance of the affective or emotional life, that these human forces and energies must be directed somewhere, and that they may even be channelled into apparently rational social structures. There is, in other words, no such thing as a post-religious secular modernity; rather, the danger to society lies in the failure to acknowledge the need for these energies to be given an outlet. Such a society might be the modern world, and thus when Weber (at the chilling end of *Politics as a Vocation*) said that 'Not summer's bloom lies ahead of us, but rather a polar night of icy darkness and hardness, no matter which group may triumph eternally now', it is hard to resist the temptation to believe that he foresaw the triumph of fascism.

References

Gerth, H.H., and Mills, C. Wright (1991) *From Max Weber: Essays in Sociology*, new edn, London: Routledge.
Weber, Marianne (1975) *Max Weber: A Biography*, New York: John Wiley.
Weber, Max (1930) *The Protestant Ethic and the Spirit of Capitalism*, London: Allen & Unwin.
—— (1978) *Economy and Society*, Berkeley: University of California Press.

Further reading

Horowitz, Asher and Maley, Terry (eds) (1994) *The Barbarism of Reason: Max Weber and the Twilight of Enlightenment*, Toronto: University of Toronto Press.
Lehmann, Hartmut and Roth, Guenther (eds) (1987) *Weber's Protestant Ethic: Origins, Evidence, Contexts*, Cambridge: Cambridge University Press.
Roth, Guenther and Schluchter, Wolfgang (1979) *Max Weber's Vision of History: Ethics and Methods*, Berkeley: University of California Press.
Turner, Bryan S. (1996) *For Weber: Essays on the Sociology of Fate*, 2nd edn, London: Sage Publications.
Schluchter, Wolfgang (1996) *Paradoxes of Modernity*, Stanford, CA: Stanford University Press.

SEE ALSO: historiography and the idea of progress; Kierkegaard, Søren; Marx and Marxism; Nietzsche, Friedrich; Simmel, Georg; social theory and sociology in the nineteenth century; Tönnies, Ferdinand

DAN STONE

WELLS, H.G. (1866–1946)

Herbert George Wells was born in Bromley, Kent, on 21 September 1866. His father, Joseph, was a small-shopkeeper and professional cricketer, and his mother, Sarah, was a housewife. In 1880, following the disablement of Joseph three years earlier that ended his cricketing career, Sarah became a housekeeper at Up Park in Sussex. Joseph, following seven years of impoverishment, moved to a cottage in Nyewoods, Sussex, in 1887 where he lived on an allowance from his wife until she joined him there in 1893. It was precisely during this period of familial disruption that Wells's early education came to an abrupt end and he was thrust into the world of employment.

Wells's early education took place at Mrs Knott's Dame School (*c.*1872–4) and Thomas Morley's Academy (1874–80) in Bromley, before he was apprenticed at the age of 14 to the drapery trade. Between 1880 and 1883, he worked in two drapery emporia (Windsor and Southsea), as a pupil-teacher in Wookey and as a chemist's assistant in Midhurst.

In 1883 Wells returned to education as a pupil-teacher at Midhurst Grammar School where he became a prize student, winning a scholarship to the Normal School of Science in South Kensington. It was as a result of his education at the Normal School (1884–7) that Wells developed as an independent thinker, progressing over the next 30 years from being a religious sceptic and an unaffiliated socialist, to being an advocate of Darwinian evolution, a statist socialist, a reform-eugenicist and a propagandist for world government.

Wells's arrival in South Kensington brought him into contact with two key influences that left their impressions on him for the rest of his life: Darwinism (see DARWIN, CHARLES) and socialism.

Although Wells only studied under T.H. HUXLEY at South Kensington for three months in 1884, he claimed on more than one occasion that Huxley had a profound influence on the way he viewed the world, and he expressed the opinion that Huxley was the greatest man he had ever met. As well as introducing Wells to Darwinian evolution, Huxley infused Darwin's theory with an ethical code that convinced Wells not only that humankind was able to influence the course of its own evolution, but also that humanity had a duty to see that its evolution was progressive and for the benefit of the species as a whole. Thus, unique amongst socialists of the nineteenth and early twentieth centuries, Wells arrived at a collectivist philosophy from a biological perspective.

As well as discovering Huxley's theory of 'ethical evolution' at South Kensington, Wells also donned a red tie within months of his move to the capital, reading Henry George's *Progress and Poverty* (1879) and Plato's *Republic* (360 BCE), and attending socialist lectures. He was an occasional visitor to Kelmscott House, hearing the likes of WILLIAM MORRIS and GEORGE BERNARD SHAW as well as other socialist speakers, and on at least two occasions, in 1886 and 1889, he presented papers to the Debating Society of the Normal School, defending socialism and advocating state control of 'production, distribution and defence'.

Although Wells's socialism and Darwinism were fairly naïve during the 1880s, he nonetheless applied them as best he could to his early literary efforts. In 1884 he founded and edited a college magazine, the *Science Schools Journal*, in which were published the abstracts of his aforementioned Debating Society papers on socialism. In addition, in 1887, he published a fragment of

a text entitled 'The Chronic Argonauts' that addressed both the possibilities and fears of science, and, in a later draft of the story, retitled *The Time Machine* (1895), he merged evolutionary theory and socialism to project a class-ridden, devolving society doomed to ultimate extinction as a result of its rejection of 'ethical evolution' and the class harmony inherent in Huxley's philosophy.

In 1887 Wells left the Normal School of Science, having failed his science degree, and took a job as an assistant schoolmaster at Holt Academy in north Wales. After four months, however, he departed that post, having suffered a crushed kidney in a footballing accident. After a year of convalescence in which he earned an income by drawing biological diagrams and doing occasional supply teaching, Wells took up a second assistant master's post, at Henley House School in Kilburn, in January 1889.

His return to the capital enabled Wells to take up his studies once again, and he enrolled for the relevant examinations to become a Licentiate of the College of Preceptors. His work for the licentiate was also useful preparation for his second attempt at gaining his bachelor's degree in science, which he passed in 1890 with first-class honours in Zoology and second-class honours in Geology, earning himself a fellowship in the Zoological Society.

In 1890 Wells quit his post at Henley House School, and became a tutor with the University Correspondence College, 'coaching' students to pass university examinations in Biology and Geology. Simultaneously, he continued to study, now for a Fellowship of the College of Preceptors, which he acquired in December 1890, winning the Doreck Scholarship Prize for his work on the theory and practice of education.

From 1891 Wells combined his academic knowledge of educational and biological philosophy with an eloquent literary style and began producing a stream of essays that he published in both popular and specialist journals throughout the 1890s, including the *Pall Mall Gazette*, the *Saturday Review* and the *Educational Times*. His first literary success occurred with the publication of 'The Rediscovery of the Unique' in the *Fortnightly Review* in February 1891. Although his follow-up essay, 'The Universe Rigid', was rejected a few months later by the *Fortnightly*'s editor, Frank Harris, nonetheless this break into paid journalism proved to be the beginning of a fabulously lucrative career.

Not only were Wells's fears of poverty put behind him from 1891, but also his concentration on essay-writing allowed him to apply his evolutionary philosophy to daily life. Thus, 'The Rediscovery of the Unique' argued against the common late-Victorian practice of classification, asserting that all things are unique and that classification ought only to be a rough guide for generalizing, inapplicable to the individual. This assertion of the unique became a fundamental tenet of Wells's philosophy and one that he reiterated throughout his life in such works as *The Discovery of the Future* (1902), 'Skepticism of the Instrument' (1904), *First and Last Things* (1908), *The Conquest of Time* (1942) and 'The Illusion of Personality' (1944).

Another important aspect of Wells's thought developed through his journalism was evolution and humanity's control over its own change, both mental and physical. In 'The Limits of Individual Plasticity' (1895), Wells argued that improvements in surgical and educational techniques meant that there was no limit to the changes that doctors and teachers could achieve to the physical and mental structure of a human being. Wells cites skin grafting, blood transfusion and hypnotism as preliminary examples of what might ultimately lead to the transformation of the human species. His belief in the power of such physical and mental manipulation was reasserted in his essays 'The Province of Pain' (1894), 'Human Evolution, an Artificial Process' (1896) and 'Morals and Civilisation' (1897), as well as in such later writings as *The Way the World is Going* (1927) and *The Science of Life* (1930) in which he discusses Pavlov's and Metchnikoff's very different experiments in Russia. Wells's late-Victorian interest in human evolution also clearly fed into his later thoughts on eugenics, to be discussed below.

Although Wells was a declared socialist from 1884 (even considering joining the Fabian Society five years later), he was careful not to write overtly ideological essays during his journalistic apprenticeship of the 1890s. Nonetheless socialistic thinking can be detected in some his writing. An early example is 'Ancient Experiments in Co-operation', published in 1892, in which he argues that evolutionary success has largely come to those species that practice a high degree of co-operation. Wells later applied this analysis, showing the

consequences of its opposite, in *The Time Machine* in which the Time Traveller initially assumes a successful communist society when he encounters the Eloi, a species free from toil and living in seeming peace, equality and plenty, only to be disappointed to learn that the Eloi are farmed and devoured by the Morlocks, the underworld heirs of the working class who have risen against their erstwhile middle-class exploiters. Not only does *The Time Machine* demonstrate the desirability of social harmony, but also it suggests, with the death of the planet at the close of the novella, that class division will ultimately lead to the extinction of the species.

Wells implicitly attacks social division in several of his other early science fiction novels, demonstrating the benefits of co-operation to defeat terrorism in *The Invisible Man* (1897) and portraying the evils of class division in *The First Men in the Moon* (1901) and *When the Sleeper Wakes* (1899). Class fusion leading to social harmony is also portrayed in such works as *The World Set Free* (1914) and *The Shape of Things to Come* (1933), in which scientific advance is harnessed for the benefit of human progress, and *The Labour Unrest* and *The Great State* (both 1912), which argue for class co-operation to end the contemporary labour unrest and achieve a classless 'great state' based on labour conscription and industrial guilds.

If such notions of class harmony seem antithetical to late nineteenth- and early twentieth-century socialism, it was absolutely fundamental to Wells's own political philosophy. Although no believer in automatic progress, Wells understood that human improvement could only be achieved through harnessing the power of science and applying it to human needs. The mechanical progress achieved during the nineteenth century suggested to Wells that further scientific advance could result in not so much the reconstitution of class relations as the dissolution of class altogether. In Wells's opinion, there was no longer a need for a toiling class and he abhorred the existence of a leisure class. For him, the future belonged to the technical-scientific class of mechanics and engineers. This did not mean the emergence of a new elite, but the synthesis of all the old classes into a society of purpose differentiated by temperamental differences alone. Such temperamental differences would be reflected in artistic expression and personal taste, and would also determine educational preference and occupational choice.

Wells presented his notions of temperamental classification (applicable to groups but never, in such a fluid society as he envisaged, to the individual) in such works as *Anticipations* (1901), *A Modern Utopia* (1905) and *Phoenix* (1942).

Although the basis of Wells's social and political thought can be identified in his late-Victorian journalism and in his early scientific romances, it was with the publication of *Anticipations of the Reaction of Scientific and Mechanical Progress upon Human Life and Thought* in 1901 that he began applying his ideas to the question of social reform. And, significantly, in *Anticipations* Wells also considered for the first time the possible application of eugenics to social reform.

In *Anticipations*, Wells cites overpopulation, and more particularly the abundance of 'poor quality' births, as a major problem for the twentieth-century statesman. Wells argues that 'efficiency' ought to be the test of parentage and he excludes a wide span of the population from reproduction. Thus, 'congenital invalids', habitual drunkards, the long-term unemployed and the mentally ill ought to be prevented from procreating through sterilization, and children that are born to them ought either to be taken into care or destroyed, depending upon their condition. Beyond these recommendations, Wells says little in *Anticipations* about social reform. Two years later, in *Mankind in the Making* (1903), Wells heavily revises his eugenic position. In that work, he argues for the expansion of educational opportunities to all in society, and believes poor parents ought to be offered training in parenthood. Furthermore, he cites low pay, underemployment and poor-quality housing as the prime reasons for the stunted growth (both mental and physical) of many working-class children. Wells rejects out of hand the possibilities of positive eugenics but he avoids the question of negative eugenics altogether. This is put right in his next work to discuss social conditions, *A Modern Utopia*. There Wells reasserts the need for improved education, and advocates state regulation of housing conditions and a minimum wage. He suggests the possibility of voluntary eugenics through the maintenance of state files on all individuals, accessible by potential spouses, and he suggests that marriage ought to be illegal until individuals earned a minimum wage and were proved free of transmissible diseases and had expurgated their criminal offences. By 1908, with the publication of his socialist opus,

New Worlds for Old (which Wells wrote as an alternative to the *Fabian Essays* following his unsuccessful attempt to reform the Fabian Society between 1903 and 1906), eugenics has been entirely superseded in Wells's thought by social reform proposals centred on education, health, employment and housing. (Eugenics does re-emerge in Wells's thought in the early 1930s with the publication of *The Science of Life* (1930) and *The Work, Wealth and Happiness of Mankind* (1932), only to be finally rejected in *The Rights of Man* (1940).) The major factors in Wells's social reform proposals of the Edwardian period were the establishment of a minimum wage, the 'endowment of motherhood', compulsory education to the age of 16, slum clearance and greater regulation of housing.

Although social reform and political theory were important aspects of Wells's thought during the Edwardian period, he is best remembered for his internationalism, which developed from 1901 and absorbed much of his energy during the 1920s, 1930s and 1940s. In *Anticipations* Wells prophesied that by the year 2000 there would be five major power blocs in the world; an Anglo-Saxon grouping, a union of the 'Latin' peoples, an East Asian union, a European union and a 'Slavic' union. Although Wells favoured such transnational developments, he saw them as simply being steps towards the emergence of a 'world state at peace within itself'. In 1905, he presented a model of what such a world state might ultimately look like in *A Modern Utopia*, and in *The World Set Free* he presented a possible scenario of how such a world state might come about. Throughout the rest of his life, Wells became more and more insistent on the need for a world state, even declaring that the nation-state was the cause of many of the world's problems and would have to be totally superseded in the ultimate global settlement. As a result of the Great War, therefore, Wells's internationalism gave way to a more comprehensive cosmopolitanism, and from 1923, with the publication of *Men Like Gods*, he rejected any notion of a world parliament in favour of a functional model of world order, based on global corporations having complete sovereignty over their specific functions, though with no corporation becoming dominant over several functions. The only supplements Wells made to this model of global order between 1923 and his death in 1946 were the creation of a world encyclopedia to supply all citizens with instantaneous information about anything they desired to know (see *The Work, Wealth and Happiness of Mankind*), the advocacy of a 'Rights of Man' charter to protect human rights in the face of potential corporate tyranny (see *The Rights of Man*) and the establishment of multi-tiered juries (from local to global) to consider the organization of affairs and outlaw practices that ran counter to the 'Rights of Man' charter (see *Phoenix*).

Wells always maintained that his thought was not original but that his special role was as a synthesizer and popularizer of ideas. Nonetheless, it is possible to argue that Wells made an important contribution to late nineteenth- and twentieth-century thought. He was the first thinker to arrive at a collectivist socialist philosophy through the interpretation of Darwinian evolution. He rejected the notion of 'races' and believed that human advance could only be achieved through a focus on the human race as a whole. Although he rejected the notion of automatic progress, he firmly believed that scientific advance was central to the creation of a peaceful, equalitarian world state. And finally, scorning racial and class division in favour of global harmony, he recognized the futility of socialism based upon class-war and nationalism, and favoured a regulated corporatism in a global service economy, in which education, human rights and popular juries would ensure the protection of individual interests in a world efficiently managed by global corporate bodies.

Despite a lifetime of campaigning for his unique brand of global socialism, Wells died a frustrated man on 13 August 1946. His last published volume, *Mind at the End of its Tether* (1945), is often cited as an example of his ultimate despair with humanity and its future.

Further reading

Partington, J.S. (2003) *Building Cosmopolis: The Political Thought of H.G. Wells*, Aldershot: Ashgate.
Smith, D.C. (1984) *H.G. Wells: Desperately Mortal. A Biography*, New Haven: Yale University Press.
Wagar, W.W. (1961) *H.G. Wells and the World State*, New Haven: Yale University Press.
Wells, H.G. (1934) *Experiment in Autobiography: Discoveries and Conclusions of a Very Ordinary Brain (since 1866)*, 2 vols, London: Gollancz/Cresset Press.

SEE ALSO: Darwin, Charles; democracy, populism and rights; Galton, Francis; ideas of war and peace; intellectuals, elites and meritocracy; Social Darwinism; theories of the state and society: the nation, nationalism and the national principle; novels, poetry and drama; the science of politics; utopianism; Sidney and Beatrice Webb

JOHN S. PARTINGTON

Index

Note: Page numbers in **bold** refer to main subject entries. Bold page numbers after a person's name indicate entries written by this person.